A HISTORY OF WESTERN MUSIC

TENTH EDITION

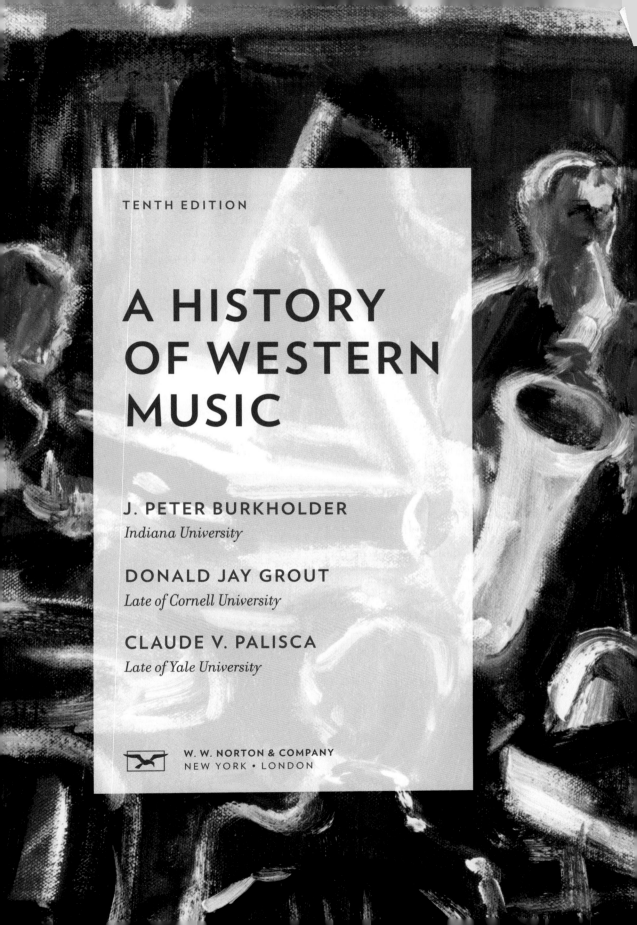

TENTH EDITION

A HISTORY OF WESTERN MUSIC

J. PETER BURKHOLDER
Indiana University

DONALD JAY GROUT
Late of Cornell University

CLAUDE V. PALISCA
Late of Yale University

W. W. NORTON & COMPANY
NEW YORK · LONDON

W. W. NORTON & COMPANY has been independent since its founding in 1923, when William Warder Norton and Mary D. Herter Norton first published lectures delivered at the People's Institute, the adult education division of New York City's Cooper Union. The firm soon expanded its program beyond the Institute, publishing books by celebrated academics from America and abroad. By mid-century, the two major pillars of Norton's publishing program—trade books and college texts—were firmly established. In the 1950s, the Norton family transferred control of the company to its employees, and today—with a staff of four hundred and a comparable number of trade, college, and professional titles published each year—W. W. Norton & Company stands as the largest and oldest publishing house owned wholly by its employees.

Editor: Christopher Freitag
Manuscript Editor and Project Editor: Michael Fauver
Electronic Media Editor: Steve Hoge
Electronic Media Assistant: Eleanor Shirocky
Assistant Editor: Julie Kocsis
Marketing Manager: Trevor Penland
Director of Production, College: Jane Searle
Photo Editor: Agnieszka Czapski
Permissions Managers: Megan Schindel and Bethany Salminen
Page Layout: Carole Desnoes
Book Designer: Jillian Burr
Music Typesetter: David Botwinik
Indexer: Marilyn Bliss
Copyeditor: Jodi Beder
Proofreader: Debra Nichols
Composition: Graphic World
Manufacturing: Transcontinental Printing—Beauceville

Library of Congress Cataloging-in-Publication Data
Names: Grout, Donald Jay, author. | Burkholder, J. Peter (James Peter) author. | Palisca, Claude V. author
Title: A history of western music / J. Peter Burkholder, Donald Jay Grout, Claude V. Palisca.
Description: Tenth edition. | New York : W. W. Norton, [2019] | Includes index.
Identifiers: LCCN 2018044161 | ISBN 9780393623949 (hardcover)
Subjects: LCSH: Music – History and criticism.
Classification: LCC ML160 .G872 2019 | DDC 780.9–dc23 LC record available at https://lccn.loc.gov/2018044161

W. W. Norton & Company, Inc., 500 Fifth Avenue, New York, NY 10110
wwnorton.com
W. W. Norton & Company, Ltd., 15 Carlisle Street, London W1D 3BS

1 2 3 4 5 6 7 8 9 0

In memory of
my parents
Donald L. and Jean A. Burkholder
and my colleagues
Donald Jay Grout and Claude V. Palisca

CONTENTS

PART ONE

THE ANCIENT AND MEDIEVAL WORLDS   2

PART TWO

THE RENAISSANCE   134

PART THREE

THE SEVENTEENTH CENTURY   276

PART FOUR

THE EIGHTEENTH CENTURY   400

PART FIVE

THE NINETEENTH CENTURY   552

PART SIX

THE TWENTIETH CENTURY AND AFTER   754

MAPS

GUIDE TO NAWM SELECTIONS

PREFACE TO THE TENTH EDITION

THE STORY OF *A HISTORY OF WESTERN MUSIC*

The science fiction writer Ursula K. LeGuin once wrote, "The story—from Rumple-stiltskin to War and Peace—is one of the basic tools invented by the human mind, for the purpose of gaining understanding. There have been great societies that did not use the wheel, but there have been no societies that did not tell stories."

A History of Western Music is a story about where music in the Western tradition came from and how it has changed over the centuries from ancient times to the present. The story naturally focuses on the musical works, styles, genres, and ideas that have proven most influential, enduring, and significant. Yet it also encompasses a wide range of music, from religious to secular, from serious to humorous, from art music to popular music, and from Europe to the Americas. In telling this tale, I have tried to bring several themes to the fore:

> the people who created, performed, heard, and paid for this music;
> the choices they made and why they made them;
> what they valued most in the music; and
> how these choices reflected both tradition and innovation.

We study music history in part because it gives greater understanding to all music, past and present. It may be surprising to discover how much and how often musicians from ancient times to the present have borrowed from musical traditions of other lands or earlier eras. Repertoires from Gregorian chant to recent vocal and instrumental music represent a fusion of elements from many regions, and musicians in Europe and the Americas have been trading ideas for more than half a millennium. Composers from the Renaissance to the twenty-first century have drawn inspiration from ancient Greek music. Bach, Mozart, Beethoven, Brahms, Schoenberg, and many composers living today all borrow ideas from music written long before they were born. It may be even more surprising to learn that jazz artists have used harmonies they heard in music by Debussy and Ravel, or that the multiple simultaneous melodic and textual layers in hip hop were first tried out in the thirteenth-century motet. It is not that there is nothing new under the sun, but that almost anything new is a fresh twist on what has become traditional. Sometimes what seems newest is actually borrowed in part from music of the distant past.

We may also be surprised to learn that things we take for granted about music have not always been around. Pop music aimed at teenagers first emerged after World War II. Most wind and brass instruments assumed their current form in the mid-nineteenth century or later. Concerts of music from the past, which are standard features of today's musical life, first appeared in the eighteenth century and were rare before the nineteenth. Tonality, our common musical language of major and minor keys, is not even as old as New York City. Knowing the origins of these and other aspects of musical life increases our understanding.

Many questions about music can only be answered historically. Why do we use a seven-note diatonic scale? Why do we have a notation system with lines, staffs, clefs, and noteheads? Why do operas have recitatives? Why is the music of Haydn and Mozart called "classical"? Why do Bach and Schumann often use the same rhythmic figure in measure after measure, while Mozart and Schoenberg rarely do? How did jazz change from being a popular form of dance music to a kind of art music? None of these has a common-sense answer, but all can be answered by tracing their history. As a rule, if something does not make sense, there is a historical reason for it, and only knowing its history can explain it.

It is with these themes in mind that I have written the new Tenth Edition of *A History of Western Music*. The text is structured in short chapters and arranged in six parts corresponding to broad historical periods—**The Ancient and Medieval Worlds**, **The Renaissance**, **The Seventeenth Century**, **The Eighteenth Century**, **The Nineteenth Century**, and **The Twentieth Century and After**. The parts are further divided into subperiods, each treated in one to three chapters. The first chapter in each chronological segment begins with a summary of the times in order to orient you to some of the most important themes of the era. In addition, each chapter starts with an overview of the music that will be discussed and ends with a sketch of its reception and ongoing impact. By structuring the narrative of music history in this fashion, I have attempted to establish a social and historical context for each repertoire and to suggest its legacy and its significance today. The heart of each chapter explores changing musical styles, the primary composers, genres, and works, and the tension between tradition and innovation, always trying to make clear what is important, where it fits, why it matters, and who cares. Each part, each chapter, and each section tells a story that is in some ways complete in itself but also connects to all the others, like pearls on a string, to form a single narrative thread rooted in human choices and values.

USING THE BOOK

A History of Western Music, Tenth Edition, is designed for maximum readability. The narrative is accompanied by many features to assist you:

- **Part introductions** highlight the most important themes in each period.
- **Chapter overviews and summaries** establish social and historical context at the outset and reception history and musical legacy at the end of each chapter to facilitate an understanding of each period and musical repertoire.

- **In Performance** sidebars trace the careers of major performers, illustrating what it was like to be a professional singer or instrumentalist from ancient times to the present, and highlight issues relevant to performers today, including ornamentation, improvisation, historically informed performance, and bel canto.

---

652 CHAPTER 27 ❖ Romantic Opera and Musical Theater to Midcentury

Italy 653

IN PERFORMANCE

The Bel Canto Diva

The art of bel canto fostered the rise of a new breed of opera singers in the first half of the nineteenth century. Like today's pop superstars, female virtuosos like Giuditta Pasta, Angelica Catalani, Giulia Grisi, Henriette Sontag, and Jenny Lind were more than mere singers; they were larger-than-life cultural icons. The term used to describe them, *diva* (Italian for "goddess"), reflects the semidivine status ascribed to them by their legions of admirers.

The Spanish mezzo-soprano Maria Malibran (1808–1836), shown in Figure 27.4, epitomizes the dazzling aura of the bel canto diva. Born into a celebrated musical family, she made her London debut in 1825 as Rosina in *The Barber of Seville*, first of many Rossini roles with which she would be closely identified. She repeated her success a few months later in New York City, appearing with a touring company organized by her father, the tenor Manuel García, and went on to take France and Italy by storm in works by Rossini, Bellini, Mozart, Meyerbeer, Donizetti, and other composers. Malibran's exceptional vocal range of nearly three octaves was matched by her dramatic powers. She was at the height of her fame when she died at the age of twenty-eight as a result of a riding accident in Birmingham, England, shortly after her marriage to the Belgian violinist Charles de Bériot.

Malibran was also remarkable for her versatility, being equally at home in Rossini's frothy comedies and in tragic roles like Bellini's Norma. Both kinds of music allowed her to show off her prowess in adorning melodies with improvised embellishments, a

FIGURE 27.4 *A portrait of Maria Malibran by Italian artist Luigi Pedrazzi (1802–1845).*

practice that was as intrinsic to bel canto idiom as it was in eighteenth-century opera (see Chapter 21). Malibran and other divas often wrote down their ornamented versions of popular arias, both for teaching purposes and for sale as sheet music. Not all of their elaborations bore the composer's stamp of approval, however. Once, after suffering through an overwrought performance of Rosina's aria *Una voce poco fa* by the soprano Adelina Patti, Rossini remarked cattily: "Very nice, my dear, and who wrote the piece you have just performed?"

It was to guard against such excesses that Rossini and other composers began, in the second decade of the century, to notate ornaments

even more painstakingly in their scores. Although these written-out embellishments were meant as suggestions rather than prescriptions, there is evidence that many singers followed them faithfully, if not slavishly. One such manuscript, preserved in the library of the Conservatory "Giuseppe Verdi" in Milan, contains a tastefully ornamented version of Rosina's *Una voce poco fa* in Rossini's hand, excerpted in Example 27.1 (compare with

the unadorned melody shown in Example 27.2d, which comes between the passages shown here). Although penned many years after the 1816 premiere of *The Barber of Seville*, and tailored for another singer's voice, the soaring cadenza, liquid runs, and pert grace notes in the final cabaletta section of the aria convey a sense of pyrotechnics that seventeen-year-old Maria Malibran displayed in New York's Park Theater on November 29, 1825.

EXAMPLE 27.1 *Two passages from Gioachino Rossini's ornamented version of Una voce poco fa, from The Barber of Seville*

Types of Instrumental Music 261

MUSIC IN CONTEXT

Social Dance

Dancing is essential in a well-ordered society, because it allows males and females to mingle and observe one another. How else does a lady decide whom to marry? Through dancing, she can tell whether someone is shapely and fit or unattractive and swine, whether he is of good health or has unpleasant breath, and whether he is graceful and attentive or clumsy and awkward.

So writes the Renaissance dancing master Thoinot Arbeau (pen name for the cleric Jehan Tabourot) in his *Orchésographie* (1589), the best-known and most detailed dance treatise of the Renaissance. He offers these views to a young man who has just returned home from a big city where he devoted many years to studying law but where, as he confesses with some regret, he did not make time to learn how to dance. Belatedly, the young man has realized that, far from being a frivolous pastime, dancing is a pleasant and profitable activity, one that confers and preserves health provided it is practiced in moderation at suitable times and in appropriate places. It is especially recommended for those who lead sedentary

lives, such as students intent upon their books and young women who spend long hours at knitting and needlework.

Most dances of the Renaissance were performed by couples who arranged themselves in rows or circles. Some, like the pavane, were elegant and dignified, involving a series of gliding steps in a stately procession. Others, like the various branles, were executed with sideways or swaying motions. Still others were much more vigorous; for example, the galliard included rapidly executed kicks, leaps, and landings, shown in Figure 12.5, with a new motion on every beat.

As the dancing master went on to suggest to his new pupil, dancing is also a kind of mute rhetoric by which persons, through movement, can make themselves understood and persuade onlookers that they are gallant or comely and worthy to be acclaimed, admired, and loved. Such attitudes help to explain the importance of social dance in the Renaissance. And although the steps may be different, the place of dance in society today remains remarkably unchanged.

FIGURE 12.5 *Figures from Thoinot Arbeau's Orchésographie showing steps used in a galliard. The dancer is to hop on the left foot and kick the right foot forward (left image); hop on the right foot and kick the left foot forward (center image); repeat both motions again; leap in the air; and land on both feet with the left foot forward (right image). All these movements take only two measures in a fast triple meter.*

THOINOT ARBEAU, ORCHÉSOGRAPHIE, FOLIO 44V AND 45R, AS REPRODUCED IN ALBERT CZERWINSKI, DIE TÄNZE DES 16. JAHRHUNDERTS (1879).

- **Composer biographies** highlight composers' lives and works.

- **Music in Context** sidebars emphasize the importance of music in the daily life of people at every level of society, showing what they valued in it and how they produced and consumed it.

- **Innovations** sidebars—one for each part, plus one for the twenty-first century—focus on key technological or sociological innovations that significantly changed the dissemination, performance, and consumption of music.

500   CHAPTER 22 ❖ Instrumental Music: Sonata, Symphony, and Concerto

Genres and Forms   501

FORMS AT A GLANCE

Binary Form and Its Relatives

Binary form is one of the most fruitful and widely adapted forms in the history of music. In the eighteenth century, there were three main types of binary form, shown in Figure 22.5 In all three types, there are two repeated sections, the first typically moving from the tonic to the dominant (or relative major) and the second working its way back to the tonic. The three types differ in the relationship between the two sections.

In *simple binary form*, the music in the second section is new or only somewhat related to the first section. In *balanced binary form*, the material first presented in the dominant at the end of the first section returns at the end of the second section in the tonic. And in *rounded binary form*, the opening of the first section reappears when the tonic returns in the second section, often followed by the material that first appeared in the dominant, now transposed into the tonic.

SIMPLE BINARY FORM	‖: A :‖: B :‖ I - V V - I
BALANCED BINARY FORM	‖: A B :‖: A B :‖ or ‖: A B :‖: X B :‖ I - V V - I I - V V - I
ROUNDED BINARY FORM	‖: A B :‖: X A B :‖ or ‖: A B :‖: X A :‖ I - V mod I - I I - V mod I

FIGURE 22.5 *Three types of binary form.*

All three types could be used as the form of an entire movement, such as a minuet; could be paired with another binary form, as in a *minuet and trio*; or could serve as the form for the theme of a *rondo* or set of *variations* (see pp. 502–3).

In addition, binary form was developed into what was then called *first-movement form*, renamed *sonata form* in the nineteenth century. As shown in Figure 22.6, eighteenth-century writers recognized that sonata form was an expansion of binary form, but nineteenth-century musicians came to regard it as a three-part form.

EIGHTEENTH-CENTURY VIEW: EXPANDED BINARY FORM

FIRST SECTION		SECOND SECTION	
One Main Period		First Main Period	Second Main Period
KEY: ‖: I - V :‖		‖: V - on V	I - I :‖

NINETEENTH-CENTURY VIEW: THREE-PART FORM

EXPOSITION	DEVELOPMENT	RECAPITULATION
KEY: ‖: I - V :‖	X on V	I - I ‖

COMPARISON

KOCH'S MODEL		NINETEENTH-CENTURY VIEW	
First Section		Exposition	
First and second phrases	I	First theme	I
Third phrase	mod to V	Transition	mod to V
Fourth phrase	V	Second theme	V
Appendix	V	Closing theme	V
Second Section		Development	
First Main Period			
Free	mod, often to vi, ii, iii	Develops ideas from exposition	mod
Preparation for return	on V	Retransition	on V
Second Main Period		Recapitulation	
First and second phrases	I	First theme	I
Third phrase	mod	Transition	mod
Fourth phrase	I	Second theme	I
Appendix	I	Closing theme	I

FIGURE 22.6 *Views of first-movement form.*

- **Forms at a Glance** sidebars describe and diagram important musical forms in a straightforward, visual format for maximum clarity.

- **Key Terms** are highlighted in ***boldface italics*** throughout and are defined, for easy reference, in the **Glossary** at the back of the book.

- **Source Readings** offer pithy and colorful excerpts from writings by people at the center of the story, allowing you to hear directly from the composers, performers, and patrons in their own words.

- **Timelines** in every chapter set the music in a social and historical context, facilitating a clear view of the interrelationship between musical and historical events—what happened when.

- **Four-color maps** establish a location and context for the musical events and works.

334   CHAPTER 15 ❖ Music for Chamber and Church in the Early Seventeenth Century

SOURCE READINGS

Frescobaldi on Instrumental Expression

In the prefaces to his collections of keyboard works, Girolamo Frescobaldi encouraged performers to vary the speed and manner of performance in order to express the changing moods or affections (*affetti*). His advice suggests that he saw instrumental music as akin to vocal music in conveying the affections, and that he sought to reflect a variety of feelings through frequent changes of figuration.

❧

In the course [of performing] take care to distinguish the passages, playing them more or less quickly according to the difference of their *effetti* [*affetti*], which are made evident as they are played.

Girolamo Frescobaldi, foreword to his Primo Libro di Toccate [First Book of Toccatas, 1615].

Having seen how accepted the manner of playing with singable *affetti* and diversity of passages is, I have seen it fit to show myself equally in favor of

it, as well as fond of it, with these feeble efforts of mine, presenting them in print with the guidelines below. . . .

First, that this way of playing must not be subject to the beat—just as we see in modern madrigals which, though difficult, are made more manageable by [altering] the beat, making it now languid, now quick, and occasionally suspending it in mid-air, according to their *affetti*, or the sense of the words.

2. In the toccatas I have taken care . . . that they be rife with a variety of passages, and of *affetti*.

Frescobaldi, foreword to the 1616 reprint of his Primo Libro di Toccate.

In those matters which do not appear to be regulated by the use of counterpoint, one must foremost seek the *affetto* of that passage and the Author's goal, as far as the pleasing of the ear and the way of playing is concerned.

Frescobaldi, foreword to his Capricci (1624). Translations by Andrew Dell'Antonio.

TIMELINE

❧

1517 Martin Luther posts his 95 Theses, beginning the Reformation

1519–56 Reign of Holy Roman emperor Charles V

1519–21 Hernán Cortés conquers Aztecs

1523–24 Luther and Johann Walter write first chorales

1526 Luther's *Deudsche Messe* published

1533 Francisco Pizarro defeats Incas in Peru

1534 Church of England separates from Rome

1534 Society of Jesus (Jesuits) founded

1539 First French psalter published

1544 Georg Rhau publishes *Newe deudsche geistliche Gesenge*

1545–63 Council of Trent

1549 *Book of Common Prayer*

1551–94 Giovanni Pierluigi da Palestrina in Rome

1553–58 Reign of Mary I of England, restores Catholicism

1558 Gioseffo Zarlino, *Le istitutioni harmoniche*

1558–1603 Reign of Elizabeth I of England, restores Church of England

1562 First complete French psalter published

1567 Palestrina's *Pope Marcellus Mass* published

1572 William Byrd appointed to Chapel Royal

1579 Orlande de Lassus, *Cum essem parvulus*

- **Vivid artwork and photographs** throughout provide essential cultural context and highlight important ideas, architecture, people, and events, including portraits of many of the composers and performers discussed.

- **Detailed diagrams** clarify forms of musical works and genres to help you grasp some of the essential structures of music.

- **Cross-references to the accompanying scores and recordings** are found throughout the text. The scores are identified by their numbers in the *Norton Anthology of Western Music* (NAWM), Eighth Edition.

- **For Further Reading**, available online at digital .wwnorton.com/hwm10, provides an up-to-date bibliography corresponding to each part, chapter, and section.

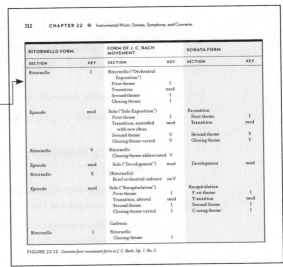

512　　CHAPTER 22 ✲ Instrumental Music: Sonata, Symphony, and Concerto

RITORNELLO FORM		FORM OF J. C. BACH MOVEMENT		SONATA FORM	
SECTION	KEY	SECTION	KEY	SECTION	KEY
Ritornello	I	Ritornello ("Orchestral Exposition")			
		First theme	I		
		Transition	mod		
		Second theme	I		
		Closing theme	I		
Episode	mod	Solo ("Solo Exposition")		Exposition	
		First theme	I	First theme	I
		Transition, extended with new ideas	mod	Transition	mod
		Second theme	V	Second theme	V
		Closing theme varied	V	Closing theme	V
Ritornello	V	Ritornello			
		Closing theme abbreviated	V		
Episode	mod	Solo ("Development")	mod	Development	mod
Ritornello	X	(Ritornello)			
		Brief orchestral cadence	on V		
Episode	mod	Solo ("Recapitulation")		Recapitulation	
		First theme	I	First theme	I
		Transition, altered	mod	Transition	mod
		Second theme	I	Second theme	I
		Closing theme varied	I	Closing theme	I
		Cadenza			
Ritornello	I	Ritornello			
		Closing theme	I		

FIGURE 22.12 *Concerto first-movement form in J. C. Bach, Op. 7, No. 5.*

USING THE ANTHOLOGY AND RECORDINGS

Although this book stands on its own as a narrative history, your understanding will be enriched by using it in tandem with the accompanying anthology and recordings:

- Available in three spiral-bound volumes, the *Norton Anthology of Western Music* (NAWM), Eighth Edition, by J. Peter Burkholder and Claude V. Palisca (Volume 1: Ancient to Baroque; Volume 2: Classic to Romantic; Volume 3: The Twentieth Century and After), provides a comprehensive collection of scores, illustrating the most significant musical trends, genres, and national schools in the Western world from antiquity to the present. Thirty-six pieces are new or expanded in this edition, including six selections written since the year 2000, offering unprecedented access to recent music.

- Each piece is followed by commentary that relates the piece's origins; describes its form, contents, and important stylistic traits; and addresses issues of the edition and performance when appropriate. In addition, all foreign-language texts are accompanied by English translations.

- The **recordings** that accompany the anthology include outstanding performances of the entire NAWM repertoire by some of the best musicians and ensembles working today (see pp. xiv–xxiv). Thirty-six performances are new to this edition. The recordings are available in streaming form as part of Total Access and available for separate purchase; consult your Norton representative or wwnorton.com for additional details.

USING TOTAL ACCESS

The Total Access program unlocks a full suite of media resources with every new book, including:

- **Streaming recordings** of the entire *Norton Anthology of Western Music* repertoire.
- NEW **Audio Timelines** that facilitate the use of recordings with the scores in NAWM.
- Stunning **Metropolitan Opera video** of scenes from selected operas discussed in the text.
- An **interactive ebook** that allows the reader to take notes, highlight, and listen to audio examples at the tap of a finger or click of a mouse.
- NEW **adaptive assessment** activities powered by **InQuizitive** to help students learn and review the history within and across each era.
- NEW **Musicology Skill Builders** for score reading, critical listening, and primary source study.

To access these resources and more, go to digital.wwnorton.com/hwm10 and register using the code in the front of this book.

TO THE INSTRUCTOR

ABOUT THE TEXT The new Tenth Edition of *A History of Western Music* offers the most current, authoritative scholarship available. Every chapter has been revised and updated to reflect recent research and incorporate myriad suggestions from reviewers and instructors.

Among the many changes, the text now offers more coverage of the music of France and Spain from the sixteenth to twentieth centuries, increased attention to the music of Russia before the appearance of Glinka, and deeper treatment of the historical contexts for music in the twentieth century. Revisions in the medieval and Renaissance chapters improve discussion of chant, fifteenth-century counterpoint, improvisation, the sixteenth-century French chanson, and instrumental music. The Baroque chapters include more on performance practice and a more nuanced discussion of seventeenth-century Venetian opera and its social, literary, and theatrical contexts. The eighteenth-century chapters include a revised and expanded discussion of galant style, based on work by Daniel Heartz and Robert O. Gjerdingen, and add discussion of schema theory alongside topic theory and other recent approaches to this repertoire. The final chapter on music in the twenty-first century, first added in the Ninth Edition, features updated discussions of music and technology. Throughout the text there is continued emphasis on performers and performance, including In Performance sidebars on issues ranging from historically informed performance to the changing relationships between opera singers and composers.

ABOUT THE ANTHOLOGY AND RECORDINGS Responding to extensive feedback from instructors and students, I have expanded the repertoire in the Eighth Edition of the *Norton Anthology of Western Music* from 220 to 229 works. Among the thirty-six new additions, a choral work by Mozart, a Beethoven string quartet, several songs from Robert Schumann's song cycle *Dichterliebe*, a Schubert impromptu, and movements from a Mendelssohn oratorio, Robert Schumann's First Symphony, and César Franck's Violin Sonata enhance the already extensive selections by major composers from the eighteenth and nineteenth centuries. A Spanish zarzuela by Francisco Asenjo Barbieri and Amy Beach's *Gaelic* Symphony broaden the representation of nineteenth-century opera and symphony. The twentieth century is represented by more than sixty pieces, including new works by Ravel, Falla, Holst, Sibelius, Stravinsky, Ives, and Reich. Examples of jazz now include innovative works by Miles Davis and John Coltrane. The repertoire of twenty-first-century music has grown to encompass movements from Caroline Shaw's *Partita for 8 Voices* and from the Violin Concerto by Thomas Adès. Coverage of early music is expanded with more examples of medieval tropes and sequences; additional movements from Victoria's *Missa O magnum mysterium*; and new selections by Isaac, Janequin, Gastoldi, Morley, Charpentier, and Padilla. New excerpts from operas by Cavalli, Sartorio, and Rousseau help to illustrate the history of opera in the seventeenth and eighteenth centuries, and a piano sonata by Baldassare Galuppi and a complete symphony by Giovanni Battista Sammartini showcase the Italian roots of the classical style.

The anthology emphasizes complete works or movements. Each work selected is a good teaching piece—representative of its period, genre, and composer. Major composers such as Machaut, Landini, Du Fay, Josquin, Byrd, Gabrieli, Monteverdi, Alessandro Scarlatti, J. S. Bach, Handel, Haydn, Mozart, Beethoven, Schubert, Mendelssohn, Chopin, Robert Schumann, Brahms, Richard Strauss, Schoenberg, Stravinsky, Bartók, Ives, John Cage, and John Adams are represented by multiple works, reflecting the composers' range of style. Other pieces reveal chains of development, including genres, conventions, forms, and techniques, from the mass to sonata form and from counterpoint to serialism. Selections encompass not only the standard canon but also music from Spain, eastern Europe, and the Americas; music of the African American tradition; music by women; and music by living composers.

The newly expanded recorded anthology features updated recordings from some of the best performers and ensembles working today alongside classic recordings by great artists, including:

- Early music ensembles Academy of Ancient Music, Altramar, Les Arts Florissants, Artek, Chapelle Royale, Chiaroscuro, Circa 1500, Concerto Cologne, Concerto Vocale, Dunedin Consort and Players, Early Music New York, English Baroque Soloists, Ensemble de' Medici, Ex Cathedra, Gabrieli Consort, The Harp Consort, Hilliard Ensemble, His Majestys Sagbutts & Cornetts, Les Musiciens du Louvre, Lionheart, London Baroque, Martin Best Medieval Ensemble, Orlando Consort, Sequentia, Trinity Baroque, and La Venexiana.

- Singers Elly Ameling, Bryan Asawa, Julianne Baird, Bethany Beardslee, Ian Bostridge, Montserrat Caballé, Paul Elliott, Gerald Finley, Dietrich Fischer-Dieskau, Renée Fleming, Ellen Hargis, Paul Hillier, Lorraine Hunt, Emma Kirkby, Guillemette Laurens, Evelyn Lear, Christa Ludwig, Ethel Merman, Birgit Nilsson, Nigel Rogers, Renata Scotto, Bessie Smith, Joan Sutherland, and Furio Zanasi.

- Harpsichordists Olivier Beaumont, Gustav Leonhardt, Byron Schenkman, Geneviève Soly, and Colin Tinley.

- Lutenists and guitarists Lex Eisenhardt, Paul O'Dette, Hopkinson Smith, and Benjamin Verdery.

- Violinists James Ehnes, Augustin Hadelich, Gidon Kramer, Sigiswald Kuijken, Ingrid Matthews, and Jaap Schröder.

- Cellist Yo-Yo Ma.

- Pianists Pierre-Laurent Aimard, Leif Ove Andsnes, Vladimir Ashkenazy, Malcolm Bilson, Aldo Ciccolini, Henry Cowell, Jörg Demus, Simone Dinnerstein, Marc-André Hamelin, Scott Joplin, Lili Kraus, Jelly Roll Morton, Matteo Napoli, Ursula Oppens, Sergei Rachmaninoff, Artur Rubenstein, Rudolf Serkin, Yuji Takahashi, and Joyce Yang.

- Atlanta Symphony Orchestra, Berlin Philharmonic, Chicago Symphony Orchestra, Concertgebouw Orchestra, Detroit Symphony Orchestra, London Philharmonic Orchestra, London Symphony Orchestra, New World Symphony, New York Philharmonic, Orchestre Revolutionnaire et Romantique, Prague Chamber Orchestra, San Francisco Symphony, members of the Simón Bolivár Youth Orchestra of Venezuela, Tafelmusik Baroque Orchestra, and Vienna Philharmonic.

- Conductors Claudio Abbado, Marin Alsop, Herbert Blomstedt, Karl Böhm, Pierre Boulez, William Christie, Aaron Copland, Colin Davis, John Eliot Gardiner, Bernard Haitink, Philippe Herreweghe, René Jacobs, Neeme Järvi, Paavo Järvi, Erich Leinsdorf, James Levine, Sir Charles Mackerras, Kent Nagano, Seiji Ozawa, Robert Shaw, Robert Spano, Igor Stravinsky, and Michael Tilson Thomas.

- Bayreuth Festival Opera, Deutsche Oper Berlin, Kirov Opera, and Royal Opera House at Covent Garden.

- Artemis Quartet, Coull Quartet, Ensemble InterContemporain, Kodály Quartet, The Lindsays, Pavel Haas Quartet, and Yuval Trio.

- Anonymous 4, Gothic Voices, His Majestie's Clerks, Robert Shaw Chamber Singers, Roomful of Teeth, Tallis Scholars, and Theatre of Voices.

- The Royal Artillery Band and Central Band of the Royal Air Force.

- Jazz artists Louis Armstrong, John Coltrane, Miles Davis, Duke Ellington, Dizzy Gillespie, Earl (Fatha) Hines, Charlie Parker, and Bud Powell.

USING THE INSTRUCTOR'S RESOURCES You have a lot to do in your course. Norton wants to make it easy for you to find the support you need, and find it quickly.

- **Coursepacks**, working within your learning-management system (LMS), are customizable and include chapter and listening quizzes to help your students prep for exams.

- The **Test Bank** includes over 2,000 multiple choice, true/false, short answer, and essay questions. Each question is identified with a topic, question type (factual, conceptual, or applied), and difficulty level.

- The **Instructor's Manual** includes detailed teaching advice for new and experienced instructors alike. In addition to suggested syllabi, the manual includes an overview and list of learning objectives, lecture suggestions and class activities, discussion questions, and a comprehensive annotated bibliography.

- The **Interactive Instructor's Guide** combines image files and instructor's manual materials in a searchable online database. Search for items by subject, chapter, or type and show them immediately in class or further customize your lecture materials.

- **PowerPoint Lecture Slides,** available for each chapter, combine bullet points from the outlines with artwork and charts.

ACKNOWLEDGMENTS

No work of this magnitude can be written without a legion of help. My profound thanks to all who have contributed to the preparation of this Tenth Edition.

I have been assisted at every stage by the members of the Editorial Advisory Board: Michael Alan Anderson, C. Matthew Balensuela, Joanna Biermann, David Brodbeck, James W. Buhler, John Michael Cooper, Don Fader, Lisa Feurzeig, Andrew Flory, Kunio Hara, John Howland, Julie Hubbert, Nicholas Mathew, Stefano Mengozzi, David Metzer, Margaret Notley, S. Alexander Reed, John A. Rice, Stephanie P. Schlagel, and Hendrik Schulze. Members of the Board read and commented on chapters; proposed changes to this book and to NAWM; pointed me to relevant scholarship; answered individual queries; and suggested ideas or turns of phrase, many of which I have incorporated. Their help has made this a much better book, and I am deeply grateful.

Several others assisted directly with research and writing. Barbara Haggh-Huglo offered extensive corrections and suggestions for Chapters 1–12. Gary Towne shared his class handouts for medieval and Renaissance music, furnishing a useful check on what to include. Matthew Leone provided background research on tropes and sequences for Chapter 3. Giovanni Zanovello gave advice on revisions to Chapters 7–9. Mollie Ables suggested ideas for reorganizing Chapter 7. Patrick Domico assisted as a special consultant and researcher for the new sections on Russian music in Chapters 16 and 21. Christine Wisch was a special consultant and researcher for Chapters 16 and 28, providing background on the Mexican villancico and Spanish zarzuela. Matthew Leone, Julie Kocsis, and Chris Freitag offered many fruitful ideas for Chapter 39, and Chris Freitag and Michael Fauver drafted portions of the sidebar on music technology. Katherine Baber, Chelsey Belt, Paul Borg, Drew Edward Davies, Jessie Fillerup, Gina Gillie, Drew Massey, Alison Mero, Pamela F. Starr, Scott A. Stewart, Kristen Strandberg, and Paul van Emmerik offered suggestions for improvements, from content to wording. Antonia Banducci and her music history students at the University of Denver contributed queries about Renaissance dance tempos that led me down one of the many enjoyable rabbit holes I explored in the course of this revision.

My colleagues at Indiana University, especially David Cartledge, Judah Cohen, Giuliano Di Bacco, Phil Ford, Halina Goldberg, Roman Ivanovitch, Thomas J. Mathiesen, Daniel R. Melamed, Kristina Muxfeldt, Massimo Ossi, Ayana O. Smith, and Giovanni Zanovello, answered queries and offered ideas. More than three hundred instructors provided extensive feedback about the previous edition and suggestions for changes. Matthew Leone assisted with several new musical examples. Nicolette van den Bogerd, Sarah McDonie, and Matthew Leone helped to update the bibliography, which is now online. Marilyn Bliss created the index. The staff of the Cook Music Library at Indiana University offered help at every turn. The staff at FedEx Office in Bloomington were always friendly and helpful, especially Roberto and Jason. Many thanks for their contributions. In addition, I remain indebted to the many people who assisted in preparing the Seventh, Eighth, and Ninth Editions, whose ideas continue to play a significant role in this new edition. In particular, several of the sidebars in this edition are adapted from sidebars originally drafted for earlier editions by Barbara Russano Hanning, Harry Haskell, Gretchen Peters, Devon Nelson, and Nathan Landes.

Special thanks to the talented authors who created the digital media resources for this edition: Rebecca Marchand (Music History Skill Builders and InQuizitive activities); Elizabeth Hoover (chapter and listening-quiz revisions); Melissa Lesbines (Test Bank and chapter outlines); Roger Hickman (Instructor's Manual); and Joseph Ovalle, Jordyn Keller Middleton, Hannah Durham, and John Husser (Audio timelines).

It has been a great pleasure to work with the staff at W. W. Norton. Chris Freitag, music editor, has been a constant source of ideas, support, enthusiasm, and editorial suggestions, and our weekly phone calls have helped to sustain my energy and focus over the past two and a half years. Michael Fauver, project editor, has guided the book's many components through the editorial process and kept the book on schedule. Jodi Beder served as copyeditor, and Debra Nichols served as proofreader; both have made many helpful suggestions and saved me from numerous errors and infelicities. Megan Schindel and Bethany Salminen secured permissions for this book and for NAWM. Julie Kocsis provided editorial assistance. Agnieszka Czapski was the photograph editor. Jane Searle oversaw production and magically kept the process moving. Jillian Burr contributed the beautiful design, David Botwinik did the elegant music typesetting, and Carole Desnoes the attractive layout. Steve Hoge designed and produced the electronic media accompanying the book. I cannot thank them all enough for their skill, dedication, and counsel.

I would also like to thank Nick D'Angiolillo and his staff at Naxos for their diligence and hard work on the recording package that accompanies NAWM.

Thanks finally but most of all to my family, especially my late parents Donald and Jean Burkholder, who introduced me to the love of music; my brother Bill and his wife Joanne and daughter Sylvie Burkholder, whose enthusiasm renewed my own; and P. Douglas McKinney, my husband for over a quarter century, whose unending patience, encouragement, and support have sustained me through four editions. My father, who passed away during the final stages of preparing the Ninth Edition, was always my biggest fan, showing my previous editions of this book to every visitor and giving copies to anyone he thought would enjoy it. My mother, who passed away in the midst of my revisions for this edition, kept the Ninth Edition on the shelf by her bed until the day she died. This edition is dedicated to the memory of my parents and of my two predecessors as authors of this book. I owe more to all four of them than I can express.

—*J. Peter Burkholder*
October 2018

ABBREVIATIONS

BCE   Before Common Era (equivalent to BC)

CE   Common Era (equivalent to AD)

SR   *Source Readings in Music History*, rev. ed., ed. Oliver Strunk, gen. ed. Leo Tre-
itler (New York: W. W. Norton, 1998). Readings in SR are cited by their item number
and page numbers in the entire collection and, when different, their volume and
item number in the individual paperback volumes published separately: vol. 1, *Greek
View of Music,* ed. Thomas J. Mathiesen; vol. 2, *The Early Christian Period and the Latin
Middle Ages,* ed. James McKinnon; vol. 3, *The Renaissance,* ed. Gary Tomlinson; vol.
4, *The Baroque Era,* ed. Margaret Murata; vol. 5, *The Late Eighteenth Century,* ed. Wye
Jamison Allanbrook; vol. 6, *The Nineteenth Century,* ed. Ruth Solie; and vol. 7, *The
Twentieth Century,* ed. Robert P. Morgan. Thus "SR 14 (2:6)" means number 14 in the
single-volume hardback and number 6 in volume 2 of the paperbacks.

PITCH DESIGNATIONS

In this book, a note referred to without regard to its octave register is designated by
an uppercase letter (A). A note in a particular octave is designated in italics, using the
following system:

 *C to B*   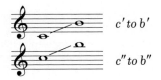 *c′ to b′*

c to b   *c″ to b″*

A HISTORY OF WESTERN MUSIC

TENTH EDITION

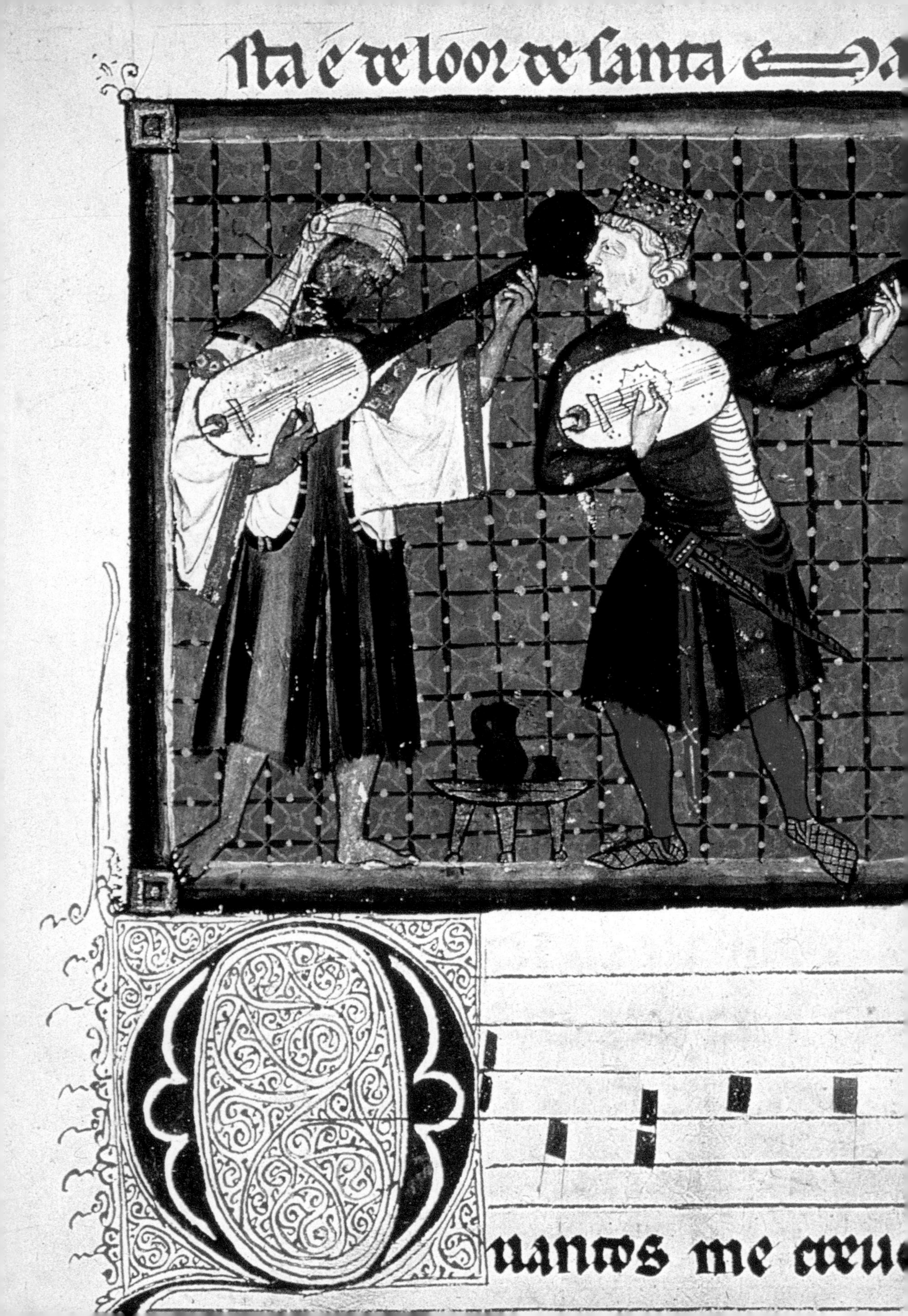
sta e de loor de santa
uantos me creu

PART ONE

THE ANCIENT AND MEDIEVAL WORLDS

Every aspect of today's music has a history, and many fundamental elements can be traced back thousands of years. Prehistoric societies developed instruments, pitches, melody, and rhythm. Early civilizations used music in religious ceremonies, to accompany dancing, for recreation, and in education—much as we do today. Ancient writers directly influenced our ways of thinking about music, from concepts such as notes, intervals, and scales, to notions of how music affects our feelings and character. Medieval musicians contributed further innovations, devising systems for notating pitch and rhythm that led to our own, creating pedagogical methods that teachers continue to use, and developing techniques of polyphony, harmony, form, and musical structure that laid the foundation for music in all subsequent eras. Church musicians sang chants that are still used today; court poets and musicians composed songs whose themes of love's delights and torments are reflected in songs of our time; and both church and secular musicians developed styles of melody that have influenced the music of later periods.

The music and musical practices of antiquity and the Middle Ages echo in our own music, and we know ourselves better if we understand our heritage. Yet only fragments survive from the musical cultures of the past, especially the distant past. So our first task is to consider how we can assemble those fragments to learn about a musical world of long ago.

PART OUTLINE

MUSIC IN ANTIQUITY

The culture of Europe and the Americas—known as Western culture to distinguish it from the traditional cultures of Asia—has deep roots in the civilizations of antiquity. Our agriculture, writing, cities, and systems of trade derive from the ancient Near East. Our mathematics, calendar, astronomy, and medicine grew from Mesopotamian, Egyptian, Greek, and Roman sources. Our philosophy is founded on Plato and Aristotle. Our primary religions, Christianity and Judaism, arose in the ancient Near East and were influenced by Greek thought. Our literature grew out of Greek and Latin traditions and drew on ancient myth and scripture. Our artists imitated ancient sculpture and architecture. From medieval empires to modern democracies, governments have looked to Greece and Rome for examples.

The music of Western culture, known as Western music, also has roots in antiquity, from the scales we use to the functions music serves. The strongest direct influence comes through Greek writings, which became the foundation for European views of music. The influence of ancient music itself is more difficult to trace. Little notated music survived, and few if any European musicians before the sixteenth century could read the ancient notation. Yet some musical practices continued, passed down through oral tradition.

These echoes of ancient music in the Western tradition are reason enough to begin our survey by examining the roles of music in ancient cultures, the links between ancient practices and those of later centuries, and the debt Western music owes to ancient Greece. Starting with ancient music also lets us consider how we can learn about music of the past and what types of evidence we can use to reconstruct the history of music from any age.

Music is sound, and sound by its nature is impermanent. What remains of the music from past eras are its historical traces, of four main types: (1) *physical remains* such as musical instruments and performing spaces; (2) *visual images* of musicians, instruments, and performances; (3) *writings* about music and musicians; and (4) *music itself*, preserved in notation, through oral tradition, or (since the 1870s) in recordings. Using these traces, we can try to reconstruct what music of a past culture was like, recognizing that our understanding will always be partial and will be influenced by our own values and concerns.

We are most confident of success when we have all four types of evidence in abundance. But for ancient music, relatively little remains. Even for Greece, by far the best-documented ancient musical tradition, we have only a small portion of the instruments, images, writings, and music that once existed. For other cultures we have no music at all. By examining what traces survive and what we can conclude from them, we can explore how each type of evidence contributes to our understanding of music of the past.

THE EARLIEST MUSIC

The earliest evidence of music-making lies in surviving instruments and representations. In the Stone Age, people bored finger holes in animal bones and mammoth ivory to make whistles and flutes. Figure 1.1 shows one of the oldest and most complete bone flutes yet found in Europe, dating from about 40,000 BCE. Paleolithic cave paintings appear to show musical instruments being played. Pottery flutes, rattles, and drums were common in the Neolithic era, and wall paintings in Turkey from the sixth millennium BCE show drummers playing for dancers and for the hunt, to drive out game. Such images provide our primary evidence for the roles music played in these cultures. Once people learned to work with metal, in the Bronze Age (beginning in the fourth millennium BCE), they made metal instruments, including bells, jingles, cymbals, rattles, and horns. Plucked string instruments appeared around the same time, as shown on stone carvings; the instruments themselves were made of perishable materials, and few have survived.

Although we can learn about various facets of prehistoric musical cultures from images and archaeological remains, our understanding is severely limited by the lack of any written record. The invention of writing, which marked the end of the prehistoric period, added a new type of evidence, and it is with these accounts that the history of music properly begins.

MUSIC IN ANCIENT MESOPOTAMIA

Mesopotamia, the land between the Tigris and Euphrates Rivers (now part of Iraq and Syria), was home to a number of peoples in ancient times. The map in Figure 1.2 shows several of the most important civilizations that developed there and in nearby regions over a span of more than two thousand years. Here in the fourth millennium BCE, the first true cities and civilizations emerged—from Nagar and Hamoukar in the north to Uruk in the south—and the Sumerians developed one of the first known forms of writing, using cuneiform (wedge-shaped) impressions on flat clay tablets. This system was adopted by

SASHA SCHUERMANN/AFP/GETTY IMAGES

FIGURE 1.1 *Front view of a bone flute made from the radius (wing bone) of a griffon vulture, unearthed in 2008 at Hohle Fels Cave in the Ach Valley in Swabia (southwestern Germany) and estimated to date from about 40,000 to 42,000 years ago. With five finger holes, it is the most complete of the early flutes yet recovered.*

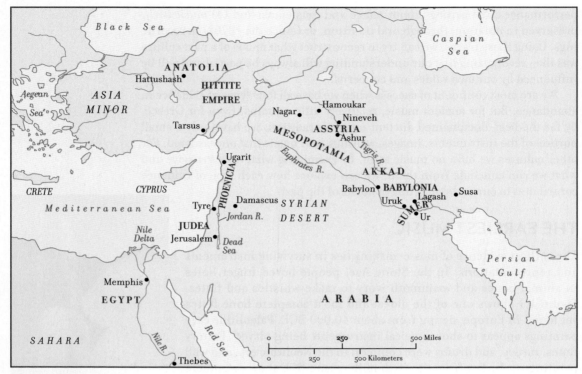

FIGURE 1.2

The ancient Near East, showing the location of the main cities and civilizations of Mesopotamia and Egypt.

later civilizations, including the Akkadians and the Babylonians. Many tablets have been deciphered, and some mention music.

Archaeological remains and images are still crucial for understanding the music of this time. Pictures show how instruments were held and played and in what circumstances music was used, while surviving instruments reveal details of their construction. For example, archaeologists exploring the royal tombs at Ur, a Sumerian city on the Euphrates, found several ***lyres*** and ***harps***, two kinds of plucked string instruments, as well as pictures of them being played, all from ca. 2500 BCE. In a lyre, the strings run parallel to the resonating soundboard, passing over a bridge that transmits their vibrations, and attach to a crossbar supported by two arms; in a harp, the strings are in a plane that is perpendicular to the soundboard, and the neck that supports them is attached directly to the soundbox. Figure 1.3 is a reconstruction of one of the instruments from Ur: a *bull lyre*, a distinctively Sumerian lyre whose soundbox features a bull's head, which had religious significance. Figure 1.4 is part of an inlaid panel depicting a musician playing a bull lyre at a victory banquet. The player holds the lyre, supported by a strap around his neck, perpendicular in front of him and plays it with both hands. Together image and instrument reveal that the lyre had a variable number of strings running from a bridge on the soundbox to the crossbar, where they were knotted around sticks that could be turned to change the tension and thus the tuning of each string. Other instruments of the period included lutes, pipes, drums, cymbals, clappers, rattles, and bells.

Written records   Combining written records with images of music-making allows a much fuller understanding of how Mesopotamian cultures used music, showing that their repertories included wedding songs, funeral laments, military music, work songs, nursery songs, dance music, tavern music, music for entertaining at feasts, songs to address the gods, music to accompany ceremonies and processions, and epics sung with instrumental accompaniment. All but the last of these are uses that continue today. As is true for every era until the nineteenth century, we find the best evidence for music of the elite classes, primarily rulers and priests, who had the resources to induce artisans to make instruments, musicians to make music, artists to depict it, and scribes to write about it.

Written sources also provide a vocabulary for music and some information on musicians. Word lists from ca. 2500 BCE on include terms for instruments, tuning procedures, performers, performing techniques, and **genres** or types of musical composition. The earliest composer known to us by name is Enheduanna (fl. ca. 2300 BCE), an Akkadian high priestess at Ur, who composed **hymns** (songs to a god) to the moon god Nanna and moon goddess Inanna; their texts, but not her music, survive on cuneiform tablets.

Around 1800 BCE, Babylonian musicians began to write down what they knew instead of passing it on by word of mouth only. Their writings describe tuning, intervals, improvisation, performing techniques, and genres, including love songs, laments, and hymns. Here again we find many aspects of music that continued into later times.

Among the writings are instructions for tuning a string instrument that indicate the Babylonians used seven-note **diatonic** scales. They recognized seven scales of this type, corresponding to the seven diatonic scales playable on the white keys of a piano. These scales have parallels in the ancient Greek musical system as well as in our own, suggesting that Babylonian theory and practice influenced that of Greece, directly or indirectly, and thus European music.

The Babylonians used their names for intervals to create the earliest

FIGURE 1.3
Reconstruction of a Sumerian bull lyre from the Royal Cemetery at Ur, ca. 2500 BCE.

FIGURE 1.4 *Inlaid panel from Ur, ca. 2600 BCE, showing a bull lyre being played at a victory banquet.*

FIGURE 1.5 *Clay tablet from Ugarit, ca. 1400–1250 BCE, with text and musical notation for a hymn to Nikkal, a wife of the moon god. The words are written above the double line, the music below.*

known musical **notation**. The oldest nearly complete piece, from ca. 1400–1250 BCE, is on a tablet shown in Figure 1.5 that was found at Ugarit, a merchant city-state on the Syrian coast. Scholars have proposed possible transcriptions for the music, but the notation is too poorly understood to be read with confidence. Despite the invention of notation, most music was either played from memory or improvised. Musicians most likely did not play or sing from notation, as modern performers do, but used it as a written record from which a melody could be reconstructed, as cooks use a recipe.

FIGURE 1.6 *Greece and Greek settlements about 550 BCE (shown in blue). The main centers of Greek population and culture were the Greek peninsula, the Aegean Islands, the west coast of Asia Minor (modern Turkey), and southern Italy and Sicily, known to the Romans as Magna Graecia (Greater Greece).*

OTHER CIVILIZATIONS For other ancient cultures we also have instruments, images, and writings that testify to their musical practices. India and China developed independently from Mesopotamia and were probably too distant to affect Greek or European music. Surviving sources that shed light on Egyptian musical traditions are especially rich, including many artifacts, paintings, and hieroglyphic writings preserved in tombs. Archaeological remains and images that relate to music are relatively scant for ancient Israel, but music

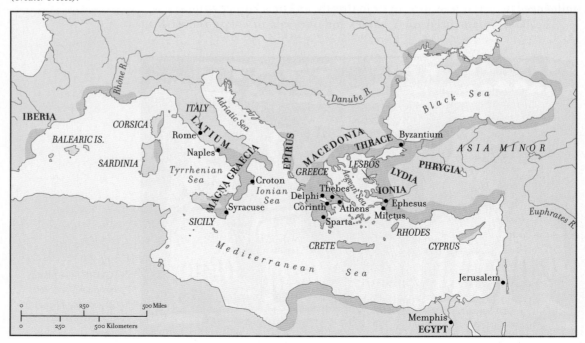

in religious observances is described in the Bible. Although some scholars have tried to discover and decipher musical indications in Egyptian hieroglyphics and wall paintings and in ancient copies of the Bible, no consensus has been reached that musical notation is even present. Through physical remains, images, and writings about music we can gain a sense of a vibrant musical life in the ancient Near East, but without actual music to perform, it remains almost entirely silent.

MUSIC IN ANCIENT GREECE

Ancient Greece is the earliest civilization that offers us enough evidence to construct a well-rounded view of musical culture, although there are still many gaps. As shown in Figure 1.6, Greek civilization encompassed not only the Greek peninsula but islands in the Aegean, much of Asia Minor, southern Italy and Sicily, and colonies ringing the Mediterranean and Black Seas. From this ancient culture, we have numerous images, a few surviving instruments, writings about music's roles and effects, theoretical writings on the elements of music, and over forty examples of music in a notation we can read.

INSTRUMENTS AND THEIR USES We know about ancient Greek instruments and how to play them from writings, archaeological remains, and hundreds of images on clay pots. The most important instruments were the **aulos** (pl. *auloi*), **lyre**, and **kithara**. The Greeks also used harps, panpipes, horns, an early form of organ, and a variety of percussion instruments such as drums, cymbals, and clappers.

The aulos was a pipe typically played in pairs, as pictured in Figure 1.7. Each pipe had finger holes and a mouthpiece fitted with a reed. No reeds survive, but written descriptions suggest that they were long tubes with a beating tongue. Images of auloi being played show both hands in the same finger position, leading most scholars to conclude that the two pipes were played in unison, with slight differences in pitch creating a plangent sound. But modern reconstructions based on surviving auloi can also be played to produce parallel octaves, fifths, or fourths, or a drone or separate line in one pipe against a melody in the other, so that these methods cannot be ruled out.

The aulos was used in the worship of Dionysus, god of fertility and wine. Links to fertility and wine explain its presence in the drinking scene in Figure 1.7; the instrument is played by a woman who was likely a prostitute as well as a musician. The great tragedies by Aeschylus, Sophocles, and Euripides, created for the Dionysian festivals in Athens, have choruses and other musical portions that were accompanied by or alternated with the aulos.

Lyres usually had seven strings and were strummed with a plectrum, or pick. There were several forms of lyre, the most characteristic of which used as a soundbox a tortoise shell over which oxhide

TIMELINE

ca. 3500–3000 BCE Rise of Sumerian cities

ca. 3100 Cuneiform writing established

ca. 2500 Royal tombs at Ur

ca. 2300 Enheduanna composes her hymns

ca. 1800 Babylonian writings about music

ca. 1400–1250 Oldest nearly complete piece in notation

ca. 800 Rise of Greek city-states

ca. 800 Homer, *Iliad* and *Odyssey*

753 Rome founded

ca. 500 Roman Republic begins

586 Sakadas of Argos, *Pythic Nomos*

408 Euripides, *Orestes*

ca. 380 Plato, *Republic*

ca. 330 Aristotle, *Politics*

ca. 330 Aristoxenus, *Harmonic Elements*

146 Greece becomes province of Rome

128–127 Second Delphic Hymn to Apollo composed

29–19 Virgil, *Aeneid*

27 Rome becomes empire under Augustus

1st century CE *Epitaph of Seikilos*

98–117 CE Roman Empire reaches its peak

ca. 127–48 Claudius Ptolemy, *Harmonics*

ca. 2nd century Cleonides, *Harmonic Introduction*

4th century Aristides Quintilianus, *On Music*

FIGURE 1.7 *Greek red-figure drinking cup showing a scene at a symposium, or drinking party, where a woman plays the double aulos. A drinking cup, like the one on which this painting appears, is seen on the lower right. On the left is the player's aulos bag, with a smaller bag attached to it that held the reeds for the aulos.*

FIGURE 1.8 *Greek red-figure drinking cup showing a lyre lesson. The teacher (left) has just strummed the strings using the plectrum in his right hand. Viewing the student's lyre from the back, we can see the tortoise-shell sound box, the strap around the left wrist, and the fingers of the left hand touching the strings.*

was stretched. As shown in Figure 1.8, the player held the lyre in front, resting the instrument on the hip and supporting it by a strap around the left wrist. The right hand strummed with the plectrum while the fingers of the left hand touched the strings, perhaps to produce harmonics or to dampen certain strings to prevent them from sounding.

The lyre was associated with Apollo, god of light, prophecy, learning, and the arts, especially music and poetry. Learning to play the lyre was a core element of education in Athens. Both men and women played the lyre, which was used to accompany dancing, singing, or recitation of epic poetry like Homer's *Iliad* and *Odyssey*; to provide music for weddings; or to play for recreation.

The kithara was a large lyre, used especially for processions and sacred ceremonies and in the theater, and normally played while the musician was standing. Figure 1.9 shows a kitharode, a singer accompanying himself on the kithara (see In Performance: Competitions and Professional Musicians).

Images from ancient Greece rarely show performers reading from a scroll or tablet while playing. It is clear from this and from the written record that the Greeks, despite having a well-developed form of notation by the fourth century BCE (see pp. 17–18), primarily learned music by ear; they played and sang from memory or improvised using conventions and formulas.

GREEK MUSICAL THOUGHT More writings about music survive from ancient Greece than from any earlier civilization. As a result, we know a great deal about Greek thought concerning music. There were two principal kinds of writings on music: (1) philosophical doctrines on the nature of music, its effects, and its proper uses; and (2) systematic descriptions of the materials of music, what we now call music theory. In both realms, the Greeks achieved insights and formulated principles that have remained important to this day. The most influential writings on the uses and effects of music are passages by Plato (ca. 429–347 BCE) in his *Republic* and *Timaeus* and by Aristotle (384–322 BCE) in his *Politics*. Greek music theory evolved continually from followers of Pythagoras (d. ca. 500 BCE) to Aristides Quintilianus (fourth century CE), its last important writer. As we might expect in a tradition lasting nearly a millennium, writers expressed differing views, and the meanings of many terms changed. The following emphasizes the features that were most characteristic of Greek music and most important for the later history of Western music.

In Greek mythology, music's inventors and earliest practitioners were gods and demigods, such as Apollo, Hermes, Amphion, and Orpheus. The word *music* (Greek *mousikē*) derives from the word for the Muses and originally denoted any of the arts associated with them, from history to dance. For the Greeks, music was both an art for enjoyment and a science closely related to arithmetic and astronomy. It pervaded all of Greek life, from work, the military, schooling, and recreation to religious ceremonies, poetry, and the theater.

Music, religion, and society

Music as a performing art was called *melos,* from which the word **melody** derives. The surviving Greek music is **monophonic**, consisting of a single melodic line, but that does not mean it was always performed that way. We know from pictures that singers accompanied themselves on lyre or kithara, but we do not know whether they sounded notes in the melody, played a variant of the melody (creating **heterophony**), or played an independent part

Music, poetry, and dance

IN PERFORMANCE

Competitions and Professional Musicians

From the sixth century BCE or earlier, the aulos and kithara were played as solo instruments, and competitions were held for the best performers. Contemporary accounts related that Sakadas of Argos won the prize for solo aulos playing at the Pythian Games in 586, 582, and 578 BCE, performing the *Pythic Nomos,* a virtuoso composition that portrayed Apollo's victory over the serpent Python. One writer attributes the piece to Sakadas, making him the earliest composer of instrumental music whose name we know.

Contests of kithara and aulos players, as well as festivals of instrumental and vocal music, became increasingly popular after the fifth century BCE. Indeed, the image in Figure 1.9 is from an amphora, a jar for wine or oil, awarded as a prize to the winner of a competition.

As instrumental music grew more independent, the number of virtuosos rose and the music became more complex and showy. When famous artists appeared, thousands gathered to listen. Some performers accumulated great wealth through concert tours or fees from rich patrons, particularly after they garnered fame by winning competitions. Among the musicians acclaimed for their performances were a number of women, who were excluded from competitions. But outside the

FIGURE 1.9 *Kitharode singing to his own accompaniment on the kithara, with his head tilted back, the fingers of his left hand touching some of the strings, apparently to dampen them, and the right hand holding the plectrum, which he has just strummed across the strings. Greek red-figure amphora from the fourth century BCE, attributed to the Berlin Painter.*

competitions, most professional performers were of low status, often slaves.

(creating **polyphony**). Melos could denote an instrumental melody alone or a song with text, and "perfect melos" was melody, text, and stylized dance movement conceived as a whole. For the Greeks, music and poetry were nearly synonymous. In his *Republic,* Plato defined melos as a blend of text, rhythm, and *harmonia* (here meaning relationships among pitches). In his *Poetics,* Aristotle enumerated the elements of poetry as melody, rhythm, and language, and noted that there was no name for artful speech, whether prose or verse, that did not include music. "Lyric" poetry meant poetry sung to the lyre; "tragedy" incorporates the noun *ōdē,* "the art of singing." Many other Greek words for different kinds of poetry, such as *hymn,* were musical terms.

Music and number   For many Greek writers, numbers were the key to the universe, and music was inseparable from numbers. Rhythms were ordered by numbers, because each note was some multiple of a primary duration. Although there is no evidence that Pythagoras himself knew or wrote anything about music, later writers attributed to him the discovery that the octave, fifth, and fourth, long recognized as consonances, are also related to numbers. These intervals are generated by the simplest possible ratios: for example, when a string is divided, segments whose lengths are in the ratio $2:1$ sound an octave, $3:2$ a fifth, and $4:3$ a fourth.

Harmonia   Because musical sounds and rhythms were ordered by numbers, they were thought to exemplify the general concept of **harmonia**, the unification of parts in an orderly whole. Through this flexible concept—which could encompass mathematical proportions, philosophical ideas, or the structure of society as well as a particular musical interval, scale type, or style of melody—Greek writers conceived of music as a reflection of the order of the universe.

Music and astronomy   Music was closely connected to astronomy through this notion of *harmonia.* Indeed, Claudius Ptolemy (fl. 127–48 CE), the leading astronomer of antiquity, was also an important writer on music. Mathematical laws and proportions were considered the underpinnings of both musical intervals and the heavenly bodies, and certain planets, their distances from each other, and their movements were believed to correspond to particular notes, intervals, and scales in music. Plato gave this idea poetic form in his myth of the "music of the spheres," the unheard music produced by the revolutions of the planets. This notion was invoked by writers throughout the Middle Ages and later, including Shakespeare in *The Tempest* and John Milton in *Paradise Lost,* and underlay the work of Johannes Kepler (1571–1630), the founder of modern astronomy.

MUSIC AND *ETHOS* Greek writers believed that music could affect **ethos**, one's ethical character or way of being and behaving. This idea was built on the view of music as a system of pitch and rhythm governed by the same mathematical laws that operated in the visible and invisible world. *Harmonia* in music reflected, and could therefore influence, *harmonia* (usually translated "harmony") in other realms. The human soul was seen as a composite whose parts were kept in harmony by numerical relationships. Because it reflected this orderly system, music could penetrate the soul and restore its inner harmony.

The doctrine of imitation   Through the doctrine of imitation outlined in his *Politics,* Aristotle described how music affected behavior: music that imitated a certain ethos aroused that ethos in the listener (see Source Reading). The imitation of an ethos was accomplished partly through the choice of *harmonia,* in the sense of a scale type or style of melody. While later centuries would interpret him

SOURCE READING

Aristotle on the Doctrine of Imitation, Ethos, and Music in Education

Music's importance in ancient Greek culture is shown by its appearance as a topic in books about society, such as Aristotle's *Politics*. Aristotle believed that music could imitate and thus directly affect character and behavior, and therefore should play a role in education.

❊

[Melodies] contain in themselves imitations of ethoses; and this is manifest, for even in the nature of the harmoniai there are differences, so that people when hearing them are affected differently and have not the same feelings in regard to each of them, but listen to some in a more mournful and restrained state, for instance the so-called Mixolydian, and to others in a softer state of mind, for instance the relaxed harmoniai, but in a midway state and with the greatest composure to another, as the Dorian alone of the harmoniai seems to act, while the Phrygian makes men divinely suffused; for these things are well stated by those who have studied this form of education, as they derive the evidence for their theories from the actual facts of experience. And the same holds good about the rhythms also, for some have a more stable and others a more emotional ethos, and of the latter some are more vulgar in their emotional effects and others more liberal. From these considerations therefore it is plain that music has the power of producing a certain effect on the ethos of the soul, and if it has the power to do this, it is clear that the young must be directed to music and must be educated in it. Also education in music is well adapted to the youthful nature; for the young owing to their youth cannot endure anything not sweetened by pleasure, and music is by nature a thing that has a pleasant sweetness.

Aristotle, *Politics* 8.5, trans. Harris Rackham, in SR 3, p. 29.

as attributing such effects to a mode or scale alone, Aristotle probably also had in mind the melodic turns and style characteristic of a *harmonia* and the rhythms and poetic genres most associated with it.

Plato and Aristotle both argued that education should stress gymnastics (to discipline the body) and music (to discipline the mind). In his *Republic,* Plato insisted that the two must be balanced, because too much music made one weak and irritable while too much gymnastics made one uncivilized, violent, and ignorant. Only certain music was suitable, since habitual listening to music that roused ignoble states of mind distorted a person's character. Those being trained to govern should avoid melodies expressing softness and indolence. Plato endorsed two *harmoniai*—the Dorian and Phrygian, because they fostered temperance and courage—and excluded others. He deplored music that used complex scales or mixed incompatible genres, rhythms, and instruments. In both his *Republic* and *Laws,* Plato asserted that musical conventions must not be changed, since lawlessness in art and education led to license in manners and anarchy in society. Similar ideas have been articulated by governments and guardians of morality ever since, and ragtime, jazz, rock, punk, and hip hop have all been condemned for these very reasons.

Music in education

Aristotle, in his *Politics,* was less restrictive than Plato. He held that music could be used for enjoyment as well as education and that negative emotions such as pity and fear could be purged by inducing them through music and drama. However, he felt that children of free citizens should not seek professional training on instruments or aspire to the virtuosity shown by performers in competitions because it was menial and vulgar to play solely for the pleasure of others rather than for one's own improvement.

GREEK MUSIC THEORY No writings by Pythagoras survive, and those of his followers exist only in fragments quoted by later authors. The earliest theoretical works we have are *Harmonic Elements* and *Rhythmic Elements* (ca. 330 BCE) by Aristoxenus, a pupil of Aristotle. Important later writers include Cleonides (ca. second or third century CE), Ptolemy, and Aristides Quintilianus. These theorists defined concepts still used today, as well as ones specific to ancient Greek music. Their writings show how much the Greeks valued abstract thought, logic, and systematic definition and classification, an approach that has influenced all later writing on music.

Rhythm   Only part of Aristoxenus's *Rhythmic Elements* survives, but enough remains to show us that rhythm in music was closely aligned with poetic rhythm. Aristoxenus defines durations as multiples of a basic unit of time. This scheme parallels Greek poetry, which features patterns of longer and shorter syllables, not stressed and unstressed syllables as in English.

Note, interval,   In *Harmonic Elements*, Aristoxenus distinguishes between *continuous*
and scale   movement of the voice, gliding up and down as in speech, and *diastematic* (or *intervallic*) movement, in which the voice moves between sustained pitches separated by discrete intervals. A melody consists of a series of ***notes***, each on a single pitch; an ***interval*** is formed between two notes of different pitch; and a ***scale*** is a series of three or more different pitches in ascending or descending order. Such simple definitions established a firm basis for Greek music and all later music theory. By contrast, Babylonian musicians apparently had no name for intervals in general, but had names only for intervals formed between particular pairs of strings on the lyre or harp. The greater abstraction of the Greek system marked a significant advance.

Tetrachord   Unique to the Greek system were the concepts of ***tetrachord*** and ***genus***
and genus   (pl. *genera*). A tetrachord (literally, "four strings") comprised four notes spanning a perfect fourth. There were three genera (classes) of tetrachord, shown in Example 1.1: ***diatonic***, ***chromatic***, and ***enharmonic***. The outer notes of the tetrachord were considered stationary in pitch, while the inner two notes could move to form different intervals within the tetrachord and create the different genera. Normally the smallest intervals were at the bottom, the largest at the top. The diatonic tetrachord included two whole tones and a semitone. In the chromatic, the top interval was a tone and a half (equal to a minor third) and the others semitones. In the enharmonic, the top interval was the size of two tones (equal to a major third) and the lower ones approximately quarter tones. All these intervals could vary slightly in size, giving rise to "shades" within each genus.

EXAMPLE 1.1 *Tetrachords*

Aristoxenus remarked that the diatonic genus was the oldest and most natural, the chromatic more recent, and the enharmonic the most refined and difficult to hear. Indeed, we have seen that the Babylonian system, which predated the Greek by more than a millennium, was diatonic.

Since most melodies exceeded a fourth, theorists combined tetrachords to cover a larger range. Two successive tetrachords were **conjunct** if they shared a note, as do the first two tetrachords in Example 1.2a, or **disjunct** if they were separated by a whole tone, as are the second and third tetrachords. The system shown in Example 1.2a, with four tetrachords plus an added lowest note to complete a two-octave span, was called the **Greater Perfect System**. The outer, fixed tones of each tetrachord are shown in open notes, the movable inner tones in black notes.

The Greater Perfect System

Each note and tetrachord had a name to indicate its place in the system. As we see in Example 1.2a, the middle note was called "mese" (middle), the tetrachord spanning a fourth below it "meson," the lowest tetrachord "hypaton" (first), and those above the mese "diezeugmenon" (disjunct) and "hyperbolaion" (of the extremes). The lowest note was called "proslambanomenos." There was also a *Lesser Perfect System*, shown in Example 1.2b, spanning an octave plus a fourth, with only one conjunct tetrachord ("synemmenon," conjunct) above the mese. The system was not based on absolute fixed pitch but on the intervallic relationships of notes and tetrachords to each other. The transcription here in the range *A–a'* is purely conventional.

In his *Harmonic Introduction*, Cleonides noted that in the diatonic genus the three main consonances of perfect fourth, fifth, and octave were subdivided into tones (T) and semitones (S) in only a limited number of ways, which he called **species**. This concept has proven useful in understanding Greek melody, medieval chant, Renaissance polyphonic music, and even twentieth-century music, so it is worthy of special attention. A fourth contains two tones and one semitone, and there are only three possible arrangements or species, illustrated in Example 1.3a: with the semitone at the bottom (as in *B–c–d–e*), on top (as in *c–d–e–f*), or in the middle (as in *d–e–f–g*). Example 1.3b shows the four species of fifth.

Species of consonances

The seven species of octave, shown in Example 1.3c, are combinations of the species of fourth and fifth, a division of the octave that became important in medieval and Renaissance theory. Cleonides identified the species by what "the ancients" supposedly called them. The first octave species, represented by the span from *B* to *b*, was Mixolydian, followed by Lydian (*c–c'*), Phrygian (*d–d'*), Dorian (*e–e'*), Hypolydian (*f–f'*), Hypophrygian (*g–g'*), and

EXAMPLE 1.2 *Scale systems*

a. The Greater Perfect System   *b. The Lesser Perfect System*

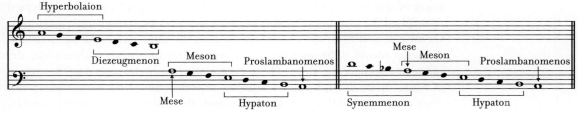

EXAMPLE 1.3 *Cleonides's species of consonances*

T = Tone   S = Semitone

a. Species of fourth

1.
S   T   T

2.
T   T   S

3.
T   S   T

b. Species of fifth

1.
S   T   T   T

2.
T   T   T   S

3.
T   T   S   T

4.
T   S   T   T

c. Species of octave

1. Mixolydian

S   T   T   S   T   T   T
1   1

4. Dorian

S   T   T   T   S   T   T
1   1

2. Lydian

T   T   S   T   T   T   S
2   2

5. Hypolydian

T   T   T   S   T   T   S
2   2

3. Phrygian

T   S   T   T   T   S   T
3   3

6. Hypophrygian

T   T   S   T   T   S   T
3   3

7. Hypodorian

T   S   T   T   S   T   T
4   1

Hypodorian (*a–a′*). These seven octave species parallel the seven diatonic tunings recognized by the Babylonians, suggesting a continuity of practice and perhaps of theory. As we will see in Chapter 2, some medieval theorists later adopted these names for their modes, but the latter do not match Cleonides's octave species, and the octave species lack one defining aspect of mode: a principal note on which a melody is expected to end.

Tonoi   The names Cleonides used for the octave species also had other associations. Dorian, Phrygian, and Lydian were ethnic names originally associated with styles of music practiced in different regions of the Greek world (see map in Figure 1.6). Plato and Aristotle used these names for *harmoniai,* in the sense of scale types or melodic styles. The addition of prefixes (such as Hypo-) multiplied the number of names in use. Later writers, including Aristoxenus, Cleonides, and Aristides Quintilianus, used the same names for up to fifteen different **tonoi**, defining a *tonos* as a scale or set of pitches within a specific range or region of the voice. These essentially involve transposing the system of tones up or down by some number of semitones. Like *harmoniai,* tonoi were associated with character and mood, the higher tonoi being energetic and the lower tonoi sedate.

We should not presume that all music from the Dorian region (southern Greece) used the Dorian octave species, Dorian *harmonia,* and Dorian tonos, or that these three concepts were equivalent or even closely related. Rather, it appears that writers over a span of almost a thousand years were applying familiar terms to new uses. This tendency for musicians to use old terms in new ways is common to all eras, and we will see it many times in other chapters. It can be frustrating when learning the history of music, since definitions seem always to be changing. What is most important here is to recognize that not all uses of words such as "harmonia" and "tonos" or of names such as "Dorian" mean the same thing, and to seek to understand how each is used in context.

ANCIENT GREEK MUSIC About forty-five pieces or fragments of ancient Greek music survive, ranging from the fifth century BCE to the fourth century CE. Most are from relatively late periods, composed to Greek texts when Greece was dominated by Rome, and most were recovered only in the twentieth century. All employ a musical notation in which letters and other signs are placed above the text to indicate notes and their durations. The earliest examples are two fragmentary choruses from plays by Euripides (ca. 485–406 BCE) with music that is probably by Euripides himself. Later pieces are more complete, including two Delphic hymns to Apollo, the second from 128–127 BCE; a short verse or epigram by Seikilos inscribed as an epitaph on a tombstone from around the first century CE; and four hymns by Mesomedes of Crete from the second century CE. Consistencies among these surviving pieces of music and the theoretical writings reveal a close correspondence between theory and practice.

The *Epitaph of Seikilos* (NAWM 1), inscribed on the tombstone in Figure 1.10, is shown in Example 1.4 in original notation and modern transcription. Over the modern notation appear alphabetical signs for the notes, and above those are marks

EXAMPLE 1.4 *Seikilos song in original notation (above the staff) and transcription*

As long as you live, be lighthearted. Let nothing trouble you. Life is only too short, and time takes its toll.

FIGURE 1.10 *Tomb stele from Tralles, near Aydin in southern Turkey, probably first century CE. It is inscribed with an epitaph by Seikilos with pitch and rhythm notation, transcribed in Example 1.4 and NAWM 1.*

indicating when the basic rhythmic unit should be doubled or tripled. The melody is diatonic, covers an octave in range, and uses the Phrygian octave species. The notation indicates the tonos called Iastian by the theorists, in which the system shown in Example 1.2a is transposed up a whole step (resulting in F♯ and C♯). The text balances extremes, counseling us to be lighthearted even while acknowledging death. This is consistent with the Iastian tonos, which is near

FIGURE 1.11 *Papyrus fragment, ca. 200 BCE, with part of a chorus from Euripides's Orestes, transcribed in NAWM 2.*

the middle of the fifteen tonoi in terms of range and thus suggests moderation. The melody seems similarly moderate in ethos, neither excited nor depressed, but balancing the rising fifth and thirds that begin most lines of the poem with falling gestures at the end of each line.

The fragment from *Orestes* (NAWM 2) by Euripides survives on a scrap of papyrus from about 200 BCE, shown in Figure 1.11. There are seven lines of text with musical notation above them, but only the middle portion of each line survives. The notation calls for either the chromatic or enharmonic genus along with the diatonic and for instrumental notes interspersed with the vocal. Both traits are noted in descriptions of Euripides's music, suggesting that this music is indeed by him.

In this choral ode, the women of Argos implore the gods to have mercy for Orestes, who has murdered his mother Clytemnestra for her infidelity to his father, Agamemnon. The poetry, and therefore the music, is dominated by a rhythmic pattern (the dochmaic foot) used in Greek tragedy for passages of intense agitation and grief. The music reinforces this ethos through small chromatic or enharmonic intervals, stark changes of register, and truncated lines filled in by instrumental notes.

These examples conform to the descriptions we have of Greek music and show (1) the role of instruments in supporting vocal music; (2) the idea that music imitates ethos; (3) the importance of poetic rhythm and structure in shaping melody; and (4) the use of diatonic, chromatic, and enharmonic genera as well as notation, tonoi, and octave species. While many questions remain, we can understand the musical culture of ancient Greece through the four types of evidence we have examined in this chapter.

MUSIC IN ANCIENT ROME

We know less about music in ancient Rome. There are plenty of images, some instruments, and thousands of written descriptions, but no settings of Latin texts survive from the Roman period.

The Romans took much of their musical culture from Greece, especially after the Greek islands became a Roman province in 146 BCE. As in Greece, lyric poetry was often sung. The *tibia* (Roman version of the aulos) played important roles in religious rites, military music, and theatrical performances, which included musical preludes and interludes, songs, and dances. The *tuba,* a long straight trumpet derived from the Etruscans (earlier residents of the Italian peninsula), was used in religious, state, and military ceremonies. The most characteristic instruments were a large G-shaped circular horn called the *cornu* and a smaller version, the *buccina.* Music was part of most public ceremonies and was featured in private entertainment and education. Cicero, Quintilian, and other writers state that cultivated people should be educated in music.

During the great days of the Roman Empire in the first and second centuries CE, art, architecture, music, philosophy, and other aspects of Greek culture were imported into Rome and other cities. Ancient writers tell of famous virtuosos, large choruses and orchestras, and grandiose musical festivals and competitions. Many of the emperors supported and cultivated music; Nero even aspired to personal fame as a musician and competed in contests. But with the economic decline of the empire in the third and fourth centuries, production of music on the large and expensive scale of earlier days ceased. Whatever direct influence Roman music may have had on later European developments seems to have left almost no traces.

THE GREEK HERITAGE

Although many details remain uncertain, we know that in the ancient world (1) melody was intimately linked with the rhythm and meter of words; (2) musicians relied on their memories and on knowledge of conventions and formulas, rather than reading from notation; and (3) philosophers conceived of music as an orderly system interlocked with the system of nature and as a force in human thought and conduct. To these elements the Greeks contributed two more: (4) an acoustical theory founded on science, and (5) a well-developed music theory.

Many of these characteristics continued in later Western music. Much vocal melody is shaped by the rhythm and meter of the words. Although notation became increasingly important in Western music from the ninth century on, many musical traditions still depend on memory and conventions. Notions of music as an orderly system and an influence on human behavior continue to this day. Plato's concern that changes in musical conventions threaten anarchy in society has been voiced repeatedly by those who resist change, and it echoes today among those lamenting current tastes in popular music.

Despite the virtual disappearance of ancient Greek music until its recovery in recent centuries, aspects of Greek musical thought influenced medieval church music and music theory. Musicians in the Renaissance and Baroque periods revived Greek concepts and joined them to modern ones to create new approaches, procedures, or genres, including rhetorical devices, expression of mood, chromaticism, monody, and opera, while citing Plato and Aristotle in defense of their innovations. Opera composers such as Peri in the seventeenth century, Gluck in the eighteenth, and Wagner in the nineteenth looked back to Greek tragedies for models of how to use music to convey drama. Twentieth-century composers such as Olivier Messiaen and Harry Partch revived Greek rhythms and tuning systems. And although ancient music is still little known, current musical concepts continue those addressed by ancient Greek writers, from diatonic scales to the use of music in educating the young and debates about the ethical and moral effects of music. The Greeks are still very much with us, and we will encounter them again and again as we explore the Western musical tradition.

Further Reading is available at digital.wwnorton.com/hwm10

THE CHRISTIAN CHURCH IN THE FIRST MILLENNIUM

The history of music in medieval Europe is intertwined with the history of the Christian church, the dominant social institution for most of the Middle Ages. Religious services were mostly sung or intoned rather than spoken. Many aspects of Western music, from notation to polyphony, first developed within church music. Most schools were part of the church, and most composers and writers on music were trained there. Moreover, because notation was invented for church music, that type of medieval music is the best preserved today.

This chapter traces the development of the church in the West and of its music, including the traditions and values that shaped how music was used and regarded, attempts to standardize liturgy and music as unifying forces, and the development of notation as a tool for specifying and teaching melody. The church drew on Greek philosophy and music theory, but also fostered practical theory for training musicians.

THE DIFFUSION OF CHRISTIANITY

Jesus of Nazareth, whose life and teachings gave rise to Christianity, was both a Jew and a subject of the Roman Empire. His teachings drew from Hebrew Scripture, yet his charge to "make disciples of all nations" (Matthew 28:19) sparked a movement that spread throughout the Roman world from Jerusalem, site of the Last Supper with his disciples and of his crucifixion, burial, and resurrection. St. Peter (d. ca. 64–68 CE), St. Paul (ca. 10–ca. 67 CE), and other apostles traveled the Near East, Greece, and Italy proclaiming Christianity as a religion open to all. The promise of salvation in the afterlife, and a strong sense of community and of equality between social classes, drew many converts. Women were attracted to Christianity and played major roles in its growth.

Roman subjects were allowed to practice their own religions as long as they also worshipped the Roman gods and emperors. But any group that worshipped a single god, denying all others, and sought to convert people of all nationalities was a threat to the state religion and thus to the state. Christians were at times persecuted; they had to gather in secret, and some were martyred. Yet Christianity gained adherents, even among leading Roman families.

Emperor Constantine I (r. 310–37) was introduced to Christianity by his mother Helena, and in 313 he issued the Edict of Milan, which legalized Christianity and allowed the church to own property. By then, Christianity was firmly established in most cities of the empire. In 392, Emperor Theodosius I r. 374–95) made Christianity the official religion and suppressed others, except for Judaism. The church organized itself on the model of the empire, with territories called dioceses and a hierarchy of local churches, bishops, and archbishops headed by patriarchs in Jerusalem, Rome, Constantinople, Antioch, and Alexandria. By 600, virtually the entire area once controlled by Rome was Christian, as we see in Figure 2.1.

Legalization and establishment

THE JUDAIC HERITAGE

Christianity sprang from Jewish roots, and some elements of Christian observances reflect those origins, chiefly the chanting of Scripture and the singing of **psalms**, sacred poems of praise from the Hebrew Book of Psalms.

The second Temple of Jerusalem, built in the late sixth century BCE on the site of the original Temple of Solomon and expanded by Herod the Great in 19–20 BCE, was a place for public worship until its destruction by the Romans in 70 CE. Observances centered around a sacrifice—usually of a lamb—performed by priests, assisted by Levites (members of the priestly class, including musicians), and witnessed by lay worshippers. Depending on the occasion, priests and sometimes worshippers ate some of the offering. Sacrifices were celebrated twice daily, with additional services on festivals and the Sabbath. During the ritual, a choir of Levites sang psalms assigned to that day, accompanied by harp and psaltery. Trumpets and cymbals were also used.

Temple rites

FIGURE 2.1 *The diffusion of Christianity.*

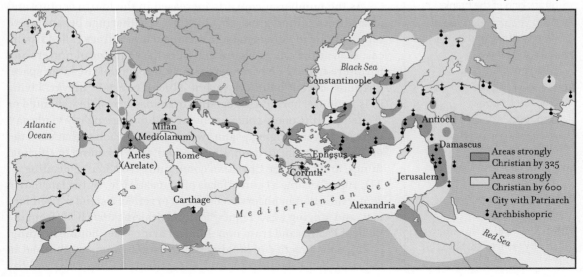

TIMELINE

In ancient times, synagogues were centers for readings and homilies rather than worship. Public reading from Scripture was probably performed in chant, as in later centuries, employing a system of ***cantillation*** (chanting of sacred texts) based on melodic formulas that reflected the phrase divisions of the text. Certain readings were assigned to particular days or festivals.

There are parallels between the Temple rites and the Christian Mass of later centuries (described in Chapter 3), including a symbolic sacrifice in which worshippers and priests partake of the body and blood of Christ in the form of bread and wine. Singing psalms assigned to certain days became a central element of all Christian observances, as did the synagogue practice of gathering in a meeting house to hear readings from Scripture and public commentary upon them. Yet the Christian services arose independently, with no direct derivation from either the Temple or the synagogue. The most immediate link to Jewish practice lies in the Mass, which commemorates the Last Supper Jesus shared with his disciples and thus imitates the festive Passover meal. Whether the melodies Christians used for singing psalms and chanting Scripture were drawn from those used in Jewish observances cannot be known, since none were written down until many centuries later.

MUSIC IN THE EARLY CHURCH

The earliest recorded musical activity of Jesus and his followers was singing hymns (Matthew 26:30, Mark 14:26). The apostle Paul exhorted Christian communities to sing "psalms and hymns and spiritual songs" (Ephesians 5:19, Colossians 3:16). In about 112, Pliny the Younger, governor of a Roman province in Asia Minor, reported the Christian custom of singing "a song to Christ as if to a god." Christians often met for communal evening meals at which they sang psalms and hymns.

As the number of converts increased in the fourth century and official recognition grew, small informal gatherings began to give way to public meetings in large rectangular buildings called basilicas, such as the one in Figure 2.2. Here the chanting of prayers and Scripture helped carry the text clearly throughout the large space. The most devout believers sought a life of constant prayer. Living in isolation as hermits or together in monasteries, they chanted or recited psalms many times each day and during nightly vigils as a form of prayer. Singing psalms was seen as a practice that used the pleasures of music to discipline the soul, turn the mind to spiritual things, and build the Christian community (see Source Reading, p. 24), and it became a central focus of monastic life. By the late fourth century, Christian observances began to reflect a standardized format, and singing was a regular feature, drawing texts both from the Book of Psalms and from non-biblical hymns (see Source Reading, p. 25). This practice of singing psalms and hymns was codified in the rites of the medieval church (described in Chapter 3) and has continued to this day, in modified forms, among Christians worldwide.

While songs of praise were encouraged, some early church leaders rejected other aspects of ancient practice. Influential Christian writers such as St. Basil (ca. 330–379), St. John Chrysostom (ca. 345–407), St. Jerome (ca. 340–420), and St. Augustine (354–430), known today as "the church fathers," interpreted the Bible and set down principles to guide the church. Like the ancient Greeks, they believed the value of music lay in its power to influence the ethos of listeners, for good or for ill. St. Augustine was so deeply moved by the singing of psalms that he feared the pleasure it gave him, while approving its ability to stimulate devout thoughts (see Source Readings, p. 24). Most church fathers rejected the idea of cultivating music simply for enjoyment and held to Plato's principle that beautiful things exist to remind us of divine beauty. This view underlay many pronouncements about music by church leaders and by later theologians of the Protestant Reformation.

FIGURE 2.2 *Interior view of the basilica Emperor Constantine built as a throne room and audience hall in Treveris (now Trier in Germany), then western capital of the Roman Empire, where he resided between 306 and 316. As Christians grew in number, they met for worship in basilicas like this one, where sung words carried better and more clearly throughout the large, resonant space than did spoken words.*

For early church leaders, music was the servant of religion, and only music that opened the mind to Christian teachings and holy thoughts was worthy of hearing in church. Believing that music without words cannot do this, most church fathers condemned instrumental music. The many references to harp, trumpet, and other instruments in the Book of Psalms and other Hebrew Scriptures were explained away as allegories. Although Christians may have used lyres to accompany hymns and psalms in their homes, instruments were not used in church. For this reason, the entire tradition of Christian music for over a thousand years was one of unaccompanied singing. Moreover, early converts associated elaborate singing, large choruses, instruments, and dancing with pagan spectacles. Avoiding such music helped to set off the Christian community from the surrounding pagan society and to proclaim the urgency of subordinating the pleasures of this world to the eternal welfare of the soul.

DIVISIONS IN THE CHURCH AND DIALECTS OF CHANT

Disputes about theology and governance led to several divisions among Christians during the first millennium. The most significant began in 395 with the partition of the Roman Empire into two parts. The Western Empire, ruled from Rome or Milan, suffered repeated invasions by Germanic tribes until it collapsed in 476. The Eastern Empire was centered at Constantinople (formerly Byzantium, now Istanbul), which Constantine rebuilt as his capital. Later known as the Byzantine Empire, it lasted over a thousand years, until Constantinople fell to the Turks in 1453.

St. Basil on Psalms and St. Augustine on the Usefulness and Dangers of Music

St. Basil (ca. 330–379) was a theologian, bishop of Caesarea (in modern-day central Turkey), and a strong advocate of communal monasticism. He extolled psalm-singing as a method that used the pleasure of music to convey a religious message and a sense of community.

❀

When the Holy Spirit saw that mankind was ill-inclined toward virtue and that we were heedless of the righteous life because of our inclination to pleasure, what did he do? He blended the delight of melody with doctrine in order that through the pleasantness and softness of the sound we might unawares receive what was useful in the words, according to the practice of wise physicians, who, when they give the more bitter draughts to the sick, often smear the rim of the cup with honey. For this purpose these harmonious melodies of the Psalms have been designed for us, that those who are of boyish age or wholly youthful in their character, while in appearance they sing, may in reality be educating their souls. For hardly a single one of the many, and even of the indolent, has gone away retaining in his memory any precept of the apostles or of the prophets, but the oracles of the Psalms they both sing at home and disseminate in the marketplace. And if somewhere one who rages like a wild beast from excessive anger falls under the spell of the psalm, he straightway departs, with the fierceness of his soul calmed by the melody.

A psalm is the tranquillity of souls, the arbitrator of peace, restraining the disorder and turbulence of thoughts, for it softens the passion of the soul and moderates its unruliness. A psalm forms friendships, unites the divided, mediates between enemies. For who can still consider him an enemy with whom he has sent forth one voice to God? So that the singing of psalms brings love, the greatest of good things, contriving harmony like some bond of union and uniting the people in the symphony of a single choir.

. . . Oh, the wise invention of the teacher who devised how we might at the same time sing and learn profitable things, whereby doctrines are somehow more deeply impressed upon the mind!

St. Basil, *Homily on the First Psalm*, trans. William Strunk Jr., Oliver Strunk, and James W. McKinnon, in SR 9 (2:1), pp. 121–22.

St. Augustine (354–430) is one of the most significant thinkers in the history of Christianity and of Western philosophy. In his *Confessions*, often considered the first modern autobiography, he expresses the tension between music's abilities to heighten devotion and to seduce with mere pleasure.

When I recall the tears that I shed at the song of the Church in the first days of my recovered faith, and even now as I am moved not by the song but by the things which are sung—when chanted with fluent voice and completely appropriate melody—I acknowledge the great benefit of this practice. Thus I waver between the peril of pleasure and the benefit of my experience; but I am inclined, while not maintaining an irrevocable position, to endorse the custom of singing in church so that weaker souls might rise to a state of devotion by indulging their ears. Yet when it happens that I am moved more by the song than by what is sung, I confess sinning grievously, and I would prefer not to hear the singer at such times. See now my condition!

St. Augustine, *Confessions* 10:33, trans. James W. McKinnon, in SR 13 (2:5), p. 133.

In the Eastern Empire, the church was under the control of the emperor. But as the Western Empire declined and collapsed, the bishop of Rome gradually asserted control of the church in the West. The Eastern Church continued to use Greek, the language of the early Christian apostles, but after the third

A Christian Observance in Jerusalem, ca. 400

In ca. 400 CE, a Spanish nun named Egeria on pilgrimage to Jerusalem described the services there, noting the psalms and hymns sung between prayers and Bible readings. Her eyewitness report is a crucial document of early Christian practices. This excerpt describes the Sunday morning Vigil, which became the service called Matins.

⸙

As soon as the first cock crows, straightway the bishop comes down and enters the cave in [the church of] the Anastasis [the site of the burial and resurrection of Jesus]. All the gates are opened, and the entire throng enters the Anastasis, where already countless lamps are burning, and when the people are within, one of the priests sings a psalm and all respond, after which there is a prayer. Then one of the deacons sings a psalm, similarly followed by a prayer, and a third psalm is sung by some cleric, followed by a third prayer and the commemoration of all. When these three psalms have been sung and the three prayers said, behold censers are brought into the cave of the Anastasis, so that the entire Anastasis basilica is filled with the smell. And then as the bishop stands behind the railings, he takes the Gospel book and goes to the gate and the bishop himself reads the Resurrection of the Lord. When the reading of it has begun, there is such moaning and groaning among everybody and such crying, that even the hardest of hearts could be moved to tears because the Lord has suffered so much for us. When the Gospel has been read, the bishop leaves and is led with hymns to the Cross, accompanied by all the people. There, again, one psalm is sung and a prayer said. Then he blesses the people, and the dismissal takes place. And as the bishop goes out, all approach to kiss his hand.

From *Itinerarium Egeriae* xxiv, 9–11, in *Music in Early Christian Literature*, ed. James W. McKinnon (Cambridge: Cambridge University Press, 1987), 115.

century, Latin, the language of the Roman Empire, was used in Rome and the West. Growing theological differences intensified the division until 1054, when it became permanent. The Western Church became the Roman Catholic Church, and the bishop of Rome was known as the pope (from *papa*, "father" or "bishop"). The Byzantine Church is the ancestor of the present-day Orthodox churches.

Early services were not rigidly determined but followed patterns common among Christian churches as a whole. As Christianity diversified, each branch or region evolved its own **rite**, consisting of a **church calendar**, or schedule of days commemorating special events, individuals, or times of year; a **liturgy**, or body of texts and ritual actions, assigned to each service; and a repertory of **plainchant**, or **chant**, unison song with melodies for the prescribed texts. The different regional repertories are called *chant dialects* by analogy to language. We will focus on the chant dialect most important for the history of Western music, **Gregorian chant**, with a brief discussion of **Byzantine chant** and mention of other dialects.

Rite, calendar, liturgy, and music

BYZANTINE CHANT Byzantine services included Scriptural readings—which were chanted using formulas that reflected the phrasing of the text—and psalms and hymns sung to fully developed melodies. Melodies were classed into eight modes or **echoi** (sing. *echos*), each with its own characteristic melodic formulas and scale type, which served as a model for the eight modes of the Western Church (see pp. 36–39).

The most characteristic Byzantine chants were hymns, which became more prominent in the liturgy and more highly developed in Eastern churches than in the West, with many different types. Hymn melodies were notated in books from the tenth century on, and many are still sung in Greek Orthodox services. Byzantine missionaries took their rite north to the Slavs starting in the ninth century, resulting in the establishment of the Russian and other Slavic Orthodox churches. The Greek texts were translated into local languages and the melodies adopted faithfully, but over time the traditions diverged.

WESTERN DIALECTS After the Western Empire disintegrated, control of western Europe was distributed among several peoples, including Celts, Angles, and Saxons in the British Isles; Franks in Gaul (approximately modern-day France) and western Germany; Visigoths in Spain; and Ostrogoths and Lombards in northern Italy. All eventually converted to Christianity and adopted the doctrines of the Western Church. A number of local and regional rites emerged, each with its own liturgy and body of chant. Besides the tradition of Rome, these included a variety of usages in Gaul, collectively known as Gallican chant; Celtic chant in Ireland and parts of Britain; Mozarabic or Old Hispanic in Spain; Beneventan in southern Italy; and Ambrosian in Milan.

Attempts at standardization From the eighth century through the eleventh century, popes and secular rulers allied with them tried to consolidate their authority by attempting to standardize what was said and sung in church services. In this process liturgy and music were valued not only for their religious functions but also as means of asserting centralized control, in parallel to the unified liturgy and church in the East under the Byzantine emperor. Over time, many of the local chant dialects disappeared or were absorbed into a single practice with authority emanating from Rome, although local variants in liturgy and chant melodies continued into modern times.

THE CREATION OF GREGORIAN CHANT The codification of liturgy and music under Roman leaders, helped by the Frankish kings, led to the repertory known as ***Gregorian chant***. The Schola Cantorum (School of Singers), the choir that sang when the pope officiated at observances, was established by the late seventh century and may have played a role in standardizing chant texts. By the middle of the eighth century, particular liturgical texts were assigned to services throughout the year in an order that was added to but not essentially changed until the sixteenth century.

Dissemination of the Roman chant to the Franks Between 752 and 754, Pope Stephen II sojourned in the Frankish kingdom with a retinue that may have included the Schola Cantorum. As a result of this visit, Pippin the Short (r. 751–68), who had become king of the Franks with the support of the previous pope, sought to import the Roman liturgy and chant and have them performed throughout his domain. The alliance between pope and king strengthened both, and in seeking to impose a common liturgy and body of music Pippin sought to consolidate his diverse kingdom, serving goals that were as much political as religious. His son Charlemagne (Charles the Great, r. 768–814), whose conquests expanded his territory throughout modern-day France, Belgium, the Netherlands, western Germany, Switzerland, and northern Italy, continued this policy, sending for singers from Rome to teach the chant in the north. Ties between Rome and the Franks were strengthened when Pope Leo III crowned Charlemagne emperor in Rome on Christmas 800, initiating what later became known as the Holy Roman Empire. Figure 2.3 shows Charlemagne with the pope, and Figure 2.4 a map of his empire.

We cannot be certain what melodies were brought from Rome to the Frankish lands, since they were not yet written down. Simple chants and melodies later preserved in almost identical form in multiple sources over a wide area may be very ancient. Some chants were probably altered by the Franks, either to suit northern tastes or to fit them into the system of eight modes imported from the Byzantine Church. Some melodies that became widely used were probably drawn from Gallican chant. Furthermore, many new melodies were developed in the north after the eighth century.

Books of liturgical texts from this time, which still lacked musical notation, attributed the developing repertory of chant used in Frankish lands to Pope Gregory I (St. Gregory the Great, r. 590–604), leading to the name *Gregorian chant*. But there is no evidence from his own time that Gregory played any role in composing or standardizing chant. The attribution of the chant repertory to Gregory may have arisen among the English, who adopted the Roman rite shortly before the Franks. They revered Gregory

FIGURE 2.3

Charlemagne wearing his crown as emperor, with Pope Leo III on the right. Gold funerary sculpture (ca. 1215) from the Palatine Chapel in the cathedral in Aachen, Charlemagne's capital.

FIGURE 2.4

Charlemagne's empire around 800.

FIGURE 2.5 *Pope Gregory the Great (r. 590–604) alternately listens to the dove (symbolizing the Holy Spirit) reveal the chants to him and dictates them to a scribe. Such manuscript illustrations arose from the legend that Gregory codified the chant that has been named for him and disseminated it in writing. So far as we know, chant was first notated more than two centuries later. Illumination from a twelfth-century French manuscript.*

as the founder of their church and consequently attributed their liturgy and its music to him. The legend arose that the chants were dictated to Gregory by the Holy Spirit in the form of a dove, as depicted in Figure 2.5. Both the ascription to a revered pope and this legend enhanced the perception of the chant as old, authentic, and divinely inspired, and thus facilitated its adoption. This is a fascinating development: it shows the desire to establish as traditional a repertory that was relatively new in this form and also the use of propaganda to do so.

After Charlemagne and his successors promulgated Gregorian chant throughout their lands, it gradually spread across almost all of western Europe, ultimately serving as the common music of a more unified church despite a great deal of local variation. It became one of the central tasks of monastery and cathedral schools to teach choirboys and future clerics the entire chant repertoire, following a similar curriculum and fostering a shared musical culture from Italy to England and from Poland to Spain. A final push to suppress most regional traditions and impose Gregorian chant throughout the Western Church came from popes in the eleventh century, aided by a new technology: a musical notation that could be read at sight.

THE DEVELOPMENT OF NOTATION

ORAL TRANSMISSION We can trace the development of the liturgy of the Western Church because the words were written down. Yet the melodies were learned by hearing others sing them, a process called oral transmission, leaving no written traces. We have only one fragment of Christian music before the ninth century—a hymn to the Trinity from the late third century found on a papyrus at Oxyrhynchos in Egypt and written in ancient Greek notation. But this notation had been forgotten by the seventh century, when Isidore of Seville (ca. 560–636) wrote that "Unless sounds are remembered by man, they perish, for they cannot be written down."

Oral composition and transmission

How chant melodies were created and transmitted without writing has been a subject of much study and controversy. Recent studies of memory and oral transmission suggest that medieval singers composed new songs by singing aloud, drawing on existing conventions and formulas, and fixed the melodies in their minds through repetition. Chant was learned by rote and sung from memory, requiring singers to retain hundreds of melodies, many sung only once a year. Chants that were simple, were sung frequently, or were especially distinctive and memorable may have been passed down with little change. Other chants may have been improvised or composed orally within strict conventions, following a given melodic contour and using opening, closing, and ornamental formulas appropriate to a particular text or place in the liturgy. This process resembles other oral traditions; for example, epic singers from the Balkans recited long poems seemingly by rote but actually using formulas associating themes, syntax, meters, line endings, and other elements.

EXAMPLE 2.1 *The second phrases of the first four verses of the Tract* Deus, Deus meus

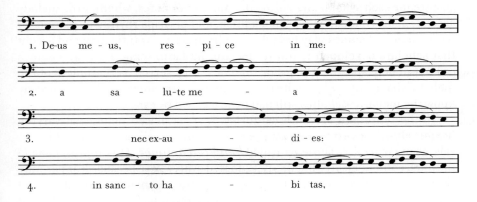

We can find evidence for such oral composition in the chants themselves. Example 2.1 compares parallel phrases from the first four verses of *Deus, Deus meus,* a Tract (for the categories of chant, see Chapter 3). Each phrase hovers around F, then descends to close with the same cadential figure at the mid-point of the verse. No two verses are exactly the same, but each features the same fund of formulas, which also appear in many other Tracts. Since Tracts were originally performed by a soloist, it seems likely that over the centuries singers developed a standard pattern, consisting of a general melodic contour and a set of formulas to delineate the phrases in each verse, and varied it to fit the syllables and accentuation of the particular text for each verse or chant. When the melodies were written down, these variations were preserved.

Traces of oral composition

STAGES OF NOTATION Individual variation was not suitable if the chants were to be performed in the same way each time in churches across a wide territory. During the eighth century, attempts were made to bring Roman chants to the Frankish lands and to train Frankish singers how to reproduce them. But as long as this process depended on memory and on learning by ear, melodies were subject to change, and accounts from both Roman and Frankish perspectives tell of melodies being corrupted as they were transmitted to the north. What was needed to stabilize the chants was **notation**, a way to write down the music. The earliest surviving books of chant with music notation date from the late ninth century, but their substantial agreement suggests to some scholars that notation may already have been in use in Charlemagne's time or soon thereafter. We have some written testimony to support this view, though scholars differ in interpreting the evidence, and the first definitive references to notation date from about 850. Whenever notation was invented, writing down the melodies was an attempt to ensure that from then on each melody would be sung in essentially the same way each time and in each place it was sung. Thus notation was both a result of striving for uniformity and a means of perpetuating that uniformity.

Notation developed through a series of innovations, each of which made the melodic outline more precise. The significant historical steps are shown in Figures 2.6–2.8, with modern equivalents in Examples 2.2–2.3. All show the Gradual *Viderunt omnes* from the Mass for Christmas Day (NAWM 3d).

In the earliest notations, signs called **neumes** (Latin *neuma,* meaning *Neumes* "gesture") were placed above the words, as in Figure 2.6, to indicate the melodic gesture for each syllable, including the number of notes, whether the melody ascended, descended, or repeated a pitch, and perhaps rhythm or manner of performance. Neumes may have derived from signs for inflection and accent that scholars developed to aid in declaiming Latin texts. Because neumes did not denote specific pitches or intervals, they served as reminders of the melodic shape but could not be read at sight by someone who did not already know the melody. Melodies still had to be learned by ear.

Heighted neumes   In the tenth and eleventh centuries, scribes placed neumes at varying heights above the text to indicate the relative size as well as direction of intervals, as in Figure 2.7. These are called ***heighted neumes***. This approach made the pitch contour clearer but was not adopted everywhere because it apparently sacrificed the more subtle performance indications in neumatic notation.

Lines, clefs, staff   The scribe of this manuscript scratched a horizontal line in the parchment corresponding to a particular note and oriented the neumes around that line. This was a revolutionary idea: a musical sign that did not represent a sound, but clarified the meaning of other signs. In other manuscripts, the line was labeled with a letter for the note it represented, most often F or C because of their position just above the semitones in the diatonic scale; these letters evolved into our clef signs, and with them each pitch in the melody was clear. The eleventh-century monk Guido of Arezzo (ca. 991–after 1033) suggested an arrangement of lines and spaces, using a line of red ink for F and of yellow ink for C and scratching other lines into the parchment. Letters in the left margin identify each line. This scheme was widely adopted, and the neumes were reshaped to fit the arrangement, as shown in Figure 2.8. From this system evolved a staff of four lines a third apart, the ancestor of our modern five-line staff.

Reading music   The use of lines and letters, culminating in the staff and clefs, enabled scribes to notate pitches and intervals precisely. In practice, pitch was still relative, as it had been for the Greeks; a notated chant could be sung higher or lower to suit the singers, but the notes relative to each other would form the same intervals. The new notation also freed music from its dependence on oral transmission. With his notation, Guido demonstrated that a singer could "learn a verse himself without having heard it beforehand" simply by reading the notes. This achievement was as crucial for the history of Western music as the invention of writing was for the history of language and literature.

Notation and   Music could now be made visible in notation, but it was still a sounding
memory   art. Oral transmission of music continued alongside written transmission, as it does today. Church choirs in many places continued to sing most chant from memory for centuries. Notation proved a valuable tool for memorization, because it is easier to remember words and music if we visualize them in our mind's eye. Moreover, notation made it possible to memorize music exactly, by fixing each note in a document that we can check if our memory fails us. Thus notation did not replace memory but enabled singers to learn hundreds of chants more quickly and to reproduce them verbatim each time.

Rhythm   Staff notation with neumes conveyed pitch but not duration. Some manuscripts contain signs for rhythm, but scholars have not agreed on their meaning. One modern practice is to sing chants as if all notes had the same basic value; notes are grouped in twos or threes, and these groups are flexibly combined into larger units. This interpretation, worked out in the late nineteenth and early twentieth centuries by the Benedictine monks of the Abbey of

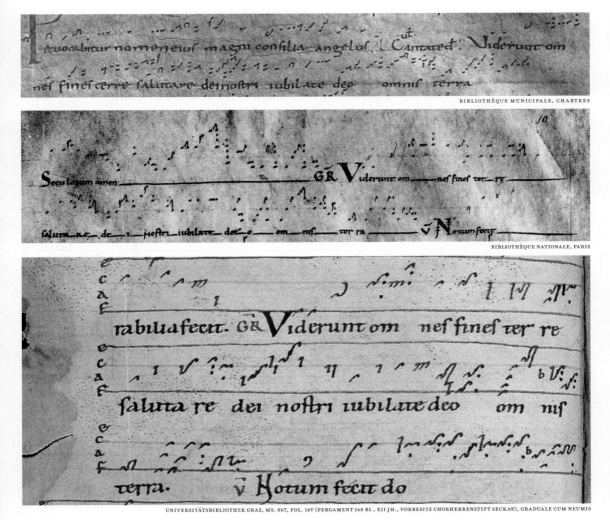

FIGURE 2.6 (TOP) *The Gradual* Viderunt omnes *in neumatic notation, from one of the earliest notated Graduals (books of chants for the Mass), copied in Brittany around 900. The neumes indicate melodic direction, but not precise notes or intervals.*

FIGURE 2.7 (MIDDLE) *The Gradual* Viderunt omnes *in heighted neumes, from the Gradual of St. Yrieix, near Limoges in southern France, copied in the second half of the eleventh century. The relative height of the neumes over the text indicates the relative pitch. A line scratched in the manuscript identifies the note A.*

FIGURE 2.8 (BOTTOM) *The Gradual* Viderunt omnes *in Guidonian notation, from a Gradual from Klosterneuberg, copied ca. 1150. In accordance with Guido's recommendations, the note F (low or high) is indicated with a red line, C with a yellow line, and lines and spaces are identified with letters in the left margin (F, A, C, and E).*

Solesmes in France under Dom Joseph Pothier and Dom André Mocquereau, was approved by the Catholic Church as conforming with the spirit of the liturgy. Whatever differences in duration there may have been in early practice, chant was almost certainly relatively free rather than metered in rhythm. Its movement has been compared to the flow of sand through an hourglass, the medieval standard for timekeeping, as opposed to the ticking of a clock.

SOLESMES CHANT NOTATION The Solesmes monks prepared modern editions of chant, which Pope Pius X proclaimed in 1903 as the official Vatican

EXAMPLE 2.2 *The Gradual* Viderunt omnes *in Solesmes chant notation*

All the ends of the earth have seen the salvation of our God: sing joyfully to God, all the earth. (Psalm 97:3–4 [98:3–4].) Verse: The Lord has made known His salvation; He has revealed His justice in the sight of the peoples. (Psalm 97:2 [98:2])

editions. Intended for use in church rather than historical study, they use a modernized form of chant notation. Examples 2.2 and 2.3 show the Gradual *Viderunt omnes* in Solesmes notation and in transcription, to facilitate comparison with each other and with the medieval neumatic notations in Figures 2.6–2.8. The staff in chant notation has four lines, one of which is designated by a clef as either middle C (𝄡) or the F below middle C (𝄢), like our modern C clefs and bass clef.

Reading chant notation   The notes and note groups are called neumes. A neume may carry only one syllable of text. Neumes are read left to right, except that when one note is below another the lower note is sung first; thus the melody on "fines" in Example 2.2 is c'–d'–c'–a. (Compare Figures 2.7 and 2.8, in which vertically stacked notes are sung from the top down instead of from the bottom up.) An *oblique neume* (◣) indicates three notes, so that "terrae" begins c'–a–c'. Diamond-shaped notes appear in descending patterns, as on "omnes," as a way to save space; they may receive the same values as square ones, although their name (*currentes*, meaning "running") suggests some quickening. The

EXAMPLE 2.3 *The Gradual* Viderunt omnes *transcribed in modern notation*

small notes indicate partially closing the mouth on a voiced consonant at the end of a syllable, as on the "n" in "Viderunt" in the first staff. The wavy line in ascending figures (∾, called *quilisma*), as on "omnis" in the third staff, may have indicated a vocal ornament. The only accidentals used are flat and natural signs, which can appear only on B. Unless it appears in a signature at the beginning of a line, a flat is valid only until the beginning of the next word or vertical division line; thus in "omnis terra" in the third staff of Example 2.2, the first word features B♭ (marked on "-mnis") and the second B♮ (because the flat has been canceled by beginning a new word).

The Solesmes editions include interpretive signs that are not in the medieval manuscripts. A dot doubles the value of a note, and a horizontal dash indicates a slight lengthening, as on "fines." Vertical lines of varied lengths show the division of a melody into sections (double barline), periods (full barline), phrases (half-barline), and smaller units (a stroke through the uppermost staff line). An asterisk in the text shows where the chorus takes over from the soloist.

MUSIC THEORY AND PRACTICE

THE TRANSMISSION OF GREEK MUSIC THEORY The chant repertory drew on sources in ancient Israel and in Christian communities from Syria and Byzantium in the East to Milan, Rome, and Gaul in the West. But for their understanding of this music, church musicians also drew on the music theory and philosophy of ancient Greece. During the early Christian era, this legacy was gathered, summarized, modified, and transmitted to the West, most notably by Martianus Capella and Boethius.

Martianus Capella   In his widely read treatise *The Marriage of Mercury and Philology* (early fifth century), Martianus described the seven liberal arts: grammar, dialectic, rhetoric, geometry, arithmetic, astronomy, and harmonics (music). The first three, the verbal arts, came to be called the *trivium* (three paths), while the last four, the mathematical disciplines, were called the *quadrivium* (four paths) by Boethius. The section on music is a modified translation of *On Music* by Aristides Quintilianus. Such heavy borrowing from earlier authorities was typical of scholarly writing and remained so throughout the Middle Ages.

Boethius (ca. 480–ca. 524) was the most revered authority on music in the Middle Ages. Born into a patrician family in Rome, Boethius became consul and minister to Theodoric, Ostrogoth ruler of Italy, and wrote on philosophy, logic, theology, and the mathematical arts. His *De institutione musica* (The Fundamentals of Music), written when Boethius was a young man and widely copied and cited for the next thousand years, treats music as part of the quadrivium. Music for Boethius is a science of numbers, and numerical ratios and proportions determine intervals, consonances, scales, and tuning. Boethius compiled the book from Greek sources, mainly a lost treatise by Nicomachus and the first book of Ptolemy's *Harmonics*. Although medieval readers may not have realized how much Boethius depended on other authors, they understood that his statements rested on Greek mathematics and music theory.

The most original part of his book is the opening chapters, where Boethius divides music into three types, depicted in Figure 2.9. The first type he calls **musica mundana** (the music of the universe), the numerical relations controlling the movement of stars and planets, the changing of the seasons, and the elements. Second is **musica humana** (human music), which harmonizes and unifies the body and soul and their parts. Last is **musica instrumentalis** (instrumental music), audible music produced by instruments or voices, which exemplifies the same principles of order, especially in the numerical ratios of musical intervals.

Boethius emphasized the influence of music on character. As a consequence, he believed music was

FIGURE 2.9 *Thirteenth-century manuscript illumination showing the three types of music Boethius described: at the top,* musica mundana, *the mathematical order of the universe, represented by stars, planets, and the four elements (fire, air, water, and earth); in the middle,* musica humana, *the harmony of the human body and soul, with men representing the four temperaments; and at the bottom,* musica instrumentalis, *audible music.*

important in educating the young, both in its own right and as an introduction to more-advanced philosophical studies. He valued music primarily as an object of knowledge, not a practical pursuit. For him music was the study of high and low sounds by means of reason and the senses; the philosopher who used reason to make judgments about music was the true musician, not the singer or someone who made up songs by instinct.

PRACTICAL THEORY Treatises from the ninth century through the later Middle Ages were more oriented toward practical concerns than were earlier writings. Boethius was mentioned with reverence, and the mathematical fundamentals of music that he transmitted still undergirded the treatment of intervals, consonances, and scales. But discussions of music as a liberal art did not help church musicians notate, read, classify, and sing plainchant or improvise or compose polyphony. These latter topics now dominated the treatises.

Among the most important treatises were the anonymous ninth-century *Musica enchiriadis* (Music Handbook) and an accompanying dialogue, *Scolica enchiriadis* (Comments on the Handbook). Both are directed at students who aspired to enter clerical orders, the former focusing on training singers, the latter combining such practical matters with mathematical approaches as a bridge to the quadrivium. *Musica enchiriadis* describes eight modes (see pp. 36–39), provides exercises for locating semitones in chant, and explains the consonances and how they are used to sing in polyphony (see Chapter 5). The most widely read treatise after Boethius was Guido of Arezzo's *Micrologus* (ca. 1025–28), a practical guide for singers that covers notes, intervals, the eight modes, melodic composition, and improvised polyphony. It was commissioned by the bishop of Arezzo, shown with Guido in Figure 2.10.

Musica enchiriadis and Micrologus

The medieval tone-system was based on the Greater and Lesser Perfect Systems of ancient Greece in the diatonic genus (see Chapter 1, pp. 14–15 and Example 1.2). Early medieval theorists used the Greek names for notes. In the late tenth century, a northern Italian treatise, *Dialogus de musica* (Dialogue on Music), introduced a simpler letter notation that was adopted by Guido of Arezzo and became the basis for our modern practice of naming notes using the letters A to G in every octave. As shown in Example 2.4, uppercase letters (A–G) were used for the bottom seven notes of the Greater Perfect System, lowercase letters (a–g) for the next octave, and double letters above that. The note a whole step below A was written Γ (the Greek letter *gamma*, equivalent to G), and Guido extended the range up to $_{d}^{d}$, beyond the two octaves of the Greek system. One difference between the Greater and Lesser Perfect Systems was whether the note above the mese (a) was a whole tone or a semitone higher, and the new letter notation accommodated both possibilities with two forms of the letter b: ♮ ("square b"), indicating a whole tone above a, and ♭ ("round b"), a semitone above a. The former sign evolved

Letter names for notes

EXAMPLE 2.4 *Guido of Arezzo's letter names for the notes of the tone-system*

FIGURE 2.10 *Guido of Arezzo (left) with his sponsor Theodaldus, bishop of Arezzo in northern Italy, calculating the string lengths for the notes in the medieval tone-system. Guido dedicated his* Micrologus *to the bishop. Twelfth-century manuscript of German origin.*

into our ♮ and ♯ signs, and the latter into our ♭ sign. The new letter system was easy to learn and to use, and it has been part of musical training ever since Guido.

THE CHURCH MODES An essential component of the curriculum for church musicians was the system of eight **modes**, adapted from the eight *echoi* of Byzantine chant (see pp. 25–26). Each chant was assigned to a particular mode, and learning the modes and classifying chants by mode made it easier to learn and memorize chants. Beginning in the late eighth century, books called *tonaries* grouped chants by mode. Characteristic melodic gestures associated with each mode also gave musicians a clear sense of mode. The modal system evolved gradually, and writers differed in their approaches. In its complete form, achieved by the tenth century, the system encompassed eight modes identified by number. Example 2.5a shows the important characteristics of each mode, especially its *final*, *range*, and *reciting tone*.

The modes are differentiated by the arrangement of whole and half steps in relation to the **final**, the main note in the mode and usually the last note in the melody. Each mode is paired with another that shares the same final. There are four finals, each with a unique combination of tones and semitones surrounding it, as shown in Example 2.5a, and outlined here:

Modes	Final	Interval below final	Intervals above final
1 and 2	D	tone	tone, semitone
3 and 4	E	tone	semitone, tone
5 and 6	F	semitone	tone, tone
7 and 8	G	tone	tone, tone

Because pitch is relative rather than absolute in chant, it is the intervallic relationship to the surrounding notes that distinguishes each final, not its absolute pitch.

Authentic and plagal modes

Modes that have the same final differ in **range**. The odd-numbered modes are called **authentic** and typically cover a range from a step below the final to an octave above it, as shown in Example 2.5a. Each authentic mode is paired with a **plagal** mode that has the same final but is deeper in range, moving from a fourth (or sometimes a fifth) below the final to a fifth or sixth above it. Because Gregorian chants are unaccompanied melodies that typically use a range of about an octave, the effect of cadencing around the middle of that octave in the plagal modes was heard in the Middle Ages as quite distinct from closing at or near the bottom of the range in the authentic modes. Modern

EXAMPLE 2.5 *The church modes*

目 = Final
O = Reciting Tone
T = Tone
S = Semitone

a. Modes with final, range, and reciting tone   *b. Modes with species of fifth and*
                                                           fourth and Greek names

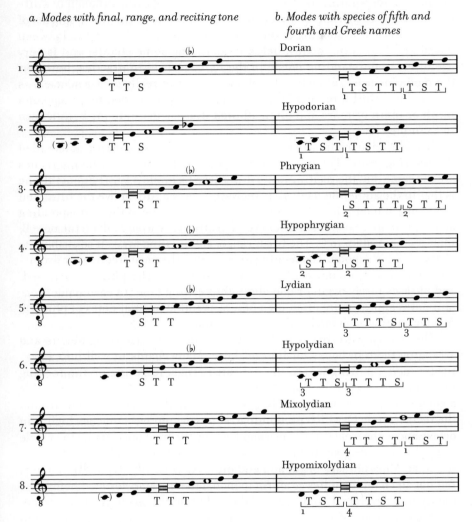

listeners may find this difference hard to understand, since we consider both *Row, Row, Row Your Boat* and *Happy Birthday* to be in the major mode, despite the different ranges of their melodies in respect to the tonic. But to medieval church musicians, the combination of different intervals around each final with different ranges relative to the final for authentic and plagal modes gave each of the eight modes an individual sound.

Only one chromatic alteration was normally allowed: B♭ often appears in place of B in chants that give prominence to F, as chant melodies in modes 1, 2, 4, 5, and 6 frequently do.

Use of B♭

Some theorists applied to the modes the species of fifth and fourth described by Cleonides (see Chapter 1 and Example 1.3), as diagrammed in

*Species of fifth
and fourth*

Example 2.5b. They divided each mode into two spans, marked by brackets in the example: a fifth rising from the final, and a fourth that is above the fifth in the authentic modes and below the final in the plagal modes. The arrangement of whole tones and semitones above each of the four finals is unique, corresponding to Cleonides's four species of fifth, although in a different order; each scale is then completed with one of the three species of fourth. This way of looking at the modes clarifies the relationship between plagal and authentic modes, helps in analyzing some chants, and is very useful for understanding music in the Renaissance. In practice, however, the modes as used in medieval melodies were not really octave species, as the diagrams in Example 2.5b might suggest, but extended to a range of a ninth or tenth or more and often allowed B♭ as a substitute for B, as shown in Example 2.5a.

Reciting tone   In addition to the final, each mode has a second characteristic note, called the **reciting tone**. The finals of corresponding plagal and authentic modes are the same, but the reciting tones differ (see Example 2.5). The general rule is that in the authentic modes the reciting tone is a fifth above the final, and in the plagal modes it is a third below the reciting tone of the corresponding authentic mode, except that whenever a reciting tone would fall on the note B, then it is moved up to C. The final, range, and reciting tone all contribute to characterizing a mode. The reciting tone is often the most frequent or prominent note in a chant, or a center of gravity around which a phrase is oriented, and phrases rarely begin or end above the reciting tone. In each mode, certain notes appear more often than others as initial or final notes of phrases, further lending each mode a distinctive sound.

Modal theory   The modes were first codified as a means for classifying chants and
and chant   arranging them in books for liturgical use. Many chants fit well into a particular mode, moving within the indicated range, lingering on the reciting tone, and closing on the final. *Viderunt omnes* in Example 2.3 on page 33 is a good example. In mode 5, it begins on the final F; rises to circle around the reciting tone C, which predominates in most phrases; touches high F an octave above the final three times and E below the final once, using the whole range of the mode; uses both B and B♭, as allowed in this mode; and closes on the final. Most phrases begin and end on F, A, or C, as is typical of mode 5. But not all chant melodies conform to modal theory. Many existed before the theory was developed, and some of these do not fit gracefully in any mode. Chants composed after the modes were codified in the tenth century often have a very different style from older ones, making the mode clear from the outset and using few if any of the standard melodic figures associated with each mode in older chants.

Application of   Beginning in the ninth century, some writers applied the names of the
Greek names   Greek scales to the church modes, as shown in Example 2.5b. Misreading Boethius, they mixed up the names, calling the lowest mode in the medieval system (*A–a*) Hypodorian, the highest in Cleonides's arrangement of the octave species (*a–a'*), and moving through the other names in rising rather than descending order (compare Example 2.5b with Example 1.3c). In the resulting nomenclature, plagal modes had the prefix Hypo- (Greek for "below") added to the name of the related authentic mode. Although medieval treatises and liturgical books usually refer to the modes by number, the

EXAMPLE 2.6 *Hymn,* Ut queant laxis

That thy servants may freely sing forth the wonders of thy deeds, remove all stain of guilt from their unclean lips, O Saint John.

Greek names are often used in modern textbooks and in discussions of modern music and jazz.

The attempts by medieval theorists to link their music to ancient Greek theory, despite the poor fit between the modes (which were based on final, reciting tone, and ranges exceeding an octave) and the Greek system (which was based on tetrachords, octave species, and tonoi), show how important it was for medieval scholars to ground their work in the authoritative and prestigious Greek tradition.

SOLMIZATION To facilitate sight-singing, Guido of Arezzo, the inventor of the musical staff and author of the *Micrologus* (see p. 35), introduced a set of syllables corresponding to the pattern of tones and semitones in the succession C–D–E–F–G–A. He noted that the first six phrases of the hymn *Ut queant laxis,* shown in Example 2.6, began on those notes in ascending order, and he used their initial syllables for the names of the steps: *ut, re, mi, fa, sol, la.* These **solmization** syllables (so called from *sol-mi*) are still used, although the most common version of the set substitutes *do* for *ut* and adds *ti* above *la.*

Singers used solmization syllables then as they do now, to help form mental sound images of the intervals and apply them when singing. Within this set of six syllables are all the intervals singers were likely to find in chant melodies: the step between *mi* and *fa* is a semitone, and the other steps are whole tones; there are two minor thirds (*re–fa* and *mi–sol*) and two major thirds (*ut–mi* and *fa–la*); and all the fourths and fifths are perfect. Learning to associate these intervals with particular syllables made it easier to sing the intervals correctly.

Later theorists mapped the solmization syllables onto the entire range of notes used in medieval music. Because the semitones E–F, B–C, and A–B♭ must be solmized with the semitone *mi–fa*, the six-syllable pattern may be placed in seven different positions in this range, as shown in Example 2.7. (The chromatic semitone B♭–B♮ does not occur in chant.) A singer who had memorized these positions was ready to sing any melody using the syllables. Within this range, each specific note in the tone-system was named by its letter and the solmization syllables used with that note in that octave. For any note in Example 2.7, its medieval name can be found by reading its letter and syllables from bottom to top. Thus the lowest note was called *gamma ut,* from which comes our word *gamut,* and middle C was *c sol fa ut.*

Using solmization to learn a melody that exceeded a six-note range   *Mutation*

EXAMPLE 2.7 *Solmization syllables in the medieval gamut*

EXAMPLE 2.8 *End of Gradual* Viderunt omnes *in solmization syllables*

re re fa fa re mi ut re fa=sol mi fa re=sol fa mi fa sol la sol fa sol la=mi sol mi re ut re mi sol sol re fa mi ut
4   3   2   3

required shifting the syllable set to different positions. For example, in the passage from *Viderunt omnes* in Example 2.8, no position can be found that contains all the notes: the first ten can be sung with the syllable set beginning on G (position 4 in Example 2.7), but the singer has to shift one position down to accommodate the B♭, shift down again for the low E, and shift back up for the C and B♭ in the cadential phrase. Shifting positions was done through a process called *mutation*, in which a singer renamed a note to fit the new syllable set, as shown in the example.

Guidonian hand   Followers of Guido developed a pedagogical aid called the "Guidonian hand," shown in Figure 2.11. Pupils were taught to sing intervals as the teacher pointed with the index finger of the right hand to the different joints of the open left hand. Each joint stood for one of the notes in the tone-system; any other note, such as F♯ or E♭, was considered to be "outside the hand."

Using solmization and staff notation, Guido boasted that he could "produce a perfect singer in the space of one year, or at the most in two," instead of the ten or more it usually took teaching melodies by rote. No statement more pointedly shows the change from three centuries earlier, when all music was learned by ear and the Frankish kings

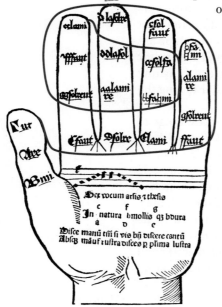

FIGURE 2.11 *The "Guidonian hand," a mnemonic device used for locating the pitches of the tone-system shown in Example 2.7 by pointing to the joints of the left hand. Although credited to Guido, the hand was probably a later application of his solmization syllables. The notes are laid out in a counterclockwise spiral, beginning with the lowest note (gamma ut) at the tip of the thumb, moving down the thumb, across the base of each finger, up the little finger, across the tips, down the index finger, and around the middle joints, then to the back knuckle of the middle finger. (The red line has been added to show this spiral.)*

struggled to make the chant consistent across their lands, or more clearly illustrates how innovations in church music sprang from the desire to carry on tradition.

ECHOES OF HISTORY

The stories in this chapter bear witness to astounding continuities and to the transformation of traditions by new circumstances. Although we do not have any music from the ancient Jews or early Christians, their musical customs resonated through the Middle Ages and beyond to the present. The texts of the psalms sung in the Temple and the Scripture chanted in the synagogue are still in use in both Jewish and Christian services. The monastic practice of singing psalms became a central focus of Christian observances. Early church leaders, drawing on Greek views of music while rejecting pagan customs, elevated worship over entertainment and singing over instrumental music, attitudes that held sway for centuries and persist today. Attempts by popes and secular rulers to consolidate control and unify their realms led to standardized liturgies and fixed melodies that were assigned to certain texts and days. The adoption by the Western Church of the eight church modes, based on the Byzantine echoi, shows both a link to the Eastern Church and a desire to systematize and classify the vast repertory of chant, which helped to make it easier to memorize. Promoting and preserving that repertory in turn led to notation and solmization, which developed over time and are still part of musical life. Many particular features of Western notation have been around for a millennium, including staff lines, clefs, and notes placed above the text and arranged so that higher notes indicate higher pitches. The invention of a notation that could record pitches and intervals precisely and could be read at sight was decisive in the later evolution of Western music, which more than other musical traditions is not just played and heard, but written and read. Indeed, notation is the very reason why we have a thousand years of music we can still perform and hear, and why books like this can be written.

Almost as important, the codification of Gregorian chant and its diffusion in notation made it the basis for much new music from the ninth through the sixteenth centuries. That these events took place under the Franks was significant, since Charlemagne's empire was the political and cultural center of western Europe. From his day through the fourteenth century, the most important developments in European music took place in the area he once ruled.

Further Reading is available at digital.wwnorton.com/hwm10

ROMAN LITURGY AND CHANT

Gregorian chant is one of the great treasures of Western civilization. Like Romanesque architecture, it stands as a memorial to religious faith in the Middle Ages, embodying the community spirit and artistic sensibility of the time. This body of chant includes some of the oldest and most beautiful melodies, and it served as the basis for much later music.

As beautiful as the chants are, they cannot be separated from their ceremonial context. We saw in Chapter 2 how Gregorian chant was codified and notated after centuries of development as an oral tradition and how it played a unifying role in the Western Church. In this chapter, we will relate chant to liturgy and see how each chant is shaped by its role, text, and manner of performance. We will also see how new chants and types of chant were added to the authorized liturgical chant during a wave of creativity around the margins of the repertory.

THE ROMAN LITURGY

Gregorian chant is music for Christian religious observances. Tunes vary from simple recitation to elaborate melodies, depending on their role in the liturgy. Thus understanding chant requires some knowledge of the services in which it is used. The Roman liturgy is complex, resulting from a long history of addition and codification that was largely unknown to those who participated in services. This historical framework can help us comprehend both the shape of the liturgy and the diversity of chant.

PURPOSE OF THE LITURGY The role of the church was to teach Christianity and to aid in saving souls. Over the centuries, as missionaries spread the faith across Europe from Spain to Sweden, they taught the precepts of church doctrine: the immortality of each person's soul; the Trinity of Father, Son, and Holy Spirit; Jesus's crucifixion, resurrection, and ascension into heaven; salvation and eternal heavenly life for those judged worthy; and damnation in hell for the rest. One purpose of religious services was to reinforce these lessons for worshippers, making clear the path to salvation through the church's teachings. This purpose was served chiefly by the liturgy, the texts that were spoken or sung and the rituals that were performed during each service. The role of music was to carry those words, accompany those rituals, and inspire the faithful.

At the same time, the words, prayers, and singing were directed to God, who was in some respects the primary audience. The daily cycle of services in monasteries and convents, attended only by the participants, reflected the belief that humans on earth, like the angels in heaven, should offer unceasing praises to God. Thus the liturgy and music of the Roman Church had dual aims: addressing God and reinforcing the faith of those in attendance.

CHURCH CALENDAR Part of teaching Christianity was repeating the stories of Jesus and of the saints, exemplary Christians whom the church raised up as models of faith or action. Every year, the church commemorated each event or saint with a feast day, in a cycle known as the ***church calendar***. The most important feasts are Christmas (December 25), marking Jesus's birth, and Easter, celebrating his resurrection and observed on the Sunday after the first full moon of spring. Both are preceded by periods of preparation and penitence: Advent begins four Sundays before Christmas, and Lent starts on Ash Wednesday, forty-six days before Easter. Although much of each religious service is the same at every observance, other aspects change with the day or season.

MASS The most important service in the Roman Church is the ***Mass***, which evolved from commemorations of the Last Supper of Jesus with his disciples (Luke 22:14–20). The central act, shown in Figure 3.1, is a symbolic reenactment of the Last Supper in which a priest consecrates bread and wine, transformed in essence into the body and blood of Christ, and offers them to worshippers in communion. This ritual fulfills Jesus's commandment to "do this in remembrance of me" (1 Corinthians 11:23–26) and reminds all present of his sacrifice for the atonement of sin. Over time, other ritual actions and words were added, including prayers, Bible readings, and psalm-singing. The Mass is performed every day in monasteries, convents, and major churches, on Sundays in all churches, and more than once on the main feast days.

The Mass as it stood by the eleventh century is described in Music in Context: The Experience of the Mass (pp. 44–45). (For the complete Mass for Christmas Day, see NAWM 3.) The most important musical items, each sung to an independent melody by the choir and its soloists, are shown in red in Figure 3.2. The other items were either intoned (recited to a simple melodic formula) or spoken by the priest or an assistant.

The texts for certain parts of the Mass vary from day to day and are collectively called the ***Proper of the Mass***. The texts of other parts, called the ***Ordinary of the Mass***, do not change, although the melodies may vary. The Proper chants are called by their function, the Ordinary chants by their initial words. The sung portions of the Ordinary were originally performed by the congregation, but were later taken over by the choir, which was all male (or, in convents, all female).

FIGURE 3.1 *A priest consecrates the wine and bread for communion, the central ritual of the Mass, in an eleventh-century German ivory carving.*

Proper and Ordinary

The Experience of the Mass

The Mass was the focal point of medieval religious life. For the largely illiterate populace, it was their main source of instruction, where they were told what to believe and how to live. It was up to the church to present those fundamental truths in a way that would engage and inspire, gripping not only the mind but also the heart.

The building where Mass was celebrated was designed to evoke awe. Whether a simple church or a grand cathedral, it was likely to be the tallest structure most people would ever enter. The high ceiling and windows drew the eye heavenward. Pillars and walls were adorned with sculptures, tapestries, or paintings depicting pious saints, the life of Jesus, or the torments of hell, each image a visual sermon. In these resonant spaces, the spoken word was easily lost, but singing carried words clearly to all corners.

European Christians, especially in central and northern Europe, were not long removed from old pagan customs of propitiating the gods to ensure good crops or prevent misfortune, and they looked to Christian observances to serve the same role. Life for most was hard, and with the constant threat of disease, famine, and war, average life expectancy was under thirty years. Worship in a well-appointed church, conducted by clergy arrayed in colorful vestments, using chalices, crosses, and books bedecked with gold, and singing heavenly chants, offered not only an interlude of beauty, but a way to please God and secure blessings in this life and the next.

In such a space, the Mass begins with the entrance procession of the celebrant (the priest) and his assistants to the altar, incense wafting through the air. The choir sings a psalm, the *Introit* (from Latin for "entrance"). After all are in place, the choir continues with the *Kyrie*, whose threefold invocations of *Kyrie eleison* (Lord have mercy), *Christe eleison* (Christ have mercy), and *Kyrie eleison* capture the hopes of the worshippers and symbolize the Trinity of Father, Son, and Holy Spirit. The Greek words and text repetitions reflect the Kyrie's origins in a Byzantine processional litany, a form in which participants repeat a short prayer in response to a leader. On Sundays and feast days (except in Advent and Lent), there follows the *Gloria*, or *Greater Doxology*, a formula of praise to God that encapsulates the doctrine of the Trinity and again asks for mercy. The priest then intones the Collect, a prayer on behalf of all those present.

After these introductory items, the next section of the Mass focuses on Bible readings, florid chants, and church teachings. Here the service offers instruction, familiarizing worshippers (at least, those who understand Latin) with the Scriptures and central tenets of the faith. First the subdeacon intones the Epistle for the day, a passage from the letters of the apostles. Next come two elaborate chants sung by a soloist or soloists with responses from the choir: the *Gradual* (from Latin *gradus*, "stairstep," from which it was sung) and the *Alleluia* (from the Hebrew *Hallelujah*, "praise God"), both based on psalm texts. These chants are the musical high points of the Gregorian Mass, performed when no ritual is taking place and text and music are the center of attention. On some days in the Easter season, the Gradual is replaced by another Alleluia as a sign of celebration; during Lent, the joyful Alleluia is omitted or replaced by the more solemn *Tract*, a florid setting of several verses from a psalm. On some occasions the choir sings a *sequence* after the Alleluia. The deacon then intones the Gospel, a reading from one of the four books of the New Testament that relate the life of Jesus. The priest may offer a sermon. On Sundays and important feast days, this section of the Mass concludes with the *Credo*, a statement of faith summarizing church doctrine and telling the story of Jesus's incarnation, crucifixion, and resurrection.

Next the priest turns from words to actions. As he prepares the bread and wine for communion, the choir sings the *Offertory*, a florid chant on a psalm. There follow spoken prayers and the

Secret, read in silence by the priest. The Preface, a dialogue between priest and choir, leads into the **Sanctus** (Holy, holy, holy), whose text begins with the angelic chorus of praise from the vision of Isaiah (Isaiah 6:3). The priest speaks the Canon, the core of the Mass that includes the consecration of bread and wine. He sings the Lord's Prayer, and the choir sings the **Agnus Dei** (Lamb of God), which like the Kyrie was adapted from a litany. In the medieval Mass, the priest then takes communion, consuming the bread and wine on behalf of all those assembled, rather than sharing it with everyone as was the custom earlier (and again today). After communion, the choir sings the **Communion**, based on a psalm. The priest intones the Postcommunion prayer, and the priest or deacon concludes the service by singing *Ite, missa est* (Go, it is ended), with a response by the choir; from this phrase came the Latin name for the entire service, *Missa*, which became the English "Mass." When the Gloria is omitted, *Ite, missa est* is replaced by *Benedicamus Domino* (Let us bless the Lord).

Throughout the Mass, the music serves both to convey the words and engage the worshippers.

FIGURE 3.2 *The Mass.*
Red: Sung by choir   Blue: Intoned   Green: Spoken

	PROPER	ORDINARY
Introductory section	1. Introit	
		2. Kyrie
		3. Gloria
	4. Collect	
Readings and psalms	5. Epistle	
	6. Gradual	
	7. Alleluia (or Tract)	
	8. Sequence (on major feasts)	
	9. Gospel	
	10. Sermon (optional)	
		11. Credo
Prayers and communion	12. Offertory	
		13. Prayers
	14. Secret	
	15. Preface	
		16. Sanctus
		17. Canon
		18. Pater noster (Lord's Prayer)
		19. Agnus Dei
	20. Communion	
	21. Postcommunion	
		22. Ite, missa est

Evolution of the Mass

Early forms of the ceremony that became the Mass fell into two parts. The community heard prayers, readings from the Bible, and psalms, often followed by a sermon. Then the catechumens, those receiving instruction in Christian beliefs but not confirmed in the church and thus unable to receive communion, were dismissed, ending the first part. The faithful offered gifts to the church, including bread and wine for the communion. The priest said prayers of thanksgiving, consecrated the bread and wine, and gave communion, accompanied by a psalm. After a final prayer, he dismissed the faithful.

From this outline, the Mass gradually emerged (see Music in Context: The Experience of the Mass). The opening greeting was expanded into an introductory section. The first part of the early Mass became a section focused on Bible readings and psalms; the final part centered on offerings and prayers leading to communion. The main musical items of the Ordinary—the Kyrie, Gloria, Credo, Sanctus, and Agnus Dei—were relatively late additions. Ironically, these are now the portions most familiar to musicians, because their texts do not change and because almost all compositions called "mass" from the fourteenth century onward are settings of these portions only.

PROPER FOR CHRISTMAS MASS While the Ordinary chants are a familiar part of every Mass, it is the Proper that links the service to a particular day of the church year and gives it a more specific meaning. For example, in the Mass for Christmas Day (NAWM 3), each element of the Proper addresses the nativity of Jesus or places it in a broader theological context. Some of the texts are drawn from psalms or other books of the Hebrew Scriptures, and it is through their juxtaposition with each other and with New Testament passages that a Christian message emerges. The Introit (NAWM 3a) announces the birth of a child who shall rule, using words from Isaiah 9:6 that Christians understood to prophesy Jesus's birth, and continues with a celebratory psalm verse. The Gradual (NAWM 3d) uses verses from the same psalm that declare the revelation of salvation to all peoples, and the Alleluia (NAWM 3e) hails this sanctified day when a great light descended to earth. These elaborate and florid chants come between the two main readings in this Mass; the Epistle, from the letter to the Hebrews (1:1–12), relates the importance of Jesus as the son of God, and the Gospel, from John 1:1–14, depicts Jesus as the Word of God born into human form. The Offertory (NAWM 3g) sets psalm verses that acknowledge God's dominion over heaven and earth, and the Communion (NAWM 3j) returns to the opening words of the Gradual. Together, these chants celebrate Jesus's birth and summarize the Christian theology that regards him as Savior, Lord, son of God, Word of God, and light of the world.

THE OFFICE Early Christians often prayed and sang psalms at regular times throughout the day and night, in private or public gatherings. These observances were codified in the **_Office_**, a series of eight services that since the early Middle Ages have been celebrated daily at specified times, as shown in Figure 3.3. The Office was particularly important in monasteries and convents, where Mass and Office observances occupied several hours every day and night. All members of the community sang in the services. Figure 3.4 depicts this central focus of monastic life.

Monasteries and convents in the Roman Church followed the liturgy for the Office codified in the *Rule of St. Benedict* (ca. 530), a set of instructions on running a monastery. The Office liturgy for churches outside monasteries differed in some respects, and both texts and music varied considerably

FIGURE 3.3 *The Office.*

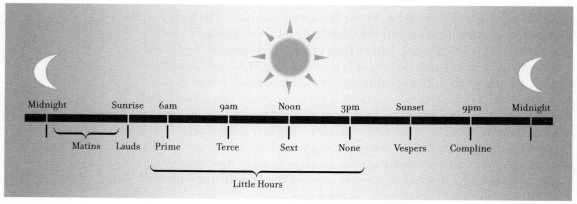

over time and from place to place, resulting in a less stable and more local repertory of chants for the Office than for the Mass. Office observances include several psalms, each with an **antiphon**, a chant sung before and after the psalm; lessons (Bible readings) with musical responses called **responsories**; hymns; **canticles**, poetic passages from parts of the Bible other than the Book of Psalms; and prayers. Over the course of a normal week, all 150 psalms are sung at least once. The most important Office services, liturgically and musically, are Matins, Lauds, and Vespers.

LITURGICAL BOOKS Texts and music for services were gathered in books, copied by scribes in the Middle Ages and later printed under church authority. Texts and some music for the Mass are in the *Missal,* and the chants sung by the choir in the *Gradual.* Texts and some music for the Office are collected in the *Breviary,* and the music for the choir in the *Antiphoner.*

In the late nineteenth and early twentieth centuries, monks of the Benedictine Abbey of Solesmes (see pp. 30–31) prepared modern editions of the *Gradual* and *Antiphoner* and issued the *Liber usualis* (Book of Common Use), which contains the most frequently used texts and chants for the Mass and Office. The Solesmes

COURTESY THE BRITISH LIBRARY

FIGURE 3.4 *Monks and choirboys singing in the choir, celebrating one of the many services that took up most of each day in a monastery. Late-medieval manuscript illumination.*

editions were adopted as the official books for use in services and are used in most recordings of Gregorian chant. Although these editions reflect a modern standardization of a repertory that varied over time and from place to place, they provide a good introduction to Gregorian chant and will serve as the basis for the discussion here and in NAWM 3 (Mass) and NAWM 4 (Vespers).

CHARACTERISTICS OF CHANT

Gregorian chants are very diverse in style, with varying approaches to performance, treatment of the text, and melodic character. These stylistic differences reflect the disparate functions and histories of the items in the liturgy, and will help guide us through the genres of chant.

Singers use three manners of performance for chant: **responsorial** (from "response"), in which a soloist alternates with the choir or congregation; **antiphonal** (from Greek for "sound-returning"), in which two groups or halves of the choir alternate; and **direct**, without alternation. Certain genres of chant are traditionally associated with each manner of performance, although the way some chants are sung has changed over time.

Manner of performance

There are also three styles of setting texts. Chants in which almost every syllable has a single note are called **syllabic**. Chants in which syllables carry one to six notes or so—generally one neume per syllable—are **neumatic** (from "neume"). Long melodic passages on a single syllable are **melismas**, and chants that feature them are **melismatic**. Not every chant can be neatly

Text setting

TIMELINE

between 4th and 7th century
Introit added to Mass

ca. 530 *Rule of St. Benedict*,
guide for monasteries in
the West, codifies liturgy
for the Office

9th to 11th centuries
Trope composition
flourishes in monasteries

884 Notker Balbulus
completes *Liber hymnorum*

late 10th century *Quem
queritis in presepe*, liturgical
drama for Christmas

1000–1300 European
population triples

1014 Last major item
(Credo) added to Mass

ca. 1020–50 Wipo, *Victimae
paschali laudes*

ca. 1025 Tropes to Mass for
Christmas Day copied into
manuscript for abbey near
Limoges

1054 Final split between
Roman and Byzantine
churches

1066 Battle of Hastings:
England falls to Normans

1095–99 First Crusade

1098–1146 Adam of St.
Victor active in Paris at
Notre Dame and Abbey
of St. Victor

ca. 1151 Hildegard of
Bingen, *Ordo virtutum*

1215 Magna Carta approved
by King John of England

ca. 1210–50 Thomas of
Celano, *Dies irae*

1562–63 Council of Trent
bans tropes and most
sequences

classified, because some chants mix styles, and chants that are mainly in one style may use another at various points.

Some parts of the Mass and Office are chanted to ***recitation formulas***, simple melodic outlines that can be used with many different texts. Other parts of the liturgy are sung to fully formed melodies. The two categories are not entirely separate, as even complex melodies may be elaborations of an underlying formula.

MELODY AND DECLAMATION Simple or ornate, chant melodies are vehicles for declaiming the words. The creators of chant made no attempt to express emotions or depict images, as in later opera or song, but their melodies reflect the shape of the text. Every chant melody is articulated into phrases and periods corresponding to those of the text. Most phrases resemble an arch, beginning low, rising into a higher range, lingering there, then descending. This parallels the way Latin was spoken. Accented syllables are often set to higher notes. Some syllables are given more notes, lending emphasis through length. But sometimes the reverse is true; melismatic chants may include long melismas on weak syllables and emphasize important words and accents with syllabic settings that stand out in contrast.

All of these features can be seen in *Viderunt omnes* in Example 2.3 (p. 33). Most phrases are archlike. The accented first syllable of "Dominus" (Lord), the most important word in the verse, is highlighted with the longest melisma and highest note in the chant. By contrast, "jubilate" (sing joyfully) is set almost syllabically, making it easy to hear, and both parts of the chant close with long melismas on unaccented syllables (on "terra" and "suam").

GENRES AND FORMS OF CHANT

Given the varied styles and histories of the chants for the Mass and Office, it will be helpful to treat them in broad categories, beginning with syllabic types, proceeding to neumatic and melismatic ones, and considering the Mass Ordinary chants separately at the end. (For a discussion of chant types in liturgical order and context, see the commentary for NAWM 3 and NAWM 4.) Each type of chant has a distinctive form in both text and music, and a particular way to perform it. While examining the chants, we should not lose sight of who sings them and in what places in the liturgy, since these factors explain the differences in musical style.

RECITATION FORMULAS The simplest chants are the formulas for intoning prayers and Bible readings, such as the Collect, Epistle, and Gospel. Here the music's sole function is to project the words clearly, without embellishment, so the formulas are spare and almost entirely syllabic. The text is chanted on a reciting note, usually A or C, with brief motives marking the ends of phrases, sentences, and the entire reading; some formulas also begin phrases with a rise to the reciting note. These recitation formulas are quite old, predating the system of modes, and are not assigned to any mode. They are sung by the priest or an assistant, with occasional responses from the choir or congregation. Priests were not necessarily trained singers, and they had a lot of text to recite, so it makes sense that their melodies were simple and in a very limited range.

PSALM TONES Slightly more complex are the ***psalm tones***, formulas for singing psalms in the Office. These are designed so they can be adapted to fit any psalm. There is one psalm tone for each of the eight modes, using the mode's reciting tone as a note for reciting most of the text. These psalm tones are still used today in Catholic, Anglican, and other churches, continuing a practice that is well over twelve hundred years old.

Example 3.1 shows the first psalm for Vespers on Christmas Day, *Dixit Dominus* (Psalm 109 in the Latin Bible, 110 in the Hebrew Scriptures and most modern translations), using the tone for mode 1 (NAWM 4a). As the example illustrates, each psalm tone consists of an *intonation,* a rising motive used only to begin the first verse; recitation on the reciting tone of the mode; the *mediant,* a cadence for the middle of each verse; further recitation; and a *termination,* a final cadence for each verse. The structure of the music exactly reflects that of the text. Each psalm verse is composed of two statements, the second echoing or completing the first. The mediant marks the end of the first statement, and the termination signals the end of the verse; both introduce melodic motion around the last one or two accented syllables of the phrase. The last verse of the psalm is followed by the ***Lesser Doxology***, a formula of praise to the Trinity (Father, Son, and Holy Spirit), sung to the same psalm tone and shown here as verses 9–10. The addition of this brief text puts the psalm, from the Hebrew Scriptures, firmly into a Christian framework. Somewhat more elaborate variants of the psalm tones are used for canticles in the Office and for the psalm verse in the Introit at Mass (NAWM 3a).

EXAMPLE 3.1 *Office psalm,* Dixit Dominus, *Psalm 109 (110)*

Intonation	Reciting tone	Mediant	Reciting tone	Termination
1. Di-xit	Dominus	Dó-mi-no mé - o:	Sede a	dex-tris mé - is.
2.	Donec ponam ini -	mí - cos tú - os,	scabellum pe -	dum tu - ó - rum.
3.	Virgam virtutis tuae emittet Domi-nús	ex Sí - on:	dominare in medio inimico-rum tu - ó - rum.
9.	Gloria	Pá-tri, et Fí-li-o,	et Spiri -	tu - i Sánc - to.
10.	Sicut erat in principio, et	núnc et sém - per,	et in saecula saecu -	lo - rum. Á - men.

1. *The Lord says to my Lord: Sit at my right hand.*

2. *Until I make Thy enemies Thy footstool.*

3. *The Lord sends the rod of Thy strength forth from Zion: rule in the midst of Thy enemies.*

. . .

9. *Glory be to the Father, and to the Son, and to the Holy Spirit.*

10. *As it was in the beginning, is now, and ever shall be, world without end. Amen.*

EXAMPLE 3.2 *Office antiphon,* Tecum principium

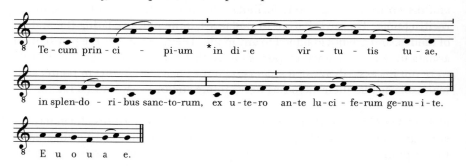

Thine shall be the dominion in the day of Thy strength in the brightness of the Saints: from the womb before the day star I begot Thee. (Psalm 109:4 [110:3])

OFFICE ANTIPHONS An Office psalm or canticle is not complete in itself, but is preceded and followed by an antiphon. Since the cycle of the 150 psalms is sung every week while the antiphon varies with each day in the church calendar, each psalm is framed by many different antiphons during the year. The text of the antiphon, whether from the Bible or newly written, often refers to the event or person being commemorated that day, placing the words of the psalm in a specific ceremonial context. On Christmas Day, the first psalm at Vespers is paired with the antiphon *Tecum principium,* shown in Example 3.2 (NAWM 4a). Here the text for the antiphon is the fourth verse of the psalm, whose images of dominion, strength, the womb, and divine parentage were understood by Christians to herald the birth of Jesus, being celebrated at this Vespers service.

Mode and psalm tone   The mode of the antiphon determines the mode for the psalm tone. The antiphon is in mode 1, so the psalm tone for mode 1 must be used for the psalm, as in Example 3.1. Because antiphons begin in various ways, medieval singers developed several terminations for each psalm tone, to lead appropriately to different opening notes or gestures. The termination to be used with a particular antiphon is shown at the end of the antiphon, using the vowels for the last six syllables of the Doxology, *E u o u a e* (for *saEcUlOrUm AmEn*), as in Example 3.2. The termination does not necessarily end on the first note of the antiphon, as long as the succession is smooth; here, the medieval musicians chose G as the most suitable ending note to lead back to the antiphon's opening notes, E–C–D. Thus the psalm tone need not close on the final of the mode, but the antiphon does.

Performance   The manner of performing psalms and canticles with antiphons has varied over time. Early descriptions include direct performance by soloists, responsorial alternation between a soloist and choir or congregation, and antiphonal alternation between two singers or groups. In medieval monastic practice, the entire community of monks or nuns was divided into two choirs singing the psalm antiphonally, alternating verses or half-verses; the antiphon could be sung by soloists, reading from the *Antiphoner,* or by all, singing from memory. Antiphonal performance was suggested by the division of each psalm verse into two parts and encouraged by the layout of medieval churches, with the choir arranged in two sets of stalls flanking the altar, as shown in Figure 3.5.

In most modern performances, the ***cantor***, the leader of the choir, sings the opening words of the antiphon to set the pitch (up to the asterisk in modern editions), and the full choir completes the antiphon; the cantor sings the first half of the first psalm or canticle verse, and half the choir completes it; the two half-choirs alternate verses or half-verses; and the full choir joins together for the reprise of the antiphon.

Office antiphons are simple and mostly syllabic, reflecting their historical association with group singing and the practical fact that over thirty are sung each day, making great length burdensome. Yet they are fully independent melodies. *Tecum principium* (Example 3.2) illustrates the elegance of even simple Gregorian chants. Text phrases and accents are clearly delineated. Each phrase centers around and cadences on important notes of the mode while tracing a unique arch. The opening phrase circles around the final D, leaps dramatically to the reciting tone A, then meanders down to D; the last two phrases both hover around F, then sink to encircle and close on D. Antiphon and psalm tone combine to create a piece with two contrasting styles, free melody and recitation, in which the outer sections emphasize the final, the longer central section the reciting tone.

FIGURE 3.5 *A mid-fifteenth-century manuscript illumination showing monks singing a memorial service. The choir is seated in two sets of stalls that face each other across the chancel, the area of the church around the altar. Two monks—presumably the cantor, or choir leader, and an assistant—stand in front, leading the singing and probably performing the solo portions.*

OFFICE HYMNS Hymns are the most familiar type of sacred song, practiced in almost all branches of Christianity from ancient times to the present. The choir sings a hymn in every Office service. Hymns are **strophic**, consisting of several stanzas that are all sung to the same melody. Stanzas may be four to seven lines long, and some include rhymes. Melodies often repeat one or more phrases, producing a variety of patterns.

The hymn *Christe Redemptor omnium,* sung at Vespers on Christmas Day (NAWM 4b) and shown in Example 3.3, welcomes the birth of Christ as redeemer, begotten by God and born of the Virgin Mary, who took on human form and came to save the world. Like most Gregorian hymns, it has one note on most syllables with two or three notes on others. It is in mode 1, and each

EXAMPLE 3.3 *Hymn,* Christe Redemptor omnium

Christ, redeemer of all, One with the Father, [who] alone, before the beginning, was born of the Father, [in a way] that cannot be expressed.

phrase and the melody as a whole have a shapely rise and fall. The first phrase ascends from C to G and falls to the final D; the second climbs to high C and cadences on the reciting tone A; the third phrase steps down to low C and rises back to E; and the final phrase repeats the first, to close on D. This kind of contour, moving mostly by seconds and thirds to a peak and descending to a cadence, has been typical of western European melodies ever since.

ANTIPHONAL PSALMODY IN THE MASS *Psalmody*, the singing of psalms, was part of the Mass as well as the Office. In the early Mass, psalms sung antiphonally with antiphons were used to accompany actions: the entrance procession and giving communion. These became the Introit and the Communion respectively. Over time, the opening procession of the Mass was shortened and the faithful came to receive communion less frequently. Eventually both chants were shifted to come after the rituals rather than accompanying them. Both chants were abbreviated, the Communion to the antiphon alone, the Introit to the antiphon, one psalm verse, Lesser Doxology, and the reprise of the antiphon (see NAWM 3a).

Because the greater solemnity of the Mass called for greater musical splendor, Mass antiphons are more elaborate than Office antiphons, typically neumatic with occasional short melismas. We can see this in Example 3.4, the Communion from Mass for Christmas Day, *Viderunt omnes* (NAWM 3j), where most syllables are sung with one to five notes. Although short melismas of eight or nine notes occur on two syllables, they are brief in comparison with the long melismas of melismatic chants like the Allelulia in Example 3.5, so the overall style of the Communion chant is neumatic. Neumatic chants are more ornate than syllabic ones, yet the characteristics of previous examples are still apparent: articulated phrases; motion mostly by steps and thirds; and arching lines that rise to a peak and sink to the cadence, circling around and closing on important notes in the mode (again mode 1). Here higher notes and longer note groups emphasize the most important accents and words.

RESPONSORIAL PSALMODY IN OFFICE AND MASS Early Christians often sang psalms responsorially, with a soloist performing each verse and the congregation or choir responding with a brief refrain. The responsorial psalms of Gregorian chant—the Office responsories and the Gradual, Alleluia, and Offertory in the Mass—stem from this practice. As we will see in later eras, singers and instrumental virtuosos, given the opportunity, would often add embellishments and display their skill through elaborate passagework. So it should come as no surprise that over the centuries of oral transmission these chants assigned to soloists became the most melismatic. They are the musical peaks of the service, moments when the words for once seem secondary to the expansive melody filling the church.

The different genres of responsorial psalm assumed different configurations. The text was usually shortened to a single psalm verse with a choral ***respond*** preceding and sometimes following the verse.

Office responsories   Office responsories take several forms, but all include a respond, a verse, and a full or partial repetition of the respond. Matins, celebrated between midnight and sunrise, includes nine Bible readings, each followed by a Great Responsory that ranges from neumatic to melismatic. Several other Office

EXAMPLE 3.4 *Communion,* Viderunt omnes

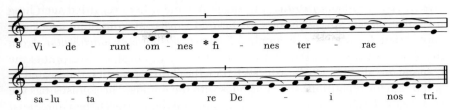

Vi - de - runt om - nes * fi - nes ter - rae
sa - lu - ta - re De - i nos - tri.

All the ends of the earth have seen the salvation of our God. (Psalm 97:3 [98:3])

EXAMPLE 3.5 Alleluia Dies sanctificatus

Al - le - lu - ia. _____ * ij.
Verse: Di - es sanc - ti - fi - ca - tus
il - lu - xit no - - - - bis:
ve - - - ni - te gen - tes,
et a - do - ra - te Do mi - num: qui - a ho - di - e
de - scen - dit lux ma - - - - gna *
su - per ter - ram. _____

Alleluia. Alleluia. Verse: A sanctified day has shone upon us; come people, and adore the Lord; for this day a great light has descended upon the earth.

services include a brief Bible reading followed by a Short Responsory that is neumatic rather than melismatic.

Graduals are considerably more melismatic than responsories. *Viderunt omnes,* the Gradual for Christmas Day (Example 2.3 and NAWM 3d), contains a melisma of fifty-two notes on "Dominus" and three other melismas ten to twenty notes long. In some Graduals, the music at the end of the verse repeats or varies the end of the respond. In performance, the cantor begins the respond and the choir completes it; then one or more soloists sing the verse, and the choir joins in on the last phrase. *Graduals*

Alleluias include a respond on the word "alleluia," a psalm verse, and a *Alleluias* repetition of the respond. The final syllable of "alleluia" is extended by an effu-sive melisma called a ***jubilus***. St. Augustine and others regarded such long melismas as an expression of a joy beyond words, making them especially appropriate for Alleluias. Example 3.5 shows *Alleluia Dies sanctificatus,* from the Mass for Christmas Day (NAWM 3e). The soloist sings the first part of the respond on "alleluia" (to the asterisk), then the choir repeats it (as indicated by *ij,* the sign for repetition) and continues with the jubilus. The soloist sings the verse, with the choir joining on the last phrase (at the asterisk), then the soloist repeats the first part of the respond, and the choir joins at the jubilus. In many Alleluias, the music at the end of the verse repeats all or part of the respond melody; here, there is instead a varied repetition of the opening of the verse (at "quia hodie descendit lux magna").

Despite the longer and more effusive melody, the characteristics seen in other chants are evident, including articulated phrases, motion primarily by steps and thirds, and gently arching contours. This Allelulia is in mode 2, the plagal mode on D. It ranges an octave from low A to high A, centers on the reciting tone F in several places, cadences most often on D, and ends both respond and verse on D. There are several long melismas, most focused around F and D, and some passages that resemble recitation on a single note, as at "sanctificatus" and "et adorate." But underneath the intricacies is the same sense of a melodic curve as in syllabic and neumatic chants.

Offertories   Offertories are as melismatic as Graduals but include the respond only (see NAWM 3g). In the Middle Ages, they were performed during the offering of bread and wine, with a choral respond and two or more very ornate verses sung by a soloist, each followed by the second half of the respond. When the ceremony was curtailed, the verses were dropped.

Tracts   Tracts (from Latin *tractus,* "drawn out") are the longest chants in the lit-urgy, with several psalm verses set in very florid style. Though now often performed like Graduals, they were originally direct solo psalmody, with no responses and thus no respond. Instead, each verse combines recitation with florid melismas. All Tracts are in mode 2 or mode 8, and the sequence of cadences, the melodic outline, and many of the melismas are shared between verses and between different Tracts in the same mode, indicating that the written melodies resulted from a tradition of oral composition based on for-mulas (see Chapter 2 and Example 2.1).

In all these chants derived from responsorial or direct psalmody, we see the hallmarks of solo performance: long, virtuosic melismas that display the voice, and passages that resemble improvised embellishment of a simple melodic outline. All but the Offertory are attached to Bible readings, orna-menting and thereby honoring that most holy text in a musical parallel to the colorful illuminations that decorate medieval Bible manuscripts.

CHANTS OF THE MASS ORDINARY The sung portions of the Mass Ordinary were originally performed by the congregation to simple syllabic melodies. But over the centuries, liturgical Latin became harder for members of the congre-gation to understand or speak, as the language of daily life gradually evolved from Latin into new vernacular tongues, such as Italian, French, Spanish, and Portuguese. Perhaps because of this linguistic gulf, church leaders reduced the congregation's participation in the Mass, and the choir took over singing the Ordinary chants. From the ninth century on, church musicians composed many new melodies for the Ordinary that were more ornate, suitable for performance by trained singers. These chants tend to be in a later style than most Proper chants, with clearer pitch centers, strong projection of the mode, more melodic repetition, a more individual melodic profile, and little or no recitation on a single note. The musical forms used in Ordinary chants vary, but often reflect the shape of their texts.

Gloria and Credo

The Credo (see NAWM 3f) was always set in syllabic style because it has the longest text and because, as the statement of faith, it was the last to be reassigned to the choir. The Gloria also has a long text, but most settings are neumatic (see NAWM 3c). Gloria and Credo melodies often feature recurring motives but have no set form. In both cases, the priest intones the opening words and the choir completes the chant.

Sanctus and Agnus Dei

Most melodies for the Sanctus and Agnus Dei are neumatic. Their texts include repetition, so melodies composed for them often have musical repetition as well. The Sanctus (see NAWM 3h) begins with the word "Sanctus" (Holy) stated three times, and the third statement often echoes the music for the first. The second and third sections of the text both end with the phrase "Hosanna in excelsis" (Hosanna in the highest) and often are set to variants of the same music (producing the form ABB′) or use the same melody for the Hosanna (creating the form A BC DC). The Agnus Dei (see NAWM 3i) states a prayer three times, altering the final words the last time. Some settings use the same music for all three statements (AAA); others are in ABA form or close all three sections with the same music (AB CB DB).

Kyrie

The Kyrie text is even more repetitive, with three statements each of "Kyrie eleison," "Christe eleison," and "Kyrie eleison." The brief text invites a florid setting, and most Kyrie melodies have melismas on the last syllables of "Kyrie" and "Christe" and the first syllable of "eleison." The text repetition is reflected in a variety of musical forms, such as AAA BBB AAA′, AAA BBB CCC′ (as in NAWM 3b), or ABA CDC EFE′. The Kyrie is usually performed antiphonally, with half-choirs alternating statements. The final "Kyrie" is often extended by a phrase, allowing each half-choir to sing a phrase before both join on the final "eleison."

Cycles of Ordinary chants

Starting in the thirteenth century, scribes often grouped Ordinary chants in **cycles**, with one setting of each text except the Credo. Similar cycles appear in the *Liber usualis*. Although there were many melodies for *Ite, missa est* in the Middle Ages, in the *Liber usualis* cycles this is set to the melody of the first Kyrie.

STYLE, USE, AND HISTORY Each type of chant is unique, reflecting its role and history. Recitation formulas were valued for their ability to project the words clearly in large spaces and for being easy to memorize and apply to many texts. Antiphons and hymns added melodic interest, and during Mass the neumatic chants of the choir adorned the service. Melismatic chants were valued for their decorative beauty and became the musical jewels of the liturgy, sung by soloists and choir when no ritual actions competed for attention. As the most elaborate chants in the repertory, they were used especially to embellish the readings from Scripture. When revisions in the liturgy changed the function of a chant or who performed it, musicians responded by changing its form or style, as when the Introit and

Communion were shortened, or when more-ornate melodies were written for the Ordinary chants after they were reassigned to the choir.

But all these chants also shared a common history with ancient roots. Their creators drew on psalm texts, continuing Jewish practice as adapted by early Christians; used modes and melodic formulas, as in the Jewish, Near Eastern, and Byzantine traditions; and emphasized correct phrasing and declamation of the text, borrowing from classical Latin rhetoric. Both the diversity of the chant repertory and the melodic and structural features most chants share become more apparent when we know the histories of plainchant as a whole and of the many individual types of chant.

ADDITIONS TO THE AUTHORIZED CHANTS

Even after the chant repertory began to be standardized in about the ninth century, church musicians continued to add to it. Besides composing new melodies for the Mass Ordinary and revising Office services, they supplied music whenever a new saint's day, commemoration of the Virgin Mary, or other feast was added to the calendar, creating new chants or adapting existing ones for the day's Mass Proper and Office. More than fifty composers known by name, and hundreds of anonymous ones, composed such chants, most for observances in honor of local saints. Moreover, church musicians developed three new types of chant as additions to the authorized liturgy: *tropes*, *sequences*, and *liturgical dramas*.

TROPE A *trope* expanded an existing chant in one of three ways: by adding (1) new words and music before the chant (an *introductory trope*) or before each phrase of the chant (an *intercalated trope*); (2) melody only, extending melismas or adding new ones; or (3) text only (usually called *prosula,* or "prose"), set to existing melismas. All three types increased the solemnity of a chant by enlarging it, and all offered musicians an outlet for creativity in the margins of the authorized repertory, paralleling the way medieval scholars sometimes added commentary in the margins of Bible texts. Moreover, the added words provided a gloss, an explanatory note or comment that interprets the chant text and usually links it more closely to the occasion.

Introductory trope   Examples of all three kinds of trope appear in NAWM 5, from a manuscript copied around 1025 for an abbey near Limoges in central France. The Introit antiphon from the Mass for Christmas Day (NAWM 3a) uses a text from the Old Testament, Isaiah 9:6, a passage Christians view as a prophecy of Jesus's birth. Prefacing it with an introductory trope makes this interpretation explicit. The trope is in the form of a dialogue, *Quem queritis in presepe* (NAWM 5a), shown in Figure 3.6 as it appears in an earlier manuscript from the late tenth century. Midwives attending Mary ask the shepherds whom they seek in the manger. The shepherds answer that they are looking for the Savior, the infant Christ. Told that they have found the one Isaiah foretold, the shepherds rejoice, their words (here in italics) leading directly into the Introit: "*Now truly we know that Christ was born on earth, concerning which let all sing with the prophet, saying*: A child is born to us, and a Son is given to us. . . ."

Intercalated trope   The Offertory from the same Mass, *Tui sunt caeli* (NAWM 3g), draws its text from a psalm. Adding the intercalated trope *Qui es sine principio* (NAWM

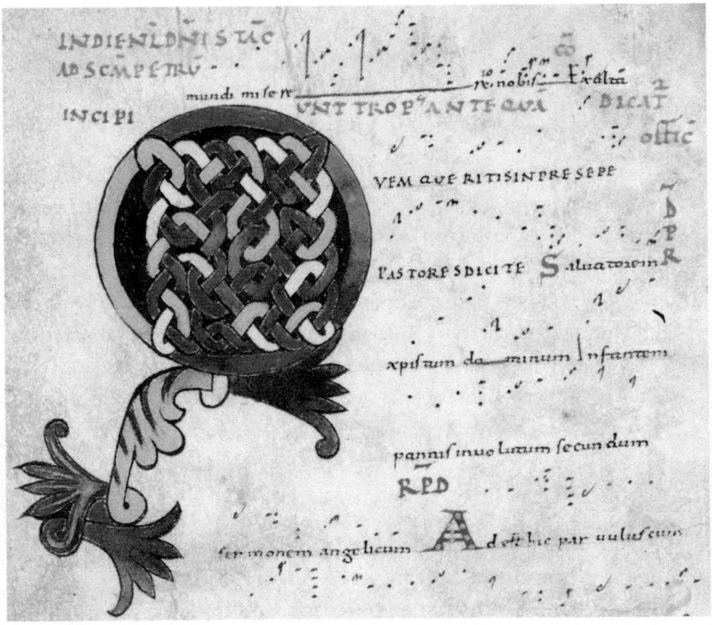

FIGURE 3.6 *The earliest surviving copy of the Christmas dramatic trope* Quem queritus in presepe, *in a manuscript from the region of Aquitaine in southwestern France. For a transcription, see NAWM 5a.*

5c), with a new phrase of music and text before each phrase of the original chant, connects the psalm directly to Christmas by addressing its words to Jesus, linking him to the other members of the Trinity, and proclaiming that "for us today, from a virgin, God was born as a man." The added phrases, which were likely sung by a soloist, are in the same mode and style as the original chant and share some melodic figures with it, so that the troped Offertory sounds like a coherent whole.

Added melisma

The manuscript also includes a textless melisma sung after the closing phrase of the Introit's antiphon (see the end of NAWM 5a), representing the second kind of trope, a purely musical addition to the chant.

Prosula

The third type, adding text to existing melismas, is illustrated by the prosula *Natus est nobis—Multis loquutionibus* (NAWM 5b), adapted from *Alleluia Multipharie olim Deus* by replacing "Alleluia" with a prose text set mostly syllabically to the music of the respond and interpolating words into the text of the verse to make it syllabic as well. The new texts relate the essence of the Christmas story. As is typical of prosulas, the vowels in the new words often match those of the syllables they replace, creating an echo of the original text that the monks singing the prosula would have readily perceived.

Rise and decline of troping

Trope composition flourished especially in monasteries during the tenth and eleventh centuries. Musicians in France, England, Germany, Italy, and Spain composed hundreds of tropes, some adopted widely but most sung only in certain locales. The use of tropes declined during the twelfth century, and all were banned by the Council of Trent (1545–63; see Chapter 11) in the interest of simplifying and standardizing the liturgy. Tropes testify to the desire among medieval church musicians to embellish the authorized chant by adding music and words. This is of crucial importance for the development of polyphony, which embodies the same impulse.

SEQUENCE The *sequence* was a genre popular from the late ninth through the thirteenth centuries in the region including France, England, Germany, Switzerland, northern Italy, and Spain. Sequences are sung after the Alleluia at Mass and are set syllabically to a text that is mostly in couplets. Early sequences are in prose, later ones more often poetic with regular meter and rhyme. Like tropes, but in more elevated language, sequences elaborate on the themes of

Notker Balbulus on Writing Sequences

The most famous early writer of sequence texts, Not-ker Balbulus ("the stammerer," ca. 840–912), a Frankish monk at the monastery of St. Gall in Switzerland, ex-plained how he learned to write words syllabically under long melismas. He appears to be describing the prac-tice of writing new texts for existing sequence melodies. Though historians once interpreted this as a description of the invention of the sequence, it is clear that Notker is refining a practice that developed elsewhere.

❈

When I was still young, and very long melodies—repeatedly entrusted to memory—escaped from my poor little head, I began to reason with myself how I could bind them fast.

In the meantime it happened that a certain priest from Jumièges (recently laid waste by the Normans) came to us, bringing with him his an-tiphonary, in which some verses had been set to sequences; but they were in a very corrupt state. Upon closer inspection I was as bitterly disappoint-ed in them as I had been delighted at first glance.

Nevertheless, in imitation of them I began

to write *Laudes Deo concinat orbis universus, qui gratis est redemptus,* and further on *Coluber adae deceptor.* When I took these lines to my teacher Iso, he, commending my industry while taking pity on my lack of experience, praised what was pleasing, and what was not he set about to improve, saying, "The individual motions of the melody should receive separate syllables." Hearing that, I immediately corrected those which fell under *ia;* those under *le* or *lu,* however, I left as too difficult; but later, with practice, I managed it easily—for example in "Dominus in Sina" and "Mater." Instructed in this manner, I soon composed my second piece, *Psallat ecclesia mater illibata.*

When I showed these little verses to my teach-er Marcellus, he, filled with joy, had them copied as a group on a roll; and he gave out different pieces to different boys to be sung. And when he told me that I should collect them in a book and offer them as a gift to some eminent person, I shrank back in shame, thinking I would never be able to do that.

Notker Balbulus, Preface to *Liber hymnorum* (Book of Hymns), trans. in Richard Crocker, *The Early Medieval Sequence* (Berkeley and Los Angeles: University of California Press, 1977), 1.

the service of which they are a part. Both tropes and sequences were additions to the liturgy, but while tropes were attached to existing chants, sequences were freestanding chants.

The origin of the sequence is uncertain, but it derives its name and place in the liturgy from an earlier practice called *sequentia* (Latin for "something that follows"), a melisma added at the end of an Alleluia. Composers of sequences sometimes drew melodic material from an Alleluia, but most melodies were newly composed. Manuscript collections of sequences customarily present them in two forms, with text and as extended melismas on "Alleluia." New texts were often written for existing sequence melodies (see Source Reading).

Form   Most sequences consist of an initial single sentence; a series of paired sentences or phrases; and a final unpaired sentence. Within each pair, the two sentences or phrases generally have the same number of syllables and are set to the same music. Both syllable count and music change for each new pair, creating the form A BB CC . . . N. The length of the paired phrases tends to rise or fall in a simple pattern. The tonal focus is usually clear, with most phrases ending on the modal final.

These characteristics are evident in the Easter sequence *Victimae paschali laudes* (NAWM 6a), attributed to Wipo (ca. 995–ca. 1050), chaplain to the Holy Roman emperor. The text emphasizes the main themes of the Easter liturgy: Christ's suffering and resurrection, the testimony of Mary and the angel that he is risen, his victory over death, and redemption for his followers. The length of verses increases from the opening through the next-to-last pair, then decreases, creating a satisfying arch. Short musical phrases, all ending on the final or reciting tone of the mode, give the music coherence, reinforced by melodic similarities at the beginning or end of some phrases.

Victimae paschali laudes

In the twelfth century, rhymed poetry in verses of even length became more common for sequences, and many sequences lacked the unpaired verses at beginning and end. The sequences by Adam of St. Victor (d. 1146), who was active in Paris, are typical in the allegorical quality of their texts, which comment on the liturgy of the day, and in their poetic form: verses of three lines in trochaic meter (alternating accented and unaccented syllables), with eight, eight, and seven syllables respectively, paired in the rhyme scheme aab ccb. The melodies are still primarily syllabic but often include short groups of two or three notes.

Later sequences

An outstanding example of the late sequence, and one of the most famous poems of the Middle Ages, is *Dies irae* (NAWM 6b), attributed to the Italian monk Thomas of Celano (ca. 1190–ca. 1260), friend and biographer of St. Francis of Assisi. The original poem is in rhymed verses of three lines, each line eight syllables long in regular trochaic meter. In the first six verses, the poet paints a vivid picture of the Day of Judgment, drawing on biblical imagery from the Psalms and Old Testament prophets through Jesus's own words in the Gospels to the letters of Peter and the book of Revelation. In the next six verses, he begs Jesus to save him, recalling that the reason Jesus came to earth and suffered on the cross was to redeem sinners like him. Then he cites Jesus's own actions and words, from the absolution he offered the sinners around him to his images of the last judgment, and pleads for mercy. The three sections of the poem are highlighted by a threefold repetition in the melody, which takes the form AA BB CC / AA BB CC / AA BB C / D E; the last two verses, in the form of a prayer, were appended when *Dies irae* was made the sequence for the Mass for the Dead (the Requiem Mass).

Dies irae

Like tropes, sequences embellished the liturgy and provided an outlet for creativity. During the heyday of sequence composition from the ninth through the twelfth centuries, church musicians composed thousands, including some of the most profound and engaging songs of the entire Middle Ages. Some sequences were widely used, but local practice varied. Seeking greater uniformity, the Council of Trent banned most sequences, retaining only four of the best known, including *Victimae paschali laudes* and *Dies irae*. The importance of the sequence as a genre of chant is masked by this later history, when all but a few of them were expunged from the repertoire.

Significance of sequences

LITURGICAL DRAMA As we have seen with the Christmas trope *Quem queritis in presepe*, some tropes took the form of dialogues, bringing long-ago events to life in the present. The earliest was the tenth-century *Quem queritis in sepulchro*, preceding the Introit for Easter. In the dialogue, the three Marys come to Jesus's tomb, and the angel asks them, "Whom do you seek in the sepulcher?" They reply, "Jesus of Nazareth," to which the angel answers, "He is not here, He is risen as He said; go and proclaim that He has risen from the grave" (Mark 16:5–7). Accounts from the period show that this dialogue was sung responsively and accompanied by appropriate dramatic action.

Such dialogues that were added to the liturgy have become known as **liturgical dramas**. They were recorded in liturgical books and performed in church, with processions and stylized actions. The Easter and Christmas dialogues were the most common and were performed all over Europe. Several other plays survive from the twelfth century and later that enact the events commemorated in the Church year, some performed within the liturgy and others staged separately. These include ten plays in a codex from the Benedictine monastery of Fleury in central France and the early-thirteenth-century *Play of Daniel* from Beauvais (north of Paris). The music for these plays consists of a number of chants strung together, sometimes joined by songs in more secular styles. All parts, even women's roles, were usually sung by the male clergy and choir, except in a few locales where nuns participated.

HILDEGARD OF BINGEN

Women were excluded from the priesthood, and as the choir took over the singing in services, women were silenced in church. But in convents—separate communities of celibate religious women—they could hold positions of leadership, except for officiating at Mass, and participate fully in singing and composing music. As in monasteries, convent life revolved around singing the eight daily Office services and Mass. Here women learned to read Latin and music and had access to an intellectual life available to few women outside convent walls.

In this context, Hildegard of Bingen (1098–1179) achieved great success as abbess of her own convent and as a writer and composer (see Figure 3.7 and biography). There are more surviving chants by Hildegard than by any other composer from the entire Middle Ages. Most of her songs, for which she composed both words and music, praise the Virgin Mary, the Trinity, or local saints. Her works, mostly composed for Office services, vary from syllabic hymns to highly melismatic responsories. Her sequences are unusual in that the paired lines often differ in syllable count and accent, and Hildegard varies the music accordingly. Her melodies often exceed the range of an octave by a fourth or fifth. She repeatedly uses a small repertoire of melodic figures in constant variation. Some patterns derive from chant, such as a rising fifth and stepwise descent, or circling around a cadential note; others are extraordinary, such as successive leaps and other patterns that quickly span an octave or more. The music serves to prolong the words, encouraging contemplation of their meaning through sung prayer.

Ordo virtutum   Hildegard's most extended musical work is *Ordo virtutum* (The Virtues, ca. 1151), a sacred music drama in verse with eighty-two songs. It is a morality play with allegorical characters, including the Prophets, the Virtues, the Happy Soul, the Unhappy Soul, and the Penitent Soul, in which the female Virtues lead the fallen soul back to the community of the faithful. All sing in plainchant except the Devil, who can only speak; the absence of music symbolizes

HILDEGARD OF BINGEN

(1098–1179)

Born to a noble family in Bermersheim in the Rhine region of Germany, Hildegard at age eight was consecrated to the church by her parents. Six years later she took vows at the Benedictine monastery of Disibodenberg, and was elected magistra of the attached convent in 1136. Led by a vision, she founded her own convent around 1150 at Rupertsberg near Bingen, where she was abbess.

Famous for her prophecies, Hildegard corresponded with emperors, kings, popes, and bishops and preached throughout Germany. Her many prose works include *Scivias* (Know the Ways, 1141–51), an account of twenty-six visions, and books on science and healing, *Physica* and *Causae et Curae*, which present a holistic approach using natural medicines for many ailments.

Hildegard wrote religious poems as well as prose, and by the 1140s she was setting them to music. Her songs, primarily antiphons and responsories for the Office and sequences for Masses dedicated to local saints, are preserved in two manuscripts organized in a liturgical cycle, with indications that many were sung in her convents and nearby monasteries and churches. Her *Ordo virtutum* (The Virtues, ca. 1151) is the earliest surviving music drama not attached to the liturgy. In a male-dominated church with a prescribed liturgy and repertory of chant, Hildegard had to make a place in the margins, for herself and for her compositions.

PHOTO: ERICH LESSING/ART RESOURCE, NY

FIGURE 3.7 *Hildegard of Bingen with Volmar, a monk who assisted her in recording her visions, in an illustration from* Scivias.

MAJOR WORKS *Ordo virtutum*, 43 antiphons, 18 responsories, 7 sequences, 4 hymns, 5 other chants

his separation from God. The final chorus of the Virtues and Souls (NAWM 7) is typical of Hildegard's expansive and individual melodies.

Hildegard claimed that her songs, like her prose writings, were divinely inspired. At a time when women were forbidden to instruct or supervise men, having a reputation for direct communication from God was the only way she could be heard outside the convent. She was renowned as a visionary, but her music, like that of countless other composers, was apparently known only locally. Her writings were edited and published in the nineteenth century, her music only in the late twentieth century when she was rediscovered in the search to reclaim the history of music by women. She quickly became the most recorded and best-known composer of sacred monophony, and one of very few known to have written both the music and the words.

Reputation

THE CONTINUING PRESENCE OF CHANT

Gregorian chant was important in itself and for its influence on other music. It was used in Christian services throughout central and western Europe until the Reformation and in Catholic areas after that. Most people in these areas heard it at least weekly. It remained the principal activity of professional singers until the end of the sixteenth century; musicians we know primarily as composers, such as Leoninus, Du Fay, Ockeghem, Josquin, and Palestrina, spent most of their time singing and directing the performance of chant. Chant was reformed in the late sixteenth and early seventeenth centuries and again in the late nineteenth and early twentieth centuries. But the Second Vatican Council of 1962–65, in an effort to engage congregations more directly in worship, permitted holding Catholic services in local languages rather than in Latin. Chant was no longer prescribed, and it has virtually disappeared from regular Catholic services, replaced by new tunes with vernacular texts. By the late twentieth century, chant was practiced mostly in monasteries and convents or performed in concerts, and was known mainly through recordings. One recording by the Benedictine monks of Santo Domingo de Silos in Spain, titled simply *Chant,* was the best-selling CD in Europe for more than six months in 1993 and was a best seller in the United States as well. The trend continues in the twenty-first century: music in the style of chant is used in Halo and other video games, and in 2008, the monks of Heiligenkreuz (Holy Cross) Abbey in Austria released an album titled *Chant: Music for Paradise* that became a top-ten hit and went gold or platinum in the United Kingdom, Germany, Austria, Belgium, and Poland. Music by Hildegard of Bingen and other composers of chant, once heard only in their own locales, is performed, recorded, and heard around the world.

From the ninth through the thirteenth centuries, chant formed the foundation for most polyphonic music, and it continued to play a leading role in polyphonic sacred music well into the sixteenth century. The diversity already inherent in chant, from the contrast between syllabic and melismatic styles to the various modes, was reflected in similar diversity in later service music. From the beginning of the Reformation, composers adapted many chants for use as chorale or hymn tunes in the Protestant churches, and melodies derived from chant are still used today in Lutheran, Anglican, and other churches. During the nineteenth and twentieth centuries, composers frequently used chant melodies, in secular as well as sacred music.

Yet the importance of Gregorian chant for later music goes beyond its presence in pieces directly based on it. Chant was part of the musical world of most Europeans for over a thousand years, and it deeply influenced their sense of how melodies should be shaped and how music should go. All later music in the Western tradition bears its imprint.

Further Reading is available at digital.wwnorton.com/hwm10

SONG AND DANCE MUSIC TO 1300

❖

Gregorian chant was a revered tradition, preserved in notation, taught in church schools, and discussed in treatises. Outside the church, few in the Middle Ages read music, and except among the educated elites, secular music was seldom written down or written about. For most people, music was purely aural, and most of the secular and nonliturgical music they heard, sang, and played has vanished. What survives are several hundred monophonic songs, many poems sung to melodies now lost, a few dance tunes, descriptions of music-making, pictures of musicians playing various instruments, and a few actual instruments. From these we can learn how music was used and can identify several important repertories, including the songs of the troubadours and trouvères in France and the Minnesingers in Germany; the Italian lauda and Spanish cantiga; and dance music. In these songs and dances we can see reflections of medieval society and discover traits common in European music ever since.

EUROPEAN SOCIETY, 800–1300

Medieval music was shaped by currents in the wider society: political developments, linguistic regions, economic growth, social class, and support for learning and the arts.

By the ninth century, three principal successors to the Roman Empire emerged. The most direct successor was the Byzantine Empire in Asia Minor and southeastern Europe. The strongest and most vibrant was the Arab world, which from the founding of the Islamic religion around 610 by Muhammad (ca. 570–632) rapidly expanded to conquer a vast territory from modern-day Pakistan through the Middle East, North Africa, and Spain. The weakest, poorest, and most fragmented of the three was western Europe. In this context, Charlemagne's coronation in 800 as emperor in Rome marked an assertion of continuity with the Roman past, independence from the Byzantine East, and confidence in the future of civilization in western Europe.

FIGURE 4.1
Europe in 1050.

European culture owes much to all three empires. The Byzantines preserved Greek and Roman science, architecture, and culture. Most writings that survive from ancient Greece exist only because Byzantine scribes recopied them. The Arabs extended Greek philosophy and science, fostered trade and industry, and contributed to medicine, chemistry, technology, and mathematics. Arab rulers were patrons of literature, architecture, and other arts. Charlemagne also promoted learning and artistic achievement. He improved education, encouraging primary schools in monasteries and cathedral towns throughout his realm. By sponsoring scholarship and the arts, Charlemagne and his son Louis the Pious (r. 814–43) made their courts into centers for intellectual and cultural life, setting a pattern for Western rulers that endured for a thousand years.

The changing map of Europe   After Louis's death, his empire was divided. Over the next few centuries the countries of modern Europe began to emerge, although their boundaries changed frequently. Figure 4.1 shows the situation around 1050.

The western part of the empire became France. Until about 1200, the French king was relatively weak, directly ruling only the area around Paris, while other regions were governed by nobles who owed nominal allegiance to the king but often acted independently. Their courts provided opportunities for poets and musicians, nurturing the troubadours and trouvères (see p. 69). Among the most important of these regions for music was the duchy of Aquitaine in southwestern France, home to important traditions of Latin songs, troubadour songs, and early polyphony (see Chapter 5).

In the eastern part of the empire, German kings claimed the title of emperor as Charlemagne's successors. Their realm, eventu-

FIGURE 4.2 *Miniature from the Book of Hours (ca. 1480) of Jean, Duke of Berry. On the lower left, the duke receives the book. The other panels show the three classes or "estates" of medieval society: the first estate, the clergy, who prayed (upper left); the second estate, the nobility, who governed and waged war (upper right); and the third estate, commoners, who worked in trades or on the land controlled by the nobles.*

ally known as the Holy Roman Empire, included non-German lands as well, from the Netherlands to northern Italy. The regional nobility and cities in the empire had considerable autonomy, and by 1250 real power lay in the hands of hundreds of local princes, dukes, bishops, and administrators. They competed for prestige by hiring the best singers, instrumentalists, and composers, which fueled the development of music until the nineteenth century.

Outside the former Frankish lands, a centralized kingdom emerged in England in the late ninth century and continued after the Norman Conquest of England in 1066. Poland and Hungary were also unified kingdoms. Italy remained fragmented among several rulers including the pope, ruler of the Papal States, and Spain was divided between Christian kingdoms in the north and Muslim lands in the south. The Crusades, a series of campaigns between 1095 and 1270 to retake Jerusalem from the Turks, ultimately failed but showed the growing confidence and military power of western Europe.

Amid these political developments, western Europe saw remarkable economic progress. Technological advances in agriculture and an expansion of lands under cultivation led to great growth in production. Increasing the food supply raised the standard of living and allowed the population to triple between 1000 and 1300. From about 1050 on, water-powered mills and windmills provided mechanical power for milling grain, manufacturing goods, and other uses, further boosting productivity. By 1300, western Europe had surpassed the Byzantine Empire and the Islamic world in economic strength.

Social classes

The medieval economy was largely agricultural, and the population mostly rural. Society was organized into three broad classes, as shown in Figure 4.2: priests, monks, and nuns, who prayed; the nobility and knights, who controlled the land and fought the wars; and commoners, the vast majority of the population, most of whom were peasants who worked the land and served the nobles. But by the twelfth century, trade in food and other products promoted the growth of markets, towns, and cities, although the largest cities were still small in modern terms: in 1300, Paris had about 200,000 residents; London about 70,000; and Venice, Milan, and Florence about 100,000 each. In every city, independent artisans made products from shoes to paintings, organizing themselves into groups called *guilds* to protect their interests by regulating production, pricing, apprenticeship, and competition. Together with doctors, lawyers, and merchants, these artisans constituted a new middle class, between nobles and peasants, and participated in town governance by mayors and town councils.

Prosperity provided resources for learning and the arts. Guilds organized apprentice systems for painters, sculptors, and musicians, both men and women. From 1050 to 1300, the center of influence in the church moved from rural monasteries led by abbots to urban cathedrals presided over by bishops, and cathedral schools were established throughout western and central Europe, teaching future church officials Latin grammar, rhetoric, and music. After 1200, independent schools for laymen spread rapidly as well, fostering a more secular culture and a tremendous rise in literacy. Women were excluded from most schools, but many were taught to read at home. From the twelfth century on, universities were founded in Bologna, Paris, Oxford, and other cities, teaching liberal arts, theology, law, and medicine. Works of Aristotle and other important writers were translated from Greek and Arabic into Latin. Scholars such as Roger Bacon and St. Thomas Aquinas made new contributions to science and philosophy. Writers in Latin and vernacular languages wrote epic, lyric, and narrative poems that grew increasingly independent from ancient models. Much of this poetry was sung, forming the repertories of medieval song.

LATIN AND VERNACULAR SONG

One type of Latin song, called ***versus*** (sing. and pl.), was normally sacred and sometimes attached to the liturgy. Typical topics included Jesus's birth, his mother Mary, and the miracles of the Virgin Birth and the Incarnation. The poetry was rhymed and usually followed a regular pattern of accents. Monophonic versus were composed from the eleventh century through the thirteenth, particularly in Aquitaine, and they influenced two other repertories from the same region, troubadour songs (see p. 69) and Aquitanian polyphony (see Chapter 5). A related type, ***conductus*** (sing. and pl.), originated in the twelfth century in northern France as a serious Latin song on a sacred or secular subject with a rhymed, rhythmical text, akin to a sequence but without the paired phrases. Both versus and conductus were set to newly composed melodies not based on chant.

Latin was no longer anyone's native tongue but was taught in schools, and many people spoke and understood it. Latin songs were composed for performance outside religious contexts, including settings of ancient poetry, laments for Charlemagne and other notables, and satirical, moralizing, or amorous songs. The music, when preserved at all, is usually in staffless neumes that cannot be transcribed unless the melody appears elsewhere in more precise notation.

Among medieval Latin songs are the so-called ***goliard songs*** from the late tenth through thirteenth centuries, associated with wandering students and clerics known as *goliards*. Topics vary from religious and moral themes to satire and celebrations of love, spring, eating, drinking, and other earthly pleasures. The poems show breadth of learning and address an educated audience, and poets who can be identified include respected teachers and courtiers; this suggests that the dissolute way of life celebrated by some songs may be more fiction than reality.

Goliard songs

VERNACULAR SONG   Many songs were composed in medieval French, English, German, Italian, Spanish, and various other vernacular languages, but most of these pieces are lost. Outside the churches and legal system, most of medieval society was nonliterate. Because the common people did not read or write, their work songs, dance songs, lullabies, laments, and other songs have disappeared. There are almost no descriptions of musical life in rural areas, where about ninety percent of the population lived. A few street cries and folk songs are preserved, like flies in amber, only because they were quoted in polyphonic music written for educated audiences.

One type of vernacular poem that survived is the epic, a long heroic narrative. Many were transmitted orally before being written down. The ***chanson de geste*** ("song of deeds") was an epic in the northern French vernacular recounting the deeds of national heroes and sung to simple melodic formulas. The most famous chanson de geste is the *Song of Roland* (ca. 1100), about Charlemagne's battle against the Muslims in Spain. About one hundred other chansons de geste exist, most from the twelfth century, but little of the music was preserved. Epics in other lands, like the Old English *Beowulf* (eighth century), the Norse eddas (ca. 800–1200), and the German *Song of the Nibelungs* (thirteenth century), were likely also sung, but the music was never written down.

Epics

MINSTRELS AND OTHER PROFESSIONAL MUSICIANS   As in any era, many people in the Middle Ages must have sung and played music for their own enjoyment or for their friends. Yet there were also professional musicians of various kinds. Poet-singers, called ***bards*** in Celtic lands, sang epics at banquets and other occasions, accompanying themselves on harp, fiddle, or another string instrument. ***Jongleurs*** (from the same root as English "jugglers") were lower-class itinerant musicians who traveled alone or in groups, earning a precarious living by performing tricks, telling stories, and singing or playing instruments. By the thirteenth century, the term ***minstrel*** (from Latin *minister,* "servant") was used for musicians who were more specialized, many of whom were employed at a court or city for at least part of the year (see Music in Context: Minstrels in Medieval French Cities, and Figure 4.3). Unlike jongleurs, minstrels came from varied backgrounds, ranging from former clerics to sons or daughters of merchants, craftsmen,

MUSIC IN CONTEXT

Minstrels in Medieval French Cities

Minstrels were an integral and prominent part of the late medieval French city. They contributed to a sense of civic identity by saluting the inauguration of the city council, sanctifying relics of saints in processions, and welcoming visiting nobility; they provided order to the day by marking the opening and closing of town gates, making official proclamations, warning citizens of danger, and announcing weddings; and they provided entertainment at dances, bathhouses, and taverns.

The world of the urban minstrels was not preserved in music manuscripts, because the music they performed was created and passed down aurally. But their world can be reconstructed with archival records, through a research process similar to putting together an enormous jigsaw puzzle for which pieces are scattered far and wide, with many irretrievably lost. Some of the valuable pieces in this puzzle include city contracts that define duties, ordinances that describe (and often restrict) common activities, partnership contracts, and guild statutes that delineate professional obligations (see Source Reading).

Although civic patronage varied significantly from city to city, musicians throughout France were hired to participate in civic ritual and customs. The major city of Montpellier, for instance, which had a population as high as 40,000, regularly contracted in the mid-fourteenth century a five-member wind band with two reed instruments, two trumpets, and a small kettledrum to precede the city council in processions, as well as two trumpeters to function as watchmen, and another to serve as public crier. Displaying

expensive livery and banners adorned with the coat of arms of the city, these musicians showcased the prosperity and political independence of the city. Reflecting this close association between musicians and civic authority, the bishop of Albi, who was the city's overlord, retaliated after a revolt by the townspeople by insisting that the public crier's silver trumpet be "nailed to the pillory" and by requiring all civic announcements to be made on a crude horn, a degrading change in ritual for the city.

FIGURE 4.3 *Jongleur or minstrel playing a* vielle *(medieval fiddle) at court, with city rooftops in the distance. Illumination from manuscript of the* Cantigas de Santa María, *from late-thirteenth-century Spain.*

or knights. Beginning around the twelfth century, professional musicians, both men and women, began to organize themselves into guilds, which provided legal protections, established guild members' exclusive rights to perform within a city or region, and laid out rules for conduct (see Source Reading). Formerly viewed as outcasts, musicians gained greater social acceptance through such guilds, the ancestors of modern musicians' unions and professional organizations.

TROUBADOUR AND TROUVÈRE SONG

The most significant body of vernacular song in the Middle Ages was the lyric tradition cultivated in courts and cities under aristocratic sponsorship. The tradition began in the twelfth century with the **troubadours** (from Occitan *trobador,* feminine **trobairitz**), poet-composers in southern France whose language was Occitan, and spread north to the **trouvères**, whose language was Old French. The two languages, whose regions are shown in Figure 4.4, were also called *langue d'oc* and *langue d'oïl* after their respective words for "yes" (*oïl* = *oui*, yes); *trobar* and *trover* were their words for "to compose a song," which later came to mean "to invent" or "to find."

SOURCE READING

The Paris Minstrels' Guild

In 1321, musicians in Paris organized the Confrérie of St.-Julien des Menestriers, a guild that regulated standards and behavior for professional musicians. Their 1341 statutes, signed by thirty-seven musicians, both men and women, forbade the hiring of inferior musicians, discouraged competition between members, and guaranteed that only guild members could perform for pay in Paris.

Know that we, by common accord, the *menestrels* and *menestrelles, jongleurs* and *jongleresses* [male and female minstrels and jongleurs] living in the city of Paris whose names are here signed, have ordained the points and articles contained and set forth below for the reformation of our craft and the common profit of the city of Paris. The persons named below have testified and affirmed by their oaths that they will be profitable and valuable to their avowed profession and to the community of the city, as indicated by the following points and articles:

(1) No *trompéeur* [trumpeter] of the city of Paris may enter into a contract at a feast for anyone except himself and his companion, or for any other *jongleur* or *jongleresse* of any other guild than his own, for there are some who . . . take inferior musicians and ignore the better players; even though they perform less well

the same salary is demanded. Because of this good people are deceived and the reputation and common profit of the profession are damaged.

(2) *Trompéeurs* or other minstrels who have been hired to play for a function must wait until it ends before they move on to another engagement.

(3) Those who have agreed to play are not to send a substitute, except in case of illness, imprisonment, or other emergency. . . .

(6) When a prospective customer appears in the *rue aus jongleurs* [street of the jongleurs] he is to be allowed to approach whatever performer he wishes to engage without interference from rivals.

(7) Apprentices must observe the same rules as fully accredited members of the profession.

(8) and (9) All minstrels, whether Parisian or from other areas of France, must swear to obey the statutes. Any outside minstrel arriving in Paris, either master or apprentice, is required to swear to the provost of St.-Julien that he will obey the statutes or else be banished for a year and a day. . . .

Translated by Kay Brainerd Slocum, "*Confrérie, Bruderschaft* and Guild: The Formation of Musicians' Fraternal Organisations in Thirteenth- and Fourteenth-Century Europe," *Early Music History* 14 (1995): 264–65.

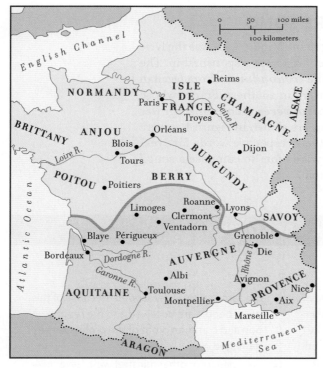

FIGURE 4.4 *Linguistic boundary between Occitan* (langue d'oc) *in the south of France and Medieval French* (langue d'oïl) *in the north.*

The many castles and courts throughout France supported the troubadours and trouvères. Their lives are recounted in somewhat fanciful biographies called *vidas* (lives), often our only source of information about them. Some were nobles themselves, such as the first troubadour whose songs we have, Guillaume IX, duke of Aquitaine and count of Poitiers (1071–1126), and the trobairitz Comtessa de Dia (Countess of Dia, fl. late twelfth and early thirteenth centuries). Some were born to servants at court, as was Bernart de Ventadorn (?ca. 1130–ca. 1200), one of the best-known and most influential troubadours, shown in Figure 4.5. Son of a baker or servant at the castle of Ventadorn, Bernart learned poetry and music from his noble patron there, then in the 1150s entered the service of Eleanor of Aquitaine (1122–1204), granddaughter of Guillaume IX and one of the most powerful women of the twelfth century as duchess of Aquitaine, queen of France (1137–52) by marriage to Louis VII, and later duchess of Normandy and queen of England (1154–89) by marriage to Henry II. Through his sojourn with Eleanor in northern France and possibly England, Bernart brought the troubadour tradition to the north and inspired the development of trouvère songs. Other troubadours and trouvères came from families of merchants, craftsmen, or even jongleurs, accepted into aristocratic circles because of their accomplishments in poetry and music and their adoption of the value system and behavior practiced at court.

FIGURE 4.5 *Portrait of Bernart de Ventadorn on a horse, from a thirteenth-century French manuscript.*

The songs were preserved in manuscript anthologies called **chansonniers** (songbooks). About 2,600 troubadour poems survive, a tenth with melodies; by contrast, two-thirds of the 2,100 extant trouvère poems have music. Whether the melody was composed by the poet is not always clear. Some poems appear with more than one melody, and some poets created new words to existing melodies, a process called **contrafactum**. Variants of text and music in the manuscripts suggest that both poems and melodies were composed orally rather than on paper, memorized by rote, and transmitted orally for a time before being written down. All the surviving manuscripts date from the mid-thirteenth century or later, well after the troubadours' own lifetimes, and appear to be the result of a conscious attempt to preserve their poetry and music retrospectively, so that we do not know whether any of the troubadours were

able to read and write music. Some troubadours and trouvères sang their own songs, but often the performance was entrusted to a jongleur or minstrel.

POETRY The songs of the troubadours and trouvères were the fountainhead of all Western vernacular poetry. Notable for their refinement, elegance, and intricacy, the poems vary in subject, form, and treatment. Love songs predominate, joined by songs on political, moral, and literary topics, dramatic ballads and dialogues, and dance songs. Most are strophic, and dance songs often include a *refrain*—a recurring phrase or verse with music—that was typically sung by the dancers. There are several particular genres of the troubadours, such as the ***canso*** (love song), *alba* (dawn song), *balada* (dance song), *planh* (lament), and *tenso* (debate song).

A central theme is ***fin' amors*** (Occitan), or ***fine amour*** (French), meaning "refined love" (sometimes called ***courtly love***, a term coined in the nineteenth century, because of its association with aristocratic courts). This was not a mutual love between equals, but a formal, idealized love through which the lover was himself refined. The object was a real woman of noble birth, usually another man's wife, but she was adored from a distance, with discretion, respect, and humility. Indeed the language of adoration in these songs can border on the language of devotional songs to the Virgin Mary. The lady is depicted as so lofty and unattainable that she would step out of character if she condescended to reward her faithful lover. Thus Bernart de Ventadorn writes in his canso *Can vei la lauzeta mover* (NAWM 8), one of the most widely disseminated troubadour songs, the classic complaint of unrequited love:

Fin' amors *and* fine amour

> Alas! I thought I knew so much
> of love, and I know so little;
> for I cannot help loving a lady
> from whom I shall never obtain any favor.
> She has taken away my heart and myself,
> and herself and the whole world;
> and when she left me, I had nothing left
> but desire and a yearning heart.

Such poetry evokes the longing and fluctuating moods familiar from later portrayals of unfulfilled romantic love. But it also serves another purpose: by playing on common themes in fresh ways through artfully constructed lyrics, the poet demonstrates his refinement and eloquence. Since these traits were the two principal requirements for success in aristocratic circles, the entire genre of poetry and song was more fiction than fact, addressed as much to other men as to women, and rewarded not by love but by social status.

Women poets adopted similar language, yet their poems can seem more direct and realistic. *A chantar* (NAWM 9), shown in Example 4.1, is the only song by a trobairitz to survive with music. In it, the Comtessa de Dia laments her lover's deception while defending her own virtue, intelligence, courtesy, and beauty.

MELODIES Troubadour and trouvère songs are strophic, setting each stanza to the same melody. Text setting is mostly syllabic with occasional groups of

EXAMPLE 4.1 *Comtessa de Dia,* A chantar

To sing I must of that which I would rather not,
so bitter I am towards him who is my love:
for I love him more than anyone;
my kindness and courtesy make no impression on him,
nor my beauty, my virtue, or my intelligence;
so I am deceived and betrayed,
as I should be if I were unattractive.

notes, especially on the penultimate syllable of a line. The melodic range is narrow, seldom over a ninth. Melodies move mostly by step with occasional skips of a third. Phrases are generally arch-shaped, rising to a peak and gradually descending to a close. Although the aristocrats and courtiers who composed the melodies were likely not trained in church schools and may have known nothing about the church modes, no doubt they heard chant all their lives and were familiar with its modal character, so it is appropriate to apply the modes to their music. While some melodies do not fit within any mode, most do, with modes 1 and 7 especially common. Many songs make their mode clear throughout, while in others it may remain ambiguous until the end. Most troubadour melodies have new music for each phrase in the stanza, but Bernart de Ventadorn often repeats one or more phrases, and AAB form occurs in some troubadour melodies and most trouvère songs. As we shall see, it remained the most common form for German medieval song, and many other song forms resulted from adding a refrain to one or more verses in AAB form (see Forms at a Glance).

A chantar illustrates these characteristics. It is mostly syllabic, with two or three notes on some syllables. (A notehead with a tail attached, called a

AAB

Most medieval songs are strophic, with several stanzas that are sung to the same melody. The melody can take many forms, but the most common pattern is AAB, either alone or with a refrain.

In AAB form, a section of one or more phrases is sung twice, with new text the second time, followed by a contrasting section. Two of the songs in NAWM take this form, as shown in Figure 4.6. In both cases, the A and B sections end with the same musical phrase, producing a musical rhyme that is a frequent feature of AAB form.

Two other songs add to this basic structure refrains, recurring lines of text always sung to the same music. By convention, when a song form has a refrain, the repetition of both text and music is shown by uppercase letters, and the repetition of music with new lines of text is shown by lowercase letters. *Robins m'aime* has only one stanza, preceded and followed by a two-line refrain that uses the same two musical phrases as the stanza. *Non sofre Santa María* has several stanzas, each preceded and followed by a refrain that uses only the last section of music from the stanza; because the refrain appears first, it is given the letter A, and the stanza is shown as bba rather than aab.

	REFRAIN	STANZA	REFRAIN
A chantar (NAWM 9)		A A B	
Palästinalied (NAWM 11)		A A B	
Robins m'aime (NAWM 10)	A B	a a b	A B
Non sofre Santa María (NAWM 12)	A	b b a	A

FIGURE 4.6 *Four songs with stanzas in AAB form, with or without a refrain.*

plica, stands for two notes, the second a step below or above the first.) The poem's seven-line stanzas are set to phrases in the pattern ab ab cdb, for an AAB form in which A and B share a musical rhyme. Melodic motion is mostly stepwise within an octave range, with frequent high points on the note A and cadences on D clearly indicating mode 1.

Except in some late manuscripts that use the rhythmic notation described in the next chapter, troubadour and trouvère melodies were written down using the notation developed for chant, which makes each pitch clear but does not indicate rhythm. Some scholars maintain that the melodies were sung in a free, unmeasured style; others that each note or each syllable should have a roughly equal duration; and still others that the songs were sung metrically, with long and short notes corresponding to the accented and unaccented syllables, although there is disagreement on how to apply meter to syllables with more than one note or to the frequent cases where accentuation differs between stanzas. Thus the treatment of rhythm varies considerably between editions, and performers can choose from a range of approaches. Most likely the dance songs were sung metrically, while the elevated love songs may have been sung more freely.

Rhythm

The songs were written as unaccompanied melodies, but pictures and

Accompaniment

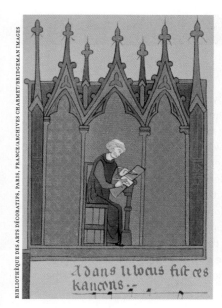

FIGURE 4.7 *Adam de la Halle as de-picted in a miniature from the* Chansonnier d'Arras, *which contains six of his chansons. The text says "Adam the hunchback made these songs."*

accounts of performance suggest that at least sometimes and perhaps most of the time singers were accompanied by instruments, especially plucked or bowed string instruments (see Medieval Instruments, pp. 76–78). The instrumentalists may have played the melody in unison, variations of the melody (producing heterophony), drones, or improvised counterpoints. Some scholars have suggested that serious or elevated genres of song like the canso were more often sung unaccompanied, while dance songs would more likely use instruments, including percussion.

MUSICAL PLAYS Musical plays were built around narrative pastoral songs (songs in idealized rural settings). The most famous was *Jeu de Robin et de Marion* (The Play of Robin and Marion, ca. 1284) by the trouvère Adam de la Halle (ca. 1240–?1288), shown in Figure 4.7. Adam was the first vernacular poet-composer whose complete works were collected in a manuscript, showing the great esteem in which he was held. The play does not exalt the lofty theme of *fin' amors,* in which a noblewoman is adored discreetly from afar, but draws on the tradition of the *pastourelle,* a song about a shepherdess and a knight who seeks to seduce or abduct her. Women of the peasant class were not venerated, nor wooed through courtly manners or poetry, so these songs either celebrate the pleasures of love or depict the wiles of a shepherdess who is able to evade unwanted advances. In this play, the shepherdess Marion enjoys the love of the shepherd Robin, and both work to resist a knight who tries to force himself upon her.

In the opening song, *Robins m'aime* (NAWM 10), Marion sings of Robin's love for her. This is a ***rondeau***, a dance song with a refrain in two phrases whose music is also used for the verse, here in the pattern ABaabAB (where uppercase letters indicate the refrain). This form is clearly related to the AAB form that we have already encountered; the verse is in that form, framed by a refrain based on the same music.

DISSEMINATION The origins of the troubadour tradition are unclear. Possible sources or influences include Arabic songs, known in southern France since the ninth century, which have themes of idealized love similar to *fin' amors*; the versus (see p. 66), which was a prominent genre in the same region of Aquitaine and southern France; and secular Latin songs. From southern France the tradition spread to the trouvères of northern France by the late twelfth century, in large part through the influence of Bernart de Ventadorn, and on to England, Germany, Italy, and Spain. In 1208, Pope Innocent III declared a crusade against the Albigensians, a heretical Christian sect centered in southern France, and the northern French joined the crusade as a way to pursue political goals of dominating the south. The war lasted for two decades until the aristocracy, courts, and wealth that supported the troubadours collapsed. The troubadours dispersed, spreading their influence into neighboring lands and remaining active in Italy until the fourteenth century. The trouvères in northern France continued through the thirteenth century. They admired the troubadours and preserved their art; indeed, most extant manuscripts of troubadour song were copied in northern France in the middle to late thirteenth century.

SONG IN OTHER LANDS

The troubadour and trouvère tradition inspired types of lyric song in other tongues, spanning subjects from love to religion.

ENGLISH SONG After the Norman Conquest of 1066, French was the language of the kings and nobility in England. The English king, as duke of Normandy and later also duke of Aquitaine, held lands in France, and he participated in French politics and culture. The royal house sponsored troubadours and trouvères, including Bernart de Ventadorn. King Richard I (the Lionheart, 1157–1199), the son of Eleanor of Aquitaine, was himself a trouvère and composed his songs in French.

Few melodies survive for songs in Middle English, the language of the lower and middle classes. Indeed, we have little secular music for these social strata from anywhere in Europe, showing how much our view of medieval music depends on the interest the religious, economic, and intellectual elites had in preserving their own music. But most surviving poems in Middle English, from narrative ballads to secular and religious lyrics, were no doubt meant to be sung, and they suggest a rich musical life.

MINNESINGERS The troubadours were the model for the German knightly poet-musicians known as *Minnesingers*, who flourished between the twelfth and fourteenth centuries and wrote in Middle High German. The love (*Minne*) of which they sang in their *Minnelieder* (love songs) was even more spiritual than *fin' amors*, with an emphasis on faithfulness, duty, and service that reflected the loyalty that knights and nobles owed to their king and that Christians owed to the church. Most songs are strophic, and the most common melodic form is AAB, called *bar form* by scholars of German music since the nineteenth century. Each A section, or *Stollen*, uses the same poetic meter, rhyme scheme, and melody. The B section, or *Abgesang*, is usually longer and may end with all or the latter part of the melody for the Stollen. The rhythm is seldom clear in the notation, raising the same issues as in troubadour song. Genres parallel those of the troubadours, including the crusade song, recounting the experiences of those who renounced worldly comfort to travel on the Crusades. A famous example is the *Palästinalied* (Palestine Song, NAWM 11) by Walther von der Vogelweide (?ca. 1170–?ca. 1230), perhaps the best-known Minnesinger, shown in Figure 4.8.

LAUDE The lyric songs of troubadours and trouvères were sung at courts throughout Italy, and poets writing in Italian drew on them for subject matter, form, and style, creating a new tradition. Yet only a few secular songs in Italian from before 1300 survive with music. Much more numerous are several dozen

FIGURE 4.8 *Walther von der Vogelweide as depicted in a fourteenth-century Swiss manuscript. Vogelweide means "bird-meadow," and his shield, shown in the upper left, includes a caged bird.*

laude (sing. *lauda*), sacred Italian monophonic songs. Composed in cities rather than at court, laude were strophic devotional songs, often with refrains, mostly syllabic, in a style that blends influences from chant, hymns, and troubadour and trouvère song. They were sung in processions of religious penitents and in confraternities, associations of citizens who gathered for prayer and mutual support. The lauda tradition continued for several centuries. From the late fourteenth century on, most laude were polyphonic.

FIGURE 4.9

Illustration from a French Bible from about 1250 showing a feast with musicians playing (from left to right) a vielle, hurdy-gurdy, harp, and psaltery.

CANTIGAS One of the treasures of medieval song is the *Cantigas de Santa María,* a collection of over four hundred *cantigas* (songs) in Galician-Portuguese in honor of the Virgin Mary. The collection was prepared about 1270–90 under the direction of King Alfonso el Sabio (the Wise) of Castile and León (northwest Spain) and preserved in four beautifully illuminated manuscripts. Whether Alfonso wrote some of the poems and melodies is uncertain. Most songs in the collection relate stories of miracles performed by the Virgin, the object of increasing veneration from the twelfth century on; after nine such tales, every tenth cantiga is a hymn of praise for Mary. Cantiga 159, *Non sofre Santa María* (NAWM 12), tells of a cut of meat, stolen from some pilgrims, that Mary caused to jump about, revealing where it was hidden. The songs all have refrains, perhaps sung by a group alternating with a soloist singing the verses. Songs with refrains were often associated with dancing, a possibility reinforced by illustrations of dancers in the *Cantigas* manuscripts. In most of the songs the verses are in the by now familiar AAB form, with music for the B section also used for the refrain; because the refrain appears first, and it is customary to label the sections of a piece in alphabetical order beginning with the first section, the musical form is written A bba A bba . . . A.

MEDIEVAL INSTRUMENTS

The songs described in this chapter were notated as single melodic lines, but may sometimes have been accompanied by instruments playing in unison or improvising accompaniments. Illustrated manuscripts depict the wide variety of medieval instruments.

String instruments

A miniature from a thirteenth-century French Bible, in Figure 4.9, shows four musicians playing at a feast. On the left is a *vielle* or fiddle, the principal medieval bowed instrument and predecessor of the Renaissance viol and modern violin. Although vielles varied in shape and size, the typical thirteenth-century vielle had five strings tuned in fourths and fifths so the melody could be supported by one or more drones on open strings. Next is a *hurdy-gurdy*, a three-stringed vielle sounded by a rotating wheel inside the instrument

FIGURE 4.10 *Illustrations from the* Cantigas de Santa María *(ca. 1250–80) showing musicians playing (clockwise from upper left) transverse flutes, shawms, pipes and tabors, and trumpets. The hand positions shown for the flutes and shawms are opposite from the positions used on modern flutes and oboes, but that may be the result of artistic license rather than performance tradition.*

turned by a crank at one end; the player presses levers to change pitches on the melody string while the other strings sound drones, creating a texture similar to a bagpipe. The third musician plays a harp of a type that apparently originated in the British Isles. On the right is a ***psaltery***, played by plucking strings attached to a frame over a wooden sounding board; it is a remote ancestor of the harpsichord and piano.

Miniatures from the *Cantigas de Santa María* in Figure 4.10 show musicians playing wind and percussion instruments of the time. The ***transverse flute*** was similar to the modern flute, but made of wood or ivory and without keys. The ***shawm*** was a double-reed instrument, similar to the oboe. The medieval trumpet was straight and lacked valves, so it could play only the harmonic series. The ***pipe and tabor*** featured a high whistle fingered with the left hand while the right hand beat a small drum with a stick.

Other instruments familiar to us today were already in use. The universal folk instrument was the bagpipe, whose player inflated a bag (often made from an animal skin or bladder) that in turn forced an unbroken stream of

Wind and percussion instruments

Bagpipes, bells, and organs

Dancing as Described in the *Romance of the Rose*

The *Romance of the Rose* (ca. 1235) is the best known of the medieval romances, long narrative poems on heroic subjects. It includes a valuable description of the *carole*, danced to the accompaniment of a *retrouenge*, a song with a refrain, and of jongleurs and minstrels playing instruments.

Now see the carole go! Each man and maid
Most daintily steps out with many a turn
And arabesque upon the tender grass.
See there the flutists and the minstrel men,
Performers on the fiddle! Now they sing
A retrouenge, a tune from old Lorraine;
For it has better songs than other lands.
A troop of skillful jongleurs thereabout
Well played their parts, and girls with
    tambourines
Danced jollily, and, finishing each tune,
Threw high their instruments, and as these fell
Caught each on finger tip, and never failed.

Guillaume de Lorris, *Roman de la rose*, trans. Harry W. Robbins (New York: Dutton, 1962), 16 (lines 753–64).

air through the chanter and one or more drone pipes, all sounded by reeds. Bells were played in church and used as signals. By 1100, monastic churches began to have early forms of the organ, and by 1300, organs were common in cathedrals as well. Besides church organs, there were two smaller types. The **portative organ** was small enough to be carried (*portatum*) or suspended by a strap around the neck. It had a single set of pipes, and the right hand played the keys while the left worked the bellows. The **positive organ** had to be placed (*positum*) on a table to be played, and required an assistant to pump the bellows.

Most of these instruments came into Europe from Asia, through either the Byzantine Empire or the Arabs in North Africa and Spain. Their early history is obscure and their nomenclature inconsistent. But in them we can recognize the variety of bowed and plucked strings, winds, brass, percussion, and organs familiar from later eras, and understand that medieval musicians already had a rich palette of instrumental color in their hands.

DANCE MUSIC

Dancing in the Middle Ages was accompanied by songs or instrumental music, usually not written down but performed from memory, so that few melodies survive. To judge from written accounts and pictures, the most popular social dance in France from the twelfth through the fourteenth centuries was the **carole**, a circle dance that was usually accompanied by a song sung by one or more of the dancers. The dancers were sometimes also joined by instrumentalists (see Source Reading). Despite the carole's popularity, only about two dozen melodies are extant.

Instrumental dances   About fifty instrumental dance tunes survive from the thirteenth and fourteenth centuries, most monophonic, some set in polyphony for a keyboard instrument. These dances are the earliest notated instrumental music and must have been preserved because they were particularly admired. Like European dance music ever since, they are marked by a steady beat, clear meter, repeated sections, and predictable phrasing. Although in most cases only the melody was written down, these dances could be performed by several players, including drum and other improvised accompaniments.

Estampie   Of the surviving medieval instrumental dances, the most common form is the **estampie**. It has several sections, each played twice with two different endings, the first with an **open** (*ouvert*) or incomplete cadence and the second with a **closed** (*clos*) or full cadence. The same open and closed endings are usually employed throughout. A late-thirteenth-century chansonnier called *Le manuscrit du roi* (The Manuscript of the King) includes eight "royal estampies" (the fourth is NAWM 13). All French estampies are in triple meter and consist of relatively short sections. A fourteenth-century Italian relative, the *istampita,* uses the same form but is in duple or compound meter, with longer sections and more repetition between sections.

THE LOVER'S COMPLAINT

The lyric songs of the troubadours and their successors share traits typical of European songs ever since. These medieval songs are strophic, diatonic, and primarily syllabic, moving mostly stepwise in a range of about an octave, usually with a clear pitch center. They have short musical phrases, roughly equal in size, each typically rising to a high point and falling to a cadence. Often one or more phrases of music are repeated to different words within each stanza, and some songs have a refrain after every verse. The most common subject, a pure, usually unattainable love, and the themes and imagery of these songs—especially the complaints of lovers whose faithful devotion goes unrewarded—also have many echoes in later music, including popular songs. Equally enduring are the images of the minstrel—the itinerant musician—and the troubadour—the poet-composer—and the structures of professional life and training embodied by musicians' guilds.

The songs themselves continued to be sung for a few years or even decades, and many were preserved in writing. Some melodies were borrowed for new songs, sometimes in other languages. Eventually, most of the songs passed from the scene along with the society that gave them birth, replaced by new styles. Dance melodies met a similar fate. In the eighteenth and nineteenth centuries, a new concern for each nation's cultural heritage led to renewed interest in the Middle Ages and the collection and publication of medieval poetry and some trouvère songs arranged with piano accompaniment. Adam de la Halle's musical works were transcribed and published in 1872, and editions of other medieval song repertories followed in the twentieth century. Recent decades have brought a revival of medieval secular and nonliturgical song and instrumental dances in concert and recordings, both in performances that try to reconstruct the sounds of medieval voices and instruments and in new guises such as the "medieval rock" arrangements of Walther von der Vogelweide's *Palästinalied*.

Further Reading is available at digital.wwnorton.com/hwm10

POLYPHONY THROUGH THE THIRTEENTH CENTURY

During Europe's economic growth between 1050 and 1300, the church prospered. Pious donors funded hundreds of new monasteries and convents, filled by rising numbers of men, women, and children seeking a religious life. St. Francis, St. Dominic, St. Clare, and others founded new religious orders. In the eleventh and early twelfth centuries, builders erected large Romanesque churches that used the principles of the Roman basilica and the round arch, and artists decorated these buildings with frescoes and sculptures. By the mid-twelfth century, craftsmen created a new style of church architecture, later called Gothic, which emphasized height and spaciousness with soaring vaults, pointed arches, slender columns, flying buttresses, large stained-glass windows, and intricate tracery (see Figure 5.3, p. 87). As scholars revived ancient learning, St. Anselm, St. Thomas Aquinas, and others associated with the intellectual movement called Scholasticism sought to reconcile the classical philosophy of Aristotle and others with Christian doctrine through commentary on authoritative texts.

These developments found parallels in *polyphony*, music in which voices sing together in independent parts. At first, polyphony was a style of performance, a manner of enriching chant with one or more added voices. Those who sang and heard polyphony valued it as a means of praising God, for its beautiful sounds, and as decoration, a concept central to medieval art. Polyphonic performance heightened the grandeur of chant and thus of the liturgy itself, just like art and architectural decoration ornamented the church and thus the service. The added voices elaborated the authorized chants through a musical gloss, resembling both the monophonic trope (see Chapter 3) and Scholastic commentary on Scripture. New developments in theory and notation during the eleventh to thirteenth centuries allowed musicians to write down polyphony and to develop styles that grew progressively more elaborate, in genres such as *organum* and *motet*.

The rise of written polyphony is of particular interest, as it inaugurated four concepts that have distinguished Western music ever since: (1) **counterpoint**, the combination of multiple independent lines; (2) **harmony**, the regulation of simultaneous sounds; (3) the centrality of **notation**; and (4) the idea of **composition** as distinct from performance. These concepts changed over time, but their presence in this music links it to all that followed.

Polyphony began as a manner of performance, became a practice of oral composition, and developed into a written tradition. It is easy for us to conceive of polyphony as essentially a tradition of written composition, as music historians used to do, because that is what we see in the manuscripts. But we must remember that what was written down was only a small part of the polyphony that was sung, and it requires historical imagination to understand the oral polyphony that existed only in the throats of singers, the ears of listeners, and the minds and memories of performers and composers.

EARLY ORGANUM

Europeans probably performed music in multiple parts long before it was described. The simplest type, singing or playing a melody against a **drone**, is found in most European folk traditions and many Asian cultures, suggesting it dates from antiquity or even prehistoric times. Drones typically sustain the modal final, sometimes joined by the fifth above. For a listener, drones ground the melody in its tonal center and heighten the sense of closure when the melody cadences on the final.

Another way to enrich a melody, doubling it in parallel perfect intervals, was apparently already an old practice when first explained and illustrated in the ninth-century treatise *Musica enchiriadis*. Examples are transcribed in Example 5.1 and NAWM 14a–b.

The treatise uses the term **organum** for two or more voices singing different notes in agreeable combinations according to given rules. This term was used for several styles of polyphony from the ninth through thirteenth centuries. The resulting piece is always called "an organum" (pl. *organa*), but in referring to the style it is best to add a modifier.

Organum

The type shown in Example 5.1 is known today as **parallel organum**. The original chant melody is the **principal voice**, the other the **organal voice**, moving in exact parallel motion a fifth below. Fifths were consonances, considered both perfect and beautiful. Although parallel fifths would later be forbidden in Renaissance counterpoint, to medieval ears they added resonance and magnificence to an otherwise bare unison. In early organum, the organal voice is normally sung below the principal voice. Either or both voices may be doubled at the octave to create an even richer sound (see NAWM 14b).

Parallel organum

EXAMPLE 5.1 *Parallel organum at the fifth below, from* Musica enchiriadis

Principal voice
Organal voice

Tu   pa – tris   sem – pi – ter – nus   es   fi – li – us.

You of the Father are the everlasting Son.

Mixed parallel and oblique organum

We might expect parallel organum at the fourth below to be as straightforward as parallel fifths, and it may once have been so in practice. But the scale system described in *Musica enchiriadis* contained augmented fourths (or tritones), such as *B♭–e* and *f–b,* and the adjustments necessary to avoid them produced organum that was not strictly parallel. To prevent these tritones from occurring, the writer of the treatise prohibits the organal voice from moving below *c* when a segment of chant includes *e* or below *g* when it includes *b*. The singers performing the organal added voice must remain on one note until they can proceed in parallel fourths without sounding a tritone. The result, illustrated in Example 5.2 (NAWM 14c), combines oblique motion, like a melody moving over a drone, with parallel motion, and thus this style is called **mixed parallel and oblique organum**. Figure 5.1 shows how this example appears in one manuscript copy of the treatise.

Avoiding tritones in this manner had significant effects. When the organal voice is stationary, harmonic major seconds and thirds may result, but they were not considered consonant; if either would occur on the last note of a phrase, the organal voice must move up to a unison with the principal voice. Converging on the unison emphasizes the cadences and phrasing of the original chant. This break away from simple drones and parallel motion raised the possibility of polyphony as a combination of independent voices.

From performance to composition

The styles of organum described in *Musica enchiriadis* were ways for singers to adorn chant in performance based on strict rules for deriving added voices from the chant. They were not methods of composition. But the next theorist to describe organum, Guido of Arezzo in his *Micrologus* (ca. 1025–28), allowed a range of choices that could result in a variety of organal voices combining oblique and parallel motion, and with choice comes the possibility of composition. In most cases, we can assume these organal voices were composed orally, either improvised by a soloist or worked out in rehearsal. We have evidence for such oral composition both from theorists and from a few practical sources in which organal voices were written down. The largest

EXAMPLE 5.2 *Mixed parallel and oblique organum, from* Musica enchiriadis

King of Heaven, Lord of the roaring sea,
Of the shining Titan (the Sun) and the squalid earth,
Your humble servants, worshipping you with pious melodies,
Beseech you, as you command, to free them from diverse ills.

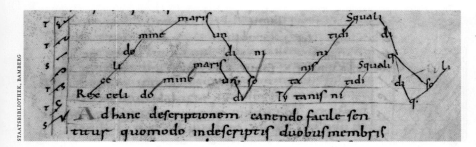

FIGURE 5.1 *Excerpt from a manuscript of* Musica enchiriadis, *showing the first two phrases of* Rex caeli domine *(Example 5.2) in mixed parallel and oblique organum. The shapes on the left are signs for pitches, with "T" and "S" in the margin indicating which steps are tones and which are semitones. The height of each syllable indicates its pitch, and the motions in each voice are shown by lines linking the syllables, until the two voices unite on the last two syllables in each phrase. The scribe has not worried about aligning the parts vertically, assuming the reader will understand that the voices will declaim the words together.*

source is the Winchester Troper, a manuscript of tropes and other liturgical music from a monastery in Winchester, England. It contains 174 organa for the Mass and Office, perhaps by Wulfstan of Winchester (fl. 992–996), the cantor there. Only the organal voices are notated; the monks would have known the chants by heart, and in all probability the organal voices were composed and transmitted orally and were written down as an aid to memory. The scribe's concern to fix them in writing shows that organum was becoming a form of composition as well as a manner of performing chant.

The new possibilities did not entirely displace the old, however. Later theorists, such as Elias Salomo in the late thirteenth century and Jacobus de Ispania (Jacques de Liège) in about 1330, describe singing in parallel fourths and fifths as a current practice. Indeed, as each new style of polyphony described in this chapter was introduced, older ones continued in other places or were used alongside the new, often for different occasions or purposes.

NOTE-AGAINST-NOTE ORGANUM As possible ways to add an organal voice multiplied, musicians must have sensed an opportunity to decorate the chants of the service, in the same way that sculptors, painters, and tapestry makers decorated the walls of the churches. By the late eleventh century, singers were improvising and scribes were recording a new style of organum, known today as ***note-against-note organum***, in which the organal voice is more independent and prominent.

Rules for improvising or composing in the new style are preserved in *Ad organum faciendum* (On Making Organum, ca. 1100), which gives as examples the solo sections of *Alleluia Justus ut palma* (NAWM 15). As shown in Example 5.3, the added voice now usually lies above the chant rather than below it (though the parts may cross), perhaps because that allows a wider range of motion. The organal voice moves against the chant, mostly note for note, in a free mixture of contrary, oblique, parallel, and similar motion while forming consonant harmonic intervals with it. The consonances remain the unison, fourth, fifth, and octave, with cadences on the unison or octave, sometimes preceded by a third or sixth to allow stepwise motion. The organal voice is more disjunct than the chant because of the limited number of harmonic intervals from which the singer may choose. Yet this style of organum offers much more freedom than its predecessors, allowing singers and composers to show their artistry while embellishing the liturgical chant.

During the next several centuries, polyphony was primarily the responsibility of soloists, not the choir. This arrangement makes sense in several ways. By long tradition the most ornate chants, the responsorial psalms, were

Ad organum faciendum

Soloists

EXAMPLE 5.3 *Note-against-note organum from* Ad organum faciendum

The righteous [shall flourish] like a palm tree.

mainly sung by soloists, and it was appropriate for them to take the lead in any further musical elaboration of the service. Soloists typically sang the tropes, and polyphony was analogous to troping as an addition to the authorized chants. Most important, only a soloist could improvise a free organal line against a given chant, so that when note-against-note organum came to be written down it was already associated with solo performance. Thus, although older styles of organum could be sung by choirs and used for any chant, note-against-note organum and later styles were used only where soloists sang, primarily in the solo portions of Graduals, Alleluias, and Office responsories and in troped sections of the Mass Ordinary. Polyphony did not stand alone; rather, soloists singing polyphonic sections alternated with monophonic chant sung by the choir.

AQUITANIAN POLYPHONY

Early in the twelfth century, singers and composers in France developed a new, more ornate type of polyphony. It is known today as **Aquitanian polyphony** because the main sources are three manuscripts once held in the Abbey of St. Martial at Limoges in the duchy of Aquitaine and copied in Aquitanian notation. The provenance of these manuscripts suggests that this style of polyphony emerged in Aquitaine, in the same region and around the same time as the early troubadours (see Chapter 4). A manuscript with similar works, the Codex Calixtinus, was prepared nearby in central France and brought by 1173 to the Cathedral of Santiago de Compostela in northwest Spain. These manuscripts contain the written traces of a primarily oral tradition. Most polyphony was improvised using conventions and formulas developed by singers and recorded in treatises of the time, and even the pieces that scribes preserved in notation were most likely composed orally and fixed in memory rather than worked out on paper.

Polyphonic versus   Aquitanian polyphony includes settings of chant, such as sequences and Benedicamus tropes. But most of the repertory comprises settings of *versus*—rhyming, metric Latin poems—which were also set monophonically (see Chapter 4).

Discant and   Some theorists of the time described two main polyphonic styles, both
organum   evident in Aquitanian polyphony. **Discant** style occurs when both parts move at about the same rate, with one to three notes in the upper part for each

note of the lower voice. *Organum style* now refers to a texture in which the upper voice sings note groups of varying lengths above each note of the lower voice, which accordingly moves much more slowly than the upper; this style is known today as ***florid organum*** because of the florid upper part. In both styles, the lower voice holds the principal melody and is called the ***tenor*** (from Latin *tenere,* "to hold"; this term did not come to mean "high male voice" until centuries later). And in both styles, the upper part elaborates an underlying note-against-note counterpoint with the tenor.

These styles are illustrated in two passages from *Jubilemus, exultemus* (NAWM 16), a versus whose tenor was apparently newly composed. The section in Example 5.4a uses the style of florid organum, with melismas of three to fifteen notes in the upper part for most notes in the tenor. (A note followed by a grace note indicates a plica, explained in Chapter 4.) Example 5.4b shows a passage in discant style, with one to three notes in the upper part for each tenor note until the penultimate syllable, which typically has a longer melisma. In both excerpts, contrary motion is more common than parallel, and most note groups in the upper voice begin on a perfect consonance

EXAMPLE 5.4 *Florid organum and discant styles in* Jubilemus, exultemus

FIGURE 5.2 *Jubilemus,*
exultemus, a two-voice
versus, in Aquitanian score
notation. The two voices
are written above the words
and separated from each
other by a red line. The
coordination between the
parts is not always clear.

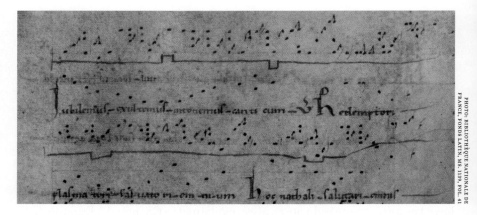

with the tenor. The lower staff in each example shows the underlying note-against-note polyphony between the voices that is embellished by the more florid motion of the upper part. As in note-against-note organum, phrases end on octaves or unisons, heightening the sense of closure.

Both florid organum and discant exemplify their medieval creators' love of decoration, ornamenting the syllabic tenor line with varied melodic gestures in the upper voice and changing harmonies between the parts. By alternating these two styles, musicians provided variety and gave their pieces shape.

Score notation *Jubilemus, exultemus* appears in the manuscript in **score notation**, as
and rhythm shown in Figure 5.2. The voices are written above the text, the top voice above the tenor, separated by a red line. We presume both voices sang the words. Both are in heighted neumes, so the pitches are reasonably clear but not always certain. The vertical alignment of parts indicates approximately which notes are sung together, yet there are ambiguities. Durations are not indicated, leaving many questions: Should the tenor proceed at a steady pace while the upper voice moves more or less quickly to fit? Or the reverse, in which case the tenor in most florid passages loses its character as a tune and becomes a series of sustained pitches? Or were both coordinated through a meter or rhythmic convention understood at the time or conveyed orally but not apparent in the notation? These uncertainties may worry historians, but they open opportunities for interpretation by modern editors and performers, who vary considerably in the solutions they offer.

NOTRE DAME POLYPHONY

Musicians in and around Paris developed a still more ornate style of polyphony in the late twelfth and early thirteenth centuries. The creators of this style were associated with the University of Paris, which furthered the intellectual atmosphere for this new style and where several of them had studied, and with the new Cathedral of Paris, Notre Dame ("Our Lady," the Virgin Mary), shown in Figure 5.3. They may also have enjoyed patronage from the kings of France. One of the grandest Gothic cathedrals, Notre Dame took almost a century to build: the foundations were begun around 1160, the apse and choir completed in 1182, the first Mass celebrated in 1183, the transept and nave finished around 1200, and the façade completed about 1250. During this time, musicians at or connected to Notre Dame and in the region of Paris created a new repertory of unprecedented grandeur and complexity, including the first body of music for more than two independent voices. Such elaborate music was valued for its artistry in decorating the authorized chant, making important services more impressive, and paralleling in sound the stunning size and beautiful decoration of the building itself.

This repertory stemming from Notre Dame was sung for more than a century, from the late twelfth century to the fourteenth, and was disseminated and imitated across much of Europe, from Spain to Poland and from Italy to Scotland. Music historians long regarded it as the first polyphony to be primarily composed in writing and read from notation rather than improvised or orally composed. But recent research complicates that view. According to records of ceremonies at Notre Dame, neither chant nor polyphony was performed from notation. The earliest surviving manuscripts of Notre Dame polyphony date from the 1240s, decades after the repertory began to be created. The musical text of individual pieces can vary considerably from one manuscript to the next, in a manner that suggests oral rather than (or alongside) written transmission. A treatise copied in Paris in the early 1200s, now preserved at the Vatican in Rome, describes how to improvise organum in Notre Dame style, including numerous melodic gestures that are present throughout the repertory. All this evidence indicates a fluid body of polyphony developed by singers and preserved in memory before it was written down. How such a vast and complex repertory was remembered, and how it was written down, are aspects that make this music especially significant in music history.

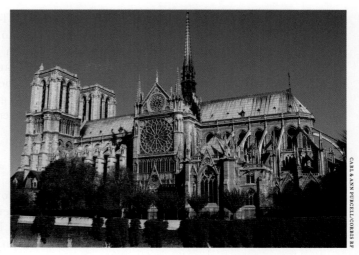

FIGURE 5.3 *Notre Dame Cathedral of Paris, built ca. 1160–1258. Its great height, elaborate decoration, and innovative architecture have parallels in the unprecedented length, intricacy, and carefully worked-out structure of the music that composers created to sing in the cathedral.*

THE RHYTHMIC MODES Musicians at Notre Dame developed the first notation since ancient Greece to indicate duration, a step of great importance for later music. In its final form, their system was described in a thirteenth-century treatise attributed to Johannes de Garlandia. Instead of using note shapes to show relative durations, as in modern notation, they used combinations of note groups, or **ligatures**, to indicate different patterns of **longs** (long notes) and **breves** (short notes). According to Garlandia, there were six basic patterns called "modes," known today as the **rhythmic modes**. These were identified by number and are shown here both as patterns of longs (L) and breves (B) and in modern transcription:

1. LB ♩ ♪   3. LBB ♩. ♪♪   5. LL ♩. ♩.
2. BL ♪♩   4. BBL ♪♪♩.   6. BBB ♪ ♪ ♪

The basic time unit (**tempus**, pl. *tempora*), here transcribed as an eighth note, was always grouped in threes, as in a modern meter of $\frac{3}{8}$ or $\frac{6}{8}$. This grouping resulted naturally from the alternation in modes 1 and 2 of a long (two tempora) and a breve (one tempus). To preserve the groups of three in modes 3, 4, and 5, the long was lengthened to three tempora, and the second breve in modes 3 and 4 was doubled in length. Modes 1 and 5 were most common and apparently the oldest. Mode 4 was rarely employed, and Garlandia may have included it primarily to round out the system, which he apparently modeled on a set of six poetic meters listed in an earlier treatise on Latin grammar.

Variety   In theory, a mode 1 melody would consist of repetitions of the pattern, each phrase ending with a rest:

But such a melody could be monotonous, and in practice the rhythm was more flexible. Notes could be broken into shorter units, or two notes of a pattern could be combined into one. In some pieces, the mode changes from one phrase to the next, and many pieces combine mode 5 in the tenor with another mode in the upper voice.

Notation   To indicate which rhythmic mode was in force, scribes used ligatures, signs derived from the neumes of chant notation that denoted groups of notes. When a melody was written as in Example 5.5a, with one three-note ligature followed by a series of two-note ligatures, it signaled the singer to use mode 1, as in the transcription in Example 5.5b. Because ligatures are the key features of the rhythmic notation, they are represented in modern editions by horizontal brackets over the notes, as here. In this mode, each ligature ends with a long, and all but the first have the same rhythmic pattern, making the notation easy to read once it becomes familiar. The other rhythmic modes were shown in similar ways, with a different combination of ligatures for each mode. Departures from the prevailing pattern, changes of mode, or repeated tones (which could not be included in ligatures) required modifications.

Rhythmic modes and memory   Writing the music down preserved the repertory, served as a memory aid, helped singers learn new pieces, and made it possible to transmit the music from Notre Dame to other centers across Europe. But the rhythmic modes were not only a notational device. The repeating rhythmic patterns gave shape to the music and made it easier to memorize and recall, in the same way that verse is often more memorable than prose.

THE *MAGNUS LIBER ORGANI* Thanks to a treatise from about 1285 known as Anonymous IV, we know the names of two musicians associated with creating polyphony for Notre Dame, Leoninus and Perotinus (see Source Reading). Leoninus (or Léonin, fl. 1150s–ca. 1201) served at the Cathedral of Paris in many capacities, beginning in the 1150s, before the current building was begun. He was a canon at Notre Dame, became a priest, and was affiliated with the monastery of St. Victor. As a poet, he wrote a paraphrase of the first eight

EXAMPLE 5.5 *Use of ligatures to indicate a rhythmic mode*

SOURCE READING

Anonymous IV on the *Magnus liber organi*

In the late thirteenth century, an Englishman who apparently studied at the University of Paris wrote a treatise that has become known as Anonymous IV because it was the fourth anonymous treatise in C.-E.-H. de Coussemaker's collection of medieval treatises. In the context of a discussion on notation, the writer mentions musicians associated with the creation of Notre Dame polyphony. He seems to ascribe the whole repertory to Leoninus and Perotinus, but it is far more likely that they were leading figures among successive generations of singers who collectively created the music over several decades.

These rules [for notational signs] are used in many old books, and this from the time of Perotinus the Great (and in his own time) . . . and similarly from the time of Leo[ninus] to a certain extent. . . . And note that Master Leoninus was an excellent *organista* [singer or composer of organum], so it is said, who made the great book of organum [*magnus liber organi*] on the gradual and antiphonary to enrich the Divine Service. It was in use up to

the time of Perotinus the Great, who edited it and made many better clausulae or puncta, being an excellent *discantor* [singer or composer of discant], and better [at discant] than Leoninus was. (This, however, is not to be asserted regarding the subtlety of organum, etc.)

Now, this same Master Perotinus made the best *quadrupla* [four-voice organa], such as *Viderunt* and *Sederunt,* with an abundance of musical *colores* [melodic formulas]; likewise, the noblest *tripla* [three-voice organa], such as *Alleluia Posui adiutorium* and [*Alleluia*] *Nativitas,* etc. He also made three-voice conductus, such as *Salvatoris hodie,* and two-voice conductus, such as *Dum sigillum summi patris,* and also, among many others, monophonic conductus, such as *Beata viscera,* etc. The book or, rather, books of Master Perotinus were in use up to the time of Master Robertus de Sabilone in the choir of the Paris cathedral of the Blessed Virgin [Notre Dame], and from his time up to the present day.

Translation adapted from Edward H. Roesner, "Who 'Made' the *Magnus liber?*," *Early Music History* 20 (2001): 227–28.

books of the Bible in verse and several shorter works. Little is known about Perotinus (or Pérotin, fl. late twelfth and early thirteenth centuries), but he must have held an important position at the cathedral. The treatise's reference to both as "master" suggests that both earned the master of arts degree at the school that would become the University of Paris, a center of intellectual innovation intertwined with Notre Dame Cathedral since the last decades of the twelfth century.

Anonymous IV calls Leoninus an excellent *organista*, meaning a singer or composer of organum, and credits him with compiling a *Magnus liber organi* ("great book of polyphony"). This collection contained two-voice settings of the solo portions of the responsorial chants (Graduals, Alleluias, and Office Responsories) for the major feasts of the church year. To undertake such a cycle, elaborating the chants that were the central musical focus of the year's most important services, shows a vision as grand as that of those building Notre Dame Cathedral. But Leoninus did not undertake it alone, despite Anonymous IV's testimony. Like building the cathedral, creating this repertory was a collective project. We cannot be certain what

Magnus liber organi

Leoninus's role was, though we may guess that he was a leading figure in its creation or preservation.

Layers of adaptation   No "great book" survives from Leoninus's lifetime, and it is not even certain whether the music was written down then. But the repertory he helped to develop is contained in later manuscripts, primarily two now in Wolfenbüttel, Germany, and one in Florence, Italy. We do not know how much of the surviving music is by Leoninus. The many variants that occur between versions of the same piece suggest that much of the music was transmitted orally. Moreover, it is clear that musicians during and after Leoninus's time freely altered and added to the collection. The manuscripts offer different settings for the same passages of chant, often presenting several alternatives, and include organa for two, three, or four voices as well as pieces in the newer genres of conductus and motet (see pp. 95–97). Clearly the "great book" was not a fixed canon, but a fluid repertory from which material could be chosen for each year's services.

By comparing different settings of a single chant, we can see this process of revision and substitution in action and can trace changes in style. An ideal example is *Viderunt omnes,* the Gradual for Christmas Day, already familiar from our discussion of chant in Chapters 2 and 3 (see NAWM 3d and Examples 2.2 and 2.3) and elaborated polyphonically by Leoninus, Perotinus, and their colleagues (NAWM 17–19).

ORGANUM IN THE STYLE OF LEONINUS The version of *Viderunt omnes* in the earlier Wolfenbüttel manuscript (NAWM 17), which also appears in virtually the same form in the Florence manuscript, may be the earliest surviving setting of this melody in the Notre Dame repertory. Although we cannot ascribe it to Leoninus with certainty, we assume it resembles the polyphony he sang. It is in two voices and features two different styles of polyphony, organum and discant, paralleling the contrast we observed in Aquitanian polyphony. Only the solo portions of the chant, the intonation of the respond and most of the verse, were sung polyphonically. The choir sang the remaining portions in unison, so that three styles—plainchant, organum, and discant—were heard side by side.

Organum style   The opening intonation on "Viderunt," shown in Example 5.6, exemplifies organum style (also called *organum purum*, "pure organum"). The chant melody appears in the tenor in unmeasured long notes, like a series of drones. Over these sustained tones the upper voice, called the **duplum** (Latin for "double"), sings expansive melismas, moving mostly stepwise, often lingering on dissonances with the tenor, and cadencing from time to time on an octave, fifth, or unison followed by a rest. Ligatures in the original notation are shown here by horizontal brackets; descending neumes by dashed slurs; and plicas by small notes slurred to the preceding note. The notation does not clearly indicate any rhythmic mode, suggesting that the duplum should be sung in free rhythm, although some scholars and performers have applied modal rhythms.

Discant style   Most of this setting is in organum style, but it is punctuated by passages in discant style where both voices move in modal rhythm, the tenor usually in mode 5 and the duplum primarily in mode 1. The longest discant passage in *Viderunt omnes* is on the syllable "Do-" of "Dominus," shown in part

EXAMPLE 5.6 *First section of* Viderunt omnes *in organum duplum*

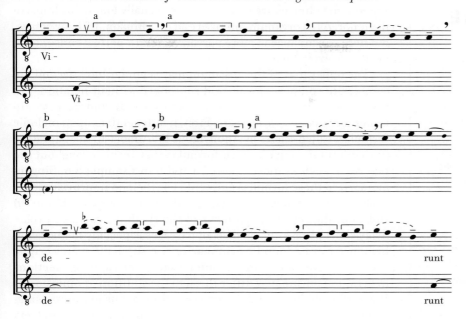

EXAMPLE 5.7 *Discant section on "Do-" of* Viderunt omnes

in Example 5.7. In the original chant, this was by far the longest melisma. Scholars have suggested that Leoninus and his colleagues set the long melismas in discant style because organum, with its elongated tenor notes, would have made the music too long. Thus changes of style in the polyphony, from organum to discant and back, occur precisely where, in the chant, the style changes from neumatic text setting to melismatic and back. In this section, the phrases are relatively short, usually four or six longs in the tenor. As in organum, phrases end on a unison, fifth, or octave, but here consonance is more pervasive, with a perfect consonance on almost every long.

The upper part of this organum may seem far too long and too complex to compose, learn, and reproduce without notation, but several factors suggest that it was composed orally and was easier to remember than it first appears. First, it is dependent upon melodic formulas, called *colores* by Anonymous IV. Almost all the figuration in the duplum is made from formulas that recur throughout the repertory, such as those marked a and b in Example 5.6. Singers memorized these formulas and could use them to improvise, compose, and remember long organa, without recourse to notation. In addition, the repeating patterns of the rhythmic modes in relatively short phrases made discant passages especially memorable. Evidence can be found by comparing the surviving manuscripts, where sections in discant are often exactly the same but sections in organum purum may differ through the addition or omission of standard melodic formulas. Long-standing habits of improvising, composing orally, and memorizing large amounts of music and text make it likely that all of the Notre Dame repertory, including the three- and four-voice organa, conductus, and motets discussed later in this chapter, could have been conceived orally before being written down.

The organa of Leoninus and his colleagues were in their day by far the longest and most elaborate settings of chant ever created. In weaving intricate strands of melody around the liturgical chant, they were worthy musical analogues to the sculptures and figuration that adorned Notre Dame Cathedral, then still under construction, or the Scholastic theologians' detailed commentary on Scripture. They must have filled the cathedral with sound, overpowering the sense of hearing just as the tall columns, stained-glass windows, and delicate stonework overwhelmed the sense of sight, and moving worshippers to deeper devotion. But they would not be the last word.

SUBSTITUTE CLAUSULAE Anonymous IV writes that Perotinus edited the *Magnus liber* and "made many better clausulae." By **clausula**, the Latin word for a clause or phrase in a sentence, he meant a self-contained section of an organum, setting a word or syllable from the chant and closing with a cadence. Since organa consisted of a series of such sections, it was possible to write new clausulae designed to replace the original setting of a particular segment of chant. Most of these new clausulae, known today as **substitute clausulae**, are in discant style, which may reflect a growing preference for discant. Hundreds appear in the same manuscripts as the organa themselves; all are unattributed, so we cannot know which are by Perotinus, if any. The Florence

EXAMPLE 5.8 *Two substitute clausulae on "Dominus" from* Viderunt omnes

manuscript includes ten clausulae on the word "Dominus" from *Viderunt omnes,* any of which could be used at Christmas Mass. The openings of two of them are shown in Example 5.8 (NAWM 18).

Both clausulae exhibit a trait found in many discant sections: the tenor repeats a rhythmic motive based on a rhythmic mode, here mode 5 in the first clausula and mode 2 in the second. Some clausulae tenors also repeat the melody (over a much longer span than the rhythmic figure). In both forms of repetition, the composer uses musical means to create a sense of coherence for an extended passage, giving it shape and structure and making it easier to follow and to remember. These two kinds of repetition in the tenor, of rhythm and of melody, became very significant in the motet of the thirteenth and fourteenth centuries (see pp. 96–102 and Chapter 6).

Repetition and structure

PEROTINUS ORGANUM Perotinus and his contemporaries also created organa for three or even four voices. A two-voice organum was called an **organum duplum** ("double"); a three-voice organum an *organum triplum,* or simply **triplum** ("triple"); and a four-voice organum a **quadruplum** ("quadruple"). The voices above the tenor were likewise named in ascending order **duplum**, **triplum**, and **quadruplum**. The upper voices all use the rhythmic modes, allowing exact coordination among them, and move in similar ranges, crossing repeatedly.

Anonymous IV tells us Perotinus composed tripla and quadrupla and names two of each, including a four-voice setting of *Viderunt omnes.* Fortunately, such a setting survives (NAWM 19), apparently created in 1198 at the request of the bishop of Paris, and we presume it is by Perotinus, although it may represent the collective work of many singers and scribes. Like other tripla and quadrupla, it begins in a style of organum with measured phrases in modal rhythm in the upper voices above very long notes in the tenor, as shown in Figure 5.4 and Example 5.9. As in the two-voice setting, such passages alternate with sections of discant, of which the longest is again on "Dominus" (not shown here).

Perotinus's Viderunt omnes

To give long sections in organum style both coherence and variety, Perotinus uses several repetitive and harmonic devices in constantly changing

FIGURE 5.4 *Opening of Perotinus's setting of* Viderunt omnes *in organum quadruplum. The upper three voices are in modal rhythm over a sustained tenor note. For a transcription, see Example 5.9 and NAWM 19.*

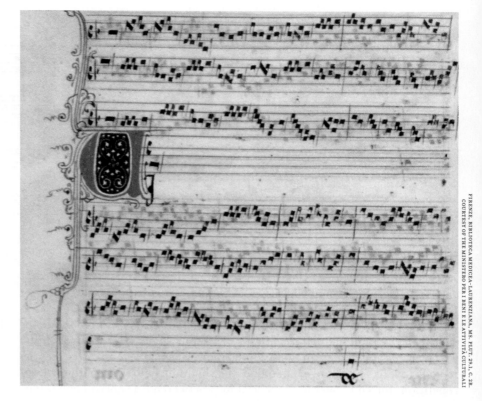

ways. He may repeat a phrase in one voice (see the quadruplum, phrases a and c) while the other voices change, or restate a phrase at a new pitch level (quadruplum, phrases a and a′; duplum, phrases d and d′). Especially characteristic is repetition of a phrase in another voice (phrases b and c throughout the example), including ***voice exchange***, where voices trade phrases (as the duplum and triplum do with phrases b and c). Each phrase emphasizes striking dissonances before resolving to the fifth and octave above the tenor, using harmonic tension to reinforce the consonance while sustaining the listener's interest. In the passage shown here, phrases are short and all voices stop together. In the next section (not shown), voices rest at different times, producing longer spans. Each new section introduces and varies new motives in seemingly endless decoration.

Through such means Perotinus and his colleagues created polyphonic works of unprecedented length, even more grandiose than those of Leoninus's generation, though they served the same liturgical roles. Just as the vastness of Notre Dame Cathedral depended upon a carefully designed structure of pillars, arches, and flying buttresses to support the weight of the roof and walls, allowing great height and large stained-glass windows that create an awesome impression, the organa of Perotinus's time were the most intricately structured music yet composed, using techniques of musical elaboration to sustain great spans of time. This music sounds glorious, evoking the awe appropriate to its religious setting, but the skill of its creators as architects in tones is just as impressive.

EXAMPLE 5.9 *Perotinus,* Viderunt omnes, *opening, with repeating elements indicated by letter*

POLYPHONIC CONDUCTUS The Notre Dame composers and others in France, England, and elsewhere also composed numerous polyphonic ***conductus***. These were settings for two to four voices of the same types of text used in the closely related genres of monophonic conductus (see Chapter 4) and Aquitanian polyphonic versus (see p. 84): rhymed, rhythmic, strophic Latin poems on a sacred or serious topic.

The conductus differs from other Notre Dame polyphony in musical features as well as in its nonliturgical poetic text. First, the tenor melody is newly composed, not borrowed from chant. Second, all voices sing the text together in essentially the same rhythm. Third, the words are set syllabically for the most part. Some conductus are largely syllabic throughout, but most feature melismatic passages, called **caudae** (sing. *cauda,* "tail"), at the beginning and end and before important cadences. Conductus with caudae are generally through-composed, although caudae often feature phrase repetitions and voice exchange. Conductus without caudae tend to be simpler in style and strophic in form. Thirteenth-century theorists said conductus were sung using rhythmic modes. The caudae are written in modal notation, but syllabic sections lack the clear patterns of ligatures that specify the mode; most scholars presume that singers chose a mode that fit the meter of the poetry.

MOTET

Musicians at Notre Dame created a new genre in the early thirteenth century by adding newly written Latin words to the upper voices of discant clausulae, analogous to the way earlier musicians had added texts to chant melismas to create sequences and textual tropes (see Chapter 3). The resulting piece was called a **motet** (Latin *motetus,* from French *mot,* "word"; the duplum of a motet could also be called *motetus*). Over the course of the century, poets and composers developed new forms of the motet, including some with French words, secular topics, three or more voices, or rhythmic patterns increasingly free of the rhythmic modes. As organum and conductus gradually fell out of fashion in the middle of the century, the motet became the leading polyphonic genre for both sacred and secular music, evolving from a textual trope of a clausula to a newly composed piece valued for its complex patterns and multiple layers of meaning.

EARLY MOTETS A typical early motet is *Factum est salutare/Dominus* (NAWM 20a), shown in Example 5.10 and based on the discant clausula in Example 5.8a. (Because motets usually have a different text in each voice, they are identified by a compound title comprising the first words of each voice from highest to lowest.) Since the poet fit words to the existing duplum melody, the varying number of notes in each short phrase required him to write a poem with irregular line lengths, accentuation, and rhyme scheme. Like many early Latin motets based on clausulae, this text is a kind of trope on the original chant text, elaborating its meaning and drawing on its words or sounds. The poem ends with the word "Dominus" (Lord), on which the tenor melody was originally sung, and incorporates several other words from the chant (underlined in the example), some of which are echoed in subsequent rhymes. The discant clausula, a musical decoration of a word, is here in turn embellished by the addition of words, like a gloss upon a gloss, both referring back to the original chant and its words, drawn from a psalm. The resulting motet is an

EXAMPLE 5.10 Factum est salutare/Dominus

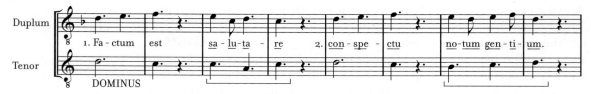

Salvation was made known in the sight of the people.

ingenious composite artwork with multiple layers of borrowing and of meaning. In an ecclesiastical culture that treasured commentary, allegory, and new ways of reworking traditional themes, such pieces must have been highly esteemed for their many allusions.

This motet would not be inappropriate for performance at Mass as part of the Gradual *Viderunt omnes,* like the original clausula, and its presence in one of the main manuscripts of Notre Dame polyphony suggests that it may have played a liturgical role. But it could also be sung on other occasions, even for entertainment. Musicians soon regarded the motet as a genre independent of church performance. The tenor lost its liturgical function and became raw material for composition, its melody serving as a supporting framework for the upper voice or voices while, in many cases, its text related to the texts of the upper voices in meaningful ways.

Motet as independent genre

This change in the role of motets raised new possibilities. Composers reworked existing motets in several ways: (1) writing a different text for the duplum, in Latin or French, often on a secular topic; (2) adding a third or fourth voice to those already present; (3) giving the additional parts texts of their own, to create a *double motet* (with two texts above the tenor) or *triple motet* (with three); or (4) deleting the original duplum and writing one or more new voices, each with its own text, to go with the existing tenor. Composers also wrote motets from scratch, by laying out one of the tenor melodies from the Notre Dame clausula repertory in a new rhythmic pattern and writing new voices to fit it.

New approaches

The two motets in Examples 5.11 and 5.12 illustrate some of these possibilities. *Fole acostumance/Dominus* (NAWM 20b) features the same tenor as *Factum est salutare/Dominus* (Example 5.10), in both melody and rhythm, but states it twice and substitutes a new, more quickly moving duplum melody for the original one. The doubled length and faster motion accommodate a much longer text, a secular French poem complaining that envy, hypocrisy, and deception have ruined France. Such a motet, with its bitter but amusing text in the vernacular, can only have been intended for entertainment.

French motets

The composer of *Super te Ierusalem/Sed fulsit virginitas/Dominus* (NAWM 20c), on the other hand, did not take a tenor unchanged from a clausula, but used the first half of the same chant melisma on "Dominus" (minus its first two notes) with a different rhythmic pattern. The top two voices set the first and second halves respectively of a Latin poem on the birth of Jesus to the Virgin Mary, appropriate to the feast of Christmas on which the tenor melody was originally sung; such a motet could have been sung in private devotions in that season. The poem was apparently written before the music, to judge from its regular line lengths. As in most motets with more than two voices, the upper parts rarely rest together or with the tenor, so that the music moves forward in an unbroken stream. This motet exists in two variants: the Montpellier Codex (late thirteenth century), a major French motet manuscript, has a version for three voices (NAWM 20c), shown in Example 5.12, and one of the English manuscripts known as the Worcester fragments includes an untexted fourth voice. Such alternate versions show that motets, like the clausulae and organa that spawned them, were regarded not as immutable works but as common property open to reworking. (In this and later examples, a slash through the stem indicates the second note of a plica.)

Motets for three or four voices

EXAMPLE 5.11 Fole acostumance/Dominus

Foolish custom makes me sing,

EXAMPLE 5.12 Super te Ierusalem/Sed fulsit virginitas/Dominus

Triplum: *Over thee, Jerusalem, from the virgin mother has arisen in [Bethlehem]*
Duplum: *Rather, her virginity received its splendor from the Holy Spirit; therefore, pious [Lord]*

Performance When, where, and how motets were performed are interesting questions. Sacred motets might have been performed in services, but we presume that secular ones were not, although the language of love often resembled the vocabulary of devotion. Motets were almost certainly music for an educated elite, including clerics, teachers, university students, poets, musicians, and their patrons. Since the words in the tenor no longer needed to be sung, the tenor part may have been played on an instrument, but there is no clear evidence to indicate whether this was customary.

Reception The elite audience must have enjoyed motets for their complex interweaving of familiar borrowed material and new elements, in both music and words. Although it is difficult for modern listeners to imagine how two texts were heard at once in a double motet, the clever interrelationships between topically related poems were part of the appeal, building on the early motet tradition of writing words for the duplum that amplify the meaning and echo the sounds of the tenor's text. Often certain vowels or syllables appear in all voices, so that similarities of sound reinforce the interplay of ideas. This was music for refined and discerning listeners who treasured witty texts, skillful composition, and intriguing juxtapositions.

MOTETS IN THE LATER THIRTEENTH CENTURY By about 1250, three-voice motets were the rule, with two texts on related topics in Latin or French, or occasionally one in each language. After midcentury, composers drew motet tenor melodies from sources other than Notre Dame clausulae, including other chants and secular music. The tenor became simply a *cantus firmus*, a term introduced around 1270 by the theorist Hieronymus de Moravia to designate an existing melody, usually a plainchant, on which a new polyphonic work is based.

The further motet composers moved away from adding text to a clausula, the more they needed a new rhythmic notation. The rhythmic modes were notated through patterns of ligatures. Except for the tenor, motets were predominantly syllabic; each syllable required a separate note, so ligatures could no longer be used to indicate rhythm. Scribes notated early motets in two versions, with words and without (that is, as clausulae), and only the latter showed the rhythm. Later motets followed the rhythmic modes less closely, in part by subdividing many notes, and their increasing rhythmic variety and complexity called for a new notational system.

Composer and theorist Franco of Cologne codified the new system, now called ***Franconian notation***, in his *Ars cantus mensurabilis* (The Art of Measurable Music), written around 1280. For the first time, relative durations were signified by note shapes, a characteristic of Western notation ever since. This is such an important innovation, and it had such an impact on what musicians could notate, that we should pause to examine how Franco's system worked.

Franconian notation

There were four signs for single notes:

double long   ⌐   long ⌐   breve ▪   semibreve ◆

Like the rhythmic modes, Franconian notation is based on ternary groupings of the basic unit, the tempus (now normally transcribed as a quarter note rather than an eighth, as is customary for Notre Dame polyphony; see pp. 87–88 and Examples 5.5 and 5.7–5.9). Three tempora constitute a **perfection**, akin to a measure of three beats. As in the rhythmic modes, a long may last two or three tempora, and a breve is normally one tempus but can last two tempora (as in modes 3 and 4) if needed to fill a perfection. A double long has the value of two longs, and a tempus may contain two or three **semibreves**. Signs for rests and for ligatures indicate durations in a similar manner. What we would transcribe as ties across the barline were not possible to notate, except for double longs. Figure 5.5 shows some of the possibilities. Figure 5.6 shows a manuscript in this notation, transcribed in Example 5.13.

Changes in motet style and notation led to a new way of laying out the music. Scribes wrote

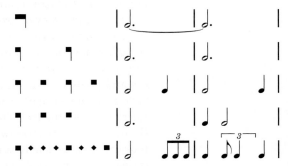

FIGURE 5.5 *Franconian notation and modern equivalents.*

FIGURE 5.6 *Page from the Montpellier Codex in choirbook format, showing the beginning of Adam de la Halle's* De ma dame vient/Dieus, comment porroie/Omnes *and the end of the previous motet. The triplum is in the left column, the motetus (duplum) on the right, and the tenor is written across the bottom. Compare the transcription in Example 5.13.*

the earliest motets in score, like the clausulae from which they were derived. But the upper voices, with each syllable needing a separate note, took up much more room on the page than the tenor, which had fewer notes and could be written in ligatures. In a score, there would be long vacant stretches in the tenor staff, a waste of space and parchment. And since the upper voices sang different texts, it seemed natural to separate them. So, in a three-voice motet, the triplum and motetus came to be written either on facing pages or in separate columns on the same page, with the tenor extending across the bottom, as in Figure 5.6. This format, which allowed all the singers to read their parts from the same opening, is known as *choirbook format*. It remained the customary way of notating polyphony from 1280 until the sixteenth century.

Franconian motet   Franconian notation allowed composers to achieve more rhythmic freedom and variety, both between and within voices. This new type of motet, in which each upper voice has a distinctive rhythmic shape, is sometimes called a *Franconian motet*, after Franco of Cologne. Whereas upper voices in early motets tend to conform closely to the rhythmic modes and repeat the same patterns frequently, this is no longer as true in a motet like Adam de la Halle's *De ma dame vient/Dieus, comment porroie/Omnes* (NAWM 21), shown in Example 5.13 and Figure 5.6. Here the upper voices tend to differ in rhythm, and the same pattern rarely repeats from one measure to the next in either voice. The duplum moves faster than the tenor, and the triplum often moves faster still, creating a hierarchy of proportions. Differences between the voices reinforce the contrast of texts, the triplum voicing the complaint of a man separated from his lady and the duplum the woman's thoughts of him. The texts themselves are very much in the manner of trouvère poetry, showing that composers and poets were combining in their motets the secular, originally courtly style and subject matter of the trouvères with the polyphonic tradition of the Notre Dame Cathedral. The tenor reiterates the melody for "omnes" from the Gradual *Viderunt omnes* twelve times, using three different rhythmic patterns four times each. The first rhythmic mode underlies the rhythm in each voice, transcribed here as alternating half and quarter notes, but is now more like a shared meter than a strict pattern. The tempo is not indicated by the notation

EXAMPLE 5.13 *Adam de la Halle,* De ma dame vient/Dieus, comment porroie/Omnes

Triplum: *From my lady comes the grievous pain which I bear and of which I will die, if hope does not keep me alive . . .*
Duplum: *God, how can I find a way to go to him, whose [lover I am?]*

but must have been slower than in earlier motets, to accommodate the many semibreves in the upper parts. Phrases may last any number of perfections, and the voices rarely cadence together. The resulting motet is a highly individual composition, no longer part of a common stock of clausulae and motets available for reworking.

The rhythmic variety of the Franconian motet was extended by Petrus de Cruce (Pierre de la Croix, mid-thirteenth to early fourteenth century). His motet *Aucun ont trouvé/Lonc tans/Annuntiantes* (NAWM 22), shown in Example 5.14, is a good illustration of his style. The tenor moves in longs (dotted half notes in transcription) and the duplum has no more than three semibreves per tempus, as in Franco's system, but the triplum may have as many as seven semibreves in a tempus, performed as equal subdivisions of the breve. To accommodate the smallest notes, the tempo must have been even slower than in a Franconian motet. The three voices move at quite different paces, producing a highly stratified texture with the tenor as harmonic foundation and the slow duplum as accompaniment to the voluble triplum.

Petrus de Cruce

The harmonic vocabulary of the motet changed less during the thirteenth century than did the rhythmic structure. By the time of Adam and Petrus, a fifth, an octave, or both together were expected at the beginning of each perfection, although thirds were allowed and dissonances appeared occasionally. A fourth above the lowest note, still used as a consonance early in the century (see Example 5.10), was now treated more often as a dissonance. The typical cadence featured the tenor descending by step and the upper voices rising by

Harmonic vocabulary

EXAMPLE 5.14 *Petrus de Cruce,* Aucun ont trouvé/Lonc tans/Annuntiantes

Triplum: *Some compose their songs out of habit, but Love gives me a reason to sing,*
he who so fills my heart with joy that I have to make a song; . . .
Duplum: *I have long refrained from singing, . . .*

EXAMPLE 5.15 *Cadence forms*

step to form a 1–5–8 sonority, as shown in Example 5.15. This type of cadence remained standard for the next two centuries.

Tradition and innovation

The motet had an astonishing career in its first century. What began as a work of poetry more than of musical composition, fitting a new text to an existing piece of music, was developed by generations of composers into the leading polyphonic genre, home to the most complex interplay of simultaneous different rhythms and texts yet conceived. The approach of Adam, Petrus, and other late-thirteenth-century composers reflects a new value placed on the distinctiveness of each piece, heralding an increased interest in the individual that became characteristic of the fourteenth century.

ENGLISH POLYPHONY

After the Norman Conquest of England in 1066, English culture and music were closely allied to those of France. We saw these links in secular song, with English trouvères such as Richard the Lionheart, and it is true as well for organum, conductus, and motet. English composers wrote in all the Notre Dame genres, as well as discant settings of sequences and of troped chants for the Mass Ordinary. They focused on sacred Latin texts and tended to prefer the relatively homorhythmic style and regular phrasing of the conductus.

A distinctive musical dialect emerged when English composers began to extend certain aspects of Continental practice. Most significant was their use of imperfect consonances, often in parallel motion. Harmonic thirds were allowed in the Notre Dame repertory, as we have seen, but were much more common in English music. This apparently reflects the influence of folk polyphony. Writing about 1200, Gerald of Wales described improvised partsinging in close harmony in Wales and northern Britain, and a twelfth-century *Hymn to St. Magnus,* patron saint of the Orkney Islands, features parallel thirds.

One element of Notre Dame style that particularly intrigued English composers was voice exchange, the technique we observed in Perotinus's organum in which voices trade segments of melody. An elaborate form of this was the ***rondellus***, in which two or three phrases, first heard simultaneously, are each taken up in turn by each of the voices:

FIGURE 5.7 Sumer is icumen in *(ca. 1250) in its original notation. The upper parts have a secondary Latin text, written in red ink below the English words. The* pes *is shown at the bottom of the page.*

Triplum	a b c
Duplum	c a b
Tenor	b c a

Since the three voices are in the same range, the listener hears a threefold repetition of the polyphonic phrase, but with voice parts traded. Rondellus sections appear frequently in English conductus from the later thirteenth century. There are also independent rondellus and rondellus-motets, such as *Fulget coelestis curia/O Petre flos/Roma gaudet* from the Worcester fragments, which has two three-voice rondellus sections framed by an introduction and coda.

Closely related to the rondellus is the ***rota***, a perpetual canon or round at the unison. The most famous is *Sumer is icumen in* (NAWM 23) from about 1250, shown in Figure 5.7 and Example 5.16. Two voices sing a *pes* (Latin for "foot," or "ground"), a repeating melody that serves as a tenor; since the second half of each *pes* is the first half of the other, they form a two-voice rondellus. Above this, two, three, or four voices enter in canon, singing in praise of summer. All the voices have similar rhythms in the first or fifth rhythmic modes, producing an effect of alternating F–A–C–F and G–B♭–D sonorities.

The distinctive qualities of English polyphony, particularly the preference

Rota

EXAMPLE 5.16 Sumer is icumen in

Summer is come, sing loud, cuckoo! The seed grows and the meadow blooms,
and now the wood turns green.
Pes: Sing, cuckoo, now; sing, cuckoo!

for imperfect consonances and for relatively simple, syllabic, and periodic
melodies, exercised an important influence on fifteenth-century Continental
composers and contributed to the development of a new international style in
the fifteenth century (see Chapter 8).

A POLYPHONIC TRADITION

The emergence in the eleventh through thirteenth centuries of complex
polyphony, whether improvised, composed and transmitted orally, or written down, was a major turning point in Western music. The coordination of
multiple parts, interest in vertical sonorities, and use of counterpoint and

harmony to create a sense of direction, tension, and resolution became characteristics of the Western tradition that set it apart from almost all others. In this sense, medieval polyphony was of enormous historical importance. Moreover, the notation that composers developed for polyphony introduced two features that became fundamental to later Western notation: vertical placement to coordinate multiple parts, as in Aquitanian and Notre Dame organum and modern scores, and different note shapes to indicate relative duration, pioneered in Franconian notation and continued in our whole, half, quarter, and eighth notes and rests.

For all the contributions made by singers, composers, and theorists of medieval polyphony, their music seldom outlived them by more than a generation or two. As new repertories of written polyphony were created, older ones fell out of fashion, sometimes persisting for a time in local practice or in distant regions but eventually replaced by newer styles. When music historians rediscovered and transcribed it in the eighteenth and nineteenth centuries, polyphony of the ninth to thirteenth centuries was regarded as crude and harsh, its open harmonies, casual dissonance, and parallel fifths and octaves lacking the full, sweet, controlled sound of Renaissance music. In the early twentieth century, editions of thirteenth-century motets and Notre Dame polyphony began to appear, but little was performed, and the music at first found few listeners.

In the late nineteenth and early twentieth centuries, composers began to draw on medieval music as an exotic element, distant in time rather than geography. Parallel organum found an echo in the parallel chord streams of Debussy and others. As composers explored sonorities based on fourths, fifths, and seconds, partly inspired by medieval harmony, listeners grew accustomed to such sounds, and polyphony before 1300 began to seem less crude and more appealing. Some techniques of medieval polyphony have contemporary parallels, showing their continued relevance if not direct influence: the repetition of short rhythmic and melodic ideas in minimalist music has echos of the modal rhythm and repeated motives of Perotinus's organa, and the layering of new texts over borrowed material in hip hop resembles that in thirteenth-century motets.

In the late twentieth century, medieval polyphony experienced a revival in concert and recording. What were once seen as defects—its differences from common-practice harmony and counterpoint, lack of instruments, uncertain rhythmic notation, and unfamiliarity—became strengths, offering new sounds, pure vocal beauty, performer freedom, and freshness. Its new role is illustrated by recordings like clarinetist Richard Stolzman's 1991 CD that featured part of Perotinus's *Viderunt omnes* alongside pieces by twentieth-century composers Charles Ives, Andrew Lloyd Webber, and Steve Reich. Music once employed to add solemnity to religious services or to entertain clerics and intellectuals has now found a small but permanent niche in modern musical life, divorced from its original context but valued for its unique sounds and styles.

Further Reading is available at digital.wwnorton.com/hwm10

NEW DEVELOPMENTS IN THE FOURTEENTH CENTURY

After the comparative stability of the thirteenth century, the fourteenth saw disruption and turmoil. The economy and population of western Europe declined, ravaged by famine, war, and plague. Conflicts and scandals tarnished the church, and revolts challenged secular authorities. Yet the fourteenth century was also a period of remarkable creativity. The desire to understand and control nature spurred advances in science and technology, and an increasing interest in the world, the individual, and human nature led to art and literature that was more true to life and more eager to please its audience. The polyphonic music of the time is characterized by an interplay between structure and pleasure, the former evident in the rhythmic and melodic patterning known as *isorhythm* and in standardized forms for secular song, and the latter in engaging melodies, chromatic inflections, more frequent imperfect consonances, and new possibilities in notating rhythm and meter.

EUROPE IN THE FOURTEENTH CENTURY

The rising economic tide of the previous three centuries reversed in the 1300s. Cooler weather reduced agricultural production, leading to a prolonged economic slump. Floods in northwestern Europe brought famine in 1315–22, and one person in ten perished. In 1347–50 the Black Death, a combination of bubonic and pneumonic plagues, marched across Europe, wiping out a third of the population; almost everyone infected died in agony within days, and many of those left alive fled the cities and towns. The resulting disruptions in agriculture, manufacturing, and trade deepened the economic problems. So did frequent wars, especially the Hundred Years' War (1337–1453) between France and England. Poverty, war, taxes, and political grievances combined to spark peasant and urban rebellions in France, England, Flanders (modern-day Belgium), Germany, Italy, and Spain.

The church was also in crisis. In the thirteenth century, Europeans viewed the church as the supreme authority not only in matters of faith but to a large extent in intellectual and political affairs; now its authority, especially the supremacy of the pope, was widely questioned. In 1305, King Philip IV (the Fair) of France engineered the election of a French pope, Clement V, who never went to Rome because of hostility there to foreigners. From 1309 until 1377, the popes resided at Avignon in southeastern France, under the virtual control of the French king. This period, known as the Babylonian Captivity of the papacy, was succeeded by the Great Schism: from 1378 to 1417, there were rival claimants to the papacy in Rome, in Avignon, and later in Pisa. This state of affairs, compounded by the often-corrupt life of the clergy, drew sharp criticism, expressed both in writings and in the rise of popular heretical movements.

FIGURE 6.1 *Giotto (ca. 1266–1337), Wedding procession. This fresco (wall painting done in wet plaster) is one of a series on the life of the Virgin Mary painted around 1305 in the Chapel of the Madonna della Carità de Arena, known as the Scrovegni Chapel after the banker Enrico Scrovegni, who built the chapel on the site of a Roman amphitheater. Mary (with halo) leads a group of virgins, while a vielle player and two pipers provide music. The large-leaf branch jutting from the window is a sign of the Virgin's pregnancy.*

Thirteenth-century Europeans could generally reconcile revelation and reason, the divine and human realms, and religion and politics. But in the fourteenth century, people began to separate science from religion and to see different roles for church and state, notions still held today. William of Ockham (ca. 1285–1349) and his followers argued that knowledge of nature and of humanity should rest on the experience of the senses rather than on reason alone and should seek natural rather than supernatural explanations. Without denying the claims of religion, this view laid the foundations for the modern scientific method and made way for a growing secular culture. New technologies brought social change: eyeglasses enabled the aging to read, the magnetic compass allowed ships to venture farther from land, and mechanical clocks began to change the way people experienced time, from a daily cycle of tasks and events marked by the sounding of local bells to a universal measure of discrete, proportional, arithmetical units. This crucial shift was reflected in musical practice, especially in fourteenth-century systems of notation.

Scientists' reliance on the senses had parallels among artists and writers, in their pursuit of realism and in their focus on pleasing their audience. The Florentine painter Giotto (ca. 1266–1337) achieved more naturalistic representation, as seen in the facial expressions, posture, and garments in the painting shown in Figure 6.1. He created a sense of depth by placing figures and objects on different planes of the pictorial space, and the beauty of the faces and the symmetry of the composition show an interest in pleasing the eye. The growth of literacy among the public encouraged writers to produce works in the vernacular, including Dante Alighieri's *Divine Comedy* (1307), Giovanni Boccaccio's *Decameron* (1348–53), and Geoffrey Chaucer's *Canterbury Tales* (ca. 1387–1400). The latter two, written to entertain rather than elevate the reader, reflect daily life and portray people of all social classes more realistically than earlier literature had done.

The secular interests of the fourteenth century are well represented in music. The best-known composers of the time, Guillaume de Machaut and

Sacred and secular music

FIGURE 6.2 *In this miniature from the* Roman de Fauvel, *a poem by Gervès du Bus, a charivari, or noisy serenade, awakens Fauvel and Vain Glory after their wedding. This manuscript from about 1317, probably prepared at the royal court, includes many interpolated pieces of music.*

Francesco Landini, focused on secular music, and even the papal court at Avignon was a center for secular song. But composition of sacred music, both chant and polyphony, continued to flourish.

The flavor of the times is captured in the *Roman de Fauvel,* an allegorical narrative poem satirizing corruption in politics and the church, apparently written as a warning to the king of France and enjoyed in high political circles at court. Fauvel, a horse who rises from the stable to a powerful position, symbolizes a world turned upside down, in which the king outranks the pope and France is defiled. Fauvel embodies the sins represented by the letters of his name: Flattery, Avarice, Villainy ("U" and "V" were interchangeable), Variété (fickleness), Envy, and Lâcheté (cowardice). He ultimately marries and produces little Fauvels who destroy the world. A beautifully decorated manuscript from around 1317, shown in Figure 6.2, has 169 pieces of music interpolated within the poem. These constitute a veritable anthology of works from the thirteenth and early fourteenth centuries, some written for this collection, others chosen for their relevance to the poem's message. Most are monophonic, from Latin chants to secular songs. But thirty-four are motets, many with texts that denounce the lax morals of the clergy or refer to political events. Among these motets in the *Roman de Fauvel* are the first examples of a new style, known today as the Ars Nova.

THE ARS NOVA IN FRANCE

Philippe de Vitry (1291–1361), French composer, poet, church canon, administrator for the duke of Bourbon and the king of France, and later bishop of Meaux, is named by one writer as the "inventor of a new art"—in Latin, *ars nova.* Several versions of a treatise from ca. 1320 representing Vitry's teaching, though perhaps not written by him, end with the words "this completes the *Ars nova* of Magister Philippe de Vitry," implying that *Ars nova* (New Art or New Method) is the title of the treatise and Vitry its author. The term **Ars Nova** has come to denote the new French musical style inaugurated by Vitry in the 1310s and continued through the 1370s.

ARS NOVA NOTATION The "new art" proceeded from two innovations in rhythmic notation, described in the *Ars nova* treatise and in treatises by Jehan des Murs, a mathematician and astronomer as well as music theorist. The first innovation allowed duple ("imperfect") division of note values along with the traditional triple ("perfect") division; the second provided for division of the semibreve, formerly the smallest possible note value, into **minims**. The resulting system offered new meters and allowed much greater rhythmic flexibility, including, for the first time, syncopation. Around 1340, des

Murs discussed another innovation, **_mensuration signs_**, symbols that are the ancestors of modern time signatures. Understanding the new rhythmic profile of fourteenth-century French music requires some knowledge of the notation itself, described in Innovations: Writing Rhythm (pp. 110–11).

The effects of the new notational system were profound and enduring. For the first time, notation was so specific and unambiguous for both pitch and rhythm that a piece of music could be written down in one city, carried to another, and performed there with the precise notes, rhythms, and alignment of parts that the composer intended, by singers who had nothing but the manuscript to work from. Such a piece could be as fixed and permanent as a poem, and perhaps for that reason composers began more often to attach their names to their works and take pride in their authorship, as poets had done for centuries.

Opponents as well as supporters acknowledged the new art. The Flemish theorist Jacobus de Ispania (also called Jacques de Liège) vigorously defended the "ancient art" (*ars antiqua*) of the late thirteenth century against the new innovations (see Source Reading). This marks the first well-documented dispute since ancient times between advocates of newer and older musical styles, a type of argument that has recurred often and always reflects differences in what is valued in music. When Jacobus complained that in the new music "perfection is brought low, [and] imperfection is exalted," he was objecting that the "imperfect" duple division was now equally as valid as the "perfect" threefold division, which carried associations with the Trinity. He may also

Arguments against the Ars Nova

SOURCE READING

Jacobus de Ispania Rails Against the Ars Nova

Jacobus de Ispania (ca. 1260–after 1330) apparently was a native of Liège in modern Belgium and studied at the University of Paris. His *Speculum musicae* (The Mirror of Music, ca. 1330) is the longest surviving medieval treatise on music. In the last of its seven books, he argued that the old style of the thirteenth century was more pleasing and more perfect than the new art of the younger generation.

I do not deny that the moderns have composed much good and beautiful music, but this is no reason why the ancients should be maligned and banished from the fellowship of singers. For one good thing does not oppose another.

In a certain company in which some able singers and judicious laymen were assembled, and where new motets in the modern manner and some old ones were sung, I observed that even the laymen were better pleased with the ancient motets and the ancient manner than with the new. And even if the new manner pleased when it was a novelty, it does so no longer, but begins to displease many. So let the ancient music and the ancient manner of singing be brought back to their native land; let them come back into use; let the rational art flourish once more. It has been in exile, along with its manner of singing; they have been cast out from the fellowship of singers with near violence, but violence should not be perpetual.

Wherein does this lasciviousness in singing so greatly please, this excessive refinement, by which, as some think, the words are lost, the harmony of consonances is diminished, the value of the notes is changed, perfection is brought low, imperfection is exalted, and measure is confused?

From *Speculum musicae* (ca. 1330), Book 7, Chapter 48, trans. James McKinnon, in SR 35 (2:27), p. 277.

Writing Rhythm

What made the new musical style of the Ars Nova possible was a set of innovations in notating rhythm, innovations that underlie our modern system of whole, half, quarter, and eighth notes and rests.

The new notation required a rethinking of musical time. Remember that a century or so earlier, musicians of the Notre Dame school had conceived of musical rhythm in terms of certain repeating patterns of long and short notes—the rhythmic modes (see Chapter 5). All six modes fit a framework in which the basic time unit, or tempus, was always grouped in threes, like a measure of triple time. Franconian notation, introduced in the late thirteenth century, made it possible to escape the rigid mold of the rhythmic modes by using the shapes of notes to indicate their durations, yet still relied on the same threefold groupings, called perfections. As long as theorists insisted on seeing musical time as a succession of perfections, each of which could only be divided in certain ways, many rhythms simply could not be written down, including anything in duple meter.

In Ars Nova notation, units of time could be grouped in either twos or threes, at several different levels of duration, allowing a much wider variety of rhythms to be written. The long (▮), breve (■), and semibreve (◆) could each be divided into either two or three notes of the next smaller value, as shown in Figure 6.3. The division of the long was called **mode** (*modus*), that of the breve **time** (*tempus*), and that of the semibreve **prolation** (*prolatio*). Division was **perfect** or **major** ("greater") if triple, **imperfect** or **minor** ("lesser") if duple. The terms "mode," "tempus," "perfect," and "imperfect" are all derived from Notre Dame and Franconian notation and applied here to new but closely related uses (see Chapter 5). A new type of note was introduced to indicate one-half or one-third of a semibreve: the **minim** (♦), meaning "least" in Latin.

The addition of smaller values was associated with a slowing of the tempo, so that for fourteenth-century music the breve rather than the long is typically transcribed as a measure in modern notation. The four possible combinations of time and prolation, shown in Figure 6.4, produce in effect four different meters, comparable to four in use today. Later in the century, time and prolation were indicated with **mensuration signs** that are the ancestors of modern time signatures: a circle for perfect time or incomplete circle for imperfect, with a dot for major prolation or no dot for minor. The incomplete circle C without a dot has come down to us as a sign for $\frac{4}{4}$ time (equivalent to imperfect time, minor prolation), showing the link between these four "prolations" and modern conceptions of meter.

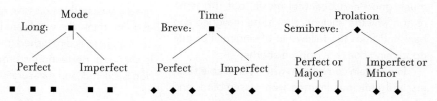

FIGURE 6.3 *Divisions of the long, breve, and semibreve in Ars Nova notation.*

In Ars Nova notation, note shapes could indicate certain durations that remained unchanged by the notes around them. Such specificity made it possible for the first time to notate syncopation, a prominent feature in melodies of composers from the fourteenth century on. Indeed, Jehan des Murs wrote of the new system, "whatever can be sung can be written down." That was certainly not true of rhythmic notation in the thirteenth century, which greatly limited what could be composed and preserved in written form.

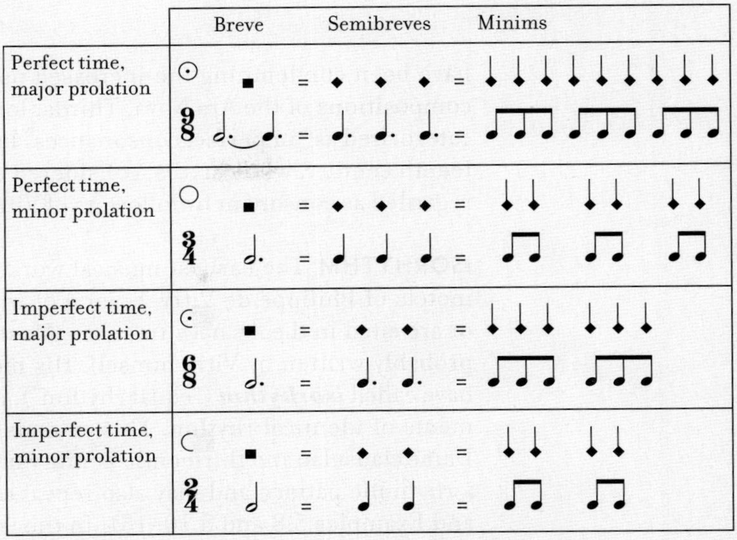

Our modern notation system is the direct descendant of Ars Nova notation, as shown in Figure 6.5. The note shapes of Ars Nova notation are the same as those of Franconian notation, with the addition of the minim. In both systems, ligatures continued to be used for certain combinations of longs and breves, as had been true since Notre Dame notation. About 1425, scribes began to write all these forms with open noteheads (sometimes called "white notation") rather than filling each in with ink ("black notation"). This change may have occurred at that time because scribes shifted from writing on parchment (scraped sheepskin or goatskin) to paper; filling in black notes on rough-surfaced paper increased the chance of spattered ink or bleed-through and thus a ruined page. Renaissance composers added still shorter note values, each half the duration of the next higher value, by filling in the notehead of a minim to create a *semiminim* and adding one or two flags to the semiminim to produce a *fusa* and a *semifusa*. Toward the end

of the sixteenth century, the diamond-shaped notes of Renaissance notation changed to the round noteheads we use now, and ligatures fell out of use. With the addition of barlines in the seventeenth century, rhythmic notation had evolved from its first manifestations to its modern form in a little over four hundred years.

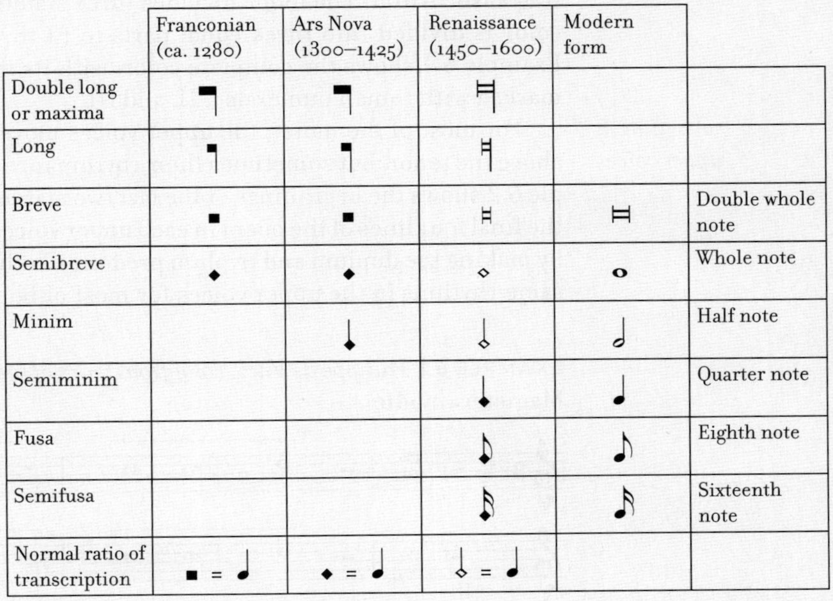

	Breve	Semibreves	Minims
Perfect time, major prolation			
Perfect time, minor prolation			
Imperfect time, major prolation			
Imperfect time, minor prolation			

FIGURE 6.4 *The four combinations of time and prolation, with modern equivalents.*

	Franconian (ca. 1280)	Ars Nova (1300–1425)	Renaissance (1450–1600)	Modern form	
Double long or maxima					
Long					
Breve					Double whole note
Semibreve					Whole note
Minim					Half note
Semiminim					Quarter note
Fusa					Eighth note
Semifusa					Sixteenth note
Normal ratio of transcription					

FIGURE 6.5 *Comparison of notation systems.*

have been condemning the increased use of the imperfect consonances in compositions of the Ars Nova. Thirds, long considered dissonant, were first categorized as "imperfect consonances" by Johannes de Garlandia in the thirteenth century, while sixths, considered dissonant by earlier theorists, were regarded as consonant by followers of Vitry and Jehan des Murs.

ISORHYTHM   The earliest musical works to exemplify the Ars Nova are the motets of Philippe de Vitry, several of which appear in the *Roman de Fauvel* or are cited in the *Ars nova* treatises. Most are in three voices with Latin texts probably written by Vitry himself. His motets use a device modern scholars have called ***isorhythm*** ("equal rhythm"), in which the tenor is laid out in segments of identical rhythm. This extends the practice we observed in Notre Dame clausulae and thirteenth-century motets, where the tenor often repeats a rhythmic pattern and may also repeat a segment of melody (see Chapter 5 and Examples 5.8 and 5.10–13). In the isorhythmic motet of the fourteenth century, the rhythmic patterns are longer and more complex, and the tenor tends to move so slowly in comparison to the upper voices that it is heard less as a melody than as a foundation for the entire polyphonic structure.

Talea and color   Theorists of the time recognized two recurring elements in motet tenors, rhythmic and melodic. They called the repeating rhythmic unit the ***talea*** (pl. *taleae*) and the recurring segment of melody the ***color***. The color and talea could be the same length, always beginning and ending together, but most often the color extended over two, three, or more taleae. In some motets, the endings of the color and talea do not coincide, so that repetitions of the color begin in the middle of a talea. Upper voices may also be organized isorhythmically, in whole or part, to emphasize the recurring rhythmic patterns in the tenor.

Vitry's motet *Cum statua/Hugo, Hugo/Magister invidie* (NAWM 24) illustrates isorhythm. The tenor includes three statements of the color, and each color is divided into three equal parts to fit three statements of the talea. Example 6.1 shows the complete color, with its three statements of the talea marked with roman numerals I, II, and III.

Isorhythm in   For most of the motet, the upper voices move in ever-changing rhythms
upper voices   above the tenor, but sometimes their rhythms are coordinated as well. Example 6.2 shows the beginnings of the last two statements of the talea, which set the final four lines of the poem in each upper voice. Vitry pairs these two taleae by making the duplum and triplum predominantly isorhythmic, featuring the same rhythms in the upper voices for most of both taleae. This effect is used

EXAMPLE 6.1 *Philippe de Vitry, color from tenor of* Cum statua/Hugo, Hugo/ Magister invidie

EXAMPLE 6.2 *Opening measures of the last two taleae, showing parallel rhythms in all voices*

in many isorhythmic works to make recurrences of the talea more audible. In this transcription, the $\frac{6}{8}$ meter in the upper voices reflects the duple division of the breve (the measure) and triple division of the semibreve (dotted quarter note), or imperfect time and major prolation (see Figure 6.4, p. 111). The longer measures in the tenor, each corresponding to three measures of the upper parts, reflect the triple division of the long into three breves, or perfect mode (see Figure 6.3, p. 110).

The upper voices in Example 6.2 exemplify a technique called ***hocket*** (French *hoquet,* "hiccup"), in which two voices alternate in rapid succession, each resting while the other sings. Passages in hocket appear in some thirteenth-century conductus and motets and are frequently used in fourteenth-century isorhythmic works in coordination with recurrences of the talea, as in this Vitry motet. Pieces that use hocket extensively were themselves called *hockets*. Most were untexted and could be performed either by voices or by instruments.

Hocket

The basic idea of isorhythm—arranging durations in a pattern that repeats—was not new in the fourteenth century, but it was applied in ever more extended and complex ways. The rhythmic and melodic repetitions gave coherence to long compositions, building upon the delight in structure we noticed in discant clausulae and thirteenth-century motets. Using isorhythmic structures helped composers at every stage of composition, from overall planning and laying out sections to filling in the upper voices over the tenor. Singers could see the repeating patterns at a glance, especially in the original notation, helping them to grasp the shape of the music and commit it to memory. Although some listeners may hardly notice the interlocked repetitions of color and talea, the recurring rhythmic patterns are evident to the performers and are not difficult to hear if one knows to listen for them, especially when the composer uses isorhythm in all voices to mark significant points in the cycle of the talea.

Usefulness of isorhythm

Audience   Such motets were composed primarily for performance before musically and textually literate audiences, from clergy to students to courtiers, and no doubt many in the audience understood and appreciated the structure. As in earlier motets, intricate webs of meaning and sound link the texts. The complex interrelationships in both text and music were aimed at educated listeners who treasured the search for meaning, whether in motets, in allegories such as the *Roman de Fauvel,* or in interpretations of the Bible itself.

GUILLAUME DE MACHAUT

The most important composer and poet of the French Ars Nova period was Guillaume de Machaut (ca. 1300–1377; see biography and Figure 6.6). His support by royal and aristocratic patrons allowed Machaut time to produce over 140 musical works, mostly settings of his own poetry, along with almost three hundred other poems. From about 1350 on, he gathered all his works in manuscripts prepared for his patrons. These collections show Machaut's awareness of himself as an individual creator and his desire to preserve his creations for posterity. He composed in most of the genres then current, from motets to secular songs, and a survey of his music also serves to introduce us to the main types of Ars Nova composition.

MOTETS Most of Machaut's twenty-three motets date from relatively early in his career. Twenty are isorhythmic, based on tenors from chant, and three use secular songs as tenors. Like other motets of the time, Machaut's are longer and more rhythmically complex than earlier examples and often include hocket and isorhythmic passages in the upper voices.

MASS Machaut's *La Messe de Nostre Dame* (Mass of Our Lady) was one of the earliest polyphonic settings of the Mass Ordinary, probably the first polyphonic mass to be written by a single composer and conceived as a unit. Machaut apparently composed the work in the early 1360s for performance at a Mass for the Virgin Mary celebrated every Saturday at an altar of the cathedral in Reims. After his death, an oration for Machaut's soul was added to the service, and his mass continued to be performed there well into the fifteenth century.

Polyphonic settings   As we saw in Chapter 5, through the thirteenth century chants from the
of the Ordinary   Mass Proper were set polyphonically much more often than Ordinary chants. But in the fourteenth century, there are numerous settings of Ordinary texts by English, French, and Italian composers, some composed for the papal chapel at Avignon, others for Masses celebrated on special occasions deserving of added solemnity. Most were set as individual pieces that could be freely combined with others in a service, some were composed as pairs of movements (such as a Sanctus and Agnus Dei), and a few were gathered into anonymous cycles. Settings were typically in one of three styles: isorhythmic, with a chant tenor; songlike, with a decorated chant in the upper voice; or homophonic, with all parts moving together. Machaut's mass builds on this tradition, but treats the six texts of the Ordinary as one composition rather than separate pieces. The movements are linked together by similarities of style and approach and by a tonal focus on D in the first three movements and on F in the last three. All six movements are for four voices, with the motetus (duplum) and triplum above the tenor and a second supporting

GUILLAUME DE MACHAUT
(ca. 1300–1377)

Machaut was the most important composer and poet in fourteenth-century France. He exercised a profound influence on his contemporaries and later artists, and his music has come to typify the French Ars Nova.

Much of what we know about Machaut's life and career comes from his own narrative poems, many of which describe events in the lives of himself and his patrons. He was born in the province of Champagne in northeastern France, probably to a middle-class family. He was educated as a cleric, probably in Reims, and later took Holy Orders. Around 1323, he entered the service of John of Luxembourg, king of Bohemia, as a clerk, eventually becoming the king's secretary. In that role, he accompanied John on his travels and military campaigns across Europe, describing these exploits in his poetry. From 1340 until his death in 1377, Machaut resided in Reims as canon of the cathedral, an office whose liturgical duties left ample time for poetry and composition. Machaut had close ties to royalty all his life, always moving in elite circles. Other patrons included John of Luxembourg's daughter Bonne; the kings of Navarre and France; and the dukes of Berry and Burgundy.

Machaut was among the first composers to compile his complete works and to discuss his working methods, both signs of his self-awareness as a creator. He addressed *Le livre du voir dit* (The Book of the True Poem, 1363–65) to Peronne, a young woman with whom Machaut had fallen in love in his sixties. In it he says he typically writes his poems before setting them to music and is happiest when the music is sweet and pleasing.

The strong support of his patrons gave him the resources to supervise the preparation of several illuminated manuscripts containing his works, but the choice to do so seems to have been his own, inspired by a sense of his own worth as an artist and a desire to preserve his music and poetry for future generations. Such attitudes, commonplace today, remained rare among composers before the nineteenth century.

MAJOR MUSICAL WORKS *La Messe de Nostre Dame* (Mass of Our Lady), *Hoquetus David* (hocket), 23 motets (20 isorhythmic), 42 ballades (1 monophonic), 22 rondeaux, 33 virelais (25 monophonic), 19 lais (15 monophonic), 1 complainte, and 1 chanson royale (both monophonic)

POETICAL WORKS *Remede de Fortune* (Remedy of Fortune), *Le livre du voir dit*, numerous other narrative poems, over 280 lyric poems

FIGURE 6.6 *In this miniature from the last manuscript of Guillaume de Machaut's works prepared during his lifetime (ca. 1372), the elderly Machaut is visited in his study by Love, who introduces his three children, Sweet Thoughts, Pleasure, and Hope.*

voice, called the **contratenor** ("against the tenor"), in the same range as the tenor, sometimes below it and sometimes above.

The Kyrie (NAWM 25a), Sanctus, Agnus Dei, and Ite, missa est are iso-rhythmic. In each of these movements, the tenor carries a cantus firmus, the melody to a chant on the same Ordinary text, divided into two or more taleae. (The melody is not repeated, so there is only one statement of the color, unlike

Isorhythmic movements

in the motets of Vitry and Machaut.) The contratenor is also isorhythmic, coordinated with the tenor, and together they form the harmonic foundation. Example 6.3 shows the opening of the Christe, including the first two statements of the seven-measure talea, marked by roman numerals. The upper two voices move more rapidly, with syncopation typical of Machaut. They are also partly isorhythmic; during the second statement of the talea, the rhythms in the upper voices closely parallel those in the first, and are virtually identical in all but the second and sixth measures of each talea. The rhythmic

EXAMPLE 6.3 *Guillaume de Machaut,* La Messe de Nostre Dame, *beginning of Christe*

EXAMPLE 6.4 *Machaut,* La Messe de Nostre Dame, *excerpt from Gloria*

⌐‾‾⌐ = ligature in original notation

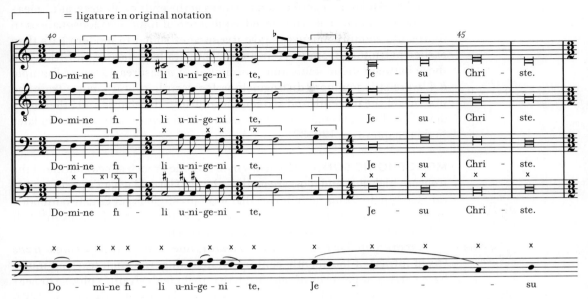

Lord, the only begotten Son, Jesus Christ.

repetition in the upper voices makes the recurring talea more evident. So does the alternation of sustained notes on the first and fifth measures of each talea with lively rhythms in the other measures. Such contrast of rhythmic rest and activity is characteristic of Machaut's blocklike construction, and it suggests an architectural parallel, like the alternation of solid pillars and filigreed stained-glass windows along the wall of a Gothic cathedral. To generate rhythmic activity, Machaut often relies on repeating figuration; for example, the descending figure in the second measure of the triplum, echoed later in both motetus and triplum, recurs frequently throughout the mass, serving not as a unifying motive but as a way to create movement.

Discant-style movements

The Gloria (NAWM 25b) and Credo, with their much longer texts, are set in the style of discant or conductus: essentially syllabic and largely homorhythmic, rapidly declaiming the words in all voices, as illustrated in Example 6.4. The words "Jesu Christe" (Jesus Christ) in the Gloria and "ex Maria Virgine" (of the Virgin Mary) in the Credo are set in relief with long-sustained chords, a musical equivalent to the tradition in medieval paintings of depicting Mary and Jesus as much larger than the figures around them, to emphasize their importance. The Gloria is based on a monophonic chant Gloria that is paraphrased at times in different voices, most often the tenor and contratenor. As shown by the notes marked with x in Example 6.4, the chant melody in this passage is paraphrased first in the contratenor (the lowest voice), shifts to the tenor, and returns to the contratenor. The Credo is apparently not based on chant. Both movements end with elaborate passages on the word "Amen," marked by hocket and syncopation in the Gloria and isorhythm in the Credo.

Harmony

The excerpts from Machaut's mass in Examples 6.3 and 6.4 illustrate the greater prominence of imperfect consonances in the Ars Nova style, in contrast to earlier polyphony. Most of the vertical sonorities include thirds or sixths, resolving to perfect consonances at the ends of phrases, as in measure 46 of Example 6.4. The more frequent use of imperfect consonances in fourteenth-century music can give it a sweeter sound to modern ears than earlier polyphony from the Continent. Yet parallel octaves and fifths, like those between the motetus and contratenor in measures 42–46 of Example 6.4, were still common, distinguishing fourteenth-century music from the practice of the fifteenth and sixteenth centuries. The sharps and other accidentals in Examples 6.3 and 6.4 are examples of *musica ficta,* discussed later in this chapter (pp. 129–32).

MONOPHONIC SONGS Machaut's monophonic French songs continued the trouvère tradition, and most are on the subject of love. Machaut's poetic ambition led him to compose in forms that were prestigious yet largely outmoded by his time: the *chant royal,* the *complainte,* and the most technically difficult of French poetic forms, the *lai,* a long form akin to the sequence.

Virelais   A more popular genre was the **virelai**, one of the three **formes fixes** (fixed forms) of fourteenth-century French song, in which text and music have particular patterns of repetition that include a refrain, a phrase or section that repeats both words and music (see Forms at a Glance, p. 120). Twenty-five of Machaut's virelais are monophonic, and eight are polyphonic.

One of the most attractive of his monophonic virelais is *Douce dame jolie* (NAWM 26), which illustrates Machaut's blend of the trouvère tradition in poetry with up-to-date musical style. The poem continues the themes of *fine amour,* pleading for mercy from a lady who reigns over the poet like a lord over his vassals, and like many troubadour and trouvère poems it demonstrates the poet's virtuosity by using only two rhymes, repeated throughout all the stanzas (as in NAWM 8). Machaut emphasizes the poetic rhymes with musical ones, short motives whose frequent repetitions and variations make the melody memorable. Together with the syncopations and strong duple meter made possible by Ars Nova notation, the result is a playful, catchy melody that reflects Machaut's notion of the virelai as a *chanson baladée,* or "danced song." Figure 6.7 shows an illumination from a manuscript of his compositions, in which a singer (perhaps Machaut himself) performs a monophonic virelai while he and several companions dance in a circle.

FIGURE 6.7 *Miniature from the earliest manuscript of Machaut's collected works (ca. 1350), showing five couples dancing in a circle. The dancer farthest to the right is singing to accompany the dance. The singer resembles Machaut as pictured in the later manuscript in Figure 6.6, at a younger age. The music under the picture is a monophonic virelai by Machaut, which we may assume is the song being performed in the picture.*

POLYPHONIC SONGS A major innovation of the Ars Nova period was the development of polyphonic songs, or **chansons** (French for "songs"), in *treble-dominated style*. In this style the upper voice carrying the text, called the **cantus** (Latin for song), or **treble**, is the principal line, supported by a slower-moving tenor without text. To this essential two-voice framework may be added one or two other untexted voices: a contratenor in the same range as the tenor or, less often, a fast-moving triplum in the treble range. That Machaut wrote the cantus before the tenor, reversing the normal order of composition in earlier polyphony, is indicated by the appearance of one of his virelais, *Mors sui se je ne vous voy*, as a monophonic song in an early manuscript and joined with a tenor in later ones. It is confirmed by Machaut's statement in a letter to his beloved Peronne (see biography, p. 115) that he had composed a song to which he would soon add a tenor and contratenor.

As is true of Machaut's monophonic songs, his polyphonic chansons are settings of his own poems. Most are in the form of a **ballade** or **rondeau** (pl. *rondeaux*), the other two *formes fixes* along with the virelai (see Forms at a Glance and Figures 6.8a–c, p. 120). The three genres tended to differ somewhat in subject matter as well as in form: ballades were the most serious, appropriate for philosophical or historical themes or for celebrating an event or person, as well as the most serious love songs; rondeaux centered on themes of love; and virelais often related descriptions of nature to feelings of love.

Ballades and rondeaux

All the *formes fixes* were derived from genres associated with dancing, as evident by their use of refrains (see Chapter 4). As we have seen, Machaut's monophonic virelais could still be danced to and often have a dancelike character. But Machaut's polyphonic chansons, like Bach's gigues and Chopin's waltzes, were highly stylized and not used for dancing. Often the repetitions of the refrain lines were invested with fresh meanings or contexts by the preceding words.

Machaut wrote ballades with two, three, and four parts, but his typical settings were for high male voice with lower voices on the untexted tenor and contratenor. (For an example of the form, see the ballade by Philipoctus de Caserta discussed on pp. 121–23.) Most rondeaux are for two or three voices.

Machaut's *Rose, liz, printemps, verdure* (NAWM 27) is exceptional in having four voices; its triplum, lacking in one early manuscript, was probably added later. But it is typical of Machaut's style in the varied rhythms, supple syncopations, and mostly stepwise flow of its melody, all designed to make it appealing to the listener. Also characteristic are long melismas near the beginnings and sometimes in the middle of poetic lines. Since these melismas often fall on unimportant words or unaccented syllables, their function is formal and decorative rather than serving to emphasize the text.

Rose, liz, printemps, verdure

REPUTATION Machaut was widely esteemed in his own time and for several decades after his death, exercising an influence on poets (including Chaucer) and composers alike. His works loom large because they survive, which Machaut ensured they would by having them copied into numerous manuscripts. Too much music by Vitry and other contemporaries has been lost, so we cannot evaluate Machaut's true place. His modern reputation as the most important composer of his time may rest at least in part on his desire that his body of work be preserved as a whole rather than left to the vicissitudes of fortune.

FORMS AT A GLANCE

The *Formes Fixes*

Most French songs of the fourteenth century are in one of the three *formes fixes* (fixed forms): **ballade**, **rondeau**, and **virelai**. All three *formes fixes* add a refrain to a stanza in AAB form. Each does so in a different way, resulting in a distinctive form. By convention, the repetition of both text and music in the refrains is shown in uppercase letters, and the repetition of music with new words is shown in lowercase letters. The number of lines of poetry for each section of music may vary.

Ballade

A ballade typically consists of three stanzas, each sung to the same music and each ending with the same line of poetry, which serves as a refrain. The form of each stanza is aabC, with two couplets sung to the same music followed by contrasting music that culminates in the refrain. Often the two a sections have different endings, the first open and the second closed, as in an estampie. The refrain may repeat the closing passage of the second a section to create a musical rhyme.

FIGURE 6.8a
Ballade.

STANZA			REFRAIN	STANZA			REFRAIN	STANZA			REFRAIN
a	a	b	C	a	a	b	C	a	a	b	C

Rondeau

A rondeau has only one stanza, framed by a refrain that includes both sections of music used for the stanza. In addition, the first half of the refrain returns midway through the piece between the a sections, creating a very distinctive form:

FIGURE 6.8b
Rondeau.

REFRAIN		STANZA BEGINS	HALF REFRAIN	STANZA CONTINUES	REFRAIN	
A	B	a	A	a	b	A	B

In practice the refrain is so closely integrated with the other lines of poetry that the entire poem functions as a single stanza with repeating lines whose impact deepens with each repetition. Typically, the A section cadences without finality, akin to an open ending. The B section may echo the final passage of the A section, but closes conclusively on the tonal center.

Virelai

The typical virelai has three stanzas, each preceded and followed by a refrain. As in the cantiga we saw in Chapter 4 (see pp. 73 and 76), the refrain uses the same music as the last section of the stanza melody; because the refrain appears first, it is given the letter A, so that the stanza is shown as bba rather than aab. The b sections often have open and closed endings, like the a sections of a ballade.

FIGURE 6.8c
Virelai.

REFRAIN	STANZA			REFRAIN	STANZA			REFRAIN	STANZA			REFRAIN
A	b	b	a	A	b	b	a	A	b	b	a	A

THE ARS SUBTILIOR

Composers in the later fourteenth century continued and extended the genres and traditions of the Ars Nova. In a paradox typical of the century, the papal court at Avignon was one of the main patrons of secular music. There and at other courts across southern France and northern Italy, a brilliant chivalric society allowed composers to flourish. Their music consisted chiefly of polyphonic songs in the *formes fixes*, especially ballades. These chansons were intended for a sophisticated audience—aristocrats, clerics, courtiers, and connoisseurs who esteemed this music because it developed every possibility of melody, rhythm, counterpoint, and especially notation, which made everything else possible. The composers' fascination with technique and their willingness to take a given procedure to new extremes led music historian Ursula Günther to term this repertory ***Ars Subtilior*** (the more subtle manner). She derived the phrase from a treatise on notation attributed to Philipoctus de Caserta (fl. 1370s), a theorist and composer at the Avignon court, which observes that composers of the day had devised a "more subtle manner" (*artem magis subtiliter*) than the aging Ars Nova. The refined and elevated style of these songs is matched by their sumptuous appearance in some of the manuscripts, including fanciful decorations, intermingled red and black notes, ingenious notation, and occasional caprices that include a love song written in the shape of a heart or a canon in the shape of a circle.

Caserta and others introduced new notational signs and practices, including the vertical combination of different mensurations. As a result, some songs from this period feature remarkable rhythmic complexities, reaching a level not seen again until the twentieth century. Voices move in contrasting meters and conflicting groupings; beats are subdivided in many different ways; phrases are broken by rests or held in suspense through chains of syncopations; and harmonies are purposely blurred through rhythmic disjunction. Whatever the notation allowed, someone would try.

Caserta's ballade *En remirant vo douce pourtraiture* (NAWM 28) exemplifies the Ars Subtilior. The original notation appears in Figure 6.9, and a transcription of the opening in Example 6.5. (Note the *partial signature* in the example, in which lower voices have a key signature with one flat, while the cantus does not; we will see this in several pieces from the late fourteenth and fifteenth centuries.) The prevailing meter is $\frac{9}{8}$—perfect time and major prolation, with threefold divisions of both the breve (the measure) and the semibreve (the beat)—and is marked off by steady dotted quarters (semibreves) in the tenor. But in the cantus, two eighth rests at the beginning of the second measure shift the following phrase off the beat, and interpolated single notes keep it so, producing a series of syncopations transcribed here as ties across the beat. Red notes, marked by broken brackets in the transcription, indicate duple divisions instead of triple and are used to

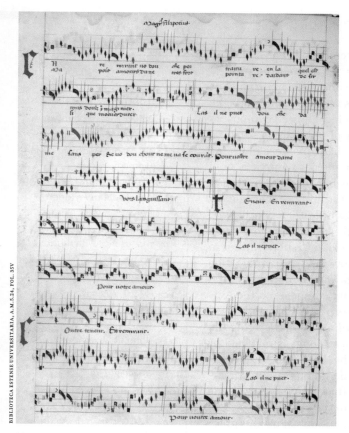

FIGURE 6.9 *Philipoctus de Caserta's* En remirant vo douce pourtraiture *in a manuscript from ca. 1410. The texted cantus (staves 1–4) is followed by the textless tenor (starting middle of the fourth staff) and contratenor (staves 7–10). The red notation indicates changes from triple to duple subdivision, such as from a dotted quarter to a quarter. Changes of meter and proportion are indicated by mensuration signs—small circles or partial circles with or without dots between the staff lines. Both red notation and mensuration signs were used in earlier Ars Nova notation, but here the changes occur much more frequently. A new feature is the profusion of small notes with stems down (third staff) or both up and down (end of second staff), allowing four notes in the space of three.*

create hemiola effects in the contratenor (measures 1–2) and cantus (measure 6). A change of mensuration sign (the backwards C) indicates the equivalent of $\frac{2}{8}$ meter in the contratenor in measures 3–5 and 6. By superimposing different meters, hemiolas, and extensive syncopation, Caserta creates a texture in which notes in different voices most often do not coincide, heightening the sense of independence between the parts. As the music continues, mensuration signs change frequently and new rhythmic arrangements are continually introduced, so that each phrase has a distinctive profile, which helps to articulate the form of the piece. Despite the elaborate compositional techniques and the virtuosic demands this song makes on its performers, the aural effect is quite attractive, with interesting melodies and many sweet consonances.

Ars Subtilior music was intended for professional performers and cultivated listeners. Its formidable rhythmic and notational complexities were in fashion for only about a generation. At the same time, guilds of musicians from northern France created a simpler type of secular polyphony. Their poems and music had a popular character: instead of polished courtly sentiments, the texts offered realistic scenes of the hunt and the marketplace, and the music imitated the straightforward rhythms of folk song. Although few examples are preserved, this simpler art may ultimately have proven more influential on later musicians.

ITALIAN TRECENTO MUSIC

Unlike France, which had a monarchy, Italy in the late Middle Ages was a collection of city-states, each with its own political, cultural, and linguistic traditions. Italians refer to the fourteenth century as the ***Trecento*** (from "mille trecento," Italian for 1300), and Italian music of the period has a distinctive character.

Social roles for Italian music

From writings of the time, we learn how music accompanied nearly every aspect of Italian social life. In Boccaccio's *Decameron*, for example, a group of friends who have retreated to the country from plague-ridden Florence pass

EXAMPLE 6.5 *Philipoctus de Caserta, beginning of* En remirant vo douce pourtraiture

the time by telling stories, dancing, singing, and playing instruments (see Source Reading, p. 124). But they never refer to notated music, and indeed most Italian music of the fourteenth century was never written down. Secular music for many levels of society was purely aural. The only music of the people to have come down to us in manuscripts is the lauda repertory (see Chapter 4). Church polyphony was mostly improvised, either by a soloist singing in discant style over the written notes of a chant, or by an organist adding a line of counterpoint above the chant while alternating phrases of the Mass Ordinary with a choir singing plainchant. What Italian church polyphony survives in notation, mostly from late in the century, includes primarily settings of Mass Ordinary texts (especially Glorias and Credos) for two to four voices or for keyboard, along with some other liturgical settings and motets.

The largest surviving body of Italian music from the time is the repertory of secular polyphonic songs, composed and sung as a refined entertainment for literate audiences in courts and cities. These songs grew out of the flowering of Italian poetry itself in the fourteenth century; until Dante wrote his epic poem *The Divine Comedy* (1307) in his native Tuscan dialect and established it as the Italian literary language, Italian courts had preferred poetry in Occitan, the language of the troubadours. The principal centers of Trecento polyphony were Bologna, Padua, Modena, Milan, Perugia, Naples, and above all Florence, an important cultural center from the fourteenth through the sixteenth centuries, and home to both Dante and Boccaccio.

Italian secular polyphony

The Italian notational system differed from that of the French Ars Nova. The most significant differences are that the breve can be broken into two,

Italian notation

Music-Making in the *Decameron*

Giovanni Boccaccio (1313–1375) was one of the great fourteenth-century writers whose use of the local dialect of Tuscany, around Florence, made that dialect into the national literary language of Italy. His masterpiece is the *Decameron* (1348–53), a collection of one hundred witty and sometimes ribald stories, told over a ten-day period by ten friends who have fled to the country to avoid the Black Death ravaging Florence. The evening before the first day of storytelling, they enjoy dinner, dancing, and music.

❄

The tables having been cleared away, the queen commanded that instruments be brought in, for all the ladies knew how to dance the carole [round dance], and the young men too, and some of them could play and sing very well. Upon her request, Dioneo took a lute and Fiammetta a viol, and they began sweetly to play a dance. Then the queen, having sent the servants out to eat, formed a circle with the other ladies and the two young men and struck up a round dance with a slow pace. When this was finished, they began to sing charming and merry songs. They continued in this way for a long time, until the queen thought it was time to go to sleep.

From Giovanni Boccaccio, *Decameron*, Day One, Introduction.

three, four, six, eight, nine, or twelve equal semibreves or various patterns of unequal ones, and that groupings of semibreves are marked off by dots, akin to the modern barline. This kind of notation, particularly convenient for florid melodic lines, served Italian music well until the later part of the century. By then it was supplemented and eventually replaced by the French system, which had proved itself better adapted to the musical style of the time.

Very few examples of Italian secular polyphony from before 1330 have survived, but after that date there are several manuscripts. The most copious source, unfortunately late and not altogether reliable, is the richly decorated Squarcialupi Codex, named for its former owner, the Florentine organist Antonio Squarcialupi (1416–1480). This collection, copied at the monastery of Santa Maria degli Angeli in Florence in about 1410–15, contains 354 pieces, mostly for two or three voices, by twelve composers of the Trecento and early Quattrocento (1400s). A miniature portrait of each composer appears at the beginning of the section containing his works, as shown in Figure 6.10. Three types of secular Italian pieces appear in this and other manuscripts: *madrigal, caccia,* and *ballata.*

THE FOURTEENTH-CENTURY MADRIGAL The fourteenth-century **madrigal** (not to be confused with the better-known sixteenth-century madrigal) is a song for two or three voices without instrumental accompaniment. All the voices sing the same text, usually an idyllic, pastoral, satirical, or love poem. Madrigals consist of two or more three-line stanzas, each set to the same music, followed by a closing pair of lines, called the **ritornello**, set to different music with a different meter. The form is charted in Figure 6.11. Jacopo da Bologna's madrigal *Non al suo amante* (NAWM 29), setting a poem by the great Italian lyric poet Francesco Petrarca (1304–1374), exhibits the characteristic rhythmic variety and fluidity of the earlier Trecento style. One difference from the French Ars Nova is that here the two voices are relatively equal, occasionally engaging in hocket-like alternation. As is typical of the Italian style, the first and last accented syllables of each line of poetry are set with long melismas, somewhat more florid in the upper voice, while the syllables in between them are set mostly syllabically in relatively rapid declamation to make the text clear. The long melismas are clearly decorative, like the fanciful illuminations that decorate the margins of manuscripts as in Figure 6.10.

THE CACCIA The *caccia* (pl. *cacce*) parallels the French *chace,* in which a popular-style melody is set in strict canon to lively descriptive words. The Italian caccia, in fashion chiefly from 1345 to 1370, features two voices in canon at the unison; unlike its French and Spanish counterparts, it usually has a free untexted tenor in slower motion below. Cacce are irregular in poetic form, although, like madrigals, many have ritornellos, which are not always canonic. *Caccia* and *chace* mean "hunt," referring to the pursuit of one voice after the other. In some cases it also applies to the subject matter of the text. For example, Gherardello da Firenze's caccia *Tosto che l'alba* describes a hunt, and the musical imitations of calling the dogs and sounding the hunting horn are both high-spirited and comic, especially when treated in canon. Besides hunting, cacce may describe other animated scenes, such as a bustling marketplace, a fire, or a battle. The music adds vivid details such as bird songs, shouts, or dialogue, often with hocket or echo effects between the voices. In Francesco Landini's caccia *Così pensoso* (NAWM 30), the narrator hears voices shouting back and forth; as he draws closer, it becomes clear that he is overhearing a group of young women and men on the bank of a pond trying to catch crabs and fish with their hands. The canonic echoing between voices in the music evokes the excited dialogue between the participants.

FIGURE 6.10 *A page from the richly illustrated Squarcialupi Codex, an early-fifteenth-century manuscript named for its fifteenth-century owner Antonio Squarcialupi, showing Francesco Landini playing a portative organ. The portrait is set inside the initial letter M of Landini's madrigal* Musica son *(I am music). The decorative border features pictures of other instruments, including (counterclockwise from upper left) lute, vielle, cittern or citole, harp, psaltery, three recorders, portative organ, and three shawms.*

FIGURE 6.11
Fourteenth-century Italian song forms.

	STANZA	STANZA	RITORNELLO
MADRIGAL			
Sections of music:	a	a	b
Lines of poetry:	1 2 3	4 5 6	7 8

	RIPRESA	STANZA PIEDI	VOLTA	RIPRESA
BALLATA				
Sections of music:	A	b b	a	A
Lines of poetry:	1 2 3	4 5 6 7	8 9 10	1 2 3

THE BALLATA The polyphonic ***ballata*** (pl. *ballate*) beame popular later than the madrigal and caccia and showed some influence from the treble-dominated French chanson style. The word "ballata" (from *ballare,* "to dance") originally meant a song to accompany dancing. Thirteenth-century ballate (of which no musical examples are known today) were monophonic dance songs with choral refrains, and in Boccaccio's *Decameron* the ballata was still associated with dancing. Although a few early fourteenth-century monophonic examples have survived, most ballate in the manuscripts are for two or three voices and date from after 1365.

As shown in Figure 6.11, polyphonic ballate have the form AbbaA, like a single stanza of a French virelai. A *ripresa,* or refrain, is sung before and after a stanza consisting of two *piedi* (feet), couplets sung to the same musical phrase, and the *volta,* the closing lines of text, sung to the same music as the ripresa.

FRANCESCO LANDINI The leading composer of ballate and the foremost Italian musician of the Trecento was Francesco Landini (ca. 1325–1397; see biography and Figure 6.12). Of his 140 ballate, 89 are for two voices, 42 for three, and 9 survive in both two- and three-part versions. Those for two voices, evidently somewhat earlier works, resemble madrigals in texture, with two texted parts. Many of the three-part ballate are in a treble-dominated style, featuring solo voice with two untexted accompanying parts that were most likely sung, as in Machaut's chansons. Example 6.6 shows the opening of a ballata in this later style, Landini's *Non avrà ma' pietà* (NAWM 31).

EXAMPLE 6.6 *Francesco Landini, beginning of* Non avrà ma' pietà

She will never have mercy, this lady of mine, . . . / Perhaps by her [the flames] would be extinguished in me.

FRANCESCO LANDINI

(ca. 1325–1397)

Landini was born in northern Italy, probably in Florence or nearby Fiesole. The son of a painter, he was blinded by smallpox during childhood and turned to music, becoming an esteemed performer, composer, and poet. A master of many instruments, he was especially known for his skill at the organetto, a small portative organ. According to a fourteenth-century Florentine chronicler, Filippo Villani, Landini played the organetto "as readily as though he had the use of his eyes, with a touch of such rapidity (yet always observing the measure), with such skill and sweetness, that beyond all doubt he excelled all organists within memory."

Landini was organist at the monastery of Santa Trinità in 1361–65, then became a chaplain at the church of San Lorenzo, where he remained until his death. He apparently wrote no sacred music, and is best known for his ballate. Landini is a principal character in Giovanni da Prato's *Paradiso degli Alberti,* a narrative poem from around 1425 that records scenes and conversations in Florence from the year 1389. Prato includes a legendary incident that testifies to Landini's skill as a performer:

> Now the sun rose higher and the heat of the day increased. The whole company remained in the pleasant shade, as a thousand birds sang among the verdant branches. Someone asked Francesco [Landini] to play the organ a little, to see whether the sound would make the birds increase or diminish their song. He did so at once, and a great wonder followed. When the sound began many of the birds fell silent and gathered around as if in amazement, listening for a long time. Then they resumed their song and redoubled it, showing inconceivable delight, and especially one nightingale, who came and perched above the organ on a branch over Francesco's head.

MAJOR WORKS 140 ballate, 12 madrigals, 1 caccia, 1 virelai

From Filippo Villani, *Le Vite d'uomini illustri fiorentini,* ed. G. Mazzuchelli (Florence, 1847), 46: Giovanni da Prato, *Il Paradiso degli Alberti,* ed. A. Wesselofsky (Bologna, 1867), 111–13.

FIGURE 6.12 *The tombstone of Francesco Landini. The blind composer plays a portative organ, accompanied by two angel musicians. The Latin inscription around the perimeter reads "Francesco, who was deprived of sight but whose mind was skillful at [composing] songs and [playing] melodies on the organ, whom alone Music brought to birth for all the world, has left his ashes here on earth, but his soul beyond the stars. 2 September 1397."*

One of the charms of Landini's music is the sweetness of the harmonies. Sonorities containing thirds and sixths are plentiful, though they never begin or end a section or piece. Equally charming are his graceful vocal melodies, arranged in arching phrases and moving most often by step, decorated with varied and often syncopated rhythms but ultimately smoother in both pitch contour and rhythm than most melodies by Machaut. Melismas on the first and penultimate syllables of a poetic line are characteristic of the Italian style, as is the clear, almost syllabic declamation between melismas. The end of every line, and often the first word and the midpoint, or caesura, of a line, is marked by a cadence. Most are of the type known as a **_Landini cadence_**, in which, as the tenor descends by step, the upper voice decorates its ascent by first descending to the lower neighbor and then skipping up a third (see Example 6.6, measures 3–4, 5–6, and 10–11). It is named after Landini because he was the first to use it consistently, although it occurs occasionally in earlier Italian music. It became ubiquitous in both French and Italian music of the late fourteenth and early fifteenth centuries.

FRENCH INFLUENCE Toward the end of the fourteenth century, the music of Italian composers began to lose its specific national characteristics and to absorb the contemporary French style. Italians wrote songs to French texts and in French genres, and their works recorded in late-fourteenth-century manuscripts often appear in French notation. The blending of national traditions became an increasingly frequent practice in the fifteenth century, when northern musicians took up positions in Italy, and traits of French, Italian, Flemish, Netherlandish, and English music were integrated into an international musical style (see Chapter 8).

PERFORMING FOURTEENTH-CENTURY MUSIC

Fourteenth-century music manuscripts left a great deal unspecified that we expect scores today to tell us, from how loud or soft the music should be to more basic information such as whether a part is vocal or instrumental, which instruments might be used, and when notes should be inflected by accidentals. Reconstructing the performing practice of seven centuries ago is no easy matter, because we have no living tradition, and evidence can be hard to find and even harder to interpret.

For example, Figure 6.13 shows a singer reading from a manuscript and accompanied by an organist, but we do not know what they are performing; is it a monophonic song for which the organist improvises an accompaniment, or is she playing one or two parts from a polyphonic setting? There has been a lively debate among scholars and performers about whether all parts in fourteenth-century polyphony were sung or some were played on instruments (see In Performance: Voices or Instruments?, p. 130). Given current knowledge, it seems likely that church polyphony was only sung, usually with one voice per part, and that secular polyphony was typically sung by soloists but could also be played by instrumentalists. We may never know for sure, and it may be that performances varied according to circumstances, depending on tastes and preferences and on the singers or players at hand.

INSTRUMENTS Musicians in the fourteenth through sixteenth centuries distinguished between instruments based on their relative loudness, using **_haut_** (French for "high") and **_bas_** ("low") for volume rather than pitch. The most common low instruments were harps, vielles, lutes, psalteries, portative organs, transverse flutes, and recorders. Among the high instruments were shawms, trumpets, and **_cornetts_** (wooden wind instruments with finger holes and a brass-type mouthpiece). Percussion instruments, including kettledrums, small bells, and cymbals, were common in ensembles of all kinds. To judge from representations in the art of the time, instruments of contrasting timbres were often grouped together. Music played outdoors, for dancing, or for especially festive or solemn ceremonies called for relatively larger ensembles and louder instruments.

Keyboard instruments became more practical and widely used in the fourteenth and fifteenth centuries. In addition to the portative organ, shown in Figures 6.10 and 6.12, positive organs like that in Figure 6.13 were employed in secular music, and large, unmovable organs were installed in many churches. Pedal keyboards were added to church organs in Germany in the late 1300s. A mechanism of **stops** enabling the player to select different ranks of pipes and the addition of a second keyboard were both achievements of the early fifteenth century. Although the earliest keyboard instruments of the harpsichord and clavichord type were invented in the fourteenth century, they were not commonly used until the fifteenth.

FIGURE 6.13 Tapestry from the Low Countries (ca. 1420), showing a man in courtly dress singing from a manuscript. He is accompanied by a woman playing a positive organ, the type that is portable but must be placed on a table to be played, rather than resting on a lap like the portative organ played by Landini in Figures 6.10 and 6.12. A boy stands behind the organ, pumping the bellows to force air through the pipes and produce the sounds.

INSTRUMENTAL MUSIC Little purely instrumental music survives from the fourteenth century. Vocal pieces were sometimes played instrumentally throughout, with added embellishments in the melodic line. Instrumental arrangements were largely improvised, but some for keyboard were written down. The Robertsbridge Codex from about 1325 includes organ arrangements of three motets, and the Faenza Codex from the first quarter of the fifteenth century contains keyboard versions of ballades by Machaut and madrigals and ballate by Landini and others, as well as keyboard pieces based on chants for Mass. We can assume that there was also a large repertory of instrumental dance melodies, but as these pieces were generally either improvised or played from memory, few written examples have been preserved. There are about fifteen surviving instrumental dances from fourteenth-century Italy, all monophonic and most in the Italian form of the estampie, the *istampita*. Other pieces from Italy include a Lamento and four tenor lines for group improvisation.

Together the instrumental works that survive from the fourteenth century suggest a vibrant performing tradition that has left few traces. Echoes of this vibrancy can be heard in the varied approaches of modern performers to playing these dances, especially the *istampita*. Tracking the realizations of this music through generations of concert-hall and folk artists over the last hundred years would provide a fascinating acoustical survey of the modern reinvention of medieval music.

MUSICA FICTA Just as the choice of instruments was normally left to the performers, so was the use of certain chromatic alterations known as **musica ficta**. Musicians from the fourteenth through sixteenth centuries often raised

IN PERFORMANCE

Voices or Instruments?

How were fourteenth-century polyphonic pieces performed? One voice on each part, or many? Instruments on some parts? If so, which instruments? The manuscripts that contain this music do not specify performing medium. What evidence can we use to answer these questions?

In his book *The Modern Invention of Medieval Music*, Daniel Leech-Wilkinson traces changes in scholarly opinion and in the practice of modern performers. Nineteenth-century scholars generally assumed medieval polyphonic music was performed by voices on every part. But in the early 1900s, Hugo Riemann and other influential musicologists asserted that untexted tenors and contratenors were instrumental, by analogy to the instrumental accompaniments for nineteenth-century songs, and some argued that the elaborate melismas in Ars Nova and Trecento songs were too complex to have been sung and thus must have been played by instruments.

From such assertions, built on little primary evidence, grew a decades-long tradition of performing medieval music with instruments on the untexted parts, often doubling the voice on texted parts as well. Performers based their choice of instruments on medieval pictures of angels making music, which often show plucked and bowed string instruments alongside wind and brass instruments and singers. A heterogeneous sound, with a different timbre on every line, came to be considered typical for medieval music.

But in the 1970s and 1980s, a new generation of scholars, led by Christopher Page and David Fallows, presented fresh evidence to show that fourteenth-century polyphony was performed by voices without instruments. Evidence included pay records showing that singers, but not instrumentalists, were paid to perform in church and that the typical cohort for singing church polyphony was one voice per part in the fourteenth century and two to six voices per part in the fifteenth; separate training systems for singers and instrumentalists, so that the latter were unlikely to read music; ordinances that excluded instrumentalists from playing in church; literary accounts of three-voice chansons performed by three singers without instruments; no accounts of voices and instruments performing composed polyphony together; and the presence of texts for the tenor and contratenor parts in more pieces and manuscripts than had been realized. Page's singing group Gothic Voices made numerous recordings that demonstrated the viability and pleasing homogeneous sound of one voice per part, without instruments (including the performances of Machaut's *Rose, liz, printemps, verdure* and Landini's *Così pensoso* on the recordings that accompany NAWM), and other performers followed suit. The combination of solid evidence and winning recordings led to a new consensus that fourteenth-century polyphony was normally sung with one voice on a part, although performance by instruments was also possible.

But this was not the last word. A 2011 article by Peter Urquhart and Heather de Savage argued that the contratenors in some fifteenth-century chansons were conceived for a plucked string instrument, using three kinds of evidence: these parts are melodically angular, with more large leaps than other parts, making them harder to sing; sustained notes in these contratenors create dissonances and other problems in counterpoint that disappear if the part is played on a plucked instrument (whose sounds decay rapidly) rather than being sung by a voice; and some contratenors are notated with more than one note sounding at once, impossible for a voice but suitable for a harp or lute. If their view is confirmed for chansons in the fifteenth century, could it also be true for fourteenth-century chansons? Stray dissonances in the contratenor of Philipoctus de Caserta's ballade *En remirant vo douce pourtraiture* suggest it might (see the commentary on NAWM 28). Stay tuned.

or lowered notes by a semitone to avoid the tritone F–B in a melody, to make a smoother melodic line, to avoid sounding an augmented fourth or diminished fifth above the lowest note, or to provide "a sweeter-sounding harmony" at cadences, as the theorist Prosdocimo de' Beldomandi observed (see Source Reading). This practice was called *musica ficta* ("feigned music"), because most altered notes lay outside the standard gamut. The medieval tone-system permitted semitones, pronounced *mi–fa* in solmization syllables, between B and C, E and F, and A and B♭. This was the realm of *musica recta* (correct music), the gamut of notes sung in liturgical chant and mapped on the Guidonian hand (see Example 2.7 and Figure 2.11 on p. 40). A note outside this realm was considered "outside the hand," "false," or "feigned" (*ficta*), because it involved putting the syllables *mi* and *fa* on notes where they would not normally go.

Musica ficta was often used at cadences. Theorists, composers, and singers agreed that a sixth expanding to an octave should be major rather than minor, and a third contracting to a unison should be minor rather than major, because, in Prosdocimo's words, "the closer the imperfect consonance

Cadences

SOURCE READING

Prosdocimo de' Beldomandi on *Musica ficta*

Fourteenth-century musicians avoided tritones and smoothed the harmony and melody by raising or lowering notes a semitone according to a set of rules, a practice called *musica ficta*. One of the best explanations of these rules is by Prosdocimo de' Beldomandi (d. 1428), a doctor and professor at the University of Padua. Since musicians of the time were trained to distinguish whole from half steps through solmization syllables (see Example 2.7 and pp. 39–40), he used the syllables to explain *musica ficta*.

✥

Musica ficta is the feigning of [solmization] syllables or the placement of syllables in a location where they do not seem to be—to apply *mi* where there is no *mi* and *fa* where there is no *fa*, and so forth. Concerning musica ficta, it is necessary to know first of all that it is never to be applied except where necessary, because in art nothing is to be applied without necessity. . . .

3. It must be known, too, that the signs of musica ficta are two, round or soft b [which became the modern ♭] and square or hard ♮ [modern ♮ or ♯]. These two signs show us the feigning of syllables

in a location where such syllables cannot be. . . .

6. Last, for understanding the placement of these two signs, round b and square ♮, it must be known that these signs are to be applied to octaves, fifths, and similar intervals as it is necessary to enlarge or diminish them in order to make them good consonances if they earlier were dissonant, because such intervals ought always to be major or consonant in counterpoint. But these signs are to be applied to imperfectly consonant intervals—the third, the sixth, the tenth, and the like—as is necessary to enlarge or diminish them to give them major or minor inflections as appropriate, because such intervals ought sometimes to be major and sometimes minor in counterpoint; . . . for you should always choose that form, whether major or minor, that is less distant from that location which you intend immediately to reach. . . . There is no other reason for this than a sweeter-sounding harmony. . . . This is because the closer the imperfect consonance approaches the perfect one it intends to reach, the more perfect it becomes, and the sweeter the resulting harmony.

From *Contrapunctus* [Counterpoint, 1412], Book 5, Chapters 1–6, trans. Jan Herlinger (Lincoln: University of Nebraska Press, 1984), 71–85.

EXAMPLE 6.7 *Alterations at cadences*

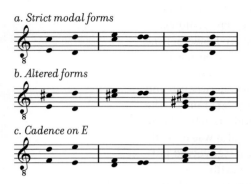

a. Strict modal forms

b. Altered forms

c. Cadence on E

approaches the perfect one it intends to reach, the more perfect it becomes, and the sweeter the resulting harmony." Thus the strictly modal cadences in Example 6.7a were typically altered as shown in Example 6.7b; the last of these, in which both upper notes resolve upward by a half step, is known as a ***double leading-tone cadence*** and is a characteristic sound in fourteenth- and fifteenth-century music. Cadences on G and C were altered in similar fashion, and cadences on F naturally featured double leading tones. In cadences on E, however, the penultimate intervals were already the right size, as shown in Example 6.7c, so no alteration was required. Cadences like these, in which the lower voice descends by a semitone and the upper voice rises a whole tone, are called ***Phrygian cadences***, since they occur naturally in the Phrygian mode; they may also occur on B or A.

Omission of accidentals in notation

Such alterations would present no difficulty to modern performers if composers and scribes had consistently entered the appropriate signs in the manuscripts: what we think of as accidentals (which they used to indicate the unexpected appearance of *mi* or *fa,* as Prosdocimo explains). But often they did not, and when they did they were inconsistent, as the same passage may appear in different manuscripts with different written accidentals. This was no mere carelessness, for it accorded with the theoretical framework of the time. Singers were trained to recognize situations in which a note should be altered to produce a smoother melody or progression of intervals and would work out such changes in rehearsal. It was unnecessary to specify an accidental where a skilled musician would have known to make an alteration. Moreover, many contrapuntal situations have more than one possible resolution, and performers had the option to choose the solution they preferred. Thus a composer like Machaut would place accidentals in his manuscripts only where he wanted a note to be altered for the sake of beauty (as in Example 6.3, measure 31 in the cantus and 39 in the contratenor) and the change could not be assumed from the rules. Modern editions of this music generally place only those accidentals found in the original sources in front of the notes to which they apply and indicate above the staff the additional alterations the editor believes the performers should supply (see Examples 6.2–6.4 and 6.6). The term musica ficta is now often used for any such alterations that are suggested by context rather than notation, even when notes outside the Guidonian gamut are not involved.

ECHOES OF THE NEW ART

Fourteenth-century approaches to music had a profound and continuing impact on music and musical life in later centuries. Perhaps most significant was the invention of a precise and unambiguous notation that could record a wide variety of rhythms and allowed music to be distributed in writing and performed accurately wherever it went. We now take this for granted when we play from notation and sight-read through unfamiliar music, but it was a remarkable innovation in the fourteenth century. Among its effects was that composers could fix their music exactly as they wished it to be performed, as poets had long been able to set down their poems, leading them to take pride in authorship as few composers had done before Machaut. The increased interest in the individual and in satisfying the human senses that was characteristic of the age grew stronger in the fifteenth and sixteenth centuries and has remained important ever since. Future composers would claim credit for their work more readily and would remain anonymous much less often than was true before 1300. Apparently a piece by Machaut or Landini was esteemed more highly, simply because it was by such a famous composer. This is of course still true today, for composers as disparate as Beethoven, Irving Berlin, Count Basie, the Beatles, Björk, Justin Bieber, or Beyoncé.

The interplay between structure and pleasure so typical of fourteenth-century music has also had a continuing resonance. Specific structural devices of the time, such as isorhythm and the *formes fixes,* lasted only to the late fifteenth century, but ideas of musical structure continued and diversified. French structure, Italian smoothness of melody and clarity of declamation, and the growing use in both traditions of prominent harmonic thirds and sixths all contributed to the international style of the fifteenth century. The meters and rhythmic combinations made possible by Ars Nova notation, from common time to syncopation, are still part of music today. The creation of a polyphonic style centered on a melodious topmost voice rather than built around the tenor, exemplified in Machaut's chansons, undergirded many later developments. More recently, many modern composers have drawn on music of the fourteenth century for sounds, techniques, and ideas. The structural artifice of Ars Nova isorhythmic motets and the notational and proportional wizardry of Ars Subtilior songs influenced composers in the second half of the twentieth century such as Olivier Messiaen and György Ligeti.

The music itself did not fare as well. Fourteenth-century styles fell out of use, and figures like Machaut became best known as poets, while their music came to be considered old-fashioned in comparison to the new fifteenth-century style. When first rediscovered in the nineteenth century, fourteenth-century polyphony seemed harsh in its harmonies and crude in allowing parallel fifths and octaves, forbidden in counterpoint since the fifteenth century. But twentieth-century music used a wider range of sounds and techniques and helped to make fourteenth-century music sound fresh in comparison to common-practice harmony. Interest in reviving fourteenth-century music led to editions of the complete works of Machaut, Vitry, Landini, and others, many of them first appearing after World War II. Now pieces by Machaut, Landini, and others from the fourteenth century are again regularly performed and recorded, both by early music specialists and by mainstream popular artists, including Judy Collins's rendition of a Landini ballata on her album *Wildflowers* (2007), Panda Bear's sampling of Machaut's rondeau *Rose, liz, printemps, verdure* in his song "I'm Not" (2005), and the blend of medieval, jazz, and pop styles in the recording of Machaut's *Douce dame jolie* by Music 4 a While (2014). Through modern media, the music of these fourteenth-century composers is heard by many times more people today than in their own lifetimes.

Further Reading is available at digital.wwnorton.com/hwm10

THE
RENAISSANCE

Europeans in the fifteenth and sixteenth centuries combined a rediscovery of ancient learning with new discoveries and innovations to produce a flowering of culture and the arts that became known as the Renaissance. Changes in music were far-reaching. Responding to a growing interest in pleasing the senses, musicians developed a new kind of counterpoint, featuring strict control of dissonances and pervasive use of sweet-sounding sonorities. They devised new methods for writing polyphonic music that included greater equality between the voices, more varied textures featuring imitation or homophony, and new ways of reworking borrowed material of every kind from chants to polyphonic pieces. Composers of vocal music endeavored to reflect in their melodies the accents, inflections, rhythms, and meanings of the words. Reading ancient Greek texts that extolled music as part of education, that expected every citizen to sing and play music, and that described the power of music to evoke emotions and instill character, writers and musicians in the sixteenth century sought the same roles and effects for the music of their times. The invention of music printing in the early sixteenth century made written music more widely accessible and created a market for music that amateurs could sing or play for their own entertainment, alone or as a social activity. The demand stimulated new kinds of secular song and a great increase in notated instrumental music. Not least important, growing interest in the individual artist and artwork brought a new prominence to composers and the concept of the musical work.

All of these developments have affected music ever since. From the very language of music to our belief that music expresses feelings, we are the heirs of the Renaissance.

PART OUTLINE

MUSIC AND THE RENAISSANCE

The fifteenth and sixteenth centuries were a period of great change for European culture, literature, art, and music. To some at the time, it seemed that the arts had been reborn after a period of stagnation. In his 1855 *Histoire de France* (History of France), Jules Michelet crystallized this notion in the term **Renaissance** (French for "rebirth"), and soon historians of literature, art, and music were using it to designate the period after the Middle Ages. The idea of rebirth captures the aims of scholars and artists to revive the learning, ideals, and values of ancient Greece and Rome. But writers, artists, and musicians did far more than recover the old. Currents already strong in the late Middle Ages continued, innovations emerged in every field, and new technologies such as the printing press brought radical changes.

In music, these centuries are better understood as a time of continual and overlapping changes than as a period characterized by a single style throughout. New genres emerged, from the polyphonic mass cycle in the mid-fifteenth century to the sonata in the late sixteenth, and old genres like the motet and chanson were transformed. From the early fifteenth century on, musicians frequently held positions outside their native regions. Their encounters with music and musicians from other parts of Europe led to the creation of a new international style drawing on elements of French, Italian, and English traditions. This new idiom featured new rules for polyphony based on strict control of dissonance, marking a distinct break from previous eras. These rules for counterpoint and dissonance treatment were followed by composers throughout the fifteenth and sixteenth centuries, and this shared practice unites these centuries as a coherent historical period in music despite numerous other changes of style and practice. The greater use of thirds and sixths required new tuning systems. The late fifteenth century saw the emergence of two principal textures that would predominate in sixteenth-century music—***imitative counterpoint*** and ***homophony***. In the late fifteenth and sixteenth centuries, the revival of classical learning had many parallels in music, including a renewed interest in ancient Greek theory and ideals for music and a new focus on setting words with correct declamation while reflecting the meanings and emotions of the text. The development of music printing in the early sixteenth century made notated music available to a wider public. Amateurs bought music to perform for their own entertainment, encouraging composers to produce new and more popular kinds of music, especially songs in vernacular languages and music for instruments, and fostering the spread of many new genres of vocal and instrumental music. The Reformation brought new forms of religious music for Protestant churches and, in reaction, new styles for Catholic music. All of these changes have affected music in fundamental ways ever since.

These developments will be taken up individually in the next five chapters. Here we will set the stage by placing the changes in music in the wider context of the Renaissance, showing some parallels with the other arts.

EUROPE FROM 1400 TO 1600

The fifteenth century saw the end of two long-standing conflicts: the Great Schism in the church was resolved in 1417 with the return to a single pope in Rome, and the Hundred Years' War concluded with the expulsion of the English from France in 1453. That same year, Constantinople fell to the Ottoman Turks, ending the Byzantine Empire. New conflicts emerged in their place, as the Turks conquered the Balkans and Hungary over the next century, and the Roman Church was splintered by the Reformation, a movement that began in 1517 as a debate about church practices but quickly led to the formation of new Protestant denominations and more than a century of theological disputes and religious wars.

Most significant in the long run was the rise of Europe as a world power. Larger ships, better navigational aids, and more powerful artillery helped Europeans expand their influence beyond the Mediterranean and northern Atlantic. During the fifteenth century, the Portuguese established colonies and trade routes extending around Africa to India and the East Indies. Columbus's encounter with the New World in 1492 led to Spanish and Portuguese colonies in the Americas, to be followed in the early seventeenth century by the French, English, and Dutch. These events would ultimately lead to the expansion of European culture, including its music, throughout the Americas and across Africa and Asia and to a transatlantic musical culture that blended genres, rhythms, styles, and traditions from Europe, the Americas, and Africa.

European expansion

After the economic turmoil of the fourteenth century, the European economy stabilized around 1400 and began to grow. Regions specialized in different agricultural and manufactured products and traded with each other across great distances. Towns and cities prospered from trade, and many city-dwellers accumulated wealth through commerce, banking, and crafts. The middle class of merchants, artisans, doctors, lawyers, and other independent entrepreneurs continued to increase in numbers, influence, and economic importance, seeking prosperity for their families, property and beautiful objects for themselves, and education for their children. Rulers, especially in the small principalities and city-states of Italy, sought to glorify themselves

Economy and support for the arts

and their realms by erecting impressive palaces decorated with new artworks and newly unearthed artifacts from ancient civilizations; by lavishly entertaining their subjects and neighboring potentates; and by maintaining ensembles of talented singers and instrumentalists. These conditions laid the economic and social foundations for a flowering of the arts.

THE RENAISSANCE IN CULTURE AND ART

The notion of the Renaissance has been debated ever since the term was introduced. Any historical periodization is an abstraction, imposed by later generations as a way to organize a mass of details into a coherent picture, and different historians have suggested varying approaches. Some begin the Renaissance in the fourteenth century with Giotto, Dante, Petrarch, and Trecento music, others in the early fifteenth century or later; some see it ending by the mid-sixteenth century, while others continue it well into the seventeenth century. Still other historians do away with the concept of a Renaissance period altogether, arguing that the fifteenth century is best regarded as the late Middle Ages and that a new era, the Early Modern, begins with the sixteenth. Those who emphasize the revival of ancient Greek and Roman writings and art and its effects on European culture find the idea of rebirth a powerful metaphor, but others argue that this revival directly affected only the elite and does not explain many changes in this era, even in the arts.

For our purposes in studying music history, it makes sense to consider the fifteenth and sixteenth centuries as a unit, because the new approach to counterpoint that emerged in the early 1400s marked a decisive change from the previous century and remained the essential foundation for music until around 1600. But what shall we call this period? The idea of "rebirth" seems especially problematic for music, because unlike writers, sculptors, and architects, musicians had no ancient classics to imitate; not until the late sixteenth century were the first examples of ancient Greek music rediscovered and transcribed. The closest music came to a literal Renaissance was through the rediscovery of ancient Greek writings about music, which influenced music theorists and then composers in their turn. Yet musicians did not revive ancient practices; rather, at times they used ideas from ancient writers as inspiration or as justification for new approaches to such issues as text setting or the modes.

Despite its problems, "Renaissance" is still a useful term for the period between about 1400 and 1600, in music as in the other arts, if we remember that the idea of rebirth is a metaphor and that it captures only one aspect of a complex era. In every field, a conscious looking-back to Greece and Rome was combined with elements continued from the Middle Ages and with entirely new developments. What seems most characteristic of the period is a spirit of discovery and invention in all aspects of life, from examining ancient writers to exploring other parts of the planet, dissecting the human body to see how it works, inventing new manufacturing processes, or devising a new way to paint more realistically or to compose a more compelling piece of music.

HUMANISM The idea of a Renaissance is most directly applicable to the realm of letters. Scholars and thinkers of the time had broader access to Greek and Roman literature and philosophy than their predecessors. Ottoman attacks on Constantinople beginning in 1396 prompted many Byzantine scholars to flee to Italy, taking with them numerous ancient Greek writings. They taught the Greek language to Italian scholars, some of whom traveled eastward to collect manuscripts of works unknown in western Europe. Soon the Greek classics were translated into Latin, making most of Plato and the Greek plays and histories accessible to western Europeans for the first time. In the early fifteenth century, scholars rediscovered complete copies of works on rhetoric by Cicero and Quintilian. Later that century, other texts from Roman antiquity came into circulation, including works by Livy, Tacitus, and Lucretius.

The increasing availability of ancient writings was complemented by new ways of approaching them. The strongest intellectual movement of the Renaissance was *humanism*, from the Latin phrase "studia humanitatis," the study of the humanities, things pertaining to human knowledge. Humanists sought to revive ancient learning, focusing on classical Latin and Greek writings, and to broaden intellectual life and the university curriculum. In opposition to Scholasticism, with its emphasis on logic and metaphysics and its reliance on authority, humanists emphasized the study of grammar, rhetoric, poetry, history, and moral philosophy. They believed these subjects developed the individual's mind, spirit, and ethics, prepared students for lives of virtue and service, and fostered effective and persuasive communication, all crucial for participation in the civic life and governance of cities in Italy and beyond. Alongside their belief in Christian doctrine, humanists had faith in the dignity and nobility of humans, in human reason, and in our capacity to understand reality through our senses and to improve our condition through our own efforts. The role of the church was not diminished; rather, the church borrowed from classical sources, sponsored classical studies, and supported thinkers, artists, and musicians. Typical of the Renaissance, humanism represented a new approach that synthesized ancient learning with Christian ideas inherited from the Middle Ages and applied both to present-day problems.

Humanism had both direct and indirect influences on music. Following Aristotle and Quintilian, humanists considered music an essential part of education. The recovery of ancient texts included writings on music, and writers from the late fifteenth century on incorporated these earlier ideas (see pp. 152–54). More broadly, the focus of the humanists on rhetoric—the art of oratory, including the ability to persuade listeners and to organize a speech in a coherent manner—influenced composers to apply ideas from rhetoric in their music, a movement that gathered strength during this period and remained forceful for centuries to come. The traditional connection of music to mathematics did not disappear, but the immediate perception of music, and the ways it resembled a language, became increasingly important.

Effects on music

Moreover, humanists came to see meaning as emerging from language itself, through acts of persuasion, the formulation of arguments, and reasoning by means of dialectic and dialogue. In a similar way, by the end of the Renaissance musicians and listeners came to understand music as innately expressive, a view most still hold today.

SCULPTURE, PAINTING, AND ARCHITECTURE Art in the Renaissance shows striking contrasts with medieval art and parallels with new developments in scholarship and music.

Classical models and naturalism The revival of classical antiquity in new guise is embodied in the bronze statue of *David* by Donatello (ca. 1386–1466), shown in Figure 7.1, the first freestanding nude since Roman times. It depicts David moments after he has slain Goliath, the champion of the Philistines (1 Samuel 17). Nakedness in the Middle Ages was used to show shame, as in paintings of the expulsion of Adam and Eve from the Garden of Eden. Here nudity shows the beauty of the human figure, as in the Greek and Roman sculptures Donatello used as models, and thereby proclaims the nobility of the biblical hero. Thus classical means are used to convey a religious theme, paralleling the church's use of classical and humanistic studies. This combination is truly new, and characteristic of the Renaissance.

Donatello's statue is rhetorically conceived, designed to have an impact on the viewer and convey meaning. David stands with his foot on his enemy's severed head, the stone that felled the giant in his left hand, Goliath's sword in his right. The contrasts between the slender youth and the giant's bearded face, the smooth skin and the textured helmets, the living flesh and the dead foe, all emphasize David's unexpected triumph and thus the power of God, whom David said would give him the victory. In similar ways, Renaissance composers used contrasts of texture, sonority, melody, rhythm, and flow to have an impact on the listener and support the meaning of the words they set.

Donatello's naturalism—his attempt to reproduce nature realistically—is also in tune with humanists' endeavor to see and understand the world as it really is. The naturalism and idealized beauty of this statue are typical of Renaissance art and have parallels in music, as composers sought to please the ear with beautiful sonorities, more pervasive consonance, greater control of dissonance, and seemingly natural rather than contorted melodies and rhythms.

Italian painters had been pursuing greater realism since Giotto in the early 1300s (see Chapter 6 and Figure 6.1). But far more lifelike representations were made possible in the early 1400s through two innovations: *perspective*, a method for representing three-dimensional space on a flat surface, creating a sense of depth, and *chiaroscuro*, the naturalistic treatment of light and shade. A comparison of two paintings will illustrate both concepts. Figure 7.2 shows a fourteenth-century fresco of a city scene. Individual parts of the painting look realistic, but the whole does not look real. This is especially true of the use of light, for some buildings are better lit to the right side, others to the left, which cannot happen with natural

FIGURE 7.1 David *(ca. 1440s), by Donatello. David, clad in helmet and leggings but otherwise nude, stands astride the head of the slain Goliath. This bronze statue was commissioned in the mid-fifteenth century by Cosimo de' Medici, the most powerful citizen and de facto ruler of Florence, for the Palazzo Medici.*

MUSEO NAZIONALE DEL BARGELLO, FLORENCE, ITALY. PHOTO: NIMATALLAH/ART RESOURCE, NY

FIGURE 7.2 *A panel from* The Effects of Good and Bad Government in the Town and in the Country *(1337–39), a fresco by Ambrogio Lorenzetti painted in the Palazzo Pubblico (public palace) in Siena, a city in Tuscany in northern Italy. The subject of the painting illustrates the new humanist concern with government and civic virtues. Yet the technique is still medieval in many respects. While objects farther away are depicted as behind and somewhat smaller than those closer to the viewer, there is no true perspective.*

FIGURE 7.3 *Idealized View of the City (ca. 1480) by a painter from the school of Piero della Francesca, in the ducal palace in Urbino, northern Italy. The scene looks realistic because of the use of perspective and attention to lighting. All the lines that in three-dimensional reality would be parallel to each other, like the lines in the pavement or on the sides of buildings, converge toward a single vanishing point, just under the top of the doorway of the central building. The sun's light is coming from the left and somewhat behind the viewer, since left-facing surfaces are brightest, surfaces facing the viewer somewhat darker, and right-facing surfaces darker still.*

sunlight. The buildings seem piled on top of one another, their distance from the viewer unclear. The late-fifteenth-century painting of an ideal city in Figure 7.3, by contrast, uses perspective, in which all parallel lines converge to a single vanishing point, and objects of the same size appear smaller in exact proportion as they grow more distant. This reflects how we actually see, creating the illusion of depth. In addition, the light falls on all surfaces as if coming from a single source. The overall effect is much more natural and realistic.

The later picture is also more orderly, with clean lines, symmetry, and little clutter. The decorative elements on the buildings make their structure clear, highlighting the floors, pillars, and arches. This preference for clarity, typical of Renaissance architecture, contrasts markedly with Gothic decoration, such as the ornate and whimsical filigree on Notre Dame Cathedral in Figure 5.3. The use of columns with capitals on the center and leftmost buildings shows the Renaissance interest in imitating ancient architecture.

Clarity and classical models in architecture

FIGURE 7.4 *Masaccio,* Holy Trinity with the Virgin, St. John, and Donors *(ca. 1425–28), fresco in the church of Santa Maria Novella in Florence. The artist used perspective to create a sense of depth and of height, placing the vanishing point at eye level as one faces the painting, below the foot of the cross. The three members of the Trinity are shown: Jesus the Son on the cross in the center, God the Father above him, and the Holy Spirit as a dove flying between them. The colors create a subtle, almost symmetrical pattern of red, gray, and cream, leading the eye from one figure to the next.*

The fresco by Masaccio (Tommaso Cassai, 1401–1428) in Figure 7.4 illustrates all these characteristics and adds another, an interest in individuals. One of the first paintings to use perspective, it creates an impressive sense of depth. The vanishing point is at the base of the cross, at eye level, so the lines in the ceiling and walls converge exactly as they would appear to do if an actual chapel stood there instead of a flat wall. Faces, bodies, drapery, and poses are natural; contrasting colors and shadings reinforce the impression of space while creating a clear and pleasing composition; and classical influence is reflected in the Greek columns with Ionic and Corinthian capitals, the arches, and the ceiling modeled after that of the Pantheon in Rome. Kneeling on either side are the painting's donors, identified as Lorenzo Lenzi and his wife. Their presence and Masaccio's lifelike portrayal of them reflect the heightened interest in individuals during the Renaissance: not for this well-to-do couple the anonymity of the donors, masons, and artisans who contributed to the Notre Dame Cathedral of Paris two centuries earlier. The many portraits painted in the Renaissance testify to the desire of patrons to be memorialized in art and the ability of artists to capture the personality of each subject.

The painting is also addressed to the individual viewer, using the rhetoric of art to persuade each person to join the community of believers. When you stand in front of it, the perspective creates lines of sight that draw you into the painting and show the way to salvation. Nearest to you are the donors, people like you who have committed themselves to the Church and exemplify contrition, devotion, and prayer. Next are the Virgin Mary and St. John, who intercede on behalf of the faithful. At the center of the painting and deeper into its imagined space is Jesus, who sacrificed himself on the cross to save humanity. Above and behind him soars the Holy Spirit in the form of a dove, and highest and farthest back is God the Father. The progression through space links the three members of the Trinity to each other, to the saints, to the donors, and to you. The perspective and realism make the image more believable. The fresco is not just beautiful and technically accomplished; it also conveys a message.

Like the ideals of beauty and naturalism discussed on page 140, chiaroscuro, clarity, perspective, and interest in individuals also have parallels in music. Composers expanded the range of their pieces to include lower and higher pitches than before, and they employed contrasts between high and low registers and between thin and full textures that recall the contrasts of light and dark in contemporary painting. Many composers sought to make the musical structure clear through such contrasts, through frequent cadences, and by other means, akin to the clarity of line and function in Renaissance architecture. Perspective, while unique to painting and drawing, is analogous to aspects of Renaissance music that orient the listener's experience around a single point of reference, such as the increasing focus on making the mode of a polyphonic work clear by having all or most phrases cadence on the main notes of the mode, especially its final and reciting tone, in the same way the receding lines in Figures 7.3 and 7.4 all lead to the vanishing point. We will encounter a few pieces that, like Masaccio's fresco, memorialize individuals, but even more important is the rising significance of composers as individual artists, celebrated in their sphere as were Donatello and Masaccio in theirs. The notion of a unique personal style in music is rare before the fifteenth century, but becomes typical of the Renaissance and later periods. Moreover, just as Masaccio's fresco targets the individual viewer, so too is Renaissance music aimed at individual listeners, carrying messages that vary from religious to erotic, while forging a sense of community.

Musical parallels

MUSIC IN THE RENAISSANCE

The broad intellectual and artistic currents of the Renaissance affected music deeply, yet in many respects music followed its own path.

PATRONAGE AND THE TRAINING OF MUSICIANS One key to developments in music in the fifteenth and sixteenth centuries lies in musicians' employment, training, and travels. Outside the church, most musicians were employed in courts and cities, the main centers of political and economic power. Few worked only as musicians; as in the Middle Ages, most had other duties as servants, administrators, or clerics.

At most courts, musicians served in one of three divisions: the **chapel**, clerics and singers responsible for religious services; the **chamber**, musicians and domestic servants who served the ruler's personal needs and family; and the public court, officials and servants responsible for public events and ceremonies, including trumpeters and dance bands. The activities in each division conveyed messages about the ruler, for whom magnificence was a way to project power and nobility.

Music at court

It was important for rulers to be seen to be pious, and a magnificent way to demonstrate their devotion—and to compete with each other for acclaim—was to offer masses and other services with lavish decoration and beautiful singing. This explains why rulers all over Europe established permanent

Court chapels

FIGURE 7.5 *Philip the Good, duke of Burgundy, at Mass. Philip is in the center of the picture. The celebrant (the priest officiating at Mass) and deacon are at lower left, the singers in the chapel at lower right, and members of the court at the rear. Miniature by Jean le Tavernier (ca. 1457–67).*

musical chapels, beginning with King Louis IX of France and King Edward I of England in the thirteenth century and spreading over the next two centuries to other aristocrats and church leaders. Members of the chapel served as singers, composers, and scribes, furnishing music for church services. Figure 7.5 shows the chapel of Philip the Good, duke of Burgundy, at Mass. These musicians also contributed to court entertainment, composing secular songs as well as sacred music, and accompanied their ruler on journeys.

Instrumentalists were associated with the chamber if they played *bas* (soft) instruments, such as lute or flute, and with the public court if they played *haut* (loud) instruments like trumpet or shawm. Music of the chamber—the origin for the term ***chamber music***, music for relatively small ensembles and audiences—highlighted the cultural refinement of the ruler, while trumpets and other *haut* instruments used in public ceremonies conveyed political and military power. Both *haut* and *bas* instruments were used to accompany dancing.

Musicians in cities   Musicians in cities fulfilled functions similar to those at court, while serving a wider range of patrons. Cathedrals and other churches were staffed by clerics and singers. Groups of shawms, trumpets, and other instrumentalists performed in public ceremonies, accompanying city councils and other city officers as symbols of political power. Heralds played trumpets to signal the hours or attract an audience to hear the news. Players of both *haut* and *bas* instruments were essential at weddings, dances, and other festivities. Guilds, confraternities, and other groups, fostered by the growing merchant classes in urban centers, developed their own musical practices that became essential to their identities.

Training of   Whether employed at court or in cities, professional instrumentalists
instrumentalists   typically came from families of musicians and were trained in the apprentice system, usually through musicians' guilds. Some had long-term positions, but many were independent contractors hired when needed by churches, officials, civic groups, or private citizens. There were also nonprofessional musicians who were recruited for specific events but made their living in another job, such as barber. Pictures from the time generally do not show instrumentalists reading from notation, and it seems likely

that most were unable to read or write music. Nor did they need to in most cases; the music they performed, from dances to military calls, was primarily created and transmitted by ear, until the development of music printing in the early sixteenth century began to foster a new tradition of notated instrumental music.

However, singers were taught to read and write musical notation, and from their ranks come most of the composers whose names we know. Most fifteenth- and sixteenth-century composers were trained as choir boys in cathedral or church schools and hired as singers for churches or court chapels. Choir schools taught not only singing and how to perform sacred music but also music theory, the modes, improvising counterpoint, composition, reading, writing, Latin grammar, mathematics, basic theology, and other subjects. Northern cities such as Cambrai, Bruges, Antwerp, Paris, and Lyons, shown on the map in Figure 7.6, were the centers most renowned for their musical training in the fifteenth century, producing musicians who took positions all over Europe; later they were joined by Rome, Venice, and other Italian cities. This helps to explain why the most prominent composers of the fifteenth and early sixteenth centuries, such as Du Fay, Ockeghem, and Josquin, came from Flanders, the Netherlands, and northern France, while Italian composers became more prominent from the mid-sixteenth century on. Because only male children were admitted into choirs, women did not have this educational opportunity or the chance to make careers in public churches and princely courts. Nuns and novices in convents did receive musical instruction, and a few distinguished themselves as composers. There were also civic schools and private instructors that taught music, including singing, counterpoint, and composition, outside the guild system and cathedral schools; these were part of the provision that cities made to educate their citizens.

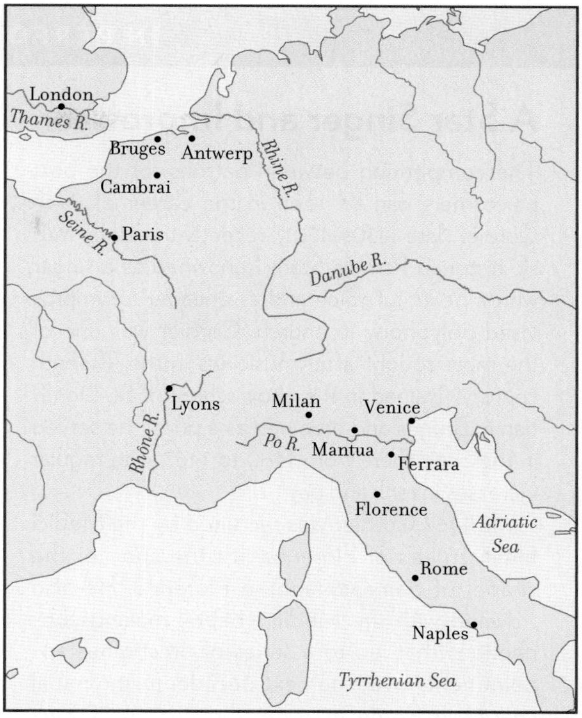

Many rulers avidly supported music and competed with each other for the best composers and performers (see In Performance: A Star Singer and Improviser). Like fine clothes and impressive pageantry, excellent music was both enjoyable in itself and valuable as a way to display wealth and power to audiences at home and abroad. The kings of France and England and the dukes of Burgundy and Savoy were especially notable patrons in the fifteenth century, but most striking is the breadth and depth of patronage in Italy. Italian rulers brought to their cities the most talented musicians from France, Flanders, and the Netherlands. One of the first northerners to make his career in Italy was Johannes Ciconia (ca. 1370–1412), born and trained in Flanders, who served in Rome, Pavia, and Padua. The Medici, the leading family in Florence, sponsored Franco-Flemish musician Jacques Arcadelt (ca. 1507–1568)

FIGURE 7.6 *Major centers for training musicians or for musical patronage in the Renaissance.*

Patronage for music

IN PERFORMANCE

A Star Singer and Improviser

The competition between patrons for the best performers can be seen in the career of Jean Cordier (late 1430s–1501), recently traced by music historian Pamela Starr. Renowned as a singer with a beautiful voice and as a leader for improvised polyphony in church, Cordier was one of the most sought-after musicians in the fifteenth century. Trained in the choir school of St. Donatian in Bruges and ordained as a priest, he served in the choir there from 1460 to 1467, with regular increases in rank and pay.

In 1467 Cordier was recruited by the Medici family, rulers of Florence, for the choir of the chapel of San Giovanni in Florence. He also traveled with the Medici chapel, making connections that led to a series of prestigious appointments over the next decade: to the papal chapel in Rome in 1468; the chapel of Ferrante, king of Naples, in 1472; and the chapel of Galeazzo Sforza, duke of Milan, in 1474. The move to Milan came only after an extended battle for Cordier's services that almost led to war between Naples and Milan. Each new appointment brought a raise in salary and other rewards, including benefices (lifetime salaried church appointments without duties) from the Vatican and land in Milanese territories.

In 1477 he returned north, and in 1481 he joined the chapel at the Burgundian court. Two years later he was appointed canon at St. Donatian in Bruges, where his career had begun, and he stayed there until his death, with an occasional leave to visit courts in Italy.

Cordier's career moves, and the competition for his services, let us glimpse what patrons most valued in their musicians. Contemporary accounts praised his exceptionally appealing voice, a quality that still today can lead to an international career. Beyond this, he was esteemed for his abilities in singing and directing polyphony, especially improvised polyphony in church. His position in every chapel was as a *tenorista*, the singer who performed the tenor part in polyphony. Most church polyphony in the fifteenth century was improvised over a cantus firmus from chant, and it was the *tenorista* who sang the cantus firmus and coordinated the other singers, shaping the improvised counterpoint like a composer. It was his beautiful voice and skill in leading group improvisation—things we value today in a wide variety of musical traditions—that were so highly prized.

In studying music history, we spend most of our time focused on composers and compositions, because until the late nineteenth century there was no way to record music except to write it down. But Cordier's career reminds us that performers and improvisers have always been important, perhaps more important than composers, and that even the Renaissance composers whose works we study spent most of their time—and earned their paychecks—primarily as performers.

as well as native Italian painters and sculptors like Donatello, Botticelli, and Michelangelo. In the 1480s both Josquin Desprez (ca. 1450–1521), the leading composer of his generation, and Leonardo da Vinci, the leading artist, worked for members of the Sforza family, rulers of Milan. The court of Ferrara under the Este family hosted Josquin and Netherlandish composers Jacob Obrecht (1457/8–1505), Adrian Willaert (ca. 1490–1562), and Cipriano de Rore (1515/16–1565). Mantua, ruled by the Gonzaga family, was another center of patronage, thanks to the presence of Isabella d'Este (wife of marquis Francesco II Gonzaga), who had studied music seriously.

Popes and cardinals were as committed as secular rulers to a high stan-   *Benefices*
dard of cultural activity and patronage. Indeed, church officials developed
the primary system through which they and secular rulers could recruit the
best singers and composers. In church practice, a ***benefice*** granted a priest
a stipend in exchange for regularly celebrating Mass or other duties in a certain place. The pope could allow a priest to hold a benefice, or more than one,
without residing in that place; the priest would then hire someone else to
perform his duties at lesser pay and keep the difference, thus supplementing his pay as a member of a court chapel. Because benefices were ultimately
controlled by the pope, the Papal Chapel usually attracted the best singers, but
by the fifteenth century many rulers had collected benefices they could use to
actively compete for talent. Most major composers in the Renaissance were
priests, because they could hold benefices. Since women and married men
could not serve as priests, they could not benefit from this system.

MOBILE MUSICIANS AND THE INTERNATIONAL STYLE The presence at
courts of musicians from many lands allowed composers and performers to
learn styles and genres current in other regions. Many composers changed
their place of service, exposing them to numerous types of music. Guillaume
Du Fay (ca. 1397–1474), for example, served at the Cathedral of Cambrai in
the Burgundian lands, at courts in Pesaro (northern Italy) and Savoy (southeastern France), and in the pope's chapel in Rome, Florence, and Bologna
(see Chapter 8). Mobility among musicians encouraged the dissemination
of new genres, such as the polyphonic mass cycle on a single cantus firmus,
developed by English composers in the early fifteenth century and taken up
by composers like Du Fay on the Continent.

The exchange of national traditions, genres, and ideas fostered the devel-   *International style*
opment of an international style in the fifteenth century, synthesizing elements from English, French, and Italian traditions. The synthesis of this
international style, described in Chapter 8, was the watershed event that set
music of the fifteenth century apart from that of the fourteenth and undergirded most other developments.

THE NEW COUNTERPOINT The core of the international style was a new
counterpoint, based on a preference for consonance, including thirds and
sixths as well as perfect fifths and octaves; on strict control of dissonance; and
on avoidance of parallel fifths and octaves. This new approach to counterpoint
reflects the high value musicians placed on beauty, order, and pleasing the
senses, attitudes that closely parallel contemporary trends in art. Yet, like
perspective in painting, it is an invention of the early fifteenth century, not
a revival of an ancient technique. More than anything else, it is this contrapuntal practice that binds the fifteenth and sixteenth centuries into a single
period of music history we call the Renaissance.

The distinction between new and older practice is starkly expressed in *Liber*   *Johannes Tinctoris*
de arte contrapuncti (A Book on the Art of Counterpoint, 1477) by Johannes
Tinctoris (ca. 1435–1511), one of the leading counterpoint treatises of the
fifteenth century. Tinctoris deplored "the compositions of older musicians,
in which there were more dissonances than consonances," and proclaimed

Johannes Tinctoris on the Music of His Time

Johannes Tinctoris was a Flemish composer who settled in Naples at the court of King Ferrante I in the early 1470s. There he wrote a dozen treatises on musical topics. He was an enthusiastic supporter of the northern composers from his own generation and the previous one, and he observed a sharp break between their music and that of previous eras.

✿

It is a matter of great surprise that there is no composition written over forty years ago which is thought by the learned as worthy of performance. At this very time, whether it be due to the virtue of some heavenly influence or to a zeal of constant application I do not know, there flourish, in addition to many singers who perform most beautifully, an infinite number of composers such as Johannes Okeghem, Johannes Regis, Anthonius Busnois, Firminus Caron, and Guillermus Faugues, who glory that they had as teachers in this divine art Johannes Dunstable, Egidius Binchois, and Guillermus Dufay, recently passed from life. Almost all these men's works exhale such sweetness that, in my opinion, they should be considered most worthy, not only for people and heroes, but even for the immortal gods. Certainly I never listen to them or study them without coming away more refreshed and wiser. Just as Virgil took Homer as his model in his divine work, the *Aeneid*, so by Hercules, do I use these as models for my own small productions; particularly have I plainly imitated their admirable style of composition insofar as the arranging of concords is concerned.

Johannes Tinctoris, *The Art of Counterpoint (Liber de arte contrapuncti)*, trans. and ed. Albert Seay (American Institute of Musicology, 1961), 14–15.

that nothing written before the 1430s was worth hearing (see Source Reading). His sympathy with humanism is shown by his references to numerous Greek and Roman writers, but lacking examples of ancient music, he claims only the composers of the last two generations as models worth imitating. Nothing could more vividly show the difference between music on the one hand and literature, art, and architecture on the other in their relation to the arts of antiquity. Drawing on the practice of the composers he names, Tinctoris describes strict rules for introducing dissonances, limiting them to passing and neighbor tones on unstressed beats and to syncopated passages (what we call **suspensions**) at cadences. Parallel fifths and octaves, common even in fourteenth-century styles, were now forbidden. These rules were further refined in later treatises and synthesized by Gioseffo Zarlino (1517–1590) in *Le istitutioni harmoniche* (The Harmonic Foundations, 1558).

NEW COMPOSITIONAL METHODS AND TEXTURES The rules for consonance and dissonance treatment remained fairly consistent throughout the fifteenth and sixteenth centuries and distinguish the music of this period from that of the preceding and following eras. Yet styles and textures changed from each generation to the next, as we will see in subsequent chapters.

Number of voices   One aspect has already been mentioned: an expansion of range, both in each voice and overall. The number of voices also grew. During the fifteenth century, the prevailing three-voice texture was replaced by a four-voice texture, with a bass line added below the tenor. This became the new standard, still familiar today. But composers in the sixteenth century often added to it, and the use of five, six, or more voices became common.

A striking change occurred during the second half of the fifteenth century, when composers moved away from counterpoint structured around the cantus (top line) and tenor and toward greater equality between voices. Since its origins, polyphony had been conceived as the addition of voices to an existing melody: in organum, adding an organal voice below or above a chant; in thirteenth-century motets, adding one or more voices above a tenor; in fourteenth-century chansons, composing a tenor to fit with the cantus, then adding a third and sometimes a fourth voice around this two-voice framework. Through the mid-fifteenth century, composers apparently worked as their predecessors had, devising the essential counterpoint between tenor and cantus and then adding the other voices around that framework. Most likely they proceeded phrase by phrase, at times even sonority by sonority, but always attended first to the cantus and tenor and then fit the other voices around them. As a result, it was hard to avoid dissonances or frequent awkward leaps in the other voices (see the contratenors in Examples 8.4 and 8.6, pp. 168 and 171). As composers in the later fifteenth century sought to make each part smooth and gratifying to sing, they increasingly worked out all the parts at the same time in relation to each other. The cantus-tenor framework was replaced by a more equal relationship in which all voices were essential to the counterpoint. This change in approach was described in the early sixteenth century by the theorist Pietro Aaron (see Source Reading, p. 150). Despite this change in style, evidence suggests that composers continued to work out polyphonic music in their minds, relying on their training and memory, without needing to use writing to visualize the counterpoint.

Equality of voices

Associated with this new approach was the emergence of two kinds of musical texture that came to predominate during the sixteenth century. In **imitative counterpoint**, voices **imitate** or echo a motive or phrase in another voice, usually at a different pitch level, such as a fifth, fourth, or octave away. In **homophony**, all the voices move together in essentially the same rhythm, the lower parts accompanying the cantus with consonant sonorities. Both textures allowed composers more freedom than the older approach of layering voices.

Imitation and homophony

PERFORMANCE In the late fifteenth and sixteenth centuries, the new textures and greater equality of voices fostered a growing preference for a homogeneous blend of sound. Singers can do this naturally, as can instruments of the same kind in different registers, and during the sixteenth century ensembles of like instruments, such as recorders, became more common. Still, as in the fourteenth century, the choice of performing forces for secular music was left to the performers; parts in ensemble music were not designated for specific instruments until around 1600, and a piece could be sung with one or more voices on each part, or played by instruments, or performed with a mix of singers and players. Vocal sound was the musical ideal; pacing and phrasing were determined by what was suitable for singers, and instruments were often conceived as imitating the quality of voices.

In other respects, performance practice resembled that of the fourteenth century. The notation was similar, changing around 1425 to open noteheads

SOURCE READING

A New Harmonic Conception

Pietro Aaron (ca. 1480–ca. 1550) was a priest, composer, and theorist who wrote some of the first musical treatises in Italian. His writings are particularly revealing about the practices of his time. Here he describes a change from the old linear approach to composition, in which the top line and tenor formed the structural framework, to a new harmonic conception, in which each voice had a more equal role.

❖

Many composers contended that first the cantus should be devised, then the tenor, and after the tenor the contrabass. They practiced this method, because they lacked the order and knowledge of what was required for creating the contralto. Thus they made many awkward passages in their compositions, and because of them had to have unisons, rests, and ascending and descending skips difficult for the singer or performer. Such

compositions were bereft of sweetness and harmony, because when you write the cantus or soprano first and then the tenor, once this tenor is done, there is no place for the contrabass, and once the contrabass is done, there is often no note for the contralto. If you consider only one part at a time, that is, when you write the tenor and take care only to make this tenor consonant [with the cantus], and similarly the contrabass, the consonance of every other part will suffer.

Therefore the moderns have considered this matter better, as is evident in their compositions for four, five, six, and more parts. Every one of the parts occupies a comfortable, easy, and acceptable place, because composers consider them all together and not according to what is described above.

From Pietro Aaron, *Toscanello in musica* (Venice, 1524), Book II, Chapter 16.

for minims and longer notes and adding smaller units of rhythm (see p. 111 and Figure 6.5). Each singer or player read from an individual part, rather than following a score, and was expected to apply musica ficta as needed, especially at cadences (see pp. 129–32).

TUNING AND TEMPERAMENT A crucial issue in performance was how to tune harmonic intervals. The new emphasis on harmonic thirds and sixths posed a challenge to music theory and systems of tuning, both of which had to yield to changing practice.

Pythagorean intonation   Medieval theorists defined only the octave, fifth, and fourth as consonant, because these were generated by the simple ratios Pythagoras was thought to have discovered, respectively 2:1, 3:2, and 4:3. In **Pythagorean intonation**, the tuning system used throughout the Middle Ages, all fourths and fifths were perfectly tuned, but thirds and sixths had complex ratios that made them dissonant by definition and out of tune to the ear; for example, the major third had the ratio 81:64, sounding rough in comparison with the pure major third (5:4 or 80:64). This tuning works very well for medieval music, in which only fourths, fifths, and octaves need to sound consonant.

Just intonation   Around 1300, the English theorist Walter Odington observed that the major third and minor third could be considered consonant if tuned using the simple ratios 5:4 and 6:5. But not until 1482 did Bartolomé Ramis de Pareia, a Spanish mathematician and music theorist residing in Italy, propose a tuning system that produced perfectly tuned thirds and sixths. Systems like Ramis's became known as ***just intonation***. Performers had probably been using forms of just intonation for many years, as Odington testifies to the use of justly tuned thirds in England by 1300.

There are at least two problems with just intonation. First, in order to bring most thirds into tune, Ramis de Pareia's diatonic scale had to include one fourth, one fifth, and one third that were out of tune, making some sonorities unusable unless the performers adjust the pitch. Second, as musicians increasingly used notes outside the diatonic scale, keeping the fifths and thirds pure meant that notes such as G♯ and A♭ were different in pitch, causing difficulties for keyboard players and for instruments with frets, such as lutes. These and other problems meant that in practice just intonation could only be used by singers or by players of fretless string instruments, who could slightly raise or lower each pitch to keep every harmonic interval pure. Some keyboard players sought to preserve the pure intervals by developing organs and harpsichords with separate keys for G♯ and A♭ and for other such pairs of tones.

More common were compromise tuning systems called ***temperaments***, in which pitches were adjusted to make most or all intervals usable without adding keys. Most keyboard players in the sixteenth century used what later was called ***mean-tone temperament***, in which the fifths were tuned small so that most major thirds could sound pure or nearly so. Various kinds of mean-tone and modified temperaments continued to be used on most keyboard instruments through the late nineteenth century. The temperament best known today is ***equal temperament***, in which each semitone is exactly the same. Although it only came into widespread use after the mid-nineteenth century, equal temperament was apparently invented in the sixteenth. First described by theorists in the late 1500s, it may have been approximated before then by performers on fretted string instruments such as lutes and viols, for whom any nonequal tuning is likely to result in out-of-tune octaves. In equal temperament, all intervals are usable, because all approximate their mathematically pure ratios; but although the fourths and fifths are nearly pure, the thirds and sixths are off by a seventh of a semitone, and only the octave is exactly in tune, showing that no tuning system is flawless. Indeed, equal temperament is ill-suited to most vocal music of the Renaissance era, because the sound of perfectly tuned fifths and thirds is part of its glory.

Temperaments

The new tuning systems reflect musicians' reliance on what pleased the ear rather than on received theory. This parallels the focus of humanists on human perception, rather than on deference to past authority.

WORDS AND MUSIC Paralleling the interest among humanists and artists in communication and clarity, composers developed new ways to project the texts they set to music. The medieval idea of music as a decoration for the text gradually gave way to a desire to convey the words clearly. Composers paid increasing attention to accents and meter in setting poetic texts. The *formes fixes* fell out of fashion during the late fifteenth century, and texts for both secular and sacred music became highly varied. Composers responded by using the organization and syntax of a text to guide them in shaping the structure of the musical setting and in marking punctuation with cadences that express different degrees of finality (see Chapter 8). By the late fifteenth century, following the rhythm of speech and the natural accentuation of syllables became the norm (see Chapter 9). The new textures of imitative counterpoint and homophony were useful here: in both cases all the voices in a polyphonic work could declaim the words in the same rhythm. Where previously singers often had leeway in matching syllables to the notated pitches and rhythms, by the early sixteenth century composers took charge, seeing the purpose of their music as serving the words.

Emotion and expression

For all the emotions expressed in medieval poetry from the troubadours on, there are few signs that composers sought to convey those emotions through their music. The issue was little discussed, and it is difficult to draw connections between particular emotions and particular musical elements. But by the late fifteenth century and throughout the sixteenth, composers sought to dramatize the content and convey the feelings of the texts, often using specific intervals, sonorities, melodic contours, contrapuntal motions, and other devices to do so.

Influence of ancient writings

The new concern for text declamation and text expression was reinforced by the rediscovery of ancient writings. Discussions of rhetoric by Quintilian and Cicero supported the goals of declaiming words naturalistically and with the appropriate feelings, in order to move and persuade the listeners. Descriptions by ancient writers of the emotional effects of music were cited as authority for the new ways composers found to express through music the feelings suggested by the words they set.

REAWAKENED INTEREST IN GREEK THEORY Perhaps the most direct impact of humanism on music lay in the recovery of ancient music treatises. During the fifteenth century, Greeks emigrating from Byzantium and Italian manuscript hunters brought the principal Greek writings on music to western Europe, including the treatises of Aristides Quintilianus, Claudius Ptolemy, and Cleonides, the eighth book of Aristotle's *Politics*, and passages on music in Plato's *Republic* and *Laws* (all discussed in Chapter 1). By the end of the fifteenth century, all of these were translated into Latin.

Franchino Gaffurio

Franchino Gaffurio (1451–1522) read the Greek theorists in Latin translations and incorporated much of their thinking into his writings. Gaffurio's treatises were the most influential of his time, reviving Greek ideas and stimulating new thought on matters such as the modes; consonance and dissonance; tuning; the relations of music and words; and the harmony of music, of the human body and mind, and of the cosmos.

Tinctoris

The church modes, like the ancient Greek tonoi, were devised for monophonic music, but if they were to be applied to music of the fifteenth and sixteenth centuries they needed to be reconceived to fit polyphony. In a 1476 treatise, Tinctoris argued that polyphonic music could be understood as modal, analyzing the mode of any piece as that suggested by the tenor, especially as it forms cadences with the top voice.

Heinrich Glareanus

Building on Tinctoris, Swiss theorist Heinrich Glareanus (1488–1563) in his book *Dodecachordon* (The Twelve-String Lyre, 1547) added four new modes to the traditional eight, using names of ancient Greek tonoi: Aeolian and Hypoaeolian with the final on A, and Ionian and Hypoionian with the final on C. With these additions, he made the theory of the modes more consistent with the current practice of composers, who frequently employed tonal centers on A and C. In using terms borrowed from ancient culture to modify his medieval heritage, Glareanus was typical of his age.

NEW APPLICATIONS OF GREEK IDEAS We have seen that ancient ideas about rhetoric and about music's power to affect the emotions were taken up by writers and musicians in the Renaissance and applied in new ways. So too were other aspects of ancient practice.

Ancient writers from Plato to Quintilian maintained that music should be part of every citizen's education, and Renaissance writers echoed their call. Gentlemen and ladies were expected to read music, to sing from notation at sight, and to play well enough to join in music-making as a form of entertainment, as others might play cards or tell stories. Even the preference ancient writers expressed for the lyre over the aulos as the instrument for educated citizens was reflected in the expectation that courtiers would play a plucked string instrument such as the lute, rather than the bowed string or wind instruments.

Music as social accomplishment

Both Plato and Aristotle insisted that each of the Greek *harmoniai*, or scale types, conveyed a different ethos and that musicians could influence a listener's emotions by their choice of *harmonia* (see Chapter 1). The stories that Pythagoras calmed a violent youth by having the piper change from one *harmonia* to another, and that Alexander the Great suddenly rose from the banquet table and armed himself for battle when he heard a Phrygian tune, were told countless times. Theorists and composers assumed that the Greek *harmoniai* and tonoi were identical to the similarly named church modes (for the confusion, see Chapter 2) and that the latter could have the same emotional effects. Composers sometimes chose to set a text in a certain mode based on the emotions that ancient writers associated with the *harmonia* or tonos of the same name. Through this practice, the notion that certain scales reflect certain moods came to be widely accepted, a concept echoed in the later idea that the major and minor modes suggest different feelings, or that certain keys have specific associations, such as E♭ major with nobility.

Power of the modes

Another new idea inspired by ancient Greek practice was **chromaticism**, the use of two or more successive semitones moving in the same direction. European music from Gregorian chant through the early sixteenth century was essentially diatonic. Although some accidentals were notated, and other alterations were called for by musica ficta (see Chapter 6), direct chromatic motion, such as from B to B♭, was never used. But the chromatic genus of ancient Greek music offered a model (see Chapters 1 and 10), and in the mid-sixteenth century composers began to use direct chromatic motion as an expressive device.

Chromaticism

These four ideas—music as servant of the words and conveyor of feelings, music as a social accomplishment every genteel person should have, the expressive power of modes, and the use of chromaticism—seem to have little in common, ranging from social custom to musical procedure. Yet each is a distinctive new element in the late fifteenth or sixteenth century, and each was reinforced by or originated in imitation of ancient practice as described in classical writings. While less direct than imitations of Greek and Roman literature, architecture, or sculpture, these concepts show music's participation in the Renaissance movement.

THE MUSICAL WORK Another concept that emerged in the Renaissance was the notion of a piece of music as a work of art. Not until the early seventeenth century did composers begin to label their publications with the word *opus* (Latin for "work"), and not until the nineteenth did performers treat compositions as inviolable texts of which not a note should be changed. But in the fifteenth and early sixteenth centuries several factors came together that made it possible to think of musical works as artworks akin to poems or paintings. They were fixed in notation so clear that their pitches and rhythms could be reproduced exactly. They were distinctive enough to be recognized as individuals, thanks to a new aesthetic appreciation for variety. They were valued in themselves, not simply for the service they rendered to a ritual or social event. They were preserved and collected in books, which were themselves prized by collectors. They were linked to their creators: musicians gained status as composers by writing works, a piece was valued more if it was by a famous composer, and composers won fame by creating works that others regarded highly. They were praised, studied, and emulated; Tinctoris analyzed works by his contemporaries, and Glareanus commented on musical works he admired by Josquin and others. Many of these currents began before the fifteenth century, but they came together then in the concept of the musical work, which endures to this day and underlies much of our experience with music.

NEW CURRENTS IN THE SIXTEENTH CENTURY

The trends discussed so far in this chapter all continued through the sixteenth century, and many only reached their fullest realization then. But there were also new currents beginning after 1500 that set the sixteenth century apart from the fifteenth.

MUSIC PRINTING The most significant of these was a technological breakthrough: the introduction of music printing from movable type (see Innovations: Music Printing, pp. 156–57). Music printing brought changes that were as revolutionary for music in the sixteenth century as the development of notation had been for the Middle Ages.

Dissemination of written music   By making possible much wider dissemination of written music, printing made notated music available to a broader public and thus fostered the growth of musical literacy. Instead of a few precious manuscripts copied by hand and liable to all kinds of errors and variants, a plentiful supply of new music in copies of uniform accuracy was now available—not exactly at a low price, but much less costly than equivalent manuscripts. Throughout Europe and the Americas, printed music spread to a broader audience the works of composers who otherwise would have been known to only a small circle.

Amateur music-making   Printed music was marketed to amateurs as well as to professional musicians. Indeed, from this point through the nineteenth century, the fashion for amateurs making music to entertain themselves or friends and family became an increasingly significant force driving the development of music.

Printing also provided a new way for composers to make money, either *New outlet for* directly by sale of their works to a publisher, or indirectly by making their *composers* names and compositions better known and potentially attracting new patrons. Moreover, the existence of printed copies has preserved many works for performance and study by later generations.

NEW REPERTORIES AND GENRES Music printing also encouraged the rise of new repertories and genres of music that remained of central importance in later centuries as well.

After the synthesis of a new international style in the early fifteenth cen- *National styles* tury, the sixteenth saw a proliferation of regional and national styles. This was true especially in secular vocal music, with separate traditions emerging in Spain, Italy, France, Germany, England, and elsewhere (see Chapter 10). This development began in the late fifteenth century but was hastened by the new market for printed music for amateurs, many of whom preferred to sing in their own language. These new vocal repertories varied from simple homophonic songs to more elevated works and from secular to sacred, each finding its own niche. Among the new vocal genres were the Spanish *villancico,* the Italian *frottola* and *madrigal,* and the English *lute song.* The rising interest in music in vernacular languages paralleled a growing interest in vernacular literature, including classics like Niccolò Machiavelli's political treatise *Il principe* (The Prince, 1532), Ludovico Ariosto's epic poem *Orlando furioso* (1532), François Rabelais's novels *Gargantua et Pantagruel* (1532–62), and the plays of Lope de Vega in Spain and of Christopher Marlowe, Ben Jonson, and William Shakespeare in England.

The market for printed music also encouraged the first widespread devel- *Instrumental music* opment of notated instrumental music (see Chapter 12). Except for a few prized pieces copied into manuscripts, most instrumental music had long been improvised or learned by ear. Now works in improvisational style were written down and published, alongside dance music, arrangements of vocal music, and works for ensemble that served many functions, from entertainment to use in church services. The result was a profusion of new instrumental genres, including *variations, prelude, toccata, ricercare, canzona,* and *sonata.*

REFORMATION One final trend in the sixteenth century drew on humanism, printing, and the creation of new repertories alike. Applying humanist principles to study of the Bible led Martin Luther and others to challenge church doctrines. The resulting Reformation beginning in 1517 ended a century of church unity since the resolution of the Great Schism. When much of northern Europe split from the Roman Church to become Lutheran, Calvinist, or Anglican, each branch of the church developed its own music for services and fostered new genres, including *chorale, metrical psalm,* and *anthem* (see Chapter 11). Church leaders sought to win adherents not only through the written word but with art and music, all made easier to distribute by the recent invention of printing. The Catholic response, known as the Catholic Reformation or Counter-Reformation, produced some of the most glorious music of the century, and one of its composers, Palestrina, became the model for sixteenth-century counterpoint for generations to come.

Music Printing

> A great number of gentlemen and merchants of good account [were entertained] by the exercise of music daily used in my house, and by furnishing them with [printed] books of that kind yearly sent me out of Italy and other places.

So wrote Nicholas Yonge—a London clerk with enough means and social position to support an active amateur musical life—in the dedication to his 1588 madrigal collection *Musica transalpina* (see Chapter 10). His words tell us how the music printing and publishing business completely changed the way people used and enjoyed notated music during the sixteenth century, allowing it to be cultivated not only in churches and noble courts but also in ordinary households as recreation. Until that time, only the very wealthy could think of purchasing a book of music, because the music had to be copied laboriously by hand. But the printing press made it possible to produce many copies relatively quickly with much less labor, making music available to many more people at a much lower price.

Printing from movable type, known in China for centuries and perfected in Europe by Johann Gutenberg around 1450, was first used for music in the 1470s, in liturgical books with chant notation. Using movable type meant that notes could be assembled in any order, rearranged, and reused.

In 1501, Ottaviano Petrucci (1466–1539) in Venice brought out the first collection of polyphonic music printed entirely from movable type, the *Harmonice musices odhecaton A* (One Hundred Polyphonic Pieces, though it actually contained ninety-six; "A" indicated it was the first book in a series). Figure 7.7, a page from this collection, shows the elegance of his work. Petrucci used a triple-impression process, in which each sheet went through the press three times: once to print the staff lines, another time to print the words, and a third to print the notes and the florid initials. His method was time-consuming, labor-intensive, and costly, but his results were models of clarity and accuracy.

Petrucci was no less clever as a businessman than he was as a craftsman. Before setting up shop, he

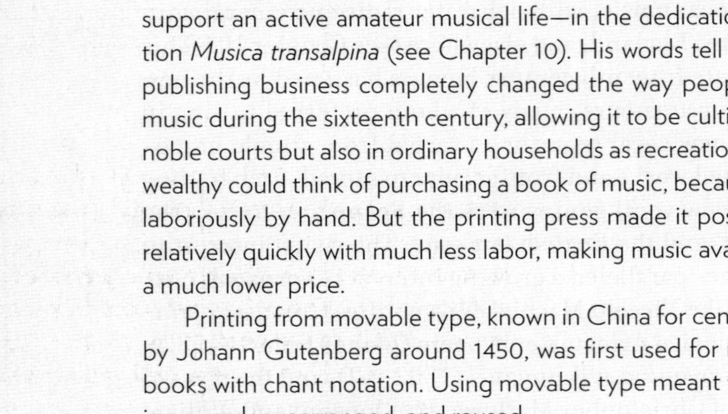

FIGURE 7.7 *Loyset Compère's chanson* Royne de ciel, *from* Harmonice musices odhecaton A, *published by Ottaviano Petrucci in 1501. The incipit of the text appears under the cantus part. The music uses the "white notation" of the Renaissance. The notes that look like diamond-shaped whole notes are semibreves; open notes with stems (akin to half notes) are minims; black notes with stems (like quarter notes) are semiminims; and flags are added to the semiminim to indicate shorter durations. The resemblance to common-practice notation is clear, except that no barlines or ties are used.*

FIGURE 7.8 *First portion of the superius part for the motet* Laudate Dominum *by Pierre de Manchicourt, as printed in Pierre Attaingnant's* Liber decimus quartus XIX musicus cantiones *(Paris, 1539). Attaingnant printed in a single impression, using type in which each note, rest, clef, or other sign includes the portion of the staff on which it sits.*

had procured a patent on his process and a "privilege" that effectively guaranteed him a monopoly on music printing in Venice for twenty years. His first volume, intended for instrumental ensembles, was an anthology of instrumental pieces and songs without their texts underlaid, including what he judged to be among the best of his own and the preceding generations. The pieces were small works for three or four parts that could be performed at home or in the company of friends. He followed up with two more collections, *Canti B* in 1502 and *Canti C* in 1504, allowing Petrucci to corner the market for the most up-to-date and popular secular music of the day. By 1523, he had published fifty-nine volumes (including reprints) of vocal and instrumental music.

Printing from a single impression—using pieces of type that printed staff, notes, and text together in one operation—was apparently first practiced by John Rastell in London about 1520 and first applied on a large scale in 1528 by Pierre Attaingnant (ca. 1494–1551/52) in Paris. Although more efficient and less costly than Petrucci's triple-impression method, the process produced much less elegant results because the staff lines were no longer continuous but part of each piece of type; inevitably, the lines were imperfectly joined and therefore appeared broken or wavy on the page, as seen in Figure 7.8. Nevertheless, the practicality of the method ensured its commercial success. Attaingnant's process set the standard for all printed music until copper-plate engraving became popular in the late seventeenth century.

Most ensemble music published in the sixteenth century was printed in the form of oblong **partbooks**—one small volume for each solo voice, so that a complete set was needed to perform any piece. Partbooks were used by professionals in church and by amateurs at home or in social gatherings, as depicted in Figure 7.9.

The economics of supply and demand for printed music grew in ever-widening circles. Printing stimulated the desire for music books and increased their affordability, which in turn spurred the development of music printing and competition among publishers. By the end of the sixteenth century, Rome, Nuremberg, Lyons, Louvain, Antwerp, and London had joined Venice and Paris as centers of music publishing, and publishers and printed music had become indispensable parts of musical life.

FIGURE 7.9 *Title page of Sylvestro Ganassi's instruction book on recorder playing,* Opera intitulata Fontegara *(1535). A recorder consort and two singers perform from printed partbooks. In the foreground are two cornetti, and on the wall are three viols and a lute.*

THE LEGACY OF THE RENAISSANCE

The Renaissance era had a profound and enduring effect on music. In direct and indirect ways, developments in music paralleled those in scholarship and in the other arts. The growing European economy, patronage for musicians, and the development of music printing laid the economic foundation for an increase in musical activity that continued into later centuries. Humanism and the rediscovery of ancient texts fostered a reexamination of musical aesthetics, encouraging a growing preference for musical styles that focused on consonance, clarity, direct appeal to the listener, natural declamation of words, and emotional expressivity. The musical language forged in this period lasted for generations and undergirds the treatment of dissonance, consonance, voice-leading, and text setting in most later styles. The new tunings and temperaments created for music in the fifteenth and sixteenth centuries were used through the mid-nineteenth century, when equal temperament began to predominate. Notions about music that developed during the Renaissance have become widely shared expectations, so that pieces that do not seek to convey emotion or appeal to a broad audience, as in some twentieth-century styles, have struck some listeners as violating basic assumptions about what music is and what it should do.

Throughout much of the seventeenth and eighteenth centuries, sixteenth-century styles endured, especially in Catholic church music, alongside newer, more dramatic styles. Training in sixteenth-century counterpoint was an accepted part of learning music composition from the seventeenth century through much of the twentieth. Many composers, including Bach and Beethoven, imitated sixteenth-century polyphonic style in their choral music or in other works as a device to suggest austerity, solemnity, or religiosity. In the late nineteenth and early twentieth centuries, music of the fifteenth and sixteenth centuries itself was revived, and scholars began the long process of transcribing into modern notation, editing, and publishing the thousands of surviving works. Now pieces by Du Fay, Josquin, Palestrina, and other composers of the era are staples of the vocal repertoire, and the music of hundreds of their contemporaries is performed and recorded.

Further Reading is available at digital.wwnorton.com/hwm10

ENGLAND AND BURGUNDY IN THE FIFTEENTH CENTURY

❖

In about 1440, French poet Martin Le Franc lauded two composers, Guillaume Du Fay and Gilles Binchois, whose beautiful melodies and "new practice of making lively consonance" made their music better than that of all their predecessors in France (see Source Reading, p. 160). He attributed the "marvelous pleasingness" of their music to their adoption of what he called the ***contenance angloise*** (English guise or quality) and their emulation of English composer John Dunstable. A generation later, Johannes Tinctoris looked back to these same three composers as the founders of a new art (see Source Reading in Chapter 7). The influence of English music on Continental composers in the early fifteenth century has become a central theme of music history of this era, alongside the synthesis of a new international style of polyphony and the development of the polyphonic mass cycle, both indebted to English influence. In this chapter, we will explore these three themes, focusing on the music of Dunstable, Du Fay, and Binchois, who from their time to ours have been considered the greatest composers of their generation. Along the way, we will examine what English elements were taken over into Continental music, what changes in values this adoption reflects, and what made the music of these three composers so appealing to their age.

ENGLISH MUSIC

The impact of English music on Continental composers in the first half of the fifteenth century had both political and artistic roots. Throughout the later Middle Ages, the kings of England held territories in northern and southwestern France as dukes of Normandy and of Aquitaine. When King Charles IV of France died in 1328, his most direct heir was his nephew King Edward III of England, the son of Charles's sister, but a cousin of Charles's assumed the throne instead. In 1337, war broke out between France and England, and Edward laid claim

The *Contenance Angloise*

Martin Le Franc (ca. 1410–1461) was a poet, cleric, and secretary to Amadeus VIII, duke of Savoy, who also employed Guillaume Du Fay as master of the court chapel. At the wedding of the duke's son Louis in 1434, Du Fay and Le Franc had occasion to meet Gilles Binchois, who was in the retinue of the duke of Burgundy. In his poem *Le champion des dames* (The Champion of Women, 1440–42), Le Franc praised the music of Du Fay and Binchois and linked them to English composers, especially John Dunstable, in terms that have shaped our view of fifteenth-century music history ever since. Dunstable may have spent time in France in the service of John of Bedford, regent of France and later duke of Normandy, but it is not known whether he knew Du Fay or Binchois personally.

Tapissier, Carmen, Cesaris	Tapissier, Carmen, Cesaris
Na pas longtemps si bien chanterrent	not long ago sang so well
Quilz esbahirent tout paris	that they astonished all Paris
Et tous ceulx qui les frequenterrent;	and all who came to hear them.
Mais oncques jour ne deschanterrent	But never did they discant
En melodie de tels chois	such finely wrought melody—
Ce mont dit qui les hanterrent	so I was told by those who heard them—
Que G. Du Fay et Binchois.	as G. Du Fay and Binchois.
Car ilz ont nouvelle pratique	For they have a new practice
De faire frisque concordance	of making lively consonance
En haulte et en basse musique	in both loud and soft music,
En fainte, en pause, et en muance	in feigning, in rests, and in mutations.
Et ont prins de la contenance	They took on the guise
Angloise et ensuy Dunstable	of the English and follow Dunstable
Pour quoy merveilleuse plaisance	and thereby a marvelous pleasingness
Rend leur chant joyeux et notable.	makes their music joyous and remarkable.

French poem quoted in Charles Van den Borren, *Guillaume Du Fay: son importance dans l'évolution de la musique au XVe siècle* (Brussels, 1926), 53–54.

to the French crown. The ensuing conflict lasted over a century and became known as the Hundred Years' War. During the war, especially after English king Henry V's victory at the famous battle of Agincourt in 1415, the English were intensely involved on the Continent. Henry married Catherine of Valois, daughter of French king Charles VI, and persuaded Charles to name him heir to the French throne. When both kings died in 1422, Henry's infant son succeeded him as Henry VI, while his brother John, duke of Bedford, served as regent in France. The war finally ended in 1453 with the defeat of the English and their expulsion from France.

During their long sojourn in France, the English nobility brought musicians with them, significantly increasing the numbers of English performers and composers on the Continent and of English pieces copied into Continental manuscripts. Moreover, the English sought alliances and trade with Burgundy and other lands. Cities like Bruges and Antwerp in modern-day

Belgium were teeming with English diplomats and merchants, and thus the Low Countries as well as France became pathways for importing English music to the Continent.

The mere presence of English musicians and compositions might not have been enough to effect a major change in style, had Continental composers not noticed something distinctive about English music. This was the ***contenance angloise***, or "English quality," referred to by Martin Le Franc. It consisted especially in the frequent use of harmonic thirds and sixths, often in parallel motion, resulting in pervasive consonance with few dissonances. Other common features included a preference for relatively simple melodies, regular phrasing, primarily syllabic text setting, and homorhythmic textures. We observed these tendencies in thirteenth-century English polyphony (see Chapter 5), and they became even stronger in English music of the fourteenth and early fifteenth centuries.

The contenance angloise

POLYPHONY ON LATIN TEXTS The largest surviving repertory of English music from this period consists of sacred music on Latin texts, composed for religious services. One common style used a chant, sometimes lightly embellished, in the middle voice of a three-voice texture. The chants were most often from the Sarum rite, the distinctive chant dialect used in England from the late Middle Ages to the Reformation. As shown in Example 8.1, a passage from a Credo of about 1330 based on an English variant of the Credo melody in NAWM 3f, the lower voice usually moves a third below the chant, opening to a fifth at cadences and at other points for variety, while the upper voice mostly parallels the middle voice a fourth above it. The resulting sound consists primarily of $\frac{6}{3}$ sonorities (that is, a sixth and a third above the lowest note) moving in parallel motion, interspersed with open fifth-and-octave sonorities, especially at the ends of phrases and words. Parallel fifths, common throughout medieval music, are now avoided, and every vertical sonority is consonant.

The contrapuntal style shown in Example 8.1 evolved into a practice of improvised polyphony known as ***faburden***, in which a plainchant in the middle voice was joined by an upper voice a perfect fourth above it and a lower voice singing mostly in parallel thirds below it, beginning each phrase and ending phrases and most words on a fifth below. Faburden was first referred to by name in about 1430 but was in use earlier, and it continued to be practiced

Faburden

EXAMPLE 8.1 *Passage from an anonymous English Credo (ca. 1330)*

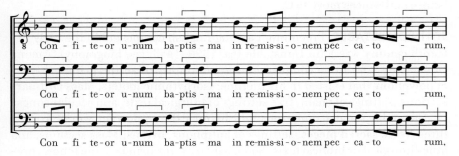

Con - fi - te - or u-num ba-ptis - ma in re-mis-si - o-nem pec - ca-to - rum,

Con - fi - te - or u-num ba-ptis - ma in re-mis-si - o-nem pec - ca-to - rum,

Con - fi - te - or u-num ba-ptis - ma in re-mis-si - o-nem pec - ca-to - rum,

I acknowledge one baptism for the remission of sins.

until the English Reformation over a century later. Although some examples were written down, it was primarily a rule-based system for producing correct, sonorous polyphony that could be used even by monks and clerics who could not read polyphonic notation or compose complex counterpoint. The term "faburden" may derive from the solmization syllable *fa* plus "burden," an English term for the lowest voice (used in other contexts to mean "refrain"), since the system frequently required the singers to use B♭("B-*fa*") to harmonize with F in the chant. Faburden inspired the somewhat different Continental practice known as *fauxbourdon* (described on p. 172).

Cantilenas, motets, and settings of Mass Ordinary texts

The characteristic consonances of faburden were also found in more sophisticated genres of English polyphony. **Cantilenas**, like their apparent ancestor the conductus, were freely composed, mostly homorhythmic settings of Latin texts, not based on existing chant melodies. In these pieces, parallel $\frac{6}{3}$ chords are interspersed with other consonant sonorities in a texture as appealing as faburden but more varied (see NAWM 33, discussed on p. 164). The most elevated genre was the motet, with the isorhythmic motet gradually replacing other types by 1400. By the end of the fourteenth century, settings of Mass Ordinary texts became the most common type of English polyphony, in styles from simple cantilenas to isorhythmic structures.

THE CAROL The English sound is also evident in the polyphonic **carol**, a distinctively English genre. Derived from the medieval *carole*, a monophonic dance-song with alternating solo and choral sections (see Chapter 4), the fifteenth-century English carol was a setting for two or three voices of a poem in English, Latin, or a mixture of the two. Most carols are on religious subjects, particularly the Christmas season and the Virgin Mary. A carol consists of a number of stanzas, all sung to the same music, and a **burden**, or refrain, with its own musical phrase, sung at the beginning and then repeated after each stanza. When, where, and by whom carols were sung is not certain, but they may have been used at religious festivals or to accompany processions.

Many carols feature contrasts of texture between two- and three-part and unison writing. An example is *Alleluia: A newë work* (NAWM 32), which includes two burdens, for two and three voices respectively. The second burden, shown in Example 8.2, shows a common English texture: the top voice is most rhythmically active, while the lower voices mostly parallel it in $\frac{6}{3}$ sonorities, moving out to the octave and fifth at cadences. After an almost unbroken flow of consonance, the final cadence features a **suspension**, as the descent of the lowest voice to D creates a seventh with the top voice that must resolve before both voices move to C.

JOHN DUNSTABLE Preeminent among English composers in the early fifteenth century was John Dunstable (ca. 1390–1453; see biography). Among Dunstable's sixty or so compositions are examples of all the principal types of polyphony that existed in his lifetime: isorhythmic motets, Mass Ordinary sections, settings of chant, free settings of liturgical texts, and secular songs.

Three-voice sacred works

Dunstable's most numerous and historically important works are his three-voice sacred pieces, settings of antiphons, hymns, Mass sections, and other liturgical or biblical texts. Some have a cantus firmus in the tenor, serving as the structural foundation for the upper voices. In others, a chant is

EXAMPLE 8.2 *Second burden (refrain) from the carol* Alleluia: A newë work

elaborated in the top voice using a technique now called **_paraphrase_**, in which the melody is given a rhythm and ornamented by adding notes around those of the chant. Example 8.3 shows such a passage from Dunstable's *Regina caeli laetare*. In Dunstable's supple style no two measures in succession have the same rhythm. The melody moves mostly by step or steps mixed with thirds, sometimes outlining a triad. While following the general contour of the chant,

JOHN DUNSTABLE [DUNSTAPLE]

(ca. 1390–1453)

Dunstable was the most highly regarded English composer of the fifteenth century. He composed in all polyphonic genres of the time and exercised a great influence on his contemporaries and successors.

Dunstable's birthplace and early training are unknown. He was a mathematician and astronomer as well as a musician, recalling the medieval grouping of music with the mathematical sciences of the quadrivium. Apparently not a priest, he served a number of royal and noble patrons. He is listed as having been in the service of John, duke of Bedford, probably while the latter was regent of France beginning in 1422. In about 1427–37, his patron was Joan, dowager queen of England, and subsequently he served Humphrey, duke of Gloucester.

Dunstable may have spent much of his career in France, where he inherited part of Bedford's lands in 1437. He is the English composer most often cited as influencing Continental composers, and his compositions are preserved chiefly in manuscripts copied on the Continent. Indeed, characteristics typical of English composers in general were often credited to him by later generations.

MAJOR WORKS Up to 3 polyphonic mass cycles, 2 Gloria-Credo pairs, 15 other Mass Ordinary movements, 12 isorhythmic motets, 6 plainchant settings, 20 other Latin sacred works, 5 secular songs

EXAMPLE 8.3 *Cantus from John Dunstable's* Regina caeli laetare *compared with original plainchant*

it repeatedly arches up to a peak, then descends to a cadence with graceful undulations and quickening rhythms whose gentle syncopations seem to suggest $\frac{6}{8}$ meter in place of the $\frac{3}{4}$ meter at the beginning of each phrase. Dunstable transforms the chant into a varied, fetching melody in up-to-date style, treating it like the melody of a chanson instead of as a foundation in the tenor.

Quam pulchra es   Many of Dunstable's works, such as his *Quam pulchra es* (NAWM 33), are not based on an existing melody. The three voices in this piece are similar in character and nearly equal in importance. They move mostly in the same rhythm and usually pronounce the same syllables together. The form of the piece is not predetermined, nor structured by repeating rhythmic patterns as in an isorhythmic motet, but is influenced by the phrases and sections of the text. Dunstable uses naturalistic rhythmic declamation of the text to call attention to significant words and thus to their meanings, an approach that remained characteristic of music throughout the Renaissance. The vertical sonorities are consonant, except for brief suspensions at cadences, yet show considerable variety. The streams of $\frac{6}{3}$ sonorities found in faburden appear only in a few phrases, leading into a cadence.

REDEFINING THE MOTET As a free, mostly homorhythmic setting of a Latin text, *Quam pulchra es* could be classified as a cantilena, but in the fifteenth century it could also be called a ***motet***. This term, coined in the thirteenth century for pieces that added text to the upper part of a discant clausula, gradually broadened in meaning to encompass any work with texted upper voices above a cantus firmus, whether sacred or secular. By the early fifteenth century, the isorhythmic motet was an old form, used for only the most important ceremonial occasions, and by 1450 it disappeared. Meanwhile, the term *motet* was applied to settings of liturgical texts in the newer musical styles of the time, whether or not a chant melody was used. The term came to designate almost any polyphonic composition on a Latin text other than a mass Ordinary cycle (see pp. 173–79), including settings of texts from the Mass Proper and the Office. Since the late sixteenth century, the term *motet* has also been used for some sacred works in German and, more recently, in other languages. The changing meanings of "motet" in different eras, summarized in Figure 8.1, provide another example of musicians using familiar terms for new types of music.

EARLY 1200s	Polyphonic piece derived from discant clausula, with words added to the upper voice
1200s–1300s	Polyphonic piece with one or more upper voices, each with sacred or secular text in Latin or French, above tenor from chant or other source
CA. 1310–1450	Isorhythmic motet: tenor structured by isorhythm
1400s ON	Used for polyphonic setting of a Latin text, usually sacred or ceremonial, other than a mass cycle
CA. 1600 ON	Also used for some polyphonic settings of sacred texts in German and (much later) in other languages

FIGURE 8.1
The changing meanings of "motet."

THE ENGLISH INFLUENCE English music of the early fifteenth century shows a range of styles, from improvised faburden and carols in popular style through sophisticated isorhythmic motets, chant paraphrases, and free compositions. The carols and much of the functional music for religious observances were used only in England, but the sound they exemplified, of three voices joined in a euphonious progression of sonorities dominated by thirds and sixths, pervaded other English music as well. As the works of Dunstable and others and the practice of faburden became known on the Continent, this sound strongly influenced other types of composition. The English sound steered composers toward homorhythmic textures and helped win acceptance for conspicuous third and sixth sonorities in the harmonic vocabulary. It also led to the emergence on the Continent of a new way of writing for three parts: the upper voice, which has the principal melodic line as in fourteenth-century chansons, is coupled with a tenor as if in a duet, and the two parts—and eventually the contratenor as well—are more nearly equal in importance, in melodic quality, and in rhythm. In these ways, English influence was an essential element in the international style of the middle to late fifteenth century. As we will see, English composers also pioneered the polyphonic mass, the largest and most prestigious musical genre of the Renaissance.

MUSIC IN THE BURGUNDIAN LANDS

On the European mainland, musicians connected with the court of Burgundy or trained in Burgundian lands played a particularly important role in the development of an international musical idiom in the fifteenth century.

THE DUCHY OF BURGUNDY The duke of Burgundy was a feudal vassal of the king of France, granted rule over the duchy in return for service to the king, yet for a time virtually equaled the king in power. During the late fourteenth and fifteenth centuries, successive dukes acquired large territories, partly through political marriages and diplomacy that took advantage of their kings' distress in the Hundred Years' War; indeed, for a time (1419–35) Burgundy was allied with the English against the French king. Thus to their original fiefs, the duchy and county of Burgundy in east-central France, the dukes added most of modern-day Netherlands, Belgium, northeastern France, Luxembourg, and Lorraine, as shown in Figure 8.2. The dukes of Burgundy ruled over the whole as virtually independent sovereigns until 1477. Though their nominal capital was Dijon, the dukes had no fixed city of residence but sojourned at various places in their dominions. The main orbit of the Burgundian court by the mid-fifteenth century was around Lille, Bruges, Ghent, and especially Brussels, an area comprising modern Belgium and northeastern France. Most of the leading composers of the late fifteenth century came from the Burgundian territories, and many of them were connected with the Burgundian court.

Burgundian chapel and minstrels

The first duke of Burgundy, Philip the Bold (r. 1363–1404), established a chapel in 1384, and it soon became one of Europe's largest and most resplendent. Under Philip the Good (r. 1419–67), it reached twenty-three singers by 1445, surpassed only by the king of England's chapel. At first, musicians were recruited chiefly from northern France. But because Philip the Good and his successor, Charles the Bold (r. 1467–77), spent more time in the north than in Dijon, most of their musicians came from Flanders and the Low Countries (modern-day Belgium and the Netherlands). In addition to his chapel, Philip the Good maintained a band of minstrels—players of trumpets, drums, vielle, lute, harp, organ, bagpipes, and shawms—which included musicians from France, Italy, Germany, and Portugal. The painting in Figure 8.3 depicts singers and instrumentalists performing at one of Philip's lavish entertainments. Charles the Bold was particularly keen on music, being an amateur instrumentalist and composer. His death in 1477 left Burgundy with no male heir. The duchy itself was absorbed by the French king, but Charles's daughter Mary of Burgundy and her son Philip the Fair continued to reign over the Burgundian territories in the Low Countries and maintained the chapel.

COSMOPOLITAN STYLE The cosmopolitan atmosphere of fifteenth-century courts was constantly renewed by visits from foreign musicians. In addition, members of the chapel themselves were continually changing, moving from one court to another in response to better opportunities. These circumstances, along with increasing trade across the Continent, fostered a common musical style, as we will see in the music of Binchois and Du Fay. The prestige of the Burgundian court was such that the music cultivated there influenced other European musical centers: the chapels of the pope at Rome, of the emperor in Germany, of the French and English kings, and of the various Italian courts, as well as cathedral choirs.

FIGURE 8.2 *The growth of Burgundian possessions, 1363–1477.*

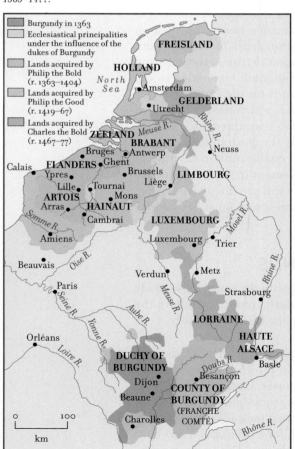

GENRES AND TEXTURE Composers in the mid-fifteenth century produced four principal types of polyphonic composition: secular chansons with French texts; motets; Magnificats; and settings of the Mass Ordinary. Most pieces were for three voices, in a combination resembling the fourteenth-century French chanson or Italian ballata but with slightly larger ranges for each voice, the cantus spanning about a tenth or twelfth (around *a* to *c″* or *e″*) and tenor and contratenor both in a range about a sixth lower (usually *c* to *e′* or *g′*). As in fourteenth-century music, each line has a distinct role, with the main melody in the cantus, contrapuntal support in the tenor, and harmonic filler in the contratenor.

BINCHOIS AND BURGUNDIAN CHANSONS In the fifteenth century, the term *chanson* encompassed any polyphonic setting of a French secular poem. Chansons most often set stylized love poems in the courtly tradition of *fine amour* (see Chapter 4), and most followed the form of the rondeau (ABaAabAB). Ballades were written for ceremonial occasions, but gradually went out of fashion.

Gilles Binchois, the most important composer at the court of Philip the Good (see biography and Figure 8.4 on p. 168), was particularly esteemed for his chansons. His well-known rondeau *De plus en plus* (NAWM 34), from around 1425, exemplifies the Burgundian chanson and Binchois's blend of French and English traits. Example 8.4 shows the opening phrase.

FIGURE 8.3 *An outdoor entertainment at the court of Duke Philip the Good of Burgundy. Musicians play and sing for the duke (center) and his company, while in the background hunters are chasing game. Detail from a sixteenth-century copy of an anonymous fifteenth-century painting.*

Most compositions from this era are in the equivalent of either $\frac{3}{4}$ or $\frac{6}{8}$ *Meter and rhythm* meter; duple meter was used mainly in subdivisions of longer works, to provide contrast. *De plus en plus* is in $\frac{6}{8}$, with occasional cross-rhythms of three quarter notes, an effect called **hemiola** (see measure 3). Like Dunstable, Binchois varies the rhythm from measure to measure, enlivening it with dotted figures and subtle syncopations. Yet the result is much less intricate than rhythms in chansons by Machaut or Ars Subtilior composers.

The cantus declaims the text clearly. As in most chansons of the time, the *Music and text* setting is mostly syllabic, especially at the beginning of each line of poetry. Groups of two to four notes provide variety, and longer melismas appear only at the most important cadences, in contrast to the more frequent melismas in fourteenth-century songs.

The main melody in the cantus moves as often by skip as by step, outlining an ascending triad (as it was later called) and then descending the scale *Melody and counterpoint* to create a fluid, gently arching line. The tenor is slower but traces a similar arch, alternating skips and steps, and the two voices form good two-part counterpoint, mostly in sixths and thirds. The contratenor, by comparison, is full

GILLES BINCHOIS [GILLES DE BINS]
(ca. 1400–1460)

Gilles de Bins, known as Binchois, was along with Dunstable and Du Fay one of the three most important composers of his generation. At a time when the Burgundian court was a focus of musical activity, Binchois stood at the center of the court's musical life. His works were widely recopied and emulated by many other composers.

Binchois was probably born and trained in Mons, where he was a chorister and organist. He went to live in Lille in 1423, and apparently spent some time in the service of William Pole, earl of Suffolk, who was with the English forces occupying France. He joined the chapel of Philip the Good, duke of Burgundy, by 1427, and served at court until retiring in 1453 on a generous pension. Like other musicians of his generation, he was paid principally to perform at the chapel services and court entertainments of his patron, and only secondarily to compose. His direct contact with English musicians and his three-decade career at the

FIGURE 8.4 *Binchois, holding a harp (on the right), and Guillaume Du Fay, next to a portative organ, in a miniature from Martin Le Franc's poem* Le champion des dames *(1440–42).*

Burgundian court made him a central figure in the creation of a Burgundian style that incorporates English influences.

MAJOR WORKS 28 mass movements (some in Gloria-Credo or Sanctus-Agnus pairs), 6 Magnificats, 29 motets, 51 rondeaux, 7 ballades

EXAMPLE 8.4 *Gilles Binchois,* De plus en plus, *opening phrase*

More and more renews again, my [sweet lady]

of skips and leaps, jumping between notes chosen to fill out the harmony. Like the contratenors of fourteenth-century chansons, it sounds at times above the tenor and at other times below it. The music is almost wholly consonant, with only a few dissonances, all carefully introduced as passing tones, neighbor tones, or suspensions. The upbeat opening, the full consonant harmony, the many melodic thirds, and the triadic skips in cantus and contratenor reflect the influence of English music, while the strong contrasts of character between the voices continue the French tradition.

The preferred cadence formula in the mid-fifteenth century was still a major sixth expanding to an octave between cantus and tenor, often decorated in the cantus with a Landini cadence (see Example 6.6). The end of the phrase in Example 8.4 illustrates a newer version of this cadence, in which the contratenor sounds a fifth below the penultimate tenor note, then leaps up an octave to a fifth above the tenor's final note. Modern ears may hear the effect of the lowest note rising a fourth, as in the common-practice dominant-to-tonic cadence.

Cadences

GUILLAUME DU FAY

Guillaume Du Fay (ca. 1397–1474; see biography on p. 170 and Figures 8.4 and 8.5) was the most famous composer of his time. He was associated with the Burgundian court, although his appointment to the ducal chapel was probably honorary. Trained at the Cathedral of Cambrai in northern France, he often traveled south, serving as a chapel musician in Italy and Savoy (now in southeastern France), but he frequently returned to Cambrai, where he spent his later career. His many travels exposed him to a wide variety of music, from his French and Italian predecessors to his English and Burgundian contemporaries and younger composers such as Johannes Ockeghem (see Chapter 9), and he absorbed many of their stylistic traits into his own music, sometimes combining contrasting styles in a single piece. His music represents well the international style of the mid-fifteenth century.

CHANSONS AND THE INTERNATIONAL STYLE Du Fay's blending of national traits can be traced in his chansons. He wrote *Resvellies vous* (NAWM 35) in 1423 while in Italy at the court of Rimini and Pesaro, to celebrate his patron's wedding. This chanson shows an early stage in Du Fay's synthesis of styles, drawing on fourteenth-century French and Italian elements but not yet on English traits. French characteristics include the ballade form (aabC), many long melismas, frequent syncopation, and some free dissonances. Example 8.5 shows one phrase with cross-rhythms between the parts and several dissonant ornamental notes, more akin to those

EXAMPLE 8.5 *Guillaume Du Fay,* Resvellies vous

* = dissonant note

All lovers who love gentleness

GUILLAUME DU FAY [DUFAY]

(ca. 1397–1474)

Du Fay was the leading composer of his time and one of the most widely traveled. Patrons competed for his services, and the positions he held in Italy, France, and the Lowlands acquainted him with a wide range of musicians and styles. He excelled in every genre, and his music was known and sung throughout Europe.

The son of a priest and an unmarried woman, Du Fay was born in modern-day Belgium, probably in Beersel, near Brussels. He trained in music and grammar in the cathedral school of Cambrai in northeastern France, where he became a choirboy in 1409. He sojourned with a patron at the Council of Constance (1414–18) in southern Germany, which ended the Great Schism between rival popes, then returned to Cambrai as subdeacon at the cathedral. In 1420 he entered the service of Carlo Malatesta at Rimini, on the Adriatic coast of northern Italy. He returned north in 1424, then worked during 1426–28 for Cardinal Louis Aleman in Bologna, where he became a priest.

Du Fay served two periods in the papal chapel, in 1428–33 at Rome and again in 1435–37 during the pope's exile in Florence and Bologna. Alternating with his service to the pope, he was chapelmaster in 1433–35 and 1437–39 at the court of Amadeus VIII, duke of Savoy, whose territories included parts of southeastern France, northwestern Italy, and western Switzerland. When in 1439 a church council deposed the pope and elected Amadeus pope, Du Fay escaped the conflict between his two major patrons by returning to Cambrai, by then under Burgundian

control. He served as an administrator at Cambrai Cathedral and enjoyed at least an honorary appointment to the chapel of Duke Philip the Good. After the papal schism was resolved, Du Fay returned to Savoy in 1452–58 as honorary chapelmaster for Duke Louis. He spent his last years at Cambrai as canon of the cathedral, living in his own house and enjoying considerable wealth.

Du Fay's music survives in almost one hundred manuscripts copied between the 1420s and the early sixteenth century in regions from Spain to Poland and from Italy to Scotland, attesting to his popularity and fame as a composer.

MAJOR WORKS At least 6 masses, 35 other Mass movements, 4 Magnificats, 60 hymns and other chant settings, 24 motets (13 isorhythmic, 11 freely composed), 34 plainchant melodies, 60 rondeaux, 8 ballades, 13 other secular songs

MUSÉE DES BEAUX-ARTS, LILLE. PHOTO: RÉUNION DES MUSÉES NATIONAUX/ART RESOURCE, NY

FIGURE 8.5 *Bas-relief from Du Fay's funeral monument, showing the composer kneeling in prayer (lower left).*

in fourteenth-century polyphony than to later fifteenth-century practice influenced by English music. Some passages recall the Ars Subtilior, with rapid notes in various divisions of the beat, including triplet-like figuration. Italian elements include relatively smooth vocal melodies, melismas on the

EXAMPLE 8.6 *Du Fay,* Se la face ay pale

If my face is pale, the cause is love, that is the principal reason,

last accented syllable of each line of text, and a meter change for the b section, paralleling the change of meter at the ritornello in the Italian madrigal.

Se la face ay pale (NAWM 37a), a ballade Du Fay wrote about ten years later while at the court of Savoy, shows the strong influence of English music, as seen in Example 8.6. Both tenor and cantus are equally tuneful, an English trait, while the contratenor leaps around to fill in the harmony, lying sometimes above and sometimes below the tenor, like those in earlier French chansons. The cantus and tenor melodies are graceful, mostly stepwise, and primarily syllabic with brief melismas, drawing on both Italian and English characteristics while leaning toward the latter with relatively brief, clearly demarcated phrases. The rhythmic energy of the French Ars Nova is still present, in frequent syncopation and constantly varying rhythmic patterns, but overall the rhythm is smoother and more directed, gradually increasing in density to shape a phrase and then relaxing at the cadence. The harmony is consonant throughout, with prominent thirds, sixths, and full triads (as they were later called), and very few dissonances, all carefully controlled as suspensions or ornamental tones. Finally, the chanson is no longer in the fixed form of the ballade (aabC), but is freely composed, although the poem itself is clearly a ballade with three stanzas, each ending with a refrain line. The English contribution is essential, yet the music is not merely English in sound; rather, it represents a blending of characteristics from all three national traditions to form a new international musical language.

MOTETS AND CHANT SETTINGS Du Fay wrote sacred music in a variety of styles and for a variety of purposes, from plainchant for a new feast, to polyphonic settings of a chant or liturgical text, to motets that enhanced a special occasion by supplementing the ritual at points where music was not required.

FIGURE 8.6

The Cathedral of Santa Maria del Fiore in Florence. Du Fay wrote the isorhythmic motet Nuper rosarum flores *for the consecration in 1436 of the dome, designed by Filippo Brunelleschi.*

Much of his polyphonic music, like that of his contemporaries, was linked to the Virgin Mary, who was venerated daily and regarded as the saint who could most effectively intercede with Christ on behalf of worshippers. His sacred polyphonic works drew on French, English, and Italian elements, including the English cantilena and the Italian lauda traditions. Most works were in three voices in a texture resembling the chanson, with the main melody in the cantus. The cantus might be newly composed, as in Du Fay's cantilena motets, but in many cases it was an embellished paraphrase of chant, reworked into a melody in up-to-date chanson style with the kinds of rhythmic variety and cadential figuration we have seen in chansons by Binchois (NAWM 34) and Du Fay himself (NAWM 37a).

Fauxbourdon   Du Fay and other continental composers of the second quarter of the fifteenth century became fascinated with successions of thirds and sixths through hearing music imported from England. Twenty-four pieces by Du Fay and over a hundred by other composers use a technique called **fauxbourdon**, which was inspired by English faburden although the procedure is different. Only the cantus and tenor were written out, moving mostly in parallel sixths and ending each phrase on an octave. A third voice, unwritten, sang in exact parallel a fourth below the cantus, producing a stream of $\frac{6}{3}$ sonorities ending on an open fifth and octave, as in faburden. The technique was used chiefly for settings of the simpler Office chants: hymns, antiphons, psalms, and canticles. Du Fay's setting of the hymn *Christe, redemptor omnium* (NAWM 36) uses fauxbourdon, paraphrasing the chant in the cantus. Only the even-numbered stanzas were sung polyphonically, alternating with the others in plainchant.

Isorhythmic motets   In addition to motets in the modern chanson style and pieces using fauxbourdon, Du Fay and his contemporaries still wrote isorhythmic motets for solemn public ceremonies, following the convention that an archaic musical style, like an archaic literary style, was especially suitable for ceremonial and state occasions. Du Fay's *Nuper rosarum flores*, performed in 1436 at the dedication of Filippo Brunelleschi's magnificent dome for the Cathedral of Santa Maria del Fiore in Florence, shown in Figure 8.6, was such a work. Du Fay's use of two isorhythmic tenors, both based on the same chant, may have been an allusion to Brunelleschi's use of two vaults to support the dome. Du Fay wrote the motet while serving in the chapel of Pope Eugene IV, who officiated at the dedication. Another of his motets, *Supremum est mortalibus bonum* (1433), written to commemorate the meeting of Pope Eugene with King Sigismund of Hungary, emperor-elect of the Holy Roman Empire, alternates sections in isorhythm, fauxbourdon, and free counterpoint in a masterful combination of these strongly contrasting styles.

THE POLYPHONIC MASS

Like their English colleagues, composers on the Continent wrote polyphonic settings of Mass Ordinary texts in increasing numbers during the late fourteenth and early fifteenth centuries. Until about 1420, the various items of the Ordinary were usually composed as separate pieces (Machaut's mass and a few others excepted), though occasionally a compiler would group them together. During the fifteenth century, it became standard practice for composers to set the Ordinary as a coherent whole. Leading this development were English composers, notably Dunstable and Leonel Power (d. 1445).

At first composers linked only two sections together, typically a Gloria *Paired movements* and Credo—the two movements that framed the readings and responsorial chants, which were the high point of the first half of Mass—or a Sanctus and Agnus Dei, which framed the preparations for communion in the second half. Movements were paired by having the same arrangement of voices (indicated by clefs), the same modal center, similar musical material, or other common elements.

Gradually composers broadened the practice to include all five main *Polyphonic mass* items of the Ordinary—Kyrie, Gloria, Credo, Sanctus, and Agnus Dei—in a *cycles* work called a *polyphonic mass cycle*, or simply a **mass**. (In common usage, although the church service—the Mass—is capitalized, the musical genre is not.) Except for the Kyrie and Gloria, which were sung back to back, the items in the Ordinary were dispersed throughout the Mass liturgy, with a great deal of chant between them. Linking the Ordinary items through impressive polyphony gave a musical shape to the whole service, appropriate for the most important occasions.

MUSICAL LINKS IN MASS CYCLES Grouping music for the Mass Ordinary into cycles, with one setting for each text, goes back to the thirteenth century with cycles of plainchants for each Ordinary item except the Credo (see Chapter 3). Scribes occasionally grouped polyphonic settings into cycles in the fourteenth century. But such cycles were not necessarily musically related. Composers in the fifteenth century devised a variety of means to link the separate sections of a mass to each other.

In the context of a liturgy that was mostly sung in plainchant, some sense *Stylistic coherence* of connection resulted simply from composing all five parts of the Ordinary in the same general style, whether freely composed, based on paraphrased chants in the upper voice, or using a cantus firmus in the tenor.

When the composer based each movement on an existing chant for *Plainsong mass* that text (the Kyrie on a Kyrie chant, and so on), the mass gained coherence because the borrowed melodies were all liturgically appropriate, although not related musically. A mass that uses chant in this way is called a *plainsong mass*. Many plainsong masses, including Machaut's, were written to be sung during a Lady Mass, a special service dedicated to the Virgin Mary.

Composers could create a more noticeable musical connection by using the same thematic material in all movements of the mass. A frequent strategy early in the fifteenth century consisted of beginning each movement with the same melodic motive, in one or all voices. A mass that uses such a **head motive** as its primary linking device is called a **motto mass**.

CANTUS-FIRMUS MASS The use of a head motive was soon combined with (and sometimes superseded by) another way of linking movements: constructing each one around the same cantus firmus, normally placed in the tenor. This type of mass has become known as a **cantus-firmus mass** or *tenor mass*. English composers wrote the earliest such masses, but the practice was quickly adopted on the Continent, and by the second half of the fifteenth century it became the principal type of mass.

The tenor cantus firmus was written in long notes and usually in an isorhythmic pattern, as in the isorhythmic motet. When this melody was a chant, a rhythm was imposed on it. When the borrowed melody was a secular tune, as was frequently the case after the 1450s, the song's original rhythm was normally retained, but in successive appearances the pattern could be made faster or slower in relation to the other voices. Often composers used the tenor of a polyphonic chanson, and when they did so, they typically borrowed some elements from the other voices as well; such a mass is sometimes called a **cantus-firmus/imitation mass** because it imitates more than one voice of the source. The mass usually derived its name from the borrowed melody. One of the melodies used most frequently was *L'homme armé* (The armed man), a well-known popular song in the fifteenth century. Most major composers for more than a century, including Du Fay, Ockeghem, Josquin, and Palestrina, wrote at least one *Missa L'homme armé*, showing that writing a mass on this cantus firmus had become a venerable tradition, perhaps serving as a test of composers' ability to create something new from familiar material.

Early cantus-firmus masses were for three voices. Placing the borrowed melody in the tenor followed the motet tradition but created compositional problems. The sound ideal of the fifteenth century needed the lowest voice to function as a harmonic foundation, particularly at cadences. Letting the lowest voice carry a melody that could not be altered limited the composer's ability to provide such a foundation.

The solution was to add a fourth voice below the tenor. This innovation was apparently introduced by the anonymous English composer of *Missa Caput*, a mass from the 1440s. The cantus firmus, chosen for theological reasons (see Music in Context: Masses and Dragons), lay in a high range, making it appropriate to add another voice below. Other composers soon adopted the same

Masses and Dragons

The choice of a cantus firmus for a mass often conveyed meanings through the words associated with the borrowed melody, as was true for isorhythmic motets. Three famous masses composed between 1440 and 1490 use as a cantus firmus a long melisma on the word *caput* (head). Anne Walters Robertson has linked these masses to the theological view of Jesus crushing the head of Satan, depicted as a dragon or serpent.

The image goes back to Genesis 3:15, in which God says to the serpent who tempted Eve, "I will put enmity between you and the woman, and between your seed and her seed; he [her seed] shall crush your head, and you shall bruise his heel." Other biblical passages equate dragons to sin. Jesus was often depicted in medieval and fifteenth-century art as stepping on a dragon at his resurrection or at the Last Judgment. In cities all over England, France, and the Lowlands, in the days leading up to Easter and to Ascension (celebrating Jesus's ascent into heaven), churches and outdoor processions displayed effigies or banners of a dragon, symbolizing the evil that Jesus defeated.

The first *Missa Caput* was composed by an unknown Englishman (possibly Dunstable), probably for use in a Mass for Ascension linked to just such a celebration. The melisma was drawn from an English chant for Maundy Thursday, the Thursday before Easter, that described Jesus's washing the feet of his disciples on the eve of his crucifixion. Using this chant as a source joined the idea of Jesus crushing the dragon's head (from the word *caput*) to the events that led up to his resurrection and to the symbolic washing away of sin.

Jean de Ockeghem and Jacob Obrecht (see Chapter 9) wrote their *Caput* masses not only in emulation of the earlier mass (as has long been assumed) but no doubt for the same reason, to create a mass appropriate for this festival. The connection to dragons is explicit in the manuscript of Ockeghem's mass in Figure 8.7, which shows a warrior fighting a dragon.

As is often true with music, knowing the historical background for a piece helps us understand aspects that we would otherwise miss. In Ockeghem's *Missa Caput,* the cantus firmus is notated in the tenor range but with instructions to push it down an octave, making it the lowest voice; this symbolizes in musical terms Jesus pressing down the head of the dragon. Placing the cantus firmus in the lowest voice for all five movements was unique among four-voice masses, and here it creates another musical symbol. The note B occurs often in the cantus firmus, and Ockeghem misses few chances to emphasize the interval of a tritone between B in the bassus and F in a higher voice. The tritone, normally avoided, could be regarded as a corruption of a perfect fifth or fourth. Its prominence in this mass may be a musical image for the evil being trampled by Christ.

FIGURE 8.7 *Illumination of a warrior and dragon accompanying Ockeghem's* Missa Caput *in a manuscript copied in about 1498. The text following the music instructs the singer to lower the* caput *cantus firmus an octave.*

approach for their cantus-firmus masses, recognizing it as a way to achieve greater control of the harmony. The widespread use of four-voice texture, which spread from cantus-firmus masses to other genres by the end of the century, changed music forever.

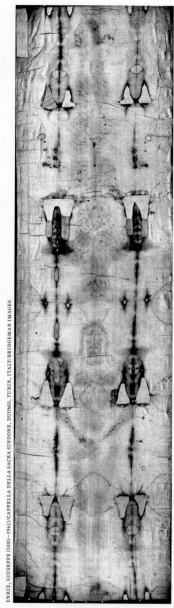

FIGURE 8.8 *The Holy Shroud, now known as the Shroud of Turin after the city where it has been since 1578. Although its history can only be traced with certainty since 1390, it was widely believed to be the burial shroud of Jesus on which somehow his image was preserved, showing wounds to the hands, feet, forehead, and side consistent with accounts of his crucifixion. The front image is on the lower portion of the Shroud, the back above it and upside down, reflecting the way the cloth was wrapped around the body.*

The voice below the tenor was called at first **contratenor bassus** (low contratenor) and later simply **bassus**, the source of our English term **bass** for a low male voice. Above the tenor sounded a second contratenor called **contratenor altus** (high contratenor), later **altus**, hence **alto**. The highest part, the cantus (melody), was also called *discantus* (discant) or **superius** (highest); from the latter (through Italian) comes our term **soprano**. These four voice parts became standard by the latter fifteenth century and remain so today.

Du Fay's *Missa Se la face ay pale* is one of the most celebrated cantus-firmus masses and the earliest known complete mass to use a secular tune for a cantus firmus. He used the tenor of his own ballade *Se la face ay pale* (see Example 8.6) in the tenor of the mass. He apparently wrote the mass in the 1450s while at Savoy and may have borrowed the ballade, written two decades earlier for the same court, to honor the Holy Shroud, acquired by the duke of Savoy in 1453. The Shroud, shown in Figure 8.8, was believed to be Jesus's burial shroud and was one of the most prized relics of his crucifixion. As Anne Walters Robertson has recently argued, the images in Du Fay's ballade of a pale face and suffering for the sake of love can be understood to refer to Christ's death on the cross for the loving redemption of human souls, making the ballade a fitting basis for a mass sung at a service to honor the Shroud. Du Fay's use of a secular chanson as a cantus firmus in this mass launched a century-long tradition of masses based on secular songs, and it seems likely that in most or all cases there was a similar symbolic meaning to the choice of song.

In *Missa Se la face ay pale*, Du Fay applied the method of the isorhythmic motet on a larger scale. The rhythmic pattern of the tenor melody from his ballade, shown in Example 8.7a, is preserved in the tenor of the mass, but subjected to **augmentation**. In the Kyrie, Sanctus, and Agnus Dei, the duration of each note from the ballade is doubled. In the Gloria (NAWM 37b) and Credo, the cantus firmus is heard three times. In Example 8.7b, we see the opening of the song's tenor in the tenor of the Gloria at "Adoramus te," sung at triple the original duration; that is, each beat of the original tenor part corresponds to three beats here, or an entire measure in the other parts. When the ballade melody repeats, at "Qui tollis" in Example 8.7c, the original note values are doubled (two beats for each original beat). Only when the melody appears a third time, at "Cum sancto spiritu" in Example 8.7d, is the melody easily recognized, because it is heard at its normal tempo. At the closing Amen, as the tenor sings the final melisma from the ballade tenor, portions of the ballade's other voices are borrowed as well, making the allusion even more recognizable. Borrowing from multiple voices makes the work a cantus-firmus/imitation mass. In addition, the movements are linked through a shared head motive, as is often true for cantus-firmus and cantus-firmus/imitation masses.

Throughout, each voice has a distinctive function and character. The upper two voices, the superius and contratenor altus, move mostly stepwise with skips interspersed, proceed in constantly varying rhythm, and occasionally exchange motives. The tenor is the main structural voice, while the more angular contratenor bassus provides

EXAMPLE 8.7 *Du Fay,* Missa Se la face ay pale, *Gloria*

a. Original tenor melody

Se la face ay pa - le, La cause est a-mer,

b. Cantus firmus at three times original duration

We adore thee. We glorify thee.

c. Cantus firmus at twice original duration

have mercy on us. Thou who takest away the sins of the world

d. Cantus firmus at original duration

a harmonic foundation. Contrasts of sonority between textures of two, three, and four voices provide variety and help the listener perceive the shape of each movement.

The music proceeds as a chain of phrases, some thinner in texture and some thicker, some slower in pace and some quicker, some longer and some shorter, each closing with a cadence that may be more or less conclusive, but in most cases overlapping with the next phrase to sustain momentum. In Example 8.7 and throughout the mass, each voice has a melody that is diatonic and relatively simple in pitch contour yet also shapely, individual, and a pleasure to sing and hear. The constant rhythmic play between voices, sometimes complementing each other but often contrasting, creates a surprisingly rich tapestry of sound. From the pleasing surface to the intriguing cantus-firmus structure, the music engages both the senses and the intellect, using tools of artistry and rhetoric to draw listeners into the religious experience embodied in the words and rituals of the Mass.

Why the cantus-firmus mass?   Why did the cantus-firmus mass develop and become so widespread? Since the nineteenth century, music historians have suggested that composers sought to unify the five movements of the mass into an integrated whole, akin to the cyclic symphonies of the nineteenth century, and found that using the same cantus firmus in each movement was an ideal way to do so. Such a view privileges composers' initiative and musical unity, both more highly valued in the nineteenth century than in the fifteenth. More recently, scholars have shown that institutions and private patrons in the fifteenth century often commissioned settings of the Mass Ordinary for specific occasions or devotional services, just as Machaut's setting served for a Mass offered to the Virgin Mary. A particular chant or secular song used as a cantus firmus could refer to the saint to whom the mass was addressed, as in Power's *Missa Alma redemptoris Mater* on a chant to the Virgin Mary, or to an institution, family, individual, or event for whose benefit the mass was composed, as in Du Fay's *Missa Se la face ay pale*, linked to his Savoy patrons and to the Holy Shroud. The unusually high cantus firmus for *Missa Caput* was chosen for the imagery associated with its text, suiting the mass for the feast of the Ascension and its attendant rituals (see Music in Context: Masses and Dragons, p. 175). Similarly, the tradition of masses on *L'homme armé* may be connected to the Order of the Golden Fleece, an association of knights at the Burgundian court, to calls for a new crusade after the fall of Constantinople to the Turks, and to images of Christ (or a particular patron) as an armed warrior battling sin. Musical unity resulted from using the same cantus firmus throughout, but it may not have been the main impetus for using a cantus firmus. Moreover, the concern for diversity was at least as strong; writers such as Tinctoris praised composers for producing variety between movements, even when each was based on the same melody.

The cantus-firmus mass met multiple needs: as service music; as a conveyer of meaning through musical allusions to its source tune and its text; and as a work that connoisseurs such as Tinctoris could appreciate. The cyclic mass began its career as a piece written for a specific occasion or patron, replacing in many respects the function of the isorhythmic motet, and many structural elements from the latter were taken over in the cantus-firmus mass. As it gained in importance, the mass became the most prestigious genre of the time. The traditions that developed, in which many composers used the same melody as a cantus firmus, suggest that the mass became a proving ground for composers' abilities. We, who typically hear this music in concert or on recordings rather than in its original liturgical environment, are likely to approach a mass as we would other music, admiring the glorious sounds and composers' skill in reworking borrowed material in many varied ways.

AN ENDURING MUSICAL LANGUAGE

The polyphonic mass cycle was the largest, most complex, and most prestigious musical genre of the fifteenth century and remained so throughout the sixteenth century, until the invention of opera around 1600. The cantus-firmus mass created by English composers and adopted by Du Fay and others on the Continent would later be joined by other types, notably the *paraphrase mass* and *imitation mass*, as we will see in Chapters 9 and 11. The mass as a genre has endured to the present day, including masses by Monteverdi, Bach, Haydn, Mozart, Beethoven, Bruckner, and other major composers, gradually changing its primary role from service music to concert music.

The new sound of the fifteenth century represented an even more profound change. The music of Dunstable, Binchois, Du Fay, and their contemporaries was regarded by Tinctoris in the 1470s as the oldest music worth listening to, and it still marks the earliest polyphonic music many Westerners may hear as familiar rather than alien. Du Fay and other composers working between the 1420s and the 1450s helped to forge a cosmopolitan musical language that blended French concern for structure and rhythmic interest, Italian emphasis on lyrical melodies, and English preference for smooth counterpoint, avoidance of parallel fifths and octaves, pervasive consonance, prominent thirds and sixths, and carefully controlled dissonance. All of these ingredients became fundamental to the musical language of the fifteenth and sixteenth centuries, enduring as common elements even as new styles emerged with each new generation and with diverging national traditions in the sixteenth century. They remained important elements of music through the nineteenth century and beyond, and their presence in fifteenth-century music is what makes it sound more familiar to modern ears than most medieval music does.

The musical idiom continued to evolve throughout Du Fay's career, as four-voice textures and equality between the voices became increasingly common. After his death, Du Fay was remembered as the leading composer of his era. Yet in the late fifteenth century, styles and tastes changed relatively quickly, and by the early sixteenth century, performances of the music of Du Fay or his contemporaries were rare. Their music lay unperformed and untranscribed for centuries, until rising musicological interest during the late nineteenth century led to editions and performances in the twentieth. Now works by Du Fay and others of his time are regularly performed and recorded, so that we can experience for ourselves the "marvelous pleasingness" Martin Le Franc heard in their music almost six centuries ago.

Further Reading is available at digital.wwnorton.com/hwm10

FRANCO-FLEMISH COMPOSERS, 1450–1520

The latter fifteenth and early sixteenth centuries saw the continuing prominence of composers from northern France, Flanders, and the Netherlands, who served courts and cities throughout France, the Low Countries, Italy, Spain, Germany, Bohemia, and Austria. The generation born around 1420 and active until the 1490s inherited the international language and characteristic genres of the Du Fay generation—chanson, motet, and cyclic mass—along with some surviving medieval traits, such as the *formes fixes,* cantus-firmus structure, and stratified counterpoint based on a structural tenor. Their newer style was marked by wider ranges, greater equality between voices, and increased use of imitation. The next generation, born around 1450 and active to about 1520, continued these trends and brought new ones: an end to the *formes fixes,* growing interest in imitative and homophonic textures, and a new focus on fitting music to words with appropriate declamation, imagery, and expression.

POLITICAL CHANGE AND CONSOLIDATION

Musicians in the late fifteenth and early sixteenth centuries depended as before on the support of patrons. Political and economic changes influenced the market for musicians and the flow of music.

Defeated in the Hundred Years' War in 1453, England withdrew from France and entered a period of relative insularity marked by civil war (the Wars of the Roses). But other major powers were gaining ground on the Continent, as shown in the map in Figure 9.1. After the death in 1477 of Charles the Bold, the duchy of Burgundy came under the control of the king of France, the first of several acquisitions over the next fifty years that consolidated France into a strong, centralized state. The Burgundian possessions in the Low Countries passed to Charles's daughter Mary of Burgundy, whose 1478 marriage to Maximilian of Hapsburg united her lands with his in Austria and Alsace. The marriage of Queen

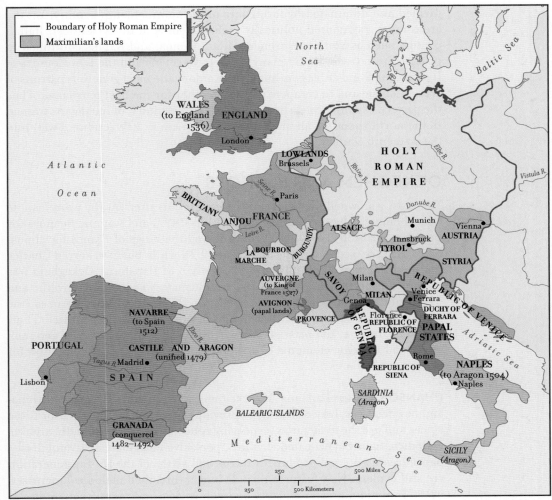

FIGURE 9.1 *Western Europe around 1500. By this time, the Spanish rulers Isabella and Ferdinand had united Spain; the kings of France controlled some former quasi-independent fiefdoms within their borders, including Burgundy, Anjou, Brittany, and Provence; and Maximilian I, king of Germany and Holy Roman emperor, ruled directly over Austria, Alsace, and the Low Countries.*

Isabella of Castile and Léon (northern and central Spain) to King Ferdinand of Aragon (eastern Spain, Sardinia, and Sicily) joined the two realms to create the modern kingdom of Spain. In the eventful year of 1492, Isabella and Ferdinand conquered the southern Spanish kingdom of Granada, controlled by the Islamic Moors; forcibly expelled the Jews from Spain, ending centuries of coexistence and mutual influence between Muslims, Jews, and Christians in Spain; and sponsored Christopher Columbus's voyage west over the Atlantic Ocean, which led to the European encounter with and colonization of the New World. The marriage of Ferdinand and Isabella's daughter to the son of Mary and Maximilian (who was by then Holy Roman emperor) ultimately brought about the unification of Austria, the Low Countries, southern Italy, Spain, and Spanish America under the Hapsburg emperor Charles V (r. 1519–1556), the most powerful European ruler since Charlemagne.

Sandwiched in between these major powers were dozens of small states and cities in Germany and Italy. When the French invaded Italy in 1494, the Italian states were unable to unite against them. The region remained divided and dominated by foreigners until the nineteenth century. Yet the areas most fragmented politically included some of the wealthiest. Italian centers such as Venice, Florence, Milan, Genoa, and Naples continued to prosper from trade, as did many cities in Germany and the Low Countries. Italian courts and cities continued to be among the most generous patrons of art and music and to compete with each other for the best musicians. Thus the pattern established earlier in the fifteenth century, of musicians trained in the north spending all or part of their careers in Italy, endured well into the sixteenth century.

OCKEGHEM AND BUSNOYS

The most renowned musicians of the generation after Du Fay were Jean de Ockeghem (or Johannes Okeghem, ca. 1420–1497) and Antoine Busnoys (or Busnois, ca. 1430–1492). Ockeghem served the kings of France for almost half a century (see biography and Figure 9.2), while Busnoys served Charles the Bold, Mary of Burgundy, and Maximilian of Hapsburg. Ockeghem was esteemed especially for his masses, and Busnoys was the most prolific and widely praised chanson composer of his time. Tinctoris lauded them as "the most outstanding and most famous professors of the art of music." Their chansons, motets, and masses were widely distributed, performed, and imitated, and the new elements of style they practiced laid the foundation for later generations.

CHANSONS   The chansons of Ockeghem and Busnoys blend traditional and new features. Like chansons of previous generations, most are for three voices and use the *formes fixes,* especially rondeau form. The smooth, arching melodies, lightly syncopated rhythms, pervasive consonance, careful dissonance treatment, and prominent thirds and sixths of the Du Fay generation are still evident. New features include longer-breathed melodies, increased use of imitation, greater equality between voices, and more frequent use of duple meter.

Je ne puis vivre   These traits are evident in Busnoys's virelai *Je ne puis vivre* (NAWM 38). The refrain is in triple meter, the b section in duple. As shown in Example 9.1a (see p. 184), the refrain opens with a long, arching melody that combines smooth, mostly scalar motion with constantly changing rhythms. Each line of poetry begins with syllabic text setting, then flowers into a more melismatic style. The most striking contrast with earlier chansons is the prevalence of imitation. The opening phrase is imitated in the contratenor and again somewhat later in the tenor. Imitation between tenor and cantus over free counterpoint in the contratenor continues throughout the chanson, varied with brief homophony to open the b section. The contratenor moves primarily by steps and thirds with relatively few leaps, making it much more similar in style to the other voices than are the contratenors in Du Fay's chansons. Although the cantus and tenor still form good two-part counterpoint and would sound well alone, the contratenor plays a significant role in shaping the musical flow. In measures 9–10, the cantus and tenor form a cadence on C, but the contratenor elides the cadence by moving to A and thus maintains momentum. The cadence at the end of the phrase is formed between cantus and contratenor instead of with the tenor. And in the final phrase of

JEAN DE OCKEGHEM [JOHANNES OKEGHEM]

(ca. 1420–1497)

Ockeghem was celebrated as a singer (he is said to have had a fine bass voice), as a composer, and as the teacher of many leading composers of the next generation.

Ockeghem was born and trained in the province of Hainaut in northeastern France, served briefly in Antwerp, and spent several years in France with the chapel of Charles I, duke of Bourbon. He is most closely identified with the French royal court, where he served three kings over a span of more than four decades. He was a member of the royal chapel from 1451 on, first chaplain from 1454, and master of the chapel from 1465. He was also treasurer at the royal church of St. Martin in Tours from 1458, and became a priest around 1464. Both his career and his music are notably less cosmopolitan than those of Du Fay. He returned to his native region on occasion, where he was in touch with Du Fay, Binchois, and Busnoys, and traveled to Spain on a diplomatic mission for King Louis XI around 1470. But he seems never to have gone to Italy, and his music shows little Italian influence.

Ockeghem's known output was relatively small for a composer of his renown. Most of his works cannot be dated with any certainty. In some respects his music continues elements from previous generations, in others it typifies his time, but in certain ways it is unique,

FIGURE 9.2 *This miniature from a French manuscript of about 1530 shows Ockeghem (right foreground) and eight musicians of the French royal chapel singing from a large manuscript choirbook on a lectern, the custom of the time. Ockeghem is wearing glasses, still unusual in his day.*

perhaps because his long service in one place encouraged the development of an individual idiom.

MAJOR WORKS 13 masses, Requiem Mass, at least 5 motets, 21 chansons

---

the refrain, shown in Example 9.1b, as the upper voices cadence twice on C (at measures 24–25 and at the end), the contratenor drops a fifth from G to C. Such cadences with a suspension in an upper voice and a falling fifth (or rising fourth) in the lowest voice were the most emphatic cadences in the latter fifteenth and sixteenth centuries, and are the forebears of the common-practice dominant-to-tonic cadence. The music of Busnoys and Ockeghem marks a transition between the older counterpoint, in which cantus and tenor form the essential structure for the other voices, and the approach that emerged by the late fifteenth century, in which all voices play more similar roles and all are essential for the counterpoint.

One trait that is typical of Busnoys, but not of Ockeghem, is the clear tonal direction of the melody. The modal center is C, and in Example 9.1a the cantus arches up a tenth from C to E, cascades down an octave, begins again on the upper C, and descends to E and then to low C, confirmed by a cadence.

EXAMPLE 9.1 *Antoine Busnoys,* Je ne puis vivre

a. Opening

I cannot live this way forever unless I have, in my grief, [some comfort.]

b. Conclusion of the refrain

[Loyal]ly will I serve Love until death.

The turning points in the melody emphasize C, E, and G, which are also the only notes approached by skip in this mostly stepwise melody. The mode and melodic direction are unmistakable and the next cadence easy to anticipate. As we will see, Ockeghem's melodic style is more diffuse and meandering, its tonal direction less clear, and its course harder to predict.

Popularity and reworkings   Many chansons by Busnoys and Ockeghem were quite popular, appearing frequently in manuscripts and prints from many different countries. Chansons at this time were freely altered, rearranged, and transcribed for instruments. Some tunes were adapted in new settings by numerous composers or were used as the basis for cantus-firmus masses. The large number of reworkings of chansons by these composers testifies to their popularity.

Range   **MASSES** Most of Ockeghem's thirteen masses and both of Busnoys's two surviving masses are for four voices, as are most of Du Fay's. Yet in the masses of

EXAMPLE 9.2 *Comparison of ranges in masses by Du Fay and Ockeghem*

a. Du Fay, Missa Se la face ay pale

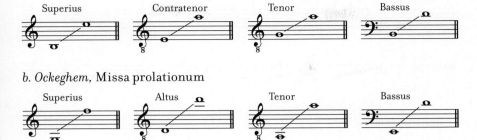

b. Ockeghem, Missa prolationum

Ockeghem and Busnoys, the voice parts cover wider ranges than in Du Fay's. The bassus, which before 1450 was rarely notated below *c,* now extends downward to *G* or *F,* and sometimes lower. Each voice now typically extends a twelfth, thirteenth, or more, rather than a ninth, tenth, or eleventh as in earlier polyphony. Example 9.2 compares the vocal ranges of Du Fay's *Missa Se la face ay pale* (NAWM 37b) with those of Ockeghem's *Missa prolationum* (NAWM 39), showing the expansion in the compass of individual voices, mostly into lower ranges. Through these changes Ockeghem creates a fuller, darker texture than we find in Du Fay's works. But like Du Fay, he varies the sonority in his masses by writing some passages or sections as trios or duets, often contrasting upper and lower voices in pairs.

Seven of Ockeghem's masses and both of Busnoys's use a cantus firmus, often deployed in a highly individual manner. For example, Ockeghem's *Missa De plus en plus* takes as its cantus firmus the tenor of Binchois's chanson *De plus en plus* (NAWM 34). Ockeghem follows custom by placing the cantus firmus in the tenor but freely paraphrases it, changing the rhythm, adding notes, and giving the tenor a character much closer to the other voices than we find in Du Fay's cantus-firmus masses. Such use of paraphrase recalls the plainchant paraphrases in Dunstable's *Regina caeli laetare* (see Example 8.3) and Du Fay's hymns in fauxbourdon (see NAWM 36), only now the paraphrased melody is in the tenor rather than the cantus. Most of Ockeghem's other masses are motto masses, unified by a common head motive; one is a plainsong mass, as is his Requiem (Mass for the Dead).

Cantus-firmus masses

Two of Ockeghem's masses show exceptional compositional virtuosity. *Missa cuiusvis toni* (Mass in any mode) can be sung in mode 1, 3, 5, or 7 by reading the music according to one of four different clef combinations and using musica ficta to avoid tritones. His *Missa prolationum,* a technical tour de force, is notated in two voices but sung in four, using the four prolations of mensural notation (see Chapter 6). Example 9.3a shows the original notation and 9.3b the transcription for the opening of the second Kyrie (the full Kyrie is in NAWM 39). Each singer observes the pertinent clef and mensuration sign at the beginning of one of the two written parts. A soprano sings the notes of the superius part in the soprano clef (C clef on the lowest staff line) in the mensuration ₵ (imperfect time and minor prolation, like modern duple meter), while an alto reads the same line using the mezzo-soprano clef (C clef on the second-to-lowest line) in the mensuration ○ (perfect time, minor prolation, like modern triple meter), to produce the top two lines in

Missa cuiusvis toni and Missa prolationum

EXAMPLE 9.3 *Jean de Ockeghem, opening of Kyrie II from* Missa prolationum

a. Original notation

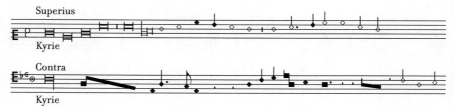

b. Transcription

Example 9.3b. The tenor and bass read the contra part in a similar fashion to produce the bottom two lines.

Canon   Deriving two or more voices from a single notated voice is known as **canon** (Latin for "rule"). The instruction or rule by which these further parts were derived was also called a canon. The rule might instruct the second voice to sing the same melody starting a certain number of beats or measures after the original at the same or a different pitch, as in the kind of canon most familiar today; the second voice might be the **inversion** of the first (moving by the same intervals but in the opposite direction); or it might be the original voice in **retrograde** (backward). The type of canon used in *Missa prolationum,* in which two voices simultaneously sing from the same part but use differing durations because they are applying different mensuration signs, is known as a **mensuration canon**. Each movement is also a *double canon,* with two canons sung or played simultaneously.

Musicians valued canonic works for the ingenuity and skill they displayed. But the techniques were often artfully hidden, unlikely to be noticed by most who heard the music. *Missa prolationum* has been prized for over five hundred years for addressing two audiences simultaneously and spectacularly well: the singers and other musical connoisseurs (including patrons who received presentation manuscripts), who enjoy puzzling out the canons from the written music; and listeners, who may be largely unaware of the canons but hear a beautiful succession of sounds.

The passage in Example 9.3 illustrates a characteristic feature of Ockeghem's music: phrases are often long, and cadences are frequently elided or overlapped by other voices, creating a more continuous flow than is typical of Du Fay's music. For instance, near the end of the example the superius and tenor form a cadence on A decorated by a suspension, but the altus elides it by moving to F. By contrast, Du Fay's *Missa Se la face ay pale* is frequently articulated by cadences. Ockeghem's melodies are also more diffuse than those of Du Fay or Busnoys; in comparison with the clear melodic direction of the cantus in Busnoys's *Je ne puis vivre* in Example 9.1a, Ockeghem's superius in Example 9.3b gives no hint that its final cadential goal is F, and it is harder to predict what the next note will be, where the next phrase will end, or on what note. What he emphasizes instead is decoration and drive, especially the rhythmic intensification that moves his counterpoint forward toward the final cadence of a piece or section.

SOURCE READING

In Memory of Ockeghem

It was customary in the fifteenth century to compose laments on the death of famous musicians. The best known is Jean Molinet's lament for Ockeghem, set to music by Josquin Desprez, which portrays Ockeghem as the "good father" of the next generation of composers, including Josquin, Pierre de la Rue, Antoine Brumel, and Loyset Compère.

Nymphs of the woods, goddesses of the
    fountains,
Skilled singers of all nations,
Change your voices so clear and proud
To sharp cries and lamentations.
For Death, terrible despot,
Has ensnared your Ockeghem in his trap.
True treasurer of music and masterpiece,
Learned, elegant in appearance, and not
    stout;
Great pity that the earth should cover
    him.
Dress yourselves in clothes of mourning,
Josquin, Piersson, Brumel, Compère,
And weep great tears from your eyes:
For you have lost your good father.
Requiescat in pace [rest in peace]. Amen.

Jean Molinet, Déploration sur le trépas de Jean Ockeghem.

INFLUENCE Busnoys and especially Ockeghem profoundly influenced the next generation of composers (see Source Reading). The new features in their music, including greater equality of voices, more use of imitation, and expansion of range, were extended by their successors and became characteristic of the sixteenth century. Older elements, such as the *formes fixes* and reliance on a structural tenor or cantus-tenor scaffolding, disappeared in the next generation, replaced by new methods that were themselves made possible by the changes Ockeghem and Busnoys had introduced.

THE GENERATION OF 1480–1520

The three most eminent figures in the generation of Franco-Flemish composers born around the middle of the fifteenth century were Jacob Obrecht (1457/8–1505), Henricus Isaac (or Heinrich Isaac, ca. 1450–1517), and

Josquin Desprez (ca. 1450–1521). All were born and trained in the Low Countries. All traveled widely, working at courts and churches in different parts of Europe, including Italy. Their careers illustrate the lively interchange between Franco-Flemish and Italian centers, and their music combines northern and southern elements: the serious tone, focus on structure, intricate polyphony, rhythmic variety, and flowing, melismatic melodies of the north with the lighter mood, homophonic textures, more dancelike rhythms, and more clearly articulated phrases typical of Italian music in the decades around 1500. Traits of this generation can be illustrated with works by Obrecht and Isaac before considering the career and music of Josquin at greater length.

GENERAL CHARACTERISTICS Composers active around 1480–1520 shared many elements of style. The structure of vocal works was now largely determined by the text. Four-voice texture was now standard, and five or six voices were sometimes employed as well, with all voices similar in melodic style and nearly equal in importance. Imitative counterpoint and homophony were the most common textures. When imitation appeared, it typically involved most or all voices.

The preference for full harmonies, smooth melodies, and motivic relationships between voices made it necessary to compose all the parts phrase by phrase, rather than layering voices around the framework of a cantus-tenor duet. The foundational role of the tenor was gradually replaced by the bass, as the lowest voice in the harmony. Full triadic sonorities predominated throughout and began to replace open fifths and octaves at cadences. Borrowed melodies were still used frequently but were often distributed among the voices, rather than confined to the tenor or superius. The mass and motet continued to be the predominant sacred genres. Breaking away from the *formes fixes*, composers cast chansons in new shapes. Pieces without text and apparently conceived for instruments became more common (see Chapter 12), although they were still far outnumbered by vocal works. Hidden structural devices gave way to immediately perceptible forms based on a succession of clearly articulated phrases, whether imitative or homophonic in texture. These trends gave composers greater flexibility and allowed them to communicate with a wide audience.

FIGURE 9.3 *Jacob Obrecht in a portrait from 1496 by an anonymous Flemish painter.*

KIMBELL ART MUSEUM/ART RESOURCE, NY

JACOB OBRECHT Obrecht, shown in Figure 9.3, was the son of a trumpeter for the city of Ghent and the Burgundian court, who probably trained him in improvised counterpoint. After becoming a priest, Obrecht worked at churches in Bergen op Zoom, Bruges, and Antwerp. In 1504 he was appointed *maestro di cappella* (master of the chapel) for Duke Ercole d'Este at Ferrara, who unfortunately died the next year, followed by Obrecht himself. Obrecht composed about thirty masses, twenty-seven motets, and numerous chansons, songs in Dutch, and instrumental pieces. Each mass is based on a cantus firmus (sometimes two or more in combination), and he treats the borrowed material in a great variety of ways.

EXAMPLE 9.4 *Jacob Obrecht, opening of Gloria from* Missa Fortuna desperata

And on earth peace to men of good will.

Like other composers of his generation, Obrecht used imitation more fre- | *Imitation*
quently and extensively than did earlier composers. Example 9.4 shows the
opening of the Gloria of his *Missa Fortuna desperata,* in which three voices
enter at two-measure intervals with the same melody in three different
octaves, each singing the same text, then continue with free counterpoint.
Such a series of imitative entrances is called a ***point of imitation***. Throughout the mass, imitative passages at the octave, fifth, and fourth are interspersed with nonimitative ones.

The music is remarkable for its clarity and comprehensibility. The tonal | *Clarity*
center on F is clear at the outset and confirmed by a series of cadences (measures 7, 9, and 11). The melodic ideas are relatively short and well defined. The
text is clearly declaimed with appropriate accentuation and is repeated in each
voice, making it easier to understand. The voices enter at even time intervals,
reinforcing the meter. The rhythm is at first regular, then quickens with smaller
values and mild syncopation. The counterpoint is smooth and consonant,
enlivened by suspensions and passing and neighbor tones, and the last cadence
is adorned by a brief run in parallel sixths (measures 11–12). All of these factors
give the music immediate appeal and help to make its structure and shape easily apparent to the listener, in contrast to the concealed canons and overlapped
cadences we noted in Ockeghem's music. We can draw a parallel between the
clearly audible structure in music like this and the tendency in Renaissance
architecture to make the structure of buildings apparent to an observer by highlighting their floors, pillars, and arches (see Figure 7.3).

ROLE OF IMITATION Comparing this passage from Obrecht to earlier pieces reveals the development of imitation during the fifteenth century. Brief moments of imitation appear in Du Fay's *Resvellies vous* and *Missa Se la face ay pale* (see the commentary in NAWM 35 and 37b), but they are short, typically involve only two voices, may occur in the middle of a phrase, and remain incidental to the fixed form of the ballade and to the cantus-firmus structure of the mass. In the generation of Busnoys and Ockeghem, when imitation occurs it is often more extensive, sometimes involving all voices and longer phrases as in the opening of Busnoys's virelai *Je ne puis vivre* (NAWM 38 and Example 9.1a), but it is still not the primary creator of the form. For Obrecht and his contemporaries, points of imitation in all voices are frequent, and stringing together a series of them interspersed with other textures became a common way of organizing a piece and remained so throughout the sixteenth century.

According to recent research by Julie Cumming, Peter Schubert, and others, the growing prominence of imitation resulted from musicians' training and changes in taste. Choirboys and apprentice instrumentalists learned how to improvise counterpoint, and theoretical descriptions from the time combined with the patterns evident in notated music suggest that they were taught rules for what intervals to use to craft melodies that could be imitated at the octave, fifth, or fourth. Composers trained in this improvisatory tradition could create imitative passages readily, without using a score to coordinate the parts. At the same time, an increasing preference for intelligibility and repetition rather than complexity and change gave imitation a new role, as a way to repeat motives, highlight text, and weave longer sections by varying a small amount of material.

Imitation is related to canon, which we have seen since the thirteenth-century rota *Sumer is icumen in* (NAWM 23) and the fourteenth-century caccia, and which Renaissance and later composers continued to use, often in ingenious ways. Yet imitation differs from canon in that the voices are similar but not the same; they may be identical for a few notes or a whole phrase, but at some point the melodies diverge, creating variety and allowing cadences or changes of texture, as in Example 9.4. Canons can be hard to follow by ear if the canonic melody is long, like that in Landini's caccia *Così pensoso* (NAWM 30), or if the relationship between voices is complex, as in the mensuration canons in Ockeghem's *Missa prolationum*. But imitation is immediately audible, a way of repeating a phrase of text and music in various voices, helping it become familiar to the listener, and elaborating it into a larger unit of music. This is why it became one of the principal tools for composers in Obrecht's generation and remained so throughout the Renaissance.

HENRICUS ISAAC Isaac worked as singer and composer at three institutions in Florence—the Cathedral, the Baptistery of San Giovanni, and the Church of Santissima Annunziata—from about 1484 to 1492 and as court composer for Holy Roman emperor Maximilian I at Vienna and Innsbruck beginning in 1497, later returning to Florence. His familiarity with Italian and German music as well as French, Flemish, and Netherlandish idioms made his output more pan-European than that of his contemporaries. His sacred works include about thirty-five masses, fifty motets, and *Choralis Constantinus,* a monumental three-volume cycle of settings of the texts and melodies of the Proper for most of the church year, comparable in its scope to the *Magnus* *liber organi* (see Chapter 5). Alongside his sacred music, Isaac wrote a large number of songs with French, Italian, and German texts and many short, chanson-like pieces that appear without words in the sources and are presumably for instrumental ensemble.

Puer natus est (NAWM 40) from *Choralis Constantinus* is based on the text and melody of the Introit from the Mass for Christmas Day (NAWM 3a). Comparing Isaac's motet to the settings of the Gradual *Viderunt omnes* by Leoninus (NAWM 17) and Perotinus (NAWM 19) demonstrates a totally different conception of how to elaborate a chant. Where the Notre Dame composers set in polyphony only the portions sung by soloists, leaving the choral portions as plainchant, Isaac does the reverse: the opening phrases of the antiphon and psalm verse are sung in chant by the cantor, and the rest is treated polyphonically. And in the polyphonic portions, instead of placing the chant in long notes in the tenor and adding more-active lines above it, Isaac paraphrases each phrase of the chant in turn and treats it in a point of imitation. We have seen paraphrase before, in settings of chant by Dunstable (Example 8.3) and Du Fay (NAWM 36). What is new here is the presence of the source melody in all four voices, suffusing the texture. Example 9.5 shows the second phrase of the chant compared with the beginning of Isaac's motet, where each voice in turn states the melody for "et filius" in even notes and then the bottom three voices repeat it in slightly embellished paraphrase, using imitation at the unison, octave, and fifth. The motet continues as a series of overlapping phrases, mostly points of imitation between three or all four voices, while constantly varying the time intervals and pitch intervals between imitative entries.

In Florence, Isaac encountered songs in predominantly homophonic style,

Choralis Constantinus

Homophony

EXAMPLE 9.5 *Henricus Isaac,* Puer natus est

a. Chant melody

and a Son is given to us:

b. Opening of motet

EXAMPLE 9.6 *Canto carnascialesco (carnival song)*, Orsu, orsu, car' Signori

Come on, come on, dear sirs, whoever wants his documents done quickly, [come to us, for we are scribes.]

such as the *canti carnascialeschi* (carnival songs) used in the festive processions and pageants that marked the holiday seasons. Florentine trade guilds promoted their products in tuneful verses sung from elaborate floats. In an early example of the singing commercial, the scribes of Florence advertised their services in the anonymous *Orsu, orsu, car' Signori*. As shown in Example 9.6, the voices mostly sing the words together, with occasional suggestions of imitation as in the tenor at measure 3.

Isaac later adapted this simple Italian style for some of his German **Lieder** (songs), four-part settings of popular songs or newly composed melodies in similar style. In his setting of *Innsbruck, ich muss dich lassen* (NAWM 41) shown in Example 9.7, the melody is in the superius and the other parts move in very similar rhythm, as in the Italian songs. Rests separate the phrases, and cadences resolve to full triads rather than open sonorities. The clear structure and sweet harmony of Isaac's Lied make it immediately appealing.

Homophonic texture became an important part of sixteenth-century polyphonic music, alongside and often alternating with the imitative texture we have seen in Obrecht's mass and Isaac's motet. It is no paradox that the music of this and later generations is both more imitative and more often homophonic than that of Ockeghem's generation; both imitation and homophony were facilitated by the greater freedom available to composers, as the traditional layering of voices around a cantus-tenor duet was replaced by composition of all voices in relation to one another.

TEXT SETTING The pieces by Obrecht and Isaac discussed here exemplify the great concern that composers of their generation had for fitting music to the words. They carefully matched accents in the music to those in the text and wanted the words to be heard and understood. This meant that the task of aligning the words with the music could no longer be left to singers during a performance, as in earlier music, and thus that parts had to have the text underlaid (positioned under the music) clearly and completely. The florid lines of Ockeghem and his contemporaries gave way to mostly syllabic settings, in which a phrase of text could be grasped as an uninterrupted thought.

EXAMPLE 9.7 *Isaac,* Innsbruck, ich muss dich lassen, *opening*

Innsbruck, I must leave you, I travel on my way to a foreign land.

JOSQUIN DESPREZ

Few musicians have enjoyed higher renown or exercised greater influence than Josquin Desprez (ca. 1450–1521; see biography and Figure 9.4 on p. 194). He held a series of prestigious positions at courts and churches in France and Italy. His compositions appeared in a larger number of manuscripts and printed collections than any other composer before 1550. Ottaviano Petrucci, the first printer of polyphonic music, published three books of Josquin masses and reprinted each to meet the demand; no other composer received more than a single volume from Petrucci. Contemporaries hailed Josquin as "the best of the composers of our time" and "the father of musicians." In 1538, Martin Luther proclaimed that "Josquin is the master of the notes. They must do as he wills; as for the other composers, they have to do as the notes will." A generation after his death, writers praised his music for expressing emotions, and humanist scholars compared him to Virgil and Michelangelo as an artist without peer in his art (see Source Readings, p. 195). Such praise reflects not only on Josquin but on his time, for it shows the greatly increased interest during the Renaissance in the individual artist and artwork and in the power of music to express feelings and ideas, a topic to which we will return (see pp. 199–200).

Composers from his time through the late sixteenth century emulated

JOSQUIN DESPREZ [JOSSEQUIN LEBLOITTE DIT DESPREZ]

(ca. 1450–1521)

Josquin (known by his given name rather than by his family name) is regarded as the greatest composer of his time. His motets, masses, and songs were widely sung, praised, and emulated in his lifetime and for decades after his death.

Josquin's biography has been clarified by recent research, but there are still gaps. Historians recently discovered his family name, Lebloitte, from a will leaving him a house and land in Condé-sur-l'Escaut, now in Belgium. He was born near Ath in the county of Hainaut, where his father and grandfather were policemen, and was trained as a choirboy in Condé and Cambrai. He served in the chapel of René, duke of Anjou, at Aix-en-Provence in the late 1470s. After René's death in 1480, his singers transferred to the service of King Louis XI at Sainte Chapelle in Paris, and Josquin may have been among them.

Josquin spent several years in Italy, serving members of the Sforza family, rulers of Milan (1484–85 and 1489), and in the Sistine Chapel choir in Rome (1489–94 or later). Evidence for his whereabouts in the next few years is scant. He was appointed maestro di cappella to Duke Ercole I d'Este in Ferrara in 1503 at the highest salary in the history of that chapel. A recruiter for the duke had recommended Isaac instead, noting that although Josquin was a better composer,

FIGURE 9.4 *Josquin Desprez, in a woodcut from Petrus Opmeer,* Opus chronographicum *(Antwerp, 1611). Opmeer based his portrait on an oil painting that once stood in Ste. Gudule church in Brussels but was destroyed in the 1570s.*

he demanded a higher salary and composed only when he wanted to and not when asked; the duke hired Josquin anyway, no doubt aware of the prestige to be gained by employing the best musician available. Josquin left after a year, apparently to escape the plague. From 1504 until his death in 1521, he resided at Condé-sur-l'Escaut, where he was provost at the church of Notre Dame.

MAJOR WORKS At least 18 masses, more than 50 motets, about 65 chansons (about 10 for instruments), and numerous doubtfully attributed works

and reworked Josquin's music. Some works were recopied, published, and performed for almost a century after his death, a rare honor at a time when most music more than a few decades old was unavailable or deemed unworthy of performance. His music was so esteemed and popular that publishers and copyists often attributed works of other composers to him, prompting one wag to comment that "now that Josquin is dead, he is putting out more works than when he was alive." Historians are still sorting out which pieces are truly his.

CHANSONS Josquin's chansons show the characteristics of the late-fifteenth-century style seen in Obrecht and Isaac, including clarity in phrasing, form, and pitch organization; fluid and tuneful melodies; use of imitation

Praise for Josquin

Josquin had a remarkably lofty reputation throughout the sixteenth century. Decades after his death, German publisher Hans Ott praised Josquin's ability to move the feelings of the listener, music theorist Heinrich Glareanus compared him to the Latin epic poet Virgil, and humanist scholar Cosimo Bartoli compared him to Michelangelo, saying both were without peer.

❖

All will easily recognize Josquin as the most celebrated hero of the art of music, for he possesses something that is truly inimitable and divine. Nor will a grateful and honest posterity begrudge him this praise.

In the earlier of the books we put forth Psalm 51 [Josquin's motet *Miserere mei, Deus*]. I beg whether anyone can listen so carelessly as not to be moved in his whole spirit and whole intellect towards contemplating the message of the Prophet more carefully, since the melodies conform to the feelings of one who is burdened by the magnitude of his sin, and [since] the very deliberate repetition by which [the sinner] begs for mercy does not permit the soul either to reflect idly or to fail to be moved toward hope of assurance.

Hans Ott, introductions to *Novum et insigne opus musicum* (1537) and *Secundus tomus novi operis musici* (1538). Translations from Stephanie Schlagel, "The *Liber selectarum cantionum* and the 'German Josquin Renaissance,'" *Journal of Musicology* 19 (Fall 2002): 590–91.

❖

No one has more effectively expressed the passions of the soul in music than this symphonist, no one has more felicitously begun, no one has been able to compete in grace and facility on an equal footing with him, just as there is no Latin poet superior in the epic to Maro [Virgil]. For just as Maro, with his natural facility, was accustomed to adapt his poem to his subject so as to set weighty matters before the eyes of his readers with close-packed spondees, fleeting ones with unmixed dactyls, to use words suited to his every subject, in short, to undertake nothing inappropriately, as Flaccus says of Homer, so our Josquin, where his matter requires it, now advances with impetuous and precipitate notes, now intones his subject in long-drawn tones, and, to sum up, has brought forth nothing that was not delightful to the ear and approved as ingenious by the learned, nothing, in short, that was not acceptable and pleasing, even when it seemed less erudite, to those who listened to it with judgment.... His talent is beyond description, more easily admired than properly explained.

From Heinrich Glareanus, *Dodecachordon* (Basel, 1547), Book 3, Chapter 24. Trans. Oliver Strunk, in SR 70 (3:35), p. 430.

❖

I know well that Ockeghem was, so to speak, the first who in these times rediscovered music, which had almost entirely died out—not unlike Donatello, who in his times rediscovered sculpture—and that Josquin, Ockeghem's pupil, may be said to have been, in music, a prodigy of nature, as our Michelangelo Buonarotti has been in architecture, painting, and sculpture; for, just as there has not yet been anyone who in his compositions approaches Josquin, so Michelangelo, among all those who have been active in these arts, is still alone and without peer. Both of them have opened the eyes of all those who delight in these arts or will delight in them in the future.

Cosimo Bartoli, *Ragionamenti accademici* (Venice, 1567). Trans. adapted from Gustave Reese, *Music in the Renaissance*, rev. ed. (New York: W. W. Norton, 1959), 259–60.

and homophony; and careful declamation of the text. Composers of his generation virtually abandoned the *formes fixes,* choosing instead strophic texts and brief four- or five-line poems. Rather than three voices, most chansons now have four, five, or six voices, all meant to be sung. Instead of a layered counterpoint with the cantus-tenor pair providing the skeleton and the other voices filling in, as in chansons from Machaut through Ockeghem, all the parts are now of equal melodic interest and essential to the counterpoint.

A look at two examples can only begin to suggest the variety of Josquin's chansons. *Faulte d'argent* (NAWM 42), from the late 1490s or early 1500s, is a five-voice setting of an existing popular monophonic song. This may be one of Josquin's earliest songs to use five voices, helping to set a trend for songs for five or six voices that continued throughout the sixteenth century. The text is brief and humorous, complaining that lack of money brings sorrow without equal, whereas having money will attract even a sleeping woman. The source melody appears in a canon between the tenor and the *quinta pars* (fifth voice), which follows it a fifth below. Around these canonic voices weave the other three parts, which participate in points of imitation on phrases of the borrowed tune and accompany it with new contrapuntal lines that are at times themselves treated in imitation. Josquin varies the number and grouping of voices to create almost constant changes of texture. The presence of the borrowed melody in all voices, whether exact or in paraphrase, and the almost constant use of imitation give this song a very different sound and style from earlier settings that use a borrowed tune as a cantus firmus. Throughout, Josquin freely repeats phrases of text, a practice that became customary in the sixteenth century, and for the most part sets the text syllabically, with some melismas at the ends of phrases.

Mille regretz (NAWM 43) is a four-voice chanson attributed to Josquin that has become one of his most frequently performed works, although his authorship has been questioned by some scholars. He apparently composed it for emperor Charles V around 1520 and presented it personally. The texture alternates between homophony and imitation and features ever-changing combinations of two, three, or four voices. Each phrase of text receives its own particular treatment, as illustrated in Example 9.8: four-voice homophony for "Jay si grand dueil"; a pair of voices answered by another pair for the next phrase; and four-voice imitation for "Quon me verra."

MOTETS Like his chansons, Josquin's more than fifty motets exemplify the diversity of his style. While masses always set the same words, texts for motets were quite varied, drawn from the Mass Proper or other sources, and invited a variety of treatment. Like chansons and masses, motets could be based on borrowed material or newly composed, and many of the same techniques appear in all three genres, from imitation and homophony to cantus firmus and paraphrase.

We can see Josquin's approach in *Ave Maria . . . virgo serena* (NAWM 44) from about 1485, one of his earliest and most popular motets. The words are drawn from three different texts, all addressed to the Virgin Mary: the opening lines of a sequence, a

EXAMPLE 9.8 *Josquin,* Mille regretz

Jay si grand dueil et pai - ne dou-lou-reu - se,

se, Jay si grand dueil et pai - ne dou-lou-reu - se,

se, Jay si grand dueil et pai - ne

se, Jay si grand dueil et pai - ne

Quon me ver - ra brief mes jours def -

Quon me ver - ra brief mes jours

dou-lou-reu - se, Quon me ver - ra

dou-lou-reu - se, Quon me ver - ra

I feel so much sadness and such painful distress, that it seems to me my days will soon dwindle away.

hymn in five stanzas hailing the five major feasts for Mary observed each year, and a prayer asking for her aid. The music is perfectly crafted to fit the words. Josquin delineates the form of the text by giving each segment a unique musical treatment and a concluding cadence on the pitch center C.

The texture is constantly changing, as illustrated in Example 9.9. The motet opens with several overlapping points of imitation in which all four voices paraphrase each phrase of the chant sequence melody in turn. When the hymn text begins, the music is no longer based on borrowed material, and the texture shifts to two, three, and all four voices in relatively homophonic phrases. As seen in Example 9.9c, there is diversity even in the styles of homophony: "Ave, cuius conceptio" is set with parallel $\frac{6}{3}$ sonorities that recall fauxbourdon, a style that by the 1480s was several decades old, yet the next phrase is in an up-to-date homophonic style typical of Josquin's own time. Later passages are equally varied. The closing prayer is particularly striking, set in the plainest chordal homophony in long notes, as if to capture the humility and simplicity of sincere prayer. Throughout, the words are declaimed naturally, giving the most accented syllables longer and higher notes in most cases (as at "*ple-*na gaudio") and sometimes emphasizing them with short melismas (as at "*gra*-tia *ple-*na") or syncopation (as at "con-*cep*-tio").

This motet is excellent in many ways at once, with clear projection of the pitch center, clearly delineated phrases and sections, elegant and beautiful counterpoint, variety in texture and style, and sensitive declamation and

EXAMPLE 9.9 *Josquin,* Ave Maria . . . virgo serena

a. Sequence melody

A - ve   Ma - ri - a,   gra - ti - a ple - na.   Do - mi - nus te - cum,   Vir - go se - re - na.

Hail Mary, full of grace, the Lord is with you, serene Virgin.

b. Opening of motet

x = note from sequence

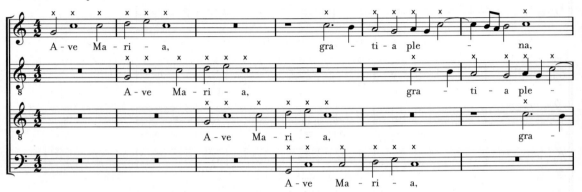

c. Measures 18–22

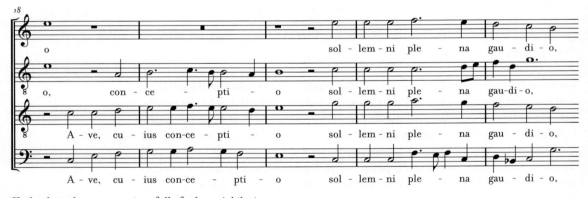

Hail to her whose conception, full of solemn jubilation,

projection of the text. It is no wonder that such music established Josquin as a composer worthy of performance and emulation in his own time and in later generations.

MASSES Josquin's eighteen masses are as varied as his motets and chansons and abound in technical ingenuity. Nine use a secular tune (either monophonic or drawn from a polyphonic chanson) as a cantus firmus. In *Missa L'homme armé super voces musicales,* Josquin transposed the familiar tune *L'homme armé* to successive degrees of the scale—C for the Kyrie, D for the Gloria, and so on—and included a mensuration canon in the Agnus Dei. He also composed masses based on chant, on freely composed double canons, and on subjects derived from solmization syllables. He wrote *Missa Hercules dux Ferrariae* to honor Ercole (Hercules) I, duke of Ferrara, probably while serving the ducal court in 1503–4. He used as a cantus firmus a *soggetto cavato dalle vocali,* a "subject drawn from the vowels" of a phrase by letting each vowel indicate a corresponding solmization syllable:

Her –	cu –	les	dux	Fer –	ra –	ri –	e
re	ut	re	ut	re	fa	mi	re
D	C	D	C	D	F	E	D

Missa Pange lingua (excerpted in NAWM 45) was one of the last masses Josquin composed. He based it on the plainchant hymn *Pange lingua glorioso.* But instead of using the hymn melody as a cantus firmus in the tenor, Josquin paraphrased it in all four voices, in whole or in part, in each movement. We have seen how he used paraphrase in points of imitation at the opening of his motet *Ave Maria . . . virgo serena,* and here he applies the same idea to the mass. Phrases from the hymn melody are adapted as motives that are treated in points of imitation, as in the Kyrie (NAWM 45a) and at the beginning of each movement of the mass. Occasionally, phrases of the hymn are also paraphrased in homophonic declamation, as in the setting of "Et incarnatus est" in the Credo (NAWM 45b). Each movement resembles a motet of Josquin's time, featuring a series of independent phrases in imitative or homophonic textures without a cantus firmus. A mass like this, based on a monophonic melody that is paraphrased and appears in all voices of the mass rather than just in the tenor or superius, has come to be known as a **paraphrase mass**.

Missa Pange lingua

MUSIC AS EXPRESSIVE OF FEELINGS AND IDEAS Writers a generation after Josquin praised him for creating melodies that "conform to the feelings" expressed by the text and for "expressing the passions of the soul in music" (see Source Readings, p. 195). This idea of the expressive powers of music is familiar to us now and was central to music's development from the sixteenth century on, but it was hardly mentioned in the centuries before Josquin. It is worth pausing to consider what musical expression entails and how his music exemplified it.

There are two principal ways that music can reflect the meaning of the words, both of which became common in the sixteenth century: through **text depiction**, using musical gestures to reinforce visual images in the text, and through **text expression**, conveying through music the emotions or overall mood suggested by the text. In the next two chapters, we will see cases of each that are unmistakable and clearly intentional. Can we find them in Josquin? And how will we know we are not reading into music of the past ideas that are foreign to it?

Text depiction and text expression

For a musical gesture or characteristic to be understood as meaningful, it must be marked as somehow different from its surroundings or from other pieces of music in a way that calls for interpretation. The points of imitation on paraphrased melodies that open Josquin's *Ave Maria . . . virgo serena* and suffuse the Kyrie from *Missa Pange lingua* are beautiful to the ear, and may inspire reverence by dwelling on a chant melody, but they do not seem markedly more expressive of emotions or suggestive of an image than other music we have encountered; rather, they appear to be applications of compositional techniques that were common at the time and used in many contexts. But there are passages that stand out.

At the end of *Faulte d'argent*, there is a surprising turn of harmony to close on D instead of the expected G, and it seems to parallel the surprising ironic turn in the text at the same point (see commentary in NAWM 42). In *Mille regretz*, the descending lines in all voices at "paine douloureuse" (painful distress) in Example 9.8 and at several other points in the chanson reflect the sadness expressed in the poem through a musical gesture whose declining energy and darkening timbres evoke the depths of grief. In the prayer at the end of *Ave Maria . . . virgo serena*, and in the "Et incarnatus" in *Missa Pange lingua*, the slow, simple, chordal homophony is starkly different from the surrounding fast imitative counterpoint, and seems to signal the focused, quiet feeling of deep prayer.

Some passages suggest visual images as well. In *Mille regretz*, the poetic line that ends with "habandonner" (to abandon or desert you) is left dangling without a proper cadence, as if it had been abandoned. In *Ave Maria . . . virgo serena*, the first time all four voices sing together in rhythmic unison is at the words "solemni plena gaudio" (full of solemn jubilation), and the suddenly full chordal texture evokes fullness (see Example 9.9c). In the Credo of *Missa Pange lingua*, a new burst of energy brings the music back to life at "Et resurrexit" (and was resurrected), with imitative entrances of a triadic figure after a phrase in calm homophony, and "Et ascendit in caelum" (and ascended into Heaven) is set with a point of imitation on an ascending melodic line.

We have to be careful not to read into music of the past our own expectations, formed by our experience of much later music. But it does seem that in these passages, and throughout his music, Josquin uses text expression and text depiction. We will see in forthcoming chapters how both become central themes of the next several centuries.

How new?   Exactly how new were text depiction and text expression in Josquin's time is hard to determine. In some earlier pieces, the music seems to illustrate an image in the text, but so few examples of this survive that we risk hearing something in the music that the composer did not intend, based on our familiarity with later music that does depict the words. Likewise, the idea that music is expressive of emotions is today commonplace and was well known to the ancient Greeks. But it is hard to prove that composers before Josquin meant to evoke emotions through musical rather than poetic means. We have seen that some composers created meanings by singling out certain words for emphasis, as in Dunstable's *Quam pulchra es,* or by using a borrowed melody in a certain way, as in Ockeghem's *Missa Caput* (see Chapter 8), and certainly much sacred polyphony was calculated to inspire awe. Yet before the late fifteenth century there was no consistent method (at least, none we know about) for suggesting happiness, grief, or other emotions through music. The link we now take for granted between music and feelings may have been a contribution by Josquin and his generation, codified in the sixteenth century by musicians and writers influenced by humanist ideals and by ancient ideas of music's emotional effects.

MASSES ON BORROWED MATERIAL

We saw in the previous chapter that composers often based masses on borrowed material, including chant, monophonic songs such as *L'homme armé,* and polyphonic works. Before Josquin's generation, the typical practice was to place the borrowed tune in the tenor of the mass as a cantus firmus, resulting in a cantus-firmus mass. When that tune was drawn from a polyphonic work, the composer had the option of borrowing from other voices as well, as Du Fay did in his *Missa Se la face ay pale,* a type known as a cantus-firmus/imitation mass.

Paraphrase mass

With the change in musical structure near the end of the fifteenth century, from music organized around a structural tenor or cantus-tenor framework to a texture in which all voices were essential to the counterpoint and similar in style, new options opened up for reworking borrowed material without relying on a cantus-firmus structure. Josquin's paraphrase mass *Missa Pange lingua* illustrates a way to rework a monophonic melody in the context of the new style, paraphrasing it in all voices in a series of points of imitation alternating with homophonic passages.

Imitation mass

At the same time that Josquin composed his *Missa Pange lingua,* some of his younger contemporaries developed a new approach to basing a mass on a polyphonic work. Instead of using *one* voice as a cantus firmus, the composer borrows extensively from *all* voices of the model, reworking the model's characteristic motives, points of imitation, and general structure in each movement of the mass. This approach is especially apt when basing a mass on a motet or chanson in the new, predominantly imitative or homophonic styles of Josquin's generation, because in such works the tenor is not the main structural voice, and no one voice would function well as a cantus firmus. Typically, the resemblance to the model is strongest at the beginning and end of each movement, and the composer's craft is demonstrated by the new combinations and variations he can achieve with the borrowed material. A mass composed in this manner is termed an **imitation mass** (or *parody mass*), because it imitates another polyphonic work.

Among the first examples of this new approach is *Missa Ave Maria* by Antoine de Févin (ca. 1470–1511/12), based on Josquin's motet *Ave Maria . . . virgo serena.* From an aristocratic family, Févin was a priest, singer, and composer at the French royal court of Louis XII, where Josquin may also have served, and was described by Glareanus as an emulator of Josquin. At the start of each movement of *Missa Ave Maria,* he reworks the initial points of imitation from Josquin's motet in a different way, so that each offers a new variation on the motet's opening phrases, sometimes at great length. Comparing the beginning of his Agnus Dei in Example 9.10a to the opening of the motet in Example 9.9b, we see that here Févin directly borrows the notes of Josquin's first point of imitation in each voice (marked with x), transposing the bassus up a fourth and moving it earlier, but then more distantly paraphrases the second point of imitation (marked with o). Example 9.10b shows a passage in Févin's Gloria that reworks the homophonic material from Josquin's motet in Example 9.9c into a short imitative duet between the two lower voices—a creative transformation of fauxbourdon style into imitation—followed by fully homophonic declamation. If he was indeed a student or follower of Josquin, Févin learned his lessons well.

Both paraphrase masses and imitation masses feature a series of

EXAMPLE 9.10 *Antoine de Févin,* Missa Ave Maria

a. Opening of Agnus Dei

x = note from Josquin's first point of imitation

o = note from his second point of imitation

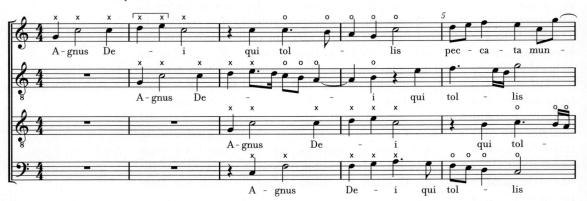

Lamb of God, who takes away the sins of the world

b. Excerpt from Gloria

x = note from Josquin's motet

Lord God, King of Heaven, God the Father almighty. Lord, the only begotten Son

TYPE	CANTUS-FIRMUS MASS	CANTUS-FIRMUS/ IMITATION MASS	PARAPHRASE MASS	IMITATION MASS
EXAMPLE	Anonymous, *Missa Caput*	Du Fay, *Missa Se la face ay pale*	Josquin, *Missa Pange lingua*	Févin, *Missa Ave Maria*
BORROWED MATERIAL	Chant or other melody	Tenor plus parts of other voices from polyphonic work	Chant melody	All voices from polyphonic work
WHERE IS IT USED?	Tenor of mass	Tenor in tenor of mass, others in other voices	All voices of mass	All voices of mass
HOW IS IT USED?	In long notes, as structural cantus firmus	Tenor used as structural cantus firmus, others reworked	Paraphrased and with notes added	Motives, points of imitation, or other elements reworked
MAIN TEXTURE	Stratified, with tenor as structural voice	Stratified, with tenor as structural voice	Imitative, with some homophonic passages	Imitative, with some homophonic passages

FIGURE 9.5 *Approaches to composing masses based on borrowed material.*

independent phrases in imitative or homophonic textures without a structural cantus firmus, but they differ in their source material. Figure 9.5 provides a comparison of these two approaches to the mass with each other and with cantus-firmus and cantus-firmus/imitation masses. Cantus-firmus, paraphrase, and imitation of a polyphonic model are all compositional techniques that were used in motets and chansons as well as in masses, but they can be particularly interesting in masses, where composers have five movements in which to rework their borrowed material in different ways.

Although composers continued to write cantus-firmus masses in the sixteenth century, they turned increasingly to imitation and paraphrase masses because they preferred imitative textures to the structural scaffolding of cantus-firmus technique, which came to be seen as archaic. It is likely that the source material for any mass was chosen for reasons parallel to those for the cantus-firmus mass: to suit a particular religious observance, institution, or saint; to honor a patron; to convey meanings by alluding to the original words of the chanson or motet in the context of the mass; or perhaps, in the case of an imitation mass, to pay homage to another composer through emulation.

OLD AND NEW

The music of the late fifteenth and early sixteenth centuries interweaves old and new elements. In some ways, Ockeghem and Busnoys represent the last climax of medieval thinking in their use of the *formes fixes,* in their long, winding phrases, and in such feats as the mensuration canons in *Missa prolationum.* Yet their music's expanded range, greater equality of voices, increased use of imitation, and freer treatment of borrowed material exemplify new traits that became typical of the next century. Building on these achievements, Josquin and his generation worked with new freedom in a polyphonic idiom based on equal, vocally conceived lines, moving now in points of imitation, now in homophony, responding to the shape, accentuation, and meaning of the text. At the same time, they continued to draw on tradition, further developing the established genres of mass, motet, and chanson and finding new applications for inherited techniques from canon to cantus firmus, paraphrase, and other methods for reworking existing music.

Ockeghem, Busnoys, Obrecht, Isaac, and Josquin were all acclaimed in life and after death. Yet only a few of Ockeghem's works were known in the middle to late sixteenth century, chiefly virtuoso canonic works like *Missa prolationum* cited in theoretical treatises. The music of Obrecht, Isaac, and Josquin continued in circulation for longer, in part because the stylistic changes they helped to introduce made earlier music sound old-fashioned. Josquin's works were performed and emulated through the end of the sixteenth century, aided by the new technology of music printing that emerged when he was at the peak of his career. He was less well known in the next two centuries but was never entirely forgotten, perhaps the first composer for whom that was true. Even when his music was no longer performed, it continued to be cited by theorists, and he figured prominently in histories of music written in the late eighteenth and nineteenth centuries. His complete works were transcribed and published beginning in 1921, stimulating a growing number of performances and a constant stream of scholarship. His music is now frequently performed and recorded, and he is viewed as the central composer of his time. The music of his contemporaries, from Ockeghem and Busnoys through Obrecht and Isaac, has also appeared in modern editions, performances, and recordings.

In some respects the musical language of Josquin and his generation is still with us, present in the attentive text setting, imitative and homophonic textures, and rules of counterpoint and voice-leading practiced by composers over the next several centuries. The emotional expressivity and vivid imagery of their music set the standard for succeeding generations, so much so that the history of music from their time to the early twentieth century is more than anything else a history of musical expressivity. It is also, at least in part, the history of exemplary composers and their music. In this too we are heirs of the Renaissance, whose interest in the individual artist is shown in the way Josquin's music was singled out for praise.

Further Reading is available at digital.wwnorton.com/hwm10

MADRIGAL AND SECULAR SONG IN THE SIXTEENTH CENTURY

If fifteenth-century composers forged an international idiom, six-teenth-century musicians cultivated a new flowering of national styles, especially in secular vocal music. Encouraged by patrons at courts and in urban centers, poets and composers in different linguistic regions naturally developed distinctive genres and forms. Music printing fostered the creation and dissemination of music for amateurs to sing for their own pleasure. This music was usually in the vernacular, further encouraging the growth of national styles.

Among the significant national genres of the sixteenth century were the Spanish *villancico*, the Italian *frottola*, and several new types of French chanson. The genre that proved most significant in the long run was the Italian *madrigal*, in which Renaissance composers brought to a peak their intense interest in realizing in music the accents, images, and emotions of the text. Besides influencing later French chansons and German Lieder, madrigals became fashionable in England, joined around the end of the century by the *lute song*. Through the madrigal, Italy and Italian composers became the leading forces in European music for the first time, a role they would maintain for the next two centuries.

THE FIRST MARKET FOR MUSIC

The development of music printing in 1501 (described in Chapter 7) was a technological breakthrough that reduced the labor, and therefore the cost, of producing notated music in multiple copies. This made possible a much wider dissemination of music, but it also changed the economics of music. Prior to this, music was preeminently a service provided by musicians. Now for the first time music, in printed form, could be sold as a commodity.

The new supply of printed music dovetailed with a growing demand for notated music that amateurs could perform for their own enjoyment. People have always made music to entertain themselves and their

FIGURE 10.1 *This anonymous sixteenth-century painting shows a vocal quartet singing from partbooks. The rich costumes suggest that these are aristocratic amateurs performing for their own pleasure in the privacy of an idyllic island.*

friends, but for most of human history they did so without using notation. When notation was invented, it was used for church music and secular music of the aristocracy, as we have seen, leaving few written traces of the music-making of the general populace. In the sixteenth century, first at courts, then among the urban middle classes, the ability to read notation and perform from printed music became an expected social grace. In Baldassare Castiglione's influential *Book of the Courtier* (1528), several speakers praise those who can sing and play from notation (see Source Reading). Paintings from the time, such as the one in Figure 10.1, show singers or instrumentalists reading from published music, usually in the form of partbooks (described in Chapter 7). In such settings, music served as a kind of social glue, an activity friends and family could join in together.

The combination of music printing with the demand for music that amateurs could sing and play created the first market for music, which ranged from relatively elite to more popular genres, styles, and forms. Published music was of course bought by professional musicians for their own use, but music suited to amateur performance sold particularly well, and composers and publishers worked to meet that demand. In vocal music, amateurs were most interested in singing in their own language, reinforcing an already evident trend toward diverse national genres and styles.

SPAIN

THE VILLANCICO In the late fifteenth century, during Ferdinand and Isabella's campaign to unify and invigorate Spain, Ferdinand and others at Spanish courts encouraged the development of a uniquely Spanish music. They especially cultivated the ***villancico***, which became the most important form of secular polyphonic song in Renaissance Spain. The name is a diminutive of *villano* (peasant), the texts were usually on rustic subjects, and the form

On Reading and Performing Music

Baldassare Castiglione (1478–1529) was a courtier, ambassador, and poet. His most influential work was *The Book of the Courtier* (1528), a manual on proper behavior at court in the guise of conversations at the ducal palace in Urbino. The ability to sing and play from notation was expected.

✿

The Count began again: "Gentlemen, you must know that I am not satisfied with our Courtier unless he be also a musician, and unless, besides understanding and being able to read music, he can play various instruments. For, if we rightly consider,

no rest from toil and no medicine for ailing spirits can be found more decorous or praiseworthy in time of leisure than this; and especially in courts where, besides the release from vexations which music gives to all, many things are done to please the ladies, whose tender and delicate spirits are readily penetrated with harmony and filled with sweetness. Hence, it is no wonder that in both ancient and modern times they have always been particularly fond of musicians, finding music a most welcome food for the spirit."

Baldesar Castiglione, *The Book of the Courtier*, trans. Charles S. Singleton (Garden City, NY: Doubleday, 1959), 74.

and style of the poetry had antecedents in popular songs, yet villancicos were composed for the aristocracy. Short, strophic, syllabic, and mostly homophonic, they reflect a growing preference for simplicity and for what were considered more-authentic representations of Spanish culture.

The form of the villancico varies in its details but always includes a refrain *Form and* (*estribillo*) and one or more stanzas (*coplas*). The stanzas typically begin with *performance* a new section (*mudanza*, "change") with two statements of a contrasting idea and conclude with a return to the music of the refrain (*vuelta*), following the AAB stanza structure that we have seen in so many types of song since the Middle Ages. Most often, only the last line of the refrain text recurs at the end of each stanza. The principal melody is always in the top voice; the others may have been sung or performed on instruments. During the sixteenth century, publishers issued many collections of villancicos in arrangements for solo voice with lute. In later centuries, the form was often used for sacred compositions (see Chapter 16).

Juan del Encina (1468–1529), the first Spanish playwright, was a leading *Juan del Encina* composer of villancicos. Like other poets and dramatists of his time, Encina was interested in **pastoral** themes borrowed from ancient Greek and Roman literature, depicting an idealized world of shepherds and other rustic figures in benign and beautiful rural landscapes. His *eclogues,* one-act pastoral plays that mark the beginning of Spanish secular drama, each include villancicos at the midpoint and at the end. His *Oy comamos y bebamos* (NAWM 46) concludes a play performed on the day before Lent begins, in which shepherds prepare and eat a feast. In this final villancico, they exhort each other and their listeners to eat, drink, and sing because tomorrow begins a season of fasting. The music is simple in melody and harmony, with dancelike rhythms marked by frequent hemiolas.

ITALY

THE FROTTOLA An Italian counterpart to the villancico was the *frottola* (pl. *frottole*), a four-part strophic song set syllabically and homophonically, with the melody in the upper voice, marked rhythmic patterns, and simple diatonic harmonies consisting almost entirely of what we would call root-position triads. The genre included several subtypes, of which some had fixed forms while others were free. The music of the frottola was essentially a tune for singing the poetry, marking the end of each line with a cadence, with the lower parts providing a harmonic foundation. Indeed, the frottola grew out of a tradition of singing poetry to an improvised melody while accompanying oneself by playing a tenor line on an instrument. The change to a notated genre made songs available to those not able to improvise their own, and at the same time allowed expansion to a four-part musical texture.

Like villancicos, frottole featured simple music and earthy and satirical texts, but were neither folk nor popular songs. Rather, they were mock-popular songs written for the amusement of the courtly elite. Frottole were cultivated in the late fifteenth and early sixteenth centuries at Italian courts such as Mantua, Ferrara, and Urbino, whose rulers encouraged musical settings of Italian poetry. They were composed almost exclusively by Italian composers, chief among them Marchetto Cara (ca. 1465–1525) and Bartolomeo Tromboncino (ca. 1470–after 1534), both active at the Mantuan court. Isabella d'Este, wife of the marquis of Mantua, was an especially important patron: she encouraged the development of the frottola, corresponded with Italian poets, and spurred musicians at her court to set their poems to music. Figure 10.2 shows a drawing of Isabella prepared by Leonardo da Vinci for an intended portrait. Petrucci published thirteen collections of frottole between 1504 and 1514, testifying to the vogue for the genre among his well-to-do customers.

Performance Usually the top voice was sung, while the other parts were either sung or played on instruments. Beginning in 1509, Francisco Bossinensis published collections of frottole by various composers in arrangements for voice and lute. With the lute carrying the lower parts, the solo singer could improvise melismatic flourishes at principal cadences.

SCALA/ART RESOURCE, NY

FIGURE 10.2 *Isabella d'Este as depicted by Leonardo da Vinci.*

THE ITALIAN MADRIGAL

More enduring than the frottola was the **madrigal**, the most important secular genre of sixteenth-century Italy and arguably of the entire Renaissance. What made the madrigal so appealing in its time and so influential on later generations was the emphasis composers placed on enriching the meaning and impact of the text through the musical setting. In the madrigal, composers explored new effects of declamation, imagery, expressivity, characterization, and dramatization that paved the way for future dramatic forms such as opera. Through the madrigal, Italy became the leader in European music for the first time in history.

The term *madrigal* was used from about 1530 on for musical settings of Italian poetry of various types, from sonnets to free forms. Most madrigal texts consist of a single stanza with seven- or eleven-syllable lines and either a standard or free rhyme scheme. There are no refrains or repeated lines, distinguishing the sixteenth-century madrigal from the frottola, from the old *formes fixes*, and from the fourteenth-century madrigal (described in Chapter 6), which it resembles in name only. The typical sixteenth-century madrigal is **through-composed**, that is, with new music for every line of poetry.

Definition and form

Composers frequently chose texts by major poets, including Francesco Petrarca (1304–1374), Ludovico Ariosto (1474–1533), Torquato Tasso (1544–1595), Giovanni Battista Guarini (1538–1612), and Giovan Battista Marino (1569–1625). The subject matter was sentimental or erotic, with scenes and allusions borrowed from pastoral poetry. Madrigals were a form of social play, and the best poems interwove vivid imagery and description with themes of love, sex, and wit that could charm, surprise, amuse, and entertain.

Poetry

Composers dealt freely with the poetry, using a variety of homophonic and contrapuntal textures in a series of overlapping sections, each based on a single phrase of text, with all voices playing essentially equal roles. In these respects, madrigals resemble motets of the same era. Most important, madrigal composers aimed to match the artfulness of the poetry and to convey its ideas, images, and emotions to the performers and listeners. Text expression was of paramount importance, and text depiction reached new heights, ranging from witty to profound and from obvious to subtle.

Music

Most early madrigals, from about 1520 to 1540, were for four voices. By midcentury five voices became the rule, and six or more were not unusual. When voices were added to the traditional cantus, altus, tenor, and bassus, they were usually labeled by number in Latin: *quintus* for the fifth voice, *sextus* for the sixth. The word "voices" should be taken literally: a madrigal was a piece of vocal chamber music intended for performance with one singer to a part. As always in the sixteenth century, however, music could be adapted to the forces available, and instruments often doubled the voices or took their place. The painting by Caravaggio in Figure 10.3 shows what must have been a common manner of performing madrigals: a young man sings one line while improvising a lute accompaniment from what he remembers of the other parts, using the bass part as a guide.

Voices

Madrigals were chiefly sung for the enjoyment of the singers themselves, typically in mixed groups of women and men at social gatherings, after meals, and at meetings of academies (societies organized to discuss literary, scientific, or artistic matters). The demand for madrigals was great: counting reprints and new editions, some two thousand collections were published between 1530 and 1600, and their popularity continued well

FIGURE 10.3 *Michelangelo Merisi da Caravaggio (1571–1610),* The Lute Player, *painted 1595–96 for Vincenzo Giustiniani, a Roman nobleman who wrote an important* Discourse on the Music of His Times *(1628). The young man appears to be singing while accompanying himself on the lute. The bass partbook is open to* Voi sapete, *from Arcadelt's first book of madrigals (1538).*

into the seventeenth century. In addition to amateur performances, by 1570 some patrons had begun to employ professional singers to perform madrigals for audiences at court. Madrigals also appeared in plays and other theatrical productions.

EARLY MADRIGAL COMPOSERS The most important early madrigalist was Philippe Verdelot (ca. 1480/85–?1530), a French composer active in Rome and Florence, where the madrigal originated in the 1520s. Verdelot's four-voice madrigals are mostly homophonic, with line endings marked by cadences, as in the frottola. His madrigals for five and six voices are more motet-like, with frequent imitation, varying voice-groupings, and overlapping parts at cadences.

Jacques Arcadelt   A style mixing homophony with occasional imitation is evident in the madrigals of Jacques Arcadelt (ca. 1507–1568), a Franco-Flemish composer who worked in Florence and Rome for almost three decades before returning to France in 1551. Arcadelt's *Il bianco e dolce cigno* (NAWM 47), published in his first book of madrigals in 1538, is among the most famous of the early madrigals. The text contrasts a swan's mournful death with the speaker's "death that in dying fills me fully with joy and desire." Referring to such deaths, the poem closes with the line, "with a thousand deaths a day

EXAMPLE 10.1 *Jacques Arcadelt,* Il bianco e dolce cigno

If when I die no other pain I feel, with a thousand deaths a day I would be content.

I would be content." This image may refer to the Neoplatonic idea, promoted by writers in Florence, that falling in love feels like dying and—if the love is reciprocated—being reborn in the beloved. Alternatively, it may be a witty allusion to sexual climax, known in the sixteenth century as "the little death." However we read the poem, Arcadelt's setting is simple and ingenious. The swan's sad death is depicted with a plaintive rising and falling half step. At the end of the poem, shown in Example 10.1, a lilting descending line suggests contentment, while the "thousand deaths a day" ("mille mort' il dì") are evoked through multiple imitative entrances, especially noticeable after the largely homophonic setting of the rest of the poem.

THE PETRARCHAN MOVEMENT The development of the madrigal was linked to currents in Italian poetry. As we have seen, in Florence, madrigal poetry reflected local themes and concerns, such as Neoplatonic philosophy. Another current was the Petrarchan movement, which was especially influential in Venice, where many of the leading madrigal composers were centered in the mid-sixteenth century. Led by poet and scholar Cardinal Pietro Bembo (1470–1547), poets, readers, and musicians returned to the sonnets and canzoni of Petrarch (Francesco Petrarca) and the ideals embodied in his works. In editing Petrarch's *Canzoniere* in 1501, Bembo noted that Petrarch often revised the sound of the words without changing the imagery or meaning. Bembo identified two opposing qualities that Petrarch sought in his verses: *piacevolezza* (pleasingness) and *gravità* (severity). In the pleasing category Bembo included grace, sweetness, charm, smoothness, playfulness, and wit, while in the severe he grouped modesty, dignity, majesty, magnificence, and grandeur. Rhythm, distance of rhyme, number of syllables per line, patterns of accents, lengths of syllables, and the sound qualities of the vowels and consonants all contributed to making a verse either pleasing or severe. Composers became sensitive to these sonic values. Many of the early madrigalists set Petrarch's poetry. Later composers preferred his imitators and other modern poets, almost all of whom worked in Petrarch's shadow.

Adrian Willaert

How composers translated Bembo's theory into musical terms can be seen in settings of Petrarch by Adrian Willaert (ca. 1490–1562) and in the writings of Willaert's student Gioseffo Zarlino (see Source Reading, p. 213). Born in Flanders, Willaert spent most of his career in Italy, culminating in thirty-five years as maestro di cappella at the principal church in Venice, St. Mark's, where he trained many eminent musicians including Cipriano de Rore, Nicola Vicentino, and Andrea Gabrieli (see pp. 213–16 and Chapter 12). In the sonnet *Aspro core e selvaggio,* Petrarch expressed his beloved Laura's "harsh and savage heart" in a severe line, filled with double consonants and clipped, harsh sounds; he then described her "sweet, humble, angelic face" in a contrasting pleasing line made up of liquid, resonant, and sweet sounds. For the first line of his remarkable setting from the mid-1540s, shown in Example 10.2a, Willaert emphasized melodic motion in whole steps and major thirds along with harmonies featuring major thirds and sixths above the bass. These major intervals were considered harsher and more severe than semitones and minor thirds or sixths, in part because their greater size rendered melodies less smooth and harmonies brighter or sharper. For the second line, in Example 10.2b, he used more semitones and minor thirds in

EXAMPLE 10.2 *Adrian Willaert,* Aspro core e selvaggio

a. First line

Harsh heart and savage, and a cruel will

b. Second line

In a sweet, humble, angelic face

his melodies and chose minor thirds and minor sixths for the harmony. These intervals gave smoother and thus more charming melodies, and minor thirds and sixths were regarded as sweet harmonic intervals.

What may be surprising for modern readers, accustomed to a later convention that links major keys and triads to happiness and minor ones with sadness, is that Willaert and Zarlino associated major thirds and sixths with harshness and bitterness, and minor intervals with sweetness as well as with grief. This may remind us that the emotional qualities of music are a result

Suiting the Music to the Words

Le istitutioni harmoniche (The Harmonic Foundations) by Gioseffo Zarlino (1517–1590) was the most respected treatise of the mid-sixteenth century. His advice to composers on how to express emotions corresponds almost exactly to the practice of his teacher, Adrian Willaert.

❦

When a composer wishes to express harshness, bitterness, and similar things, he will do best to arrange the parts of the composition so that they proceed with movements that are without the semitone, such as those of the whole tone and ditone [major third]. He should allow the major sixth and major thirteenth, which by nature are somewhat harsh, to be heard above the lowest note of the concentus [ensemble], and should use the suspension of the fourth or the eleventh above the lowest part, along with somewhat slow movements, among which the suspension of the seventh may also be used. But when a composer wishes to express effects of grief and sorrow, he should (observing the rules given) use movements which proceed through the semitone, the

semiditone [minor third], and similar intervals, often using minor sixths or minor thirteenths above the lowest note of the composition, these being by nature sweet and soft, especially when combined in the right way and with discretion and judgment.

It should be noted, however, that the cause of the various effects is attributed not only to the consonances named, used in the ways described above, but also the movements which the parts make in singing. These are two sorts, namely, natural and accidental. Natural movements are those made between the natural notes of a composition, where no sign or accidental note intervenes. Accidental movements are those made by means of the accidental notes, which are indicated by the signs ♯ and ♭. The natural movements have more virility than the accidental movements, which are somewhat languid. . . . For this reason the former movements can serve to express effects of harshness and bitterness, and the latter movements can serve for effects of grief and sorrow.

Gioseffo Zarlino, *Le istitutioni harmoniche* (1558), Book III, Chapter 31, trans. Vered Cohen in Zarlino, *On the Modes,* ed. Claude V. Palisca (New Haven: Yale University Press, 1983), 95.

of association, convention, and tradition, not of acoustics alone, and that in trying to understand music of an earlier time or another culture we must seek to know how those who made the music understood it, not to impose our own codes of meaning.

MIDCENTURY MADRIGALISTS By the mid-sixteenth century, most madrigals were for five voices, with frequent changes of texture. Composers freely alternated homophony and imitative or free polyphony.

The leading madrigal composer at midcentury was Cipriano de Rore   *Cipriano de Rore* (1516–1565), shown in Figure 10.4. Flemish by birth, Rore worked in Italy, chiefly in Ferrara and Parma, and succeeded his teacher Willaert at St. Mark's in Venice. Rore's madrigals show his profound interest in capturing the sounds, emotions, and images of his texts.

Da le belle contrade d'oriente (NAWM 48) was published posthumously in 1566, in Rore's last madrigal collection. Rore imbued every detail of the music with the rhythm, sense, and feeling of the poem, a sonnet modeled on Petrarch. Throughout, accented syllables receive longer notes than do

EXAMPLE 10.3 *Cipriano de Rore,* Da le belle contrade d'oriente

sweet desire, you go, alas! Alone you leave me! Farewell! What will [become of me?]

unaccented syllables, sometimes creating syncopation, as at "dolce" and "lasci" in Example 10.3.

In the passage shown here, a woman expresses sorrow that her lover is about to depart. The combination of voices changes every word or two, suggesting the breathlessness of grief through frequent rests. The composer chose intervals associated with sadness and reflected natural speech inflection through the melodic contours: rising semitones for "T'en vai" (You go); falling minor thirds, semitones, and minor seventh for "haime" (alas!); and (in two of the voices) falling minor thirds on "addio" (farewell). The phrase "sola mi lasci" (alone you leave me) is sung by a single high voice, symbolizing "alone" while evoking the woman's plaintive cry. This phrase also uses two successive semitones, A–B♭–B♮, to convey grief.

Direct chromatic motion—from B♭ to B♮, or any semitone between notes with the same letter name but different signs—was not possible in the Guidonian system of solmization (see Chapter 2). Indeed, we have not seen direct chromatic motion since ancient Greek music, where it was part of the chromatic tetrachord (see Chapter 1 and NAWM 2). It was forbidden—perhaps scarcely imagined—in polyphony before Rore's generation, and its

FIGURE 10.4 *Cipriano de Rore, in a portrait by Hans Muelich.*

transgression against expected norms made it a powerful means for expressing grief. Zarlino approved of chromatic motion, along with other uses of
accidentals to move temporarily beyond the notes of the diatonic mode, as
ways to express sorrow (see Source Reading, p. 213). Rore frequently introduces notes outside the mode, so much so that the passage in Example 10.3
includes all twelve notes of the chromatic scale in a very brief compass.

Rore may have regarded chromaticism primarily as an expressive device,
but for others it provided a link back to the ancient Greeks. Composer and
theorist Nicola Vicentino (1511–ca. 1576) proposed reviving the chromatic
and enharmonic genera of Greek music in his treatise, *L'antica musica ridotta
alla moderna prattica* (Ancient Music Adapted to Modern Practice, 1555).
Many of his contemporaries scoffed at his ideas and his music. Yet a number
of his madrigals reach a high level of artistry, among them *L'aura che 'l verde
lauro*, on a Petrarch sonnet (published 1572). At one point, shown in Example
10.4, he incorporated the Greek chromatic tetrachord, descending a minor
third and two semitones, as a motive for imitation on the word "soavemente"

Nicola Vicentino

EXAMPLE 10.4 *Nicola Vicentino,* L'aura che 'l verde lauro

[The breeze, which the green laurel and her golden hair] gently sighing moves

(gently). Here, direct chromatic motion is not a sign of grief but an evocation of classical antiquity and thus of an idyllic pastoral scene.

In the madrigals of Rore and Vicentino, chromaticism was a special effect, startling (and therefore effective) because of its unfamiliarity. But by the end of the century, as other composers adopted it with a wider range of meanings, chromaticism gradually became part of the common musical language.

WOMEN AS COMPOSERS AND PERFORMERS Madrigals were written for mixed groups of men and women to sing in social gatherings. Yet the poets and composers were mostly male, and most madrigal texts were written from the male perspective. Professional opportunities were closed to most women, who were expected to be proper, obedient wives, servants, or nuns. Despite these limitations, several women, including Vittoria Colonna, Veronica Franco, and Gaspara Stampa, achieved fame as poets in the sixteenth century.

Female composers were comparatively rare. The first woman whose music was published, and the first to regard herself as a professional composer, was Maddalena Casulana (ca. 1544–ca. 1590s). In the dedication to her *First Book of Madrigals* (1568), Casulana wrote that she was publishing them not only to honor her dedicatee, the duchess of Bracciano, but also "to expose to the world, insofar as it is given me to do so in the profession of music, the vain error of men who esteem themselves such masters of high intellectual gifts that they think women cannot share them too." Her madrigals show inventive use of all the typical devices of midcentury madrigals, including text depiction, chromaticism, surprising harmonies, and dramatic contrasts of texture.

Women could more easily win renown as singers, and many did. Some were daughters and wives of the nobility, who sang in private concerts for invited audiences of their social peers, while others pursued professional careers. For example, at Ferrara in the 1570s, sisters Lucrezia and Isabella Bendidio, noblewomen by birth and marriage, won plaudits for their singing in musical evenings at court. In 1580, Duke Alfonso d'Este established the *concerto delle donne* (women's ensemble), a group of trained singers (Laura Peverara, Anna Guarini, and Livia d'Arco). Their performances at court, alone or with male singers, attracted so much attention and praise that the Gonzagas of Mantua and the Medici of Florence formed ensembles to rival that of Ferrara. Descriptions of performances by these groups (see Source Reading) make clear that the professional singers often introduced vocal ornaments and dramatized the words with appropriate gestures. These singers were praised both for their virtuoso technical abilities and for their expressivity in conveying the words and feelings. Here the madrigal has been transformed, from social music for the enjoyment of the singers themselves to concert music for the pleasure of an audience.

SOURCE READING

Women's Vocal Ensembles

Vincenzo Giustiniani (1564–1637) was a well-to-do musical amateur who described contemporary musical life in *Discorso sopra la musica de' suoi tempi* (Discourse on the Music of His Times, 1628). His description of the women's vocal ensembles at Ferrara and Mantua in the 1570s reveals their manner of performance and some of the reasons they were so greatly esteemed.

❖

These dukes [of Ferrara and Mantua] took the greatest delight in such music, especially in gathering many important gentlewomen and gentlemen to play and sing excellently. So great was their delight that they lingered sometimes for whole days in some little chambers they had ornately outfitted with pictures and tapestries for this sole purpose. There was a great rivalry between the women of Mantua and Ferrara, a competition not only in the timbre and disposition of their voices but also in ornamentation with exquisite runs joined opportunely and not excessively. . . . There was competition even more in moderating or enlarging the voice, loud or soft, attenuating it or fattening it as was called for, now drawing

it out, now breaking it off with the accompaniment of a sweet interrupted sigh, now giving out long runs, distinct and well followed, now turns, now leaps, now long trills, now short ones, now sweet runs sung quietly, to which sometimes one suddenly heard an echo respond; and more still in the participation of the face, and of the looks and gestures that accompanied appropriately the music and conceits of the poetry; and above all, without any indecorous motions of body, mouth, or hands that might have diminished the effect of their songs, in enunciating the words so well that each one could be heard down to the last syllable and was not interrupted or overwhelmed by the runs and other ornaments. And many other particular artifices could be observed in these singers and recorded by one more expert than I. And in such noble situations these excellent singers strove with all their might to win grace from their masters, the princes, and also fame for them—wherein lay their usefulness.

Vincenzo Giustiniani, *Discorso sopra la musica de' suoi tempi* (Discourse on the Music of His Times, 1628), ed. in Angelo Solerti, *Le origini del melodramma* (Turin: Fratelli Bocca, 1903), 107–8. Trans. Gary Tomlinson, in SR 54 (3:19), pp. 353–54.

LATER MADRIGALISTS Important composers of madrigals in the later sixteenth century include several northerners. Orlande de Lassus (see pp. 222–23) and Philippe de Monte (1521–1603) both began writing madrigals while in Italy early in their careers and continued doing so during their long tenures at northern courts, Lassus in Bavaria and Monte under the Hapsburg emperors in Vienna and Prague. Lassus's madrigal collections were published in Antwerp, Nuremberg, and Munich as well as in Rome and Venice, testifying to a fashion for Italian madrigals even in the north. Giaches de Wert (1535–1596), born near Antwerp, spent most of his life in Italy. Building on Rore's approach, Wert developed a dramatic style full of bold leaps, recitative-like declamation, and extravagant contrasts.

But the leading madrigalists were native Italians. Chief among them was Luca Marenzio (1553–1599), who depicted contrasting feelings and visual details with the utmost artistry. One of his most celebrated madrigals is *Solo e pensoso* (NAWM 49), based on a Petrarch sonnet and published in 1599 in Marenzio's last book of madrigals. The opening image, of the pensive poet walking alone with deliberate and slow steps, is unforgettably portrayed in

Luca Marenzio

EXAMPLE 10.5 *Carlo Gesualdo,* "Io parto" e non più dissi

["Ah, may I never cease to pine away] in sad laments." Dead I was, now I am alive,
[for my spent spirits returned to life at the sound of such pitiable accents.]

the top voice by a slow chromatic ascent of over an octave, moving one half step per measure. Later, "flee" and "escape" are depicted with quickly moving figures in close imitation.

Such striking musical images, evoking the text almost literally, were so typical of madrigals that they later became known as **madrigalisms**. Although disparaged by those who preferred a naturalistic expression of feelings to the depiction of individual words, such word-painting at its best can be both clever and deeply meaningful, and it has reappeared in many kinds of vocal music over the past four centuries.

Carlo Gesualdo   One of the most colorful figures in music history was Carlo Gesualdo, prince of Venosa (1566–1613). He is unusual among composers because he was an aristocrat, and it was rare for nobility to compose or to seek publication for their music. He was also a murderer: when he discovered his wife in bed with her lover, he killed them both. Gesualdo survived the scandal to marry Leonora d'Este, niece of Duke Alfonso II of Ferrara, in 1593.

In his madrigals, Gesualdo preferred modern poems full of strong images that provided opportunities for amplification through music. He dramatized and intensified the poetry through sharp contrasts between diatonic and chromatic passages, dissonance and consonance, chordal and imitative textures, and slow-moving and active rhythms, often breaking up poetic lines to isolate striking words that he captured in brilliant musical images. Example 10.5 shows a passage from *"Io parto" e non più dissi* (NAWM 50), published in 1611 in his last book of madrigals, that exhibits all these types of contrast. Slow, chromatic, mostly chordal music touched with dissonance portrays the laments of the woman whose lover is about to depart. When her plaintive cries arouse him again, his return to life ("vivo son") after his "little death" is shown by a turn to faster, diatonic, imitative figures.

VILLANELLA, CANZONETTA, AND BALLETTO Alongside the relatively serious madrigal, Italian composers also cultivated lighter kinds of song. The *villanella*, a lively strophic piece in homophonic style, usually for three voices, first appeared in the 1540s and flourished especially in Naples. Composers often deliberately used parallel fifths and other harmonic crudities to suggest a rustic character and sometimes mocked the correct, more sophisticated madrigals.

Toward the end of the sixteenth century, two other light genres gained prominence: the *canzonetta* (little song) and *balletto* (little dance). They were written in a vivacious, homophonic style, with simple harmonies and evenly phrased sections that were often repeated. The canzonetta combined elements of the madrigal and the villanella. The first composer to use the term was Orazio Vecchi (1550–1605), who published six books of canzonette between 1580 and 1597. Balletti, as the name suggests, were intended for dancing as well as singing or playing. They are identifiable by their dance-like rhythms and "fa-la-la" refrains and are usually in AABB form, adopting the repeated strains of dance music (see Chapter 12). Giovanni Giacomo Gastoldi (ca. 1554–1609) launched the genre with collections of balletti for five voices (1591) and for three voices (1594). Both genres were imitated by German and English composers. We will see how Thomas Morley, a leading English madrigalist, modeled a work of his own on Gastoldi's balletto *A lieta vita* (NAWM 55a).

THE LEGACY OF THE MADRIGAL These lighter genres continued the tradition of social singing for the pleasure of the singers themselves. While the madrigal also served this role, its purposes widened over the century to include madrigals for performance in private concerts or theatrical productions. Such venues encouraged increasing virtuosity and dramatization.

Yet a continuous thread was the ideal of conveying the text well: shaping melody and rhythm to follow the inflections and rhythms of natural speech, reflecting the poetic imagery through striking musical figures, and suiting all musical elements to the emotions in the text. The techniques developed by madrigal composers led directly to opera and other seventeenth-century forms of dramatic music. Most of our assumptions about what music should do when setting poetry were established in and for the sixteenth-century madrigal.

This emphasis on matching every aspect of the text profoundly

HERMITAGE, ST. PETERSBURG, RUSSIA. PHOTO: SCALA/ART RESOURCE, NY

FIGURE 10.5 Three Musicians (*or* The Concert), *by the Master of Female Half-Lengths, illustrates the variety of ways in which sixteenth-century songs could be performed. The music is Sermisy's chanson* Joyssance vous donneray. *The flutist reads from the superius partbook, the singer sings the tenor part, and the lutenist adds the other voices from memory or perhaps improvises an accompaniment.*

differentiates the madrigal from earlier secular songs, such as the chansons of the fourteenth and fifteenth centuries, and it reflects the deepening impact of humanism on musical culture over the course of the Renaissance. That we still find madrigals so engaging today suggests the continuing importance of that humanist influence for our own culture and music.

FRANCE

During the long reign of Francis I (r. 1515–47), composers in France developed three new types of chanson—lyric, narrative, and descriptive—in a lighter, more popular style. They were stimulated by a new style of French poetry cultivated by Clément Marot (ca. 1496–1544), the most influential French poet of his time. Blending popular and courtly traditions, Marot set aside the elevated language and formal artifice he had been taught in favor of simple language, direct expression, brevity, and freely spontaneous rhyme schemes and forms, all touched by elegance and wit. Composers responded with equally straightforward music, marked by tuneful melodies in short phrases, simple and pleasing rhythms, and clear articulation.

Such pieces were easy and satisfying to sing and ideally suited for amateurs. Between 1528 and 1552, Pierre Attaingnant (ca. 1494–ca. 1552), the first French music printer, brought out more than fifty collections of such chansons, about 1,500 pieces, and other publishers soon followed. The great number of chansons printed in the sixteenth century, including hundreds of arrangements for voice and lute or for lute alone, testifies to their popularity.

Sermisy and Janequin   Chief among practitioners of this new style were Claudin de Sermisy (ca. 1490–1562) and Clément Janequin (ca. 1485–1558). Sermisy was active in the French royal chapel and at Sainte-Chapelle in Paris. Although he composed 12 masses and about 100 motets, he is best known for his chansons, some 175 of them. Janequin spent most of his career in Bordeaux, where he became a priest, and Angers, where he headed the cathedral chapel and composed most of his 250 chansons. He spent his last decade in Paris, eventually earning the title *compositeur ordinaire du roi* (composer to the king). Several of Sermisy's and Janequin's chansons were so popular that they were reprinted for decades and adapted into many new forms, from dance melodies to psalm tunes. Some even showed up in paintings, as in Figure 10.5.

Lyric chansons   Lyric poems typically speak in the first person and describe an emotion, usually about love, ranging from pleasant, amorous situations to more serious sentiments. Chansons on these texts set them syllabically, usually in duple meter, in clearly articulated balanced phrases. The principal melody is in the highest voice, and the musical texture is largely homophonic, with occasional short points of imitation or echoes between voices. Verse forms vary, but most

EXAMPLE 10.6 *Claudin de Sermisy,* Tant que vivray

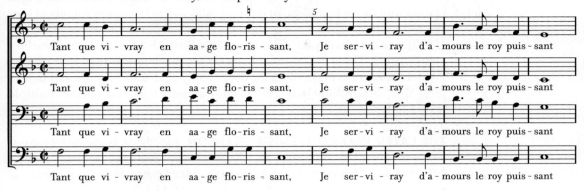

As long as I am able-bodied, I shall serve the potent king of love

pieces are in short sections that repeat in an easily grasped pattern, such as AABC, ABCA, or AABB'.

Sermisy's *Tant que vivray* (NAWM 51), shown in Example 10.6, is typical. The text by Marot is a lighthearted and optimistic love poem, far afield from the old tradition of courtly love. As in a frottola or villancico, the melody is in the top voice, and the harmony consists of thirds and fifths with only an occasional sixth above the bass. The four voices mostly declaim the text together. One result is that accented dissonances appear where earlier chansons would have featured a syncopated suspension before a cadence, as on the third quarter note of measure 3 in the top voice. The opening long-short-short rhythm is common. The end of each line of text is marked by a relatively long note or repeated notes, emphasizing the form of the poetry. Overall the song is as graceful, clear, simple, and seemingly spontaneous as the poetry, neatly matching Marot's marriage of courtly and popular styles.

Narrative poems tell a story, often including dialogue. The characters are usually from lower social classes, rustic or urban, and the situations most often are humorous, sometimes even bawdy. Musical settings treat the poetry line by line, usually in points of imitation that converge into homophony and cadence before the next line begins, so that the phrase structure remains clear. Despite the imitation, sometimes phrases or sections repeat. Each voice sings a similar rhythm, closely matching the accentuation of the words, and often declaiming the text so fast that it approaches the patter of eighteenth- and nineteenth-century comic opera.

Narrative chansons

All these characteristics are evident in Janequin's *Martin menoit son pourceau* (NAWM 52), set to a poem by Marot. Martin is taking his pig to market with Alice when she suggests they "do the sin" in the middle of the field. She ties the pig to her leg to keep it from running off, but while they are engaged in the act the pig takes fright, and Alice shouts that it is dragging her away. The text is funny but elegant, a tale of lustful rustic characters told in two neatly shaped five-line stanzas with a symmetrical rhyme scheme (ababb ccdcd). The music is equally artful, combining learned imitative counterpoint, gracefully shaped melodies, and logical harmonic structure with patter-like declamation, sudden contrasts, rhythmic jolts, and surprising turns of events.

Descriptive chansons

Janequin was particularly celebrated for his descriptive chansons, which feature imitations of bird calls, hunting calls, street cries, and sounds of war. His most famous chanson was *La guerre* (War), about the battle of Marignan (1515). *Le chant des oiseaux* (The Song of the Birds) is filled with vocal warbles and chirping. These descriptive chansons are much longer than lyric or narrative chansons, to make room for the panoply of sounds they present in textures that vary from homophony to contrapuntal combinations of multiple texts and figurations.

THE LATER FRANCO-FLEMISH CHANSON Alongside these new types of chanson, northern composers such as Nicolas Gombert and Jacobus Clemens (discussed in Chapter 11) maintained the older Franco-Flemish tradition of the contrapuntal chanson.

Orlande de Lassus

Traditions mix in the chansons of Orlande de Lassus (ca. 1532–1594), reflecting his cosmopolitan background. Also known as Orlando di Lasso (the Italian version of his originally French name), Lassus was one of the most important and prolific composers of the sixteenth century (see biography and Figure 10.6). While some of his chansons are in the new lyric or narrative styles, others show the influence of the Italian madrigal or grow from the Franco-Flemish tradition, using a tight polyphonic texture with close imitation and sudden changes of pace. His range of subject matter was equally wide; no one was more accomplished at writing humorous and bawdy chansons, but he also wrote songs of impressive seriousness. Lassus was always acutely attuned to the text and made sure that the music fit its rhythm, reflected its imagery, and conveyed the appropriate feelings.

Lassus's *La nuict froide et sombre* (NAWM 53) sets words by Joachim du Bellay (1522–1560), one of a group of young French poets called the Pléiade who criticized Marot and sought to create a new style of French poetry modeled on ancient Greek and Latin writers. Lassus chose two stanzas from du Bellay's ode *De l'inconstance des choses* (On the Inconstancy of Things) and matched the serious subject with a beautiful and evocative setting. Blending madrigal and chanson traditions, the music captures the overall mood—contrasting somber night and sweet sleep to the shining day that brings activity and varied colors—and depicts vivid images in the poem, from the contrast of earth and sky to the weaving of a tapestry of light.

MUSIQUE MESURÉE Another distinctive style of chanson emerged from the desire among some French poets and composers to imitate the rhythm of Greek poetry, resulting in ***musique mesurée*** (measured music). Members of the Académie de Poésie et de Musique (Academy of Poetry and Music), formed in 1570, sought to unite poetry and music as in ancient times and revive the ethical effects of ancient Greek music. By imposing their music on the general public, they hoped to improve society, an effort reminiscent of Plato.

The poet Jean-Antoine de Baïf, cofounder of the Académie, wrote strophic French verses in ancient Greek and Latin meters, which he called *vers mesurés à l'antique* (measured verse in ancient style). Ancient Greek and Latin poetry had accents of quantity (length of vowel or syllable) rather than stress accents as in modern languages. Since French lacked the long and short vowels of ancient languages, Baïf assigned French vowels durations, roughly equating

ORLANDE DE LASSUS
[ORLANDO DI LASSO]

(ca. 1532–1594)

In both his career and his compositions, Lassus was one of the most cosmopolitan figures in the history of music. He was prolific in all genres and was a particularly imaginative composer of chansons and motets.

Lassus was born in Mons in Hainaut, the region where Binchois, Ockeghem, and Josquin were also born and trained. Little is known of Lassus's family or early education. Beginning at a young age, he served Italian patrons at Mantua, Sicily, Milan, Naples, and Rome, allowing him to become thoroughly familiar with Italian styles. By the age of twenty-four he had already published books of madrigals, chansons, and motets. In 1556, he entered the service of Duke Albrecht V of Bavaria. He became maestro di cappella for the ducal chapel in Munich in 1563 and remained in that post until his death in 1594. He was good friends with his patron and especially with Albrecht's son, who became Duke Wilhelm V in 1579; letters from the composer to Wilhelm reveal a witty personality capable of making jokes in four languages.

Although Lassus served almost four decades in one post, he traveled frequently and kept abreast of developments in Flanders, France, and Italy. His total production amounted to more than two thousand

FACULTY OF MUSIC COLLECTION, OXFORD UNIVERSITY/BRIDGEMAN IMAGES

FIGURE 10.6 *Orlande de Lassus.*

pieces. His music was published by printers in Italy, Paris, Germany, and the Low Countries and was known all over Europe. He was granted rights to control the dissemination of his music by French king Charles IX and by the Holy Roman emperor, making him the first composer to hold the equivalent of copyright on his compositions. The principal collection of his motets, the *Magnum opus musicum* (Great Work of Music), was published by his sons in 1604, ten years after his death.

MAJOR WORKS 57 masses, over 700 motets, 101 Magnificats, hundreds of other liturgical compositions, about 150 French chansons, 200 Italian madrigals, and 90 German Lieder

---

stress accent with length. In setting this poetry, composers such as Claude Le Jeune (ca. 1528–1600), the leading exponent of this style, gave each long syllable a long note and each short syllable a note half as long. The variety of verse patterns produces a corresponding variety of musical rhythms in which duple and triple groupings alternate freely, as in Le Jeune's *Revecy venir du printans* (NAWM 54).

Musique mesurée was too artificial to become popular. But the experiment introduced irregular rhythms into the ***air de cour*** (court air), a genre of song for voice and accompaniment which became the dominant type of French vocal music after about 1580. Though the chanson in the fifteenth century had been a central genre of the international style, the lyric, narrative, and descriptive chansons of Sermisy and Janequin and the musique mesurée of Le Jeune were truly national, as French as the madrigal was Italian or the villancico was Spanish.

GERMANY

German secular song in the sixteenth century exhibits a fascinating mixture of styles. The **Meistersingers** (master singers) preserved a tradition of unaccompanied solo song, derived from the Minnesingers (see Chapter 4), that continued even as styles changed around them. The Meistersingers were urban merchants and artisans who pursued music as an avocation and formed guilds for composing songs according to strict rules and singing them in public concerts and competitions. The movement began in the fourteenth century, peaked in the sixteenth, and endured until the last guild dissolved in the nineteenth century. Most poems were written to fit an existing *Ton* (pl. *Töne*), a metric and rhyme scheme with its own melody. All *Töne* use bar form, and many were taken from Minnelieder. The best-known Meistersinger was Hans Sachs (1494–1576), a shoemaker in Nuremberg who composed thousands of poems and thirteen new *Töne*.

Composers in Germany continued to cultivate the German polyphonic Lied, with a popular song or leading melody in the tenor or cantus and free counterpoint in the other voices, as in the Lieder of Isaac's student Ludwig Senfl (ca. 1486–1542/3). Many collections of German Lieder were published in the first half of the century, chiefly at Nuremberg, a leading center of German culture at this time. After 1550, German taste veered toward Italian madrigals and villanelle, and the Lied declined in importance or took on Italianate characteristics. Once again a leading figure was Lassus, who composed seven collections of German Lieder. Most are madrigals in style if not in language, with close attention to the accentuation and expression of the text, alternating homophonic and imitative passages, and all parts equally important in the interplay of motives.

FIGURE 10.7 *Title page of Thomas Morley's book* A Plaine and Easie Introduction to Practicall Musicke *(1597). Music, in the lower right corner, is linked to the other members of the medieval quadrivium: astronomy (above music), geometry, and arithmetic (see Chapter 2). As announced in the center of the page, the treatise is in three parts, covering three skills: singing from notation, improvising or composing a descant to a given voice, and composing in three or more voices.*

ENGLAND

England had its own native tradition of secular music in the sixteenth century. Both Henry VIII and his second wife, Anne Boleyn, were musicians and composers. Manuscripts from his reign (1509–47) contain a variety of songs and instrumental pieces in three and four parts that reflect many facets of court life.

From this environment, around mid-century, emerged the **consort song**, a distinctively English genre for voice accompanied by a consort of viols (a string ensemble; see Chapter 12). The master of the consort song was William Byrd (see Chapter 11), who raised the technical level of the medium with skillful imitative counterpoint in his collection *Psalmes, Sonets and Songs* (1588). This collection was so successful that it was reprinted four times, and Byrd's consort song *Lulla lullabye* from this collection remained his most famous piece for more than a century. Composers wrote consort songs well into the seventeenth century, and although today the English madrigal and lute song are better known, the consort song remained an important genre until the viol consort itself was superseded by other ensembles in the early eighteenth century.

ENGLISH MADRIGALS The late sixteenth century brought to England a fashion for Italian culture, art, and music. The products of this influence most familiar today are Shakespeare's plays set in Italy, including *The Taming of the Shrew* (1593), *The Two Gentlemen of Verona* (1594), *Romeo and Juliet* (1594), *The Merchant of Venice* (1596), and *Othello* (1604). But everything from manners to clothing was affected, and music was in the vanguard.

Italian madrigals began to circulate in England in the 1560s and were sung in the homes of aristocrats and the middle class alike. In 1588, Nicholas Yonge published *Musica transalpina,* a collection of Italian madrigals translated into English. According to Yonge's preface, the anthology encompassed the repertoire sung by gentlemen and merchants who met daily at his home. This and similar collections created a vogue for singing madrigals, which spurred native composers to cash in on the trend by writing their own. Leading English madrigalists include Thomas Morley (1557/8–1602), Thomas Weelkes (ca. 1575–1623), and John Wilbye (1574–1638).

Morley was the earliest and most prolific of the three. Alongside his madrigals, he wrote **canzonets** and **balletts**, borrowing the lighter Italian genres of canzonetta and balletto. He modeled his ballett *Sing we and chant it* (NAWM 55b) on Gastoldi's balletto *A lieta vita* (NAWM 55a), and a comparison of the two illustrates how English composers drew on their Italian predecessors. Typical of their genre, both pieces are strophic, each verse is in two repeated sections (AABB), and each section begins with a homophonic setting of poetic couplets and concludes with a "fa-la-la" refrain. Morley borrows elements of Gastoldi's rhythm, melody, and harmony in the first part of each section, but in the "fa-la-la" refrains he enriches the texture with contrasting rhythms in the different voices and with brief imitation and motivic interplay between the parts. The dancelike rhythms, varied textures, and occasional contrapuntal challenges made such works particularly satisfying to sing.

Thomas Morley

Morley described the madrigal, canzonet, ballett, and other vocal and instrumental genres in *A Plaine and Easie Introduction to Practicall Musicke* (1597). Unlike most earlier treatises, this manual was aimed at the broad public interested in music, its title inviting even the most unlearned amateur to pick it up and learn about music. The title page, shown in Figure 10.7, lists the topics to be covered: singing from notation, adding a descant to a given voice, and composing in three or more voices.

In 1601, Morley published a collection of twenty-five madrigals by twenty-three composers, modeled after a similar Italian anthology called *Il trionfo di Dori* (The Triumphs of Dori, 1592). He called his collection *The Triumphes*

The Triumphes of Oriana

of Oriana, and each madrigal in it ends with the words "Long live fair Oriana." Although it was long assumed that "Oriana" referred to Queen Elizabeth, recent research suggests that Morley intended the collection to honor Anna of Denmark, wife of King James VI of Scotland (who later succeeded Elizabeth in 1603 as James I of England), and altered it to suit Elizabeth only when the political situation made it necessary.

Thomas Weekles   One of the most famous madrigals in the collection is Weelkes's *As Vesta was* (NAWM 56), on his own poem. Since word-painting was a strong tradition in the madrigal, Weelkes as poet provided numerous opportunities for musical depiction, and Weelkes the composer capitalized on all of them: rising scales for "ascending," falling scales for "descending" and "running down," a melodic peak for "hill," and one, two, three, or all voices for "alone," "two by two," "three by three," and "together" respectively. Most striking, and less conventional, is Weelkes's treatment of the final phrase. "Long live fair Oriana" is set to a motive that enters almost fifty times, in all voices and in all transpositions possible in the mode, suggesting the acclamation of a vast people; the passage lasts a long time and includes augmentations of the motive to four and eight times its original length, all witty symbols of the long life they wish for their queen. The treatment is both clever and meaningful, exemplifying the mixture of wit, wordplay, sentiment, contrapuntal skill, melodiousness, and sheer pleasure for the singers that characterizes the best madrigals, English or Italian.

Performance   Like their Italian counterparts, English madrigals, balletts, and canzonets were written primarily for unaccompanied solo voices, though many printed collections indicate that the music is "apt for voices and viols," presumably in any available combination. This flexibility made these publications ideal for informal gatherings, and the music was perfectly suited for amateurs. Ability to read a vocal or instrumental part in such pieces was expected of educated persons in Elizabethan England, as it was on the Continent.

LUTE SONGS In the early 1600s, the solo song with accompaniment became more prominent, especially the **lute song** (or **air**). The leading composers of lute songs were John Dowland (pronounced "Doe-lend," 1563–1626) and Thomas Campion (1567–1620). The lute song was a more personal genre than the madrigal, with more serious and literary texts and with none of the madrigal's aura of social play. The music generally reflects the overall mood, with much less word-painting than is typical of madrigals. The lute accompaniments support the vocal melody but have considerable rhythmic and melodic independence.

Alternate formats   Lute songs appeared in books rather than in partbooks, as madrigals did. The voice and lute parts are vertically aligned, allowing singers to accompany themselves. In some collections the songs are also printed in an alternative version, shown in Figure 10.8, in which the lute accompaniment is written out for three voices with each part arranged on the page so that performers sitting around a table could all read their parts from the same book. The lute part is in **tablature**, a notational system that tells the player which strings to pluck and where to place the fingers on the strings, rather than indicating what pitches will result.

Flow, my tears   The Dowland lute song best known to his contemporaries, *Flow, my tears*

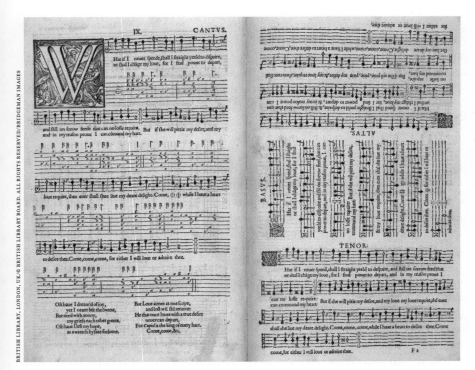

FIGURE 10.8 *John Dowland's song* What if I never speede, *as printed in his* Third and Last Book of Songs or Aires *(London, 1603). The song may be performed as a solo with lute accompaniment, reading from the left-hand page, or as a four-part arrangement, with or without lute accompaniment. The altus, tenor, and bassus are so arranged that singers around a table can read from a single book.*

(NAWM 57) from his *Second Booke of Songs or Ayres* (1600), was adapted from a lute piece by Dowland that spawned a whole series of variations and arrangements. It is in the form of a pavane, a sixteenth-century Italian processional dance, with three repeated strains. The performer sings the first two stanzas of the poem to the first strain, the next two to the second, and the final stanza twice to the third strain, resulting in the musical pattern aabbCC. The repeats minimize the opportunity for depiction or expression of individual words and phrases, but Dowland's music matches the dark mood of the poetry.

The fashion in England for madrigals and lute songs was intense but relatively brief, lasting only into the 1620s. The lute song's focus on a single singer with accompaniment links it to the growing interest in solo song in the early seventeenth century, which we will explore in Chapters 14 and 15.

THE MADRIGAL AND ITS IMPACT

Italian madrigals, French chansons, German Lieder, and English madrigals were laboratories for exploring the declamation, expression, and depiction of words. In this respect they reflect the growing influence of humanism on music over the course of the Renaissance. The importance of the text and its dramatic expression through music, especially in Italian madrigals, led directly into opera around 1600. More broadly, madrigals introduced the idea of music as a dramatic art, and over the next two centuries this concept broadened to include instrumental as well as vocal music. These developments led to the dominance of Italian music throughout the Baroque era, so that the madrigal truly made Italy the leader in European music for the first time.

The code of expression worked out by Willaert's generation is different in many respects from later codes but is the main taproot for them. More important than the specific correspondence of certain intervals to certain moods or characters that Zarlino outlines is the broader notion that melody, harmony, rhythm, and pacing all directly communicate feelings, and that the emotions they suggest must correspond to those of the text being set. The devices that composers of operas, ballets, tone poems, and film scores have used to suggest a character's mood or manipulate the feelings of the audience have long histories, reaching back in concept and often in specific detail to the procedures that sixteenth-century composers used in their madrigals.

Madrigals themselves have varied in popularity, along with other sixteenth-century secular songs. The vogue for social singing declined after 1600 but was maintained to some extent in England. Visiting London in the 1790s, Joseph Haydn heard English madrigals and wrote some of his own. The growth of amateur choral societies in the nineteenth century helped inaugurate a revival of madrigal singing, and new editions popularized English madrigals in the twentieth century, especially in schools. For the millions who have sung in school choirs or madrigal groups in Britain or North America, madrigals are often the oldest music they have performed.

From the English repertory, the revival spread to encompass Italian madrigals and French chansons. German and Spanish songs are heard less often but in recent years have begun to be performed and recorded more frequently than before, as have some other repertories such as frottolas and consort songs. Of the thousands of secular songs published in sixteenth-century partbooks, many have not been issued in modern editions and most have never been recorded. Sixteenth-century songs still serve their function admirably when amateurs sing through music together for their own pleasure, but such gatherings are rarer than they once were, and singers today have numerous repertories from more recent eras to draw on. Like the popular songs of later times, the secular songs of the sixteenth century are known today chiefly through a few dozen hits, which are sung and reprinted repeatedly. For the avid fan, there are thousands more to explore.

Further Reading is available at digital.wwnorton.com/hwm10

SACRED MUSIC IN THE ERA OF THE REFORMATION

❖

When the sixteenth century began, Christians from Poland to Spain and from Italy to Scotland shared allegiance to a single church centered in Rome and supported by political leaders. By midcentury, this unity of belief and practice was shattered. So was the peace. European society was disrupted by the Protestant Reformation, as central and western Europe entered a century of religious wars.

Sacred music was profoundly affected. Leaders of the Reformation sought to involve worshippers more directly, through congregational singing and services presented in the vernacular rather than in Latin. These changes led to new types of religious music in each branch of Protestantism, including the *chorale* and chorale settings in the Lutheran Church, the *metrical psalm* in Calvinist churches, and the *anthem* and *Service* in the Anglican Church. The Catholic Church also undertook reforms, but continued to use Gregorian chant and polyphonic masses and motets in styles that extended the tradition of Josquin's generation. Jewish service music remained distinctive, yet absorbed some outside influences. In each tradition, the genres and styles of sacred music were determined by people's religious beliefs and aims as much as by their musical tastes.

THE REFORMATION

The Reformation began as a theological dispute and mushroomed into a rebellion against the authority of the Catholic Church. It started in Germany with Martin Luther, then spread to most of northern Europe, as shown in Figure 11.1. There were three main branches: the Lutheran movement in northern Germany and Scandinavia, the Calvinist movement led by Jean Calvin that spread from Switzerland and the Low Countries to France and Britain, and the Church of England, organized by King Henry VIII for political reasons but ultimately influenced by Reformation ideals. The theology and circumstances of each branch determined its values and choices concerning music, so knowing the religious and political issues behind each movement will help us understand why their music takes the forms it does.

MARTIN LUTHER The instigator of the Reformation was Martin Luther (1483–1546), shown in Figure 11.2, a professor of biblical theology at the University of Wittenberg. His approach to theology was influenced by his humanistic education, which taught him to rely on reason, on direct experience, and on his own reading of Scripture rather than on received authority. Study of the Bible, notably St. Paul's view that "the just shall live by faith" (Romans 1:17), led Luther to conclude that God's justice consists not in rewarding people for good deeds or punishing them for sins, but in offering salvation through faith alone. His views contradicted Catholic doctrine, which held that religious rituals, penance, and good works were necessary for the absolution of sin.

FIGURE 11.1 *Religious divisions in Europe around 1560.*

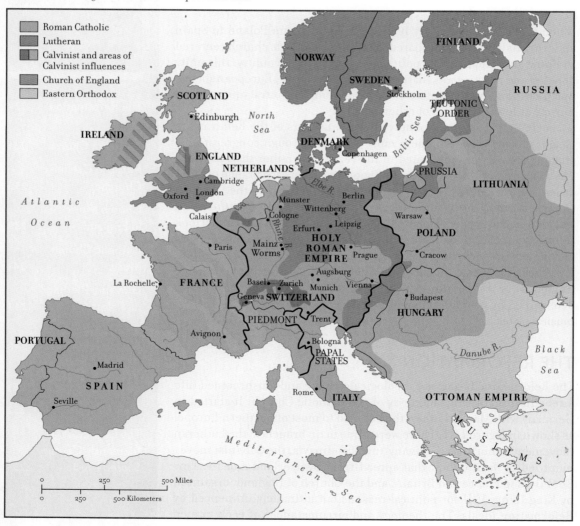

Luther also insisted that religious authority was derived from Scripture alone, so that if a belief or practice had no basis in the Bible it could not be true. This notion challenged the authority of the Church, which had developed a rich tapestry of teachings and practices that rested on tradition rather than Scripture.

One such practice was the sale of indulgences, credits for good deeds done by others, which one could purchase to reduce the punishment for sin. This practice raised money for the Catholic Church, but it had no Scriptural basis and violated Luther's principle that salvation was granted through faith alone, not works. So on October 31, 1517, intending to start a dialogue that could lead to reform within the Church, he sent to the Archbishop of Mainz a list of ninety-five theses (points or arguments) opposing indulgences and the doctrine that lay behind them and challenging the pope's role in granting them.

FIGURE 11.2 *Martin Luther, in a portrait by Lucas Cranach the Elder.*

He posted copies in Wittenberg, and soon his theses were printed and disseminated widely, making Luther famous. When pressed to recant, he instead affirmed the primacy of Scripture over the Catholic hierarchy. In response, the pope charged him with heresy in 1519 and excommunicated him in 1520. By then, Luther had numerous followers in German universities and among the populace. He organized a new Evangelical Church, known in English as the Lutheran Church. Many German princes supported him and made Lutheranism the state religion, freeing them from control by Rome.

MUSIC IN THE LUTHERAN CHURCH

In creating his church, Luther sought to give the people a larger role. He made the services easier to understand by increasing the use of the vernacular. Yet he retained some Latin, which he considered valuable for educating the young. He kept much of the Catholic liturgy, some in translation and some in Latin. Similarly, Lutheran churches continued to employ a good deal of Catholic music, both chant and polyphony, whether with the original Latin texts, German translations, or new German words.

Music assumed a central position in the Lutheran Church because of Luther's own appreciation for it. He was a singer, performer on flute and lute, and composer, and he greatly admired Franco-Flemish polyphony, especially the music of Josquin. Like Plato and Aristotle, he believed strongly in the educational and ethical power of music. Through singing together, worshippers could unite in proclaiming their faith and praising God. For these reasons, he wanted the entire congregation to sing in the services, not just the celebrants and choir, as Catholic custom dictated (see Source Reading, p. 232).

Luther and music

Luther never intended any formula to prevail uniformly in Lutheran churches, and various compromises between Roman usage and new practices could be found throughout sixteenth-century Germany. Large churches with trained choirs generally kept much of the Latin liturgy and its polyphonic music. Smaller churches adopted the *Deudsche Messe* (German Mass) published by Luther in 1526, which followed the main outlines of the Roman Mass

SOURCE READING

Martin Luther on Congregational Singing

In early Christian services, all those present had sung hymns and psalms (see Chapter 2), but by the late Middle Ages music in Catholic services was assigned to the celebrants and choir alone. When he established his new church, Luther sought to restore the congregation's role.

✤

I also wish that we had as many songs as possible in the vernacular which the people could sing during Mass, immediately after the Gradual and also after the Sanctus and Agnus Dei. For who doubts that originally all the people sang these which now only the choir sings or responds to while the bishop is consecrating the Host? The bishops may have these congregational hymns sung either after the Latin chants, or use the Latin on one Sunday and the vernacular on the next, until the time comes that the whole Mass is sung in the vernacular.

Martin Luther, "Order of Mass and Communion for the Church at Wittenberg" (1523), trans. Paul Zeller Strodach, in *Luther's Works*, vol. 53 (Philadelphia: The Fortress Press, 1965), 36.

but differed from it in many details and replaced most elements of the Proper and Ordinary with German hymns.

THE LUTHERAN CHORALE The most important form of music in the Lutheran Church was the congregational hymn, known since the late sixteenth century as the ***chorale*** (from *Choral*, the German for "chant"). During each service, the congregation sang several chorales, fulfilling Luther's aim of increasing worshippers' participation through music.

Chorales are known today primarily in four-part harmonized settings, but they originally consisted of only a metric, rhymed, strophic poem and a melody in simple rhythm sung in unison, without harmonization or accompaniment. In Luther's time, the congregation was led in its singing by a monophonic choir. Of course, chorales, like plainchants, could be enriched through harmony and counterpoint and reworked into large musical forms. Just as most medieval and Renaissance Catholic church music was based on chant, so Lutheran church music of the sixteenth through eighteenth centuries largely grew out of the chorale.

Luther and his colleagues worked quickly to provide chorales suitable for every Sunday of the church year. Luther wrote many of the poems and melodies himself. Four collections of chorales were published in 1524, and over two hundred followed in the next fifty years. The printing press played as large a role in disseminating chorales as it had in the spread of Luther's message.

Sources for chorales   In addition to composing new tunes, Luther and his followers fashioned chorales by adapting Gregorian chants, German devotional songs, and secular songs. Recycling existing music had practical advantages: it was a fast way to produce a large number of chorales and gave congregants familiar melodies to sing, reducing the amount of new music they had to learn. But it also served other purposes. Using Gregorian melodies and German religious songs asserted a sense of continuity with past Christian traditions. At the same time, converting Catholic songs into Lutheran ones was an act of appropriation that proclaimed the superiority and vibrancy of the new church and challenged the old order. Likewise, remaking secular songs into religious ones symbolized the supremacy of religion in daily life even while appealing to the broadest popular taste.

Adaptations of chant   Example 11.1 shows the chant hymn *Veni redemptor gentium* (NAWM 58a) and Luther's adaptation of it as a chorale, *Nun komm, der Heiden Heiland* (NAWM 58b). Luther's poem is a rhymed, metrical translation of the Latin

EXAMPLE 11.1 *Martin Luther's adaptation of a chorale from a chant hymn*

a. Hymn, Veni redemptor gentium

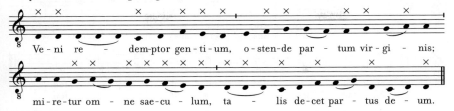

Come, Savior of nations, display the offspring of the Virgin. Let all ages marvel that God granted such a birth.

b. Luther's chorale Nun komm, der Heiden Heiland

Now come, peoples' Savior, known as Child of the Virgin, at which all the world marvels that God such a birth for him ordains.

text. The notes that are shared are marked with an x, showing that Luther took over most of the melody yet made several significant alterations. Changing the first and last note in the middle phrases gives the melody a new contour with a single high point for each phrase. Although the first and last phrases in the chant hymn differ from each other, in the chorale they are the same, heightening the sense of closure. Most important, the chorale has a distinct rhythmic profile of long and short notes. The changes recast the melody in an appealing, up-to-date style that was easier for lay worshippers to sing. The transformation of a chant into a current style is akin to the paraphrases we have seen by Du Fay, Isaac, and Josquin (NAWM 36, 40, 44, and 45).

Religious songs in German had circulated since the ninth century, and Luther and his colleagues adapted many as chorales. For example, the first stanza of *Nun bitten wir den Heiligen Geist* (Now we pray to the Holy Spirit) is from the thirteenth century and its tune from the fifteenth; Luther added three stanzas and slightly modified the tune.

German devotional songs

Luther and his colleagues also used familiar secular tunes for chorales, substituting religious words. The practice of replacing the original words of a song with new ones is called **contrafactum**. The texts were most often wholly new, but sometimes included clever reworkings of the existing poem, as in the anonymous chorale *O Welt, ich muss dich lassen* (O world, I must leave you), a contrafactum of Isaac's Lied *Innsbruck, ich muss dich lassen* (NAWM 41).

Contrafacta

Finally, Luther and other composers wrote many new tunes for chorales. The best known is Luther's *Ein feste Burg* (NAWM 58c), shown in Example 11.2,

New melodies

EXAMPLE 11.2 *Luther,* Ein feste Burg

Ein fe - ste Burg ist un - ser Gott,
Er hilft uns frei aus al - ler Not,

ein gu - te Wehr und Waf - fen.
die uns jetzt hat be - trof - fen.

Der alt bö - se Feind, mit Ernst ers jetzt meint;

gross Macht und viel List sein grau - sam Rü - stung ist;

auf Erd ist nicht seins Glei - chen.

A sturdy fortress is our God, a good defense and weapon. He helps us free from all afflictions that have now befallen us. The old, evil enemy now means to deal with us seriously; great power and much cunning are his cruel armaments; on Earth is not his equal.

which became the song most identified with the Reformation. Luther was very concerned with proper setting of text, and this chorale shows his attention to the expression and declamation of the words. The dynamic repeated opening notes and descending scale vividly convey the images of power in the poem, which Luther adapted from Psalm 46. The original rhythm features alternating long and short notes to suit the stresses of the text. Since the eighteenth century, an altered, more even rhythm has become more common.

POLYPHONIC CHORALE SETTINGS Lutheran composers soon began to write polyphonic settings for chorales. These served two purposes: group singing in homes and schools, and performance in church by choirs. Early published collections of chorale settings were aimed at providing music for young people to sing that was "wholesome" and could "rid them of their love ditties and wanton songs," as Luther wrote in the foreword to one such collection. These same chorale settings could also be sung in church by the choir, sometimes doubled by instruments, alternating stanzas with the congregation singing in unison without accompaniment. Such ways of performing chorales added variety and interest to the music of the services.

Composers used a variety of approaches borrowed from existing genres. Many settings adopted the traditional technique of German Lieder, placing the unaltered chorale tune in the tenor and surrounding it with three or more free-flowing parts, as in the setting by Luther's collaborator Johann Walter (1496–1570) in Example 11.3a (NAWM 58d). More elaborate settings, known as **chorale motets**, borrowed techniques from the Franco-Flemish motet. Some treated the chorale as a cantus firmus in relatively long notes surrounded by free or imitative polyphony. Others developed each phrase of

EXAMPLE 11.3 *Two settings of* Ein feste Burg

a. Johann Walter, from Geistliches Gesangbüchlein

b. Lupus Hellinck, from George Rhaw's collection Newe deudsche geistliche Gesenge *(1544)*

the chorale imitatively in all voices, as in Isaac's *Puer natus est* (NAWM 40). An example of such a chorale motet is Example 11.3b, in which each voice paraphrases the chorale, some more closely than others.

By the last third of the century, influenced by Calvinist psalm-tune harmonizations in chordal homophony (see pp. 238–39), Lutheran composers most often arranged chorales with the tune in the highest voice, accompanied by block chords with little contrapuntal figuration. This is called ***cantional style***, after its use in chorale collections called *Cantionale* (Latin for "songbook"). Although such settings were often sung in parts, after 1600 it became customary to have all the parts played on the organ while the congregation sang the melody in unison for all the verses of the tune. This style of harmonization and performance has continued to the present and is embodied in hymnbooks for almost all branches of Protestantism.

THE LUTHERAN TRADITION By 1600, Lutherans had a rich fund of over seven hundred chorale melodies and a great variety of pieces based upon them, from simple settings to complex chorale motets. Chorales were also elaborated in organ works of various types (discussed in Chapter 12). The Lutheran Church had quickly gained musical independence and established a strong heritage on which later composers like Heinrich Schütz and Johann Sebastian Bach would build.

MUSIC IN CALVINIST CHURCHES

Outside Germany and Scandinavia, Protestantism took different forms. The largest branch was led by Jean Calvin (1509–1564). Like Luther, he rejected papal authority and embraced justification through faith alone. But Calvin believed that some people are predestined for salvation, others for damnation. He also held that all aspects of life should fall under God's law as given in the Bible, requiring of his followers lives of constant piety, uprightness, and work. From his center at Geneva, missionaries spread Calvinism across Switzerland and to other lands, establishing the Dutch Reformed Church in the Netherlands, the Presbyterian Church in Scotland, the Puritans in England, and the Huguenots in France.

Seeking to focus worship on God alone, Calvin stripped churches and services of everything that might distract worshippers with worldly pleasures, including decorations, paintings, stained-glass windows, vestments, colorful ceremony, incense, organs and other musical instruments, and elaborate polyphony. Figure 11.3 shows how spare Calvinist churches were. Like Luther, however, Calvin valued congregational singing for its ability to unite worshippers in expressing their faith and praising God.

METRICAL PSALMS Calvin insisted that only biblical texts, especially psalms, should be sung in church (see Source Reading, p. 238). But psalms had verses of varying lengths, making them difficult for congregations to sing. The solution was to recast them as ***metrical psalms***—metric, rhymed, strophic translations of psalms in the vernacular that were set to newly composed melodies or tunes adapted from chant or other sources. Among the first to translate psalms into metrical French verse was Clément Marot, whom we met in Chapter 10 as a writer of lyric love poems and bawdy narrative poems (see NAWM 51 and 52). His simple, direct, and elegant style was perfectly suited to metrical psalms, and he produced more than fifty, at first for the French court and then at Calvin's request.

Metrical psalms were published in collections called ***psalters***. Calvin issued several in French, beginning in 1539. After Marot died in 1544, Théodore de Bèze continued the project of translating every psalm, and a complete French psalter containing all 150 psalms in their translations was published in 1562. Tens of thousands of copies were printed in several cities simultaneously, a sign of the growing importance of printing as a means for disseminating music. The psalms were sung in church in unaccompanied unison. The melodies move mostly by step, giving them an austere simplicity. The most widely known melody is the tune for Psalm

BIBLIOTHÈQUE PUBLIQUE ET UNIVERSAIRE, GENEVA. PHOTO: ERICH LESSING/ART RESOURCE, NY

FIGURE 11.3 *The Calvinist Temple at Lyon, in a 1564 painting that shows the austerity of Calvinist churches. The preacher wears no elaborate vestments, there is no choir, the focus is on the pulpit rather than the altar, and the only decorations are coats of arms in the windows and above the pulpit.*

134 (NAWM 59a), by Loys Bourgeois (ca. 1510–ca. 1561), shown in Example 11.4. This tune was used in English psalters for Psalm 100, becoming known as "Old Hundredth" (see NAWM 59b).

From Switzerland and France, metrical psalms spread widely. Translations of the French psalter appeared in Germany, Holland, England, and Scotland, and the Reformed churches in those countries took over many of the French tunes. In Germany, many psalm melodies were adapted as chorales, and Lutherans and Catholics published metrical psalters to compete with the Calvinists. The French model influenced the most important English psalter of the sixteenth century, that of Thomas Sternhold and John Hopkins (1562). In 1620, dissenters from the Church of England called Separatists emigrated to New England, establishing the Plymouth Colony (the term "Pilgrim" is a

Dutch, English, Scottish, and American psalters

EXAMPLE 11.4 *Loys Bourgeois, Psalm 134, Or sus, serviteurs du Seigneur*

Arise, you servants of the Lord, you who by night in his honor serve him in his house, praise him, and lift up his name.

SOURCE READING

Jean Calvin on Singing Psalms

In his preface to the psalter published at Geneva in 1542, Calvin detailed his views for how music should be used in services, and why only psalms sung by the entire congregation were appropriate.

❀

We know by experience that song has great force and vigor to move and inflame people's hearts to invoke and praise God with a more vehement and ardent zeal. Care must always be taken that the song be not light and frivolous but have weight and majesty, as Saint Augustine says, and there is likewise a great difference between the music one makes to entertain people at table and in their homes, and the psalms that are sung in the Church in the presence of God and the angels.

. . . It is true that, as Saint Paul says, every evil word corrupts good manners, but when it has the melody with it, it pierces the heart much more strongly and enters within; as wine is poured into

the cask with a funnel, so venom and corruption are distilled to the very depths of the heart by melody. Now what is there to do? The solution is to have songs not merely honest but also holy, which will be like spurs to incite us to pray and praise God, and to meditate on God's works in order to love, fear, honor, and glorify God. Now what Saint Augustine says is true—that we cannot sing songs worthy of God save what we have received from God. Wherefore, although we look far and wide and search in every land, we will not find better songs nor songs better suited to that end than the Psalms of David, which the Holy Spirit made and uttered through him. And for this reason, when we sing them we may be certain that God puts the words in our mouths as if God sang in us to exalt God's glory.

Jean Calvin, "Epistle to the Reader," in the Geneva Psalter (1542). Adapted from the translation by Oliver Strunk, in SR 57 (3:22), pp. 365–67.

modern construction). They brought with them French and Dutch traditions of psalm singing acquired during a thirteen-year sojourn in Holland and embodied in the psalter issued by Henry Ainsworth in Amsterdam in 1612. The first book-length publication in British North America was a psalter, the *Bay Psalm Book* of 1640. Some tunes from sixteenth-century psalters are still used today, appearing in hymnals all over the world.

POLYPHONIC PSALM SETTINGS Although singing in Calvinist churches was at first unaccompanied and monophonic, psalm tunes were set polyphonically for devotional use at home or in gatherings of amateur singers. Settings were typically in four or five parts, with the tune in either the tenor or the superius, and ranged from simple chordal style to motet-like settings in cantus-firmus style or imitation. French composers of psalm settings included Loys Bourgeois, Claude Goudimel (ca. 1520–1572), and Claude Le Jeune, and Flemish or Dutch composers included Jacobus Clemens (ca. 1510–ca. 1555) and Jan Pieterszoon Sweelinck (1562–1621). There were also settings of psalm tunes for voice and lute, for organ, and for other combinations. All told, the repertory of Calvinist polyphonic psalm settings numbers in the thousands, about as large as that of Lutheran chorale settings or of Italian madrigals, as composers and printers responded to a demand for religious music that amateurs could perform for their own enjoyment and edification. If monophonic metrical psalms were church music, these polyphonic settings resembled popular music with a religious message, like modern Christian popular music.

CHURCH MUSIC IN ENGLAND

The third major branch of Protestantism in the sixteenth century was the Church of England, whose origins lay more in politics than in doctrine. King Henry VIII (r. 1509–47), shown in Figure 11.4, was married to Catherine of Aragon, daughter of Ferdinand and Isabella of Spain. Henry desired a male heir, but their only surviving child was a daughter, Mary. With Catherine past childbearing age, in 1527 Henry sought an annulment so he could marry Anne Boleyn. The pope could not grant this without offending Catherine's nephew, Emperor Charles V, so in 1534 Henry persuaded Parliament to separate from Rome and name Henry head of the Church of England.

FIGURE 11.4 *Henry VIII, in a portrait by Hans Holbein the Younger.*

The Church of England remained Catholic in doctrine under Henry. But during the brief reign of Edward VI (r. 1547–53), Henry's son by his third wife, Jane Seymour, the Church adopted Protestant doctrines, reflecting Edward's Protestant upbringing and the views of the regents who governed in his name. English replaced Latin in the service, and in 1549 the *Book of Common Prayer* was adopted as the only prayer book permitted for public use. Edward's early death at the age of fifteen brought to the throne his half-sister Mary (r. 1553–58). Loyal to her mother, Catherine, and to the pope, she restored Catholicism, but met considerable resistance. She was succeeded by Elizabeth I (r. 1558–1603), Henry's daughter by Anne Boleyn, who again broke from the papacy and brought back the liturgical reforms instituted under Edward, yet tolerated Catholicism so long as its adherents conducted their services in private and remained loyal to her as queen. She sought to steer a middle course, compromising enough on doctrine to make the Church of England hospitable to some Catholics as well as Protestants. The present-day Anglican Church (including the Episcopal Church in the United States) continues to blend Catholic and Protestant elements in theology, ritual, and music.

All these events had repercussions for church music. New forms were created for services in English, but Latin motets and masses were composed during the reigns of Henry, Mary, and even Elizabeth. Although most services during her reign were in English, Elizabeth provided for the use of Latin in some churches and of Latin hymns, responds, and motets in her own royal chapel, where they served political needs for international diplomacy in a Europe dominated by hostile Catholic powers. Some Protestants valued the tradition of Latin sacred polyphony in itself, for its links to the past and its musical splendors. And Catholics continued to hold services in private households, often in secret, for which new Latin works were composed.

Church music

After the Church of England adopted English as its liturgical language, two principal forms of Anglican music developed: the **Service** and the ***anthem*** (from Latin "antiphon"). A Service consists of the music for certain portions

Service and anthem

of Matins (corresponding to Catholic Matins and Lauds), Holy Communion (Mass), and Evensong (Vespers and Compline). A contrapuntal and melismatic setting of these portions is called a *Great Service*. A *Short Service* sets the same texts, but in a syllabic, chordal style. An anthem is a polyphonic work in English, like a motet, usually sung by the choir near the end of Matins or Evensong. Many anthems set texts from the Bible or *Book of Common Prayer*.

Thomas Tallis   The most important English composer of sacred music in the mid-sixteenth century was Thomas Tallis (ca. 1505–1585), who served in the Chapel Royal for over forty years under every sovereign from Henry VIII to Elizabeth I. While Tallis apparently remained Catholic, his works encompass Latin masses and hymns, English service music, and other sacred works that reflect the religious and political upheavals in England during his lifetime.

Tallis's *If ye love me* (NAWM 60) exemplifies the early anthem. Among the first pieces of music composed for the new liturgy in English around 1547, it balances the demands of the Anglican Church for clear, comprehensible setting of the words with musical qualities of beauty and variety. The four-part choir of men and boys begins with simple homophony followed by four brief points of imitation, each different in construction. The text setting is syllabic and perfectly matched to the spoken rhythm of the words, and the light texture and repetitions keep the words intelligible even in the imitative sections. At the same time, every phrase in every part is an attractive melody. Tallis's music strikes the listener as an interplay not of abstract musical lines but of voices—so closely is the melodic curve wedded to the natural inflection of speech, and so naturally does it lie for the singer.

WILLIAM BYRD The leading English composer in the late sixteenth and early seventeenth centuries was William Byrd (ca. 1540–1623; see biography and Figure 11.5). Although a Catholic, Byrd served the Church of England and was a member of the royal chapel. In addition to secular vocal and instrumental music (discussed in Chapters 10 and 12), he wrote both Anglican service music and Latin masses and motets.

Anglican music   Byrd composed in all the forms of Anglican church music, including a Great Service, three Short Services, psalms, and anthems. He was the first English composer to absorb Continental imitative techniques so thoroughly that he could apply them imaginatively and without constraint. In his *Sing joyfully unto God* (NAWM 61), an energetic and vivid anthem for six voices, points of imitation succeed one another, occasionally interspersed with homophony. The imitation is handled freely, often with changes of interval and rhythm.

Latin masses and   Byrd's Latin masses and motets are his best-known vocal compositions.
motets   He probably intended his earlier motets for the royal chapel or for private devotional gatherings. But in the 1590s he began to write music for liturgical use by Catholics who celebrated Mass in secret. His two books titled *Gradualia* (1605 and 1607) contain complete polyphonic Mass Propers for the major days of the church year, a cycle as ambitious and impressive as the *Magnus liber organi* and Isaac's *Choralis Constantinus*. With these motets and his three masses, one each for three, four, and five voices (ca. 1593–95), Byrd provided almost all the polyphonic music his Catholic countrymen would need.

Byrd was a Catholic in an Anglican state, a loyal subject of and servant to Queen Elizabeth, protected by her from prosecution for his religious practices and yet committed to providing music for his friends and patrons

WILLIAM BYRD

(ca. 1540–1623)

Byrd, the most important English composer between Dunstable and Purcell, was a master of almost all major genres of his time, from music for Anglican and Catholic services to secular vocal and instrumental music.

He was probably a student of Thomas Tallis and a choirboy with the Chapel Royal in London under both the Protestant Edward VI and the Catholic Queen Mary. He was a Catholic, yet he served the Church of England as organist and choirmaster at Lincoln Cathedral (1563–72) and enjoyed the patronage of Queen Elizabeth, returning to the Chapel Royal for over five decades (1572–1623). In 1575, he and Tallis were granted a twenty-one-year monopoly for the printing of music in England, and Byrd continued publishing music after Tallis's death in 1585.

In trouble from time to time for his Catholic practices, Byrd nonetheless composed Latin masses and motets for Catholic use alongside his less controversial music, winning admiration among Catholics as a self-sacrificing advocate for their faith. That he avoided a worse fate is a sign of how valuable his other music was to the Anglican Church and to the state. Indeed,

FIGURE 11.5 *William Byrd.*
LEBRECHT MUSIC AND ARTS PHOTO LIBRARY/ALAMY STOCK PHOTO

Elizabeth understood that he was the chief adornment of her Chapel Royal, and she used his reputation as a composer to raise hers as a monarch and that of England as a cultured nation.

MAJOR WORKS Over 180 motets, 3 masses, 4 Services, dozens of anthems, secular partsongs, consort songs, fantasias and other works for viol consort, and variations, fantasias, dances, and other works for keyboard

to use in their clandestine services. His prolific output of both Anglican and Catholic service music, and the way he sought to make space for the latter in the face of a sometimes hostile environment, embody on a personal level the religious divisions throughout Europe.

CATHOLIC CHURCH MUSIC

How music was used in the Catholic Church was changed relatively little by the religious turbulence of the sixteenth century. Although the Church undertook some reforms, including major changes in liturgy and chant, the primary response to the Reformation was to stiffen the Church's resolve and reaffirm its doctrines, traditions, and practices. Church leaders did not translate services into the vernacular or invite worshippers to participate in the liturgy through singing. Instead, we find continuity in the roles played by music and in the genres and forms that were used, from chant to polyphonic masses and motets. Tradition, splendor, and a projection through music of the power and leadership of the church were valued over congregational participation.

THE GENERATION OF 1520–1550 Flemish composers remained prominent in the generation active between 1520 and 1550, working in positions all over Europe. Among the best known were Adrian Willaert, Nicolas Gombert (ca. 1495–ca. 1560), and Jacobus Clemens. All were born in Flanders but took posts elsewhere, extending a century-old tradition: Willaert was at St. Mark's in Venice, Clemens served churches in the Netherlands, and Gombert spent most of his career in the chapel of Emperor Charles V, working in Madrid, Vienna, and Brussels.

General style features

Catholic composers in this period shared several characteristics. They preserved the careful dissonance treatment and equality of voices of the preceding generation. They expanded the typical number of voices from four to five or six, which allowed a greater variety of contrasting combinations. They defined the mode of polyphonic works clearly through frequent cadences and melodic profiles in the superius and tenor voices that fit the range of the mode, whether authentic or plagal. Most works were in duple meter, sometimes with brief, contrasting passages in triple meter. The prevailing texture continued to be imitative polyphony, but now voices often varied motives as they imitated them. Phrases tended to overlap, with one or more voices beginning a new idea while others cadenced, producing an almost continuous flow articulated only by strong cadences at the ends of sections. The imitation mass became the most common type of mass, followed by the paraphrase mass, although cantus-firmus masses continued to be written. Chant melodies, usually treated freely through paraphrase in all voices, served as subjects for motets as well as masses. Canons and other intricate structural devices appeared much less often than they had in previous generations.

Gombert's Ave regina caelorum

We can see several of these traits in Gombert's five-voice motet *Ave regina caelorum* (NAWM 62), based on a chant with the same words. Each phrase of text is treated in a separate point of imitation, using a melodic idea paraphrased from the chant. As each point of imitation cadences on the modal final, the next has already begun. The succession of interlocking points of imitation continues throughout the work, creating a seamless flow that lacks the clear breaks and strong contrasts that were typical of Josquin, with whom Gombert was said to have studied. At each new phrase, the voices enter in a different order and after a different interval of time, providing endless variety within a unified structure. The music reflects the value Gombert placed on combining continuity with constant variation, and the lesser value he placed on the rhetorical effects Josquin achieved through contrasts of character, texture, and figuration and through word-painting. As we shall see, the pendulum swung back from sheer beauty to rhetorical expressivity in motets composed in the later sixteenth century.

Willaert and humanism

Although they shared many characteristics, composers at this time also developed individual styles. Willaert, with his long career in Italy, was most affected by the humanist movement. He carefully suited his music to the accentuation, rhetoric, and punctuation of the text. He never allowed a rest to interrupt a word or thought within a vocal line, and he placed a strong cadence in all voices only at significant breaks in the text. Willaert was one of the first composers to insist that syllables be printed precisely under their notes and that scrupulous attention be paid to the stresses of Latin pronunciation.

CATHOLIC RESPONSE TO THE REFORMATION As the Protestant Reformation spread, the Catholic Church responded with a series of initiatives, called the Counter-Reformation or Catholic Reformation. The loss or threatened loss of England, the Netherlands, Germany, Austria, Bohemia, Poland, and Hungary made this campaign urgent. Pope Paul III (r. 1534–49) and his successors brought austerity and asceticism to a church hierarchy formerly known for profligacy and excess. Simultaneously, Saint Ignatius Loyola (1491–1556) organized the Society of Jesus, known as the Jesuits, in 1534. Swearing strict obedience to the pope, the Jesuits founded schools, promoted Catholic education, and proselytized among Protestants in Europe and non-Christians in Asia and the Americas. Their work helped to restore Poland and large areas of France and Germany to Catholicism.

THE COUNCIL OF TRENT From 1545 to 1563, with numerous interruptions, a church Council met at Trent in northern Italy to consider how to respond to the Reformation. Figure 11.6 shows the final session. After discussing possible compromises, the Council reaffirmed the doctrines and practices that Luther and Calvin had attacked. However, the Council did pass measures aimed at purging the Church of abuses and laxities, such as the use of benefices to support absent priests, a practice that had fostered the careers of many musicians (see Chapter 7).

Liturgy and chant

Among the most significant changes for music resulted from a move to suppress variation in local practices in favor of a uniform liturgy. Over the centuries, most churches and many monasteries and convents had developed a substantial distinctive repertory of sequences, tropes, and Offices for saints, often locally composed. The Council eliminated nearly all tropes and sequences, leaving only four of the most widely used sequences, including *Victimae paschali laudes* and *Dies irae* (NAWM 6a and 6b). They also imposed the Roman rite on all churches that were not at least 200 years old; older churches were permitted to keep their historic liturgy, but many Offices of saints that they celebrated had to be revised, and some were removed entirely. Giovanni Pierluigi da Palestrina (see pp. 244–48) and a colleague were commissioned

FIGURE 11.6 *The Council of Trent, shown at its final session in 1563, led by Pope Pius IV. Painting attributed to Titian.*

to revise the official chant books to conform to the revised liturgy and purge the chants of "barbarisms, obscurities, contrarities, and superfluities." Their edition, completed by others after Palestrina's death, was published in 1614 and remained in use until the Solesmes editions of the early twentieth century (see Chapter 2). Yet because the reforms advocated by the Council were left to local bishops to enforce, some dioceses did not accomplish

them until the eighteenth century, and in some churches the medieval tropes, sequences, and saints' Offices continued to be sung until then.

Polyphony   Polyphonic church music took up only a small part of the Council's time. Some reformers sought to restrict polyphonic music, complaining that basing a mass on a secular chanson profaned the liturgy or that complicated polyphony such as that of Gombert's generation made it impossible to understand the words. Some sought to eliminate polyphonic music from convents entirely. Others argued strongly for retaining music without restrictions, noting that it had been part of Christian worship from the beginning.

In the end, the Council said little about polyphonic music. The only policy adopted regarding polyphonic music was this statement of 1562 that could be read to suggest a ban on masses based on vernacular songs: "Let them keep away from the churches compositions in which there is an intermingling of the lascivious or impure, whether by instrument or by voice." It was left to local bishops to regulate music in the services. Some bishops, notably in Rome and Milan, did restrict music in convents or insist that in polyphonic works the text must always be intelligible. The prominence of their efforts led to the belief among some contemporaries and some later historians that the Council of Trent indeed had declared that polyphony was allowed only if the words remained comprehensible to all.

GIOVANNI PIERLUIGI DA PALESTRINA

The controversy around the intelligibility of words in polyphonic music became linked to Giovanni Pierluigi da Palestrina (1525/6–1594; see biography and Figure 11.7), the leading Italian composer of church music in the sixteenth century. According to a legend already circulating soon after his death, Palestrina saved polyphony from condemnation by the Council of Trent by composing a six-voice mass that was reverent in spirit and did not obscure the words. The work in question was the *Pope Marcellus Mass* (Credo and Agnus Dei I in NAWM 63), published in Palestrina's *Second Book of Masses* in 1567. While the legend is probably false, Palestrina noted in his dedication to this collection that the masses it contained were written "in a new manner," no doubt responding to the desire of some for greater clarity in setting the text.

THE PALESTRINA STYLE Palestrina has been called "the Prince of Music" and his works the "absolute perfection" of church style. His sober, elegant music captured the essence of the Catholic response to the Reformation in a polyphony of utter purity. Yet his music is also remarkably varied in its melodies, rhythms, textures, and sonorities and acutely sensitive to the text, making it profoundly satisfying to hear.

Masses   Palestrina's style is exemplified in his 104 masses. Fifty-one are imitation masses based on polyphonic models. Thirty-four are paraphrase masses, almost all on chant, with the borrowed melody paraphrased in all voices. Eight masses use the old-fashioned cantus-firmus method, including the first of two he wrote on *L'homme armé*. Also reminiscent of the older Flemish tradition are a small number of canonic masses. Six masses, including the *Pope Marcellus Mass*, are free, using neither canons nor borrowed material.

Melody   Palestrina's melodies have a quality almost like plainchant. The melodic lines in the first Agnus Dei from the *Pope Marcellus Mass* (NAWM 63b), shown

GIOVANNI PIERLUIGI DA PALESTRINA

(1525/1526–1594)

Palestrina was renowned especially for his masses and motets. His music became a model for later centuries of church music and of counterpoint in strict style.

Palestrina was named after his presumed birthplace, a small town near Rome. He served as a choirboy and received his musical education at the Church of Santa Maria Maggiore in Rome. After seven years as organist and choirmaster in Palestrina (1544–51), he returned to Rome under the patronage of Pope Julius III. He spent most of his career as choirmaster at the Julian Chapel at St. Peter's (1551–55 and 1571–94) and at two other important churches in Rome, St. John Lateran (1555–60) and Santa Maria Maggiore (1561-66). He briefly sang in the papal chapel (1555) but had to relinquish the honor because he was married. He also taught music at the new Jesuit seminary. He declined two offers that would have taken him away from Rome: one from Emperor Maximilian II in 1568 and another in 1583 from the duke of Mantua.

Most of Palestrina's music was sacred, and he wrote more masses than any other composer. His main secular works are madrigals. Late in life, he wrote that he "blushed and grieved" to have written music for love poems.

Palestrina married Lucrezia Gori in 1547, and they had three sons. After two died of plague in the 1570s, followed by Lucrezia in 1580, Palestrina considered

FIGURE 11.7 *Giovanni Pierluigi da Palestrina, in a contemporary painting.*
ISTITUTO DEI PADRI DELL'ORATORIO, ROME. PHOTO: SCALA/ART RESOURCE, NY

becoming a priest. Instead, in 1581 he married Virginia Dormoli, an affluent widow whose financial resources allowed him to publish his own music. His reputation as a composer, already high in his lifetime, grew after his death until he became an almost legendary figure.

MAJOR WORKS 104 masses, over 300 motets, 35 Magnificats, about 70 hymns, many other liturgical compositions, about 50 spiritual madrigals with Italian texts, and 94 secular madrigals

---

in Example 11.5, are typical: long-breathed, rhythmically varied, easily singable lines that trace a natural, elegant curve. The voices move mostly by step, with few repeated notes. Most leaps greater than a third are smoothed over by stepwise motion in the opposite direction to fill in the gap.

Palestrina's counterpoint conforms in most details with the teachings of Willaert as transmitted by Zarlino in his *Le istitutione harmoniche*. The music is almost entirely in duple meter. The independent lines meet in a consonant sonority on each beat (each half note in Example 11.5), except when there is a suspension, shown by S in the example, which occurs at almost every cadence. Dissonances between beats may occur if entered and left by step, as in the passing (P) and neighbor (N) tones marked in the example. In addition, Palestrina often used the ***cambiata*** (Italian for "changed"), as it was later

Counterpoint and dissonance treatment

EXAMPLE 11.5 *Opening of Agnus Dei I from Giovanni Pierluigi da Palestrina's* Pope Marcellus Mass

called. In this figure, marked C in Example 11.5, a voice skips down a third from a dissonance to a consonance instead of resolving by step. Where one might expect two passing tones between consonant notes, as between D and A in the cantus at measure 6, the second passing tone—here, B—is omitted, only to become the next note in the melody. This elegant gesture delays, encircles, and thus emphasizes the note of resolution.

Sonority   The smooth diatonic lines and discreet handling of dissonance give Palestrina's music transparency and serenity. At the same time, despite what might seem a limited harmonic vocabulary, he achieves an astonishing variety in sonority through different arrangements of the same few notes. For instance, in the passage in Example 11.5, each time the notes G–D or G–B–D are combined vertically their spacing is unique. These combinations, shown in Example 11.6, illustrate Palestrina's ability to produce many subtly different shadings and sonorities from the same simple harmonies, sustaining the listener's interest.

Text declamation   Palestrina strove to accentuate the words correctly and make them intelligible, in accordance with the goals of reformers. In Example 11.5, each voice declaims "Agnus Dei" clearly, with one note on each syllable except for the accented "De-," which is emphasized by an upward leap and long melisma. In the movements with longer texts, the Gloria and the Credo, Palestrina set many passages in homophony so that the words could be easily understood. Example 11.7 shows one such passage, from the Credo of the *Pope Marcellus Mass* (NAWM 63a). As a result, there is a contrast in style between these largely homophonic movements and those with shorter texts—the Kyrie, Sanctus, and Agnus Dei—which use imitative polyphony throughout.

Texture   To achieve variety, Palestrina typically gave each new phrase to a different combination of voices, reserving the full six voices for climaxes, major

EXAMPLE 11.6 *Varied spacings in Palestrina's Agnus Dei*

EXAMPLE 11.7 *From the Credo of Palestrina's* Pope Marcellus Mass

Begotten, not made, being of one substance with the Father: by whom all things were made.

cadences, or particularly significant words. In Example 11.7, "Genitum, non factum" (Begotten, not made) and "consubstantialem" (being of one substance) are sung by two different groups of four voices, "Patri" (with the Father) by three voices, and "per quem omnia facta sunt" (by whom all things were made) by all six. Subtle text depiction abounds: the phrase on "consubstantialem" is a variation of the previous one and thus is "of one substance" with it; "the Father" is sung by three voices, symbolizing the Trinity; and "all" in the last phrase is emphasized as all six voices sing together for the first time in the Credo.

Rhythm   The rhythm of sixteenth-century polyphony comprises both the rhythms of the individual voices and a collective rhythm resulting from the harmonies on the beats. Within each voice, there is a great variety in durations, and no two successive measures feature the same rhythm. In imitative passages, such as the opening of the Agnus Dei in Example 11.5, the individual lines are rhythmically quite independent, each emphasizing different beats through long notes and high notes. But when the passage is performed, we perceive a fairly regular succession of measures in duple meter, projected by changes in harmony and suspensions on strong beats. Palestrina often uses syncopation to sustain momentum and link phrases. In Example 11.7, each phrase begins with a syncopated sonority that enters half a beat earlier than expected, just after the previous phrase cadences, and thus maintains forward motion until the end of the sentence in the text.

In all of these respects, Palestrina's music combines elegance, clarity, pleasingness, variety, and close attention to the words, all features that were highly valued in the sixteenth century. Accordingly, his works earned praise as the pinnacle of church music.

PALESTRINA AS A MODEL Palestrina's style was the first in the history of Western music to be consciously preserved and imitated as a model in later ages. Seventeenth-century theorists and composers looked to him as the ideal of the *stile antico* (old style). Counterpoint books from Johann Joseph Fux's *Gradus ad Parnassum* (Steps to Parnassus, 1725) to recent texts have aimed at teaching young musicians how to compose in this style. During the eighteenth and nineteenth centuries, through his role as a pedagogical model and the legend that his *Pope Marcellus Mass* saved church polyphony, Palestrina's reputation eclipsed almost all other sixteenth-century composers. Only since the late nineteenth century, when his music and that of his contemporaries has been studied, edited, and more widely performed, have we begun to see Palestrina in context and to understand how his style represents just one important strand in a vast and colorful tapestry.

SPAIN AND THE NEW WORLD

In Spain, the Catholic Church was closely identified with the monarchy. Queen Isabella and King Ferdinand, joint rulers from 1479, were called the "Catholic monarchs," and they strongly promoted Catholicism in their realm. In 1480, Ferdinand launched the Spanish Inquisition, which sought to root out heresy and enforce belief in Catholic doctrine. After conquering the Moors in Granada in 1492, Ferdinand and Isabella forced Jews (and later Muslims) to accept baptism as Christians or leave Spain. Later Spanish kings Charles I (r. 1516–56, and 1519–56 as Holy Roman emperor Charles V) and his son Philip II (r. 1556–98) were equally fervent Catholics, and together with Jesuit missionaries they made sure that the Church and its music prospered in Spain and its possessions in the Americas.

CATHOLIC MUSIC IN SPAIN Royal family ties to the Low Countries brought Flemish musicians such as Gombert to Spain, and the Franco-Flemish tradition deeply influenced Spanish polyphony. There were also close links to Italy, through Spain's possessions in southern Italy, and directly to Rome, particularly after the election of a Spaniard as Pope Alexander VI (1492–1503). The most eminent Spanish composer of the first half of the sixteenth century, Cristóbal de Morales (ca. 1500–1553), had links to both Flemish and Italian traditions. Morales acquired fame in Italy as a member of the papal chapel between 1535 and 1545, and his masses drew on works by Josquin, Gombert, and other Franco-Flemish composers as well as on Spanish songs. Among the most widely performed Spanish composers was Morales's student Francisco Guerrero (1528–1599), chapelmaster at the Seville Cathedral, whose smooth, singable melodies made his music popular throughout Spain and Spanish America.

Tomás Luis de Victoria (1548–1611) was the most famous Spanish composer of the sixteenth century. All of his music is sacred and intended for Catholic services. He spent two decades in Rome, where he almost certainly knew Palestrina and may have studied with him. Victoria was the first Spanish composer to master Palestrina's style, yet his music departs from it in several respects. Victoria's works tend to be shorter, with less florid melodies, more frequent cadences, more chromatic alterations, and more contrasting passages in homophony or triple meter. All of these characteristics are evident in his best-known work, *O magnum mysterium* (NAWM 64a). In this motet, Victoria uses a variety of motives and textures to express successively the mystery, wonder, and joy of the Christmas season.

Tomás Luis de Victoria

Most of Victoria's masses are imitation masses based on his own motets, including *Missa O magnum mysterium*, based on this motet. In comparison with the generous length of Palestrina's Credo (NAWM 63a), each movement is relatively brief, typical of Spanish masses. As we saw in Chapter 9, writing an imitation mass lets the composer show how existing material can be used in new ways. In each movement of the mass, Victoria reworks a different set of passages and motives from his motet and reshapes them into new configurations, exemplifying the high value placed on variety that was a consistent feature of polyphonic mass cycles. At the beginning of the Kyrie (NAWM 64b), Victoria preserves the paired entrances that open the motet but changes them from almost exact imitation into a dialogue between two subjects, each a distinctive variant of the motet's opening motive. The second Kyrie reworks a later point of imitation, and the Christe remakes a homophonic passage into an imitative one. The Gloria (NAWM 64c) begins by reworking a later, homophonic passage from the motet, then presents a patchwork of motives drawn from various points in the motet and recast in various ways. The Sanctus (NAWM 64d) starts with a new variant of the motet's opening, then weaves new points of imitation out of motives from the motet. The result is a kaleidoscopic meditation on ideas from *O magnum mysterium* that simultaneously evokes its text and spirit and demonstrates the skill of the composer.

Imitation mass

MUSIC IN THE SPANISH NEW WORLD Soon after Columbus landed in the New World, Spanish *conquistadores* claimed much of its territory for Spain.

A Spaniard's Description of Aztec Festivals

Fray Toribio de Benavente (ca. 1495–ca. 1565) was one of twelve Franciscan missionaries who went to Mexico in 1524 to convert the indigenous people to Christianity. Called Motolinia ("he suffers") by the Aztecs, he admired their skill in music and described their rituals in detail. Ironically, the Church he served sought to end those rituals and to replace the Aztec music with its own.

❋

Songs and dances were very important in all this land, both to celebrate the solemn festivals of the demons they honored as gods, whom they thought well served by such things, and for their own enjoyment and recreation. . . . And because in each town they put much stock in these things, each chieftain had a chapel in his house with his singers who composed the dances and songs; and these leaders sought out those who knew best how to compose songs in the meter and verses they practiced. . . .

The singers decided some days before the festivals what they would sing. In the larger towns there were many singers, and if there were to be new songs and dances they gathered in advance so there would be no imperfections on the festival day. On the morning of that day they put a large mat in the middle of the plaza where they set up their drums. Then they gathered and dressed at the house of the chieftain; from there they came singing and dancing. Sometimes they began their dances in the morning, sometimes at the hour when we celebrate High Mass. At night they returned singing to the palace, there to end their song early in the night, or when the night was well advanced, or even at midnight.

Fray Toribio de Benavente, called Motolinia (ca. 1495–ca. 1565), *Memoriales de Fray Toribio de Motolinia*, ed. Luis García Pimentel (Mexico: Casa del Editor, 1903), 339–40. Trans. Gary Tomlinson, in SR 77 (3:42), pp. 496–97.

Leading small bands of adventurers, Hernán Cortés overthrew the Aztec empire in present-day Mexico (1519–21), and Francisco Pizarro conquered the Incas in Peru (1527–33). The Spanish brought with them Catholic missionaries, who sought to convert the native peoples to Christianity.

Aztec and Inca music

The Aztecs and Incas had rich musical traditions, with songs in a variety of styles and a wide array of instruments, from drums to flutes. Much of their music was associated with dancing, whether for recreation or as part of religious rituals and festivals. Accounts by Spanish witnesses speak of particularly elaborate music and dances, sometimes lasting all day and into the night, to mark special occasions (see Source Reading).

Catholic music

Catholic missionaries exploited the native peoples' interest in music to spread the message of the new religion. They brought over the music used in Spanish churches and taught native musicians to sing polyphonic masses and motets and to play European instruments. The masses of Morales, Victoria, and Palestrina were sung often in New World cathedrals, and the works of Guerrero were especially popular, remaining in use for centuries. Spanish musicians moved to the Americas to serve as cathedral musicians, and many composed music for services, creating the first written music in the New World. Some of this sacred music was in local languages, including the first polyphonic vocal work published in the Americas, *Hanacpachap cussicuinin,* a processional in the Quechua language of Peru printed in Lima in 1631 by Juan Pérez de Bocanegra (?1598–1631), who may have composed it. Figure 11.8

shows the music and open-
ing stanza of this four-voice
work. The power of music to
win converts, well known to
Luther and Calvin, was used
here to spread Catholicism
on the other side of the globe.

The use of music to prop-
agate the various branches
of Christianity is one of the
central themes of music history in the sixteenth century,
and it lay behind the spread
of European music all over
the Americas. From this
time forward, what was the
European musical tradition
became a transatlantic tradition. Influences soon began
to flow in both directions, making what was going on in the Americas as much
a part of our story as developments in Europe.

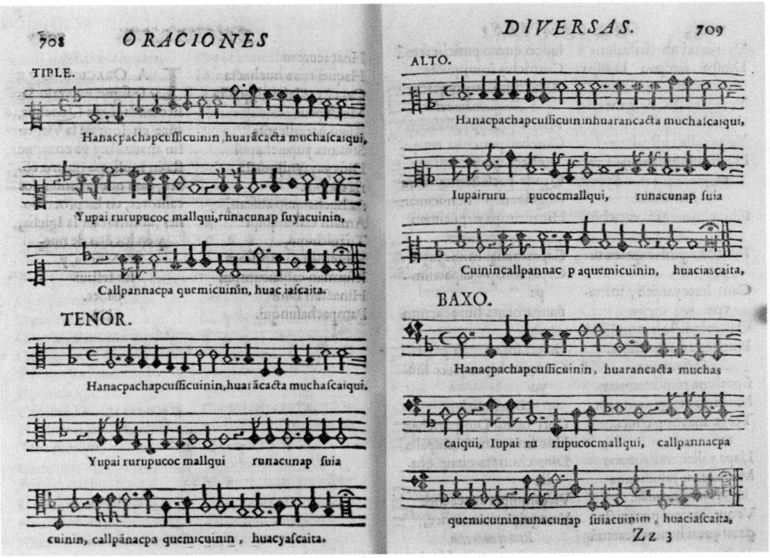

FIGURE 11.8 Hanac-
pachap cussicuinin,
from Ritual formulario,
e institución de curas, *a
manual for priests serving
Inca parishes, published
by Juan Pérez de Bocanegra
in 1631 in Lima, Peru. The
treble and tenor are on the
left, the altus and bassus
on the right. These pages
show the music and first
stanza, followed by nine-
teen more stanzas on the
next three pages.*

GERMANY AND EASTERN EUROPE

Much of central and eastern Europe remained Catholic after the Reformation, including southern Germany, Austria, Bohemia, and Poland. Music in
these areas reflected developments in Flanders, France, and Italy. Influences
came from Franco-Flemish and Italian musicians serving at courts in the
region and from local musicians trained in Italy or France. The leading eastern European composers of Catholic church music were Wacław of Szamotuł
(ca. 1524–ca. 1560) in Poland and Jacob Handl (1550–1591) in Bohemia.
Szamotuł's career reflects the religious tumult of the time in much the same
way as Tallis's or Byrd's. For the Catholic chapel of King Sigismund II August of
Poland, he composed Latin motets in imitative counterpoint like those of his
Flemish contemporaries. But after 1550 he became involved with the Protestant movement in Poland and wrote pieces in Polish for Protestant services in
a simpler, more homophonic style.

The music of Josquin and other Franco-Flemish composers circulated in
Germany beginning early in the sixteenth century, and German composers
adopted their style or blended it with local traditions. The leading German
composer of the late Renaissance was Hans Leo Hassler (1564–1612), who
studied with Andrea Gabrieli in Venice and then held various positions at
Augsburg, Nuremberg, Ulm, and Dresden. The range of his works typifies
the eclecticism of German composers at the time, from settings of Lutheran
chorales to Latin masses and motets for Catholic services, secular partsongs
in German and Italian, and pieces for instrumental ensemble and keyboard.

Germany

ORLANDE DE LASSUS Chief among the Franco-Flemish composers in Germany was Orlande de Lassus (see Chapter 10). Lassus ranks with Palestrina
among the great composers of sacred music in the sixteenth century. Whereas

Motets

Palestrina became a model of the restrained church style and of strict counterpoint, Lassus was equally influential as an advocate of emotional expression and the depiction of text through music, drawing on his experience as a composer of madrigals and chansons.

Lassus wrote fifty-seven masses, but his chief glory lies in his more than seven hundred motets. In each motet, Lassus's rhetorical, pictorial, and dramatic interpretation of the text determines both the overall form and the details. Especially vivid is the six-voice motet *Cum essem parvulus* (NAWM 65), composed in 1579 to words from St. Paul's first epistle to the Corinthians (1 Corinthians 13:11–13). Lassus set the opening words, "When I was a child," as a duet between the two highest voice parts, representing the child through the thin texture and the high vocal range sung by the boys in the choir, alternating with phrases in the four lower voices, representing Paul speaking as an adult. Lassus sets the text "Now we see as if through a mirror in riddles" with enigmatic counterpoint full of suspensions and a brief mirror figure between the bassus and other voices. The promise that eventually we will see "face to face" is a moment of revelation that Lassus portrays with the only fully homophonic passage in the motet, as all six voices declaim the words together in rhythmic unison. Throughout, the words prompt every gesture in the music, from changes of texture and the placement of cadences to the rhythm, accents, and contours of the musical motives.

More than any other sixteenth-century composer, Lassus synthesized the achievements of an era. He was so versatile that we cannot speak of a "Lassus style." He was master of Flemish, French, Italian, and German styles, and every genre from high church music to the bawdy secular song. His motets were especially influential, particularly on German Protestant composers. Lassus's creative use of musical devices to express the emotions and depict the images in his texts led to a strong tradition of such expressive and pictorial figures among German composers, as we will see with Heinrich Schütz (Chapter 15) and Johann Sebastian Bach (Chapter 19).

JEWISH MUSIC

The small but vibrant Jewish community in Europe had its own musical traditions, primarily oral rather than written. Singing was an important part of worship in the home and at meals. Synagogue services included singing hymns (*piyyutim*) and chanting psalms to traditional formulas, usually performed responsorially by a leader and the congregation. Readings from Hebrew Scripture were chanted by a soloist using a system of cantillation. Melodies were not written down, but beginning in the ninth century a notation called *te'amim* was developed for cantillation to indicate accents, divisions in the text, and appropriate melodic patterns. The singer was expected to improvise a melody from the notation, drawing on melodic formulas and practices handed down through oral tradition, and freely adding embellishments.

The hazzan

During the sixteenth century, Jewish communities began to appoint a specific person to perform the chants. This person, called the *hazzan* (later also called *cantor* in some regions), became an integral part of the community as well as of the synagogue structure. Although the position was essentially that of a professional musician, the hazzan typically did not receive formal musical training until the nineteenth century.

Over the centuries, the Ashkenazi Jews of Germany and eastern Europe and the Sephardic Jews of Spain absorbed elements from other music in their regions, and the sound and style of their music gradually diverged. Some Ashkenazi hymns and chants, for example, show melodic elements from Gregorian chant and German Minnelieder, while Sephardic music drew on Arab sources. Thus the threads of borrowing continued to weave through the tapestry of European music: just as early Christian chant borrowed from Jewish sources, and Lutherans based chorale tunes on Gregorian chants and German secular songs, European Jews blended styles of melody from the surrounding society with elements from their ancestral tradition.

Blending borrowed and traditional elements

THE LEGACY OF SIXTEENTH-CENTURY SACRED MUSIC

The religious divisions of the early sixteenth century changed Europe forever. Their echoes are still present in ongoing conflicts between Protestants and Catholics in Northern Ireland and elsewhere. Ironically, in October 1999, on the 482nd anniversary of Luther's ninety-five theses, the Lutheran and Catholic churches signed a declaration ending their dispute. But the genie is long out of the bottle, and there is no going back to the relative uniformity of doctrine and practice of fifteenth-century western Europe.

So too, the Reformation and the Catholic response utterly changed church music. The Lutheran Church developed chorales that have been sung and adapted in myriad ways for almost five hundred years. Their use as the basis for organ and choral works by Bach and other German composers has given chorales a significance for Baroque and later music equal to that of Gregorian chant. Many of the psalm tunes written for the Calvinist Reformed churches are still in use, and several, such as Old Hundredth, are sung in a wide range of Protestant churches. The Church of England and its offspring, including the Episcopal Church, continue to use the Service and anthem; those of Tallis, Byrd, and other sixteenth-century composers are still sung, and new music is written each year in the same genres. The reformed liturgy and chant that resulted from the Council of Trent remained in use in the Catholic Church until later reforms in the twentieth century. Palestrina established a style for church music that has been emulated in all later centuries, although his music faded from regular use in the seventeenth century until its revival and publication in the nineteenth and twentieth centuries. The Palestrina revival was followed by rediscoveries of Lassus, Victoria, and others who represent different musical flavors of the sixteenth century. Only recently have we begun to hear music of this time from the Spanish New World.

In the various musical responses to theological and political disputes as described in this chapter, the political and religious content of particular musical styles is especially clear. To sing *Ein feste Burg* or a Palestrina mass is still an act potent with meaning, even after half a millennium. This should remind us that other pieces, which we now hear simply as music, once carried equally strong associations—associations that we can learn only by studying the historical circumstances from which they emerged.

Further Reading is available at digital.wwnorton.com/hwm10

CHAPTER

12

THE RISE OF INSTRUMENTAL MUSIC

Our story so far has focused on vocal music, since the great majority of pieces that survive from before the sixteenth century are for voices, alone or with instruments. Dances, fanfares, and other instrumental pieces were of course played throughout the Middle Ages and early Renaissance. But since performers played from memory or improvised, little of this music survived in notation. Instrumental music was functional: people welcomed it to accompany dancing or dining, but seldom listened to or played it for its own sake, and thus it was valued less highly than vocal music.

This limitation began to lift after 1480 and especially during the sixteenth century, when churches, courts, cities, and musical amateurs increasingly cultivated instrumental music. The growth in music for instruments is partly an illusion: it simply means more was being written down. But that change in itself shows that music without voices was now more often deemed worthy of preservation and dissemination in writing. It also suggests that instrumental performers were more often musically literate than in earlier eras.

The rise of instrumental music during the Renaissance is evident in new instruments, genres, and styles and in the growing supply of written music for instruments, including many published collections. As in earlier times, musicians performed, improvised, and composed dance music, instrumental versions of vocal works, and settings of existing melodies. Yet they also developed new genres that were not dependent on dancing or singing, including *variations*, *prelude*, *fantasia*, *toccata*, *ricercare*, *canzona*, and *sonata*. For the first time, composers were writing instrumental music that was as interesting and challenging as vocal music. This development set the stage for later periods, when instrumental music became increasingly important.

INSTRUMENTS AND ENSEMBLES

The appearance of books that describe instruments and give instructions for playing them testifies to the growing regard for instrumental music in the sixteenth century. Writers addressed the practicing musician, whether professional or amateur, so they wrote in the vernacular instead of in Latin. From these books we learn about pitch, tuning, and the art of embellishing a melodic line, as well as about instruments themselves (see In Performance: Embellishing Sixteenth-Century Music, p. 256).

Books on instruments

The first such book was Sebastian Virdung's *Musica getutscht* (Music Explained, 1511). Others followed in increasing numbers. One of the richest, the second volume of *Syntagma musicum* (Systematic Treatise of Music, 1618–20) by Michael Praetorius, contains descriptions of instruments then in use, illustrated by woodcuts like the one in Figure 12.1.

Renaissance musicians played an astonishing variety of instruments, some of which are pictured in Figures 12.1 and 12.2. Unlike modern performers, who typically specialize in a single instrument, professional musicians were expected to be adept at several broadly related ones, such as all the fingered wind instruments. As we saw in Chapter 7, Renaissance musicians maintained the distinction between *haut* (high) and *bas* (low) instruments, or relatively loud and soft instruments, that began in the Middle Ages, and cities and courts employed players of both types of instrument.

Wind and string instruments were often built in sets or ***instrumental families***, so that one uniform timbre was available throughout the entire range from soprano to bass. An ensemble of three to seven instruments became known in England as a ***consort***. From the late fifteenth century on, musicians and listeners enjoyed the sound of a homogeneous ensemble, in which all the instruments were from the same family, but mixed ensembles

Instrumental families and consorts

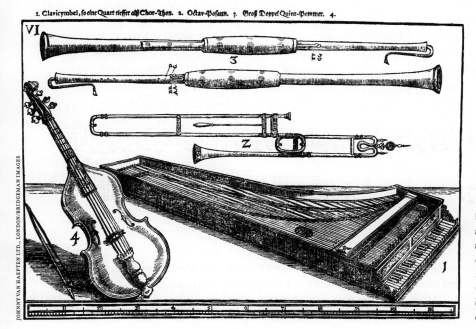

1. Clavicymbel, so eine Quart tieffer alß Chor-Thon. 2. Octav-Posaun. 3. Groß Doppel Quint-Pommer. 4.

VI

JOHNNY VAN HAEFTEN LTD., LONDON/BRIDGEMAN IMAGES

FIGURE 12.1 *Instruments illustrated in Michael Praetorius,* Syntagma musicum, *vol. 2 (Wolfenbüttel, 1618–20): (1) harpsichord; (2) sackbut or trombone; (3) bass shawm; (4) bass viola da gamba.*

IN PERFORMANCE

Embellishing Sixteenth-Century Music

Modern performers of classical music are accustomed to playing or singing the music as written. But sixteenth-century performers were expected to embellish the music, decorating a given melody with passing tones, neighbor tones, runs, and other figurations. Because these decorative figures divided up relatively long notes into several shorter ones, they were called "diminutions" or "divisions." Through tasteful use of diminutions, performers could shape and direct the flow of the music, impel the melody forward to the next note, make the rhythm more lively, and keep listeners intrigued.

Typically these embellishments were applied to the top line of a piece for vocal or instrumental ensemble, but performers of the lower parts could use them as well if they were careful to coordinate with each other, making sure not to conflict with other lines or to break the rules of counterpoint by introducing parallel fifths or other forbidden motions. Diminutions were also part of the improvisatory stock-in-trade of performers on polyphonic instruments such as the lute and harpsichord.

We assume such embellishments have a performing tradition that extends at least as far back as the fourteenth century. The earliest surviving manuscript of keyboard music, the Robertsbridge Codex of about 1360, contains *intabulations* (see p. 264) of vocal pieces from the time, highly decorated with diminutions.

The methods for ornamenting melodies were passed down orally for generations, no doubt changing over time. In the sixteenth century, several musicians published books that included guides for how to add diminutions for a given melody. The earliest book was Sylvestro Ganassi's *Opera intitulata Fontegara*, a manual for playing recorder (see Figure 7.9 on p. 157 for the title page). Modern performers rely on Ganassi and on later books such as Heinrich Finck's *Practica musica* (1556) and Lodovico Zacconi's *Prattica di musica* (1596) to learn how to apply such embellishments in instrumental and vocal music of the time.

Following a pedagogical tradition extending back to the Middle Ages, Ganassi offers hundreds of examples of how one might ornament specific motions of the melody. Playing through these examples, and memorizing many of them, gives the performer a repertoire of figures to use and models to follow in creating new embellishments. Example 12.1 shows seven of his examples for decorating a rising second. In all of these, the diminutions of the first note B begin and end with B, which helps to ensure that the motion of this voice in relation to the others is preserved, and no contrapuntal errors such as parallel fifths or octaves are introduced. In other examples, he allows the performer to move more freely, as long as each new note of the original melody is reached by step.

EXAMPLE 12.1 *Dimunitions of a rising second, from Sylvestro Ganassi's* Fontegara

were also common. The choice was up to the players; until the end of the sixteenth century, composers did not specify instruments.

Wind instruments   Most Renaissance wind instruments were already in use by the Middle
and ensembles   Ages (see Chapters 4 and 6): recorders, transverse flute, shawms, cornetts,

FIGURE 12.2 *Hans Burgkmair,* Maximilian I Surrounded by His Court Musicians and Instruments, *woodcut for the emperor's memoirs* Weisskunig (1514–16). *Clockwise from top left, the instruments include a cornett being played; on the table, viol, clavichord (or virginal), transverse flute, crumhorn (the curved wind instrument), three recorders, and another cornett (extending off the table); in the lower right, tromba marina (a bowed string instrument), sackbut, kettledrum, military drum with drumsticks, and lute (in its case); harp; and positive organ, being played while an assistant works the bellows.*

and trumpets. New in the Renaissance were keys to extend the range of wind instruments; the **sackbut**, the early form of the trombone, made possible by the invention of bent tubing and slide tubing; and the **crumhorn**, whose double reed is enclosed in a cap so the player's lips do not touch it, producing a sound like a soft bagpipe (see Figures 12.1 and 12.2). A typical wind ensemble of the fifteenth and early sixteenth centuries was the **alta** (from Italian "alta musica," loud music) or *alta cappella*, which played for dances, celebrations, and other occasions. At first the standard combination was two shawms and a sackbut or slide trumpet. As music in four or five parts became common after 1450, altas added more players and the instrumentation grew more varied. Courts and cities employed wind ensembles, including the town *waits* of England and the *Stadtpfeifer* (town pipers) of Germany (see Chapter 17), and independent musicians formed groups to play for private citizens, confraternities, and civic organizations.

Percussion instruments also continued from the Middle Ages, often with new refinements, including the tabor, side drum, kettledrums, cymbals, triangles, and bells. Parts were never written for percussion, but performers improvised or played rhythmic patterns from memory.

Percussion

The most popular household instrument in the sixteenth century was the **lute** (from the Arabic *al-oud*, "the oud"), shown in Figure 12.3 (see also Figures 10.3 and 10.5). Lutes had been known in Europe for more than five hundred years, introduced by the Arabs into Spain. (The *oud*, the ancestor of the

Plucked strings

FIGURE 12.3 Mary Magdalene Playing Lute
*(ca. 1550), by an unknown Flemish artist. The music
is written in tablature, a notation that shows which
strings to play and where to put the fingers on the frets to
produce the right pitches.*

lute, is still the primary instrument in Arab countries.)
The standard lute was pear-shaped, with a rounded back,
flat fingerboard, and pegbox (where the strings attached
to tuning pegs) turned back at a right angle. It had one
single and five double strings, usually tuned G–c–f–a–
d′–g′, which were plucked with the fingers. Frets, made
of strings of leather or gut wound around the neck,
marked where the player stopped the string with the fingers of the left hand to raise the pitch one or more semitones. A skilled player could produce a great variety of
effects, from melodies, runs, and ornaments of all kinds
to chords and counterpoint. Lutenists performed solos,
accompanied singing, and played in ensembles. Closely
related to the lute was the Spanish *vihuela*, which had a
flat back and guitar-shaped body.

The *viol* or *viola da gamba* (leg viol) was developed
in Spain in the mid-fifteenth century, was taken up by
Italian musicians a generation later, and quickly became
the leading bowed string instrument of the sixteenth
century. Figure 12.4, from the title page of a manual on
playing the viol, shows a consort of three viols in the three
most common sizes, a bass in the middle, a tenor to our
right, and a treble to the left. As seen in the illustration,
the player held the instrument on or between the legs and bowed underhand.
The tone, played without vibrato, was more delicate and less penetrating than
a modern violin or cello. Like lutes, viols had frets, and the six strings were
tuned a fourth apart with a major third in the middle; for instance, the tenor
viol was tuned G–c–f–a–d′–g′, the standard lute tuning.

FIGURE 12.4 *Consort
of viols as shown on the title
page of Sylvestro Ganassi's
manual on viol playing,*
Regola rubertina *(1542).*

A distant cousin to the viol was the **violin**, a bowed, fretless instrument tuned in fifths rather than fourths and apparently descended from the medieval fiddle. The violin first appeared in the early sixteenth century as a three-string instrument used primarily to accompany dancing. During the seventeenth century, the violin and its relatives the viola and violoncello gradually displaced the viols, in part because of their brighter tone.

The organ had already been widely used in the Middle Ages but changed over time as organ builders added stops (ranks of pipes) with distinctive timbres, many resembling wind instruments. By about 1500, the large church organ was essentially like the instrument we know today, although the pedal keyboard was employed only in Germany and the Low Countries and was adopted much later in other countries. The medieval portative organ had gone out of fashion, but small positive organs like the one in Figure 12.2 were common.

Keyboard instruments

There were two main types of keyboard string instrument by the sixteenth century, the **clavichord** and the **harpsichord**. The clavichord (see Figure 12.2) was a solo instrument suitable for small rooms, while the harpsichord (see Figure 12.1) served both solo and ensemble playing in spaces of moderate size. In a clavichord, pressing a key raises a brass blade that strikes a string, making it vibrate, and remains in contact with it, sustaining the tone until the player releases the key. The position of the blade on the string determines the sounding length of the string and thus its pitch. The tone is very soft, but within limits the performer can control the volume and even effect a vibrato by changing pressure on the key. In instruments of the harpsichord family, the key moves a quill that plucks the string. Harpsichords came in different shapes and sizes and had various names, including **virginal** in England, **clavecin** in France, and *clavicembalo* in Italy. The tone was more robust than a clavichord's but could not be shaded by varying the pressure on the key. A builder could achieve different timbres and degrees of loudness by adding a second keyboard or a stop mechanism that allowed coupling with another string, usually tuned an octave higher.

Each instrument described here has qualities particularly suited to the music performed on it. Renaissance instruments are not imperfect versions of modern ones but are ideal vehicles for the music of that time. This does not mean we should not play lute music on guitar or Renaissance ensemble music on modern brass instruments, for that would deprive performers of much glorious music—and even at the time, musicians freely substituted one instrument for another. But knowing something of the sound, playing techniques, and other properties of the instruments a composer may have had in mind can shed light on the special qualities of the music itself and how to perform it.

Renaissance instruments and music

TYPES OF INSTRUMENTAL MUSIC

Instrumental music served many roles in the Renaissance: as accompaniment to dancing, as part of a public ceremony or religious ritual, as background to other activities, or as music for the entertainment of a small group of listeners or of the players themselves. Just as music printing created a market for music for amateur singers, it also fostered the composition and dissemination of

TIMELINE

instrumental music for amateurs to perform. Professionals also used printed music in their work, from playing for dances to playing in church.

We can divide Renaissance instrumental music into five broad categories:

- dance music
- arrangements of polyphonic vocal music
- settings of existing melodies
- variations
- abstract instrumental works

DANCE MUSIC Social dancing was widespread and highly valued in the Renaissance, and cultured people were expected to be expert dancers. In addition to providing healthy exercise, dancing was a way to meet people, interact with them in a formal setting, judge their fitness and social skills, and show off one's own abilities (see Music in Context: Social Dance). With dancing a central part of social life, it is no surprise that musicians played and composed a great deal of dance music. In writing dance pieces, which owed little to vocal models, sixteenth-century composers began to develop a distinctive instrumental style.

Performers frequently improvised dance music or played dance tunes from memory, as in earlier times. Several fifteenth-century manuscripts contain dances, typically in the form of tenor lines over which treble instruments would improvise. But in the sixteenth century, many dance pieces were printed in collections issued by Petrucci, Attaingnant, and other publishers, for ensemble, lute, or keyboard. These written works tell us much about improvisatory practice, showing that sixteenth-century performers often improvised by ornamenting a given melodic line or by adding one or more contrapuntal parts to a given melody or bass line.

Published dances also show that dance music served two very different purposes in the Renaissance. Most dances for ensemble were functional music, suitable for accompanying dancers, although they were also marketed to amateur performers. In these pieces, the beat, meter, rhythm, and phrasing tend to be very clear, making the music easy for the dancers to follow. The principal melody is typically in the uppermost part, sometimes highly ornamented, but often left plain for the performer to add embellishments. The other parts are mostly homophonic, with little or no contrapuntal interplay. Most dance pieces for solo lute or keyboard, on the other hand, are stylized or abstracted, intended for the enjoyment of the player or listeners rather than for dancing. These pieces often include more counterpoint or written-out decoration, and may feature syncopation, metric ambiguity, irregular phrase lengths, or other ways of creating interest by playing against

MUSIC IN CONTEXT

Social Dance

Dancing is essential in a well-ordered society, because it allows males and females to mingle and observe one another. How else does a lady decide whom to marry? Through dancing, she can tell whether someone is shapely and fit or unattractive and lame, whether he is in good health or has unpleasant breath, and whether he is graceful and attentive or clumsy and awkward.

So writes the Renaissance dancing master Thoinot Arbeau (pen name for the cleric Jehan Tabourot) in his *Orchésographie* (1589), the best-known and most detailed dance treatise of the Renaissance. He offers these views to a young man who has just returned home from a big city where he devoted many years to studying law but where, as he confesses with some regret, he did not make time to learn how to dance. Belatedly, the young man has realized that, far from being a frivolous pastime, dancing is a pleasant and profitable activity, one that confers and preserves health provided it is practiced in moderation at suitable times and in appropriate places. It is especially recommended for those who lead sedentary lives, such as students intent upon their books and young women who spend long hours at knitting and needlework.

Most dances of the Renaissance were performed by couples who arranged themselves in rows or circles. Some, like the pavane, were elegant and dignified, involving a series of gliding steps as in a stately procession. Others, like the various branles, were executed with sideways or swaying motions. Still others were much more vigorous; for example, the galliard included rapidly executed kicks, leaps, and landings, shown in Figure 12.5, with a new motion on every beat.

As the dancing master went on to suggest to his new pupil, dancing is also a kind of mute rhetoric by which persons, through movement, can make themselves understood and persuade onlookers that they are gallant or comely and worthy to be acclaimed, admired, and loved. Such attitudes help to explain the importance of social dance in the Renaissance. And although the steps may be different, the place of dance in society today remains remarkably unchanged.

FIGURE 12.5 *Figures from Thoinot Arbeau's* Orchésographie *showing steps used in a galliard. The dancer is to hop on the left foot and kick the right foot forward (left image); hop on the right foot and kick the left foot forward (center image); repeat both motions again; leap in the air; and land on both feet with the left foot forward (right image). All these movements take only two measures in a fast triple meter.*

THOINOT ARBEAU, *ORCHÉSOGRAPHIE*, FOLIO 45V AND 47R, AS REPRODUCED IN ALBERT CZERWINSKI, *DIE TÄNZE DES 16. JAHRHUNDERTS* (1879).

DANCE	METER	FORM	CHARACTER
Basse danse	Duple or triple	Repeated phrases	Five steps in various set patterns; stately, graceful
Pavane	Duple	AABBCC	Stately, gliding steps
Galliard	Triple or $\frac{6}{4}$	AABBCC	Lively, with hops, kicks, and leaps
Allemande	Duple	2 or 3 repeated strains	Moderate, simple steps, begins with upbeat

FIGURE 12.6 *Four Renaissance dances.*

expectations. The use of a very social kind of music for solitary music-making is intriguing; perhaps the pleasure of solo performance was enhanced by incorporating the familiar rhythms of dance, which carried associations with social interaction or with the physical motions of dancing. Whatever the reason, from the Renaissance to now, many instrumental works have been stylized dances.

Meter and form   Each dance follows a particular meter, tempo, and form, which are reflected in pieces composed for it. This distinguishes each type of dance from the others and gives all dance music a character unlike other kinds of music. Dance pieces feature distinct sections, usually repeated, with two, three, or more sections depending on the dance. Usually the phrase structure is clear and predictable, often in four-measure groups, so that dancers can follow it easily. The combination of regular structure with contrasting phrases and sections provided aural cues for the dancers, helping them to remember and recognize dance patterns and to know when to change steps. Figure 12.6 shows the meter, form, and character of four types of court dance.

Basse danse   The favorite courtly dance of the fifteenth and early sixteenth centuries was the ***basse danse*** (low dance), a stately couple dance marked by gracefully raising and lowering the body. The dance featured five different kinds of steps in various combinations. The music can be in triple or duple meter and is usually in four-measure phrases to suit the patterns of steps in the dance. Several published collections of dances for ensemble begin with numerous basse danses, including Tielman Susato's *Danserye*, published in Antwerp in 1551.

Dance pairs   Renaissance musicians often grouped dances in pairs or threes. A favorite combination was a slow dance in duple meter followed by a fast one in triple meter on the same tune, the music of the second dance being a variation of the first. One such pair, the ***pavane*** (or *pavan*) and ***galliard***, was a favorite in sixteenth-century Italy (where both dances originated), France, Germany, and England. Example 12.2 presents the melody of a pavane and galliard pair by Claude Gervaise, published in 1555. The pavane was a stately dance in three repeated strains (AABBCC), and the more lively galliard follows the same form with a variant of the same melody. Susato's *Danserye* contains two such pairs, including Pavane and Galliard *La dona* (NAWM 66a and 66b). Figure 12.7 shows three couples dancing a pavane, clearly more reserved and less vigorous than the galliard shown in Figure 12.5. A similar pairing of dances in

EXAMPLE 12.2 *Claude Gervaise,* Pavane d'Angleterre *and* Galliard

Gaillard

slow duple and fast triple meter was the *passamezzo* and *saltarello,* popular in Italy, and German and Polish sources also feature such pairs.

Susato's *Danserye* also includes *La morisque* (NAWM 66c), a melody for a *moresca.* This lively type of dance, apparently named for and associated with the Moors of Spain and northern Africa, was performed by men only, often with small bells on their leggings that were set to ringing by the motions of the dance. A close relative is morris dancing, an English tradition that dates back to the fourteenth century.

Moresca

By the late sixteenth century, dances were a core part of the instrumental repertoire for soloists and ensembles alike. Anthony Holborne's *The Night Watch* and *The Fairie-round* exemplify the abstract dances composed around the end of the century for amateurs to play for their own enjoyment. *The Fairie-round* is a galliard, and *The Night Watch* is an *almain,* the English word

Anthony Holborne

FIGURE 12.7 *Three couples dance a stately pavane at a party in the court of Duke Albrecht IV in Munich. The dancers are accompanied by a flute and drum visible in the left balcony, while the right balcony holds a kettledrum player and two trumpeters, whose instruments are hung up. In the background the duke and a lady play cards. Engraving by Matthäus Zasinger, ca. 1500.*

for ***allemande*** (French for "German dance"), a stately couple dance in $\frac{4}{4}$ meter that begins with an upbeat. Both of Holborne's dances exist in versions for solo lute, but he also arranged them for a consort of five instruments (NAWM 67a and 67b) and published them in 1599 in *Pavans, Galliards, Almains and Other Short Aeirs*, the largest surviving collection of English consort music from that time. They are ideal consort music, playable on viols or recorders or other combinations, with constantly varying rhythms and melodies, motives that are tossed back and forth between the players, syncopations and other metric effects, and brilliant counterpoint. Their musical complexity puts them in the category of stylized dance music, entertaining for the players and engaging for listeners, but not easy for dancers to follow.

ARRANGEMENTS OF POLYPHONIC VOCAL MUSIC   Another major source for instrumental music was, paradoxically, polyphonic vocal music. Instruments frequently doubled or replaced voices in polyphonic compositions. Instrumental ensembles often played vocal works, reading from the vocal parts and adding their own embellishments. We have seen that the first book of music published from movable type, Petrucci's *Odhecaton*, was primarily a collection of vocal works without their texts, presumably intended for instrumental performance. Indeed, polyphonic vocal music, printed in great quantities and often labeled "for singing and playing," represented the bulk of what instrumentalists played when they were not improvising or accompanying singers or dancers.

Intabulations   Lutenists and keyboard players made arrangements of vocal pieces, either improvised or written down. These arrangements were often written in tablature (see Chapter 10), so they became known as ***intabulations***. Great numbers of intabulations were published during the sixteenth century, testifying to their popularity. Since plucked instruments lack the sustaining power of voices, arrangers had to recast the original work in a manner idiomatic to the instrument. The intabulations for vihuela by Spanish composer Luys de Narváez (fl. 1526–49) demonstrate that such works are much closer to inventive variations than to simple transcriptions, making intabulations another instance of the Renaissance tendency to rework existing music. In his version of Josquin's *Mille regretz* (NAWM 68a), published in 1538, Narváez preserves the four-voice texture of the original (NAWM 43) but introduces runs, turns, and other figures, called "divisions" or "diminutions" in the terminology of the time, that enliven the rhythm and sustain the listener's interest.

SETTINGS OF EXISTING MELODIES   Instrumental music, like vocal music, sometimes incorporated existing melodies. Composers in the late fifteenth and early sixteenth centuries wrote many settings of chanson melodies for instrumental ensembles; these pieces, among the first written instrumental chamber music, could be played as background music for other activities or by amateurs for their own pleasure. Church organists often improvised or composed settings of Gregorian chant or other liturgical melodies for use in services, replacing portions that were normally sung.

Chant settings and   In Catholic churches, chants traditionally performed by two half-choirs
organ masses   alternating segments or verses, such as Kyries and hymns, could instead

EXAMPLE 12.3 *Girolamo Cavazzoni, opening of Kyrie I from* Missa Apostolorum

alternate between the choir singing chant and the organ playing a cantus-firmus setting or paraphrase. Such settings of short segments of chant were called *organ verses* or *versets.* Example 12.3 shows the beginning of a Kyrie by organist-composer Girolamo Cavazzoni with the chant melody (from NAWM 3b) paraphrased in the upper voice; later other voices carry phrases of the chant as well. This Kyrie is part of an ***organ mass***, a compilation of all the sections of the mass for which the organ would play.

In Lutheran churches, verses of chorales could alternate between the congregation singing in unison and a polyphonic setting for choir or organ. Organists typically improvised their verses, but from the 1570s on, collections of chorale settings for organ appeared. These pieces varied in style, from harmonizations to more elaborate cantus-firmus settings or paraphrases.

Organ chorales

The way musical genres develop through composers imitating each other is exemplified by the *In Nomine.* Sixteenth- and seventeenth-century English composers wrote over two hundred pieces for consort or keyboard titled *In Nomine,* all but a few setting the same cantus firmus. The source for the tradition was the section on "in nomine Domini" from the Sanctus of *Missa Gloria tibi trinitas* by John Taverner (ca. 1490–1545), which he transcribed for instruments and titled *In Nomine.* He was apparently seeking a secular use for the music at a time when England was no longer Catholic and masses were not performed. Others then wrote settings of the same melody (the chant *Gloria tibi trinitas*), and eventually *In Nomines* became one of the most popular genres of English music for viol consort, lasting through Henry Purcell's settings in about 1680. By then the origins of the tune and the name were long forgotten.

In Nomines

VARIATIONS Improvising on a tune to accompany dancing has ancient roots, but the form known as ***variations*** or ***variation form*** is a sixteenth-century invention, used for independent instrumental pieces rather than as dance accompaniment. Variations combine change with repetition, taking a given ***theme***—an existing or newly composed tune, bass line, harmonic plan, melody with accompaniment, or other subject—and presenting an uninterrupted series of variants on that theme. The goal was to showcase the variety that could be achieved in embellishing a basic idea. Variations served both to entertain the listener or amateur performer with fresh and interesting ideas and to demonstrate the skill of the performer and composer. In all these ways, playing variations paralleled an orator elaborating on a theme,

EXAMPLE 12.4 *Luys de Narváez,* Diferencias sobre "Guárdame las vacas"

a. Structural outline of melody and bass for Guárdame las vacas

b. First variation

c. Second variation

d. Third variation

e. Fourth variation

suggesting a link to the Renaissance interest in the ancient art of rhetoric (see Chapter 7).

Types of variations   Written variations on pavane tunes first appeared in 1508 in the lute tablatures of Joan Ambrosio Dalza, published by Petrucci, featuring either a varied repetition of each strain (AA′BB′CC′) or several variants of a single strain. Composers and performers wrote and improvised variations on **ostinatos**, short repeated bass lines. Several basses were used for dancing, such as the *passamezzo antico* and *passamezzo moderno,* both derived from the pavane. Composers also created sets of variations on standard airs for singing verses, such as the Spanish *Guárdame las vacas,* its Italian equivalent the *romanesca,* and the Italian *Ruggiero,* which all feature a spare melodic outline over a standard bass progression.

Example 12.4 shows the main melody and bass for *Guárdame las vacas* and the opening of each variation from a set of four variations (called *diferencias* in Spanish) by Narváez (NAWM 68b). His 1538 collection of works for vihuela, *Los seys libros del Delphín* (The Six Books of the Dauphin), contains the first published sets of variations, including this one. In these first examples of the genre, ideas that would characterize variation form for the next five centuries are already in place: each variation preserves the phrase structure, harmonic plan, and cadences of the theme, while recasting the melody with a new figuration that distinguishes it from the other variations.

Other major Spanish composers of variations are the organist Antonio de Cabezón (ca. 1510–1566) and the lutenist Enríquez de Valderrábano (fl. mid-1500s). Comparing their variations on *Guárdame las vacas* with those of Narváez gives a sense of emerging differences in what was idiomatic for performers on vihuela, lute, and keyboard.

Variations enjoyed an extraordinary flowering in the late sixteenth and early seventeenth centuries among a group of English keyboard composers known as the English virginalists, after the name of their instrument. Works by William Byrd (see Chapter 11), John Bull (ca. 1562–1628), and Orlando Gibbons (1583–1625) appear in the first published collection of music for virginal, *Parthenia* (1613), shown in Figure 12.8. In addition to variations,

FIGURE 12.8 *Title page of* Parthenia, or The Maydenhead, *a collection of music for virginal by William Byrd, John Bull, and Orlando Gibbons presented to Princess Elizabeth and Prince Frederick on their wedding in 1613.* Parthenia *were Greek maidens' choral dances, so both title and subtitle allude whimsically to the virgin bride, the instrument's name, and the fact that this was the first such collection ever printed.*

this collection contains dances, preludes, fantasias, and other genres.

The English virginalists typically used dances or familiar songs of the time as themes for variation. Their interest in varying melodies distinguishes the English from earlier Spanish and Italian composers, who focused more on bass patterns and bare melodic outlines. The songs used were generally short, simple, and regular in phrasing. The melody may be presented intact throughout an entire set of variations, passing at times from one voice to another, or it may be broken up by decorative figuration, so that its original profile is only suggested. Each variation typically uses one type of figuration, and in most variation sets the rhythmic animation increases as the work progresses, though with intermittent quieter interludes and often a slower final variation.

An example of English variation technique is Byrd's variations on *John come kiss me now* (NAWM 69), a popular song of the time. The song melody is present in every variation, most often in the treble but sometimes in a middle voice or the bass. The tune is occasionally embellished, but usually what varies is the setting. Each variation introduces a new motivic idea or rhythmic

The Power of Instrumental Music

Writers in the sixteenth century attributed great emotional powers to music, echoing the ideas of the ancient Greek writers whose works were being rediscovered and more widely read (see the excerpt from Aristotle in Chapter 1). This reminiscence by a French traveler of a banquet in Milan testifies both to the abilities of Francesco da Milano (1497–1543) as an improviser and to the emotional impact of his playing. That the diners stopped conversing and listened intently demonstrates the growing esteem for purely instrumental music.

❁

Among other pleasures and rare things assembled for the satisfaction of these select people was Francesco da Milano, a man considered to have attained the goal (if it is possible) of perfection in playing the lute. The tables having been cleared, he took up a lute and as though testing the tuning of his strings, sitting near one end of the table, began to search out a fantasia. He had only moved the air with three plucked sounds when his music interrupted the conversations that had begun between the guests. And having compelled them to turn their faces to him, in whole or part, he continued with such ravishing zeal, making the strings

faint under his fingers through his divine manner of playing, that little by little he transported all those who listened in such a gracious melancholy that—one resting his head in his hand supported by his elbow; another stretched out relaxed with his limbs in a careless arrangement; another, with mouth open and eyes more than half closed, fixing his gaze (one judged) on those strings; and another, with his chin fallen on his chest, concealing his face that revealed the saddest reticence one had ever seen—his listeners remained deprived of all sensations but that of hearing, as if the soul, having abandoned all the seats of the other senses, had retired to the ears in order to enjoy more at her ease such a ravishing symphony. And I believe (said Monsieur de Ventemille) that we would be there still, had not he himself, I know not how, revived the strings, and little by little invigorating his playing with a gentle force, returned our souls and our senses to the place from which he had stolen them—not without leaving as much astonishment in each of us, as if we had been picked up by an ecstatic transport of some divine frenzy.

From an account by Jacques Descartes de Ventemille as reported by Pontus de Tyard, *Solitaire second ou Prose de la musique* (Lyons: Jan de Tournes, 1555), 114–15.

figure in the other voices, sometimes derived from the source tune, and most variations change figuration midway. There is a gradual quickening of the pace from quarter to eighth to sixteenth notes, climaxing with three variations in triplets and sextuplets. The final two variations relax the pace, creating a satisfying conclusion, while introducing unexpected changes in the bass line and harmony.

ABSTRACT INSTRUMENTAL WORKS The instrumental genres we have seen so far are all based on dance patterns or derived from song, the two traditional wellsprings of music. But beginning in the late fifteenth and early sixteenth centuries, for the first time in history, composers wrote down several types of instrumental music that were truly independent of dance rhythms or borrowed tunes. Most of these developed from habits of improvisation on polyphonic instruments such as lute or keyboard, while others drew on imitative textures derived from vocal music. Although some such pieces were used as

EXAMPLE 12.5 *Johannes Martini,* La Martinella, *excerpts*

x = note from opening figure

a. Opening

b. Beginning of second half

interludes in church or as background music for dining or conversation, they could also be played or listened to for their own sake, and improvisers and composers frequently employed unusual or highly expressive effects to attract listeners' attention (see Source Reading).

Ensemble works

Alongside instrumental ensemble settings of chanson melodies, composers in the fifteenth and early sixteenth centuries wrote pieces in a similar style with no known source in vocal music. Typically based on imitation mixed with free counterpoint, as in chansons of the time (see Example 9.1), these pieces represent the first body of instrumental music to be written down that was truly independent of dances and of song melodies. One of the most widely distributed such works was *La Martinella* by Johannes Martini (ca. 1440–1497), an older contemporary of Isaac and Josquin who worked in Milan and Ferrara. The piece unfolds in a series of phrases, most featuring imitation between two voices (usually superius and tenor) while the third voice rests or adds a free counterpoint. The opening figure returns in various guises throughout the piece, including in varied inverted form at the midpoint, as shown in Example 12.5.

Introductory and improvisatory pieces

Performers on keyboard and lute often had reason to improvise: to introduce a song, to fill time during a church service, to establish the mode of a subsequent chant or hymn, to test the tuning of a lute, or to entertain themselves or an audience. Compositions that resemble such improvisations appeared early in the sixteenth century, especially in Spain and Italy, and became mainstays of the repertoire for solo players. Such pieces were given a variety of names, including **prelude**, **fantasia**, or **ricercare**. Not based on any preexisting melody, they unfold freely, with varying textures and musical ideas. They served the same function as an introduction to a

EXAMPLE 12.6 *Claudio Merulo, Toccata IV in the 6th Mode, excerpts*

a. Opening

b. Central imitative section

c. Closing

speech, preparing the listener and establishing the pitch center and mode for what followed. The fantasias of Spanish composer Luis Milán (ca. 1500–ca. 1561) in his collection for vihuela entitled *El Maestro* (Valencia, 1536), for example, are each in the same mode as the following vocal piece, using rapid scale passages or other figuration to add tension and suspense before a strong cadence on the final of the mode.

Toccata   The **toccata** was the chief form of keyboard music in improvisatory style during the second half of the sixteenth century. The name, from the Italian *toccare* ("to touch"), refers to touching the keys, reminding us of the player's body and actions. The toccatas by the organist Claudio Merulo (1533–1604) exemplify the genre. His Toccata IV in the 6th Mode from his second book of toccatas (1604), excerpted in Example 12.6, shows a variety of textures and figuration. In the opening succession of slowly changing harmonies, Merulo takes advantage of the organ's power to sustain tones. The numerous suspensions and prolonged and repeated dissonances are idiomatic to the organ. Embellishments on the most active tones and scale passages in freely varied rhythms animate the texture. A contrasting middle section develops four short subjects in turn through imitation; the first of these is shown in Example 12.6b. The last third of the piece is again free, like the opening, but with more spacious harmonies and even more fantastic play of brilliant running passages. The majestic slowing down of the chordal changes coupled with the increased liveliness and ever wider sweep of the runs makes an impressive climax. The closing measures appear in Example 12.6c. Pieces of this sort did not always contain imitative sections, nor were they uniformly labeled toccatas; they were also called *fantasia, prelude,* and *intonazione* (intonation).

One type of prelude, the **ricercare** or *ricercar,* evolved into a motet-like *Ricercare* succession of imitative sections. Ricercare is an Italian verb meaning "to seek out," and its application to music probably comes from lutenists' jargon for picking out notes on the instrument and testing the tuning. The earliest ricercari, for lute, were brief and improvisatory. When transferred to the keyboard, the genre acquired occasional passages of imitation. By 1540, the ricercare consisted of successive themes, each developed in imitation and overlapping with the next at the cadence—in effect, a textless imitative motet, but with embellishments that were typically instrumental. Such ricercari were written for ensemble as well as keyboard or lute. By the early 1600s, the ricercare was an extended imitative piece on a single subject (see Chapter 15).

The Italian **canzona** or *canzon* became one of the leading genres of con- *Canzona* trapuntal instrumental music in the late sixteenth century, alongside the fantasia and ricercare, but had a different origin. The earliest pieces called *canzona* were intabulations of French chansons, after which the canzona was named. By midcentury, composers such as Girolamo Cavazzoni were writing canzonas that thoroughly reworked chansons rather than simply embellishing them. Newly composed canzonas in the style of an imitative French chanson appeared by 1580, first for ensemble and then for organ. Canzonas were light, fast moving, and strongly rhythmic, with a fairly simple contrapuntal texture. From the chanson, composers adopted the typical opening rhythmic figure that occurs in most canzonas: a single note followed by two notes of half the value, such as a half note followed by two quarter notes. Like chansons, canzonas often feature a series of themes that differ from one another in melodic outline and rhythm. Each is worked out in turn, resulting in a series of contrasting sections.

MUSIC IN VENICE

Instrumental performance and composition reached a particularly high level in Venice in the late sixteenth and early seventeenth centuries. Music in Venice exemplifies traits of the late Renaissance and also of the early Baroque period (see Chapters 14 and 15), so it may serve as a point of transition between the two eras.

ACADEMIA, VENICE, ITALY. PHOTO: ERICH LESSING/ART RESOURCE, NY

FIGURE 12.9 Procession in Piazza San Marco *(1496) by Gentile Bellini, showing a religious or civic procession with singers and instrumentalists, with St. Mark's Church in the background.*

VENICE Venice, the second most important Italian city after Rome, was an independent state with its own empire. Nominally a republic, it was actually an oligarchy run by several important families, with an elected leader called the doge (Venetian for "duke"). Because Venice was a city of traders and the chief port for European trade with the Near East and Asia, it had accumulated enormous wealth, power, and splendor by the fifteenth century. Wars and other misfortunes reduced its position in the sixteenth century, but it still controlled extensive territories on the Italian peninsula and along the Adriatic coast from Croatia to Greece.

The government had plenty of money and spent lavishly on public spectacle, music, and art. This was cultural propaganda on a grand scale: although the empire had shrunk, the arts could still project Venice's lingering glory, and sumptuous public displays of wealth and confidence could rally the public behind the state and intimidate potential enemies at home or abroad.

CHURCH OF ST. MARK The center of Venetian musical culture was the great eleventh-century Church of St. Mark, or Basilica San Marco, whose Byzantine domes, spacious interior, bright gold mosaics, and ostentatious Pala d'Oro, an altarpiece of solid gold and precious jewels, proclaimed the city's wealth and close links to the Near East. Like Venice itself, St. Mark's was independent: it was the private chapel of the doge, essentially the state church of the republic, and thus was not controlled by the church hierarchy. Many civic and religious ceremonies took place each month in the church and in the vast piazza in front of it, like the procession depicted in Figure 12.9. On each occasion, Mass and Vespers were celebrated with great pomp and elaborate music.

Music in St. Mark's was supervised by officials of the state, sparing no expense. The position of chapelmaster, the most coveted musical post in all Italy, was held by Willaert, Rore, and Zarlino in the sixteenth century and by Claudio Monteverdi in the early seventeenth. Renowned artists, chosen after stringent examination, served as organists, including Claudio Merulo, Andrea Gabrieli (ca. 1532–1585), and his nephew Giovanni Gabrieli (ca.

GIOVANNI GABRIELI
(ca. 1555–1612)

Gabrieli was one of the leading composers of the late Renaissance and early Baroque periods, known today primarily for his instrumental works but equally accomplished in sacred music.

Little is known about Gabrieli's early life and training. In his teens and early twenties, he was in the service of Duke Albrecht V in Munich, where he studied with Orlande de Lassus. In 1585, he won appointment as second organist at St. Mark's, serving alongside his uncle Andrea Gabrieli until the latter's death that August. That same year, the younger Gabrieli also was elected organist to the Scuola Grande di San Rocco, one of the most prominent of the scuole (schools), or charitable confraternities, of Venice. The scuole sponsored religious observances and performances, participated in civic celebrations, and strove to outdo each other in pageantry and music, giving Gabrieli ample opportunity to compose lavish music for large forces. At St. Mark's, he was the main composer of ceremonial music, producing about a hundred motets, most for multiple choirs. As second organist, Gabrieli supervised the instrumentalists, and his ensemble

FIGURE 12.10 *Portrait of Giovanni Gabrieli by Annibale Carracci (1560–1609).*

canzonas and sonatas were no doubt written for them. He served both St. Mark's and San Rocco until his death in 1612.

MAJOR WORKS About 100 motets, over 30 madrigals, 37 ensemble canzonas, 7 sonatas, and about 35 organ works, including ricercares, canzonas, toccatas, and intonazioni

---

1555–1612). Beginning in 1568, a permanent ensemble of first-rate instrumentalists was assembled, centering on cornetts and sackbuts but including violin and dulcian, forerunner of the bassoon. Additional players were hired on major feast days, when as many as two dozen instrumentalists performed, alone or together with the choir of twenty to thirty voices.

GIOVANNI GABRIELI The rich musical environment of Venice shaped the music of Giovanni Gabrieli. He served St. Mark's for almost three decades as organist, composer, and supervisor of the instrumentalists (see biography and Figure 12.10). His compositions used all the resources available at the church, resulting in works for multiple choirs and the earliest substantial collections of pieces for large instrumental ensemble.

The glory of Venetian church music is manifest in its ***polychoral motets***, works for two or more choirs, usually performed with one to four singers on each vocal line. From before the time of Willaert, composers in the Venetian region had often written for divided choirs, or *cori spezzati*. Willaert published a collection of psalms for double choir in 1550 that sparked a fashion for polychoral works across Europe over the next several decades. Palestrina,

Polychoral motets

Victoria, and Lassus wrote polychoral motets for use on special ceremonial occasions. The vogue reached a peak in the 1560s when Alessandro Striggio (ca. 1536–1592) composed a mass for forty voices divided into eight choirs for performance in Florence during a visit of the Holy Roman emperor Maximilian II in 1567, and a performance in England of his motet for the same forces, *Ecce beatam lucem*, inspired Thomas Tallis to write another motet for eight five-voice choirs, *Spem in alium*.

In Venice, polychoral music was a regular diet rather than a special treat. Andrea Gabrieli wrote numerous polychoral works for important state and church ceremonies, and the medium reached new heights in the polychoral music of his nephew Giovanni Gabrieli. In the latter's music, two to five choirs, each with a different combination of high and low voices, mingled with instruments of diverse timbres, answered one another antiphonally, and joined together in massive sonorous climaxes. Sometimes the choirs were separated spatially, with groups in the two organ lofts, one on each side of the altar, and another on the floor. Gabrieli's use of contrasting forces was a major influence on Baroque church music, especially in Germany. We will examine one of his later polychoral motets in Chapter 15.

Ensemble canzonas

Gabrieli and other Venetian composers applied the idea of divided choirs to instruments. The *Canzon septimi toni a 8* (Canzona in Mode 7 in Eight Parts, NAWM 70) from Gabrieli's *Sacrae symphoniae* (Sacred Symphonies, 1597) resembles a double-chorus motet for two groups of four instruments, with organ accompaniment. Like other canzonas, it presents a series of contrasting sections, some imitative, others more homophonic. The two instrumental groups alternate long passages, engage in more rapid dialogue, and sometimes play together, especially at the end. The form is defined by a refrain, partly in triple meter, that appears three times.

Sonatas

The Venetian **sonata** (Italian for "sounded") was a close relative of the canzona, consisting of a series of sections each based on a different subject or on variants of a single subject. Both canzonas and sonatas were used at Mass or Vespers as introductions or postludes or to accompany significant rituals. The *Sonata pian' e forte* from Gabrieli's *Sacrae symphoniae* has earned a prominent place in music history because it is among the first instrumental ensemble pieces to designate specific instruments in the printed parts: in the first choir, cornett and three sackbuts, and in the second, a violin and three sackbuts. Another innovation in the printed music was indicating passages as *pian* (piano, meaning "soft") or *forte* ("loud"), one of the earliest instances of dynamic markings in music. Through contrasts of one instrumental choir against the other, single choir with both together, loud versus soft, and slow homophonic passages with faster motion and points of imitation, Gabrieli created a purely instrumental work with as much interest, variety, and depth of content as a madrigal or motet. Such pieces were the foundation from which independent instrumental music developed over the next two centuries.

INSTRUMENTAL MUSIC GAINS INDEPENDENCE

The sixteenth century saw the rise of instrumental music that was cultivated for its own sake, whether derived from dance music, related to vocal music, or conceived as abstract music independent of dance or song. The abstract types would ultimately have the most significance, leading to the sonatas and symphonies of later centuries, but links to vocal music and dance remain in later instrumental music. Some genres of sixteenth-century instrumental music were regularly cultivated in the Baroque era and beyond, including stylized dances, organ settings of sacred tunes, variations, and preludes. The traditions of improvising and embellishing instrumental music also continued to develop, and the figurations players used increasingly influenced written music as composers began to specify the figures and ornamentation they desired. Instrumental music continued to gain independence, until by the nineteenth century it reached a level of prestige higher than most vocal music. Moreover, the tradition of playing instrumental music for one's own pleasure, alone or with friends, was well established by the end of the sixteenth century and has endured to this day.

Instrumental works were published in great numbers in the sixteenth century, and some were played for a generation or more until tastes changed and the old books were shelved, replaced by music in newer styles. The oldest instrumental works most listeners know today are Gabrieli's canzonas and sonatas, which were rediscovered in the early nineteenth century and have become part of the standard repertoire for modern brass instruments. The revival of most other Renaissance instrumental music had to wait until the twentieth century, when artisans began to reconstruct Renaissance instruments from pictures and surviving examples and to produce them in increasing numbers. Scholars have transcribed a good deal of Renaissance instrumental music, but it is still far less often studied or performed than vocal music, in part because relatively few can read the complex tablatures developed for keyboard and plucked strings, which varied from each instrument to the next and from one region to another. Only in recent decades have Renaissance dances and lute pieces begun to appear on recordings and classical radio stations, as performers and listeners have rediscovered the instruments, sounds, and appeal of this once very popular music.

Further Reading is available at digital.wwnorton.com/hwm10

THE
SEVENTEENTH
CENTURY

Western culture for the last four hundred years has lived off the intellectual capital created in the seventeenth century. From discoveries about the solar system to the invention of calculus, from notions of political equality to the economic system of capitalism, Europeans in the 1600s laid the groundwork for scientific and social developments for generations to come.

The same is true in music. Familiar musical genres invented in the seventeenth century include opera, oratorio, cantata, overture, concerto, solo sonata, trio sonata, keyboard sonata, suite, fugue, chaconne, and passacaglia. During that century, Italian composers created the first recitatives, musicians in Paris and Rome organized the first orchestras, Venetian singers became the first divas, an entrepreneur in London originated the idea of public concerts, and a French girl became the first celebrated child prodigy in music. Composers and performers in the seventeenth century responded to their contemporaries' interest in drama, theater, and spectacle by creating music that was more dramatic and spectacular than any before. Highly expressive styles developed for the stage found their way into music for religious services, forever changing the character of church music, and into instrumental music, which began for the first time to rival vocal music in importance and emotional content. Tonality, the system of major and minor keys oriented around a central pitch, emerged as the fundamental musical language of Europe, remaining so for over two centuries. These and other aspects of music first introduced in the seventeenth century are among those we encounter most often and take most for granted, making the history of that era especially interesting.

PART OUTLINE

NEW STYLES IN THE SEVENTEENTH CENTURY

Italian musicians living around 1600 knew they were inventing new ways of making music. They devised new idioms, such as **basso continuo**, **monody**, and **recitative**; new styles, marked by unprepared dissonance, greater focus on the solo voice or instrument, and idiomatic playing; and new genres, including **opera**. This generation saw the most deliberate cultivation of the new in music since the Ars Nova in the early 1300s.

In retrospect, we have come to see this outpouring of innovation as the beginning of a new period often called the **Baroque**. The term was employed by art historians in the nineteenth century, but only in the twentieth century did music historians apply it to the period from about 1600 to about 1750. There are certainly elements that composers of the early seventeenth century such as Peri and Monteverdi share with early-eighteenth-century composers like Vivaldi and Bach, notably their focus on moving the **affections** (emotions). But the seventeenth century was also a period of its own, marked by continuous invention of new genres, styles, and methods, the gradual diffusion of Italian ideas, and, in response to them, the development of independent national idioms. Whichever view we take, the innovations around 1600 launched a new era in music, in which opera and theatrical styles played leading roles.

This chapter will contrast the Baroque period with its predecessor, the Renaissance. Chapter 14 traces the invention and early spread of opera in Italy. Chapter 15 takes up church, chamber, and instrumental music in the first half of the seventeenth century, and Chapters 16 and 17 chart developments after midcentury.

EUROPE IN THE SEVENTEENTH CENTURY

The interest in innovation among musicians paralleled new ideas in science, politics, and economics. The effects of war, varying political structures, and relative wealth made circumstances for musicians different in each part of western Europe, influencing the music cultivated in the different regions.

Europe, shown in Figure 13.1, was in the midst of a scientific revolution, led by a new breed of investigators who relied on mathematics, observation, and practical experiments to extend knowledge beyond received opinion. Johannes Kepler showed in 1609 that the planets, including the earth, move around the sun in elliptical orbits at speeds that vary with their distance from the sun. During the following decade, Galileo Galilei demonstrated the laws that control motion and used the newly invented telescope to discover sunspots and moons orbiting Jupiter. Sir Francis Bacon argued for an empirical approach to science, relying on direct observation rather than on ancient authorities. Balancing Bacon's inductive method, René Descartes put forth a deductive approach that explained the world through mathematics, logic, and reasoning from first principles. These two strands joined in the work of Sir Isaac Newton, whose law of gravitation, developed in the 1660s, combined acute observation with mathematical elegance, and whose invention

The scientific revolution

FIGURE 13.1 *Europe around 1610.*

TIMELINE

of calculus created new methods in mathematics and engineering. These scientists did not entirely abandon the traditions they inherited—Kepler published an elaborate account of the harmony of the spheres, harking back to Plato (see Chapter 1), and Newton was an alchemist as well as a physicist—but their focus on experimentation and observation and their integration of physics with mathematics set the pattern for scientific methods for centuries to come. The same interest in what is useful and effective, often in combination with what is hallowed by tradition, is apparent in seventeenth-century music of all kinds. Perception and perceived effect lay at the heart of the new styles in art and music around 1600, including the *second practice* (see pp. 287–90) and recitative, and in the new genres developed throughout the century, from opera, *cantata*, and *oratorio* to *solo sonata*, *trio sonata*, *suite*, *overture*, and *concerto*.

The century also saw new thinking about politics, ranging from the English Levellers, who advocated democracy with equal political rights for all men, to Thomas Hobbes, whose *Leviathan* (1651) argued for an all-powerful sovereign state. Such debates were stimulated in part by struggles for power or disputes over religion that sometimes broke out into war. Some long-standing conflicts were resolved around the turn of the seventeenth century. In France, Henri IV issued the Edict of Nantes in 1598 guaranteeing some freedom to Protestants while confirming Catholicism as the state religion. Protestant England and Catholic Spain ended decades of war in 1604, and the Calvinist Netherlands gained independence from Spain in 1609 and became a republic. But religious conflict combined with struggles for political advantage within the Holy Roman Empire precipitated the Thirty Years' War (1618–48), which devastated Germany, reducing the population in some areas by more than half. The English Civil War (1642–49), primarily a battle for power between the king and Parliament, resulted in a temporary end to the monarchy, followed by its restoration in 1660. Most wars were purely political, as Spain, France, England, and other major powers jockeyed for superiority, often involving other regions such as Italy and the Low Countries in their conflicts. Almost everywhere, the authority of the state grew. All these political and religious conflicts directly affected music, chiefly because rulers and church authorities remained important patrons.

Meanwhile, Europeans were expanding overseas. During the seventeenth century the British, French, and Dutch established colonies in North America, the Caribbean, Africa, and Asia, in competition with Spain and Portugal. Especially lucrative imports were sugar and tobacco, new luxury items for Europe, grown on plantations in the Americas. These crops required intensive labor provided by the cruel trade in human life that brought Africans to the New World as slaves. Europeans who settled in the Western hemisphere brought their traditions with them, including Catholic service music and villancicos to the Spanish colonies and metric psalmody to British North America.

Britain, the Netherlands, and northern Italy prospered from capitalism, a *Capitalism* system in which individuals invested their own money (capital) in businesses designed to return a profit. An important innovation was the joint stock company, which pooled the wealth of many individuals while limiting their risk. Stock companies were formed to finance opera houses in Hamburg, London, and other cities. Capitalism put money in the hands of individuals, who would invest or spend it locally and thus boost the economy. The capitalist system proved a better economic engine than concentration of money in the hands of the state or the privileged few, as was the practice in Spain, France, and many smaller principalities. Among the effects on music were the rise of public opera and public concerts, as well as an increased demand from the upper and middle classes for published music, musical instruments, and music lessons.

Musicians continued to depend on patronage from court, church, or city, *Patronage* and the types of music that won support varied from region to region. Musicians were best off in Italy, which was wealthy from trade yet still divided between Spanish control in the south, the papal states around Rome, and several independent states in the north (see Figure 13.1). Rulers, cities, and leading families supported music and the arts as a way of competing for prestige. Aristocrats in Florence sponsored a brilliant series of musical and theatrical innovations around 1600, spawning similar efforts by the dukes of Mantua, churchmen in Rome, and the citizens of Venice. Their support continued Italy's reign as the dominant influence in European music through the mid-eighteenth century.

In France, power and wealth became more concentrated in the king. Louis XIV (r. 1643–1715) controlled the arts, including music, and used them to assert his glory. During the seventeenth century, France replaced Spain as the predominant power on the Continent; partly as a result, French music was imitated widely, while the music of Spain had little influence beyond its borders. Civil war and parliamentary prerogative limited the wealth of the English royalty, but their patronage strongly influenced national tastes. The calamity of the Thirty Years' War sapped treasuries throughout the Holy Roman Empire, but after midcentury, German courts and free city-states built up their musical establishments, drawing on influences from both Italy and France. The church continued to support music, although its role was less important than it had been in previous centuries, after the reform of benefices by the Council of Trent deprived churches and court chapels of a major source of funding and of talent.

Along with aristocratic, civic, and ecclesiastical patronage, many cities had "academies," private associations that, among other functions, sponsored musical activities. Public opera houses were established in many cities, beginning in Venice in 1637. Public concerts to which one subscribed or paid admission first occurred in England in 1672, but the practice did not become widespread in Europe until the later 1700s.

FROM RENAISSANCE TO BAROQUE

THE BAROQUE AS TERM AND PERIOD How the term *baroque*, meaning bizarre, exaggerated, or in bad taste, came to be applied to the art and music of several generations is a story of changing tastes and values. The word is

FIGURE 13.2 *Detail of the Pamphili Palace (now Doria-Pamphili) in Rome, completed ca. 1739. Writing around 1755, Charles de Brosses criticized as "baroque" the delicate, detailed decoration of the sort he considered more suitable for silverware than for a building. His is thought to be the first use of the word in relation to one of the visual arts.*

French, from the Portuguese *barroco,* a misshapen pearl. It was first applied pejoratively to music and art in the mid-eighteenth century by critics who preferred a newer, simpler style. The older, "barocque" music was deemed by one critic to be dissonant and unmelodious, with capricious and extravagant changes of key and meter, and by another as aiming "to surprise by the boldness of its sounds." Travel writer Charles de Brosses applied the term to architecture, complaining that the Pamphili Palace in Rome, shown in Figure 13.2, was decorated with filigree better suited to tableware than to buildings.

When nineteenth-century art critics began to appreciate the ornate, dramatic, and expressive tendencies of seventeenth-century painting and architecture, *baroque* took on a positive meaning. Music historians since the 1920s saw many of the same qualities of extravagance, decoration, and focus on drama and expression in much music of the times, and by the 1950s *Baroque* was well established as a name for the period of about 1600 to around 1750. Recognizing that these 150 years encompassed a diversity of styles too great to be embraced by one word, we will speak of a Baroque period, but not a Baroque style. The boundary dates must be taken as rough approximations for a time when composers and listeners shared ideals for music and accepted common conventions for how it should behave. Most important, they prized music for its dramatic power and its capacity to move the affections (see pp. 286–87).

THE DRAMATIC BAROQUE The most striking aspect of seventeenth-century literature, art, and music is its focus on the dramatic. Not since ancient Greece were there so many playwrights among the leading authors, including William Shakespeare (1564–1616) and Ben Jonson (ca. 1572–1637) in England and Pierre Corneille (1604–1684), Jean Racine (1639–1699), and Jean Baptiste Molière (1622–1673) in France. Poetry of the time often had theatrical qualities (see Source Reading, p. 284), and vivid images and dramatic scenes in the poems of John Donne (1572–1631), the epic *Paradise Lost* of John Milton (1608–1674), and the novel *Don Quixote* by the Spaniard Miguel de Cervantes (1547–1616) at times suggest the intensity of staged performance.

Baroque art   In art and architecture, as in music, the Baroque began in Italy. The theatricality of Baroque art is seen in the sculptures of Gian Lorenzo Bernini (1598–1680), who worked for the church and other patrons in seventeenth-century Rome. Contrasting Michelangelo's famous *David* (1501–4), in Figure 13.3, with Bernini's *David* (1623) in Figure 13.4 shows the change from Renaissance to Baroque goals. Michelangelo evokes ancient Greek statuary with his standing nude, celebrates the nobility and beauty of the human figure through balance and proportion, and portrays his hero as contemplative and still, with only a furrowed brow to suggest the coming battle with Goliath. Bernini shows David winding up to sling the stone, his body dynamic, his muscles taut, his

FIGURE 13.4
Gian Lorenzo Bernini's David (1623), embodying the Baroque virtues of drama, dynamism, and emotional expression.

FIGURE 13.3 *Michelangelo Buonarotti's David (1501–4), which evokes ancient Greek statuary and is endowed with the ideal traits of Renaissance humanism, including intelligence, nobility, balance, and calm.*

lips and face tense with exertion. Instead of contemplation and balance, Bernini emphasizes motion and change. The effect is dramatic, making the viewer respond emotionally rather than with detached admiration.

Even more stunning is Bernini's *Ecstasy of St. Teresa* (1645–52), shown in Figure 13.5. Teresa of Avila, a sixteenth-century Spanish nun, mystic, and leader in the Catholic Reformation, had a vision of an angel's arrow piercing her heart, overwhelming her with both pain and joy. Bernini captures that moment of transformation, with the saint in rapture, her robes moving wildly about her, borne upward on a cloud toward a light from Heaven. The use of material is virtuosic: the heavy marble statue, fastened to the wall, seems to float in midair, lit from a hidden window above, with golden rays behind it. These were theatrical effects, designed to astonish viewers and arouse strong feelings. As shown in Figure 13.6, Bernini heightened the theatricality by placing on the side walls of the chapel sculptures that depict members of the Cornaro family, who commissioned the chapel, looking at St. Teresa and discussing the scene as if they were in a box at the theater watching the enactment of her ecstasy on stage. The Catholic Church saw such art as a persuasive instrument in its campaign to keep its flock faithful and to counteract the Reformation.

Baroque architecture could be equally theatrical, using ancient and Renaissance elements in new and astounding ways. Bernini's dramatic design for the square in front of St. Peter's Basilica at the Vatican, shown in Figure 13.7, features two semicircular colonnades, four columns deep, that seem to

Baroque architecture

SOURCE READING

The Dramatization of Poetry

Baroque theatricality infused poetry as well as art and music. This poem uses the image of the poet as a fortified city attacked by the enemy, Love. Written by Giulio Strozzi (1583–1652) and set by Claudio Monteverdi in his *Eighth Book of Madrigals* (1638), the poem is witty in its theatricality: at the end of each stanza, as the crisis grows more intense, the protagonist shouts to his imagined companions.

❖

The insidious enemy, Love, circles
The fortress of my heart.
Hurry up, for he is not far away.
Arm yourselves!

We must not let him approach, so he can scale
Our weak walls,
But let us make a brave sally out to meet him.
Throw on the saddles!

His weapons are no fakes, he draws nearer
With his whole army.
Hurry up, for he is not far from here.
Everyone to his post!

He intends to attack the stronghold of my eyes
With a vigorous assault.
Hurry up, for he is here without any doubt.
Everyone to his horse!

There's no more time, alas, for all of a sudden he
Has made himself the master of my heart.
Take to your heels, save yourselves if you can.
Run!

My heart, you flee in vain, you are dead.
And I hear the arrogant tyrant,
The victor, who is already inside the fortress,
Crying "Fire, slaughter!"

Giulio Strozzi, *Gira il nemico insidioso.*

enfold the observer, symbolizing the Church's claim to embrace the world. While the columns, capitals, lintels, portals, and other components are traditional and based on ancient classical models, the length and curve are unprecedented, and the height, width, and open space add to the spectacular effect.

Music becomes dramatic

Just as the central impulse of Baroque art is dramatization, the quintessential music of the Baroque era is dramatic, centered in opera but extending to songs, church music, and instrumental music. All kinds of motion and change in music—from rhythmic motions and melodic rise and fall to contrasts of harmony, texture, and style—were used with a new intensity to convey emotions and suggest dramatic action.

Performing for the public

Drama requires an audience, and it is in the seventeenth century that the concept of "the public" in the modern sense began to emerge. Until then, even when music's sole purpose was to entertain, performers and listeners were near to each other, and the performer could quickly turn into a listener and vice versa, as in the convivial music-making at court and in private homes that fostered the vogue for the madrigal and other secular songs (see Chapter 10). But during the seventeenth century, performers became professionals (see Innovations: The Impresario and the Diva, pp. 312–13), and the listener was no longer a co-participant but became a passive recipient whose feelings performers sought to move. This century saw the first public opera houses, the first public concerts, and other new venues for music in which the audience was more distant physically than had been typical in earlier eras.

FIGURE 13.5 *Bernini's* The Ecstasy of St. Teresa *(1645–52), in the Cornaro Chapel, church of Santa Maria della Vittoria, Rome.*

FIGURE 13.6 *Part of the right wall of Bernini's Cornaro Chapel, with life-size sculptures of members of the Cornaro family observing and commenting on the ecstasy of St. Teresa.*

FIGURE 13.7 *St. Peter's Square and Basilica at the Vatican in Rome, with colonnades designed by Gian Lorenzo Bernini in 1657.*

THE AFFECTIONS Composers of the Baroque period sought musical means to express or arouse the ***affections***, also called *affects* (pronounced AF-fects) or *passions*. These were rationalized emotions such as sadness, joy, anger, love, fear, excitement, or wonder.

Aristotelian view

In his *Metaphysics*, Aristotle described affections as states of the soul that are caused by specific acts and inspire reactions in turn. Actions are associated with the body, the active subject, and passions with the soul, the passive object. Life—or the plot of a drama—is a series of events in which an action (whether by me or someone or something else) causes a passion in my soul, which causes me to take another action that affects others in turn, in an ongoing chain. In this view, which predominated through the mid-seventeenth century, affections are individual responses to specific situations. Painters, poets, and dramatists sought to convey the affections of the individuals they depicted, and composers aimed to heighten through music the affections expressed in the words they set.

Descartes on affections

René Descartes introduced a new view in his influential treatise *The Passions of the Soul* (1649), an attempt to analyze and catalogue the affections. For Descartes, the body and soul were separate, and the affections were objective and relatively stable states of the soul, each caused by a certain combination of "spirits" in the body. Once these spirits were set in motion by external stimuli through the senses, they conveyed their motions to the soul, thus bringing about emotions. Descartes posited a simple mechanical theory to explain their cause: for every motion stimulating the senses there is a particular emotion evoked in the soul. Grief, joy, and other affections are universal experiences, not specific to an individual; they are more like colors, an objective reality that can be described, than like taste, which may differ from person to person.

The affections in art and music

Descartes's view came to predominate in the latter seventeenth and eighteenth centuries. Since all the arts sought to move the emotions and conjure the passions, it became a matter of interest to codify the affections and ways to stimulate each one. In an essay on expression in painting, French painter and designer Charles Le Brun (1619–1690) portrayed and labeled an entire gallery of emotions and their corresponding facial gestures, including those in Figure 13.8, to serve as examples for artists. Writers about music made similar attempts to isolate and catalogue the affections and to describe how to arouse them. In so doing, they reflected the practice of composers and performers, who developed new methods for representing emotions in music, many of which became enduring conventions.

It was widely believed that experiencing a range of affections through music could bring the spirits in the body into better balance, promoting physical and psychological health, so that both vocal and instrumental works typically offered a succession of contrasting moods. Composers did not try to express their personal feelings; rather, in instrumental music, they sought to portray the affections in a generic sense, using specific conventional techniques, and in vocal music they sought to convey the emotions of the text, character, or dramatic situation. Thus composers of opera displayed a musical gallery of emotions in writing a series of arias in every act, each for a particular character and situation on stage, seeking to render a psychological portrait of that character aroused by a certain emotion. By imitating the emotion in musical gestures—such as melodic and rhythmic motives, harmonic motion,

FIGURE 13.8 *Charles Le Brun 1619–1690), who dominated seventeenth-century French painting as head of the Royal Academy of Painting and Sculpture, drew these facial expressions to illustrate various emotions ranging from alarm, fear, and anger to hope, sorrow, and joy. They were published in 1698 as "Method for Learning How to Draw the Passions" in his Conférence . . . sur l'expression générale et particulière.*

bass lines, meter, and figuration—the composer expected to cause the listener to experience the corresponding affection.

Such theories were reinforced by the scientific discoveries of the era. Galileo's observations through the telescope and experiments with the laws of motion had shown that the senses as well as reason were instruments of learning. Placed in the service of human knowledge, the eyes and ears could be conduits through which to influence emotions and behavior.

It was in the very nature of Baroque expression to place the arts on an equal footing as valid interpreters of human experience and to foster their association with each other. Their combined powers enhanced their individual effect, as exemplified by the combined impact of the sculpture, architecture, and lighting brought together in Bernini's chapel (Figures 13.5 and 13.6), or the music, poetry, theater, stage design, and costumes synthesized in an opera (see Chapters 14 and 16–17). All the arts in the seventeenth century sought to move the affections, and that goal licensed painters, sculptors, poets, and musicians to transcend previously established limits in order to imitate and penetrate the invisible realm of the soul.

THE SECOND PRACTICE One tool for expression was to break the rules of music deliberately in order to convey the poetic text. A classic example is the madrigal *Cruda Amarilli* (NAWM 71) by Claudio Monteverdi (1567–1643; see biography and Figure 14.3 on p. 305). Its opening is shown in Example 13.1. Numerous dissonances (marked by **x** in the example) violate the rules of counterpoint, which require suspensions to be resolved before the bass moves again (see canto, measures 2 and 6), forbid passing tones from falling on strong beats (see measures 2 and 6), and require dissonances to be entered and left by step (see canto, measure 13). Here the rule-breaking and striking dissonances serve as a rhetorical device, highlighting the words "Cruda"

EXAMPLE 13.1 *Claudio Monteverdi*, Cruda Amarilli

x = unprepared or incorrectly resolved dissonances

Cruel Amaryllis, who with your very name [teach bitterly] of love, alas,

(cruel) and "ahi lasso" (alas) and forcing the listener of Monteverdi's time to interpret the rule-breaking music in light of the text. Precisely because the music does not follow its expected path, we are wrenched in a way that dramatizes the emotions expressed in the text, and we recognize and empathize with those feelings.

Artusi-Monteverdi   Monteverdi's madrigal was criticized in Giovanni Maria Artusi's *L'Artusi*
debate   *overo Delle imperfettioni della moderna musica* (The Artusi, or Of the Imperfections of Modern Music, 1600), not for its dissonances but for needlessly breaking the rules. Artusi points out, for example, that the dissonances in measure 13 would be allowed if the cantus moved by step (G–A–G–F–E) and asks why the rules are deliberately flaunted. Monteverdi wrote a brief response in 1605, filled out with more detail by his brother Giulio Cesare Monteverdi two years later (see Source Readings). They distinguished between a

Music as the Servant of the Words

Change to new styles often creates conflicts. One of the most famous disputes is Giovanni Maria Artusi's attack in 1600 on Claudio Monteverdi's *Cruda Amarilli* for needless violations of the rules of counterpoint. In response, Monteverdi placed the madrigal first in his *Fifth Book of Madrigals* (1605) and included a brief preface suggesting that there is a "Second Practice" beyond the traditional rules. He promised a full explanation that never appeared, but his brother Giulio Cesare Monteverdi elaborated in the preface to Claudio's *Scherzi musicali* (1607), saying that in the Second Practice the music serves the meaning of the words, rather than following its own rules as in the First Practice codified by Zarlino.

❈

[These passages] are contrary to what is well and good in the institution of harmony. They are harsh to the ear, rather offending than delighting it; and to the good rules left by those who have established the order and the bounds of this science, they bring confusion and imperfection of no little consequence. . . .

I do not deny that discovering new things is not merely good but necessary. But tell me first why you wish to employ these dissonances as they employ them? . . . If the purpose can be attained by observing the precepts and good rules handed down by the theorists and followed by all the experts, what reason is there to go beyond the bounds to seek out new extravagances?

From Giovanni Maria Artusi, *L'Artusi overo Delle imperfettioni della moderna musica* (Venice, 1600), trans. Oliver Strunk, rev. Margaret Murata, in SR 82 (4:2), p. 532.

❈

Studious Readers,

Be not surprised that I am giving these madrigals to the press without first replying to the objections that Artusi made against some very minute portions of them. Being in the service of his Serene Highness of Mantua, I am not master of the time I would require. Nevertheless I wrote a reply to let it be known that I do not do things by chance, and as soon as it is rewritten it will see the light under the title, *Second Practice, or the Perfection of Modern Music*. Some will wonder at this, not believing that there is any other practice than that taught by Zarlino. But let them be assured concerning consonances and dissonances that there is a different way of considering them from that already determined, which defends the modern manner of composition with the assent of reason and of the senses. I wanted to say this both so that the expression "second practice" would not be appropriated by others and so that men of intellect might meanwhile consider other second thoughts concerning harmony. And have faith that the modern composer builds on foundations of truth.

Claudio Monteverdi, preface to *Il quinto libro de madrigali a cinque voci* (Venice, 1605), trans. Claude V. Palisca, "The Artusi-Monteverdi Controversy," in *The New Monteverdi Companion*, ed. Denis Arnold and Nigel Fortune (London and Boston: Faber & Faber, 1985), 151–52, in SR 83 (4:3), p. 543.

❈

My brother says that he does not compose his works by chance because, in this kind of music, it has been his intention to make the words the mistress [i.e., the ruler] of the harmony and not the servant. . . .

But in this case, Artusi takes certain portions, or, he calls them, "passages," from my brother's madrigal "Cruda Amarilli," paying no attention to the words [i.e., the meaning and impact of the text], but neglecting them as though they had nothing to do with the music. . . . By passing judgment on these "passages" without the words, his opponent implies that all excellence and beauty consist in the exact observance of the aforesaid rules of the First Practice, which make the harmony mistress of the words. This my brother will make apparent, knowing for certain that in a kind of composition such as this one of his, . . . the harmony, from being the mistress becomes the servant of the words, and the words the mistress of the harmony. This is the way of thinking to which the Second Practice, or modern usage, tends.

Giulio Cesare Monteverdi, "Dichiaratione," in Claudio Monteverdi, *Scherzi musicali* (Venice, 1607), trans. Oliver Strunk, in SR 83 (4:3), p. 538.

prima pratica, or **first practice**, the sixteenth-century style of vocal polyphony codified by Zarlino, and a **seconda pratica**, or **second practice**, used by modern Italians. They explained that in the first practice the music had to follow its own rules and thus dominated the verbal text, while in the second practice the music serves to heighten the effect and rhetorical power of the words, and voice-leading rules may be broken and dissonances may be used more freely to express the feelings evoked in the text. In Monteverdi's music, the music and the words are equal partners in conveying the emotion that prompted the words; here, the unprepared dissonances suggest the cruelty of Amaryllis, whose very name entwines love (*amare*) with bitterness (*amaro*). The second practice did not displace the first, but each was used where appropriate.

Style classifications   The distinction between first and second practices was only the first of many to be made during the 1600s. It was a century of classifications, of naming and ordering everything from the affections (as in the treatises by Descartes and Le Brun mentioned on pp. 286–87) to the various musical styles required for different purposes. Monteverdi himself enumerated a wide array of options available to the composer beyond the first and second practices, including styles for different types of affections—relaxed, moderate, or excited—and distinct musical languages appropriate to music's differing functions—church, chamber, theater, and dance. In each case, composers sought to match the style to the music's function and to the appropriate affection.

GENERAL TRAITS OF BAROQUE MUSIC

Beyond interest in drama and in moving the affections, music of the Baroque era tends to share several traits that distinguish it from music of other periods.

The prevailing texture of sixteenth-century music is a polyphony of independent voices. By contrast, the new seventeenth-century styles typically feature prominent bass and treble lines, with written-out or improvised inner parts filling in the harmony. Melody with accompaniment was not itself new; something like it appears in chansons of the fourteenth and fifteenth centuries and in homophonic partsongs in the sixteenth. What was new around 1600 was a polarity between bass and treble as the two essential lines.

Related to this polarity was the system of notation called **basso continuo** (Italian for "continuous bass") or simply **continuo**. In this system, the composer wrote out the melody or melodies and the bass line but left it to the performers to fill in the appropriate chords or inner parts. The bass and chords were played on one or more **continuo instruments**, typically harpsichord, organ, lute, or

FIGURE 13.9 *The Five Senses, a painting by Theodoor Rombouts from ca. 1630. The sense of hearing is represented by a man playing a theorbo, a type of lute with long, unstopped bass strings in addition to shorter strings across a fretted fingerboard, often used in accompanying singers. The alternate Italian name, chitarrone (large kithera), reflects Italians' interest in ancient Greek music. The instrument's first known appearance was in the Florentine intermedi of 1589 (described in Chapter 14), whose theme was the power of Greek music; the theorbo may have been invented for the occasion.*

FLORENCE: MARESCOTTI, 1601/2

FIGURE 13.10 *Giulio Caccini's solo madrigal* Vedrò 'l mio sol, *as printed in* Le nuove musiche. *In this early example of figured bass notation, the bass is figured with the exact intervals to be sounded in the chords above it, such as the dissonant eleventh (11) resolving to the major tenth (♯10) in the first measure. In later practice, the precise octave was left to the player, so 4 and ♯ would be used instead of 11 and ♯10. A flat or sharp without a number indicates a minor or major third respectively, as in the middle of the third system.*

theorbo (also called *chitarrone*), a large lute with extra bass strings as shown in Figure 13.9. By the later seventeenth century, the bass line was sometimes reinforced by a melody instrument such as viola da gamba, cello, or bassoon, although this may not have been as common a practice as historians believed a generation ago. When the chords to be played were other than common triads in root position, or if nonchord tones (such as suspensions) or accidentals were needed, the composer usually added figures—numbers or flat or sharp signs—above or below the bass notes to indicate the precise notes required, as shown in Figure 13.10. Such a bass line is called a ***figured bass***.

The ***realization***—the actual playing—of such a bass varied according to the type of piece and the skill and taste of the player, who had considerable room for improvisation. The performer might play only chords, or add passing tones or melodic motives that imitated the treble or bass. Example 13.2 shows two possible realizations of the first phrase of Figure 13.10—one in mostly chordal style, the other with moving parts and an embellished suspension. In choosing how to realize the bass, the continuo player was free to aid the interpretations and differing emphases of various soloists. Some modern editions of works with continuo print an editor's realization in

EXAMPLE 13.2 *Two possible continuo realizations for the opening of* Vedrò 'l mio sol

a. Chordal style

b. With figuration

I will see my sun.

smaller notes, which clarifies the harmony for those who do not read figured bass notation (compare Figure 13.10 with its realization in NAWM 72). Yet many editors and performers regard such printed realizations as limiting and consider it the responsibility of the performer to master both the notation and the style in order to create the most suitable realization.

Not all pieces used basso continuo; because its purpose was accompaniment, it was unnecessary in solo lute and keyboard music. Then again, old-style unaccompanied motets and madrigals were sometimes published with a continuo part, to conform with the new practice.

The concertato medium

Seventeenth-century composers frequently combined voices with instruments that played different parts. The result was called the **concertato medium** or **concertato style** (*stile concertato*, from Italian *concertare*, "to reach agreement"). In a musical **concerto**, contrasting forces are brought together in a harmonious ensemble. Today we think of concertos as pieces for soloists and orchestra, but the meaning was broader in the seventeenth century, embracing such genres as the **concerted madrigal** for one or more voices (sometimes with melody instruments) and continuo and the **sacred concerto**, a sacred vocal work with instruments. The use of diverse timbres in combination became characteristic of the Baroque era, in contrast to the sixteenth-century preference for homogeneous ensembles.

Mean-tone and equal temperaments

Joining voices and string instruments with keyboards and lutes created problems of tuning. As noted in Chapter 7, sixteenth-century musicians used a variety of tuning systems. Just intonation was preferred by singers and violinists, who could make the slight pitch adjustments needed to keep harmonic intervals perfectly in tune. Keyboard players could not adjust pitch while performing, so they used mean-tone temperaments, in which the major triads from E♭ major to E major were in tune or nearly so, but those further to the flat or sharp side were out of tune, and chromatic semitones (such as B♭–B) were much smaller than diatonic semitones (such as B–C). Fretted instruments, like lutes and viols, tended to use approximations of equal temperament to avoid out-of-tune octaves, although players could adjust the pitch with their fingers. The combination of these three incommensurate tuning systems provoked some of Artusi's most bitter complaints against modern music.

In practice, performers worked out compromises. As harpsichord and organ became the most widely used continuo instruments, various kinds of mean-tone temperaments came to predominate, although tunings closer to equal temperament were sometimes used to allow a wider range of keys.

Chords and dissonance

Basso continuo composition led naturally to thinking of consonant sounds as chords rather than as sets of intervals over the bass. This idea, in turn, led to a view of dissonance less as an interval between voices than as a note that does not fit into a chord. As a result, a greater variety of dissonances was tolerated, though by the mid-seventeenth century, conventions governed how they could be introduced and resolved.

Chromaticism

Chromaticism followed a similar development, from experimentation around the turn of the century to freedom within an orderly scheme by mid-century. Chromaticism was used especially to express intense emotions in vocal works, to suggest harmonic exploration in instrumental pieces, and to create distinctive subjects for treatment in imitative counterpoint.

Harmonically driven counterpoint

The nature of counterpoint changed during the Baroque era. Treble-bass polarity and the use of continuo altered the balance among the parts, replacing the polyphony of equal voices typical of the sixteenth century with an emphasis on the bass. Even in imitative counterpoint the individual melodic lines were subordinated to a succession of chords implied by the bass, producing a counterpoint driven by harmony.

Music in the Baroque period was either very metric or very free. Composers used flexible rhythms for vocal recitative (see Chapter 14) and improvisatory solo instrumental pieces like toccatas and preludes (see Chapter 15). For other music, regular rhythms such as those found in dance music became ever more pervasive. Barlines, used in tablatures since the fifteenth century, became common in all kinds of music in the seventeenth century. At first these barlines simply demarcated phrases of equal or unequal length. But by midcentury they were used in the modern sense to mark off **measures**, recurring patterns of strong and weak beats, with the value and number of beats indicated by time signatures. The two types of rhythm, flexible and metric, were often used in succession to provide contrast, as in the pairing of recitative and aria, or toccata and fugue.

Regular and flexible rhythm

Sixteenth-century polyphony, performable by any combination of voices and instruments, tended to equalize vocal and instrumental styles. The prominent role of the soloist in the seventeenth century encouraged composers to make music idiomatic for a particular medium, such as violin or solo voice. The development of the violin family was especially important because the forceful overhand bowing, in contrast to the underhand bowing on viols, produced a distinctive, penetrating sound. Lutes and keyboard instruments had their own idiomatic styles suited to each instrument and its playing technique. Technical improvements in wind instruments made them suitable for exposed solo performance. Famous singers and voice teachers promoted new standards of virtuosity, color, and projection. Styles for voice and for each family of instruments gradually diverged, eventually becoming so distinct that composers could consciously borrow vocal idioms to use in instrumental writing and vice versa.

Idiomatic styles

The idiomatic quality of much Baroque music relates to another trait: this music is centered on the performer and performance, not the composer and the work. Singers and other professional musicians thought of themselves in the way actors do: their job was to interpret the music and words and to bring them alive for an audience. To do this, they first had to determine what affection a piece projected, based on their familiarity with the musical language, and then they employed a whole toolbox of expressive techniques, from musical nuance to physical gestures, to convey this meaning. This expectation that each performer will interpret and dramatize the music, bringing it to life as an actor inhabits a character, is why music of the time rarely features the expressive marks composers since the nineteenth century have added to guide (and constrain) performers, and why a performance of this music is likely to differ from what is on the page.

The centrality of performance

As part of their embodiment of the music, musicians in the Baroque era regarded written music as a basis for performance, not as an unalterable text. Performers were expected to add to what was written. Continuo players improvised chords, melodies, and even counterpoint above the given bass. Vocal and instrumental soloists ornamented melodies while performing. The choices they made varied from one performer or performance to another, but tended to fall within a range of performance practices typical of their region

EXAMPLE 13.3 *Monteverdi,* Possente spirto, *from* L'Orfeo, *Act III*

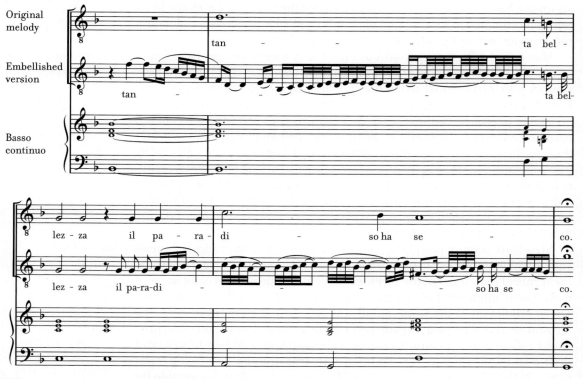

[wherever there is] so much beauty as hers is paradise.

and generation. Modern scholars and performers have tried to reconstruct these practices based on written accounts and transcribed improvisations, a task that remains complex and controversial (see In Performance: Historically Informed Performance and Its Controversies).

Ornamentation   For us the word **ornamentation** may suggest merely adding decoration, but Baroque musicians saw it as a means for moving the affections. They recognized two principal ways of ornamenting a melodic line:

- Brief formulas called **ornaments**, such as trills, turns, appoggiaturas, and mordents, were added to certain notes to emphasize accents, cadences, and other important points in the melody. Special signs sometimes—though not always—indicated their placement.

- More-extended embellishments, such as scales, arpeggios, and the like, were added to create a free and elaborate paraphrase of the written line. This process, sometimes called *division, diminution,* or *figuration* (see p. 256), was especially appropriate to melodies in slow tempo.

Example 13.3 shows an excerpt from an aria in Monteverdi's opera *L'Orfeo* (see Chapter 14) that was published with the original melody (top staff) in the tenor register joined by an embellished version that represents the kind of ornamentation added by a singer, presumably indicating the way it was sung at the first performance.

IN PERFORMANCE

Historically Informed Performance and Its Controversies

How should we perform music of the past? Composers in the late nineteenth and twentieth centuries often gave guidance in their scores for every aspect of their music, from the notes themselves to precise tempo, dynamics, articulation, and phrasing, and expected performers to render the music as faithfully as possible. But musicians in earlier times took part in traditions where a written piece of music was a platform for performance, not an inviolate text, and where many aspects of performance were not notated because it was assumed that performers would know what to do. For this music, simply following the score is not sufficient.

The problem for performers today who sing or play music of the seventeenth and eighteenth centuries is that the tradition of how to perform it, once passed down orally from teacher to student, has been lost over time. Like other aspects of past music, this performing tradition has to be reconstructed from its traces, the historical evidence left behind. Through historically informed performance, we can attempt to re-create how a piece of music might have sounded to its composer, and perhaps understand better what listeners of the time valued.

While much cannot be known about how music sounded in previous eras, there are many resources scholars and performers can use to piece together as much information as possible. By playing instruments of the time or reconstructions of period instruments, performers not only can produce a sound similar to what listeners of the era might have heard but also can discover the unique character of each instrument. For example, the phrasing and articulation that result from using a seventeenth-century violin and bow are very different from the style natural to a modern violin with wire strings and higher tension on the bowhairs. These differences affect how performers play violin music of the time, as is apparent in the period instrument recordings of sonatas by Biagio Marini (NAWM 84) and Arcangelo Corelli (NAWM 96) on the accompanying recordings. Performance treatises and other primary sources describe tuning systems, playing techniques, ornamentation, vocal timbre, and how to realize a basso continuo, all of which help us re-create the technical and stylistic practices of the period.

Yet there are limits to what we can know, and heated debates over what the goals of historically informed performance should be. In his book *The Early Music Revival*, Harry Haskell identified as a central issue the sizable gap between what can be known about past music and everything the music is. Richard Taruskin sparked controversy in the 1980s by arguing that trying to re-create the sounds the composer would have heard is a false goal, because we can never know when we have succeeded; that it is a historically misleading goal, because there has always been a range of options and of opinions among performers; and that it is a bad goal as well, because it devalues the creative music-making that is the hallmark of good performance. So what should be our aim in performing music of the past?

For performers trained on modern instruments, learning about past practices can be like learning a new language. Perhaps most important, studying past practices can open up new ways of thinking about and conceiving music in performance. For example, learning the variety of ways in which performers in earlier centuries departed from the written notes—embellishing melodies, filling in harmonies, adding ornamentation—can empower performers today to unleash their own creativity within the range of available options. From this perspective, knowing the history of performance is liberating, and just as applicable to performers on modern instruments and of any repertory.

Alterations   Performers were free not only to add embellishments to a written score but also to change it in other ways. Singers often added **cadenzas**—elaborate passages decorating important cadences—to arias. Arias were omitted from operas, or different arias substituted, to suit the singers. Church organ works could be shortened to fit the service. Sections of variation sets and movements of suites could be omitted or rearranged as desired. Title pages of ensemble collections encouraged players to choose which instruments and even how many to use for a performance. In every respect, the written music was regarded as a script that could be adapted to suit the performers.

From modal   If the elements discussed so far tend to characterize the entire Baroque
to tonal music   period, one aspect of music that did not hold constant is harmonic organization. Musicians in the early seventeenth century still thought of themselves as working within the eight church modes or the expanded system of twelve modes codified by Glareanus (see Chapter 7). By the last third of the century, Corelli, Lully, and other composers were writing music we would unhesitatingly call **tonal**, operating within the system of major and minor keys familiar from music of the eighteenth and nineteenth centuries. Jean-Philippe Rameau's *Treatise on Harmony* in 1722 (see Chapter 18) offered the first complete theoretical formulation of the new system, which by then had existed in practice for over half a century.

Like the Renaissance version of the modal system, **tonality** evolved gradually. The long-standing use of certain techniques—standard cadential progressions, bass movement by a fourth or fifth, conventional bass patterns, the use of suspensions to create forward motion—eventually bred a consistent set of routines that could be codified in a theory. But the presence of such techniques does not mean that a work is tonal, and music in the first half of the seventeenth century often shows the continuing influence of the modes.

ENDURING INNOVATIONS

Many innovations of the seventeenth century endured for centuries, and some are still with us. Several characteristics described in this chapter remained typical of eighteenth- and nineteenth-century music, including interest in dramatic effect, emotional expressivity, rule-breaking as a rhetorical device, treble-bass polarity, chordal harmony, chromaticism, idiomatic writing, and tonality.

Others, such as basso continuo, passed from use by the end of the eighteenth century. The performer's role as the music's "co-composer" diminished in the course of the nineteenth and early twentieth centuries when the composer came to be more important than the performer. Of course, there were star performers, but many of them also composed the music they played. In the twentieth century, faithfulness to the composer's score became a paramount virtue for music of earlier times.

Engaging with Baroque music requires us to accept, at least for a time, the values and preferences held by those who made and heard this music. Chief among them was the focus on drama and moving the affections, embodied in the development of a new genre: opera, the topic of the next chapter.

Further Reading is available at digital.wwnorton.com/hwm10

THE INVENTION
OF OPERA

❖

The quintessential art of the seventeenth century is **opera**, a union of poetry, drama, music, and stagecraft, all brought to life through performance. An opera (Italian for "work") consists of a text or **libretto** ("little book"), a play usually in rhymed or unrhymed verse, combined with continuous or nearly continuous music, and is staged with scenery, costumes, and action.

There are two ways to tell the tale of its creation. In one sense, opera was a new invention, an attempt to re-create in modern terms the experience of ancient Greek tragedy: a drama, sung throughout, in which music conveys the emotional effects. Yet in another sense, opera was a blend of existing genres, including plays, theatrical spectacles, dance, madrigals, and solo song. Both views are correct, because the creators of early operas drew on *ideas* about ancient tragedy and on the *content* of modern genres.

After its origins around 1600 as a court entertainment, opera was reinvented in Venice in the mid-seventeenth century as a theatrical production for the ticket-buying public. With support from patrons and the public, opera became the leading genre of the seventeenth and eighteenth centuries, and it has remained important ever since. What made it successful in the long run was the development of new modes of production that made opera feasible and profitable in a public theater, and of operatic conventions that made the genre accessible to a wide audience.

Opera was conceived as drama. Plato and Aristotle distinguished between three kinds of poetry: *epic*, a story told by a narrator, though at times characters may speak; *drama*, a story acted out on stage, told entirely through the words and actions of the characters; and *lyric*, a brief expression of a feeling or image. In this classification, well known in the sixteenth and seventeenth centuries, opera is drama. Yet sources for opera included both epic and lyric poetry, and part of opera's appeal was its absorption of elements from both into drama. The characters

tell us how they are feeling—a function of lyric—but also relate aspects of the story that we may not see for ourselves and that explain their actions—a function of narrative. The music can serve both to deepen the expression of their feelings, enhancing the lyric aspect, and to set the scene, comment on events, or even undercut how the characters present themselves, acting as an authorial voice or omniscient narrator, as in an epic. The interplay between action and affection—as one character's act provokes an emotion in another and generates a reaction in turn—is intrinsically dramatic, driving the plot forward and creating opportunities for music that heightens the drama and is expressive of feelings. The ways all these elements are balanced can vary greatly from one period in opera's history to another, and they make opera a rich and fascinating art.

FORERUNNERS OF OPERA

Although the earliest operas date from around 1600, the association of music with drama goes back to ancient times. The choruses and principal speeches in the plays of Euripides and Sophocles were sung (see NAWM 2). Medieval liturgical dramas were sung throughout (see NAWM 5), and the religious mystery and miracle plays of the late Middle Ages included some music. Renaissance plays often incorporated songs or offstage music, as do many plays of Shakespeare.

RENAISSANCE ANTECEDENTS One source for opera was the ***pastoral drama***, a play in verse with music and songs interspersed. In a tradition derived from ancient Greece and Rome, pastoral poems told of idyllic love in rural settings peopled by rustic youths and maidens as well as mythological figures. Simple subjects, bucolic landscapes, nostalgia for classical antiquity, and yearning for an unattainable earthly paradise made pastoral themes attractive to poets, composers, and patrons. In this imaginary world, song seemed the natural mode of discourse. The first pastoral poem to be staged was Angelo Poliziano's *Favola d'Orfeo,* on the legend of Orpheus, produced in Florence in 1471. As we saw in Chapter 10, in the late fifteenth century Juan del Encina wrote pastoral plays called *eclogues* for Spanish courts. Pastoral dramas and eclogues became increasingly popular at Italian courts and academies during the sixteenth century. Their subject, style, mythological character types, and use of music and dance were all adopted by the earliest opera composers.

Another influence on opera was the madrigal. Although intrinsically a lyric genre, some madrigals were miniature dramas, using contrasting groups of voices to suggest dialogue between characters (see NAWM 48 and 50). Madrigal composers' experience in expressing emotion and dramatizing text through music laid the foundation for opera. Occasionally, composers grouped madrigals in a series to represent a succession of scenes or a simple plot, a

FIGURE 14.1 *Set and costumes designed by Bernardo Buontalenti for the first intermedio for* La pellegrina, *performed in Florence in 1589.*

genre known as ***madrigal comedy*** or ***madrigal cycle***. The best known was *L'Amfiparnaso* (The Slopes of Parnassus, 1594) by Orazio Vecchi (1550–1605).

Perhaps the most direct source for opera was the ***intermedio*** (pl. *intermedi*), a musical interlude on a pastoral, allegorical, or mythological subject performed between acts of a play. The genre arose from a practical need: Renaissance theaters lacked curtains that could close between acts, so something was needed to mark divisions and suggest the passage of time. Intermedi served this function. Usually there were six, performed before, between, and after a play's five acts and often linked by a common theme. Some intermedi were brief, but those for important occasions were elaborate productions that combined dialogue with choral, solo, and instrumental music, dances, costumes, scenery, and stage effects: in sum, almost all the ingredients of opera except a plot and the new style of dramatic singing (see pp. 302–4).

Intermedio

The most spectacular intermedi were those for the comic play *La pellegrina* (The Pilgrim Woman) at the 1589 wedding in Florence of Grand Duke Ferdinand de' Medici of Tuscany and Christine of Lorraine. Several artists who were later involved in the earliest operas worked on these intermedi, including their producer, composer and choreographer Emilio de' Cavalieri (ca. 1550–1602); poet Ottavio Rinuccini (1562–1621); and singer-composers Jacopo Peri (1561–1633) and Giulio Caccini (ca. 1550–1618). The unifying theme, conceived by Florentine count Giovanni de' Bardi (1534–1612), was the power of ancient Greek music, a consuming interest of his circle. Figure 14.1 shows the set and costumes of the first intermedio, on the harmony of the spheres, giving a sense of how lavish the production was.

The 1589 intermedi

GREEK TRAGEDY AS A MODEL These musical and theatrical genres provided materials that composers incorporated in early operas, but opera might never have emerged without the interest of humanist scholars, poets, musicians, and patrons in reviving Greek tragedy. They hoped to generate the ethical effects of ancient Greek music by creating modern works with equal emotional power. Their discussions, at first abstract and entirely theoretical, led to experiments that ultimately culminated in the first operas. In this sense, opera fulfilled a profoundly humanist agenda, a parallel in dramatic music to the emulation of ancient Greek sculpture and architecture.

Music in Greek tragedy   Renaissance scholars disagreed about the role of music in ancient tragedy. One view, that only the choruses were sung, was put into practice in a 1585 performance in Vicenza of Sophocles's *Oedipus Rex* in Italian translation. For that production, Andrea Gabrieli cast the choruses in a homophonic declamatory style that emphasized the rhythm of the spoken word.

Girolamo Mei   A contrary view, that the entire text of a Greek tragedy was sung, was expressed by Girolamo Mei (1519–1594), a Florentine scholar who edited several Greek dramas. While working in Rome as a cardinal's secretary, Mei embarked on a thorough investigation of Greek music, particularly its role in the theater. After reading in Greek almost every ancient work on music that survived, he concluded that Greek music consisted of a single melody, sung by a soloist or chorus, with or without accompaniment. This melody could evoke powerful emotional effects in the listener through the natural expressiveness of vocal registers, rising and falling pitch, and changing rhythms and tempo.

THE FLORENTINE CAMERATA Mei communicated his ideas to colleagues in Florence, notably Count Bardi and Vincenzo Galilei (ca. 1520s–1591), a theorist and composer and the father of astronomer Galileo. From the early 1570s, Bardi hosted an academy where scholars discussed literature, science, and the arts and musicians performed new music. Galilei and Giulio Caccini (and perhaps also Jacopo Peri) were part of this group, which Caccini later called the ***Camerata*** (association). Mei's letters about Greek music often appeared on the agenda as part of a wider interest in classical antiquity, fostered by the ruling family of Florence, the Medici, as a way to reinforce their image of themselves as the "Caesars of their age" and their goals of political empire.

Vincenzo Galilei   In his *Dialogo della musica antica et della moderna* (Dialogue of Ancient and Modern Music, 1581), Galilei used Mei's doctrines to attack vocal counterpoint. He argued that only a single line of melody, with pitches and rhythms appropriate to the text, could express a given line of poetry. When several voices simultaneously sang different melodies and words, in different rhythms and registers, some low and some high, some rising and others descending, some in slow notes and others in fast, the resulting chaos of contradictory impressions could never deliver the emotional message of the text. Word-painting, imitations of sighing, and the like, so common in madrigals, he dismissed as childish. Only a solo melody, he believed, could enhance the natural speech inflections of a good orator or actor.

MONODY, ARIA, AND SOLO MADRIGAL Galilei was advocating a type of ***monody***, a term used by modern historians to embrace all the styles of accompanied solo singing practiced in the late sixteenth and early seventeenth centuries (as distinct from monophony, which is unaccompanied melody). Solo singing was not new; soloists sang epics and other strophic poems to standard formulas with light accompaniment, composers wrote songs for voice and lute, and it was common to sing one part of a polyphonic madrigal while instruments played the other parts. But the Camerata's discussions of Greek music led several members down new paths.

Caccini wrote numerous songs for solo voice with continuo in the 1580s and 1590s and published them in 1602 under the title *Le nuove musiche* (The New Music). Those with strophic texts he called **arias** (Italian for "airs"), which at this time could mean any setting of strophic poetry. The others he called madrigals, showing that he considered these to be the same type of piece as polyphonic madrigals: through-composed settings of nonstrophic poems, sung for one's own entertainment or for an audience. Today we use the term **solo madrigal** to distinguish the new type from the madrigal for several voices.

In his foreword, Caccini boasted that the madrigal *Vedrò 'l mio sol* (NAWM 72 and Figure 13.10) was greeted in Bardi's Camerata "with affectionate applause." Caccini set each line of poetry as a separate phrase ending in a cadence, shaping his melody to the natural accentuation of the text. He wrote into the music the kind of embellishments that singers would usually have added in performance. Faithful to the goals of the Camerata, he placed ornaments to enhance the message of the text, not just to display vocal virtuosity. His foreword to *Le nuove musiche* includes descriptions of the vocal ornaments then in use, providing a valuable resource for scholars and singers today.

Caccini's Le nuove musiche

THE FIRST OPERAS

After Bardi moved to Rome in 1592, discussions about new music—and performances of such works—continued under the sponsorship of another nobleman, Jacopo Corsi (1561–1602). Among the participants were two veterans of the 1589 intermedi, poet Ottavio Rinuccini and singer-composer Jacopo Peri, shown in Figure 14.2. Convinced that Greek tragedies were sung in their entirety, they set out to re-create the ancient genre in modern form. Peri's setting of Rinuccini's pastoral poem *Dafne* was performed in October 1598 at Corsi's palace. Although only fragments of the music survive, this was the first opera, modeled on the Greek plays: a staged drama, sung throughout, with music designed to convey the characters' emotions. (It was not *called* an "opera," however; that did not become the common term for such works until later, when the genre was well established.)

Meanwhile, Emilio de' Cavalieri, who was in charge of theater, art, and music at the Florentine ducal court, mounted smaller scenes with his own music in a similar style. In February 1600, he produced in Rome his musical morality play *Rappresentatione di anima et di corpo* (Representation of the Soul and the Body), at that time the longest entirely musical stage work. These works typify the search for new expressive means that could match the power ancient writers ascribed to Greek music.

FIGURE 14.2 *Jacopo Peri, in a costume designed by Bernardo Buontalenti, as the legendary singer Arion in Peri and Christofano Malvezzi's fifth intermedio of 1589. Arion, returning from concerts in Corinth, sings an echo aria just before he plunges into the sea to escape his mutinous crew.*

L'EURIDICE In 1600, Peri set to music Rinuccini's pastoral drama *L'Euridice*. The subject demonstrates music's power to move the emotions: through his singing, Orfeo (Orpheus) makes even the denizens of the underworld weep and persuades them to restore his wife Euridice to life.

L'Euridice was performed in Florence that October for the wedding of Maria de' Medici, niece of the grand duke, to King Henri IV of France. Cavalieri directed, and Peri sang

SOURCE READING

Peri's Recitative Style

In the preface to his opera *L'Euridice*, Jacopo Peri described his search for a new kind of musical setting, midway between speech and song, that could convey a character's emotions as forcefully as did the music of ancient Greek dramas. This new style, known as recitative, became an essential part of the new genre of opera.

✿

Putting aside every other manner of singing heard up to now, I dedicated myself wholly to searching out the imitation that is owed to these poems. And I reflected that the sort of voice assigned by the ancients to song, which they called diastematic (as if to say sustained and suspended), could at times be hurried and take a moderate course between the slow sustained movements of song and the fluent and rapid ones of speech, and thus suit my purpose (just as the ancients, too, adapted the voice to reading poetry and heroic verses), approaching that other [voice] of conversation, which they called continuous and which our moderns (though perhaps for another purpose) also used in their music.

I recognized likewise that in our speech certain sounds are intoned in such a way that a harmony can be built upon them, and in the course of speaking we pass through many that are not so intoned, until we reach another that permits a movement to a new consonance.

Keeping in mind those manners and accents that serve us in our grief and joy and similar states, I made the bass move in time with these, faster or slower according to the affections. I held the bass fixed through both dissonances and consonances until the voice of the speaker, having run through various notes, arrived at a syllable that, being intoned in ordinary speech, opened the way to a new harmony. I did this not only so that the flow of the speech would not offend the ear (almost stumbling upon the repeated notes with more frequent consonant chords), but also so that the voice would not seem to dance to the movement of the bass, particularly in sad or severe subjects, granted that other more joyful subjects would require more frequent movements.

From Peri, *Le musiche sopra l'Euridice* (Florence, 1601), trans. in Claude V. Palisca, *Humanism in Italian Renaissance Musical Thought* (New Haven: Yale University Press, 1985), 428–32.

the role of Orfeo. Although the event looms large in music history as the first performance of the earliest surviving opera, the work was only a small part of the wedding entertainment, eclipsed at the time by more established forms such as a horse ballet. The production incorporated sections of another setting of the libretto, this one by Caccini, who would not allow his singers to perform music composed by others. Both versions were soon published, and they remain the earliest surviving complete operas. Of the two settings, Caccini's is more melodious and lyrical, resembling the arias and madrigals of *Le nuove musiche*. But Peri claimed that his was better suited to the drama, because he found a new way to imitate speech and varied his approach according to the dramatic situation.

Recitative style For dialogue, Peri invented a new idiom, soon known as **recitative style**. In his preface to *L'Euridice* (see Source Reading), Peri recalled the distinction made in ancient Greek theory between continuous changes of pitch in speech and intervallic, or "diastematic," motion in song (see Chapter 1). He sought a kind of speech-song that was halfway between them, similar to the style that scholars thought the Greeks used for reciting epic poems. By holding steady the notes of the basso continuo while the voice moved freely through both consonances and dissonances, he liberated the voice from the harmony enough so that it simulated free, pitchless declamation of poetry. When a syllable arrived that would be stressed in speaking—in his words, "intoned"— he formed a consonance with the bass.

Example 14.1 shows how Peri followed his own prescription for the new style. The vertical boxes identify the syllables that are sustained or accented in speech and the consonant harmonies that support them. The horizontal boxes contain the syllables that are passed over quickly in speech and may be set with either dissonances (marked by asterisks) or consonances against the bass and its implied chords. The ways dissonances are introduced and left often violate the rules of counterpoint, but the effort to imitate speech exempts these notes from normal musical conventions. This combination of speechlike freedom and sustained, harmonized accented syllables realized Peri's idea of a medium halfway between speech and song.

Two excerpts from *L'Euridice* illustrate contrasting types of monody used by Peri. Tirsi's aria, or strophic song (NAWM 73a), sets a short lyric poem with music that is rhythmic and tuneful, resembling a canzonetta or dance song. It is introduced by a brief *sinfonia*, a term used throughout the seventeenth century for an abstract ensemble piece, especially one that serves as a prelude. An instrumental refrain called a *ritornello* (Italian for "small return") follows each stanza; here the ritornello echoes the introductory sinfonia.

Aria

The speech in which Dafne narrates Euridice's death (NAWM 73b and Example 14.1) uses recitative. The bass and chords have no rhythmic profile or formal plan and are there only to support the voice's recitation, which is

Varied styles of recitative

EXAMPLE 14.1 *Jacopo Peri, narrative recitative from* Euridice

But the lovely Eurydice dancingly moved her feet on the green grass, when—O bitter, angry fate!—a snake, cruel and merciless, [that lay hidden in the grass, bit her foot.]

EXAMPLE 14.2 *Peri, expressive recitative from* Euridice

I do not weep and I do not sigh, O my dear Eurydice, for to sigh, to weep I cannot.

free to imitate the inflections and rhythms of poetic speech. This moment of narration is more like epic than drama, telling a story rather than acting it out. For more lyric moments, Peri heightens the expressivity of his recitative, using methods from the madrigal tradition to convey a character's feelings. When Orfeo first reacts to the news of Euridice's death, as shown in Example 14.2, his breathless shock is conveyed by frequent rests (measures 1–3), and his grief by suspensions (measure 4), unprepared dissonance (measure 5), chromaticism (measures 4–6), and unexpected harmonic progressions (measures 5–6). The range from narrative recitative to expressive recitative shows that Peri's new idiom could encompass both the epic and the lyric sides of early opera, as well as being used for dialogue.

A blend of new and older styles   In *L'Euridice*, Peri devised an idiom that met the demands of dramatic poetry. Although he and his associates knew they had not revived Greek music, they claimed to have realized a speech-song that was close to what had been used in ancient theater but was also compatible with modern practice. At the same time that it introduced a new style based on ancient models, Peri's opera also borrowed from the traditions of the madrigal, aria, pastoral drama, and intermedio, using what was most appropriate for each moment of the drama.

THE IMPACT OF MONODY The various styles of monody, including recitative, aria, and madrigal, quickly made their way into all kinds of music, both secular and sacred. Monody made musical theater possible because it could convey in music everything from narration to dialogue to soliloquy, with the immediacy and flexibility needed for truly dramatic expression. The stylistic diversity Peri introduced was continued and expanded in all later opera, as composers followed his lead in suiting their music to the dramatic situation.

CLAUDIO MONTEVERDI

It is sometimes not the originator of an idea, but the first person to show its full potential, who secures for it a permanent place in human history. So it appears with opera, whose first widely renowned composer was not Peri or Caccini but Claudio Monteverdi (see biography and Figure 14.3).

CLAUDIO MONTEVERDI

(ca. 1567–1643)

FIGURE 14.3 *Claudio Monteverdi, in a portrait by Bernardo Strozzi.*

LANDESMUSEUM FERDINANDEUM, INNSBRUCK, AUSTRIA. PHOTO: ERICH LESSING/ART RESOURCE, NY

The most innovative and imaginative composer of his day, Monteverdi wrote only vocal works, including sacred pieces, madrigals, and operas. His music is always perfectly suited to the text. He was particularly inventive in creating expressive devices and combining styles and genres to capture feelings and personalities in music.

Monteverdi was born in Cremona, in northern Italy. Trained by the cathedral's music director, he was a prodigy as a composer, publishing two volumes of sacred music by age sixteen and three books of madrigals in his early twenties.

Monteverdi was an accomplished viol and viola player by 1590, when he entered the service of Vincenzo Gonzaga, duke of Mantua. He married a court singer, Claudia Cattaneo, and in 1601 was appointed master of music in the ducal chapel.

The Gonzagas commissioned Monteverdi's first operas, *L'Orfeo* (1607) and *L'Arianna* (1608; only the heroine's much-praised lament survives). Between the two premieres, Claudia died, leaving him with three small children. Overworked and poorly paid, he suffered a nervous breakdown, then complained bitterly to the duke that he was being mistreated. He was rewarded with an annual pension in 1609 and a generous salary increase. His *Vespro della Beata Vergine* (Vespers of the Blessed Virgin), published in 1610, may have been intended as self-advertisement, as he was unhappy in Mantua and was seeking a new position. The collection features a range of styles from modern vocal display to severe counterpoint.

The new duke dismissed Monteverdi in 1612, but the following year he became maestro di cappella at St. Mark's in Venice, the most prestigious musical post in Italy, where he remained until his death thirty years later. He wrote a great deal of sacred music for St. Mark's and for the confraternities that were an important part of Venetian life. In 1632, he became a priest.

Throughout his career, however, Monteverdi remained drawn to the madrigal, publishing no fewer than 250 in nine collections over five decades. He helped to transform the genre from the witty, polyphonic, a cappella partsongs of the late Renaissance to powerful explorations of the concertato medium and updated its language with emotionally charged, unprepared dissonances and declamatory melodies.

His operas *Il ritorno d'Ulisse* (The Return of Ulysses, 1640) and *L'incoronazione di Poppea* (The Coronation of Poppea, 1643), written in his seventies, use a varied mixture of styles to portray the characters and their emotions.

After his death at the age of seventy-six, Monteverdi was lauded in poetry and music. His influence spread through the circulation of his published works and the operas of his younger contemporaries.

MAJOR WORKS 3 surviving operas, *L'Orfeo, Il ritorno d'Ulisse*, and *L'incoronazione di Poppea*; 9 books of madrigals; 3 other volumes of secular songs; *Vespro della Beata Vergine*; 3 masses; 4 collections of sacred music

L'ORFEO Monteverdi's first opera, *L'Orfeo*, was commissioned by Francesco Gonzaga, heir to the throne of Mantua, and produced there in 1607. It was modeled on *L'Euridice* in subject and mixture of styles, but Monteverdi drew on an even wider range of styles and genres and used the contrasts to shape both the music and the drama. The librettist, Alessandro Striggio, organized the drama into five acts, each centered around a song by Orfeo and ending with a vocal ensemble that comments on the situation, like the chorus in a Greek tragedy. Monteverdi brought to opera his experience composing madrigals known for expressive text setting and dramatic intensity. He also used a larger and more varied group of instruments than Peri; the score, published in 1609, calls for recorders, cornetts, trumpets, trombones, strings, double harp, and several different continuo instruments, including a regal (a buzzy-sounding reed organ) for the scenes in the underworld.

Monody   Monteverdi followed Peri in using several kinds of monody from songlike aria to recitative. His Prologue is a declamatory aria with ritornello in which Monteverdi wrote out each strophe, varying the melody and the duration of the harmonies to reflect the accentuation and meaning of the text, a procedure called ***strophic variation***. He used the same approach for the work's centerpiece, Orfeo's Act III aria *Possente spirto*, and included in the published score a florid ornamentation of the first four strophes (see Example 13.3). Monteverdi's recitative is more varied than Peri's, moving from narrative to songfulness to agonized expression as the drama warrants.

Ensembles   In addition to monody, Monteverdi included duets, dances, and ensemble madrigals and balletos, providing a range of contrasting styles to reflect the varying moods in the drama. The ritornellos and choruses help to organize scenes into schemes of almost ceremonial formality. For example, Act I is an arch, framed by strophic variations in the Prologue and at the end of the act. Two choruses, a madrigal and a balletto, alternating with recitatives, precede the central impassioned recitative of Orfeo, followed by a response from Euridice and then the same balletto and madrigal in reverse order.

Act II   If Act I is a static arch, appropriate to a wedding ceremony, Act II (excerpted in NAWM 74) is a dramatic rush forward. Orfeo and his companions salute the happy day in a series of arias and ensembles, each with its own ritornello, strung together without a break. The series culminates with a strophic aria for Orfeo, *Vi ricorda* (NAWM 74a), in which he recalls his unhappiness turning to joy as he won Euridice. The form and the lighthearted style parallel Peri's canzonetta for Tirsi, and the hemiola rhythms give it a dancelike lilt.

Ironically, at the peak of joy, a Messenger arrives to bring the tragic news that Euridice has died from a snakebite. A sudden change of continuo instrument to an organ with wooden pipes and of tonal area from Ionian mode (C major) to Aeolian (A minor) marks the Messenger's cry, *Ahi, caso acerbo* (Ah, bitter event; NAWM 74c), in an impassioned recitative. At first, Orfeo's companions do not understand and keep singing in their own tonal and timbral world as they wonder what is wrong. But after the Messenger relates her story, a shepherd repeats her opening cry, which becomes a recurring refrain for the rest of the act, as the other characters join her in grief. This use of tonal area, timbre, and formal organization to deepen the dramatic impact shows Monteverdi's skill in using all the resources at hand for expression.

Orfeo's lament *Tu se' morta* (NAWM 74d) attains a new height of lyricism

EXAMPLE 14.3 *Claudio Monteverdi, Orfeo's lament, from* L'Orfeo, *Act II*

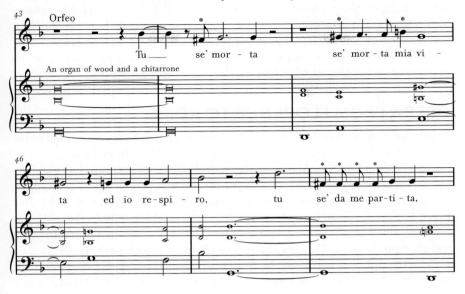

You are dead, my life, and I still breathe? You have departed from me,

for recitative that leaves the first monodic experiments far behind. In the opening passage, shown in Example 14.3, each phrase of music, like each phrase of text, builds on the preceding one, intensifying it through pitch and rhythm. The dissonances against sustained chords, marked with asterisks, not only enhance the illusion of speech but also express Orfeo's bitter feelings. The raw passage from an E-major to a G-minor chord (measures 45–46) underscores the irony that he still lives when Euridice—his "life"—is dead.

LATER DRAMATIC WORKS *Orfeo* was so successful that Duke Vincenzo Gonzaga commissioned a second opera, *L'Arianna*, from Monteverdi for the next year. It won great renown, but only a fragment survives: Arianna's lament. Both *Orfeo* and *Arianna* were staged in other cities as much as three decades later, an unusual longevity for operas at the time, when most were produced only once.

L'Arianna

Monteverdi moved to Venice in 1613 as maestro di cappella at St. Mark's. Alongside church and vocal chamber music (described in Chapter 15), he continued to write operas and other dramatic works. Especially significant is *Combattimento di Tancredi e Clorinda* (The Combat of Tancred and Clorinda, 1624), a short work blending music and mime. The text, an excerpt from Torquato Tasso's epic *Gerusalemme liberata* (Jerusalem Delivered, 1575), describes the combat between the crusader knight Tancred and the armored pagan heroine Clorinda. Most of the poem is narration, which Monteverdi assigned to a tenor in recitative. The few short speeches of Tancred and Clorinda are sung by a tenor and soprano, who also mime the actions during the narrative. The instruments (strings with continuo) accompany the voices and play interludes that suggest the action, such as galloping horses and clashing swords. To convey anger and warlike actions, Monteverdi devised the **concitato genere** or **stile concitato** (excited style), characterized by rapid

Combattimento di Tancredi e Clorinda

reiteration on a single note, whether on quickly spoken syllables or in a measured string tremolo. Other composers imitated this device, and it became a widely used convention.

Venetian operas　　Near the end of his life, Monteverdi composed three operas for the new public theaters in Venice. We will consider them below (see pp. 311–14) after first tracing what happened to opera in the intervening decades.

OPERA FROM FLORENCE TO ROME

Operas were expensive and remained relatively rare, yet they continued to be produced in Florence and Mantua and slowly spread to other cities.

Marco da Gagliano　　Florentine composer Marco da Gagliano (1582–1643) composed a widely praised new setting of Rinuccini's *Dafne* for the Mantuan court in 1608, then returned to Florence as maestro di cappella at both the cathedral and the Medici court. For the Medicis, he wrote several operas, of which only *La Flora* (1628) survives, along with other stage works. Opera had not yet gained preeminence, and the court preferred ballets and intermedi to glamorize state events.

Francesca Caccini　　The flexibility of genres at the time is illustrated by *La liberazione di Ruggiero dall'isola d'Alcina* (The Liberation of Ruggiero from the Island of Alcina, 1625), with music by Francesca Caccini (1587–ca. 1645), staged for the visit of a Polish prince. Based on an episode in Ludovico Ariosto's epic *Orlando furioso* (1532) and billed as a ballet, the work had all the trappings of opera: opening sinfonia, prologue, recitatives, arias, choruses, ritornellos, dances, and elaborate staging, as shown in Figure 14.4. Commissioned by the archduchess, the work explores the theme of women and power, with a good sorceress and an evil sorceress, delineated by contrasting musical styles, contending over the young knight Ruggiero.

Caccini had a brilliant career as a singer, teacher, and composer, becoming the highest-paid musician employed by the grand duke of Tuscany. She

FIGURE 14.4 *Stage design by Giulio Parigi for the second change of scene in Francesca Caccini's* La liberazione di Ruggiero, *produced in 1625 at the Medici Villa of Poggio Imperiale. The setting is the enchanted island of the sorceress Alcina, who holds the crusader Ruggiero captive there. Engraving by Alfonso Parigi.*

ALFONSO PARIGI

came from a musical family: her father was Giulio Caccini, and she sang frequently with her sister Settimia and stepmother Margherita in a *concerto delle donne* rivaling that of Ferrara (see Chapter 10). She composed music for at least fourteen dramatic entertainments, making her among the most prolific composers of dramatic music at the time.

ROME In the 1620s, the center for new developments in opera moved to Rome, where wealthy prelates vied with each other in offering lavish entertainments. When Maffeo Barberini was elected Pope Urban VIII in 1623, his nephews were put in an advantageous position, and they became ardent sponsors of opera.

Subjects expanded from pastoral and mythological plots to include the epics of Torquato Tasso and Ludovico Ariosto, the lives of saints, and the first comic operas. The most prolific librettist was Giulio Rospigliosi (later Pope Clement IX), who helped create libretto writing as a distinct craft. His most famous libretto, *Sant' Alessio* (1632), based on the life of the fifth-century Saint Alexis, was set to music by Stefano Landi (1587–1639). Operas often emphasized spectacular stage effects; for example, in the 1634 revival of *Sant' Alessio,* the devils and demons are consumed in flames. *Librettos and spectacle*

In Roman operas, solo singing increasingly fell into two clearly defined types, recitative and aria. The recitatives were more speechlike than Peri's or Monteverdi's, and the arias were melodious and mainly strophic. Domenico Mazzocchi (1592–1665) enlivened the recitatives in his opera *La catena d'Adone* (1626) by interleaving short, tuneful passages that he called *mezz'arie* (half-arias) and were later termed **arioso**, indicating a style somewhere between recitative and aria style. Roman operas often included vocal ensembles, developed from the madrigal tradition, and extended finales for each act, with choral singing and dancing, following the models of classical plays. Many Roman operas open with a sinfonia in two parts, a slow chordal section followed by a lively imitative canzona. Opening sinfonias of this kind became standard for seventeenth-century operas. *Music*

Because women were prohibited from performing on stage in Rome, female roles were sung by **castrati** (sing. *castrato*), males who were castrated before puberty to preserve their high vocal range. Castrati were already singing church music there; women were not allowed to sing in Catholic churches, and from the mid-sixteenth century on castrati sang the high parts in some church choirs in Italy, including the papal choir. Later in the seventeenth and eighteenth centuries, castrati also sang in operas outside Rome, most often in male rather than female roles (see Chapter 18). *Castrati*

PUBLIC OPERA IN VENICE

A decisive step in the history of opera was taken in 1637 with the opening in Venice of the first public opera house, Teatro San Cassiano. Until then musical theater depended on individual aristocratic or ecclesiastical patrons, but now it was presented for and supported in part by the paying public, with financial backing from wealthy and prominent families. That combination of private underwriting with income from ticket sales has continued to the present, and the operatic conventions and modes of production established in Venice

Audience

underlie the history of opera ever since. Without these changes, opera might not have endured.

Venice was ideal for public opera. Each year during Carnival season, which ran from the day after Christmas to the day before Lent, almost as many people came to Venice as lived there year-round, attracted by the mixing of social classes, freedom from religious and social constraints, and extravagant entertainments typical of the season. This large, diverse, and eager audience provided a favorable environment for opera. The first opera staged in Venice, Francesco Manelli's *Andromeda* on a libretto by Benedetto Ferrari, premiered during Carnival in 1637 and was an immediate success. Both Manelli and Ferrari had worked in Rome, as had most of their troupe, so opera was a Roman transplant. Their success led them to collaborate again the next year. Then in 1639 both composed operas as a second theater opened, and soon the new genre was a regular feature of Carnival.

Theaters

If the enthusiastic audience was crucial for the success of public opera, no less important were the theaters themselves and the funding that sustained them. Venice was an oligarchy controlled by rich merchant families, several of whom financed the building or remodeling of theaters for opera, seeing them as vehicles both for enhancing their prestige and for turning a profit. Nine theaters were competing by 1678, when Teatro San Giovanni Grisostomo, shown in Figure 14.5, opened as the last new theater of the century. Wealthy families and individuals could lease boxes, and anyone could rent a seat on the ground level for a single performance. Everyone, including box holders, had to buy admission tickets. With steady financing and a guaranteed audience, those engaged in putting on an opera could count on multiple performances during the Carnival season, and many in the audience would attend the same opera numerous times.

Impresarios and singers

Theater owners contracted with an ***impresario*** to produce the season's operas, including hiring the librettists, composers, singers, and production staff. Singers were as important in attracting the public as the drama

FIGURE 14.5 *A view of the Teatro San Giovanni Grisostomo in Venice, showing the stage with sets in place, the orchestra in front of the stage, and several tiers of boxes, which offered both a better view and greater prestige for audience members than seating on the main floor. Engraving from 1709.*

and spectacle, and usually more important than the composer or librettist, so impresarios competed for the most popular singers by paying them high fees. The singers Signora Girolama and Giulia Masotti earned two to six times as much for an opera's run as the composer received for writing it. Naturally, singers—especially women and castrati—were drawn to Venice to further their careers. The vogue of the operatic *diva* was inaugurated by Anna Renzi, who came from Rome and conquered the Venetian stage in 1641 (see Innovations: The Impresario and the Diva and Figure 14.6, pp. 312–13), and composers wrote parts expressly for her talents.

Alongside operas on mythological themes, Venetian librettists drew subjects from the epics of Homer, Virgil, Tasso, and Ariosto, and from Roman history. Plots were chosen with an eye for a wide range of emotions, dramatic conflicts, and striking stage effects, from magical transformations to clouds that carried singers. Three acts (plus a prologue) rather than the five of earlier times were now typical. Instead of the epic style of narration we saw in early opera, exemplified in descriptions of Euridice's death, librettists sought to tell the story through drama itself, using the interactions of characters to move the plot along. The number of arias increased to fifty or sixty in an opera. To keep the focus on the drama and the principal singers, choruses and dances were mostly eliminated or used only at the end of an act. As shown in Figure 14.5, the stage sets created a sense of a three-dimensional room or landscape with a series of painted flats on each side. In a marvel of stagecraft, these could be removed and replaced in seconds, using a system of ropes, levers, and pulleys. Drama, spectacle, and comic episodes all helped operas appeal to the broad and diverse audience in the theaters, which encompassed visitors from across Europe and Venetians from every social class.

Librettos and staging

After the initial successes of Manelli and Ferrari, one of the first to compose operas for Venice was Monteverdi, already renowned for *Orfeo* (1607) and *Arianna* (1608). He had come to Venice in 1613 as maestro di cappella at St. Mark's and continued to compose dramatic works for private performance, such as *Combattimento di Tancredi e Clorinda* (see p. 307). He turned to the public stage in 1640 with a revision of *Arianna*, followed by three new operas. Two survive: *Il ritorno d'Ulisse in patria* (The Return of Ulysses to His Homeland, 1640), based on the last part of Homer's *Odyssey*, and *L'incoronazione di Poppea* (The Coronation of Poppea, 1643), a historical opera on the Roman emperor Nero's illicit affair with the ambitious Poppaea Sabina, whom he eventually married.

Monteverdi's Venetian operas

Poppea is often considered Monteverdi's masterpiece. Because it was written for a commercial theater rather than a wealthy court, it lacks the varied instrumentation of *Orfeo*; operas in Venice were typically performed with harpsichords, theorbos, and a bowed bass instrument playing continuo, plus two solo violins and a viola for ritornellos and sinfonias. Yet *Poppea* surpasses *Orfeo* in depiction of human character, emotions, and interpersonal drama.

L'incoronazione di Poppea

The scene between Nerone (Nero) and Poppea in Act I, Scene 3 (NAWM 75), exemplifies Monteverdi's willingness to change styles frequently to reflect the actions and passions of the characters: expressive recitative inflected with dissonance and chromaticism as Poppea begs Nerone not to leave; simpler recitation for dialogue; arias with ritornellos, often in triple meter, for declarations of love; and ariosos for highlighting brief expressions of specific feelings. Thus the stylistic variety in *Poppea*, though even greater

The Impresario
and the Diva

❧

From its very beginnings, opera was a complicated, costly, even extravagant affair requiring the collaboration of the librettist, the composer (who held a decidedly lower status than the author of the words), and the artists whose performances engaged the audience directly. In addition, it demanded the services of a vast array of craftspeople and providers who worked behind the scenes. Among these silent and unseen participants—including stage managers, carpenters, painters, costume designers, tailors, hairdressers, and copyists—none was more crucial than the *impresario*, who was roughly equivalent to the modern producer. Transferred into English from the Italian, the word *impresario* acquired its distinctive meaning with the rise of public opera in Venice. The theater's owner, head of one of the noble families of Venice, entrusted the impresario with managing the theater successfully for one season at a time, which meant bringing in a profit after all the production expenses and artists' fees were paid. Naturally, the economic outcome depended in good measure on the impresario's decisions about how many and which operas were to be performed in a given season. Competition was fierce, so the impresario also had to consider the financial risks involved in mounting spectacular scenic effects or hiring the most highly paid singers, and measure these costs against the potential gains of attracting larger audiences.

This volatile commercial atmosphere fostered, among other things, the phenomenon of the operatic *diva* (or star). Impresarios went to great lengths and expense to secure effective performers because they realized that a singer could make or break an entire opera season no matter what work was being produced. Although the power of singers had been a theme in opera from its beginnings—think of Orfeo, whose legendary song persuaded supernatural beings to return his spouse to life—that power now resided with the singers themselves rather than with the characters they portrayed. Sopranos, especially those who were able to win favor through virtuosic ornamentation and persuasive interpretation, quickly achieved stardom. Once having made it to the top, a diva could demand that composers and librettists alter roles to suit her particular vocal talents and range. In so doing, she not only exercised her star power but actually influenced the development of opera in ways that eventually affected its dramatic structure as well as its musical values.

The career of Anna Renzi, leading lady of the Venetian operatic stage in the 1640s, is a case in point and illustrates the rise in stature of the female singer. Renzi was only about twenty when her teacher brought her from Rome to Venice to perform the title role in *La finta pazza* (The Feigned Madwoman), the work that was scheduled to open the newest public opera house in that city, the Teatro Novissimo, in 1641. The composer, Francesco Sacrati, undoubtedly tailored the role specifically to her in order to

Intima si cantum simulat præcordia mulcet,
Ipsam animam sensim si canit Anna rapit.

Iacobus Picinus Venetus faciebat Ven:

FIGURE 14.6 *The famous opera singer Anna Renzi, in an engraving from Giulio Strozzi's adulatory book* The Glories of Signora Anna Renzi the Roman.

capitalize on her particular talents. That she played a woman pretending to be afflicted with madness on that occasion and then, two years later, created the role of Nerone's spurned empress Ottavia in Monteverdi's *L'incoronazione di Poppea* speaks to her capabilities as an actress, one who could impart a certain dramatic intensity to her characters. Although her powers as a performer were by all accounts splendid, her meteoric ascent was at least in part a product of "media hype." The librettist of *La finta pazza*, Giulio Strozzi, anxious to prove that public opera employed singers as divine as those of the wealthiest courts, published a special volume of adulatory poetry in her honor in 1644. The engraving of her likeness seen in Figure 14.6 comes from that volume.

In an introductory essay, Strozzi describes Renzi's stage presence and vocal qualities, stressing the apparently spontaneous nature of her movements and gestures: "Our Signora Anna is endowed with such lifelike expression that her responses and speeches seem not memorized but born at the very moment. In sum, she transforms herself completely into the person she represents." He goes on to praise her diction and vocal delivery, extolling her "fluent tongue, smooth pronunciation, not affected, not rapid, a full, sonorous voice, not harsh, not hoarse." He also remarks on her stamina and resilience, her ability to "bear the full weight of an opera no fewer than twenty-six times, repeating it virtually every evening . . . in the most perfect voice." Finally, Strozzi approaches Renzi's offstage attributes and portrays her as a person of "great intellect, much imagination, and a good memory . . .; of melancholy temperament by nature [she] is a woman of few words, but those are appropriate, sensible, and worthy." Although she did not have what might be called a "classic beauty," Renzi's qualities essentially set the standard for the **prima donna** (Italian for "first lady," the lead soprano in an opera).

Divas became larger-than-life heroines with lucrative international careers. Following her memorable Venetian years, Renzi performed roles in other Italian cities and in Innsbruck, where Queen Christina of Sweden, who was then visiting the Austrian court, acknowledged her stunning skills by making her a present of her own medal and chain. Other prima donnas (and leading male singers) enjoyed similarly close relationships with patrons, composers, librettists, and impresarios in whose homes they sometimes lived when they were on the road. Not surprisingly, they frequently exploited these ties by exerting their influence on such matters as the selection of a plot, the number and length of arias written for their parts, and the casting of supporting roles. Occasionally a singer even refused to participate in a production unless a particular composer was commissioned to write the music.

Singer power and singer worship, then, ultimately played a big part in the direction that opera took in the seventeenth century. But the story does not end there. After taking hold of the Venetian imagination, the glamorous world of opera and its stars went on to captivate all of Europe and eventually the Americas. Even today, the powerful personalities of divas and their equivalents outside of opera—rock stars and film icons—are the driving force behind much of the entertainment industry.

*Quotations from Giulio Strozzi are taken from Ellen Rosand, *Opera in Seventeenth-Century Venice: The Creation of a Genre* (University of California Press, 1991), 228–35.

than in *Orfeo*, serves the same dramatic goals. Monteverdi freely reorders text in the libretto to make speeches into dialogue, intensifying the drama, and sometimes uses aria style even for sections not in strophic verse. Throughout, he exploits conventions of form, genre, texture, and expressive gesture to depict the characters and at the same time comment on them, inserting his authorial voice.

Francesco Cavalli

The leading composer of opera in Venice was Francesco Cavalli (1602–1676), who was probably Monteverdi's student and certainly his colleague at St. Mark's, beginning as a singer in 1616, then serving as organist from 1639 and as maestro di cappella from 1668 until his death. From 1639 to 1673, Cavalli composed almost thirty operas for Venice plus others for Naples, Milan, Florence, and Paris. He was the most successful and best-paid opera composer of the time, but he also looms large in opera history because he preserved his own scores for posterity.

Operatic conventions

In ten operas from 1642–52, Cavalli and librettist Giovanni Faustini established the essential structural, poetic, and musical conventions of Venetian opera. Whether based on history, epic, or myth or on newly created characters, the plots center on two pairs of noble lovers, who are united at the end after conflicts, intrigues, and misunderstandings keep them apart. One pair, called **prima donna** (first lady) and *primo uomo* (first man), typically outrank the other, have larger roles, and were often cast with the most popular singers (whose regal behavior led to the modern meaning of *prima donna*). The female nobles are sopranos, and the males are castrati. They are joined by advisors, often including a bass who lends a sense of gravity, and by servants in comic roles, usually played by male singers for both male and female parts.

Recitatives are in *versi sciolti*, free verse in seven- or eleven-syllable lines, and aria texts in regular meter and rhyme. The characters convey the drama through soliloquies and conversations, narrating any events that we do not witness directly. Both recitative and aria are part of the story, as each action by a character produces an affection or emotion in another, prompting action in response, in accord with the Aristotelian notion of the affections that prevailed at the time (see Chapter 13). Cavalli's music captures the actions and passions of each character with empathy and insight, using speechlike inflection and syllabic declamation to convey the words and the feelings behind them. The recitatives reflect the drama through changes of pacing, style, and harmonic treatment, and the arias, mostly in triple meter, unfold in graceful, melodious, smoothly flowing phrases supported by simple harmonies. Following these conventions let librettists and composers create operas quickly while allowing infinite variation in details and a wide range of plots. The combination of predictability and freshness gave their operas broad appeal.

Artemisia

After Faustini's death in 1651, Cavalli worked most often with librettist Nicolò Minato. Their second collaboration, *Artemisia* (1657), exemplifies midcentury Venetian opera. Artemisia, ruler of Caria, is a historical figure, whose elaborate tomb for her husband Mausolus gave us the word *mausoleum*. Everything else in the opera is invented. Artemisia is secretly in love with a commoner, who is actually a visiting prince, Meraspe, in disguise. She has vowed to put to death the man who killed her husband; since Meraspe did so accidentally in a tournament, he cannot reveal his identity or his love for her. Their inability to be honest with each other produces a series of misunderstandings that drive the plot.

EXAMPLE 14.4 *Francesco Cavalli,* Artemisia, *Act I, Scene 3, opening aria*

certain is the pain, but hope is doubtful.

In Act I, Scene 3 (NAWM 76), Meraspe muses on his feelings in a lyrical strophic aria with a refrain ("certain is the pain, but hope is doubtful") and a ritornello for two solo violins and continuo (NAWM 76a). Example 14.4 shows the last phrase of the aria and the beginning of the ritornello. Cavalli subtly depicts the emotions and images of the text, capturing pained certainty with a repeated note, the uplift of hope with a stepwise rising motive stated twice in succession (anticipated in the continuo in the previous two measures), and doubt with the descending tritone that links the two motives. The ritornello is a conventional part of the form, but it also provides a pause for reflection and a further glimmer of hope with its rising figure, echoed and repeated by the two violins.

Then the opera's second pair enter: Ramiro and Artemia, nobles from Meraspe's homeland. In recitative dialogue sometimes heightened with arioso (NAWM 76b), their conversation reveals that Ramiro loves Artemia, who is not interested, and she in turn loves Meraspe, who advises her to return Ramiro's love. After Meraspe leaves, Ramiro pleads for pity and Artemia refuses, conversing through a duet in aria style framed by a ritornello (NAWM 76c).

Throughout the scene, Cavalli follows the conventions he helped to establish, while neatly capturing in melody each personality and emotion, all in his typically direct and lyrical style. The continuo and ritornellos sometimes comment on the actions and feelings of the characters, inserting a narrator's authorial voice, as in the continuo's anticipation of the figure associated with hope in Example 14.4, and in a later passage its use of a lament bass (see Chapter 15) to suggest the characters' deep pain.

ITALIAN OPERA ABROAD The conventions that made Venetian operas a success at home also made those operas, and the genre itself, successful exports throughout Italy and Europe. From Venice, touring companies took opera to Bologna, Naples, Lucca, Genoa, and other Italian cities. In the 1650s, permanent opera houses were established in Naples and Florence, and others soon followed.

Meanwhile, Italian opera began to reach other lands. Italian operas were staged in Paris in the 1640s, culminating in a commission to Roman composer Luigi Rossi (1597–1653) for a new version of *Orfeo* (1647). Cavalli wrote *Ercole amante* for Paris (staged in 1662), and a copy of a Cavalli opera reached England, though no performance is known. Austria became a center of Italian opera. In Innsbruck, the archduke of Tyrol had a Venetian-style opera house built in 1654, and Antonio Cesti (1623–1669) wrote four operas for that theater, including *Orontea* (1656), which became one of the most frequently performed operas of the century. The French turned to their own style of opera in the 1670s (although it was devised by an Italian immigrant; see Chapter 16), but Italian opera reigned in German-speaking lands through the early nineteenth century.

OPERA AS DRAMA AND AS THEATER

Opera began as an effort to re-create the ancient Greek union of music and drama, linking the new Baroque era with the first musical culture we studied in Chapter 1. Yet it also had sources in theatrical spectacles like intermedi and in various types of solo song. These roots proved strong, and spectacular staging and solo singing were part of opera's appeal, contributing to what might be called the theatrical side of opera alongside the dramatic. This combination of drama, spectacle, and vocal display has continued in all later opera and musical theater. Many operatic reform movements, including those around Gluck in the eighteenth century and Wagner in the nineteenth, sought to tip the balance in favor of drama, once again looking back to Greek tragedies for inspiration. But love of the theatrical has been a constant theme, from the elaborate costumes and dances of French Baroque opera, to the virtuosic singing of nineteenth-century Italian opera, to modern musical theater events like *Cats* that emphasize everything from costumes to dancing over plot.

Most seventeenth-century operas lasted only a single season. Those that were still performed two or three decades after their composition were exceptional. Almost inevitably, a new production brought new singers and revisions to the score, often by other hands. Historians and musicians have tended to value Monteverdi most highly, and other early opera is rarely heard today. But the methods developed in Venice by Cavalli and his collaborators endured, from the very nature of opera as a collaborative art to the conventions and modes of production they created. We will return to opera many times in subsequent chapters, for it has continually evolved while remaining one of the most important and influential genres through our own day.

Meanwhile, styles nurtured in opera also appeared in church music, vocal chamber music, and instrumental music, as we will see in the next chapter. The use of music for dramatic or theatrical effect, pioneered in the early operas, has been a constant feature of musical life ever since. Today such uses for music surround us, in songs, films, television, websites, video games, and even commercials, and most of the emotional and dramatic effects they employ have their source in opera.

Further Reading is available at digital.wwnorton.com/hwm10

MUSIC FOR CHAMBER AND CHURCH IN THE EARLY SEVENTEENTH CENTURY

Seventeenth-century musicians were acutely aware of style and its relationship to the social functions music serves. Theorists of the time distinguished between church, chamber, and theater music, recognizing different styles appropriate for each. Composers continued to cultivate and expand on the forms, genres, and idioms characteristic of sixteenth-century vocal and instrumental music, giving music in each category a distinctive flavor. Yet the new styles and techniques that were developed for monody and opera quickly spread, as composers infused dramatic elements into other types of music. Thus the chamber, church, and instrumental music of 1600–1650 reveals both continuities with the past and influences from the modern theatrical style.

ITALIAN VOCAL CHAMBER MUSIC

Although opera by midcentury had become the focus of musical life in Venice, elsewhere it was still an extraordinary event. Most secular music involved ensembles with voices and was performed in private music-making or by amateurs for their own enjoyment. Different kinds of secular vocal music were cultivated in different regions and by different social groups. In Italy, canzonettas, ballettos, villanellas, and other light genres of strophic songs continued to be popular with the musically literate public (see Chapter 10). Vocal chamber music for the elites appeared in many forms and styles, often combining elements of the madrigal, monody, dance songs, dramatic recitative, and aria. The concertato medium (see p. 292) allowed varying textures, and composers used ritornellos, repeating bass patterns, and contrasts of style to create large-scale forms and enrich the expressive resources of their music. The following brief summary cannot do justice to the variety of song in the early seventeenth century, but it does focus on the three developments in Italy that had particular significance for the future: concertato works, **basso ostinato**, and the **cantata**.

SECULAR WORKS IN CONCERTATO STYLE Italian composers turned out thousands of pieces for solo voice or small vocal ensemble with basso continuo, sometimes including other instruments. These pieces were widely sung and were published in numerous collections. Most works were written for one to three voices, though some featured six or more. Forms and genres included madrigals, canzonettas and other strophic songs and arias, strophic variations, dialogues, and recitatives. Many of these compositions were more widely known than any of the operas, which were performed only a few times for restricted audiences, and several of the innovations crucial to opera were popularized through secular song.

Concerted madrigals   The importance of the concertato medium can be gauged by its impact on the madrigal. We can trace the change from the unaccompanied polyphonic madrigal to the **concerted madrigal** with instrumental accompaniment in Monteverdi's fifth through eighth books of madrigals. Beginning with the last six madrigals of Book 5 (1605), all include a basso continuo, and some call for other instruments as well. Solos, duets, and trios are set off against the vocal ensemble, and there are instrumental introductions and ritornellos. The seventh book, titled *Concerto* (1619), includes strophic variations and canzonettas as well as through-composed madrigals. Book 8, *Madrigali guerrieri et amorosi* (Madrigals of War and Love, 1638), features a remarkable variety, encompassing madrigals for five voices; solos, duets, and trios with continuo; large pieces for chorus, soloists, and instrumental ensemble; and short dramatic works. Styles range from imitative polyphony and homophonic declamation, typical of sixteenth-century madrigals, to operatic recitative and *stile concitato* (excited style).

OSTINATO BASSES Many works used a **basso ostinato** (Italian for "persistent bass"), or **ground bass**, a pattern in the bass that repeats while the melody above it changes. Most ostinato basses were in triple or compound meter, usually two, four, or eight measures long. There was a well-established tradition in Spain and Italy of popular songs, composed or extemporized, that were sung to familiar basso ostinato patterns such as *Guárdame las vacas* (see NAWM 68b), its close relative the *romanesca,* and the *Ruggiero* (see Chapter 12). Such basses underlay many songs and instrumental works of the early seventeenth century.

Descending tetrachord   Another common pattern was a descending tetrachord, a stepwise descent spanning a fourth, which Monteverdi used in his *Lamento della ninfa* (Lament of the Nymph) in his eighth book of madrigals. Its falling contour and constant repetition are suited to a lament, conveying a sense of inescapable sorrow. In the passage in Example 15.1, the recurring bass establishes a pitch center on A and regular phrasing, while the vocal melody conveys the nymph's distress through strong dissonances (marked with x) and phrases of six or seven measures that overlap the four-measure groupings of the bass. Notes that were dissonant in the singer's first phrase become consonant in her varied repetition and vice versa. Three male singers introduce and comment on her lament, turning this madrigal into an unstaged drama. Many composers used various forms of the descending bass pattern, especially in opera, for over a century (see NAWM 76, 77, 80, and 90 for examples).

Chacona   An opposite emotion was conveyed by bass patterns adapted from the **chacona** (Italian **ciaccona**), a vivacious dance-song imported from the Spanish colonies in the Americas into Spain and then into Italy. The chacona was one of the first types of music to be brought from the New World to Europe, where it became widely influential. The refrain followed a simple

EXAMPLE 15.1 *Monteverdi,* Lamento della ninfa, *with descending tetrachord bass*

fa che ri - tor - ni   il mio a - mor co - m'ei pur fu,   o —

o tu m'an - ci - di ch'i - o   non mi tor - ment - ti   più.

[Spoken to Love:] *Make my love return as he once was, or kill me yourself so that I will not torment myself any longer.*

EXAMPLE 15.2 *Monteverdi,* Zefiro torna e di soavi accenti, *with chacona bass*

a. Chacona bass

Harmony: I   V   vi   V

b. Zefiro torna e di soavi accenti

Ze - fi-ro ze - fi - ro   ze - fi-ro ze - fi - ro

Ze - fi-ro tor - na   ze - fi-ro tor - na

Zephyr [the gentle breeze] returns.

repeating pattern of chords played on the ***guitar***, which had become the most popular plucked or strummed instrument in Spain and the Spanish colonies. Example 15.2 shows the original repeating bass pattern and its adaptation in Monteverdi's madrigal *Zefiro torna e di soavi accenti,* published in his *Scherzi musicali* (Musical Jests) of 1632. Monteverdi repeats the rising, lightly syncopated figure (indicated by a bracket) fifty-six times in succession

EXAMPLE 15.3 *Barbara Strozzi,* Lagrime mie

La — — — gri-me mi - e,

My tears, [what holds you back?]

while two tenors provide vivid imagery suggesting happy feelings inspired by breezes, flowers, and scenes of nature, then ironically depict the abandoned lover's torment in slow, expressive recitative.

CANTATA A new genre of vocal chamber music emerged in Italy in the seventeenth century: the ***cantata***, meaning a piece "to be sung." The term was applied before 1620 to a published collection of arias in strophic variation form. By midcentury, *cantata* meant a secular composition with continuo, usually for solo voice, on a lyrical or quasi-dramatic text, consisting of several sections that included both recitatives and arias. Most cantatas were composed for private performances in the homes of aristocratic patrons and are preserved only in manuscripts. Some of the leading cantata composers of the mid-seventeenth century were Luigi Rossi and Antonio Cesti (see Chapter 14); Giacomo Carissimi (1605–1674), remembered today for his oratorios (see p. 325); and Barbara Strozzi (1619–1677; see biography and Figure 15.1).

Strozzi's Strozzi's *Lagrime mie* (NAWM 77), published in her *Diporti di Euterpe* (Plea-
Lagrime mie sures of Euterpe, 1659), is representative of the solo cantata in presenting successive sections of recitative, arioso, and aria, and of Strozzi in its focus on unrequited love. In the opening measures of the recitative, shown in Example 15.3, the long descending line, hesitations on dissonant notes (D♯, A, and F♯) over the opening E-minor harmony, and the augmented second from D♯ to C♮ portray the weeping and sobbing lover. Throughout the cantata, Strozzi changes style and figuration frequently to capture the moods and images of the text. The overall effect, combining contrasting musical elements and emotions, is typical of the concerted style at midcentury.

CATHOLIC SACRED MUSIC

Just as Gian Lorenzo Bernini used theatrical effects for his religious sculpture and architecture (see Chapter 13), so Catholic composers adopted the theatrical idiom for church music, setting religious texts in ***sacred concertos*** that incorporated basso continuo, the concertato medium, monody, and operatic styles from recitative to aria. The stimulus was the same in both cases: using a dramatic, powerful art medium to convey the church's message in the most persuasive and rhetorically effective way.

Stile antico Yet the church did not abandon polyphony. Indeed, Palestrina's style

BARBARA STROZZI

(1619–1677)

Strozzi was a rarity among Baroque composers, both as a woman and as a musician whose performances were intended for intimate, private gatherings rather than for large, public audiences.

She was born in Venice, the adopted (and perhaps biological) daughter of poet and librettist Giulio Strozzi. Her father nurtured her ambitions as a composer and introduced her to the intellectual elite of Venice. From her teens, she sang at the Strozzi home for gatherings of poets and other writers, formalized in 1637 as the Academy of the Unisoni. She studied with Francesco Cavalli, the leading Venetian opera composer and a student of Monteverdi's. Unlike Anna Renzi (see Chapter 14) and other female singers, Strozzi did not perform in public and perhaps could not because of her high social class. She was supported financially by her father, by the noble patrons to whom she dedicated her publications, and probably by Giovanni Paolo Vidman, the apparent father of at least three of her four children.

Between 1644 and 1664, Strozzi published eight collections of vocal music (one is now lost). Her publications contain over one hundred madrigals, arias, cantatas, and motets, placing her among the most prolific composers of vocal chamber music of the century. Indeed, she published more cantatas than any other composer of the time. Her choice to publish her music is unusual for women musicians in the seventeenth century and may reflect the feminist sympathies of her

GEMÄLDEGALERIE STAATLICHE KUNSTSAMMLUNGEN, DRESDEN, GERMANY. PHOTO: ERICH LESSING/ART RESOURCE, NY

FIGURE 15.1 Female Musician with Viola da Gamba, *almost certainly a portrait of Barbara Strozzi around 1637, painted by Bernardo Strozzi (perhaps a relative). Her seductive costume, the flowers in her hair, and the musical attributes (instruments and songbook) suggest that the subject is a personification of La Musica (Music), allegorized as an invitation to sensual love.*

father and his circle or (since publication was expensive) her relative wealth. Perhaps her choice to publish was a way for her to be "heard" beyond the private gatherings in which she sang.

MAJOR WORKS 3 collections of cantatas and arias, 2 of arias, and 1 each of madrigals and motets

became the supreme model for church music, bringing associations of age, tradition, reverence, purity, and sanctity. Composers were routinely trained to write in the old contrapuntal style, known from midcentury on as the ***stile antico*** (old style), which coexisted alongside the ***stile moderno*** (modern style). A composer might utilize both styles, sometimes in a single piece, as Monteverdi did on several occasions. Over time, the stile antico was modernized. Composers added a basso continuo and regularized rhythms, and church modes gave way to major-minor tonality. Johann Joseph Fux codified this quasi-Palestrinian counterpoint in his famous treatise *Gradus ad Parnassum* (Steps to Parnassus, 1725), which remained the most influential textbook on counterpoint for the next two centuries.

LARGE-SCALE SACRED CONCERTO Major feast days—at least in the large, wealthy churches—were celebrated on a grand scale. For such observances, composers wrote Vespers, psalms, mass movements, and other works for many voices with instruments, often using *cori spezzati* (divided choirs). Giovanni Gabrieli wrote polychoral motets for St. Mark's in Venice and for the confraternity of San Rocco that included two or more choirs, vocal soloists, an instrumental ensemble, and one or more organs playing continuo. One of his most spectacular large-scale sacred concertos is *In ecclesiis* (NAWM 78), written for an annual celebration in Venice and published posthumously in 1615. Here Gabrieli combined four vocal soloists, a four-part chorus, a six-part instrumental ensemble, and organs in a kaleidoscope of styles from modern arias and instrumental canzonas to Renaissance imitative polyphony, slowly building to a massive sonorous climax.

SMALL SACRED CONCERTO Few places had the resources to support large polychoral works, but the **small sacred concerto**, with one or more soloists accompanied by continuo and often by one or two violins, was within the means of even small churches.

Lodovico Viadana

Lodovico Viadana (ca. 1560–1627) pioneered the small vocal concerto for church music, and his 1602 collection *Cento concerti ecclesiastici* (One Hundred Church Concertos) was the first volume of sacred vocal music printed with basso continuo. Viadana adapted the melodic style and imitative textures of sixteenth-century polyphony to the reduced forces of one to four singers with continuo. *Exsultate Deo,* shown in Example 15.4, is typical in suggesting more voices than are actually present. The voice imitates the bass, then both bass and voice repeat the same figure at another pitch level, creating an effect of four independent voices entering in succession. The continuo player may add further voices, as shown in the example. The presence of continuo assured a full harmony, making it unnecessary to double or replace any vocal parts with instruments; indeed, the pieces for two to four singers sound complete even if one voice is omitted. This adaptability made Viadana's collection usable by almost any church and contributed to its popularity.

Alessandro Grandi

Alessandro Grandi (1586–1630), Monteverdi's deputy at St. Mark's in Venice in the 1620s, composed many solo motets that used the new styles of monody. His *O quam tu pulchra es* (NAWM 79), published in 1625, blends elements from recitative, solo madrigal, and lyric aria. The changing styles reflect the moods of the text, drawn from the Song of Songs, a book in the Hebrew

EXAMPLE 15.4 *Lodovico Viadana,* Exsultate Deo

Exult in God our helper

EXAMPLE 15.5 *Contrasting styles in Alessandro Grandi's* O quam tu pulchra es

a. Recitative style

Oh how beautiful you are.

b. Aria style

Arise, hasten, arise, my bride.

Scriptures whose dialogue between two lovers was taken as a metaphor for God's love for the church. As shown in Example 15.5, the wonder of the opening line, "Oh how beautiful you are," is captured in recitative style by a sustained note in the voice, a skip to a dissonance in the bass, and a quick descent to a resolution in the voice, while parts of the text suggesting action are set in aria style in triple meter. The use of modern musical styles and the language of love parallels Bernini's sensuous depiction of St. Teresa in ecstasy (see Chapter 13) in suggesting the intensity of communion with the divine. No doubt many more people encountered the modern vocal styles in church services and devotional music than in opera or in private concerts of secular vocal music.

MUSIC IN CONVENTS Music in convents was mostly unheard by the public. Church administrators in Rome and some other cities put many obstacles in the way of convents trying to develop a full musical life for nuns and novices. These administrators would not allow experienced male music directors, composers, or outside musicians to enter the convents for the purpose of instructing singers or joining them in rehearsals.

Despite the many regulations that made serious musical activity a clandestine operation, a lively musical culture developed in the convents throughout Italy. At Santa Cristina della Fondazza in Bologna, the nuns fought for a level of music-making equal to the standards and styles outside the convent walls. Lucrezia Vizzana (1590–1662) entered Santa Cristina as a child and was trained there by an aunt, an organist, and by the convent's music master. Her *Componimenti musicali* (Musical Compositions), published in Venice in 1623,

Lucrezia Vizzana

TIMELINE

contains twenty motets, most for one or two soprano voices with basso continuo. They incorporate elements of theatrical monody, including elaborate vocal ornamentation, declamatory phrases, and expressive use of unprepared or unresolved dissonance.

Although the church officially restricted music in convents, some establishments thrived because of sympathetic male church officials who believed that the angelic voices of nuns could have a crucial role in the salvation and spiritual edification of the communities that surrounded and supported the convents. One such convent was Santa Radegonda in Milan, where the public could attend services in the public half of the church and the nuns' music-making on feast days was known all over Europe. Margarita Cozzolani (1602–ca. 1677), daughter of a wealthy merchant, entered the convent in 1619 and took the name Chiara. Between 1640 and 1650 she published four collections of sacred concertos, including an extended dialogue on Mary Magdalene at Jesus's tomb and a large-scale Vespers that alternates polychoral antiphony with solos and duets in up-to-date aria and declamatory styles. Cozzolani's settings are marked by variety in style and scoring, by reorderings of liturgical texts, and by frequent use of refrains, sequences, repeating bass lines, and other structural devices.

ORATORIO Italy had a long tradition of religious music outside church services, such as the lauda. In seventeenth-century Rome, a new genre of nonliturgical religious music emerged, combining narrative, dialogue, and commentary. Such sacred dramatic works, at first relatively brief but soon growing to twenty minutes or more in length, were performed at meetings of lay societies who gathered to pray, hear sermons, and sing laudas and other devotional songs. By midcentury, a piece of this type came to be known as an **oratorio**, after the Italian word for the building where such devotions were held. From Rome, the practice of writing and performing oratorios spread across Italy and into Vienna, Germany, and France in the latter seventeenth century, then into Spain and England in the eighteenth.

Like operas, oratorios used recitatives, arias, duets, and instrumental preludes and ritornellos. But oratorios differed from operas in several ways: their subject matter was religious; they were not staged; action was described or suggested rather than played out; there was often a narrator; and the chorus—usually an ensemble of several voices singing one to a part—could take various roles, from participating in the drama to narrating or meditating on events.

Early oratorio librettos were in Italian or in Latin, and despite general similarities the two types served somewhat different purposes. Since they were in the vernacular, Italian oratorios were a useful tool for the Catholic Church to spread its message of faith to commoners and noblemen alike. Italian oratorios were longer than Latin ones, sometimes lasting as long as an hour, usually in two parts with a sermon in the middle. They resembled operas in style and could provide a high-minded alternative to the theatrical form that was at times condemned as sinful by the church. Often the same singers were hired to sing opera and oratorio, helping to blur the stylistic differences between the genres. However, especially early on, the Italian oratorio repertory was not as carefully preserved, since it was considered functional music to spread the faith. The Latin oratorio, on the other hand, was more cherished by the church elites, because like early operas for aristocratic courts, it was presented by invitation only, with the most sophisticated resources available, sparing no expense. Latin oratorios were usually in one extended part. Both Latin and vernacular oratorios came to be performed most often in Lent, the penitential season before Easter, when operas were not staged.

The leading composer of Latin oratorios was Giacomo Carissimi. His *Historia di Jephte* (ca. 1648) exemplifies the midcentury oratorio. The libretto is based on Judges 11:29–40, with some paraphrasing and added material. In recitative, the narrator introduces the story. Then Jephtha, an Israelite general, vows that if the Lord gives him victory in the impending battle, he will sacrifice whatever creature first greets him on his return home. Jephtha's victory over the Ammonites is recounted by the ensemble of six singers, with appropriate effects including *stile concitato.* The narrator relates in recitative how Jephtha returns home in triumph, but the first to greet him is his daughter, so he must sacrifice her. Songs of rejoicing for victory are set as solo arias, duets, and ensembles, followed by a dialogue in recitative between father and daughter. The chorus tells how the daughter goes to the mountains with her companions to bewail her approaching death. In the final scene (NAWM 80), she sings a lament, a long, affecting recitative. Two sopranos, representing her companions, echo some of her cadential flourishes. The response by the chorus of six voices employs both polychoral and madrigalistic effects, including the descending tetrachord bass associated with laments.

Giacomo Carissimi

In the sacred concertos of Gabrieli, Grandi, Vizzana, and Cozzolani, the oratorios of Carissimi, and other Catholic sacred music, we see composers using a wide range of styles with both secular and religious origins to convey the church's message to their listeners. Rhetorical effectiveness was prized far above stylistic purity. In these works, the primacy of the text and its dramatic declamation was central.

LUTHERAN CHURCH MUSIC

In German-speaking regions, composers in both the Catholic and Lutheran churches soon took up the new monodic and concertato techniques. Sacred music in Austria and Catholic southern Germany remained under strong Italian influence, with Italian composers particularly active in Munich, Salzburg, Prague, and Vienna. Composers in the Lutheran central and northern regions employed the new media, sometimes using chorale tunes or texts. Alongside compositions in modern style, Lutheran composers continued to write polyphonic chorale motets and motets on biblical texts.

Many biblical motets by Hans Leo Hassler, Michael Praetorius, and others in the early seventeenth century were in the large-scale concerto medium, showing Germans' admiration for the Venetian fashion. The small sacred concerto was even more common. Here the most influential figures were Viadana, whose works circulated in German-speaking lands, and Johann Hermann Schein (1586–1630), who published two important collections in

Sacred concerto in Germany

1618 and 1626 at Leipzig, both titled *Opella nova* (New Little Works). The first book consists chiefly of duets with continuo on chorales, freely paraphrasing the chorale melodies, inserting vocal embellishments, and dividing phrases among the voices. In these works Schein blends the Lutheran chorale tradition with the modern Italian style. The second book includes more chorale duets, but most pieces are on biblical texts and the settings are more varied, often using one or more solo instruments and contrasting solo with ensemble sections. Schein's sacred concertos set a precedent for a long series of similar works by Lutheran composers.

HEINRICH SCHÜTZ   Heinrich Schütz (1585–1672) was a master at applying the new Italian styles to church music. He studied in Venice with Giovanni Gabrieli, visited again during Monteverdi's years there, and brought both composers' approaches back to Germany, where he was chapelmaster at the Saxon court in Dresden (see biography and Figure 15.2). He is particularly renowned for writing music that captures the meanings and imagery of the text. Although he was a Lutheran composer at a Lutheran court, he seldom used chorale melodies in his sacred music, preferring to create motets and sacred concertos on texts from the Bible and other sources.

Early sacred works   Schütz published most of his sacred works in a series of collections that show a remarkable variety. The first, *Psalmen Davids* (Psalms of David, 1619), combines sensitive treatment of German texts with the magnificence of the Venetian large-scale concerto for two or more choruses, soloists, and instruments, following the model of Gabrieli. *Cantiones sacrae* (Sacred Songs, 1625) contains polyphonic Latin motets, enlivened by harmonic novelties and madrigal-like word-painting. The first book of *Symphoniae sacrae* (Sacred Symphonies, 1629) presents concerted Latin motets for various small combinations of voices and instruments. Published in Venice during Schütz's second sojourn there, it shows the strong influence of Monteverdi and Grandi, combining recitative, aria, and concerted madrigal styles.

Kleine geistliche Konzerte   Schütz wrote the pieces in his *Kleine geistliche Konzerte* (Small Sacred Concertos, 1636 and 1639) during the 1630s for church services at Dresden. As he mentions in his preface (see Source Reading, p. 328), the chapel had been greatly reduced in size due to the Thirty Years' War (1618–48) then raging through Germany and draining his patron's treasury, so he scored the concertos for only one to five solo voices, fewer singers than in most of his previous works, and used no instruments beyond the continuo. These two collections were quite popular throughout Germany because they met the need for small works suitable for performance in Lutheran churches.

Symphoniae sacrae II and III   Two more books of *Symphoniae sacrae*, featuring sacred concertos in German, appeared in 1647 and 1650. The last installment included the large-scale concerto *Saul, Saul was verfolgst du mich* (NAWM 81), which calls for two choirs doubled by instruments, six solo voices, two violins, and continuo and combines the polychoral style of Gabrieli with the dissonant rhetoric and modern style of Monteverdi and Grandi. It brings to life the moment when Saul, on the way to Damascus to fetch Christian prisoners, is stopped by a blinding flash of light and the voice of Christ calling to him, "Saul, why do you persecute me?" (Acts 9:1–9 and 26:12–18). The experience led him to convert to Christianity, change his name to Paul, and devote himself to spreading the Gospel. Although it was not published until 1650, Schütz composed this

HEINRICH SCHÜTZ

(1585–1672)

Schütz is known especially for his church music and for his singular genius at conveying the meaning of words.

The son of an innkeeper, Schütz showed an early talent for music. Although his family did not want him to pursue music as a career, his singing at age twelve so impressed Moritz, the Landgrave of Hesse, that the nobleman insisted on bringing Schütz to Kassel and sponsoring his education in music and other subjects.

Schütz entered the University of Marburg to study law, but Moritz persuaded him to go to Venice in 1609 and study composition with Giovanni Gabrieli. There Schütz published his first work, a collection of five-part Italian madrigals. After Gabrieli's death in 1612, he returned to Kassel as court organist, but the elector of Saxony pressured Moritz first to lend and ultimately to grant him the young musician, showing not only that Schütz was greatly esteemed as a musician, but also that musicians were essentially servants, not entirely free to decide their own destinies.

From 1615 to his death in 1672, Schütz was chapel-master for the elector's court in Dresden, although he took leaves to visit Italy and work briefly at other courts. He petitioned for reduction of his duties beginning in 1645, at age sixty, a request granted only after the elector's death in 1657.

Schütz wrote music for all major ceremonies at court, secular and sacred. The former included the first German opera (1627), several ballets, and other stage works, although almost none of this music survives. He apparently did not write independent instrumental music. What remains is a great quantity and variety of church music. Some had personal resonance:

FIGURE 15.2 *Heinrich Schütz at about age seventy, in a portrait by Christoph Spetner.*

his first sacred collection, *Psalmen Davids,* was published shortly before his 1619 wedding to Magdalena Wildeck, and her death in 1625 prompted simple four-part settings of a German psalter (published 1628). His *Musikalische Exequien* (1636) was funeral music for a friend and patron. But most was simply service music, each piece perfectly suited to the text at hand and the musicians at his disposal.

MAJOR WORKS   *Psalmen Davids* (German polychoral psalms), *Cantiones sacrae* (Latin motets), *Symphoniae sacrae* (Sacred Symphonies, 3 volumes), *Musikalische Exequien* (funeral music), *Kleine geistliche Konzerte* (Small Sacred Concertos, 2 volumes), *The Seven Last Words of Christ, Christmas History,* 3 Passions

sacred concerto during the Thirty Years' War, for a Vespers service in 1632 held to celebrate a victory by Saxony and its Protestant ally Sweden over Catholic forces. By dramatizing the moment when Jesus intercedes to halt Saul's persecution of the early Christians, the concerto draws an implicit parallel to the situation of Schütz's Lutheran listeners, who saw themselves as persecuted by the Catholic Church and regarded their military triumph as the result of divine intervention.

This work typifies Schütz's use of ***musical figures*** to convey the meaning of the words. Schütz's student Christoph Bernhard (1627–1692) was one

Use of musical figures

SOURCE READING

The Effects of the Thirty Years' War

The Thirty Years' War (1618–48) devastated Germany and depleted the treasuries of the rulers involved. After Saxony entered the war in 1631, the elector of Saxony, Heinrich Schütz's employer, could no longer afford to keep many musicians. In response, Schütz composed and published his *Kleine geistliche Konzerte* (Small Sacred Concertos, 1636 and 1639), which could be performed with the reduced forces available. His preface acknowledged the effects of the war.

✾

The extent to which, among other liberal arts, so also praiseworthy Music has not only gone into a great decline but in many places has been altogether destroyed by the still continuing course of the war in our beloved German homeland, is clear to many eyes, along with the general ruinous conditions and deep-seated unrest which unhappy war is wont to bring with it. I myself am experiencing this with regard to several of my musical compositions, which I have had to hold back for lack of publishers up to this time and even now, until perhaps the Almighty will graciously grant us better times in which to thrive. But meanwhile, so that my God-given talent in this noble art does not remain totally idle but can create some small offering, I have composed a few small concerted pieces and have now published them as a foretaste, as it were, of my musical work in God's honor.

Heinrich Schütz, Dedication to Part One, trans. Stanley Appelbaum, in *Kleine geistliche Konzerte*, ed. Philipp Spitta (Mineola, NY: Dover, 1996), 3.

of many German theorists to catalogue figures that break the rules of traditional counterpoint but are useful to composers in interpreting the text. For example, at the end of the opening phrase, shown in Example 15.6a, the top voice leaps down from a dissonant A to a dissonant E (both against a G-minor triad). The two voices emphasize the dissonant second through length and repetition, then move in parallel seconds, the bottom voice resolving the suspension, D–C♯, at the same time the top voice anticipates the resolution by moving to D. These unusual dissonances at the cadence are what Bernhard called *cadentiae duriusculae* (harsh cadential notes), conveying the harshness of Jesus's words, "Why do you persecute me?" Later, in Example 15.6b, a solo voice leaps down a sixth from an unresolved dissonance, a *saltus duriusculus* (harsh leap), to suggest the hard road ahead for Saul if he resists. Such figures have their roots in the text-painting of Renaissance madrigals and motets, while the attempt to codify them reflects the desire of German theorists to reconcile theory with practice.

Historia   A prominent genre in the Lutheran tradition was the **historia**, a musical setting based on a biblical narrative. In *The Seven Last Words of Christ* (1650s?), Schütz set the narrative portions as solo recitative or for chorus with continuo, while the words of Jesus, in free, expressive monody, are accompanied by strings and continuo. The whole is introduced by a short chorus and instrumental sinfonia and ends with a repetition of the sinfonia and a closing chorus. His *Christmas History* (1664) features recitatives for the narrative interspersed with scenes in the concertato medium, including arias and choruses with instrumental accompaniment.

Passions   The most common type of historia was a **Passion**, a musical setting of the story of Jesus's crucifixion. Schütz wrote three in 1666, following the accounts

EXAMPLE 15.6 *Heinrich Schütz,* Saul, Saul was verfolgst du mich

a. Opening, with cadentiae duriusculae

Saul, why do you persecute me?

b. Solo, with saltus duriusculus

It will be hard for you to kick against the goads.

of Matthew, Luke, and John. For these he used not concertato style but the older German tradition of treating the narrative in plainsong and the words of the disciples, the crowd, and other groups in polyphonic motet style.

During his lifetime, Schütz's music was known mainly in Lutheran areas of Germany, and after his death it faded from the repertoire until revived in the nineteenth and twentieth centuries. Yet he helped to establish Germany as a central part of the European tradition rather than as a peripheral region. His synthesis of German and Italian elements helped to lay the foundation for later German composers, from Bach through Brahms.

Legacy

JEWISH MUSIC

The new developments in the seventeenth century extended even to Jewish music, which was among European faiths the one most bound by tradition. Musical practices in synagogues had remained remarkably stable for centuries, but this began to change in the early 1600s. Although cantillation was still the primary form of music in the Jewish liturgy, new techniques came into use. We know this because of several rabbinical declarations denouncing the use of popular non-Jewish tunes as the basis for improvised passages. Because of the oral nature of cantillation, no music survives to show how these secular melodies were used, but written descriptions suggest practices that resemble those still used today in Orthodox Jewish synagogues.

Polyphony   The seventeenth century also saw the introduction of polyphony into synagogue services. Through the efforts of Leon Modena (1571–1648), who was a humanist scholar as well as a rabbi and cantor, improvised polyphony was performed at the synagogue in Ferrara as early as 1604. In 1607, Modena became hazzan (cantor) at the Venice synagogue and continued to promote the use of polyphony.

Salamone Rossi   Among Modena's writings on music is the preface to the first published book of polyphonic Jewish liturgical music, whose title page is shown in Figure 15.3. The thirty-three settings of Hebrew psalms, hymns, and synagogue songs were written by the Mantuan composer Salamone Rossi (ca. 1570–ca. 1630), and the collection was titled *Hashirim asher lish'lomo* (The Songs of Solomon, 1622–23), a pun on Rossi's first name. The style is that of Rossi's secular music, incorporating the influences of Monteverdi and other northern Italian composers of the time. There are also elements of Italian Jewish chant, which is the only factor, other than Hebrew texts, that identifies these works as Jewish. Rossi is equally well known for his madrigals, including the first published collection of continuo madrigals. Despite his evident skills as a composer, Rossi's Jewish faith limited his professional opportunities, and he never achieved a permanent court position. His remained one of the few attempts to write Jewish liturgical polyphony until the nineteenth century.

FIGURE 15.3 *Title page of the first publication of Jewish liturgical music in polyphony, Salamone Rossi's* Hashirim asher lish'lomo, *printed in Venice in 1622–23.*

INSTRUMENTAL MUSIC

The interaction of tradition and innovation typical of the first half of the seventeenth century is apparent in music for instruments as well as for voices. Instrumental music continued to gain independence from vocal music, becoming the latter's equal in both quantity and quality. Composers still practiced most sixteenth-century types of instrumental music but focused on abstract genres while deemphasizing those most dependent on vocal models, such as transcriptions. At the same time, instrumental composers borrowed many elements typical of the new vocal idioms, including employment of the basso continuo, interest in moving the affections, focus on the soloist, and use of virtuosic embellishment, idiomatic composition, stylistic contrast, and even specific styles such as recitative and aria. Performers on the violin, which rose to prominence in the seventeenth century, emulated the solo voice and absorbed many vocal techniques into their vocabulary.

TYPES OF INSTRUMENTAL MUSIC There are several ways to categorize Baroque instrumental music. Four overlapping approaches are particularly helpful: by performing forces, venue, nationality, and type of composition.

In considering performing forces, we find solo works, for keyboard, lute, theorbo, guitar, or harp; chamber works, for soloist or chamber group with continuo; and large-ensemble works, for two or more players on a part. The last becomes significant only after 1650, but some earlier ensemble works may have been performed with multiple players on each part.

Baroque instrumental music can also be categorized by venue or social function. Like vocal music, instrumental works served in all three social arenas: church (for example, organ and ensemble music in religious services), chamber (such as solo and small ensemble music for private entertainments and public pageants), and theater (including sinfonias, dances, and interludes in ballets and operas).

A third way is by nationality. Italian, French, German, English, and Spanish composers differed in the genres and stylistic elements they preferred. Part of the fascination of Baroque music is learning which traits are common in each region and watching composers borrow and blend characteristics from other lands.

Finally, a fourth way is by type of work. Until 1650, the following broad categories prevailed, many of them continuing from the sixteenth century (see Chapter 12).

Performing forces

Venue

Nationality

Types of pieces

- keyboard or lute pieces in improvisatory style, called *toccata*, *fantasia*, or *prelude*;
- fugal pieces in continuous imitative counterpoint, called *ricercare*, *fantasia*, *fancy*, *capriccio*, or *fugue*;
- pieces with contrasting sections, often in imitative counterpoint, called *canzona* or *sonata*;
- settings of existing melodies, as in an *organ verse* or *chorale prelude*;
- pieces that vary a given melody (*variations*, *partita*), chorale (*chorale variations*, *chorale partita*), or bass line (*partita*, *chaconne*, *passacaglia*);
- *dances* and other pieces in stylized dance rhythms, whether independent, paired, or linked together in a *suite*.

In the second half of the century, composers more often specified the exact instrumentation, and the mix of preferred genres changed. The principal types of keyboard composition after 1650 were the prelude, toccata, fugue, chorale or chant setting, variations, and suite. Works for ensemble fell into two broad categories: sonata and related genres, and suite and similar genres. Large-ensemble music encompassed suites, sinfonias, and the new genre of the instrumental concerto (see Chapters 16 and 17).

Elements of one style or genre often appear in another. The process of varying an idea can be found in ricercares, canzonas, and dance suites as well as in variations. Toccatas may include fugal sections, and canzonas may have sections in improvisatory style. For listeners at the time, the differences between national styles, between dances, or between toccata and fugal textures were as apparent as the differences between hip hop and country music

Mixing textures and styles

are to modern listeners. Composers exploited these differences, using contrasts of style and texture as elements of form and expression.

TOCCATA Toccatas and other improvisatory pieces were played on the harpsichord (as chamber music) or the organ (as church service music). Although some differences can be observed between toccatas intended for organ and harpsichord, notably greater reliance on sustained tones and unusual harmonies in those for organ, most toccatas could be played on either instrument.

Girolamo Frescobaldi   The most important composer of toccatas was Girolamo Frescobaldi (1583–1643; see biography and Figure 15.4), organist at St. Peter's in Rome. Toccata No. 3 from his first book of toccatas for harpsichord (1615; NAWM 82) is typical in featuring a succession of brief sections, each focused on a particular figure that is subtly varied. Some sections display virtuoso passagework, while others pass ideas between voices. Each section ends with a cadence, weakened harmonically, rhythmically, or through continued voice movement in order to sustain momentum until the very end. According to the composer's preface, the various sections of these toccatas may be played separately, and the player may end the piece at any appropriate cadence, reminding us that in the Baroque era written music was a platform for performance, not an unchangeable text. Frescobaldi indicated that in his toccatas the tempo is not subject to a regular beat but may be modified according to the mood or character of the music. He also sought to convey a variety of affections or moods in each toccata (see Source Readings, p. 334).

Fiori musicali   The role of the toccata as service music is illustrated by those in Frescobaldi's *Fiori musicali* (Musical Flowers, 1635), a set of three **organ masses**, each containing examples of the music Frescobaldi suggests an organist could play at Mass. All three include a toccata before Mass and another at the Elevation of the Host before Communion, and two add another toccata before a ricercare. These toccatas are shorter than his ones for harpsichord but just as sectional, and they feature the sustained tones and harmonic surprises often found in organ toccatas. He published this collection in open score, as shown in Figure 15.5, rather than on two staves, the usual notation for keyboard music, arguing in his preface that playing from a score "serves to distinguish the true gold of the actions of virtuosos from those of the ignorant."

Johann Jacob Froberger   Frescobaldi's most famous student was Johann Jacob Froberger (1616–1667), organist at the imperial court in Vienna. Froberger's toccatas tend to alternate improvisatory passages with sections in imitative counterpoint. His pieces were the model for the later merging of toccata and fugue, as in the works of Buxtehude (see NAWM 97), or their coupling, as in Bach's toccatas or preludes and fugues (see NAWM 102).

RICERCARE AND FUGUE The seventeenth-century ricercare was typically a serious composition for organ or harpsichord in which one **subject**, or theme, is continuously developed in imitation. Sometimes there is also a **countersubject**, a secondary melody designed to make good counterpoint with the subject. The Ricercare after the Credo from Frescobaldi's *Mass for the Madonna* in *Fiori musicali* (NAWM 83) is remarkable for the skillful handling of chromatic lines and the subtle use of shifting harmonies and dissonances, revealing a quiet intensity that characterizes much of Frescobaldi's organ music. As shown in Example 15.7, the subject has a strong profile marked by

GIROLAMO FRESCOBALDI

(1583–1643)

As one of the first composers of international stature to focus primarily on instrumental music, Frescobaldi helped to put it on a par with vocal music. He is best known for his keyboard music, but he also wrote vocal works and ensemble canzonas.

Born in Ferrara, Frescobaldi was trained there in organ and composition. In 1608, he became organist at St. Peter's in Rome. He supplemented his income serving noble patrons and teaching keyboard, giving him an outlet for harpsichord and other chamber music. He published collections of keyboard works with dedications to various patrons. In 1628, he became organist to the Grand Duke of Tuscany in Florence, then returned to Rome and St. Peter's in 1634 under the patronage of the Barberini family, nephews of the pope. By then, his music was celebrated in France, Flanders, and Germany.

After his death, Frescobaldi remained widely admired across Europe. His keyboard music was a model for composers from his time through J. S. and C. P. E. Bach's, particularly his toccatas because of their free fantasy and his ricercares and other imitative works because of their learned counterpoint.

MAJOR WORKS Keyboard toccatas, fantasias, ricercares, canzonas, and partitas; *Fiori musicali*, with 3 organ masses; ensemble canzonas; madrigals, chamber arias, motets, and 2 masses

---

leaps and a slow chromatic ascent, making it easy to hear the subject on each entrance, while the faster diatonic countersubject offers contrast.

In the early seventeenth century, some composers, especially in Germany, began to apply the term **fugue** (from the Italian *fuga,* "flight"), formerly used for the technique of imitation itself, as the name of a genre of serious pieces that treat one theme in continuous imitation. As we will see in Chapters 17 and 19, fugues became increasingly important in the late seventeenth and early eighteenth centuries.

Fugue

FANTASIA The keyboard fantasia, an imitative work on a larger scale than the ricercare, had a more complex formal organization. The leading fantasia

FIGURE 15.5 *Toccata before* Mass for Sundays, *from Frescobaldi's* Fiori musicali *(1635), as it appeared in the original print. Frescobaldi published the work in open score, rather than on two staves as was usual for Italian keyboard music, because he considered it of great importance for performers to know how to play from open score.*

SOURCE READINGS

Frescobaldi on Instrumental Expression

In the prefaces to his collections of keyboard works, Girolamo Frescobaldi encouraged performers to vary the speed and manner of performance in order to express the changing moods or affections (*affetti*). His advice suggests that he saw instrumental music as akin to vocal music in conveying the affections, and that he sought to reflect a variety of feelings through frequent changes of figuration.

In the course [of performing] take care to distinguish the passages, playing them more or less quickly according to the difference of their *effetti* [*affetti*], which are made evident as they are played.

Girolamo Frescobaldi, foreword to his *Primo Libro di Toccate* [First Book of Toccatas, 1615].

Having seen how accepted the manner of playing with singable *affetti* and diversity of passages is, I have seen it fit to show myself equally in favor of

it, as well as fond of it, with these feeble efforts of mine, presenting them in print with the guidelines below. . . .

First, that this way of playing must not be subject to the beat—just as we see in modern madrigals which, though difficult, are made more manageable by [altering] the beat, making it now languid, now quick, and occasionally suspending it in mid-air, according to their *affetti,* or the sense of the words.

2. In the toccatas I have taken care . . . that they be rife with a variety of passages, and of *affetti*.

Frescobaldi, foreword to the 1616 reprint of his *Primo Libro di Toccate.*

In those matters which do not appear to be regulated by the use of counterpoint, one must foremost seek the *affetto* of that passage and the Author's goal, as far as the pleasing of the ear and the way of playing is concerned.

Frescobaldi, foreword to his *Capricci* (1624). Translations by Andrew Dell'Antonio.

EXAMPLE 15.7 *Girolamo Frescobaldi, Ricercare after the Credo, from* Mass for the Madonna, *in* Fiori musicali

composers in this period were the Dutch organist Jan Pieterszoon Sweelinck (1562–1621) and his German pupil Samuel Scheidt (1587–1654). In Sweelinck's fantasias, a fugal exposition usually leads to successive sections with different countersubjects, sometimes treating the subject in rhythmic augmentation or **diminution** (in shorter durations). Scheidt's *Tabulatura nova* (New Tablature, 1624) includes several monumental fantasias. He called it new, because instead of using traditional German organ tablature, Scheidt adopted the modern Italian practice of writing out each voice on a separate staff. The works of Scheidt, and his influence as a teacher, were the foundation of a remarkable development of North German organ music in the Baroque era.

In England, music for viol consort was a mainstay of social music-making in the home. The leading genre was the imitative fantasia, often called *fancy,* which could treat one or more subjects. Popular composers included Alfonso Ferrabosco the Younger (ca. 1575–1628), son of an Italian musician active at Queen Elizabeth's court, and John Coprario (ca. 1570–1626), whose Italianized name (he was born Cooper) exemplifies the English fashion for things Italian.

English consort fantasias

CANZONA As in the sixteenth century, the canzona was an imitative piece for keyboard or ensemble in several contrasting sections, played either as chamber music or in church. Canzonas featured markedly rhythmic themes and a more lively character than ricercares. We can see in Frescobaldi's organ masses the role canzonas played in services: all include a canzona after the Epistle, and two have another after Communion. In some keyboard and most ensemble canzonas, each section treats a different theme in imitation or offers a nonimitative texture for contrast. In another type, called the *variation canzona,* transformations of a single theme appear in successive sections.

SONATA The term *sonata* was often used early in the seventeenth century to refer broadly to any piece for instruments. It gradually came to designate a composition that resembled a canzona in form but had special characteristics. Sonatas were often scored for one or two melody instruments, usually violins, with basso continuo, while the ensemble canzona was written in four or more parts and could be played without continuo. Sonatas often exploited the idiomatic possibilities offered by a particular instrument and imitated the modern expressive vocal style, while the typical canzona displayed more of the formal, abstract quality of Renaissance polyphony.

The traits of the seventeenth-century sonata can be highlighted by examining one of the earliest sonatas for solo violin and continuo, by Biagio Marini (1594–1663). Marini served for a time as violinist at St. Mark's under Monteverdi, and then held various posts in Italy and Germany. He published twenty-two collections of vocal and instrumental music, designating each collection as an **opus** (Latin for "work") and numbering them; later composers followed his lead and designated opus numbers for their published works, whether collections or individual pieces. His *Sonata IV per il violino per sonar con due corde,* from Op. 8 (NAWM 84), published in 1629, is an early example of what may be called "instrumental monody." Like the canzona, it has contrasting sections, but almost every one features idiomatic violin gestures, including large leaps, double stops, runs, trills, and embellishments. Marini's sonata opens with an expressive melody, shown in Example 15.8, that is reminiscent of a Caccini solo madrigal, then turns almost immediately to violinistic sequential figures. Rhapsodic and metrical sections alternate, recalling the contrasts of recitative and aria styles in Strozzi's cantatas and

Biagio Marini

EXAMPLE 15.8 *Biagio Marini,* Sonata IV per il violino per sonar con due corde

Schütz's sacred concertos. One section features double stops, first in singing style and then in imitation; others include leaps as large as two octaves.

By the middle of the seventeenth century the canzona and sonata had merged, and the term *sonata* came to stand for both.

SETTINGS OF EXISTING MELODIES As in the sixteenth century (see Chapter 12), organists improvised or composed settings of liturgical melodies for use in church services. These works include organ verses on Gregorian chant, like the Kyrie and Christe settings in Frescobaldi's organ masses, and various kinds of chorale settings known collectively as *organ chorales* or ***chorale preludes***. Composers in middle and northern Germany produced chorale settings in large numbers and in a great variety of forms after midcentury, but examples already appear in Scheidt's *Tabulatura nova* and in the works of Sweelinck.

VARIATIONS Keyboard and lute composers wrote sets of variations on borrowed or newly composed themes. These works were known as ***variations*** or ***partite*** (parts or divisions). The most common techniques for variations were the following:

- The melody is repeated with little change but is surrounded by different contrapuntal material in each variation and may wander from one voice to another. This type is sometimes called ***cantus-firmus variations*** and was practiced by Sweelinck and the English virginalists (see Chapter 12).

- The melody, usually in the topmost voice, receives different embellishment in each variation while the underlying harmonies remain essentially unchanged.

• The bass or harmonic progression, rather than the melody, is held constant while the figuration changes. Sometimes, as in the case of the romanesca, a melodic outline is associated with the bass but may be obscured in the variations.

Of the last type, the genres most familiar to modern listeners are the **chaconne** and **passacaglia**, the former ultimately deriving from the Latin American chacona and the latter from the Spanish *passacalle,* a ritornello improvised over a simple cadential progression and played before and between strophes of a song. The earliest known keyboard variations on the chacona and passacalle are Frescobaldi's *Partite sopra ciaccona* and *Partite sopra passacagli,* both published in his second book of toccatas and partitas in 1627. Each of the first several variations from *Partite sopra ciaccona* features a different variant in the bass line, as shown in Example 15.9, indicating that Frescobaldi considered the I–V–vi–V harmonic progression to be the constant element, not the bass itself. Within a generation, *chaconne* and *passacaglia* were used in France, Germany, and elsewhere as terms for variations over a ground bass, whether traditional or newly composed, usually four measures long, in triple meter and slow in tempo. Chaconnes and passacaglias appeared in solo keyboard music, chamber music, and theatrical dance music. By about 1700, the distinctions between the two faded, and the terms became interchangeable.

Chaconne and passacaglia

DANCE MUSIC Dances were composed for social dancing, for theatrical spectacles, and in stylized form for chamber music for lute, keyboard, or ensemble. Dance music was so central to musical life that dance rhythms permeated other instrumental and vocal music, secular and sacred alike.

The idea of linking two or three dances together, such as pavane and galliard, was now extended to create a **suite** of several dances, used either for dancing or as chamber music. Johann Hermann Schein's *Banchetto musicale* (Musical Banquet, 1617) contains twenty suites for five instruments with continuo, each having the sequence padouana (pavane), gagliarda (galliard), courante, allemande, and tripla, the last a triple-meter variation of the allemande. Some of the suites build on one melodic idea that recurs in varied form in every dance, and others are linked by subtle melodic similarities.

Suites

EXAMPLE 15.9 *Frescobaldi,* Partite sopra ciaccona, *first three variations*

A SEPARATE TRADITION As composers focused increasingly on abstract genres—including toccata, prelude, ricercare, fantasia, canzona, sonata, and ground bass variations—instrumental music gained stature as a tradition separate from vocal music and worthy of attention for its own sake. The toccatas, ricercares, and variations of Frescobaldi have been compared to orations, holding the listener's attention while ideas are presented and developed. This is a new role for music without words, moving beyond decoration and diversion to encompass levels of intellectual and expressive communication formerly reserved for vocal music. It was on this foundation that the fugues, sonatas, and symphonies of later generations were built.

TRADITION AND INNOVATION

The extraordinary burst of innovation in the early seventeenth century is as apparent in the chamber, church, and instrumental music of the time as in opera. Yet, like opera, these other kinds of music also drew deeply on sixteenth-century traditions, redefining existing genres and approaches by combining them with new styles and techniques.

This period is of lasting importance because it set the pattern for several generations, creating new genres such as cantata, sacred concerto, oratorio, sonata, partita, chaconne, passacaglia, and dance suite; establishing techniques such as basso continuo, the concertato medium, and ground bass; and fostering new expressive devices and an increasingly separate instrumental tradition. One especially noteworthy development was the recognition that different styles were appropriate for different purposes. Thus the older style (stile antico) was preserved and practiced alongside newer ones, useful for its associations with sacred music and with pedagogy. At the same time, most styles could be used outside their original contexts for expressive ends, so that, for example, theatrical styles were used in church.

But the fascination with the new that energized the music of this period implicitly guaranteed its impermanence. As tastes and styles rapidly changed, virtually all this music fell out of fashion by the end of the century. Some, like Frescobaldi's keyboard music, was known to composers but rarely played.

The music of the early seventeenth century was rediscovered in the late nineteenth century and throughout the twentieth, and much of it has been published in scholarly editions and recorded. Although nowadays performances and recordings of works by Monteverdi, Schütz, Frescobaldi, and other early-seventeenth-century composers are relatively frequent, until recent decades their music was not as well known as that of Palestrina, Vivaldi, or Bach. Perhaps seventeenth-century music sounds less familiar in part because in the music of Monteverdi, Schütz, and their contempories styles are more fluid and the routines of melody, rhythm, harmony, and counterpoint are less fixed than in sixteenth- or eighteenth-century music, so that the listener may not know what to expect. But that element of exploration is also one of the great charms of this music, as composers, thoroughly trained in the now out-of-date idiom of the sixteenth century, invented new styles at every turn, feeling their way forward in the dark to a new musical world.

Further Reading is available at digital.wwnorton.com/hwm10

FRANCE, ENGLAND, SPAIN, THE NEW WORLD, AND RUSSIA IN THE SEVENTEENTH CENTURY

The last two chapters focused largely on genre: how new and old ideas combined in opera, and how theatrical styles affected chamber, sacred, and instrumental music, fostering new genres such as cantata, sacred concerto, oratorio, and solo sonata. Without neglecting genre as a way of focusing our historical narrative, it becomes more useful in the middle and late Baroque period to highlight the distinctive national and regional styles that developed, including trends within a nation's music and borrowings across borders.

National style was influenced by politics as well as by culture. The Italian peninsula remained the leading musical region, but France, a centralized monarchy whose king used the arts for image-building and social control, emerged as Italy's chief competitor. Under the king's sponsorship, musicians forged a new French idiom marked by elegance and restraint, a counterbalance to the virtuosic, expressive music of Italy. Musicians in England and German-speaking lands then absorbed elements from both French and Italian styles, combining them with native traditions. The English monarch was an important musical patron but did not dominate the scene as in France, leaving room for direct support of music by the public and the invention of the public concert. Rulers of the many small German states adopted French fashions in music as in literature, art, architecture, and manners, but Italian musicians and genres remained influential. Spain and its American colonies supported a thriving musical life and developed a unique style of theater music marked by syncopated rhythms. In Russia, long isolated culturally and musically from western Europe, musicians, religious leaders, and the tsar himself began to absorb western European ideas and practices, from notation and theory to styles and genres.

This chapter explores the impact of politics on music in France and England, the adaptation of Italian genres in France, the rise of a distinctive French style, English assimilation of French and Italian elements, Spanish traditions at home and in the New World, and the

FIGURE 16.1 *Louis XIV in his sixties, in a portrait by Hyacinthe Rigaud from around 1700. The king is surrounded by images that convey his grandeur: a red velvet curtain, multicolor stone column, impressive wig, and enormous ermine robe covered on one side with gold fleurs-de-lis, the symbol of French royalty. His crown is by his side, shadowed and partially obscured, as if he did not need to emphasize the sign of his power, even while his hand and staff draw the eye to it. His elongated, upright stature and exposed, perfectly shaped legs proclaim his physical strength and remind the viewer of his renown as a dancer.*

opening of Russian music to western European influences. Italy and Germany are the focus in Chapter 17. We will follow the same categories as in the previous two chapters: theatrical music, vocal chamber music, church music, and instrumental music.

FRANCE

The special qualities of French Baroque music were shaped by the centrality of dance and the role of the arts in a strong, centralized monarchy. These in turn reflect the personality and policies of King Louis XIV, whose seven-decade reign changed the culture of Europe.

LOUIS XIV Louis XIV (r. 1643–1715) succeeded to the throne at age five on the death of his father. Until he was twenty-three, however, France was ruled by his mother, Anne of Austria, and her prime minister Cardinal Mazarin, an Italian. Resentment against the rule of foreigners provoked a series of revolts known as the Fronde. When Louis took the reins of state after Mazarin's death in 1661, he remembered those years of tumult and resolved to assert his personal authority.

To maintain power, Louis projected an image of himself as in supreme control, using the arts as tools. The portrait in Figure 16.1 is a fitting example: an almost theatrical performance, depicting Louis as an imposing physical specimen, surrounded by symbols of power and majesty, in complete command.

The Sun King   Louis styled himself "the Sun King," an ideal symbol for the monarch as giver of light. He identified himself with Apollo, the Greek sun god. Apollo was also the god of music, learning, science, and the arts, and Louis wanted to be seen as the chief patron in all those fields. He centralized the arts and sciences, establishing royal academies of sculpture and painting (1648), dance (1661), literature (1663), the sciences (1669), opera (1669), and architecture (1671) and granting each academy authority to oversee endeavors in its field.

Versailles   Louis rebuilt the Louvre, the great palace in Paris (now a remarkable museum), and constructed a vast palace in the country at Versailles. Figure 16.2 shows only one part of this huge building. The gardens are equally expansive, stretching for miles. Figure 16.3 illustrates the sculpted gardens near the palace, where the beds are laid out in elaborate symmetrical geometric

FIGURE 16.2 *Garden façade of the Palace of Versailles, designed by Louis Le Vau and built 1661–90. The columns and arches echo classical architecture, and the mythological statuary throughout the building and grounds reinforced the links Louis XIV sought to make between his reign and Greek and Roman civilizations. The sheer size of the building, emphasized by the reflecting pool, was meant to impress, but was also practical, because the entire French nobility and their entourages spent much of the year here.*

FIGURE 16.3 *Part of the south garden at Versailles, with fleurs-de-lis. The carefully trimmed plantings convey an image of control over nature, and the way each garden leads to the next suggests a limitless space.*

patterns, like the palace itself. Everything is ordered and disciplined, creating both logic and beauty, and no plant is out of place or allowed to grow wild. It is a perfect image for the centralized monarchy, where all have their roles in the orderly state ruled by a single vision, and even nature must submit to the will of the king.

Versailles proclaimed Louis's power and also served a practical purpose. The nobility were partly independent and could be dangerous, as they were in the Fronde rebellions. By keeping the aristocracy at Versailles for large parts of the year, away from their lands and focused on court ceremonies, etiquette, and entertainment, he kept them under his firm control.

DANCE AT COURT Dance, both social and theatrical, was particularly important in French culture and to Louis. The upper classes of society were expected to set an example for others of self-control, composure, serenity, grandeur, tenderness, grace, and vitality, and dancing provided a means to practice and embody these qualities. Social dancing at court took place at parties, masquerades, and formal balls. The balls typically began with dances performed by all the couples lined up in order by rank, followed by a series of *danses à deux* (dances for two), each couple dancing in turn while the others watched, and ended with other dances for couples in sets or lines.

Court ballet   A distinctive French genre was the ***court ballet*** or *ballet de cour*, a musical-dramatic work, staged with costumes and scenery, that featured members of the court alongside professional dancers. A typical court ballet had a series of *entrées* (entries) that included solo songs, choruses, and instrumental dances in styles suited to the characters portrayed by the dancers. Ballets had flourished at court since the *Ballet comique de la reine* (The Queen's Dramatic Ballet, 1581). Louis XIII (r. 1610–43) regularly took part in music and dance at court. His son Louis XIV won a reputation as a brilliant dancer, performing in ballets from the age of thirteen. His roles included Apollo in the *Ballet des fêtes de Bacchus* (Ballet of the Festivals of Bacchus, 1651) and the Rising Sun in the *Ballet de la nuit* (Ballet of the Night, 1653), establishing his identity as the Sun King.

Both ballroom dances and the theatrical dances of the court ballet were elaborate, including a great variety of steps in patterns designed by dancing masters that required discipline, skill, and practice to execute well. In the late 1670s, Louis XIV asked Pierre Beauchamp, director of the Royal Academy of Dance, to devise a notation for dance. As part of his work, Beauchamp established five basic positions for the feet, still used in ballet today. In 1700, Raoul Auger Feuillet published a system of dance notation adapted from Beauchamp's in *Chorégraphie, ou l'art de décrire la danse par caractères, figures, et signes démonstratifs* (Choreography, or The Art of Describing Dance with Demonstrative Characters, Figures, and Signs), the first complete method for recording dance steps and gestures. Feuillet's book gave its name ***choreography*** (from the Greek words for "dance" and "write") to the art of designing dance. Figure 16.4 shows Feuillet's choreography for a gigue (see p. 356) danced by a couple, with a complex series of steps and gestures in a pattern as geometric and symmetrical as the gardens of Versailles. The invention of notation changed dance as it had changed music centuries before, making it possible to preserve and disseminate in writing an art that previously had been as ephemeral as the wave of a hand.

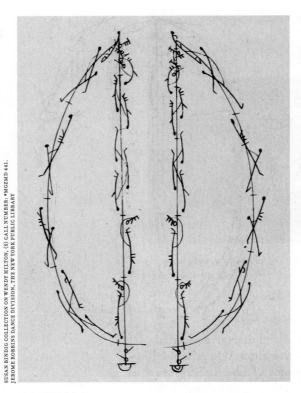

FIGURE 16.4 *Raoul Auger Feuillet's choreography for a gigue to be danced by a couple. The pattern begins at the bottom of the page. The man is on the left, the woman on the right. Each starts with one foot in front of the other, both feet pointing out at a diagonal, and executes a sequence of steps that mirrors their partner in perfect symmetry.*

Dance reinforced the state by offering a model of discipline, order, refine-   *Dance and*
ment, restraint, and subordination of the individual to a common enterprise.   *political control*
Requiring aristocrats to participate in social dancing and ballets kept them
busy and provided a ritualized demonstration of the social hierarchy, with the
king at the top. It is no wonder that French Baroque music, so centered on
dance, is marked by refinement, elegance, and restraint, in strong contrast to
the individuality and showmanship typical of Italian music at the time.

MUSIC AT COURT   Music for the king was as hierarchically organized as the
state itself. There were 150 to 200 musicians in three divisions like those we
saw in Renaissance courts (see Chapter 7): the Chapel, the Chamber, and the
Great Stable. The Music of the Royal Chapel included singers, organists, and
other instrumentalists who performed for religious services. The Music of
the Chamber, primarily solo singers and string, lute, harpsichord, and flute
players, provided music for indoor entertainments. The Music of the Great
Stable comprised wind, brass, and timpani players, who played for military
and outdoor ceremonies and sometimes joined the chapel or indoor music,
adding instrumental color (see Music in Context and Figure 16.5, p. 344).
Louis's wind ensemble profoundly influenced the development of wind and
brass music by encouraging improved instruments and playing techniques
and by nurturing generations of performers, among them families of wind
players such as the Hotteterres and Philidors.

Although the French often preferred the viol for chamber and solo music,   *String orchestras*
they created the first large ensembles of the violin family. These became the
model for the modern ***orchestra***—an ensemble whose core consists of strings
with more than one player on each part. Louis XIII established the Vingt-
quatre Violons du Roi (Twenty-Four Violins of the King), which typically
played in a five-part texture: six soprano violins, tuned like modern violins,
on the melody; twelve alto and tenor violins tuned like modern violas, divided
among three inner parts; and six bass violins, tuned a whole tone lower than
modern cellos, on the bass line. In 1648, the Petits Violons (Small Violin
Ensemble), with eighteen strings, was created for Louis XIV's personal use.
These two groups accompanied ballets, balls, the king's supper, and other
court functions. By the 1670s, the term "orchestra" was used for such ensembles, after the area in front of the stage in a theater, where the musicians were
usually placed for operas and other events.

JEAN-BAPTISTE LULLY AND FRENCH OPERA   For over three decades,
Louis XIV's favorite musician was Jean-Baptiste Lully (1632–1687; see biography and Figure 16.6, p. 345). Lully wrote music for ballets and religious
services at court but earned his greatest success with dramatic music. In the
1670s, with Louis's support, Lully created a distinctive French kind of opera
that persisted for a century.

Cardinal Mazarin had tried to establish Italian opera in France, commis-   *Influences on*
sioning Luigi Rossi's *Orfeo* in 1647 and Francesco Cavalli's *Ercole amante* in   *French opera*
1662. But the operas, which were sung in Italian, met opposition on political
and artistic grounds. Lully learned operatic styles from both operas, especially from *Ercole amante,* to which he contributed ballet music. After Cavalli's
departure, Lully collaborated with comic playwright Jean-Baptiste Molière to

The Music of the Great Stable

Louis XIV's musicians of the Great Stable played at all manner of events that took place outdoors: processions occasioned by royal weddings and funerals, fireworks displays commemorating royal births, visits by foreign dignitaries, military reviews, hunts, and other types of games and pageants. Like the uniformed trumpeters who always preceded the king's coach when he rode out from his palace, stable musicians often mounted horses on these occasions, which helps to explain their association with the stable. These musicians were Louis XIV's best wind and brass players. They performed ceremonial music on instruments such as fifes and drums, oboes and bassoons, cornetts and trumpets, all of which could easily be heard in the open air. Stable musicians were relatively well paid and, like other members of Louis's household, could pass their position on to a son with the permission of the king.

Because employment as a stable musician offered status and job security, the institution of the Great Stable became a proving ground for several important families of wind players. A member of one such family, Jean Hotteterre (ca. 1610–ca. 1692), experimented with the construction of several kinds of wind instruments. Fashioning them out of wood, he sometimes included elegant ornamental details in ivory and ebony, signs that his instruments were highly prized and appreciated at court. The inclusion of woodwinds in orchestras for the opera also became a factor in their improvement, stimulating their makers and players to strive for a sweeter, more refined sound.

Wind players and instrument makers at the French court are believed to have created the modern oboe. This instrument differed from its predecessor, the shawm, in having longer and thinner reeds, producing less volume and allowing for greater control of intonation and tone quality. Instead of being constructed out of a single piece of wood, the oboe had three sections fitted together in a way that facilitated the most delicate adjustments in tuning. It also had an expanded, two-octave range, and the instrument's improved design and smaller fingerholes allowed the player to produce chromatic pitches more accurately. Thus the Great Stable initiated the rise to prominence of woodwind instruments in today's orchestras.

CHATEAU DU GRAND TRIANON, VERSAILLES, FRANCE/BRIDGEMAN IMAGES

FIGURE 16.5

Perspective view from the Chateau of Versailles of the Place d'Armes and the Stables, 1688 (oil on canvas) by Jean-Baptiste Martin (1659–1735). The musicians of the Grand Ecurie (Great Stable) provided music for the pomp and ceremony of all manner of events under Louis XIV.

JEAN-BAPTISTE LULLY

(1632–1687)

Lully was the most powerful force in French music in the seventeenth century, renowned for creating a French type of opera, pioneering the French overture, and fostering the modern orchestra. Ironically, he was Italian, though he lived in France throughout his adult life.

Born in Florence, Lully came to Paris at age fourteen as Italian tutor to a cousin of Louis XIV. In Paris he completed his musical training and studied dance. His dancing in the *Ballet de la nuit* (1653) so impressed Louis that he appointed Lully court composer of instrumental music and director of the Petits Violons. In 1661, Lully became Superintendent of Music for the King's Chamber, taking over the Vingt-quatre Violons du Roi as well as the Petits Violons, and became a French citizen. His marriage the next summer to Madeleine Lambert, daughter of composer Michel Lambert, was witnessed by the king and queen, showing how high Lully had risen at court.

Lully composed music for numerous court ballets and sacred music for the royal chapel. He turned to comédies-ballets in 1664, then in 1672 to opera, where he gained his greatest fame.

The discipline Lully imposed on his orchestra, enforcing uniform bowing and coordinated use of ornaments, won admiration, was widely imitated, and became the foundation for modern orchestral practice. Although Lully conducted with a long staff or cane

CHURCH OF NOTRE-DAME-DES-VICTOIRES, PARIS, FRANCE. PHOTO: GIRAUDON/BRIDGEMAN IMAGES

FIGURE 16.6 *Jean-Baptiste Lully, in a bronze bust by Antoine Coyzevox placed on Lully's tomb in the church of Notre Dame des Victoires in Paris.*

instead of a baton, the tradition of dictatorial leadership he introduced, modeled on the king's own absolute power, has been continued by later conductors.

Lully's close relationship with Louis XIV was clouded by scandal in 1685 when the king learned that Lully had seduced a young male page in his service. Lully remained rich and powerful but had to rely on other patrons. He died in 1687 after he hit his foot with his staff while conducting his *Te Deum* and the injury turned to gangrene.

MAJOR WORKS *Alceste, Armide,* and 13 other operas; 14 comédies-ballets; 29 ballets (most in collaboration with other composers); numerous motets and other liturgical music

---

create a series of successful *comédies-ballets,* which blended elements from ballets, spoken plays, and operas. But Lully did not yet contemplate full opera. The ballet tradition seemed too strong, as did French spoken tragedy, represented by dramatists Pierre Corneille (1606–1684) and Jean Racine (1639–1699). French literary culture demanded that poetry and drama be given priority on the stage, and the French found the idea of characters having long conversations in recitative ridiculous. The domination of music and singing in Italian opera therefore seemed unsuitable for France.

In time, successful experiments by others convinced Lully that opera in French was viable. In 1672, with Louis XIV's support, he purchased a royal privilege granting him the exclusive right to produce sung drama in France and established the Académie Royale de Musique. Together with his librettist,

Tragédie en musique

playwright Philippe Quinault (1635–1688), Lully reconciled the demands of drama, music, and ballet in a new French form of opera, ***tragédie en musique*** (tragedy in music), later named ***tragédie lyrique***.

Quinault's librettos   Quinault's five-act dramas combined serious plots from ancient mythology or chivalric tales with frequent ***divertissements*** (diversions), long interludes of dancing with solo and choral singing. He cleverly intermingled episodes of romance and adventure with adulation of the king, glorification of France, and moral reflection. His texts were overtly and covertly propagandistic, in tune with Louis's use of the arts. Like Italian operas from Peri through Cavalli, each of Quinault's opera librettos began with a prologue, usually with allegorical characters singing the king's praises literally or through analogy. The plots exemplified the virtue of overcoming one's passions, offering a model of self-control for nobles and others to follow, and the mythological characters and settings reinforced the parallels Louis sought to draw between his regime and ancient Greece and Rome. The librettos also provided opportunities for spectacles to entertain the audience, including singing and dancing, supernatural beings flying down from the clouds, and conflagrations, as in Figure 16.7.

French overtures   Lully's music projected the formal splendor of Louis's court. Each opera began with an ***ouverture*** (French for "opening"), or ***overture***, marking the entry of the king (when he was present) and welcoming him and the audience to the performance. Lully's overtures were appropriately grand and followed a format that he had already used in his ballets, known today as a ***French overture***. There are two sections, each played twice. The first is homophonic and majestic, marked by dotted rhythms and figures rushing toward the downbeats. The second section is faster and begins with imitation, then usually returns at the end to the tempo and figuration of the first section. The overture to Lully's opera *Armide* (1686; NAWM 85a) exemplifies the genre.

Divertissements   A divertissement usually appeared at the center or end of every act, and it was the job of the librettist to link it to the surrounding plot. These extended episodes, which continued the French ballet tradition, offered opportunities for songs, choruses, and instrumental dances, each with colorful costumes and elaborate choreography. The songs in divertissements, and other lyrical moments in Lully's operas, were cast as ***airs***, songs with a rhyming text and regular meter and phrasing. Less elaborate and effusive than Italian arias, airs were typically syllabic or nearly so, with a tuneful melody, repetitive form, and no melismas or virtuosic display.

An example of a divertissement is in the second act of *Armide* (excerpt in NAWM 85b). The sorceress Armide has commanded her demons to bring the warrior Renaud to her so she can put him to death. Renaud arrives and, bewitched by their music, he falls asleep on the grass. In the divertissement, demons disguised as nymphs, shepherds, and shepherdesses sing solo airs and choruses praising the pleasures of love, interspersed with instrumental dances during which they cast a spell on Renaud and entwine him with garlands of flowers. The presence of supernatural beings provided opportunities for spectacular stage effects, and the singing and dancing were especially appealing to the public. Dances from Lully's ballets and operas became so popular that they were arranged in independent instrumental suites, and many new suites were composed imitating his divertissements.

Adapting recitative   To project drama, Lully adapted Italian recitative to French language and
to French   poetry. This was no simple task, since the style of recitative typical in Italian

opera of the time was not suited to the rhythms and accents of French. Lully is said to have solved the problem by listening to celebrated French actors and closely imitating their declamation. Certainly the timing, pauses, and inflections often resemble stage speech, but Lully did not aspire to create the illusion of speech as in a recitative by Peri, and the bass is often more rhythmic and the melody more songful than in Italian recitative.

In his recitatives, Lully followed the general contours of spoken French while shifting the metric notation between duple and triple meter to allow the most natural and expressive declamation of the words. Thus Lully's recitatives continue the French tradition, dating back to musique mesurée (see Chapter 10), of using irregular metric groupings to reflect the rhythms of the text. Some scholars distinguish between two styles of recitative, one metrically fluid and one more measured, but in reality Lully's recitative spans a flexible continuum between metric fluidity and regularity, varying as appropriate to the poetry and the emotions of his characters. The terms *récitatif simple* (simple recitative) and *récitatif mesuré* (measured recitative), often used for this distinction, were coined only in the latter eighteenth century and used inconsistently by French critics, making it problematic to apply them to Lully.

FIGURE 16.7 *Design for Lully's opera* Armide *(1686), in an ink-wash by Jean Bérain. It shows the burning of Armide's palace, which she ordered in a fury over her failure to win Renaud's love and over his escape from her power. In the foreground, Renaud, in armor, bids farewell to Armide.*

Armide's monologue in Act II, Scene 5, of *Armide* (NAWM 85c) illustrates Lully's mixture of styles to create drama. The scene begins with a tense orchestral prelude suffused with dotted rhythms and rapid scale figures called *tirades* that were often associated with powerful or supernatural characters such as Armide. The sorceress, dagger in hand, stands over her captive, the sleeping warrior Renaud. In recitative, she speaks of her determination to kill him as revenge for freeing her captives, but she cannot bring herself to stab him because she realizes she loves him. Measures of four, three, and two beats are intermixed, permitting the two accented syllables in each poetic line to fall on downbeats. Rests follow each line and are also used dramatically, as when Armide vacillates between hesitation and resolve in the excerpt shown in Example 16.1a (see p. 349). When she finally decides to use sorcery to make him love her, her new determination is reflected in more regularly measured recitative. This leads to an air in a relatively fast triple meter, shown in Example 16.1b. It is accompanied only by continuo but is introduced by an orchestral interlude that presents the music of the entire air.

Armide's monologue

Armide's monologue illustrates the power of Lully's operas and reflects his aim to present the drama as naturally as music can. Time does not stop for an aria as it does in Italian opera of the late seventeenth or eighteenth

Focus on drama

French Writers on Nature and Expression

French writers of the seventeenth and eighteenth centuries praised the "natural" in art and music, including the naturalistic representation of human emotions. Among them were François Fénelon, a rhetorician and theologian, and Jean-Laurent Lecerf de la Viéville, a magistrate and writer of several works on music, including a biography of Lully.

To successfully paint the passions, you must study the movements that they inspire. For example, observe what the eyes do, what the hands do, what the entire body does, and what its posture is; what the voice does when it is overcome by sorrow, or struck by the sight of a shocking thing. There nature reveals herself to you; you have only to follow her.

François Fénelon, *Dialogue sur l'éloquence et Oposcules académique* (1679).

Nature and expression are the two primary qualities of music; ornamentation, the harmonic contentment of the ears . . . will be the third. . . . I have told you that the melody must travel to the auditor's heart. But how does it get there? By way of the ear. The ear is, in music, the door to the heart. To open this door wide, to flatter the ear, is thus the musician's third task; but it is only the third. The requirements of being natural and being expressive come first.

Jean-Laurent Lecerf de la Viéville, *Comparaison de la musique italienne et de la musique française* (1704–6). Translations by Jonathan Gibson.

century; instead, the music moves seamlessly between vocal and instrumental passages in contrasting styles to fit the natural rhythm of speech and the flow of the drama. The succession in this scene from irregular to more metric recitative and the mixture of recitative, air, and orchestral interludes allowed Lully to convey Armide's intense, rapidly changing feelings of tension, vengeance, doubt, and love through simple but effective means, dramatizing her lack of control over her passions, which ultimately leads to her downfall.

The contrast between the raw emotions starkly depicted in this scene and the stylized divertissement that directly precedes it embodies an aesthetic dichotomy typical of French Baroque art and music, between refined elegance and the desire to convey human passions in a way that was true to nature. Although the political structure and court culture of France favored refinement and emotional restraint, French writers praised the emulation of nature in a true expression of feelings (see Source Readings). Lully's balance between the values of elegance and naturalism made his operas successful both politically and dramatically.

Some typically French elements cannot be seen in the notation but were added in performance. Passages notated in even, short durations, like the eighth notes in the bass line of Example 16.1b, were often rendered by alternating longer notes on the beat with shorter offbeats, producing lilting rhythms like triplets or dotted figures; this practice is called **notes inégales** (unequal notes) and was considered a matter of expression and elegance, left to the players' discretion. A related practice is **overdotting**, in which a dotted note is held longer than its notated value—according to the performer's taste—while the following short note is shortened. These changes accentuate the beats and sharpen the rhythmic profile. Although the elaborate embellishments of Italian singers were considered in bad taste, performers were expected to use brief ornaments called **agréments**, whether notated or added by the performer, to emphasize cadences and other important notes and to enhance the emotional affect of the music. Agréments were fixed types of ornament that decorated a single note, such as trills and appoggiaturas, and could be performed and combined in a variety of ways depending on the context.

EXAMPLE 16.1 *Jean-Baptiste Lully, excerpts from Armide's monologue in* Armide

a. Recitative

What makes me hesitate? What in his favor does pity want to tell me? Let us strike . . . Heavens! Who can stop me? Let us get on with it . . . I tremble! Let us avenge . . . I sigh!

b. Air

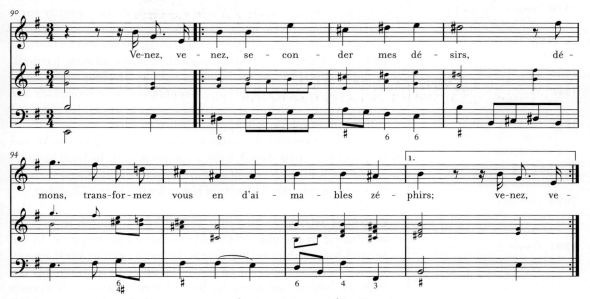

Come, come, support my desires, demons, transform yourselves into friendly zephyrs.

Lully's music is **tonal**, in the new system of major and minor keys, rather than modal, the system still common earlier in the century. The excerpts in Example 16.1 feature harmonic progressions that are typical of tonal music, moving forward in a predictable manner to close on a dominant-tonic cadence. Lully sometimes evades the cadence by using a first-inversion tonic triad (as in measure 39) to prolong the harmonic tension and make the ultimate resolution even more satisfying. This technique depends on the listener's expectations for tonal music.

Lully's followers continued to write operas that imitated his style while introducing an occasional aria in Italian style, expanding the divertissements, intensifying the harmony, and increasing the complexity of the texture. Lully's own operas were performed well into the eighteenth century, in France and other countries, and his style influenced opera and instrumental music in England, Germany, and elsewhere. The French overture, which he did not invent but helped to popularize, was used across Europe through the mid-eighteenth century to introduce ballets, operas, oratorios, and instrumental works such as suites and sonatas, including the overtures of J. S. Bach and the operas and oratorios of Handel. Effects he popularized, such as associating dotted rhythms and tirades with powerful characters or ideas, continued to be used for more than a century. French dances were fashionable throughout Europe, and Lully's dance music was the epitome of the French tradition. If every princeling, king, and emperor wanted his own Versailles, he also wanted his own Lully, and echoes of Lully's style and of his special relationship with his patron are evident through the late eighteenth century.

SONG The air was the leading genre of vocal chamber music in France, as it had been since the late sixteenth century. Composers wrote airs in a variety of styles and types, from courtly vocal music to songs of a popular cast. The air de cour gradually went out of fashion, replaced by other types like the *air sérieux* (serious air) and *air à boire* (drinking song), the former on love, pastoral, or political topics, and the latter on light or frivolous topics. Both types were typically syllabic and strophic and were scored for one to three voices with lute or continuo accompaniment. Hundreds of collections of such songs were published in Paris.

The most prolific and influential composer of airs was Michel Lambert (ca. 1610–1696), Lully's father-in-law. In 1660 he published the first collection of airs with basso continuo, and the next year he was appointed Master of Music for the King's Chamber.

CHURCH MUSIC Until about 1650, French church music was dominated by the old style of Renaissance counterpoint. In the second half of the century, in sacred as in secular vocal music, French composers borrowed genres invented in Italy, notably the sacred concerto and oratorio, but wrote in distinctively French styles. Their vocal and organ music was flavored by many of the stylistic elements found in French opera, including agréments, notes inégales, and overdotting.

Composers in the royal chapel produced numerous motets on Latin texts. These were of two main types: the ***petit motet*** (small motet), a sacred concerto for few voices with continuo, and the ***grand motet*** (large motet) or *motet à grand choeur* (motet with large chorus) for soloists, contrasting large and small choruses, and orchestra, corresponding to the large-scale concertos of Gabrieli and Schütz. Grand motets featured several sections in different meters and tempos, encompassing preludes, vocal solos, ensembles, and choruses. Among the grandest is Lully's *Te Deum* (1677; conclusion in NAWM 86), scored for soloists, large and small choruses, full string orchestra, trumpets, and timpani and performed by as many as 150 musicians.

Petits motets and grands motets

Marc-Antoine Charpentier (1643–1704) introduced the Latin oratorio into France, drawing on the model of Carissimi and combining Italian and French styles. He was the most significant French composer of the seventeenth century to incorporate Italian dissonance and chromatic counterpoint, setting himself apart from the Lully tradition and providing many composers with an alternative model. In the mid-1660s, he went to Rome, where he learned the current Italian style and where oratorios were often performed at institutions associated with the Jesuit religious order (the Society of Jesus). When he returned to Paris in 1670, he brought back copies of several oratorios and motets by Carissimi and other Roman composers. He spent his career outside the royal sphere of influence, which allowed him the freedom to compose in a unique manner that combines French and Italian qualities. By the 1680s he was serving Jesuit churches, including as chapelmaster at Collège de Clermont and as master of music at Saint Louis, the principal Jesuit church in Paris. For them he composed masses, motets, oratorios, and other works that incorporated the styles and approaches he had encountered in Rome.

Marc-Antoine Charpentier

Charpentier's oratorio *Le reniement de Saint Pierre* (The Denial of Saint Peter; NAWM 87) is a masterpiece of musical dramatization enacting the story of the disciple Peter's threefold denial that he knows Jesus, just before Jesus's crucifixion. Accompanied by basso continuo, five singers narrate and play the parts, alternating ensemble singing with recitative and arioso. The closing chorus depicts Peter's tears with dissonant suspensions in almost every measure, a series of ravishing clashes far from Lully's style but reminiscent of Carissimi's.

In the later years of his reign, Louis XIV's favorite sacred composer was Michel-Richard de Lalande (1657–1726), whose more than seventy motets reveal a masterly command of the resources of the grand motet: syllabic solos, homophonic and imitative choruses, and operatic airs and duets, with frequent contrasts of texture and mood. De Lalande worked as an organist at the Church of Saint Louis under Charpentier early in his career, and he incorporated into his motets elements of Italian style such as aria-like solos and dissonant counterpoint.

Michel-Richard de Lalande

A distinctive French school of organ music emerged in the seventeenth century, consisting mostly of music for church services, such as organ masses, alongside pieces resembling the overtures and expressive recitatives of French opera. National traits include the use of agréments and an interest in the coloristic possibilities of the organ, often specified in the title or in the score itself by indicating the combinations of organ stops to be used in order to produce

Organ music

FIGURE 16.8 *Harpsichord with two manual keyboards, built by Michel Richard, Paris, 1688.*

distinct tonal colors. This music incorporated the colorful sounds of the outdoor wind ensembles, with stops imitating oboes, crumhorns, trumpets, and cornetts, along with sounds unique to the organ. Timbre as a compositional resource is a constant thread in French music, from these organ works and the operas of Lully to the program music of Berlioz (Chapter 26) and the impressionism of Debussy and Ravel (Chapter 32).

LUTE AND KEYBOARD MUSIC Lute music flourished in France during the early seventeenth century and left a permanent mark on French style. The leading lute composer was Denis Gaultier (1603–1672), whose two published collections instructed amateurs on how to play the lute. During the seventeenth century, the *clavecin* (French for "harpsichord"), shown in Figure 16.8, displaced the lute as the main solo instrument, while harpsichord music absorbed many characteristics of lute style. Important harpsichord composers, or *clavecinists*, included Jacques Champion de Chambonnières (1601/2–1672), Jean Henry D'Anglebert (1629–1691), Elisabeth-Claude Jacquet de la Guerre (1665–1729; see biography and Figure 16.10, p. 354), and François Couperin (1668–1733; see Chapter 18). All of them served Louis XIV in various capacities but are best known today for their printed collections of harpsichord music, marketed to a growing public of well-to-do amateur performers.

Agréments   Lutenists and harpsichordists developed the use of agréments to emphasize important notes and give the melody shape and character. Both instruments are played by plucking strings, the lute with fingers and the harpsichord with quills operated from the keyboard, resulting in a strong attack and a relatively quick decay on each note. Adding an ornament animates the note through repetition and embellishment and can convey a sense of forward momentum akin to a sustained tone. Since the harpsichord mechanism plucks each string with the same force, the player cannot achieve differences in dynamics or color by striking the keys with more or less pressure, as piano players can do, yet similar variety can be attained through ornaments; because agréments involve multiple plucks in relatively quick succession, they sound louder and thus more accentuated than unornamented notes. By combining agréments with the clear articulation innate to plucked strings, lute and harpsichord players can achieve a great variety of effects, from stressing the strong beats in a dance rhythm to making a melodic line more prominent and expressive.

Agréments became a fundamental element of all French music, and the proper use of ornaments was a sign of refined taste. Agréments were often left to the discretion of the player, but composers also worked out ways of notating them. Figure 16.9 shows the table of agréments in D'Anglebert's *Pièces de clavecin* (Harpsichord Pieces, 1689), the most comprehensive of many such tables published in collections of harpsichord music.

Style luthé   Lute style also strongly influenced the texture of harpsichord music. On

FIGURE 16.9 *Table of ornaments from* Pièces de clavecin (1689) *by Jean Henry D'Anglebert, showing for each ornament its notation, name, and manner of performance. "Autre" indicates another way to notate or perform the preceding ornament.*

a plucked string instrument like the lute or harpsichord, players can extend the sound of a chord and give it dynamic shape by arpeggiating it rather than playing all the notes at once. Thus lutenists often struck only one note at a time, sketching in the melody, bass, and harmony by sounding the appropriate tones—now in one register, now in another—and relying on the listener's imagination to supply the continuity of the various lines. This technique, the **style luthé** (lute style), sometimes called by the modern term **style brisé** (broken style), was imitated by harpsichord composers and became an intrinsic part of French harpsichord style. Like agréments, aspects of the style luthé were sometimes notated by composers, as seen in Examples 16.2 and 16.3 (see pp. 355 and 357), but were also regularly added by performers; for example, players could arpeggiate chords in different directions and at different speeds to shape the music at their discretion.

DANCE MUSIC Dances formed the core of the lute and keyboard repertory, reflecting their importance in French life. Composers arranged ballet music for lute or harpsichord and composed original music in dance meters and

ELISABETH-CLAUDE JACQUET DE LA GUERRE

(1665–1729)

Women continued to play an active role in the music of the seventeenth century, from singers and composers to patrons of art, as well as hostesses at the salons where music was actively cultivated. One such extraordinary woman was the French composer Elisabeth-Claude Jacquet de la Guerre, born into a family of musicians and instrument makers. Trained by her father, she was the original child prodigy in music, of which Mozart is the most famous example. From the age of five, she sang and played the harpsichord at Louis XIV's court, supported by the king's mistress. In 1677, the Paris journal *Mercure galant* gushed:

> There is a prodigy who has appeared here for the last four years. She sings at sight the most difficult music. She accompanies herself, and others who wish to sing, on the harpsichord, which she plays in an inimitable manner. She composes pieces and plays them in any key one suggests.

Some years later the same writer called her "the marvel of our century."

In 1684, she married the organist Martin de la Guerre and moved permanently to Paris. There she taught harpsichord and gave concerts that won her wide renown. She enjoyed the patronage of Louis XIV and dedicated most of her works to him, including the first ballet (1691, now lost) and first opera (*Céphale et Procris*, 1694) written by a French woman.

PRIVATE COLLECTION, LONDON

FIGURE 16.10 *Portrait of the composer by François de Troy (1645–1730).*

Jacquet de la Guerre is best known for her two published collections of harpsichord pieces (1687 and 1707) and three books of cantatas, two on biblical subjects (1708 and 1711) and one secular (1715). Her violin and trio sonatas show an interest in the Italian instrumental style. Her output was small but encompassed a wide variety of genres, and she was recognized by her contemporaries as one of the great talents of her time.

MAJOR WORKS *Céphale et Procris* (opera), 3 books of cantatas, 2 books of *Pièces de clavecin*, 8 violin sonatas, 4 trio sonatas

forms. Most dance music for lute or keyboard was intended not for dancing but for the entertainment of the player or a small audience. Composers used the rhythms and forms of dances, but played with the characteristic features of each dance to make the music more challenging to musicians and more intriguing for listeners. Paired two- and four-measure phrases are frequent, matching the patterns of many dance steps.

Binary form   Earlier dances had assumed a variety of forms, such as the three repeated sections of the pavane or the repeating bass of the passamezzo. Most seventeenth-century dances were in **binary form**: two roughly equal sections, each repeated, the first leading harmonically from the tonic to close on the dominant (sometimes the relative major), the second returning to the tonic. This form was widely used for dance music and other instrumental genres over the next two centuries.

Many of Denis Gaultier's dances for lute are contained in a sumptuous manuscript of his lute music titled *La rhétorique des dieux* (The Rhetoric of the Gods, ca. 1650). Typical of his style is *La coquette virtuose* (The Virtuous Coquette; NAWM 88), whose title may have been given by the compilers of the manuscript rather than by the composer himself. This is a *courante,* a dance in binary form in a moderate triple or compound meter (see p. 356). Example 16.2 shows the first section, which moves from tonic to dominant as expected. Gaultier did not notate any agréments, leaving them to the performer. Characteristic of the style luthé are the many broken chords; whether simply arpeggiated (as in measures 3 and 7) or embellished by neighbor tones (as in the succession of chords in measures 5 and 6), each chord is presented in a different way, creating an irregular, unpredictable, and ever-changing surface garb for a straightforward underlying progression. Also characteristic are the syncopations in the melody in measures 4–6, where melody notes often lag just behind the changes of harmony, and the changes in texture between two, three, or more contrapuntal voices.

Denis Gaultier lute dances

French composers often grouped a series of dances into a **suite**, as did their German counterparts (see Chapter 15). Each dance had a unique character and affect, determined in part by its individual meter, tempo, characteristic rhythm, and national origin, providing strong contrasts between movements. Figure 16.11 shows the most common dances in suites. Although none of the movements of a keyboard suite would have been used for dancing, the steps and associations of the dances were known to the listeners and influenced the rhythm and style of the music.

Suites

A look at excerpts from Jacquet de la Guerre's Suite No. 3 in A Minor from her *Pièces de clavecin* (1687; NAWM 89), shown in Example 16.3, illustrates both the structure of a typical suite and the most common types of dance. All but two movements, the prelude and a chaconne, are in binary form.

Many suites begin with a prelude in the style of a toccata or other abstract work. Here it is an **unmeasured prelude**, a distinctively French genre whose non-metric notation allows great rhythmic freedom, as if improvising (NAWM 89a).

Prelude

EXAMPLE 16.2 *Denis Gaultier,* La coquette virtuose

DANCE	TEMPO	METER	AFFECTIVE CHARACTER	NATIONAL ORIGIN	COMMON RHYTHMS
Allemande	Moderately slow	$\frac{4}{4}$	Serious	German	Pickup, running sixteenths
Courante	Moderate	$\frac{6}{4}, \frac{3}{2}, \frac{3}{4}$	Witty	French	Pickup, hemiola
Sarabande	Slow	$\frac{3}{4}, \frac{3}{2}$	Tender, proud, noble	Spanish/ New World	Stress on second beat, ♩ ♩. ♪ (in $\frac{3}{4}$)
Gigue	Fast	$\frac{6}{4}, \frac{6}{8}, \frac{12}{8}$	Lively	English/Irish	𝅗𝅥 ♩, ♩ ♩ ♩, and ♩. ♪♩ (in $\frac{6}{4}$)

FIGURE 16.11 *Four dances that were common in suites.*

In Example 16.3a, the whole notes indicate arpeggiated chords, the black notes show melodic passages, and the slurs show groupings or sustained notes.

Allemande
The ***allemande*** (French for "German"), was usually in a moderately slow $\frac{4}{4}$ meter beginning with an upbeat. Rarely danced in the latter seventeenth century, the allemande had become among the most contrapuntal and rhythmically varied of dances, elaborated for the enjoyment of players and listeners. As shown in Example 16.3b (NAWM 89b), all voices participate in almost continuous movement, and agréments appear often, emphasizing notes that seek resolution and reinforcing forward motion in the melodic line. Signs of the style luthé include the opening arpeggiation of the tonic chord in the bass and staggered rhythms between the voices.

Courante
The ***courante*** (French for "running" or "flowing") also begins with an upbeat but is in a moderate triple or compound meter ($\frac{3}{2}$ or $\frac{6}{4}$) or shifts between the two. The interplay between the two meters is highlighted in Example 16.3c by the agréments and chords, which sometimes appear on the fourth quarter note in a measure, suggesting $\frac{6}{4}$, and sometimes stress the third and fifth quarter notes, suggesting $\frac{3}{2}$ (NAWM 89c). The steps of the dance were dignified, with a bend of the knees on the upbeat and a rise on the beat, often followed by a glide or step.

Sarabande
The ***sarabande*** was originally a quick, lascivious type of dance-song from Central America, accompanied by guitar and percussion. It came across the Atlantic to Spain in the late sixteenth century and was the most popular dance there for decades, then spread to Italy and France. In France, it lost its associations with the New World and was transformed into a slow, dignified dance in triple meter with an emphasis on the second beat, reinforced in Example 16.3d by agréments and chords (NAWM 89d). The melodic rhythm in the first measure is especially common.

Gigue
The ***gigue*** (French for "jig") originated in the British Isles as a fast solo dance with rapid footwork. In France it became stylized as a movement in fast compound meter such as $\frac{6}{4}$ or $\frac{12}{8}$, with wide melodic leaps and continuous lively triplets. Sections often begin with imitation, as in Example 16.3e, where agréments and longer notes on the strong beats emphasize the lilting meter (NAWM 89e).

Other dances
Numerous other dances could appear in suites. Jacquet de la Guerre's suite continues with a chaconne in the form of a ***rondeau***, in which a refrain

EXAMPLE 16.3 *Elisabeth-Claude Jacquet de la Guerre,* Pièces de clavecin, *Suite No. 3 in A Minor*

a. Prelude

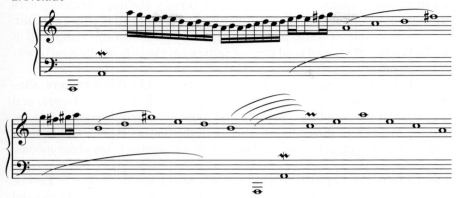

b. Allemande

c. Courante

d. Sarabande

e. Gigue

f. Minuet

alternates with a series of contrasting periods called **couplets**, then returns to close the movement (NAWM 89f). A **gavotte** follows, a duple-time dance with a half-measure upbeat and a characteristic rhythm of short-short-*long* with the long note on the downbeat (NAWM 89g). The suite ends with a **minuet**, an elegant couple dance in moderate triple meter, shown in Example 16.3f (NAWM 89h). The dance used various patterns of four steps within each two-measure unit.

German versus French suites

In Germany, the suite assumed a standard order like that seen here: allemande, courante (or *corrente*, an Italian dance in $\frac{3}{4}$ time), sarabande, and gigue, often preceded by a prelude and augmented with optional dances. French composers allowed more variety in the dances chosen and in their order, and often gave movements fanciful titles referring to people or moods.

EMULATION OF FRENCH STYLE France was the leading power in Europe after the Thirty Years' War ended in 1648. Louis XIV was the most powerful monarch and the model for artistic patronage. French tastes, manners, and arts were widely regarded as the most refined and highly developed. Both admiring and envious, the English, Germans, Austrians, Poles, Russians, and others imitated French architecture, decorative arts, and music. From the 1660s through the mid-eighteenth century, there were two dominant national styles of music in Europe: Italian, associated with opera and with abstract instrumental genres from sonata to toccata, and French, associated with dances, suites, and overtures and with Lully's operas, characterized by their use of dance and chorus and the close integration of recitative and air into seamless and continuous scenes. French style was almost as influential as Italian style, and the integration of the two became one of the themes of the eighteenth century.

ENGLAND

English music drew inspiration from both Italy and France, in combination with native traditions. Royal patronage exercised a major influence, as in France, but music for the public grew increasingly important.

Limited monarchy

Unlike France, England was a limited monarchy, whose king shared rule with Parliament. After Elizabeth I died in 1603, her cousin James VI of Scotland succeeded her as James I of England, uniting the two kingdoms. His son Charles I (r. 1625–49) sought to increase royal power, provoking the Civil War (1642–49). He was executed and the monarchy was abolished in 1649, succeeded by a Commonwealth and Protectorate under Oliver Cromwell (1599–1658). Preferring limited monarchy to military rule, Parliament restored the monarchy in 1660 but reserved to itself the right to pass laws and levy taxes. Charles II (r. 1660–85) agreed to respect Parliament but gradually returned to his father's policy of enlarging royal power. The religious and political policies of James II (r. 1685–88), a Catholic, provoked the Glorious Revolution, which installed as sovereigns James's Protestant daughter Mary II (r. 1689–94) and her Dutch husband William of Orange (r. 1689–1702). A Bill of Rights passed in 1689 guaranteed civil liberties and subjected the monarch to the rule of law. From then on, Parliament controlled the collection and allocation of public funds. As a result, the royal house had considerably less money than the French kings to spend on music.

MUSICAL THEATER Despite attempts to introduce opera, the English monarchs, aristocracy, and public preferred native genres of dramatic music.

A favorite court entertainment since Henry VIII was the ***masque***. Masques shared many aspects of opera, including instrumental music, dancing, songs, choruses, costumes, scenery, and stage machinery, but were long collaborative spectacles akin to French court ballets rather than unified dramas with music by one composer. A highly elaborate masque, *The Triumph of Peace* (1634), included music by William Lawes (1602–1645) and others. Shorter masques were produced by aristocrats and in theaters or private schools.

Cromwell was a Puritan, part of a movement inspired by Calvinist theology that sought to purify the Church of England and English culture. His government prohibited public performances of stage plays, but not concerts or private musical entertainments. This policy allowed the production of the first English "operas," not operas in the Italian sense, but mixtures of elements from spoken drama and the masque, including dances, songs, recitatives, and choruses. From this period comes the only seventeenth-century masque whose music survives complete, *Cupid and Death* (1653), with music by Matthew Locke (ca. 1621–1677) and Christopher Gibbons (1615–1677).

After the Restoration in 1660, audiences eagerly returned to the theaters, where plays often included masques or similar musical episodes, as illustrated in Figure 16.12. Charles II had spent his exile in France, and French music and court ballet became increasingly influential in England after his return. But an attempt to introduce French opera in the 1670s failed, and there was little interest in dramas set to continuous music. Only two dramas sung throughout met any success, both composed for private audiences rather than for the public: John Blow's *Venus and Adonis* (ca. 1683) and Henry Purcell's *Dido and Aeneas* (ca. 1687–88).

John Blow (1649–1708) was organist of Westminster Abbey and organist and composer in the Chapel Royal. He wrote *Venus and Adonis* to entertain Charles II, and it featured Charles's former mistress Mary Davis as Venus and their daughter Mary Tudor as Cupid. Called a masque, it resembles an unpretentious pastoral opera whose charming and moving music combines elements of Italian, French, and English styles. The overture and prologue are modeled on those of French operas; many of the airs and recitatives adopt the emotionally expressive style of the Italian lyric aria; other songs have English rhythms and melodic traits; and the dances and choruses stem from the masque tradition. The final chorus, *Mourn for thy servant*, is typically English in its naturalistic setting of the text, clear part writing, and frequent harmonic audacities.

Venus and Adonis

FIGURE 16.12 *Scene from "The Masque of Orpheus," with music by Matthew Locke. This masque, telling the story of Orpheus and Euridice, comprises part of Act IV of Elkanah Settle's play* The Empress of Morocco, *produced in 1673 at the Dorset Garden Theatre in London. Engraving by William Dolle.*

HENRY PURCELL'S DRAMATIC MUSIC Henry Purcell (1659–1695) was England's leading composer (see biography and Figure 16.13), renowned for his dramatic music, songs, and anthems.

Dido and Aeneas Purcell composed *Dido and Aeneas* by 1688, according to a recently discovered letter by an acquaintance. The first known performance took place at an exclusive girls' boarding school, but the work may have been intended for court. It is a masterpiece of opera in miniature: there are only four principal roles, and the three acts take only about an hour to perform. As Blow did in *Venus and Adonis,* which must have served as his principal model, Purcell combines elements of the English masque and of French and Italian opera.

French and Italian elements The overture and homophonic choruses resemble those of Lully, and the typical scene structure also follows Lully's example, with solo singing and a chorus leading to a dance. The most notable Italian element is the presence of several arias, rare in French opera or English masque. Three arias are built entirely over ground basses, an important type in Italian opera. The last of these, and one of the most moving arias in all opera, is Dido's lament, *When I am laid in earth* (NAWM 90b). It follows the Italian tradition of setting laments over a descending tetrachord (see Chapter 15), and Purcell heightens the pathos by adding chromaticism to the bass line, using sighing figures in the voice and violins, and rearticulating suspended notes on strong beats, intensifying the dissonance.

English elements Amid these foreign influences, the English traits are still strong. The use

HENRY PURCELL

(1659–1695)

FIGURE 16.13
Henry Purcell in 1695, in a portrait by John Closterman.
BY COURTESY OF THE NATIONAL
PORTRAIT GALLERY, LONDON

Purcell's entire career was supported by royal patronage. His father, a member of the Chapel Royal, died just before his son's fifth birthday. Purcell joined the Chapel Royal as a choirboy and proved to be a gifted prodigy as a composer, publishing his first song at the age of eight. When his voice broke, he was apprenticed to the keeper of the king's keyboard and wind instruments. In 1677, he succeeded Matthew Locke as composer-in-ordinary for the violins. Purcell held a number of prestigious positions simultaneously throughout his life, including organist of Westminster Abbey (1679), organist of the Chapel Royal (1682), and, the following year, organ maker and keeper of the king's instruments as well as composer to the court. He died at the young age of thirty-six, and his funeral was held in the hallowed Westminster Abbey, where he was also buried. He was celebrated after his death as "the British Orpheus."

Throughout his brief life, Purcell wrote enormous amounts of music in almost all genres. His primary focus was vocal music: he composed songs for home performance, choral music for Anglican services and royal ceremonies, and music for the theater. Purcell's greatest gift lay in setting English words in ways that sounded both natural and emotionally expressive.

MAJOR WORKS *Dido and Aeneas* (opera), 5 semi-operas, incidental music for 43 plays, 65 anthems, 6 Services, numerous odes, songs, and catches, and chamber and keyboard music

EXAMPLE 16.4 *Henry Purcell, recitative from* Dido and Aeneas

of dance for dramatic purposes owes less to Lully than to the masque tradition. Many solos and choruses use the style of the English air: tuneful, diatonic, in the major mode, with simple, catchy rhythms. The closing chorus, *With drooping wings* (NAWM 90c), was modeled on the final chorus of *Venus and Adonis*. Equally perfect in workmanship, it is longer and conveys a more profound depth of sorrow. Descending minor-scale figures portray the "drooping wings" of cupids, and arresting pauses mark the words "never part."

English recitatives

In the recitatives, Purcell draws on precedents from Locke and Blow to fashion melodies flexibly molded to the accents, pace, and emotions of the English text. Example 16.4 shows a recitative from Act I in which Dido praises Aeneas to Belinda, her confidante. Where Lully might use naturalistic declamation to convey emotions, Purcell composed florid passages to illustrate the text, as in Italian recitatives: upward rushes on "storms" and "fierce," and martial dotted rhythms on "valour." Descending lines filled with semitones suggest the sighs of love at "mix'd with Venus' charms, How soft in peace." Purcell catches the rhythms of English exactly with figures on "so much" and "did he" that reflect the tendency of English speakers to shorten accented syllables. Dido's final recitative, *Thy hand, Belinda* (NAWM 90a), portrays the dying Dido through a slow, stepwise, meandering descent tinged with chromaticism.

Semi-operas

For public theaters, Purcell wrote incidental music for almost fifty plays, most in the last five years of his life. During this period, he also wrote the music for five works in the mixed genre called **dramatic opera** or **semi-opera**, a spoken play with an overture and four or more masques or substantial musical episodes, including *The Fairy Queen* (1692), based on Shakespeare's *A Midsummer Night's Dream*.

MUSIC IN ENGLISH SOCIETY Music historians' fascination with opera in the seventeenth century has tended to obscure England, which did not develop a robust native tradition of opera until the nineteenth century. But England had a lively musical culture, worth noting in its broad outlines.

Vocal music

The royal family often commissioned large works for chorus, soloists, and orchestra for ceremonial or state occasions, such as royal birthdays, the king's return to London, or holidays. Purcell's magnificent *Ode for St. Cecilia's Day* (1692) was influenced by the French genre of the grand motet and in turn became a direct ancestor of Handel's English oratorios (see Chapter 19). In addition to hundreds of theater songs, Purcell wrote a large number of vocal solos, duets, and trios, all published for home performance. A specialty of Purcell and other English composers in this period was the ***catch***, a round or canon with a humorous, often ribald text. Catches were sung unaccompanied by a convivial group of gentlemen, in an elevated, musically intellectual parallel to the bawdy songs and coarse jokes of other all-male gatherings.

Anglican church music

Under Cromwell, Puritans sought to purge the Church of England of practices held over from its Catholic heritage, including church organs, musical instruments, and the singing of any music other than psalms, and they dissolved institutions for church music and music education. After the Restoration, such practices were revived, and anthems and Services again became the principal genres of Anglican church music. During his exile in France, Charles II had grown familiar with French grand motets by Lully and others, and therefore he favored solo singing and orchestral accompaniments. Accordingly, Blow, Purcell, and their contemporaries produced many anthems for soloists with chorus. Coronation ceremonies inspired especially elaborate works. Purcell also set nonliturgical sacred texts for one or more voices with continuo, evidently for private devotional use.

Instrumental music

The English continued to enjoy playing viol consort music, particularly *In Nomines* and fantasias. This was music for well-to-do amateurs to play for their own entertainment. The leading composer for viol consort at mid-century was John Jenkins (1592–1678). The principal later composers for viols were Locke and Purcell, whose viol fantasias and *In Nomines*, written about 1680, are the last important examples of both genres. Purcell also wrote numerous dances and other pieces for harpsichord, as well as chamber sonatas that show some Italian influences.

FIGURE 16.14 *Title page of the first edition of* The English Dancing Master, *published by John Playford.*

Social dancing was an important part of English life, with strong dance traditions at court, in cities, and in rural areas. The London publisher John Playford (1623–1687) collected the tunes most commonly used for traditional English country dances and published them, along with instructions for the dances, in *The English Dancing Master* (1651). Playford's title page for his first edition is shown in Figure 16.14. This was one of the first printed collections to include a large number of genuine folk melodies and popular airs. For us, it represents a valuable source for music that would otherwise have gone undocumented; at

The English Dancing Master:

OR,

Plaine and easie Rules for the Dancing of Country Dances, with the Tune to each Dance.

LONDON,

Printed by *Thomas Harper*, and are to be sold by *John Playford*, at his Shop in the Inner Temple neere the Church doore. **1651.**

The First Public Concerts

Concerts that anyone can attend for the price of a ticket are so much a part of modern musical life that it is hard to imagine they are only three and a half centuries old. The public concert is an English invention, inspired by the presence in London of excellent musicians with inadequate salaries and of middle-class audiences eager to hear music but without means to employ their own musicians. The first concert series was advertised in the *London Gazette* in December 1672:

These are to give notice, That at Mr *John Banisters* House (now called the Music-School) over against the *George Tavern* in *White Fryers,* this present Monday, will be Music performed by excellent Masters, beginning precisely at 4 of the clock in the afternoon, and every afternoon for the future, precisely at the same hour.

✳

Roger North, a writer and critic, recalled the concerts:

But how and by what steps Music shot up into such request, as to crowd out from the stage even comedy itself, and to sit down in her place and become of such mighty value and price as we now know it to be, is worth inquiring after. The

first attempt was low: a project of old Banister, who was a good violin, and a theatrical composer. He opened an obscure room in a public house in Whitefriars, filled it with tables and seats, and made a side box with curtains for the music. 1^S [one shilling] apiece, call for what [food and drink] you please, pay the reckoning [the bill], and *Welcome gentlemen.*

✳

Elsewhere, North noted that Banister was "one of the [King's] band of violins" whose "course of life was such as kept him poor" and who started the concert series "by way of project to get a little money." The performers, "the best hands in town," were

the mercenary teachers, chiefly foreigners, who attended for a sportula [a gift or share of the proceeds] at the time. Sometimes consort, sometimes solos, of the violin, flageolet (one of Banister's perfections), bass viol, lute, and song *all'Italiana,* and such varieties diverted the company, who paid at coming in.

Roger North on Music, ed. John Wilson (London: Novello, 1959), 302–3 and 352. Spelling and punctuation modernized.

the time, it marked the spread of an oral tradition into urban settings where amateur performance from printed music had been fashionable since the sixteenth century. It was one of the best-selling musical publications of the Baroque era, with new editions appearing frequently through 1728.

Perhaps more important in the long run than the music composed in seventeenth-century England was an institution pioneered there: the public concert open to anyone who pays the price of admission. Until the 1670s, concerts were private affairs, given for an invited audience by amateurs, by performers employed by a patron, or by learned academies. Then in London several trends came together: a middle class interested in listening to music, a large number of excellent musicians in the service of the royal court and the London theaters, and the inability of the king to pay his musicians well, which encouraged them to find means of supplementing their income. Impresarios rented rooms in taverns, charged an entrance fee, and paid the performers out of the proceeds (see Source Readings). Soon the first commercial concert halls were built, and modern concert life began. Public concerts gradually

The public concert

spread to the Continent, reaching Paris in 1725 and major German cities by the 1740s, and to the British colonies in North America, with public concerts in cities up and down the east coast from the 1730s on.

SPAIN AND THE NEW WORLD

The third great monarchy in western Europe was Spain. By 1600, the flood of silver from its New World colonies had made Spain the richest country in Europe. It was the most powerful nation on earth, with an empire that included Portugal (annexed in 1580), half of Italy and the Netherlands, the Philippine Islands, enclaves in India and Africa, almost all of Central and South America, and much of North America. The early seventeenth century was the climax of Spain's Golden Age in literature, theater, and the arts, marked especially by the appearance of Miguel de Cervantes's world-famous novel *Don Quixote* (1605 and 1615), the poems and plays of the prolific Lope de Vega, and the paintings of Diego Velázquez, court painter to Philip IV (r. 1621–65), pictured in Figure 16.15. Yet much of Spain's great wealth was wasted on military adventures in Europe, leading to economic and political decline midcentury. In the 1640s, Spain suffered defeat by France during the Thirty Years' War and revolutions in Catalonia (northeastern Spain), Portugal, and southern Italy. Although Spain reestablished control in Catalonia and southern Italy, Portugal regained its independence, taking Brazil with it.

Spanish colonies   Spain still ruled vast colonies in the Americas, stretching from present-day Chile and Argentina through Florida, Texas, and California. More than a century of colonization had produced an ethnically diverse society, encompassing a wide range of native peoples, Spanish immigrants and their descendants, slaves brought from Africa to work the mines and plantations, and people of mixed race. Each group had its own music but also borrowed elements from other groups, a habit that has characterized music in the Americas ever since. Musicians in the Spanish colonies drew directly on Spanish and wider European traditions; in turn, dances, songs, rhythms, and musical traits popular in the colonies found eager listeners in Spain, Italy, France, and elsewhere in Europe, as we saw with the spread of the chacona and sarabande. For these reasons, it makes sense to consider the music of Spain and the Spanish New World together, while recognizing the different circumstances of the home country and the colonies.

OPERA, ZARZUELA, AND SONG Spain developed its own national types of opera and musical theater. An opera in Spanish modeled on the early Florentine operas was presented at the royal court in 1627, but the style did not catch on. In 1659–60, for celebrations of peace with France and the wedding of Spanish princess Maria Teresa to Louis XIV, dramatist Pedro Calderón de la Barca and composer Juan Hidalgo (1614–1685) collaborated on two operas that inaugurated a distinctively Spanish tradition. The music survives only for the second opera, *Celos aun del aire matan*; it consists mostly of syllabic, strophic airs in Spanish styles and dance rhythms, with recitative monologues reserved for the most dramatic moments. Hidalgo also wrote music for many plays. Together with Calderón, he devised the distinctly Spanish **zarzuela**, the predominant genre of musical theater in Spain for several centuries, which

originally was a light, mythological play in a pastoral setting that alternates between sung and spoken dialogue and
various types of ensemble and solo song. Hidalgo was for
Spain what Lully was for France, the founder of enduring
traditions for the nation's musical theater and a composer
who knew how to appeal both to his royal patrons and to a
broader public.

The characteristics of Spanish Baroque opera are seen
in *La púrpura de la rosa* (The Blood of the Rose; excerpt in
NAWM 91), the first opera produced in the New World. It
was staged in 1701 at the court of the viceroy of Peru in Lima
to celebrate the accession to the Spanish throne of Philip V,
grandson of Louis XIV and the first Bourbon king of Spain.
The libretto was adapted from that of Calderón and Hidalgo's first opera. The music was by Tomás de Torrejón y
Velasco (1644–1728), who may have studied with Hidalgo in
Spain, went to Peru in 1667, and became *maestro di capilla*
of the Lima cathedral and the most famous composer in the
Americas. As was traditional in Spanish lyric theater of the
time, most of the roles were played by women. The story
centers on love between Venus and Adonis, threatened by
the jealousy of Mars. Example 16.5 illustrates the distinctly
Spanish practice of setting the dialogue not in recitative, but
rather to a strophic song. Venus and Adonis converse in the
first strophe, shown in the example; then Venus sings three

FIGURE 16.15 *Portrait
of King Philip IV of Spain,
painted ca. 1631–32 by
Diego Velázquez.*

strophes to the same music, and the fifth strophe is again in dialogue. The
syncopations are typical of Spanish song. The scene closes with a five-part
chorus of nymphs welcoming Adonis to Venus's garden with dance and song,
marked by even greater syncopations. The sound of the accompaniment was
also distinctive, since the continuo in Spanish works was usually played by
harps, guitars, and viols rather than by lute or keyboard as in Italy and France.

Many songs from theatrical productions also circulated in manuscript
throughout Spain and Spain's possessions in Italy and the Americas. So did
independent songs in genres such as the *romance*, scored for two to four
voices or for solo voice with guitar or harp accompaniment, and the *tonada*, a
solo song. The many variants between manuscripts give evidence for a strong
Spanish tradition of treating music as common property suitable for reworking and improvisation. Relatively few Spanish pieces were published because
Spain lacked music printers, which discouraged the growth of a strong amateur performing tradition as in England or France.

Songs

CHURCH MUSIC In Spain and the Spanish colonies, many liturgical works,
especially masses, continued to be composed in imitative polyphony well
into the eighteenth century. But the most distinctive and vibrant genre of
sacred music was the villancico, sung especially at Christmas, Easter, and
other important feasts. Scored for one or more choirs, soloists with choir,
or solo voice with continuo, and in the vernacular rather than Latin, these
works brought into church the concertato medium and the rustic style of the
secular villancico (see Chapter 10) and helped to attract large numbers of

EXAMPLE 16.5 *Tomás de Torrejón y Velasco,* La púrpura de la rosa

Venus: *What old-fashioned flattery!*
Adonis: *Pardon me, but I have to go forth following your beauty.*
Venus: *To what end? If in my garden,*

worshippers to services. The form resembled that of villancicos of the previous century, with a refrain (*estribillo*) that precedes and follows one or more stanzas (*coplas*), but the proportions were often greatly enlarged.

A colorful example is the Christmas villancico *Albricias pastores* (NAWM 92) by Juan Gutiérrez de Padilla (ca. 1590–1664). Padilla was born and trained in Málaga, Spain, and was chapelmaster of the Cádiz cathedral. In 1622 he became cantor at the cathedral of Puebla in present-day Mexico, one of the most prominent musical centers in Spanish America, and served there as chapelmaster from 1629 until his death. He composed masses, motets, hymns, and other service music in stile antico, often using double choirs and antiphonal effects. Many of his villancicos are also for double choir, including *Albricias pastores*, where the two choirs alternate passages, engage in dialogue, and join together at the ends of sections in the *estribillo*, then take turns singing the *coplas*. The text announces to the shepherds the good news of Jesus's birth, celebrates him as a child who brings love that is stronger than castles or weapons, and tells of the three kings who travel to give him their hearts and their treasures. The music blends rhythms of popular dances with the resources of church music, from divided choirs to imitative polyphony, and thus merges listeners' everyday experiences with a religious spirit and message.

INSTRUMENTAL MUSIC Few instrumental ensemble pieces survive from seventeenth-century Spain, but there were vibrant traditions of solo music for organ, harp, and guitar.

Organ music   Spanish organ music is characterized by strong contrasts of color and texture, particularly in the **tiento**, an improvisatory-style piece that often featured imitation, akin to the sixteenth-century fantasia. A striking example is the *Tiento de batalla* (Battle Tiento) of Juan Bautista José Cabanilles (1644–1712), which imitates trumpet calls resounding from opposite sides of a battlefield. Cabanilles was the leading Spanish composer for organ, and he left us over a thousand works, including tientos, hymn settings, and toccatas.

The main chamber instruments were harp and guitar, and their reper- *Harp and guitar music*
tory centered around dances and variations on familiar dance tunes, songs,
bass ostinatos, or harmonic patterns. Compositions included the sarabande,
chacona, passacalle, and other dance types that became the most widely disseminated contributions of Spain and its American colonies to European
music as a whole. But apart from these instrumental dances, Spanish music
remained relatively little known in the rest of Europe.

RUSSIA

Russia has not been part of our story so far, because since its founding in the
Middle Ages Russia was culturally isolated from western Europe, and musical life there followed its own traditions. That began to change in the second
half of the seventeenth century, inaugurating a process of absorbing influences from Italy, Germany, and France that lasted two centuries. This process
culminated in the nineteenth century in a vibrant new Russian tradition that
burst onto the international scene and became in turn an important influence
on music in western Europe and the Americas.

Through the seventeenth century, the dominant institution in Russia was *Russian Orthodox*
the Russian Orthodox Church, which derived from the Byzantine branch of *Church*
Christianity rather than the Catholic (see Chapter 2). The Church was conservative in doctrinal, liturgical, and musical matters, banning instruments
from church services, and the leaders of the Church in Moscow sought to suppress other forms of music-making, such as the wedding and funeral music
of traditional Russian minstrels known as the *skomorokhi*. Liturgical music
consisted of monophonic chant, known as *znamenny* chant after its notation. In the sixteenth century, simple three-voice polyphony came into use
alongside the chant, and by 1600 both the patriarch of Moscow (the head of
the Church) and the tsar (the ruler of the Russians) were supporting choirs,
initiating what would become a great Russian tradition of unaccompanied
choral singing. Musical innovations happening elsewhere on the Continent,
from imitative counterpoint to monody and concertato styles, did not find a
foothold in Moscow.

Significant change came in the 1650s with the introduction of musical *Western European*
notation, theory, styles, and genres from western Europe, brought by a grow- *influence*
ing influx of musicians from the western periphery of the Russian empire. The
new patriarch appointed in 1652, Nikon, had been the top church official in
Novgorod in western Russia, where he encountered western European styles,
and he opened the Russian Orthodox Church to greater musical influence
from western Europe. Musicians brought five-line staff notation and western
European practices of harmony and counterpoint. An important figure in this
process was Nikolay Diletsky (ca. 1630–after 1680), a composer and author of
a monumental treatise on music theory, *Idea grammatikii musikiyskoy* (An Idea
of Musical Grammar, 1679), which includes the earliest known description of
a complete circle of fifths.

The most prestigious genre in the new style inaugurated by Diletsky was *Kontserty*
the *kontsert* (plural *kontserty*), adapted from the sacred concerto but for voices
alone without instruments, since the Russian Orthodox Church did not use
instruments in services. Also known as *partesnoe penie* (partsong), such pieces

were typically composed for many parts, up to twelve or more, with textures alternating between soloists or small groups and the whole ensemble. Texts were drawn from the Bible, especially the Psalms, or less often from the liturgy. Kontserty were employed in religious services, in secular ceremonies, and as musical entertainments.

Following in Diletsky's footsteps, a new generation of composers in Moscow took up the kontsert. Chief among them was Vasiliy Titov (ca. 1650–ca. 1715), a singer with the tsar's choir, whose musical language is tonal with simple triadic harmonies often tinged by the relative minor. Example 16.6 shows the beginning of Titov's kontsert *Beznevestnaya Devo* (O Unbetrothed Virgin), where the tenors and bass 1 repeat the first two words of the text as a refrain, answered

EXAMPLE 16.6 *Vasiliy Titov,* Beznevestnaya Devo

O Unbetrothed Virgin, who indescribably conceived God in the flesh, O Unbetrothed Virgin, Mother of God in the highest,

by the entire choir or smaller subgroups. The setting is mostly homorhythmic, with some dialogue between groups, as at the end of the example.

A more popular genre was the *kant* (plural *kanty*), a three-voice song that was short, simple, and easy to sing. Texts could be sacred or secular but were never liturgical. The top two voices typically move in parallel thirds over an independent bass, resembling the texture in the first two measures of Example 16.6, and harmonies are diatonic. Titov was renowned for *Psaltir' rifmovannaya* (1686), his setting as kanty of all 150 psalms in the Russian translation by Simeon Polotsky. Kanty were enormously popular and widely distributed. Hundreds of kanty from the seventeenth and eighteenth centuries survive, and the genre retained its popularity into the nineteenth century.

Kanty

Near the end of the seventeenth century, tsar Peter the Great (r. 1682–1725) succeeded to the throne and pursued a dual agenda of westernizing Russian society and reducing the political power of the Church. In 1700, the patriarch died and Peter refused to appoint a successor; by the end of his reign he had replaced the office of the patriarch with a Holy Synod controlled by the tsar. Peter visited western Europe on diplomatic missions in 1697–98 and again in 1716–17, and he brought back to Russia western European ideas, technology, and customs, from shipbuilding to music and theater. He founded St. Petersburg in 1703, made it the capital of Russia in 1712, and forced the aristocracy to move there and participate in courtly life modeled on what he had seen in western European courts, notably concerts and theatrical entertainments that often included kanty and other music. Although not a fan of Italian opera, he enjoyed music as an accompaniment to state and military ceremonies and as part of religious services. During his reign, kanty and kontserty were frequently employed in celebrations of military victories and other notable occasions, and both genres became more musically sophisticated.

Peter the Great

NATIONAL STYLES AND TRADITIONS

Although France, England, Spain, and Russia were all monarchies, France and its king were the most powerful and influential. French music was imitated throughout Europe, and Lully's operas were performed for more than a century after his death, a remarkable legacy for the time. The elegant manner cultivated by French composers remained strong in the eighteenth century and contributed to the distinctive flavor of later French works. The suite remained an important genre for almost a century and was revived in the late nineteenth and twentieth centuries. Several of the dances, especially the minuet, had long careers in other instrumental music.

Purcell represented a high-water mark for English music, but in the century that followed, foreigners dominated English musical life. Because there are no modern institutions devoted to the performance of masques or semi-operas, English dramatic music of the seventeenth century has languished in obscurity. In part because historians have focused so intently on opera in telling the story of seventeenth-century music, *Dido and Aeneas* is renowned and widely performed, while other English music of the time is less well known. Meanwhile, the public concert, an English innovation, became one of the cornerstones of musical life.

In Spain and the New World, distinctive national traditions such as Spanish opera, zarzuela, dance-songs, and villancicos continued into the next century. But influences from Italy and France became increasingly important, and Spanish music came to reflect a blending of native, New World, and more broadly European trends. The mixture of European, native American, and African characteristics in Spanish colonial music presaged later developments in the nineteenth and twentieth centuries, culminating in the worldwide enjoyment of American, Cuban, and Brazilian popular music that blends elements from all four continents.

In Russia, the kontsert and the kant endured as significant genres into the nineteenth century, and the choral tradition has continued to thrive until today. The trickle of musicians and musical styles and genres from western Europe into Russia gradually increased to a broad current, and from the nineteenth century onward Russian composers have made major contributions to the repertoire of opera, ballet, and instrumental music.

In the late nineteenth and twentieth centuries, French, English, Spanish, and Russian musicians looked back at their respective Baroque traditions as native sources independent of the German tradition, which by then had become dominant. The works of Lully, Purcell, Hidalgo, Titov, and others were edited and published, valued for their intrinsic musical worth and as proof of a vibrant national musical heritage that predated Bach. Only recently have works from the New World been rediscovered, published, and appreciated for showing the early transplantation of European culture in the Americas. By the late twentieth century, Lully's operas were again being staged, and a widening range of French, English, Spanish, New World, and Russian music was performed and recorded. While politics played a role in the revival of this music, as in its creation, its ability to move and entertain us is what sustains its continuing presence.

With these revivals came new questions about how to perform this music. Should Baroque operas be staged with historically accurate scenery, stage machinery, costumes, gestures, and dancing, in order to represent the work as seventeenth-century audiences would have experienced it, as in a recent production of Lully's *Cadmus et Hermione* by Martin Fraudreau with Poème Harmonique, or should directors and designers be as creative with this repertory as with more recent operas, like the staging of *Armide* with Les Arts Florissants? Similar questions arise for Latin American music, now typically performed with percussion instruments that add exoticism and are familiar markers for modern Latin American popular music but would not have been used in the seventeenth century. As we have seen, such questions of how to perform music of the past arise for almost every repertory, but they become especially pressing for music that is less widely known or newly revived.

Further Reading is available at digital.wwnorton.com/hwm10

ITALY AND GERMANY IN THE LATE SEVENTEENTH CENTURY

❖

Unlike the centralized monarchies of France, England, Spain, and Russia, Italy and Germany were each divided into numerous sovereign states. Musical life was not concentrated in one royal court or capital city, as in Paris and London, but was supported by many rulers and cities, each competing for the best musicians. Like bees pursuing pollen, performers and composers often traveled from one center or patron to another seeking better employment, and both regions provided rich environments for exchanging ideas. In Italy, the influences were mostly native. Composers developed genres pioneered in the early seventeenth century, such as opera, cantata, and sonata, and devised the instrumental concerto. Here the story is one of stylistic evolution within an established tradition and of codifying new conventions, including the **da capo aria** and tonality. In German-speaking lands, by contrast, composers drew deeply on both French and Italian styles, blending elements from each with homegrown traditions. From this melting pot would come the great German and Austrian composers of the eighteenth century, from Bach and Handel to Haydn and Mozart.

ITALY

In Italy, opera continued to be the leading musical genre, and the cantata was the most prominent form of vocal chamber music. Yet the Italian musical works from this time that are most often performed today are instrumental, particularly the sonatas and concertos of Arcangelo Corelli and his contemporaries.

Figure 17.1 shows the main musical centers of Italy around 1650. Politically, the peninsula was divided among Spanish dominions in the south and in the region around Milan; territories governed by the pope, stretching from Rome up to Bologna and Ferrara; and numerous small states in the north. Paradoxically, the political splintering of northern Italy bred economic and musical strength. Outside of Rome, seat of the pope, and Naples, capital of the southern Spanish possessions, all the major developments in Italian music throughout the seventeenth and eighteenth centuries took place in the north.

OPERA As opera spread across Italy and outward to other countries, the principal Italian center remained Venice, whose public opera houses were famous all over Europe. By the late 1600s, opera was also well established in Naples and Florence, and its importance was growing in Milan and other major cities.

New view of the affections

In early and midcentury operas, composers such as Monteverdi and Cavalli portrayed the dramatic action through a flexible alternation of recitative, arioso, and aria styles, in accord with the Aristotelian concept of the affections as states of the soul caused by specific events (see Chapters 13 and 14). But by the late 1660s, librettists and composers began to adopt the view of René Descartes that the passions were relatively stable and objective emotional states that were widely shared and recognized, not specific to an individual person or situation. What mattered was not how a character came to be in a particular emotional state but how that state could be captured in music that stimulated a specific emotional response in the listener. This new view of the affections is associated with a greater separation between recitatives, where the action of the drama took place, and the arias, where characters reflected on their feelings.

FIGURE 17.1 *Italy around 1650, showing the cities that were the main centers for music.*

In this process, the arias became the most vital part of any opera. It was in the arias that the depths of human emotions could be expressed. Often the meaning of the text was conveyed through musical motives in the melody or accompaniment that matched the affection being represented. For example, a composer might imitate trumpet figures or a march to portray a martial or vehement mood, or use a dance rhythm to suggest feelings traditionally associated with that dance. The associations these figures acquired through their use in opera could then be used in turn to suggest moods in instrumental music, leading to a language for conveying the affections through musical conventions.

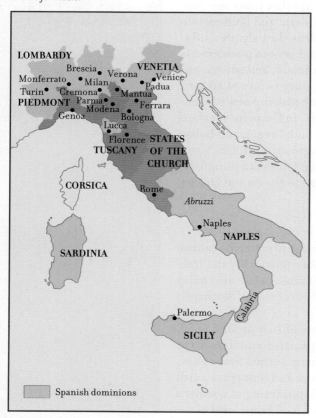

As the emotional content of opera moved into the arias, it was increasingly the arias and the star singers who performed them, rather than the drama itself, that attracted the public and assured the success of an opera production. Audiences loved the beauty of a solo voice singing an elegant melody, supported by ingratiating harmonies, and conveying a familiar emotion with an intensity that could elicit their empathy.

Librettists responded to the demand for

arias by writing more verse in poetic meters and forms suitable for arias. Composers outdid them by indulging in aria-like lyrical expansions whenever a few lines of dialogue or a situation provided an opportunity. The typical number of arias in an opera increased from two dozen around 1640 to sixty by the 1670s. Common forms included the strophic song, in which two or three stanzas were sung to the same music, as well as ground-bass arias, three-part ABB' and ABA or ABA' forms, and rondo arias in ABACA or ABAB'A forms. Many arias had a refrain, one or more lines of text that recurred with the same music. By the end of the century, the dominant form was the **da capo aria**, which takes its name from the words "Da capo" (from the head) placed at the close of the second section, instructing the performers to return to the beginning and repeat the first section to produce an ABA form. In all of these forms, any repetition gave the singer a chance to ornament the melody with new embellishments and impressive vocal display.

A characteristic Italian opera of the 1670s is *Giulio Cesare in Egitto* (Julius Caesar in Egypt), composed in 1676 by Antonio Sartorio (1630–1680) for Teatro San Salvatore in Venice. Like most of his contemporaries, Sartorio conceived of opera as a theatrical spectacle and of arias as the primary vehicles for achieving an emotional impact on the audience. Known for the variety of his arias and for introducing new effects, he was the first to use a trumpet in arias, establishing a type in which the trumpet signifies the heroic. Among its sixty-five arias and duets, *Giulio Cesare in Egitto* includes four trumpet arias, three drawing on the military associations of the instrument and the last a virtuosic competition between soprano and trumpet of high notes and sustained tones.

Antonio Sartorio

Scenes 3–4 in Act II (NAWM 93), in which Cleopatra woos Cesare while disguised as her handmaiden Lidia, illustrate Sartorio's approach, alternating recitative with a variety of aria forms. The recitatives, where almost all the dramatic action takes place, are more functional than expressive (NAWM 93a). This sort of recitative, with many repeated notes, mostly chord tones, and modulating harmonies with frequent secondary dominants, became standard for over a century. Then the action stops for an aria, each one a lyrical statement projecting a character's emotion.

Many arias in the opera follow da capo form, as does Nireno's *Se qualcuna mi bramasse* (NAWM 93b). But in others Sartorio writes out the repetition of the A section to add phrases or variants, as in Cesare's *Son prigioniero* (NAWM 93c), and more than twenty arias combine strophic form with an ABA form within each stanza, as does Cesare's *Alla carcere d'un crine* (NAWM 93e). At times Sartorio and his librettist play with the expectations of the audience, such as when Cleopatra, offstage, sings what is essentially a da capo aria, but each of the three sections is preceded and followed by recitative dialogue between Nireno and Cesare (NAWM 93d); the effect wonderfully conveys the impression of overhearing music nearby, music Cesare finds so enchanting that he cannot help but respond.

VOCAL CHAMBER MUSIC The cantata had become the leading form of vocal chamber music in Italy, and the center of cantata composition was Rome. There, wealthy aristocrats and diplomats sponsored gatherings and academies for the elite, where the entertainment often included a cantata written

FIGURE 17.2 *Alessandro Scarlatti, in an oil painting by an unknown artist.*

SCALA/ART RESOURCE, NY

expressly for the occasion. Because cantatas were meant for performance before a small audience of musically knowledgeable amateurs in a room without a stage, scenery, or costumes, they invited elegance, refinement, and playful wit that would be lost in a performance for a broader public audience in a spacious opera house. The demand for a new cantata at frequent intervals offered poets and composers regular work and chances to experiment.

Cantatas around 1650 featured many short, contrasting sections, as we found in Barbara Strozzi's *Lagrime mie* (NAWM 77). By the 1690s, poets and composers settled on a pattern of alternating recitatives and arias, normally two or three of each, totaling eight to fifteen minutes. Most cantatas were written for solo voice, usually a soprano or castrato, with continuo, though some featured two or more voices. The text, usually pastoral love poetry, took the form of a dramatic narrative or soliloquy. Such musical settings of Italian pastoral poetry had a long tradition, going back to madrigals in the sixteenth century and operas in the early seventeenth. Like these predecessors, cantata texts idealize nature and the simple life, a world where shepherds customarily sing and are at once rustic and innately noble, and where a lover's complaints often have a kind of bittersweet, tongue-in-cheek quality.

Scarlatti cantatas   The more than six hundred cantatas of Alessandro Scarlatti (1660–1725), shown in Figure 17.2, mark a high point in this repertory. His *Clori vezzosa, e bella* is typical of the solo cantata around 1690–1710, with two recitative-aria pairs in which a shepherd expresses his passionate love for a nymph. He vows that he loves only her, with a burning passion, and then—a bit overeager—says he suffers for her sake yet welcomes the torment as a way to prove his devotion. Italian cantata audiences relished such a witty and ironic antithesis of joy and pain. Depicting these pangs of love, the second recitative (NAWM 94a) exemplifies Scarlatti's mature style in using a wide harmonic range, chromaticism, and diminished chords. The passage in Example 17.1 moves first to the flat side, reaching an F-minor triad at "affanni miei" (my troubles), then to the sharp side, passing through A-major and E-major triads over a chromatic ascent in the bass, before cadencing on A minor. Scarlatti often used diminished seventh chords, rare for the time, to convey strong emotions or add bite to a cadence. Here a diminished seventh chord at the cadence on "il martire" (that torture) serves both purposes.

Da capo arias   The most common form of aria in Scarlatti's operas and cantatas is the da capo aria. Although his earlier cantatas and operas feature da capo arias like those of Sartorio, in which both the A and the B sections tend to present their texts once (with some repetition of words or of the last line) and each normally stays in a single key, those Scarlatti composed after about 1690 are more elaborate. Typically the A section includes two different settings of the same text, framed by instrumental ritornellos, the first vocal statement modulating to a new key and the second leading back to the tonic (see Forms at a Glance, p. 376). The B section also now usually features more text repetition and more than one key, and the whole form is more expansive.

EXAMPLE 17.1 *Alessandro Scarlatti,* Clori vezzosa, e bella, *recitative*

Because if I think that you alone are the cause of so many of my troubles, it becomes my joy, that suffering and that torture,

In Scarlatti's hands, the da capo aria was the perfect vehicle for sustaining a lyrical moment through a musical design that expressed a single sentiment, often joined with an opposing or related one in the contrasting middle section. In *Sì, sì ben mio* (NAWM 94b), the second aria from *Clori vezzosa, e bella*, the sprightly gigue rhythm of the ritornello and vocal line in the A section contrasts ironically with the lover's request for "more torments for my heart." The B section offers contrast in turning to a major key and more hopeful sentiments sung to a new but related melody.

The da capo aria in this expanded format, with two vocal statements in the A section, became the standard aria form in the eighteenth century for opera and cantata alike because it offered great flexibility in expression. *In voler ciò che tu brami,* from Scarlatti's last opera, *La Griselda* (1720–21; NAWM 95), exemplifies the rich contrasts the composer achieved in his later arias both between and within sections. The A section shows two sides of Griselda's character as an obedient wife, combining dignity and strength with tenderness and love for her husband despite his public rejection of her, while in the B section, she adamantly insists that she will never stop loving him. Part of the appeal of the da capo form for composers, singers, and audiences alike was its combination of contrast with coherence: the music of the B section could be as similar or different as the poetry required, while the form guaranteed contrasts of key, a sense of departure and return, and harmonic and thematic closure. Singers typically introduced new embellishments on the repetition of the A section, providing the perfect opportunity to display their artistry.

Midway between cantata and opera stood the ***serenata***, a semidramatic piece for several singers and a small orchestra, usually written for a special

Serenata

FORMS AT A GLANCE

Da Capo Aria

The text for a da capo aria is in two brief poetic stanzas that express complementary or conflicting thoughts. The overall form is ABA, setting the first stanza in the A section and the second in the B section in a contrasting key, but this is only part of the story.

In early examples, such as *Se qualcuna mi bramasse* (NAWM 93b) from Sartorio's opera *Giulio Cesare in Egitto*, each section typically states its text once, sometimes with repetition of the last line, and stays in a single key. A ritornello may introduce the aria.

In arias from the late seventeenth and eighteenth centuries, the form is longer and more complex.

The A section features two vocal statements, each a setting of the first stanza of poetry, and each is typically preceded and followed by an instrumental ritornello. The first vocal statement (A1) modulates from the tonic to another key, and the second vocal statement (A2) modulates back to the tonic. In each case, the following ritornello confirms the new key.

The B section sets the second stanza once or twice but typically lacks the orchestral ritornellos that punctuate the A section. To emphasize the contrasting ideas between the two stanzas, the B section is in one or more contrasting keys and introduces new or varied musical material. Then the A section is repeated.

The precise structure can vary, as illustrated by two Scarlatti arias, diagrammed in Figure 17.3. *Sì, sì ben mio* (NAWM 94b), from his cantata *Clori vezzosa, e bella*, lacks the ritornello at the end of the A section, while all three ritornellos are present in *In voler ciò che tu brami* (NAWM 95), from his opera *La Griselda*. Other da capo arias may lack the ritornello between the two vocal statements, or omit the opening ritornello when the first section repeats.

These two arias differ in other ways as well. In *Sì, sì ben mio*, the voice takes up the musical ideas introduced by the ritornello, which are varied throughout both parts of the aria. *In voler* features different material in the A and B sections, and the vocal melody is entirely distinct from the ritornello. The choice of contrasting keys for the A and B sections is also different, as shown in Figure 17.3. The da capo form was conventional, but it would not have been used so widely and for so many decades if it were not flexible and variable.

SECTION	A						B	A REPEATS
Sì, sì ben mio	Ritornello	A1		Ritornello	A2		B	
KEY:	Dm	Dm→Gm		Gm	Gm→Dm		FM→Am	Dm
	i	i→iv		iv	iv→i		III→v	i
In voler	Ritornello	A1		Ritornello	A2	Ritornello	B	
KEY:	B♭	B♭→Cm		Cm	Cm→B♭	B♭	Gm→Dm	B♭
	I	I→ii		ii	ii→I	I	vi→iii	I

FIGURE 17.3 *Da Capo aria form.*

occasion. Except for their secular subject matter, serenatas resembled Italian oratorios and were cultivated by the same patrons, high-level clergy and nobility in Rome and other cities. Alessandro Stradella (1639–1682), an innovative composer of operas and cantatas, was one of the first to write serenatas.

CHURCH MUSIC AND ORATORIO Italian church composers in the second half of the seventeenth century continued to cultivate the old contrapuntal style modeled on Palestrina alongside the newer concerted styles featuring basso continuo and solo singers, sometimes juxtaposing the two in the same work. We can see this stylistic diversity in the nearly fifty collections of sacred vocal music published by Maurizio Cazzati (1616–1678), music director at Bologna's Church of San Petronio from 1657 to 1671. At one end of the spectrum, his *Messa a cappella* (Unaccompanied Mass) of 1670 is in stile antico. His *Magnificat a 4* of the same year, however, alternates florid duets in the modern style with choruses in the older style. In other works he plays soloists against a full choir, as in the later instrumental concerto (see pp. 383–86).

San Petronio was also an important center for instrumental ensemble music, which was often played during church services. Cazzati published numerous collections of sonatas suited for use in church, including the first sonatas to include trumpet. His early sonatas are imitative and in brief contrasting sections, like those of Gabrieli; later ones feature separate movements, with longer themes, more homophonic passages, and greater use of dance rhythms and fanfare-like motives. Italian organists, like their colleagues in Spain and in Catholic regions of Germany, continued to compose in existing genres, such as ricercares, toccatas, variation canzonas, and chant settings.

Although oratorios were still performed in oratories, they were also presented in the palaces of princes and cardinals, in academies, and in other institutions. They were a ready substitute for opera during Lent or at other times when the theaters were closed. Most oratorios were now in Italian rather than Latin, had librettos in verse, and had two sections, leaving room for a sermon or, in private entertainments, an intermission with refreshments.

INSTRUMENTAL CHAMBER MUSIC In instrumental chamber music, as in opera and cantata, Italians remained the undisputed masters and models. The late seventeenth and early eighteenth centuries were the age of the great violin makers of Cremona in northern Italy: Nicolò Amati (1596–1684), Antonio Stradivari (Stradivarius, 1644–1737), and Giuseppe Bartolomeo Guarneri (1698–1744), all famed for instruments of unrivaled excellence, such as the Stradivarius shown in Figure 17.4 (see Music in Context, p. 378). It was also the age of great string music in Italy, of which the two leading genres were the sonata and the instrumental concerto.

Sonatas in the first half of the seventeenth century consisted of several sections differentiated by musical material, texture, mood, character, and sometimes meter or tempo, as in the Biagio Marini sonata examined in Chapter 15 (NAWM 84). In the second half of the century, composers made these sections longer and more self-contained, and finally separated them into distinct movements with pauses between them. Thus the sonata became

TIMELINE

1647 Johann Crüger, *Praxis pietatis melica*

1648 Thirty Years' War ends

1655 First regular newspaper in Berlin

1657 Francesco Cavalli, *Artemisia*

1657–71 Maurizio Cazzati at San Petronio in Bologna

1658–1705 Leopold I reigns as Holy Roman emperor

1668 Dieterich Buxtehude appointed organist at Lübeck

1673 Buxtehude begins *Abendmusiken*

ca. 1675 Heinrich Biber, *Mystery Sonatas*

1676 Antonio Sartorio, *Giulio Cesare in Egitto*

1678 Hamburg opera house opens

1679 Alessandro Scarlatti's first opera in Rome

1681 Arcangelo Corelli, Op. 1 Trio Sonatas

1682 Biber, *Missa salisburgensis*

1688 Louis XIV invades Holy Roman Empire

1692 Giuseppe Torelli publishes first concertos

1695 Georg Muffat, *Florilegium*, vol. 1

1696 Johann Kuhnau, *Frische Clavier Früchte*

1700 Corelli, 12 Violin Sonatas, Op. 5

1705 Johann Sebastian Bach hears Buxtehude's *Abendmusiken*

1720–21 Alessandro Scarlatti, *La Griselda*

MUSIC IN CONTEXT

The Stradivarius Violin Workshop

During the seventeenth century, Italian composers created new instrumental genres—solo sonata, trio sonata, and concerto—which called on the violin to imitate the expressivity and virtuosity of the singing voice. Not surprisingly, it was also the Italians—specifically, a few families of instrument builders in the northern Italian town of Cremona—who developed the art of violin making to a peak that has never been surpassed. During their heyday, the violin became the new agent of that artistic power which had previously resided only in the voice.

Antonio Stradivari (ca. 1644–1737) was the most prominent member of his universally renowned family of instrument makers. He was possibly a pupil of Nicolò Amati, founder of another dynasty of violin makers. During his long life, Stradivari made or supervised the production of more than 1,100 instruments—including harps, guitars, violas, and cellos—about half of which survive and are still being used today by some of the world's leading string players.

Most of his violins have been rebuilt into modern violins, with a longer fingerboard, higher bridge, and neck angling further from the body. Figure 17.4 shows one of the few Stradivari violins that has been restored to its original seventeenth-century form. Thousands of violins were made in tribute to Stradivari and modeled on his superior construction design; with no intention to deceive, these instruments bear the label "Stradivarius," although they were produced neither by the master nor his workshop.

What was involved in making a "Strad" and why are these instruments so highly prized? To

begin with, Stradivari selected woods of the highest possible quality, using pine for the front and sides, and maple for the back of the instrument. Then he proceeded to carve the pieces, taking care to get just the right degree of arching because the body of the instrument is not flat but slightly rounded, and arrive at just the right amount of thickness because even the tiniest variation in the thickness of the wood will affect the instrument's resonance. Next he cut the elegantly shaped f-holes into the front piece to optimize the vibrations and maximize the sound. Finally, he applied the varnish to protect the instrument from dirt and moisture. In addition to its practical function, the varnish added to the beauty of the instrument by giving it a radiant, orange-brown sheen and highlighting the grain patterns on the wood's surface.

In an effort to explain the extraordinarily rich and powerful tone of a Stradivarius violin, a popular theory held that its varnish had some sort of "magic" ingredient. However, historical research has shown that the varnish is no different from that used by furniture makers when Stradivari was alive. Other theories suggest that the wood was first soaked in water and then specially seasoned before being carved, or that the grain of the wood used is tighter than modern woods. But so far, scientists have been unable to ascertain any measurable qualities that set these instruments apart. Even if such properties are discovered, the intrinsic superiority of a Stradivarius remains a matter not only of science but also of a long-lost art.

FIGURE 17.4 *Violin, 1693, by Antonio Stradivari, restored to its original form.*
IMAGE COPYRIGHT © THE METROPOLITAN MUSEUM OF ART. IMAGE SOURCE: ART RESOURCE, NY

a work with several movements that contrasted in tempo, meter, and affect. These contrasts were in sympathy with the theory of the affections, which held that music stimulated the bodily humors and could keep them in balance by offering a diversity of moods. Some composers maintained thematic similarities between movements, as in the older variation canzona (see Chapter 15), but thematic independence of movements became more common.

By about 1660, two main types of sonata had emerged. The **sonata da camera**, or **chamber sonata**, had a series of stylized dance movements, often beginning with a prelude. The **sonata da chiesa**, or **church sonata**, had mostly abstract movements, often including one or more that used dance rhythms or binary form but were not usually titled as dances. Church sonatas could be used in church services, substituting for certain items of the Mass Proper or for antiphons for the Magnificat at Vespers, and both types were played for entertainment in private concerts.

Chamber sonatas and church sonatas

The most common instrumentation after 1670 for both church and chamber sonatas was two treble instruments, usually violins, with basso continuo. Such a work is now called a **trio sonata** because of its three-part texture, but a performance can feature four or more players if more than one is used for the basso continuo, such as a cello performing the bass line and a harpsichord, organ, or lute doubling the bass and improvising a harmonic accompaniment. Indeed, Arcangelo Corelli's church sonatas were published with two bass parts, one for organ and a second for cello or archlute; the latter, although mostly identical to the organ part, occasionally has more rapid figuration. The texture of the trio sonata, with two high melody lines over basso continuo, served many other types of solo music, both vocal and instrumental.

Trio sonatas

Solo sonatas, for violin or another instrument with continuo, were less numerous than trio sonatas in the late seventeenth century but gained in popularity after 1700. Composers also wrote sonatas for larger groups, up to eight instrumental parts with continuo, as well as a few for unaccompanied string or wind instruments.

Solo and ensemble sonatas

ARCANGELO CORELLI'S SONATAS The trio and solo sonatas of Arcangelo Corelli (1653–1713) were the most famous and widely played chamber works of the seventeenth century. Trained in Bologna, active in Rome, and renowned as violinist, teacher, and composer (see biography and Figure 17.5, p. 380), Corelli had an unparalleled influence on performers and composers alike. Most composers of instrumental music in the early eighteenth century learned from his music, including Handel, Bach, Telemann, and Couperin. The latter two paid homage to him, Telemann in his *Sonates Corellisantes* (Corellian Sonatas) and Couperin in *Le Parnasse, ou L'apothéose de Corelli* (Parnassus, or The Apotheosis of Corelli). Corelli's pervasive influence brought about a standardization of form, style, and harmonic practice that became the international language of eighteenth-century instrumental music.

In his trio sonatas, published in four sets of twelve (church sonatas in Opp. 1 and 3 and chamber sonatas in Opp. 2 and 4), Corelli emphasized lyrical conversation over virtuosity. He rarely used extremely high or low notes, fast runs, or difficult double stops. The two violins frequently cross and exchange music, interlocking in suspensions that give his works a decisive forward

Corelli's trio sonatas

ARCANGELO CORELLI
(1653–1713)

Corelli left no vocal music, and fewer than ninety piec-es of his survive, almost all in three genres: trio sonata, solo violin sonata, and concerto grosso. Yet he helped to establish standards of form, style, harmony, and playing technique that influenced several generations.

Born into a well-to-do family in Fusignano, a small town in northern Italy, he studied violin and composition in Bologna beginning in 1666, com-pletely assimilating the craft of the Bolognese mas-ters. By 1675, Corelli was living in Rome, where he quickly became a leading violinist and composer, enjoying the support of Queen Christina of Sweden and other rich patrons. As a violinist, teacher, and en-semble director, he helped to raise performance stan-dards to a new level. He organized and led some of the first orchestras in Italy, which became a model for oth-ers. Like Lully, he required string players in each section to use the same bowing, creating a unity of sound that became standard. His teaching was the foundation of most eighteenth-century schools of violin playing; his impact is evident in the many prominent violinists who were his students, including Francesco Geminiani (1687–1762), who wrote the first major treatise on violin performance, *The Art of Playing on the Violin* (1751). The technique required by Corelli's multiple stops and

FIGURE 17.5

A portrait of Arcangelo Corelli (ca. 1700) by Hugh Howard.

FACULTY OF MUSIC COLLECTION, OXFORD UNIVERSITY/BRIDGEMAN IMAGES

polyphonic writing for the violin made his solo sonatas standard pieces for study.

Beginning in 1681, Corelli published a series of collections of trio sonatas, violin sonatas, and concerti grossi that were disseminated across Europe, bringing him international fame. His renown was as lasting as it was widespread; his collections were reprinted dozens of times over more than a century.

MAJOR WORKS 6 published collections known by opus (work) number: Op. 1 (1681), 12 trio sonatas (sonate da chiesa); Op. 2 (1685), 12 trio sonate da camera (one is a chaconne); Op. 3 (1689), 12 trio sonate da chiesa; Op. 4 (1695), 12 trio sonate da camera; Op. 5 (1700), 12 solo violin sonatas; Op. 6 (1714), 12 concerti grossi; 6 other trio sonatas and 3 quartets for three instruments and basso continuo

momentum. In the church sonatas, the two soloists tend to be treated alike, engaging in a dialogue between equals, while in the chamber sonatas they often play similar rhythms in parallel thirds or sixths or the first violin part is more active than the second. Example 17.2 shows a passage from the first movement of his Trio Sonata in D Major, Op. 3, No. 2 (NAWM 96a), that fea-tures several typical traits of Corelli's style: a ***walking bass***, with a steadily moving pattern of eighth notes, under free imitation between the violins; a chain of suspensions in the violins above a descending sequence in the bass; and a dialogue between the violins as they leapfrog over each other to progres-sively higher peaks.

The church sonatas   Most of Corelli's church trio sonatas consist of four movements, often in two pairs, in the order slow–fast–slow–fast. Although there are many exceptions to this pattern, it gradually became a norm for Corelli and later composers, and the sequence of movements and their typical characteristics became conventions of the sonata in the early eighteenth century. The first

EXAMPLE 17.2 *Arcangelo Corelli, Trio Sonata in D Major, Op. 3, No. 2, first movement*

slow movement usually has a contrapuntal texture and a majestic, solemn character. The Allegro that follows normally features imitation, with the bass line a full participant. This movement is the musical center of gravity for the church sonata, and it retains elements of the canzona in its use of imitation, of a subject with a marked rhythmic character, and of variation at later entrances of the subject. The subsequent slow movement most often resembles a lyrical operatic duet in triple meter. The fast final movement usually features dancelike rhythms and often is in binary form. All of these traits are true of Op. 3, No. 2 (NAWM 96). We have seen in Example 17.2 the contrapuntal web of suspensions and imitations in the first movement. The opening of the second movement (NAWM 96b) features exact imitation between first violin and bass, while the second violin inverts and truncates the subject. Such variation is typical of chamber music in this period, which is more about witty play with expectations and possibilities than about presenting a strict learned composition. The next movement (NAWM 96c) is songlike with some imitation. As became conventional for slow third movements of sonatas in major keys, it is in the relative minor and closes with a Phrygian cadence on the dominant, leaving it harmonically open and presenting an opportunity for ornamentation. The finale (NAWM 96d) is an imitative gigue in binary form whose subject often appears in inversion, offering the same playful approach to counterpoint as in the second movement.

Corelli's chamber sonatas usually begin with a prelude, after which two or three dances may follow as in the French suite. Often the first two movements resemble those of a church sonata, a slow movement and an imitative Allegro. Some of the first movements feature dotted rhythms, recalling the French overture. The dance movements are almost always in binary form, with each section repeated, the first section closing on the dominant or relative major

The chamber sonatas

FIGURE 17.6 *The opening of the first movement of Corelli's Sonata in C Major, Op. 5, No. 3, in an edition printed by Estienne Roger in Amsterdam. In the slow movements, the violin part is given both as originally published and in an embellished version claimed to represent the way Corelli himself performed it.*

SONATE A VIOLINO E VIOLONE O CIMBALO DI ARCANGELO CORELLI DA FUSIGNANO, OPERA QUINTA, PARTE PRIMA (AMSTERDAM: ESTIENNE ROGER, 1710), 22; REPRINTED IN ARCANGELO CORELLI, SONATE A VIOLINO E VIOLONE O CIMBALO, ARCHIVUM MUSICUM 21 (FLORENCE: STUDIO PER EDIZIONI SCELTE, 1979)

and the second making its way back to the tonic. Rather than sharing an almost equal role as in the church sonatas, the bass line in the chamber sonatas is almost pure accompaniment.

Corelli's solo sonatas   Corelli's solo violin sonatas are also divided between church and chamber sonatas, following similar patterns of movements but allowing considerably more virtuosity. In the Allegro movements, the solo violin sometimes employs double and triple stops to simulate the rich three-part sonority of the trio sonata and the interplay of voices in a fugue. There are fast runs, arpeggios, extended perpetual-motion passages, and cadenzas—elaborate solo embellishments at a cadence, both notated and improvised. The slow movements were notated simply but were meant to be ornamented freely and profusely with musical passagework between the main notes of the original melody. This Italian style of decoration, quite different from French agréments, has roots in the performing traditions of the sixteenth century (see Chapter 12). In 1710, the Amsterdam publisher Estienne Roger reissued Corelli's solo sonatas, showing for the slow movements both the original solo parts and embellished versions that, Roger claimed, represented the way the composer played the sonatas, as in Figure 17.6. The embellishments surely reflect the practice of Corelli's time, and probably of the composer himself.

Thematic   In Corelli's sonatas, each movement tends to be based on a single subject
organization   stated at the outset. The music unfolds in a continuous expansion of the opening subject, with variations, sequences, brief modulations to nearby keys, and fascinating subtleties of phrasing. This steady spinning out of a single theme, in which the original idea seems to generate a spontaneous flow of musical thoughts, is highly characteristic of the later Baroque era from about

the 1680s on. Often there are subtle connections between movements; for instance, in Op. 3, No. 2 (NAWM 96), each movement begins with a variant of the same opening motive.

Tonal organization

Corelli's music is tonal, marked with the sense of direction or progression that, more than any other quality, distinguishes tonal music from modal music. Indeed, Jean-Philippe Rameau, the first theorist to describe the tonal system (see Chapter 18), used Corelli's musical language as the basis for his rules of functional tonality. Example 17.2, for instance, features several series of chords whose roots move down the circle of fifths, falling by a fifth or rising by a fourth (see measures 8–10 and 10–14). This is the normal direction for chord progressions in tonal music, whereas modal music may move up the circle of fifths as easily as down. In tonal progressions, the chord root also may rise by step or fall by a third before again rising by a fourth (see measures 14–15). Chord series whose roots primarily move down by a fourth or second and up by a fifth or third suggest modal thinking, as in Example 14.3 from Monteverdi's *Orfeo*. The increasing use, over the course of the seventeenth century, of directed progressions like Corelli's led gradually from modal practice to the new functional harmony we call tonality.

Corelli often relied on chains of suspensions and on sequences to achieve the sense of forward harmonic motion on which tonality depends. Measures 10–12 in Example 17.2 display both suspensions in the violins and a sequence in the bass, resulting in a progression down the circle of fifths. Corelli's music is almost completely diatonic; beyond secondary dominants (as in measures 8 and 12 in Example 17.2), we find only a rare diminished seventh chord or Neapolitan sixth at a cadence. His modulations within a movement—most often to the dominant and the relative minor or major—are logical and straightforward and are frequently propelled by sequences. He either kept all movements of a sonata in the same key or, in major-key sonatas, cast the second slow movement in the relative minor.

Influence and reputation

Corelli's sonatas served as models that composers followed for the next half century. The motivic techniques and principles of tonal architecture he helped to develop were extended by Vivaldi, Handel, Bach, and other composers of the next generation. He has been called the first major composer whose reputation rests exclusively on instrumental music, and along with Frescobaldi he was one of the first to create instrumental works that became classics, continuing to be played and reprinted long after his death.

Music for orchestra

THE CONCERTO Toward the end of the seventeenth century, musicians began to distinguish between music for chamber ensemble, with only one instrument for each melodic line, and music for orchestra, in which each string part was performed by two or more players. We have seen that Louis XIII of France (r. 1610–43) established a string ensemble, essentially the first orchestra, with four to six players per part. Louis XIV had two such ensembles, and as their leader Lully instituted what is now standard orchestral discipline, enforcing uniform bowing and forbidding improvised ornamentation. By the 1670s, similar ensembles were formed in Rome and Bologna, followed by others in Venice, Milan, and elsewhere. For special occasions in Rome, Corelli often led a "pickup" orchestra of forty or more, gathered from players employed by patrons throughout the city. While some pieces, like the overtures, dances, and interludes of Lully's operas, were clearly intended for orchestra, and others, like Corelli's solo violin sonatas, could be played only as chamber music, a good deal of seventeenth- and early-eighteenth-century music could be performed either way. For instance, on a festive occasion or in a large hall, each line of a trio sonata might be played by several performers.

Instrumental concertos

In the 1680s and 1690s, Italian composers created a new kind of orchestral work that became the most prestigious type of Baroque instrumental music and helped to establish the orchestra as the leading instrumental ensemble. In the long tradition of adapting old terms to new uses, the new genre was called **concerto**. Like the vocal concerto, it united contrasting forces into a harmonious whole, in an instrumental version of the concertato medium. It combined this texture with other traits favored at the time: florid melody over a steadily moving bass; musical organization based on tonality; and multiple movements with contrasting tempos, moods, and figuration. Concertos were closely related to sonatas and served many of the same roles: they were played at public ceremonies, entertainments, and private musical gatherings, and they could substitute for portions of the Mass.

Types of concerto

By 1700, composers were writing three kinds of concertos. The **orchestral concerto** was a work in several movements that emphasized the first violin part and the bass, distinguishing the concerto from the more contrapuntal texture characteristic of the sonata. The other two types systematically played on the contrast in sonority between many instruments and one or only a few. The **concerto grosso** set a small ensemble (*concertino*) of solo instruments against a large ensemble (*concerto grosso*). The concertino normally comprised two violins accompanied by cello and continuo, the same forces needed to play a trio sonata, although it could consist of other groupings of solo string or wind instruments. In essence, a concerto grosso resembles an ensemble sonata in which some passages are reinforced with multiple players on each part. The third and most common type, simply called **concerto**, contrasts one or more solo instruments with the large ensemble. The large group was almost always a string orchestra, usually divided into first and second violins, violas, and cellos, with basso continuo and double bass either doubling the cellos or playing their own part. In both the concerto grosso and the concerto for one or more soloists, the full orchestra was designated **tutti** (all) or **ripieno** (full).

Predecessors of concerto style

The practice of contrasting solo instruments with a full orchestra goes back to Lully's operas, where some of the dances included episodes for solo wind trio; to oratorio and opera arias by Stradella; and to sonatas for solo trumpets with string orchestra, popular in Bologna and Venice. The melodic style idiomatic to the natural trumpet, marked by triads, scales, and repeated notes, was imitated by the strings and became characteristic of concertos.

Corelli's concertos

Since orchestras in Rome were typically divided between concertino and ripieno, Roman composers favored the concerto grosso. Corelli's *Concerti grossi,* Op. 6, written in the 1680s and published in revised form in 1714, are essentially trio sonatas, divided between soli and tutti. The larger group echoes the smaller, fortifies cadential passages, or otherwise punctuates the structure through doublings. Corelli's approach was widely imitated by later composers in Italy, England, and Germany. Indeed, one of the best descriptions of the Corellian concerto grosso is by a German, the composer Georg Muffat (1653–1704), introducing a collection of his own pieces that can be played either as trio sonatas or as concerti grossi (see Source Reading).

Georg Muffat on Converting Sonatas into Concertos

Georg Muffat played a major role in introducing both Italian and French styles and genres into Germany. In the early 1680s he visited Rome, where he heard Corelli's concertos. On his return to Salzburg in 1682, he published a set of five pieces playable as sonatas but intended for full realization as concerti grossi. When he republished them in 1701 in a set of twelve concerti grossi, his foreword explained his method, making clear the roots of the concerto in the sonata.

❧

Friendly reader:

It is very true that the beautiful concertos of a new kind that I enjoyed in Rome gave me great courage and reawakened in me some ideas that perhaps will not displease you. If nothing else, at least I tried to serve your convenience, since you may concert these sonatas in various manners with the following conditions:

1. They may be played with only three instruments, namely two violins and a cello or bass viol as a foundation. . . .

2. They may be played by four or five instruments. . . .

3. If, further, you wish to hear them as full concertos with some novelty or variety of sonority, you may form two choirs in this way. Make a small ensemble [*concertino*] of three or two violins and a cello or viola da gamba, which three solo parts, not doubled, will play throughout. From these parts you will draw the two [solo] violins as well as the violins to be doubled for the large ensemble [*concerto grosso*] when you find the letter *T*, which signifies "tutti." You will have these rest at the letter *S* [soli], when the small ensemble will play solo. The middle violas will be doubled in proportion to the other parts of the large ensemble with which they will play, except when you find the letter *S*, when it will be enough that this part be played solo and not doubled. I went to all this trouble to achieve this opportune variety.

From the Italian in *Ausserlesene Instrumental-Music* (Passau, 1701), *Denkmäler der Tonkunst in Österreich* XI/2, vol. 23 (Vienna, 1904), 118.

Giuseppe Torelli

While Roman practice treated the orchestra as an expansion of the concertino, in northern Italy the soloists were adjuncts to the orchestra. Composers there focused first on the orchestral concerto, then on the concerto for one or more soloists and the concerto grosso. Giuseppe Torelli (1658–1709), a leading figure in the Bologna school, composed all three types, including the first concertos ever published (his Op. 5, 1692). In his concertos we can see a new notion of the concerto develop. He wrote trumpet concertos for services in San Petronio, and his Op. 6 (1698) includes two solo violin concertos, perhaps the first by any composer. Six more violin concertos and six concerti grossi appeared as his Op. 8 (1709). Most of these works follow a three-movement plan in the order fast–slow–fast, taken over from the Italian opera overture. This scheme, introduced to the concerto by Venetian composer Tomaso Albinoni (1671–1750) in his Op. 2 (1700), became the standard pattern for concertos.

Framing ritornellos

In the fast movements of his violin concertos, Torelli often used a form that resembles and may have been modeled on the structure of the A section of a da capo aria (see pp. 374–76). There are two extended passages for the soloist, framed by a ritornello that appears at the beginning and end of the movement and that recurs, in abbreviated form and in a different key, between the two solo passages. The solos present entirely new material, often exploiting the virtuosity of the soloist, and modulate to closely related keys, providing contrast and variety. The return of the ritornello then offers stability and resolution. Torelli's approach was developed by Antonio Vivaldi into *ritornello form*, the standard pattern for eighteenth-century concertos, as we will see in the next chapter.

THE ITALIAN STYLE In the last third of the seventeenth century, Italian music in all genres shared common features. Composers sought to make their music pleasing to the ear, emotionally expressive, gratifying to perform, and able to show off the performers to best advantage. Both voices and instruments drew on a variety of melodic styles, from lyrical song to trumpet-call arpeggiations to virtuoso passagework. The emphasis on soloists, characteristic since early in the century, continued in both vocal and instrumental music. Sacred choral music and trio sonatas featured equal voices in collaboration, but arias and solo sonatas highlighted the virtuosity and expressivity of an individual, and concertos incorporated the contrast between individual and collective voices. What we now call tonality became a strong organizing force, and many pieces followed a similar pattern of establishing the tonic, departing from it, exploring nearby keys, and returning to the tonic at the end. In arias, concertos, and other forms, the final tonic was often emphasized by a reprise of the opening material, which became a basic principle of form for the next two centuries. From all the influences across genres and among a variety of musical centers, there emerged a vibrant, exuberant, identifiably Italian style that was widely imitated and became the foundation for developments in the eighteenth century.

GERMANY AND AUSTRIA

At the end of the Thirty Years' War in 1648, much of Germany was ruined and impoverished. The Holy Roman emperor was weak, and the empire encompassed almost three hundred essentially independent political units, from self-governing free cities such as Hamburg and Nuremberg to territories ruled by princes, dukes, counts, landgraves, margraves, electors, bishops, and archbishops. The map in Figure 17.7 can only suggest the complexity. Because states were relatively small and power decentralized, cities were smaller than those in France or Britain. The great majority of the people were farmers. Germany had neither the state-controlled industries of France, nor the robust capitalism of England and the Netherlands, and was further limited by the strong system of professional guilds left over from the Middle Ages, which discouraged innovation.

Court, city, and church musicians

But the situation was hardly bleak for music. Rulers jealously guarded their sovereignty, and many imitated Louis XIV's use of the arts as a way to assert power and status. Numerous courts eagerly hired singers, instrumentalists, and composers, though the number at any one court could not rival the French court.

Cities and churches also supported music. In a tradition derived from the Renaissance wind ensembles known as *alta* or *alta cappella* (see Chapter 12), most cities employed town musicians, called **Stadtpfeifer** ("town pipers"),

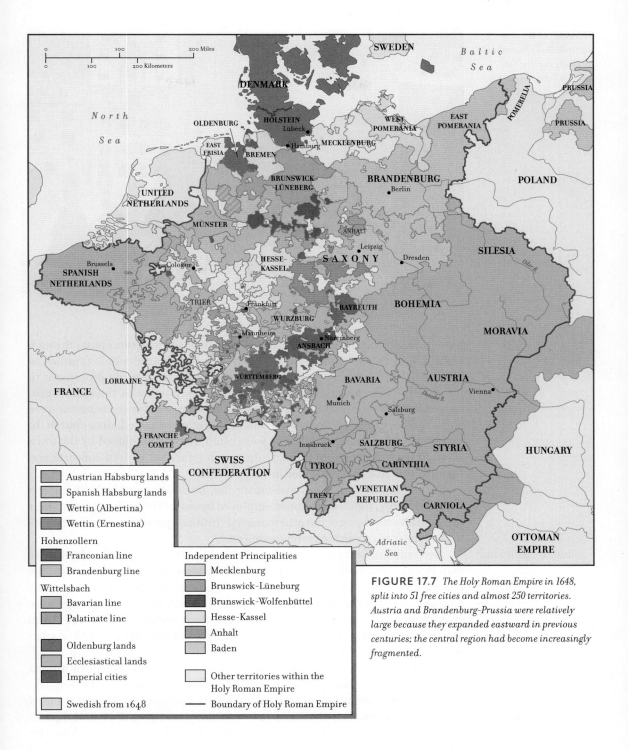

FIGURE 17.7 *The Holy Roman Empire in 1648, split into 51 free cities and almost 250 territories. Austria and Brandenburg-Prussia were relatively large because they expanded eastward in previous centuries; the central region had become increasingly fragmented.*

who had the exclusive right to provide music in the city. They performed at public ceremonies, parades, weddings, and other festivities and supervised the training of apprentices. Figure 17.8 shows a small troupe in Nuremberg sounding in the New Year. Stadtpfeifer were jacks-of-all-trades, proficient at

FIGURE 17.8
Stadtpfeifer *in Nuremberg heralding the New Year. Detail of a drawing by an unknown sixteenth-century artist.*

numerous wind and string instruments, and typically won their posts through auditions or family connections. The system encouraged whole families to make music their trade, among them the Bach family, already prominent in the seventeenth century and about to reach new heights in the eighteenth. In some places, chorales or sonatas called *Turmsonaten* (tower sonatas) were played daily on wind instruments from the tower of the town hall or church. In Lutheran areas, church musicians were often directly employed by the town through the town council. Some Lutheran churches sponsored concerts and recitals, as well as having music during services.

Among all these professional musicians, those at courts had the highest social standing, followed by those employed by major cities. Some spent their careers in a single place, but others moved from one position to another seeking the most advantageous circumstances.

Amateur musicians

Amateur music-making was a prominent part of social life. Many German towns had a **collegium musicum**, an association of amateurs from the educated middle class who gathered to play and sing together for their own pleasure or to hear professionals in private performances. Such groups were also organized in schools, and some drew their members primarily from university students. In the eighteenth century, some collegia gave public concerts (see Chapter 19).

Cosmopolitan styles

German musicians and composers played and wrote music in almost all genres of the time, whether imported or homegrown. Like the English, composers in Germany drew on Italian, French, and native styles and blended them in new ways. The circulation of musicians from post to post, the presence of many foreign-born musicians, and the influence of Germans who traveled or studied abroad all combined to produce a cosmopolitan musical life that would characterize German-speaking areas for the next two centuries. As in Italy, the music in Germany from this period that is best known today is primarily instrumental, especially the great tradition of North German organ music.

OPERA As we saw in Chapter 14, Italian composers were welcomed at Austrian and German courts, where opera in Italian became central to musical life. In addition to Italian composers who made opera careers in Germany—such as Carlo Pallavicino (1630–1688), who worked chiefly in Dresden, and Agostino Steffani (1654–1728), active in Munich and Hanover—German composers also took up the genre. In the eighteenth century, several of the most successful composers of Italian opera were German, from Handel and Hasse to Gluck and Mozart (see Chapters 19, 21, and 23).

After scattered experiments, opera in German found a home in Hamburg with the opening in 1678 of the first public opera house in Germany. In this prosperous commercial center, the opera house was a business venture designed to turn a profit through year-round productions of works that would appeal to the middle class. In deference to Lutheran authorities, who opposed such entertainment, many operas in the early years concerned biblical subjects. Local poets translated or adapted librettos from Venetian operas and wrote new ones that were similar in subject matter and general plan. Composers adopted the recitative style of Italian opera but were eclectic in their arias. In addition to Italianate arias, usually in da capo or modified da capo form, and free ariosos, they occasionally wrote airs in the French style and in the rhythms of French dances. Also common in early German opera, especially for lower-class or comic characters, are short strophic songs in the popular style of northern Germany, displaying brisk, syllabic melodies and straightforward rhythms. The foremost and most prolific of the early German opera composers was Reinhard Keiser (1674–1739), who wrote almost sixty works for the Hamburg stage.

Opera in German

SONG AND CANTATA Keiser and his German contemporaries wrote individual songs and arias as well as cantatas in Italian and in German. The most notable song and cantata composer was Adam Krieger (1634–1666) of Dresden. His arias were mostly strophic melodies in a charmingly simple popular style with short orchestral ritornellos common in German solo songs.

CATHOLIC CHURCH MUSIC In sacred music, composers in Catholic and Lutheran areas followed largely separate paths, responding to the very different liturgies and traditions of the two churches.

The southern German-speaking area, which included Munich, Salzburg, and Vienna (the seat of the imperial chapel), was largely Catholic. The four emperors who reigned there from 1637 to 1740 not only supported music financially but further encouraged it by their interest and actual participation as composers. Like their Italian counterparts, Catholic composers of vocal music cultivated both the older contrapuntal style and the newer concerted styles. In their masses and other liturgical works, composers at the richest courts and cathedrals intermingled orchestral preludes and ritornellos, magnificent choruses, and festive solo ensemble sections, all supported by full orchestral accompaniment. Polychoral music was especially encouraged at Salzburg, where the new cathedral had four choir lofts. For the 1,100th anniversary of the archbishopric of Salzburg in 1682, illustrated in Figure 17.9, Heinrich Biber (1644–1704) composed the monumental *Missa salisburgensis,* with sixteen singers and thirty-seven instrumentalists, each performing

FIGURE 17.9 *Interior view of the Salzburg Cathedral in 1682, during the ceremony celebrating the 1,100th anniversary of the archbishopric of Salzburg, founded in 582 by St. Rupert. Engraving by Melchior Küsel.*

a separate line of music, arranged in seven groups around the cathedral.

LUTHERAN VOCAL MUSIC After the ravages of the Thirty Years' War, churches in the Lutheran territories of Germany quickly restored their musical forces. However, two conflicting tendencies had arisen within the church, and they inevitably affected music. Orthodox Lutherans, holding to established doctrine and public forms of worship, favored using all available resources of choral and instrumental music in their services. In contrast, Pietists emphasized private devotions and Bible readings, distrusted formality and high art in worship, and preferred simple music and poetry that expressed the emotions of the individual believer.

Lutherans possessed a common heritage in the chorale (see Chapter 11). New poems and melodies continued to be composed, many of them intended not for congregational singing but for use in home devotions. The most influential Lutheran songbook of the time was Johann Crüger's *Praxis pietatis melica* (Practice of Piety in Song), issued in 1647 and reprinted in over forty editions during the next half century. Crüger set the melodies over figured bass and added accidentals to the old modal chorale melodies to make them fit emerging conventions of triadic harmony.

Orthodox Lutheran centers provided a favorable environment for developing the sacred concerto. The backbone was the concerted vocal ensemble on a biblical text, as established by Schein, Schütz, and others in the early and middle seventeenth century. Of more recent vintage was the solo aria, normally in Italian style, on a strophic, nonbiblical text. The chorale was the most traditional and characteristically German ingredient, set either in the concertato medium or in chordal harmonies. Composers often drew on these elements in various combinations to create multimovement works. Today such works are usually referred to as cantatas, but their composers called them concertos, sacred concertos, or simply "the music" for a service.

Dieterich Buxtehude   An example of the concertato chorale is the setting of *Wachet auf* by Dieterich Buxtehude (ca. 1637–1707), one of the best-known Lutheran composers of the late seventeenth century (see biography). In this work, the accompanying instruments, strings, bassoon, and continuo begin with a short festive sinfonia on motives from the chorale. Then each stanza of the chorale text is set to a new paraphrase of the melody, distinct from the others

DIETERICH BUXTEHUDE

(ca. 1637–1707)

Buxtehude was renowned as an organist as well as a composer of organ music and sacred vocal works. His pieces for organ, with attention-grabbing themes and virtuosic playing for both hands and the pedals, had a powerful influence on J. S. Bach and other composers.

The son of a German organist working in Denmark, Buxtehude was likely trained by his father and at the Latin School in Elsinore. He played organ in a German church there from 1660 to 1668, when he succeeded Franz Tunder as organist at St. Mary's Church in Lübeck, one of the most important and lucrative musical posts in northern Germany. He later married Tunder's younger daughter Anna Margarethe, apparently as a condition of his employment.

Buxtehude remained at St. Mary's for the rest of his life. He played for the principal services, including morning and afternoon on Sundays and feast days, and composed music to suit: organ solos as preludes to chorales and other parts of the service, and organ, ensemble, and vocal pieces for performance during Communion.

Buxtehude was famed for his *Abendmusiken*, public concerts of sacred vocal music at St. Mary's on five Sunday afternoons each year before Christmas. Admission was free, subsidized by local merchants. The *Abendmusiken* attracted musicians from all over Germany. The twenty-year-old J. S. Bach attended in 1705, and is said to have walked more than two hundred miles just to hear them.

Buxtehude's works are catalogued in Georg Karstädt's *Buxtehude-Werke-Verzeichnis* (Buxtehude Works Catalogue), abbreviated BuxWV.

MAJOR WORKS About 120 sacred vocal works, about 40 chorale settings for organ, 22 organ preludes and toccatas, 19 harpsichord suites, numerous other keyboard pieces, 20 ensemble sonatas

---

in vocal range, figuration, rhythm, texture, and relation to the original tune. The result is a series of chorale variations, a frequent procedure at the time.

LUTHERAN ORGAN MUSIC Organ music enjoyed a golden age in the Lutheran areas of Germany between about 1650 and 1750. In the north, Buxtehude at Lübeck and Georg Böhm (1661–1733) at Lüneburg continued the tradition of preludes, imitative works, and chorale-based compositions established by Sweelinck and Scheidt. A central group in Saxony and Thuringia included Johann Christoph Bach (1642–1703) of Eisenach, first cousin of J. S. Bach's father. One of the most notable German organ composers was Johann Pachelbel (1653–1706) of Nuremberg, composer of the now-famous canon for three violins and continuo.

German organ builders of the late seventeenth and early eighteenth centuries drew on elements of French and Dutch organs, much as German composers blended Italian, French, and northern styles. The best-known builders were Arp Schnitger (1648–1718), who built the organ in Figure 17.10, and Gottfried Silbermann (1683–1753), who emulated the colorful stops used in France to play solos and contrapuntal lines. They and their colleagues adopted the Dutch practice of dividing the pipes into a main group and subsidiary groups, each with its own keyboard and pipes having a particular character and function. The main group, the *Hauptwerk*, or Great organ, sits high above the player. Other groups may include a *Rückpositiv*, mounted on the outside of the choir balcony rail behind the organist's back;

The Baroque organ

FIGURE 17.10 *Organ built in 1710–11 by Arp Schnitger in the Martinikerk in Sneek, a city in the northern Netherlands. The upper chest of pipes is the* Hauptwerk, *or Great organ. The tall pipes in the center and around the sides produce the lowest notes, played by the pedals. Below the* Hauptwerk *is the* Brustwerk, *and below that, unseen in this photograph, are the manual keyboards, the pedal keyboard, and the organist's bench. In the foreground is the* Rückpositiv, *mounted on the railing behind the organist.*

a *Brustwerk,* directly above the music rack in front of the player; an *Oberwerk,* high above the Great; and the pedal organ, whose pipes are usually arranged symmetrically on the sides of the Great. Only the largest German organs had all of these components. Even on a modest instrument with two manual keyboards and one pedal keyboard, an organist could create a great variety of sounds combining variously voiced principal, flute, and reed pipes, as well as mixtures, in which pipes sounding upper harmonics add brilliance to the fundamental tone.

Functions of organ music

Most of the organ music written for Protestant churches served as a prelude to something else: a chorale, a scriptural reading, or a larger work. Such pieces were often chorale settings, or they were toccatas or preludes that contained fugues or culminated in them.

Buxtehude's toccatas typify those of seventeenth-century German com-   *Toccatas and*
posers in presenting a series of short sections in free style that alternate with   *preludes*
longer ones in imitative counterpoint, expanding on the similar juxtapositions of styles in Frescobaldi's toccatas (see NAWM 82). Filled with motion
and climaxes, Buxtehude's toccatas display a great variety of figuration and
take full advantage of the organ's idiomatic qualities, including its huge
range, rapid articulation, sustained tones, varied timbres, and wide-ranging
dynamics, offering more contrasting colors, textures, dynamic levels, and
layers than any other instrument. The capricious, exuberant character of his
toccatas made them ideal vehicles for virtuosic display at the keyboard and
on the pedals. The toccata as a genre and its focus on imitative counterpoint
were fostered by Johann Jacob Froberger (see Chapter 15), who studied with
Frescobaldi and whose keyboard works had a deep impact on later German
composers.

The free sections simulate improvisation by contrasting irregular rhythm
with steadily driving sixteenth notes, by using phrases that are deliberately
irregular or have inconclusive endings, and by featuring abrupt changes of
texture, harmony, or melodic direction. Example 17.3 shows a passage that is
typical of toccata style, from Buxtehude's Praeludium in E Major, BuxWV 141
(NAWM 97). The virtuoso part for the pedals (the lowest staff in the score)
includes long trills played by quickly alternating between the feet; when
the pedal sustains a tone, the two hands erupt in rapid passagework with
unpredictable changes of speed, direction, and figuration. At the opposite
extreme is a later, slow-paced free section marked by suspensions and passing changes of key.

In the Praeludium in E, there are five free sections, of which the first two
are the longest, the next two relatively brief transitions, and the last a climactic coda. These sections in toccata style frame four fugal sections, each

EXAMPLE 17.3 *Dietrich Buxtehude, Praeludium in E Major, BuxWV 141, toccata section*

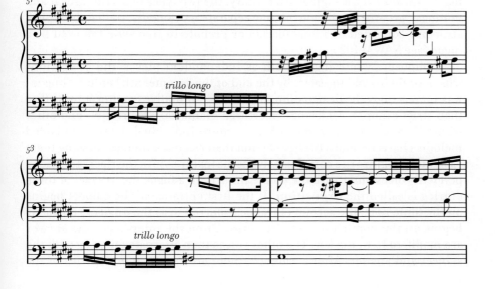

EXAMPLE 17.4 *Fugue subjects from Buxtehude's Praeludium in E Major*

on a different subject and in a different meter or tempo. The treatment is different in each case, from full-scale fugues in four voices with pedals for the first and last fugal sections, to less rigorous fugal imitation in three voices without pedals in the inner two. All four blend into the following free section.

The four subjects are shown in Example 17.4. They all share family resemblances, recalling the variation canzonas of Frescobaldi and the keyboard fantasias of Sweelinck and Scheidt, which apply variation to their fugal subjects. Here the relationships are rather subtle; while the melodic contours are similar, as shown by the vertical alignment of notes, and similar figures recur (marked a and b in the example), Buxtehude reverses the order of a motive (see notes marked x), fills in leaps (as in the third subject), and uses other devices to provide both unity and variety.

In the seventeenth century, such keyboard pieces were called "toccata," "prelude," "praeludium," or some similar name, even though they included fugal sections. In the eighteenth century, the two types of section, fugal and nonfugal, grew in length and became separate movements, so that the typical structure consisted of a long toccata or prelude in free style followed by a fugue (see NAWM 102).

Fugue   Composers wrote fugues both as independent pieces and as sections within preludes and toccatas. By the end of the seventeenth century, "fugue" was increasingly the designation for pieces in imitative counterpoint (other than strict canons), replacing "ricercare," "fantasia," "capriccio," and other terms. Fugue subjects tend to have a more individual, sharply chiseled melodic character and a livelier rhythm than ricercare themes, making them easier to recognize in a complex polyphonic texture. As in the ricercare, independent voices enter with the theme in turn. In a fugue the first set of these entries is called the **exposition**. If the first entrance of the subject begins on the tonic note, the second entrance, referred to as the **answer**, normally begins on the dominant, and vice versa. Often the intervals of the answer are modified to fit the key. The other voices then alternate entering with the subject and answer. After a cadence, there are several more entries of the subject, alone or in points of imitation, each differentiated from the others by the order of entries, pitch level, or some other aspect. Seventeenth-century fugues may have short ***episodes***—periods of free counterpoint between statements of the subject.

While toccatas, preludes, and fugues remained independent of vocal music, organ compositions based on chorales used the melodies in different ways. In *organ chorales,* the tunes were enhanced by harmony and counterpoint. A tune could serve as a theme for a set of *chorale variations,* also called *chorale partita,* or as the subject for a *chorale fantasia.*

Chorale settings

Another genre based on a chorale tune was the ***chorale prelude***. This term, often applied to any chorale-based organ work, will be used here to denote a short piece in which the entire melody is presented just once in readily recognizable form. This type of chorale setting appeared in the mid-seventeenth century. The name suggests an earlier liturgical practice in which the organist played through the tune, with improvised accompaniment and ornaments, as a prelude to the congregation's or choir's singing of the chorale. Later, when they were written down, such pieces were called "chorale preludes" even if they did not serve the original purpose.

Chorale prelude

In effect, a chorale prelude is a single variation on a chorale, which may be constructed in any of the following ways:

- Each phrase of the melody serves in turn as the subject of a point of imitation.

- Phrases appear in turn, usually in the top voice, in long notes with relatively little ornamentation. Each phrase is preceded by a brief imitative development in the other voices of the phrase's beginning, in diminution.

- The melody appears in the top voice, ornamented in an imaginative manner, and the accompanying voices proceed freely with great variety from phrase to phrase.

- The melody is accompanied in one or more of the other voices by a motive or rhythmic figure not related motivically to the melody itself.

An example of the third type is Buxtehude's chorale prelude on *Nun komm, der Heiden Heiland* (compare Example 11.1b). The opening phrase, shown in Example 17.5a, is decorated with passing and neighbor tones and with short trills that resemble French agréments in sound and function. Each phrase is progressively more elaborate in its embellishment. The last phrase, which in the original chorale is the same as the first phrase, is here presented with florid Italianate ornamentation that includes dramatic octave leaps and striking runs, shown in Example 17.5b. In combining a German chorale with styles of melody and elaboration from France and Italy, this brief piece nicely illustrates the tendency for German composers to blend elements from all three regions.

OTHER INSTRUMENTAL MUSIC By the late seventeenth century, German organists had assimilated what they could learn from Italian and French

EXAMPLE 17.5 *Buxtehude, chorale prelude on* Nun komm, der Heiden Heiland

a. Opening phrase, compared with original chorale

Nun komm, der Hei - den Hei - land,

b. Final phrase

x = note from chorale melody

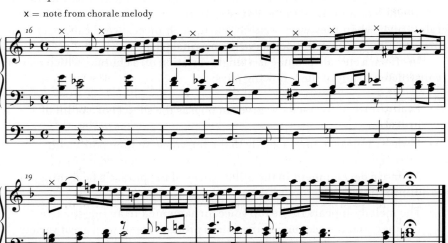

models, developed a distinctive style of their own, and established themselves as leaders in organ composition. In other realms of instrumental music, the process of assimilation was still under way, the genres practiced still largely those of Italy or France.

Harpsichord suites   The French harpsichord style was carried to Germany by Froberger, who helped to establish the allemande, courante, sarabande, and gigue as standard components of dance suites. Manuscript copies of Froberger's suites end with the sarabande, a slow dance. In a later, posthumous publication of 1693, the order was revised so that each suite ends with a lively gigue, which had by then become the standard close for German suites. Many German composers, including Buxtehude, J. S. Bach, and Handel, wrote suites.

Orchestral suites   Impressed by the high standards of performance in Lully's orchestra and by the French musical style he cultivated, many German musicians sought to introduce these traits into their own country. One result of this effort was a fashion in Germany between about 1690 and 1740 for a new type of **orchestral suite**. The dances of these suites, patterned after those of Lully's ballets and operas, did not appear in any standard number or order. Among the early collections of orchestral suites were two publications titled *Florilegium* (1695 and 1698) by Georg Muffat, who pioneered in introducing Lully's style into Germany as he had Corelli's a decade earlier. Muffat included an essay with musical examples about the French system of bowing, the playing of the agréments, and similar matters.

Although Muffat, Buxtehude, and other German composers took up the trio sonata, the solo sonata attracted more interest. The solo violin sonata had always been the prime vehicle for experiments in special bowings, multiple stops, and all kinds of difficult passagework. Twelve sonatas by Johann Jakob Walther (ca. 1650–1717), published in 1676 under the title *Scherzi*, built on the tradition of Biagio Marini but surpassed all others in technical brilliance. The most famous German sonatas of the seventeenth century are Heinrich Biber's *Mystery Sonatas* (or *Rosary Sonatas*) for Violin (ca. 1675), which represent meditations on episodes in the life of Christ. These works make considerable use of *scordatura,* unusual tunings of the violin strings to facilitate the playing of particular notes or chords. Biber was esteemed as a violin virtuoso as well as composer at the court of the archbishop of Salzburg, and he probably composed and played the sonatas as music for services at the Salzburg Cathedral, which centered each October on the Mysteries of the Rosary. Both Walther and Biber often interspersed rhapsodic movements or toccata-like sections in their sonatas, and both wrote many of their longer movements in the form of a passacaglia or theme and variations, as in Biber's Passacaglia for unaccompanied solo violin.

Violin sonatas

Seventeenth-century sonatas were strictly ensemble music until Johann Kuhnau (1660–1722) transferred the genre to the keyboard in 1692. His *Frische Clavier Früchte* (Fresh Keyboard Fruits, 1696), a title apparently calculated to herald a new genre, consists of seven multimovement sonatas. The elaborate title page, shown in Figure 17.11, was clearly designed to catch the attention of the amateur keyboard player. His six "Biblical" sonatas (1700), bearing titles such as *Saul's Madness Cured by Music* and *The Combat Between David and Goliath,* represent stories from the Old Testament cleverly and sometimes humorously told in music.

Keyboard sonatas

THE GERMAN SYNTHESIS Germans had imported musical fashions from France since troubadour songs and from Italy since the sixteenth-century madrigals, each time remaking the foreign style to suit local tastes. In the seventeenth century, this trend continued with the adopted genres of opera, polychoral and concerted church music, toccata, suite, and sonata. As they mastered the styles and genres of other nations and added elements from their own traditions, composers in German-speaking lands laid the foundations for the extraordinary developments of the eighteenth century, when German and Austrian composers would play key roles in developing the sonata and concerto as vehicles for advanced musical thought and in forging a new international musical language.

FIGURE 17.11 *Engraved title page of Johann Kuhnau's* Frische Clavier Früchte, oder Sieben Suon-aten, von guten Invention und Manier auff dem Claviere zu spielen *(Fresh Keyboard Fruits, or Seven Sonatas, of Good Invention and Manner, to Be Played on the Keyboard, Leipzig, 1696). In the middle we see a clavichord, the preferred instrument for home performance. Around it is an elaborate garland of grain, grapes, apples, peppers, and other fruits of the field, vine, and garden, illustrating the title.*

SEEDS FOR THE FUTURE

In the second half of the seventeenth century, Italian music reached new heights, and Germanic composers began to come into their own. Cities and courts all over Italy and Germany sponsored Italian opera, which continued to be the most prestigious musical genre throughout the eighteenth century. The da capo aria, especially in its extended format with two vocal statements in the A section, became a convention for operas and other vocal works and lasted for almost a century. The trio sonata, solo violin sonata, and concerto, all originated by Italians, became the leading genres of ensemble music in both nations through the mid-eighteenth century. German composers also emulated French styles in vocal music and in suites for keyboard or orchestra. By the closing decades of the century, Lutheran organist-composers had surpassed their Italian and French colleagues, perhaps the first time that Germany led other nations in any field of music. It would not be the last: German musicians in the eighteenth century would make a virtue of their eclecticism and gradually outshine their Italian counterparts in the increasingly important genres of instrumental music.

This half-century also saw other developments of enduring significance. Tonality as exemplified in Corelli's sonatas proved of fundamental importance for music ever since. Among other things, the clear direction and predictable expectations characteristic of tonal music made possible more complex harmonic structures and thus longer forms and more adventurous storytelling in instrumental music. The sonata and the concerto were the first multimovement instrumental genres not based on stringing together smaller pieces, as in a suite of dances. By engaging the listener's interest for a relatively long time without the support of a text, these forms paved the way for the concert works of later centuries, designed to be listened to with complete attention.

Many pieces from this time were written for specific occasions, for local use as entertainment, or for church services, and usually received at most a few performances. These circumstances were especially true for vocal music, which was fueled by a constant demand for new operas, cantatas, and church music in preference to the old. Instrumental music had a somewhat longer life. The sonatas and concertos of Corelli continued to be played throughout the eighteenth century and influenced many composers, including Handel. German organists continued to play music of Buxtehude and his contemporaries for some time, and younger composers like J. S. Bach emulated their predecessors. But by the end of the eighteenth century, even Corelli was rarely heard. In the second half of the nineteenth century, the respect Bach and Handel showed their late-seventeenth-century forebears aroused the interest of musicians and scholars, leading to performances and editions of the music of Corelli, Buxtehude, and others from their era. Since the early twentieth century, Corelli's sonatas and concertos have found a permanent place in the repertoire, and music of the North German organists is frequently played. Other late-seventeenth-century music remains less familiar than the music of the eighteenth or even the sixteenth century but is gradually finding a wider audience as it becomes available in good editions and recordings.

Further Reading is available at digital.wwnorton.com/hwm10

PART FOUR

THE EIGHTEENTH CENTURY

With few exceptions, the standard concert repertoire begins in the early eighteenth century with Vivaldi, Bach, and Handel. Yet there was no major change around 1700 to mark a new style, as there had been at 1300, 1400, and 1600. Rather, the new generation that reached maturity then was marked by consolidation, integrating and developing ideas and trends introduced over the previous century.

In stylistic terms, it is customary to divide the eighteenth century at 1750, regarding the first half as the late Baroque period and the second half as the Classic period, culminating in the music of Haydn and Mozart. But looked at in another way, the eighteenth century can be regarded as a period in its own right, marked not by consistency in style but by winds of change. Reading the music journals and composers' writings, one comes to see the 1700s as a century-long argument about what is most valuable in music—a contest between musical tastes. Elements of what would become the Classical style were already present at the start of the century, and echoes of Baroque styles were still heard at the end.

However we view it, this century was one of the most remarkable times in the history of music. Musicians cultivated many new genres, including keyboard concerto, opera buffa, ballad opera, symphony, and string quartet, and developed new forms such as sonata form and rondo. From Vivaldi's concertos, Bach's fugues, and Handel's oratorios through Haydn's string quartets and symphonies and Mozart's piano sonatas and operas, composers of the era created exemplary works that defined their genres and today lie at the heart of the classical repertoire.

PART OUTLINE

THE EARLY EIGHTEENTH CENTURY IN ITALY AND FRANCE

Composers around 1700 were not inventing new techniques, styles, and genres at the pace of their predecessors a century earlier. Rather, they continued and extended well-established traditions, taking for granted the approaches developed during the seventeenth century: the doctrine of the affections, basso continuo, the concertato medium, tonality, and the genres of opera, cantata, concerto, sonata, and suite.

Influential and original composers of the early eighteenth century such as Vivaldi, Couperin, Rameau, Telemann, J. S. Bach, and Handel established individual styles by combining elements from seventeenth-century traditions in new ways. It is fitting that we focus on them and on the patrons, institutions, tastes, and values that shaped their music, treating each composer's story as a case study of musical life at the time. This chapter will discuss Vivaldi, Couperin, and Rameau, representatives of Italy and France, still the leading musical nations at the dawn of the eighteenth century. In Chapter 19, we will turn to Telemann, Bach, and Handel, typical of German-speaking musicians in their synthesis of elements from several national traditions. As we will see in Chapters 20–22, even while these composers were at the peak of their careers, currents were beginning that would lead in new directions, making this the last generation of Baroque composers.

EUROPE IN A CENTURY OF CHANGE

In political and social terms, as in music, the eighteenth century moved from continuity with the past, through new currents, to radical change, culminating in revolutions at the end. When the century began, a balance of power was emerging in Europe among several strong centralized states, each supported by a professional military and government bureaucracy. France had the biggest army, but Louis XIV's lavish spending on wars abroad and spectacles at home was depleting the treasury, and his expansionist ambitions were checked by other nations. Great Britain, formed by the union of England and Scotland in 1707, had the most powerful navy and used it to wrest India, Canada, and several Caribbean islands from France during the Seven Years' War in 1756–63. Having won back Hungary from the Turks in the late seventeenth century, Austria was increasing its influence, reflected by the emergence in the late eighteenth century of its capital Vienna as the leading musical city in Europe. A new power emerged when Prussia became a kingdom in 1701 and developed one of the Continent's largest and best-trained armies. Late in the century, Poland—where the nobles had resisted consolidation of power under the king—fell victim to the centralized states around it; Prussia, Russia, and Austria divided Poland's territories among themselves and erased it from the map for over a century. By then, the American Revolution (1775–83) and the French Revolution (1789–99) were bringing winds of change that would remake the political culture of Europe and the Americas.

The population of Europe expanded rapidly, especially after 1750. The new mouths were fed by a growing food supply made possible through improved agricultural methods, such as crop rotation and intensive manuring, and new crops like the potato, introduced from the New World, whose widespread adoption ended the frequent famines that plagued Europe in the previous centuries. Roads were gradually improved, making travel faster and more comfortable; a hundred-mile trip that took fifty hours in 1700 (four days with stops for refreshment and sleep) took only sixteen hours in 1800. As a result, intercity postal service became more efficient and less expensive. Trade increased, both within Europe and with Asia and the New World. As manufacturing and trade became more lucrative, the urban middle class grew in size and economic clout, while the landed aristocracy became less important, though they still occupied the top of the social ladder.

Economic expansion

As the continent became more urbanized, nature was increasingly idealized. The aristocracy's nostalgia for rural life was perfectly captured in paintings by Jean-Antoine Watteau (1684–1721), such as *Embarkation for Cythera* in Figure 18.1. Pastoral themes were also prominent in musical works, from Scarlatti's cantatas (see NAWM 94) and Vivaldi's concertos *The Four Seasons* near the beginning of the century to Gluck's opera *Orfeo ed Euridice* (NAWM 113) and Haydn's oratorio *The Seasons* near its end.

Idealization of nature

Many new schools were founded, both for the governmental elite—teaching the traditional Greek and Latin—and for the middle classes, providing a more practical education. King Frederick the Great of Prussia (r. 1740–86) and Empress Maria Theresa of Austria (r. 1740–80) sought to require primary school for every child, although they were only partially successful. By 1800, half the male population of England and France was literate, and women, usually taught at home, were catching up. Daily newspapers began publishing in London in 1702 and quickly spread to other cities. From cheap paperbacks to leather-bound tomes, more and more books were published, purchased, read, and passed around. Novels became the most popular form of literature, including Daniel Defoe's *Robinson Crusoe* (1719) and Henry Fielding's *Tom Jones* (1749). At public coffeehouses, meetings of learned societies, and salons, gatherings in private homes hosted by well-to-do women, people avidly discussed current events, ideas, literature, and music. Amid this broadening interest in learning, thinkers such as Voltaire (1694–1778)

Education and learning

MUSÉE DU LOUVRE, PARIS. PHOTO: ERICH LESSING/ART RESOURCE, NY

FIGURE 18.1 *Jean-Antoine Watteau's* Embarkation for Cythera *(1717) was one of the most famous paintings of the eighteenth century. The setting is in an imagined Arcadian paradise of nature populated by winged infants (perhaps cupids or angels) and muscular boatmen, on the left. On the right, nearer the viewer, are several amorous couples in fashionable, modern, courtly dress. Nature is depicted by Watteau as a theater for leisure and pleasure, far from the constraints of urban society, but equally far from the reality of rural life for the poor peasants who made up most of the population of France.*

sought to analyze social and political issues through reason and science, spreading the intellectual movement known as the Enlightenment (discussed in Chapter 20).

Demand for new music   In London, Paris, and other large cities, support from the middle class became increasingly important for musicians and composers. The growth of the middle class and the broadening of education meant that more and more people were interested in hearing and playing music, buying music to perform, and attending concerts. This resulted in expanding markets for printed music and instruments and growing opportunities for musicians as teachers and performers. The public constantly demanded new music. Few works of any kind were performed for more than two or three seasons, and composers were expected to furnish new pieces for almost every occasion. Such unceasing pressure accounts for the vast output of many eighteenth-century composers and the phenomenal speed at which they worked.

Changing styles   The demand for new music also helps to explain the changing fashions in musical style. The eighteenth century is often divided between Baroque and Classic styles, but the two overlapped in time, as we will see in the next several chapters. Indeed, the history of this century's music can be seen as a long argument about taste and style, often literally argued in newspapers, journals, salons, and coffeehouses. Changes in audiences and venues for music across the century contributed to the development of new styles, which in turn inspired debates between partisans of "new" and "old" styles. As in our own day, these discussions about musical style were often rooted in deeper

arguments about other issues, such as class or politics; for example, supporters of aristocratic values promoted music that was simple, witty, and expressive and criticized music preferred by the middle class for what they regarded
as bad taste, excessive complexity, or empty show.

MUSIC IN ITALY

In Italy, opera remained the most prestigious—and most expensive—type of
music, but instrumental music, especially the concerto, was gaining ground.
Principal centers for music included Naples, Rome, and Venice, which were
the capitals of the most powerful states on the peninsula and therefore were
the most fashionable cities, had the wealthiest patrons and most developed
musical life, and attracted the most renowned and original composers.

NAPLES Southern Italy, a Spanish possession since 1503, came under Aus-   *Conservatories*
trian control in 1707, then in 1734 became an independent kingdom ruled
by the son of the Spanish king. Its capital Naples had four **conservatories**,
homes for orphaned and poor boys, that specialized in teaching music. Over
the years, musical instruction gradually became as important as the original
charitable purpose, and the conservatories took on paying students as well.
Their pupils made musical careers all over Europe, helping to spread Italian
opera and Italian instrumental music across the Continent.

Most conservatory students were singers, many of them castrati. By the   *Castrati*
late seventeenth century, the leading male roles in operas were almost always
written for castrati, whose increased lung capacity made them ideal soloists
and whose powerful, agile voices were much prized. Although most castrati
remained church musicians, hundreds sang on opera stages across Europe.
A few became international superstars and commanded huge fees, including
Carlo Broschi (1705–1782), known as Farinelli, who was raised and trained in
Naples (see Music in Context: The Voice of Farinelli and Figure 18.2, p. 406).

Opera was at the center of Neapolitan musical life, thanks to the support   *Opera*
of its rulers and other patrons. Alessandro Scarlatti, who wrote one or more
operas almost every year, was its leading composer (see Chapter 17). While
new types of comic opera, sung in the Neapolitan dialect, gained popularity
and inspired imitators across Europe (see Chapter 21), a new kind of serious Italian opera also emerged in the 1720s, codified by the librettist Pietro
Metastasio (1698–1782). Both comic and serious opera of the time continued
standard practices of Baroque opera, alternating recitatives and da capo arias.

ROME Opera was less central in Rome because of support for other genres
and occasional papal strictures against the secular genre of opera. The popes
also forbade women from appearing on stage, so that female roles had to be
sung by castrati when operas were performed in Rome. Rich patrons regularly
sponsored academies, where their musicians performed cantatas, serenatas,
sonatas, and concertos. The support of wealthy patrons attracted instrumentalists from all over Italy and Germany, making Rome a training ground for
performers. Among them were violin virtuosos Francesco Geminiani (1687–
1762) and Pietro Locatelli (1695–1764), who came to Rome in their teens,
absorbed the Corelli tradition of performance and composition, and then

MUSIC IN CONTEXT

The Voice of Farinelli

The castrato voice resulted from the same impulse that motivates today's athletes to take hormones and steroids: the desire to control and manipulate nature in order to enhance a performer's abilities. The ever-increasing demand by opera audiences for virtuosic superstars and the rise of certain castrato soloists to fame and fortune in turn stimulated the production of castrati throughout Italy, especially among poor families who saw it as a possible way of improving their miserable circumstances.

However, although thousands aspired to stardom, only a few ever achieved the fame of a Farinelli, whose career took him from triumph to triumph in all the operatic capitals of Europe. He was legendary for his vocal range, spanning more than three octaves, and for his breath control, which enabled him to sustain a note for a full minute before having to inhale. Such capacities allowed him to execute the most rapid and difficult passagework and most engaging embellishments, winning him acclamation from audiences.

The painting in Figure 18.2 depicts Farinelli as he appeared in 1734, the year of his debut in London with the Opera of the Nobility—the company that rivalled Handel's own (see pp. 444–46)—led by Nicola Porpora, who had been Farinelli's teacher in Naples. The portrait gives us a good idea of the physical characteristics that were typical of castrati: somewhat effeminate facial features, including a smallish head and a smooth pale skin with no beard, a large chest, well-rounded hips, and narrow shoulders. Contemporary writers also commented on castrati's fairly tall stature, which was unusual in the eighteenth century, and their tendency for obesity. In addition to illustrating these general characteristics, the portrait presents Farinelli, the singular virtuoso, as a commanding presence, exquisitely outfitted in brocade, fur-trimmed velvet, and lace, his right hand resting on a harpsichord as if acknowledging what must have been the principal tool of his training. We may assume from his authoritative, even arrogant, pose that he had already reached the height of his powers. In fact, he retired from the stage only three years later, at age thirty-two, having been invited to Madrid, where he spent the next two decades in the service of Spanish kings.

ROYAL COLLEGE OF MUSIC/BRIDGEMAN IMAGES

FIGURE 18.2 *Farinelli, the most famous and widely admired of the castrato singers, in a portrait by Bartolomeo Nazari from 1734.*

made their careers in London and Amsterdam respectively, deepening the already strong impact of Corelli's style on northern Europe.

VENICE At the beginning of the eighteenth century, Venice was declining in political and economic power but remained the most glamorous city in Europe. Travelers attracted to its colorful, exuberant life returned home full of stories about the city and its music and often carried some of that music with them, thus spreading its influence across Europe from England to Russia. In Venice, musicians sang on the streets and canals; gondoliers had their own repertory of songs; amateurs played and sang in private academies; and opera impresarios competed for the best singers and composers.

Public festivals, more numerous in Venice than elsewhere, remained occasions of musical splendor. The city had long taken pride in its church music, chamber music, and opera. In the eighteenth century, Venice never had fewer than six opera companies, which together played thirty-four weeks of the year. Between 1700 and 1750, the Venetian public heard an average of ten new operas annually, and the count was even higher in the second half of the century.

ANTONIO VIVALDI

The best-known Italian composer of the early eighteenth century was Antonio Vivaldi (1678–1741), who was born and spent most of his career in Venice (see biography and Figure 18.3, p. 408). A virtuoso violinist, master teacher, and renowned composer of opera, cantatas, and sacred music, he is known today primarily for his concertos, which number around five hundred.

Vivaldi's main position from 1703 to 1740 was as teacher, composer, conductor, and superintendent of musical instruments at the Pio Ospedale della Pietà. The Pietà was one of four "hospitals" in Venice, homes for orphaned, illegitimate, or poor boys and girls, which were run like restrictive boarding schools and provided excellent instruction in music to those girls who showed talent. These institutions paralleled the Naples conservatories, except that careers as instrumentalists or church musicians were not open to women, and before the girls were allowed to leave they had to agree never to perform in public. Educating the girls in music served other purposes: to occupy their time; to make them more desirable as prospects for marriage or prepare them for convent life; and to earn donations for the hospitals through regular performances, such as the concert pictured in Figure 18.4. Services with music at the Pietà and other places of worship in Venice attracted large audiences, and travelers wrote about these occasions with enthusiasm (see Source Reading, p. 409).

The Pietà

Vivaldi's position required him to maintain the string instruments, teach his students to play, and constantly compose new music for them to perform. He wrote oratorios and music for Mass and Vespers, including the well-known Gloria in D major, but most of his works for the Pietà were instrumental, primarily concertos for church festivals. Concertos were uniquely well suited for players of varying abilities because the best performers could show off their skill in the solo parts, while those of lesser ability could play in the orchestra.

VIVALDI'S CONCERTOS Vivaldi's concertos have a freshness of melody, rhythmic verve, skillful treatment of solo and orchestral color, and clarity of form that won them wide renown in his time and have made them perennial favorites in ours. Working at the Pietà, having skilled performers at his disposal, and being required to produce music at a prodigious rate provided Vivaldi with a workshop for experimenting with the concerto. The secret of Vivaldi's success, and of the profound influence he exercised on other

ANTONIO VIVALDI

(1678–1741)

Vivaldi was one of the most original and prolific composers of his time, and his influence on later composers was profound.

Born in Venice, the eldest of nine children of a violinist at St. Mark's, Vivaldi trained for both music and the priesthood, a combination that was not unusual at the time. Due to his red hair, he was known as *il prete rosso* (the red priest).

In 1703, the year he was ordained, he became master of violin at the Pio Ospedale della Pietà, a home for poor or orphaned children. He was later appointed master of the concerts, a position of greater responsibility, and he remained at the Pietà until 1740, with some breaks in service.

Like most of his contemporaries, Vivaldi composed every work for a definite occasion and for particular performers. For the Pietà, he composed oratorios, sacred music, and especially concertos. He also fulfilled forty-nine opera commissions, most for Venice and a few for Florence, Ferrara, Verona, Rome, Vienna, and elsewhere. Between 1713 and 1719, the theaters of Venice staged more works of his than of any other composer. He usually supervised the production of his operas in person, and was often absent from the Pietà for long periods. During a two-year sojourn in Rome (1723–24), he was asked by the Pietà's governors to compose two new concertos a month for a fee, which he did for the next six years; this arrangement is one of the most direct signs of Vivaldi's value to them as a composer, distinct from his roles as

FIGURE 18.3 *Antonio Vivaldi, in an engraving by François Morellon La Cave from around 1725.*

teacher and performer. He also wrote sonatas and concertos on commission and for publication.

In the 1720s, Vivaldi took the contralto Anna Girò as his singing pupil (and, some gossiped, his mistress, although he denied it). In 1737, he was censured for conduct unbecoming a priest. By then his popularity with the Venetian public had sunk, and he increasingly sought commissions elsewhere, traveling to Amsterdam in 1738 and Vienna in 1740. He earned enormous sums of money from his music, but spent almost all of it, and when he died in Vienna in 1741, he was given a pauper's funeral.

MAJOR WORKS About 500 concertos (including *The Four Seasons*), 16 sinfonias, 64 solo sonatas, 27 trio sonatas, 21 surviving operas, 38 cantatas, and about 60 sacred vocal works

composers, was a simple but flexible recipe that allowed him to achieve extraordinary variety through ever-changing combinations of a few basic elements.

Instrumentation   Vivaldi achieved a remarkable range of colors and sonorities through different groupings of solo and orchestral instruments. His orchestra at the Pietà probably consisted of twenty to twenty-five string instruments, with harpsichord or organ for the continuo. The strings were divided in what was becoming the standard arrangement of violins I and II, violas, cellos, and double bass (usually doubling the cellos). This was always the core group, though in many concertos Vivaldi also called for flutes, oboes, bassoons, or horns, any

FIGURE 18.4 *Female singers and string players (upper left), thought to be from the Pio Ospedale della Pietà, give a concert in Venice honoring Archduke Paul and Mary Fedorov of Russia. Painting by Francesco Guardi (1712–1793).*

ALTE PINAKOTHEK, MUNICH, GERMANY/GIRAUDON/BRIDGEMAN IMAGES

SOURCE READING

Concerts at the Pio Ospedale della Pietà

The Frenchman Charles de Brosses toured Italy in 1739–40 and wrote his impressions in letters to friends, later collected for publication. His account of concerts at the Pio Ospedale della Pietà, where Vivaldi had long overseen instrumental music, gives us a sense of the institution and of the concerts performed by its residents. De Brosses was mistaken when he called them girls; most were young women, but some residents remained and performed at the Pietà most of their lives.

A transcendent music here is that of the hospitals [orphanages]. There are four, all made up of illegitimate or orphaned girls or girls whose parents are not in a condition to raise them. They are reared at public expense and trained solely to excel in music. So they sing like angels and play the violin, the flute, the organ, the violoncello, the bassoon. In short no instrument is large enough to frighten them. They are cloistered in the manner of nuns. They alone perform, and each concert is given by about forty girls. I swear to you that there is nothing so charming as to see a young and pretty nun in her white robe, with a bouquet of pomegranate flowers over her ear, leading the orchestra and beating time with all the grace and precision imaginable. Their voices are admirable for their character and lightness, because here they don't know the heavy, drawn-out French sound. . . .

The hospital I go to most often is that of the Pietà, where one is best entertained. It is also first for the perfection of the instrumental pieces. What a precise performance! It is only there that you hear the first stroke of the bow [the first chord of a piece attacked as one by the strings] of which the Opéra in Paris falsely boasts.

Charles de Brosses, *L'Italie il y a cent ans ou Lettres écrites d'Italie à quelques amis en 1739 et 1740*, ed. M. R. Colomb, vol. 1 (Paris: Alphonse Levavasseur, 1836), 213–14.

of which might be used as solo instruments or in the ensemble. He also used special coloristic effects, like pizzicato and muted strings.

About 350 of Vivaldi's concertos are for orchestra with one solo instrument—over two-thirds of them for violin, but many also for bassoon, cello, oboe, flute, viola d'amore, recorder, or mandolin. The concertos for two violins give the soloists equal prominence, producing the texture of a duet for two high voices. The concertos that call for several solo instruments are not concerti grossi like Corelli's, in which the orchestra serves to double and reinforce the concertino of two violins and cello; rather, they feature the same opposition between virtuoso soloists and orchestra as in Vivaldi's solo concertos. There are also about sixty orchestral concertos (without solo instruments).

Three-movement structure

With occasional exceptions, Vivaldi followed the three-movement plan introduced by Albinoni: an opening fast movement; a slow movement in the same or closely related key (relative minor or major, dominant, or subdominant); and a final fast movement in the tonic, often shorter and livelier than the first. By using this format so consistently and creatively, Vivaldi helped to establish it as the standard for concertos over the next three centuries.

Ritornello form

We saw in Chapter 17 that Torelli structured the fast movements of his concertos like the A section of a da capo aria, with a ritornello at the beginning, middle, and end framing two long episodes for the soloist. Vivaldi's concertos expand on this pattern, producing what is now known as ***ritornello form***. This is less a formal mold than it is an approach, or set of guidelines, that allows a great deal of variety:

- Ritornellos for the full orchestra alternate with episodes for the soloist or soloists.
- The opening ritornello is composed of several small units, typically two to four measures in length, some of which may be repeated or varied. These segments can be separated from each other or combined in new ways without losing their identity as the ritornello.
- Later statements of the ritornello are usually partial, comprising only one or some of the units, sometimes varied.
- The ritornellos are guideposts to the tonal structure of the music, confirming the keys to which the music modulates. The first and last statements are in the tonic; at least one (usually the first to be in a new key) is in the dominant; and others may be in closely related keys.
- The solo episodes feature virtuosic, idiomatic playing, sometimes repeating or varying elements from the ritornello, but often presenting scales, arpeggiations, or other figuration. Many episodes modulate to a new key, which is then confirmed by the following ritornello. Sometimes the soloist interrupts or plays some part of the closing ritornello.

All these points are illustrated by the two fast movements in Vivaldi's Concerto for Violin and Orchestra in A Minor, Op. 3, No. 6 (NAWM 98), whose forms are diagrammed in Figure 18.5 (see p. 412). Example 18.1 shows the opening ritornello of the first movement. Each of the segments, denoted in the example by letter, has a strikingly individual character that makes it easy

EXAMPLE 18.1 *Antonio Vivaldi, Concerto in A Minor, Op. 3, No. 6, first movement, opening ritornello*

to remember. Each is a separate harmonic unit, enabling Vivaldi to separate and recombine the segments later on. In both movements, later statements of the ritornello are only partial, and some vary motives from the original ritornello, as do some of the solo episodes. One ritornello in the finale even changes keys, which in most movements only happens during episodes. New figurations are introduced in the episodes, as shown in Example 18.2, providing even more variety within a clearly understood structure. These solo passages often exploit the open strings of the violin (tuned g–d'–a'–e'') to facilitate rapid passagework, as in Examples 18.2a and d, or impressive leaps, as in Example 18.2c, where the bottom note in each downward leap is played

FIRST MOVEMENT

SECTION	RIT	EPI	RIT	EPI	RIT	EPI	RIT	EPI	RIT	EPI	RIT
Motives	ABCC′	A, A′	A″	new, A′	ABA‴	new	A	new	C′	B′	CC′
Key	a	mod	a	mod	e	mod	a	mod	a	a	a
Measure	1	13	21	24	35	45	58	60	68	71	75

THIRD MOVEMENT

SECTION	RIT	EPI	RIT	EPI	RIT	EPI	RIT	EPI	RIT (w/ solos)	EPI	CADENCE
Motives	ABABCDEF	AB′, new	AA	C′	DEF′	F′, new	AAC′F′AAC	new	ABC′DEF″	new	end of F″
Key	a	mod to C	e	e	a	mod to C	C, e, a	a	a	a	a
Measure	1	30	50	55	62	71	91	109	115	138	143

FIGURE 18.5 *Ritornello forms in Vivaldi's Concerto in A Minor, Op. 3, No. 6.*

EXAMPLE 18.2 *Examples of figuration in solo episodes in the first movement*

on an open string. Typical of Vivaldi, the alternation between tutti and solo does not stop when the music returns to the tonic near the end of the movement; in the first movement, further episodes appear between successive units of the ritornello, and in the finale, the orchestra and soloist alternate in presenting segments of the final ritornello.

The result in each case is a movement unique in form, yet the overall strategy is clearly the same. Far from following a textbook plan, Vivaldi's ritornello structures show almost infinite variety in form and content.

Slow movements   Vivaldi was the first concerto composer to make the slow movement as important as the fast ones. His slow movement is typically a long-breathed, expressive, cantabile melody, like an adagio operatic aria or arioso, to whose already rich figuration the performer was expected to add embellishments. Some slow movements are through-composed, and others use a simplified ritornello or two-part form. The slow movement in Op. 3, No. 6 (NAWM 98b) is unusual in that the bass instruments and continuo are silent, and the soloist is accompanied only by the upper strings playing sustained tones.

Vivaldi once claimed he could compose a concerto faster than a copyist could write out the score and parts. One reason he could compose rapidly was that ritornello form allowed him to spin out relatively long movements from a small amount of material that he repeated, transposed, varied, and recombined. In both fast and slow movements, he frequently used sequences, generating several measures from a short motive while dramatizing a strong chord progression, as in the second segment (B) of Example 18.1, built on a progression around the circle of fifths.

Economy and variety

Despite his reliance on formulas, what is most striking about Vivaldi's concertos is their variety and range of expression. His works were known for their spontaneous flow of musical ideas; clear formal structures; assured harmonies; varied textures; and forceful rhythms. He established a dramatic tension between solo and tutti, not only giving the soloist contrasting figuration, as Torelli had already done, but also letting the soloist stand out as a musical personality.

Vivaldi composed many of his concertos for the Pietà, where they served as the ideal combination of two roles: as exciting concert music to engage listeners and as teaching pieces for his students, with flashy soloistic work to challenge the best players, rapid orchestral passages to develop control, and less difficult inner parts, all perfectly crafted to cultivate the playing style of the time (see In Performance: Performing Vivaldi, p. 414). But he also wrote on commission and earned money from publications. Through distribution in printed collections and in manuscript copies, Vivaldi's concertos became tremendously popular across Europe, heard at private and public concerts and played by amateurs for their own pleasure. Nine collections of his concertos (Opp. 3–4 and Opp. 6–12) were published in Amsterdam, the last seven apparently printed at the publisher's expense instead of being subsidized by the composer or a patron as was common; this shows Vivaldi's value to his publisher and reflects the immense popularity of his concertos, especially in northern Europe. Several of these collections were given fanciful titles, in part to attract buyers: Op. 3, *L'estro armonico* (Harmonic Inspiration, 1711); Op. 4, *La stravaganza* (Extravagance, 1716); Op. 8, *Il cimento dell'armonia e dell'inventione* (The Test of Harmony and Invention, 1725); and Op. 9, *La cetra* (The Kithara, 1727), evoking ancient Greece. Some individual concertos were also given titles and even programs. Most famous are the first four concertos in Op. 8, known as *The Four Seasons*. Each of these is accompanied by a sonnet, perhaps written by Vivaldi himself, that describes the season, and the concertos cleverly depict the images in the poetry, taking advantage of the variety possible in ritornello forms.

Publications, titles, and programs

VIVALDI'S POSITION AND INFLUENCE Vivaldi's music reflects the stylistic changes of the first half of the eighteenth century. At the conservative

Range of styles

IN PERFORMANCE

Performing Vivaldi

Although they can be (and often are) played on modern instruments, Vivaldi's concertos were ideally suited to the instruments, bows, and playing style of the time. String instruments were strung with gut strings, which give a more mellow and less penetrating sound than modern wire strings. As shown in Figure 18.6, the Baroque bow was somewhat shorter than bows of today and curved slightly away from the bowhairs instead of toward them, producing less tension on the hairs that touch the strings. As a result the Baroque bow was quick to respond, producing a less forceful sound but allowing greater agility.

Using such a bow, the solo and orchestral string players of Vivaldi's time could cleanly articulate each note with a separate bowstroke without taking the hair off the string, because the lesser tension on the bowhairs let the string sound soften and stop momentarily each time the bow changed directions. This nonlegato style of playing allows a light and clear sound and a variety of instrumental color that can be emulated by today's performers, whether using modern instruments and bows or reconstructions of historical ones. In addition, performers of the time emphasized the downbeat and other strong beats of each measure, keeping the meter clear and the momentum driving forward. The

passages in Examples 18.1 and 18.2c sparkle with brilliance when played with such clear articulation; a modern legato style of playing with more equal emphasis on each note is heavy and unvaried by contrast.

The slurs in Example 18.2a, b, and d indicate that the notes under each slur are to be played in a single stroke of the bow. Using that more legato playing style groups the notes into a single gesture, and the Baroque bow gives groups played with a downbow a rounding decrescendo. The result can be energetic in fast passages like these, as each group bounces off the higher notes played on the main beats, yet supremely lyrical in slow movements.

Another difference in performance style is that vibrato was used only as an ornament in the eighteenth century, and most tones were played without vibrato. Modern string performers tend to play with constant vibrato, which took hold in the 1930s at least in part because it sounded better on recordings of that era.

While Vivaldi's concertos can be convincingly performed on modern instruments, it is no surprise that they sound especially fresh, dynamic, and compelling when played on the instruments he knew, with the bows he used and the playing style he taught.

CHRIS STOCK/LEBRECHT

FIGURE 18.6 *Comparison of a late-seventeenth Baroque violin bow (top) and a modern bow (bottom), based on a design by François Tourte from ca. 1785. The curve of the Baroque bow results in less tension on the bowhairs, and the shorter length makes it lighter and more agile. The modern bow shown here, modeled after Dominique Peccatte from the mid-nineteenth century, allows the performer a combination of flexibility and strength, suitable for a wide range of stylistic responses.*

extreme are his trio and solo sonatas, which emulate the style of Corelli, and his cantatas and serenatas, which resemble those of Scarlatti. Most of his concertos were part of the stylistic mainstream, responding to and often creating contemporary trends. His operas reflected the conventions and trends of his time, but their rhythmic vitality, thematic invention, and individual style gave them wide appeal, earning him commissions from Rome to Prague. His sacred music was influenced by current operatic styles and by his concertos; his *Beatus vir* for chorus and orchestra is in ritornello form with vocal soloists in the episodes, and his Gloria in D features several movements whose instrumental ritornellos sound like those of a concerto, interspersed with standard arias and choral fugues. At the progressive extreme are the solo concerto finales, the orchestral concertos, and most of the sixteen sinfonias—works that establish Vivaldi as a founder of the Classic symphony (see Chapter 22).

Vivaldi's influence on instrumental music equaled that of Corelli a generation earlier. His codification of ritornello form provided a model for later concerto composers. His successors admired and emulated his concise themes, clarity of form, rhythmic drive, and logical flow of musical ideas. Among those who learned from Vivaldi was J. S. Bach, who made keyboard arrangements of at least nine Vivaldi concertos, including five from Op. 3. Later in the eighteenth century, concerto composers adopted and developed Vivaldi's dramatic conception of the soloist's role as an individual personality in dialogue with the orchestra.

MUSIC IN FRANCE

While Italy had many cultural centers, France had only one: Paris, the capital and by far the largest city. Musicians in the provinces dreamed of careers in Paris, where patrons, publishers, and an eager public waited to hear and see the latest music. Only there could a composer achieve true success and a national reputation. The Académie Royale licensed theaters in several provincial cities to perform operas that had already been staged in the capital, but only in Paris could new operas be premiered. In addition to the main opera theater, the royally supported Opéra, Paris also had the Comédie-Française and Comédie-Italienne, both subsidized by the king, and the private Opéra-Comique, which presented plays with spoken dialogue interspersed with songs based on popular tunes. Although other cities had concert series in which amateurs could perform, Paris was home to the most prestigious concert organizations like the Concert Spirituel, a public concert series founded in 1725. The royal court of Louis XV (r. 1715–74) continued to support musicians but no longer dominated musical life as had the court of his great-grandfather Louis XIV. In its place a wider range of patrons and institutions supported musicians and composers.

RECONCILING FRENCH AND ITALIAN STYLE Since the seventeenth century, Italian music in France had been viewed as a foreign influence, welcomed by some and resisted by others. The latest Italian music could be heard in Paris, particularly the sonatas

FIGURE 18.7 *François Couperin around 1695, by an unknown French painter.*

and concertos of Corelli, Vivaldi, and others, and the relative merits of French and Italian styles were discussed constantly in salons and in print. Many French composers sought to blend the two musical styles, especially in genres pioneered in Italy. Louis Nicolas Clérambault (1676–1749), who published five books of cantatas between 1710 and 1726, alternated recitatives in the manner of Lully with Italianate arias. Jean-Marie Leclair (1697–1764), the principal French composer of violin sonatas, combined what he considered the classic purity of Corelli with French grace and sweetness of melody, perfect clarity of texture and form, and tasteful decoration.

FRANÇOIS COUPERIN Among the most active proponents of blending French and Italian tastes was François Couperin (1668–1733), shown in Figure 18.7. His career reflects the growing diffusion of patronage in France: he was organist to the king and at the church of St. Gervais in Paris, but earned much of his money teaching harpsichord to members of the aristocracy and publishing his own music. His output reflected the venues for which he composed: organ music for St. Gervais, convents, and other churches; elaborate motets for the royal chapel; chamber music for the gatherings in Paris salons that became fashionable during the reign of Louis XV; and harpsichord music for his students and for publication. His book *L'art de toucher le clavecin* (The Art of Playing the Harpsichord, 1716), a guide he wrote for his students, is one of the most important sources for performance practice of the French Baroque.

Chamber music   Couperin synthesized French with Italian styles. Through the titles, prefaces, and choice of contents for his published collections of chamber music, he proclaimed that the perfect music would be a union of the two national styles. He admired the music of both Lully and Corelli, and celebrated them in suites for two violins and harpsichord: *Parnassus, or The Apotheosis of Corelli* (1724) and *The Apotheosis of Lully* (1725). In the second work, Lully is represented as joining Corelli on Mt. Parnassus to perform a French overture and then a trio sonata. Couperin was the first and most important French composer of trio sonatas, beginning in 1692. His collection *Les nations* (The Nations, 1726) contains four *ordres*, each consisting of a sonata da chiesa in several movements followed by a suite of dances, thus combining the most characteristic genres of Italy and France in a single set. Within each ordre, he combined French and Italian style traits, for example using French agréments to ornament passages based on the sequences, walking basses, and circle-of-fifth harmonic progressions typical of Corelli sonatas. He also wrote twelve suites he called *concerts* for harpsichord and various combinations of instruments, each consisting of a prelude and several dance movements. He titled the first four *Concerts royaux* (Royal Concerts, published 1722), because they were played before Louis XIV. Couperin published the last eight in a collection titled *Les goûts-réünis* (The Reunited Tastes, 1724), signifying that they joined French and Italian styles.

Harpsichord suites   Couperin collected his harpsichord pieces in twenty-seven suites, or ordres, published in four books between 1713 and 1730. Each ordre was a

EXAMPLE 18.3 *Excerpts from François Couperin,* Vingt-cinquième ordre

a. La visionaire

b. Les ombres errantes

loose grouping of pieces intended as recreation for amateur performers. Most works were in dance meters and binary form, but as in earlier suites Couperin extended and elaborated the basic characteristics of each dance to create music that challenged players and engaged listeners.

By now there was a long tradition, stretching back to the Renaissance, of music for solo keyboard incorporating the familiar rhythms of dance music, bringing its associations with physical gestures and social interaction into the solitary activity of playing music for one's own pleasure. What is new in Couperin's harpsichord pieces is that many of them are *pièces de caractère,* or **character pieces**, works with evocative titles that are depicted in the music, often suggesting a mood, scene, or personality, like a character in a play. The fashion for character pieces, which Couperin helped to establish in the early eighteenth century, built on the tradition of fanciful titles attached to works in the previous generation, such as Denis Gaultier's *La coquette virtuose* (NAWM 88), but in a character piece the music explicitly illustrates the title.

Character pieces

Couperin's *Vingt-cinquième ordre* (Twenty-Fifth Order, 1730), for example, opens with *La visionaire* (The Visionary, or The Seer; NAWM 99a), a piece in the form and style of a French overture in which the dotted rhythms in the slow first section and the end of the second section are combined with *tirades* (fast scale figures), as in Example 18.3a. In French operas such as Lully's *Armide,* the combination of French overture style with tirades was associated with powerful or supernatural characters (see NAWM 85c), and these and other aspects of the music suggest a whimsical image of a mystic visionary or seer. Reflecting Couperin's interest in blending the French and Italian styles, this movement combines elements from Lully with the sequences, seventh chords, and driving harmonic progressions typical of Corelli. The fourth piece in the suite, *La muse victorieuse* (The Victorious Muse; NAWM 99b), uses triple meter, a quick tempo, leaping figures, and changes of register to depict the victory dance of a muse—perhaps the amateur player herself, conquering the music's technical challenges. The final piece, *Les ombres errantes* (The Errant Shades, or The Lost Souls; NAWM 99c), captures the title image through a languid tempo, descending lines, sighing figures, plangent dissonances, and chromaticism. As shown in Example 18.3b, Couperin tweaks the

Vingt-cinquième ordre

style brisé of an earlier generation into a more linear counterpoint, sustaining the first note of his eighth-note figures to create three voices (with the outer voices in imitation in measures 6–7), and then sustaining the offbeat eighth notes to create a syncopated inner voice in a four-voice texture suffused with suspensions typical of Corelli. Here again Couperin combines French and Italian elements, exemplifying his mixed style as well as the new genre of the character piece.

JEAN-PHILIPPE RAMEAU

Jean-Philippe Rameau (1683–1764) had an unusual career, spending two decades as an organist in the provinces, then moving to Paris, winning recognition as a music theorist around the age of forty, and achieving fame as a composer only in his fifties (see biography and Figure 18.8). Attacked then as a radical, he was assailed twenty years later as a reactionary. His writings founded the theory of tonal music, and his operas established him as Lully's most important successor.

THEORY OF HARMONY Music theory engaged Rameau throughout his life. Inspired by works of Descartes and Newton, Rameau approached music as a source of empirical data that could be explained on rational principles. He described his methodology in *Traité de l'harmonie* (Treatise on Harmony, 1722), one of the most influential theoretical works ever written.

Acoustics and chords   Rameau's debt to Descartes can be seen in his search to ground the practice of harmony in the laws of acoustics. He considered the triad and seventh chord the primal elements of music, and derived both from the natural consonances of the perfect fifth, major third, and minor third.

The fundamental bass   In Rameau's approach, each chord has a fundamental tone, equivalent in most cases to what is today called its root (the lowest note when the chord is arranged as a series of thirds). In a series of chords, the succession of these fundamental tones is the *fundamental bass*. In modern terms, Rameau was asserting that a chord keeps its identity through all its inversions and that the harmony of a passage is defined by the root progression rather than by the actual lowest note sounding. These concepts, now staples of music theory, were revolutionary at the time. Example 18.4 shows the fundamental bass for a passage from Rameau's opera *Hippolyte et Aricie* of 1733 (NAWM 100).

Tonal direction   For Rameau, music was driven forward by dissonance and came to rest in consonance. Seventh chords provided dissonance, triads consonance. He coined the terms **tonic** (the main note and chord in a key), **dominant** (the note and chord a perfect fifth above the tonic), and **subdominant** (the note and chord a fifth below the tonic); established those three chords as the pillars of tonality; and related other chords to them, formulating the hierarchies of functional tonality. The strongest progression between two chords in his system is from a seventh chord on the dominant to a triad on the tonic, with the dissonant notes resolving by step and the fundamental bass falling a fifth (or rising a fourth). Other falling-fifth progressions are almost as strong, and indeed motion by falling fifth is more common than any other. Through such progressions, the fundamental bass gives music coherence and direction and helps to define the key. Note in Example 18.4 that all but two of the motions in the fundamental bass are by falling fifth

JEAN-PHILIPPE RAMEAU

(1683–1764)

Practically unknown before the age of forty, Rameau emerged late in life as the most significant music theorist of his era and the leading composer in France. In his fifties and sixties, he wrote the operas and ballets that made him famous.

Rameau was born in Dijon, in Burgundy (east central France), the seventh of eleven children. From his father, an organist, Rameau received his first and, as far as we know, only formal musical instruction. He attended a Jesuit school, then visited Italy briefly as a teenager.

After two decades holding positions as organist at Clermont, Paris, Dijon, and Lyons, he moved permanently to Paris in 1722, seeking better opportunities. His pathbreaking *Traité de l'harmonie* (Treatise on Harmony), published that year, quickly won him renown as a theorist. He made a living teaching harmony and playing continuo but could not find another position as organist until 1732. In 1726, aged forty-two, he married a nineteen-year-old singer and harpsichordist, Marie-Louise Mangot, and over the next two decades they had four children.

Success as a composer came gradually and late. He published some cantatas and two books of harpsichord pieces in the 1720s. He found patrons who helped to support him, including the Prince of Carignan. His first opera, *Hippolyte et Aricie* (1733), began to build his reputation as a composer, followed by four other operas and opera-ballets in the next six years. In the mid-1730s, he won the patronage of the rich tax collector Alexandre-Jean-Joseph Le Riche de la Pouplinière, whose gatherings attracted aristocrats, artists, literary figures (Voltaire and Jean-Jacques Rousseau), adventurers (Casanova), and musicians. Rameau served his patron as organist and in various capacities until 1753, and members of La Pouplinière's

FIGURE 18.8 *Jean-Philippe Rameau in about 1725. Portrait by Jacques André Joseph Aved.*

circle became enthusiastic backers of Rameau. In 1745, the king of France granted Rameau an annual pension. The next few years were his most productive and successful, with eleven dramatic works by 1749. Given his late start at the age of fifty, it is remarkable that over twenty-five of his ballets and operas were staged, more than by any other French composer of the eighteenth century.

Polemical writings and theoretical essays occupied Rameau's closing years. He died in Paris in 1764, at the age of eighty-one. Feisty to the end, he found strength even on his deathbed to reproach the priest administering the last rites for bad chanting.

MAJOR WORKS 5 tragédies en musique (*Hippolyte et Aricie, Castor et Pollux, Dardanus, Zoroastre*, and *Les Boréades*), 6 other operas, *Les Indes galantes* and 6 other opera-ballets, 7 ballets, harpsichord pieces, trio sonatas, cantatas, and motets

(marked by brackets), helping to establish the local tonics of C minor and Bb major, and that seventh chords keep the music moving forward until the cadence is reached. Rameau recognized that a piece could change key, a process called **modulation**, but considered that each piece had one principal tonic to which other keys were secondary.

EXAMPLE 18.4 *Jean-Philippe Rameau, recitative from* Hippolyte et Aricie, *with fundamental bass*

Ah! if you are fair-minded, do not thunder any more at me! The glory of a hero whom injustice oppresses demands your rightful aid.

Rameau's impact   Rameau's theories have become commonplaces learned by every music student, so it takes an exercise of historical imagination to grasp how important they were at the time. Most of the elements had been described by earlier theorists, but Rameau was the first to bring them together into a unified system. Living at a time when the notion of universal laws of nature was fashionable, Rameau found in the music of some of his contemporaries—Corelli foremost among them—harmonic practices that could be described according to universal laws. Other writers popularized his ideas, and by the late eighteenth century his approach was the primary paradigm for teaching musicians.

INSTRUMENTAL WORKS As a composer, Rameau first made his mark with three published collections of harpsichord pieces (published 1706, 1724, and ca. 1729–30). The first contains a single suite of dances, and each of the others has two suites, one mostly containing dance movements and the other almost entirely character pieces. Among the latter are evocations of mood, nature, and the theater, such as *Les soupirs* (The Sighs), *La poule* (The Hen), and *Les sauvages* (The Savages), the last inspired by dances of Louisiana Indians that Rameau had seen in Paris. As he noted in the preface of his second collection, Rameau's harpsichord pieces feature virtuosic scales and figuration rarely if ever found in earlier French keyboard pieces. These brilliant textures, along with the harmonic adventures of such pieces as *L'enharmonique* (Enharmonic Progressions), distinguished his keyboard music from his predecessors'.

Also distinctive is his last collection, *Pièces de clavecin en concerts* (Concerted Harpsichord Pieces, 1741), a set of five suites for harpsichord accompanied by violin (or flute) and bass viol (or second violin). Unlike a trio sonata, here the harpsichord has the leading part, with the other instruments at times in dialogue with it and at times accompanying.

STAGE WORKS Although his keyboard music was widely circulated and influential, and he also composed some sacred and secular vocal music, Rameau attained his greatest fame as a composer of stage works. From a young age he aspired to compose opera, but the monopoly of the Académie Royale de Musique made it almost impossible to produce new operas except in Paris. When he moved there in 1722, he wrote airs and dances for a few musical comedies, pieces with spoken dialogue performed at the Opéra-Comique. Finally, in 1733, his opera *Hippolyte et Aricie* was produced in Paris, establishing his reputation as a composer. A string of successes followed, including the opera-ballet *Les Indes galantes* (The Gallant Indies, 1735) and the opera *Castor et Pollux* (1737), often considered his masterpiece. After a relatively fallow period in the early 1740s came his most productive years, from the comedy *Platée* (1745) to the tragic operas *Zoroastre* (1749), the most important of Rameau's later works, and *Les Boréades* (The Boreades, 1763), rehearsed when Rameau was eighty but not performed in his lifetime.

Comparison with Lully

Rameau's theater works resemble Lully's in several ways: both composers exhibit realistic declamation and precise rhythmic notation in the recitatives; both mix recitative with more tuneful, formally organized airs, choruses, and instrumental interludes; and both include long divertissements. But within this general framework, Rameau introduced many changes.

Melodic and harmonic style

The melodic lines offer one notable contrast. Rameau the composer constantly practiced the doctrine of Rameau the theorist that all melody is rooted in harmony. Many of his melodic phrases are plainly triadic and make clear the harmonic progressions that must support them. Orderly relationships within the tonal system of dominants, subdominants, and modulations govern the harmony. Rameau drew from a rich palette of chords and progressions, including chromatic ones, diversifying his style much more than Lully's and achieving dramatic force through expressive, highly charged dissonances that propel the harmony forward.

Instrumental music

Rameau made his most original contribution in the instrumental sections of his operas—overtures, dances, and descriptive symphonies that accompany the stage action. The French valued music for its powers of depiction, and Rameau was their champion tone painter. His musical pictures range from graceful miniatures to broad representations of thunder (*Hippolyte et Aricie,* Act I) or earthquake (*Les Indes galantes,* Act II). The depiction is often enhanced by novel orchestration, especially independent woodwind parts.

Airs and choruses

Like Lully and other French composers, Rameau made less of a contrast between recitative and air than did Italian composers. He often smoothly moved between styles to suit the dramatic situation. Often the most powerful effects are achieved by the joint use of solo and chorus. Choruses remained prominent in French opera long after they were no longer used in Italy, and they were numerous throughout Rameau's works.

Combination of elements

The closing minutes of Act IV of *Hippolyte et Aricie* (NAWM 100) illustrate the high drama Rameau could achieve by combining all these elements. In this scene complex, the action and music are nonstop: one type of musical setting leads to another, echoing the line of the plot and creating a sense of realism or naturalness as in life, not as in the conventions of Italian opera. A divertissement of hunters and huntresses is suddenly followed by tragedy, so fast that the audience has little time to adjust. Throbbing strings depict a rough sea, while rushing scales in the flute and violins evoke high winds. A monster appears, and the chorus begs for aid from the goddess Diana, singing over the orchestra. Hippolyte steps up to fight the monster, as his beloved Aricie trembles in fear; they too sing over the orchestra, in a texture of accompanied recitative borrowed from contemporary Italian opera. The monster breathes flame and smoke, then disappears, and the orchestra stops abruptly. When the smoke clears, Aricie mournfully sees that Hippolyte is gone, and the chorus comments on the tragedy in stirring, richly dissonant homophony. The rapid juxtaposition of styles continues as Phèdre, Hippolyte's stepmother, enters, hears the news from the chorus, and laments his death, for which she feels responsible. Although no full-breathed air appears—indeed, one would be inappropriate—short segments of air-like melody are intermixed with measured and unmeasured recitative, with and without the orchestra, over varying styles of accompaniment, each element perfectly placed for maximum dramatic effect.

Lullistes versus Ramistes

From the first, Rameau's operas stirred up a storm of critical controversy. The Paris intelligentsia divided into two noisy camps, one supporting Rameau and the other attacking him as a subverter of the good old French opera tradition of Lully. The Lullistes found Rameau's music difficult, forced, grotesque, thick, mechanical, and unnatural—in a word, baroque—because of its complex and dissonant harmony, dense orchestration, and demanding writing for instruments, all of which they felt violated their preference for the simple and natural. Rameau protested, in a foreword to his opera-ballet *Les Indes galantes,* that he had "sought to imitate Lully, not as a servile copyist but in taking, like him, nature herself—so beautiful and so simple—as a model." As the quarrel of the Lullistes and Ramistes raged, Rameau's increasing popularity sparked many parodies of his operas—light-handed imitations or adaptations of the originals. Eventually his newer style became widely accepted, and critics and the public acknowledged that it took time to get to know his music and appreciate it; this was an interesting lesson for an audience to learn in the early eighteenth century, when immediate appeal was so highly valued. By the

1750s, during the battle between critics on the relative merits of French and Italian music known as the *Querelle des bouffons* (Quarrel of the Comic Actors; see Chapter 21), Rameau had become the most eminent living French composer, exalted as the champion of French music by the very faction that twenty years earlier had castigated him for not writing like Lully.

A VOLATILE PUBLIC

With the spread of public opera houses and public concerts, audiences in the eighteenth century were opinionated as never before, expressing their views of operas and concert works through ticket sales, diary entries, letters, and the new medium of newspapers and journals as well as through applause or other immediate reactions. Changes in musical fashion, taste, and style flowed from the opinions and reactions of critics and the public, from the vogue for Vivaldi's concertos to the new approaches to opera and instrumental music throughout the century.

By the time Vivaldi died in 1741, tastes had begun to change, the public turned elsewhere, and his music passed from the scene. In the later eighteenth century, he was virtually forgotten. But his influence on Bach was noted by nineteenth-century scholars, and his importance in the evolution of the concerto was demonstrated in the early twentieth century. Interest in Vivaldi's music, especially his concertos, was intensified by the discovery in the 1920s of what must have been Vivaldi's own collection of scores. The prominent Italian publishing house Ricordi began publishing his complete instrumental music in 1947, motivated in part by a desire to reclaim the glorious Italian Baroque tradition that had been obscured by later German composers. Vivaldi is now considered a master composer alongside Bach and Handel, and a central figure in our image of music from the Baroque period. His concertos seem almost inescapable, from concerts to recordings to film and advertising scores to the training of young string players. His operas and other music are beginning to be revived, although they are still seldom heard.

Couperin's harpsichord music was well known in his lifetime, in England and Germany as well as in France, then slowly fell out of fashion. Rameau died famous, with several of his operas still in the repertory, but tastes changed in the 1770s and his operas gradually passed from the stage. His harpsichord music remained in circulation and was widely performed over the next several generations. In the late nineteenth and early twentieth centuries, Couperin and Rameau's works, especially for keyboard, were edited and revived as exemplars of French music that could rival the music of the German composers Bach and Handel. A complete edition of Rameau's music was issued between 1895 and 1924, followed by Couperin's complete works in 1932–33. Their music is less omnipresent than Vivaldi's but has found a secure and enthusiastic band of devotees, especially in France. Meanwhile, Rameau's reputation as a theorist never waned, and his approach became the foundation for most writings on and teaching of music theory from his day to the present.

Further Reading is available at digital.wwnorton.com/hwm10

GERMAN COMPOSERS OF THE LATE BAROQUE

In the eighteenth century, for the first time in history, the leading composers in Europe came from German-speaking lands. Telemann, Handel, members of the Bach family, Haydn, and Mozart all rose to prominence not by inventing new genres, as the Italians had done in the previous two centuries, but by synthesizing elements from Italian, French, German, and other national traditions in new, rich ways. The German secret was a balance of tastes between native trends and foreign influences. The Italians and the French generally resisted foreign ideas, and no composer in either country matched the international reputation of Vivaldi or Rameau until the nineteenth century. England became a virtual colony for foreign musicians, and it remained so until the twentieth century. But German and Austrian composers consistently sought wide appeal by combining the best traits of several nations.

This chapter will focus on J. S. Bach and Handel, the best-known German-speaking composers of the early eighteenth century. Using them as case studies to explore conditions for music in Germany and England, we will examine how each found patronage from a variety of sources; made choices among competing tastes, values, and styles in music; and met with both success and failure.

CONTEXTS FOR MUSIC

In the eighteenth century, German-speaking central Europe continued to be divided among hundreds of political entities, from the large states of Austria, Saxony, and Brandenburg-Prussia to tiny principalities and independent cities. Each of these supported music. Some rulers followed Louis XIV's example of displaying their power and wealth through patronage of the arts, as did the Holy Roman emperors in Vienna, the electors of Saxony in Dresden, and King Frederick the Great of Prussia in Berlin. City governments were also significant employers of musicians, especially in Lutheran areas, where the town council was often responsible for hiring music directors for the churches.

One interesting phenomenon in eighteenth-century Germany is the number of aristocrats who pursued music avidly as performers and as composers. Johann Ernst, prince of Weimar (1696–1715), was a violinist who composed instrumental works, of which six concertos were published. Frederick the Great, shown in Figure 19.1, regularly performed flute sonatas and concertos at private concerts in his chambers and composed flute concertos, arias, and other music. His sister Anna Amalia, princess of Prussia (1723–1787), played harpsichord and organ, composed vocal and instrumental music, and collected a large library of scores. Her niece Anna Amalia, duchess of Saxe-Weimar (1739–1807), was a keyboard player, composer, and important patron of music and literature. Her major works are two Singspiels (spoken plays with music) with librettos by Johann Wolfgang von Goethe (1749–1832), the leading German poet, novelist, and dramatist of his age. Many other aristocrats were enthusiastic amateur performers, and they often made particularly generous patrons.

Aristocratic musicians

Britain was a unified kingdom, but since the revolutions in the seventeenth century the power and wealth of the monarch were quite limited. At times even the relatively low salaries of the court musicians went unpaid. In order to keep musicians in service, the king had to allow them to earn extra money outside official duties. The presence of highly skilled, underpaid, and underutilized performers in London led to the growth of the public concert. The nobility also supported music. Many noblemen had visited Italy as young men to learn its language, arts, and culture. On their return to England, they emulated Italian aristocrats in employing household musicians and helping to fund Italian opera.

English patrons

Musicians supplemented their salaried appointments through public concerts, an increasingly important part of musical life in Germany as well as

Concerts and publishing

NATIONALGALERIE, STAATLICHE MUSEEN, BERLIN, GERMANY. PHOTO: B.P.K./ART RESOURCE, NY

FIGURE 19.1 *King Frederick II (the Great) of Prussia performing as flute soloist in a concerto, accompanied by a small orchestra, with Carl Philipp Emanuel Bach at the harpsichord. Painting by Adolph von Menzel, 1852.*

in England, and through the sale of their compositions to publishers. Earnings from publishing were still quite limited; the system of paying royalties on sales had not yet developed, so a composer would simply receive a set fee from a publisher for all rights to a score. Moreover, copyright laws were weak, and publishers often copied and issued pieces without paying the composer. Under these circumstances, no one could earn a living by composing alone. Indeed, there was as yet no notion of "composer" as a separate career; all those who composed music professionally did so as musicians who also performed, copied, supervised, and directed their own music and that of others. It is only because their compositions survived, while their performances were ephemeral, that we remember them primarily as composers.

MIXED TASTE: GEORG PHILIPP TELEMANN For centuries, Germans had been interested in music from other nations: Flemish polyphony; Dutch and English keyboard music; Italian madrigals, operas, and concertos; and French operas, orchestral suites, and harpsichord and lute music. German musicians were often trained in more than one style. Composers studied music from other countries when they could and imported foreign genres, styles, and techniques. This diverse background allowed German composers great flexibility to draw elements from various traditions and adapt or blend them to suit any purpose or audience. More than any other trait, this synthesis of traditions gave the music of eighteenth-century German composers its broad appeal.

A paragon of this stylistic eclecticism was Georg Philipp Telemann (1681–1767), shown in Figure 19.2, regarded by his contemporaries as one of the best composers of his era. He was also the most prolific, with over three thousand works to his credit. Writing in every genre, he produced thirty operas, forty-six Passions, over a thousand church cantatas, and hundreds of overtures, concertos, and chamber works. In 1729, he described his style as a mixture of many:

> What I have accomplished with respect to musical style is well known. First came the Polish style, followed by the French, church, chamber and operatic styles, and [finally] the Italian style, which currently occupies me more than the others do.

Almost every current style can be found in Telemann's music. He helped to establish the characteristic German style of his time, a synthesis of German counterpoint with traits from the other nations he mentions.

Among Telemann's most popular and original works are the twelve quartets for flute, violin, viola da gamba (or cello), and continuo, his so-called *Paris* Quartets, published in two sets of six pieces each (1730 and 1738). These quartets differ from trio-sonata scoring in that the viola da gamba part is largely independent from the continuo and plays a role as soloist alongside the flute and violin. Throughout, all three instruments share equally in the thematic material, often interchanging ideas. The first set exemplifies Telemann's mixed taste by including two Italian-style concertos, two sonatas in the German style, and two suites in the French style, and by mixing styles and genres within each work. The opening piece, titled *Concerto primo* (First Concerto; excerpts in NAWM 101), includes a Presto in ritornello form and a short slow movement in concerto style, but the work closes with an Allegro in gigue rhythm and French *rondeau* form. The Presto ritornello features three simultaneous melodies treated in invertible counterpoint, like the subjects of a triple fugue. The mixture of French and Italian forms, German counterpoint, and themes and figuration reminiscent of all three traditions is typical of the stylistic blending in music by Telemann and by most of his German contemporaries.

FIGURE 19.2 *Georg Philipp Telemann, in an engraving by Georg Lichtensteger.*

Telemann aimed to please varied tastes and write for the abilities of good amateur or middle-level professional players, giving his music wide appeal. He was his own publisher in Hamburg, helping to establish the principle that a piece of music was the intellectual property of its composer, and he issued the first music periodical in Germany, *Der getreue Music-Meister* (The True Music-Master, 1728–29), which made his music and that of other German composers available to amateurs and students. His works were published in Paris as well as in Germany, and bought by musicians from Italy to England and from Spain to Scandinavia. Telemann's preference for relative simplicity helped make him much more popular in his time than J. S. Bach, but he was then ignored and belittled in the nineteenth century. His music was gradually revived in the twentieth century, and he is slowly regaining his stature as one of the great composers of his age.

JOHANN SEBASTIAN BACH

Posterity has raised Johann Sebastian Bach (1685–1750) to the pinnacle of composers of all time in the Western tradition. His current position contrasts with his reputation in his own day, when he was renowned in Protestant Germany as an organ virtuoso, keyboard composer, and writer of learned contrapuntal works, but comparatively little of his vocal, chamber, or orchestral music was published or circulated in manuscript, in part because he focused on composing for professional performers. In the course of his career, Bach embraced all the major styles, forms, and genres of his time (except opera), blended them in new ways, and developed them further. The result is music of an unprecedented richness. Although some eighteenth-century listeners found his music cluttered or forced, and it was regarded as old-fashioned by the time he died, it was always esteemed by connoisseurs. The revival and publication of his works in the nineteenth century brought him legions of admirers, performers, and listeners, from the leading musicians of the day to the general public.

BACH AT WORK   Bach was a working musician who composed primarily to fulfill the needs of the positions he held (see biography and Figure 19.3). When he was a church organist at Arnstadt (1703–7) and Mühlhausen (1707–8) and

JOHANN SEBASTIAN BACH

(1685–1750)

Now considered one of the greatest composers in the Western music tradition, Bach regarded himself more modestly, as a conscientious craftsman doing his job to the best of his ability. He was a virtuoso organist and keyboard player, a skilled violinist, and a prolific composer in almost every genre then current except opera.

Bach came from a large family of musicians in the region of Thuringia in central Germany. Over six generations, from the late sixteenth to the nineteenth century, the Bach family produced an extraordinary number of good musicians and several outstanding ones. Johann Sebastian was born in Eisenach and attended the Latin school there, receiving a solid grounding in theology and humanistic studies. He must have learned violin from his father, a court and town musician who died just before Bach's tenth birthday. He then lived and studied music with his older brother Johann Christoph Bach, organist in Ohrdruf. Bach spent 1700–1702 in school at Lüneburg, where he encountered the organist Georg Böhm and experienced the French repertoire and style of the local orchestra.

Bach's first positions were as a church organist at Arnstadt in 1703, when he was eighteen, and then at Mühlhausen in 1707. That year he married Maria Barbara Bach, his second cousin, with whom he had seven children before her death in 1720. His second wife, Anna Magdalena Wilcke, a court singer from a family of musicians, whom he married a year later, bore him thirteen children (seven died in infancy). From his time at Mühlhausen to the end of his life, Bach tutored private students in performance and composition, including several of his own sons, and served as an organ consultant.

In 1708, Bach became a court musician for the duke of Weimar, first as organist and later as concertmaster. He was appointed Kapellmeister (music director) at the court of Prince Leopold of Anhalt in

FIGURE 19.3 *Johann Sebastian Bach in a portrait by Elias Gottlob Haussmann (a 1748 copy of a 1746 original). Shown in Bach's hand is the manuscript of his triple canon for six voices, BWV 1076.*

Cöthen in 1717. After a stay of six years, Bach moved to Leipzig to become cantor of St. Thomas's School and civic music director, one of the most prestigious positions in Germany.

After a lifetime of hard work, Bach's last two years were marked by disease (probably diabetes), vision problems, and severe eye pain. At his death after a stroke, he left a small estate, split between his nine surviving children and his wife, who died in poverty ten years later.

Bach's works are identified by their number in Wolfgang Schmieder's catalogue of his works, abbreviated BWV for Bach-Werke-Verzeichnis (Bach Works Catalogue).

MAJOR WORKS *St. Matthew Passion, St. John Passion*, Mass in B Minor, about 200 church cantatas and 20 secular cantatas, about 200 organ chorales and 70 other works for organ, *Brandenburg Concertos, The Well-Tempered Clavier, Clavier-Übung, Musical Offering, The Art of Fugue*, and numerous other keyboard, ensemble, orchestral, and sacred compositions

court organist at Weimar (1708–14), he composed mostly for organ. When he became concertmaster at Weimar (1714–17), he also wrote cantatas for the court chapel. As court music director at Cöthen (1717–23), where he had no formal church music duties, he turned out mostly solo or ensemble music for domestic or court entertainment, along with some pedagogical works. At Leipzig (1723–50), in charge of music at four churches, he produced cantatas and other church music. His appointment in 1729 as director of the Leipzig collegium musicum led him to write concertos and chamber works. Numerous pieces for organ or harpsichord also date from the Leipzig period, including teaching pieces for his many private students.

Oft-told anecdotes of Bach's life remind us that musicians were not free agents but were subject to the wishes of their employers. When Bach accepted the position at Cöthen, the duke of Weimar would not let him leave at first, and imprisoned him for a month before allowing him to go. As cantor of St. Thomas's School and director of music in Leipzig, Bach was an employee of the town council, and in his contract he had to pledge himself to lead an exemplary life and not to leave town without permission from the mayor. He was the council's third choice, after Telemann, who used the offer to leverage a raise from his bosses in Hamburg, and Christoph Graupner, whose employer in Darmstadt refused to accept his resignation but increased his pay. On many occasions, Bach clashed with the council about what he saw as the prerogatives of his office, sometimes defying their authority in a bid to preserve his independence.

The position of musicians

Bach's working conditions in Leipzig illustrate the multiple demands on musicians in an era when no one worked solely as a composer. Leipzig was a flourishing commercial city of about 30,000, a center for publishing, and home to Germany's leading university, founded in 1409. St. Thomas's School, shown in Figure 19.4, took in both day and boarding pupils. It provided between fifty and sixty scholarships for boys and youths chosen for their musical and scholastic abilities. In return, they sang or played in the services of the four main Leipzig churches and fulfilled other musical duties. Bach's position as cantor obliged him to teach Latin and music four hours each day and to compose, copy, and rehearse music for the church services. He directed the top choir and supervised the other three, conducted by older students who were his assistants. He trained some of the best students on instruments and directed them in the church instrumental ensemble, which also included performers from the town and university. In his early years, he composed at least one major work for church each week, then gradually lessened his pace. He had further duties providing music for town ceremonies and at the university, and he received additional fees to compose and lead music for weddings, funerals, and other special occasions. For all this he was paid a comfortable

Conditions in Leipzig

FIGURE 19.4 *St. Thomas's Church in Leipzig, where Bach regularly directed the music for services. At the far end of the square, past the fountain, is St. Thomas's School (after it was enlarged in 1732), where Bach taught.*

middle-class income and provided with an apartment for his family in one wing of the school, including a personal study for composing and for housing his professional library.

The craft of composition

Bach learned composition primarily by copying or arranging the music of other composers, a habit maintained throughout his career. Among his pieces are adaptations of music by Torelli, Vivaldi, Telemann, and numerous others. In this way he became familiar with the methods of the foremost composers in Italy, Germany, Austria, and France.

According to his son Carl Philipp Emanuel, Bach typically composed away from the keyboard, then tested the result by playing through it. The most important step was inventing the principal theme or subject, on which Bach then elaborated using established conventions of genre, form, and harmonic structure. When working with a text, as in a recitative or aria, he wrote the vocal melody first, fitting it to the accentuation and meaning of the words. Bach's manuscripts show that he continually sought to improve his music, making small revisions as he copied out a score or performing parts, and revising afresh when he performed a piece again. He also frequently reworked his own existing pieces for new forces, new uses, or new words; many of his cantata movements are adapted from earlier cantatas, instrumental works, or other music (see Figure 19.6, p. 436).

ORGAN MUSIC As a church organist, Bach focused on the genres used in Lutheran services: chorale settings, played before each chorale and sometimes used to accompany the congregation as they sang; and toccatas, fantasias, preludes, and fugues, featured as preludes or interludes during the service and suitable also for recitals. (See Source Reading, p. 435, for the place of "preluding" in a Lutheran service.) From a young age, Bach was acquainted with a wide variety of organ music, by North Germans like Buxtehude and Böhm, central and southern Germans such as Pachelbel and Froberger, Italians like Frescobaldi, and French organists. While working in Arnstadt, he traveled on foot and by postal coach to hear Buxtehude in Lübeck, a journey of about 225 miles. By blending and then transcending his models, he developed a personal and distinctive style, marked by prolific imagination, mastery of counterpoint, virtuosity, and extensive use of the pedals. He was renowned as an improviser and was often called upon to test new or rebuilt organs.

Preludes and fugues

Buxtehude had written freestanding fugues as well as preludes that alternated sections of free fantasia with fugues (see NAWM 97). By 1700, some composers were prefacing fugues with separate preludes (or toccatas or fantasias), a practice that became standard for Bach.

Vivaldi's influence

While at Weimar, Bach became fascinated by the music of Vivaldi. He arranged several Vivaldi concertos for organ or harpsichord solo, writing out the ornaments and occasionally reinforcing the counterpoint or adding inner voices. As a consequence, Bach's own style began to change. From Vivaldi he learned to write concise themes, to clarify the harmonic scheme, and to develop subjects into grandly proportioned formal structures based on the ritornello idea.

Vivaldi's influence is evident in Bach's preludes and fugues composed at Weimar, such as the Prelude and Fugue in A Minor, BWV 543 (NAWM 102). In the prelude, violinistic figuration resembling that of concerto solos, as

EXAMPLE 19.1 *Johann Sebastian Bach, Prelude and Fugue in A Minor, BWV 543, opening and fugue subject*

a. Opening of prelude

b. Fugue subject

in Example 19.1a, alternates with toccata sections. Contrasting textures, sequences, circle-of-fifth progressions, clear tonal structure, and returns of the opening material in new keys all recall Vivaldi's typical procedures. The fugue subject, shown in Example 19.1b, is again violinistic, featuring the rapid oscillation between a repeated note and a moving line that on a violin is accomplished by alternating strings. Typical of Bach fugues, the form closely resembles a concerto fast movement. The fugue subject functions like a ritornello, returning in related keys as well as the tonic. Between these statements are episodes that have the character of solo sections in a concerto, often marked by lighter texture, sequences, or a change of key.

Chorale settings

Bach wrote over two hundred chorale settings for organ, encompassing all known types in a constant search for variety. At Weimar, he compiled a manuscript collection, the *Orgelbüchlein* (Little Organ Book), containing forty-five short chorale preludes. These served in church as introductions before the congregation sang the chorale. But this book, like several of his other collections, also had a pedagogical aim. The title page reads "Little Organ Book, in which a beginning organist is given guidance in all sorts of ways of developing a chorale, as well as improving his pedal technique, since in these chorales the pedal is treated as completely obbligato [essential, not optional]." In each prelude, the chorale tune is heard once through, but otherwise the settings vary greatly. The melody may be treated in canon, elaborately ornamented, or accompanied in any number of styles. Some preludes symbolize the visual images or underlying ideas of the chorale text through musical figures, in a tradition extending back through Schütz to the Italian madrigalists. In *Durch Adams Fall* (Through Adam's Fall), BWV 637 (NAWM 103), shown in Example 19.2, while the top line carries the chorale tune, jagged descending leaps in the bass depict Adam's fall from grace, the twisting chromatic line in the alto portrays the sinuous writhing of the serpent, and the downward-sliding tenor combines with both to suggest the pull of temptation and the sorrow of sin.

Bach conceived his later organ chorales in grander proportions, replacing the vivid expressive details of the earlier works with more generalized emotion and extensive musical development of ideas.

EXAMPLE 19.2 *Bach, chorale prelude on* Durch Adams Fall

HARPSICHORD MUSIC Bach's music for harpsichord includes masterpieces in every current genre, including suites; preludes, fantasias, and toccatas; fugues; and variation sets.

Suites Bach's harpsichord suites show the influence of French, Italian, and German models. He wrote three sets of six: the *English Suites,* the *French Suites,* and the Partitas. The designations "French" and "English" for the suites are not Bach's own, and both collections blend French and Italian qualities in a highly personal style. In line with German tradition, each suite contains the standard four dance movements—allemande, courante, sarabande, and gigue—with additional short movements following the sarabande. Each of the *English Suites* opens with a prelude, in which Bach transferred Italian ensemble idioms to the keyboard. The prelude of the third *English Suite,* for example, simulates a concerto fast movement with alternating tutti and solo.

The Well-Tempered Clavier Bach's best-known keyboard works are the two books titled *The Well-Tempered Clavier* (1722 and ca. 1740). Each book consists of twenty-four prelude and fugue pairs, one in each of the major and minor keys, arranged in rising chromatic order from C to B. Both sets were designed to demonstrate the possibilities of playing in all keys on an instrument tuned in near-equal temperament, then still novel for keyboards. The eighth pair in Book I, the Prelude in E♭ Minor and Fugue in D♯ Minor (NAWM 104), shows the capacity of the new tuning system to accommodate key signatures with more than four sharps or flats (here six flats and six sharps respectively), in which most triads would be out of tune in the mean-tone temperaments traditional for keyboard instruments. Bach adapted these and several other pieces in both books from existing works, sometimes transposing them in order to cover unusual keys; for example, the fugue in D♯ minor was based on an earlier version in D minor.

Bach had pedagogical aims as well. The typical prelude gives the player one or more specific technical tasks, so that the piece functions as an étude. In addition, the preludes illustrate various keyboard performance conventions and compositional practices. For example, Nos. 2 and 21 of Book I evoke the style of toccatas, No. 8 (NAWM 104a) a concerto slow movement, No. 17 a concerto fast movement, and No. 24 a trio sonata. The fugues constitute a compendium of fugal writing, from two to five voices and from an archaic ricercare in Book I, No. 4 in C♯ minor to an up-to-date style in No. 24 in B minor, featuring a subject with all twelve chromatic notes and long episodes with sequences and circle-of-fifth progressions reminiscent of Vivaldi. Fugue No. 8 in D♯ Minor from Book I (NAWM 104b) illustrates several of Bach's fugal techniques, including inversion, augmentation, and **stretto** (overlapping

EXAMPLE 19.3 *Bach, theme from the* Musical Offering

EXAMPLE 19.4 *Bach, theme from* The Art of Fugue

entrances of the subject). As in the organ fugues, each subject has a clearly defined musical personality that unfolds throughout the entire fugue.

Variety also marks the *Goldberg Variations* (1741), which raised the genre of keyboard variations to a new level of artfulness. All thirty variations preserve the bass and harmonic structure of the theme, a sarabande. Every third variation is a canon, the first at the interval of a unison, the second at a second, and so on through the ninth. The noncanonic variations take many forms, including fugue, French overture, slow aria, and bravura pieces for two manuals. The result is a unique piece that draws on many existing types, like a summation of the music of his time. It is also the most technically demanding keyboard work composed before the nineteenth century, and its combination of compositional and performing virtuosity exemplifies an essential aspect of Bach.

The systematic, comprehensive approach shown in the *Goldberg Variations* is evident in many of Bach's works. He often wrote several pieces of the same type in a short time, like the chorale preludes of the *Orgelbüchlein,* or sought to work out all the possibilities of a genre, technique, or idea, as in the preludes and fugues of *The Well-Tempered Clavier.* This systematic tendency is clear in two unusual works from his last years. The *Musical Offering* contains a three- and a six-part ricercare for keyboard and ten canons, all based on a theme proposed by Frederick the Great of Prussia and shown in Example 19.3. Bach improvised on the theme while visiting the king at Potsdam in 1747 and then wrote these fugues and canons to demonstrate its potential. He added a trio sonata for flute (Frederick's instrument), violin, and continuo, in which the theme also appears, had the set printed, and dedicated it to the king. *The Art of Fugue,* composed in the final decade of Bach's life, systematically demonstrates all types of fugal writing. Written in score though intended for keyboard performance, it consists of eighteen canons and fugues in the strictest style, all based on the subject in Example 19.4 or one of its transformations, and arranged in a general order of increasing complexity. The last fugue, left incomplete at Bach's death, has four subjects, including one spelling Bach's name: B♭–A–C–B♮, or B–A–C–H in German nomenclature, B and H being the German terms for B♭ and B♮, respectively.

CHAMBER MUSIC Bach's chief compositions for chamber ensemble are fifteen sonatas for solo instruments and harpsichord: six each for violin and flute, and three for viola da gamba. Most have four movements in slow–fast–slow–fast order, like the sonata da chiesa. Indeed, most are virtual trio sonatas, since the right-hand harpsichord part is often written out as a melodic

Goldberg Variations

Musical Offering and The Art of Fugue

Sonatas

line in counterpoint with the other instrument. These are now believed to be products of Bach's Leipzig years, when he directed the collegium musicum.

Works for unaccompanied instruments

Bach's six sonatas and partitas for violin alone, six suites for cello alone, and partita for solo flute are unusual, although not unprecedented, in featuring melody instruments without accompaniment. In these works, Bach created the illusion of a harmonic and contrapuntal texture by requiring the performer to play on several strings at once or jump between registers.

Brandenburg Concertos

ORCHESTRAL MUSIC Bach's best-known orchestral works are the six *Brandenburg Concertos,* dedicated in 1721 to the Margrave of Brandenburg—who had requested some pieces—but composed during the previous ten or so years. For all but the first, Bach adopted the three-movement, fast–slow–fast order of the Italian concerto, as well as its triadic themes, steady driving rhythms, ritornello forms, and overall style. The third and sixth feature multiple string parts with continuo, and the others pit solo instruments in various combinations against the body of strings and continuo; all six can be played either with one player per part (as Bach may have performed them at Cöthen) or with string orchestra. In typical Bach fashion, he also expanded on his model, introducing more ritornello material into the episodes, featuring dialogue between soloists and orchestra within episodes, and enlarging the form with devices such as the astonishing long cadenza for the harpsichord (normally a continuo instrument!) in the fifth concerto.

Collegium musicum

Most of Bach's other orchestral music was written in the 1730s when he directed the Leipzig collegium musicum, made up mostly of university students. By the early eighteenth century, such organizations often presented public concerts, like the outdoor concert shown in Figure 19.5; Leipzig's collegium had done so since its founding by Telemann in 1704. Bach apparently wrote his two violin concertos and Concerto in D Minor for Two Violins for such concerts. He was one of the first to write—or arrange—concertos for one or more harpsichords and orchestra, which he no doubt led in performance from the keyboard.

FIGURE 19.5 *Outdoor concert by the collegium musicum of the University of Jena in the 1740s. Bach led a similar group in Leipzig in the 1730s.*

The concerto for four harpsichords and orchestra is an arrangement of a Vivaldi concerto for four violins, and most or all of the others are arrangements of concertos by Bach or perhaps by other composers. Bach also wrote four orchestral suites, once again balancing Italian influences with French ones.

CANTATAS In 1700, Lutheran theologian and poet Erdmann Neumeister (1671–1756) introduced a new kind of sacred text for musical setting, which he called by the Italian term *cantata*. Throughout the seventeenth century, Lutheran composers had set biblical, liturgical, and chorale texts. Neumeister added poetic texts, intended to be set as recitatives, arias, and ariosos, that brought home the meaning of the day's Gospel reading. The new church cantata found widespread acceptance among Lutherans. Its poetry brought together their faith's Orthodox and Pietistic tendencies, blending objective and subjective as well as formal and emotional elements. Its musical scheme incorporated all the great traditions of the recent past—the chorale, the solo song, the concertato medium—and added to these the dramatically powerful elements of operatic recitative and aria. Although Bach set only five of Neumeister's texts, many of his cantatas follow a similar format.

The church cantata figured prominently in the Lutheran liturgy of Leipzig. At the two main churches, St. Nicholas's and St. Thomas's, the principal Sunday service included a motet, a Kyrie, chorales, and a cantata on alternate Sundays (see Source Reading). Bach directed the first choir, with the best

Role in church services

SOURCE READING

Music in Lutheran Church Services

In his first year as cantor and music director in Leipzig, Bach wrote out the order of events, particularly the musical ones, for the main morning service on the first Sunday in Advent. The main musical item was the cantata, which Bach refers to here as "the principal composition." The subject for the cantata was usually linked to the Gospel reading that immediately preceded it, and the sermon would often be on a similar theme. The choir also sang a motet and the Kyrie, the congregation sang chorales, and each musical item was preceded by a prelude, often improvised, on the organ.

❦

1. Preluding
2. Motet
3. Preluding on the Kyrie, which is performed throughout in concerted manner
4. Intoning before the altar

5. Reading of the Epistle
6. Singing of the Litany
7. Preluding on [and singing of] the Chorale
8. Reading of the Gospel
9. Preluding on [and performance of] the principal composition [cantata]
10. Singing of the Creed [Luther's Credo hymn]
11. The Sermon
12. After the Sermon, as usual, singing of several verses of a hymn
13. Words of Institution [of the Sacrament]
14. Preluding on [and performance of] the composition [probably the second part of the cantata]. After the same, alternate preluding and singing of chorales until the end of the Communion, *et sic porrò* [and so on].

From *The New Bach Reader: A Life of Johann Sebastian Bach in Letters and Documents*, ed. Hans T. David and Arthur Mendel, rev. and enl. by Christoph Wolff (New York: W. W. Norton, 1998), 113.

FIGURE 19.6 *Bach's autograph manuscript of the serenata (or secular cantata)* Durchlauchtster Leopold *(Most Serene Highness Leopold), BWV 173a, written for the birthday of his patron, the prince of Anhalt-Cöthen, probably in 1722. Bach soon reused the music for his church cantata* Erhöhtes Fleisch und Blut *(Exalted Flesh and Blood), BWV 173, adding the new text beneath the original words. In the third through fifth measures, he also revised the vocal melody to better suit the revamped text and the new singer.*

singers, at the church whose turn it was to hear the cantata, while a deputy conducted the second choir at the other important church. The third and fourth choirs, made up of the less experienced singers, took care of the modest musical requirements in the two remaining churches. A 1730 memorandum from Bach to the town council set the ideal minimum requirements as twelve singers for each of the first three choirs, which sang polyphonic music, and eight for the fourth choir, which sang only monophonic chants. For the cantatas, he specified a soloist and two or three *ripienists* (from the Italian *ripieno,* "full") for each voice part (soprano, alto, tenor, and bass); the soloists sang the solo movements and were joined by the ripienists on the choral movements. Surviving performing parts suggest that Bach often performed cantatas with only four or eight singers total. The small orchestra that accompanied the cantata included strings with continuo, two or three oboes, and one or two bassoons, sometimes augmented with flutes or, on festive occasions, trumpets and timpani.

Altogether, the Leipzig churches required fifty-eight cantatas each year, in addition to Passion music for Good Friday, Magnificats at Vespers for three festivals, an annual cantata for the installation of the city council, and occasional music such as funeral motets and wedding cantatas. Between 1723 and 1729 Bach composed at least three and possibly four complete annual cycles of about sixty cantatas each. Cantatas written during the 1730s and early 1740s may be part of a fifth cycle, but if so, many of these and of the fourth cycle have not survived. Approximately two hundred of his church cantatas have been preserved, most newly written for Leipzig, others for earlier positions at Mühlhausen or Weimar. In addition, we have about twenty secular cantatas written at Weimar, Cöthen, and Leipzig to celebrate birthdays of his patrons or other festive events. Since these typically could be performed only on a single occasion, Bach often reused the music for church cantatas, as shown in Figure 19.6.

Chorale cantatas   Although no single example can suggest the breadth and variety of Bach's cantatas, *Nun komm, der Heiden Heiland,* BWV 62 (NAWM 105), composed in 1724 for the first Sunday in Advent, illustrates some of his typical procedures. This work was part of his second cycle for Leipzig, which consisted of cantatas whose words and music were based on chorales. The unknown poet who wrote the texts of these cantatas used the first and last stanzas of a chorale for the opening and closing choruses and paraphrased the middle stanzas in poetry suitable for recitatives and arias. Bach then based the opening chorus on the chorale melody, ended the work with a four-part harmonization of the chorale for its closing stanza, and set the middle movements as recitatives and arias in operatic style for the soloists, with few if any references to the chorale melody. For this cantata, Bach and the librettist used Luther's Advent chorale *Nun komm, der Heiden Heiland* (see NAWM 58b and Example 11.1b).

As we often find in Bach's choral works, the opening chorus displays an ingenious mixture of genres—here, concerto and chorale motet. The orchestra begins with a sprightly ritornello that would be at home in a Vivaldi concerto, yet features the chorale as a cantus firmus in the bass. Repeated rising figures evoke the sense of welcome and anticipation in the chorale's text, which heralds the coming of the Savior. As in a concerto, this ritornello serves as a frame for the movement, recurring three times in shortened or transposed form before its full reprise in the tonic at the end. But instead of episodes, Bach presents the four phrases of the chorale in the chorus, set in cantus-firmus style; the sopranos, doubled by the horn, sing each phrase in long notes above imitative counterpoint in the other three parts, while the orchestra continues to develop motives from the ritornello. The first and fourth phrases are preceded by the lower voices in a point of imitation based on the chorale, a procedure called *fore-imitation*. Example 19.5 shows the fore-imitation and subsequent soprano entrance for the first chorale phrase, with phrases from the ritornello in the orchestra. The mixture of secular and sacred models, and of old-style counterpoint and cantus firmus with modern Italianate style, is characteristic of Bach, creating a depth of meanings through references to many familiar types of music.

The four solo movements set sacred texts in operatic idioms. A da capo aria for tenor muses on the mystery of the Incarnation; as if to show Jesus's embodiment as a human being, Bach wrote the aria in the style of a minuet with predominantly four-measure phrasing, evoking the physical body through dance. Next are a recitative and aria for bass, praising the Savior as a hero who conquers evil. The recitative includes word-painting, such as a run on "laufen" (run). The aria follows the operatic conventions for heroic or martial arias, with the orchestra playing in unison throughout, and the figuration emphasizing rapid motions, large leaps, and jumping arpeggios. The soprano and alto join in an accompanied recitative, moving in sweet parallel thirds and sixths as they express awe at the nativity scene. The closing chorale verse is a doxology, praising Father, Son, and Holy Spirit.

OTHER CHURCH MUSIC   Bach's church music was not confined to cantatas but included motets, Passions, and Latin service music. Most important are his Passions and his Mass in B Minor.

Bach wrote two surviving Passions, telling the story of Jesus's crucifixion, for performance at Vespers on Good Friday in Leipzig. Both the *St. John Passion* (1724, later revised), based on the account of John 18–19, and the *St. Matthew Passion* (1727, revised 1736), on Matthew 26–27, employ recitatives, arias, ensembles, choruses, chorales sung by the chorus, and orchestral accompaniment. This type of setting, drawing on elements from opera, cantata, and oratorios, had replaced the older type composed by Schütz and

Passions

EXAMPLE 19.5 *Entrance of the first phrase of the chorale in* Nun komm, der Heiden Heiland, *BWV 62*

a. Beginning of fore-imitation in alto, tenor, and bass

b. Cantus firmus in soprano, doubled by the horn

Now come, savior of the gentiles

others, which combined plainsong narration with polyphony (see Chapter 15). In both Passions, a tenor narrates the biblical story in the style of recitative, soloists play the parts of Jesus and other figures, and the chorus sings the words of the disciples, the crowd, and other groups. At other times the chorus comments on events, like the chorus in a Greek drama. The interpolated recitatives, ariosos, and arias serve a similar purpose, reflecting on the story and relating its meaning to the individual worshipper.

The excerpt from the *St. Matthew Passion* in NAWM 106 relates two dramatic episodes in the Passion story: the judgment of Jesus's guilt, and his disciple Peter's denials that he knows Jesus. Both evoke high emotions. The first ends with the anger and violence of the priests, scribes, and elders against Jesus, which Bach captured in short, agitated choruses marked by rapid imitative entrances and alternation between voices. There follows a contemplative chorale expressing the reactions of the congregation listening to Bach's Passion, who sympathize with Jesus. The story of Peter's threefold denials has a similar arc, beginning with simple narration but moving to highly expressive recitative for Peter's bitter tears when he realizes that he has betrayed his friend, just as Jesus prophesied he would do. Peter's remorse is then reflected in one of Bach's most moving arias, whose drooping figures, sighing gestures, long-spun phrases, and continuous form capture the overwhelming grief of one who feels remorse and cries for God's mercy. After this outburst, a chorale expresses confidence that God's grace is greater than the believer's sin. By dramatizing the events in the story, then expressing the reactions of a contemporary believer, Bach's Passion setting pulled his listeners emotionally into the Gospel account and helped them experience it directly.

Although they are often performed with a large choir and orchestra, recent research on the performance parts suggests that Bach's Passions were intended for just four solo and four ripieno singers, who divided the roles among them and joined together for the choral movements. Thus the same singers portrayed the roles in the Gospel story and commented on it in solo movements and chorales, embodying in themselves the identification of modern believers with the ancient events that the Passion was meant to promote.

Bach assembled the Mass in B Minor, his only complete setting of the Catholic Mass Ordinary, between 1747 and 1749. He drew most of it from music he had composed much earlier. He had already presented the Kyrie and Gloria in 1733 to the Catholic elector of Saxony, in hopes of getting an honorary appointment to the electoral chapel, which he did receive three years later. The Sanctus was first performed on Christmas Day 1724. He adapted some of the other sections from cantata movements composed between 1714 and 1735, replacing the German text with the Latin words of the Mass and reworking the music. Of the newly composed sections, the opening of the Credo and the *Confiteor* (a later passage of the Credo) are in stile antico, the *Et incarnatus* (also in the Credo) and *Benedictus* (from the Sanctus) in modern styles.

Mass in B Minor

Throughout the work, he juxtaposed contrasting styles, making the Mass in B Minor a compendium of approaches to church music. Since the mass was never performed as a whole during Bach's lifetime, and is too long to function well as service music, he may have intended it as an anthology of movements, each a model of its type, that could be performed separately. As a collection of exemplary works, the Mass in B Minor stands with *The Well-Tempered Clavier,*

A Critique of Bach's Style

The composer and critic Johann Adolph Scheibe (1708–1776) considered Bach unsurpassable as an organist and keyboard composer. However, he found much of the rest of Bach's music overly elaborate and confused, preferring the more tuneful and straightforward styles of younger composers such as Johann Adolf Hasse (see Chapter 21). Scheibe's critique is only one volley in the long argument between advocates of Baroque styles and partisans of the new galant style.

❈

This great man would be the admiration of whole nations if he had more *Annehmlichkeit* [pleasantness or charm], if he did not take away the natural element in his pieces by giving them a turgid and confused style, and if he did not darken their beauty by an excess of art. Since he judges according to his own fingers, his pieces are extremely difficult to play; for he demands that singers and instrumentalists should be able to do with their throats and instruments whatever he can play on the clavier. But this is impossible. Every ornament, every little grace, and everything that one thinks of as belonging to the method of playing, he expresses completely in notes; and this not only takes away from his pieces the beauty of harmony but completely covers the melody throughout. All the voices must work with each other and be of equal difficulty, and none of them can be recognized as the principal voice. In short, he is in music what Mr. [Daniel Casper] von Lohenstein was in poetry. Turgidity has led them both from the natural to the artificial, and from the lofty to the somber; and in both one admires the onerous labor and uncommon effort—which, however, are vainly employed, since they conflict with Nature.

From an anonymous letter by "an able traveling musician" published in Scheibe's periodical review, *Der critische Musikus*, May 14, 1737, translated in *The New Bach Reader*, ed. Hans T. David and Arthur Mendel, rev. and enl. by Christoph Wolff (New York: W. W. Norton, 1998), 338.

The Art of Fugue, and the *Musical Offering* as witness to Bach's desire to create comprehensive cycles that explore the furthest potential of a medium or genre.

BACH'S SYNTHESIS Bach absorbed into his works all the genres, styles, and forms of his time and developed hitherto unsuspected potentialities in them. In his music, the often conflicting demands of harmony and counterpoint, and of melody and polyphony, are brought into equilibrium. Many qualities give his works deep and lasting appeal: memorable themes, copious musical invention, balance between harmonic and contrapuntal forces, rhythmic drive, clarity of form, grand proportions, imaginative use of pictorial and symbolic figures, intensity of expression always controlled by a ruling architectural idea, and attention to every detail.

This recipe was too rich for some of his contemporaries, who preferred less complex, more tuneful music (see Source Reading). Throughout the 1720s and 1730s, the very decades during which Bach composed some of his most important works, the new style emanating from the opera houses of Italy invaded Germany and the rest of Europe (see Chapters 20–22), making his music seem old-fashioned. Never entirely forgotten, he was rediscovered and achieved enormous popularity in the nineteenth century, when music that could please both amateurs and connoisseurs and could keep its appeal through many performances was highly prized. Perhaps only a composer who spent most of his life teaching, wrote excellent music for students at every level from beginning to advanced, worked in positions that constantly demanded new music for immediate performance, embraced a wide variety of genres and approaches, and aspired to explore all the possibilities of every kind of music he encountered, could achieve the central position Bach now occupies in the Western musical tradition.

GEORGE FRIDERIC HANDEL

Unlike Vivaldi, Rameau, and Bach, who rarely traveled outside their countries, George Frideric Handel (1685–1759) moved comfortably between German-, Italian-, and English-speaking cities (see biography and Figure 19.7, pp. 442–43). His German music teacher gave him a thorough education in organ, harpsichord, counterpoint, and current German and Italian idioms. When he was a young man, three years at the Hamburg opera house and four years in Italy helped to lay the foundations of his style. He matured as a composer in England, the country then most hospitable to foreign composers. Moreover, England provided the choral tradition that made Handel's oratorios possible. Vivaldi's influence on the musical world was immediate, although he died almost totally forgotten; Rameau's was felt more slowly, and then mainly in the fields of opera and music theory; and Bach's work lay in comparative obscurity until the nineteenth century. But Handel won international renown during his lifetime, and his music has been performed ever since, making him the first composer whose music has never ceased to be performed.

Handel's music was enormously popular. When his *Music for the Royal Fireworks* was given a public rehearsal in 1749, it attracted an audience of over 12,000 people and stopped traffic in London for three hours. How could a composer gain such popularity, and why should it be Handel? The answer to the first question is that for virtually the first time, a composer was working for the public—not just for a church, a court, or a town council—and it is the public that bestows popularity. And why Handel? He had a keen business sense and was supremely adaptable, able to measure and serve the taste of the public. He could do this because of his cosmopolitan and eclectic style, drawing on German, Italian, French, and English music.

Handel's popularity

HANDEL AND HIS PATRONS Although Handel achieved his greatest fame writing music for public performance, he was no freelancer. From his early years in Italy to the end of his life, he enjoyed the generous support of patrons. Their wishes often determined what he composed, yet their support also allowed him freedom to write operas and oratorios for the public.

In Italy, Handel's chief patron was Marquis Francesco Ruspoli, who employed the young musician as keyboard player and composer in Rome and at his country estate. There Handel wrote Latin motets for church performances and numerous chamber cantatas for Ruspoli's weekly private music-making.

Italy

Hired in 1710 as court music director for the elector of Hanover in north central Germany, Handel used the position to establish himself in London. This is less odd than it may seem: the elector was heir to the British throne,

Hanover and London

GEORGE FRIDERIC HANDEL [GEORG FRIEDERICH HÄNDEL]

(1685–1759)

Handel, recognized since his own time as one of the greatest composers of his era, was a master of all types of vocal and instrumental music. He is best known for his English oratorios, a genre he invented, and for his Italian operas.

Handel was born in Halle, Germany, the son of a barber-surgeon at the local court. His father wanted him to study law, but he practiced music secretly. His organ playing at the age of nine impressed the duke, who persuaded Handel's father to let him study with Friedrich Wilhelm Zachow, composer, organist, and church music director in Halle. Under Zachow, Handel became an accomplished organist and harpsichordist, studied violin and oboe, mastered counterpoint, and learned the music of German and Italian composers by copying their scores. He entered the University of Halle in 1702 and was appointed cathedral organist. The following year, he abandoned the cantor's career for which Zachow had prepared him and instead

FIGURE 19.7 *George Frideric Handel at his composing desk, in a portrait by Philippe Mercier.*

and the incumbent, Queen Anne, was in precarious health, so it was only a matter of time before Handel's patron would be in England himself. Handel spent the 1710–11 season in London, drawing his Hanover salary while he wrote *Rinaldo* for the new public opera house. When he came to London a second time in 1712, he found a supportive patron in the earl of Burlington, in whose house he lived and for whom he wrote Italian cantatas and other works. In 1717–19 he served a similar role for James Brydges, earl of Carnarvon, later duke of Chandos, composing during that period the large-scale Chandos Anthems for church services.

British monarchs   Handel's most important patrons were the British monarchs. In 1713, Queen Anne commissioned several ceremonial choral works, including a *Te Deum* and *Ode for Queen Anne's Birthday,* for which Handel took Purcell's compositions as his model. The Queen granted Handel a pension of £200 a year (roughly twice what Bach made in Leipzig). After she died in 1714 and the elector of Hanover was crowned King George I, he doubled Handel's pension to £400. George's daughter-in-law, the future Queen Caroline, increased it to £600 around 1724, when Handel undertook the musical education of her daughters. For the rest of his life, Handel could depend on this sizable income

moved to Hamburg, the center for German opera. There he played violin in the opera house orchestra and wrote his own first opera, *Almira,* performed with great success in 1705, when Handel was just nineteen.

The following year, Handel traveled to Italy at the invitation of Prince Fernando de' Medici. Winning recognition as a promising young composer, he associated with the leading patrons and musicians of Florence, Rome, Naples, and Venice. While in Italy, Handel wrote a large number of Italian cantatas, two oratorios, several Latin motets, and the operas *Rodrigo* (1707) for Florence and *Agrippina* (1709) for Venice.

After a brief period at the court in Hanover, Germany, Handel spent the rest of his life in London, where he adopted the English version of his name, served aristocratic patrons, and enjoyed the lifelong support of the British royal family. In the 1730s, after three decades of writing Italian operas for the London theaters, Handel turned to oratorios in English, mostly on sacred subjects. He also published a considerable amount of instrumental music, from solo and trio sonatas to concertos and orchestral suites, including *Water Music* and *Music for the Royal Fireworks.*

Handel never married. In Italy and London, he lived with various patrons until 1723, when he leased a house in an upper-class neighborhood where he stayed the rest of his life. There were rumors of brief affairs with sopranos, but none has been substantiated. Recently, scholars have noted that several of his patrons moved in social circles where same-sex desire was common, and that the texts of the cantatas Handel wrote for these patrons often allude to love between men in coded terms. Whether Handel himself had intimate relationships with anyone of either sex remains open to question.

Handel's imperious, independent nature made him a formidable presence, but the rougher sides of his personality were balanced by a sense of humor and redeemed by a generous and honorable approach to life. Experiencing both successes and failures, criticism as well as praise, Handel suffered physical ailments as he aged, notably a paralytic stroke in 1737 (from which he recovered) and cataracts in his final years. By the end of his life he ranked as one of the most revered figures in London, and some three thousand people attended his funeral at Westminster Abbey.

MAJOR WORKS *Messiah, Saul, Samson, Israel in Egypt,* and about 20 other oratorios; *Giulio Cesare* and about 40 other Italian operas; numerous odes, anthems, and other sacred vocal music; about 100 Italian cantatas; about 45 concertos, 20 trio sonatas, 20 solo sonatas, numerous keyboard pieces, and the well-known *Water Music* and *Music for the Royal Fireworks*

despite minimal responsibilities, a situation that contrasted with Bach's. In 1723, he won honorary appointment as composer to the Chapel Royal. He continued to supply music for important state occasions; for the coronation of King George II in 1727 he wrote four splendid anthems, including *Zadok the Priest,* performed at every British coronation since. But while he was closely identified with the royal house, most of his activities were in the public sphere, writing and producing operas and later oratorios and composing for publication.

OPERAS Handel devoted thirty-six years to composing and directing operas, which contain much of his best music. In an age when opera was the main concern of ambitious musicians, Handel excelled among his contemporaries.

Handel's blending of national styles is evident from his first opera, *Almira* (1705), premiered in Hamburg when he was nineteen. He kept to the local fashion of setting the arias in Italian and the recitatives in German, so the audience could follow the plot. Imitating Reinhard Keiser, the dominant opera composer in Hamburg, Handel patterned the overture and dance music after French models, composed most of the arias in the Italian manner, and

International style

incorporated German elements in the counterpoint and orchestration. In Italy, he learned from Scarlatti's cantatas and operas how to create supple, long-breathed, rhythmically varied melodies that seem naturally suited for the voice, amply demonstrated in Handel's *Agrippina* (Venice, 1709). Ever after, his operatic style was uniquely international, combining French overtures and dances, Italianate arias and recitatives, and German traits, notably the tendency to double the vocal line with one or more instruments.

London operas

Handel's *Rinaldo* (1711) was the first opera in Italian composed for London. Interest there in Italian opera had been stimulated by the success of Thomas Clayton's *Arsinoe* (1705), an opera in Italian style based on an English translation of an Italian libretto, so Handel arrived at the perfect time, fresh from his experiences in Italy. His brilliant music, combined with elaborate stage effects, made *Rinaldo* a sensation and helped establish Handel's public reputation in England. The arias were published by John Walsh, bringing Handel additional revenue. He wrote four more operas in the 1710s, and with revivals of *Rinaldo*, a Handel opera was staged almost every season.

LONDON METROPOLITAN ARCHIVES, CITY OF LONDON/BRIDGEMAN IMAGES

FIGURE 19.8 *Entryway to the King's Theatre in London, where most of Handel's operas were performed. From the entrance, stairs led upward to the lobby of a sumptuous auditorium, many times larger than one might expect from this street view. Engraving from ca. 1780.*

In 1718–19, about sixty wealthy gentlemen, with the support of the king, established a joint stock company for producing Italian operas. They called it the Royal Academy of Music. The operas were staged at the King's Theatre in the Haymarket, the public opera house that opened in 1705, shown in Figure 19.8. Handel was engaged as the music director. He traveled to Germany to recruit singers, mostly Italians performing in Dresden and other courts. Perhaps his biggest catch was the arrogant but widely celebrated castrato Senesino (Francesco Bernardi, 1686–1758). Giovanni Bononcini (1670–1747) was brought from Rome to compose operas and to play cello in the orchestra. Later, the eminent sopranos Francesca Cuzzoni (1696–1778) and Faustina Bordoni (1697–1781) joined the group. For this company, which flourished from 1720 to 1728, Handel composed some of his best operas, including *Radamisto* (1720), *Ottone* (1723), *Giulio Cesare* (Julius Caesar, 1724), *Rodelinda* (1725), and *Admeto* (1727). The subjects of Handel's operas were the usual ones of the time: episodes from the lives of Roman heroes freely adapted to include the maximum number of intense dramatic situations, or tales of magic and marvelous adventure revolving around the Crusades.

Recitative styles

The action developed through dialogue rendered in the two distinct types of recitative that emerged in Italian opera in the early eighteenth century. One type, accompanied only by basso continuo, set stretches of dialogue or monologue in as speechlike a fashion as possible (as in the Scarlatti recitative in Example 17.1). It would later be called *recitativo semplice*, or ***simple*** *recitative*, and eventually *recitativo secco* (dry recitative). The other type, called *recitativo obbligato* and later *recitativo accompagnato,* or **accompanied recitative**, used stirring and impressive orchestral outbursts to dramatize tense situations (see Example 19.7 on p. 448). These interjections reinforced the rapid changes of emotion in a character's monologue and punctuated the singer's phrases.

Solo da capo arias allowed the characters to respond lyrically to their situations. Each aria represented a single specific mood or affection, or sometimes two contrasting but related affections in the A and B sections. At the singers' insistence, the arias had to be allocated according to the importance of each member of the cast and had to display the scope of each singer's vocal and dramatic powers. The *prima donna* ("first lady"), the soprano singing the leading female role, normally demanded the most and the best arias (hence the modern meaning of that phrase). Handel wrote for specific singers, seeking to show off their abilities to the best advantage.

Arias

Handel's scores are remarkable for the wide variety of aria types. They range from brilliant displays of florid ornamentation, known as **coloratura**, to sustained, sublimely expressive songs of pathos or grief, such as *Se pietà* in *Giulio Cesare.* Arias of regal grandeur with rich contrapuntal and concertato accompaniments contrast with arias whose simple, folklike melodies suggest the French or German air. The pastoral scenes are noteworthy examples of eighteenth-century nature painting. Some arias feature the tone color of a particular instrument to set the mood, as the horn does in Cesare's aria *Va tacito e nascosto* from *Giulio Cesare,* in which both voice and instrument imitate a hunting horn.

In several operas, Handel used instrumental sinfonias to mark key moments in the plot such as battles, ceremonies, or incantations, and a few of his operas include ballets. The orchestra is usually fuller than for Scarlatti operas, with more use of winds, as in French operas. Vocal ensembles larger than duets are rare, as are choruses.

Instrumental sections

One or both types of recitative are sometimes freely combined with arias, ariosos, and orchestral passages to make larger scene complexes that recall the freedom of earlier Venetian and French operas and foreshadow the methods of later composers such as Gluck (see Chapter 21). Instead of presenting the plot in recitative, then the aria with orchestral ritornello as a static moment, Handel interleaves these elements so that the plot continues to move forward.

Scene complexes

Several such scenes occur in *Giulio Cesare,* on a libretto adapted from the one Sartorio set in *Giulio Cesare in Egitto* (NAWM 93). In Act III, Scene 4, Cesare finds himself on a deserted shore to which he swam to escape enemy troops. The scene begins with a ritornello evoking the sea breezes, but instead of an aria Cesare sings an accompanied recitative, asking himself where he can turn for help. Then he begins the aria we expect, asking the breezes for pity and comfort, and the sea breeze music returns, serving as the ritornello. In the contrasting B section, he implores the breezes to tell him the fate of his beloved Cleopatra. Just when we expect the da capo repetition, he again turns to accompanied recitative to express the helplessness of his situation, before finally turning back to the A section. By upending our expectations, and keeping us wondering what will happen next, Handel achieves a sense of realism and suspense.

A similar scrambling of elements occurs in Act II, Scenes 1–2 (NAWM 107), paralleling the intermixing in Sartorio's setting (NAWM 93d) in more sophisticated ways. After dialogue in simple recitative, Cleopatra's da capo aria *V'adoro, pupille* is interwoven with other elements. Cesare has been brought to a grove where he overhears Cleopatra singing. An orchestral sinfonia, essentially the opening ritornello, introduces the aria's principal motive. From his hiding place, Cesare unexpectedly breaks in, expressing awe at the ravishing music in a brief recitative. Cleopatra sings the first and middle sections of the aria, then stops; transfixed, Cesare again comments in recitative, wondering at the beauty of the song. Only then does Cleopatra take up the repetition of the A section, now not just a conventional formal device but something more profound, because we know of Cesare's entrancement.

Throughout the opera, Handel's characteristic combination of national elements is apparent. Cleopatra's aria, shown in Example 19.6, is in French sarabande rhythm, arousing that dance's associations with nobility, tenderness, and love. Yet the da capo form of the aria is Italian, the voice is doubled by instruments in the German manner, and the orchestra is divided as in an Italian concerto, with soloists accompanying the voice and the full orchestra offering punctuation.

Handel as impresario
Stressed by rising salaries for the singers, the Royal Academy dissolved in 1729. Although the collapse has sometimes been linked to a dispute between the sopranos Cuzzoni and Bordoni or to the popular success in 1728 of *The Beggar's Opera,* John Gay's English ballad opera (see Chapter 21), which satirized opera and the Academy, the main causes were financial. Handel and a partner took over the theater, formed a new company, and had several great successes with Senesino in the major roles. But Senesino found Handel dictatorial; he left in 1733 and soon joined a competing company, the Opera of the Nobility, which featured the Neapolitan composer Nicola Porpora (1686–1768) and the highest-priced singers in Europe. The two companies spent so much on singers and staging and so completely divided the London public that by 1737 both were nearly bankrupt, and the Opera of the Nobility closed that summer. Although Handel continued to write and produce operas until 1741, none matched his earlier successes.

ORATORIOS In the 1730s, Handel devised a new genre that would reward him as richly as opera had and bring him his greatest popularity: the English oratorio. As we have seen, Italian oratorios resembled operas in style, telling their story through a series of recitatives, arias, and choruses, but were on a sacred subject, usually from the Bible, and were presented in concert or as part of religious devotions rather than on stage, usually in a church hall or in a patron's residence. Handel had written such a work, *La resurrezione* (The Resurrection, 1708), during his stay in Rome. In his English oratorios, he continued aspects of the Italian tradition by setting dialogue in recitative and lyrical verses as arias. The latter resemble his opera arias in form, style, the nature of musical ideas, and techniques for expressing the affections. But Handel and his librettists brought into their oratorios elements that were foreign to Italian opera, taken from French classical drama, ancient Greek tragedy, the German Passion, and especially the English masque and anthem.

EXAMPLE 19.6 *George Frideric Handel,* V'adoro pupille, *from* Giulio Cesare

I adore you, pupils, Cupid's darts. Your sparks are welcome to the heart.

Handel's most important innovation in the oratorios was his use of the   *Use of chorus*
chorus. Italian oratorios had at most a few ensembles. Handel's experience
with choral music led him to give the chorus much more prominence. His
early training had made him familiar with Lutheran choral music and with
the south German combination of chorus with orchestra and soloists. He was
especially influenced by the English choral tradition, which he had absorbed
and extended in his Chandos Anthems and works for the Chapel Royal. Thus,
in his oratorios, the chorus makes a crucial contribution. It plays a variety
of roles, participating in the action, narrating the story, or commenting on

events like the chorus in Greek drama or in Bach's Passions. The grand character of his choral style, drawn from the English tradition, fits the oratorio's emphasis on communal rather than individual expression.

In his choruses, Handel was a dramatist, a master of effects. He wrote for chorus in a style simpler and less consistently contrapuntal than Bach's. He alternated passages in open fugal texture with solid blocks of harmony and often set a melodic line in sustained notes against one in quicker rhythm. Everything lies well for the voices, and the orchestra usually reinforces the vocal parts, making his choral music a pleasure to sing—one factor in its enduring popularity.

Saul   Handel's first oratorio in English was *Esther,* revised from a masque of about 1718. Like his operas but unlike oratorios in Italy, Handel's oratorios were usually performed in theaters. *Esther,* which premiered at the King's Theatre in 1732, was the first in a series of oratorios Handel put on in almost every subsequent Lenten season as a way to extend his earnings from opera, which could not be staged during Lent. But the decisive move to oratorio began when subscriptions to the 1738–39 opera season were insufficient, so instead of a new opera, Handel composed the oratorio *Saul* to a libretto by Charles Jennens for a three-month season of choral works in early 1739.

The closing scene of Act II (NAWM 108) illustrates the blending of genres in Handel's oratorios. Saul, king of Israel, sees the young military hero David as a rival. In an accompanied recitative in martial style (NAWM 108a), shown in Example 19.7, Saul resolves to have David killed. Dialogue between Saul and his son Jonathan, David's beloved friend, is rendered in simple recitative (NAWM 108b). After these two numbers in styles borrowed from opera, Handel presents not an aria, but a chorus that reflects on the morality of the situation: *O fatal consequence of rage* (NAWM 108c). It comprises a series of three fugues, each ending with a majestic homorhythmic passage. In typical Handelian style, the chorus is filled with rhetorical figures that convey the

EXAMPLE 19.7 *Accompanied recitative from Handel's* Saul, *Act II, Scene 10*

meaning of the text. In the opening section, a falling tritone to express sorrow in the fugue subject and the use of rapid repeated notes to express rage both recall techniques first introduced by Monteverdi (see Chapter 14).

Saul was well received, but Handel continued to compose and produce operas. He committed himself fully to the new genre only after remarkable success during the winter of 1741–42 with a series of oratorios and other concerts in Dublin, Ireland. The trip culminated in performances of a new oratorio, *Messiah* (1741), which would become Handel's most famous work. Its libretto, also by Jennens, is unusual: instead of telling a story, it unfolds as a series of contemplations on the Christian idea of redemption using texts drawn from the Bible, beginning with Old Testament prophecies and going through the life of Christ to his resurrection. However, the music of *Messiah* is typical of Handel, full of his characteristic charm, immediate appeal, and mixture of traditions, from the French overture to the Italianate recitatives and da capo arias, the Germanic choral fugues, and the English choral anthem style.

Messiah

Handel and a collaborator leased a theater in London to present oratorios every year during Lent. As an added attraction at these performances, the composer played an organ concerto or improvised at the organ during intermissions. Figure 19.9 shows a contemporary sketch of an oratorio performance, perhaps led by Handel, with a chorus and orchestra each numbering about twenty. Oratorios needed no staging or costumes and could use English singers, who were a good deal less expensive than Italian ones, so it was much easier to turn a profit. Oratorios also appealed to a potentially large middle-class public that had never felt at home with the aristocratic entertainment of opera in Italian. The English public's enthusiastic response to these concerts laid the foundation for the immense popularity that made Handel's music the prevailing influence in British musical life for more than a century.

Performing oratorios

Oratorios were not church music; they were intended for the concert hall and were much closer to theatrical performances than to church services—indeed, *Messiah* was advertised as a "sacred entertainment." But stories from the Bible were well known to middle-class Protestant listeners, much more so than the historical or mythological plots of Italian opera, so most of Handel's oratorios were based on the Old Testament or Apocryphal books. Moreover, such subjects as *Saul, Israel in Egypt* (1739), *Judas Maccabaeus* (1747), and *Joshua* (1748) had an appeal based on something beyond familiarity with the ancient sacred narratives: in an era of prosperity and expanding empire, English audiences felt a kinship with the ancient Israelites whose heroes triumphed with the special blessing of God.

FIGURE 19.9 *Drawing of an oratorio performance in London around the middle of the eighteenth century, showing about twenty singers and some twenty instrumentalists. Handel may be the figure on the right or the player at the harpsichord.*

Borrowing and reworking   We have seen that Bach often borrowed and reworked music by himself or by other composers. This practice was common at the time, but Handel borrowed more than most. Three duets and eleven of the twenty-eight choruses of *Israel in Egypt,* for example, were taken in whole or in part from the music of others, while four choruses were arrangements from earlier works by Handel himself. When such instances of borrowing were discovered in the nineteenth century, Handel was charged with plagiarism, because audiences and critics of that time valued originality and demanded original themes. In Handel's time, simply presenting another composer's work as one's own was condemned, but borrowing, transcribing, adapting, rearranging, and parodying were universal and accepted practices. When Handel borrowed, he more often than not repaid with interest, finding new potential in the borrowed material.

Indeed, Handel borrowed from others or reused his own music only when the material was well suited for its new role. As illustrated in Example 19.8, one of the best-known choruses in *Messiah* was adapted from an Italian duet that Handel had recently composed, but the music is perfect for its new text. The chorus sings "All we like sheep" as a group, then "have gone astray" as single, diverging melodic lines; "we have turned" is set to a rapidly twisting, turning figure that never gets away from its starting point; and "every one to his

EXAMPLE 19.8 *Handel's reworkings in* All we like sheep have gone astray, *from* Messiah

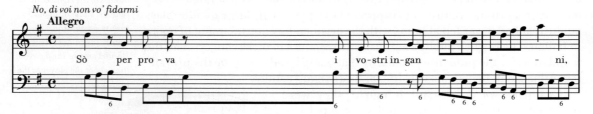

I know through experience your deceptions,

two tyrants you are every hour,

own way" is rendered with stubborn insistence on a single repeated note. The first motive is substantially recast, but the others are essentially unchanged. It is hard to imagine that these musical ideas were conceived for any other text, but Handel originally composed them for the words of a lover complaining about his beloved's deceit. The composer's cleverness is revealed in how well he makes them work in the new context. The only wholly new material in the movement appears in the last few measures, where the point of the chorus is revealed suddenly, with dramatic force, in a slow, solemn, minor-mode setting of the words "And the Lord hath laid on Him the iniquity of us all."

INSTRUMENTAL WORKS Although Handel made his reputation with vocal works, he wrote a great deal of instrumental music. Much of it was published by John Walsh in London, earning Handel extra income and keeping his name before the public in their home music-making. There were also unauthorized prints by other publishers, for which Handel received nothing. His keyboard works include two collections of harpsichord suites that contain not only the usual dance movements but also examples of most keyboard genres current at the time. Handel composed some twenty solo sonatas and almost as many trio sonatas for various instruments. Corelli's influence can be heard in these works, but the sophisticated harmonies and vivacious fast movements reflect a later Italian style.

Handel's most popular instrumental works are his two collections of suites *Ensemble suites* for orchestra or winds, both composed for the king and intended for outdoor performance. *Water Music* (1717) contains three suites for winds and strings, played from a boat during a royal procession on the river Thames for the king. *Music for the Royal Fireworks* (1749), for winds (although Handel later added strings), was composed to accompany fireworks set off in a London park to celebrate the Peace of Aix-la-Chapelle.

Handel's concertos mix tradition and innovation but tend toward a ret- *Concertos* rospective style. His six Concerti Grossi, Op. 3 (published 1734), feature woodwind and string soloists in novel combinations. He invented the concerto for organ and orchestra, which he performed during the intermissions of his oratorios and published in three sets (1738, 1740, and 1761). His most significant concertos are the Twelve Grand Concertos, Op. 6, composed during one month in 1739 and published the next year. Instead of following Vivaldi's model, Handel adopted Corelli's conception of a sonata da chiesa for full orchestra, although he often added a movement or two to the conventional slow–fast–slow–fast pattern. The serious, dignified bearing and the prevailing full contrapuntal texture of these concertos hark back to the early part of the century, when Handel was forming his style in Italy.

HANDEL'S REPUTATION The English came to regard Handel as a national institution, and with good reason. He spent all his mature life in London, becoming a naturalized British citizen in 1727, and wrote all his major works for British audiences. He was the most imposing figure in English music during his lifetime, and the English public nourished his genius and remained loyal to his memory. When he died in 1759, he was buried with public honors in Westminster Abbey, and three years later his monument, shown in Figure 19.10, was unveiled there.

FIGURE 19.10 *Handel memorial in Westminster Abbey, London, sculpted by Louis-François Roubiliac. The music shows the soprano aria* I know that my Redeemer liveth *from* Messiah.

Handel's music aged well because he adopted the devices that became important in the new style of the mid-eighteenth century. His emphasis on melody, harmony, and contrasting textures, as compared to the more strictly contrapuntal procedures of Bach, allied him with the fashions of his time. As a choral composer in the grand style he had no peer. He was a consummate master of contrast, not only in choral music but in all types of compositions. In the oratorios he deliberately appealed to a middle-class audience, recognizing social changes that would have far-reaching effects on music. The broad, lasting appeal of his oratorios made some of them the earliest pieces by any composer to enjoy an unbroken tradition of performance from their premieres through the present day.

AN ENDURING LEGACY

The careers of Bach and Handel were almost as interesting in death as in life. Burial and resurrection describe the history of Bach's music. Only a few pieces were published in his lifetime, almost all for keyboard; the rest remained in handwritten copies. Musical taste changed radically in the mid-eighteenth century, and Bach's work was quickly left behind. Bach's sons Carl Philipp Emanuel Bach and Johann Christian Bach were influenced by him but went their own ways, and for a time their fame eclipsed his. Yet his music was always known to a core of musicians and connoisseurs. Some of the preludes from *The Well-Tempered Clavier* were printed, and the whole collection circulated in manuscript copies. Haydn owned a copy of the Mass in B Minor. Mozart knew *The Art of Fugue* and studied the motets on a visit to Leipzig in 1789. Citations from Bach's works appeared frequently in the musical literature of the time, and the important periodical, the *Allgemeine musikalische Zeitung* (General Musical Journal), opened its first issue (1798) with a Bach portrait.

A fuller discovery of Bach began in the nineteenth century with the publication of a biography by Johann Nikolaus Forkel in 1802. In part for reasons of nationalism, Bach was promoted by German musicians. The revival of the *St. Matthew Passion* by the composer and conductor Carl Friedrich Zelter and its performance at Berlin under Felix Mendelssohn's direction in 1829 did much to inspire interest in Bach's music. The Bach-Gesellschaft (Bach Society), founded by Robert Schumann and others in 1850 to mark the centenary of Bach's death, published a collected edition of Bach's works, completed by 1900. By the late nineteenth century, Bach had reached almost godlike status, and his reputation has only increased since then. His music is now everywhere, studied by every student of Western music. When twenty-seven pieces of recorded music representing the world's peoples were placed on Voyager 1 and 2, the first human-made objects to travel beyond the solar system, eight were of European classical music, and (despite the reported objection that "that would be bragging") three of those were by Bach: movements from a *Brandenburg Concerto, The Well-Tempered Clavier,* and a violin partita. Composers such as Mozart, Mendelssohn, Schumann, and Brahms have emulated Bach, and he has exercised an enduring influence on modern composers as diverse as Schoenberg and Ives, Bartók and Stravinsky, Villa-Lobos and Webern.

Whereas Bach was resurrected, Handel never left. Some of his oratorios have been performed continually since they were written. Annual choral festivals at cathedrals in London, Salisbury, and elsewhere had begun in the late seventeenth and early eighteenth centuries, and from the late 1740s on their repertory increasingly centered on Handel's oratorios, odes, and other works. In 1784, the twenty-fifth anniversary of his death was commemorated with a massive Handel festival; organized by the directors of the Concerts of Ancient Music and supported by the nobility and King George III, it consisted of a series of five concerts at Westminster Abbey that included a performance of *Messiah* by 525 performers before an audience of 4,500. In the late eighteenth and nineteenth centuries, amateur choral societies sprang up throughout English- and German-speaking Europe, and Handel's oratorios became the core of their repertoire. Through this development, Handel became the first classical composer, the first to attain a permanent place in the performing repertoire. His other music passed from the scene for awhile, then was revived, with his orchestral suites and concertos gaining a broad popularity and works in other genres receiving frequent performances. Finally, Handel's operas are now getting the attention they merit, with successful and critically acclaimed productions of *Giulio Cesare* leading the way. For many listeners today, Bach and Handel *are* the Baroque.

Further Reading is available at digital.wwnorton.com/hwm10

MUSICAL TASTE AND STYLE IN THE ENLIGHTENMENT

Beginning in the 1720s, composers created a new musical language made up of readily comprehensible gestures arranged in songful, **periodic** melodies over light accompaniment. First developed in Italian vocal music, especially opera, this new idiom reflected a growing taste for music that was "natural," expressive, and immediately appealing. This new language, called the ***galant style***, emerged during an era when many types and styles of music coexisted and the merits of each were fiercely debated. Taught in Italian conservatories and by master teachers, the new idiom spread from courtly entertainments and urban theaters to concerts and amateur domestic music-making throughout most of Europe and the Americas. It won the day because it reached a wide audience, met the taste of the growing public for music that was pleasurable and easily understood, and suited the intellectual tenor of the times, marked by the broad movement known as the Enlightenment.

    This chapter will sketch the social and intellectual background for the new musical language and describe its central traits. The next three chapters will trace its development in opera and vocal music; examine how composers applied the new idiom to instrumental music, including several new genres and forms; and show how Haydn and Mozart enriched it with elements of other styles to create enduring musical works in what has become known as the ***classical style***.

EUROPE IN THE ENLIGHTENMENT

Eighteenth-century Europe was dominated politically by the great powers, centralized states with large military establishments. In the west, France had succeeded Spain as the dominant force by 1650 but was outclassed in the Seven Years' War (1756–63) by Britain's more powerful navy and more vibrant economy. In central and eastern Europe,

absolutist monarchies in Prussia, Austria, and Russia competed for influence and expanded their territories. The smaller states in Italy and Germany
maintained their independence as best they could. By the end of the century,
revolutions in America and France brought changes that would eventually
transform political and social life throughout Europe and the Americas and
change the foundations of musical culture in the nineteenth century.

Improvements in agriculture boosted food production and made possible   *Economic change*
a rapid increase in population across Europe and North America. Capitals and
other large cities expanded especially rapidly, and growth in manufacturing
and trade stimulated the economy in new directions. The urban middle class
rose in numbers, wealth, and social prominence. The poor often suffered
dislocation from the land and overcrowding in the cities, victims of the very
progress that helped the well-born and the lucky.

The eighteenth century was a cosmopolitan age. Partly because of mar-   *A cosmopolitan*
riages between powerful families, foreign-born rulers abounded: German   *society*
kings in England, Sweden, and Poland; a Spanish king in Naples; a French
duke in Tuscany; a German princess (Catherine the Great) as empress of
Russia. Intellectuals and artists traveled widely. The Frenchman Voltaire
sojourned at the French-speaking court of Frederick the Great of Prussia,
the Italian poet Metastasio worked at the German imperial court in Vienna,
and the German writer F. M. von Grimm gained prominence in Parisian literary and musical circles. Shared humanity and culture mattered more than
national and linguistic differences.

Musical life reflected this international culture. Italian opera composers   *International*
and singers worked in Austria, Germany, France, Spain, England, and Russia,   *musical style*
and German composers were active in Paris, London, and North America.
Johann Joachim Quantz proposed in 1752 that the ideal musical style blended
the best features of music from all nations, and by 1785 this mixed style was
so universally adopted that, in the words of a French critic, there was only
"one music for all of Europe" (see Source Readings, p. 456). Yet *nationalism*,
a major theme in the nineteenth century, was already beginning to emerge by
the end of the eighteenth century, especially in a growing preference for opera
in the vernacular rather than exclusively in Italian.

THE ENLIGHTENMENT The most vibrant intellectual movement of the
eighteenth century was the Enlightenment, whose central themes were reason, nature, and progress. The scientific advances of the previous century
led many intellectuals to believe that people could solve all kinds of problems, including social and practical ones, by reasoning from experience and
from careful observation. This approach was now applied to the study of the
emotions, social relations, and politics. Belief in natural law led to the idea
that individuals had rights and that the role of the state was to improve the
human condition. Those who subscribed to the Enlightenment valued individual faith and practical morality over the church, preferred naturalness to
artificiality, and promoted universal education and a growing social equality.

The leaders of the Enlightenment were French thinkers such as Voltaire,   *The philosophes*
Montesquieu, and Jean-Jacques Rousseau. Known as *philosophes*, they were
among the principal contributors to Denis Diderot's monumental *Ency-
clopédie*, a compendium of everything then known and a key text of the

The Merging of National Styles

Throughout the seventeenth and early eighteenth centuries, Italy and France were the leading musical nations, and their distinctive styles were admired and imitated in other countries. But by the mid-eighteenth century, musicians, audiences, and critics increasingly preferred music that mixed national characteristics. German flutist and composer Johann Joachim Quantz (1697–1773), writing in his *Essay on Playing the Transverse Flute* (1752), argued that the ideal music blended the best elements of many nations and appealed to the widest audience. Not surprisingly, he noted that this mixed taste was typical of German composers.

✵

In a style that consists, like the present German one, of a mix of the styles of different peoples, every nation finds something familiar and unfailingly pleasing. Considering all that has been discussed about the differences among styles, we must vote for the pure Italian style over the pure French. The first is no longer as solidly grounded as it used to be, having become brash and bizarre, and the second has remained too simple. Everyone will therefore agree that a style blending the good elements of both will certainly be more universal and more pleasing. For a music that is accepted and favored by many peoples, and not just by a single land, a single province, or a particular nation, must be the very best, provided it is founded on sound judgment and a healthy attitude.

Johann Joachim Quantz, *Versuch einer Anweisung, die Flöte traversiere zu spielen* (Berlin: J. F. Voss, 1752), Chapter 18, § 89.

✵

Three decades later, French composer and critic Michel-Paul-Guy de Chabanon (ca. 1729–1792) observed that a single musical idiom, grounded in the Italian style, prevailed throughout Europe. His description of music as a "universal language" resonated through the next two centuries and contributed to the growing prestige of purely instrumental music.

✵

In the [present] state of civilization and mutual communication between all the peoples of Europe, there exists a commerce of the fine arts, of taste, intelligence, and enlightenment which makes the same discoveries, principles, and methods ebb and flow from one end of the continent to the other. In this free circulation, the arts lose something of their *indigenous* character; they alter it by blending it with other foreign characteristics. In this regard Europe might be considered as a mother-land of which all the arts are citizens; they all speak the same language; they all obey the same customs.

In applying what I have just said especially to music, an even more incontestable degree of truth will be found in it. There is no more than one music for all of Europe since France has overthrown the barriers of ignorance and bad taste. This universal language of our continent at the most undergoes some differences in pronunciation from one people to another, which is to say, in the manner of performing music.

From Harry Robert Lyall, "A French Music Aesthetic of the Eighteenth Century: A Translation and Commentary on Michel Paul Gui de Chabanon's *Musique considérée en elle-même et dans ses rapports avec la parole, les langues, la poésie, et le théâtre*" (Ph.D. dissertation, North Texas State University, 1975), 155–56.

Enlightenment. The philosophes were social reformers more than philosophers. In response to the terrible inequalities between the common people and the privileged classes, they developed doctrines about individual human rights. Some of these doctrines were incorporated into the American Declaration of Independence, Constitution, and Bill of Rights; indeed, Thomas Jefferson, Thomas Paine, Benjamin Franklin, and other founders of the United States were as representative of the Enlightenment as were their French predecessors.

In general, the Enlightenment was a humanitarian movement, whose adherents were interested in promoting the welfare of humankind. Rulers not only patronized arts and letters, they also promoted social reform. The century's enlightened monarchs, such as Frederick the Great of Prussia, Catherine the Great of Russia, and Holy Roman emperor Joseph II, exercised centralized power in their realms as had Louis XIV (see Chapter 16) but sought to use it for the betterment of their subjects, including programs to expand education and care for the poor. In addition, humanitarian ideals and a longing for universal brotherhood were fundamental to a popular movement known as Freemasonry, the teachings of the secret fraternal order of Masons. Founded in London early in the eighteenth century, it spread rapidly throughout Europe and North America and numbered among its adherents monarchs (Frederick the Great and Joseph II), statesmen (Washington), poets (Goethe), and composers (Haydn and Mozart).

Humanitarianism

The pursuit of learning and the love of art and music became more widespread, particularly among the expanding middle class. This growing interest made new demands on writers and artists that affected both the subject matter and its manner of presentation. Philosophy, science, literature, and the fine arts all increasingly addressed a general public as well as patrons, experts, or connoisseurs. Popular treatises were written with an eye to bringing culture within the reach of all, while novelists and playwrights increasingly depicted common people in everyday situations.

Popularization of learning

SOCIAL ROLES FOR MUSIC While courts, city governments, and churches continued to sponsor music-making as they had for centuries, musicians drew increasing support from the public. There were now public concerts in many cities (see Innovations: The Public Concert, pp. 458–59), offering opportunities for performers and composers to supplement their incomes and to reach a wider audience. Many musicians also earned money as teachers to amateur performers.

With an expanding economy, a steadily growing middle class, and more leisure time, the number of amateurs making music continued to increase. Women were welcome to participate at amateur performances, especially at the keyboard, as in Figure 20.3 (see p. 460), but they were excluded from almost all professional roles other than as singers; to perform in front of men for money was to put oneself in the courtesan class, which would have been a catastrophic loss of status for any middle- or upper-class woman. Men in the middle and upper classes also often participated in amateur music-making, and young people, especially girls, usually received music lessons. Amateur musicians naturally bought music that they could understand and play, and music publishers catered especially to them. Most of the published music for keyboard, chamber ensemble, or voice and keyboard was designed for amateurs to perform at home for their own pleasure. In addition, from mid-century on, many amateur groups formed to sing choral music for their entertainment and for public performance, and these groups provided publishers with a rich new market. The growing enthusiasm for music as a leisure activity also fostered the development of informed listeners who cultivated a taste for

Musical amateurs and connoisseurs

The Public Concert

During the eighteenth century, public concerts and concert series arose in many cities alongside the private concerts and academies that had long been presented by wealthy individual patrons and clubs. Private concerts were by invitation only, and the aristocratic patrons who sponsored them normally assumed all the costs. Public concerts, by contrast, were usually moneymaking ventures for which tickets were sold. Tickets were offered by subscription to a series or for an individual event, and anyone who could pay the price could attend. But ticket prices were not readily affordable for most people, so the audience for public concerts came mostly from the upper-middle and wealthy leisure classes.

Concert halls and concert societies flourished in London starting in 1672 and especially after 1720. At pleasure gardens such as Vauxhall, shown in Figure 20.1, the public paid an entrance fee to enjoy music and other entertainment outdoors. A remarkable institution for the day was the Academy of Ancient Music, devoted to the performance of sixteenth- and seventeenth-century sacred music and madrigals and other music of earlier times; its founding in 1726 inaugurated concerts of music from the past, which became increasingly popular over the next three centuries. By the second half of the eighteenth century, musical life in London centered around public concerts, including an annual subscription series put on from 1765 to 1781 by Johann Christian Bach and Carl Friedrich Abel. Similar societies were formed in other British and North American

FIGURE 20.1 *Outdoor concert at Vauxhall pleasure gardens in London. Mrs. Weischel sings from the balcony of the "Moorish-Gothick temple," accompanied by the orchestra behind her, while the writer Samuel Johnson and his companions eat in the supper box below. Watercolor (ca. 1784) by Thomas Rowlandson.*

Dimanche 25 Mars 1781,
CONCERT SPIRITUEL,
Au Bénéfice de M. RAYMOND, Maître de Muſique du Spectacle.

1°. Une Symphonie à grand Orchestre, de M. RAYMOND.
2°. Une Ariette, par M. l'Abbé d'AUVILLIERS.
3°. Une Ariette, par Mlle. LACOUR.
4°. La Chaſſe de l'Amoureux de quinze ans, par M. PAULMIER.
5°. Un Concerto de Hautbois, par M. CASIMIR.
6°. L'Ariette des traîneaux dans les Souliers mordorés, par M. STE-FOIX.
7°. La grande Ariette de l'Amant jaloux, par Mademoiselle DUCHAUMONT.

8°. Une Ariette.
9°. Un Concerto de Clavecin, par un Amateur de cette Ville.
10°. Une Ariette, par M. l'Abbé CROISI.
11°. Une Ariette.
12°. Une Ariette, par M. l'Abbé QUESNEL.
13°. Une Symphonie concertante de Baſſon, Alto, &c., par MM. LACROIX & ROUSSEL.
14°. La grande Ariette de la Belle Arſène, par Mademoiselle DUCHAUMONT.

LE FRANÇOIS AU COMBAT,
Ariette Militaire, à grand Orchestre, de M. RAYMOND, chantée par M. GAGNEROT.

Le Concert ſera terminé par
LA RÉSURRECTION,
Oratoire à grand Orchestre, mis en Muſique par M. RAYMOND.

AUX DAMES.

SEXE CHARMANT, à qui je cherche à plaire,
Viens embellir le ſéjour des talens;
Par ta préſence échauffe mes accens:
Un ſeul de tes regards & m'anime & m'éclaire.
Eh! que m'importe à moi ce Laurier ſi vanté
Dont le génie ſe couronne,
Ce ſceau de l'immortalité,
Si ce n'eſt point la Beauté qui le donne.

On prendra Trente ſols par Perſonne. On commencera à ſix heures préciſes.
C'eſt à la Salle du Concert de MM. les Amateurs.

FIGURE 20.2 *Handbill for a benefit concert held in March 1781, probably in Paris.*

cities, including the Edinburgh Musical Society in Scotland (1728) and the St. Cecilia Society in Charleston, South Carolina (1766).

In Paris, the composer and oboist Anne Danican Philidor founded the Concert Spirituel series in 1725, which lasted until 1790. The repertoire encompassed new music from France and other nations, with performers from across the continent. The presentation of sonatas and concertos by Vivaldi and other Italians fostered a growing taste for Italian music in France, and from midcentury on, performances of symphonies by German and Austrian composers spurred French composers to cultivate the symphony.

Later in the century, the movement toward public concerts spread to German-speaking lands as well. In 1763, J. A. Hiller began a concert series in Leipzig, which continued after 1781 in the new concert hall at the Gewandhaus (Clothiers' Exchange); the Gewandhaus Orchestra still exists and has become one of the most famous orchestras in the world. Similar concert organizations were founded in Vienna (1771) and in Berlin (1790).

Public concerts were advertised by word of mouth and through handbills, posters, notices in newspapers, and other printed media. Figure 20.2 shows a handbill for a 1781 benefit concert that offers a wealth of information about the concerts of the time. The concert was presented "for the benefit of M[onsieur] Raymond, Master of Music for the performance," meaning

that he directed the concert and received whatever profits were left over after paying the musicians, the hall rental, and other expenses. The price, given at the bottom of the poster, was thirty sols per person, steep enough that only the well-to-do were likely to attend. The concert was to begin "precisely at six o'clock." To judge from the announced program, it lasted about three hours, which was typical at the time.

We are accustomed today to concerts made up entirely of a single type of music, such as orchestral works, piano music, or songs. But concerts in the eighteenth and early nineteenth centuries, public or private, typically presented a variety of vocal and instrumental genres for various ensembles, as "pops" concerts do today. The program listed here includes a symphony, two concertos, a symphonie concertante, numerous arias, and an oratorio. The composer is given only for pieces by Raymond; in other cases, the name by each piece is that of the featured performer, showing that the performer was in most cases more important than the composer. Listed ninth is "A Harpsichord Concerto, [performed] by an Amateur of this City." The unnamed amateur who played the keyboard may have been a woman, since women were not yet accepted as professional instrumentalists.

An eighteenth-century concert was a social occasion as well as an opportunity to hear music. Audience members could stroll around and converse, paying attention only to the music that interested them, without being considered rude; the silent, motionless audience was an invention of the nineteenth century. The presence of women of the right social class was essential for making the event a social success, so Raymond made sure they felt welcome by including a poem at the bottom of the poster:

To The Ladies.
Charming sex, whom I seek to please,
Come embellish the abode of our talents;
By your presence warm up my accents:
Just one of your looks brings me to life and
lights me up.
Eh! what does it matter to me, this much
vaunted Laurel
With which genius is crowned,
This seal of immortality,
If it is not Beauty who gives it.

FIGURE 20.3 *A private performance by a chamber ensemble consisting of a singer, two violins, viola, cello, and harpsichord. The presence of a woman at the keyboard and the similarity of dress and wigs worn by the musicians and listeners indicate that the performers were most likely skilled amateurs rather than professionals, who would have been dressed in servants' livery. Engraving from 1769 by Daniel Nikolaus Chodowiecki.*

ERICH LESSING/ART RESOURCE, NY

the best in music; the term ***connoisseur*** was coined in the early eighteenth century to describe such listeners. Concert life and amateur music-making reinforced each other; connoisseurs were often amateur performers themselves, and amateurs were often avid concertgoers.

Musical journals and histories   As the musical public broadened, more people became interested in reading about music and discussing it. By midcentury, magazines devoted to musical news, reviews, and criticism began to appear, catering to both amateurs and connoisseurs. The public's curiosity about music extended to its origins and past styles, addressed in the first universal histories of music: Charles Burney's *A General History of Music* (1776–89), John Hawkins's *A General History of the Science and Practice of Music* (1776), and Johann Nikolaus Forkel's *Allgemeine Geschichte der Musik* (General History of Music, 1788–1801).

MUSICAL TASTE AND STYLE

Many musical styles coexisted in the eighteenth century, each supported by strong adherents and criticized by detractors. Every country had distinctive traditions and developed a national form of opera. Works in new styles, such as the operas of Pergolesi and Hasse (see Chapter 21), were written at the same time as works in late Baroque styles, such as Rameau's operas, Handel's oratorios, and Bach's *Art of Fugue*. Writers and musicians still recognized distinctions between styles appropriate for theater, chamber, and church, and composers were trained in all three.

Values for music   Despite the variety of styles, leading writers in the middle and late eighteenth century articulated the prevailing view of what was most valued in music. Instead of the contrapuntal complexity and spun-out instrumental melody of Baroque music, audiences preferred and critics praised music that featured a vocally conceived melody in short phrases over spare accompaniment. Writers held that the language of music should be universal,

Nature and the Arts

Charles Batteux (1713–1780) was a professor of philosophy in Paris. His widely read book *Les beaux-arts réduite à un même principe* (The Fine Arts Distilled to a Common Principle, 1746) distinguished the fine arts from the practical arts (which serve functional purposes) and argued that the fine arts must imitate and idealize nature, which music does by expressing the passions.

✤

It is man who created the arts; he has done so to satisfy his own needs. Finding the pleasures of simple nature too monotonous, and finding himself moreover in a situation in which he could enhance his pleasure, he created out of his own native genius a new order of ideas and feelings, one that would revive his spirits and enliven his taste. For what could the man of genius do? . . . He had necessarily to direct his entire effort to a selection from nature of her finest elements, in order to make from them an exquisite, yet entirely natural whole, one that would be more perfect than nature herself. . . .

From this I conclude, first, that genius—the father of the arts—must imitate nature. Secondly, that genius may not imitate nature just as she is.

Thirdly, that taste, for which the arts are made and by which they are judged, finds satisfaction when the artistic choice and imitation of nature has been well managed.

Music speaks to me in tones: this language is natural to me. If I do not understand it, art has corrupted nature rather than perfected her. . . .

Thus, although the learned musician may congratulate himself if he so wishes on having reconciled, by means of mathematics, sounds that seemed to be irreconcilable, unless those sounds mean something they may be compared to the gestures of an orator which do no more than show that the speaker is alive; they may similarly be compared to verses that are nothing but measured sounds, or to the mannerisms of a writer that are nothing but frivolous ornament. The worst kind of music is that which has no character. There is not a musical sound that does not have its model in nature, and which may not at least be the beginnings of expression, just as is a letter or syllable in speech.

Charles Batteux, *Les beaux-arts réduits à un même principe* (Paris 1746), in *Music and Aesthetics in the Eighteenth and Early-Nineteenth Centuries*, ed. Peter le Huray and James Day (Cambridge: Cambridge University Press, 1981), 44–45 and 48–49.

rather than limited by national boundaries, and should appeal to all tastes at once, from the connoisseur to the untutored. The best music should be noble as well as entertaining; expressive within the limits of decorum; and "natural"—free of technical complications and capable of immediately pleasing any sensitive listener.

These values for music, especially the preference for the "natural," related directly to the central ideas of the Enlightenment. In the realm of knowledge, Enlightenment thinkers rejected the supernatural claims of traditional religion in favor of direct observations of nature, the evidence they could see and hear with their own senses and understand through human reason. In art, they rejected artifice and complexity, which they regarded as unnatural, and preferred direct communication. In his influential book *Les beaux-arts* (The Fine Arts, 1746), philosopher Charles Batteux defined the task of the arts as imitating and even perfecting nature (see Source Reading). He asserted

TIMELINE

that if music is true to nature it will be easily understood, while learned counterpoint that conveys no meaning is empty show. Even taste—by which Batteux and his contemporaries meant not individual opinion but prevailing social norms—was governed by rational processes and subject to the laws of "artistic choice and imitation of nature." Especially striking is his claim that "it is man who created the arts; he has done so to satisfy his own needs." Just two generations earlier, in the preface to *Der edlen Music-Kunst* (The Noble Art of Music, 1691), Andreas Werckmeister had called music "a gift of God, to be used only in His honor." The contrast between these two statements illustrates the change in thought between the Baroque period and the Enlightenment, affecting music along with every other aspect of life.

TERMS FOR STYLES: GALANT, EMPFINDSAM, CLASSICAL
These new values for music led to the development of a new musical idiom known today as the ***classical style***. Several terms have been used to describe this style and its close relatives, and writers, both today and then, sometimes use these words with somewhat different meanings.

During the eighteenth century, the most common term for the new style was ***galant***, a French term for the manners and attitudes cultivated at courts and in polite society, including charm, wit, sophistication, attentiveness, proper behavior, fashionable dress, and the ability to perform music as amateurs and to listen to it with discernment. Galant men and women expected the music they heard and played to be likewise charming, witty, sophisticated, fashionable, and comprehensible on first hearing. The galant style met their requirements with attractive, winning melodies paired with bass lines that led the ear to the next harmonic goal.

Writers distinguished between the learned or strict style of contrapuntal writing—what we would call Baroque—and the freer, more songlike, homophonic, galant style (see Source Reading). The latter emphasized melody made up of short-breathed, often repeated gestures organized in phrases of two, three, or four measures. These phrases combined into larger units, lightly accompanied with simple harmony and punctuated by frequent cadences. The learned style was still considered appropriate for church music, where an old and elevated style conveyed solemnity and tradition, but even in sacred music the galant style became the primary style.

Despite its French name, the galant style originated in Italian operas and instrumental music, and the term was apparently coined in 1721 by the German composer and theorist Johann Mattheson, showing the international reach of the new style. It emerged in the opera houses of Naples and Venice, was cultivated at courts throughout Italy and Germany where Italian-trained musicians served, and spread to cities across Europe and the Americas. Like many other musical traditions, from Renaissance counterpoint to jazz, the galant style was developed and disseminated by a network

A View of the Galant Style

Keyboard teacher and composer Daniel Gottlob Türk (1750–1813) aimed his *Klavierschule* (School of Clavier Playing, 1789) at the amateur who needed instruction in taste and style as well as method. He described the differences between "strict" and "free" styles—that is, between the older learned style and the new galant style.

A strict (contrapuntal) style is the one in which the composer follows all the rules of harmony and modulation in the strictest manner, mixing in artful imitations and many tied notes, working out the theme carefully, and the like, in short, allowing

more art to be heard than euphony. In the free (*galant*) manner of composition, the composer is not so slavishly bound to the rules of harmony, modulation, and the like. He often permits bold changes, which could even be contrary to the generally accepted rules of modulation, assuming that the composer in doing this proceeds with proper insight and judgment, and with it is able to attain a certain goal. In general, the free style of writing has more expression and euphony rather than art as its chief purpose.

Daniel Gottlob Türk, *School of Clavier Playing*, trans. Raymond H. Haggh (Lincoln: University of Nebraska Press, 1982), 399. In SR 132 (5:11), p. 891.

of musicians who learned from each other and shared a set of routines that could be used to create new pieces, whether improvised or written down. It was a music of stock figures and gestures deployed in endless combinations, akin to the improvised plays of the *commedia dell'arte* (see Chapter 21). Musicians with a deep knowledge of the style could improvise a minuet or sonata movement by playing on these gestures, which typically comprised an outline of melody and bass, and composition was putting together (com-posing) these figures into convincing successions and embellishing them with taste and individuality. Listeners familiar with these routines took pleasure in hearing them elegantly presented in new combinations, anticipating what would come next and enjoying the surprises, delays, and fulfillment along the way. The style was nurtured in the conservatories of Naples and Venice and passed down through teachers all over Europe, ultimately becoming the foundation for the musical idiom of the middle to late eighteenth century.

A close relative of the galant style was the *empfindsamer Stil* (German for "sensitive style") or **empfindsam style**. Characterized by surprising turns of harmony, chromaticism, nervous rhythms, and rhapsodically free, speech-like melody, the empfindsam style is most closely associated with fantasias and slow movements by Carl Philipp Emanuel Bach (see Chapter 22).

Empfindsam style

The term "classical" is used at times for art music of all periods and at other times more narrowly for the style of the late eighteenth century. There is a historical reason for this ambiguity. In the nineteenth century, works of J. S. Bach, Handel, Haydn, Mozart, and Beethoven were regarded as classics of music, akin to classics of literature or art, and they formed the core of what became known as the classical repertoire (see Chapter 26). During the nineteenth and twentieth centuries, the classical repertoire expanded beyond its original core, so that now **classical music** is a tradition that covers many

Classical music and classical style

centuries and a multitude of styles. By the mid-twentieth century, the music of Bach and Handel was called "Baroque" rather than "classical," leaving the latter as the term for the late-eighteenth-century style. Thus, from an original single meaning, "classical" evolved through use to mean two very different things in relation to music.

What is the classical style?

Some writers apply the term "classical style"—or its variant, "classic"—only to the mature music of Haydn and Mozart, while others use it more broadly for the entire period from the 1720s or 1730s to around 1800 or 1815. The term as applied to music came by way of analogy to Greek and Roman art. At its best, classical music possessed the qualities of noble simplicity, balance, formal perfection, diversity within unity, seriousness or wit as appropriate, and freedom from excesses of ornamentation and frills. It is almost impossible to use the term without making value judgments. Is it to apply only to Haydn, Mozart, and Beethoven, in whom these qualities abound and whose works have been judged classics? Or also to their contemporaries, no matter how little known? Should it also apply to their midcentury predecessors who used a similar musical language? The latter are sometimes called *preclassic*, an unfortunate term that suggests their only value was to pave the way for Haydn and company.

The Classic period

The solution adopted in this book is to regard the era from about 1730 to 1815 as the **Classic period**, to use *Classic music* (rather than "classical style") as the all-embracing term for music of the period, and to use terms such as galant, empfindsam, and "the Haydn idiom" to identify different styles or trends current at the time. This period could with more justice be called the *Galant period*, since the term *galant* was used at the time (unlike *classic* or *classical*) and both the empfindsam style and the idiom of Haydn and Mozart are outgrowths of the galant style; but modern musicians and audiences are so accustomed to the term *Classic* for this period that it seems unlikely to be displaced. The boundaries of the Classic period overlap with the Baroque and Romantic periods, just as boundaries blur between Medieval and Renaissance and between Renaissance and Baroque, since the language, genres, and customs of music change only gradually and at different times in different places.

MELODY, HARMONY, PHRASING, AND FORM The focus on melody in the new styles reflects a musical syntax quite different from the continuous motivic variation of earlier styles. J. S. Bach, for example, would typically announce at the outset of a movement the musical idea, a melodic-rhythmic subject embodying the basic affection. This idea was then spun out, using sequential repetition as a principal constructive device, within a generally irregular phrase structure marked by relatively infrequent cadences.

Periodicity

In contrast, the newer styles were marked by **periodicity**, in which frequent resting points break the melodic flow into segments that relate to each other as parts of a larger whole. Musical ideas, rather than being persistently spun out, were articulated through distinct phrases, typically two or four measures in length but sometimes three, five, or six measures. Two or more phrases were needed to form a **period**, a complete musical thought concluded by a full cadence, and a composition was made up of two or more periods in succession. This technique creates a structure delineated by frequent cadences and integrated through small motivic correspondences.

The terminology of phrases and periods was borrowed from rhetoric, the art of oration. Eighteenth-century theorists frequently compared a melody to a sentence or a musical composition to a speech. The most thorough guide to melodic composition based on rhetorical principles appears in volume 2 of the *Versuch einer Anleitung zur Composition* (Introductory Essay on Composition, published in three volumes in 1782, 1787, and 1793) by Heinrich Christoph Koch (1749–1816), one of several treatises written for amateurs who wished to learn how to compose. Here the student learns how to construct a melody by joining short melodic segments (Koch calls them *incises*, or clauses) to form phrases, and phrases to form periods. Clauses, phrases, and periods differ in their endings, which create resting points of varying strength that Koch compares to melodic punctuation, like the commas, semi-colons, and periods in a text: a segment or clause contains an incomplete idea, ending with the musical equivalent of a comma; a *phrase of partial close* requires another phrase to follow it; and a *closing phrase* has a full cadence that can end a period. Koch states that this kind of organization is necessary to make a melody intelligible and capable of moving our feelings, just as the sentences and clauses that break up a speech make it easier to follow the train of thought.

Musical rhetoric

In Example 20.1a (see p. 466), Koch's approach is used to show the structure of the theme of a variations movement by Baldassare Galuppi (1706–1785), the finale of his Keyboard Sonata in D Major, Op. 2, No. 1 (NAWM 116c), from about 1750. Galuppi was the most famous opera composer of the mid-eighteenth century, and his contemporaries likely would have named him if asked who was the greatest composer of their time.

Phrasing and rhetoric in a theme by Galuppi

Galuppi's theme is a small binary form, with two periods of eight measures, each repeated. Each period comprises two four-measure phrases, a phrase of partial close followed by a closing phrase. The opening phrase has two two-measure segments: the first closes weakly with a rising appoggiatura, and the second completes the phrase with a more emphatic falling appoggiatura ornamenting a half cadence. Though there is a clear articulation between them and the second segment introduces a new rhythmic figure (x), the two segments are linked by similar bass lines, similar overall rhythm, the motion in each segment from tonic to dominant, and the overarching melodic contour that rises from d'' to a'' then falls back to e''. The closing phrase that follows is continuous, without a resting point in the middle; it begins by echoing the end of the first phrase, continues with a descending figure in a new rhythm (y), and then repeats the rhythmic figure x while presenting the most definitive cadence so far, providing a fit conclusion to the phrase and to the entire first period. This phrase features a gradual descent from the melodic peak to the cadential note, and an accelerating harmonic rhythm, changing chords first on every half note, then every quarter note in measure 6 and every eighth note in measure 7.

The second period begins with a variant of the theme's opening segment, repeated in a rising sequence to complete the phrase. Like the first phase of the first period, there is an articulation between the two segments, and the harmony changes every two beats. The second phrase varies that of the first period, again featuring rhythmic figures x and y, tracing a mostly stepwise descent, and accelerating the harmonic rhythm, leading to a conclusive full

EXAMPLE 20.1 *Baldassare Galuppi, theme from finale of Keyboard Sonata in D Major, Op. 2, No. 1*

a. Analyzed by segment, phrase, and period

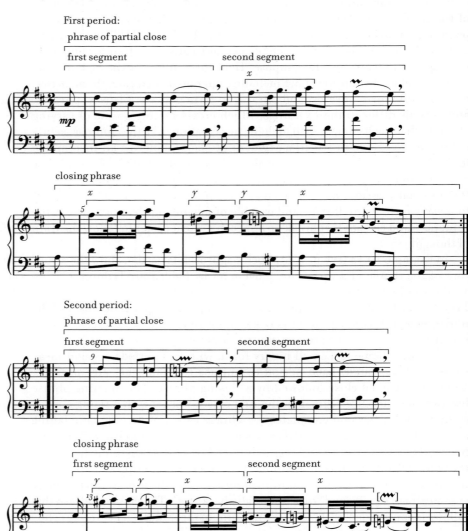

cadence on the tonic. A rest in the bass separates the two segments of this phrase, but they are linked by the unbroken flow in the melody.

The theme is beautifully constructed, each segment of the melody varying material that has come before. Like a skilled orator, Galuppi holds to his subject, reinforcing it with repetition, variation, and new arguments, and carefully arranges his thoughts to make them intelligible, persuasive, and moving.

Harmony   The division of the melody into phrases and periods is supported by the harmony. There is a hierarchy of cadences, with the weakest marking off internal phrases, stronger ones closing periods, and the strongest reserved

b. Analyzed by schema

for the ends of sections and movements. There is also a hierarchy of harmonic motions, with the small-scale I–V–I in a single phrase (seen here in measures 1–3) subsumed within a large-scale modulation from tonic to dominant and back over the course of the theme or an entire movement.

Finally, the coherence of late-eighteenth-century music was made possible by the differentiation of musical material according to its function. Each segment of music was immediately recognizable as a beginning, middle, or ending gesture. The first two measures of Example 20.1a serve well as the beginning of a phrase, period, or movement, but could not be an ending. By contrast, measures 7–8 offer an emphatic ending, but would sound out of place at the beginning of a phrase or period. Measure 6 serves well in the middle of a phrase, repeating a motive and rhythm in sequence, but would not serve as a good beginning and could not be followed by a rest, as is the

Form

ending gesture in measures 7–8, without sounding as if the music had been interrupted midstream. Within these categories, there are levels of relative strength. The segment in measures 13–14 can begin a phrase but not a movement, since it starts in midair over an inverted chord and thus has the quality of being in the middle of a thought. Measures 3–4 are strong enough to end a phrase but not a period, as the cadence feels incomplete. The cadence in measures 7–8 is stronger, marking the end of the period, but is on the dominant, and thus cannot close the theme or an entire movement. Such distinctions allowed composers to make clear at every turn where we are in the musical form, just as an orator varies the use of emphasis, inflections, and pauses to mark the beginnings and ends of sentences, paragraphs, sections, and the entire speech.

COMPOSING WITH SCHEMATA Koch's description of music as a kind of oration makes sense to us, and we still speak of music in terms of phrases and periods. But Koch was writing for amateurs—which in a sense is what we are today when we encounter a musical tradition from the past. Professional composers of the eighteenth century learned from other composers in a living tradition. Through practice and repetition, they absorbed the trade secrets of their time, a lore for how music goes that allowed them to compose fluently and create pieces that would please and entertain their audience. Koch teaches us how to think *about* music; professionals were trained to think *in* music.

Schema   Music theorist and historian Robert O. Gjerdingen has sought to reconstruct this tradition by studying the training composers received in the conservatories of Naples and Venice or from Italian-trained master composers. He argues that they learned a common set of formulas combining motion of the melody and of the bass line—he calls such a formula a ***schema*** (pl. *schemata*)—and strategies for joining them into logical successions and elaborating them with pleasing grace. Through constant use, these schemata became conventions that were recognized by performers and listeners acquainted with the galant style, who enjoyed hearing these gestures in new guises and combinations and could use their familiar outlines to follow the progress of the music.

Schemata in Galuppi's theme   Example 20.1b shows Galuppi's theme as a series of such formulas, using Gjerdingen's name for each schema. It begins with a *Do-Re-Mi,* a decorated progression of scale degrees 1, 2, and 3 in the melody over 1–7–1 in the bass, and concludes the first phrase with a *Half Cadence,* scale degrees 3 and 2 over 5 in the bass. The second phrase modulates to the key of the dominant using a *Prinner,* a melodic progression of scale degrees 6–5–4–3 in the new key over 4–3–2–1 in the bass, and concludes with a *Complete Cadence* in the new key, 4–5–5–1 in the bass under 4–3–2–1 in the melody. The second period begins with a *Monte,* a rising modulating sequence featuring 5–4–3 in the melody over 7–1 in the bass, first in G major (the key of the subdominant) and then in A major (the dominant). The final phrase returns to D major with a *Sol-Fa-Mi* (5–4–3 in the melody over 1–2–7–1 in the bass) and concludes with a Complete Cadence in the tonic. All of these melodic outlines are elaborated and decorated, creating a pleasing and individual piece of music.

Schema and function   Each schema has a clear function in this theme. The Do-Re-Mi is one of several schemata that can begin a piece, period, or section, and it serves that function here. Such opening gambits are frequently followed by a Prinner, which cannot serve as a beginning but works well as a response to an opening gesture and is often deployed to effect a modulation to the dominant, as is true here. The Monte is commonly used to begin the second half of a binary form, as in this theme, and Complete Cadences naturally mark the ends of periods. Each schema is a module that fits together with the others to make a complete and convincing whole.

We do not know whether most of these schemata were given names in the eighteenth century; only a few were described or named in writings from that time (among them the Monte, meaning "mount"), suggesting that they were absorbed not from textbooks but from practice. But musicians learned all of these and many more, along with strategies for stringing them together and decorating them to create new pieces of music. They internalized them through exercises such as filling in upper parts above a bass designed for instructional purposes (called a *partimento*) and adding a bass and middle voices to an instructional melody (called a *solfeggio*). Knowing these schemata and strategies allowed eighteenth-century musicians to improvise coherently and to write long works quickly.

Learning schemata

Both Koch and Gjerdingen give us insight into music of the middle to late eighteenth century. Koch's guide for amateur composers helps us understand the style of the era, using terminology not so different from our own, and get a sense of why it was comprehensible to such a wide range of listeners. Gjerdingen's approach is an attempt to reconstruct how musicians of the time thought in music itself. Like training in twelfth-century polyphony or twentieth-century jazz, the focus of a professional composer's education in the eighteenth century was on memorizing what to do in specific situations, rather than articulating general rules (an approach more typical of amateurs or scholars). For Gjerdingen, it is these schemata and strategies that constitute the galant style, the common musical language of composers working between about 1720 and 1780, an idiom used to create a play of expectation, permutation, combination, deception, and fulfillment that cultivated listeners could follow with pleasure.

Schema and style

EMOTIONAL CONTRASTS One of the most striking characteristics of Classic music resulted from a new view of human psychology. Descartes and others in the seventeenth century believed that once an emotion, such as anger or fear, was aroused, a person remained in that affection until moved by some stimulus to a different emotional state. Accordingly, composers in the Baroque era sought to convey a single mood in each movement, or at most to contrast conflicting moods in self-contained sections, such as the two parts of a da capo aria or the ritornello and episodes of a concerto movement. But deeper knowledge of blood circulation, the nervous system, and other aspects of human physiology led to a new understanding that feelings were constantly in flux, jostled by associations that might take unpredictable turns.

New view of psychology

The new notion that emotions were not steady states, but were constantly changing and sometimes contradictory responses to one's experiences and thoughts, undermined the Baroque approach of conveying a single feeling in a movement or section. Instead, composers began to introduce contrasting moods in the various parts of a movement or even within the themes themselves.

Form and content

We will see in the next chapter (pp. 474–76) how Pergolesi portrayed the shifting moods of a character in *La serva padrona* through an aria whose musical material changes from nervously jumpy to lyrical to slow and deliberate, and in Chapter 23 how Mozart infused both his vocal and his instrumental music with strong contrasts of style, texture, and mood. The possibilities for contrasts were heightened by the nature of the new music, with its many short phrases and its dependence on differences in the material to articulate the form.

THE ENDURING ENLIGHTENMENT

We are in many ways children of the Enlightenment, often taking for granted its central themes: that humans can know the natural world through our senses, understand it through our reason, and make progress in science and culture. These ideas are still strong today. Yet the intervening centuries have also seen waves of reaction to the Enlightenment that have challenged its ideals, such as the nineteenth-century Romantic interest in fantasy and the supernatural, the twentieth-century loss of faith in reason and progress—in response to two world wars and nuclear weapons—and recent postmodernist challenges to the very concepts of reason, nature, and progress.

In music too, many of our most enduring and often unquestioned assumptions can be traced back to the Enlightenment, including the ideas that music serves human needs, that its primary purpose is pleasure rather than religious or social ends, that music is a universal language, that ideally music should appeal to a wide audience, that we should be able to understand a piece of music on first hearing, and that the feelings music suggests may change as quickly as our own emotions do. Many of our musical institutions and forums stem from the same period, such as public concert organizations, amateur choirs, music journalism, and books on music history like this one.

Alongside ideas and institutions, many aspects of musical style from the era of the Enlightenment have continued through the past 250 years. The tradition of teaching the schemata at the core of the galant style continued not only in Italy but elsewhere as well, especially in Paris, where Italian composers and their students taught at the conservatory and in private studios well into the nineteenth century. Even composers outside this pedagogical tradition absorbed elements of the galant style through their familiarity with music influenced by it. More broadly, much of the music composed since 1800 shares essential characteristics with that of the middle to late eighteenth century, from a texture of melody with accompaniment to a periodic structure of phrases and periods. Music that meets these expectations is for most of us the music we encounter most often and find most normal. Music that does not, whether a Baroque fugue, a Renaissance madrigal, or an electronic or minimalist work of the late twentieth century, is distinctive by comparison and may become all the more intriguing for that reason. The galant style hailed by eighteenth-century writers suited the tastes of its time, but the arguments about which types and styles of music are best have only grown more intense since then.

Further Reading is available at digital.wwnorton.com/hwm10

OPERA AND VOCAL MUSIC IN THE EARLY CLASSIC PERIOD

❈

The new musical idiom hailed by Enlightenment writers had its roots in vocal music, where direct and natural expression of feeling was especially appropriate. Many traits that became typical of Classic-era music originated in Italian opera, beginning in the 1720s and 1730s. A key development was the emergence around 1700 of separate traditions of comic and serious opera. Because tradition weighed less heavily on comic opera, it was more hospitable to innovations than was serious opera; emotions that were expressed through conventions in serious opera could be portrayed in more unexpected and naturalistic ways in comic opera. But composers, singers, and audiences for both kinds of opera nurtured elements that would become crucial in the new style, through the value they placed on the beauty of melody and on the ability of music to portray complex characters and rapidly changing emotions.

National styles of comic opera emerged as well in France, England, and German-speaking lands, each appealing to a wide public through simple and direct musical expression. After midcentury, composers and librettists introduced reforms into serious opera to reflect Enlightenment ideals. Alongside the arena of opera, which included performances of arias in public concerts, new trends also emerged in vocal music for chamber and church. A growing interest in amateur music-making at home fostered new national traditions of song with keyboard accompaniment. Music for church blended older styles, hallowed with use, with current styles borrowed from secular music.

ITALIAN COMIC OPERA

Italian opera, cultivated throughout Italy and at some twenty German and Polish courts by the 1690s, spread even more widely in the eighteenth century, finding homes from Madrid and London in the west to St. Petersburg in the east and Denmark and Sweden in the north. Renewed interest in the views of drama found in Aristotle and other classical writers led librettists to eliminate comic elements from serious opera. In response, beginning in Naples and Venice during the first decade of the eighteenth century, poets, composers, and entrepreneurs developed new independent genres of comic opera that offered social criticism and appealed to a wider audience.

NEAPOLITAN COMIC OPERA　Terms used in eighteenth-century Italy for comic opera included **opera buffa** (comic opera), *dramma giocoso* (jesting drama), *dramma comico* (comic drama), and *commedia per musica* (comedy in music). Today *opera buffa* is often used to encompass all these kinds of opera, but in the eighteenth century it represented a distinct type (see pp. 476–77).

Italian comic operas were sung throughout, unlike comic operas in other languages. Comic opera originated in Naples, staged at the Teatro de' Fiorentini and other public theaters and aimed at a primarily middle-class audience. It spread north to Rome, across northern Italy, and throughout most of Europe by the middle of the eighteenth century, often carried by traveling troupes of performers. Plots centered on ordinary people in the present day, in contrast to the stories from myth or history in serious opera. Comic opera entertained and served a moral purpose by caricaturing the foibles of aristocrats and commoners, vain ladies, miserly old men, awkward and clever servants, deceitful husbands and wives, pedantic lawyers, know-it-all doctors, and pompous military commanders. These derive from the stock characters of the *commedia dell'arte*, the improvised comedy popular in Italy since the sixteenth century that was performed by touring companies of professional actors, but the characters in comic operas are often more fully rounded, placed in specific locales and situations that reflect everyday life. The comic cast was often complemented by serious characters, including a pair of young lovers, around whom the main plot revolved and who interacted with the comic characters, particularly in amorous intrigues. The dialogue was set in rapidly delivered recitative accompanied by continuo, often keyboard alone.

The arias in comic operas are typically in galant style, made up of short tuneful phrases, often repeated or varied, organized into periods, and accompanied by simple harmonies and figuration. One of the pioneers of this style was Leonardo Vinci (ca. 1696–1730). His *Li zite 'ngalera* (The Lovers on the Galley), with a libretto in Neapolitan dialect, premiered in Naples in 1722. Many of the arias are substantial, in da capo form, and accompanied by four-part string ensemble, while others are brief and supported only by continuo. One of the latter type, shown in Example 21.1, is the aria *T'aggio mmidea*, which opens a scene between Belluccia, a woman disguised as a man, and Ciommatella, a young woman who has fallen in love with "him." It begins with two one-measure phrases in an antecedent-consequent pair, repeated when the voice enters, which establishes periodic phrasing as the norm. But later phrases

EXAMPLE 21.1 *Leonardo Vinci,* T'aggio mmidea, *from* Li zite 'ngalera, *Act I, Scene 11*

Bellucia: *I envy you, beautiful bird! You disport yourself among the branches, you sing, you want to hide. And I dress up in feathers.*
Ciommatella: *Why in feathers?*
Bellucia: *Ciomma, what's the use? I told you why*

are extended (measures 6–7 and 10) or truncated (measure 9), creating a dynamic melody that cleverly evades expectations. The surprises continue: after the usual modulation to the dominant, a deceptive cadence (measure 12) leads to a dialogue in recitative. The result is a witty musical setting that perfectly fits the text and moves the drama forward.

INTERMEZZO Another important type of Italian comic opera in the early eighteenth century was the **_intermezzo_**, which was performed in two or three segments between the acts of a serious opera or play. The genre originated in Naples and Venice around 1700 when comic scenes were purged from serious operas, and the comic characters were given their own separate story in the intermezzo. These intermezzi contrasted sharply with the grand and heroic manners of the principal drama, sometimes even parodying its excesses. The plots usually presented two or three people in comic situations, and the action proceeded in alternating recitatives and arias, as in serious opera. Because of their role as adjunct to serious opera, intermezzi were accepted by aristocratic patrons and were performed at court as well as in public opera houses. Figure 21.1 shows an intermezzo performed in Venice.

Pergolesi's
La serva padrona

Giovanni Battista Pergolesi (1710–1736) was one of the most original composers of his day but died young of tuberculosis. He is best known for his intermezzo *La serva padrona* (The Maid as Mistress, 1733), a classic example of opera in miniature, with only three characters: Uberto (bass), a rich bachelor; his

FIGURE 21.1 *Performance of an intermezzo, a short comic work given between the acts of an opera seria. This Venetian painting shows not only how such works were staged, but also how audiences behaved. Some are seated, others standing, and only some are paying attention to the performers on stage, while several are engaged in conversations. The silent attentiveness now expected of audiences for operas and classical concerts was a creation of the nineteenth century.*

EXAMPLE 21.2 *Giovanni Battista Pergolesi,* Son imbrogliato io già, *from* La serva padrona

a. Opening

Son im-bro-glia - to i-o giá, son im-bro-glia - to i-o giá, son im-bro-glia - to i-o

giá!   Ho un cer - to che nel co - re,   che dir per me non so, ___

I am all mixed up! I have a certain something in my heart; truly, I cannot tell [whether it's love or pity.]

b. Later passage

U - ber - to,   pen - sa a   te,   pen - sa a   te!

[I hear a voice that tells me:] Uberto, think of yourself!

maid, Serpina (soprano); and his mute valet, Vespone. Typical of comic opera, the social hierarchy is questioned as Serpina manipulates her master into proposing marriage by inventing a rival suitor (in fact, Vespone in disguise).

The scene after Serpina tells Uberto that she will marry another (NAWM 109) displays the extraordinary aptness and nimbleness of Pergolesi's music. As is typical of both comic and serious opera, the dialogue is rendered in simple recitative, accompanied only by the harpsichord and usually a sustaining bass instrument, with the words set to lively, speechlike rhythms over freely modulating harmonies. After Serpina leaves, Uberto descends into confusion when the thought of marrying her battles with concern over their difference in social class. His mutterings are rendered in accompanied recitative, in which voice and orchestra alternate freely. In serious opera, this style was reserved for the most dramatic situations; knowing this convention, Pergolesi's audience understood the effect here as comic, elevating Uberto's bewilderment to high drama.

As was customary, his feelings culminate in a da capo aria (see Chapter 17, pp. 373–76). Neither the main nor the middle section of the aria develops a single musical motive, as in a Scarlatti or Handel aria. Rather, there are as many melodic ideas as there are shifting thoughts and moods in the text. In the first line, shown in Example 21.2a, Uberto complains that he is confused. The melody reflects his state with a nervous, jumpy motive with wide leaps that are typical of comic opera style, and its threefold repetition suggests his mental paralysis. Uberto then realizes that something mysterious is stirring in his heart (measure 15) and waxes lyrical as he asks himself whether it is love that he feels. But a sober voice within checks his ardor: he should think of himself, guarding his independence and his own interests. Here the melody, shown in Example 21.2b, is slow and deliberate, exploiting the bass's low F to suggest a deep pensiveness, and both melody and harmony turn to F minor. Like the earlier comic reference to accompanied recitative, this dark moment—a voice from out of the depths, speaking to him in second person with a warning conveyed in a slow melody with a chromatic tinge—wittily evokes a style from serious opera, known as *ombra* (Italian for "shadow") and used for scenes with ghosts, gods, or other supernatural beings. The implication that Uberto experiences his nagging fears as some sort of divine intervention arousing both awe and terror is a classic case of humor through exaggeration. In this scene and throughout the opera, Pergolesi's depiction of character and emotion through highly contrasting melodic ideas over light accompaniment made his music particularly successful and influential.

Carlo Goldoni

OPERA BUFFA From the late 1740s on, Venetian dramatist Carlo Goldoni (1707–1793) drew on his experience writing intermezzi, serious opera librettos, and spoken comedies to become the most highly regarded librettist for *opera buffa*, a term he apparently coined. Unlike an intermezzo, an opera buffa was full-length, usually in three acts, and featured six or more singing characters. Goldoni's librettos are full of lifelike dialogue, keen observations of everyday life, and gentle mocking of the fads and foibles of his day, setting the tone for most later comic opera. The comedy springs from the situation as much as from the characters, and the plots include surprises, spectacle, and a variety of material, giving composers ample room for creativity.

Baldassare Galuppi

Beginning with *L'Arcadia in Brenta* in 1749, Goldoni collaborated on more than a dozen comic operas with Baldassare Galuppi (see Chapter 20), who was already among the most prominent composers of serious Italian opera. Galuppi was a master of timing, making music the chief agent of the drama through carefully planned intensification and release. Their works were staged successfully all over Europe and helped to establish the model for opera buffa in the second half of the century, which in turn led to the increasing prominence of comic opera.

Ensemble finales

Goldoni and Galuppi operas featured an opening ensemble to set the scene, diverse aria types and forms, and frequent duets and trios. Especially significant were their extensive ensemble finales, which became a characteristic feature of Italian comic opera. At the end of an act, all the characters were gradually brought on stage while the action continued, becoming more and more animated until it reached a climax with all the singers taking part. These ensemble finales were unlike anything in serious opera, and in writing them composers had to follow the rapidly changing action of the scene without losing coherence in the musical form. Galuppi's finales unfold as a series of sections for different combinations of singers, contrasting in mood, texture, theme, key, meter, and tempo but linked by continuous orchestra playing and a logical key scheme. Such finales are significant because they use music not only to depict emotional states, as opera had long done, but to convey dramatic action, a role that became increasingly important over the next two centuries in opera and in instrumental music as well.

Contributions of Italian comic opera

The periodic phrasing, tuneful melodies, simple harmonies, and spare accompaniment typical of Italian comic opera derived in large part from the galant style in which Vinci, Pergolesi, and Galuppi were all trained, as did their use of standard galant schemata (see Chapter 20). But other traits characteristic of Italian comic opera became its distinctive contributions to the international idiom of the later eighteenth century, including representation of dramatic action, direct expression, emotional fluidity, strong stylistic contrasts, and amusing mixtures of elements.

OPERA SERIA

The transparent and charming style of Vinci and Pergolesi soon invaded serious Italian opera, which became known around midcentury as *opera seria* in contrast to opera buffa.

Serious opera received its standard form from the Italian poet Pietro Metastasio (1698–1782), shown in Figure 21.2. His dramas were set to music hundreds of times by many eighteenth-century composers, including Galuppi, Gluck, and Mozart. His success in Naples, Rome, and Venice led to an appointment in 1729 as court poet in Vienna, where he remained the rest of his life. Despite his aristocratic connections, Metastasio was from a poor background. In his youth, he improvised poetry on the streets of Rome, attracting crowds that one day included lawyer and literary figure Giovanni Vincenzo Gravina, who was so impressed that he adopted the boy and sponsored his education.

Pietro Metastasio

Metastasio's heroic operas present conflicts of human passions, often pitting love against duty, in stories based on ancient Greek or Latin tales. His operas were intended to promote morality through entertainment and to present examples of merciful and enlightened rulers, in tune with Enlightenment thought. Metastasio's favorite characters are magnanimous tyrants, such as the Roman emperor Titus in *La clemenza di Tito* (The Clemency of Titus). His librettos did not include allegorical prologues extolling a monarch, as did Quinault's librettos for Lully at the court of Louis XIV (see Chapter 16), but the noble behavior of rulers like Titus was understood as an implicit compliment to Metastasio's patron, Holy Roman emperor Charles VI, flattering him as an exemplar of the grand and merciful leader. The same implication is evident in countless dedications of opera seria librettos to patrons. The support opera seria gave to the image and legitimacy of rulers was a central reason for its cultivation at courts across Europe.

FIGURE 21.2 *Pietro Metastasio, in a portrait by Pompeo Batoni.*

COLL. MURRAY, MONTEBUONI, ITALY. PHOTO: SCALA/ART RESOURCE, NY

Metastasio's librettos employ a conventional cast of two pairs of noble lovers surrounded by other characters. The action provides opportunities for introducing varied scenes—pastoral or martial episodes, solemn ceremonies, and the like. The resolution of the drama, which rarely has a tragic ending, often turns on a deed of heroism or sublime renunciation by one of the principal characters. Metastasio's dramas, like Quinault's operas (which he knew well), extol the virtues of overcoming one's passions and exemplifying self-control.

An opera seria's three acts consist almost without exception of alternating recitatives and arias. Recitatives develop the action through dialogues and monologues, set either as simple recitative or, at the most dramatic moments, as accompanied recitative with orchestra. Each aria is a virtual dramatic soliloquy in which a principal character expresses feelings or reacts to the preceding scene. There are occasional duets, a few larger ensembles, and rare, simple choruses. Except in the overture, the orchestra serves mainly to accompany the singers, with the violins often doubling the vocal line, although as the century progressed the role of the orchestra became increasingly important.

THE ARIA   The musical interest of Italian opera is centered in the arias, which were created by eighteenth-century composers in astounding profusion and variety.

Da capo aria

The favored form in the first half of the century remained the da capo aria (see Chapter 17), a basic ABA scheme that permitted enormous variation in detail. Metastasio's two-stanza aria texts set the standard for the da capo aria of the 1720s through 1740s.

Abbreviated da capo

For some arias, composers shortened the repetition of the first section by omitting the opening ritornello, altering the direction "da capo" (from the beginning) to "dal segno" (from the sign, indicating that only part of the first section is repeated), or writing out an abridged return. Some arias lacked the contrasting second section (B) and instead followed a format like a da capo aria's first section, with two vocal statements (A1 and A2) framed by ritornellos.

New features

Arias written in the first decades of the century by composers like Alessandro Scarlatti (see Chapter 17, pp. 374–76) had usually projected a single affection, or mood, through the development of a single motive, or presented contrasting affections in the A and B sections. Beginning in the 1720s and 1730s, composers started to express a succession of moods, using a variety of musical material that ranged from lighthearted to tragic. Often two keys are contrasted in the first vocal statement (A1), then the material in the second key is recapitulated in the tonic at the close of the second vocal statement (A2). This repetition in the tonic of material first heard in another key became a central principle of form later in the century, in both vocal and instrumental music. The vocal melody dominates the music and carries it forward, and the orchestra provides harmonic support to the singer rather than adding independent contrapuntal lines. The melodies are usually in short units, most often in two- or four-measure antecedent and consequent phrases, with occasional expansions to create tension or offer variety.

Johann Adolf Hasse (1699–1783), shown in Figure 21.3, was one of the most popular and successful opera composers in Europe from the 1720s to the 1770s. Acknowledged by contemporaries as a great master of the opera seria, he symbolizes the genre's international character. Born near Hamburg, he directed music and opera at the court of the elector of Saxony in Dresden for most of his life, but he spent many years in Italy, married the celebrated Italian soprano Faustina Bordoni, and became so thoroughly Italian in his musical style that the Italians nicknamed him "il caro Sassone" (the dear Saxon). The great majority of his eighty operas use Metastasio librettos, some of which he set two or three times, and his music is the perfect complement to Metastasio's poetry.

The famous aria *Digli ch'io son fedele* (Tell him that I am faithful) from Hasse's *Cleofide* (1731), his first opera for Dresden (NAWM 110), illustrates the elegant and judicious qualities of his music. The first vocal statement

FIGURE 21.3 *Johann Adolf Hasse, in a pastel portrait by Felicitas Hoffmann.*

is shown in Example 21.3 both as he wrote it and in embellished form (see In Performance: The Art of Vocal Embellishment, pp. 480–81). Hasse set the opening lines with a graceful
motive that follows the natural rhythms and inflections of the
text, highlights the parallelism between the first two lines,
and reflects the earnest optimism of Cleofide, queen of India.
These and several later phrases end with accented suspensions
on the last stressed syllable, creating both a natural accentuation of the words and a musical sigh that conveys the feeling behind them. After the opening rhythmic motive appears
three times, Hasse introduces syncopations and scales in measures 13–14 and reverse-dotted rhythms (called Lombardic
rhythms or Scotch snaps) in measure 15. These gently desta-
bilizing elements give the melody interest and expressivity
without sacrificing elegance. The slowly pulsing bass line stays
in the background, its steadiness throwing the irregularities
of the melody into relief. The aria was a perfect embodiment
of the early galant style, and both the aria and its composer
became famous across Europe.

FIGURE 21.4 *Faustina Bordoni in a pastel portrait by female artist Rosalba Giovanni Carriera (1675–1757).*

The title role of Cleofide was created by Hasse's wife, Faustina Bordoni
(1700–1781), shown in Figure 21.4. Universally admired as one of the great
singer-actresses of her age, she established her reputation in Venice while
still in her teens, enjoyed success at Munich and Vienna in the 1720s, and
sang in Handel's London opera company later that decade (see Chapter 19).
She married Hasse in 1730 and starred in most of his operas for Dresden, but
also performed throughout Italy until her retirement from the stage in 1751.
She was particularly known for her fluent articulation, trills, embellishments,
and expressive power.

Faustina Bordoni

OPERA IN OTHER LANGUAGES

While opera seria maintained its character across national boundaries from
Italy to England, comic opera took different forms in different countries. It
usually represented people from the middle or lower classes in familiar situations and required relatively modest performing resources. Comic-opera
librettos were written in the national tongue, and the music tended to accentuate national musical idioms. From humble beginnings, comic opera grew
steadily in importance after 1750, and before the end of the century many of
its characteristic features had been absorbed into the mainstream of operatic composition. The historical significance of comic opera in languages
other than Italian was twofold: it reflected the widespread demand for simple, clear, and "natural" singing in the second half of the eighteenth century,
and it encouraged the growth of separate national traditions of opera, which
became prominent in the Romantic period.

FRANCE In Paris, long-simmering critical opposition to the old-fashioned,
state-subsidized French opera erupted in 1752–54 in a pamphlet war known
as the *Querelle des bouffons* (Quarrel of the Comic Actors). The dispute was
prompted by the presence in Paris of an Italian comic opera troupe that for
two seasons enjoyed sensational success with its performances of opere

Querelle des
bouffons

Jean-Jacques Rousseau

buffe and intermezzi, including *La serva padrona.* Many French intellectuals took part in the quarrel, partisans of Italian opera on one side and friends of French opera on the other.

One of the most vehement voices arguing for the merits of Italian opera was Jean-Jacques Rousseau (1712–1778), who praised Italian composers' emphasis on melody and their ability to express any emotion through melody (see Source Reading, p. 482). Shortly before the Italian troupe came to Paris, Rousseau wrote a charming little opera, *Le devin du village* (The Village Soothsayer, 1752), with airs and recitatives inspired by the new Italian melodic style. The opera's opening air, *J'ai perdu tout mon bonheur* (NAWM 111), shown in Example 21.4 (p. 483), exhibits the balanced two-measure phrases, plain harmonies, primacy of melody, and subordinate accompaniment that Rousseau

IN PERFORMANCE

The Art of Vocal Embellishment

In the eighteenth century, singers in opera seria were not expected to perform their melodies exactly as written. The music was a platform for their performance, and shaping the melody in an individual way was a fundamental aspect of both their acting and their singing.

As actors, they sought to embody the character they were portraying, capture that character's feelings, and convey to the audience the affections (that is, the emotions) represented in the music. At the same time, as singers, they were the stars of the show, and listeners came to the opera primarily to hear them sing.

Both for expressive reasons and to showcase their beautiful sound and vocal agility, opera seria singers embellished the written vocal line,

EXAMPLE 21.3 *Johann Adolf Hasse,* Digli ch'io son fedele, *from* Cleofide, *with embellished vocal line as sung by Porporino*

lauded in Italian opera, all of which became typical features of music in the second half of the eighteenth century. The scene continues with recitative that blends aspects of Italian and French recitative style and a partial reprise of the air. The opera also combines the two national traditions in other ways, with an overture in Italian form and style alongside French traits such as dances, a chorus, and a divertissement. With its direct appeal and pleasing combination of elements from both traditions, *Le devin du village* became one of the most successful and frequently performed operas of the eighteenth century.

The native French version of opera with spoken dialogue, known as **_opéra_** **_comique_**, began around 1710 as a popular entertainment at suburban fairs. Until midcentury, the music consisted almost entirely of songs setting new words to popular tunes, known as *vaudevilles,* or simple melodies imitating

Opéra comique

particularly in the da capo repetition of an aria's A section. The top line of Example 21.3 shows such an elaborated reprise for Cleofide's aria *Digli ch'io son fedele*. This version, as sung by Porporino (Antonio Uberti), a famous castrato of the day, survives in the hand of King Frederick the Great of Prussia, an avid musical amateur. The music is ablaze with trills, grace notes, rapid turns, appoggiaturas, scales, triplets, and arpeggios, at times departing considerably from the original contour while preserving its phrasing and overall shape. In this example, the most ornate decoration appears

in the middle of phrases while the opening melodic gesture and cadential motion of each phrase are retained, making it easier to hear this as a varied performance of Hasse's melody.

Each singer was expected to create their own ornamented version of the melody, whether worked out in advance or improvised on the spot—most likely a bit of both. Such elaborate embellishments remind us that the center of attention in an opera seria was not the composer, drama, plot, or scenery, but the singers, and their vocal acrobatics were certain to please the audience.

Tell him that I am faithful, tell him that he's my darling;
[tell him] to love me, that I adore him, that he should not yet despair.

SOURCE READING

The Merits of Italian Opera

Jean-Jacques Rousseau was a leader of the Enlightenment in France and a major influence on Romanticism. In the debate between advocates of French and of Italian opera, he supported the latter, finding it truer to nature and more moving because of its emphasis on expressive melody. His preference for lightly accompanied melody and his disdain for counterpoint were widely shared in the latter eighteenth century.

On first acquaintance with Italian melody, one finds in it only graces and believes it suited only to express agreeable sentiments, but with the least study of its pathetic and tragic character, one is soon surprised by the force imparted to it by the art of the composer in their [the Italians'] great pieces of music. It is by the aid of these scientific modulations, of this simple and pure harmony, of these lively and brilliant accompaniments that their divine performances harrow or enrapture the soul, carry away the spectator, and force from him, in his transports, the cries with which our placid operas were never honored.

How does the musician succeed in producing these grand effects? Is it by contrasting the movements, by multiplying the harmonies, the notes, the parts? Is it by heaping design upon design, instrument upon instrument? Any such jumble, which is only a bad substitute where genius is lacking, would stifle the music instead of enlivening it and would destroy the interest by dividing the attention. Whatever harmony several parts, each perfectly melodious, may be capable of producing together, the effect of these beautiful melodies disappears as soon as they are heard simultaneously, and there is heard only a chord succession, which one may say is always lifeless when not animated by melody; so that the more one heaps up inappropriate melodies, the less the music is pleasing and melodious, because it is impossible for the ear to follow several melodies at once, and as one effaces the impression of another, the sum total is only noise and confusion. For a piece of music to become interesting, for it to convey to the soul the sentiments which it is intended to arouse, all the parts must concur in reinforcing the impression of the subject: the harmony must serve only to make it more energetic; the accompaniment must embellish it without covering it up or disfiguring it; the bass, by a uniform and simple progression, must somehow guide the singer and the listener without either's perceiving it; in a word, the entire ensemble must at one time convey only one melody to the ear and only one idea to the mind.

Jean-Jacques Rousseau, *Letter on French Music* (1753), trans. William Strunk Jr. and Oliver Strunk, in SR 133 (5:12), pp. 900–901.

such tunes. The presence in Paris of Italian comic opera in the 1750s stimulated the production of opéras comiques in which original airs (called *ariettes*) in a mixed Italian-French style were introduced along with the older vaudevilles. The vaudevilles were gradually replaced by the ariettes until, by the end of the 1760s, all the music in an opéra comique was freshly composed. Like all the national variants of comic opera except the Italian, opéra comique used spoken dialogue instead of recitative.

Serious plots   By the later eighteenth century, librettists and composers of opéra comique were using serious plots, some based on the social issues that agitated France before and during the years of the Revolution. Many such works were produced at the Théâtre de l'Opéra-Comique in Paris, which became one of the principal competitors of the royally supported Opéra. The leading French opera composer of the late eighteenth century was the Belgian-born André Ernest Modeste Grétry (1741–1813). His *Richard Coeur-de-Lion* (Richard the

EXAMPLE 21.4 *Jean-Jacques Rousseau,* J'ai perdu tout mon bonheur, *from* Le devin du village

I have lost all my joy, I have lost my servant. Colin forsakes me.

Lion-Hearted, 1784) inaugurated a vogue for "rescue" operas around the turn of the century—Beethoven's *Fidelio* was one (see Chapter 24)—in which the hero, in imminent danger of death for two and a half acts, is finally saved through a friend's devoted heroism. The opéra comique remained extremely popular in France throughout the Revolution and the Napoleonic era and into the nineteenth century.

ENGLAND In England, the popular form of opera in the local language was ***ballad opera***. Like the early opéra comique, a ballad opera consisted of spoken dialogue interspersed with songs that set new words to borrowed tunes, including folk songs and dances, popular songs, and well-known airs and arias from other works for the stage. The fashion for ballad operas peaked in the 1730s, but they continued to be composed and staged over the next several decades in Britain, in its North American colonies, and later in the United States. Over time, ballad opera composers borrowed less and wrote more original music, in a development parallel to that of opéra comique.

 The genre was spawned by the tremendous success of *The Beggar's Opera* (1728; excerpted in NAWM 112), with libretto by John Gay (1685–1732) and music arranged probably by Johann Christoph Pepusch (1667–1752). Gay's play satirized London society by replacing the ancient heroes and elevated sentiments of traditional opera with modern urban thieves and prostitutes and their crimes, as shown on the ticket in Figure 21.5. The poetry and music sometimes spoof opera or use operatic conventions to create humor through incongruous juxtapositions. When the main character Macheath likens his roaming heart to a bee in *My heart was so free* (NAWM 112a), contemporary listeners would have been reminded both of the naive popular

Ballad opera

The Beggar's Opera

FIGURE 21.5 *A ticket for a performance of* The Beggar's Opera *at the Theatre Royal at Covent Garden in London. The evening's receipts were to be paid to Thomas Walker, the actor playing the central character, the notorious thief and murderer Macheath. In the engraving by renowned satirist William Hogarth (1697–1764), Polly and Lucy, both in love with Macheath, plead for his release from prison.*

LEBRECHT MUSIC & ARTS PHOTO LIBRARY

courting song whose tune he sings and of the noble *simile arias* of serious operas, which compare a character's situation to a vivid image portrayed in the music. Rather than equate his heart with a ship tossed upon stormy seas, as in an opera seria aria, Macheath compares it to a buzzing little insect and makes no attempt to illustrate the bee in the music, deflating audience expectations. As he and his wife Polly pledge their constancy in *Were I laid on Greenland's coast* (NAWM 112b), a sentiment which would have been set with great earnestness in Italian opera, the audience could not help but notice the tune, whose original text tells of a lad "run mad" by his lass, and be amused at the contrast of mood.

Singspiel

GERMANY AND AUSTRIA Serious operas in German had been composed and produced since the seventeenth century, and a few composers continued to write such works throughout the eighteenth century, generally adopting the style and format of Italian opera mixed with French and native elements. But much more popular was the new genre called **Singspiel** (German for "singing play"), which featured spoken dialogue, musical numbers, and usually a comic plot centered on love among common rural folk. The earliest examples appeared in the 1710s at the Kärtnertortheater in Vienna. The success of ballad operas in England inspired poets in northern Germany to translate or adapt some into German, and from the 1750s on composers were providing new music for them in a familiar and appealing melodic vein. As was true for ballad operas, Singspiels were often presented by traveling troupes of actors who could sing, accompanied by small instrumental ensembles, and the music was tuneful rather than elaborate. The principal composer of Singspiel in the 1760s and 1770s was Johann Adam Hiller (1728–1804) of Leipzig.

Many Singspiel tunes were published in German song collections, and some achieved such lasting popularity that they virtually became folk songs, transmitted orally as well as in print.

In northern Germany, the Singspiel eventually merged with early-nineteenth-century native opera. In the south, particularly in Vienna, farcical subjects and treatment became fashionable, with lively music in a popular vein influenced by Italian comic opera. The Singspiel was an important precursor of the German-language musical theater of composers such as Mozart and Weber (see Chapters 23 and 27).

RUSSIA Having spread across western Europe in the seventeenth century and to the New World in the early eighteenth, opera finally arrived in Russia in 1731 with a performance in Moscow by a visiting Italian troupe. A new fashion for Italian opera was encouraged by Tsaritsa Anna (r. 1730–40), who sought to continue the westernizing program of her uncle Peter the Great but did not share his Germanic tastes in music and saw in opera a way to establish parity with rival European courts. In 1735 Anna engaged Neapolitan composer Francesco Araja (1709–1770) as chapelmaster and court composer, and he formed a permanent Italian opera company at the imperial court in St. Petersburg with musicians recruited from Italy and Germany.

In the 1740s and 1750s, Tsaritsa Elizabeth (r. 1741–61) redoubled efforts to promote Italian opera at the imperial court. In 1755, she commissioned Araja to compose the first opera in Russian, *Tsefal i Prokris* (Cephalus and Prokris), a three-act work in the style of Italian opera seria to a libretto by Alexander Sumarokov. A second Russian opera by Hermann Raupach (1728–1778), *Altsesta* (Alceste), with the same librettist, premiered in 1758, and both operas were revived over the next few years.

Russian serious opera

Meanwhile, comic opera was coming to Russia as well. Giovanni Battista Locatelli brought his troupe of Italian opera buffa performers to St. Petersburg in 1757 at the invitation of Elizabeth, mostly performing operas by Galuppi. The next tsaritsa, Catherine the Great (r. 1762–96), supported Italian opera seria at court, employing Italians as court composer (including Galuppi himself in 1765–68), but also subsidized opera buffa. By the 1770s, French and German troupes had brought opéra comique and Singspiel to Russia, inspiring native Russian composers to create a new comic genre of opera in Russian with a similar mix of plots from daily life, spoken dialogue, and borrowed popular melodies as well as newly composed songs. These operas were performed not at court, where opera seria continued to reign, but at theaters in cities or country estates. The first such opera was *Aniuta* (1772), a one-act Singspiel to a libretto by Mikhail Popov (1742–ca. 1790); although the score is lost, it apparently featured popular folk melodies. By the end of the decade, numerous Russian composers were creating such comic operas, the most famous of which is *Melnik—koldun, obmanshchik, i svat* (The Miller Who Was a Sorcerer, a Cheat, and a Matchmaker, 1779) by Mikhail Sokolovsky (1756–after 1795). Native Russians continued to compose comic operas in this fashion well into the nineteenth century, but there was no support for serious opera in Russian until the 1830s (see Chapter 27).

Russian comic opera

OPERA AND THE PUBLIC Each of these national traditions of comic opera was at first primarily supported by the public rather than depending on well-to-do patrons, and only when already thriving did genres like opera buffa and opéra comique attract generous aristocratic patronage. As a result, each tradition developed unique features based on what pleased audiences in that region, encouraging the growth of distinct national styles, which later became one of the strongest trends of the nineteenth century. Indeed, the increasing importance of the middle-class public for music is the main economic force behind changes in musical style and the growth of new genres in the late eighteenth century and throughout the nineteenth as well. This public support also reinforced the preference of many Enlightenment intellectuals for music that was simple, clear, and direct and had wide appeal.

OPERA REFORM

Although serious Italian opera remained dependent on royal and aristocratic patronage, it also underwent changes that reflected Enlightenment thought. From midcentury on several composers, librettists, and patrons worked to bring opera into harmony with new ideals of music and drama. They sought to make the entire design more "natural"—that is, more flexible in structure, more expressive, less ornamented with coloratura, and more varied in musical resources. They did not abandon the da capo aria but modified it and introduced other forms as well. In order to move the action forward rapidly and more realistically, they alternated recitatives and arias more flexibly. To increase variety and heighten dramatic impact, they made greater use of accompanied recitative and ensembles. They made the orchestra more important as a vehicle for depicting scenes, evoking moods, and adding color and depth to accompaniments. They reinstated choruses, long absent in Italian opera. In all of these ways, they sought to assert the primacy of the drama and the music and subordinate the solo singers to this larger purpose, reversing the long-standing focus on star singers. The argument for such changes was articulated in *An Essay on the Opera* (1755) by Francesco Algarotti, who was influenced by the more integrated approach of French serious opera and by the tradition of classical Greek tragedy.

Jommelli and Traetta   Two of the most important figures in this reform were Niccolò Jommelli (1714–1774) and Tommaso Traetta (1727–1779). That these Italian composers worked at courts where French taste predominated—Jommelli at Stuttgart (1753–69) and Traetta in Parma (1758–65)—naturally influenced them toward a cosmopolitan type of opera.

Jommelli composed some one hundred stage works and achieved wide popularity. He blended Italian melody and French declamatory recitative in powerfully dramatic scenes such as the orchestrally accompanied recitative at the end of *Atillio Regolo* (1753), in which the protagonist bids a moving farewell to Rome. His later operas provided models within opera seria for a more continuous dramatic flow and gave the orchestra a more important role, including more colorful use of woodwinds and horns.

Traetta similarly aimed to combine the best of French tragédie en musique and Italian opera seria in his *Ippolito et Aricia* (1759), on a libretto translated and adapted from Rameau's *Hippolyte et Aricie* (see Chapter 18). Besides borrowing some of Rameau's dance music and descriptive orchestral interludes, Traetta included a number of choruses, common in the French tradition but rare in Italian opera. For the solo roles, he used the Italian genres of recitative and aria, but deployed several forms beyond the conventional da capo aria. In 1768, Traetta succeeded Galuppi as court composer to Catherine the Great in St. Petersburg, where he composed and staged *Antigona* (1772), widely regarded as his masterpiece. Traetta dispensed with the simile arias of earlier opera seria and tightened the drama by focusing on a small number of contrasting emotions, highlighting a limited number of keys, using key relationships to unify large scene complexes, and foregrounding a few characteristic motives that embody aspects of the plot.

CHRISTOPH WILLIBALD GLUCK Christoph Willibald Gluck (1714–1787), shown in Figure 21.6, achieved a winning synthesis of French, Italian, and German operatic styles. Born of Bohemian parents in what is now Bavaria, Gluck studied under Giovanni Battista Sammartini in Italy (see Chapter 22), visited London, toured in Germany as conductor of an opera troupe, became court composer to Emperor Charles VI at Vienna, and triumphed in Paris under the patronage of Marie Antoinette. After writing operas in the conventional Italian style, he was strongly affected by the reform movement in the 1750s and collaborated with the poet Ranieri Calzabigi (1714–1795) to produce in Vienna *Orfeo ed Euridice* (1762) and *Alceste* (1767). In a preface to *Alceste,* published two years after the premiere, Gluck (or possibly Calzabigi) expressed a resolve to remove the abuses that had deformed Italian opera and to confine music to what reformers considered its proper function—to serve the poetry and advance the plot (see Source Reading, p. 488). This he wanted to accomplish without regard either to the outworn conventions of the da capo aria or the desire of singers to show off their skill in ornamental variation. He further aimed to make the overture an integral part of the opera, to adapt the orchestra to the dramatic requirements, and to lessen the contrast between aria and recitative.

FIGURE 21.6 *A 1775 portrait of Christoph Willibald Gluck by Joseph-Siffred Duplessis.*

KUNSTHISTORISCHES MUSEUM, VIENNA. PHOTO: ERICH LESSING/ART RESOURCE, NY

Gluck aspired to write music of "a beautiful simplicity," which he achieved especially in *Orfeo ed Euridice.* In both this opera and the more monumental *Alceste,* the music is molded to the drama, with recitatives, arias, and choruses intermingled in large unified scenes. Compared to the final choruses Jommelli employed in his operas for Vienna in the early 1750s, Gluck's dance and chorus of the Furies in Act II of *Orfeo ed Euridice* (NAWM 113) is more integral to the action. In this scene, Orfeo has descended into the underworld, where the Furies challenge him in strident tones reinforced by string tremolos, horns, and trombones. He replies with pleas for mercy, accompanied by harp and plucked strings to simulate the playing of his lyre. The opposition of performing forces, timbres, keys, dynamic levels, and styles helps the music to deepen the dramatic conflict.

Orfeo ed Euridice

Gluck supervised the production of his operas, enhancing the drama with more naturalistic lighting, staging, and acting. He wanted his singers, even

Naturalistic staging and acting

Principles of Reform Opera

Christoph Willibald Gluck played a leading role in liberating opera from the conventions of opera seria and creating a new operatic style based on truly dramatic expression. In the preface to the printed score of the opera *Alceste* (1769), either Gluck or his librettist, Ranieri Calzabigi, explained the aims behind the movement for operatic reform.

❄

When I undertook to write the music for *Alceste,* I resolved to divest it entirely of all those abuses, introduced into it either by the mistaken vanity of singers or by the too great complaisance of composers, which have so long disfigured Italian opera and made of the most splendid and most beautiful of spectacles the most ridiculous and wearisome. I have striven to restrict music to its true office of serving poetry by means of expression and by following the situations of the story, without interrupting the action or stifling it with a useless superfluity of ornaments; and I believed that it should do this in the same way as telling colors affect a correct and well-ordered drawing, by a well-assorted contrast of light and shade, which serves to animate the figures without altering their contours. Thus I did not wish to arrest an actor in the greatest heat of dialogue in order to wait for a tiresome *ritornello,* nor to hold him up in the middle of a word or a vowel favorable to his voice, nor to make display of the agility of his fine voice in some long-drawn passage, nor to wait while the orchestra gives him time to recover his breath

for a cadenza. I did not think it my duty to pass quickly over the second section of an aria of which the words are perhaps the most impassioned and important, in order to repeat regularly four times over those of the first part, and to finish the aria where its sense may perhaps not end for the convenience of the singer who wishes to show that he can capriciously vary a passage in a number of guises; in short, I have sought to abolish all the abuses against which good sense and reason have long cried out in vain.

I have felt that the overture ought to apprise the spectators of the nature of the action that is to be represented and to form, so to speak, its argument; that the concerted instruments should be introduced in proportion to the interest and the intensity of the words, and not leave that sharp contrast between the aria and the recitative in the dialogue, so as not to break a period unreasonably nor wantonly disturb the force and heat of the action.

Furthermore, I believed that my greatest labor should be devoted to seeking a beautiful simplicity, and I have avoided making displays of difficulty at the expense of clearness; nor did I judge it desirable to discover novelties if it was not naturally suggested by the situation and the expression; and there is no rule which I have not thought it right to set aside willingly for the sake of an intended effect.

Dedication for *Alceste* (1769), trans. Eric Bloom. From Alfred Einstein, *Gluck* (London: J. M. Dent & Sons, 1936), 98–100. In SR 136 (5:15), pp. 933–34.

the chorus, to think of themselves as actors and to move realistically in order to bring the drama to life. The first Orfeo, Gaetano Guadagni, took as his model the great Shakespearean actor David Garrick, who pioneered a new, more natural style of acting. Guadagni so inhabited the role of Orfeo that he did not break character to acknowledge applause as other singers did.

French operas   In *Orfeo ed Euridice* and *Alceste,* Gluck amalgamated Italian melodic grace and the stately magnificence of the French *tragédie en musique.* The climax of his career was ushered in with the Paris production of *Iphigénie en*

Aulide (Iphigenia in Aulis, 1774), with a libretto adapted from the tragedy by seventeenth-century French playwright Jean Racine. Both it and its sequel, *Iphigénie en Tauride* (Iphigenia in Tauris, 1779), are works that display an excellent balance of dramatic and musical interest. Gluck used all the resources of opera—solo and choral singing, orchestra, and ballet—to produce a total effect of classical tragic grandeur.

Gluck's operas became models for many subsequent works, especially in Paris. His influence on the form and spirit of opera was transmitted to the nineteenth century through composers such as Niccolò Piccinni (1728–1800), Luigi Cherubini (1760–1842), Gasparo Spontini (1774–1851), and Hector Berlioz (1803–1869).

Gluck's influence

SONG AND CHURCH MUSIC

While opera held sway in the larger public arena, solo songs, cantatas, and other types of secular vocal chamber music often served as entertainment in smaller spaces and private gatherings throughout Europe. By this time, church music was a follower of secular styles rather than a focus of innovation, but it was still an important part of musical life.

SONG Songs for home performance were composed and published in many nations, reflecting the growing interest in amateur music-making. Increasingly the accompaniment was written for a keyboard instrument, although guitar was also used. Most songs were relatively simple, usually syllabic, diatonic, and strophic, with accompaniments easy enough to be played by the singer.

Many of the songs sung at home were religious, set in a plain hymnlike style. In addition, distinctive genres of secular song emerged in different regions. In France, the *romance* was a strophic song on a sentimental text with an expressive melody, almost entirely without ornamentation, over a plain accompaniment. In Britain, *ballads* were printed on single large sheets called broadsides or gathered in printed collections. Usually only the text was printed, typically a new poem about recent events or on a sentimental theme, meant to be sung to a familiar tune. Such songs were produced in Britain from the sixteenth through the early nineteenth centuries, and parallel genres were widespread on the European continent and in North America. English composers also wrote new songs in popular style and in the more elegant manner cultivated in concerts at the pleasure gardens in London. In the late eighteenth century, a fashion developed for Scottish and Irish folk songs, and publishers issued hundreds of them in new settings, as well as new songs written in a similar style.

The German song, or **Lied**, achieved a special prominence. Song was central to musical life and aesthetics in Germany. Publishers brought out more than 750 collections of Lieder with keyboard accompaniment during the second half of the century. German writers on music believed all music and musical instruments should emulate the singing voice, and insisted that song should be simple and expressive. Lyric poems were strophic, and composers setting them to music strove to create a single melody that would suit every stanza well, generally with one note per syllable. Songs were considered best when the melody was easy to sing, even by those untrained in music, and the

The Lied

accompaniment featured little or no figuration and was completely subordinate to the vocal line, often doubling it in the piano. This modest style, frequently (though not entirely accurately) compared to folk song, was meant to please those who performed and heard it, not to impress or astound as did the vocal display of opera.

North German composers were particularly important for song composition, including Telemann in Hamburg and C. P. E. Bach and Carl Heinrich Graun (ca. 1704–1759) in Berlin. The plain style of their Lieder contrasts sharply with their more elaborate music in other genres, and probably reflects the taste of most German consumers of music. Toward the end of the century, Johann Friedrich Reichardt (1752–1814) and other composers expanded the stylistic possibilities of the Lied, primarily by making the structure more flexible and giving the accompaniment greater independence.

The virtues of song   All these genres are marked by a lack of affectation, spare accompaniment, little if any word-painting, direct expression of feelings, and melodies that are simple, clear, and well suited to the accents, phrasing, and mood of the text. Although songs of the late eighteenth century are little known today, they embody values the Enlightenment held most dear. Song became a critically important genre in the nineteenth century, and the spirit of song pervades music from the late eighteenth century on.

CHURCH MUSIC Once the driving force in the development of new styles, church music by the middle of the eighteenth century was valued more for its traditionalism than for innovations, or else simply adopted the current prevailing styles of secular music. As a result, church music of this era has attracted much less attention from performers and scholars than opera or instrumental music.

Catholic music   Church composers in Catholic areas increasingly conformed to the prevailing secular style, especially that of the theater. A few composers carried on the stile antico tradition of Palestrina or the grand polychoral style of Gabrieli. But for the most part, church musicians took over the musical idioms and genres of opera, using orchestral accompaniment, da capo arias, accompanied recitatives, and choruses to express the sentiments in the text and inspire appropriate feelings in listeners attending services. For example, Pergolesi's *Stabat mater* (The Mother Was Standing, 1736) drew on the same vein of exuberant melody and dramatic scene-painting that the composer had mined three years earlier in his comic intermezzo *La serva padrona*. A setting for soprano, alto, and strings of a medieval poem about Mary at Jesus's crucifixion, it became one of the most popular and frequently printed sacred works of the century. A list of the leading eighteenth-century Italian church composers would be almost identical with the list of leading opera composers of the period, Galuppi chief among them. Even more than masses and motets, Italian oratorios became almost indistinguishable from operas. At the same time some composers, particularly in northern Italy, Austria, and southern Germany, affected a compromise between traditional and modern elements, blending galant traits with the older learned style. Composers were still trained in species counterpoint, imitation, and fugue, which were regarded as especially appropriate for church music, but as the newer styles became more prevalent, the learned style increasingly became a special effect used to convey a sense of the serious, solemn, sacred, or exalted.

In Lutheran areas, the Enlightenment's focus on reason, Pietism's emphasis on individual worship, and the new taste for elegant simplicity led to drastic changes in church music. The cantata and elaborate chorale-based compositions were now considered old-fashioned, and music for the service consisted primarily of congregational hymns composed in or adapted to the new galant style. The nonliturgical genre of the oratorio became the principal medium for North German composers. The best known was the Passion oratorio *Der Tod Jesu* (The Death of Jesus, 1755) by Carl Heinrich Graun, which remained popular in Germany until the end of the nineteenth century.

Lutheran music

During the reign of Catherine the Great (r. 1762–96), restrictions on Italianate influence in Russian Orthodox sacred music were relaxed, and composers were free to experiment and engage with modern styles within the ongoing tradition of unaccompanied choral singing. Galuppi, who was chapelmaster and court composer from 1765 to 1768, wrote numerous *kontserty* (sacred concertos) in Russian, in an up-to-date style. Dmitri Bortnyansky (1751–1825) sang as a boy in the Imperial Chapel Choir, where he studied with Galuppi, and spent 1769–79 in Italy, where he continued studies with Galuppi and wrote Italian operas. On his return he became chapelmaster and director of the Imperial Chapel Choir, the first Russian in generations to serve in that capacity, and became the most famous composer of sacred music for the Russian Orthodox Church.

Russian Orthodox music

In England, the enormous influence of Handel and the English interest in older music kept Baroque styles of church music alive. Composers focused on the traditional genres of Anglican music, the service and the anthem, and on hymns for church or private devotions. William Boyce (1710–1779), more famous for his theater music, served as the official composer for the Chapel Royal.

English church music

Church musicians in European settlements in the New World drew on their respective national styles. Villancicos and other choral music continued to be sung throughout the Spanish colonies, and French-Canadian churches emulated the Catholic music of France. In British North America, diverse immigrant groups brought with them elements of their religious music. For example, Anglican churches in large cities presented music that differed little from that of their English cousins, featuring organs as well as choirs of men and boys. Two groups were especially notable for their music: the Puritans of New England and the Moravians of Pennsylvania and North Carolina.

New World

The Puritans who settled New England were Calvinists, and their use of music in worship centered on metrical psalm singing. The original *Bay Psalm Book* (1640; see Chapter 11), the first book published in North America, contained no music, but the ninth edition of 1698 furnished thirteen melodies for singing the psalms. Congregations were taught and encouraged to read notes and not to depend solely on rote learning. In the eighteenth century, singing schools, often taught by traveling singing masters, trained a core of amateurs to sing psalm settings and anthems in parts. The availability of such singers became an invitation for composers to write new music.

New England hymnody

William Billings (1746–1800), the most prominent of these composers, left a significant body of music and writings. His *New-England Psalm-Singer* (1770), shown in Figure 21.7, contained 108 psalm and hymn settings and fifteen anthems and canons for chorus. His book marked two milestones—as the first published collection of music entirely composed in North America

William Billings

FIGURE 21.7 *The frontispiece to William Billings's New-England Psalm-Singer (1770). Surrounding the singers at the table is a canon for six voices with a ground bass to be sung "by three or four deep voices." Engraving by Paul Revere, later a hero of the American Revolution.*

and the first music book published in North America devoted to a single composer. Billings issued several more collections, including *The Continental Harmony* in 1794. Most of Billings's settings were "plain tunes," homophonic four-part harmonizations of his newly invented melodies, such as *Chester,* a patriotic song from the Revolutionary War period to his own words. But his later collections showed a preference for ***fuging tunes***, like *Creation* (NAWM 114) from *The Continental Harmony.* These tunes usually open with a syllabic and homophonic section, then feature a passage in free imitation before closing with voices joined again in homophony.

Billings declared his independence from the normal rules of counterpoint, writing that he had devised a set of rules better suited to his aims and method, and indeed his settings exhibit numerous parallel octaves and fifths as well as open chords without thirds. The rugged character of the music matches the colorful and eccentric personality of his writings. Yet even Billings's highly individual music reflects currents of the Enlightenment, emphasizing direct emotional expression over artifice as well as respect for experience over deference to authority, and it shares the clear phrasing and contrasting textures typical of music of its time.

Moravians   The Moravians, on the other hand, were thoroughly conversant with European trends. They were German-speaking Protestants from Moravia, Bohemia, and southern Germany who settled in Nazareth and Bethlehem in Pennsylvania, Salem in North Carolina, and surrounding areas. They embellished their church services with concerted arias and motets in current styles, whether imported from Europe or composed in America, and used organs, strings, and other instruments in church. Moravians also collected substantial libraries of music, both sacred and secular, and regularly played chamber music and even symphonies by the leading European composers of the time. Johann Friedrich Peter (1746–1813), John Antes (1740–1811, the first native-born American composer of chamber music), and other Moravians wrote sacred vocal and secular instrumental works that show familiarity with and a mastery of European styles from Handel to Haydn.

OPERA AND THE NEW LANGUAGE

The new musical idioms of the middle to late eighteenth century had their principal sources in vocal music, from opera seria to comic opera and vernacular song. In those genres, the urge to entertain a diverse audience led to a simplification of means and a striving for effective and "natural" expression. From Italian theaters the new styles spread through a cosmopolitan network of patrons, musicians, composers, and directors to other regions, stimulating new genres of opera and song that reached a wider public than ever before. Seeking to serve the growing taste for a clear and universally appealing music, composers developed a spare, logically organized flow of musical ideas that could be grasped on first hearing.

The new styles were inspired by vocal music, yet they had a tremendous impact on instrumental music, creating a new approach to melody and form, as described in Chapters 20 and 22. But the same vocal music that led the way to a new syntax and rhetoric fell victim to changing fashion. Although *La serva padrona* and *Le devin du village* were revived for several decades, and *The Beggar's Opera* lasted into the nineteenth century, other works did not fare so well. While Gluck's operas were never entirely forgotten, and *Orfeo ed Euridice* is now a permanent fixture, most other vocal music of the time quickly passed from the stage and is now little known.

Because of the way the history of music has been told, emphasizing Bach and Handel as paragons of Baroque music and Haydn and Mozart as masters of the classical style, the music of the middle eighteenth century is often seen merely as transitional. That view misunderstands the significance of the galant style that underlies the entire musical culture from the 1720s through the 1810s, a style of endlessly varying charm based on a common musical language within which Pergolesi, Galuppi, Hasse, Gluck, Haydn, Mozart, and countless other composers were trained. Much of this music is beautiful and deserves attention on its own merits. It was also of great importance to its performers and listeners, as made evident by the flood of writings and discussions about music by everyone from professional musicians to merchants to monarchs. From their own perspective, musicians of the time were engaged in a vigorous argument about musical taste and style, and in a constant search to please their growing audiences. As we encounter their music today, we would be wise to measure it against their own goals and values rather than those of an earlier or later generation.

Further Reading is available at digital.wwnorton.com/hwm10

INSTRUMENTAL MUSIC: SONATA, SYMPHONY, AND CONCERTO

The new musical idiom of the mid-eighteenth century, developed primarily in opera, became pervasive in instrumental music. Periodic phrasing, songlike melodies, diverse material, contrasts of texture and style, and touches of drama, all typical of the new idiom, made it easier to follow instrumental music and to be engaged by it. As an abstract play of gestures and moods, a drama without words, the music itself absorbed the listener's attention. Paradoxically, by borrowing from vocal music, instrumental music gained new independence, rising in the next two generations to unprecedented prominence.

Instrumental music was a form of entertainment for players and listeners alike. Pleasing the performers and appealing to a wide audience became paramount for composers, who flooded the market with instrumental music for domestic consumption. The **piano** replaced the harpsichord and clavichord as the favorite keyboard instrument, and new chamber ensembles, notably the **string quartet**, were developed for social music-making. The sonata (including similar works called by other names) became the leading genre for solo and chamber music, and the concerto and **symphony** dominated orchestral music. All these genres had deep roots in Baroque music, but the new melody-centered idiom brought new forms to the individual movements, including **sonata form** and other adaptations of binary form.

INSTRUMENTS AND ENSEMBLES

Instrumental music served a variety of social roles in the middle to late eighteenth century. Much music, including keyboard, harp, or guitar music to play alone and ensemble music to perform as a social activity, was written, purchased, and performed for the enjoyment of the players themselves. Especially among the middle and upper classes, amateurs often played for family and friends. In the houses of aristocrats and the well-to-do, musicians were employed to play during dinner or at parties. Amateur orchestras, sometimes filled out with professionals, performed in private or public concerts, and professional groups increasingly did so as well. All levels of society enjoyed music for dancing, from written-out orchestral dances for the upper echelons to folk tunes passed down by oral tradition for the peasantry.

While harpsichords and clavichords were played and manufactured until the early nineteenth century, both gradually ceded popularity to the *pianoforte* (Italian for "soft-loud"), or *piano*. Invented by Bartolomeo Cristofori (1655–1732) in Florence in 1700, the piano uses a mechanism in which the strings are struck by hammers that then drop away, allowing each string to reverberate as long as the corresponding key is held down. This differs from the harpsichord, in which strings are plucked, and from the clavichord, where they are struck by tangents that stay in contact with the strings until the key is released. The piano allowed the player to change dynamic level and expression through touch alone, creating crescendos, diminuendos, sudden contrasts, and other effects. At first the new instrument met very slow acceptance, but from the 1760s on, makers in Austria, Germany, France, and England produced pianos in increasing quantity. There were two main types. The grand piano was shaped like a harpsichord, as shown in Figure 22.1; relatively expensive, it was used in public performances and in aristocratic homes. Most domestic instruments were square pianos, in the shape of a clavichord, like the one being played in Figure 22.2. Eighteenth-century pianos are now often called *fortepianos* to distinguish them from the larger, louder forms of the piano developed in the nineteenth century.

FIGURE 22.1 *Piano made in 1792 by Johann Andreas Stein of Augsburg, whose instruments were typical of the age. The case resembles that of a harpsichord, and the strings are attached to a wooden frame, producing a lighter sound than the iron frames of nineteenth-century and modern pianos. The range is five octaves, from F′ to f‴.*

Ensemble music was written for numerous combinations. Very common were works for one or more melody instruments, such as violin, viola, cello, or flute, together with keyboard, harp, or guitar. When the latter play basso continuo, they serve as accompaniment to the melody instruments. But whenever the keyboard has a fully written-out part in the chamber music of the 1770s and 1780s, it tends to take the lead, accompanied by the other parts. The reason for this dominance lies in the role this music played in domestic music-making among middle- and upper-class families. The daughters were often skilled performers at the keyboard, since music was one of the accomplishments they were expected to cultivate, while the sons—who typically played flute, violin, or cello—devoted less time to practice. Therefore an evening's entertainment required works that would highlight the woman's greater expertise, while allowing others to participate.

Chamber ensembles

Chamber music for two to five strings alone was also common, especially the *string quartet* for two violins, viola, and cello. In these works, the first violin often carries most of the melodic substance, while the cello provides

String quartets

FIGURE 22.2
George, 3rd Earl Cow-
per, with the Family of
Charles Gore, *painting
by Johann Zoffany (1775),
showing a square piano
and a cello. Such pianos
were the main domestic
musical instrument from
the 1760s through the mid-
nineteenth century.*

YALE CENTER FOR BRITISH ART, PAUL MELLON COLLECTION/BRIDGEMAN IMAGES

the bass, and the inner voices fill out the texture. However, knowing that players enjoyed hearing themselves in extended solos of several measures, composers also wrote *concertante* quartets in which the parts are of equal importance, as well as quartets in which players exchanged shorter motives as if in musical conversation. Although now played in concerts, as they were on occasion at the time, string quartets and other chamber works were primarily intended for the enjoyment of the performers and their companions. Figure 22.3 shows a table designed for playing quartets, with a music rack for each player. The very layout, facing each other across a small table, makes clear that quartet playing was as social an activity in the late eighteenth century as card playing was in the twentieth.

The clarinet, a single-reed wind instrument, was invented around 1710, and by the 1780s took its place alongside the oboe, bassoon, and flute as the standard woodwind instruments in wind ensembles. At this time, all four were typically made of wood and had one or more keys to aid in fingering and allow pitches that were otherwise unattainable. Groups of wind players had been a regular feature of courts and military establishments since the Renaissance (see Chapter 12). French ensembles from the time of Louis XIV (see Chapter 16) often comprised only oboes, tenor oboes, and bassoons, but by the mid-eighteenth century the combination of two

KUNSTHISTORISCHES MUSEUM, VIENNA

FIGURE 22.3 *Table for playing string quartets, from about 1790. With the tabletop (in the background) removed and the music racks raised as shown here, the four players face one another, ideally positioned to listen to each other and engage in the "conversation" that string quartet playing was thought to embody.*

FIGURE 22.4 *A wind band consisting of two oboes, two clarinets, two horns, and two bassoons. This image shows a regimental band from the Netherlands army, 1751.*

oboes and/or two clarinets with two horns and two bassoons was becoming common, as in Figure 22.4. There were as yet no amateur wind ensembles, and amateurs tended not to play wind instruments other than the flute; other wind instruments were considered too difficult for amateurs and inappropriate for women because they required use of the mouth and lips.

Orchestra

The eighteenth-century concert orchestra was much smaller than today's. Haydn's orchestra from 1760 to 1785 rarely had more than twenty-five players, comprising flute, two oboes, two bassoons, two horns, about twelve to sixteen strings (violins I and II, violas, and cellos doubled by a double bass), and a harpsichord, with trumpets and timpani occasionally added. Viennese orchestras of the 1790s usually numbered fewer than thirty-five players, now often including two clarinets. In the last quarter of the eighteenth century, the basso continuo was gradually abandoned in orchestral and other ensemble music because all the essential voices were present in the melody instruments. The responsibility for directing the group, formerly the job of the harpsichord player, fell to the leader of the violins.

The typical orchestration in the mid-eighteenth century gave all essential musical material to the strings and used the winds and horns only for doubling, reinforcing, and filling in the harmonies. Sometimes in performance woodwinds and brasses might be added to the orchestra even though the composer had written no parts specifically for them. Later in the century, the wind instruments were entrusted with more important and more independent material.

GENRES AND FORMS

Many of the characteristic genres of Baroque instrumental music fell out of fashion in the Classic period, including preludes, toccatas, fugues, chorale settings, and dance suites. Composers continued to write variation sets, fantasias, and individual dances for keyboard, but the major keyboard genre became the sonata, commonly in two to four movements of contrasting mood and tempo. Multimovement works similar to the keyboard sonata were also composed for a variety of chamber ensembles. These works were called *sonata* when written for solo instrument plus keyboard and otherwise named by the number of players: *duet*, *trio*, *quartet*, *quintet*, and so on. The main orchestral genres were the concerto, an extension of the Baroque solo concerto, and the **symphony**, derived from the Italian opera overture (or *sinfonia*), the orchestral concerto, ensemble sonatas, and the orchestral suite. In works of three movements, typically the first and last were fast and the middle slow, ordinarily in a closely related key. Later symphonies and quartets often had four movements, usually adding a minuet movement after the slow movement (or before it, as in many of Haydn's string quartets). But the number and order of movements varied considerably: some symphonies had only one or two movements, others more than four; some three-movement works had a minuet in the middle, instead of a slow movement, or at the end, as a finale; some string quartets and symphonies had five movements, with two minuets. It was not until late in the eighteenth century that standard formats for most genres—three movements for sonatas, four for string quartets and symphonies—became the norm.

Continuity and change

In name at least, there was a continuity of genre with earlier generations: the concerto, the sinfonia, and the sonata for keyboard, soloist and keyboard, or chamber ensemble had all been prominent since the late seventeenth century. What was new, and quite distinct from their Baroque counterparts, was the content of each genre, including the forms used in each movement. All absorbed the new galant style that emphasized expressive melody in short phrases, arranged in periods, over light accompaniment.

Preference for major mode

Another difference from the Baroque era is the overwhelming preference for pieces in the major mode. More than a quarter of Vivaldi's concertos are in the minor mode, as are half of J. S. Bach's, but fewer than a tenth of those by Johann Christian Bach, Haydn, Mozart, or other composers active in the second half of the century are in minor. The major mode was considered more pleasing and natural, and was associated with more pleasant emotions. In addition, the focus on major for primary keys allowed composers to use closely related minor ones for contrast. The motion from happy stability—represented by a major-mode theme in a stable key and predictable phrasing—through dangers and trials—represented by minor keys, frequent modulation, and unstable phrasing—and then back to the home key and theme became a paradigm of Classic-era form.

BINARY FORMS Most forms of the Classic era are essentially harmonic, modulating from the tonic to the dominant (or, in a minor key, the relative major) and then back home, either directly or after further harmonic adventures through a point of greatest distance from the tonic. Important points in this harmonic plan are typically marked by new, repeated, or varied musical material and by changes in phrasing, texture, and other parameters.

Simple binary form

Most Classic forms are based on binary form (also called *dual reprise form*), which features two sections, each repeated, the first usually moving from tonic to dominant or relative major and the second returning to the tonic. Binary form originated as a form for dances, reaching prominence in the dances and dance suites of the Baroque period (see Chapters 16 and 18). The dances for lute by Denis Gaultier (NAWM 88) and in the keyboard suites of Elisabeth-Claude Jacquet de la Guerre (NAWM 89) use **simple binary form**, in which the two sections are roughly equal in length and feature musical material that is different or only loosely related.

In the eighteenth century, composers sought to emphasize the arrival on the dominant in the first section and the return to the tonic in the second section, producing the new types of binary form shown in Figure 22.5 (see Forms at a Glance, pp. 500–501). One common strategy was to present new material in the dominant at the end of the first section and to repeat that material in the tonic at the end of the second section, like a musical rhyme that serves to confirm the return to the home key. Such an approach heightens the contrast between tonic and dominant by associating different musical ideas with each and then resolves the harmonic tension by repeating in the tonic material that first appeared in another key. This pattern, called **balanced binary form**, appears in François Couperin's *La muse victorieuse* (NAWM 99b) and is typical of Domenico Scarlatti's sonatas (see pp. 503–4).

Balanced binary form

Another approach, known as ***rounded binary form***, highlights the return to the tonic in the second section by repeating the material that opened the first section. The double return of the opening key and opening material lends a strong sense of closure. Minuets often feature this form, as do the minuet in Jacquet de la Guerre's Suite in A Minor (NAWM 89h) and the Minuet of Haydn's Symphony No. 88 (NAWM 122c, discussed in Chapter 23).

Rounded binary form

SONATA FORM These two strategies for emphasizing the return to the tonic—reprising the opening idea and restating in the tonic material that first appeared in the dominant—are joined in the form now known as ***sonata form***. Also called *first-movement form,* this was the most common form for the first movement of a sonata, chamber work, or symphony in the Classic period. Since the nineteenth century, this form has been viewed primarily in terms of themes arranged in a three-part structure, but eighteenth-century writers understood it as a two-part form organized by phrase structure and harmony. The two views are compared in Figure 22.6 (see Forms at a Glance).

The best contemporary account of the form is in the third and final volume of Heinrich Christoph Koch's *Introductory Essay on Composition* (1782–93). Building on his discussion of phrases and periods (see Chapter 20), Koch describes first-movement form as an expanded version of binary form. There are two large sections, each of which may be repeated, the first moving from tonic to dominant (or relative major in a minor key), the second returning to the tonic. The first section has one main period, the second two.

Koch on first-movement form

- In the first section, the principal ideas are presented, organized in a series of four phrases: the first two in the tonic; the third modulating to the dominant or relative major (often closing with a half-cadence in the new key); and the fourth in the new key, confirmed by an optional "appendix" phrase.
- The first period of the second section may consist of any number of phrases. It often begins with the opening theme on the dominant, occasionally with another idea or in another key; moves through one or more

Binary Form and Its Relatives

Binary form is one of the most fruitful and widely adapted forms in the history of music. In the eighteenth century, there were three main types of binary form, shown in Figure 22.5 In all three types, there are two repeated sections, the first typically moving from the tonic to the dominant (or relative major) and the second working its way back to the tonic. The three types differ in the relationship between the two sections.

In **simple binary form**, the music in the second section is new or only somewhat related to the first section. In **balanced binary form**, the material first presented in the dominant at the end of the first section returns at the end of the second section in the tonic. And in **rounded binary form**, the opening of the first section reappears when the tonic returns in the second section, often followed by the material that first appeared in the dominant, now transposed into the tonic.

SIMPLE BINARY FORM	‖: A :‖: B :‖ I - V V - I
BALANCED BINARY FORM	‖: A B :‖: A B :‖ or ‖: A B :‖: X B :‖ I - V V - I I - V V - I
ROUNDED BINARY FORM	‖: A B :‖: X A B :‖ or ‖: A B :‖: X A :‖ I - V mod I - I I - V mod I

FIGURE 22.5 *Three types of binary form.*

All three types could be used as the form of an entire movement, such as a minuet; could be paired with another binary form, as in a **minuet and trio**; or could serve as the form for the theme of a **rondo** or set of **variations** (see pp. 502–3).

In addition, binary form was developed into what was then called *first-movement form*, renamed **sonata form** in the nineteenth century. As shown in Figure 22.6, eighteenth-century writers recognized that sonata form was an expansion of binary form, but nineteenth-century musicians came to regard it as a three-part form.

keys more distant from the tonic; and then modulates back to the tonic key by means of another melodic idea, ending on the dominant chord as preparation for the return of the tonic.

• The second period of the second section begins and ends on the tonic. It typically parallels the first section and for the most part restates the same material, except that the third phrase ends on a half-cadence in the tonic, and the fourth phrase and appendix are now in the tonic. Thus in most sonata-form movements, the return to the tonic in the second section is signaled by the return of the opening theme and emphasized by the restatement in the home key of the material first presented in the dominant, combining aspects of rounded and balanced binary form.

EIGHTEENTH-CENTURY VIEW: EXPANDED BINARY FORM

FIRST SECTION	SECOND SECTION	
One Main Period **KEY:** ||: I – V :||	First Main Period ||: V – on V	Second Main Period I – I :||

NINETEENTH-CENTURY VIEW: THREE-PART FORM

EXPOSITION	DEVELOPMENT	RECAPITULATION
KEY: ||: I – V :||	X on V	I – I ||

COMPARISON

KOCH'S MODEL		NINETEENTH-CENTURY VIEW	
First Section		Exposition	
First and second phrases	I	First theme	I
Third phrase	mod to V	Transition	mod to V
Fourth phrase	V	Second theme	V
Appendix	V	Closing theme	V
Second Section			
First Main Period		Development	
Free	mod, often to vi, ii, iii	Develops ideas from exposition	mod
Preparation for return	on V	Retransition	on V
Second Main Period		Recapitulation	
First and second phrases	I	First theme	I
Third phrase	mod	Transition	mod
Fourth phrase	I	Second theme	I
Appendix	I	Closing theme	I

FIGURE 22.6 *Views of first-movement form.*

The phrases mentioned here may be as brief as two to four measures but are often greatly expanded by repeating or varying material, inserting new material, or extending the phrase through delayed or evaded cadences. Koch notes that in symphonies, the various melodic units tend to be extended and flowing, with few perceptible pauses and cadences. In sonatas and chamber works, on the other hand, melodic units are more often separated by clear phrase endings and rests.

What Koch describes is an overall plan or set of principles for organizing a movement, not a rigid mold. His description conforms well to the great majority of first movements of the Classic period, as well as many middle movements and finales. We will see several examples in this and the next chapter.

*Later view of
sonata form*

By the 1830s, theorists and analysts looking at works from the late 1700s and early 1800s, especially the music of Beethoven (see Chapter 24), began to describe the form in somewhat different terms. Where Koch saw a binary form, they divided the movement into three sections, corresponding to Koch's three periods, but defined thematically rather than harmonically:

- An ***exposition***, usually repeated, with a *first theme* or group of themes in the tonic; a ***transition*** to the dominant or relative major; a *second theme* or group in the new key, often more lyrical; and a *closing theme* or cadential reinforcement in the same key.

- A ***development*** section, in which motives or themes from the exposition are presented in new aspects or combinations, and which modulates through a variety of keys and then works its way back toward the tonic to close on the dominant chord. The passage leading to and emphasizing the dominant is called the ***retransition***.

- A ***recapitulation***, in which the material of the exposition is restated in the original order but with all themes in the tonic.

In addition, there may be a slow introduction before the exposition, or a ***coda*** after the recapitulation that revisits one or more themes and confirms the tonic key.

*Changes in first-
movement form*

Both models serve well to describe the mature works of Haydn and Mozart. But Koch's approach, emphasizing phrase structure and a specific harmonic plan, works better for music before about 1780, while the later view, focusing more on thematic content and contrast of keys, is a better fit for music after about 1800. The change came about partly because movements grew longer, making themes the most obvious guideposts for listeners, and partly due to a growing tendency to omit the repetition of the second section, making the binary structure less apparent. By the early nineteenth century, a three-part plan seemed to better describe the presentation, development, and recapitulation of themes.

Of course, what is most interesting about any individual movement is how the composer uses the principles articulated by Koch or later theorists to create a unique piece of music. While following these principles, composers of sonata-form movements achieved a remarkable variety in form and content.

OTHER FORMS Several of the other forms used in sonatas, chamber works, and symphonies in the Classic era also expand upon binary form, in various ways.

- Many slow movements use a variant of sonata form that omits the first period of the second section and has no repeats, but otherwise follows Koch's model; this has been called ***slow-movement sonata form*** or *sonata form without development*.

- ***Variation form***, used in some slow movements and occasional first or last movements, presents a small binary form (or sometimes a single period) as a theme, followed by several embellished variants.

- *Minuet and trio form*, often present in symphonies and string quartets, joins two binary-form minuets, repeating the first after playing the second (the *trio*) to produce an ABA pattern.

- *Rondo form*, common in last movements, presents a small binary form or single period as a theme, then alternates it with other periods called *episodes*, which are often in other keys, in a pattern such as ABACA or ABACADA.

All forms of the Classic era exhibit similar compositional approaches. All depend upon grouping phrases into periods and periods into forms. All use both repetition and variation. All depend upon motion from the tonic to the dominant and back, and most confirm the tonic by restating material first presented in another key. Although expert composers scarcely had to think about these matters, it will help us to keep Koch's advice to novice composers in mind as we look at how this music is put together.

KEYBOARD MUSIC

Stimulated by the growing demand by amateur keyboard players for music that could be played at home and in private gatherings, composers of the middle and late eighteenth century produced great numbers of keyboard works, including sonatas, rondos, variations, and minuets. Sonatas were widely regarded as the most challenging and rewarding for both performer and listener, so the genre attracted composers interested in exploring new possibilities in expression, style, and form. In their music, we can find many elements of the new musical idiom.

Domenico Scarlatti

Although he was virtually unknown throughout Europe during his lifetime, Domenico Scarlatti (1685–1757), shown in Figure 22.7, was one of the most original and creative keyboard composers of the eighteenth century. The son of Alessandro Scarlatti, and a friend and exact contemporary of Handel, he composed operas, cantatas, and church music for Naples and Rome, then left Italy in 1719 to enter the service of the king of Portugal. When his pupil, the king's daughter, married Prince Ferdinand of Spain in 1729, Scarlatti followed her to Madrid, where he remained for the rest of his life in the service of the Spanish court, somewhat isolated from the rest of Europe.

Sonatas

Scarlatti published a collection of thirty harpsichord sonatas in 1738 under the title *Essercizi* (Exercises), but most of his 555 sonatas survive in scribal copies from his time. Each sonata is identified by its number in the standard index by Ralph Kirkpatrick. Most of his sonatas are paired in the sources with one or two others in the same key that contrast in tempo, meter, or mood and were designed to be performed together.

Scarlatti typically used balanced binary form in his sonatas, repeating the material from the latter part of the first section at the end of the second section, transposed into the tonic. His sonatas in major keys usually follow a distinctive scheme:

```
||: A        B   C:||: D        B   C:||
    I   —>V   v   V    V   —>I   i   I
```

DE AGOSTINI PICTURE LIBRARY/BRIDGEMAN IMAGES

FIGURE 22.7 *Domenico Scarlatti, in a portrait from about 1740 by Domingo Antonio de Velasco.*

In the first section, the arrival of the new key of the dominant is highlighted by presenting new material in the minor mode first, then proceeding to the parallel major dominant. The second section spends little or no time on the ideas presented at the outset of the movement, but reprises all the material that first appeared in the dominant, transposed into the tonic to achieve both formal and harmonic closure. In both sections, the passage in the minor mode emphasizes and dramatizes the change of key.

In Scarlatti's sonatas, the harmonic scheme is paramount, and the musical material is designed mainly to activate the texture. What sets his sonatas apart from the keyboard pieces of earlier composers is the sheer diversity of figuration. Example 22.1 shows some of the variety in the first section of Scarlatti's Sonata in D Major, K. 119 (NAWM 115), probably composed in the 1740s. After the broken-chord opening establishes the tonic (Example 22.1a), it is confirmed by a scalar idea (Example 22.1b) and a cadence, each immediately repeated. A new phrase (Example 22.1c) imitates the rhythm and effect of castanets. After a modulation, a theme appears in the dominant minor (Example 22.1d); this is the first idea in the sonata to resemble the galant texture of melody with accompaniment, and it receives the most development. Scarlatti then leads us to a striking passage that builds to a climax through trills and growing dissonance, with chords of five or even six notes (Example 22.1e). The effect recalls Spanish guitar music, with the almost constant a' sounding like an open string strummed against those being fingered. These evocations of Spanish music are featured in a number of Scarlatti's sonatas.

Other Italian composers   Scarlatti was exceptional both in his geographic isolation and in his almost exclusive focus on the keyboard sonata in his later years, but he was one of many Italians to produce sonatas. His contemporary Ludovico Giustini (1685–1743) published the first sonatas written explicitly for piano instead of harpsichord, *12 Sonate da cembalo di piano e forte* (12 Sonatas for Keyboard with Soft and Loud, 1732). Although conservative in form, resembling Baroque church sonatas or suites, they use contrasts of *piano* and *forte* to dramatic effect. Domenico Alberti (ca. 1710–1746) composed about forty keyboard sonatas, all in galant style and in two binary-form movements of contrasting character. He was the first to use frequently an accompanimental device known since the later eighteenth century as the ***Alberti bass***, in which the notes of a chord are sounded one at a time in a repeating pattern of low-high-middle-high (such as 1–5–3–5) to create a rapidly pulsating chordal background that sets off the melody to advantage.

Baldassare Galuppi   Baldassare Galuppi, shown in Figure 22.8, was best known for the enormously popular comic operas he wrote in collaboration with the playwright Carlo Goldoni (see Chapter 21) but was also a virtuoso harpsichordist who composed about 130 keyboard sonatas in one, two, and three movements. He had numerous keyboard-playing students, including daughters of the leading families of Venice, and composed his sonatas primarily for them and other amateurs to perform in their lessons and for their families and friends.

EXAMPLE 22.1 *Domenico Scarlatti, figures from Sonata in D Major, K. 119*

Galuppi embraced the galant style, spinning graceful, aria-like melodies in short phrases over largely homophonic accompaniments. All his sonatas exhibit the "vaghezza, chiarezza, e buona modulazione" (beauty, clarity, and good modulation) that he considered hallmarks of good music.

By "good modulation" Galuppi seems to have meant the pleasing arrangement of modules, the elegant flow of melody linking each phrase and schema to the next, that we observed in Chapter 20 in the theme from the finale of his Sonata in D Major, Op. 2, No. 1 (NAWM 116; see Example 20.1 and pp. 465–69). This sonata is in three movements, all in D major, and all are outstanding examples of the deft combination of schemata into tasteful, compelling, and entertaining pieces of music. Throughout all three movements, changes of figuration and texture provide contrasts that reinforce and articulate the melodic and harmonic structure.

FIGURE 22.8

Baldassare Galuppi, in a portrait dated 1751.

HERITAGE IMAGE PARTNERSHIP LTD/ ALAMY STOCK PHOTO

The slow first movement (NAWM 116a) is in balanced binary form, the opening motive alternating scalar and sighing figures and the answering phrase elaborating descending schemata (a Prinner and cadences) with an undulating, highly decorated melody. The fast second movement (NAWM 116b) is an expanded rounded binary form that strings together more than half a dozen different schemata and contrasting figurations to create a musical adventure marked by frequent surprises and artful turns of phrase that unfold in a logical and pleasing succession. In both movements, the second section begins with the opening theme in the dominant, a typical feature of larger galant binary-form movements, and ends by recapitulating in the tonic the material introduced in the dominant at the end of the first section. The finale (NAWM 116c) is a theme and variations that treats its binary-form theme to a series of rhythmic transformations: elaborating the melody with sixteenth-note and thirty-second-note figuration; energizing the accompaniment; and then featuring fast runs and arpeggios that obscure the melody while decorating the harmonic progression. As is typical of eighteenth-century variation sets, each variation has a distinctive rhythmic profile, with a gradual increase in intensity over the course of the movement.

FIGURE 22.9 *Carl Philipp Emanuel Bach, in a pastel portrait by his distant cousin Gottlieb Friedrich Bach, court organist and painter in Meiningen.*

STAATSBIBLIOTHEK, BERLIN/BRIDGEMAN IMAGES

Outside Italy, the keyboard sonata was cultivated particularly by German composers, including Carl Philipp Emanuel Bach (1714–1788). Shown in Figure 22.9, Bach was one of the most influential composers of his generation. Trained in music by his father, J. S. Bach, he served at the court of Frederick the Great in Berlin from 1740 to 1768 and then became music director of the five principal churches in Hamburg, as successor to his godfather, Georg Philipp Telemann. He composed oratorios, songs, symphonies, concertos, and chamber music, but most numerous and significant are his works for keyboard. His widely read *Essay on the True Art of Playing Keyboard Instruments* (1753–62) is an important source of information on the musical thought and practice of the period.

C. P. E. Bach's favorite keyboard instrument was the clavichord, which he prized for its delicate dynamic shadings,

EXAMPLE 22.2 *Carl Philipp Emanuel Bach, second movement from Sonata in A Major, H. 186, Wq. 55/4*

although his late keyboard works seem to have been written with the piano in mind. He published eight sets of six keyboard sonatas (1742–79) and five sets of sonatas mixed with rondos and fantasias (1780–87). His first two sets, called the Prussian (1742) and Württemberg sonatas (1744), featured a new manner of keyboard writing and exerted a strong influence on later composers. These sets helped to establish the three-movement pattern for the sonata—with the first and last movements marked fast and the slow middle movement written in a related key—and demonstrated the possibility of expressive keyboard music outside the Baroque tradition of the suite. The fast movements of his sonatas usually exhibit the typical traits of the galant style: an emphasis on melody, with clear phrasing, frequent cadences, and light accompaniment. Many of his works, especially his slow movements, exemplify the empfindsam style, which adds elements that give the music greater individuality and emotional intensity.

The main characteristics of the empfindsam style are apparent in the second movement (NAWM 117) of the fourth of his *Sechs Clavier-Sonaten für Kenner und Liebhaber* (Six Clavier Sonatas for Connoisseurs and Amateurs), composed in 1765 and published in 1779. As in the galant style, the basic texture features expressive melody in short phrases, arranged in periods, over light accompaniment. The form is slow-movement sonata form, lacking a development but otherwise conforming to Koch's description. But as shown in Example 22.2, the multiplicity of rhythmic patterns, nervously and constantly changing—turns, Scotch snaps (reverse dotted rhythms such as 𝅘𝅥𝅮𝅘𝅥), short dotted figures, triplets, asymmetrical flourishes of five and thirteen notes—gives the music a restless, effervescent quality. In the opening phrase (measures 1–3), descending lines suggest sighs, and appoggiaturas and chromatic lower neighbor tones reinforce the melancholy mood. Later, Bach exploits the element of surprise, when unusual turns of melody, rests on the beat, sudden changes of dynamic level, unexpected harmonic shifts, and a rising sequence create suspense and excitement. Bach also introduced in his instrumental works sections of musical dialogue and passages of recitative, applying the expressive tools of opera to create emotionally vibrant music.

Empfindsam characteristics

ORCHESTRAL MUSIC

Music for orchestra grew in importance during the eighteenth century, as public and private concerts became more common and more likely to include orchestral music.

SYMPHONY The major orchestral genre of the middle to late eighteenth century was the **symphony**, a work usually in three or four movements, in a primarily homophonic style, without the division between orchestra and soloists that distinguishes the concerto. It originated in Italy around 1730 and spread across Europe, performed at courts, in public concerts, and by amateurs who played for their own enjoyment. Throughout the century, a symphony was often the first item on a concert, followed by works in other genres. By the late 1700s, the symphony was considered the summit of instrumental music.

Italian origins   Like many musical genres, the symphony had more than one parent. The most obvious ancestor is the Italian *sinfonia,* or opera overture, from which the symphony takes its name. By 1700, many opera overtures used a structure of three sections or movements in the order fast-slow-fast: an Allegro, a short lyrical Andante, and a finale in a dance rhythm, such as a minuet or gigue. These overtures, as a rule, have no musical connection with the opera they introduce and could be played as independent pieces in concerts. Yet other sources for the symphony are equally important. The orchestral concertos of Torelli and other composers (see Chapter 17) also typically followed the fast-slow-fast format and were played in the same venues as concert symphonies. Eighteenth-century church sonatas in northern Italy often had the fast-slow-fast structure and homophonic style as well, without the opening slow movement and imitative fast movements typical of Corelli's church sonatas, and indeed throughout the eighteenth century symphonies were played in Catholic Church services, each movement at a different point in the Mass. Finally, the orchestral suite is one source for the binary forms that are common in the symphony. These similarities across genres suggest that multiple influences led to the symphony.

The first concert symphonies were written by composers working in Milan and the surrounding region of Lombardy in northern Italy, then an Austrian possession. Milan was a center for the Italian Enlightenment, with close cultural ties to Paris and Vienna, and it had a large number of well-to-do amateur string players whose interest in new music seems to have encouraged local composers to write symphonies. The most prominent and influential of these composers was Giovanni Battista Sammartini (ca. 1700–1775), shown in Figure 22.10, whose music was played all over Europe. His Symphony in F Major, No. 32 (ca. 1740; NAWM 118), is representative of early symphonies. It is scored for strings in four parts: violin I and II, viola, and bass, played by cellos, double bass, and probably harpsichord and bassoon (his later symphonies add winds as well). As in most early symphonies, there are three movements in the fast-slow-fast format, each relatively short; the whole piece takes less than ten minutes to play.

FIGURE 22.10
Giovanni Battista Sammartini, in an oil portrait copied in 1778 by Domenico Riccardi from a lost painting.

The opening Presto (NAWM 118a) follows the first-movement form described by Koch and is a concise thirty-eight measures. Each phrase of the form is given one or two distinctive ideas, and their diversity makes it easy to follow the form. Example 22.3 shows the first eight measures, which contain five sharply contrasting ideas: hammered octaves, a rising scale, a repeated melodic idea, rushing scalar figures, and a rising arpeggiation over a throbbing bass. The second movement (NAWM 118b) is a slow binary form in the relative minor, D minor, a restful interlude between the active outer movements. Again there are several contrasting ideas, most based on familiar galant schemata, woven together in a convincing and pleasing order. The fast triple-meter finale (NAWM 118c) is back in F major, with an opening theme marked by leaping octaves and rushing scales followed by a series of contrasting phrases. All three movements are in binary form, begin the second half with the opening material on the dominant (or relative major), signal the return of the tonic with a restatement of the opening theme, and transpose material first presented in the dominant into the tonic at the end of the second section. Typical of the galant symphony, when material returns later in the movement it is usually slightly varied, offering the listener a fresh twist alongside the pleasure of hearing a familiar theme repeat.

From Italy the symphony spread north to Germany, Austria, France, and England. Especially prominent was Mannheim, where the elector Palatine's court was one of the most active musical centers in Europe. Under the leadership of Bohemian violinist and composer Johann Stamitz (1717–1757), the Mannheim orchestra became internationally famous for its impeccable discipline and technique, leading Charles Burney to call it "an army of generals." It was renowned for its unprecedented dynamic range, from the softest *pianissimo* to the loudest *fortissimo*, and for the thrilling sound of its crescendo, both effects that Stamitz often employed in his music.

Mannheim

Stamitz was the first symphony composer to use consistently what would

EXAMPLE 22.3 *Giovanni Battista Sammartini, Symphony in F Major, No. 32, first movement, opening*

TIMELINE

1700 Bartolomeo Cristofori invents the pianoforte

ca. 1710 Clarinet invented

ca. 1730 First concert symphonies composed

1732 Ludovico Giustini, *12 Sonatas for Keyboard with Soft and Loud*

1738 Domenico Scarlatti, *Essercizi* published

1740–86 Reign of Frederick the Great of Prussia

ca. 1740 Giovanni Battista Sammartini, Symphony in F Major, No. 32

mid-1750s Johann Stamitz, Sinfonia in E-flat Major

1753–62 Carl Philipp Emanuel Bach, *Essay on the True Art of Playing Keyboard Instruments*

1759 Baldassare Galuppi, *Sonate per Cembalo*, Op. 2, published in London

1760s on Increasing numbers of pianos produced in Austria, Germany, France, and England

ca. 1770 Vogue for symphonie concertante begins in Paris

1770 Johann Christian Bach, Piano Concertos, Op. 7

1776 American colonies declare independence from Great Britain

1779 C. P. E. Bach, *Six Clavier Sonatas for Connoisseurs and Amateurs* published

1782–93 Heinrich Christoph Koch, *Introductory Essay on Composition*

1789–99 French Revolution

later become the standard plan: four movements, with a minuet and trio as the third movement, and a very fast finale, often marked Presto (quickly). He was also among the first to introduce a strongly contrasting and full-blown theme after the modulation to the dominant in the first section of an allegro movement, a practice that likewise later became standard. The first movement of his Sinfonia in E-flat Major (NAWM 119), written in the mid-1750s, follows the customary plan outlined by Koch, but without the sectional repetitions of binary form and on a much larger scale than in Sammartini's Symphony in F Major, No. 32. In addition to the four string parts, Stamitz includes two oboes and two horns, as was becoming customary. The opening phrases use several energetic ideas to emphasize the tonic. The transition to the dominant exploits the famous Mannheim crescendo, building excitement by means of string tremolos that progress from *piano* to *fortissimo*. After the arrival in the new key, a series of lyrical, graceful, and playful ideas provides a change of mood. The return of the tonic key after the development is marked not with the opening phrases but with the series of ideas that were introduced in the dominant, as in the balanced binary form of Scarlatti (NAWM 115). The opening motives reappear at the end, in reverse order, to emphasize the tonic once again.

Other centers of symphonic activity included Vienna and Paris. In Vienna, Georg Christoph Wagenseil (1715–1777) wrote three-movement symphonies that feature pleasant lyricism and good humor, as well as the contrasting first-movement theme groups that later became important characteristics of Mozart's music. Other symphony composers active in Vienna include Bohemian-born Johann Baptist Wanhal (1739–1813), who combined accessible, songlike themes with sonata-form structure, and Carl Ditters von Dittersdorf (1739–1799), who injected Greek myths and other extramusical elements into some of his symphonies. In Paris, an important center of composition and publication in the mid-eighteenth century, symphonies flowed from the city's presses, and foreign composers flocked to the city. The Belgian François-Joseph Gossec (1734–1829) came to Paris in 1751 and eventually established himself as one of France's leading composers of symphonies, string quartets, and comic operas. He became one of the most popular composers of the Revolutionary period and one of the first directors of the Paris Conservatoire (see Chapter 24).

As concert life expanded around 1770, a new genre emerged in response to the Parisian public's taste for pleasing melodies and virtuoso solos alongside big orchestral sonorities. This was the ***symphonie concertante***, a concerto-like work with two or more solo instruments in addition to the regular orchestra, in which the main material is entrusted to the soloists. The format was ideal for the new concert environment because it gave composer-performers an opportunity to show off their abilities to the public, attract students, and encourage sales of their music. Hundreds of symphonies concertantes were written, performed, and published in Paris in the 1770s and 1780s, and composers in Mannheim and elsewhere soon followed suit. Among those writing symphonies concertantes in Paris was violinist, conductor, and composer Joseph Bologne, Chevalier de Saint-Georges (1745–1799), the first composer of African descent to achieve recognition in Europe and among the first from the New World, born in Guadaloupe to a French planter and his enslaved mistress. The popularity of symphonies concertantes waned by 1830, displaced by a new focus on individual virtuosity in solo recitals and concertos.

FIGURE 22.11
Johann Christian Bach, in a portrait by the renowned English painter Thomas Gainsborough (ca. 1776).

CONCERTO Even while symphonic form gained increasing attention throughout the eighteenth century, the solo concerto remained popular as a vehicle for virtuosos, who often wrote concertos to play themselves. Giuseppe Tartini (1692–1770), the most renowned violin virtuoso in the generation after Vivaldi, founded a violin school in Padua, Italy, that attracted students from all over Europe. He composed about 135 technically innovative violin concertos and an equal number of sonatas that expanded the capabilities of his instrument.

Among the first to compose piano concertos was Johann Christian Bach (1735–1782), shown in Figure 22.11. The youngest son of J. S. Bach, Johann Christian was trained by his father and his older brother C. P. E. Bach, studied and worked in Italy, and in 1762 moved to London, where he prospered as a performer, teacher, impresario, and composer of concertos, symphonies, chamber music, keyboard music, and operas. His works, mostly galant in style, were performed all over Europe. J. C. Bach was a major influence on the young Mozart, who visited London in 1764 at age eight, met Bach, and arranged three of Bach's sonatas into concertos.

As in the early eighteenth century, concertos were typically in three movements, with two fast movements framing a slow middle movement. The slow movement and finale often used forms like those of other genres, but first movements followed a form unique to concertos.

Three-movement plan

The first movement of a typical concerto retained elements of the ritornello form of Baroque concertos, which alternates orchestral ritornellos with episodes that feature the soloist (see Chapter 18), in combination with the contrasts of key and thematic material characteristic of sonata form. As Koch describes the form, there are three solo sections, structured in a way that is equivalent to the three main periods of sonata form. These sections are enclosed between four orchestral ritornellos; the first presents all or most of the main ideas while the others are relatively short. In essence, the concerto first movement is a sonata form framed by a ritornello form.

Concerto first-movement form

To demonstrate these parallels, Figure 22.12 aligns the elements of ritornello form and of sonata form with the first movement of J. C. Bach's Concerto for Harpsichord or Piano and Strings in E-flat Major, Op. 7, No. 5 (NAWM 120), from ca. 1770. (The figure uses the more familiar nineteenth-century terminology for sonata form, although Koch's terms would be equally apt; compare Figure 22.6.) The Baroque plan of alternating ritornellos and episodes is clearly reflected in Bach's concerto, yet the three solo "episodes," in which the

RITORNELLO FORM		FORM OF J. C. BACH MOVEMENT		SONATA FORM	
SECTION	KEY	SECTION	KEY	SECTION	KEY
Ritornello	I	Ritornello ("Orchestral Exposition")			
		First theme	I		
		Transition	mod		
		Second theme	I		
		Closing theme	I		
Episode	mod	Solo ("Solo Exposition")		Exposition	
		First theme	I	First theme	I
		Transition, extended with new ideas	mod	Transition	mod
		Second theme	V	Second theme	V
		Closing theme varied	V	Closing theme	V
Ritornello	V	Ritornello			
		Closing theme abbreviated	V		
Episode	mod	Solo ("Development")	mod	Development	mod
Ritornello	X	(Ritornello)			
		Brief orchestral cadence	on V		
Episode	mod	Solo ("Recapitulation")		Recapitulation	
		First theme	I	First theme	I
		Transition, altered	mod	Transition	mod
		Second theme	I	Second theme	I
		Closing theme varied	I	Closing theme	I
		Cadenza			
Ritornello	I	Ritornello			
		Closing theme	I		

FIGURE 22.12 *Concerto first-movement form in J. C. Bach, Op. 7, No. 5.*

pianist takes the lead and the orchestra provides accompaniment and punctuation, have the shape of an exposition, development, and recapitulation of a sonata. The only long ritornello is the first, which introduces most of the movement's material in the tonic; in some modern views of concerto first-movement form, this is called the "orchestral exposition," followed by the "solo exposition" in the first episode. The later ritornellos can use any element from the first one, and here Bach mostly uses the closing theme. As is often the case, both the transition and the development introduce new ideas. Bach's concerto diverges from Koch's description in one significant aspect: the next-to-last ritornello is replaced by a brief orchestral articulation.

Cadenza   By Bach's time, it had become a tradition for the soloist to play a cadenza, usually improvised, just before the final orchestral ritornello. The cadenza had developed from the trills and runs that singers inserted, particularly before the return of the opening section in the da capo aria. By convention, concerto cadenzas are typically introduced by a weighty $^6_4$ chord, and the soloist signals the orchestra to reenter by playing a long trill over a dominant chord.

ENTERTAINMENT MUSIC Finally, a great deal of music for orchestra and other ensembles was not concert music at all. Some pieces were written for background music, to be played during a meal, a party, or other social occasion in an aristocratic or well-to-do home, or for performance in informal settings both indoors or outdoors. Genres in this category include the *divertimento, cassation,* and *serenade,* all multimovement pieces for orchestra or other combinations of winds and strings that might include a mix of dances with the types of movement common in symphonies.

THE SINGING INSTRUMENT

We saw in the sixteenth and seventeenth centuries how composers and performers of music for instruments imitated and adapted elements of vocal music, and in the process created instrumental music of greater expressivity, meaningfulness, interest, and independence than ever before (see Chapters 12 and 15–17). Musicians in the eighteenth century embraced the same idea, bringing instrumental music to new heights. Composers absorbed the new styles pioneered in opera and vocal music and blended them with existing traditions within each instrumental repertoire. New genres, including the piano sonata, string quartet, and symphony, as well as new forms like sonata form and first-movement concerto form, were consolidated and became the basis for much later instrumental music. Still, in all of them, melody was paramount.

The instrumental music of this era was designed to appeal to a wide variety of people, to be understood on first hearing, and above all to please its performers and listeners. The tremendous numbers of new pieces show that they found ready audiences among middle- and upper-class amateurs and concertgoers. These numbers also confirm that consumers were eager for new music. Most of the vast quantities of instrumental music composed and published during this time passed from the stage fairly quickly, displaced by new works and styles, like popular music of later centuries.

After overshadowing their father for a generation or two, C. P. E. Bach and J. C. Bach were in turn overshadowed by Haydn and Mozart, and their music was little played during the nineteenth century. Some of Domenico Scarlatti's sonatas circulated in the nineteenth century, and a complete edition was published early in the twentieth century. But only since the mid-twentieth century have Scarlatti, the Bach sons, Sammartini, Stamitz, Dittersdorf, and a few of their contemporaries received enough attention from scholars, performers, and listeners for us to begin to hear and understand them on their own terms, rather than as "transitional" composers between the better-known figures of Bach and Handel near the beginning of the eighteenth century and Haydn and Mozart near the end. Even today, most of their contemporaries—Alberti, Galuppi, Wagenseil, Wanhal, Dussek, Gossec, Saint-Georges, Tartini, and many who have gone unmentioned here—have been almost totally eclipsed by their more famous colleagues. Composers of the middle to late eighteenth century designed their music to charm and entertain both players and listeners, and if we seek it out and listen with open ears, it continues to invite us in, to be charmed once again.

Further Reading is available at digital.wwnorton.com/hwm10

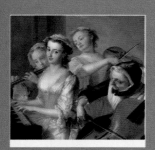

CLASSIC MUSIC IN THE LATE EIGHTEENTH CENTURY

Musicians in the late eighteenth century worked mainly for courts, cities, and churches, but they also made money by teaching, performing, and composing on commission or for publication. As popularity with the public became more important, the most successful composers wrote music that pleased everyone from connoisseurs to those with little learning.

No one was better at reaching a diverse audience than Haydn and Mozart, whose music has come to exemplify the Classic period. Their careers, though exceptional in many respects, illustrate the circumstances in which professional musicians worked. Through a synthesis of styles and traditions, they created music with immediate yet deep and enduring appeal. Working for a patron in relative isolation, Haydn forged an idiom that brought him great popularity. In later years, writing for public concerts, he honed the balance of form and expression in his music, producing a series of masterpieces. Mozart achieved fame as a child prodigy, touring Europe and mastering every kind of music he encountered. In his maturity, working as a freelance pianist and composer, he blended aspects of many styles in music of unique richness. If we view these two composers in their eighteenth-century environments, we can see more clearly the problems that confronted them and the solutions they found. Haydn secured a job with a patron and lived a life of relative stability while Mozart had to find income where he could, yet both produced music that has attracted performers and listeners for over two centuries.

JOSEPH HAYDN

Joseph Haydn (1732–1809) was the most celebrated composer of his day (see biography and Figure 23.1). Prolific in every medium, he is best remembered for his symphonies and string quartets, which set standards of quality, style, content, form, and expressivity that other composers emulated.

JOSEPH HAYDN

(1732–1809)

HAYDN! Great Sovereign of the tuneful art!
Thy works alone supply an ample chart
Of all the mountains, seas, and fertile plains
Within the compass of its wide domains.—
Is there an artist of the present day
Untaught by thee to think, as well as play?

So wrote music historian Charles Burney in 1791 on Haydn's arrival in England. Indeed, Haydn was hailed in his time as the greatest composer alive. In public life, he exemplified the Enlightenment ideals of good character, piety, and kindness. He was also an ambitious entrepreneur and skillful businessman, capable of both seriousness and humor. But above all, he had a consummate ability to satisfy his patrons and please his audiences.

Born in Rohrau, a village about thirty miles southeast of Vienna, Haydn was the son of a master wheelwright. At the age of seven he became a choirboy at St. Stephen's Cathedral in Vienna, where he learned singing, harpsichord, and violin. Dismissed at seventeen when his voice changed, Haydn barely supported himself as a freelance performer, composer, and teacher. He mastered counterpoint using Fux's *Gradus ad Parnassum*, studied the music of other composers, and took lessons from the famous Italian composer Nicola Porpora, a master of the galant style.

Haydn became music director for Count Morzin in about 1757 and probably wrote his first symphonies for the count's orchestra. Three years later, he married a wigmaker's daughter, Maria Anna Keller, although he was really in love with her sister Josepha. Josepha, however, became a nun, and his long marriage was unhappy, childless, and marked by extramarital affairs on both sides.

In 1761, Haydn found a position that determined the course of his career: he entered the service of a noble Hungarian family, the Esterházys, and continued in their employ for the rest of his life. For years Haydn was responsible for composing on demand, presenting concerts or operas weekly, and assisting with chamber music. While the position forced him to

FIGURE 23.1 *Joseph Haydn, in an oil portrait by Thomas Hardy, painted in 1791–92 during Haydn's first sojourn in London.*

compose at a prodigious rate—just the catalogue of his works, by Anthony van Hoboken, fills three hefty volumes—it allowed him to hear his music in excellent performances and to experiment with new ideas. During visits to Vienna, Haydn took part in the city's intellectual and musical life. It was there around 1784 that he met Mozart, twenty-four years his junior, and their mutual admiration blossomed.

The publication of Haydn's music brought him fame throughout Europe and generated commissions from many other patrons. He spent most of the time between 1790 and 1795 composing, giving concerts, and teaching in London, where he had long been famous. His triumphs there raised his reputation at home, and he was invited to return to Vienna as court music director for Prince Nikolaus II Esterházy in 1795, with minimal duties. He began to complain of weakness around 1799, and by 1802 had all but ceased to compose. He died a rich man at seventy-seven in 1809, still universally admired.

MAJOR WORKS 104 symphonies, 20 concertos, 68 string quartets, 29 keyboard trios, 126 baryton trios, 47 keyboard sonatas, 15 operas, 12 masses, *The Creation*, *The Seasons*, numerous other ensemble, keyboard, and vocal works

HAYDN'S PATRONS: THE ESTERHÁZY PRINCES Haydn spent most of his career serving the Esterházy family, the most powerful noble family in Hungary. Hired in 1761 by Prince Paul Anton Esterházy, a generous patron devoted to music, Haydn had to compose whatever music the prince commanded, conduct performances, train and supervise all the musical personnel, and keep the instruments in repair (see Source Reading). When Paul Anton died in 1762, his brother Nikolaus succeeded to the title; even more avid about music, he confirmed Haydn's appointment and raised his salary.

Eszterháza   At the Esterházy court, Haydn passed nearly thirty years in circumstances almost ideal for his development as a composer. Beginning in 1766, Nikolaus, whose seat was in Eisenstadt just south of Vienna, lived for most of the year at his remote country estate of Eszterháza, shown in Figure 23.2. The palace and grounds were designed to rival the splendor of Versailles. Eszterháza boasted two theaters, one for opera and one for marionette plays, and two large and

SOURCE READING

Haydn's Contract

When he entered the service of Prince Paul Anton Esterházy, Haydn was named Vice-Kapellmeister, allowing the elderly Kapellmeister to retain his title but giving Haydn sole direction of orchestral, chamber, and dramatic music. His contract, excerpted below, spells out his duties and his social standing as a house officer, higher than servants yet still required to wear the court uniform. On the death of the Kapellmeister in 1766, Haydn succeeded to the title.

2. The said Joseph Heyden [*sic*] shall be considered and treated as a member of the household. Therefore his Serene Highness is graciously pleased to place confidence in his conducting himself as becomes an honorable official of a princely house. He must be temperate, not showing himself overbearing toward his musicians, but mild and lenient, straightforward and composed. It is especially to be observed that when the orchestra shall be summoned to perform before company, the Vice-Kapellmeister and all the musicians shall appear in uniform, and the said Joseph Heyden shall take care that he and all the members of his orchestra follow the instructions given, and appear in white stockings, white linen, powdered, and with either a pigtail or a tiewig. . . .

4. The said Vice-Kapellmeister shall be under obligation to compose such music as his Serene Highness may command, and neither to communicate such compositions to any other person, nor to allow them to be copied, but he shall retain them for the absolute use of his Highness, and not compose for any other person without the knowledge and permission of his Highness.

5. The said Joseph Heyden shall appear daily in the antechamber before and after midday, and inquire whether his Highness is pleased to order a performance of the orchestra. On receipt of his orders he shall communicate them to the other musicians, and take care to be punctual at the appointed time, and to ensure punctuality in his subordinates. . . .

7. The said Vice-Kapellmeister shall take careful charge of all music and musical instruments, and be responsible for any injury that may occur to them from carelessness or neglect.

8. The said Joseph Heyden shall be obliged to instruct the female vocalists, in order that they may not forget in the country what they have been taught with much trouble and expense in Vienna, and, as the said Vice-Kapellmeister is proficient on various instruments, he shall take care himself to practice on all that he is acquainted with.

Translated in Karl Geiringer, *Haydn: A Creative Life in Music* (New York: W. W. Norton, 1946), 52–53.

FIGURE 23.2 *Eszterháza Palace, built 1762–66 as a summer residence on Lake Neusiedl by the Hungarian prince Nikolaus Esterházy, whom Haydn served for almost thirty years. The palace opera house opened in 1768 with a performance of Haydn's* Lo speziale. *Mezzotint from 1791 by János Berkeny after Szabó and Karl Schütz, showing horsemen in formation and a Roma (Gypsy) band at lower right.*

sumptuously appointed music rooms. By the 1780s, Haydn had built up the orchestra from around fourteen to about twenty-five players, giving concerts every week and operas on special occasions. In almost daily chamber music sessions in the prince's private apartments, Nikolaus played cello, viola da gamba, and especially baryton, a large string instrument with sympathetic strings, shown in Figure 23.3. Through the early 1760s, Haydn composed mostly instrumental music for the prince—from orchestral works for concerts to baryton trios. After the move to Eszterháza, he also composed sacred vocal music and operas, while continuing to produce instrumental works.

Although Eszterháza was isolated, Haydn kept abreast of current developments in music through a constant stream of distinguished visitors and through sojourns in Vienna for one or two months each winter. He had the inestimable advantages of working with a devoted, highly skilled group of singers and players and an intelligent patron, whose requirements may have been burdensome but whose understanding and enthusiasm were inspiring. As Haydn once wrote,

> My prince was pleased with all my works, I was commended, and as conductor of an orchestra I could make experiments, observe what strengthened and what weakened an effect, and thereupon improve, substitute, omit, and try new things. I was cut off from the world, there was no one around to mislead or harass me, and so I was forced to become original.

Haydn's original contract forbade him to sell or give away his composi-   *Publications*
tions, but unauthorized publications of his music in London, Paris, and elsewhere spread his reputation across Europe. A new contract in 1779 allowed

FIGURE 23.3 *This baryton, shown leaning against its case, was owned by Prince Nikolaus Esterházy. A favorite instrument of the prince's, the baryton resembled a bass viola da gamba but had an extra set of resonating metal strings that could be plucked like a harp. Haydn wrote some 165 chamber works with baryton for the prince to perform, mostly trios with viola and cello.*

Haydn to sell his music to others while continuing to direct opera and musical activities at court. He subsequently wrote most of his instrumental music with the expectation of sales to the public, in manuscript or printed copies. Since copyright at the time did not extend across national boundaries, Haydn tried to maximize his profits and to prevent pirated editions by selling the same piece simultaneously to publishers in several different countries.

As Haydn increasingly composed for publication or for other patrons, he gained a measure of independence from his employer. His freedom grew unexpectedly in 1790 when Nikolaus died and his son Anton disbanded the orchestra. Haydn was given a pension and went to live in Vienna, but the impresario and violinist Johann Peter Salomon persuaded him to come to London for two extended stays between 1791 and 1795. There Haydn conducted concerts, taught well-to-do students, and composed many new works. His last twelve symphonies, written for London, were received there with great acclaim.

HAYDN'S STYLE Haydn's style, which drew on many sources, was recognized in his time as highly individual. It was forged by his experiences trying to please his patron, his players, and the public. He sought broad and immediate appeal by devising themes that seemed familiar on first hearing and by following conventions for phrasing, form, and harmony. Yet he made his music more interesting than most by introducing the unexpected, in numerous ways (see Source Reading). In a delightful alchemy, each aspect of his style reinforced the others: the familiar was enriched by contrasts, the reliance on conventions created listener expectations that made surprises possible, the diverse content clarified the form, and the intrinsic variety allowed him to evoke the sublime or create musical humor with equal skill.

The main source for Haydn's idiom was the galant style, the predominant language of music by midcentury, marked by songful melody in short phrases, arranged in balanced periods, over light accompaniment. Into this framework Haydn brought elements of other styles. From C. P. E. Bach, whose keyboard sonatas he studied diligently, Haydn adopted the heightened expressivity of the empfindsam style and an emphasis on making the most of each musical idea through variation and development. Also important was the learned style of counterpoint, absorbed from church music, Baroque composers, and Fux's *Gradus ad Parnassum*. Other elements came from styles associated with particular genres, nations, or social classes, from opera buffa to hymns and from military fanfares to folk songs.

Simple yet sophisticated   A characteristic example of Haydn's mature style is the theme for the rondo-form finale of his String Quartet in E-flat Major, Op. 33, No. 2 (*The Joke*, 1781; NAWM 121d), shown in Example 23.1 (see p. 520). The tuneful theme—a small rounded binary form—seems simple on first hearing, but on closer examination, we find remarkable sophistication.

Economy and novelty   The theme derives entirely from a single idea presented in the first two measures (bracketed in the example). The idea contains three motives

SOURCE READING

Haydn's Recipe for Success

In a brief book called *Hints to Young Composers of Instrumental Music* (1805), English gentleman composer John Marsh (1752–1828) offered tips on the use of various instruments and on other aspects of composition. Noting the revival of Handel's music in the 1780s, he credits Haydn with breathing new life into the "modern style" of galant composers.

❋

By this revival, or rather exaltation of the ancient, it seems not improbable that the modern style would have also failed in its turn (as it was about this time degenerating into a light, trivial and uniform character) had not the great Haydn, by his wonderful contrivance, by the variety and eccentricity of his modulation, by his judicious dispersion of light and shade, and happy manner of blending simple and intelligible air with abstruse and complicated harmony, greatly improved the latter species of composition, insomuch that, instead of being able, as was before the case, to anticipate in great measure the second part of any

movement, from its uniform relation to the foregoing, it is on the contrary, in his works, impossible to conceive what will follow, and a perpetual interest is kept up, in much longer pieces than any of the same kind ever composed. . . .

To conclude; in the composition of every piece of music, containing two or more movements, as well as in the selection and arrangement of pieces for a concert, let *contrast* be always attended to, as the best means of keeping the attention alive and active. For through the common neglect to relieve loud passages with soft ones, full pieces and choruses, with quartettos, songs and glees, instrumental music with vocal, and ancient music with modern, many compositions, in other respects excellent, produce but little effect; and people become fatigued, and complain of the length of concerts, which perhaps would never tire them, were they not cloyed with too much of one thing, or too great a uniformity of style.

John Marsh, *Hints to Young Composers of Instrumental Music* (London, 1805); reprinted and ed. Charles Cudworth, *The Galpin Society Journal* 18 (1965): 57–72, quoting pp. 60 and 71.

distinguished by rhythm and articulation (marked a, b, and c), which recur in various permutations in what follows. Even when the rhythm repeats exactly (at measures 3, 9, and 11), Haydn gives it a new melodic contour, so that each phrase is both familiar and fresh. Combining economy of material with constant novelty is typical of Haydn.

The opening idea does not close on the downbeat but spills over into the second half of the measure, lending it a playful, unfinished character. When it repeats at measure 5, the rhythmic momentum carries forward to the downbeat of measure 7, allowing the last motive to close on the downbeat of measure 8. Through this expansion, Haydn creates a four-measure phrase to balance the two preceding two-measure units. Because the harmony avoids root-position cadences at measures 4 and 6, the listener does not sense a relaxation until the cadence in measure 8 closes the first period. Thus rhythm and harmony work together to sustain continuity throughout the entire period, despite its short, choppy melodic units.

Rhythm, phrasing, and harmony

After the first period repeats, the second section begins on the dominant with a complementary eight-measure period that continues to vary the opening idea. After this period cadences in measure 16, a simple reprise of the first period would bring the theme to a satisfactory conclusion. But before

Expansion, delay, and drama

EXAMPLE 23.1 *Joseph Haydn, theme from the finale of String Quartet in E-flat Major, Op. 33, No. 2*

finally granting the reprise (at measure 29), Haydn delays its arrival by inserting a long elaboration on the dominant. Louder dynamic levels, diminished
chords, diminuendos and crescendos, and a pedal point all create a sense of
drama. Even within this insertion there is expansion; measures 20–21 or
measures 23–28 could be omitted, since the former prolongs what "should"
have been a four-measure phrase and the latter confirms and extends the
cadence. Such expansion of a phrase, period, or section is a basic technique in
Haydn's music, used for both expressive and formal purposes.

Because this dramatization of the dominant seems exaggerated in the   *Wit*
context of a little rondo theme, the effect is witty. The humor is produced
through incongruity of a sort that only experienced listeners and performers
can notice, because in order to catch the joke we must understand the form,
the genre, and the conventions that underlie them. Haydn's wit makes his
music especially endearing to players and connoisseurs because he compli-
ments our perceptiveness with every joke or subtle effect he puts in his music.

This quartet earned the nickname *The Joke* because of this movement's
closing passage, shown in Example 23.2. Here Haydn inserts long rests
between phrases of his theme. Through these surprising pauses, we are made
aware of our expectations for how the music will continue. When measures
5–8 of the theme (see Example 23.1) are broken into two-measure phrases
(measures 160–62 and 164–66), we suddenly realize that such two-measure
units are what we expected at the beginning, and that Haydn's original version
was a witty variant. After the longest rest of all leads us to think that the piece
is over, the opening figure returns once more, suggesting yet another go-
around of the theme. But when the players relax, indicating that the piece is

EXAMPLE 23.2 *Closing passage from the finale of Haydn's Op. 33, No. 2*

finished, we are meant to be amused at the way Haydn played on our expectations. We may also notice that the opening figure cadences on the tonic, making it a suitable ending after all. The joke is obvious, but its fullest meaning is open only to an experienced listener.

Differentiation
of function

The anomaly of Haydn's converting an opening phrase into a final cadence points out a basic truth about the galant style: there is a strong differentiation of function between elements. Familiarity with the conventions of the style makes it easy for listeners to distinguish between musical gestures that signal the beginning, middle, or end of a phrase, period, or larger section. Even surrounded by silence, measures 164–66 clearly constitute an ending gesture, and measures 160–62 could not satisfactorily begin or end a period but must fall in the middle. Similarly, listeners can tell a theme from a transition or a cadential extension. The opening eight-measure period of Example 23.1 is immediately perceptible as thematic, marked by regular phrasing, frequent cadences, and a logical harmonic progression that stays in a single key. On the other hand, measures 17–28 could not stand alone as a theme; the relative harmonic stasis, repetitions, and continuous rhythms would sound odd in a theme but are just right for confirming a cadential arrival. Haydn exploits these differences to make his music easy to follow but also turns gestures on their heads when he wants to amuse and surprise us.

Double appeal

When we examine Haydn's music closely, we recognize how sophisticated it is. Yet it remains simple in the best sense: clear, engaging, easy to understand. It appeals at once to the least experienced listener yet rewards the connoisseur, even after repeated hearings. This double appeal is a recipe for greatness as well as popular success, an achievement that many have tried to emulate but few have equaled.

COMPOSITIONAL PROCESS As simple and natural as Haydn's music may sound, it was not produced without effort. According to his own report, he began a composition by improvising at the keyboard until he settled on an appropriate theme or idea. He then worked out the piece at the keyboard and on paper, usually writing down only the main melody and harmony on one or two staves. Figure 23.4, a page of sketches for his oratorio *The Seasons* (1799–1801), shows this type of musical shorthand. Often, he drafted sections in an order that was different from their appearance in the piece. Finally, he wrote out the completed score. This procedure combined improvisation and calculation, while Haydn first searched for something to say and then devised the most effective way to say it. The interplay of heart and mind this process embodies is reflected in his music's union of expressivity and craft.

SYMPHONIC FORM Haydn has been called "the father of the symphony," not because he invented the genre but because his symphonies set the pattern for later composers through their high quality, wide dissemination, and lasting appeal. When the classical repertoire was established in the nineteenth century, his were the oldest symphonies to receive regular performances. Thus he seemed to stand at the head of a great tradition.

Haydn's symphonies are traditionally identified by number, although the numbering (applied by a nineteenth-century publisher) does not precisely reflect the order in which they were written nor their total number of

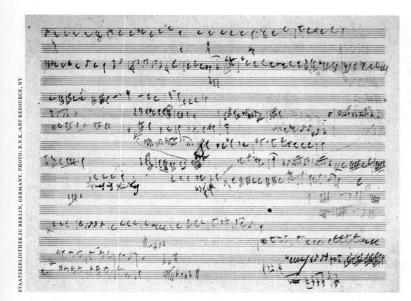

FIGURE 23.4 *A page of Haydn's sketches for his oratorio* The Seasons. *The composer notated passages in a kind of musical shorthand on one or two staves without clefs or key signatures. This was intended to jot down his thoughts, not to be read by others, and it can be difficult to follow without comparing it to the final score.*

approximately 106. Many of his symphonies that have acquired names—few of which were bestowed by the composer himself—are among the best known. His symphonies are remarkably diverse, for he seems deliberately to have made each one an individual. Yet they have enough in common that we can distill his usual practices.

Most Haydn symphonies have four movements: (1) a fast sonata-form movement, often with a slow introduction; (2) a slow movement; (3) a minuet and trio; and (4) a fast finale, usually in sonata or rondo form. All are in the same key except the slow movement, which is in a closely related key such as the subdominant or dominant. Haydn's consistent use of this format helped to make it the standard for later composers.

Four-movement structure

Haydn's Symphony No. 88 in G Major (NAWM 122) illustrates many elements that characterize his symphonic techniques. Written in 1787 for publication and performance in Paris, it has become one of Haydn's most popular and frequently performed works. After a close look at this symphony as an example, we will survey the changes in Haydn's approach to symphonic composition over the course of his career.

Symphony No. 88

As in many of Haydn's symphonies, the first movement (NAWM 122a) begins with a slow introduction, whose solemn mood makes the ensuing Allegro sound energetic by comparison. Similarly strong contrasts delineate the components of the movement's sonata form. Thematic areas are tonally stable, with balanced phrases articulated by cadences. The themes alternate with unstable passages that serve as transitions, often scored for full orchestra and characterized by loud dynamics, sequences, modulation, dramatic rushing figures, overlapping phrases, and avoidance of cadences. The contrasts between stability and instability in phrasing and key help us follow the form. Haydn often heightens these contrasts through differences in style, texture, instrumentation, or mood, so that whichever musical elements we pay attention to, we are not likely to get lost.

First-movement form

Exposition Each thematic area typically contains a variety of ideas. In the exposition of Symphony No. 88, Haydn derives each new idea from rhythmic and melodic elements already presented. Example 23.3a shows the opening theme, in which each phrase varies the first (motive a). When the theme repeats, it is accompanied by the figure in Example 23.3b (motive b), whose neighbor-tone motion in sixteenth notes echoes the theme's cadential figure (a′). The transition is suffused with variations and recombinations of parts from both motives, shown in Example 23.3c. The second theme in Example 23.3d hearkens back rhythmically to the first. A transition-like passage, with further variants of both motives, leads to the closing theme, which is typically more repetitive and cadential than the first or second themes; here it combines the first theme's rhythm with a chromatic countermelody from the second theme, as shown in Example 23.3e, followed by more figuration derived from motives a and b. Although not every Haydn exposition is so focused on such limited material, this remarkable display of variety through reworking a small number of motives is characteristic of Haydn.

Development In Haydn's development sections, motives from the exposition are varied, extended, combined, or superimposed; treated in sequence, imitation, fugato, or stretto; or made into figurations for rushing passages. In the first movement of Symphony No. 88, the development continues the focus on motives derived from the first theme, moving quickly to the distant key of A♭ and gradually returning to the home key while treating the material in sequence, fragmentation, invertible counterpoint, and a brief canon. Enriching developments and transitions with counterpoint is one way Haydn brought the older learned style into works in the modern galant style. Abrupt changes of subject, digressions, and silences are particularly characteristic of Haydn developments.

Recapitulation We are usually well prepared for the recapitulation, but Haydn sometimes disguises or plays down its actual appearance so that we may not recognize that it has begun until after the fact. Often the opening subject is rescored or extended in new ways. In the first movement of Symphony No. 88, the first theme appears as expected but with a countermelody added in the flute, introducing counterpoint where there was none in the exposition. The second and closing themes now appear in the tonic, but instead of curtailing the transition because he does not need to modulate, Haydn often prefers to intensify and animate it with a simulated modulation. He does so in this movement, where part of the closing theme unexpectedly shows up in the transition. A brief coda, based on the first theme, closes the movement.

Slow movement The second movement of a Haydn symphony usually offers an oasis of calm and gentle melody after the contrasts, drama, and complexity of the first movement. Many of the slow movements are in sonata form without repeats, and in later works Haydn often used theme and variations. In Symphony No. 88, the slow movement (NAWM 122b) combines elements of variations, rondo, and rounded binary form. The songlike theme is played by solo cello and oboe over a constantly varied accompaniment, alternating with other material. Most contrasting is a dramatic idea with trumpets and timpani, instruments with military associations whose appearance here is a complete surprise, having not been used in the first movement.

EXAMPLE 23.3 *Motivic relationships in the first movement of Haydn's Symphony No. 88*

a. First theme

b. Accompanimental figure

c. Motives in transition

d. Beginning of second theme

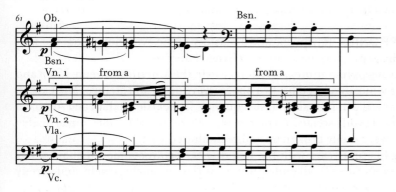

e. Beginning of closing theme

Minuet and trio   The third movement comprises a pair of stylized minuets, with the first repeated after the second (the trio) to create an ABA form for the movement as a whole. Both minuet and trio are cast in the traditional binary dance form with repeats. The trio is usually set in the same key as the minuet (possibly with a change of mode), sometimes in a closely related key, but has a lighter orchestration and character; it takes its name from the reduced texture of three parts used for such middle dances in the seventeenth century. Often, the minuet has an urban character and the trio a countrified affect, a coupling that dates back to sixteenth- and seventeenth-century dance music. The minuet movement provides relaxation, since it is shorter than the previous movements, is written in a more popular style, and has a form that is easy to follow. But its very directness allowed Haydn to introduce interest and humor. In the minuet and trio in Symphony No. 88 (NAWM 122c), for example, irregular phrasing, grace notes on offbeats, unexpected harmonies, and changes of dynamic level keep the listener off-balance, and open-fifth drones in the trio create a rustic sound.

Finale   After the easygoing minuet, the final movement closes the symphony with a further buildup of tension, climax, and release. The finale is typically faster and shorter than the first movement, overflowing with high spirits and impish surprises. The finale of Symphony No. 88 (NAWM 122d) is a rondo, in which the main theme, a small rounded binary form, alternates with episodes in the pattern ABACA plus coda. Here the episodes modulate to other keys and include variations on the main theme, evoking the character of a sonata-form exposition and development section. Many Haydn finales are in sonata form, and some are **sonata-rondos** in the pattern ABACABA, in which the A and B sections resemble the first and second themes in a sonata-form exposition, C is a modulatory development passage, and B returns near the end in the tonic. Whatever form he chose, Haydn typically gave his finales the character of a *contredanse*, a light, quick dance in duple meter.

THE SYMPHONIES Haydn showed a mastery of the symphony from his first works in the genre, but his approach changed over time.

Early symphonies,
1757–67   His earliest symphonies, written for Count Morzin between 1757 and 1761, were typically scored for two oboes, two horns, and strings. Most are in three movements in fast-slow-fast sequence, like earlier Italian and Austrian symphonies. For his sonata-form movements, he chose themes made of elements that were easily broken up and recombined.

During his first years with the Esterházys, Haydn composed about thirty symphonies (1761–67), all quite diverse, as Haydn sought novelty and variety in his offerings at court. The ensemble is often augmented with flute, bassoon, or other instruments. The best-known symphonies from this time are Nos. 6 to 8, titled *Le matin* (Morning), *Le midi* (Noon), and *Le soir* (Evening), which Haydn composed soon after entering Prince Esterházy's service in 1761. Haydn included solo passages for each instrument designed to showcase the skills of his players.

Symphonies of
1768–72   Beginning about 1768, Haydn presented his symphonies at Eszterháza in the elegant concert room shown in Figure 23.5. The twelve symphonies of the next four years show Haydn as a composer of mature technique and fertile imagination. These symphonies are longer, more rhythmically complex,

more contrapuntal, and more challenging to play. They are marked by greater extremes in dynamic level, more sudden contrasts between loud and soft, and more use of crescendos and sforzatos, all used to startling effect. The harmonic palette is richer than in early symphonies, and modulations range more widely. Several symphonies from this period, particularly the six in minor keys, have an emotional, agitated character that some scholars have associated with the literary movement known as *Sturm und Drang* (storm and stress, after a 1776 play about the American Revolution); a more direct source lies in operatic scenes from the 1760s that use tremolos, angular melodies, and other devices to depict terrifying events, such as the portrayal of the Furies in Gluck's *Orfeo ed Euridice* (NAWM 113).

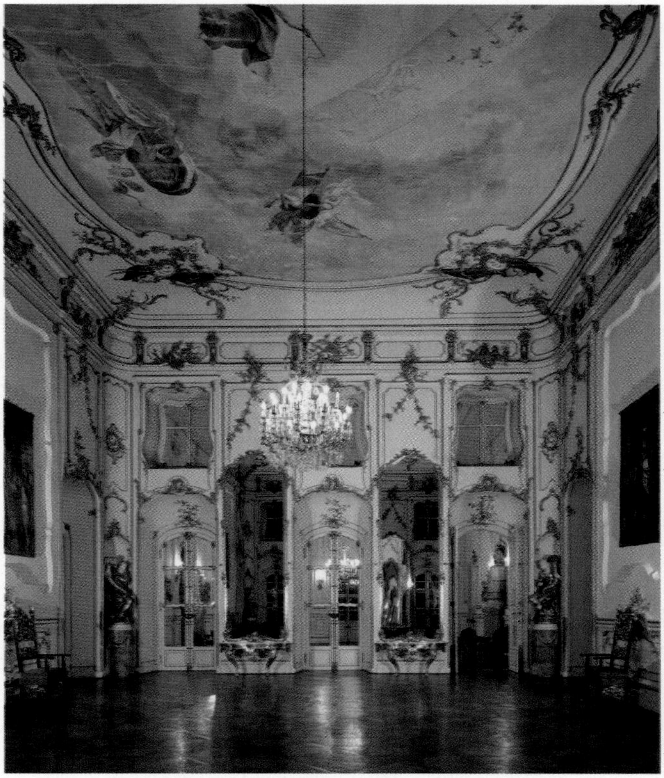

ESZTERHÁZA PALACE, FERTOED, HUNGARY. PHOTO: ERICH LESSING/ART RESOURCE, NY

FIGURE 23.5 *This hall in the Eszterháza Palace was used from around 1768 for concerts, at which Haydn presented his symphonies. Although in other centers symphonies were often accompanied by basso continuo and the keyboard player directed the ensemble, at Eszterháza there was no continuo, and Haydn led the ensemble while playing first violin.*

Beginning around 1773, Haydn turned from minor keys and experiments in form and expression to embrace a more popular style. Audiences expected symphonies to be immediately intelligible and appealing, but also serious, stirring, and impressive, and Haydn produced works that have all these traits. Symphony No. 56 in C Major (1774) is festive and brilliant, like its predecessors in the same key, but encompasses a broader emotional range, reflecting Haydn's recent experience with heightened expression. The opening theme alternates arpeggiations for the whole orchestra, suggestive of fanfares, with songlike phrases for the strings. The agitation, counterpoint, chromaticism, and dramatic surprises of *Sturm und Drang* style now serve as contrast, making the transition stand out in comparison to the themes.

Symphonies for public concerts

In the 1780s, Haydn increasingly composed for the public, selling his symphonies to patrons or publishers abroad. By now he consistently wrote for an orchestra of flute, two oboes, two bassoons, two horns, and strings, sometimes augmented by trumpets and timpani. The *Paris* Symphonies of 1785–86 (Nos. 82–87), commissioned for performance in the French capital, were his grandest so far. Queen Marie Antoinette is said to have been especially fond of No. 85, called *La reine* (The Queen). After the six symphonies were performed again in 1787, a reviewer noted how "this great genius could draw such rich and varied developments from a single subject, so different from the sterile composers who pass continually from one idea to another." Symphonies Nos. 88–92 were also composed on commission. Like the *Paris* symphonies, they offer a combination of popular and learned styles, and of

EXAMPLE 23.4 *Opening theme from the finale of Haydn's Symphony No. 104*

deep expression with masterful technique, that gave them immediate and lasting appeal.

London Symphonies   The invitation from Johann Peter Salomon in 1790 to compose and conduct symphonies for the cosmopolitan and exacting audiences of London spurred Haydn to supreme efforts. Hailed by the British as "the greatest composer in the world," he was determined to live up to what was expected of him. The twelve *London* Symphonies are his crowning achievements, with more daring harmonic conceptions, intensified rhythmic drive, and especially memorable thematic inventions. The orchestra is expanded, with trumpets and timpani now standard and clarinets in all but one of the last six. Woodwinds and double bass are used more independently than before, solo strings appear at times, and the whole sound achieves a new spaciousness and brilliance.

Haydn's shrewd appraisal of London's musical tastes is evident. There is a sudden *fortissimo* crash on a weak beat in the slow movement of Symphony No. 94 that has given this work its nickname *Surprise.* It was put there because, as Haydn later acknowledged, he wanted something novel and startling to take people's minds off the rival concert series of his former pupil Ignaz Pleyel (1757–1831). The greater tunefulness may also have been prompted by this competition, since Pleyel's strong suit was melody. Haydn turned to Slovenian, Croatian, and other peasant tunes he remembered from his youth. Symphony No. 103 displays characteristic instances of folklike melodies, and the finale of No. 104, with its imitation of the drone of a bagpipe, is particularly suggestive of a peasant dance, as shown in Example 23.4. Similar allusions are the "Turkish" band effect (triangle, cymbals, bass drum) and the trumpet fanfare in the Allegretto of the *Military* Symphony (No. 100), and the ticking accompaniment in the Andante of No. 101 (*The Clock*). Such appealing features reflect Haydn's aim to please both the music lover and the expert.

STRING QUARTETS   Haydn has been called "the father of the string quartet" with more justification than we have for the epithet "father of the symphony." Although not the first to compose quartets, he was among the earliest and was the first great master of the genre. Unlike symphonies, which were typically performed by professionals for an audience, quartets were primarily music for amateurs to play for their own pleasure. Haydn's quartets are very much addressed to the players. They are sometimes described as a conversation among the instruments: the first violin has the leading role, but the cello and inner parts often carry the melody or engage in dialogue. The evolution of his quartets parallels that of the symphonies in many respects, from early mastery, through increasing length and emotional depth, to very individual late works.

Haydn's first ten quartets resembled divertimentos and were so titled when they were published in his Opp. 1 (1764) and 2 (1766). From then on, Haydn tended to write quartets in groups of six, the most common number of works in a published collection.

Early quartets

The next eighteen quartets, Opp. 9 (ca. 1770), 17 (1771), and 20 (1772), established for the quartet the same four-movement pattern as in the symphony, but with the minuet often before instead of after the slow movement. Several of these quartets are in minor keys, like the contemporary *Sturm und Drang* symphonies, and three from Op. 20 end with fugues. The quartets of this period made Haydn famous far beyond Austria, and their expanded proportions and expressive range set the pattern for later quartets.

Opp. 9, 17, and 20

Haydn composed the six quartets of Op. 33 in 1781 and proclaimed to two admirers that they were written in a "quite new and special way." They are lighthearted, witty, and tuneful. The minuets, here titled *scherzo* (Italian for "joke" or "trick") or *scherzando* ("joking" or "playful"), play tricks with the courtly dance by breaking normal metrical patterns, as illustrated by the hemiolas and sudden silence in Example 23.5. Many of Haydn's minuets, whatever their title, feature such playful rhythmic devices. Another kind of joke, used in the minuet movement of Op. 33, No. 2 (NAWM 121b), is the sudden juxtaposition of starkly contrasting styles, gestures, or dynamics. **Scherzo** later became the term for an especially fast movement in minuet and trio form.

Op. 33

Even apart from the scherzos, Op. 33 contains some of Haydn's best strokes of humor, as we have seen with the rondo finale of No. 2 (NAWM 121d). His playfulness in the themes themselves and in the dialogue between

EXAMPLE 23.5 *Scherzo from Haydn's String Quartet in G Major, Op. 33, No. 5*

TIMELINE

1757 Joseph Haydn hired by Count Morzin

1761 Haydn hired by Prince Paul Anton Esterházy

1762 Prince Nikolaus Esterházy succeeds to title, becomes Haydn's main patron

1762–73 Wolfgang Amadeus Mozart tours as child prodigy

1765–80 Maria Theresa and Joseph II rule Austria jointly

1772 Haydn, Op. 20 string quartets

1772 Mozart named third concertmaster at Salzburg

1776 American Declaration of Independence

1780 Death of Maria Theresa; Joseph II sole Hapsburg ruler

1781 Mozart moves to Vienna

1781 Haydn, Op. 33 string quartets

1784 Mozart publishes Piano Sonata in F Major, K. 332

1786 Mozart, Piano Concerto in A Major, K. 488

1787 Haydn, Symphony No. 88 in G Major

1787 Mozart, *Don Giovanni*

1788 Mozart, *Jupiter* Symphony

1789–99 French Revolution

1790 Joseph II dies, Leopold II succeeds him as emperor

1791 Mozart, *Ave verum corpus*

1791 Haydn, first *London* Symphonies

1798 Haydn, *The Creation*

players added merriment to amateur quartet evenings in cities such as London, Paris, and Vienna, in the country estates of the nobility and upper classes, and even in monasteries. Since quartets were normally played at sight and were not published in score, many of the jokes became apparent only in performance; there is more than one story of a player cracking up with laughter at an unexpected turn of events.

The first and third movements of Op. 33, No. 2 (NAWM 121a and 121c) are more serious. The first movement exemplifies some characteristic strategies Haydn adopts in the sonata-form movements of his quartets that differ from his works in other genres. After the first theme, dominated by the first violin, he usually chooses a looser texture in which the primary motives pass from one instrument to another. In place of the orchestral tuttis that highlight the transitions in the symphonies, Haydn introduces changes of texture, here featuring dialogue between instruments, pedal points, and loud rhythmic unisons. The slow third movement presents two main ideas in alternation, the first of them in a new scoring each time, so that each instrument has a chance to shine. It is such exchanges of ideas among the players that give Haydn's quartets the character of a conversation with friends.

In his remaining years, Haydn composed thirty-four quartets. Especially noteworthy are the six quartets of Op. 76 (ca. 1796–97), which exemplify a new approach to the quartet as a genre for performance in concerts, alongside its traditional role in private music-making. In his last quartets, Haydn expanded the harmonic frontiers, foreshadowing Romantic harmony with chromatic progressions, chromatic chords, enharmonic changes, and fanciful tonal shifts. Each quartet has individual features, as if Haydn were trying to avoid repeating himself; indeed, this had become a requirement, since he was writing primarily for publication, and amateurs and audiences were most attracted to the new. Like his late symphonies, his late quartets juxtapose the serious and jocular, the artful and folklike, the sublime and the jesting.

KEYBOARD SONATAS AND TRIOS In Haydn's day, keyboard sonatas and trios were written for amateurs to play in private for their own enjoyment. Both genres usually featured three movements in fast-slow-fast format, and both focused on the expression of intimate or sentimental feelings, befitting their private character and their intended audience among the middle classes, who valued emotional expressivity. Indeed, the piano trio was essentially a piano sonata accompanied by strings, the cello doubling the bass line and the violin adding background and some contrasting themes.

VOCAL WORKS In a modest autobiographical sketch of 1776 written for an Austrian encyclopedia, Haydn named his most successful works: three operas, an Italian oratorio, and his setting of the *Stabat mater* (1767). He made no mention of the sixty symphonies he had written by then and referred to his chamber music only to complain that the Berlin critics dealt with it too harshly. In line with the aesthetic theories of the era, Haydn believed that vocal music was more important than instrumental, more effective at moving the listener, and closer to song, which he considered the natural source of all music.

Opera occupied much of Haydn's time and energy at Eszterháza. Besides six little German operas for marionettes, he wrote at least fifteen Italian operas. Most were comic, with music abounding in humor and high spirits. Of the three serious operas, the most famous was *Armida* (1784), remarkable for dramatic accompanied recitatives and arias on a grand scale. Successful in their day and full of excellent music, Haydn's operas have never attained the same level of popularity as those of Gluck or Mozart. But several have been rediscovered and staged in recent decades, notably the comic operas *Lo speziale* (The Apothecary, 1768) and *Il mondo della luna* (The World on the Moon, 1777), both on librettos by Goldoni.

Operas

Haydn's earliest surviving and last completed works were masses dating from 1749 and 1802 respectively. His last six masses (1796–1802), including *Missa in tempore belli* (Mass in Time of War, 1796), the *Lord Nelson* Mass (1798), the *Theresienmesse* (1799), and the *Harmoniemesse* (Wind Band Mass, 1802), are large-scale, festive works using four solo vocalists, chorus, and full orchestra with trumpets and timpani. Like the masses of Mozart and other south Germans, these works have a flamboyance that matches the architecture of the Austrian Baroque churches in which they were performed. Haydn's masses blend traditional elements, including contrapuntal writing for solo voices and the customary choral fugues at the conclusion of the Gloria and the Credo, with a new prominence for the orchestra and elements drawn from symphonic style and symphonic forms. The occasional criticism that his sacred music was too cheerful met with the composer's assurance that at the thought of God, his heart "leaped for joy" and his confidence that God would not reproach him for praising the Lord "with a cheerful heart."

Masses

During his stay in London, Haydn became better acquainted with Handel's oratorios, some of which he had already encountered in Vienna. At Westminster Abbey in 1791, Haydn was so deeply moved by the Hallelujah Chorus in a massive performance of *Messiah* that he burst into tears and exclaimed, "He is the master of us all." Haydn's appreciation for Handel bore fruit in the choral parts of his late masses and inspired him to compose his oratorios *The Creation* (completed 1798), on texts adapted from Genesis and Milton's *Paradise Lost*, and *The Seasons* (completed 1801). Both were issued simultaneously in German and English, in a nod both to Handel and to the English public, and both quickly became standards of the repertoire for choral societies in German- and English-speaking areas. The German texts were written by Baron Gottfried van Swieten, the imperial court librarian in Vienna and a busy musical and literary amateur.

Oratorios

Haydn's instrumental introductions and interludes in both works are among the finest examples of scene-painting in music of the time. His *Depiction of Chaos* at the beginning of *The Creation* features confusing and disturbingly dissonant harmonies. The following recitative and chorus (NAWM 123) set the opening words of the Bible in an unforgettable fashion. Darkness is

The Sublime and the Beautiful

Several writers in the eighteenth century differentiated the sublime and the beautiful. Among the most influential was Edmund Burke (1729-1797), who drew the distinction in stark terms.

❀

On closing this general view of beauty, it naturally occurs that we should compare it with the sublime, and in this comparison there appears a remarkable contrast. For sublime objects are vast in their dimensions, beautiful ones comparatively small: beauty should be smooth and polished; the great, rugged and negligent . . . : beauty should not be obscure; the great ought to be dark and gloomy: beauty should be light and delicate; the great ought to be solid and even massive. They are indeed ideas of a very different nature, one being founded on pain, the other on pleasure; and however they may vary afterwards from the direct nature of their causes yet these causes keep up

an eternal distinction between them, a distinction never to be forgotten by any whose business it is to affect the passions. . . .

The passion caused by the great and sublime in nature, when those causes operate most powerfully, is astonishment; and astonishment is that state of the soul in which all its motions are suspended with some degree of horror. In this case the mind is so entirely filled with its object that it cannot entertain any other, nor by consequence reason on that object which employs it. Hence arises the great power of the sublime, that far from being produced by them, it anticipates our reasonings and hurries us on by an irresistible force. Astonishment, as I have said, is the effect of the sublime in its highest degree; the inferior effects are admiration, reverence, and respect.

Edmund Burke, *A Philosophical Enquiry into the Origin of Our Ideas of the Sublime and the Beautiful* (London, 1757), in *Music and Aesthetics in the Eighteenth and Early-Nineteenth Centuries*, ed. Peter le Huray and James Day (Cambridge: Cambridge University Press, 1981), 70–71.

depicted through the minor key, muted strings, and soft singing. Then suddenly, at the words "and there was Light," light streams forth with an awesome choral outburst on a radiant C-major chord backed by the full orchestra, including trumpets, trombones, and timpani. This moment made a profound impression on audiences and was extolled by contemporary writers as the supreme example of the sublime in music. Philosophers of the time distinguished between the sublime, which evoked awe and astonishment, and the beautiful, which afforded pleasure (see Source Reading). This distinction helps to explain many passages in the music of Haydn, Mozart, and Beethoven, like this one in *The Creation*, that go beyond mere beauty to create an effect of overwhelming the senses. The notion of the sublime became one of the sources of Romanticism (see Chapter 25).

ACHIEVEMENT AND REPUTATION Haydn made his last public appearance for a performance of *The Creation* to celebrate his seventy-sixth birthday in 1808, as depicted in Figure 23.6. When he died the next year, he left an enormous body of music, the fruit of over half a century of hard work. His reputation rested on a small fraction of his output, primarily the symphonies and quartets of the 1770s to 1790s and the last two oratorios. These works, which were popular with performers and audiences, greatly influenced other

composers and quickly became part of the permanent repertoire. In its union of opposites, its ability to hold stark contrasts together in a coherent whole, and its balance of form and expression, Haydn's best music still elicits admiration and awe. The combination he achieved of wide appeal to the public with long-lasting rewards for the connoisseur has seldom been matched.

FIGURE 23.6 *Haydn (seated in foreground center) attends a performance of his oratorio* The Creation *in the Great Hall of the University of Vienna on March 27, 1808, put on to mark his seventy-sixth birthday earlier that month. This was Haydn's last public appearance before his death the following year. Watercolor by Balthasar Wigand.*

WOLFGANG AMADEUS MOZART

Wolfgang Amadeus Mozart (1756–1791) counted Haydn as a friend, and each admired and was influenced by the other. But their lives and careers differed fundamentally. Although Mozart was twenty-four years younger than Haydn, he achieved wide renown earlier, as a touring child prodigy in the 1760s. For most of his career, Haydn worked contentedly for the Esterházy princes, while Mozart spent his mature years as a free agent in Vienna (see biography and Figure 23.7). Yet when he died at thirty-five, Mozart was seen by many (including Haydn) as Haydn's equal, and the two have come to define the music of their era.

CHILD PRODIGY Mozart was profoundly affected by his experiences as a child prodigy. His early and thorough training gave him seemingly effortless command of the craft of composition, and his exposure at a young age to a wide range of music is reflected in his use of diverse styles to portray characters, convey moods, or heighten contrasts within a movement.

Mozart's father, Leopold Mozart (1719–1787), was a violinist for the   *Leopold Mozart*

WOLFGANG AMADEUS MOZART

(1756–1791)

Mozart composed prolifically from the age of six to his premature death at thirty-five. A master of every medium, he is widely considered one of the greatest musicians of the Western classical tradition. His piano sonatas and concertos and his mature operas, symphonies, chamber music, and choral works are mainstays of the repertoire and epitomize the classical style.

Mozart was born in Salzburg, a quasi-independent state ruled by an archbishop. His father Leopold was a violinist and composer in the archbishop's service. When Wolfgang and his older sister Nannerl showed remarkable talent at an early age, Leopold trained them in music and took them on tours across Europe, exhibiting their skills as child prodigies. And prodigy he was: by the age of three he was recognized to have perfect pitch; at five he was an accomplished harpsichord player; at six he was composing; at seven he could read at sight, harmonize melodies on first hearing, and improvise on a tune supplied to him. Though arduous, these trips exposed Mozart to an enormous

FIGURE 23.7 *Wolfgang Amadeus Mozart in an unfinished portrait from about 1789 by his brother-in-law Joseph Lange.*

archbishop of Salzburg and became deputy Kapellmeister in 1763. He was a well-regarded composer and the author of a celebrated treatise on violin playing published in 1756, the year of his son's birth. From earliest childhood the boy showed such extraordinary talent for music that his father sacrificed his own advancement and devoted himself to educating Wolfgang and his gifted elder sister Maria Anna, known as Nannerl (1751–1829), in music and other subjects. Both children became keyboard virtuosos, and Wolfgang was also an accomplished violinist. Father and children are pictured performing together in Figure 23.8 (see p. 536).

Touring   From 1762 to 1773, Leopold took his children on a series of tours through Austria-Hungary, Germany, France, England, Holland, and Italy, beginning with performances for the elector of Bavaria at Munich and Empress Maria Theresa in Vienna. During performances in aristocratic homes and in public, Wolfgang played prepared pieces, read concertos at sight, and improvised variations, fugues, fantasias, and arias. He was repeatedly tested by experts, who published reports on his performances and improvisations as if he were a wonder of nature. Meanwhile he was composing, producing his first minuets

range of musical styles. He also composed at a stupendous rate, turning out thirty-four symphonies, sixteen quartets, five operas, and over one hundred other works before his eighteenth birthday.

Mozart spent the years 1772 to 1780 in Salzburg as third concertmaster at Archbishop Colloredo's court. In 1781, he moved to Vienna, convinced that he could make a living through teaching, concertizing, and composing. He quickly established himself as the best pianist in Vienna and enjoyed a triumph with his Singspiel *Die Entführung aus dem Serail* in 1782, the same year he married Constanze Weber. Their marriage was happy and affectionate. Four children died in infancy, but two sons lived into adulthood, the younger becoming a composer.

Composing at a prodigious pace, teaching private students, performing in public and private concerts, and selling his works to publishers brought Mozart a good income and impressed his demanding father. At a quartet party in Mozart's home, Haydn told Leopold, "Before God and as an honest man I tell you that your son is the greatest composer known to me either in person or by name. He has taste and, what is more, the most profound knowledge of composition." But by the late 1780s there were money troubles, apparently due more to rising family expenses and

other factors than to declining income. In addition, relations with his father had been strained for many years, and the bitterness between father and son—as some scholars argue—contributed to a growing estrangement between Mozart and his sister Nannerl, with whom he had been so close as a child. Mozart's sudden death prompted a variety of false rumors, including that he was poisoned, but it seems to have resulted from a fever.

Mozart's more than six hundred compositions are listed and numbered chronologically in a thematic catalogue compiled by Ludwig von Köchel in 1862, whose "K." numbers are universally used to identify Mozart's compositions. The original numbers are the most familiar and are used here, but revised numbers assigned to some pieces reflect newer information about the chronology of Mozart's music.

MAJOR WORKS *Die Entführung aus dem Serail, The Marriage of Figaro, Don Giovanni, Così fan tutte, The Magic Flute*, 15 other operas and Singspiels, 17 masses, Requiem, 55 symphonies, 23 piano concertos, 15 other concertos, 26 string quartets, 19 piano sonatas, numerous songs, arias, serenades, divertimentos, dances; many other vocal and instrumental works (the traditional numbering of some Mozart works, such as symphonies 1–41 and piano concertos 1–27, assigned by publishers, excludes some compositions and includes some spurious pieces)

at age five, his first symphony just before his ninth birthday, his first oratorio at eleven, and his first opera at twelve. Nannerl also composed, but none of her music survives.

Thanks to his father's excellent teaching and to his many travels, young Mozart became familiar with every kind of music being written or heard in western Europe. At each stop, he acquired music that was unavailable in Salzburg and met musicians who introduced him to new ideas and techniques. He absorbed it all with uncanny aptitude. The ideas that influenced him not only echoed in his youthful compositions but also continued to grow in his mind, sometimes bearing fruit years later. His work became a synthesis of many styles, a mirror that reflected the music of a whole age.

Absorbing influences

In June 1763, the whole family (including Mozart's mother Anna Maria) embarked on a three-and-a-half-year tour that included lengthy stops in Paris and London. In Paris, Mozart became interested in the music of Johann Schobert (ca. 1735–1767). In his harpsichord writing, Schobert simulated orchestral effects through rapid figuration and thick chordal textures, a technique Mozart later imitated. Example 23.6 compares passages in a Schobert sonata

Paris

FIGURE 23.8 *Three Mozarts making music in about 1763: Leopold, violin; Wolfgang, age seven, keyboard; and Nannerl, age eleven, singing from a score. Watercolor by Louis Carrogis de Carmonetelle.*

for harpsichord with violin accompaniment and a Mozart piano sonata that use rapid alternating notes in the right hand to simulate orchestral string tremolos.

London   Johann Christian Bach, whom Mozart met in London, had an important and lasting influence on the boy. Bach enriched his keyboard and symphonic works with features from Italian opera: songful themes, tasteful embellishments, appoggiaturas, and harmonic ambiguities. These traits, together with Bach's consistent use of contrasting themes in concerto and sonata-form movements, appealed to Mozart and became permanent marks of his writing. In 1772, Mozart arranged three of Bach's sonatas as piano concertos (K. 107). As we will see, Mozart's approach to concerto form has significant parallels to Bach's.

Italy and Vienna   When Nannerl came of marriageable age in 1769, she bumped up against the prevailing attitude that women belonged in the home. Accordingly, her father insisted she stop performing in public, and she was left behind in Salzburg while father and son continued to travel. Mozart was familiar with Italian style through his father and J. C. Bach, but three trips to Italy between 1769 and 1773 left him more thoroughly Italianized than ever. He studied counterpoint with Padre Martini in Bologna and composed his first two opere serie (staged in Milan) and first string quartets. The influence of Sammartini and other Italian symphonists emerges in Mozart's symphonies written between 1770 and 1773. A visit to Vienna in 1773 acquainted him with current styles there, especially in the serenade, string quartet, and symphony. Although he may have encountered Haydn's quartets at this time, the six quartets he wrote in Vienna, K. 168–173, reflect local Viennese tastes more directly than they do Haydn's influence.

EXAMPLE 23.6 *Simulation of orchestral tremolos in sonatas by Schobert and Mozart*

a. Johann Schobert, Sonata Op. 2, No. 1, Allegro assai

b. Wolfgang Amadeus Mozart, Piano Sonata in A Minor, K. 310 (300d), Allegro maestoso

FREELANCING If his extraordinary childhood explains the diversity of styles and genres Mozart had at his command, his adult career illustrates the growing tension between two ways musicians were now making money: steady employment with a patron or institution, and freelancing. For a musician today, the parallel choices would be to secure a salaried position—such as playing with a major orchestra or teaching at a conservatory, college, or university—or to make a living by playing concerts, making recordings, teaching private students, or composing on commission or for publication. In Mozart's time, most successful musicians had paid positions and augmented their income through other activities. Few survived solely as free agents.

At age sixteen, Mozart was appointed unpaid third concertmaster at Archbishop Colloredo's court in Salzburg, where his duties included composing church music. Much more interested in opera and instrumental music, Mozart vainly sought a position elsewhere, traveling with his father to Italy and Vienna and with his mother through Germany to Paris. The latter trip had far-reaching emotional consequences: at Mannheim he fell in love with the singer Aloysia Weber, the sister of his future wife Constanze, and in Paris his mother took ill and died. The search outside Salzburg proved fruitless, and Mozart returned home disconsolate. *Salzburg*

After spending eight years at the Salzburg court, Mozart received a welcome commission in 1780 to write an opera seria for Munich. During his several months there to compose and supervise the production of *Idomeneo* (1781), Mozart had a taste of independence. When Archbishop Colloredo summoned him back to Salzburg, Mozart dutifully went, but chafed at being treated like a servant and soon left the archbishop's service, against his father's advice. *Gaining independence*

For the next ten years, Mozart earned his living as a freelance musician in Vienna, with several sources of income. His Singspiel *Die Entführung aus* *Vienna dem Serail* (The Abduction from the Harem, 1782) was a great success and was performed repeatedly in Vienna and other German cities, and his later operas also did well. He had all the pupils he was willing to take, from wealthy amateur pianists to talented composition students, and made them pay by the month so he would not lose money if they skipped lessons. He performed in public and private concerts, quickly winning a reputation as the finest pianist in Vienna. He sometimes served as his own impresario, putting on concerts at venues such as the Burgtheater, shown in Figure 23.9, and pocketing the proceeds after expenses. He composed copiously, for his own concerts, on commission, and also for publication, as Viennese publishers issued his piano works, chamber music, piano concertos, dances, symphonies, and songs. In December 1787, Mozart was appointed chamber music composer to Emperor Joseph II, giving him a steady if modest salary with light duties and a boost to his reputation. The emperor later said the job was meant to keep Mozart in Vienna, showing that it was in part a reward for his other activities.

Financial difficulties   However, these early successes were followed by difficult times, coinciding with a period of considerable economic and political instability in Vienna. A war with the Turks in 1788–90 led to a decline in musical patronage, reducing Mozart's public appearances as a pianist. Almost as soon as he achieved a salaried position, the emperor went off to wage war against the Ottoman Empire and all chamber concerts at court ceased. At the same time, Mozart's expenses increased as a result of a growing family, his passion for gambling, the loss of an expensive lawsuit brought against him by a prominent aristocrat, and his desire to pursue a lifestyle suitable for an imperial court composer. In response, he moved his family to cheaper quarters in 1788 and wrote begging letters to a merchant friend and brother Freemason, Michael Puchberg, who always responded generously to Mozart's appeals.

FIGURE 23.9 *St. Michael's Square in Vienna. The building in the center is the Burgtheater, where Mozart performed several of his piano concertos in the mid-1780s and where the premieres of* The Marriage of Figaro *and* Così fan tutte *took place.*

MATURE STYLE Although many notable compositions date from the Salzburg years, the works that immortalized Mozart's name were composed in Vienna, when he was aged twenty-five to thirty-five and the promise of his youth came to fulfillment. In every kind of composition he achieved an extraordinary synthesis of form and content, of the galant and learned styles, and of polish and charm with emotional depth.

Mozart's music was enriched by new influences from three of the century's greatest composers: Haydn, J. S. Bach, and Handel. Haydn spent every winter in Vienna, and whatever acquaintance Mozart may previously have had with his works was now deepened through intense study and personal friendship. Mozart was introduced to Bach's music by Baron Gottfried van Swieten, later the librettist for Haydn's last two oratorios. As Austrian ambassador to Berlin in 1771–78, van Swieten had become an enthusiast for the music of north German composers. In weekly reading sessions at van Swieten's home during 1782, Mozart became acquainted with Bach's *The Art of Fugue, The Well-Tempered Clavier,* and other works. He arranged several of Bach's fugues for string trio or quartet and composed his own Fugue in C Minor for two pianos, K. 426. Bach's deep and lasting influence is heard in the increased contrapuntal texture of Mozart's later works. Through van Swieten Mozart also became interested in Handel, whose *Messiah, Alexander's Feast, Acis and Galatea,* and *Ode for St. Cecilia's Day* Mozart reorchestrated in 1788–90 for private performances sponsored by van Swieten and other aristocratic patrons.

Influence of Haydn, J. S. Bach, and Handel

PIANO MUSIC Mozart was a virtuoso pianist, and his style is well represented in his music for piano. His sonatas, fantasias, variations, rondos, and piano duets (for two players at one piano) were written for his pupils, for domestic music-making, and for publication. The nineteen piano sonatas are among his most popular works, and almost every piano student for the last two centuries has studied them. He demonstrated his command of the genre with a set of six sonatas (K. 279–284) written in 1775 while in Munich to supervise an opera, and he wrote three more while in Mannheim and Paris in 1777–78 (K. 309–311). These already show a wide variety of keys, content, and form, as if Mozart sought to explore all the possibilities of the sonata and pose diverse challenges for the player.

Mozart's style at the beginning of his Vienna period is exemplified by the sonata-form first movement of the Sonata in F Major, K. 332 (NAWM 124), one of three sonatas composed in 1781–83 and published as a set in 1784 (K. 330–332). Especially characteristic of Mozart are his themes and his combination of heterogeneous styles. Example 23.7 shows the first theme and the beginning of the transition.

Sonata in F Major, K. 332

While Haydn built themes by varying small motives (see Example 23.1) or forming a series of contrasting gestures, Mozart's themes tend to be songlike, reflecting Italian influence and his training in the galant style. The opening idea of K. 332 (measures 1–12) is typical of his themes in seeming to unfold naturally and spontaneously, while giving evidence of careful shaping. Phrases are usually balanced between antecedent and consequent, but often the second phrase is extended—in this case through imitation between the hands. The whole melody grows out of the opening series of thirds, which are subtly paralleled in the Alberti bass accompaniment. As he often does,

Themes

EXAMPLE 23.7 *Mozart, Piano Sonata in F Major, K. 332, first movement*

Mozart introduces a contrasting idea even within the first theme area (measures 12–22), but he ties it back to the opening melody by using the same cadence (measures 19–20). Every gesture reflects grace, taste, and elegance.

Contrasting styles   All composers of the time used contrast to delineate form, convey feelings, and provide variety. But Mozart's skill in using diverse styles for these purposes was unparalleled. In Example 23.7, the following styles follow in quick succession:

- The first phrase is in singing allegro style, with a songlike melody in quick tempo over broken-chord figures.

- Its consequent (measures 5–12) introduces imitation and counterpoint, hallmarks of the learned style.

- The second idea suggests hunting style, with a melody and bass line that can be played on the natural horn, using solely the pitches of the harmonic series (see the left hand in measures 12-20).

- The transition (beginning measure 23) is in *Sturm und Drang* style, a loud and impassioned passage in minor mode with faster rhythms, full texture, chromaticism, and strong dissonances such as diminished seventh chords.

Such frequent changes of style continue throughout the movement, outlining the form and broadening the range of expression.

Modern listeners can easily miss noticing this diversity. It all sounds like Mozart's style to us, because we are not familiar with the wide range of styles that his contemporaries would have recognized. For them, the difference between galant and learned style, or hunting style and *Sturm und Drang,* would have been as immediately apparent as the differences between swing, rock, country, hip hop, and military band music are today. The differing styles in Classic-era music have been referred to as ***topics***, because they serve as subjects for musical discourse. Becoming aware of the many styles Mozart and other Classic composers invoke helps us understand their music and discover an intriguing and meaningful network of references we would otherwise miss.

CHAMBER MUSIC After composing sixteen quartets in the early 1770s, Mozart did not return to the genre until his first years in Vienna. Between 1782 and 1785, he wrote six quartets (K. 387, 421, 428, 458, 464, and 465), published in 1785 as his Op. 10. He dedicated them to Haydn in gratitude for all that he had learned from the older composer, writing in the most affectionate terms: *Mozart's* Haydn *Quartets*

> A father, having resolved to send his sons out into the great world, considers it desirable to entrust them to the protection and guidance of a very celebrated man, who happily has also been his best friend.

Mozart called these quartets "the fruit of a long and laborious effort," and the many revisions in the manuscript bear witness to his exertions. Haydn's Op. 33 quartets (1781) had fully established the technique of pervasive thematic development with substantial equality between the four instruments. Mozart's six *Haydn* Quartets show his mature capacity to absorb the essence of Haydn's achievement without becoming a mere imitator. Although the themes remain Mozartean, they are subjected to much more thorough development in an increasingly contrapuntal texture.

Many of Mozart's other chamber works are also classics, though composed for less standardized ensembles. His string quintets, for two violins, two violas, and cello, have been praised in even stronger terms than his quartets, especially the quintets in C major and G minor (K. 515–516, 1787). Shortly after composing the Quintet for Piano and Winds, K. 452, Mozart wrote to his father, "I myself think it's the best work I've written in my entire life." His six works for solo wind and strings, including three flute quartets, oboe quartet, horn quintet, and clarinet quintet, are staples in the repertoire for those instruments. *Quintets*

SERENADES AND DIVERTIMENTOS Mozart composed serenades—ever popular in Salzburg—and what are now classed as divertimentos in the 1770s and early 1780s for garden parties or outdoor performances, for weddings and birthdays, or for concerts at the homes of friends and patrons. Although sometimes intended as background music, they received serious treatment from Mozart. Some are like chamber music for strings with two or more wind instruments. Others, written for six or eight wind instruments in pairs, are meant for the outdoors, and still others approach the style of the symphony or concerto. Most share an unaffected simplicity of material and treatment, appropriate to their purpose.

The most familiar of Mozart's serenades is *Eine kleine Nachtmusik* (A Little Night-Music, K. 525; 1787), in four movements for string quintet but now usually played by a small string ensemble. The most dramatic and substantial is the Serenade in C Minor for two oboes, two clarinets, two horns, and two bassoons, K. 388 (1782/83). Essentially a full-scale four-movement symphony for winds, it is a compelling work notable for its canonic minuet and trio and lengthy finale in variation form.

PIANO CONCERTOS Although Mozart wrote piano concertos in Salzburg in the 1770s, notably the impassioned Piano Concerto in E-flat Major, K. 271 (1777), the seventeen piano concertos written in Vienna occupy a central place in his output. He composed them primarily as vehicles for his own concerts and intended them to please the entire range of listeners. As he wrote to his father on December 28, 1782, the first three Vienna concertos, K. 413–415,

> are a happy medium between what's too difficult and too easy. They are Brilliant—pleasing to the ear—Natural without becoming vacuous. There are passages here and there that only connoisseurs can fully appreciate, yet the common listener will find them satisfying as well, although without knowing why.

Each of the Vienna concertos is an individual masterpiece, and together they show Mozart at his best. Figure 23.10 shows a manuscript page from one of the Vienna concertos, K. 467. It reveals the composer's clarity and logic as well as a revision around the middle of the page, where he wanted to improve the textural distribution.

First movement   Mozart's concertos follow the traditional three-movement pattern in the sequence fast-slow-fast. The first movement blends elements of ritornello and sonata form as do the concertos of J. C. Bach, Mozart's primary model for his piano concertos. Comparing the first movement of Mozart's Piano Concerto in A Major, K. 488 (NAWM 125), composed in 1786, to the J. C. Bach concerto diagrammed in Figure 22.12, we see the same general outlines:

- The solo sections resemble the exposition, development, and recapitulation of a sonata form, with the soloist accompanied by and sometimes in dialogue with the orchestra.
- The opening orchestral ritornello introduces the movement's first theme, transition, second theme, and closing theme, but remains in the tonic.

FIGURE 23.10 *A page from Mozart's Piano Concerto in C Major, K. 467, dated February 1785. Mozart's rapid rate of composition is well known. In a letter to their mother, Mozart's sister Nannerl jokes that her brother was writing down a sonata while at the same time composing another in his head. It is believed that this particular concerto took Mozart around a month to finish—just to copy a concerto of this length (83 pages) would have taken many composers a full month to complete. K. 467 is surprisingly free of corrections and revisions, but around the middle of the page we can see where Mozart decided to revise some unbalanced scoring.*

- The ritornello returns, greatly abbreviated, to mark the end of the first solo and the end of the movement.

Like Bach, Mozart includes a cadenza for the soloist, but his cadenza usually interrupts the final ritornello, as it does here. It is also Mozart's typical practice to punctuate the long solo sections with passages for full orchestra that serve as further ritornellos. Here these include the transition in the solo exposition and recapitulation and the first two phrases of the recapitulation. The other differences are in the details that make each first movement unique. While Bach's concerto used the closing theme for later ritornellos, in K. 488 Mozart mainly uses the transition, an energetic, pulsating tutti that contrasts markedly with the quiet, lyrical themes. Mozart introduces a new idea at the beginning of the development, which becomes the focus of that section and returns at the end of the recapitulation and in the final ritornello. The resulting form follows convention in most respects yet may surprise the listener with several individual features. The movement is suffused with Mozart's characteristic wealth of melodic invention, diversity of figuration, and elegance.

The second movement of a Mozart concerto resembles a lyrical aria. It is set in the subdominant of the principal key or, less often, in the dominant or relative minor. Its form may vary—most often sonata without development,

Slow movement and finale

sometimes variations or rondo. The finale is typically a rondo or sonata-rondo on themes with a popular character; these are treated in scintillating virtuoso style with opportunities for one or more cadenzas.

Balance of elements   Although the concertos were show pieces intended to dazzle an audience, Mozart never allowed display to get the upper hand. He always maintained a balance of musical interest between the orchestral and solo portions, and his infallible ear is evident in the myriad combinations of colors and textures he draws from the interplay between the piano and orchestral instruments, especially the winds. Moreover, the goal of composing for an immediate public response did not keep him from expressing profound musical ideas.

SYMPHONIES Mozart wrote only six symphonies in the last ten years of his life, having earlier produced almost fifty (notwithstanding the traditional numbering of forty-one symphonies, introduced by a nineteenth-century publisher). The symphonies written before 1782 served most often as curtain raisers for concerts or theatrical performances; those he composed after he settled in Vienna were intended for concert programs that also included concertos and arias. Many of the early symphonies followed the older Italian three-movement format, while most of the later ones have the standard four.

Vienna symphonies   Like Haydn, Mozart approached his mature symphonies with great seriousness, and he devoted much time and thought to their composition. The *Haffner* Symphony, K. 385, written in 1782 for the elevation to nobility of Mozart's childhood friend Sigmund Haffner, and the *Linz* Symphony, K. 425, written in 1783 for a performance in that city, typify the late symphonies in their ambitious dimensions, greater demands on performers (particularly wind players), harmonic and contrapuntal complexity, and final movements that are climactic rather than light. These symphonies are in every way as artful as the London symphonies of Haydn, and some may indeed have served as models for the older composer. The others of this group—usually recognized as his greatest—are the *Prague* Symphony in D Major (K. 504), composed in 1786 for a concert in that city, and the Symphonies in E-flat Major (K. 543), G Minor (K. 550), and C Major (K. 551, nicknamed *Jupiter*), all written in the summer of 1788.

Each of the six symphonies is a masterpiece with its own special character. Their opening gestures leave an indelible impression. The *Haffner* and *Jupiter* Symphonies both begin with loud, forceful statements in octaves followed by delicate ensemble responses. Three others (K. 425, 504, and 543) have slow introductions animated by the spirit of the French overture, with its majestic dotted rhythms, intense harmony, and anacrusis figures. Rather than intimating subtly what is to come, as Haydn sometimes did, Mozart's slow introductions create suspense, tantalizingly wandering away from the key and making its return a major event. Most striking is the beginning of the Symphony in G Minor, with its *piano* undulating melody suffused with sighing gestures.

Finales   As in Haydn's late symphonies, Mozart's finales do more than send an audience away in a cheerful frame of mind. They balance the serious opening movement with a highly crafted counterweight fashioned with whimsy and humor. Most remarkable is the finale of the *Jupiter* Symphony (NAWM 126), a brilliant combination of sonata form and symphonic style with learned counterpoint and fugue. The opening theme, shown in Example 23.8, presents two

EXAMPLE 23.8 *First theme of the finale of Mozart's* Jupiter *Symphony*

contrasting ideas, as is Mozart's typical practice: an elegant singing motive in whole notes (a) and a more active response (b) marked by repeated staccato notes and sweeping gestures. They have different destinies. Motive a, drawn from a fugue example in Fux's counterpoint treatise *Gradus ad Parnassum,* gets the full contrapuntal treatment from Mozart, including all four species of strict counterpoint described by Fux plus stretto and fugue, while motive b is treated solely as a melody in a homophonic texture. Indeed, motive b is a typical galant gesture, the Prinner (see Chapter 20 and Example 20.1b), in its usual position as a riposte to the theme's opening gambit; the pairing of learned and galant style reflects not only Mozart's deep familiarity with both, stemming from his early training, but also his ability to combine disparate elements in a unified whole. Other thematic elements occupy a middle ground, presented both as accompanied melody in Classic-era style and in close imitative counterpoint. The coda then weaves all of the thematic motives but b into a five-voice fugue, revealing that they all work in counterpoint with each other. Example 23.9 shows part of this coda, with motives from the first theme (a and c), transition (d), and second theme (e and f). In this contrapuntal climax, Mozart achieves a stunning integration of the galant style and

EXAMPLE 23.9 *Excerpt from coda, showing themes in counterpoint*

a = first theme, opening idea

c = first theme, concluding idea (also appears in second theme and closing theme)

d = figure from transition (also appears in second theme)

e = second theme, opening phrase

f = countersubject to second theme

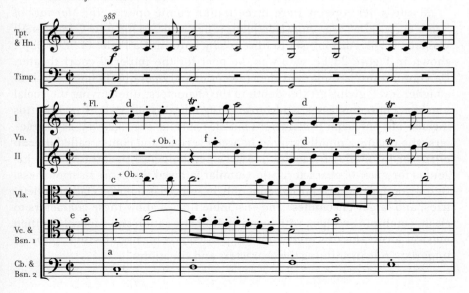

rhetoric of his own age with the fugal style of the early eighteenth century, making us hear his themes in an entirely new context. His contemporaries identified fugue with church music, so the combination is one not only of eras but of genres and social contexts, bringing associations of solemnity and the sacred into the realm of the symphony. The effect is sublime, inspiring awe and astonishment—not at Creation, as in Haydn's oratorio, but at human creativity and ingenuity.

OPERAS Opera was still the most prestigious musical genre, and Mozart eagerly sought opportunities to compose for the stage. On a visit to Vienna in 1768, the twelve-year-old composer wrote his first opera buffa, *La finta semplice* (The Pretend Simpleton, performed the following year at Salzburg), and first Singspiel, *Bastien und Bastienne.* During his trips to Italy in the early 1770s, he composed two opere serie that were produced in Milan, hoping they would lead to a permanent position. He composed two operas on commission for Munich, *La finta giardiniera* (The Pretend Gardener, 1775), an opera buffa, and *Idomeneo* (1781), the best of his opere serie. In its dramatic and pictorial music, accompanied recitatives, conspicuous use of chorus, and inclusion of spectacular scenes, *Idomeneo* shows the reformist tendencies of Traetta and Gluck (see Chapter 21) and the influence of French opera.

Die Entführung   Mozart's fame in Vienna and beyond was established by the Singspiel *Die Entführung aus dem Serail* (The Abduction from the Harem, 1782). The opera tells a romantic-comic story of adventure and rescue set in a Turkish harem. Such "oriental" settings and plots were popular, in part because they provided a taste of the exotic while making the Turks, long-standing enemies of Austria-Hungary, seem less threatening. But one reason *Die Entführung* is compelling is the humane and fully rounded nature of its Turkish characters. Mozart sets the scene in the overture by using "Turkish style," meant to suggest Turkish military band music, known as Janissary music, through the use of shrill winds, drums, and cymbals; exaggerated first beats; and deliberately simple harmonies, melodies, and textures. Mozart's music perfectly captures the characters and their feelings, as he had aimed (see Source Reading).

Da Ponte operas   Mozart's next operas were three Italian comic operas: *The Marriage of Figaro* (1786), *Don Giovanni* (Don Juan, 1787), and *Così fan tutte* (Thus Do All Women, 1790). All were set to librettos by Lorenzo Da Ponte (1749–1838), shown in Figure 23.11, who was the poet for the imperial court theater. Da Ponte's librettos followed the conventions of opera buffa but lifted it to a higher level, giving greater depth to the characters, intensifying the social tensions between classes, and introducing moral issues. All three librettos include not only comic characters but also serious ones, as well as characters who occupy a middle ground between serious and comic, called **mezzo carattere** (middle character). Mozart's psychological penetration and his genius for musical characterization similarly raised the genre's seriousness. Delineation of character occurs not only in solo arias but especially in duets, trios, and larger ensembles. The ensemble finales allow these characters to clash, combining realism with ongoing dramatic action and superbly unified musical form. Mozart's orchestration, particularly his use of winds, plays an important role in defining the characters and situations.

Mozart's Depiction of Character and Mood

In his operas, Mozart portrays the personalities of the characters and conveys their feelings so perfectly through his music that listeners can immediately understand them—sometimes better than the characters understand their own predicament. In a letter to his father written while composing *Die Entführung aus dem Serail*, Mozart described how he made the music of two arias fit the characters, the situation, and the singers who would premiere the roles.

❖

Osmin's rage will be rendered comical by the use of Turkish music. In composing the aria, I made [the singer] Fischer's beautiful deep tones really glisten. . . . The passage *Therefore, by the beard of the Prophet*, etc., is, to be sure, in the same tempo, but with quick notes—and as his anger increases more and more, the Allegro assai [a faster tempo]—which comes just when one thinks the aria is over—will produce an excellent Effect because it is in a different tempo and in a different key. A person who gets into such a violent rage transgresses every order, moderation, and limit; he no longer knows himself. In the same way the Music must no longer know itself. But because passions, violent or not, must never be expressed to the point of disgust, and Music must never offend the ear, even in the most horrendous situations, but must always be pleasing, in other words always remain Music, I have not chosen a key foreign to F, the key of the aria, but one that is friendly to it, not however its nearest relative in D minor, but the more remote A minor. Now about Belmonte's aria in A major, "Oh how anxious, oh how passionate!" Do you know how I expressed it?—even expressing the loving, throbbing heart? With two violins playing in octaves. This is the favorite aria of everyone who has heard it—it's mine too. And it was written entirely for Adamberger's voice. One can see the trembling—faltering—one can see his heaving breast—which is expressed by a crescendo—one can hear the whispering and the sighing—which is expressed by the first violins with mutes and one flute playing in unison.

Letter of September 26, 1781, from *Mozart's Letters, Mozart's Life*, selected letters edited and newly translated by Robert Spaethling (New York: W. W. Norton, 2000), 286. Punctuation and spelling have been modernized.

The plot of *The Marriage of Figaro*, which revolves around a series of amorous intrigues between commoners and nobles, was decidedly risqué by the moral standards of the time; indeed, Emperor Joseph II had banned performances of the play by Beaumarchais on which Da Ponte's libretto is based. Nevertheless, the opera was so successful in Vienna that the emperor issued an edict forbidding encores of any pieces other than solo arias.

Figaro was even more enthusiastically received in Prague, leading to the commission for *Don Giovanni*, premiered there the following year. The medieval legend of Don Juan, on which the plot is based, had been treated often in literature and music since the early seventeenth century. Da Ponte and Mozart extended the character of Don Juan, adding to his traditional image as a farcical figure, seducer, and blasphemer a new extreme as a scorner of common morality, unrepentant to the last. On the comic side, he is always in hot water, and his attempts at seduction during the opera go wildly awry. Yet his focus on pursuing his own pleasures leads him to acts of cruelty, from

The Marriage of Figaro

Don Giovanni

FIGURE 23.11 *Lorenzo Da Ponte, in a portrait by American artist Samuel Morse. Best known for the librettos to Mozart's* Marriage of Figaro, Don Giovanni, *and* Così fan tutte, *Da Ponte went to London in the 1790s and to America in 1805, where he was a grocer, private teacher, bookdealer, translator, and eventually professor of Italian at Columbia College. He became an American citizen and sought to bring Italian culture to his new nation.*

attempted rape to making a laughingstock of the one woman who actually loves him, and his blasphemy and lack of shame earn him a place in Hell. This is a character on the edge of what was conceivable at the time, which made him thrilling as well as comical.

Don Giovanni incorporates opera seria characters, situations, and styles into the comic opera, as illustrated in the opening scene (NAWM 127a). Leporello, Don Giovanni's servant, laments his sufferings in an aria in the style of opera buffa, with a touch of aristocratic horn calls when he declares his wish to live like a gentleman rather than a servant. He is interrupted by a clamor as Don Giovanni and Donna Anna emerge from her house, where he has tried to have his way with her. In furious pursuit, she sings in dramatic opera seria style and Don Giovanni replies in kind, while Leporello comments in buffo style from his hiding place. Donna Anna's father, the Commendatore, rushes in to protect her and challenges Don Giovanni to fight. They do, and the Commendatore is mortally wounded—a shocking turn of events for a comedy. In a powerful trio, he pants out his last words as Don Giovanni and Leporello comment, each in his own characteristic style. Instantly, master and servant revert to the comic banter of opera buffa in the following recitative dialogue (NAWM 127b).

Three levels of character

Throughout the opera, there are three levels of character: Donna Anna and other nobles who emote in the elevated, dramatic tone of opera seria; Leporello and other characters, mostly lower-class, marked by the buffoonery of opera buffa (though they show both cleverness and wisdom); and Don Giovanni, who, in his character as duplicitous seducer, passes easily from one world to the other. His seductive powers are on full display in his duet *La ci darem la mano* with the peasant Zerlina, whose wedding to Masetto he has just interrupted. After sending everyone else off to his castle, he gently persuades Zerlina to marry him instead; Mozart's music perfectly captures her initial uncertainty, gradual change of mind, and final agreement as they sing separately at first, then alternate in shorter phrases, and finally join together in parallel thirds. The three levels of character in the opera are highlighted in the finale of Act I, where Mozart masterfully coordinates three onstage dance bands playing simultaneously: a minuet for the nobles, a contredanse for Don Giovanni and Zerlina, and a rustic waltz for Leporello and Masetto.

Another character with a foot in both worlds is Donna Elvira, a comic character posing as a serious one. When she first enters, singing in the aria *Ah! chi mi dice mai* of a lover who has betrayed her and vowing to kill him if he will not return to her, we take her seriously. But in the background Don Giovanni overhears, senses an opportunity, and is already planning to "console" her in his usual manner, interweaving his comic music with her dramatic singing.

When he steps forward and she turns to see him, they recognize each other, for it is he who has loved and left her. The potentially romantic moment instantly turns comic as he attempts to deflect her anger, to Leporello's great amusement, and then flees, leaving Leporello to explain in the famous "Catalogue Aria" that she is only one of hundreds of women Don Giovanni has seduced and abandoned. Here Mozart uses a variety of musical styles to match the many types of women on the list, and the pairing of Donna Elvira with Leporello's comic aria marks her as a comic character.

Donna Elvira's later attempts to depict herself as a tragic heroine abandoned by Don Giovanni are hilariously undercut by Mozart's music. Her rage aria *Ah fuggi il traditor,* shown in Example 23.10, is in an out-of-date style, that of Scarlatti or Handel from more than fifty years before, as if she were reading her lines out of an old novel (as Leporello comments elsewhere), so she sounds fake rather than sincere. She tries to be dignified, shown by her choice of sarabande rhythm, but takes such a fast tempo that she sounds hysterical. Such references to other styles and departures from their conventions are crucial aspects of Mozart's depiction of characters and of their feelings. Modern audiences often miss these meanings if they do not recognize the styles and conventions Mozart is evoking.

In his last year of life, Mozart wrote two final operas: an opera seria, *La clemenza di Tito* (The Mercy of Titus), for the coronation in Prague of

The Magic Flute

EXAMPLE 23.10 *Donna Elvira's aria* Ah fuggi il traditor, *from Mozart's* Don Giovanni

Ah, flee the traitor, let him say nothing more;

Leopold II as king of Bohemia, and *The Magic Flute* (Die Zauberflöte) for a theater in Vienna. *The Magic Flute* is a Singspiel, with spoken dialogue instead of recitative and with some characters and scenes appropriate to popular comedy. Yet its action is filled with symbolic meaning, and its music is so rich and profound that it ranks as the first great German opera. The largely solemn mood of the score reflects the relationship between the opera and the teachings and ceremonies of Freemasonry. We know that Mozart valued his Masonic affiliation, not only from allusions in his letters but especially from the serious quality of the music he wrote for Masonic ceremonies in 1785 and for a Masonic cantata in 1791 (K. 623). In *The Magic Flute,* Mozart interwove threads of many eighteenth-century musical styles and traditions: the vocal opulence of Italian opera seria; the folk humor of the German Singspiel; the solo aria; the buffo ensemble; a new kind of accompanied recitative applicable to German words; solemn choral scenes; and even a revival of the Baroque chorale-prelude technique, with contrapuntal accompaniment. The reconciliation of older and newer styles is summed up in the delightful overture, which combines sonata form with fugue.

CHURCH MUSIC Given that Mozart's father worked as a musician for the archbishop of Salzburg and that Mozart himself served there as concertmaster and organist, it was natural for him to compose church music from an early age. However, with notable exceptions—his Mass in C Minor, *Ave verum corpus,* and Requiem—settings of sacred texts are not counted among his major works. The masses, like Haydn's, are for the most part in the current symphonic-operatic idiom, intermingled with fugues at certain customary places, and scored for chorus and soloists in free alternation, with orchestral accompaniment.

Ave verum corpus

Ave verum corpus, K. 618 (NAWM 128), although brief, has become one of Mozart's best-known choral works. Composed for the feast of Corpus Christi in 1791 and scored for chorus accompanied by orchestra and organ, it is restrained, serene, and mostly homophonic, beautifully conveying the words with a sense of awe and wonder.

Requiem

The Requiem, K. 626, was commissioned by a wealthy nobleman, Count Walsegg, in July 1791, but Mozart was busy with *La clemenza di Tito* and *The Magic Flute* and made little progress until the fall. Left unfinished at Mozart's death, it was completed by his pupil and collaborator Franz Xaver Süssmayr (1766–1803), who added some instrumental parts to Mozart's draft and set the Sanctus, Benedictus, and Agnus Dei, in part repeating music that Mozart had composed for an earlier section.

ACHIEVEMENT AND REPUTATION The unfinished Requiem has become a metaphor for Mozart's sudden, unexpected death, cutting off his career at the height of his abilities and just after he had been appointed to succeed the ailing Kapellmeister of St. Stephen's Cathedral, where Haydn had served his apprenticeship fifty years earlier. Mozart never took up the secure position he had so long sought, but his music eventually found a secure place among performers and listeners. His encounters with and absorption of almost every current style enabled him to extend Haydn's stylistic synthesis to an even wider range, making possible the masterful depiction of mood and character in his operas and the rich variety of his instrumental music. He equaled Haydn in balancing form and expression, and combining immediate with long-lasting appeal. Together, the two composers ranged over all the genres practiced in the late eighteenth century, and their music represents the best that the period produced.

CLASSIC MUSIC

Since the 1790s, Haydn and Mozart have been paired as the two outstanding composers of their time. Both met with great success during their lifetimes, and their music continued to be known and performed after their deaths. Haydn's and Mozart's works provided models for Beethoven and many other composers of their own generation and following ones. By the early nineteenth century, certain works of Haydn and Mozart (especially the late symphonies and some string quartets of each, Haydn's late oratorios, Mozart's piano concertos and sonatas, and the five main Mozart operas) had become classics, part of the core group of works cultured people were expected to know. Their music eventually came to be known as "classical," which in turn became the name most often used for works of the late eighteenth century. Yet among the composers of their time, only Haydn and Mozart achieved widespread and enduring fame and composed such complex and heterogeneous music. It is not easy to achieve the balance between wide and deep appeal that they accomplished, and it was the unique merits of this music that led to its continued performance in the early nineteenth century and its adoption into the permanent repertoire.

Further Reading is available at digital.wwnorton.com/hwm10

PART FIVE

THE NINETEENTH CENTURY

In the nineteenth century, the Industrial Revolution transformed the economy, bringing people from the countryside to the cities and creating a society based on mass production and distribution. The result was a large and influential middle class, who saw transformations in musical life as well. Affordable pianos and printed music broadened the market for home music, encouraging a torrent of songs and piano pieces. The audience for music expanded, and opera companies, professional orchestras, and concert halls grew in number and size.

Nineteenth-century professional musicians typically worked for the public—playing in orchestras, giving concerts, composing for publication, or teaching amateurs. One path to success was to specialize, becoming a virtuoso on one instrument or a composer for one medium. Another path was to create music that was novel, individual, evocative, spectacular, nationalist, exotic, or in some other way distinctive yet attractive. All of these traits are characteristic of Romanticism, a leading movement in the arts at the beginning of the 1800s and a term now associated with the entire century's music. Composers developed new styles to appeal to middle-class listeners, creating new kinds of instrumental music—from virtuoso showpieces to symphonic poems—and new operatic traditions in Italy, France, Germany, Russia, and elsewhere.

Two other developments had profound and lasting effects: the rise of a permanent repertoire of musical classics, and a growing rift between classical and popular music. These changes have shaped our modern musical culture, in which nineteenth-century music is still an enduring presence.

PART OUTLINE

CHAPTER

24

REVOLUTION AND CHANGE

❖

The generation born around 1770 came of age in a whirlwind of change. From the French Revolution in 1789 through the end of the Napoleonic Wars in 1815, the old political order in Europe gave way to a new one. At the same time, a new economic order began to emerge, in which the Industrial Revolution and middle-class entrepreneurship would eventually surpass the old wealth of the landed aristocracy. Along with these changes came a new sense of time associated with the idea of progress, the notion that technology, society, the arts, and other aspects of life were improving at an accelerating pace, making each new period of human history fundamentally different from past eras.

One member of that generation, Ludwig van Beethoven, grew up and was trained in the old world of court musicians; was inspired by the French Revolution and sympathetic to the idea of replacing rule by a monarch with a republic; made a successful career in Vienna by combining freelance income with support from aristocratic patrons; was angered by Napoleon's betrayal of republican ideals and isolated by increasing deafness; and suffered through war and the post-1815 economic depression and political repression. Formed by these experiences of revolution and social change, Beethoven led a revolution of like importance in the history of music. His creation of works unprecedented in their individuality, dramatic power, wide appeal, and depth of interest to connoisseurs changed society's concept of music and of composers.

REVOLUTION, WAR, AND MUSIC, 1789–1815

THE FRENCH REVOLUTION The French Revolution was inspired in part by Enlightenment ideas of equality, human rights, and social reform, but also had other causes. The first phase of the Revolution (1789–92) was reformist. Stimulated by King Louis XVI's ruinous fiscal policies and supported by popular uprisings like the assault on the

FIGURE 24.1 *Contemporary oil painting of* The Fall of the Bastille, July 14, 1789. *Citizens of Paris stormed the old fortress, a symbol of royal authority, to obtain the guns and ammunition stored there and to protect the new municipal government from attack by royal forces. The action cost almost one hundred lives but demonstrated the popular will for revolutionary change. The anniversary, July 14, is now celebrated as the French national holiday.*

Bastille shown in Figure 24.1, a National Assembly of well-to-do citizens forced the king to accept a new constitution for France. The Assembly abolished old privileges, adopted the Declaration of the Rights of Man and Citizen, and set up elected local governments. But after Austria and Prussia attacked France in 1792, seeking to restore the old regime, a more radical group came to power, declared France a republic, and executed the king. In this second phase (1792–94), as French armies fought off attacks, the government maintained control by executing tens of thousands of political opponents in a Reign of Terror. In the third phase (1794–99), the government adopted a more moderate constitution and sought to restore order, but opposition and economic hardships continued.

In 1799, Napoleon Bonaparte, an army general and war hero, became First Consul of the Republic. Ignoring the legislature, Bonaparte consolidated power and in 1804 crowned himself emperor. Through a series of military victories, he overran nearby countries, expanded French territories, ended the 840-year-old Holy Roman Empire, and created client states in Spain, Switzerland, and most of Germany and Italy, installing his own siblings as rulers. In these areas as well as France, he introduced reforms that made government more efficient, the legal system more uniform, and taxation less burdensome, carrying out some of the goals of the Revolution. But a disastrous campaign to take Moscow led to his defeat and abdication in 1814. As a congress of the major European powers met in Vienna to finalize the peace treaty, Napoleon escaped from exile in 1815, marched to Paris, and resumed power, only to suffer final defeat that summer in a battle at Waterloo in Belgium.

Napoleon Bonaparte

Though the Revolution and Napoleon's wars of conquest ultimately failed, they changed European society utterly. The Revolutionary motto "liberté, egalité, fraternité" (liberty, equality, brotherhood) attracted adherents from every stratum of French society, and French armies spread it across Europe. People everywhere saw the possibility of freedom, democratic reform, and the abolition of rank and privilege, and they sustained that vision even when its

Effects of the Revolution

TIMELINE

1789 French Revolution begins

1792 Ludwig van Beethoven arrives in Vienna

1792 French Republic declared, King Louis XVI executed

1792 Franz II becomes Holy Roman emperor

1793 Eli Whitney invents mechanical cotton gin

1793–94 Reign of Terror

1795 Paris Conservatoire founded

1797–98 Beethoven, *Sonate pathétique*

1802 Beethoven realizes his hearing loss is permanent, writes Heiligenstadt Testament

1803–4 Beethoven, Symphony No. 3 in E-flat Major (*Eroica*)

1804 Napoleon Bonaparte crowns himself Emperor Napoleon I

1806 Holy Roman Empire dissolved, Franz II continues as emperor of Austria to 1835

1809 Beethoven given lifetime annuity

1814 Napoleon defeated, exiled to Elba

1814–15 Congress of Vienna

1815 Napoleon defeated at Waterloo

1815 Postwar economic depression begins

1822–24 Beethoven, Symphony No. 9 in D Minor

1824–26 Beethoven, late string quartets

realization was delayed. Moreover, the Revolution and subsequent wars introduced a new concept of the *nation,* conceived as citizens with a common heritage and equal legal rights, not as subjects to a monarch. As the French forged an identity as a nation, so increasingly did people in Germany, Italy, Spain, and Austria, giving rise to cultural and political trends that gained force throughout the nineteenth and early twentieth centuries.

MUSIC AND THE REVOLUTION The Revolution remade every aspect of French life, including music. Popular songs carried the messages and stories of the Revolution, often setting new words to familiar melodies. Composers wrote marches and symphonies for wind band for public ceremonies, and large choral works known as *Revolutionary hymns* for government-sponsored festivals held to celebrate the Revolution. The government also supported the Opéra and Opéra-Comique, the two main opera theaters in Paris, although opera librettos were subject to censorship for political reasons. Many of the plots touched on themes of the Revolution or concerns of the time. One thrilling scenario (mentioned in Chapter 21) centered around the rescue of a hero from unjust imprisonment.

An enduring product of the Revolutionary era was the Paris Conservatoire, a music school founded by the government in 1795 as part of the new national system of education designed to make training in any field available to all citizens based on merit rather than on class, wealth, or family tradition. Combining traditional methods from the conservatories of Naples and Venice with newer approaches, the Conservatoire trained singers and instrumentalists through a standard curriculum and system of examinations and offered courses in composition, theory, and music history. As the first modern conservatory, it became the model for conservatories throughout Europe. It has been a dominant force in French musical life ever since.

THE INDUSTRIAL REVOLUTION Meanwhile, new technologies began to transform the economy from chiefly rural and agricultural, with most goods made by hand, to an urban economy based on manufacturing by machine. This gradual change, known as the Industrial Revolution, started in Britain during the late eighteenth century and spread across Europe and North America over the next hundred years. It began in the textile industry with inventions such as the flying shuttle (1733), which made weaving on a hand loom twice as fast; the spinning jenny (1764), which greatly speeded up the spinning of yarn and thread; and the mechanical cotton gin (1793), which rapidly separated cotton fiber from the seeds. Such machines led to mass production of thread and cloth in large factories powered by water mills or by the new steam engine (invented 1769). Other industries followed suit, including the rise of instrument-making firms (see Chapter 25). Mass production lowered costs and thus prices, which drove out competitors who worked by hand. Men, women, and even children came to work in the factories and the coal and iron mines that kept them running, despite long hours and often bad working conditions. The Industrial Revolution brought unprecedented prosperity, but in many ways was as disruptive as the French Revolution and Napoleonic Wars, threatening traditional ways of life and enriching the urban middle and merchant classes at the expense of the landowning aristocracy and the poor.

LUDWIG VAN BEETHOVEN

The musician whose career and music best reflect the tumultuous changes in the decades around 1800 was Ludwig van Beethoven (1770–1827; see biography and Figure 24.2). He was steeped in Enlightenment ideals; absorbed the music of Haydn and Mozart; was affected by the French Revolution; idealized and then was disillusioned by Napoleon; endured occupation and economic privation during the Napoleonic Wars; and lived his last dozen years under political repression. In his youth a promising piano virtuoso and composer, he was forced to cease performing because of deafness and in his later years became the first musician to make a living almost exclusively as a composer. His pieces placed new demands on listeners and performers, and in the process they redefined what listeners expected from and valued in music.

Shortly after Beethoven's death, a scholar divided his career and works *Three periods* into three periods, beginning a tradition that survives to this day. During the first period, which takes us from his birth in 1770 to about 1802, Beethoven mastered the musical language and genres of his time and gradually found a personal voice. In the second period, through about 1814, he developed a style that achieved a new level of drama and expression and brought him enormous popularity. In the third period, from about 1815 to his death in 1827, his music became more introspective and more difficult for performers to play and for listeners to comprehend. Such a neat framework is, of course, an interpretation, a convenient way to organize a discussion of Beethoven's career and music. But it both reflects changes in his style and marks crucial turning points in his life: a crisis in 1802 over his gradual loss of hearing and a growing isolation around 1815 caused by deafness, family troubles, and political and economic conditions.

BONN AND THE FIRST DECADE IN VIENNA Beethoven's "first period" was really two periods: his youth in Bonn and his first decade in Vienna. In Bonn, after training by his father and other local musicians, he entered the service of Maximilian Franz, elector of Cologne, and attracted notice as a virtuoso pianist and improviser (see Source Reading, p. 560). In his late teens, Beethoven began to make his mark as a composer and gained patrons among the local nobility. On a visit to Bonn, Haydn praised Beethoven's music and urged the elector to send the young man to Vienna for further study. So in November 1792, just under twenty-two years of age, Beethoven traveled from Bonn to Vienna, a five-hundred-mile journey that took a week by stagecoach and required him to pass through lines of French troops at war with Austria and Prussia.

LUDWIG VAN BEETHOVEN
(1770–1827)

For two centuries, Beethoven has dominated the world of classical music like no other composer. His symphonies, concertos, string quartets, and piano sonatas are central to the repertory, and his influence has been virtually inescapable. His perseverance in the face of deafness, combined with the sense of struggle and triumph depicted in much of his music, made him a heroic figure. His individualism and self-expression appealed to the growing middle-class audience for music and made him a model for generations of composers.

Beethoven was born in Bonn in northwestern Germany, where his grandfather and father were musicians at the court of the elector of Cologne. He grew up surrounded by ideas of the Enlightenment, enthusiastically promoted by intellectuals, the social elite, and fellow musicians in Bonn. From early childhood, Beethoven studied piano and violin with his father, Johann, who hoped to make him into a famous child prodigy like Mozart. He took the boy out of school at age eleven so that Ludwig could concentrate solely on music, which included lessons in piano, organ, theory, counterpoint, composition, and improvisation. One of his significant teachers, court organist and composer Christian

HISTORISCHES MUSEUM DER STADT WIEN/BRIDGEMAN ART LIBRARY

FIGURE 24.2 *Ludwig van Beethoven, in a portrait from around 1804 by his friend Willibrord Joseph Mähler, an amateur painter. The composer kept this painting all his life.*

Gottlob Neefe, arranged for the earliest publication of a composition by Beethoven and first called attention to the young musician in print.

Teachers, patrons, and publishers   Beethoven took lessons with Haydn, but they were interrupted when Haydn left for London in January 1794. He then studied counterpoint for a year with Johann Georg Albrechtsberger, author of a famous composition treatise, and later studied how to set Italian poetry with Antonio Salieri. Meanwhile, Beethoven quickly established himself as a pianist and composer, with the support of generous patrons. For a while, Beethoven had rooms in a house owned by Prince Karl von Lichnowsky. At private concerts sponsored by Lichnowsky and others, Beethoven's outstanding abilities as a pianist, and especially his improvisations, won great admiration. He also played in public concerts and taught well-to-do piano students. Aside from juvenilia published when he was twelve to fourteen years old, he started to sell works to music publishers in 1791, although his first work to bear an opus number did not appear until 1795. It was a set of three piano trios dedicated to Lichnowsky, and his Op. 2 of the following year, a set of three piano sonatas, was dedicated to Haydn. The piano trio and piano sonata were genres aimed at amateur performers, and thus potentially lucrative as well as prestigious.

Beethoven traveled to Vienna in 1787 and may have met Mozart, then moved to Vienna for good in 1792. His first teacher there was Haydn, with whom he studied counterpoint, at the same time cultivating patrons among the aristocracy. His compositions ranged widely, from music for amateurs to virtuoso works for himself and from private works for connoisseurs to public symphonies.

Confident in his own worth as an artist, Beethoven treated his aristocratic sponsors with independence and even occasional rudeness. His presumptions of social equality led him repeatedly to fall in love with women of noble rank, whom he as a commoner could not marry (and some of whom were already married). Especially poignant is a letter he addressed in 1812 to his "Immortal Beloved" but apparently never sent. Beethoven never established a permanent home, moving more than two dozen times during his thirty-five years in Vienna.

A gradual loss of hearing provoked a crisis around 1802, from which he emerged with new resolve to compose works of unprecedented scope and depth. The instrumental music of the next dozen years established him as the most popular and critically acclaimed composer alive. Through sales to publishers and support from patrons, notably a permanent stipend set up for him in 1809, he was able to devote himself entirely to composition and write at his own pace.

On his brother Caspar's death in 1815, Beethoven became guardian for his eight-year-old nephew Karl, giving Beethoven the family he had long desired but also bringing years of conflict with Karl's mother Johanna. Growing deafness, bouts of illness, political repression, and the death or departure of many friends and patrons led to an increasing withdrawal from society. His music became more intense, concentrated, and difficult.

His troubled relationship with Karl reached a shattering climax when the nineteen-year-old attempted suicide in 1826. But for all of Beethoven's social isolation and difficult personality, he never lost the support of a devoted circle of friends. We can eavesdrop on their discussions even now; because Beethoven was too deaf to hear them, they wrote their side of the conversations in bound notebooks for him to read and respond. These notebooks are now known as the "Conversation Books."

Beethoven died at fifty-six after years of ill health. His funeral procession was witnessed by over ten thousand people, and his popularity as a composer and as a cultural icon continues to this day.

MAJOR WORKS   9 symphonies, 11 overtures, 5 piano concertos, 1 violin concerto, 16 string quartets, 9 piano trios, 10 violin sonatas, 5 cello sonatas, 32 piano sonatas, 20 piano va riation sets, the opera *Fidelio*, *Missa solemnis*, Mass in C Major, the song cycle *An die ferne Geliebte*, over 80 songs, and numerous other works

---

Haydn was the most famous composer of both genres; that Beethoven gave both collections opus numbers and dedicated the sonatas to Haydn shows that he sought to place himself beside the older composer in the minds of the public, as Mozart had done a decade earlier in dedicating a set of quartets to Haydn (see p. 541).

Through performing, teaching, publishing, and the generosity of patrons, Beethoven was able to make a living without taking a position with a specific employer. Although he had hoped for the security of a court appointment, which did not come his way, his success as a freelance musician, backed up by a stipend from Lichnowsky, granted him an independence Haydn and Mozart did not achieve until late in their careers.

Piano sonatas

Since he was a pianist, piano works were a natural outlet for Beethoven's compositional impulses; indeed sonatas, variations, and shorter works for piano comprise the largest group of works he wrote during his first decade in Vienna. Beethoven followed the tradition of aiming solo keyboard music at the amateur market, although his early sonatas already make increasing

Beethoven's Playing and Improvising at the Piano

When Beethoven's Bonn employer, the elector of Cologne, presided over a meeting of the Teutonic Order for several weeks in 1791 at Mergentheim in southern Germany, he took his musicians along. Carl Ludwig Junker, a composer and writer on music and art, came to hear them, and published a glowing account of Beethoven's playing and improvising at age twenty.

❄

I have also heard one of the greatest of pianists—the dear, good Bethofen. . . . I heard him extemporize in private; yes, I was even invited to propose a theme for him to vary. The greatness of this amiable, light-hearted man as a virtuoso may, in my opinion, be safely judged from his almost inexhaustible wealth of ideas, the highly characteristic expressiveness of his playing, and the skill he displays in performance. I do not know that he lacks anything for the making of a great artist. I have often heard Vogler play by the hour on the pianoforte—of his organ playing I cannot speak,

not having heard him on that instrument—and never failed to wonder at his astonishing ability. But Bethofen, in addition to skill, has greater clarity and profundity of ideas, and more expression—in short, he speaks to the heart. He is equally great at an *adagio* as at an *allegro*. Even the members of this remarkable orchestra are, without exception, his admirers, and are all ears when he plays. Yet he is exceedingly modest and free from all pretension. He, however, acknowledged to me that, upon the journeys which the Elector had enabled him to make, he had seldom found in the playing of the most distinguished virtuosi that excellence which he supposed he had a right to expect. His manner of treating his instrument is so different from the usual that he gives the impression of having attained his present supremacy through a path that he discovered himself.

From Bossler's *Musikalische Correspondenz* (Speyer, November 23, 1791), adapted from the translation by Henry Edward Krehbiel in Alexander Wheelock Thayer, *Thayer's Life of Beethoven*, rev. and ed. Elliot Forbes (Princeton: Princeton University Press, 1967), 105.

demands on the performer. Relatively difficult passages or movements appear next to easier ones, perhaps to challenge the player. Like Mozart, Beethoven often used strong contrasts of style or topic to delineate the form and broaden the expressive range. He also adopted new approaches to piano composition, including the use of frequent octaves, thick textures, and abrupt changes of dynamics, techniques he may have learned from the sonatas of Muzio Clementi (1752–1832), an Italian composer active in London, and the Bohemian-born Jan Ladislav Dussek (1760–1812).

Pathétique *Sonata*   The title of Beethoven's *Sonate pathétique* (Sonata with Pathos, 1797–98, published 1799), Op. 13, announced that the work would depict suffering and a tragic mode of expression. It was also likely to attract buyers, as composers and publishers found such evocative titles a useful marketing tool, and indeed this was one of Beethoven's most popular pieces. The sonata, in C minor, has outer movements of a stormy, passionate character—which Beethoven, like his predecessors, associated with that key—framing a calm, profound slow movement in A♭ major. The first movement (NAWM 129) begins with a dramatic, fantasia-like slow introduction, a stunning depiction of grief, that is recalled before the development and again just before the end of the movement. A slow introduction is unusual for a piano sonata but common for symphonies, so its presence lends the *Pathétique* Sonata symphonic grandeur, while its unexpected reoccurrences deepen the pathos. The main themes of the movement are energetic and determined, and in the development the main motive of the introduction is transformed and assimilated into the character of the Allegro. Thus over the course of the movement, Beethoven first evokes the depths of suffering and then suggests a struggle to overcome it. The sonata-rondo finale is equally serious and intense, unlike the typically lighthearted rondos of Haydn and Mozart. Its theme recalls part of the second theme of the first movement, and its central episode is in A♭ major, the key of the second movement, creating the sort of intermovement connections that Beethoven frequently used in later works.

Beethoven waited until he was well established in Vienna and confident in his craft before composing his first string quartets and symphonies. He knew these were genres in which Haydn, then regarded as the greatest composer alive, was preeminent, and that to write pieces in these genres would invite a direct comparison with his former teacher. For that very reason they offered Beethoven a chance to prove his merits.

Op. 18 string quartets

Beethoven's first six quartets were completed in 1800, were probably first played by a quartet led by violinist Ignaz Schuppanzigh at private concerts sponsored by Prince Lichnowsky, and were published in 1801 as his Op. 18. Through these quartets, Beethoven sought to make himself the successor to Haydn and Mozart in the genre, using quartets by both as models, and thereby helped to establish the string quartet as a tradition stemming from these three composers. While he drew on their example, Beethoven's personality shows through in the individuality of every movement, the character of his themes, frequent unexpected turns of phrase, unconventional modulations, and subtleties of form. The slow movement of No. 1, which Beethoven indicated on the sketches and in conversation was inspired by the burial vault scene of *Romeo and Juliet,* is especially striking and perhaps the most dramatic—even operatic—movement yet written for string quartet. The hilarious scherzo of No. 6, shown in Example 24.1, emphasizes offbeats so convincingly that it is almost impossible for listeners to keep the beat. The finale of this quartet is a rondo with a long, intense, slow introduction labeled "La Malinconia" (Melancholy), which is recalled later in the movement. The

EXAMPLE 24.1 *Ludwig van Beethoven, String Quartet in B-flat Major, Op. 18, No. 6, scherzo*

simultaneous invocation and subversion of tradition in these quartets and the stark juxtapositions of opposing emotions and styles became characteristic of Beethoven's music.

First Symphony   Beethoven's Symphony No. 1 in C Major, premiered in 1800, shows his allegiance to the model of Haydn's and Mozart's late symphonies. Yet Beethoven sought to distinguish himself in distinctive ways: a slow introduction that avoids any definitive tonic cadence; careful dynamic shadings; unusual prominence for the woodwinds; a scherzo-like third movement; and long codas for the other movements.

Reputation and patrons   **CIRCUMSTANCES IN THE MIDDLE PERIOD** Around 1803, Beethoven began to compose in a new, more ambitious style that marks a pivotal point in his career. He was free to take this step because of his reputation, the support of patrons and publishers, and, paradoxically, the predicament created by his growing loss of hearing.

By this time, Beethoven was acknowledged in German-speaking lands as the foremost pianist and composer for piano and had begun to establish a reputation as a composer of symphonies and string quartets. He was befriended by the loftiest noble families of Vienna, and he had generous patrons. When Jérôme Bonaparte, king of Westphalia and youngest brother of Napoleon, offered Beethoven a position in Kassel in 1808, Prince Franz Joseph von Lobkowitz, Prince Kinsky, and Archduke Rudolph, brother of Emperor Franz II, joined to provide the composer a lifetime annuity just to stay in Vienna, an unparalleled arrangement that caused astonishment at the time. The strong financial backing Beethoven received from his patrons meant that he could do largely what he wished as a composer. His sponsors were connoisseurs devoted to his music; indeed, Archduke Rudolph was his student in piano and composition. The combination of financial, social, and creative support freed Beethoven to follow his own inspiration, a virtually unprecedented situation for a composer.

Publishers   Publishers competed for Beethoven's music. He drove hard bargains, got them bidding against each other, and followed Haydn's lead in publishing works in several countries at once to preserve his rights and maximize his returns. Although he wrote on commission, he often failed to meet deadlines. He could afford, as he said, to "think and think," to revise and polish a work until it suited him.

Sketches   Beethoven composed with great deliberation, one reason that he wrote so much less than his predecessors—for instance, only nine symphonies compared to Haydn's 106 and Mozart's 55. He kept notebooks of sketches in which he jotted down themes and plans for compositions, worked out the continuity of each piece, and gradually filled in details. Figure 24.3 shows a page from the sketchbook for Beethoven's Third Symphony. Thanks to these sketchbooks, we can follow the progress of his ideas through various stages until they reached final form (for an example, see the commentary for NAWM 130). By composing in this deliberate way, Beethoven created music in which the relation of each part to the whole was remarkably sophisticated, satisfying one of the central tenets of nineteenth-century aesthetics.

Deafness   While his status, financial position, and compositional methods made it possible for Beethoven to strike out in new directions, it was apparently a

FIGURE 24.3 *A page from the sketchbook Beethoven used while composing his Symphony No. 3 in E-flat Major (Eroica). For a partial transcription, see NAWM 130.*

psychological crisis that helped to make it necessary. In 1802, he realized that the hearing loss he had noticed for some time was permanent and would only get worse. A deaf musician was as inconceivable as a blind painter. In despair, Beethoven considered suicide, but resolved to continue for the sake of his art (see Source Reading, p. 564). He played in public less and less but kept on composing and, occasionally, conducting.

Beethoven's courageous resolve to continue composing in the face of calamity was translated into his music, as he sought with each piece to say something new. His compositions seem to reflect the struggle of his own life, becoming like narratives or dramas. The music gives the impression of conveying the composer's own experience and feelings rather than representing the emotions of a text or operatic character or invoking generalized affections, as was typical in earlier music. Often, the thematic material assumes the character of a protagonist who struggles against great odds and emerges triumphant. Haydn and Mozart had often introduced dramatic gestures into their music to highlight important junctures in the form or to heighten expression, giving their late music a remarkable profundity, but they did not treat their musical material like characters in a drama, as Beethoven came to do. This new conception of instrumental music as drama, extending the achievements of Haydn and Mozart while replacing earlier notions of music as entertainment or diversion, is part of what musicians and listeners have valued in Beethoven's music since his own time.

Music as drama

This interpretation and some others to follow represent only one way to view Beethoven's output after 1802. Some commentators prefer to discuss Beethoven's music in more abstract terms. But the expansiveness, dynamism, and unusual features of many of Beethoven's works create the sense of experiencing a dramatic conflict, climax, and catharsis more than any previous instrumental music.

SOURCE READING

The Heiligenstadt Testament

Beethoven began to lose his hearing by 1798, and by 1818 he could hardly hear at all. In October 1802, just before leaving his summer lodgings in the village of Heiligenstadt, he wrote about his affliction in a letter, now known as the Heiligenstadt Testament, intended to be read by his brothers after his death.

❄

For 6 years now I have been hopelessly afflicted, made worse by senseless physicians, from year to year deceived with hopes of improvement, finally compelled to face the prospect of a *lasting malady* (whose cure will take years or, perhaps be impossible). Though born with a fiery, active temperament, even susceptible to the diversions of society, I was soon compelled to withdraw myself, to live life alone. If at times I tried to forget all this, oh how harshly was I flung back by the doubly sad experience of my bad hearing. Yet it was impossible for me to say to people, "Speak louder, shout, for I am deaf." Ah, how could I possibly admit an infirmity in the *one sense* which ought to be more perfect in me than in others, a sense which I once possessed in the highest perfection, a perfection such as few in my profession enjoy or ever have enjoyed.—Oh I cannot do it, therefore forgive me when you see

me draw back when I would have gladly mingled with you. My misfortune is doubly painful to me because I am bound to be misunderstood; for there can be no relaxation with my fellow-men, no refined conversations, no mutual exchange of ideas. I must live almost alone like one who has been banished, I can mix with society only as much as true necessity demands. If I approach near to people a hot terror seizes upon me and I fear being exposed to the danger that my condition might be noticed. Thus it has been during the last six months which I have spent in the country. By ordering me to spare my hearing as much as possible, my intelligent doctor almost fell in with my own present frame of mind, though sometimes I ran counter to it by yielding to my desire for companionship. But what a humiliation for me when someone standing next to me heard a flute in the distance and *I heard nothing,* or someone heard a *shepherd singing* and again I heard nothing. Such incidents drove me almost to despair, a little more of that and I would have ended my life—it was only *my art* that held me back. Ah, it seemed to me impossible to leave the world until I had brought forth all that I felt was within me.

Trans. Henry Edward Krehbiel, in Alexander Wheelock Thayer, *Thayer's Life of Beethoven,* rev. and ed. Elliot Forbes (Princeton: Princeton University Press, 1967), 304–5.

Style characteristics　　　The music of this period continues to build on the models of Haydn and Mozart in most respects. The genres, forms, melodic types, phrasing, and textures all draw on tradition. But the forms are often expanded to unprecedented lengths or reworked in novel ways. Typically, Beethoven is economical in his material, adopting Haydn's focus on a few ideas subjected to intense development rather than Mozart's abundance of melody, yet he achieves great variety through ingenious transformations of his themes.

EROICA SYMPHONY　The first work that fully exemplifies Beethoven's new approach is his Symphony No. 3 in E-flat Major, composed in 1803–4, which he eventually named *Sinfonia Eroica* (Heroic Symphony). Longer than any previous symphony, the *Eroica* goes beyond evoking conventional moods and topics, as his First Symphony had done. The title suggests that the symphony expresses in music the ideal of heroic greatness. It has been said that the heroism it depicts is Beethoven's own: that it represents in music his experience of being almost overpowered by affliction, fighting against despair, and winning back his will to create. But it also reflects Beethoven's understanding of heroism as portrayed in the ancient Greek and Roman literature he most admired, Homer's *Iliad* and *Odyssey* and Plutarch's *Parallel Lives,* marked by nobility of character, acceptance of one's circumstances, and determination to overcome obstacles.

First movement

According to one possible interpretation, the first movement (NAWM 130) encapsulates this story of challenge, struggle, and final victory. Within an enlarged sonata form, the main motive of the first theme, shown in Example 24.2, serves as protagonist. In its original form (Example 24.2a), it is more pastoral than heroic. The movement is in the fast triple meter of the *deutsche,* the German peasant dance that evolved into the waltz, and the first three measures of the triadic motive are identical to a traditional *deutsche* melody Beethoven may have known, published in a collection of dance tunes around 1790. Moreover, the motive is first presented in a low register, in the cello, at a soft dynamic, followed by a chromatic descent to a surprising C♯. None of these characteristics suggests heroism, and the associations with a peasant dance imply that the protagonist is of common rather than noble origin.

The heroic content of this movement lies not in its opening motive, but in what happens to it. Over the course of the movement, the motive undergoes a

EXAMPLE 24.2 *Main motive and its transformations in the first movement of Beethoven's Symphony No. 3*

a. Original form

b. In rising sequence

c. Disguised as a "new theme" in the development

* = note shared with original form

d. Unison statement, striving upwards

e. Final form

number of transformations: treated in sequence, with the chromatic tail now rising (Example 24.2b); disguised as a "new theme" in minor, with stepwise motion filling in its skips and leaps (Example 24.2c); and striving upward, only to tumble back down (Example 24.2d). By the end of the movement, it has achieved a new form, no longer falling at the end but sustaining its high note in a sign of final triumph (Example 24.2e). At this point, especially given its scoring for horn, the triadic motive sounds no longer like a dance but like a fanfare, as if its potential for heroism has been realized.

Victory requires an opponent. Here the principal antagonist is another element from the first theme group: a leaping figure, shown in Example 24.3a, whose strong accents on weak beats create a forceful duple meter against the serene triple meter of the main motive. Offbeat accents appear in the transition, second theme, and closing theme, and near the end of the exposition they briefly threaten the equilibrium with a powerful assertion of duple time before a varied fragment of the main motive restores the proper meter, as shown in Example 24.3b.

In the development, the leaping figure and offbeat accents build to a terrifying, dissonant climax. Almost overcome, the main motive gradually struggles to reassert itself. First it assumes the disguised form of Example 24.2c, in the remote key of E minor. Next it returns as in Example 24.2d, a statement in three parallel octaves without accompaniment that reaches for the heights but falls back down, deflected by another offbeat accent. Finally, as shown in Example 24.4, it achieves its new form with the sustained high note. It is now accompanied by the leaping figure, which has also been transformed, in two ways: it has been stripped of its offbeat accents so that it fits into triple meter; and it has been altered so that its contour echoes that of the main motive, arpeggiating the notes of a major triad in a similar order, as can be seen by comparing it with the transposed version of the main motive in the bottom staff of Example 24.4. The transformation of both motives resolves the principal conflict of the movement in favor of the main motive. Its victory is confirmed in the recapitulation, where its return in original form (as in Example 24.2a) is immediately followed by two statements in its new form, while the leaping figure is omitted entirely. The second and closing themes unfold as before, transposed into the tonic. The long coda revisits episodes from the development, retracing the path back to victory, and reaffirms the new form of the theme. Like Beethoven in his personal crisis, the motive emerges from its struggle triumphant but changed by the experience.

This account of the movement is only one possible interpretation, and there have been many; from its first performance this symphony has been regarded as an especially challenging work. What most analyses share is an emphasis on the economy of material, the great variety of gestures drawn from a few central ideas, the expansion of the form to unprecedented length, and the sense of struggle, achievement, and progressive change over the course of the long movement. It is particularly this spirit of struggle and progress that reflects so well the temper of the times, suggesting a new conception of musical time parallel to the belief of Beethoven's contemporaries that their era differed fundamentally from the past.

Other movements   The other movements are also large and dramatic. The slow movement is a funeral march in C minor, full of tragic grandeur and pathos. A contrasting

EXAMPLE 24.3 *Leaping figure and associated rhythmic disturbances*

a. First appearance

b. Rhythmic disruption near end of exposition

EXAMPLE 24.4 *Main motive and leaping figure transformed and reconciled*

section in C major, brimming with fanfares and celebratory lyricism, is followed by further development of the march and a varied reprise, broken up with sighs at the end in a stunning musical depiction of grief. The third movement is a quick scherzo, with grandiose horn calls in the trio. The finale is a complex mixture of variations with fugal, developmental, and marchlike episodes, all based on a theme from Beethoven's ballet music for *The Creatures of Prometheus*. Thus each movement reflects a different aspect of heroism: struggle and triumph in the first movement, mourning a fallen hero in the second movement, calls to battle in the trio of the third movement, and in the finale an invocation of Prometheus, the hero who brought wisdom, science, and the arts to humanity at great cost to himself.

References to French Republic

In addition, the second movement has strong links to France during the Republic, with which Beethoven was in sympathy. Thirty-second-note upbeats in the strings imitate the roll of muffled drums used in the Revolutionary processions that accompanied heroes to their final resting place. The C-major section has the character of a Revolutionary hymn, punctuated by fanfares and drum rolls and ending in unisons.

Beethoven originally named the symphony "Bonaparte" in honor of Napoleon, whom he admired as a hero of the French Republic. But according to his student Ferdinand Ries, when Beethoven heard that Napoleon had crowned himself emperor, he angrily tore up the title page, disillusioned when his idol proved to be an ambitious ruler on the way to becoming a tyrant. The title page of a score containing Beethoven's corrections, shown in Figure 24.4, reveals that Bonaparte's name was violently scratched out, confirming the gist if not

FIGURE 24.4 *Cover page for a score of the Eroica Symphony containing Beethoven's corrections, which read "Sinfonia grande intitolata Bonaparte" (Grand Symphony entitled Bonaparte) before the last two words were scratched out. The date "1804 im August" was subsequently added in different ink. Below Beethoven's signature, in the middle of the page, he later added in pencil "Geschrieben auf Bonaparte" (composed about Bonaparte), not visible in this photograph.*

the details of the story. But Beethoven seems to have wavered in his opinion of Napoleon: that August he wrote to his publisher that the symphony's title was "Bonaparte," in 1809 he conducted the symphony in Vienna during the French occupation of the city at a concert that Bonaparte was to have attended, and in 1810 he considered dedicating his Mass in C, Op. 86, to the emperor. In any case, Beethoven's plan to honor Napoleon may explain the strong links to music of the French Republic.

At its public premiere in 1805, the *Eroica* Symphony was recognized as an important work, but its unprecedented length and complexity made it difficult for some audience members to grasp. Beethoven had tilted Haydn and Mozart's balance between learned and less-learned listeners toward the connoisseurs and had sacrificed some immediate widespread appeal in order to gain the freedom to write as he chose. This decision put Beethoven, the genre of the symphony, and indeed much music of the next two centuries on a new course, challenging listeners to engage music deeply and thoughtfully rather than merely seeking to be entertained.

Reception

Yet in another sense Beethoven's music was better suited to attract a broad and devoted public than that of his predecessors. From Baldassare Galuppi and Giovanni Battista Sammartini through Haydn and Mozart, the instrumental music of the middle to late eighteenth century was rooted in the galant style, a style whose effects depended on its audience's familiarity with a common repertoire of gestures that composers presented in ever new guises and combinations, like the characters and situations of improvised *commedia dell'arte* theater (see Chapter 20). It was a style that was nurtured in court culture and depended on insider knowledge to follow the subtle play of expectations in a Galuppi sonata or a Haydn quartet (see NAWM 116 and 121). Beethoven's music grew out of the same stylistic tradition, but instead of relying on the interplay of familiar schemata, each piece has its individual internal logic, a drama that can be understood on its own terms, even for a listener unfamiliar with the music of galant composers. The *Eroica* and Beethoven's later symphonies became the center of the symphonic tradition because someone who had never heard a symphony before could be riveted by them on first hearing, and because they could hold a listener's interest through many rehearings.

OTHER WORKS OF THE MIDDLE PERIOD Other major works over the next decade followed in the footsteps of the Third Symphony. In each, Beethoven probed new possibilities in traditional genres and forms, and several works of this period took their place among the most popular ever written in their genres.

Beethoven turned next to opera, still the most prestigious form of music. For a libretto, he borrowed from a French Revolutionary opera, *Léonore, ou L'amour conjugal* (Leonore, or Conjugal Love), in which Leonore, disguised as a man, rescues her husband Florestan from prison. Operas on rescue themes were embraced at the time both in France and in Vienna. Beethoven's opera, *Fidelio,* makes Leonore into an idealized figure of sublime courage and self-denial, and the last scene of the opera glorifies Leonore's heroism and the humanitarian ideals of the Revolution. The subject perfectly suited Beethoven's new heroic style, but it took him several tries to achieve the right balance between musical depth, broad appeal, and dramatic concision. The

Fidelio

original three-act production of 1805, called *Leonore,* was a financial failure in part because the French army occupied Vienna a week before the premiere, and Beethoven's primary supporters in the nobility and wealthy middle class had left the city. In addition, the opera's length and music overwhelmed the drama. Beethoven made cuts, but the shortened revision staged the following year was again a failure, and only in 1814 was a third version successful under the new title *Fidelio*. In contrast to Mozart, for whom writing operas seemed almost effortless, Beethoven found it a struggle and never wrote another opera. His other dramatic music consists of overtures and incidental music for plays, notably *Egmont* by Johann Wolfgang von Goethe (1749–1832), whose prominence among German writers was even greater than Beethoven's as a musician, and whom Beethoven regarded as the best living writer. He also wrote dozens of Lieder, often making the music as interesting as the poetry, as in later Romantic Lieder (see next chapter), rather than subordinate as in the eighteenth-century Lied.

Chamber music

The chamber music of the middle period abounds in fresh explorations of each genre, including five string quartets, three piano trios, two violin sonatas, and a cello sonata. Like piano sonatas, chamber music had traditionally been intended for enjoyment in the home, but, as he did in his piano sonatas, Beethoven increasingly tested the limits of amateur players, most notably in his string quartets. Beethoven dedicated the three quartets published as his Op. 59 to Count Andrey Razumovsky, the Russian ambassador to Vienna. As a compliment to the count, Beethoven introduced Russian melodies as themes in the finale of No. 1, the scherzo of No. 2, and the slow movement of No. 3. The style of these quartets was so new that musicians were slow to accept them. The first movement of No. 1, for example, is particularly charged with idiosyncrasies, including frequent changes of texture, exploitation of the instruments' extreme ranges, and fugal passages. The Op. 59 quartets were premiered by the first professional string quartet, founded in 1804 by Ignaz Schuppanzigh, whose repertoire centered on quartets by Haydn, Mozart, and Beethoven. Having professional players to work with allowed Beethoven to increase the difficulty, length, complexity, and individuality of his quartets and to write with the expectation of public performance, while still aiming to sell copies to amateurs.

Concertos

During his first decade in Vienna, Beethoven composed three piano concertos to play at his own concerts, following the pattern of Mozart a decade earlier. But the concertos of his middle period are, like the symphonies, composed on a grander scale. In the Piano Concerto No. 5 in E-flat Major, Op. 73 (the *Emperor*), and the Violin Concerto in D Major, Beethoven greatly expanded the music's expressive range and dimensions. The soloist is often coequal with the orchestra, as if playing the part of a hero in a drama. In the first movement of the *Emperor* Concerto, for example, the soloist enters with a written-out cadenza even before the orchestra's exposition begins. Such dramatic interaction between soloist and orchestra was to become a frequent feature of nineteenth-century concertos.

Fifth Symphony

Beethoven's Fifth Symphony (1807–8) can be considered the musical projection of his resolution "I will grapple with Fate; it shall not overcome me." He symbolizes his struggle for victory by passing from C minor to C major, in a grand expansion of the move from chaos to light that he found in Haydn's

EXAMPLE 24.5 *Beethoven, Symphony No. 6, Scene by the brook*

Creation (see NAWM 123). Like that moment, though on a much larger scale, Beethoven's symphony embodies an experience of the sublime. The first movement is dominated by one of the best-known motives in all of Western music: the four-note figure that is emphatically announced at the outset. The same rhythmic idea recurs in various guises in the other three movements. The transition from minor to major takes place in an inspired passage that begins with the timpani softly recalling the rhythm of the four-note motive and leading without a break from the scherzo into the triumphant finale. Here the entrance of the full orchestra with trombones on the C-major chord has an electrifying effect. The finale adds piccolo and contrabassoon as well as trombones to the normal complement of strings, woodwinds, horns, trumpets, and timpani.

The *Pastoral* Symphony, No. 6 in F Major, was composed immediately after the Fifth, and the two were premiered on the same program in December 1808. Each of the *Pastoral* Symphony's five movements bears a title suggesting a scene from life in the country, following the normal sequence of movements but with an extra movement (*Storm*) that serves to introduce the finale (*Thankful feelings after the storm*). In the coda of the Andante movement (*Scene by the brook*), flute, oboe, and clarinet join harmoniously in imitating bird calls—the nightingale, the quail, and the cuckoo—as shown in Example 24.5. The symphony is more a character piece than a work of program music (see Chapter 25 for the distinction), marked by what Beethoven called "expression of feelings rather than tone-painting."

Pastoral Symphony

By 1814, Beethoven had reached the height of his popularity. He was celebrated as the greatest living composer of instrumental music, he received a steady demand from publishers for new works, and his music was played regularly throughout Austria and Germany and increasingly across Europe from England to Russia. The heroic style evident in some of his works, a source of controversy a decade earlier when the *Eroica* Symphony and *Razumovsky* Quartets first appeared, was now widely appreciated. He had changed audience expectations for what instrumental music can do.

Peak of popularity

CIRCUMSTANCES IN THE LATE PERIOD Ironically, at the height of his renown, several factors forced Beethoven into greater isolation, slowed the pace of composition, and prompted a change in focus and style. His deafness became increasingly profound, until by 1818 he could hardly hear at all. Because it caused him to lose contact with others, he retreated into himself, becoming moody and morbidly suspicious even toward his friends. A currency devaluation in 1811 and the death of Prince Kinsky in 1812 had reduced the value of Beethoven's annuity, making him feel financially vulnerable. Family problems, ill health, and unfounded apprehensions of poverty also plagued him, and it was only by a supreme effort of will that he continued composing amid all these troubles.

Compounding these personal problems was the political and economic situation. The final defeat of Napoleon in 1815 was followed by a disastrous postwar depression, making it difficult to produce large-scale public works. That same year saw the beginning of tremendous repression instituted by Count Metternich, head of the Austrian government under the emperor. Beethoven's sympathy with the ideals of republican government as it had developed in France was now seen as a threat to the state, and he was investigated and spied on by government security forces. During these years, he did not write politically linked works like *Fidelio,* or even the *Eroica* Symphony; the heroic style itself became psychologically inappropriate. In his last dozen years of life, Beethoven produced only two large public works, the *Missa solemnis* (1819–23) and the Ninth Symphony (1822–24), both completed only after the economy began to improve in the early 1820s. Otherwise, his major focus was on the last five piano sonatas (1816–21), *Diabelli Variations* for piano (1819–22), and last five string quartets (1824–26), all in genres traditionally intended for private music-making.

FIGURE 24.5 *Title page of Beethoven's String Quartet in C-sharp Minor, Op. 131, published by Schott in 1827 and printed in score ("en partition") to make the work easier to study. Traditionally, quartets had been printed only in separate parts, one for each player, but not in score, since only parts were needed to perform quartets. Printing this work in score made it possible for musical connoisseurs to examine the piece at leisure, play through portions at the keyboard, and explore the complex interrelationships among the elements.*

CHARACTERISTICS OF THE LATE STYLE By now, Beethoven was addressing most of his compositions to connoisseurs. The publication of his late quartets in score, as in Figure 24.5, in addition to the traditional format of a set of four parts for performance, shows they were meant to be studied, not just played through for the pleasure of the performers. Indeed these quartets were too difficult for most amateurs; Beethoven composed them with the expectation of concert performance by professional string quartets, notably the quartet led by Ignaz Schuppanzigh, which premiered four of the five. The urgent sense of communication to a large public was replaced by a more introspective character, aimed at a smaller, more select audience, and the musical language became more concentrated. Classical forms remained, like the features of a landscape after a geological upheaval—recognizable under new contours, lying at strange angles beneath the new surface.

An essential element of Beethoven's late style is the high degree of contrast. Extremes meet in these pieces: the sublime and the grotesque in the *Missa solemnis* and Ninth Symphony, the profound and the apparently naive in the late quartets and sonatas, high seriousness and high comedy often side by side. Contrasts of topic become exaggerated, involving not only style, figuration, and

EXAMPLE 24.6 *Opening of Beethoven, Piano Sonata in E Major, Op. 109, first movement*

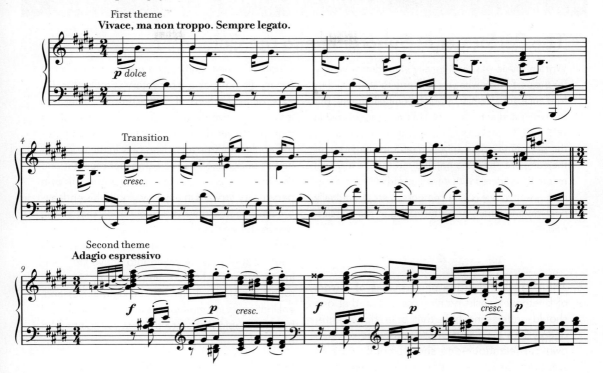

character but also meter and tempo. The two ideas presented at the beginning of the Piano Sonata in E Major, Op. 109 (1820), shown in Example 24.6, sound like they belong in entirely different movements, a light bagatelle or fast finale in duple meter and a pensive triple-meter slow movement. Yet they function as the first and second themes in a sonata-form first movement with a relatively brief exposition and recapitulation and much more extensive development and coda. Everything the music refers to is familiar, but the juxtapositions are strange, and even sympathetic listeners at the time found such pieces hard to understand.

Beethoven balanced the contrasts in his late style with an emphasis on continuity. Within movements, he achieves continuity by intentionally blurring divisions between phrases or placing cadences on weak beats. He also emphasized continuity between movements, sometimes indicating that successive movements should be played without a pause in between. His *An die ferne Geliebte* (To the Distant Beloved), Op. 98 (1816), inaugurated the genre of the **song cycle**, a group of songs performed in succession that tell or suggest a story; earlier published song collections had little or no continuity from one song to the next.

The way Beethoven used variation technique epitomizes his late style. Usually in a variations movement composers preserved the essential structure of the entire theme in each variation while introducing new embellishments, figurations, rhythms, and even meters and tempos. But Beethoven's late variations often go beyond this to reexamine the very substance of the

Continuity

Variation technique

SOURCE READING

The Performer as Subordinate to the Composer

Written music was traditionally viewed as a vehicle for the performer, who was at liberty to alter it in performance, for instance by adding embellishment. But the writer and critic E. T. A. Hoffmann suggested in 1813 that Beethoven's music was different, requiring the performer's total subordination to the vision of the composer, as if the notated music were a sacred text to be rendered with devotion and restraint. Scrupulous adherence to the composer's score gradually became a hallmark of performance in the classical tradition.

✤

The correct and fitting performance of a work of Beethoven's asks nothing more than that one should understand him, that one should enter deeply into his being, that—conscious of one's own consecration—one should boldly dare to step into the circle of the magical phenomena that his powerful spell has evoked. He who is not conscious of this consecration, who regards sacred

Music as a mere game, as a mere entertainment for an idle hour, as a momentary stimulus for dull ears, or as a means of self-ostentation—let him leave Beethoven's music alone. Only to such a man, moreover, does the objection "most ungrateful" apply. The true artist lives only in the work that he has understood as the composer meant it and that he then performs. He is above putting his own personality forward in any way, and all his endeavors are directed toward a single end—that all the wonderful enchanting pictures and apparitions that the composer has sealed into his work with magic power may be called into active life, shining in a thousand colors, and that they may surround mankind in luminous sparkling circles and, enkindling its imagination, its innermost soul, may bear it in rapid flight into the faraway spirit realm of sound.

From E. T. A. Hoffmann, "Beethovens Instrumental-Musik," *Sämtliche Werke*, ed. C. G. von Maassen, vol. 1 (Munich and Leipzig, 1908), 63–64, adapted from a review first published in March 1813. Trans. Oliver Strunk, in SR 160 (6:13), pp. 1197–98.

theme. In the slow movement of his String Quartet in C-sharp Minor, Op. 131 (1825–26), for example, only a few basic elements of the theme—a harmonic plan, a rhythmic quirk of deemphasizing the downbeat, a neighbor-note motion in the melody—are preserved through a very diverse series of variations.

New sonorities   Beethoven's search for new expressive means in his late works gave rise to new sonorities, such as the simultaneous use in all four instruments of pizzicatos or of *sul ponticello* effects (playing on the bridge to produce a thin sound) in the scherzo of the C-sharp Minor Quartet. Early critics deemed some passages unsuccessful, holding that Beethoven went too far in subordinating euphony and performability to the demands of his musical conceptions, perhaps because of his deafness. But we have no reason to believe that even with perfect hearing Beethoven would have altered a single note, either to spare tender ears or to make life easier for performers. Such insistence on the composer's vision at the expense of performer freedom and audience comfort was to become an important strain in nineteenth- and, especially, in twentieth-century music, with Beethoven as the model for later composers (see Source Reading).

Use of traditional   In his late works, Beethoven frequently used familiar styles and genres,
styles   either for expressive purposes or to reflect on tradition. For example, the slow movement of the String Quartet in A Minor, Op. 132 (1825; NAWM 131),

opens in the style of a sixteenth-century chorale setting, each phrase simply harmonized and preceded by a brief point of imitation, then alternates this style with a sprightly dance in triple meter. Beethoven composed this movement after being seriously ill and used the contrasting styles to express his personal feelings, titling the chorale section "Holy Song of Thanksgiving to the Divinity from One Who Has Recovered from Illness, in the Lydian Mode" and the dance section "Feeling New Strength"; such expression of a composer's own experience in his music, instead of a generalized emotional state or the feelings of an operatic character, was rare before Beethoven but became increasingly common during the nineteenth century. The next movement (NAWM 131b) presents a boisterous march that is suddenly interrupted by an operatic accompanied recitative for the first violin, leading into a finale (NAWM 131c) whose main theme resembles an impassioned opera aria. Other works include equally surprising references to both popular and cultivated styles.

Characteristic of Beethoven's late works is his use of imitative counterpoint, especially fugue. There are numerous canonic imitations and contrapuntal devices in all the late works, particularly in the fugatos that play a central role in development sections. Many movements or sections are predominantly fugal, such as the finales of the Piano Sonatas Opp. 106 and 110, the two double fugues in the finale of the Ninth Symphony, and the gigantic *Grosse Fuge* (Great Fugue) for String Quartet, Op. 133, first conceived as the finale for the Quartet in B-flat Major, Op. 130. The fugal finale has a long tradition extending back through Haydn's Op. 20 quartets to Corelli's trio sonatas. More unusual is Beethoven's use of a long, slow fugue as the first movement of the C-sharp Minor Quartet, Op. 131.

Imitation and fugue

Beethoven's reflections on tradition include reconceiving the number and arrangement of movements. Each of the last five piano sonatas has a unique succession of movement types and tempos, often linked without pause. The first and last of the late quartets (Opp. 127 and 135) have four movements, but Op. 132 has five, Op. 130 has six, and Op. 131 has seven played without breaks between them. The succession of movements is again unique in each, reshuffling or adding to the traditional four movements: the scherzo comes before the slow movement in Opp. 132 and 135; Op. 132 adds the march and recitative before the finale; Op. 130 features outer movements in sonata form framing a scherzo in cut time, a sonata-form slow movement, a second dance movement, and a second slow movement in the style of an aria; and Op. 131 offers a slow fugue, fast sonata-rondo, recitative, slow variations movement, scherzo (again in cut time), slow introduction, and sonata-form finale.

Reconceiving multimovement form

While Beethoven varied the traditional sequence of movements, he sought ways to integrate the movements more closely. In Op. 132, he does this through motivic and key relationships. The key scheme is symmetrical: A minor in the outer movements, A major in movements 2 and 4, and F Lydian in the central slow movement. (F Lydian has a pitch center of F but uses B♮ instead of B♭ for the fourth degree of the scale; see the discus sion of modes in Chapter 2.) F is also the key of the second theme in the first movement's exposition, forecasting its importance in the overall structure of the quartet. The notes A and F are also highlighted in the thematic material, together with their neighbors a half step below. The first movement begins with a brief slow introduction initiated by the G♯–A–F–E cello motive in

Unity

EXAMPLE 24.7 *Motivic links in the String Quartet in A Minor, Op. 132*

a. First movement, opening cello motive

b. First movement

c. End of fourth movement and beginning of finale

Example 24.7a. The same half steps are emphasized in the first theme of the Allegro, and when that theme repeats at measures 23–26 it is combined with an echo of the long-note half steps from the introduction, as seen in Example 24.7b. These same semitone pairs reappear in later movements: the theme of the second movement scherzo begins G♯–A; the chorale tune in the third movement begins F–E; and, as shown in Example 24.7c, both half steps are stressed at the end of the fourth movement and in the first theme of the fifth. These relationships between themes are subtle yet audible, and they help to draw all five movements together as a unified whole.

Appeal to connoisseurs   Like all of Beethoven's late sonatas and quartets, Op. 132 is a piece for connoisseurs. It is dramatic and emotionally rich, ranging from prayer to lightheartedness and from puckish humor to passion, so that it appeals to audiences on many levels. But only those "in the know" about music are likely to notice and appreciate the complex relationships between the whole and the individual parts, or the crafty combination of tradition and innovation, as the old and the new are inextricably intertwined. Music like this asks us to interpret it. It calls for analysis of its structure and motivic development but also of its meanings and its topical references. It draws us into its world. It poses problems—motivic problems that Beethoven addresses over the course of a movement (why this introductory motive in the cello? what does it portend?) and interpretive problems that seem never-ending (what does this music mean? how am I as a performer or listener supposed to respond?). That is why it is both difficult and satisfying, ever fresh and ever enduring.

LAST PUBLIC WORKS Like his late sonatas and quartets, the two large public works of Beethoven's final period reexamine the traditions of their respective genres.

Beethoven began his *Missa solemnis* as a mass to be performed at the elevation of Archduke Rudolph to archbishop of Olmütz in 1820, but it grew too long and elaborate for liturgical use. It is full of musical and liturgical symbols, reinterpreting traditional elements in new ways. The choral writing owes something to Handel, whose music Beethoven revered. But a Handel oratorio was a string of independent numbers, whereas Beethoven shaped his setting of the Kyrie, Gloria, Credo, Sanctus, and Agnus Dei as a unified five-movement symphony. As in the late masses of Haydn, choruses and solo ensembles freely alternate within each movement. Beethoven's setting was an idealized musical treatment of a well-loved text, not a liturgical work; like the late quartets, it was a concert piece in a genre that traditionally had a different function.

Missa solemnis

The Ninth Symphony was first performed in May 1824 on a program with one of Beethoven's overtures and three movements of the *Missa solemnis*, as advertised in the handbill in Figure 24.6. The large and distinguished audience applauded vociferously after the scherzo (the modern tradition of maintaining silence between movements had not yet been introduced); Beethoven, who was conducting, did not hear the applause, so one of the solo singers pulled his sleeve and pointed to the audience, and he turned and bowed.

The first three movements of the symphony are on a grand scale, and the whole takes more than an hour—even longer than the *Eroica* Symphony. But the most striking innovation is the use of solo voices and chorus in the finale. Just as Beethoven's mass was symphonic, and his quartets referred to vocal genres from recitatives and arias to the chorale motet, his last symphony looked to another genre, the choral

FIGURE 24.6 *Handbill for the concert of May 7, 1824, at the Kärntnertor Theater, advertising a "Great Musical Academy of Herr L. van Beethoven, Honorary Member of the Royal Academy of Arts and Sciences of Stockholm and Amsterdam and later Honorary Citizen of Vienna." The program promises "first: a grand overture; second: three grand hymns with solo and choral voices; third: a grand symphony with solo and choral voices entering in the finale on Schiller's Ode to Joy." The "hymns" were the Kyrie, Credo, and Agnus Dei of the Missa solemnis, and the symphony was the Ninth.*

ode. Beethoven had thought as early as 1792 of setting Friedrich Schiller's *Ode to Joy,* but more than thirty years went by before he decided to incorporate a choral finale on this text in his Ninth Symphony. Consistent with his ethical ideals and religious faith, he selected stanzas that emphasize universal fellowship through joy, and its basis in the love of an eternal heavenly Father.

The apparent incongruity of introducing voices at the climax of a long instrumental symphony posed an aesthetic difficulty. Beethoven's solution determined the finale's unusual form:

- tumultuous introduction, inspired by the operatic genre of accompanied recitative;
- review and rejection (by instrumental recitatives) of the themes of the three preceding movements, then proposal and joyful acceptance of the "joy" theme;
- orchestral exposition of the theme in four stanzas;
- return of the tumultuous opening;
- bass recitative: "O Freunde, nicht diese Töne!" (O friends, not these tones! Rather let us sing more pleasant and joyful ones);
- choral-orchestral exposition of the joy theme, "Freude, schöner Götterfunken" (Joy, beautiful, divine spark), in four stanzas, varied (including a march in Turkish style), and a long orchestral interlude (double fugue) followed by a repetition of the first stanza;
- new theme, for orchestra and chorus: "Seid umschlungen, Millionen!" (Be embraced, O millions!);
- double fugue on the two themes;
- a brilliant Prestissimo choral coda, bringing back the Turkish percussion, in which the joy theme is hailed in strains of matchless sublimity.

Everything here builds on tradition, but the whole is unprecedented. This combination of innovation with reverence for the past, of disparate styles, and of supreme compositional craft with profound emotional expression is characteristic of Beethoven's last period and has been seen as a measure of his greatness.

BEETHOVEN'S CENTRALITY

Having often celebrated heroism in his music, Beethoven himself became a cultural hero, a reputation that grew throughout the nineteenth century. His life story helped to define the Romantic view of the creative artist as a social outsider who suffers courageously to bring humanity a glimpse of the divine through art. The stories told about him and the images of him in art and literature reflect the mythology that grew up around him. In the twentieth century, biographers and historians began to peel back the myth and reclaim the mere human being who was Beethoven. But he has remained a central figure in music, both because of what he accomplished and because of how he has been regarded by critics and the public.

Many of Beethoven's compositions, particularly from the late 1790s through the 1810s, were immediately popular and have remained so ever since. His late works were considered idiosyncratic during his lifetime and were not absorbed into mainstream musical culture until decades after his death. But gradually they too came to be regarded as great, reflecting his inner life and consummate craft even more deeply than his more accessible music. Works of Beethoven form the core of the symphonic repertoire and are central to the repertoires for piano, for string quartet, and for other chamber ensembles. All later composers for those media, from Schubert to Schoenberg and on to our own time, have had to confront him as model and competitor. His influence has been felt not only in style and technique but also in conceptions of music and the role of the composer.

Beethoven's works invited attentive listening and probing critical interpretation. Seeking to explain his music, theorists developed new approaches in harmonic, motivic, formal, and tonal analysis, some of which have become standard and are applied to a wide range of music. The coherence and unity Beethoven achieved through development, key relationships, motivic links, and other means were highlighted in such studies and became a measure of greatness in musical art. Many composers in the classical tradition from nineteenth-century Romantics through twentieth-century modernists aspired to greatness in similar terms. But since the 1950s, the notions of what is most valuable in music that are embodied in Beethoven's works have been challenged by new values and by attempts to rediscover the values of earlier generations. Musicians, critics, and scholars have often used ideas derived from their understanding of Beethoven's work and aesthetic as a measuring rod, but doing so can be inappropriate or misleading when evaluating music of other traditions, periods, styles, or purposes.

Beethoven could afford the time to compose as he pleased, without answering to an employer. Perhaps as a result, sometimes he put his own experiences and feelings at the heart of a work, going beyond the long-standing traditions of representing the emotions of a poetic text, dramatizing those of an operatic character, or suggesting a generalized mood through conventional devices. Such self-expression was in tune with the growing Romantic movement described in the next chapter, and it came to be expected of composers after Beethoven. Modern musicians and listeners who assume that composers before Beethoven also wrote when they felt inspired and sought to capture their own emotions in music are astonished to discover that earlier composers typically created music to meet an immediate need, to please their employer, or to gratify their audience. Beethoven, and especially the critical reaction to Beethoven, changed everyone's idea of what a composer is and does. The image he fostered of a composer as an artist pursuing self-expression who composes only when inspired continues to hold sway.

Further Reading is available at digital.wwnorton.com/hwm10

THE ROMANTIC GENERATION: SONG AND PIANO MUSIC

❊

Most music that survives from the Middle Ages through the eighteenth century was composed for the church or for courts. In later centuries, genres suitable for home music-making, such as madrigals and string quartets, or for public performance, exemplified in Venetian opera, Handel's oratorios, and Haydn's late symphonies, became progressively more prominent. In the nineteenth century, music for home or public performance took center stage. The market for music to play at home and the popularity of concertgoing stimulated new styles tailored to broad musical tastes. At the same time, writers and musicians promoted new artistic ideals for music that focused on individuality, originality, fantasy, expression of pure emotion, and transcending conventional limits in pursuit of deeper truths. The new ideas and styles were called **Romantic**, an evocative term whose vagueness is part of its power. The word is now used to identify music of the entire nineteenth century, but such an overarching concept should not blind us to the great variety of styles and ideas manifest in the music of the time.

The next three chapters address music from the end of the Napoleonic Wars to the middle of the century. After outlining the economic and social settings for music and the ideas of Romanticism, this chapter will focus on songs and piano music, the mainstays of home music-making and of virtuoso piano recitals, and the Romantic styles they fostered. The following two chapters will examine music for public venues, in the concert hall and in the theater. Chapters 28–30 then address music in the second half of the nineteenth century, when Romanticism combined with other trends such as realism.

THE NEW ORDER, 1815–1848

The upheavals of 1789–1815 changed the European political landscape. The French Revolution made peasants and workers into citizens instead of subjects. Napoleon's wars swept away old political boundaries and spread the Revolutionary ideas of liberty, equality, brotherhood, and national identity across Europe. In 1814–15, the Congress of Vienna drew a new map, shown in Figure 25.1, made up of far fewer states. Although Italy and German-speaking lands were still partitioned, the inhabitants of each felt an increasing sense of belonging to a nation united by language and culture. So did the people in lands that had recently lost independence, such as Poland, or had long endured foreign domination, such as Hungary and Bohemia: to them, the independent nation-state seemed an ideal. In the Austrian Empire and elsewhere, close surveillance, censorship, and repression held aspirations for freedom in check and made it almost impossible to express political ideas directly through literature, art, or music until the stirring but largely unsuccessful revolutions of 1848–49. But interest in national culture grew, and composers incorporated national traits in song, instrumental music, and opera. The eighteenth-century cosmopolitan ideal was replaced by the expectation that composers write music true to their national identity.

The Americas saw equally radical change. In the wake of the American and French Revolutions, a revolution in Haiti began in 1791 and led to Haiti's establishment in 1804 as the second independent state in the Americas and the first nation founded by liberated slaves. After Spain and Portugal were

The Americas

FIGURE 25.1 *Europe, 1815–48.*

weakened by Napoleon's invasion, revolutions in 1810–24 brought independence to most of Latin America, and by 1838 most modern nations of the region had emerged. Between 1803 and 1848, the United States expanded west and south through purchase, treaties, and wars. The indigenous Native American peoples in many areas fought to retain control, but settlers moved west in increasing numbers. The United States began to create its own cultural identity in the tales of Washington Irving and Nathaniel Hawthorne, the novels of James Fenimore Cooper, and the songs of Stephen Foster. In Canada, French and British provinces were officially united in 1841, although the two sides continued in conflict until the Canadian Confederation was established in 1867.

THE DECLINE OF ARISTOCRATIC PATRONAGE The economic order in Europe changed along with the political, dramatically affecting musicians. War and inflation impoverished the aristocracy, and the elimination of over one hundred small states drastically reduced the number of courts supporting the arts. The typical musician no longer served a prince or church but made a living as a free agent through public performance, teaching, composing on commission, or creating music for publication. While patrons had expected their employees to play several instruments and, like Bach and Haydn, compose in most genres, musicians were now competing in an open market and often found a niche through specialization. Among the most prominent musicians of the age were ***virtuosos***—performers, such as violinist Nicolò Paganini and pianist Franz Liszt (see p. 612–15), who specialized in one instrument and dazzled audiences with displays of technical mastery. Many composers also specialized in one medium, as Fryderyk Chopin did in piano music and Giuseppe Verdi in opera.

Opportunities for careers in music broadened as well. Legal reforms begun during the French Revolution and spread across Europe by the Napoleonic Wars eliminated the privileges enjoyed by the old guilds—which set standards and controlled various crafts, including music—and opened careers to anyone with talent. Conservatories opened in cities across Europe and the Americas, providing training for students and steady income for musicians who taught them. Rising interest in music supported a growing number of music journalists and critics, including several known today primarily as composers.

As the aristocracy declined, the urban middle class grew in size and influence. The Industrial Revolution was mechanizing manufacturing, thereby reducing prices, drawing people from the country to work in factories, creating more leisure time, and allowing merchants and entrepreneurs to become the economic leaders.

MIDDLE-CLASS MUSIC-MAKING Music-making was an important outlet for the middle and upper classes, who had the money and leisure to purchase instruments and learn to play them. In many homes, evenings were a time for making music with family and friends, singing or playing piano, violin, flute, guitar, harp, or other instruments. Music released social pressures. It provided a way to express aspirations for equality and national freedom without risking censorship or imprisonment. It offered an escape from wars, depressed economies, and political repression.

Music also was a means of social control. State-sponsored opera often carried political messages. Churches established amateur choirs, and factories organized wind bands for their workers, seeking to provide entertainment, elevate taste, make working conditions more palatable, and divert the working classes from drinking and carousing (or from political organizing). And in an era of starkly differentiated gender roles, music kept women occupied at home.

Music as social control

Although many working-class women and children labored long hours in factories, women and girls of the middle and upper classes were expected to stay at home, their leisure a sign of status. The genders were assigned separate spheres: boys went to school and men to work while women and girls maintained the home, regarded as a sacred refuge in a harsh world. When possible, servants were employed to do housework, releasing the women of the family to pursue what were regarded as appropriate feminine accomplishments, from needlework to music.

Separate spheres

THE PIANO At the center of home music was the piano. Innovations in manufacturing greatly increased the availability of pianos and lowered their cost (see Innovations: Musical Instruments in the Industrial Revolution, pp. 584–85). Square pianos like that in Figure 25.2, small enough for parlors, found their way into many homes on both sides of the Atlantic, from Montreal to Moscow.

FIGURE 25.2 Family Concert in Basle *(1849) by Sebastian Gutzwiller. This painting shows a typical domestic scene of music-making: a woman performs on a square piano while other family members play the violin and flute. Others listen either with complete attention or while engaged in their own activities.*

Musical Instruments in the Industrial Revolution

The Industrial Revolution was not a single event, but a series of inventions and applications that together radically changed the way goods were manufactured. Items that had been crafted by hand for centuries, from cloth to clocks, could now be mass-produced by machine, making them much more widely available and less costly. In addition, existing products were improved and new ones developed in a continuing stream of innovation.

Musical instrument-making was one of many industries to be revolutionized. One profound change was in the sheer quantity of instruments that could be produced. In the 1770s, the output of even the largest piano manufacturers in Europe was only about twenty pianos a year, because every piece had to be made by hand. By 1800, John Broadwood & Sons of London was manufacturing about four hundred pianos a year by employing a large and specialized workforce, and by 1850 the firm was using steam power and mass-production techniques to make over two thousand pianos a year, one hundred times as fast as eighty years before. Many were grand pianos, but most were square pianos like the one in Figure 25.2. Because they were produced in such quantity, pianos became inexpensive enough for middle-class families to afford.

The design of the piano was also improved through a number of innovations. The sustaining pedal (also called the damper pedal), by holding all dampers off the strings, let tones continue after the keys were released, allowing greater resonance, closer imitation of orchestral sound, and new pianistic effects. The metal frame, introduced in England during the 1820s, allowed higher tension on the strings and thus greater volume, wider dynamic range, longer sustain, and better legato. Felt-covered hammers allowed more powerful *fortissimos* and quieter *pianissimos*. The standard range was extended to six octaves by 1820 and seven by 1850. The double-escapement action, introduced in 1821 by Parisian manufacturer Sébastien Erard, allowed quick repetition of notes and thus enabled a new level of virtuosity. All of these new capabilities were exploited by pianists and composers, and the piano became the indispensable instrument for home music-making and for public concerts. But it was clearly a modern-day machine,

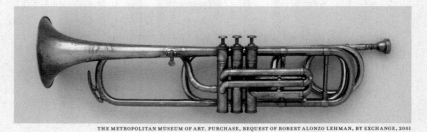

THE METROPOLITAN MUSEUM OF ART. PURCHASE, BEQUEST OF ROBERT ALONZO LEHMAN, BY EXCHANGE, 2001

FIGURE 25.3 *Trumpet with piston valves (ca. 1865) by Antoine Courtois of Paris.*

FIGURE 25.4 *Horn with rotary valves (1835) by W. Glier of Warsaw.*

with thousands of separate parts and hundreds of mechanical connections.

The same spirit of innovation was applied to other instruments. Erard's firm also played an important role in creating the modern harp. Traditionally, harps were tuned to a single diatonic scale, so that they could not play chromatic passages, and even to change keys required retuning some of the strings. Several eighteenth-century harp makers had tried to solve this problem, but harps strung with all the chromatic notes were cumbersome to play, and finding a way quickly to change tuning proved difficult. Erard's solution was a new fork mechanism, operated by a set of seven pedals, that allowed the strings to be shortened, raising the pitch by one half step. Eventually, Erard patented a harp that could be played in any key because each string could be adjusted almost instantaneously to produce any of three semitones by a double-action fork mechanism. By 1820, the firm had sold 3,500 of these instruments, whose principles are still in use by modern pedal-harp makers.

Starting in the 1810s, brass instrument makers applied the valve technology of the steam engine—in which valves controlled the flow of steam, water, or air—to the design of trumpets and horns, finally enabling these instruments to produce all the notes of the chromatic scale. Using either piston valves, as in the trumpet in Figure 25.3, or rotary valves, as on the horn in Figure 25.4, the player can open one or more lengths of pipe to extend the sounding length of the air column and thus lower the pitch one or more

semitones. Only three or four valves are needed, rather than the many holes and keys on a flute or clarinet, because brass instruments produce notes from the harmonic series, and only a few semitones separate each note in the series from the next one up or down. Many new brass instruments were invented as well, including the ***tuba***, which became the bass of the orchestral brass section.

Wind instruments also profited from a combination of new technologies, enterprising innovators, and improved manufacturing methods. Theobald Boehm established a successful flute factory in Munich in 1828. He experimented with mechanisms that would achieve uniform tone production, superior volume, and better control of tuning. By 1849, he had created the modern "Boehm-system" flute, an all-metal instrument with large holes that were closed not with the bare fingers but with padded keys, linked to each other through a series of rod-axles, levers, and clutches, as shown in Figure 25.5. Louis-Auguste Buffet, working in Paris, applied some of Boehm's ideas to the clarinet, producing a design that has remained standard to the present. Adolphe Sax used a similar system to create the ***saxophone***, a new wind instrument most familiar today in marching bands and jazz.

Similar mechanical innovations brought about by the Industrial Revolution—such as interlocking rods, gears, and screws—improved the construction and tuning methods of the timpani in the early nineteenth century. String instruments were also altered to create a bigger, more dramatic tone, with greater string tension, a higher bridge, and a tilted fingerboard. Fingerboards were lengthened to allow for higher notes. The modern bow, devised by François Tourte around 1785, had a wider, uniform band of bowhair kept taut with concave curvature of the wood and a screw tightening mechanism, which gave more control and a larger sound.

By the late nineteenth century, the piano, the harp, and the instruments of the orchestra had almost all reached their modern form, thanks to the inventors and industrialists who applied the century's new technologies to music.

FIGURE 25.5 *Boehm-system flute (1856) by Theobald Boehm.*

The years 1820–50 saw many design improvements that allowed for new pianistic effects and a greatly expanded range. On such an instrument, a pianist could express a complete musical thought almost as well as an entire orchestra, yet more personally. These characteristics made the piano the quintessential nineteenth-century instrument, ideal both for home music and for public concerts.

Women and the piano

Women, particularly, played piano, continuing a tradition of keyboard-playing for their own and others' pleasure that stretched back to the sixteenth century. Pianist-composers such as Fryderyk Chopin and Franz Liszt supported themselves in part by giving lessons to well-to-do women. Teachers expected daily practice, often for several hours, thereby keeping energetic young women occupied at home but also helping many of them achieve astonishing fluency. There were quite a few professional women pianists in the first half of the nineteenth century—such as Clara Wieck, a formidable virtuoso who was to marry Robert Schumann—and many excellent amateurs who played at a professional level. Yet for most women, music was an accomplishment, designed to attract a spouse and entertain family and friends, rather than a career. Men also played, often accompanying their wives, sisters, or daughters as they sang. A favorite format was music for two players at one piano, which offered siblings a joint recreation or a married or dating couple a structured physical and emotional intimacy.

THE MARKET FOR MUSIC AND THE NEW IDIOM All these amateurs needed music to play, creating a boom in music publishing. In the 1770s, the largest publishers in London, Paris, and Leipzig listed hundreds of items in their catalogues, already a great number in comparison to earlier decades; by the 1820s they listed tens of thousands of pieces. The number of music stores in Europe and the New World grew rapidly in the early 1800s, increasing in London from thirty in 1794 to 150 in 1824. Technology again proved crucial: lithography, invented around 1796, let publishers print music cheaply with elaborate illustrations that helped it sell. Consumers demanded a constant flood of new music, and composers supplied it. As a result, the amount of music from the nineteenth century still available to us is overwhelming, far greater than for any previous era.

The market in sheet music gave the public at large unprecedented influence over what music was produced, because publishers had to supply what their customers wanted. Composers wrote songs, piano works, and piano duets in great quantities. Arrangers transcribed orchestral and chamber works for piano solo or duet, making concert works accessible to a large public. At a time before recordings, such arrangements were the only opportunity many people had to hear most works.

The new musical idiom

Composers writing for the public sought to make their music accessible and appealing to amateur performers by writing tuneful melodies with attractive accompaniments, little counterpoint, and relatively uniform rhythm and level of difficulty from measure to measure; by using predictable four-bar phrasing, simple songlike forms, and idiomatic writing that exploited the textures, sonorities, and dynamic contrasts available on the modern piano; by interspersing familiar chords and progressions with dramatic or colorful harmonic contrasts; and by introducing strong musical and extramusical imagery, evocative titles, or national or exotic associations. The most successful music offered something novel and individual that made it stand out from the crowd. Competition for sales fostered innovations in harmony such as greater use of nonharmonic tones, unexpected progressions, chromatic chords and voice leading, distant modulations, and tonal ambiguity.

These characteristics defined a new idiom, known today as the early Romantic style. The best composers of the time deepened their music's appeal to discerning players and listeners, but their styles were rooted in this idiom. The high value placed on a beautiful melody and striking harmonies within small forms such as songs and short piano pieces carried over into larger forms as well. Originality was now marked, not by how one treated conventional material, as in the Classic era, but by the material itself.

ROMANTICISM

The new idiom, which focused on melody, emotion, novelty, and individuality, paralleled Romanticism in literature and art and came to be called **Romantic**. The term has many meanings, and tracing its history will clarify its use and implications.

The word *romantic* derived from the medieval romance, a poem or tale *"Romantic" as a term* about heroic events or persons, such as King Arthur or Charlemagne. It connoted something distant, legendary, and fantastic, an imaginary or ideal world far from everyday reality. In the late eighteenth and early nineteenth centuries, especially in German-speaking lands, writers applied the term to literature and then to art and music. Philosopher and critic Friedrich Schlegel (1772–1829) differentiated "classic" poetry—which he deemed objectively beautiful, limited in scope and theme, and universally valid—from "romantic" poetry, which mixed genres and forms, transgressed rules and limits, or expressed insatiable longing and the richness of nature. Schlegel thought of the dichotomy as a difference of character, not time period, classing as "romantic" Dante's *Divine Comedy* (1307), the plays of Shakespeare, and the relatively new genre of the novel, called *Roman* in both French and German. Like the novel, political liberalism, and idealist philosophy, Romantic art focused on the individual and on expression of the self. As the word gained currency, composers and artists who came of age in the 1820s and 1830s, such as Berlioz, Mendelssohn, Chopin, Liszt, and Robert and Clara Schumann, conceived of themselves as "romantics." By the mid-nineteenth century, Schlegel's dichotomy seemed to distinguish the elegant, natural, simple, clear, formally closed, and universally appealing (and therefore classic) music of Haydn and Mozart from the music of the second quarter of the nineteenth century, marked as Romantic because of its search for the original, interesting, evocative, individual, expressive, or extreme. The music of Beethoven was regarded as straddling the two camps, Romantic in its aspirations and individuality yet Classic in language and forms.

This distinction crystallized into the notion of two style periods, Clas- *"Romantic"* sic and Romantic, divided around the 1820s. Schlegel's original dichotomy *as a period* between artworks with different characters was now used to distinguish two eras. Some later music historians considered the whole nineteenth century "Romantic," while others saw the entire span from the mid-eighteenth through the early twentieth century as a single Classic-Romantic period in which composers shared conventions of harmony, rhythm, and form but differed in how they treated those conventions. For our purposes, the political and economic events of 1815 serve as a convenient starting point for the Romantic period because their impact on composers helps to explain the distinctive music of the era. As we will see in Chapters 28–30, music in the second half of the nineteenth century is characterized by a shifting blend of Romanticism with realism and other trends.

Romanticism as a reaction   The flowering of Romanticism after 1815 was a direct reaction to several of the themes explored in the first part of this chapter. Society was changing rapidly, driven in part by science and technology, and Romanticism sought refuge in the past, myth, dreams, the supernatural, and the irrational. As the new political concept of "nation" emerged, Romantics regarded "common folk" as the true embodiment of the nation. As people crowded into cities, Romantics valued rural life and looked to nature for refuge, inspiration, and revelation. As industrialization brought about a mass society, Romantics esteemed solitude and the individual. As people in factories, shops, and homes were bound to routine, Romantics pursued novelty, boundlessness, and the exotic. And as a new capitalist economy replaced old forms of support for artists, Romantics saw artists as pursuing not money but a higher ideal of enlightening the world through access to a realm beyond the everyday. Some of these impulses are captured in the art of Caspar David Friedrich, the leading German Romantic painter, as in his *Wanderer above the Sea of Fog* (ca. 1818), shown in Figure 25.6, which depicts solitude and the boundlessness of nature, transcending everyday experience. The same impulses suffuse the music of many Romantic composers.

FIGURE 25.6
Caspar David Friedrich, Wanderer above the Sea of Fog.

HAMBURGER KUNSTHALLE, HAMBURG, GERMANY. PHOTO: B.P.K./ART RESOURCE, NY

Romanticism encouraged composers to seek individual paths for expressing intense emotions, such as melancholy, longing, or joy. Composers respected conventions of form or harmony to a point, but their imagination drove them to trespass limits and explore new realms of sound. E. T. A. Hoffmann and other writers considered instrumental music the ideal Romantic art because it was free from the concreteness of words and visual images and thus could evoke impressions, thoughts, and feelings that are beyond the power of words to express (see Source Reading).

Such writers saw instrumental music as an autonomous art, free from earlier notions that music must serve the words of a madrigal or opera, convey an appropriate affect, or fulfill a particular social role, whether as entertainment or as accompaniment to a religious ritual or dinner party. This autonomy paralleled the composers' own freedom as independent entrepreneurs outside the old patronage system. They were no longer part of the servant class as Haydn and earlier composers had been. The autonomy of music as an art symbolized the individualism and economic independence so valued by the nineteenth-century middle class.

The idealization of instrumental music as the

The Most Romantic Art

In an influential essay, poet, novelist, critic, and composer E. T. A. Hoffmann (1776–1822) lauded instrumental music as the most Romantic art.

When we speak of music as an independent art, should we not always restrict our meaning to instrumental music, which, scorning every aid, every admixture of another art (the art of poetry), gives pure expression to music's specific nature, recognizable in this form alone? It is the most romantic of all the arts—one might almost say, the only

genuinely romantic one—for its sole subject is the infinite. The lyre of Orpheus opened the portals of Orcus [Roman god of the underworld]—music discloses to man an unknown realm, a world that has nothing in common with the external sensual world that surrounds him, a world in which he leaves behind him all definite feelings to surrender himself to an inexpressible longing.

From E. T. A. Hoffmann, "Beethovens Instrumental-Musik," *Sämtliche Werke*, ed. C. G. von Maassen, vol. 1 (Munich and Leipzig, 1908), adapted in 1813 from a review first published in July 1810. Trans. Oliver Strunk, in SR 160 (6:13), pp. 1193–94.

premier mode of artistic expression led Hoffmann, Ludwig Tieck, and other writers to formulate new distinctions among instrumental works between **absolute**, **characteristic** (or **descriptive**), and **program music**. A programmatic work recounts a narrative or sequence of events, often spelled out in an accompanying text called a **program**; a **character piece** depicts or suggests a mood, personality, or scene, usually indicated in its title; and absolute music offers instead an idealized play of sound and form. Program music was not a nineteenth-century invention. Composers in the seventeenth and eighteenth centuries expected their instrumental music to convey particular emotions, associations with everyday life (from dance rhythms to hunting horns), and in some cases even specific characters, scenes, or programs, as in Biber's *Mystery Sonatas*, Couperin's character pieces, or Vivaldi's *Four Seasons*. What is truly new in the nineteenth century is the notion of absolute music, which refers to nothing but itself—a powerful idea that lay behind numerous developments in both nineteenth- and twentieth-century music.

The esteem for instrumental music was reflected in a new concept of **organic** musical form. Eighteenth-century writers conceived of musical works as rhetorical, shaped like a speech and intended to have a certain effect on the listener (see Chapter 20). This metaphor for music can be traced back at least to the Renaissance and continued to echo throughout the nineteenth century and into the twentieth. But Goethe argued in a study of plant metamorphosis that, just as all the parts of a plant are adaptations of the same basic shape, so too artists should shape their works so that all the parts are unified by being derived from a common source. Applying this view to music, the organic relationship of the themes, sections, movements, and other parts to the whole (and to each other) becomes more important than rhetorical structure or persuasive force. In the metaphor of organicism, motivic links can contribute more to a work's unity than its harmonic plan or use of a conventional form.

Organicism

Music and
the literary   Despite the prestige of instrumental music, literature was central to the work of most composers. Many had writers as friends, and some were writers themselves: Berlioz and Schumann were professional music critics, Liszt and Wagner wrote influential essays on music, and Wagner wrote his own opera librettos. From songs to choral works and opera, several leading genres required an integration of music and text. In setting words, composers sought to draw out the inner meanings and feelings suggested in the poetry or libretto. Even many instrumental works bore inseparable links to words through a descriptive title or program. The effort to find a musical effect capable of expressing an idea or program often led to innovations in harmony, melody, and instrumental color. Such novelty appealed to middle-class consumers, and the program enhanced that appeal while justifying the unusual effects. For this reason, composers and publishers often added programs or descriptive titles after a work was composed.

SONG

The trends described in previous sections are apparent in songs of the time. Voice and piano (played by the singer or an accompanist) was the preferred medium, offering a wide expressive range with minimal forces. Texts were typically strophic poems, and the words were meant to be heard, set for the most part with one note per syllable and reserving longer gestures for special emphasis. Whether expressing a feeling or telling a story, the poem usually adopted a persona and situation—a woman in love, a man wandering in nature, an adult remembering childhood—that gave the singer an opportunity to act a part as well as sing. Songs varied from simple settings with chordal accompaniment and the same melody for every verse to artful, through-composed miniature dramas in which the accompaniment rivaled the voice in importance. Only later in the century did a firm line develop between popular songs for sale to the widest possible musical public and art songs for connoisseurs.

The most influential and prestigious repertoire of nineteenth-century song was the German Lied. The Lied was in many ways the quintessential Romantic genre: a fusion of music and poetry, centering on the expression of individual feelings, with descriptive musical imagery and aspects of folk style. The Lied influenced song composers in other nations, especially later in the century (see Chapter 30). A significant independent tradition was the British and American parlor song. Among the thousands of song composers active before midcentury, the following focuses on only a few of the most exemplary.

THE LIED The Romantic Lied built on a strong eighteenth-century tradition (see Chapter 21). The popularity of Lieder grew after 1800. The number of German song collections published increased from about one a month in the late 1700s to over one hundred a month in 1826, when the *Allgemeine musikalische Zeitung* (General Music Journal) asked "has there ever been an age more prolific in song than ours?" Changes in poetry anticipated changes in the Lied. Poets drew elements from both classical and folk traditions. A frequent theme was an individual confronting the greater forces of nature or society, vulnerable yet ennobled by the encounter; another was nature as a metaphor for human experience.

The chief poetic genre continued to be the *lyric,* a short, strophic poem on one subject expressing a personal feeling or viewpoint. The ultimate models were the lyric poets of ancient Greece and Rome, such as Sappho and Horace. Two collections of folk-song verses, Johann Gottfried von Herder's *Volkslieder* (Folk Songs, 1778–79) and Clemens Brentano and Achim von Arnim's *Des Knaben Wunderhorn* (The Boy's Magic Horn, 1805), influenced poets to adopt similar language and imagery. Both ancient lyrics and folk verses were meant to be sung, and the poetry written in imitation of them was ideal for setting to music, with short strophes and regular meter and rhyme.

The lyric

In the late eighteenth century, German poets cultivated a new form, the **ballad**, in imitation of the folk ballads of England and Scotland. Ballads might alternate narrative and dialogue and usually dealt with romantic adventures or supernatural incidents. Their greater length and wider palette of moods and events inspired composers to use more varied themes and textures. The ballad thus expanded the Lied both in form and in emotional content. In many such Lieder, the piano rose from accompaniment to equal partner with the voice in illustrating and intensifying the meaning of the poetry.

The ballad

Lieder composers often grouped their songs into collections with a unifying characteristic, such as texts by a single poet or a focus on a common theme. Beethoven's *An die ferne Geliebte* (see Chapter 24) introduced the concept of the song cycle, in which all the songs were to be performed in order, as movements of a multimovement vocal work. Using this format, composers could tell a story through a succession of songs, combining the narrative emphasis of ballads with the focused expressivity of the lyric poem.

Song collections and song cycles

FRANZ SCHUBERT The characteristics of the Romantic Lied are exemplified in the songs of Franz Schubert (1797–1828; see biography and Figure 25.7). Schubert wrote over six hundred Lieder, many of which were first performed for friends in home gatherings known as Schubertiads. In the picture of one such evening in Figure 25.8, many of the listeners seem transported, gazing into space with attentive expressions on their faces. The drawing conveys the intensely emotional engagement with music that was characteristic of the age.

Schubert set poetry by many writers, including fifty-nine poems of Goethe. Some of Schubert's finest Lieder are found in his two song cycles on poems by Wilhelm Müller, *Die schöne Müllerin* (The Pretty Miller-Maid, 1823) and *Winterreise* (Winter's Journey, 1827). When Schubert wrote a song he strove to make the music the equal of the words, not merely their frame. Through melody, accompaniment, harmony, and form, he sought to embody the person speaking, the characters described, the scene, the situation, and the emotions expressed.

Song texts

Schubert always chose forms that suited the shape and meaning of the text. When a poem sustains a single image or mood, Schubert typically uses strophic form, with the same music for each stanza, as in *Heidenröslein* (Little Heath-Rose, 1815) and *Das Wandern* (Wandering), the first song in *Die schöne Müllerin.* Most Lieder of his time were strophic and unadorned, and when Schubert deviates from that norm (as he often does), it is for expressive purposes. Contrast or change is often depicted with **modified strophic form,** in which music repeats for some strophes but others vary it or use new music; an example is *Der Lindenbaum* (The Linden Tree) from *Winterreise.* Some songs

Form

FRANZ SCHUBERT
(1797–1828)

Schubert was the first great master of the Romantic Lied and a prolific composer in all genres.

The son of a Vienna schoolmaster, Schubert grew up surrounded by music-making at home and at school. As a child he studied piano, singing, violin, organ, counterpoint, and figured bass, and took composition lessons from the court music director, Antonio Salieri. Schubert's musical talent won him a free, first-class education at a prestigious Vienna boarding school. Although trained to follow his father's profession, his heart lay in composing. For several years he taught at his father's school, all the while composing with astonishing speed and fluency; in 1815 alone he produced more than 140 songs. January 1818 saw the first publication of his music, and from then on he devoted himself entirely to composition.

By 1821, Schubert's music was widely performed in Vienna, and he was earning substantial sums from publishers. As he never secured a permanent salaried position, he gained most of his income from publication, especially of songs and piano music. Thus he was a freelance composer, largely independent of the patronage system that supported earlier composers and on which even Beethoven had depended. In the 1820s, he began to focus increasingly on larger works, including chamber music, symphonies, and operas, but most were not performed until after his death.

The last years of Schubert's life were clouded by illness. He died at thirty-one, possibly from syphilis he had contracted by 1823 or from its treatment with

FIGURE 25.7 *Franz Schubert, in a watercolor portrait from 1825 by Wilhelm August Rieder.*

mercury. His tombstone was inscribed "Music has here buried a rich treasure but still fairer hopes." Given the brevity of his career, his output of almost one thousand works is astounding.

MAJOR WORKS Over 600 songs, including the song cycles *Die schöne Müllerin* and *Winterreise*; 9 symphonies, notably No. 8 in B Minor (*Unfinished*) and No. 9 in C Major (*Great*); about 35 chamber works, including Piano Quintet in A Major (the *Trout*), String Quartet in D Minor (*Death and the Maiden*), and String Quintet in C Major; 22 piano sonatas; many short piano pieces; 17 operas and Singspiels; 6 masses; 200 other choral works

use ternary form (ABA or ABA′), as in *Der Atlas* (Atlas), or bar form (AAB), as in *Ständchen* (Serenade), both from the posthumously published collection *Schwanengesang* (Swan Song, 1828). Longer narrative songs may be through-composed, with new music for each stanza, like the ballad *Erlkönig* (The Erl-King, 1815), or combine declamatory and arioso styles as in an operatic scene, like *Der Wanderer* (The Wanderer, 1816); in either case, recurring themes and a carefully planned tonal scheme lend unity.

Melody   Schubert had a gift for creating beautiful melodies that perfectly capture a poem's character, mood, and situation. Many songs use the simple, seemingly

FIGURE 25.8 *Sepia drawing by Schubert's friend Moritz von Schwind (1868), showing Schubert at the piano accompanying the singer Johann Michael Vogl, sitting to his right. The occasion is a Schubertiad, a gathering in a private home during which Schubert would play piano and either sing his own songs or accompany a singer.*

artless quality of folk song to suggest a rural setting or uncomplicated feelings, as in *Heidenröslein* and *Das Wandern,* shown in Example 25.1a–b. Others are suffused with sweetness and melancholy, as is *Ständchen,* Example 25.1c, or are declamatory and dramatic, like *Der Atlas,* Example 25.1d.

Accompaniment

The excerpts in Example 25.1 only begin to illustrate the variety of Schubert's accompaniments. The figuration always fits the poem's mood and the personality of its protagonist, from a simple alternation of bass note and chord in *Heidenröslein* to dramatic tremolos and octaves in *Der Atlas.* The accompaniment often reflects an image in the poem, especially an image of movement, like the walking motion of *Das Wandern* or a serenader plucking a guitar in *Ständchen.*

Gretchen am Spinnrade

In *Gretchen am Spinnrade* (Gretchen at the Spinning Wheel, 1814; NAWM 132), on an excerpt from Goethe's famous play *Faust,* the piano suggests the spinning wheel by having a constant rising and falling sixteenth-note figure in the right hand, and the motion of the treadle by using repeated notes in the left hand, as shown in Example 25.2. These figures also convey Gretchen's agitation as she thinks of her beloved. Often, as here, the piano introduces the song's mood and central image in a short prelude before the voice enters. When Gretchen recalls her beloved's kiss, the accompaniment suddenly stops, then haltingly restarts. Although the words do not indicate her actions, we know from the music that she stops the wheel when she is overcome by emotion, then gradually returns to spinning as she regains her composure.

Harmony

The harmony also reinforces the poetry. The simple *Das Wandern* uses only five different chords. The sweet melancholy of *Ständchen* is evoked by alternating minor and major forms of a key or triad, an effect that is almost a trademark of Schubert's style. In other songs, he underlines the poem's dramatic qualities powerfully through complex modulations. In *Der Atlas,* he uses a diminished seventh chord to move abruptly from G minor to the distant key of B major, then gradually works his way back through E minor to G minor. This extraordinary key scheme illustrates Schubert's fondness for modulation

EXAMPLE 25.1 *Franz Schubert songs*

a. Heidenröslein

A boy saw a rosebud standing, a rosebud on the heath,

b. Das Wandern

Wandering is the miller's pleasure!

c. Ständchen

Gently my songs through the night implore you;

d. Der Atlas

I, the unlucky Atlas!

EXAMPLE 25.2 *Schubert,* Gretchen am Spinnrade

My peace is gone,

by third rather than by fifth, a trait also found in his instrumental music, as we will see. His predilection for unusual harmonic relationships reflects his use of harmony as an expressive device, since the unconventional generally carries more expressive potential than the conventional, and both aspects of his harmonic practice greatly influenced later composers.

Schubert's ability to capture the mood and character of a poem and to make the music its equal in emotive and descriptive power, along with the sheer beauty of his music and the pleasure it gives to those who perform it, have endeared Schubert's songs both to his contemporaries and to generations of singers, pianists, and listeners. His songs set the standard that later song composers strove to match.

Schubert's achievement

ROBERT AND CLARA SCHUMANN Schubert's first important successor as a Lieder composer was Robert Schumann (1810–1856), also renowned for his piano music, symphonies, and chamber music (discussed on pp. 603–5 and in Chapter 26). He wrote over 120 songs in 1840, which he called his "Lieder year." He focused on love songs, including the song cycles *Dichterliebe* (A Poet's Love) and *Frauenliebe und -leben* (Woman's Love and Life). He was inspired in part by his impending marriage to Clara Wieck, a renowned pianist and composer (see their joint biography and Figure 25.9). He turned to song to express the passions and frustrations of love, to make money from a lucrative genre, and to synthesize music and poetry, his two great interests.

Robert Schumann thought that music should capture a poem's essence in its own terms and that voice and piano should be equal partners. He often gave the piano relatively long preludes, interludes, or postludes, showing that the instrument is no mere accompaniment. He typically used a single figuration throughout to convey the central emotion or idea of the poem.

Music and poetry

His song cycle *Dichterliebe* (excerpts in NAWM 133) exemplifies these precepts. He chose sixteen poems from Heinrich Heine's *Lyrical Intermezzo* and arranged them to suggest the course of a relationship as recalled after it has ended, from longing to initial fulfillment, abandonment, and resignation.

Dichterliebe

In the first song, *Im wunderschönen Monat Mai* (In the marvelous month of May; NAWM 133a), the poet remembers the blossoming of newborn love in springtime. His tentative feelings are expressed in the harmonic ambiguity

ROBERT SCHUMANN
(1810–1856)

CLARA SCHUMANN
(1819–1896)

One of the most significant marriages in the history of music was that of Robert and Clara Schumann. He was an influential music critic and outstanding composer, especially of piano music, songs, chamber music, and symphonies, and she was among the foremost pianists of her day and a distinguished composer and teacher. Their careers intertwined, so that one is difficult to describe without the other.

Robert Schumann studied piano from age seven and soon began to compose. Son of a writer and book dealer, he had an intense interest in literature, especially Romantic writers such as Friedrich Schlegel, Jean Paul, and E. T. A. Hoffmann. After university studies in law, Schumann devoted himself to becoming a concert pianist, studying in Leipzig with Friedrich Wieck, his future father-in-law. When an injury to Schumann's right hand cut short his performing career, he turned to composition and criticism, founding and editing the Leipzig *Neue Zeitschrift für Musik* (New Journal of Music) from 1834 to 1844. In his essays and reviews, he opposed empty virtuosity, promoted the study of older music, and was among the first and strongest

FIGURE 25.9 *Robert and Clara Schumann in 1850. Daguerreotype (early photograph) by Johann Anton Völlner.*

of the opening, shown in Example 25.3, and his "longing and desire" through suspensions and appoggiaturas. The music signals that his love may remain unrequited by refusing to settle into a key and by ending on a dominant seventh. The hint of unfulfillment is not explicit in Heine's poetry, but is Schumann's creation, revealing his success in making the piano as important as the voice, the music the equal partner of the words in conveying meaning and emotions, and the composer the cocreator with the poet. The lack

EXAMPLE 25.3 *Robert Schumann,* Im wunderschönen Monat Mai

advocates of Chopin, Brahms, and the instrumental music of Schubert.

In his career as a composer, Schumann often focused on one medium at a time: piano music until 1840, then songs that year, symphonies in 1841, chamber music in 1842–43, oratorio in 1843, dramatic music in 1847–48, and church music in 1852.

Meanwhile, Friedrich Wieck was training his daughter Clara to become a concert pianist. Recognized as a child prodigy from her first public appearance at age nine, she toured Europe and earned the praise of Goethe, Mendelssohn, Chopin, Liszt, and Paganini. By the age of twenty, she was one of the leading pianists in Europe and had many published works to her credit. She was renowned for playing from memory, performing music from Bach to the present, and adhering scrupulously to the composer's text rather than adding embellishments, all traits that were new in her time. She and Robert became engaged, but Wieck opposed the relationship, and it took a lawsuit to permit their wedding in 1840.

The Schumanns concertized throughout Germany, Austria-Hungary, Russia, and the Netherlands, with Robert conducting and Clara at the piano. In 1850, Robert became municipal music director in Düsseldorf, his only salaried position as a musician, but increasing signs of mental instability forced him to resign in 1853. Syphilis, contracted early in his life, and depression, which ran in his family, doubtless contributed to episodes of strange behavior and aural hallucinations that climaxed in a suicide attempt in February 1854. He was confined to an asylum near Bonn, where he died in July 1856.

Although Clara Schumann curbed her concert touring after marrying Robert and while raising eight children, she continued to perform, teach, and write music. Robert encouraged her composing, including in larger forms such as her Piano Sonata and her Piano Trio (discussed in Chapter 26), and almost all her works were published to favorable reviews. After his death, she resumed concert tours across Europe, from Russia to England, and was a sought-after teacher, becoming the primary piano instructor at the Hoch Conservatory in Frankfurt in 1878. However, she ceased composing, turning instead to promoting and editing her husband's music, including the edition of his complete works, and often advised Brahms on his compositions. She continued to concertize until 1891 and to teach until her death in 1896.

MAJOR WORKS (Robert Schumann) Over 300 piano works, including *Papillons*, *Carnaval*, *Fantasiestücke*, *Kreisleriana*, and *Album for the Young*; about 300 songs; 75 partsongs for mixed, mens', or womens' voices; 4 symphonies; piano concerto; 3 piano trios; about 15 other chamber works; various works for orchestra, solo with orchestra, or voices with orchestra

MAJOR WORKS (Clara Schumann) Piano Trio, Op. 17; piano concerto; many piano pieces; and several collections of Lieder

of resolution at the end of the first song renders it a fragment, paralleling in music the literary fragments cultivated by Schlegel and other early Romantics, who regarded the complete expression of an idea as impossible and a fragment as the nearest one can get to expressing a truth.

The next song in the cycle, *Aus meinen Tränen sprießen* (From my tears sprout; NAWM 133b) resolves some of the ambiguities of the first, asserting the key of A major. Yet the tentativeness remains, as the voice never cadences on the tonic. The cycle continues with songs suggesting mutual love and contentment. In song 7, *Ich grolle nicht* (I am not resentful; NAWM 133c), the budding relationship turns sour; the poet says though his heart is breaking he bears no resentment, while the music's pounding bass line, throbbing chords, and sharp dissonances ironically contradict his words and make clear his true feelings of anger. There follow songs expressing his sorrow and pain. But in song 12, *Am leuchtenden Sommermorgen* (On a brilliant summer morning; NAWM 133d), the story takes another turn: whispering flowers tell him not to be angry, and descending arpeggios suggest the beginnings of acceptance and resignation, reinforced in an extended piano postlude. In the last of the sixteen songs, *Die alten, bösen Lieder* (The old, angry songs; NAWM 133e), he imagines putting his love, his anger, and the songs they inspired into a huge casket and sinking it into the sea. The resigned piano postlude from song 12 returns, and the cycle concludes on the same chord as the first song with the unresolved seventh removed. These and other links between songs unify the cycle, enhancing the expressive power of each song by making it part of a larger narrative.

Clara Schumann   Clara Schumann also wrote several collections of Lieder, including one coauthored with Robert. Her approach to song parallels her husband's, with long preludes and postludes, similar figuration throughout each song, and voice and piano as equals in conveying the images and feelings of the poem. For example, in *Geheimes Flüstern* (Secret Whispers, 1853), from her last song cycle, the poem is dominated by an image of the forest whispering to the poet. A continuous sixteenth-note arpeggiation establishes a backdrop of rustling leaves and branches, helping to express the poet's reliance on the forest as a refuge and a communicator of life's secrets.

Other composers   The German Lied had numerous other exponents, including Felix Mendelssohn, Fanny Hensel, and Franz Liszt, whose piano music is discussed later in this chapter; Johannes Brahms, Hugo Wolf, Gustav Mahler, Richard Strauss, and Arnold Schoenberg, whom we will encounter in subsequent chapters; and specialists in song, such as Louise Reichardt (1779–1826), Carl Loewe (1796–1869), Josephine Lang (1815–1880), Robert Franz (1815–1892), and Peter Cornelius (1824–1874).

Influence in other nations   The songs of Schubert became known in France in the 1830s and helped to stimulate the development of the *romance* into a French counterpart of the Lied, the **mélodie**. Hector Berlioz (discussed in the next two chapters) wrote several, but the high point of the genre came in the later nineteenth century with composers such as Jules Massenet, Gabriel Fauré, and Claude Debussy (see Chapters 28, 30, and 32). The German Lied also influenced song traditions in Bohemia, Poland, Russia, Scandinavia, and elsewhere.

Parlor songs   **BRITISH AND NORTH AMERICAN SONG** A separate tradition grew in Great Britain, where songs for home performance were called *ballads* or *drawing-room ballads,* and in the United States and Canada, where they were called **parlor songs**. As the names indicate, such songs held an important place in home music-making, but they were also sung in musical theater productions and public concerts. Songs of this type are usually strophic or in **verse-refrain form**, with piano preludes and postludes based on phrases from the tune. Their expressivity lies almost entirely in the vocal melody. The piano typically supports the singer with conventional figuration, rather than dramatizing or interpreting the text as it does in many German Lieder. Like much Baroque music (see Chapter 13), this type of song tended not to be treated as unalterable; rather, it served as a vehicle for the performers, who were free to adorn the melody and reshape the accompaniment.

Henry R. Bishop   The most famous drawing-room ballad, and probably the best-known song of the nineteenth century, was *Home! Sweet Home!* (1823) by the English composer Henry R. Bishop (1786–1855). Bishop was a renowned composer of theatrical music who is remembered today for this one song, from his opera *Clari*. It has a sentimental text in verse-refrain form, regular four-measure phrases, and the characteristic melodic style of the genre: simple, mostly diatonic, stepwise, and triadic, but also tuneful, charming, and expressive, with opportunities for embellishment.

Hundreds of composers all over the English-speaking world wrote parlor songs. The most notable song composer in Canada was Scottish-born church musician James P. Clarke (1807/8–1877), the first person to earn a Bachelor of Music degree from a North American university, whose song cycle *Lays of the Maple Leaf* (1853) was the most substantial work yet published by a Canadian.

Canada

The leading American song composer of the nineteenth century was Stephen Foster (1826–1864). Growing up in Pittsburgh, he heard German, Italian, and Irish music. He taught himself to play several instruments but had no formal training in composition. After his 1848 song *Oh! Susanna* achieved great success, he signed a contract with a New York publisher and became the first American to earn a living solely as a composer. Like Bishop, he wrote for the stage as well as the parlor; his songs for minstrel shows are treated in Chapter 27. He typically wrote his own texts, which are mostly sentimental, sometimes comic.

Stephen Foster

Foster combined elements of British ballads, American minstrel songs, German Lieder, Italian opera, and Irish folk songs. Seeking—and finding—wide popularity, he made his music easy to perform and remember. His melodies are almost wholly diatonic, mostly stepwise or pentatonic (a feature of both Irish and minstrel tunes), and in four-measure phrases. The harmony and accompaniment are deliberately simple, although the figuration often changes with each phrase to demarcate the form. *Jeanie with the Light Brown Hair* (1853; NAWM 134), one of his best-known songs, illustrates all these features. In the last phrase of the first verse, shown in Example 25.4, the harmonic and melodic simplicity makes the dissonances on "Jeanie," "floating,"

EXAMPLE 25.4 *Stephen Foster,* Jeanie with the Light Brown Hair

and "summer" more piquant and the faster progression at the end of phrase more expressive. There is even a touch of opera in the brief cadenza.

Continuum of taste   Today, nineteenth-century parlor songs are thought of as popular music, but they were written for the same middle-class market as German Lieder and share many of the same characteristics. The Lieder of Schubert and the Schumanns have an appeal to connoisseurs that was recognized at the time and led to their canonization as art songs by later generations. Yet in the early nineteenth century, the chasm between popular and serious music so typical of later eras had not yet opened, and all these songs coexisted on a continuum in which popular appeal and interest to the learned did not necessarily exclude one another.

MUSIC FOR PIANO

If song was the most popular medium of the nineteenth century, piano music ran a close second. Piano works served three overlapping purposes: teaching, amateur enjoyment, and public performance. The first category includes graded studies such as Muzio Clementi's *Gradus ad Parnassum* (Steps to Parnassus, 1817–26), consisting of one hundred exercises of increasing difficulty, and the numerous **études** (studies) and method books by Beethoven's student Carl Czerny (1791–1857), many of which are still in use today. The second category includes dances, lyrical pieces modeled on song, character pieces, and sonatas. The third category features bravura pieces for virtuosos. It is typical of the age that many pieces have more than one function; for example, amateur pieces were used in teaching, Chopin and Liszt pioneered the étude worthy of concert performance, and many concert artists included sonatas and small lyrical works on their programs alongside virtuoso vehicles.

Our look at piano music will include Franz Schubert and Robert and Clara Schumann, composers whose songs we have already encountered, and Felix Mendelssohn and his sister Fanny Hensel, all representing the German tradition. But we will also look further afield, because it was in piano music that the first internationally famous composers from Poland, Hungary, and the United States made their mark: Fryderyk Chopin, Franz Liszt, and Louis Moreau Gottschalk.

SCHUBERT Among works suitable for the amateur market, Schubert wrote dozens of marches, waltzes, and other dances. His six *Moments musicaux* (Musical Moments, 1823–28) and eight Impromptus (1827) are models of the short lyrical piece that creates a distinctive mood. The Impromptu in G-flat Major, Op. 90, No. 3 (NAWM 135) features a songlike melody over a slowly moving bass and gently murmuring accompaniment, flowing from serene elegance to a more turbulent middle section in the relative minor and back to radiant beauty, like a return to contentment. Such pieces appealed to amateurs by combining attractive sonorities, interesting harmonies, emotional expressivity, and performance challenges that were rewarding to master. Of Schubert's numerous works for piano duet, several challenge the most advanced amateurs, including the sublimely beautiful and moving Fantasy in F Minor (1828).

Schubert's most important larger works for the piano are his eleven com- Wanderer Fantasy
pleted piano sonatas and the *Wanderer Fantasy* (1822), whose virtuosity and
unusual form fascinated later composers. The fantasy's four movements are
played without breaks between them, and they combine the general shape of
a four-movement sonata—fast movement in a truncated sonata form without recapitulation, slow theme and variations, scherzo and trio, and brilliant
finale—with constant variation of a rhythmic figure taken from a phrase in
his song *Der Wanderer,* which is quoted explicitly at the beginning of the second movement. Drawing the movements together through musical continuity
and common material lent the work an organic unity. The overall key scheme
reflects Schubert's interest in harmonic relationships of a third: the movements are in C, E, Ab, and C major respectively (though the second movement
begins in the relative minor, C#). Schubert was the first to use such a complete
circle of major thirds around the octave, an idea later adopted by Liszt (see p.
615) and many other composers.

In his sonatas, Schubert wrestled with contradictions between his song- *Sonatas*
inspired style and the demands of the sonata, with its multiple movements
and extended forms. His themes typically are expansive melodies that do not
lend themselves to motivic development; instead, they recur in different environments that suggest new meanings. His sonata-form movements often
use three keys in the exposition rather than two (for example, tonic for the first
theme, mediant for the second, and dominant for the closing theme). Some
slow movements are particularly songful and resemble impromptus. His last
three sonatas, in C minor, A major, and Bb major, show a strong awareness
of Beethoven, as in the stormy first movement of the C-minor sonata. But
Schubert's lyrical style is ever present. The sonata in Bb opens with a long
singing melody, which returns throughout the movement in various guises,
major and minor, complete and fragmented, as if set to new words in conflict
with those of before. Schubert's approach to sonata form (discussed further in
Chapter 26) had a notable influence on later composers.

FELIX MENDELSSOHN One of the leading German Romantic composers was
Felix Mendelssohn (1809–1847; see biography and Figure 25.10). He blended
influences from Bach, Handel, Mozart, Beethoven, and his own contemporaries in music that combined contrapuntal skill and formal clarity with
Romantic expression, beautiful melodies, and interesting, often unpredictable rhythms. A virtuoso performer on both piano and organ, Mendelssohn
emphasized fluent technique over bravura display, preferring the older style of
virtuosity typical of Mozart and Clementi to the new virtuosity of his own day,
which he viewed as a kind of acrobatics without substance. His larger piano
works include three sonatas, variations, and fantasias. His *Seven Character
Pieces,* published in 1827, helped to popularize that term and define the genre.

Mendelssohn's best-known piano works are his *Lieder ohne Worte* (Songs Songs without
without Words), forty-eight short pieces grouped in eight books. (Mendels- Words
sohn also displayed his melodic gift in more than one hundred songs *with*
words.) In the first "song" (1830), shown in Example 25.5, the similarity
to the Lied is immediately apparent. It could be written on three staves, the
bass for the pianist's left hand, the arpeggiations for the right, and the melody for a singer. Having to cover all three lines with two hands produces

FELIX MENDELSSOHN

(1809–1847)

Mendelssohn's precocious musical talent equaled or even surpassed that of Mozart. A renowned pianist, organist, and conductor, and one of the most prominent composers of his generation, Mendelssohn wrote music that combines Romantic expressivity with Classical forms and techniques.

Mendelssohn was the grandson of Moses Mendelssohn, the leading Jewish philosopher of the Enlightenment in Germany. The family also had strong connections to Romanticism in literature; the writer Friedrich Schlegel married Felix's aunt Dorothea Mendelssohn, who was a novelist and an important figure in literary circles. Although Jews were slowly gaining legal rights as a spillover from the French Revolution, Felix's banker father, Abraham, had his children baptized as Lutherans when they were still young and then converted to Christianity himself, adding Bartholdy to the family's surname. Abraham and his wife, an amateur pianist, encouraged their children's musical interests, and both Felix and his sister Fanny were trained from an early age by excellent teachers. Thus Felix and Fanny were born into a family that was at the center of Berlin's intellectual life and received every advantage that their parents' money and position could provide.

Mendelssohn began composing seriously at age eleven. At sixteen he composed his Octet for Strings, Op. 20, and at seventeen the magical Overture to Shakespeare's *A Midsummer Night's Dream*. He continued to compose at an astonishing rate throughout

FIGURE 25.10 *Felix Mendelssohn at twenty. Watercolor portrait by Warren Childe (1829).*

his life, marked by frequent travel, concert tours as pianist and conductor, and positions as music director in Düsseldorf, music director and conductor of the Gewandhaus Orchestra in Leipzig, and in various capacities in Berlin. He married Cécile Jeanrenaud in 1837, and they had five children. In 1843, he founded the Leipzig Conservatory, whose faculty included both Robert and Clara Schumann. He died at the age of thirty-eight, after a series of strokes.

MAJOR WORKS Oratorios *St. Paul* and *Elijah*; 5 symphonies, including symphony-cantata *Lobgesang*; violin concerto; 2 piano concertos; 4 overtures; incidental music to 7 plays, including *A Midsummer Night's Dream*; numerous chamber works, including 6 string quartets, 2 piano trios, 2 cello sonatas; numerous pieces for piano and for organ; choral works; and over 100 songs

interesting pianistic problems: how to bring out the melody and bass in a smooth legato while using mainly the weaker fourth and fifth fingers, and how to share the sixteenth-note figuration evenly between the two hands. The piece exploits the piano's ability to respond to the player's varying touch, louder for the melody and bass, softer for the accompaniment, even when they are played by fingers of the same hand. Beyond these technical matters, the piece presents an engaging melody and interesting accompaniment that convey a distinct mood, like a well-crafted song. The *Songs without Words* exemplify Mendelssohn's belief that music can express feelings that words cannot (see Source Reading), reflecting the idealist philosophy that underpins Romantic thought.

Mendelssohn on the Meaning of Music

Mendelssohn regarded his *Songs without Words* as complete in themselves, needing neither lyrics nor titles to convey their meaning. When an admirer wrote to ask what some of the individual pieces meant, Mendelssohn responded with this famous statement that argues for music's ability to express thoughts that cannot be expressed in words.

❧

People usually complain that music is so ambiguous, and what they are supposed to think when they hear it is so unclear, while words are understood by everyone. But for me it is exactly the opposite—and not just with entire discourses, but also with individual words; these, too, seem to be so ambiguous, so indefinite, in comparison with good music, which fills one's soul with a thousand better things than words. What the music I love expresses to me are thoughts not too *indefinite* for words, but rather too *definite*.

Thus, I find in all attempts to put these thoughts into words something correct, but also always something insufficient, something not universal. . . . If you ask me what I was thinking of, I will say: just the song as it stands there. And if I happen to have had a specific word or specific words in mind for one or another of these songs, I can never divulge them to anyone, because the same word means one thing to one person and something else to another, because only the song can say the same thing, can arouse the same feelings in one person as in another—a feeling which is not, however, expressed by the same words.

Letter to Marc-André Souchay, October 15, 1842, trans. John Michael Cooper, in SR 161 (6:14), p. 1201.

EXAMPLE 25.5 *Felix Mendelssohn*, Song without Words, *Op. 19, No. 1*

ROBERT SCHUMANN   Robert Schumann's publications up to 1840 were all for solo piano, and they include his principal music for that instrument. Aside from a few longer works, the bulk of his piano compositions are short character pieces, often grouped in colorfully named sets such as *Papillons* (Butterflies), *Carnaval*, *Fantasiestücke* (Fantasy Pieces), *Kinderszenen* (Scenes from

Childhood), and *Kreisleriana*. Attractive little pieces for children are gathered in the *Album für die Jugend* (Album for the Young).

Titles and meanings

His titles are evocative, meant to stimulate the player's and the listener's imaginations and to suggest possible meanings for the unusual effects and striking contrasts in his music. In *Carnaval* (1834–35), for instance, he conjures up a masquerade ball in carnival season through twenty short pieces in dance rhythms, each named for a dance, a costumed figure or acquaintance at the ball (including Clara), or an interaction between revelers, such as flirtation or recognition. Among the guests are characters he had used in his own literary writings to embody different facets of his personality: the impulsive revolutionary Florestan (named after the hero of Beethoven's *Fidelio*) and the visionary dreamer Eusebius (after a fourth-century pope). The movement titles evoke strongly contrasting visual and emotional images that are paralleled in the music. *Eusebius* (NAWM 136a), shown in Example 25.6a, is a dreamy fantasy with a slow, undancelike, chromatic bass under a curving melody in septuplets. By contrast, *Florestan* (NAWM 136b), in Example 25.6b, is a fast, impassioned waltz full of angular melodies, pulsating dissonances, and offbeat sforzandos. The waltz rapidly shifts ideas but always returns to the opening figure, never finding a satisfactory cadence. Each of these movements remains a fragment, like many of Schumann's songs and piano pieces: lacking a clear harmonic conclusion, each piece remains open to extension, as if it captured a momentary thought or experience while implying that there may be more to the story. The next movement, *Coquette* (NAWM 136c), is almost as strong a contrast, still a waltz but now all lilt and charm.

One could view the music of *Carnaval* as fulfilling a program suggested by the titles. But it is truer to Schumann's intent to see the titles as a way to encourage close attention to the special features of each piece and make each one more intriguing and memorable. Indeed, he claimed that he did not

EXAMPLE 25.6 *Excerpts from Robert Schumann's* Carnaval

a. Eusebius

b. Florestan

always know the title of a piece until the music was written, making clear that the title is itself part of the composition, one that can be decided at any stage from initial conception to final polish. The main function of titles for character pieces was not to specify meanings but to indicate possible avenues for exploration, inviting the player and listener to enter the composer's musical world and become in one sense cocreators of that world by devising their own narratives to explain how the music justifies the title and vice versa. Is it any wonder that such music and such titles were so popular?

Another window into meaning is Schumann's interest in musical ciphers, representing names through notes. In *Carnaval,* many of the movements feature melodies based on motives that spell Asch, the home town of Schumann's then-fiancée Ernestine von Fricken: A–E♭–C–B♮ (in German note names, A–Es–C–H) and A♭–C–B♮ (As–C–H). The first of these is prominent in *Florestan* and *Coquette* and is more subtly present in *Eusebius,* as shown in Example 25.6. While inviting extramusical interpretation, these motives also give unity to the entire work, an organic connection between movements that underlies their surface diversity.

Ciphers and motives, unity and diversity

CLARA SCHUMANN AND FANNY HENSEL The contrasting careers of Clara Schumann and Fanny Mendelssohn Hensel (1805–1847), who was Felix Mendelssohn's sister, illustrate the prospects for and limitations on women composers in the early nineteenth century (see Music in Context: Women and the Music Profession, pp. 606–7). Both women were highly skilled pianist-composers, yet Schumann played public concerts and published much of her music, while Hensel, shown in Figure 25.11, confined her music-making almost entirely to the domestic sphere.

Clara Schumann won fame as a pianist at a young age and was at first better known than her husband, Robert. In an era when the score was often only a starting point for a performer's embellishment, she played what was written, thus focusing attention on the composer rather than the performer. In her day, this idea was pathbreaking. Her performances also provided opportunities for improvisation, a staple of nineteenth-century concerts, and for showcasing her own music and that of her husband. Her piano compositions include polonaises, waltzes, variations, preludes and fugues, character pieces, and a Sonata in G Minor (1841–42).

Clara Schumann

Fanny Mendelssohn had equally thorough training, but for the most part performed and composed in private and semiprivate settings. She studied piano from a young age, and theory and composition in her teens. She was as talented and almost as precocious musically as her brother Felix, who solicited her advice on his compositions and considered her his most reliable and helpful critic. Yet a musical career was considered inappropriate for a woman of her wealth and class. Both Felix and their father Abraham Mendelssohn opposed her performing in public or publishing her music, although Felix did publish some of her songs under his

FIGURE 25.11 *Fanny Hensel in an 1842 portrait by Moritz Daniel Oppenheim.*

Women and the Music Profession

In the nineteenth century, opportunities expanded for women as professional musicians, within limits. Many women were professional singers, and several made careers as pianists. Some were recognized as performers on other instruments, and a few composed works in large "public" genres such as symphony and opera, previously considered the exclusive preserve of male composers. Yet women were excluded from most orchestras, and men continued to dominate the field of composition. For every Clara Schumann who enjoyed the support of her father and husband in her professional career, there were scores of women who faced daunting and often insuperable obstacles.

Even Fanny Hensel, despite having virtually the same education as her brother Felix Mendelssohn, was constrained by the social mores of the time to confine her musical activities within the home, as host of an important salon. Her first published pieces were songs that appeared under Felix's name, and she waited until she was forty (the year before her death) to accept an offer from a Berlin publisher to publish her music in her own right. This minimized her impact outside her circle and limited her compositions mostly to genres appropriate for home music-making, along with a few chamber works and cantatas. Yet these circumstances, combined with the high quality of her music, have made her a focus of recent efforts to rediscover the music women composed in the face of the constraints they encountered.

The rigorous childhood training that Clara Schumann and Fanny Hensel received was exceptional. Because women were expected to be amateur musicians rather than professionals, most found it difficult or impossible to obtain a musical education comparable to that available to men. The Leipzig Conservatory, which Mendelssohn founded in 1843 (and where both Clara and Robert Schumann were on the faculty), restricted women to a two-year course in music theory "especially organized for their requirements." The Paris Conservatoire barred its doors to women composers altogether until the 1870s; singer-composer Pauline Viardot (1821–1910) studied privately with its renowned professor of counterpoint and fugue, Antoine Reicha. In most music schools, male students outnumbered women by lopsided margins. The Hoch Conservatory in Frankfurt, where Clara Schumann taught in the last years of her life, was unusual in enrolling more than twice as many women as men.

name as a way of getting them into print; when he asked Queen Victoria which of his songs she liked best, she chose *Italien,* and he had to admit that it was by his sister.

After marrying Prussian court painter Wilhelm Hensel, Fanny led a salon, a regular gathering of friends and invited guests, where she played piano, conducted choral and orchestral works, and presented her compositions. The salon met in their home in a large music room that could accommodate up to two hundred people, ranging from bankers, merchants, and politicians to writers, artists, and musicians such as Liszt and Clara Schumann. She wrote more than four hundred works, mostly in the small genres appropriate for home music-making, including at least 250 songs and 125 piano pieces. Her husband encouraged her to publish her music, but she died unexpectedly of a stroke less than a year after the publication in 1846 of her Op. 1, six songs. Only in the past fifty years or so has she become more than "Mendelssohn's sister," as scholars have discovered a trove of her works and realized the importance of her salons.

Marriage or child-rearing often interrupted even the most promising careers. The Schumanns' marriage was more equal than most, though Clara deferred to Robert by refraining from practicing while he was composing. When work and family came into conflict, it was almost always the woman who stayed home. Rare was the husband who subordinated his own career to his wife's, as Pauline Viardot's did; one of Europe's reigning opera divas, she probably earned considerably more than Louis Viardot did as director of the Théâtre Italien.

Few women, no matter how talented or ambitious, were willing to forgo the status and security of marriage for the sake of a public career. The pianist-composer Marie Pleyel (1811–1875) may have acted capriciously in jilting the up-and-coming Hector Berlioz at age twenty to marry the wealthy piano manufacturer Camille Pleyel (see Chapter 26), but it took both pluck and self-confidence to leave Pleyel four years later and strike out on her own. The Polish pianist-composer Maria Szymanowska (1789–1831) likewise launched a highly successful international career after separating from her husband.

For women who did compose, their horizons were often limited to genres associated with domestic music-making, such as songs and piano pieces. Only a few women attempted to compose symphonies, operas, and other large-scale works meant to be performed in public concert halls and theaters, which required the cooperation of many professionals to perform. The three symphonies that Louise Farrenc (1804–1875) wrote in the 1840s were played in public, but only her piano and chamber music made it into print. Farrenc had a privileged position as professor of piano at the Paris Conservatoire—the only woman to hold such an exalted post in the nineteenth century—and was the wife of music publisher Aristide Farrenc. Many of her contemporaries lacked the professional and political connections needed to secure performances and publication of their works. Others lowered their sights, unable or unwilling to compete in a man's world. Louise Bertin (1805–1877) virtually retired from composing after the failure of her fourth opera, *Esmerelda*, at the Paris Opéra in 1836.

Despite these difficulties, more women were active as professional musicians and more music by women was performed and published in the nineteenth century than in any previous era. The last fifty years have seen increasing attempts by scholars and performers to discover, edit, perform, and record their works and to gain a better sense of the roles women played as composers, performers, and patrons of music.

Hensel's masterpiece for piano is *Das Jahr* (The Year, 1841), a cycle of character pieces on the twelve months from January through December plus a postlude. The piece embodies the contradictions of Hensel's career. It is a grand conception, taking over fifty minutes to perform, featuring cyclic links between movements, and incorporating chorales relevant to the seasons: an Easter chorale in *March*, a Christmas chorale in *December* (NAWM 137), and a New Year's chorale in the postlude. The large scale and ambitious scope of the cycle elevate the genre of the character piece, associated with domestic music-making, to a more universal and public level. The first version of the piece included virtuosic passages that only players of Hensel's ability could master, but she scaled back the difficulty, rewriting the end of *December* and all of *June* to make the cycle playable for a wider range of amateurs. These changes suggest that she intended to publish it. But the final copy, neatly written out in an elegant hand, looks like a one-of-a-kind manuscript: each month is on a different color of paper and begins with a hand-drawn illustration by her husband Wilhelm Hensel. Was it intended as a private treasure

Das Jahr

FRYDERYK CHOPIN

(1810–1849)

Chopin was the Romantic composer most closely identified with the piano. His solo piano music won him enormous popularity and has been central to the repertoire ever since.

He was born near Warsaw to a French father and a Polish mother in a section of Poland that was then under Russian domination. His talent as pianist, improviser, and composer showed early, and at age seven he published his first piece and played his first public concert, as a concerto soloist. After studies at the Warsaw Conservatory, he performed in Vienna and toured Germany and Italy. His pieces with a strong Polish character were especially successful, encouraging him to write more. The national flavor of his music and its brilliant virtuosity won him a strong following in Poland. Seeking an international reputation, he returned to Vienna and to Germany in 1830. When he heard of the failed Polish revolt against Russia that November, he continued on to Paris, where he settled in 1831, never to see Poland again.

Chopin soon met the leading musicians in Paris, including Rossini, Meyerbeer, Berlioz, and Liszt, and entered the highest social circles. He became the most fashionable piano teacher for wealthy students. Their fees meant he could give up public performance and play only at private concerts and at salons hosted by the leading women of the city. In turn, the rarity of his appearances increased his cachet and allowed him

FIGURE 25.12 *Portrait of Fryderyk Chopin by Eugène Delacroix (1838).*

to charge very high fees for lessons. He also earned considerable sums from publications. He never married, but had a tempestuous nine-year affair with the novelist Aurore Dudevant, known by her pseudonym George Sand. The 1848 revolutions in Paris disrupted his teaching and forced a grueling tour of England and Scotland. By then, he was ravaged by tuberculosis, and he died in Paris in 1849.

MAJOR WORKS 2 piano concertos, 3 piano sonatas, 4 ballades, 4 scherzos, 21 nocturnes, 27 études, 27 preludes, 57 mazurkas, 17 waltzes, 15 polonaises, 4 chamber works with piano, 20 songs

for the two of them, or as an exemplar from which a publication could be engraved or lithographed, complete with illustrations? We may never know, but the revival of the piece since the 1980s has deepened our experience of Fanny Hensel as a composer and our awareness of the potentially rich legacy of nineteenth-century music we have yet to discover.

FRYDERYK CHOPIN Fryderyk Chopin (1810–1849) composed almost exclusively for piano (see biography and Figure 25.12). His entire output comprises about two hundred solo piano pieces, six works for piano and orchestra composed for his concert appearances as a young virtuoso, some twenty songs, and four chamber works. He is revered for idiomatic writing that opened new possibilities for the piano and appealed to amateurs and connoisseurs alike.

The genres he cultivated range from the étude and prelude, associated with teaching, and types suitable for amateurs, such as dances and nocturnes, to longer and more challenging works for his own performances and for other advanced players, including ballades, scherzos, and sonatas.

Chopin wrote twenty-seven études in all—twelve each in Opps. 10 (1829–32) and 25 (1832–37) and three without opus number. Because études are intended to develop technique, each one as a rule addresses a specific skill and develops a single figure. Among the problems addressed in Op. 25 are parallel diatonic and chromatic thirds (No. 6) and parallel sixths (No. 8) in the right hand, chromatic octaves in both hands (No. 10), and sixteenth-note filigree in the right hand above a vigorous march in the left (No. 11). Chopin's études were among the first with significant artistic content and as such were often played in concert, inaugurating the genre of the **concert étude**. *Études*

Chopin's twenty-four preludes of Op. 28 (1836–39), like the preludes in Bach's *Well-Tempered Clavier,* cover all the major and minor keys. They are brief mood pictures, less challenging than his études but like them in posing specific performance problems. They also illustrate the astounding inventiveness of his figuration. As shown in Example 25.7, No. 1 wraps arpeggiated chords, each sustained by the sustaining pedal, around a tenor-range melody echoed an octave above; No. 2 alternates wide two-note intervals in the left *Preludes*

EXAMPLE 25.7 *Fryderyk Chopin, Preludes, Op. 28*

a. No. 1 in C Major

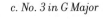

b. No. 2 in A Minor   *c. No. 3 in G Major*

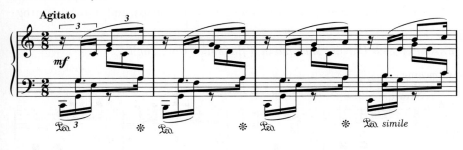

d. No. 4 in E Minor

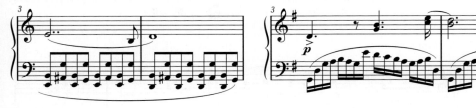

hand; No. 3 has a sweeping sixteenth-note pattern; and No. 4 features pulsating chords that sink chromatically through nonfunctional sonorities on their way to more stable chords. Such rich chromatic harmonies influenced many later composers, as did the varied textures of Chopin's piano writing.

Dances   Chopin's **waltzes**, **mazurkas**, and **polonaises** are all stylized dances, often composed for his students and dedicated to them when published. All are extremely idiomatic for piano in their figuration and fingerings. The waltzes and mazurkas, although only moderately difficult, show off an amateur's ability through brilliant passagework and expression of a mood. Part of Chopin's genius was finding ways to write music that even players of limited skill could perform with satisfaction and feelings of accomplishment.

His waltzes evoke the ballrooms of Vienna, but his mazurkas and polonaises are suffused with the spirit of Poland. The polonaise is a courtly, aristocratic dance in $\frac{3}{4}$ meter often marked by a rhythmic figure of an eighth and two sixteenths on the first beat. Chopin's go beyond the stylized polonaise of Bach's time to assert a vigorous, at times militaristic, national identity.

The mazurka was a Polish folk dance that by Chopin's time had become an urban ballroom dance popular among high society in Paris as well as in Poland. The Mazurka in B-flat Major, Op. 7, No. 1 (1831; NAWM 138), shown in Example 25.8, illustrates the genre: $\frac{3}{4}$ meter with frequent accents on the second or third beat and often a dotted figure on the first beat; simple accompaniment; and four-measure phrases combined in periods that alternate, here in ||:A:||:BA:||:CA:|| form. The melody, which is instrumental rather than vocal in style, displays elements meant to suggest the exoticism of Polish folk music, including trills, grace notes, large leaps, and slurs beginning

EXAMPLE 25.8 *Chopin, Mazurka in B-flat Major, Op. 7, No. 1*

a. Opening

b. Third section

on the last sixteenth of a beat to imitate folk bowing. When played properly, the tempo is uneven, passing quickly through the opening ascent and then allowing extra time for the sforzando, trills, and grace notes in order to suggest the longer time required for dancers to execute a turn or a lift than to take quick steps. In the third section, shown in Example 25.8b, Chopin creates an exotic sound with drone fifths, unusual harmonies, and augmented seconds while keeping the sustaining pedal on to add an unusual blur. The marking **rubato** indicates a slight anticipation or delay of the right-hand melody while the accompaniment continues in strict time, or a departure from the regular pulse in both hands at once. Like the sustaining pedal, rubato can be used in places where it is not marked, and nineteenth-century performers used both techniques freely as expressive devices.

A **nocturne** (French for "night-piece") is a short mood piece evoking night, usually with a beautiful, embellished melody above a sonorous accompaniment. Fascination with night is linked to other aspects of Romanticism, such as interest in dreams, emotions, and the irrational. Chopin's initial conception of the nocturne owed much to the nocturnes by Irish pianist-composer John Field (1782–1837), who invented the genre, and Polish pianist-composer Maria Szymanowska (1789–1831), both of whom toured widely and were active in St. Petersburg, the capital of Russia. All three composers also drew inspiration from the vocal nocturne for two or more voices with piano or harp accompaniment, so that the nocturne for piano was essentially a song without words. The style of Chopin's nocturnes draws on the *bel canto* vocal style of Bellini's opera arias (see Chapter 27 and NAWM 150). The Nocturne in D-flat Major, Op. 27, No. 2 (1835; NAWM 139), has an angular melody and a notably expansive accompaniment of arpeggiating chords left sounding by the sustaining pedal. It also includes virtuoso elements, such as parallel thirds and sixths (a texture characteristic of the vocal nocturne) in the right hand; wide leaps; and triplets, quintuplets, septuplets, and cadenza-like passagework in the right hand against steady sixteenths in the left. *Nocturnes*

Chopin's ballades and scherzos are longer and more demanding than his other one-movement piano works. Chopin was one of the first (along with Clara Schumann) to use the name **ballade** for an instrumental piece. His ballades capture the charm and fire of Polish narrative ballads, combining these qualities with constantly fresh turns in harmony and form. His scherzos are not joking or playful, as the name of the genre implies, but serious and passionate. Yet they are tricky and quirky, which the term also implies, particularly in their rhythm and thematic material. *Ballades and scherzos*

Chopin's three piano sonatas all have four movements: sonata form, minuet or scherzo, slow movement, and finale. Sonata No. 2 in B-flat Minor, Op. 35, includes as its third movement the funeral march that has become Chopin's most famous piece; orchestrated, the march was played at Chopin's funeral and has been heard by millions since. *Sonatas*

The distinctive characteristics of Chopin's music stem from his life and career: Polish nationalism, the concentration on piano music, virtuosity for public performance blended with elegant lyricism for the parlor, and originality in melody, harmony, and pianism encouraged equally by the values of the salon and by competition in the marketplace. His works were shaped by the demand for amateur compositions yet spoke to connoisseurs as well, *Chopin's achievement* giving his music broad and enduring appeal. His pieces are as gratifying to play as they are to hear. His greatest achievement was to liberate the piano from imitations of choral or ensemble textures and make it sound the way only a piano could sound, producing a whole new repertory of idiomatic sounds and figurations.

FRANZ LISZT Franz Liszt (1811–1886) was the most electrifying piano virtuoso of his era and one of its most important composers (see biography and Figure 25.13). Already a child prodigy in Hungary and Vienna, Liszt came with his family to Paris in 1823 at age twelve. There piano manufacturer Sébastien Erard gave him a seven-octave grand piano with the new double-escapement action that allowed quick repetition, opening possibilities for virtuosity that Liszt was among the first to exploit.

As a young man, Liszt frequented the salons that formed the core of Parisian intellectual and artistic life. There he met many of the most notable writers, painters, and musicians of the day. He and Countess Marie d'Agoult became lovers and lived together in Switzerland and Italy from 1835 to 1839. He recorded impressions of both countries in piano pieces collected in *Album d'un voyageur* (Album of a Traveler, 1837–38) and *Années de pèlerinage* (Years of Pilgrimage, Books 1 and 2 composed 1838–61, Book 3, 1877–82). In many of these pieces Liszt responded to a poem (three on sonnets of Petrarch, one on Dante) or work of art (a Raphael painting, a Michelangelo sculpture).

Solo recitals Between 1839 and 1847 Liszt gave over one thousand solo concerts, touring Europe from Portugal and Ireland in the west to Turkey, Romania, and Russia in the east. He was the first pianist to give solo concerts in large halls, for which he pioneered the term ***recital***, still used today. He was also the first to play a range of music from Bach to his contemporaries and to play entirely from memory, two innovations that are now long-standing traditions. His reception at times rivaled the hysteria afforded rock superstars of the twentieth century, but he insisted on quiet while he played. In 1848, Liszt ceased touring and concentrated on composition, essentially beginning a second career. His music after 1848 is described in Chapter 29.

Influences Liszt's music reflects many diverse influences. Although he did not speak Hungarian, he grew up in Hungary and wrote numerous works based on or inspired by Hungarian or Romani (Gypsy) melodies, including nineteen *Hungarian Rhapsodies* for piano. His piano style drew on the playing styles of Viennese and Parisian virtuosos, and then added his own stunning effects. After Chopin moved to Paris in 1831, Liszt adopted Chopin's melodic lyricism, rubato, rhythmic license, and harmonic innovations.

Paganini and virtuosity Perhaps Liszt's most important influence was not a pianist but the great Italian violinist Nicolò Paganini (1782–1840), one of the most hypnotic artists of the era, who raised both the technique and the mystique of the virtuoso to unprecedented heights. Stimulated by Paganini's stunning technical prowess, Liszt resolved to accomplish similar miracles with the piano. He pushed the instrument's technique to its limits both in his own playing and in his compositions.

Un sospiro *Un sospiro* (A Sigh; NAWM 140), the third of his *Three Concert Études* (1845–49), illustrates Liszt's virtuosic technique. It addresses the technical problem of how to project a slower-moving melody outside or within rapid

FRANZ LISZT

(1811–1886)

Liszt had an enormous impact on music, in a variety of roles. As the foremost piano virtuoso of his time, Liszt devised new playing techniques and textures for piano music. As a composer, he introduced innovations in form and harmony and invented the symphonic poem. As a conductor, he championed Bach, Beethoven, and other composers from the past, alongside Berlioz, Wagner, and other contemporaries. As a teacher, he invented the master class, in which students play for each other as well as for the teacher, and other approaches that remain standard practice today.

Liszt was born in a German-speaking region of western Hungary, now in Austria. His father, an official for Prince Nikolaus Esterházy and an amateur musician, taught him piano from the age of six, then moved the family to Vienna so the boy could study piano further with Carl Czerny and theory and counterpoint with Antonio Salieri. At the age of eleven Liszt played several public concerts, inaugurating a dazzling career as a virtuoso. The next year the family moved to Paris, where Liszt studied theory and composition with private teachers.

After his father's death in 1827, Liszt earned a regular income teaching piano to children of the well-to-do. For the next two decades he pursued a brilliant career as a concert virtuoso. He left the concert stage in 1848 and devoted the rest of his career to composing, conducting, and teaching. From 1848 to 1861, he was court music director at Weimar, where he encouraged new music by conducting performances of many important works, among them the premiere of Wagner's *Lohengrin* in 1850. Several well-publicized love affairs with women of elevated social status—and honors showered upon him all over Europe—added glamour to his fame as pianist, conductor, and composer. From 1861 until about 1870, Liszt resided chiefly in Rome, where, his love affairs notwithstanding, he took minor orders in the Catholic Church. The remainder of his life was divided between Rome, Weimar, and Budapest.

MAJOR WORKS *Album d'un voyageur, Années de pèlerinage,* 19 *Hungarian Rhapsodies, Funerailles,* Sonata in B Minor, and hundreds of other piano pieces; *Mazeppa, Les préludes,* and 10 other symphonic poems; *Faust Symphony;* chamber music, choral music, and songs

FIGURE 25.13 *Liszt piano recital in Berlin, as depicted in an 1842 book on the city. The adulation of the audience is supported by many contemporary accounts, but two aspects of the picture are misleading: Liszt normally played from memory rather than from the score, and he insisted the audience be quiet while he performed.*

broken-chord figurations. At the beginning, shown in Example 25.9a, the pedal sustains harmonies while the two hands brave treacherous leaps over each other to pick out a pentatonic tune. The notation makes it look as though the pianist requires three hands, but the bottom staff is taken by the left hand, the middle by the right, and the top by whichever hand is free at the time, indicating left hand by a downward stem and right by an upward stem. Later on, the melody appears in the right hand in the middle of the texture, while the left arpeggiates below and above it. At the climax, in Example 25.9b, difficult

EXAMPLE 25.9 *Franz Liszt,* Un sospiro

a. Melody at opening

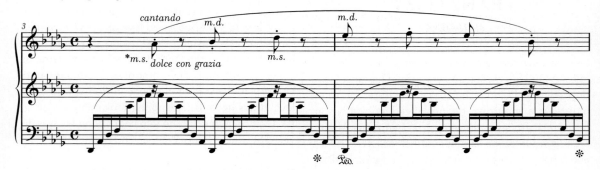

*Stems downward, left hand (*m.s.* = mano sinistra); stems upward, right hand (*m.d.* = mano destra).

b. Climax and cadenza

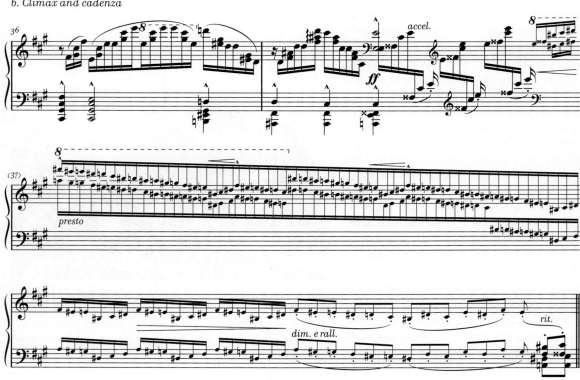

leaps and stretches show the size of Liszt's hands (he could easily span a tenth) and lead to a chromatic cadenza in parallel sixths.

Harmony   The last example also illustrates Liszt's use of chromatic harmony. Here a diminished seventh chord on the fourth beat of measure 36 moves to an augmented triad created by a suspension (D–F♯–A♯), then the following major triad moves chromatically to an augmented sixth chord (A–C♯–E–F𝄪). Chromatic movement from one chord to the next is a characteristic we already noticed in Chopin (see Example 25.7d), and it became a common element in the music of Liszt and later composers. The ensuing chromatic cadenza repeatedly decorates C♯, E, and G (F×) with their neighbor notes B♯, D♯, F♯, and A, and at the end of the cadenza those neighbor notes sound together as a diminished seventh that resolves to the augmented sixth, showing that the entire cadenza served to prolong the latter chord. Such elaborate harmonic and melodic decoration of a dissonant sonority became a typical feature in late Romantic harmony and ultimately led Liszt to experiments that virtually abandon traditional tonality by prolonging dissonant sonorities without resolving to consonance.

Liszt's harmony is also marked by his interest in third relationships, equal divisions of the octave, and nondiatonic scales. *Un sospiro* does not move from the tonic to the dominant and back, as most tonal pieces do, but instead modulates around a circle of major thirds, D♭–F–A–D♭, dividing the octave into three equal parts, a harmonic technique pioneered by Schubert in his *Wanderer Fantasy* and other works (see p. 601). Liszt often used augmented triads and diminished seventh chords, which divide the octave equally, and scales based on them, such as the whole-tone and octatonic scales (discussed in Chapter 28).

Liszt's technical innovations served both to display his skill and to allow him a vast range of expression and pictorial effects. The breadth of his poetic imagination is displayed in numerous character pieces and Lieder, often inspired by the same poetic texts. His Sonata in B Minor (1853), modeled on Schubert's *Wanderer Fantasy*, is a masterpiece of formal innovation, using four main themes in one extended sonata-form movement subdivided into three large sections analogous to the movements of a Classic-era sonata. Such a combination of single-movement and multimovement structures is known as **double-function form**. The themes are transformed and combined in a free rhapsodic order, but one that is perfectly suited to the thematic material.

Character pieces and sonata

Much of Liszt's piano music consists of arrangements, of two types. His *operatic paraphrases* (some of which he called *reminiscences*) are free fantasies on excerpts from popular operas by Mozart, Bellini, Donizetti, and Verdi, often retelling the story by varying and combining the borrowed themes. His **transcriptions** of Schubert songs, Berlioz and Beethoven symphonies, Bach organ fugues, and excerpts from Wagner operas are re-creations that brought important works to audiences who were either unacquainted with the originals or pleased to hear a familiar work transformed into a brilliant virtuoso vehicle.

Paraphrases and transcriptions

Liszt had a profound influence on performers and composers. As a piano virtuoso, he established most of the traditions of the modern recital, developed new playing techniques, and provided a model for others to emulate. His contributions as a composer were equally important, opening new possibilities in harmony and form while offering deeply felt music on subjects as varied as looking at an artwork or remembering an opera. Liszt may have embodied more of the characteristics—and contradictions—of the Romantic era than any other musician.

Liszt's reputation

LOUIS MOREAU GOTTSCHALK Another pianist and composer celebrated for his audacity and showmanship was the globe-trotting American Louis Moreau Gottschalk (1829–1869), the first American composer with an international reputation. Born in New Orleans, he showed talent at a young age and studied piano and organ from the age of five. He went to Paris in 1841 for more training, and toured France, Switzerland, and Spain in 1845–52. Chopin heard him in 1845 and predicted he would become "the king of pianists." The publication of pieces based on melodies and rhythms from his mother's Caribbean heritage made Gottschalk's reputation. His incorporation of American sounds and rhythms into piano works for the European market parallels Chopin's mazurkas and Liszt's Hungarian rhapsodies, bringing elements from the peripheries of western European culture into the mainstream of piano music for virtuosos, salons, and home music-making. Through Gottschalk's music, composers from Bizet, Offenbach, and Borodin to Debussy and Ravel came to know—and at times to imitate—the dance rhythms and syncopations of the New World. Gottschalk gave his New York debut in 1853 to wildly enthusiastic reviews, playing mostly his own compositions, and spent the rest of his life touring the United States, the Caribbean islands, and South America.

Souvenir de Porto Rico   During a Caribbean tour in 1857–58, Gottschalk wrote *Souvenir de Porto Rico* (NAWM 141), which uses a theme derived from a Puerto Rican song and features Afro-Caribbean rhythms such as the *habanera*, *tresillo*, and *cinquillo*. The piece starts soft and simple, builds to a climax full of extraordinary syncopations, and fades away, depicting a band of musicians gradually approaching, passing by, and marching off into the distance. It is a perfect example of nineteenth-century piano music designed to appeal to the middle-class audience, combining an extramusical program, an exotic subject, novel melodic and rhythmic material, virtuosic showmanship, and rewards for the amateur performer.

THE ROMANTIC LEGACY

Home music-making, the engine that drove composers to produce a constant stream of songs and piano pieces, declined in the late nineteenth and early twentieth centuries, victim of new recreations for women like bicycling and of new technologies like radio and the phonograph. Fewer young people today study piano, and family gatherings to make music have now all but died out, so that Lieder, parlor songs, and piano pieces rarely serve their original function. Some pieces disappeared with that change, others were established as art music, and a few became old favorites of popular music.

The Lieder of Schubert and Robert Schumann formed the core of the art song repertoire, paralleling the Bach fugues, Handel oratorios, Haydn string quartets, and Beethoven symphonies as works that define a genre and serve as models for later composers. Foster's songs played a similar role for American parlor and popular song. Songs of all three composers have been sung in an unbroken tradition from their time to ours, preserving the genres they represented and opening the door for modern performers and listeners to explore music by their less-well-known contemporaries.

By the 1820s, some works were already regarded as classics of piano music, including Bach's *Well-Tempered Clavier* (now played on piano rather than harpsichord) and the sonatas of Mozart and Beethoven. The Romantic generation created piano music in new genres and idioms that contrasted with earlier classics, but some of it has proven equally enduring, including Schubert's impromptus and other short lyric pieces; Mendelssohn's *Songs without Words*;

Robert Schumann's character pieces; Chopin's études, preludes, dances, nocturnes, and ballades; and Liszt's études and character pieces. Together these works redefined piano music and became central to the repertoire of permanent classics for the piano. This generation still valued the sonata and fugue as prestige genres in which composers could demonstrate their mastery of a historically important form, and the sonatas of Schubert, Chopin, and Liszt have claimed a prominent place in the repertoire. Of course, the music of the composers discussed here comprises only a small part of the piano music written for the home market or for virtuoso display during the nineteenth century. Pieces by dozens of others are also played and heard today. Yet so much was written for piano that most of it long ago fell out of fashion, as performers, critics, and historians focused on composers and works they considered to be the greatest and dismissed pieces they judged merely entertaining.

Music by women was treated differently in a century that expected musical genius only from men and regarded music as no more than a pleasing adornment for women. As these attitudes were challenged in the last decades of the twentieth century, scholars sought to unearth music by women, especially music that met the highest standards. Clara Schumann and Fanny Hensel have emerged as key figures because of their family ties to composers central to the tradition; their compositions and descriptions of their playing make clear they would have been great musicians even if Robert Schumann and Felix Mendelssohn had never been born, and their stories function almost as parables about how social attitudes nurture and hinder talent. They are far from the only women composers of interest from the period; Louise Reichardt, Josephine Lang, Pauline Viardot, Marie Pleyel, Maria Szymanowska, Louise Farrenc, and Louise Bertin have been mentioned, and others include Emilie Zumsteeg (1796–1857), Johanna Kinkel (1810–1858), and Augusta Browne (1820–1882). Current research is bringing to light music by many other talented women composers of the nineteenth century.

The melody-centered style of song and piano music affected every other genre of the nineteenth century. Never before or since were symphonies, chamber works, and choral music so full of songlike melodies. Opera composers used them too, as witnessed by, for example, Senta's ballad in Wagner's *Der fliegende Holländer* (The Flying Dutchman).

The Romantic view of music has been even more influential. We no longer view composers as artisans writing music to suit their patrons, as most earlier composers saw themselves, but regard them as artists expressing their own ideas and feelings. Originality, fostered by competition in the marketplace and inscribed by Romantic views of individual genius, became a requirement for all later composers, encouraging an ever more rapid pace of change in musical style for the next two centuries, in popular and art music alike. Romantic concepts of absolute music and of musical works as autonomous and organic remained influential throughout the twentieth century, underlying many works and innovations that were far from Romantic in style. Indeed, most of our attitudes about music, especially those we barely question, are those of the Romantic era.

Further Reading is available at digital.wwnorton.com/hwm10

ROMANTICISM IN CLASSICAL FORMS: CHORAL, CHAMBER, AND ORCHESTRAL MUSIC

Alongside the fashion for home music-making explored in the previous chapter, the nineteenth century saw phenomenal growth in public concerts. Amateur choral societies and orchestras carried amateur performance into the public sphere, and new professional orchestras, touring virtuosos, concert societies, and entrepreneurs helped to create a vibrant concert life based on ticket sales to all classes of society. Chamber music, once primarily intended for the enjoyment of the players themselves, was now often performed as concert music.

These changes were accompanied by the gradual emergence of musical classics, pieces that continued to be performed regularly long after the composer's death. From the 1780s through the 1870s, classical repertoires formed first in choral music, starting with the oratorios of Handel and Haydn, and then in chamber and orchestral music, beginning with string quartets and symphonies of Beethoven, Haydn, and Mozart. Instead of falling out of fashion after a generation, as music had always done, some pieces attained a permanent place in musical life, akin to the classics of literature or art. Living composers in these genres could aspire to similar permanence for their own music.

In part because older music for chorus, chamber ensemble, and orchestra was still being performed, nineteenth-century composers mixed retrospective genres and forms with new musical styles. They held on to their Romantic ideals—expressing feelings sincerely and projecting a distinctive personality. But composing in genres with long traditions stretching back generations, such as oratorio, string quartet, and symphony, and in traditional forms such as sonata form and fugue, prompted a more acute sense of historical awareness than is evident in the newer genres of song and piano music discussed in the previous chapter. Composers sought to balance tradition and individuality, some leaning toward innovation, others toward emulating the past. The result is a rich tension in much of this music between Romantic content and Classical genres and forms.

CHORAL MUSIC

Most nineteenth-century choral music was composed with amateur rather than professional singers in mind. Church choirs were increasingly made up of amateurs, and most choruses outside of church were organized primarily for the enjoyment of the singers themselves. In part because of their amateur status, choruses were less prestigious than orchestras and opera houses, and much of the music written for them has been neglected. The choral repertory was one of the first to be dominated by music of the past, and as a result nineteenth-century choral music is often retrospective in genre and format, though not necessarily in style.

There were three main types of choral music in the nineteenth century: *Types of choral music*

- short choral works on secular texts, usually homophonic with the melody in the upper voice, with or without accompaniment by a piano or organ;
- oratorios and similar works for large chorus and orchestra, often with one or more solo vocalists, on dramatic, narrative, or sacred texts but intended for concert rather than stage performance;
- liturgical works, anthems, hymns, and other sacred pieces written for church choirs, congregations, or home performance.

Choral music was a particularly lucrative field for publishers, since each choir member needed a separate copy of the music for every piece, and most works were also suitable for home music-making with one or two singers on each vocal part. Publishers recognized the potential of the market and issued great quantities of music for amateur and church choirs at low prices.

AMATEUR CHOIRS Amateur choruses were typically organized as ***choral societies***, with members paying dues to purchase music, pay the conductor, and meet other expenses. One of the first, the Berlin Singakademie, began as a singing class for wealthy women. In 1791 men were accepted as well, and the group gave its first concert. By 1800, under the direction of Carl Friedrich Zelter (1758–1832, who later was Felix and Fanny Mendelssohn's teacher), the chorus had quintupled in size to almost 150 members. Zelter added an orchestra to allow the group to sing oratorios, and by his death in 1832 the chorus had over 350 singers.   *Choral societies*

Similar organizations sprang up in Leipzig, Dresden, Zurich, Liverpool, Manchester, Boston, and other cities all over Germany, Switzerland, England, and the United States. All-male choruses, often composed of working-class men, were especially popular in Germany and American cities with large German populations. The choral movement in France was inspired by Guillaume Wilhem (1781–1842), who devised a system for teaching sight-singing in schools; the Parisian chorus he founded in 1833 spawned over 1,700 choral societies called *orphéons,* which became a central institution for middle-class music-making throughout France. Choral singing was seen as a way to occupy leisure time, develop a sense of unity, elevate musical tastes, and encourage spiritual and ethical values (see Source Reading). In addition, choral societies were often self-governing with elected managing boards, providing practice in democratic processes—one reason they were forbidden in autocratic Austria until later in the century.

The Value of Amateur Choirs

The choral society movement was encouraged not only by a love of music but by the belief that the right kind of music promoted ethical values, a view that goes back to Plato. Richard Wagner commented that for the English "an evening spent listening to an oratorio may be regarded as a sort of service and is almost as good as going to church." George Hogarth, secretary of the London Philharmonic Society, praised choral singing as an instrument of moral reform.

❀

The cultivation of a taste for music furnishes to the rich a refined and intellectual pursuit, which excludes the indulgence of frivolous and vicious amusements, and to the poor, a *laborem dulce lenimen* [sweet solace of labor], a relaxation from toil, more attractive than the haunts of intemperance. . . . In the densely populated districts of Yorkshire, Lancashire, and Derbyshire, music is cultivated among the working classes to an extent unparalleled in any other part of the kingdom.

Every town has its choral society, supported by the amateurs of the place and its neighbourhood, where the works of Handel, and the more modern masters, are performed with precision and effect, by a vocal and instrumental orchestra consisting of mechanics and workpeople. . . . Their employers promote and encourage so salutary a recreation by countenancing, and contributing to defray the expenses, of their musical associations; and some provide regular musical instruction for such of their workpeople as show a disposition for it. . . . Wherever the working classes are taught to prefer the pleasures of the intellect, and even of taste, to the gratification of sense, a great and favorable change takes place in their character and manners. . . . Sentiments are awakened in them which makes them love their families and homes; their wages are not squandered in intemperance, and they become happier as well as better.

George Hogarth, *Musical History, Biography and Criticism* (London, 1835), 430–31, as quoted by Henry Raynor, *Music and Society Since 1815* (New York: Schocken Books, 1976), 98.

Festivals   Large amateur choruses also played a central role at music festivals, where singers from across a region gathered to perform. The first such festivals centered on Handel's works, beginning in England in 1759, the year of his death. Festivals were held in France during the Revolutionary era, and in the nineteenth century the tradition spread across Germany, Austria, and North America. Among the most prominent and long-running festivals were the Birmingham (England) Musical Festival (founded 1784) and the Lower Rhenish Music Festival (founded 1818) in Düsseldorf. Festival choruses were even larger than local choral societies. Figure 26.1 shows the Handel Festival in London's Crystal Palace in 1857, with an immense choir and orchestra in a huge performing space. Not to be outdone, bandleader Patrick S. Gilmore organized the World Peace Jubilee (1872) in Boston with an orchestra numbering two thousand and a chorus of twenty thousand.

PARTSONGS The staple of smaller mixed, men's, and women's choirs was the ***partsong***, the choral parallel to the Lied or parlor song. Partsongs were scored for two or more voice parts and sung unaccompanied, or with the voices simply doubled on piano or organ. They could be sung by any number of voices from one on a part to a large choir, making them suitable for

FIGURE 26.1 *Handel Festival at the Crystal Palace in London in 1857, with an orchestra of over three hundred and a chorus of almost two thousand, as shown in* The Illustrated London News.

domestic music-making as well as public performance. Like Lieder and parlor songs, partsongs were mostly syllabic and were closely attuned to the poetry. Schubert, Mendelssohn, Hensel, Robert Schumann, Liszt, and nearly every other composer in central and northern Europe produced partsongs and choruses on patriotic, sentimental, convivial, and other kinds of verse. Nature was a favorite subject.

Schubert's *Die Nacht* (NAWM 142) for male voices in four parts (two tenor and two bass) is typical in using as a text a strophic, lyric poem that would serve equally well for a Lied. The poem expresses awe at the beauty of the night stars shining over the flowering fields of spring. Schubert's music captures the tranquil scene and a sense of wonder with quiet, slowly moving chords, mostly resonant major triads with occasional diminished, augmented, and seventh chords that create color and intensity. He carefully sets the text, emphasizing important words with melodic peaks and changes of dynamics. The music is perfectly suited for amateurs performing for their own pleasure. It is relatively simple and easy to sing while offering intriguing challenges, the melodies are attractive, and the lower parts also have melodic interest.

Schubert's Die Nacht

Schubert wrote about one hundred partsongs and other pieces for male voices, some accompanied by piano or guitar, making this the most common medium in his output after solo songs and piano works. Yet two centuries later his partsongs and other small choral works are little known, and the same is true for other composers. Although the most popular partsongs were sung and reprinted for decades, the amateur choruses and home music-making that supported the genre declined after the nineteenth century, and no permanent repertoire of classics developed for the partsong as there did for oratorios and Lieder. This music, however beautiful, served its immediate purpose and has been largely forgotten.

ORATORIOS AND OTHER LARGE WORKS The core of the repertory for large choruses was formed by the oratorios of Handel and Haydn, a pairing immortalized in the name of the Handel and Haydn Society, founded in Boston in 1815 and one of the oldest music organizations in the United States that is still active. Another composer was added to the repertoire in 1829, when the twenty-year-old Felix Mendelssohn conducted the Berlin Singakademie in the first performance of J. S. Bach's *St. Matthew Passion* since the eighteenth century. Bach's *St. John Passion* and Mass in B Minor followed in 1833 and 1834. These performances began the revival of Bach's vocal music, although they converted pieces Bach wrote for performance in church by eight to twelve singers and an orchestra of about fifteen into concert works for large chorus and orchestra.

Mendelssohn's oratorios   While performing music of the past, the choral societies and festivals also encouraged the composition of new works in the same mold. The most successful new oratorios were Felix Mendelssohn's *St. Paul* (1836), premiered at the Lower Rhenish Festival, and *Elijah* (1846), premiered at the Birmingham Festival, which themselves became standards of the choral repertory. Both treated biblical subjects and received great acclaim in Europe and North America. In both Mendelssohn employed a wide variety of styles and textures for choral movements, as Handel had done in his oratorios; evoked the style of chorales, which Bach had used in his Passions; and used links between movements to integrate each work into a cohesive whole, following the practice of his own time. In these ways, Mendelssohn rooted his oratorios in Baroque tradition while creating something new and up-to-date.

St. Paul   The excerpt from *St. Paul* in NAWM 143 centers on the event that precipitated Paul's conversion to Christianity, when in the midst of persecuting Christians he is stopped by a blinding light and the voice of Jesus asking, "why do you persecute me?" (Acts 9:1–6). We saw in Chapter 15 how Heinrich Schütz dramatized this moment in *Saul, Saul, was verfolgst du mich* (NAWM 81), setting only the words of Christ himself. Mendelssohn probably did not know Schütz's piece, but followed the precedent of Bach's Passions by framing the biblical narrative with movements that comment on the story and interpret its meaning for a modern audience. After an alto soloist narrates in recitative, she sings a brief aria in Lieder style, assuring the faithful that the Lord remembers his own (NAWM 143a). The flash of light is recounted by a tenor in recitative over string tremolos, and Jesus's words are set for women's chorus joined by winds and brass to suggest a heavenly sound (NAWM 143b). There follow two choral movements that reflect on the encounter. The first proclaims in majestic homophony the rising of the Lord and the coming of the light, contrasted with a long central fugue portraying darkness covering the earth (NAWM 143c). Then comes a chorale in four-part harmony, punctuated by brass fanfares (NAWM 143d). The recitatives, chorale, and fugue breathe the spirit of Bach; the interweaving of homophonic and fugal textures evokes Handel's choruses (compare NAWM 108c); setting Jesus's words for chorus recalls the opening of Haydn's *Creation* (NAWM 123); and the melodies, orchestration, and dramatic effects are of Mendelssohn's own time and style. The combination of new elements with familiar ones helped to make this work a phenomenal success, Mendelssohn's most popular piece during his lifetime.

Hector Berlioz on His Requiem

In his musical biography, Berlioz bares his Romantic soul while settling many an old score. Here he describes the qualities that made his choral music by turns overpowering and confounding to his contemporaries.

❁

The prevailing characteristics of my music are passionate expression, intense ardour, rhythmical animation, and unexpected turns. When I say passionate expression, I mean an expression determined on enforcing the inner meaning of its subject, even when that subject is the contrary of passion, and when the feeling to be expressed is gentle and tender, or even profoundly calm. This is the sort of expression that has been discovered in *L'Enfance du Christ*, the *Ciel* scene in the *Damnation de Faust*, and the *Sanctus* of the Requiem....

The musical problems I have tried to solve in these works . . . are exceptional, and require exceptional methods. In the Requiem, for example, I employ four distinct brass orchestras, answering each other at certain distances round the main orchestra and chorus. In the *Te Deum*, the organ at the end of the church answers the orchestra and two choirs, whilst a third large choir represents the mass of the people, taking part from time to time in a vast sacred concert. But it is more especially the form of the pieces, the breadth of style, and the deliberateness of certain progressions, the goal of which is not at once perceived, that give those works their strange gigantic physiognomy and colossal aspect. The result of this immensity of form is, that either one entirely misses the drift of the whole, or is crushed by a tremendous emotion. At many performances of the Requiem I have seen one man listening in terror, shaken to the very depths of his soul, while his next neighbor could not catch an idea, though trying with all his might to do so.

From *Memoirs of Hector Berlioz*, translated by Rachel (Scott Russell) Holmes and Eleanor Holmes; annotated and the translation revised, by Ernest Newman (New York: Knopf, 1932), 488–89.

The availability of large forces encouraged a grandiosity that reached a pinnacle in two choral works by French composer Hector Berlioz (see p. 638), his Requiem (*Grande Messe des morts*, 1837) and Te Deum (1855). They belong not to an ecclesiastical but to a patriotic tradition inspired by the massive music festivals of the French Revolution. Both works are of huge dimensions, not only in length and number of performers but also in grandeur of conception. The Requiem requires an orchestra of 140 players, four brass choirs distributed around the performance space, four tam-tams, ten pairs of cymbals, and sixteen kettledrums, all used to achieve brilliant musical effects from representing the thunderous clamor of the Day of Judgment to the *pianissimo* strokes of bass drum and cymbals that punctuate the *Sanctus* (see Source Reading). Berlioz also composed several large choral works on secular themes, notably *The Damnation of Faust* (1845–46), on scenes from Goethe's play, and *Lélio* (1831–32), a sequel to his *Symphonie fantastique* (see pp. 637–41).

Berlioz's Requiem and Te Deum

MUSIC FOR RELIGIOUS SERVICES Church music remained a vehicle for worship, but in some areas it also served as music for amateur singers at home and in public gatherings.

Instead of using amateur choirs for services, Catholic churches tended

Catholic music

TIMELINE

1802 St. Petersburg Philharmonic Society founded

1813 London Philharmonic Society founded

1815 Handel and Haydn Society founded in Boston

1815 End of Napoleonic Wars

1818 First steamship crosses the Atlantic

ca. 1822 Franz Schubert, *Die Nacht*

1828 Schubert, String Quintet in C Major

1829 Felix Mendelssohn conducts Bach's *St. Matthew Passion* in Berlin

1830 Hector Berlioz, *Symphonie fantastique*

1830 Revolutions in France and Belgium

1834 Victor Hugo, *The Hunchback of Notre Dame*

1836 Mendelssohn, *St. Paul*

1837 Berlioz, Requiem

1838 Photography developed

1841 Robert Schumann, Symphony No. 1

1842 Founding of New York Philharmonic and Vienna Philharmonic

1844 Mendelssohn, Violin Concerto

1844 First intercity telegraph between Baltimore and Washington

1844 First edition of *The Sacred Harp*

1846 Clara Schumann, Piano Trio in G Minor

1856 Lowell Mason, *Bethany*

to employ clerics and choirboys; women were normally excluded from performing in church, as had been true for centuries. Catholic composers continued to produce concerted liturgical music. Schubert's masses in A♭ and E♭ are exemplary settings of the Ordinary. Elaborate works like Gioachino Rossini's *Stabat mater* (1832, revised 1841) brought up-to-date operatic styles into church. But in the second quarter of the century, renewed interest in music of the past brought about a revival of the sixteenth-century choral style of Palestrina's masses and motets. The phrase *a cappella* had been used since the seventeenth century to denote the old contrapuntal style known as stile antico, but in the nineteenth century it came to mean "unaccompanied," because of the mistaken belief that it referred to the lack of any instrumental accompaniment in the papal chapel where Palestrina worked. By the mid-nineteenth century, the Catholic Church was actively promoting the composition of unaccompanied choral music in a Palestrina-inspired style. In German-speaking areas especially, the Cecilian movement, named after St. Cecilia, the patron saint of music, encouraged a cappella performances of older music and of new works in similar styles.

Protestant churches also saw new developments building on music of the past. The performances of Bach's Passions at the Berlin Singakademie took place during a general revival of Lutheran music. Lutheran composers produced a flood of new music for services or home devotions that often used Bach as a model, as in numerous psalm settings by Mendelssohn. In England, Anglican musicians recovered classics from their tradition. Among new works, the anthems of Samuel Sebastian Wesley (1810–1876) were especially acclaimed. Women, encouraged by their participation in choral societies, began to sing in church choirs, and some served as professional church organists, such as Elizabeth Stirling (1819–1895), a renowned organist and composer in London. Yet in some corners of the church the Oxford Movement, begun in 1841, sought to restore all-male choirs of boys and men and to revive sixteenth-century unaccompanied polyphony.

Music in Jewish synagogues was transformed by the Reform movement in Judaism that emerged in the early nineteenth century, when Jewish leaders influenced by the Enlightenment revised traditional beliefs, customs, and religious services. Many synagogues in Germany and elsewhere adopted practices from Protestantism, singing congregational hymns (often borrowing the melodies from Lutheran chorales) and introducing organs and choirs. The first influential composer of the movement was Salomon Sulzer (1804–1890), cantor at the Reform synagogue in Vienna, who updated traditional chants and wrote service music in modern styles for soloist and for choir. He also commissioned music from other composers, including Schubert's choral setting of Psalm 92 (1828), which used the Hebrew text.

In the United States, church music divided not only by sect but by race. African American churches developed their own styles

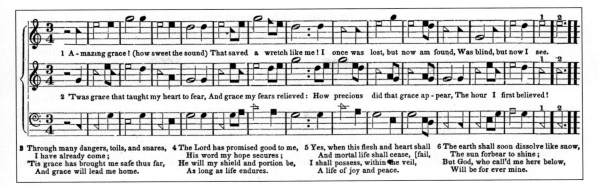

FIGURE 26.2 *The hymn tune* New Britain *(in the middle voice), set to the text "Amazing Grace" by John Newton, as it appears in the* The Sacred Harp, *3rd edition (1859).*

of music that would later have enormous influence. In the 1790s, Reverend Richard Allen organized the first congregation of the African Methodist Episcopal Church and published a hymnbook designed specifically for his all-black congregation. In the predominantly white churches, choirs sang music like their European brethren. Congregational singing continued to be central, fostering a market for hymns in a variety of styles. Two divergent trends in American hymnody were especially notable: the *shape-note* tradition in the rural South, and the European-influenced style of Lowell Mason.

Singing masters spread the music of the Yankee tunesmiths throughout the South, composed new tunes and harmonizations in a similar style, and published both old and new songs in collections such as *Kentucky Harmony* (1816), *The Southern Harmony* (1835), and *The Sacred Harp* (1844). The last, the most popular of its kind, included spiritual songs used in Southern revival meetings. The tradition of singing this music is known as **shape-note singing** after the notation used in these collections, in which the shape of the noteheads indicates solmization syllables, allowing for easy sight-reading in parts without instrumental accompaniment. This notational system is an inventive American reconception of the syllables introduced by Guido of Arezzo (see Chapter 2). Figure 26.2 shows a song from *The Sacred Harp,* which uses four syllables and shapes. The major scale is sung to the syllables *fa-sol-la-fa-sol-la-mi-fa,* using *fa* (shown with a triangle) for the notes just above a half step and *sol* (round), *la* (square), and *mi* (diamond) for the following whole steps. Ordinary folks sang from these collections in church and in local and regional gatherings, with roughly equal numbers of singers reading each part, using the solmization syllables the first time through each song and then singing all the verses.

In shape-note harmonizations, the tune is usually in the tenor (the second line from the bottom), as in Figure 26.2. Nineteenth-century hymn tunes could be used with any hymn text that featured the same pattern of lines, syllables, and accents, and so the tunes themselves were given names to identify them, often drawn from place names. Here the tune is *New Britain,* a melody of unknown origin most often sung to John Newton's poem "Amazing Grace." The harmonization is typical of the shape-note songbooks, with many open fifths (as in measures 1, 5, and 8), dissonant fourths above the bass (measures

Shape-note singing

4, 7, and 10–11), and parallel fifths and octaves (measures 4–5, 6–7, 7–8, 9, 11, and 13–14) that give this music its characteristic sound.

Lowell Mason   The style of the Yankee tunesmiths and shape-note singers was considered crude and primitive by musicians who knew European music. Especially significant was Lowell Mason (1792–1872), born in Massachusetts and trained in harmony and composition by a German emigrant musician in Savannah, Georgia. Mason returned to Boston in 1827, became president of the Handel and Haydn Society, and helped found the Boston Academy of Music to provide musical instruction for children. As superintendent of music for the Boston public schools, he introduced music into the regular curriculum, prompting other cities to follow suit and thereby establishing the American tradition of music education in schools. He deplored what he regarded as the crude music of the Yankee tunesmiths and championed a correct, modest European style, in which he composed some 1,200 original hymn tunes and arranged many others. Even today, many Protestant hymnals contain several of his melodies and arrangements. Among his most famous tunes is *Bethany* (1856), set to Sarah Flower Adams's 1841 poem "Nearer, My God, to Thee," shown in Example 26.1. The melody is largely pentatonic and in modified AABA form, like *New Britain,* but the harmony follows the rules of proper European music of the time.

THE TRADITION OF CHORAL MUSIC From Gregorian chant through the oratorios of Handel, music for choirs often led stylistic development in music.

EXAMPLE 26.1 *Lowell Mason,* Bethany

But choral music in the nineteenth century either looked back to previous eras or emulated other genres of the time, such as solo song. In histories of music that focus on the evolution of musical style, nineteenth-century choral music need hardly be mentioned. But enormous numbers of people participated in or heard choral music in concert or church, and it has exercised a significant and enduring influence on musical tastes.

CHAMBER MUSIC

In chamber music, the masterpieces of the past proved inescapable for nineteenth-century composers. Music for small instrumental ensembles continued to serve as a form of home music-making for the enjoyment of the players. Chamber music intended for home performance, called *Hausmusik* (house music) in German, was typically aimed at middle-class amateurs. Music for a variety of ensembles was also played in salons, home concerts, and other private gatherings across Europe and the Americas, serving as entertainment for guests and at times including professional performers as well as amateurs. But string quartets and other chamber works were increasingly played in public concerts by professional ensembles such as the Joachim Quartet, shown in Figure 26.3. Composers often treated chamber music as seriously as symphonies, especially in genres that were identified with Haydn, Mozart, and Beethoven, like the string quartet, violin sonata, and piano trio. These came to be seen as classical genres that required an engagement with the past, and composers increasingly aspired to match the individuality of Beethoven's middle quartets, taking his works as a defining model as much in chamber music as in the symphony and concerto.

FIGURE 26.3 *The Joachim Quartet performing in about 1872 at the Monday Popular Concert at St. James's Hall in London, with some of the audience seated on the stage behind the string quartet. Playing first violin is Wilma Norman-Neruda, one of the few women to make a career as a professional violinist in the nineteenth century.*

SCHUBERT In his teens, Schubert wrote numerous string quartets for his friends and family to play, modeling them on works by Mozart and Haydn. He achieved an individual and appealing style in the five-movement Quintet for piano, violin, viola, cello, and bass (1819), known as the *Trout* Quintet because the fourth movement presents variations on his song *Die Forelle* (The Trout). But his most important chamber works came in his last five years of life, as he undertook what John Gingerich has called "Schubert's Beethoven Project." This was his attempt to go beyond the songs, partsongs, and pieces for piano solo and piano duet that had brought him success with the Viennese public, and to master the genres that Beethoven had raised to unprecedented prestige, from string quartet to symphony, meeting—and trying to best—the elder composer on his own turf. The products of this project include Schubert's String Quartets in A Minor (1824), D Minor (1824, nicknamed *Death and the Maiden*), and G Major (1826), and the String Quintet in C Major (1828). Schubert composed them hoping that Ignaz Schuppanzigh (who had premiered most of Beethoven's quartets) would play them on his series of "classical" chamber music concerts in Vienna, where the string quartets of Haydn, Mozart, and Beethoven made up over 80 percent of the repertoire, and that they would achieve a similar prestige and immortality. All four attain the "heavenly length" Robert Schumann admired in Schubert's C-Major Symphony (see p. 636). In mood, difficulty, style, and conception, Schubert's late chamber works are intended more as dramatic pieces of concert music than as entertaining diversions for amateur players.

String Quintet   The String Quintet in C Major (first movement in NAWM 144), which Schubert composed just two months before his death, is often considered his chamber music masterpiece. To the standard four instruments of the quartet, he added a second cello, whose rich sound appealed to Romantic sensibilities. Schubert obtains exquisite effects and constantly varying textures from this combination. He treats all five instruments as equals and groups them in ever-changing ways, often with one instrument pitted against two pairs. For example, the beautiful E♭-major melody of the second theme in the first movement, shown in Example 26.2, appears first in the cellos in parallel thirds, with the viola providing a pizzicato bass line and violins an offbeat accompaniment. Later the parts exchange ideas, with the melody in the violins, and in the recapitulation, the melody appears in the first cello and viola.

There are strong contrasts of mood and of style within and between movements, from the profound slow movement to the playful finale, and from learned counterpoint to rustic vernacular styles. In the first movement (NAWM 144), the opening theme sets up oppositions between C major and minor, and between a slow, dramatic first idea and a lilting continuation, that take the entire movement to resolve. The early emphasis on C minor foreshadows the three main keys of the exposition: C, E♭, and G major, the notes of the C-minor triad. The second theme moves between E♭, G, and B major, keys whose tonics divide the octave into equal major thirds; such a key scheme is a typical device of Schubert's, which was later emulated by Robert Schumann, Liszt, Brahms, and other composers. Unusual key relationships and stylistic juxtapositions also figure in the other movements. The slow ternary second movement contrasts an ethereal E-major melody with an impassioned F-minor middle section in a style Schubert associated with

EXAMPLE 26.2 *Franz Schubert, String Quintet in C Major, first movement, opening of second theme*

Hungarian Roma (Gypsies). In the third movement, an antic C-major scherzo passes through numerous distant keys and surrounds a slow D♭-major trio that is like a calm, sweet song. The sonata-rondo finale contrasts a rustic dance with a more refined urban one and with *pianissimo* cascades that suggest a transcendent vision. Throughout, Schubert integrates the drama of Beethoven's style with the lyricism of his own, proving himself a worthy successor to Beethoven.

MENDELSSOHN Felix Mendelssohn wrote a large amount of chamber music, and in it we can trace his evolution from a talented boy, to a maturing composer testing his skill against Beethoven, to mastery on his own terms. He wrote numerous chamber works in his youth, using Haydn, Mozart, and Bach as his principal models. His first published compositions, written in 1822–25, were three piano quartets and a violin sonata. His earliest recognized masterpiece, written at the age of sixteen, was his Octet in E-flat Major for strings, Op. 20 (1825), remarkable for its symphonic conception, independent treatment of all eight instruments, and demanding string techniques; its character as a piece conceived for concert performance contrasts greatly with earlier chamber works intended primarily for the enjoyment of the players, such as Haydn's baryton trios (described in Chapter 23). The Octet's scherzo, inspired by a passage from Goethe's *Faust*, anticipated the light, sprightly style he used to depict the fairies in his overture *A Midsummer Night's Dream*, written the following year (see pp. 642–43). After the appearance of Beethoven's late quartets, Mendelssohn absorbed their influence in his String Quartets in A Minor, Op. 13 (1827), and E-flat Major, Op. 12 (1829). Following Beethoven's lead, Mendelssohn integrated the movements through thematic connections, while giving each movement a distinctive, highly contrasting character.

Mendelssohn's most characteristic chamber works are the Piano Trios in D Minor, Op. 49, and C Minor, Op. 66. Both are full of tuneful, attractive themes and idiomatic writing, and both feature slow movements in the manner of his *Songs without Words* and scherzos in his typical pixieish style.

In pieces like these, the classical genre and forms serve as vessels for the Romantic material, emphasizing expressive melody over the motivic economy and taut development typical of Beethoven.

Robert Schumann   **ROBERT AND CLARA SCHUMANN** Robert Schumann followed his "Lieder year" in 1840 and "symphony year" in 1841 with a "chamber music year" in 1842–43. After studying the quartets of Haydn and Mozart, he composed three string quartets, published together as Op. 41, followed by a piano quintet and a piano quartet. In his critical writings, he had argued that string quartets should resemble a four-way conversation, and his own quartets meet this ideal, with fluid interchange among the parts. He also insisted that quartet composers should build on the tradition of Haydn, Mozart, and Beethoven without simply imitating them, and indeed Schumann's quartets reflect the influence of these three composers more strongly than his works in other genres yet still project his own distinctive style.

Influenced by his study of Bach, Schumann introduced a new, more polyphonic approach to chamber music in 1847 with his Piano Trios No. 1 in D Minor, Op. 63, and No. 2 in F Major, Op. 80. The two contrast markedly in mood, the first somber, the second warm and cheerful, but both balance intellectual rigor in form and counterpoint with expressive depth and originality in the themes and their development. This combination of elements made them his most influential chamber works, especially for Brahms and other German composers.

Clara Schumann   Clara Schumann composed what she regarded as her best work, the Piano Trio in G Minor, in 1846, and it may have inspired her husband's trios of the following year. The first and last movements, in sonata form, combine traits from Baroque, Classic, and Romantic models: memorable songlike themes, rich polyphonic treatment, development through motivic fragmentation and imitation, fugue (in the finale's development), and rousing codas. Schumann specified minuet tempo for the second movement but labeled it Scherzo to highlight its subtle rhythmic tricks, such as Scotch snaps and syncopations. The slow third movement (NAWM 145) is outwardly simple in form, a modified ABA with a nocturne-like, somewhat melancholy first section and a more animated B section. But the effect is enriched by constantly changing textures. The opening melody appears three times, each time in a different instrument and with ever more complex accompanying figuration: alone in the piano over alternating bass notes and chords; in the violin, surrounded by flowing piano arpeggios above a bass line shared by piano and pizzicato cello; and finally in the cello, with a new arpeggio figure in the piano and pizzicato chords in the violin.

CHAMBER MUSIC AND THE CLASSICAL TRADITION By midcentury, chamber music was regarded as a conservative medium strongly linked to classical models, cultivated by those who saw themselves as continuing the classical tradition but shunned by more radical composers such as Berlioz and Liszt. Yet in creating new twists on classical forms and expressing Romantic passions in genres long associated with private music-making and intimate listening, chamber music composers in the first half of the nineteenth century offered something new and distinctive.

ORCHESTRAL MUSIC

THE NINETEENTH-CENTURY ORCHESTRA The orchestra was central to public concert life in the nineteenth century. The number of orchestras multiplied many times over, and concert societies played an increasingly significant role, from the St. Petersburg Philharmonic Society in Russia (founded 1802) to the Musical Fund Society in Philadelphia (founded 1820). Some orchestras, such as the Society of the Friends of Music in Vienna, were made up primarily of amateurs, while others were organized and staffed by professional musicians, including the London Philharmonic (founded 1813), New York Philharmonic (1842), and Vienna Philharmonic (also 1842). Playing in an orchestra gradually became a profession, as it remains today. By the end of the century, most major cities in Europe and the Americas had professional orchestras that provided regular concert series, though not necessarily full-time work for the musicians.

In addition to concert orchestras (the main subject of this section), there were orchestras in opera houses, theaters, cafés, and dance halls, like the famous Viennese dance orchestras led by Joseph Lanner (1801–1843) and Johann Strauss the elder (1804–1849).

New and redesigned instruments

Most wind and brass instruments were redesigned in the nineteenth century, and several new ones were invented. Flutes, oboes, clarinets, and bassoons acquired elaborate systems of keys by midcentury (see pp. 584–85), making the instruments easier to finger quickly and play in tune in most keys. Wind instruments with extended ranges, notably piccolo, English horn, bass clarinet, and contrabassoon, were occasionally used in orchestras, as was the tuba, invented in the 1830s. Valves were added to horns and trumpets, allowing players to reach all chromatic notes throughout the instruments' ranges, although natural horns and trumpets remained more common in orchestras until late in the century.

Wider color palette

The greater variety of instruments provided a much wider range of colors and color combinations. Composers could now treat the winds and brass more as equals to the strings, often contrasting one section with another. In some works, bass drum, triangle, or other percussion instruments joined the timpani. The new, fully chromatic pedal harp was sometimes added, often played by a woman because of the harp's long association with domestic music-making. Otherwise, orchestral players were usually men, and with rare exceptions—including a handful of all-women orchestras—that situation did not begin to change until the mid-twentieth century, after women had won some equal rights and become more integrated generally in the workforces of Europe and the Americas.

Size and composition

Orchestras grew in size from about forty players in 1800 to around fifty at midcentury, and as many as ninety by 1900. The main increase was in the number of strings, in part to fill larger concert spaces, which in turn affected the balance between strings and other instruments. Mendelssohn, Robert Schumann, and others of their generation typically wrote for an orchestra with pairs of flutes, oboes, clarinets, bassoons, and trumpets; two or four horns; alto, tenor, and bass trombone; timpani and an optional second percussionist; and around thirty strings (about eight each of violins 1 and 2 and four each of violas, cellos, and basses).

FIGURE 26.4 *Concert at Covent Garden Theatre in London, showing Louis Jullien (in the center of the picture) conducting his orchestra (in front) and four military bands (on risers in back). In the middle of the musicians, who are surrounded on three sides by the audience, Jullien conducts without a score, turning as needed to give cues—as much the virtuoso (and center of attention) as any opera star.*

CONDUCTORS Eighteenth-century orchestras were led from the harpsichord or by the leader of the violins, who might sometimes beat time with a violin bow or roll of music paper. In the nineteenth century, this role was gradually taken over by a ***conductor*** who used a baton to beat time and cue entrances. The practice of conducting developed first at the Paris Opéra, where since the seventeenth century performances had been led by beating time with a stick, sometimes audibly; by the late eighteenth century, this had evolved into silent gestures with a baton by the *chef d'orchestre* (leader of the orchestra), who not only indicated the tempo and coordinated the performers on stage and in the pit but also shaped the music's phrasing and character. German composer, violinist, and conductor Louis Spohr (1784–1859) is said to have introduced conducting with a baton into orchestral music while rehearsing the London Philharmonic in 1820, and the baton was soon adopted by Carl Maria von Weber (1786–1826), Felix Mendelssohn, and others. Although at first the conductor simply kept the orchestra together, by the 1840s conductors were drawing attention to themselves as interpreters of the music, exploiting the Romantic cult of the individual. Conductors like Louis Jullien (1812–1860), shown in Figure 26.4, formed their own orchestras and became stars on the same order as the instrumental virtuosos.

AUDIENCES AND CONCERTS Court orchestras in the eighteenth century had played to mixed audiences of nobility and city people. The new orchestras drew a primarily middle-class audience, often the same people whose enthusiasm for home music-making sustained the market for songs, piano music, and *Hausmusik*. Many orchestral pieces were available in piano transcriptions for home performance, which is often how people got to know them; the experience of hearing an orchestra was still a relatively rare event. Yet orchestral music carried a special prestige, in part because of the lasting impression of Beethoven's symphonies. The prominence given to orchestral music in this book and in most histories of music is out of proportion to the place it occupied in the activities of most musicians and all but the elite public during the nineteenth century, but the emphasis is justified by the importance accorded to it by audiences, patrons, critics, and the composers themselves.

Nineteenth-century concert programs offered a diversity of works and ensembles. For example, a concert by the London Philharmonic before 1850 typically featured a symphony, an aria or choral composition, a concerto, an instrumental solo or chamber work, another vocal piece, and a closing symphony or overture. Jullien's Promenade Concerts in London, less formal and aimed at a larger audience, included quadrilles and other dances (often performed jointly with military bands), choral music, and a symphony. The variety of performing forces and the alternation of instrumental and vocal music continued a tradition that went back to the first public concerts (see Chapters 16 and 20). The concert of music for a single medium, inaugurated by Liszt's solo piano recitals in 1839, did not become the rule until quite late in the century.

Concert programming

Balancing the taste for diverse concert programs with concerns for length, orchestras often programmed one-movement works alongside or instead of complete symphonies or concertos. Opera overtures were a perennial favorite, as were overtures to plays, such as Beethoven's *Egmont* Overture. Mendelssohn's *A Midsummer Night's Dream* (1826, discussed on pp. 642–43) helped to popularize the new genre of the **concert overture**, typically a sonata-form movement with a descriptive title that was reflected in the music, and composers from Berlioz and Schumann through Brahms and Tchaikovsky followed suit. Carl Maria von Weber pioneered the **concertino** or *Konzertstück* ("concert piece"), a one-movement concerto that fused sonata form with the traditional three contrasting movements of concertos, in his Concertino for Clarinet and Orchestra (1811) and *Konzertstück* in F Minor for piano and orchestra (1821), and his approach was emulated by Schumann, Liszt, and others.

New one-movement genres

THE RISE OF THE CLASSICAL REPERTOIRE One of the most remarkable developments in the entire history of music is the emergence in the nineteenth century of a repertoire of musical classics by composers of the past. This process happened at different times for different genres; we have seen it already for oratorios, string quartets, and other chamber works, and it is also evident in the programs of the major European orchestras. In concerts of the Leipzig Gewandhaus Orchestra, for example, about 85 percent of the pieces performed in the 1780s were by living composers; by 1820, the percentage had dropped to about 75 percent. Over the next fifty years, the situation reversed completely, so that by 1870, three-quarters of the repertoire was by composers of past generations, chiefly Beethoven, Mozart, Haydn, and the early Romantics.

Several factors lay behind this change. Haydn and Beethoven achieved such popularity during their lifetimes that their music continued to be performed after their deaths, as did some works by other composers. Music by these earlier composers was often cheaper (and thus more profitable) to publish, more readily available, and easier for amateurs to perform than the newer music. Perhaps most important, influential musicians and critics actively promoted the music of the past as a counterweight to that of the present. Virtuoso performer-composers of the 1820s to 1840s, such as Paganini and Gottschalk, gained mass appeal through spectacular showmanship and heightened expressivity, often at the expense of the musical values esteemed by connoisseurs. By contrast, Bach, Handel, Haydn, Mozart, and Beethoven had aimed their music at all listeners, seeking to provide something of value for every taste. Serious musicians now championed their works as musical classics, masterpieces that combined compositional craft with emotional depth, and immediate appeal with lasting interest.

The effect on audiences   The new seriousness of the repertoire was matched by a new seriousness in concert behavior. Increasingly, audiences were expected to be quiet and listen attentively to the music rather than be free to converse and socialize as was typical of eighteenth-century concerts. The silent audience became one of the defining traits of classical music concerts and remains so today.

The effect on performers   The movement to establish a classical repertoire was aided by conductors like Jullien, who saw that they could star as interpreters of the classics, and by younger virtuosos such as violinist Joseph Joachim (1831–1907) and pianist Anton Rubinstein (1829–1894), who helped to popularize the concertos of Beethoven, Mozart, and other older composers. Although most of these conductors and virtuosos also composed, the primary way to prove themselves as performers gradually shifted from performing their own music to playing the classics. This was a profound change that permanently altered the nature of performers' work and training.

The effect on composers: Beethoven's legacy   These changes were gradual. Orchestral concerts in the first half of the nineteenth century included much more new and recent music than is typical today. The rise of the permanent classical repertoire was just beginning in the 1820s, and its fullest effects were felt by composers in the late nineteenth and twentieth centuries, as we will see in later chapters. Yet even before 1850, composers of orchestral music strongly felt the presence of the old masterpieces. Most important was Beethoven, whose orchestral works were construed as artistic statements by the composer, not merely diverting entertainments, as most music had been regarded in earlier eras. All later composers for orchestra labored in his shadow, knowing that their works would be compared to his and thus must meet a similar standard while offering something distinctive. Indeed, the history of orchestral music in the nineteenth century can be seen as a series of varied responses to Beethoven's example, as each composer explored ways to say something new and individual within the forms Beethoven had cultivated.

THE NEW ROMANTIC STYLE: SCHUBERT One response, pioneered by Schubert in the 1820s, was to maintain the outward form of the symphony while infusing it with content derived from the new Romantic style developed in Lieder and piano pieces. This style included a greater focus on songlike melodies, adventurous harmonic excursions, innovative textures, enchanting instrumental colors, strong contrasts, and heightened emotions. For the

EXAMPLE 26.3 *Schubert,* Unfinished *Symphony, first movement*

a. First theme

b. Second theme

mature Schubert and his fellow Romantics, themes were the most important element in any form, rather than the phrase structure and harmonic structure emphasized in eighteenth-century descriptions of form (see Chapter 22). While Classic-era symphonists demonstrated their originality through the ways they treated conventional material, Schubert and his successors sought to make both their thematic material and their treatment of it as individual and memorable as possible.

Schubert wrote several symphonies in his teens and early twenties, but his first attempt at a large-scale symphony came in 1822 with the two movements now called the *Unfinished* Symphony, originally planned as a four-movement work in B minor. After a brief, mysterious introductory subject played by the strings without accompaniment, the first movement presents a soulful, undulating, singable melody, shown in Example 26.3a, that is quite different from the typical first themes of his predecessors and less easily fragmented into motives for symphonic development. Its soaring extension, full of anguish and longing, was also a departure. The second theme, shown in Example 26.3b, is a relaxed, graceful melody in the style of the Ländler, an Austrian country dance. These two themes share three rhythmic ideas—marked *x*, *y*, and *z* in the example—which dominate the extensions that follow each theme and thus unify the entire exposition into an organic whole. Instead of centering the development section and coda on these two themes, as Haydn or Beethoven might have done, Schubert focuses on the introductory subject, revealing the almost demonic potential latent in its initial mysterious appearance. In this way, Schubert was following the custom for symphonic development while devoting the main thematic areas to the presentation of memorable, lyrical melodies like those of his songs and piano works.

In his Symphony No. 9 in C Major (1825), known as the *Great*, Schubert blended his Romantic lyricism and Beethovenian drama within an expanded Classical form. The first movement opens with an unaccompanied melody in C major played softly in the horns, shown in Example 26.4. This melody

Unfinished Symphony

The Great Symphony in C Major

EXAMPLE 26.4 *Schubert,* Great *Symphony in C Major, opening of first movement*

repeats several times with varied accompaniments as in a set of variations, alternating with melodically related ideas that depart from tonic harmonies. Only in retrospect do we discover that this lyrical section is a long, slow introduction to a sonata-form Allegro, whose rhythmically charged, easily fragmented first theme shows the influence of Haydn and Beethoven. Typical of Schubert's approach to sonata form is the three-key exposition, in which the second theme begins in E minor before settling into the dominant, G major. This tonal plan combines Schubert's long-standing interest in key relationships of a third with the traditional polarity of tonic and dominant. Elements of the opening horn melody return during the second and closing themes, development, and coda, binding together the lyrical introduction and the more motivic, constantly developing Allegro.

Robert Schumann praised the C-Major Symphony's "heavenly length" (see Source Reading), appreciating the expansion of the form of all four movements to accommodate Schubert's beautiful melodies and orchestral effects.

SOURCE READING

Robert Schumann on Schubert's Symphony in C Major

When he visited Schubert's brother Ferdinand in 1839, Robert Schumann discovered the manuscript of Schubert's *Great* Symphony in C Major, which had never been performed in public. Through Schumann's intercession it was performed that same year at the Gewandhaus Concerts in Leipzig under the direction of Mendelssohn. In a review of the piece the following year, Schumann praised it as revealing both an unknown aspect of Schubert and a new approach to the symphony.

✱

I must say at once that anyone who is not yet acquainted with this symphony knows very little about Schubert. When we consider all that he has given to art, this praise may strike many as exaggerated, partly, no doubt, because composers have so often been advised, to their chagrin, that it is better for them—after Beethoven—"to abstain from the symphonic form." . . .

On hearing Schubert's symphony and its bright, flowery, romantic life, the city [Vienna] crystallizes before me, and I realize how such works could be born in these very surroundings. . . . Everyone must acknowledge that the outer world—sparkling today, gloomy tomorrow—often

deeply stirs the feeling of the poet or the musician; and all must recognize, while listening to this symphony, that it reveals to us something more than mere beautiful song, mere joy and sorrow, such as music has ever expressed in a hundred ways, leading us into regions that, to our best recollection, we had never before explored. To understand this, one must hear this symphony. Here we find, besides the most masterly technicalities of musical composition, life in every vein, coloring down to the finest gradation, meaning everywhere, sharp expression in detail, and in the whole, a suffusing romanticism that other works by Franz Schubert have already made known to us.

And then the heavenly length of the symphony, like that of a thick novel in four volumes (perhaps by Jean Paul, who was also never able to reach a conclusion), and for the best reason—to permit readers to think it out for themselves. How this refreshes, this feeling of abundance, so contrary to our experience with others when we always dread to be disillusioned at the end and are often saddened through disappointment.

From *Neue Zeitschrift für Musik* 12 (1840): 82–83, after the translation by Paul Rosenfeld in Robert Schumann, *On Music and Musicians*, ed. Konrad Wolff (New York: W. W. Norton, 1946), 108–11.

Schubert had found an orchestral voice that could stand any comparison. Unfortunately, neither the *Unfinished* Symphony nor the *Great* C-Major Symphony was publicly performed until many years after the composer's death. Yet this gave them a special cachet: the story of their posthumous discovery, first performances, and ultimate success was touchingly Romantic in itself, fitting Schubert's image as a composer who died too young and spurring the notion that his life was itself an "unfinished symphony"—which later became the title of a book and a movie about his life.

PROGRAMMATIC ROMANTICISM: BERLIOZ An approach different from Schubert's was reconceiving the symphony as a programmatic work and allowing it to assume an unconventional form to suit the program. Following Beethoven's lead in his Fifth and Sixth Symphonies, Hector Berlioz (1803–1869; see biography and Figure 26.5) shaped his symphonies around a series of emotions that tell a story.

In the *Symphonie fantastique* (Fantasy Symphony), which Berlioz wrote in 1830 while still a conservatory student and revised before its publication in 1845 (finale in NAWM 146), the composer dwells on the passions aroused by his thoughts and fantasies about a woman whose love he hopes to win. He based the story on his own infatuation with the Irish actress Harriet Smithson. Beethoven had subjected the main theme in both his Third and Fifth Symphonies to a series of exciting adventures (see Chapter 24). Berlioz followed this precedent in his device of the ***idée fixe*** (fixed idea or obsession, a term he borrowed from psychology). This was a melody that he used in each movement to represent the obsessive image of the hero's beloved, transforming it to suit the mood and situation at each point in the story.

Symphonie fantastique

To ensure that his listeners would understand the feelings and experiences that inspired the symphony, Berlioz originally titled it *Episode in the Life of an Artist: Fantasy Symphony in Five Movements* and provided it with an autobiographical program (see NAWM 146 for the program and complete idée fixe). The work is thus a musical drama whose words are not spoken or sung, but read silently; Berlioz wanted listeners to regard the program "in the same way as the spoken words of an opera, serving to introduce the musical numbers by describing the situation that evokes the particular mood and expressive character of each." The situations are depicted in the passionate prose of a young and sensitive artist. Literary influences in the program include Goethe's *Faust* and Thomas De Quincey's *Confessions of an English Opium Eater*. Musical influences, besides Beethoven, are from the opera theater: Gluck, Spontini, Rossini, Weber, and Meyerbeer (see Chapters 21 and 27). Berlioz also borrowed from himself, drawing the symphony's main theme from his cantata *Herminie* (1828), the opening melody of the slow introduction from an early song, part of the third movement from his *Messe solennelle* (Solemn Mass, 1824), the fourth movement from his opera *Les francs-juges* (1826), and perhaps also parts of the second and fifth movements from other unfinished projects.

The first movement, "Dreams and Passions," features a slow introduction followed by an Allegro that has the outward characteristics of sonata form, including contrasting themes and a repeated exposition. The idée fixe, a melody with the long, arching line of an operatic aria, serves as the first theme,

HECTOR BERLIOZ

(1803–1869)

Berlioz, who created more than a dozen works that have gained the status of musical classics and who wrote the nineteenth-century "bible" on orchestration, played flute and guitar but never learned how to play piano. Born in southeastern France, he developed a fascination for music, taught himself harmony from textbooks, and began composing in his teens. His father sent him to medical school in Paris, but Berlioz frequented the opera, studied composition at the Paris Conservatoire, and eventually abandoned medicine for a career as a composer.

After several attempts, Berlioz won the Prix de Rome in 1830, a composition prize that paid a stipend for him to live and work in Rome. By then he had become enchanted with Beethoven's symphonies, Shakespeare's plays, and the Irish actress Harriet Smithson, whom he saw play Ophelia in *Hamlet.* His obsession for her inspired his *Symphonie fantastique*, an attempt to express his feelings in the context of a Beethovenian symphony. Its premiere in 1830 established Berlioz as a leader of the radical wing of composers in France.

Smithson spurned Berlioz for good reason: they had never met, and practically all she knew of him were mad love letters he sent her. Berlioz then became engaged to a nineteen-year-old piano teacher, Camille Marie Moke, but he had hardly begun his required residence in Rome when she turned around and married piano maker Camille Pleyel. In his autobiography, Berlioz recalls his response: "I must at once proceed to Paris and kill [Camille and her mother]. After that, of course, I would have to commit suicide." He made it as far as Nice, then wisely relented and returned to Italy. Back in Paris in 1832, he courted Smithson again and they married the following year. The ideal Ophelia, however, turned into an alcoholic, and their marriage fell apart after a few years and the birth of a son.

Although Berlioz won a few fervent advocates for his compositions, his music was too radical to win steady support from the musical institutions in Paris. He turned to music criticism as his chief profession, as Robert Schumann did around the same time. He got his music played by putting on concerts himself,

FIGURE 26.5 *Hector Berlioz, in a portrait by Emile Signol painted in 1832 during Berlioz's sojourn in Rome.*

working as his own impresario, and produced a flood of important compositions.

In addition to being a brilliant prose writer, Berlioz was one of the most literary of composers. Many of his compositions were inspired by his reading of Virgil (his opera *Les Troyens*, The Trojans), Shakespeare (*Romeo and Juliet, King Lear Overture, Beatrice and Benedict*, and other works), Goethe (*La damnation de Faust*), and other writers.

In 1835 he began to conduct, and soon he became one of the first to make a career of orchestral conducting, touring across Europe presenting his own works and music by other composers.

After Smithson died in 1854, he married the singer Marie Recio, with whom he had long had an affair. In his final years, Berlioz grew ill and felt bitter at the lack of recognition for his music in France. He died at sixty-five, having outlived two wives, his son, and most of his family and friends.

MAJOR WORKS 3 operas: *Benvenuto Cellini, Les Troyens,* and *Béatrice et Bénédict*; 4 symphonies, including *Symphonie fantastique, Harold en Italie* (with viola solo), and *Roméo et Juliette* (with soloists and chorus); 4 concert overtures; over 30 choral works, including Requiem, *La damnation de Faust, Te Deum,* and *L'enfance du Christ*; orchestral song cycle *Les nuits d'été* and other songs with orchestra or piano

accompanied by an irregularly throbbing figure that imitates the artist's racing heartbeat at first sight of the woman. Example 26.5a shows the first phrase of the theme in its original form. The development presents a series of dramatic episodes, including a full statement of the main theme in the dominant, and culminates in a triumphant tutti *fortissimo* statement of the theme in the tonic that is more a resplendent apotheosis than a recapitulation. For the second movement, "A Ball," Berlioz replaced the classical minuet with a waltz, enacting a scene at a ball where the artist catches a glimpse of his beloved, embodied by the waltzlike version of her theme shown in Example 26.5b. The slow third movement, "In the Country," is a pastorale in F major with piping shepherds, birdcalls reminiscent of Beethoven's *Pastoral* Symphony (see Chapter 24), and distant thunder. As the artist walks in the country, he suddenly thinks of his beloved, interweaving phrases of her theme as in Example 26.5c—its rhythms subtly at odds with the pastoral $\frac{6}{8}$ meter—with ominous instrumental recitatives that suggest his worries about her feelings for him. In the fourth movement, "March to the Scaffold," he dreams of his own execution in a macabre orchestral tour de force. Only the opening of her motive appears, just before he is guillotined at the end. The fifth and final movement (NAWM 146) depicts a "Dream of a Witches' Sabbath," presenting transformations of the idée fixe and two other themes, first singly, then in combination. The new

EXAMPLE 26.5 *Hector Berlioz,* Symphonie fantastique, *comparing first phrase of the idée fixe in its various transformations*

a. First movement, "Dreams and Passions"

b. Second movement, "A Ball"

c. Third movement, "In the Country"

d. Fifth movement, "Dream of a Witches' Sabbath"

form of the idée fixe, in Example 26.3d, is a grotesque caricature, implying that the beloved's depravity has been revealed. One of the other themes is the chant sequence *Dies irae* (NAWM 6b), part of the Mass for the Dead; this movement inaugurated a long tradition of using the *Dies irae,* especially its opening phrase, as a symbol of death, the macabre, or the diabolical.

The outlines of a traditional symphony are still here, in movements that resemble (or perhaps allude to) a sonata with slow introduction, a dance in minuet-and-trio form, a slow quasi-rondo form, and a fast finale. But the material is constantly developing, seldom repeated exactly, and the sequence of events is so unusual that it would suggest a narrative even if none were provided. Throughout, the transformations of the main theme help to tell the story, as it assumes a wide range of contrasting characters.

Symphonie fantastique is original not only in bending the symphony to serve narrative and autobiographical purposes but also in Berlioz's astounding ability to express the emotional content of his drama in music of great communicative power. Berlioz unified the symphony by introducing a recurring theme and by developing the dramatic idea through the five movements, extending procedures Beethoven had used in his Fifth, Sixth, and Ninth Symphonies. Multimovement works in which one or more themes recur or are recollected in later movements are said to be in **cyclic form**, and Berlioz helped to establish a precedent that was followed by many later composers from Robert Schumann to Charles Ives. Equally important is the variety he created by transforming his themes and using an astonishing array of instrumental colors, which lend a distinctive character to each passage. These include muted strings to suggest dreaming, harps for the ball, English horn and an offstage oboe imitating shepherds' pipes, snare drum and cymbals for the march to the scaffold, church bells, and violins played with the wood of the bow (*col legno*) in the witches' dance, creating a brittle sound evocative of skeletons rattling. Berlioz's vivid aural imagination and his inventive orchestral sonorities shine through in nearly every measure.

Harold en Italie

For his second symphony, *Harold en Italie* (Harold in Italy, 1834), Berlioz drew the title from Lord Byron's poem *Childe Harold's Pilgrimage* and the substance from recollections of the composer's sojourn in Italy. The piece features a solo viola, though less prominently than in a concerto—one reason why Paganini, who commissioned the work as a showpiece for viola, refused to play it. A recurring theme in the viola appears in each movement and is combined contrapuntally with the other themes. The finale sums up the themes of the preceding movements, as in Beethoven's Ninth Symphony, but does not end with a triumphant chorale. Indeed, the viola, like Byron's antihero protagonist Harold, remains a largely passive observer—at least until he flings himself into the final "Orgy of the Brigands"—so that the work inverts the heroism of Beethoven's symphonies.

Later symphonies

In his later symphonies, Berlioz departed even further from the traditional model. In *Roméo et Juliette* (Romeo and Juliet, 1839, revised ca. 1847), which he called a "dramatic symphony," he combined orchestra, soloists, and chorus in an unstaged concert drama, building in its conception on the precedent set by Beethoven's Ninth Symphony. The *Grande symphonie funèbre et triomphale* (Grand Funeral and Triumphant Symphony, 1840) for military band with optional strings and chorus is one of the early masterpieces of band music.

In addition to his symphonies, Berlioz composed concert overtures following the precedent of Beethoven's overtures and Mendelssohn's *A Midsummer Night's Dream*. The two earliest, *Waverley* (1828) and *King Lear* (1831), are based on English literature, capturing the overall mood of a novel by Walter Scott and a Shakespeare play. *The Roman Carnival* (1844) is a brilliant showpiece that has become a concert favorite, and *The Corsair* (1844) depicts a fast sailing vessel at sea and conveys a sense of independence that appealed to Romantic sensibilities. *Concert overtures*

Berlioz's *Symphonie fantastique* and other symphonic works made him the leader of the Romantic movement's radical wing. All subsequent composers of program music would be indebted to him. He enriched orchestral music with new resources of harmony, color, expression, and form. The idée fixe and his use of cyclic form gave impetus to the cyclical symphony of the later nineteenth century (see Chapter 30). His orchestration initiated a new era in which instrumental color rivaled harmony and melody as an expressive tool for composers. He codified his practice in the first book on the subject, his *Treatise on Instrumentation and Orchestration* (1843). *Berlioz's achievement*

CLASSICAL ROMANTICISM: MENDELSSOHN Felix Mendelssohn's works, compared with those of Berlioz written during the same period, have a much more Classic sound. For one thing, Mendelssohn was rigorously trained in classical genres and forms in his youth, writing thirteen string symphonies that gave him a mastery of form, counterpoint, and fugue and helped to determine his personal style. For another, his mature symphonies (which are numbered by date of publication rather than composition) follow classical models, although with departures that show the strong impact of Romanticism. In line with Romantic interest in the past, he wrote his Symphony No. 5 in D Minor (*Reformation,* 1830, revised 1832) to celebrate the Protestant Reformation and concluded it with a movement based on Luther's chorale *Ein feste Burg.* In his Symphony No. 2 in B-flat Major, titled *Lobgesang* (Song of Praise, 1840), he adds solo voices, chorus, and organ, following Beethoven's Ninth Symphony in incorporating voices while blending the genres of symphony and cantata. Mendelssohn's two most frequently performed symphonies both carry geographical nicknames: No. 3 in A Minor, the *Scottish* (1829–42), and No. 4 in A Major, the *Italian* (composed 1833 and published posthumously; a revised version of 1834 was left incomplete). They preserve impressions he gained of sounds and landscapes on trips to Italy and the British Isles, which he also recorded in drawings and paintings like the one in Figure 26.6.

The *Italian* Symphony celebrates the sunny and vibrant south, with a slow movement suggesting a procession of chanting pilgrims and a finale suggesting people dancing a spirited *saltarello* and *tarantella*. Mendelssohn opens the first movement with a melody, shown in Example 26.6, whose sighing lurches, sequences, and repeated postponement of closure are inspired by Italian opera, although its wide range and many leaps lend it an instrumental rather than vocal character. The second theme is similarly constructed, giving both thematic areas more the quality of well-shaped tunes than of material for future development. Perhaps as a consequence, the development section dwells on a new melodic idea, a motive that gradually builds to a new theme in combination with the opening figure of the first theme. All three themes are Italian *Symphony*

FIGURE 26.6
*Watercolor painting by
Felix Mendelssohn, titled*
Amalfi in May 1831.
*A talented amateur artist,
Mendelssohn sketched,
drew, and painted
throughout his journeys in
Italy and Britain. This is a
view of the Gulf of Salerno
from Amalfi, near Naples,
in southern Italy.*

EXAMPLE 26.6 *Felix Mendelssohn, Symphony No. 4 (Italian), opening theme*

recalled in the recapitulation, binding the movement together. In this way, Mendelssohn neatly accommodates his tuneful themes within the developmental structure of sonata form.

Concert overtures   Mendelssohn's genius for musical landscapes is evident in his concert overtures *The Hebrides* (also called *Fingal's Cave,* 1832), on another Scottish topic, and *Meeresstille und glückliche Fahrt* (Becalmed at Sea and Prosperous Voyage, 1828–32), on two poems by Goethe. His masterpiece in the genre is *A Midsummer Night's Dream,* inspired by Shakespeare's play. Written in 1826 when he was seventeen, it set the standard for all subsequent concert overtures. It opens with a series of magical chords, as if to say "once upon a time," then depicts the fairies fluttering and dancing in a brilliant example of perpetual motion for a full orchestra trained to tiptoe like a chamber ensemble. The light, bustling string texture of this passage became a trademark of Mendelssohn's scherzos. The classical overture structure of sonata form without repeats is perfectly clear, but the listener's attention is drawn to Mendelssohn's imaginative use of musical figuration and orchestral color to evoke everything from fairy dust to the braying of the character Bottom after his head is magically transformed into that of a jackass. Seventeen years later, Mendelssohn wrote additional incidental music, including the famous *Wedding March,* for a production of the play.

A virtuoso pianist, Mendelssohn wrote four concertos for his own performances, the last two of which were published in his lifetime: No. 1 in G Minor (1831) and No. 2 in D Minor (1837). Although the showpieces composed by most virtuosos of the time revel in startling effects and technical display—more for their own sakes than for their musical inspiration—Mendelssohn emphasized the musical content, seeking to achieve the same balance of audience appeal and lasting value that connoisseurs praised in the concertos of Mozart and Beethoven. For Mendelssohn as for Beethoven, the virtuosic display of the soloist was a vehicle for the composer's expression, not a purpose in itself.

Piano concertos

The same could be said for Mendelssohn's Violin Concerto in E Minor (1844; first movement in NAWM 147). The three movements, played without pause, are linked by thematic content and connecting passages: a transition leads from the opening Allegro molto appassionato to the lyrical Andante, and an introduction to the last movement alludes to the first movement's opening theme. In the first movement, Mendelssohn has the soloist state the main theme at the outset, skipping the usual orchestral exposition, and places the cadenza just before rather than after the recapitulation. Essentially, he reworked concerto form into a variant of sonata form with a featured soloist, a reformulation that is typical of Mendelssohn and of his age in finding new ways to reinterpret yet continue tradition. The middle movement, in ABA' form, is a romance for violin and orchestra driven by a slowly unfolding melody. The finale, in sonata or sonata-rondo form, has the lightness of a scherzo. Throughout the concerto, the music for the soloist is at times lyrical and expressive, at times highly virtuosic, exhibiting the full range of what a violin can do. The violin and orchestra are partners, and the leading melodies move seamlessly from soloist to orchestra and back. Although there are plenty of opportunities for the soloist to dazzle, as was expected in a Romantic showpiece, the concerto always seems motivated by a greater poetic purpose, as Mendelssohn uses the contrasts of virtuosity with lyric expression and of solo with orchestra to delineate the form, create variety, and convey deep feelings. The resulting concerto has become one of the most popular in the repertoire.

Violin Concerto

ROMANTIC RECONCEPTIONS: ROBERT SCHUMANN In the eyes of many composers and listeners, the prestigious status that Beethoven had conferred on the symphony made it a rite of passage to full recognition. For example, Clara Schumann believed that composers were judged by their symphonies and operas, and she wrote in her diary, "My greatest wish is that [Robert] should compose for orchestra." When he did so, Robert Schumann applied the same lofty idealism as in his piano music and music criticism. His primary orchestral models were Schubert's *Great* C-Major Symphony and the symphonies and concertos of Mendelssohn, which showed how songlike themes could be integrated into developmental forms.

First Symphony   Schumann completed his First Symphony in B-flat Major in the spring of 1841 and drafted another that same year—his "symphony year," following the "Lieder year" of 1840. The music of the First, known as the *Spring* Symphony, is fresh and spontaneous and is driven by inexhaustible rhythmic energy. Reflecting his absorption in poetry during the previous year, Schumann took inspiration from a poem about spring whose every line uses the same accentual rhythm. That rhythm is echoed in the opening motto of the first movement (NAWM 148), first heard in trumpets and horns in the slow introduction, that becomes the principal figure of the first theme and pervades the development and coda. At the recapitulation, Schumann replaces the first theme with a powerful restatement of the slow introduction's opening passage, and in the coda he remakes the motto rhythm into a new, lyrical theme; both moments upend listeners' expectations and make the movement a continual adventure while drawing it into a tighter whole. The symphony was an immediate success and established Schumann as a composer of large instrumental forms.

Fourth Symphony   The other symphony from 1841, in D minor, had a mixed reception at its premiere that December, and Schumann laid it aside. After completing two more symphonies in 1846 and 1850, Schumann returned to the D minor in 1851, revising it as Symphony No. 4. It represents his most radical rethinking of symphonic form. The four movements are played without a break, joined by harmonic links and transitional passages. Moreover, many of the themes are variations of each other, unifying the work as an extended development of a small number of ideas. The whole symphony can be heard as one large sonata form, in which the first movement serves as slow introduction, exposition, and beginning of an extensive development section; the slow movement and scherzo are episodes within the development; and the finale serves as recapitulation and coda. This double-function form recalls the succession of linked movements in Schumann's *Carnaval* (see Chapter 25), yet with much stronger connections to the forms, genres, and procedures of the Classic period.

THE ROMANTIC LEGACY Schubert, Berlioz, Mendelssohn, and Robert Schumann each found a distinctive solution to the problem of how to write symphonic music after Beethoven. But while they won a place beside Beethoven in the repertory, they did not displace him, and orchestral composers in the second half of the century continued to struggle against his potentially overwhelming influence (see Chapters 29 and 30). New genres like the symphonic poem, pioneered by Liszt, offered one path, while composers like Brahms and Bruckner engaged the symphony tradition directly. All these later composers drew on models in the Romantic generation, finding in them a rich treasure of new possibilities: Berlioz's symphonies and Mendelssohn's overtures for programmatic and descriptive music, Mendelssohn and Schumann for links and continuities between movements, Berlioz and Schumann for transformation of themes, and all of them for ways to integrate the Romantic emphasis on melody, surprising harmonies, and novel orchestral effects into the symphonic tradition.

ROMANTICISM AND THE CLASSICAL TRADITION

The first half of the nineteenth century was a paradoxical age in music. The period saw extraordinary growth in concert life, music publishing, instrument manufacture, amateur music-making, touring virtuosos, and professional orchestras and chamber ensembles, all of which reinforced each other and spurred composers to produce a torrent of new music. These same factors also helped to establish a repertoire of classical masterpieces from Handel and Bach through Haydn, Mozart, and Beethoven. Composers of music for large chorus, chamber ensemble, or symphony orchestra could see this process at work and aspired to similar greatness. They competed for performances, recognition, and sales with the masters of the past—and with their contemporaries—by introducing something new and individual into genres and forms that were hallowed by tradition. In varying degrees, they blended elements of Romanticism into classical frameworks from the eighteenth century.

Many of the works they produced—including Schubert's late chamber works and *Unfinished* and *Great* C-Major Symphonies; Berlioz's Requiem and *Symphonie fantastique*; Mendelssohn's *St. Paul* and *Elijah, Italian* and *Scottish* Symphonies, and Violin Concerto; and Robert Schumann's piano quintet, piano trios, and symphonies—won wide popularity and became classics in their own right. Pieces by these and other composers of their time have become staples of the repertoire. For many of these works in eighteenth-century genres and forms, the relationship to past music is an important aspect of their meaning, part of what makes the music interesting, distinctive, and worth hearing many times over. In other compositions, the tension between new and old is no less strong, but what is innovative seems more significant than the references to tradition. As we will see in later chapters, composers defining themselves in relation to the classical tradition is a theme that grew stronger for at least the next century and produced a remarkable variety of responses.

Of course, few pieces attained a permanent place in the repertoire during their composer's lifetime. Most works were printed, performed, and eventually eclipsed by newer works, the typical fate of music in earlier centuries. But with music of the past playing an increasing role, some composers were lucky enough to find performers or critics to champion their works after their deaths, as Mendelssohn had done for Bach, Robert Schumann for Schubert, and Clara Schumann for her husband. Berlioz, for example, had to wait until the second half of the twentieth century for full acceptance, aided by recordings of his monumental works.

Meanwhile, some of the utilitarian music of the day won a surprising permanence. The orchestral waltzes and other dances of Joseph Lanner and Johann Strauss the elder, numerous hymns by Lowell Mason and his contemporaries, and the music of *The Sacred Harp* have all been performed continuously since they first appeared, sustained by living traditions in which their music is useful and even revered. As we will see in later chapters, the nineteenth and twentieth centuries spawned many such repertoires of classic works from the past, even while new styles and types of music emerged at a dizzying pace.

Further Reading is available at digital.wwnorton.com/hwm10

27

ROMANTIC OPERA AND MUSICAL THEATER TO MIDCENTURY

❖

While purely instrumental music gained prestige, opera continued to be a central part of musical life, especially in Italy and France. Opera served as elite entertainment and also as the source of music that was popular with audiences of all classes and professions. Composers followed national trends, even while they developed new forms and approaches and borrowed ideas across national boundaries. **Nationalism**, both political and musical, brought new themes into opera. Italian **bel canto** opera dominated the field, but new types of opera were cultivated in France and Germany that exercised a lasting influence, and Russian opera gained independence after a century of absorbing foreign styles. In addition, a lively operatic life emerged in the Americas, centered on the performance of European operas. At the same time, a new form of musical theater—the minstrel show—sprang up in the United States and became the first musical export from North America to Europe.

THE ROLES OF OPERA

The first half of the nineteenth century was in many ways a golden age for opera. New opera theaters were erected all over western Europe. The craze even jumped the Atlantic and took root in the New World. Most opera theaters were run for profit by an impresario, usually backed by government subsidies or private support. Members of the upper and middle classes attended fully staged opera, and for some people, being seen at the opera asserted their social status even more than their love of music. Opera was and remains big business, as the poster for the Paris premiere of Meyerbeer's *Les Huguenots* in Figure 27.1 makes clear in announcing that free passes, or *entrées de faveur,* would not be honored. Publishers such as Ricordi in Italy and Escudier in France even started their own newspapers (the *Gazetta musicale di Milano* and *La France musicale*) that mixed advertising with substantive articles about new works and reviews of important performances.

FIGURE 27.1 *Poster for the premiere of* Les Huguenots *by Giacomo Meyerbeer.*

Outside the opera house, excerpts from opera cropped up everywhere, comprising an important part of popular as well as elite culture. Individual numbers and complete scores were published in versions for voices and piano and were performed in salons and by amateurs at home; selections from operas were transcribed for piano; overtures and arias appeared on concert programs in original form or arrangements; operas were abridged and parodied in burlesques, puppet shows, and other forms of popular theater; and melodies from opera arias became staples of café orchestras and even barrel organs. All types of opera from the period embody this dual appeal to the elite and to the public at large.

Opera in elite and popular culture

Early in the century, the balance of interest in Italian opera remained focused on beautiful singing. In French and German opera, the orchestra played an increasingly significant role in depicting scenes, conveying emotions, portraying the dramatic situation, and carrying the musical continuity, and beginning in the 1840s Italian composers followed suit. Star singers were still paid more than composers, no doubt because their reputations sold tickets, as suggested by the advertisement in Figure 27.1 for *Les Huguenots,* which lists the principal singers and dancers with nary a mention of the composer. Often the composer's score was only the starting point for a performance, subject to cuts and substitutions at the insistence of the singers, the impresario, or state censors. But over the course of the century, the composer gradually became the most prominent figure in the collaborative effort of creating an opera, instead of ranking behind the librettist and singers as was typical in the eighteenth and early nineteenth centuries. New operas by the leading composers became major events, and successful ones were performed numerous times and restaged in many cities. By 1850, a permanent repertory of operas began to emerge, paralleling the classical repertoire in the concert hall. At the center of this repertory were operas by Rossini, Bellini, Donizetti, Meyerbeer, and Weber, alongside the late Mozart operas and the early operas of Verdi (discussed in Chapter 28).

Singers, orchestra, and composer

TIMELINE

1814–24 Reign of Louis XVIII as king of France

1816 Gioachino Rossini, *The Barber of Seville*

1819 Théâtre d'Orléans opens in New Orleans

1821 New Paris Opéra opens

1821 Carl Maria von Weber, *Der Freischütz*

1824–30 Reign of Charles X as king of France

1825 First Italian opera season in New York

1829 Rossini, *Guillaume Tell*

1830 "July Revolution" in France puts Louis Philippe on throne

1831 Vincenzo Bellini, *Norma*

1835 Gaetano Donizetti, *Lucia di Lammermoor*

1836 Giacomo Meyerbeer, *Les Huguenots*

1836 Mikhail Glinka, *A Life for the Tsar*

1841 Adolphe Adam, *Giselle*

1842 Giuseppe Verdi, *Nabucco*

1843 Richard Wagner, *The Flying Dutchman*

1843 Michael Balfe, *The Bohemian Girl*

1843 Virginia Minstrels debut

1845 William Henry Fry, *Leonora*

1848 Second Republic declared in France

1848–49 Gold Rush in California

1850–52 Jenny Lind tours United States

1854 Academy of Music opens in New York

1856–58 Hector Berlioz composes *Les Troyens*

Like composers in earlier eras, opera composers in the first half of the nineteenth century aimed to capture in their music the drama, emotions, and personalities on stage. Naturally, they (and the impresarios they worked for) preferred librettos with strong plots, interesting characters, and wide audience appeal. Subjects and settings for operas varied widely, from grand historical epics to folktales, and from plots with strong political overtones to stories that centered on private emotions and personal relationships. Distant lands and long-ago times had a special attraction. Like movies today, many operas were adapted from recent literary works, such as the novels of Sir Walter Scott and the plays of Friedrich Schiller and Victor Hugo, or from venerable literary masterpieces such as Shakespeare's plays. Librettists sought to reflect the concerns of the broader audience that was now attending operas, not so much by putting middle-class characters on stage—although that would become more common over the course of the century—as by addressing issues that spoke to them: how to balance love with loyalty to family (as in Meyerbeer's *Les Huguenots*) or nation (Bellini's *Norma*), women's growing desire for independence (Rossini's *Barber of Seville* and Donizetti's *Lucia di Lammermoor*), the struggle for freedom (Rossini's *Guillaume Tell* and Auber's *La muette de Portici*), and the fear of evil (Weber's *Der Freischütz*).

NATIONALISM Among the new themes were issues of national identity. The French Revolution and Napoleonic Wars had helped to spread the concept of a nation as a group of citizens with a common heritage rather than as subjects of a ruler. The influence of this idea grew throughout the nineteenth century. ***Nationalism*** in the political realm was the attempt to unify a group of people by creating a national identity through characteristics such as a common language, shared culture, historical traditions, and national institutions and rituals. Not all of these elements had to be present: the Swiss achieved a sense of nationhood through shared history and institutions despite speaking four different languages, while elsewhere people sought to create a sense of commonality based on language and culture that crossed existing political boundaries. Although later generations would take it as a given, national identity was in almost every case intentionally created and channeled to achieve social and political goals.

Nationalism could be used to support the status quo or to challenge it. In France and Russia, which had long been unified states, expressions of nationalism could rally support for the government. But Germany and Italy had been divided since the Middle Ages, and in both regions nationalist sentiment supported unification. That was not to come until the third quarter of the century, despite struggles in Italy as early as the 1820s during the Risorgimento (resurgence), which sought to unify Italy and reclaim the leading role it played in Roman antiquity and the Renaissance. The foundation for unification could be laid by creating a shared national culture through a common language, literature, music, and the other arts. Such cultural nationalism became a strong element in many, though not all, nineteenth-century operas, as well as in much other music. As we will see, opera—an expensive art form that usually relied on government support—was frequently staged within a political context and could carry political meanings on many levels, whether put there by the librettist and composer, prompted by the government itself, or imputed to the work by those who heard it.

The presence of national elements in opera and other forms of music could serve different purposes, depending on the audience. Representing the history, culture, or musical styles of a people could reinforce their group identity as a nation. For Italians, their identification with Italian opera as a national art form was so strong that making the plot or music deliberately Italian was beside the point, and librettists and composers instead relied on analogies to suggest nationalist ideas, as in Bellini's *Norma*. But for Germans, Weber's *Der Freischütz*—an opera based on German folklore, focused on German peasants as characters, and filled with references to the styles of German dances and folk songs—became a symbol of the nation that was yet to be, and thus an inspiration for nation-building as well as for many later operas.

Nationalism at home

People are curious about each other, not only about themselves, and thus the use of national elements attracted audiences from other nations. This was evident in the popularity in western Europe of Chopin's Polish dances and Gottschalk's pieces on American and Caribbean themes, tunes, and rhythms (see Chapter 25). And it was evident again in the reception of *Der Freischütz* outside Germany and of Glinka's operas outside Russia. Such interest in faraway places and peoples was part of Romanticism, and it was also reflected in the many plots set in distant lands and times and the occasional use of **exoticism**, the evocation of a foreign land or culture. Nationalism and exoticism became more prominent in the second half of the century, as we will see in the next chapter.

Nationalism abroad

ITALY

Opera had been invented and popularized in Italy, which was still home to more opera houses than any other region. Forty or more new operas were produced every year in the early nineteenth century, and dozens of composers were writing operas. Within constraints imposed by politics, state or religious censorship, the business of opera production and music publishing, and poetic and operatic traditions, librettists and composers sought to create operas with engaging plots and attractive music that appealed to listeners, moved their emotions, and conveyed the drama. Amid this ferment, Rossini, Donizetti, and Bellini created a new Italian tradition in opera, later extended by Verdi and others, and composed works that have been performed across Europe and in the New World almost every year since their first performances.

GIOACHINO ROSSINI If asked who was the most famous and important living composer, most people in Europe around 1825 would have answered not Beethoven but rather Gioachino Rossini (1792–1868; see biography and Figure 27.2). He is best known today for his comic operas such as *L'italiana in Algeri* (The Italian Woman in Algiers; Venice, 1813) and *Il barbiere di Siviglia* (The Barber of Seville; Rome, 1816). Yet Rossini's reputation during his lifetime rested as much on his serious operas such as *Otello* (Naples, 1816), *Mosè*

GIOACHINO ROSSINI
(1792–1868)

Rossini had a brilliant career as a composer of opera, producing some of the most popular ever written.

Born in Pesaro on the Adriatic coast of Italy, Rossini was the son of a horn and trumpet player and an operatic singer. He studied music as a child and performed professionally as a violist, singer, and pianist. In 1806, he enrolled in the Bologna Conservatory, where his studies of the music of Haydn and Mozart had a permanent impact on his style.

Rossini was commissioned to write his first opera in 1810, at age eighteen, and the great success three years later of *Tancredi* and *L'italiana in Algeri* established his international reputation. In 1815, he was appointed musical director of the Teatro San Carlo in Naples, and a year later his most successful opera, *The Barber of Seville*, was produced in Rome. For the next eight years, Rossini composed numerous operas for Naples and other cities. Because copyright protection did not exist in Italy, he could earn money from operas only when he participated in the performances. As a result, he constantly had to produce new works, composing very rapidly (sometimes writing an opera in a month or less), often borrowing or reworking overtures and arias from his own previous works. He always wrote for particular singers, creating music to suit their talents.

In 1822, Rossini married the soprano Isabella Colbran, with whom he had worked since coming to Naples. After *Semiramide* (1823), Rossini's last opera for Italy, they traveled to London, then settled in Paris, where he became director of the Théâtre Italien. He reworked some of his Italian operas to French librettos translated or adapted from the Italian and wrote one entirely new opera in French, *Guillaume Tell*, in 1829. Then, a rich man and not yet forty years old, he retired from writing operas.

FIGURE 27.2 *Gioachino Rossini around 1816, the year he composed* The Barber of Seville. *Painting by Vincenzo Camuccini.*

His remaining forty years of life were marred by illness, but he was financially comfortable, entertaining every Saturday night in his villa outside Paris, eating to excess, and inventing recipes that he exchanged with some of the most famous chefs in Europe. He began an affair with Olympe Pélissier in the 1830s and married her in 1846 after his first wife's death. He composed music for church and salons but published little. In his last decade, he produced witty piano pieces and songs—often parodies of other music—that influenced Saint-Saëns, Satie, and others and anticipate French neoclassicism of the twentieth century. He died in 1868, known best for music written four to six decades earlier.

MAJOR WORKS 39 operas, including *Tancredi, L'italiana in Algeri, Il barbiere di Siviglia, Otello, La Cenerentola, Mosè in Egitto, Semiramide,* and *Guillaume Tell; Stabat mater, Petite messe solennelle,* and other sacred vocal works; and smaller vocal and instrumental pieces collected in *Soirées musicales* and *Péchés de vieillesse* (Sins of Old Age)

in *Egitto* (Moses in Egypt; Naples, 1818), and *Guillaume Tell* (William Tell; Paris, 1829). He was the most popular and influential opera composer of his generation, in part because he blended aspects of opera buffa and opera seria into both his comic and his serious operas, making them all more varied, more appealing, and more true to human character. The new conventions he established for Italian opera would endure for over half a century and influence operas in France, Germany, and other nations.

Bel canto singing

In Rossini's operas, the most important element is the voice, even more than the story, orchestra, costumes, and scenery. He called for an elegant style of singing characterized by seemingly effortless technique, an equally beautiful tone throughout a singer's entire range, agility, flexibility, and control of every type of melody from long lyrical lines through florid embellishment, much of it improvised. This style is today known as **bel canto**—literally, "beautiful singing"—a term that Rossini and others used only in retrospect in order to contrast the Italian singing style of the eighteenth and early nineteenth centuries with the heavier dramatic style that dominated by midcentury (see In Performance: The Bel Canto Diva, pp. 652–53).

General style

Rossini's operas are known for their irrepressible tunefulness combining catchy melodies with snappy rhythms and clear phrases. His melodies are laced with coloratura that combines vocal display with expressivity and perceptive depiction of each character. He often repeats ideas, usually with a new twist, and shows an impeccable sense of theatrical timing. His spare orchestration supports rather than competes with the singers, while featuring individual instruments, especially winds, for color. His harmonic schemes are not complex but are often original, and he shares with other early-nineteenth-century composers a fondness for juxtaposing third-related keys. One of his characteristic devices, both simple and effective, became known as the "Rossini crescendo"—building up excitement by repeating a phrase, louder each time and often at a higher pitch, sometimes giving the effect of a world about to spin out of control.

Scene structure

The action in earlier operas was mostly confined to dry recitative dialogue, while arias were dramatically static, expressing only one or two moods. Rossini continued to use simple recitative in his comedies, but in his serious operas and some parts of comic operas Rossini and his librettists developed a scene structure that distributed the story more evenly and integrated new plot developments or changes of mood within an aria or ensemble. A continuous succession of orchestrally accompanied recitatives, solo arias, duets, ensembles, and choruses all contributed to advancing the plot, with both orchestra and chorus playing more significant roles than they had in previous Italian operas.

As shown in Figure 27.3, a typical scene begins with an instrumental introduction and a recitative section called a **scena** (Italian for "scene") that

ARIA (SOLO OR WITH CHORUS)					
Orchestral introduction	*Scena*		*Cantabile*	*Tempo di mezzo* (middle section)	*Cabaletta*
	recitative		usually slow	changes tempo, modulates; may be transition, ensemble, or chorus	usually fast

DUET OR ENSEMBLE					
Orchestral introduction	*Scena*	*Tempo d'attacco* (opening section)	*Cantabile*	*Tempo di mezzo*	*Cabaletta*

FIGURE 27.3 *Scene structures in Rossini operas.*

IN PERFORMANCE

The Bel Canto Diva

The art of bel canto fostered the rise of a new breed of opera singers in the first half of the nineteenth century. Like today's pop superstars, female virtuosos like Giuditta Pasta, Angelica Catalani, Giulia Grisi, Henriette Sontag, and Jenny Lind were more than mere singers; they were larger-than-life cultural icons. The term used to describe them, *diva* (Italian for "goddess"), reflects the semidivine status ascribed to them by their legions of admirers.

The Spanish mezzo-soprano Maria Malibran (1808–1836), shown in Figure 27.4, epitomizes the dazzling aura of the bel canto diva. Born into a celebrated musical family, she made her London debut in 1825 as Rosina in *The Barber of Seville*, the first of many Rossini roles with which she would be closely identified. She repeated her success a few months later in New York City, appearing with a touring company organized by her father, the tenor Manuel Garcia, and went on to take France and Italy by storm in works by Rossini, Bellini, Mozart, Meyerbeer, Donizetti, and other composers. Malibran's exceptional vocal range of nearly three octaves was matched by her dramatic powers. She was at the height of her fame when she died at the age of twenty-eight as a result of a riding accident in Birmingham, England, shortly after her marriage to the Belgian violinist Charles de Bériot.

Malibran was also remarkable for her versatility, being equally at home in Rossini's frothy comedies and in tragic roles like Bellini's Norma. Both kinds of music allowed her to show off her prowess in adorning melodies with improvised embellishments, a

FIGURE 27.4 *A portrait of Maria Malibran by Italian artist Luigi Pedrazzi (1802–1845).*

practice that was as intrinsic to bel canto idiom as it was in eighteenth-century opera (see Chapter 21). Malibran and other divas often wrote down their ornamented versions of popular arias, both for teaching purposes and for sale as sheet music. Not all of their elaborations bore the composer's stamp of approval, however. Once, after suffering through an overwrought performance of Rosina's aria *Una voce poco fa* by the soprano Adelina Patti, Rossini remarked cattily: "Very nice, my dear, and who wrote the piece you have just performed?"

It was to guard against such excesses that Rossini and other composers began, in the second decade of the century, to notate ornaments

is accompanied by the orchestra. The ensuing aria has two main sections, a slow, lyrical **cantabile** and a lively and brilliant **cabaletta**. The cantabile expresses relatively calm moods such as pensiveness, sadness, or hope, and the cabaletta more active feelings such as anger or joy. Part or all of the cabaletta is repeated, perhaps with improvised embellishments. Some arias, like *Una voce poco fa* from *The Barber of Seville* (NAWM 149), have these two sections only, but in most arias, we also find a middle section between the cantabile and the cabaletta called the **tempo di mezzo** (middle movement), which

even more painstakingly in their scores. Although these written-out embellishments were meant as suggestions rather than prescriptions, there is evidence that many singers followed them faithfully, if not slavishly. One such manuscript, preserved in the library of the Conservatory "Giuseppe Verdi" in Milan, contains a tastefully ornamented version of Rosina's *Una voce poco fa* in Rossini's hand, excerpted in Example 27.1 (compare with the unadorned melody shown in Example 27.2d, which comes between the passages shown here). Although penned many years after the 1816 premiere of *The Barber of Seville*, and tailored for another singer's voice, the soaring cadenza, liquid runs, and pert grace notes in the final cabaletta section of the aria convey a sense of pyrotechnics that seventeen-year-old Maria Malibran displayed in New York's Park Theater on November 29, 1825.

EXAMPLE 27.1 *Two passages from Gioachino Rossini's ornamented version of* Una voce poco fa, *from* The Barber of Seville

I allow myself to be led.

and a hundred tricks before I give in I will play!

is usually some kind of transition or interruption by other characters and in which something happens to alter the situation or the character's mood. A duet or ensemble has a similar form (as in the duet from Verdi's *La traviata* in NAWM 154), but the cantabile is usually preceded by an opening section called **tempo d'attacco** in which the characters trade melodic phrases. The finale of an act is normally an action piece that brings together most or all of the characters and is organized in many sections, employing shifts in tempo, meter, and key to accommodate the rapid changes of situation and emotion

EXAMPLE 27.2 *Changes of style in* Una voce poco fa, *from Rossini's* The Barber of Seville

a. Quasi-recitative

A voice a short while ago here in my heart resounded.

b. Patter song

The guardian will refuse, I shall sharpen my wits.

taking place on stage. The action often culminates in a fast ***stretta*** corresponding to the cabaletta in an aria or ensemble.

Rossini's basic format could be flexibly applied to suit almost any dramatic situation, and his structure created a dramatic progression from one mood or idea to another while allowing more than two contrasting moods to be presented within a coherent form. In line with the continued role of Italian opera as a vehicle for virtuoso singing, this structure also provided singers with an opportunity to show a wide range of emotions and vocal effects, from lyric beauty to sparkling pyrotechnics.

The Barber of Seville

Considered today Rossini's most popular opera, *The Barber of Seville* combines features of opera buffa with bel canto tradition. The main character, the town's barber and resident schemer, helps a count (disguised as Lindoro, a poor soldier) to win the hand of the beautiful and wealthy Rosina, who has

c. Cabaletta, lyrical opening

I am docile, I am respectful,

d. Contrasting comic style

But if they touch my weaker side, I will be a viper,

been locked away by her guardian, Dr. Bartolo—a man intent on marrying her for her inheritance. Secret messages, drunken brawls, and mistaken identities are all part of the chaotic plot.

Rosina's justly famous aria *Una voce poco fa* (NAWM 149) conveys her character through changes of style, as shown in Example 27.2. The orchestral introduction presents ideas that will reappear later. There is no opening recitative, but the first part of her cantabile—as she narrates being serenaded by and falling in love with Lindoro—is broken into small phrases punctuated by orchestral chords, a style appropriate to narration (Example 27.2a). When she swears to outwit her guardian, the style briefly changes to a comic patter song (Example 27.2b), which is preceded and followed by elaborate embellishments and runs as she vows to marry Lindoro. Rossini proceeds directly to the cabaletta, where the music reveals Rosina's true nature. She claims to be both docile and obedient—singing a winning, lyrical melody (Example 27.2c)—as well as a viper and trickster—showing off her sudden vocal leaps and rapid passagework in opera buffa style (Example 27.2d). The aria is a cunning portrayal of the different facets of Rosina's character and a masterful combination of bel canto melody, wit, and comic description.

Serious operas   The lasting appeal of Rossini's comic operas has overshadowed his serious ones, but they were equally significant in his day. Many of the serious operas have enjoyed successful revivals in recent decades, showing that his style and approach have a far wider range in delineating characters, capturing situations, and conveying emotions than are represented in the comic operas alone.

Guillaume Tell   The best known of his serious operas was his last, *Guillaume Tell*, which was written for the Paris Opéra in 1829 and had five hundred performances there during the composer's lifetime. The libretto, based on Friedrich Schiller's play *Wilhelm Tell* (1804), celebrates a folk hero who led a rebellion of three Swiss cantons against an Austrian governor. The theme was timely—revolution and struggles for national unity were in the air—but it also subjected the work to censorship in Milan, London, Berlin, and St. Petersburg. While continuing the conventions he had helped to establish in Italian opera, Rossini's setting includes many choruses, ensembles, dances, processions, and atmospheric instrumental interludes, all of which drew on French operatic traditions. This combination of elements, along with its large scale and dramatic power, made *Guillaume Tell* one of the founding examples of French grand opera (see pp. 660–62). Rossini's role in creating a new genre of French opera invites comparison to Lully, another Italian, who originated the French operatic tradition in the seventeenth century (see Chapter 16).

A new kind of tenor   Given Rossini's devotion to the bel canto style of singing, it is ironic that his *Guillaume Tell* provided the occasion for a new kind of tenor voice that would come to dominate by midcentury and foster a more dramatic, less lyrical style of singing. At the Italian premiere of the opera at Lucca in 1831, tenor Gilbert Duprez (1806–1896) sang for the first time on the operatic stage a high C in full voice (known among singers as *chest voice*), not in falsetto as had been the tradition for centuries. After great success in Italy, Duprez returned to his native Paris in 1837 and triumphed at the Opéra in *Guillaume Tell*. His new style of singing was enormously popular with audiences (though not with Rossini, who compared his high notes to a squawking chicken). Other tenors adopted his approach, and composers from Donizetti and Berlioz to Verdi and Wagner wrote for his type of voice.

Overtures   Rossini's opera overtures have found a second career in the concert hall, as gems of the orchestral repertoire. Most are in two parts: a long, slow introduction with a lyrical melody for wind instruments followed by a fast binary form without repeats, shaped like the exposition and recapitulation of a sonata form. The fast section focuses almost exclusively on the themes, with minimal transitions and a rousing Rossini crescendo at the end of each half. This formula, combining attractive melodies with a rising sense of excited anticipation, makes Rossini's overtures the perfect curtain-raisers at the opera and tasty appetizers on concert programs.

The most famous is the overture to *Guillaume Tell*. Written for Paris, it has a different shape from the Italian overtures, with four sections that present a series of genre scenes taken from the opera: a slow pastoral introduction; a musical depiction of a storm; another slow section featuring a *ranz des vaches*—a Swiss cowherd's call—played by an English horn (and later repeated throughout the opera); and a galloping allegro (used in the twentieth century as the theme for the radio and television show *The Lone Ranger*). Combining simplicity in melody, harmony, and form with vivacious rhythms, exciting dynamics, and unusual orchestral effects has made Rossini's overtures perennial favorites.

VINCENZO BELLINI Vincenzo Bellini (1801–1835) was a younger contemporary of Rossini's who came to prominence after Rossini had retired from opera composition. Bellini preferred dramas of passion, with fast, gripping action. His favorite librettist, Felice Romani, did not limit action to recitative passages but built it into the arias and provided opportunities for lyrical moments within the recitatives. Of Bellini's ten operas—all serious—the most important are *La sonnambula* (The Sleepwalker, 1831), *Norma* (1831), and *I puritani* (The Puritans, 1835).

Bellini is known for long, sweeping, highly embellished, intensely emo-   *Style*
tional melodies. Among the most famous is the cantabile section of Norma's *cavatina,* or entrance aria, *Casta diva* (Chaste goddess) from *Norma* (NAWM 150), shown in Example 27.3. The choice of subject for the opera, set in ancient Gaul after its conquest by the Romans, reflected both the Romantic fascination with distant times and places and Italian yearnings for freedom from foreign domination, especially acute after the Austrians suppressed revolts in northern Italy in 1830–31. When Norma, high priestess of the Druids, prays to the moon for peace with the Romans, her vocal line seems to be in constant motion, creating a deeply expressive and unpredictable melody. The secret of such melodies is that an underlying simple structure, often stepwise motion (A–G–F in the first phrase, A–B♭ in the second), is embellished with

EXAMPLE 27.3 Casta diva, *from Vincenzo Bellini's* Norma

Chaste goddess, who plates with silver [these sacred ancient plants]

ever-changing figuration that draws our attention and plays with our expectations. The scene follows Rossini's typical pattern, beginning with orchestrally accompanied recitative, followed by the cantabile section, a declamatory tempo di mezzo, and a brilliant cabaletta. In each section, the chorus plays an important role, responding to Norma's pleas for peace. The constant interaction of the principal protagonists with subordinate characters and the chorus creates a sense of continuous action, which Bellini reinforces through frequent changes of style, texture, and figuration.

GAETANO DONIZETTI One of the most prolific Italian composers during the second quarter of the century was Gaetano Donizetti (1797–1848), who composed oratorios, cantatas, chamber and church music, about one hundred songs, and several symphonies in addition to some seventy operas. His most enduring works were the serious operas *Anna Bolena* (Milan, 1830) and *Lucia di Lammermoor* (Naples, 1835); the comic operas *L'elisir d'amore* (The Elixir of Love; Milan, 1832) and *Don Pasquale* (Paris, 1843); and the opéra comique *La fille du regiment* (The Daughter of the Regiment; Paris, 1840).

Donizetti, like Rossini, had an instinct for the theater and for melody that effectively captures a character, situation, or feeling. His comic operas often mix sentimentality with comedy. In his serious operas, Donizetti constantly moves the drama forward, occasionally averting cadences that would entice applause and thus sustaining dramatic tension until a major scene is finished. The beginnings and endings of the formal components of a scene, such as the orchestral introduction, cantabile, and cabaletta, are sometimes disguised by choral or recitative episodes so that the music seems to possess an almost seamless continuity.

Lucia di Lammermoor

One of Donizetti's most famous operas, *Lucia di Lammermoor,* offers a prime example of this kind of transparent continuity. Based on a novel by Sir Walter Scott (1771–1832), the most popular novelist of his generation, the opera is set among the lonely cliffs and ancient feuds of the Scottish highlands, a distant place whose land, people, and culture fascinated the public and captured the imagination of Romantic writers and composers. Lucia is tricked by her brother into thinking that the man she loves, Edgardo, has been unfaithful. She reluctantly agrees to marry someone else, but on her wedding night, she murders him on their nuptial bed. Lucia then begins to hallucinate, imagining she hears Edgardo's voice calling to her. Her "mad scene" in the last act creates an unbroken flow of events through numerous entrances and tempo changes.

Reminiscence motive

The scene begins with a short chorus that comments on Lucia's deathly and disheveled appearance as she enters after murdering her husband. We then hear foreboding music that first appeared in the opera's prelude, played by a quartet of horns. Against this and a syncopated flute motive, Lucia begins an impassioned recitative, calling out to Edgardo. The flutes and clarinets recollect the theme of her love duet with him from Act I; such hearkening back to an earlier theme or motive became known as a **reminiscence motive**. Lucia's recitative continues through several tempo changes and overlaps the introduction to her cantabile, the blurring of boundaries serving as a sign of her madness. Lucia's tutor, a captain of the guards, and her brother, having learned of the murder, break in to pray for the Lord's mercy. At the tempo di mezzo, she is joined by her brother and tutor and later the chorus. After a pause and orchestral introduction, Lucia begins the cabaletta. But before she can sing the anticipated repetition, the chorus and other characters break in, joining her again as she brings the repetition to a close and faints. Such flexible adaptation of Rossini's standard scene structure to suit the course of the drama is typical of Donizetti and served as a model for Giuseppe Verdi in the next generation (see Chapter 28).

CLASSICS OF ITALIAN OPERA The most successful operas of Rossini, Bellini, and Donizetti were performed in opera houses all over Italy and at theaters in other nations that specialized in Italian opera or presented Italian operas in translation. Their most famous arias became popular tunes heard by large segments of the public, as operatic excerpts were performed widely outside the opera house and disseminated through all manner of arrangements for voice and piano, piano alone, band, and other ensembles. By midcentury, these operas were becoming part of a core repertory, staged repeatedly wherever opera was performed. Rossini's *The Barber of Seville,* Bellini's *Norma,* and Donizetti's *Lucia di Lammermoor* were among the first operas ever to reach the status of permanent classics, akin to Handel's *Messiah* or Beethoven's symphonies. In part due to the phenomenal success of these operas, Italian musical life was dominated by opera for several more generations, during which the most noted composers specialized in opera, while instrumental genres, choral music, and even solo song were overshadowed.

FRANCE

Throughout the nineteenth century, opera remained the most prestigious musical genre in France, whose musical culture was second only to Italy's in its focus on the genre.

French opera under Napoleon

From its founding by Lully in the late seventeenth century, French opera was centered in Paris and shaped by politics. The French Revolution had ended aristocratic patronage, bringing new laws that allowed anyone to open a public theater. But Napoleon again restricted theaters, allowing only three to present operas. The Opéra, which focused on tragedy, was the most prestigious, staging new works, revivals by Gluck and others, and French versions of foreign operas by composers such as Mozart. The Opéra-Comique gave operas with spoken dialogue instead of recitative; despite the name, many of these opéras comiques had serious plots. The Théâtre Italien presented operas in Italian, including works composed for Paris and older operas by Mozart and others. Other Paris theaters featured a variety of stage works that included music, from plays and comedies with incidental music to vaudevilles (comedies with songs interspersed), pantomimes (scenes acted out silently with musical accompaniment), and ballets. Although Paris was the center for producing new works, theaters and opera houses in other French cities were also active.

Restoration and the July Revolution

Following the defeat of Napoleon, the French monarchy was restored under Louis XVIII (r. 1814–24), brother of Louis XVI. Government sponsorship for the Opéra continued as before, and a new theater, shown in Figure 27.5, was built for it in 1821. Gas lighting was introduced the next year, allowing much more spectacular and subtle stage effects. The Théâtre Italien mounted operas by Rossini, who became the director there in 1824. But Charles X (r. 1824–30)

FIGURE 27.5 *The new Paris Opéra building on Rue Le Peletier, which opened August 16, 1821. The illustration shows its interior during a performance in the 1840s of Meyerbeer's* Robert le diable. *The stage scenery is of a new kind, with a curved backdrop shell designed to look more realistic than previous flat canvasses could. Lithograph by Jules Arnout.*

MUSÉE DE LA VILLE DE PARIS, MUSÉE CARNAVALET, PARIS, FRANCE/ARCHIVES CHARMET/BRIDGEMAN IMAGES

failed to gain the support of the growing and powerful middle class, and the "July Revolution" of 1830, which reduced the power of the French monarch, put his distant cousin Louis Philippe on the throne as a constitutional monarch. The government continued to subsidize opera and concerts, but now the royal family contributed informally to opera and benefit concerts rather than sponsoring them directly. The Opéra theater was leased to a businessman, Louis Véron, who found wealthy sponsors. Anyone could purchase tickets, but the boxes were rented at high prices.

GRAND OPERA With the decline of royal patronage, a new kind of opera came into being, designed to appeal to the newly well-to-do middle-class audiences who thronged the opera theaters looking for excitement and entertainment. ***Grand opera***, as this type came to be called, was as much spectacle as music, consistent with the fashion that had prevailed in France ever since Lully. Writers created librettos that focused on romantic love in the context of historical conflicts and exploited every possible occasion for ballets, stage machinery, choruses, and crowd scenes. Two early examples of grand opera, both on themes of rebellion against foreign domination, were Rossini's *Guillaume Tell* (1829), featuring an onstage lake across which Tell rows to safety, and *La muette de Portici* (The Mute Woman of Portici, 1828) by Daniel-François-Esprit Auber (1782–1871), which ends with a battle during an eruption of the volcano Vesuvius—and ironically has a title role that is danced, not sung, since she is a mute.

Eugène Scribe and Giacomo Meyerbeer

Along with Véron, the director of the Paris Opéra, the leaders of grand opera were the librettist Eugène Scribe (1791–1861) and the composer Giacomo Meyerbeer (1791–1864), shown in Figure 27.6. Scribe, who coauthored the libretto to *La muette de Portici,* created the mix of formality, spectacle, and historical, political, or religious themes that defined the new genre. Meyerbeer's *Robert le diable* (Robert the Devil, 1831, shown in Figure 27.5) and *Les Huguenots* (1836), both on Scribe librettos, set the pattern for the musical treatment, using every available technique to dramatize the action and please the public. Meyerbeer had a command of varied musical styles forged from his earlier experiences: born to a German-Jewish family in Berlin, he was a child prodigy as a pianist, then spent nine successful years as an opera composer in Italy, where he Italianized his first name (originally Jakob).

FIGURE 27.6 *Giacomo Meyerbeer in 1847. Engraving from a lithograph by Fritz Kriehuber.*

Les Huguenots is typical of French grand opera in having five acts, an enormous cast, a ballet, and dramatic scenery and lighting effects. The plot centers on events leading to the St. Bartholomew's Day Massacre of 1572, in which Catholics slaughtered hundreds of Protestants (Huguenots) in Paris. The subject was of current interest due to concerns about religious freedom and the influence of the Catholic Church on the government. Unlike earlier historical dramas that showed rulers in control, *Les Huguenots* represents a new view of history, influenced by the revolutions of 1789 and 1830, that regarded competition between groups as the principal engine driving events, beyond the control of individuals. This perspective is poignantly exemplified in the closing scene of Act II (NAWM 151), which illustrates Meyerbeer's ability to integrate the expression of deep personal feelings with crowd scenes, public ceremonies, and confrontations, using a variety of styles and gestures to convey the emotional and psychological import of events on stage. Reflecting Rossini's influence on grand opera and Meyerbeer's earlier experiences in Italy, the scene is structured like an Italian opera finale, with an orchestral introduction, opening section, slow movement (akin to a cantabile), dialogue in accompanied recitative, and fast stretta at the end.

Queen Marguerite de Valois tries to reconcile the two factions through a peacemaking marriage of a Catholic noblewoman, Valentine, to the Protestant nobleman Raoul. Before introducing the couple to each other, she asks the Protestant and Catholic gentlemen of her court to swear eternal friendship. She sings her request in an ingratiating Italianate style marked by Rossinian embellishment, far briefer than an Italian aria but long enough to convey her charming personality and happy mood. In the following slow movement, the main protagonists on each side sing an oath of peace in unison, softly, solemnly, and without accompaniment, lending it a sacred, chantlike aura. The male chorus, representing the rival groups, loudly affirms their vow, accompanied by the orchestra. Then the leaders hail the benefits of harmony among all people, in a soft unaccompanied ensemble of four voices whose texture recalls the a cappella singing of a church choir or of a partsong for men's chorus, both associated with good feelings and social harmony. Only the militant Protestant Marcel defies the others, quietly vowing to make war on Catholics.

But then Marguerite's plan goes awry. When Raoul sees Valentine, he angrily refuses to marry her in a dramatic accompanied recitative. This is heartbreaking on a personal level, because we know from Act I that they love each other and that his reaction is the result of a misunderstanding—ironically, one that resulted from Marguerite's own actions in executing her plan, since she sent Valentine on an errand that led Raoul to conclude mistakenly that Valentine was another man's mistress. Raoul's refusal ignites a firestorm, captured in the final stretta. The Catholics are inflamed to vengeance, Marguerite is furious at Raoul's disobedience, Valentine asks plaintively what she has done to merit such an insult, and Marcel, pleased with the turn of events, sings the Lutheran chorale *Ein feste Burg,* an emblem of the Protestant struggle. Except for the chorale, Meyerbeer has everyone sing the same musical ideas, expressing disbelief, fury, anguish, vengeance, and despair in turn, thereby showing that the characters on stage are experiencing similar feelings, each from their unique perspective, all powerless to resist the coming conflict. Meyerbeer keeps the tumult fresh by continually introducing new ideas and combinations, building repeatedly to powerful climaxes. This scene exemplifies the conception of grand opera as a combination of entertaining spectacle and glorious singing with a serious artistic statement.

Impact of grand opera

Meyerbeer's approach to grand opera was admired and emulated by later composers. Other grand operas, like *La Juive* (The Jewess, 1835) by Fromental Halévy (1799–1862) with a libretto by Scribe, follow a similar formula. Donizetti's *La favorite* (1840) was a grand opera written for Paris, as were Verdi's *Les vêpres siciliennes* (1855) and *Don Carlos* (1867). The genre spread, with productions in Germany, London, and elsewhere. Particularly significant is Meyerbeer's profound influence on Richard Wagner (see Chapter 28), whose *Rienzi* (1842) is grand opera pure and simple, and whose later operas were heavily influenced by *Les Huguenots*.

Berlioz, Les Troyens

Hector Berlioz's great five-act opera *Les Troyens* (1856–58, partial premiere in 1863) drew on grand opera but also on the older French opera tradition of Lully, Rameau, and Gluck. The text, by Berlioz himself, is based on the second and fourth books of Virgil's *Aeneid*. Berlioz condensed the narrative in a series of powerful scenes and used appropriate occasions to introduce ballets, processions, and other musical numbers. Like Meyerbeer's *Huguenots*, *Les Troyens* can be classified as an "epic opera"—a work in which the story of a nation competes with the passions and emotions of individual characters.

OPÉRA COMIQUE Side by side with grand opera, opéra comique continued to be fashionable. As in the eighteenth century (see Chapter 21), the technical difference between the two was that opéra comique used spoken dialogue instead of recitative. Apart from this, the differences were primarily questions of size and subject matter. Opéra comique was less pretentious than grand opera and required fewer singers and players. Its plots, as a rule, presented straightforward comedy or semiserious drama instead of the historical pageantry typical of grand opera. Two kinds of opéra comique existed in the early part of the nineteenth century, the romantic and the comic, although many works shared characteristics of both types.

BALLET Another form of musical theater popular in France was the ballet. French operas since the seventeenth century had often included ballets, but in the late eighteenth century dance troupes began to present independent ballets that had a series of dance scenes linked together by a narrative. A new style, now known as Romantic ballet and still common in modern performances, was introduced by Marie Taglioni (1804–1884), shown in Figure 27.7. In this style ballerinas became preeminent, moving with a new lightness and freedom, marked by gestures and positions that were more extended and elevated, including sprightly leaps and delicate landings. Their graceful elevation was enhanced by shoes that allowed them to rise up on their toes ("on point") and by sheer costumes that seemed to float in the air. Having triumphed in Paris and London, Taglioni performed for many years in St. Petersburg with the Imperial Ballet, where she helped to establish a lasting ballet tradition in Russia.

Composers typically wrote music for ballets after the dance had already been choreographed, so they had to fit their music to the timing, rhythms, movements, and mood of the dance. One of the highlights of Romantic ballet was *Giselle,* premiered at the Paris Opéra in 1841, with music by Adolphe Adam (1803–1856) that used recurring motives and recollection of earlier material to highlight the progress of the drama, as in an opera.

GERMANY

The interaction between music and literature, so typical of nineteenth-century Romanticism, was developed most fully by composers in the German-speaking lands, in opera as well as song and instrumental music. At the root of German opera was the Singspiel, whose composers in the early nineteenth century soaked up Romantic elements from French opera while intensifying the genre's specific national features.

CARL MARIA VON WEBER The work that established German Romantic opera was *Der Freischütz* (The Free Shooter, first performed in Berlin in 1821), by Carl Maria von Weber, depicted in Figure 27.8. What made *Der Freischütz* so daring for its time was not only Weber's unusual orchestration and harmonies, but also his idea of putting ordinary people center stage, talking and singing about their concerns, their loves, and their fears.

The libretto of *Der Freischütz* exemplifies the characteristics of German Romantic opera. Plots are drawn from medieval history, legend, or fairy tale. The story involves supernatural beings and happenings set against a background of wilderness and mystery, but scenes of humble village or country life are frequently introduced. Supernatural incidents and the natural setting are intertwined with the fate of the human protagonists. Mortal characters act not merely as individuals but as agents or representatives of superhuman forces, whether good or evil. The triumph of good is a form of salvation or redemption, a vaguely religious concept of deliverance from sin and error through suffering, conversion, or revelation. In giving such importance to the

FIGURE 27.7 *Marie Taglioni, clad in the new costume of the Romantic ballerina, with a close-fitting bodice and sheer, almost translucent skirt. Her position, rising "on point" (on the toes, in special shoes that allow this), typifies the light, airy effect ballet dancers sought to achieve. Lithograph from the 1830s by James Henry Lynch after Alfred Edward Chalon.*

FIGURE 27.8 *Carl Maria von Weber, in a portrait by Caroline Bardua.*

FIGURE 27.9 *Setting by Carl Wilhelm Holdermann for the Wolf's Glen Scene in Weber's* Der Freischütz *as performed at Weimar in 1822. In the magic circle, Caspar casts the magic bullets, while Max looks around with growing alarm at the frightening apparitions aroused by each bullet cast.*

physical and spiritual background, German opera differs sharply from contemporary French and Italian opera. But its musical styles and forms draw directly from those of other countries, while the use of simple folklike melodies introduces a distinctly German national element. German opera also displays increasingly chromatic harmony, the use of orchestral color for dramatic expression, and a more equal role for the orchestra, in contrast to the Italian emphasis on beautiful singing.

Der Freischütz   All these facets are illustrated in *Der Freischütz.* Rustic choruses, marches, dances, and airs mingle in the score with multisectional arias in a format adapted from Rossini that exhibit many of the florid vocal characteristics of the Italian style. The somber forest background is depicted idyllically by the horns at the beginning of the overture and diabolically in the eerie midnight scene in the Wolf's Glen, shown in Figure 27.9.

In a story line derived from folklore, Max, a young ranger, loves Agathe, but in order to win her hand in marriage, he must pass a test of marksmanship. He has had bad luck for a few days, failing target practice. Caspar, a fellow ranger, persuades Max that he can obtain some magic bullets, which will guarantee that Max will win the trial. In the dead of night, the two men meet in the Wolf's Glen, where Caspar casts the magic bullets. But unbeknownst to Max, Caspar is working in league with the devil, Samiel, who controls the final bullet cast and has destined it to kill Agathe. By the time of the fateful shooting trial, six of the bullets have been used and Max has only one left—that guided by Samiel. Agathe unexpectedly appears in the line of fire as Max shoots, but she is protected by an old hermit's magical wreath, and the bullet kills Caspar instead.

Wolf's Glen Scene   The Wolf's Glen Scene (finale of Act II; NAWM 152), during which the seven bullets are cast, incorporates elements of the ***melodrama***, a genre of musical theater that combined spoken dialogue with background music. Melodramas had been popular in France and in German-speaking areas since the 1770s, and scenes in melodrama had appeared in operas by Mozart, Beethoven, and others. Speaking his lines over continuous orchestral music, Caspar first invokes Samiel. Then, as he casts each bullet, with Max cowering beside him, Caspar counts *one, two, three,* and so on, while the mountains echo each count. For each casting, Weber paints a different picture of the terrifying dark forest. Throughout, he ingeniously exploits the resources of the orchestra: timpani, trombones, clarinets, and horns in the foreground, often against string tremolos. Diminished and augmented intervals and daring chromaticism depict evil, and an offstage chorus reinforces the shadowy and supernatural elements of the plot.

The entire scene centers on the notes of a diminished seventh chord, E♭–F♯–A–C. Scored in the dark lower ranges of the oboes, clarinets, and upper strings over a repeated A in the bass, this chord is a reminiscence motive linked to Samiel, first heard in the overture. The same chord recurs often in other forms throughout the scene, and its notes are the principal keynotes: F♯ minor at beginning and end; C minor through most of the rest of the scene, especially identified with Caspar; E♭ major at Max's entrance; and A minor for several supernatural visions.

Influence

Weber's association of motives and keys with particular characters or events exercised an enormous influence on later composers of opera. These ideas were especially important to Wagner (see Chapter 28), who also found in this scene a model for a continuous, through-composed musical drama based on German legend. More generally, Weber's use of tritone-related and third-related harmonies, diminished seventh chords, and string tremolos to evoke mystery, danger, and the supernatural contributed to the establishment of these associations as conventions followed by countless Romantic composers and still used by composers for film and television.

Other operas

Weber apparently did not intend to send a nationalist message or found a national school of opera with *Der Freischütz,* and his other dramatic works are quite varied in subject, including *Euryanthe* (1823), about a troubadour in medieval France, and *Oberon* (1826), which combines the supernatural world of elves and fairies, medieval knights, and the Islamic courts of Baghdad and Tunis, portrayed with authentic Turkish and Egyptian melodies. These are exoticist rather than nationalist, though equally Romantic in their appeal to distant places and times and to the supernatural. But the national sentiment in *Der Freischütz* made it Weber's most popular work.

RUSSIA

Russian nationalism

When nationalism began to affect Russian artists, opera proved valuable as a genre in which a distinctive Russian identity could be proclaimed through subject matter, set design, costumes, and music. Ironically, while nationalism was a force for unification in Germany and Italy and for liberation struggles in Austria-Hungary, in Russia it was primarily a tool of propaganda for the absolutist government under the tsar.

Mikhail Glinka

The first Russian composer recognized both by Russians and internationally as an equal of his western European contemporaries was Mikhail Glinka (1804–1857). He established his reputation in 1836 with the patriotic, pro-government historical drama *A Life for the Tsar,* the first Russian opera to gain an international audience. The plot centers on a peasant who sacrifices his own life to save the tsar from Polish invaders. Glinka drew on the major Western operatic traditions, blending Italianate melody, French drama and spectacle, and German counterpoint and idealization of peasant life and culture. Some of the melodic writing has a distinctive Russian character, attributable to modal scales, quotation or paraphrasing of folk songs, and a folklike idiom. The Poles are depicted through Polish dance rhythms, creating a strong contrast in style that reinforces the nationalist oppositions of the plot. Glinka based his second opera, *Ruslan and Lyudmila* (1842), on a poem by Russia's leading poet, Aleksander Pushkin (1799–1837). It has a magical plot, justifying Glinka's many imaginative uses of chromaticism, dissonance, and the whole-tone scale to portray his supernatural characters, which established a Russian tradition that lasted through Rimsky-Korsakov and Stravinsky (see Chapters 28 and 33).

Glinka is valued in western Europe for the Russian flavor of these operas, which satisfied tastes for both the national and the exotic. But he was more important to Russians as the first to claim a place for their country in the international musical world. The Russian operas that preceded him were suitable for consumption at home, and many featured Russian folk styles, but they could not represent Russia on the world stage because they did not aspire to the same level, musically or dramatically, as Western operas. Glinka's operas could and did, because they incorporated the best of the Western tradition together with a special Russian flavor, treating the peasants as fully rounded, heroic characters and their music as the equal of any. This paradox pervades the reception of Russian music: foreign audiences and critics often prize what is recognizably national in it above all other characteristics, which is often not what the composers themselves or their compatriots most esteemed.

THE UNITED STATES

If the history of opera composition in the first half of the nineteenth century focuses on Italy, Paris, Germany, and St. Petersburg, the history of opera performance must include London, Spain, eastern Europe, and the Americas, where opera became an important part of musical life. In London, for example, operas by Continental composers were staged both in the original language and in English adaptations. Yet the British public's long-standing preference for spoken plays with interpolated music (see Chapter 16) made it difficult to establish a native tradition of opera in English, despite attempts by critics, impresarios, and composers to create one, and the only British opera to win an international reputation in the nineteenth century was *The Bohemian Girl* (1843) by Irish composer Michael Balfe (1808–1870).

Theater companies   In North America, theater companies in major cities and touring troupes that traveled across the continent performed not only spoken plays but also ballad operas such as John Gay's *The Beggar's Opera* (see Chapter 21) and English versions of foreign-language operas, which typically replaced recitative with spoken dialogue and simplified the ensembles and arias. These companies presented operas as entertainment accessible to all, in a time before the gulf had opened up between high and low (popular) culture.

European opera   Opera in foreign languages took hold more slowly. In New Orleans, formerly a French colonial city, French operas helped to preserve a distinctive cultural identity. Active between 1819 and 1866, the Théâtre d'Orléans performed primarily French and Italian operas in the original languages, giving many American premieres and touring the East Coast several times. In New York, a European troupe presented a season of Italian operas in 1825–26, including Rossini's *Barber of Seville* (see In Performance: The Bel Canto Diva, pp. 652–53) and Mozart's *Don Giovanni*. Several attempts were made to establish a permanent Italian opera house; one in 1833 involved Mozart's librettist Lorenzo da Ponte, then professor of Italian at Columbia University. The first opera company to last more than a few years was the Academy of Music, which opened in 1854 with *Norma* and presented regular opera seasons until 1886. By the 1850s, opera in Italian and English was also established in San Francisco, newly wealthy with Gold Rush money.

While foreign-language operas attracted a relatively small, elite audience, a much wider public heard the music of opera. Overtures, arias, and other excerpts were arranged and published as sheet music, performed in parlors, and included in concerts. When Swedish soprano Jenny Lind toured the United States in 1850–52, singing before tens of thousands of people, her programs included opera overtures and Italian arias (especially Bellini's *Casta diva*) as well as familiar songs such as *Home! Sweet Home!* There were also homegrown star singers such as Elizabeth Greenfield (1824–1876), born into slavery in Mississippi but emancipated as an infant and adopted by a Philadelphia Quaker: she toured the United States and England in the 1850s singing arias by Handel, Bellini, and Donizetti alongside *Home! Sweet Home!* and Stephen Foster; became the first African American to perform for royalty when she sang before Queen Victoria in 1854; and founded an opera troupe in the 1860s. Operatic excerpts and arrangements were also widely performed by orchestras, bands, and choruses. The music and plots of operas were so well known that operatic parodies had a ready audience; for example, New York's Olympic Theater offered opera burlesques like *Mrs. Normer* (on *Norma*) and *Fried Shots* (on *Der Freischütz*). Thus, although relatively few Americans saw operas in their original form, operatic music was widespread as popular entertainment.

Opera as popular entertainment

AMERICAN OPERA American audiences that supported opera in Italian, French, or German were attracted in part by its prestige as a European art form. There was virtually no demand for American composers to produce opera on a similar scale because no local product carried the same cachet. Two ambitious attempts illustrate the difficulties of creating a native opera. William Henry Fry (1813–1864) believed that the English and American tradition of mixing spoken dialogue with arias and ensembles was a corruption of the operatic ideal. His *Leonora* (Philadelphia, 1845) was sung throughout, the first such opera by an American-born composer to be staged. Fry based his style on that of European composers, especially Bellini. There were several successful performances, but his opera soon vanished; why listen to an imitator of Bellini when one could hear the real thing? George Frederick Bristow (1825–1898) took up an American subject in his opera *Rip Van Winkle* (New York, 1855), but the style again was European, primarily influenced by Mendelssohn, and again the opera had only a few performances. Not until the twentieth century did American operas find a more secure audience.

FIGURE 27.10 *Cover of a collection of music sung in shows by Christy's Minstrels. The troupe's founder and leader, Edwin P. Christy (1815–1862), is at top, followed by scenes in which white actors, singers, and musicians made up in blackface and dressed as stylish urban blacks or as plantation slaves imitate the dances, songs, and dialogue of African Americans.*

MINSTREL SHOWS The most popular form of musical theater in the United States from the 1830s through the 1870s was ***minstrelsy***, in which white performers blackened their faces with burnt cork and impersonated African Americans in jokes, skits, songs, and dances. Figure 27.10 illustrates scenes from a typical minstrel show by one of the most successful troupes, Christy's Minstrels. These shows propagated offensive racial stereotypes, and their history is linked with the shameful history of slavery, segregation, and enduring racial inequality in the United States. Yet minstrelsy is also an early example of what Christopher J. Smith has called "the creolization of American culture," the interweaving of strands across divides of race, ethnicity, and class that have made American culture, art, literature, and music unique. Minstrelsy was the first of many forms of entertainment in which white musicians borrowed from the music of African Americans, a recurring theme in American music. The combination of minstrelsy's mixed pedigree with its popularity and its very offensiveness makes it a fascinating and even necessary subject.

Smith traces the development of minstrelsy to the boat decks, wharves, and bars along America's rivers and coasts, the main transportation routes before railroads and highways. In these areas, men from different backgrounds, including Irish, German, and African American, worked close by each other, heard each other sing and play, and absorbed aspects of each other's musical traditions, developing a common language that crossed racial lines. Smith cites the sketches and paintings of William Sidney Mount (1807–1868), which show people of both races playing music or dancing to it in ways that became identified with minstrelsy. Other scholars have drawn attention to working-class neighborhoods in urban areas such as New York, arguing that early minstrelsy owed more to European styles. Although minstrel songs were not direct imitations of African American music, performers did borrow elements characteristic of African and African American traditions, from the banjo (a folk instrument based on African predecessors) to call-and-response, in which a lead singer alternates with a chorus or with instruments.

Daddy Rice and George Washington Dixon

As stage entertainment, minstrelsy grew from the solo comic performances of Thomas Dartmouth ("Daddy") Rice (1808–1860) as Jim Crow, a naive plantation slave, and of George Washington Dixon (1808–1861) as Zip Coon, a boastful black urban dandy. Their theme songs were among the best sellers of their day: Rice's *Jump Jim Crow* (1829) was the first American piece of music to be a hit overseas, and *Zip Coon* (later adapted as *Turkey in the Straw*) was almost as popular. Rice developed a genre he called "Ethiopian opera," interspersing sketch comedy with songs, performed between or after the acts of a play. His act included imitating a cakewalk, a dance developed by blacks as a parody of the quadrilles and grand marches danced by the whites who held them in slavery; his parody of a parody is an example of the ironic blends produced by imitation across lines of race, class, and power.

The first full independent minstrel shows, consisting of dialogue, songs, banjo and fiddle playing, and dances loosely strung together, were given in 1843 by the Virginia Minstrels in New York, who then continued their shows throughout the East Coast and the British Isles. This group gave their name to the genre and made minstrelsy the first musical export from the United States to Europe, where it remained popular for over a century; "The Black and White Minstrel Show," featuring white singers in blackface, ran on British television from 1958 to 1978.

Virginia Minstrels

What was the attraction of minstrelsy? Smith suggests that minstrel shows were popular because the blended styles of music and dance they presented were already familiar from the informal performances he documents. Other scholars have argued that the portrayal of black men as uneducated but clever, free from social constraints, and ready to indulge in singing, dancing, drinking, gambling, and sex, entertained white audiences while reassuring them of their superiority. Still others have pointed to the social satire that was intrinsic to blackface. Like drag shows today, in which men dress as women and mock gendered expectations, or eighteenth-century comic operas in which servants got the better of their masters, minstrel shows explored issues of social and political power and of proper and improper behavior through inversions of normal social roles. White performers playing black characters had license to behave outside accepted norms and to comment candidly on social, political, and economic conditions.

Social roles

As minstrelsy became broadly popular, it lost many of these subversive tendencies and increasingly served to reinforce stereotypes that underlie attitudes of white supremacy. Indeed, the very name "Jim Crow" was applied to laws passed between the 1870s and the 1950s to deprive African Americans of the vote and other legal rights and render them second-class citizens. Yet there were also African Americans who were part of the minstrelsy tradition, most notably James A. Bland (1854–1911), who made a very successful career in the United States and in England and is best known for *Oh, Dem Golden Slippers* and *Carry Me Back to Old Virginny*, later named the state song of Virginia.

Although minstrel shows long ago passed out of fashion, some of the songs written for them have proven remarkably durable. The Virginia Minstrels' violinist, Dan Emmett (1815–1902), was the composer of *Dixie* (1860), whose theme of longing for the South is common in minstrel songs. Many of Stephen Foster's best-known songs were written for Christy's Minstrels, including *Oh! Susanna* (1848), *Camptown Races* (1850), *Old Folks at Home* (1851), and *My Old Kentucky Home* (1853). The first two are fast comic numbers, the latter two are slow, sentimental plantation ballads, and most share the black dialect, pentatonic melodies, and occasional syncopation that were typical of minstrel songs. *My Old Kentucky Home* is especially poignant; inspired by Harriet Beecher Stowe's antislavery novel *Uncle Tom's Cabin* (1852), Foster wrote a lament of an enslaved servant born in Kentucky who has been sold to a sugar plantation owner further south, where conditions were even more cruel. The abolitionist Frederick Douglass, who assailed minstrel shows for their demeaning portrayal

Legacy

of African Americans, hailed this song for awakening "sympathies for the slave in which antislavery principles take root and flourish." All of these were songs almost everyone in the United States knew for over a century, and they are still well known and widely sung. They are part of the heritage of minstrelsy; so too, unfortunately, are the stereotypes minstrel shows embodied and promoted.

OPERA AS HIGH CULTURE

Most musical theater in the early 1800s was aimed at mixed tastes. Composers and producers of all kinds of opera in every country could assume that their audience included wealthy elites, educated connoisseurs, musical amateurs, and the public at large. The librettists and composers of *The Barber of Seville, Norma, Lucia di Lammermoor, Les Huguenots,* and *Der Freischütz* sought to include elements that would appeal to all possible listeners.

By the middle of the nineteenth century, these and other works had become part of a repertory of operas that were performed repeatedly. In the later nineteenth and early twentieth centuries, new operas were staged less frequently, and the standard repertory came to predominate worldwide. Over time, the works that survived, and opera itself as a medium, have become increasingly associated with high culture; perhaps only in Italy, where some audience members still sing along with their favorite arias and choruses, has opera kept one foot in the world of popular music. Meanwhile, the vaudevilles, pantomimes, musical comedies, minstrel shows, and other lighter forms of musical theater from the period have been almost completely forgotten, yet their descendants—variety shows, cabarets, musicals, and the like—have formed a vital part of musical life for the last two centuries.

Opera today is a very expensive art form that depends on government support and wealthy private donors. Yet it continues to attract devoted fans from all classes of society. Nineteenth-century operas have continued to flourish in part because of their resonance and engagement with elements of twentieth- and twenty-first-century popular culture. The recording industry, television, and movie theaters have brought opera to new listeners, using technologies from wax cylinder recordings to the latest digital media, and have helped to make stars of singers whose celebrity status has transcended the confines of the opera house, from Enrico Caruso (1873–1921) to Maria Callas (1923–1977) to Anna Netrebko (b. 1971). Attending live opera still serves as an elite status symbol for some, but millions of people experience opera through radio and television broadcasts, HD simulcasts in movie theaters, performances at universities and schools of music, and programs for opera in primary and secondary schools. Institutions like the Metropolitan Opera in New York use such broadcasts and outreach programs, along with a dose of glamour and celebrity, to draw in new audiences, while using ever more sophisticated production techniques, including stage projections and digital imagery developed for film, to enhance the spectacle intrinsic to Romantic opera. Wherever opera is heard and seen, most of the operas that are performed come from the nineteenth century, eclipsing all earlier periods, and the composers discussed in this chapter are well represented.

Further Reading is available at digital.wwnorton.com/hwm10

OPERA AND MUSICAL THEATER IN THE LATER NINETEENTH CENTURY

❖

The second half of the nineteenth century saw a continuation of strong national traditions in German, Italian, and French opera, the rise of a vibrant Russian school in opera and ballet, and growing traditions of musical theater in other lands. Nationalism was an increasingly important force, linking opera to broader political and cultural currents. Exoticism and *realism* were also significant trends. Sources for plots ranged from mythology to modern love affairs, and from European history to exotic tales in foreign lands. As the market for theatrical music grew larger and more diverse, elite and popular audiences diverged and new forms of comic opera and musical theater emerged to satisfy popular tastes. Wagner and Verdi dominated German and Italian opera respectively, while composers in France, Spain, Bohemia, Russia, and elsewhere developed new national styles. The rise in status of the composer and the operatic "work" corresponded with a decline in the centrality of singers and in the arts of improvisation and embellishment.

TECHNOLOGY, POLITICS, AND THE ARTS

Europe and the United States became industrial powerhouses during the later nineteenth century. Railroads spread across both continents, transporting people and goods more rapidly. New products and technologies such as chemical soaps and dyes, steel manufacture, the electric lightbulb, and the telephone spawned new industries and altered daily life. Workers streamed to the cities to work in factories, and labor unions formed to represent their interests. With improved agriculture, sanitation, and medicine, life expectancy and population rose dramatically. Literacy also increased, and newspapers and magazines proliferated, made cheaper by advertising. With new laws that limited investors' risk to the amount they owned in stock, the modern corporation emerged, employing legions of office workers and middle

FIGURE 28.1 The Uprising (1848) by French artist Honoré Daumier. Renowned for his satirical drawings that lampooned those in power, Daumier here paints an arresting portrait of the passion that united workers (in shirt-sleeves) and middle class (in top hat) and brought together men, women, and children in the 1848 Paris revolution.

managers. Mass consumption became a driving force for the economy, evident in the new institutions of the brand name, the department store, and the mail-order catalogue.

1848 revolutions　　A growing movement for political reform in the 1840s culminated in a series of popular uprisings that swept Europe in 1848–49. The first revolution, pictured in Figure 28.1, was in France, toppling King Louis Philippe and establishing the Second French Republic. Its gains were short-lived, since the desire for order overcame the push for reform. Napoleon's nephew was elected president and in 1852 made himself Emperor Napoleon III (1852–70). Similar revolts in German, Italian, and Austro-Hungarian cities failed to produce permanent changes, due in part to disunity among revolutionary leaders and lack of support from peasants.

Political reforms　　Over the next half century, however, most European governments granted more political rights to their people, including constitutional limits on the monarch, direct election of parliamentary assemblies, greater freedom of the press, and voting rights for most men. Russia abolished serfdom in 1861, and in the United States the Civil War of 1861–65 brought the abolition of slavery. France established its Third Republic in 1875. In the 1880s, Germany granted workers national health care, limits on the length of the working day, and old-age pensions that formed a model for other countries. Beginning in 1848 with the Seneca Falls Convention in upstate New York, women began pushing for equal treatment under the law, including the rights to make contracts, get a divorce, and cast a vote. Although women in most areas would not win the vote until the twentieth century, they made substantial gains by the end of the nineteenth. But improved rights for the many coincided with exploitation of others, as expropriation of Native American lands continued in the

Americas, the Russian Empire expanded south and east, and the European powers divided up Africa and much of Asia into colonies.

The struggles for national unification in Germany and in Italy finally came to fruition. The 1848 revolutionaries in Germany tried to unify through negotiation, but failed. Then, between 1864 and 1871, Prussia under prime minister Otto Bismarck forged the German Empire through a combination of war and diplomacy. In Italy, building on earlier efforts of the Risorgimento, the 1848 revolts against foreign rule and for democratic reforms were initially successful, but by summer 1849 all the changes had been decisively reversed. Unification came in 1859–61: after the armies of Sardinia expelled Austrian rulers from northern Italy and conquered most of the papal states in central Italy, revolutionaries under Giuseppe Garibaldi overthrew the Bourbon monarchy in Sicily and southern Italy and then acknowledged the king of Sardinia, Victor Emmanuel II, as king of united Italy.

National unification

NATIONALISM, EXOTICISM, REALISM, AND FANTASY Literature, music, and the other arts played important roles in promoting nationalism, and in turn nationalism had a profound influence on the arts. In both Germany and Italy, cultural nationalism—teaching a national language in the schools rather than local dialects, creating national newspapers and journals, and cultivating a national identity through the arts—was crucial in forging a new sense of nationhood. By contrast, in Austria-Hungary, cultural nationalism worked against political unity, for the empire encompassed ethnic Germans, Czechs, Slovaks, Poles, Hungarians, Romanians, Serbs, Croats, Slovenians, and Italians, and those promoting independence for their people could buttress their case by speaking their own language, emphasizing their distinctive traditions, and creating nationalist art and music.

Cultural nationalism

In part because of these political forces, nationalism in music became more prominent during the second half of the nineteenth century. Many composers cultivated melodic and harmonic styles or chose subjects that carried associations with their own ethnic group. Sometimes this involved using native folk songs and dances or imitating their traits, but composers also invented "national" styles by introducing novel sounds or by deliberately shunning the conventions of the common international musical language. The point was dramatic effect, not authenticity. In a similar way, artists and architects looked to native handicrafts, ornamentation, and building styles to develop a distinctive national style, as in the onion domes and intricate decoration on the Russian church in Figure 28.2. Built in the late nineteenth century, the church was designed to look centuries old and specifically Russian, although both the building and its "traditional" style were newly manufactured.

FIGURE 28.2 *Church of the Resurrection in St. Petersburg, built 1883–1907.*

DAVID BALL/CORBIS DOCUMENTARY/GETTY IMAGES

Although musical nationalism began in Germany, the search for an independent native voice was especially keen in Russia and eastern Europe, where the dominance of Austro-German instrumental music and

Italian opera was felt as a threat to homegrown musical creativity. For many, composing in a recognizably national style was a sign of authenticity, part of an artist's core personality. Norwegian composer Edvard Grieg gave voice to this view when he insisted that "the spirit of my native land, which has long found a voice in the traditional songs of its people, is a living presence in all I give forth." Ironically, composers from lands outside the traditional musical powers of Italy, France, and Germany were boxed in by this viewpoint: their music *had* to be nationalist or risk being considered inauthentic, yet no merely national music could rival the claim to universality that had been part of the Austro-German tradition since the eighteenth century.

Exoticism   Exoticism, the evocation of foreign lands and cultures, also grew more common in the later nineteenth century. Many composers wrote music associated with a nation or region not their own, as when French and Russian composers wrote music on Spanish or Middle Eastern topics. As was true for nationalist music, some works borrowed actual melodies, instruments, or stylistic features in pursuit of a realistic portrayal of another culture, but authenticity was not required. More important was creating a sense of difference that combined strangeness and allure. Musical exoticism has a long history. Rameau's opera-ballet *Les Indes galantes* (1735; see p. 421) featured scenes in Persia, among the Incas in Peru, and in a forest with American Indians, and in the late 1700s Turkish-style sounds and instruments were all the rage (see Chapter 23). Exoticism reached new heights in nineteenth-century opera. The opening of Japan to Westerners in 1854 and a series of world's fairs beginning in the 1880s inspired a stream of stage works set in Japan and China, including Gilbert and Sullivan's *The Mikado* and Puccini's *Madama Butterfly* and *Turandot* (see pp. 695–96).

Realism and fantasy   The political and economic conditions in the nineteenth century stimulated another dichotomy in the arts, between **realism** and fantasy.

FIGURE 28.3 *Gustave Courbet,* A Burial at Ornans *(1849–50). This oil painting is ten feet tall and twenty-two feet wide, with room for over fifty life-size figures. The clergy, pallbearers, and men and women of the village are painted realistically, treated as human beings as important as any king.*

Realism (sometimes called *social realism*) developed first in literature and art, critiquing modern society by showing the reality of everyday life, the real suffering of the poor, and the hypocrisies of the elite and well-to-do, as in the novels of Charles Dickens, Victor Hugo, Gustave Flaubert, and Feodor Dostoevsky, the plays of Henrik Ibsen, and the paintings and illustrations of Honoré Daumier (see Figure 28.1) and Gustave Courbet. Courbet's life-size painting *A Burial at Ornans,* in Figure 28.3, treats a commonplace subject on a scale usually reserved for state ceremonies, historical figures, or heroes, showing that he considered this village funeral as important as the burial of a monarch. Realism influenced music as well, especially opera, as in Verdi's *La traviata* and Italian *verismo* operas (see pp. 690–91 and 694). But artists also offered escape from gritty reality and from modern city life through fantasy and the distant past in works by Pre-Raphaelites such as English poet and painter Dante Gabriel Rossetti, or enjoyment of the outdoors in paintings by Claude Monet, John Singer Sargent, and other impressionists. Operas likewise explored myth, fantasy, and nature, as in Wagner's *Ring* cycle and Rimsky-Korsakov's fairy-tale operas (see pp. 680–84 and 706–7).

OPERA

Throughout the later nineteenth century, opera became increasingly associated with nationalism as an ideology, whether intentionally or by circumstance. But just as many composers blended traditions.

Especially significant was a growing tendency to stage operas that had already been successful rather than gambling on new works. Improved communications and increasing intercity commerce meant that theater managers and listeners quickly learned about operas premiered elsewhere, and operas that did well in one city were often produced across Europe and the Americas. The public began to demand that popular operas be repeated, and audiences were eager to hear their favorite singers in particular roles. As in the choral, chamber, and orchestral repertoires (explored in Chapter 26), a core repertory of operas gradually emerged, varying in each country, and the number of new operas produced each year declined. Rather than working only for impresarios, as Rossini had done, composers increasingly worked for themselves, in collaboration with publishers, hoping to earn royalties from productions around the globe. No longer contracted to produce a fixed number of works in a season, composers could take more time to write each opera. With greater financial independence came new artistic freedom and new challenges; instead of following tried and true formulas, it became more important to create something individual that would stand out against the competition and be produced again and again.

Rise of the operatic repertory

As the audience for opera grew, so did the performing spaces. Orchestras became larger and louder, and singers now needed more powerful and intense voices to be heard, rather than the flexibility prized in earlier generations (see In Performance: An Original Verdi Baritone: Victor Maurel, pp. 692–93). Composers adapted to the new type of singer, writing melodies that were more syllabic and less ornamented. Perhaps seeking to contribute something new to the repertory, composers set ever more varied plots. Greater realism in many operas, focusing on the private emotional lives of common people, was

Other changes

balanced by stories based on exoticism, legend, fairy tales, or the supernatural. New genres of light opera emerged, including ***opéra bouffe*** in France and ***operetta*** in Austria, England, and the United States. Late in the century, electric lighting replaced gas, allowing new lighting effects. When electricity made it possible to dim the house lights almost completely, the traditional convivial atmosphere of opera, in which conversation was acceptable between and even during arias, was gradually replaced by dark and reverent silence. These changes, especially the creation of the permanent repertory, made the world of opera in the late nineteenth century very similar to what it is today.

RICHARD WAGNER

The outstanding composer of German opera, and one of the crucial figures in nineteenth-century culture, was Richard Wagner (1813–1883; see biography and Figure 28.4). Several of his ideas had an enormous impact on all of the arts, notably his belief in the interrelationships between the arts and his view of art as a kind of religion. All of his important compositions are for the stage and set to his own librettos. After bringing German Romantic opera to a new height, he reconceived the very nature of opera as a drama based in music but

RICHARD WAGNER
(1813–1883)

Wagner was one of the most influential musicians of all time. His emphasis on music as the servant of drama, his use of *leitmotives* as an organizing principle, and his creative manipulation of chromatic harmony had a profound and far-reaching impact on many later composers.

Wagner was born in Leipzig, Germany, the ninth child of a police actuary. Soon after Richard's birth his father died, and his mother married Ludwig Geyer, an actor and playwright whom Wagner suspected was his real father. Geyer evidently encouraged Richard's intellectual interests. His early passions were theater and music, and he was particularly inspired by Weber's operas and Beethoven's symphonies. He studied music in Dresden and Leipzig, having begun formal study in his teens, later than most composers. His student works include piano pieces, overtures, and a symphony that show a firm grasp of compositional technique and a devotion to Beethoven.

In the early 1830s, Wagner began writing operas and held positions with regional opera companies in

FIGURE 28.4 *Richard Wagner, in a portrait by Franz von Lenbach.*

southern Germany and Latvia. By then, he had met the soprano Minna Planer, whom he married in 1836.

incorporating all the other arts. In his later works, he developed a rich chromatic idiom and a system of conveying meanings through motivic associations, later termed *leitmotives*, which influenced composers for generations.

WRITINGS AND IDEAS Wagner held strong and in some ways revolutionary views about how operatic music could serve the drama. He presented his ideas in a series of essays, including *The Artwork of the Future* (1850) and *Opera and Drama* (1851, revised 1868). He believed that Beethoven had done everything that could be done in instrumental music and had shown in his Ninth Symphony the path to the future by joining music to words (see Source Reading, p. 678). Wagner saw himself—not the composers of symphonies and string quartets—as Beethoven's true successor.

Wagner believed in the absolute oneness of drama and music—that the two are organically connected expressions of a single dramatic idea. Poetry, scenic design, staging, action, and music work together to form what he called a **Gesamtkunstwerk** (total or collective artwork). His vision of a new union of music and dramatic text has been called *music drama,* although he rejected that term; instead he called his works opera, drama, or *Bühnenfestspiel* (festival stage play), and in one essay suggested the phrase "acts of music made visible."

Gesamtkunstwerk

They spent 1839–42 in Paris, where Wagner worked as a music journalist while trying to secure performances for his operas, with no success despite support from Meyerbeer. In 1842, Wagner moved back to Dresden, where his *Rienzi* was a great success, followed by *Der fliegende Holländer* (The Flying Dutchman) in early 1843. That year he was appointed second Kapellmeister for the king of Saxony in Dresden, directing the opera, conducting the orchestra, and composing for occasions at court.

Wagner supported the 1848–49 insurrection and had to flee Germany after a warrant was issued for his arrest. He settled in Switzerland, where he wrote his most important essays and began his massive cycle of four operas, *Der Ring des Nibelungen.* He was supported by a stipend from two wealthy female patrons. After several years of travel, in 1864 he found a new patron and devoted fan in the young King Ludwig II of Bavaria, who paid his debts (Wagner was a habitual gambler), granted him an annual pension, and sponsored the production of his operas *Tristan und Isolde* and *Die Meistersinger von Nürnberg* and the first two operas in the *Ring* cycle.

Although Wagner would stay married to Minna until her death in 1866, he maintained relationships with numerous other women. He channeled the energy from his affair with Mathilde Wesendonck, the wife of one of his patrons—he set five of her poems for his *Wesendonck-Lieder*—into his sensuous opera about Tristan and Isolde, whose forbidden love could not be fully consummated in life. He later formed a new union with Cosima von Bülow, daughter of Liszt and wife of the conductor Hans von Bülow, another of Wagner's ardent admirers and promoters (see Chapter 29). Wagner had three children with Cosima, but she did not marry him until 1870, after her marriage to von Bülow was annulled.

Wagner dreamed of a permanent festival of his operas, and in 1872 he began to build the festival theater at Bayreuth. The first festival was held in 1876, with the premiere of the complete *Ring* cycle, and the second in 1882, with performances of his last opera, *Parsifal.* He died the next year of a heart attack and was buried at his beloved Bayreuth, where his operas are still performed every summer.

MAJOR WORKS 13 operas, notably *Der fliegende Holländer, Tannhäuser, Lohengrin,* the four-opera cycle *Der Ring des Nibelungen (Das Rheingold, Die Walküre, Siegfried, Götterdämmerung), Tristan und Isolde, Die Meistersinger von Nürnberg,* and *Parsifal*

The Artwork of the Future

In *The Artwork of the Future* (1850), Richard Wagner argued that Beethoven strove to discover the full potential of music and found it in his Ninth Symphony by rooting his music in the word. Thus for Wagner purely instrumental music after Beethoven was sterile ("the *last* symphony had already been *written*"), and only the artwork that combined all the arts was worthwhile.

❦

This *last symphony* of Beethoven's is the redemption of music out of its own element as a *universal art*. It is the *human* gospel of the art of the future. Beyond it there can be no *progress*, for there can follow on it immediately only the completed artwork of the future, *the universal drama*, to which Beethoven has forged for us the artistic key.

Thus from within itself music accomplished what no one of the other arts was capable of in isolation. Each of these arts, in its barren independence, helped itself only by taking and egoistic borrowing; not one was capable of being *itself* and of weaving from within itself the all-uniting bond. The art of tone, by being wholly *itself* and by moving from within its own primeval element, attained strength for the most tremendous and most generous of all self-sacrifices—that of self-control, indeed of self-denial—thus to offer to its sister arts a redeeming hand. . . .

Man as artist can be fully satisfied only in the union of all the art varieties in the *collective* artwork [*Gesamtkunstwerk*]; in every *individualization* of his artistic capacities he is *unfree,* not wholly that which he can be; in the collective artwork he is *free,* wholly that which he can be.

The *true* aim of art is accordingly *all-embracing*; everyone animated by the true artistic impulse seeks to attain, through the full development of his particular capacity, not the glorification of *this particular capacity,* but the glorification *in art of mankind in general.*

The highest collective artwork is the *drama*; it is present in its *ultimate completeness* only when *each art variety, in its ultimate completeness,* is present in it.

True drama can be conceived only as resulting from the *collective impulse of all the arts* to communicate in the most immediate way with a *collective public*; each individual art variety can reveal itself as *fully understandable* to this collective public only through collective communication, together with the other art varieties, in the drama, for the aim of each individual art variety is fully attained only in the mutually understanding and understandable cooperation of all the art varieties.

From *Das Kunstwerk der Zukunft: Sämtliche Schriften und Dichtungen,* 6th ed. (Leipzig, 1912–14). Trans. Oliver Strunk, in SR 153 (6:6), pp. 1108–9 and 1112.

The last of these terms is revealing, because for Wagner the core of the drama is really in the music, and the other arts make that drama apparent. The orchestra conveys the inner aspect of the drama, while the sung words articulate the outer aspect—the events and situations that further the action and give names to the feelings and experiences suggested by the music. In a similar way, the traditional hierarchy of voice and orchestra is reversed. The orchestral web is the chief factor in the music, and the vocal lines are part of the musical texture. In a traditional opera, the voices lead and the orchestra supports, punctuates, and comments; in a Wagner drama, the dramatic thread is in the music itself, led by the orchestra, and the voices give it definition and precision through words. As he wrote in *Opera and Drama,* the dramatic singer's verse-melody is like a boat borne upon the sounding surges of the orchestra.

MUSIC IN CONTEXT

Wagner, Nationalism, and Anti-Semitism

Wagner was a musical and philosophical nationalist, claiming that German art was pure, true, spiritual, and profound, as opposed to the superficial appeal of Italian and French music. He expressed his most radical nationalism in his abhorrent anti-Semitic tract *Das Judentum in der Musik* (Judaism in Music), which appeared under a pseudonym in 1850 and under Wagner's name in 1869.

What drove him to write this essay, he explained to Liszt, was his antipathy toward Meyerbeer, whose music he once admired and who had used his influence to help Wagner. But Wagner turned against the elder composer when critics wrote how much Meyerbeer influenced his own music. Seeking to establish his independence, Wagner attacked Meyerbeer's music, arguing that it was weak because he was Jewish and therefore lacked national roots, without which a composer could not have an authentic style.

Wagner implied that the same problem affected Mendelssohn, whom he had revered in his younger days, despite Mendelssohn's conversion to Christianity. Wagner's essay drew on and strengthened an anti-Semitic strain in German culture, while attempting to obscure his deep debt to both Meyerbeer and Mendelssohn, without whose music his own would have been impossible.

In this essay, Wagner applied to music a new view of nationalism that was beginning to emerge at the time: the idea that only people who shared the same ethnicity could truly be part of a nation—for example, that Jews could never be German, no matter how many generations their families had lived in Germany, spoken German, and participated in German culture.

Whether or how Wagner's anti-Semitic views should affect our reception of his music has been debated since his own time, particularly after the National Socialists (Nazis) who ruled Germany in 1933–45 appropriated Wagner's music as a symbol of the best of German culture. Several critics have found anti-Semitic undercurrents in the operas themselves, and for decades his music was not welcome in Israel. Yet among his greatest advocates have been Jewish musicians, including conductors Hermann Levi (who conducted the premiere of *Parsifal* at Bayreuth), Gustav Mahler, and Daniel Barenboim.

Wagner's published writings address not only music but also literature, drama, and even political and moral topics. He believed that the *Gesamtkunstwerk* could help reform society and that art should not be undertaken for profit. He argued for vegetarianism and against animal experimentation. Most controversial were his views on nationalism, including anti-Semitism (see Music in Context: Wagner, Nationalism, and Anti-Semitism).

Other writings

EARLY OPERAS Before formulating his conception of the *Gesamtkunstwerk*, Wagner composed several operas that drew directly on his predecessors. His first triumph came with *Rienzi,* a grand opera in the Meyerbeer mold, performed at Dresden in 1842. The following year Dresden saw a production of *Der fliegende Holländer* (The Flying Dutchman), a Romantic opera in the tradition of Weber.

Characteristics that became typical of Wagner's later music were established in *The Flying Dutchman.* The libretto—written, like those of all his operas, by the composer himself—is based on a Germanic legend, and the hero is redeemed through the unselfish love of a heroine (in this case, Senta),

The Flying Dutchman

FIGURE 28.5 *The Bayreuth Festival Theater, designed by Otto Brückwald, incorporated Wagner's highly innovative ideals for the production of his operas. Here he was able to produce the* Ring *cycle in its entirety for the first time in August 1876.* Parsifal *(1882) was written for this theater, which continues to be the stage for the Bayreuth Festival today.*

a common theme in Romantic literature as well as for Wagner. Themes from Senta's ballad, the central number of the opera, appear in the overture and recur throughout the opera, functioning like reminiscence motives in Meyerbeer, Weber, Donizetti, and Verdi. Also like Weber is Wagner's use of musical mimicry to portray nature, here especially in depicting a powerful storm at sea.

Tannhäuser *and* Lohengrin

In *Tannhäuser* (Dresden, 1845), Wagner again adapted a Germanic legend about sin and redemption. For Tannhäuser's narrative in Act III, Wagner introduced a new kind of flexible, semi-declamatory vocal line that became his normal method of setting text. *Lohengrin,* first performed under Liszt's direction at Weimar in 1850, embodies several other elements that foreshadow the dramas that followed. In this work, Wagner's treatment of medieval legend and German folklore is both moralizing and symbolic, suffused with nationalism while aspiring to universality. Wagner's new style of declamatory melody appears more often, and the technique of recurring themes is further developed.

Der Ring des Nibelungen

THE *RING* CYCLE From 1848 to 1852, around the time he was formulating and publishing his ideas on music and drama, Wagner wrote the verse librettos for his most colossal achievement: a cycle of four dramas with the collective title *Der Ring des Nibelungen* (The Ring of the Nibelung). The music of the first two—*Das Rheingold* (The Rhine Gold) and *Die Walküre* (The Valkyrie)—and part of the third, *Siegfried,* was finished by 1857, and the entire cycle was completed with *Götterdämmerung* (The Twilight of the Gods) in 1874. The first complete performance, over four evenings, took place two years later in a theater built in Bayreuth according to Wagner's specifications, shown in Figure

LEBRECHT MUSIC & ARTS PHOTO LIBRARY

FIGURE 28.6 *The singers portraying the three Rhine maidens in the 1876 Bayreuth premiere of the* Ring *cycle were each held up and moved about by a machine, operated by several stagehands, that gave the illusion that they were swimming beneath the Rhine. The watery set and stage effect matched the wavelike music Wagner wrote for them.*

28.5. The large orchestra pit was hidden from view and extended beneath the stage, so that the sound seemed to be coming from under and around the singers, and the hall lights were dimmed to focus the audience's attention on the action. The stage effects were state-of-the-art, as in Figure 28.6. After Wagner's death, his widow Cosima established a permanent summer festival at the Bayreuth theater, devoted to productions of Wagner's operas.

The four dramas, a kind of German national epic, are woven out of stories from medieval German epic poems and Nordic legends and linked by common characters and musical motives. The cycle is largely about the value of love and people's willingness to abandon it for worldly ends. The "ring" of the title refers to a ring that the gnome Alberich fashions out of the gold he stole from the river Rhine, where it was guarded by three Rhine maidens. The ring gives its wearer limitless power. Wotan, ruler of the gods, tricks Alberich out of the ring and a hoard of gold, using both to pay two giants for building his new castle, Valhalla. Furious, Alberich puts a curse on the ring that will bring its wearer misery and death. In the course of the four dramas—about nineteen hours of music—the curse is fulfilled: Wotan's doomed empire comes to a fiery end, and the Rhine maidens reclaim the ring. Despite its fantastical setting, the themes of the *Ring* cycle—love, greed, power, innocence, passion, and betrayal, to name a few—are universal and as relevant now as then.

For the librettos, Wagner devised a kind of poetry based on the style of the medieval *Nibelungenlied,* his source for the story of the hero Siegfried. Instead of regular meter and rhymes that fall at the end of each line, as used in traditional opera (see NAWM 149–152), his poetry features vigorous, changing speech rhythms marked by *Stabreim* (alliteration), the repetition of speech sounds. For example, Alberich's curse on the ring in Scene 4 of *Das Rheingold*

Stabreim

moves rapidly through a series of repeated consonants, *g, m, n, z* (pronounced *ts*), *t,* and *d*:

Gab sein Gold	Its gold gave
mir Macht ohne Mass,	me power without measure,
nun zeug' sein Zauber	now its magic will beget
Tod dem, der ihn trägt!	death for him who wears it!

Such poetry is already rich with sound, and well suited for setting to music.

Leitmotive

Each of Wagner's later dramas—and indeed the entire *Ring* cycle as a group—is organized around numerous themes and motives that are each associated with a particular character, thing, event, or emotion. Wagner referred to these ideas as the work's principal themes, the same terminology one would use in describing a symphony. But analysts since Wagner's time have called such a theme or motive a ***Leitmotiv*** (leading motive), often rendered as ***leitmotive*** or *leitmotif* in English. The association is established by sounding the leitmotive (usually in the orchestra) at the first appearance or mention of the subject, and by its repetition during subsequent appearances or citations. Often the significance of a leitmotive can be recognized from the words to which it is first sung. Thus the leitmotive is a musical label, but it becomes much more than that through its symphonic treatment in the music drama: it accumulates significance as it recurs in new contexts; it may recall an object in situations where the object itself is not present; it may be varied, developed, or transformed as the plot develops; similar motives may suggest a connection between the things to which they refer, especially if one leitmotive morphs into another; motives may be contrapuntally combined; and, through their repetition, motives unify a scene or opera as recurrent themes unify a symphony. Leitmotives are often characterized by particular instruments, registers, harmonies, or keys, which may also suggest meanings or associations. In principle, there is a complete correspondence between the symphonic web of leitmotives and the dramatic web of the action.

Leitmotives in the Ring cycle

The creation of leitmotives, their dramatic role, and the development of one leitmotive into another can be illustrated through examples from the *Ring* cycle. Near the beginning of *Das Rheingold,* the Rhine maiden Wellgunde tells Alberich that he who fashions the Rhine gold into a ring can gain limitless power. At this, the first mention of the ring around which the whole four-opera cycle revolves, she and the reed instruments that accompany her trace a melodic outline, shown in Example 28.1a, that descends by thirds through a half-diminished seventh chord (E–C–A–F♯) and rises again. This idea seems to grow seamlessly from what comes before, but through repetition it emerges as a distinctive motive whose identification with the ring is reinforced several times in the text. By the time it is recalled in the orchestral interlude between the first and second scenes, in the new rhythmic form shown in Example 28.1b, the motive calls to mind its association with the ring, as it will continue to do throughout the entire cycle.

As the morning fog clears at the beginning of the second scene, we see Valhalla, the new castle of the gods, accompanied by a long, majestic theme that begins as in Example 28.1c. We recognize that this melody identified with Valhalla begins with a diatonic variant of the ring leitmotive. This links the

EXAMPLE 28.1 *Leitmotives from Richard Wagner's* Das Rheingold

a. The ring leitmotive's first appearance, as Wellgunde refers to the ring

Der Welt Er - be ge - wän-ne zu ei - gen, wer aus dem Rhein - gold schü-fe den Ring,

Inheritance of the world would be won as his own by he who from the Rhine gold could fashion the Ring [that would endow him with limitless power.]

b. The ring leitmotive in definitive form

c. Beginning of the Valhalla leitmotive

d. The first appearance of the curse leitmotive

Wie durch Fluch er mir ge - riet, ver - flucht sei die-ser Ring!

As through a curse it came to me, cursed be this ring!

ring and Valhalla in our minds even before we learn that their fates are inter-twined: the ring will help to pay for the castle, which will ultimately be doomed by Alberich's curse on the ring. The melodic relationship simultaneously sug-gests a parallel between Alberich and Wotan, both of whom aim for absolute power, and the difference between them, with Alberich's aspiration—a power marked as evil by the dissonant, unstable harmony outlined by the ring leit-motive and its emphasis on the tritone C–F♯—contrasting with Wotan's nobler concept of divine power, conveyed by the diatonic melody and major triads played by brass instruments. Thus the future course of the drama is suggested by the music, exemplifying Wagner's concept that the drama is in the music and that the words, scenery, and stage action make it visible.

In the fourth scene of the opera, after Wotan tricks him into surrendering the ring, Alberich curses it using the notes of the ring leitmotive but in reverse order (F♯–A–C–E), as if negating the ring. His curse leitmotive, shown in Example 28.1d, ends with E, C, and G, all notes that are dissonant over the

F♯ pedal-tone that rolls in the timpani. This high level of dissonance intensi-fies the sense of threat and foreboding associated with the curse motive. The melodic relationships between the motives make the dramatic point that the ring, the castle, and the curse are bound up with each other. At the same time, they are part of a web of dozens of such motives that bind the operas into a unified whole. As Wagner wrote to a friend in 1854 after completing *Das Rheingold,* "It has worked up to a perfect unity; there is scarcely a bar in the orchestral part which is not developed out of preceding motives."

Musical prose and endless melody

The mutability of Wagner's leitmotives distinguishes them from the remi-niscence motives appearing in operas by Weber, Meyerbeer, and Donizetti and in his own earlier operas. Moreover, his leitmotives are the basic thematic material of the score. He uses them not once in a while but constantly, in inti-mate alliance with every step of the action. Most are short and open-ended, making it possible to combine them in succession or simultaneously, in whatever ways best suit the drama. They also serve as elements for forming melodies, replacing the four-square phrases set off by rests and cadences of earlier composers. The leitmotives, their development, their restate-ments and variants, and the connective tissue linking these, form the stuff of "musical prose" Wagner used to replace the "poetic" rhythms of symmetrical phrases. The impression of "endless melody" observed by many commenta-tors results from the continuity of line, unbroken by the stops and restarts of Classic musical syntax.

Codes of meaning

Contrasts like those we have seen here, between consonance and disso-nance, major and minor or diminished harmonies, diatonic and chromatic music, tonally stable and unstable passages, and timbres of different instru-ments, were basic elements of Wagner's expressive palette. Such opposi-tions have long histories, depending on codes of meaning that stretch back to Renaissance madrigals and Baroque operas, and they make Wagner's music dramatically apt and immediately comprehensible on first hearing. His for-mulation of these oppositions was particularly powerful, even elemental. In an instant, we understand from the ponderous descending tritone identified with Alberich's son Hagen that he is evil and to be feared, from Siegfried's triadic and diatonic horn call that he is a hero, and from the undulating pentatonic leitmotive of the Rhine maidens that they are benign water creatures, embodi-ments of the beauty of nature. Equally elemental and compelling are Wagner's depictions of nature in its various guises throughout the *Ring* cycle, from the slow, powerful welling up of the river Rhine that opens *Das Rheingold,* repre-sented by a gradual rise in range, rhythmic activity, dynamic level, figuration, density of layers, and turbulence while arpeggiating a single E♭-major chord over a steady E♭ drone in the lowest reaches of the orchestra, through the vio-lent storm at the start of *Die Walküre* and the "Forest murmurs" in *Siegfried,* to the flames rising toward the heavens at the end of *Götterdämmerung,* captured in swirling waves of chromatic motion. The same can be said of his represen-tations of the supernatural, such as the storm swirls and galloping rhythms in the famous "Ride of the Valkyries" that begins Act III of *Die Walküre,* and the shimmering strings and colorfully unpredictable harmonies in the "Magic Fire Music" that ends the opera. Such stark and effective use of music to depict character, mood, and scene has had an enduring influence on later opera and on film and television scores, as has the concept of the leitmotive itself.

LATER OPERAS During two long breaks from composing *Siegfried,* Wagner wrote *Tristan und Isolde* (1857–59) and *Die Meistersinger von Nürnberg* (The Meistersingers of Nuremberg, 1862–67). In contrast to the high seriousness of the *Ring* cycle and *Tristan,* both based on medieval German legends, *Die Meistersinger* is a sunny human comedy centered on the historical figure of Hans Sachs, most famous of the Meistersingers (see p. 224). Its predominantly diatonic music contrasts markedly with the chromaticism that suffuses Wagner's other late operas, even as its evocations of an old German tradition of song serve similar nationalist ends. His final work was *Parsifal* (1882), based on the legend of the Holy Grail, which uses the opposition between diatonic and chromatic music to suggest the polarity of redemption and corruption.

Tristan, Meistersinger, and Parsifal

Beginning in the later 1850s with *Tristan und Isolde,* Wagner's dramas were influenced by the philosopher Arthur Schopenhauer (1788–1860), whose pessimistic views gained influence after the failed revolutions of 1848. In *The World as Will and Representation,* Schopenhauer argued that music was the one art that embodied the deepest reality of all human experience—our emotions and drives—and could, therefore, give immediate expression to these universal feelings and impulses in concrete, definite form without the intervention of words. Words and ideas were the product of reason, which governed only "Appearance," whereas emotions resided in the "Will," which Schopenhauer deemed the dominant and ultimate reality.

Schopenhauer's influence

Wagner embraced these views, but rejected Schopenhauer's insistence upon seeking release from the Will through contemplation. In *Tristan und Isolde,* adapted from a thirteenth-century romance by Gottfried von Strassburg, Wagner depicts the raw, vital force of the Will in the passion of two lovers whose ardor can be consummated only in death, a tragedy that serves as the gateway to the highest ecstatic fulfillment.

Embodiment in Tristan und Isolde

Desire is evoked in *Tristan und Isolde* from the very beginning of the Prelude (NAWM 153a), shown in Example 28.2, as Wagner uses chromatic harmony and delayed resolutions to convey an almost inexpressible yearning. Tonal music is based on our desire for dissonance to resolve to consonance,

Prelude

EXAMPLE 28.2 *Opening of Prelude to Wagner's* Tristan und Isolde

and for the dominant to resolve to the tonic. That desire is intensified when resolution is delayed, cadences are evaded, or the moment of resolution introduces a new dissonance, all of which Wagner does here.

The opening motive, a rising sixth followed by a chromatic descent, suggests longing. The first chord, F–B–D♯–G♯, is a striking sonority whose resolution is at first uncertain, given the lack of harmonic context; used throughout the opera and instantly recognizable whenever it appears, this chord has become known as "the Tristan chord." When the top note rises to A, we understand the chord in retrospect as an augmented sixth chord in A minor with a very long chromatic appoggiatura on G♯. The resolution to the dominant seventh of A minor in measure 3 is inflected by a piquant chromatic passing tone (A♯) in the melody, so that we hear four dissonant sonorities in a row, each of which "resolves" the previous one without itself resolving to consonance. It is hard to imagine a three-measure phrase more effective in creating a sense of yearning in the listener.

Nor does the dominant seventh resolve to A minor. After a rest, the opening phrase repeats a minor third higher and then repeats again, varied. Desire is not attenuated by granting resolution to a tonic; instead, the keys of A, C, and E (the three notes of the A minor triad) are suggested through their respective dominant chords, each left hanging in the air. We expect to hear more of all three keys, and eventually we do: A and E in the Prelude itself, and C minor and major as the keys that begin and end Act I. Yet the harmony is constantly churning, shifting keys, altering chords chromatically, and blurring progressions by means of nonchord tones. Desire and yearning are communicated unmistakably by repeatedly evoking yet evading traditional harmonic expectations.

Throughout Act I, motives and extended passages from the Prelude return and acquire significance as leitmotives through association with the words. The act takes place aboard a ship on which the knight Tristan is transporting the reluctant Isolde from Ireland to Cornwall, where she will become King Marke's bride. We learn that she is both secretly in love with Tristan and angry at him for having slain her former fiancé. In the final scene of the act (conclusion in NAWM 153b), she asks him to share a drink of atonement, intending to give them both poison. But her companion Brangäne has substituted a magical love potion. After they drink, we hear the opening section of the Prelude again, as they stare at each other, trembling, then call out to each other with longing. Here the yearning so cunningly expressed in the Prelude finds its parallel on stage, as they surrender to passionate love. But meanwhile the ship has arrived in Cornwall, and the sailors hail King Marke. Their celebratory music competes for attention with the rapture of the lovers until the curtain falls at the end of the act. Throughout, Wagner strings together his open-ended leitmotives in whatever sequence best conveys the actions and emotions of the drama, while constantly varying them to suggest the developing dramatic situation and the fluid feelings of the characters.

This scene exemplifies the intertwining of action, scenery, and music typical of Wagner's *Gesamtkunstwerk*. The deck, railings, sails, ropes, and backdrop onstage join with wave-gestures in the music and the songs of the sailors to convey the ship's journey into port. The realistic shouts of the chorus interrupt the sometimes speechlike, sometimes lyrical and passionate declamation of Tristan and Isolde. The large orchestra maintains continuity, elaborating motives that illustrate the content of the words or the underlying emotions and associations. Thus action, dialogue, musical scene-painting, and lyrical expression are not parceled out to different moments, as in traditional opera, but all constantly mingle and reinforce one another.

Intertwining of the arts

Tristan und Isolde is an extraordinary opera, focused almost entirely on the two main characters and their psychological journey. The outward activity of the plot serves largely as a backdrop to the musical manifestation of the characters' inner emotions. In this sense, this opera most completely embodies Wagner's concept of a drama in which music is the leading element: the words and action on stage are much more a representation of the music than the other way around, which had been typical of opera since its origins. *Tristan und Isolde* has become a monument of music as secular religion, a notion Wagner endorsed and one that pervades much musical activity in the later nineteenth century, from the pilgrimages Wagnerites made to hear his music at Bayreuth to the worshipful attention given to the music of the masters at concerts.

Music as secular religion

WAGNER'S INFLUENCE Wagner's music and ideas were enormously influential. His operas from *The Flying Dutchman* to *Parsifal* quickly became central to the worldwide operatic repertoire, and excerpts from the *Ring* cycle, *Tannhäuser,* and *Lohengrin* were played so often by orchestras and bands and in keyboard transcriptions that they became among the most familiar and popular pieces on the planet. More has been written about Wagner than about any other musician. His writings, and the success of his operas, regained for dramatic and representational music the prestige that some had argued belonged to absolute music alone. His ideal of opera as a drama with music, words, staging, and action all intimately linked affected virtually all later opera. Almost as important was his method of minimizing divisions within an act and charging the orchestra with maintaining continuity by developing pregnant musical motives while the voices sang in free, arioso lines rather than in the balanced phrases of the traditional aria. His use of leitmotives was imitated by many other composers of opera and later became a standard practice for film and television music. Wagner was a master of orchestral color, and here also his example bore fruit. Many musicians became Wagnerians, while others kept their distance or opposed his ideas, but few escaped his influence.

Wagner also had a tremendous impact on the other arts and on culture at large. So great was his influence that "Wagnerism" became a term for interest in his ideas in a number of fields, from politics to aesthetics. Many found in Wagner support for their own idealistic beliefs, and his unique mix of mythology and philosophy, and of the erotic with the spiritual, appealed to a wide range of followers. Paul Verlaine, Stéphane Mallarmé, and other poets associated with the symbolist movement drew on Wagner's use of leitmotives and symbols, an influence that carried over to many writers of the early twentieth century. Visual artists including Gustav Klimt and Aubrey Beardsley transferred to their realm Wagner's interest in legends and symbols, and his re-creations of national legends inspired imitators everywhere.

GIUSEPPE VERDI

Giuseppe Verdi (1813–1901; see biography and Figure 28.7) was the dominant figure in Italian music for the fifty years after Donizetti, as central to Italian opera as Wagner was to German opera. The first of his twenty-six operas was produced in 1839 when he was twenty-six, the last in 1893 when he was eighty.

Political themes   As the most popular Italian composer of his generation, Verdi came to be identified with the Italian Risorgimento. Like other opera composers, he devised ways to sidestep the ever-present threat of government censorship by camouflaging political messages in historical dramas. Italians under foreign rule found relevance in the oppressed characters and tyrants who populated Verdi's operas of the 1840s, including *Nabucco* (Nebuchadnezzar, 1842), *Giovanna d'Arco* (Joan of Arc, 1845), and *Attila* (1846). By 1859, his name had become a nationalist rallying cry: "Viva Verdi!" to Italian patriots stood for "**Viva V**ittorio **E**manuele **R**e d'**I**talia!"—Long live Victor Emmanuel, king of Italy. Even after unification, Verdi never abandoned his interest in politics as a theme. Rather, he approached it more deeply in *Simon Boccanegra* (1857, revised 1881), *Don Carlos* (1867, revised 1884), and *Otello* (1887), which explore complex rulers and the personal consequences of ego and power.

APPROACH TO OPERA Verdi's operas are first and foremost works of theater, whose impact depends on vivid characterization, sharp contrasts, and a fluid and concise dramatic and musical structure. One of his most effective tools, and a prime reason for his enduring popularity, was his ability to capture character, feeling, and situation in memorable melodies that sound both fresh and familiar. Many use a simple form such as AABA, making them easy to follow, and combine regular phrasing and plain harmony with an intriguing rhythmic and melodic motive that catches the listener's attention. So aware was Verdi of the appeal of his melodies that he strove to keep a new opera's best tunes from being leaked to the public before the premiere. But his craft did not stop at melody. He had comprehensive training in harmony and counterpoint, a wide knowledge of the music of his predecessors, and a keen ear for orchestration that adds color, atmosphere, and drama without overpowering the singers.

Librettos   Verdi usually chose the opera's subject himself. He preferred stories that had succeeded as spoken dramas, drawing on plays by authors like Shakespeare, Friedrich Schiller, and Victor Hugo. Mirroring contemporary developments in spoken theater, he expected fast action, striking contrasts, unusual characters, and strong emotional situations from his librettos. Verdi focused on tragic plots and shied away from comedy; after the failure of his first comic opera, *Un giorno di regno* (1840), which followed the deaths of his young children and wife Margherita, it was more than fifty years before he wrote another comedy, *Falstaff* (1893).

GIUSEPPE VERDI

(1813–1901)

Verdi's music has been called the epitome of Romantic drama and passion. He worked within the traditions of his predecessors but during his long life continually refined his techniques.

The son of an innkeeper in a village near Busseto in northern Italy, Verdi studied music as a child, and by age nine was a church organist. After studying privately in Milan, he returned home and took a position as music director in Busseto, where he married Margherita Barezzi in 1836.

He soon returned to Milan, aiming for a career composing operas. The success of his first, *Oberto*, won him a contract for three more operas. When his two children died in infancy, followed by Margherita's early death in 1840 and the failure of his second opera, he nearly gave up composition in despair. But his next opera, *Nabucco* (1842), was a triumph and launched Verdi as a star composer. The next eleven years were the busiest of his career, and he wrote one or two new operas each year for houses in Milan, Venice, Rome, Naples, Florence, London, Paris, and Trieste. This period culminated in *Rigoletto* (1851), *Il trovatore* (1853), and *La traviata* (1853), which quickly became mainstays of the permanent opera repertory.

During these years he met soprano Giuseppina Strepponi, who became his life partner. After spending most of 1847–49 in Paris, he acquired land near Busseto and moved back there with Strepponi, where he and his lover put up with much gossip about their unsanctioned union. In 1851, they settled on a nearby farm, where they lived for the rest of their lives, with frequent sojourns to Paris, Milan, and other cities. They married in secret in 1859.

GALLERIA NAZIONALE D'ARTE MODERNA, ROME.
PHOTO: LEBRECHT MUSIC & ARTS PHOTO LIBRARY

FIGURE 28.7 *Giuseppe Verdi at seventy-two, in a pastel portrait by Giovanni Boldoni.*

After *La traviata*, Verdi slowed his production of new operas, writing only six in the sixteen years from *Les vêpres siciliennes* (1855) to *Aida* (1871). Then he retired from the stage, focusing on his farm and living off royalties from his music, until he was persuaded to write two last operas, *Otello* (1887) and *Falstaff* (1893). Strepponi died in 1897, and Verdi followed in early 1901. A month later, escorted by a procession of thousands of admirers, his remains—along with Strepponi's—were interred in Milan at the home for retired musicians he had helped to found. According to his wishes, the funeral was a very quiet affair, "without music or singing."

MAJOR WORKS 26 operas, including *Nabucco, Macbeth, Luisa Miller, Rigoletto, Il trovatore, La traviata, Les vêpres siciliennes, Simon Boccanegra, Un ballo in maschera, La forza del destino, Don Carlos, Aida, Otello,* and *Falstaff*; Requiem and other Latin sacred choral works

Verdi always wrote with specific singers in mind, suiting his music to their voices in order to create the best possible effect, yet unlike composers of the bel canto era he demanded that singers remain subordinate to the composer and the work (see In Performance: An Original Verdi Baritone: Victor Maurel, pp. 692–93). Collaborating closely with his librettist, Verdi planned the sequence of musical forms to make sure each singer had opportunities for arias, dramatic duets, and larger ensembles. Once the libretto was complete,

Working methods

Verdi wrote out a draft with the vocal melodies and essential accompaniment, then a skeleton score with more of the elements filled in. The final step was the orchestration, usually completed after rehearsals had begun and he heard how the singers sounded in the theater. Verdi could afford to take more time to compose than his predecessors because he was better paid for each new opera and, thanks to improved copyright laws, could count on royalty income from later productions and from sales of the published scores. He used that time to calculate the most effective setting to enhance the opera's dramatic impact on the audience, increasing its chances for a successful first run and a permanent place in the repertory. His strategy worked: although he wrote fewer operas than Rossini or Donizetti, Verdi's have been far more frequently performed than theirs ever since.

STYLE Verdi's early operas built on the conventions of Rossini, Bellini, and especially Donizetti. His first great success was *Nabucco* (Milan, 1842), on the biblical story of Nebuchadnezzar; the Hebrew slaves' unison chorus *Va pensiero* became an emblem of Italian opposition to foreign oppression. After the failure of the revolutions and reforms of 1848–49, Verdi turned from historical subjects to dramas centered on interpersonal conflict and finer psychological portrayal of character, beginning with *Luisa Miller* (Naples, 1849).

Rigoletto

Musical characterization, dramatic unity, and melodic invention unite in *Rigoletto* (Venice, 1851), in which the central characters are delineated by their contrasting styles of singing and relation to musical convention. Rigoletto, a hunchback court jester at odds with the courtiers around him, sings in a declamatory arioso style and lacks a real aria, while the superficiality of his employer the Duke of Mantua is shown in tuneful arias that stick to predictable formal conventions, and Gilda—Rigoletto's daughter, who is in love with the Duke—moves between the two extremes. In the final act, Verdi captures the Duke's charming but shameless nature in the aria *La donna è mobile,* where his claim that women are fickle rings truer about himself, yet his captivating melody in a carefree waltz rhythm makes him seem irresistible. A high point of the opera is the quartet from Act III, where four characters sing, each in a different style to convey their individual personalities and moods. In a seductive, lyrical song the Duke romances a new lover, Maddalena, who coquettishly laughs at his insincerity; meanwhile, listening outside the tavern walls, Gilda sings in dramatic style of her pain at his betrayal, while Rigoletto, bent on revenge, asks in arioso if she has heard enough.

In *Rigoletto* and his next two operas, *Il trovatore* (The Troubadour; Rome, 1853) and *La traviata* (The Fallen Woman; Venice, 1853), Verdi reached new heights of dramatic compression, and all three have remained among the most popular operas ever composed. Verdi often uses reminiscence motives, as Donizetti had done in *Lucia di Lammermoor,* recalling at crucial points in the drama distinctive themes from earlier scenes in order to reinforce connections and deepen the dramatic impact. In several operas, including *Il trovatore* and *La traviata,* Verdi replaced the overture with a briefer prelude that sets the scene and introduces important themes to come.

La traviata

Many features of Verdi's mature works are embodied in *La traviata*. This was one of the first tragic operas to be set in the present rather than in the historical past. Both its setting and its subject—a woman trapped between her livelihood as a courtesan, her desire to escape that life and be loved as an equal, the social mores that keep her in her place, and the tuberculosis that threatens her life—link the opera to the contemporary trend of realism in literature and art.

The resources Verdi commanded are evident in the scene of the final act in which Violetta, the "fallen woman" of the title, and her lover Alfredo reconcile after she had left him to save his family's reputation (NAWM 154). The scene follows the structure Rossini had standardized for duets—scena (accompanied recitative), tempo d'attacco (opening section), slow cantabile, tempo di mezzo (contrasting dramatic section), and fast cabaletta—yet each element is in a new style characteristic of Verdi. Instead of recitative punctuated by the orchestra, the scena presents a complete musical texture in the orchestra, a skipping melody in four-measure phrases, over which Violetta and her maid engage in recitative-like dialogue. When Alfredo enters, their conversation is set not as recitative but as a tuneful song (the tempo d'attacco) in which they alternate phrases. The following cantabile, in which Alfredo and Violetta look forward to life together as she recovers her health, is almost as simple and direct as a popular song, both in its form (AA'BB with coda) and in the tunefulness of its A section, shown in Example 28.3. The cantabile lyricism and the light background accompaniment are familiar, but the style of the vocal line is worlds away from Rossini or Bellini (compare Examples 27.2 and 27.3, pp. 654–57). The tempo di mezzo offers a series of startling contrasts in mood and style as Violetta collapses, insists nothing is wrong, collapses again, and finally despairs that her illness will overtake her just as happiness is so near. These emotions intensify in the cabaletta, where Violetta bewails her ironic misfortune and Alfredo begs her to calm herself. This final section follows a common form for Verdi, AABA' with coda, which allows him to introduce contrast and end on an emotional climax.

As in earlier Italian opera, the focus is on the singing, but here the drama is most important and the composer is in control. The singers are not free to embellish and improvise as they would be in a Rossini opera of a generation earlier, and Verdi wrote out even the cadenzas. The orchestra remains subordinate to the singers, yet Verdi often uses contrasting colors of winds or brass to heighten the effect, doubling a vocal melody, providing punctuation, highlighting a dramatic moment onstage, or building momentum to a climax. Throughout the scene, Verdi takes every opportunity for stark contrasts, strong emotions, and catchy melodies while keeping the action moving in an almost perfect marriage of drama and music.

EXAMPLE 28.3 *Excerpt from Verdi's* La traviata, *Act III*

Paris, my dear, we shall forsake; our life, united, we shall pass together.

IN PERFORMANCE

An Original Verdi Baritone: Victor Maurel

In the second half of the nineteenth century, the relationship between composers and singers shifted as composers like Verdi and Wagner asserted control over every aspect of opera performance and production, rejected the bel canto tradition of improvisation and embellishment, and insisted that the music be performed as written. At the same time, the growing ease of travel and communication gave leading singers unprecedented opportunities to build international careers. Increasingly, this enabled them to act as free agents, independent of both composers and opera-house managements.

A good example of this trend is the French baritone Victor Maurel (1848–1923), shown in Figure 28.8 in costume for Verdi's *Falstaff*. Early in the course of a career that spanned some four decades, he joined a select group of singers who were in demand throughout Europe and the United States. His repertoire centered on operas by Verdi, Wagner, and other

APIC/GETTY IMAGES

FIGURE 28.8 *French baritone Victor Maurel as Falstaff.*

LATER OPERAS Now famous and well off, Verdi could afford to work even more carefully, writing only six new operas in the next two decades. In these operas, the action is more continuous; solos, ensembles, and choruses are more freely combined; harmonies become more daring; and the orchestra is treated with great originality. Verdi still used traditional forms but often reshaped them to suit the dramatic situation. An important influence was French grand opera, especially Meyerbeer. Verdi wrote *Les vêpres siciliennes* (The Sicilian Vespers, 1855) as a grand opera, for Paris, to a libretto by Meyerbeer's collaborator Eugène Scribe, blending French and Italian elements. This also signaled a return to historical subjects with political ramifications, coinciding with renewed interest in Italian unification. He introduced comic roles in *Un ballo in maschera* (A Masked Ball; Rome, 1859) and in *La forza del destino* (The Force of Destiny, 1862, revised 1869), composed for the imperial Russian opera in St. Petersburg. All the traits of his mature style appear in *Aida* (1871), which unites the heroic quality of grand opera with vivid character delineation, pathos, and a wealth of melodic, harmonic, and orchestral color. Commissioned for the Cairo opera, *Aida* was on an Egyptian subject, giving Verdi opportunity to introduce exotic color and spectacle.

contemporary composers, but he was also a notable interpreter of Mozart's *Don Giovanni*. Verdi chose him to premiere the roles of the villain Iago in *Otello* (1887) and of the comic title character in *Falstaff* (1893), showing his appreciation for Maurel's superior abilities and range as an actor, and he shaped the music to suit the singer's voice. Maurel also created the roles of the Indian chief Cacico in Gomes's *Il Guarany* (1870, see p. 708) and of the clown Tonio in Leoncavallo's *Pagliacci* (1892, see p. 694).

After graduating from the Paris Conservatoire in 1867, Maurel made his obligatory debut at the Opéra, singing leading roles in Meyerbeer's *Les Huguenots* and Verdi's *Il trovatore* (in French). But he quickly grew frustrated by the old guard's dominance at France's premier opera house and struck out for Italy, where he became a favorite of audiences in Florence, Rome, Naples, and Venice. He returned to Paris as an international star and later also sang at London's Royal Opera House and Covent Garden and at New York's Metropolitan Opera. His commanding portrayal of the Ethiopian king Amonasro in *Aida*, under Verdi's baton, prompted the composer to cast him in the title role of the revised version of *Simon Boccanegra* at Milan's La Scala in 1881.

Maurel shared Verdi and Wagner's conviction that the old-style bel canto singer was obsolete. He argued that modern singers needed to be accomplished actors and versed, as he was, in contemporary theater and dramatic techniques. In the old days, Maurel wrote in an essay on vocal instruction, "the singer was not expected to portray characters' emotions realistically; he was only required to produce beautiful bel canto sounds. Today, the public wants true theater and lifelike emotions; these demands have given rise to vocal difficulties that are insurmountable for students and that masters can only teach them to overcome when they themselves have learned to do so." *

Verdi declared that "there is no better singer and actor than Maurel," and particularly admired the Frenchman's clear and expressive diction. But Maurel's ego often put him into conflict with Verdi, who, by his own account, was something of a "bear" in his dealings with singers. Tensions came to a head when Maurel demanded the exclusive right to perform the title role in *Falstaff*. The composer politely but firmly demurred. Undeterred, Maurel went on to publish a staging manual for *Otello* and an essay on *Falstaff* in which he took exception with Verdi's express instructions.

*Victor Maurel, *Dix ans de carrière* (Paris, 1897), 171. Translation by Harry Haskell.

Verdi wrote only two more operas after *Aida*, highly individual master-pieces based on plays by his favorite dramatist, Shakespeare. Both feature librettos by poet and composer Arrigo Boito (1842–1918).

In 1879, Verdi's publisher Giulio Ricordi, eager for another opera, proposed adapting Shakespeare's *Othello*. Verdi began *Otello* in 1884, and it was finally produced in Milan in 1887. Like Donizetti before him, Verdi often sought continuity in music and action, and here he realized it most completely, through reminiscence motives in the orchestra and in the unbroken flow of music within each act. The traditional scheme of declamatory and lyrical solos, duets, ensembles, and choruses is still present, but the units are arranged in larger scene-complexes, and the orchestra develops themes in a more symphonic manner, often independent of the voices.

Two years after the premiere of *Otello*, Boito suggested an opera on scenes from Shakespeare's *The Merry Wives of Windsor* and *Henry IV* involving the character Falstaff, shown in Figure 28.8. If *Otello* was the consummation of Italian tragic opera, *Falstaff* (Milan, 1893) holds a parallel place in comic opera. While Verdi reshaped dramatic lyrical melody for *Otello*, for *Falstaff* he transformed that characteristic element of opera buffa, the ensemble.

Otello *and* Falstaff

Carried along over a nimble, endlessly varied orchestral background, the comedy speeds to its climaxes in the finales of the second and third acts, culminating in a fugue for the entire cast on the words "All the world's a joke. We are all born fools."

VERDI'S RECEPTION Verdi experienced phenomenal success in his own lifetime. By the 1850s, his operas were performed more often than those of any other Italian composer. In the twentieth century, even his operas that had not been performed in decades were revived, and in recent decades there have been more operas in the permanent repertory by Verdi than by any other composer.

LATER ITALIAN OPERA

Verdi was such a central figure that later Italian opera composers struggled to escape his shadow. As opera houses increasingly performed works already in the repertory rather than new ones, few operas by composers after Verdi found a permanent place there.

Verismo   Two works that did enter the repertory are the one-act operas *Caval-leria rusticana* (Rustic Chivalry, 1890) by Pietro Mascagni (1863–1945) and *Pagliacci* (Clowns, 1892) by Ruggero Leoncavallo (1858–1919), often paired with each other in performance. Both are examples of **verismo** (from Italian *vero,* "true"), an operatic parallel to realism in literature. Instead of treating historical figures or faraway places, these operas present everyday people, especially the lower classes, in familiar situations, often depicting events that are brutal or sordid. In their realism and in other respects, these composers were strongly influenced not only by Verdi's *La traviata* but also by Bizet's *Carmen* (see pp. 697–98). The music responds directly to the text, driven by vocal melody rather than by earlier operatic conventions. Although now the term "verismo" is often restricted to operas like these, in the late nineteenth and early twentieth centuries it was used more broadly for artworks, including operas, that reacted against Romantic idealism and turned away from a reliance on conventions. In this broader sense, the term embraces a wide range of operas from the late nineteenth and early twentieth centuries that introduce novel elements, whether realistic plots, unconventional scene structures, multidimensional characters, irregular versification, use of everyday language, coloristic harmony, nontraditional accompaniment, or declamatory melodic styles. By this definition, verismo includes Verdi's late operas, Arrigo Boito's *Mefistofele* (1868, revised 1875–76), Alfredo Catalani's *La Wally* (1892), and the operas of Puccini (below), among many others.

FIGURE 28.9
Giacomo Puccini in 1900.

GIACOMO PUCCINI The most successful Italian opera composer after Verdi was Giacomo Puccini (1858–1924), shown in Figure 28.9. The son of a church organist and composer, he was slated to follow in his father's footsteps but chose instead to focus on opera. After studying at the conservatory in Milan, Puccini attracted attention with his first opera, *Le villi,* in 1884. His third opera, *Manon Lescaut* (1893), catapulted him to international fame. Over the next three decades he produced nine more operas, all of which have found enthusiastic audiences around the world.

Puccini's letters show a continual search for dramatic conceptions that evoke "the spirit behind the words." He was interested in realism, embodied by diverse characters, authentic local color, lifelike stage action, and engaging visual effects. To provide these elements, he chose plots set in a place and time that inspired him, whether that be Florence in 1299 (*Gianni Schicchi*, 1918), Rome in 1800 (*Tosca*, 1900), California during the Gold Rush (*La fanciulla del West*, The Girl of the Golden West, 1910), Nagasaki at the turn of the twentieth century (*Madama Butterfly*, 1903–6), or ancient China (*Turandot*, 1926). For him, the exoticism of America, Japan, or China was just another form of realism, with the added appeal of the unfamiliar and far away.

Puccini created a highly individual personal style by blending Verdi's focus on vocal melody with elements of Wagner's approach, notably the use of recurring melodies or leitmotives, freedom from conventional operatic forms, and a greater role for the orchestra in creating musical continuity. In Puccini's operas, arias, choruses, and ensembles are usually part of a continuous flow rather than set off as independent numbers. The standard scene structure pioneered by Rossini and observed in most of Verdi's operas is replaced by a fluid succession of sections that differ in tempo, mood, and character. Musical ideas grow out of the dramatic action, blurring the distinction between recitative and aria. Puccini often juxtaposes different styles and harmonic idioms in order to suggest the diverse people in the drama, such as impoverished artists and other residents of the Parisian Latin Quarter in *La bohème* (1896); the idealistic singer Tosca and the evil Scarpia in *Tosca*; a Japanese woman and her American lover in *Madama Butterfly*; or various levels of an imaginary ancient Chinese society in *Turandot*.

FIGURE 28.10 *Cover by Leopoldo Metlicovitz for the 1906 vocal score of Giacomo Puccini's opera* Madama Butterfly, *showing Butterfly waiting for her American husband Pinkerton to return.*

All of these characteristics are evident in the scene of Butterfly's marriage to Pinkerton in *Madama Butterfly* (NAWM 155). The music moves seamlessly between dialogue and brief aria-like moments. The main continuity and many of the most important melodies are in the orchestra, which nonetheless always supports the singers. In a private dialogue before the ceremony, Pinkerton speaks in the Romantic tones of Puccini's usual style, but Butterfly moves among several different styles to present different personas to Pinkerton: conforming to Western expectations of exotic charm with a Westernized Japanese style, joining in his Western style as an equal, and at one point inadvertently letting him see a darker side of Japanese culture and of her own personal history: her father's ritual suicide. Puccini's music balances exoticism with a very human portrait of Butterfly, captured in her Act II aria *Un bel dì*, expressing her faith that Pinkerton will return to her, and also on the cover of a vocal score, shown in Figure 28.10. Through very simple

Madama Butterfly

means, Puccini responds directly to the text and the situation. His melody-centered, colorful, and emotionally direct style has won his operas a permanent place in the repertory and has exercised a strong influence on scoring for film and television.

FRANCE

In France, no one figure was as dominant as Wagner and Verdi were in their respective lands, but Paris remained the main center for the production of new works. State subsidies for the main opera houses brought with them occasional attempts to dictate policy, including an insistence on performing new works by French composers. Although these efforts to support French music have nationalist origins, few operas had overtly nationalist plots.

Particularly notable is the variety of offerings in the Parisian musical theaters, ranging from old genres to new ones and from serious to light entertainment.

Grand opera and ballet

GRAND OPERA, BALLET, AND LYRIC OPERA Grand opera continued its prominence through Meyerbeer's *L'Africaine* (1865) and Verdi's *Don Carlos* (1867)—written for the Paris Opéra—then began to fade in importance and to blend with other types of serious opera. But ballet, long a part of grand opera, grew in popularity as an independent art. The leading ballet composer was Leo Delibes (1836–1891), whose *Coppélia* (1870) and *Sylvia* (1876) were premiered at the Opéra and became standards of the ballet repertoire. Both are in three acts and constitute an evening's entertainment, like an opera, with mimed actions and solo, duet, and grouped dances linked by a romantic plot.

Lyric opera

The romantic type of opéra comique developed into a genre that might best be termed **lyric opera**, after the Théâtre Lyrique founded in 1851. Lyric opera lies somewhere between light opéra comique and grand opera. Like opéra comique, its main appeal is through melody. The subject matter is usually romantic drama or fantasy, and the scale is larger than that of the opéra comique, although not so huge as that of the typical grand opera.

Gounod's Faust

The most famous lyric opera is *Faust* by Charles Gounod (1818–1893), the most frequently performed opera in the last third of the nineteenth century. First staged at the Théâtre Lyrique in 1859 as an opéra comique (that is, with spoken dialogue), it was later arranged by the composer in its now familiar form with recitatives. Gounod restricted himself to Part I of Goethe's drama, which focuses on the tragic love affair of Faust and Gretchen. The result is a well-proportioned work in an elegant lyric style, with melodies that balance clarity with expressivity.

Other lyric operas

Other popular lyric operas include Gounod's *Roméo et Juliette* (1867), *Mignon* (1866) by Ambroise Thomas (1811–1896), and the many successful operas of Jules Massenet (1842–1912). Massenet's *Manon* (1884), *Werther* (1892), and *Thaïs* (1894) made him the most famous French composer of the time. Both Massenet and Gounod shaped their melodies around the natural speech rhythms of the French language, often resulting in asymmetrical phrases and novel contours. The suave, sensuous impression they create has come to seem characteristic of French musical style.

FRENCH EXOTICISM Several French operas exploited an interest in exoticism, including *Les pêcheurs de perles* (The Pearl Fishers, 1863) by Georges Bizet (1838–1875), set in ancient Ceylon; the biblical opera *Samson et Dalila* (1877) by Camille Saint-Saëns (1835–1921); and Delibes's *Lakmé* (1883), on the doomed relationship between an Indian priestess of Brahma and an officer in the English army occupying India.

Exoticism and realism combine in Bizet's *Carmen,* premiered at the Opéra-Comique in 1875. It was set not in Asia but in Spain, considered as exotic by Parisians despite its proximity. Originally classified as an opéra comique (although Bizet never called it that) because it contained spoken dialogue (later set in recitative by Ernest Guiraud), it was a stark, realistic drama ending with a murder. That such an opera could be called "comique" shows that the distinction between opera and opéra comique had become a mere technicality.

The Spanish flavor was embodied especially in the character of Carmen, shown in Figure 28.11 as portrayed by the singer who created the role. Carmen is a Romani (Gypsy) who works in a cigarette factory and lives only for pleasures of the moment. Her suggestive costume and behavior, her provocative sexuality and language, and Bizet's music all characterize her as outside of normal society, making her both dangerous and enticing. Bizet borrowed three authentic Spanish melodies, including Carmen's famous habanera *L'amour est un oiseau rebelle* (Love is a rebellious bird), set to the rhythm of a Cuban dance. But most of the Spanish-sounding music is Bizet's own invention, blending elements associated with Romani or Spanish music with the modern French style. As shown in Example 28.4, a motive linked to Carmen's fate emphasizes augmented

BRIDGEMAN IMAGES

FIGURE 28.11 *The first Carmen, Célestine Galli-Marié. Her costume and gestures combined with Bizet's music to evoke her exotic allure as a Spanish Romani (Gypsy).*

EXAMPLE 28.4 *Augmented second motives from Georges Bizet's* Carmen

a. Motive associated with Carmen's fate

b. Carmen's entrance motive

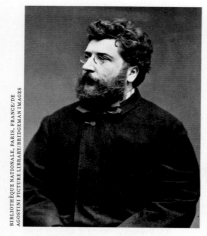

seconds, considered a trademark of Romani music, and a variant of the same motive accompanies Carmen's first entrance. She seduces Don José, an upright army corporal, by singing a seguidilla (NAWM 156), a type of Spanish song in fast triple meter. The accompaniment pattern imitates the strumming of a guitar, the vocal melody features melismas and grace notes, and the harmony includes Phrygian cadences, all features conventionally linked to Spanish music. The plot provoked outrage among some at the premiere—one critic wrote that Bizet "had sunk to the sewers of society" to create his heroine—but the opera won success and has become one of the most popular of all time.

Bizet, pictured in Figure 28.12, might have become the leading opera composer in France, with numerous other projects already underway, but died at 36 just three months after the premiere of *Carmen*. Even so, he was among the most influential of opera composers, as his blend of exoticism and gritty realism in his most famous opera had a strong impact on later composers in Italy and France and across Europe.

FIGURE 28.12 *Georges Bizet in 1875. Photograph by Étienne Carjat.*

LIGHTER FARE While the serious theaters were controlled by the government, the ***opéra bouffe*** could satirize French society more freely. This new genre emerged in the 1850s during the Second Empire and emphasized the smart, witty, and satirical elements of comic opera. Its founder was Jacques Offenbach (1819–1880), who even managed to introduce a can-can dance for the gods in his *Orphée aux enfers* (Orpheus in the Underworld, 1858). His work influenced developments in comic opera in England, Vienna, the United States, and elsewhere (see pp. 708–9). The perennial charm of Offenbach's music owes much to its appealing melody and rhythm, simple textures and harmonies, and conventional formal patterns. But the deceptively naive quality of opéra bouffe often clothes a rapier wit, satirizing operatic as well as social conventions.

Paris was also famous for its popular musical theaters. ***Cabarets*** like Chat Noir (Black Cat, opened 1881) were nightclubs that offered serious or comic sketches, dances, songs, and poetry, often with the intent to foster innovation and draw together artists

FIGURE 28.13 *Edgar Dégas's* Café-Concert aux Ambassadeurs *conveys the vibrant atmosphere of a café-concert from the perspective of an audience member looking toward the singers on stage. Some members of the small orchestra are visible in front of the stage, but the lighting keeps the focus on the singers.*

and the public. A **café-concert**, as pictured in Figure 28.13, joined the food and beverage service of a café with musical entertainment, usually songs on sentimental, comic, or political topics. The Folies-Bergère, Moulin Rouge, and other large music halls offered various kinds of entertainment including **revues**, shows that strung together dances, songs, comedy, and other acts, often united by a common theme. From grand opera to music halls, the range of offerings in Paris was vast, and listeners with broad tastes might sample the Opéra, a cabaret, and the Moulin Rouge, all in the same weekend.

SPAIN

While French writers and composers treated Spain as exotic, Spanish artists sought to create distinctive national traditions of their own. The zarzuela, a theatrical genre alternating spoken dialogue with musical numbers, was already two centuries old (see Chapter 16), yet the Spanish royalty and aristocracy supported Italian opera instead. That changed in mid-century, as a new generation of composers revitalized the zarzuela.

FIGURE 28.14
Francisco Asenjo Barbieri.

Central in the search for a national musical tradition was Francisco Asenjo Barbieri (1823–1894), shown in Figure 28.14, the most influential figure in Spanish music during the second half of the nineteenth century. Trained at the Madrid Conservatory, he sang in Italian operas and composed an Italian opera buffa before turning to zarzuelas. His first two zarzuelas, *Gloria y peluca* (Wigs and Glory) and *¡Tramoya!* (both 1850) were a great success with audiences and critics alike. The next year he cofounded a company to present zarzuelas. His *Jugar con fuego* (Playing with Fire, 1851) was the first in three acts, inaugurating the new genre of the *zarzuela grande* (large zarzuela), and was so popular that it won the support of the queen's mother, María Cristina, and other aristocrats. In 1856 Barbieri's company built a new venue, the Teatro de la Zarzuela, presenting concert series as well as zarzuelas. Some of his zarzuelas are serious dramas, notably his national epic *Pan y toros* (Bread and Bulls, 1864), a sharp political critique. Besides his work as a composer, Barbieri was a conductor, founding a concert society and conducting the first full performances of Beethoven symphonies in Spain; a critic and musicologist, supporting Spanish music through articles and books; and an editor of early Spanish music, in the pathbreaking *Cancionero musical de los siglos XV y XVI* (Musical Songbook of the Fifteenth and Sixteenth Centuries, 1890).

Francisco Asenjo Barbieri

At the height of his career, Barbieri wrote his comic zarzuela grande *El barberillo de Lavapiés* (The Little Barber of Lavapiés, 1874; NAWM 157), whose title puns on his own name and on Rossini's *The Barber of Seville* (NAWM 149). Set in 1770s Madrid, it interweaves political intrigue with the romance of two couples: one comic and middle class, the barber Lamparilla and his dressmaker girlfriend Paloma, and the other noble, the Marquesita of Bierzo and her fiancé Don Luis. The king's chief minister is Italian—historically true, but also a symbol of Barbieri's campaign against Italian influence and for an independent Spanish operatic tradition—and is suppressing dissent with night patrols by the Walloon Guards, foreigners recruited from Spain's possessions in the Low Countries. The Marquesita is part of a conspiracy against the minister, and Lamparilla and Paloma, whose shops are near her house, help to

El barberillo de Lavapiés

protect her. Near the end of Act II, Lamparilla delays the Guards from storming her house by singing and dancing a seguidilla (NAWM 157a), assisted by young men from the neighborhood. The seguidilla, one of the genres most identified with Spanish culture, contrasts with the Italian opera buffa style of the Guards, and the scene embodies Barbieri's struggle to promote a distinctly Spanish style. In the finale (NAWM 157b), the Guards enter the house while Lamparilla and his friends help the conspirators escape through the cellar, then distract the Guards by smashing the hated Italian-style street lamps the minister has imposed on the city, allowing the conspirators to get away in the dark. The continuous music of the finale underscores dialogue between all the principal characters and the chorus, creating a rousing end to the act. The roots of such finales lie in eighteenth-century opera buffa (see Chapter 21), but by the mid-nineteenth century they were part of the international operatic tradition, also common in Spain and France (see NAWM 151). Ultimately Barbieri is for Spanish music what Glinka was for Russia (see Chapter 27): foreigners value his distinctly national style, while for his compatriots he is important also for achieving a level of artistry that can represent Spain on the world stage.

Latin America and Spanish opera   The revitalized zarzuela spread to the remaining Spanish colonies (such as Cuba) and throughout Latin America, which developed its own very strong zarzuela tradition. In Spain, composers in the generation after Barbieri maintained the fashion for zarzuelas, but some also wrote operas sung throughout. Felipe Pedrell (1841–1922) continued the nationalist revival with his editions of sixteenth-century Spanish composers (including the editions of Victoria's music in NAWM 64) and his operas, chief among them *Los Pirineos* (The Pyrenees, 1891).

BOHEMIA

In Bohemia (now the Czech Republic), opera was a specifically nationalist project. Bohemia had for centuries been an Austrian crown land and in the mainstream of European music. Education was in German, the official state language and the primary language of the middle and upper classes and of city-dwellers. Opera had long been heard in the capital, Prague, but in Italian (Mozart's *Don Giovanni* was premiered there) or in German. In the 1860s, in an attempt to foster a national tradition of stage works in Czech, the provincial government established a Czech national theater, and a nobleman sponsored a contest for the best historical and comic operas in Czech.

Bedřich Smetana   The contest was won by the national theater's conductor, Bedřich Smetana (1824–1884), whose eight operas form the core of the Czech operatic repertory and whose comic opera *The Bartered Bride* (1866) secured his international reputation. Smetana chose Czech subjects, and the sets and costumes drew on national traditions. Within a personal idiom heavily influenced by Liszt, Smetana created a Czech national style by using folklike tunes and popular dance rhythms like the polka and by avoiding many of the stylistic conventions of Italian and German opera.

Antonín Dvořák   Smetana was succeeded by Antonín Dvořák (1841–1904), whose twelve operas include plots based on Czech village life, Czech fairy tales, and Slavic history. Most important are *Dmitrij* (1882, revised 1894), a historical opera influenced by Meyerbeer and Wagner, and *Rusalka* (1900), a lyric fairy-tale opera. Both Smetana and Dvořák are better known in western Europe and the Americas for their instrumental music, discussed in Chapter 30.

RUSSIA

When Russian Tsar Alexander II emancipated the serfs in 1861, he did so as part of a broader effort to modernize Russia and catch up to western Europe. There were two main approaches to modernization: the nationalists, or "Slavophiles," idealized Russia's distinctiveness, while the internationalists, or "westernizers," sought to adapt western European technology and education. This dichotomy has often been applied to schools of Russian composers, but it is misleading, because all who composed operas, ballets, symphonies, or sonatas were adopting Western genres and approaches, whatever their style. Rather, a distinction might be made between composers who pursued professional training in the western European mode and those who opposed academic study as a threat to their originality.

Among the former, a key figure was Anton Rubinstein (1829–1894), virtuoso pianist and prolific composer, who founded the St. Petersburg Conservatory in 1862 with a program of training on the Western model. His pianist brother Nikolay Rubinstein (1835–1881) founded the Moscow Conservatory in 1866 on similar lines. Their work raised the standards of musicianship all over Russia and led to a strong tradition of Russian pianists, violinists, composers, and other musicians that continues today.

Rubensteins and conservatories

PIOTR IL'YICH TCHAIKOVSKY The leading Russian composer of the nineteenth century was Piotr Il'yich Tchaikovsky (1840–1893; see biography in Chapter 30). Tchaikovsky sought to reconcile the nationalist and internationalist tendencies in Russian music, drawing models from Beethoven, Schubert, Schumann, and other western European composers as well as from Russian folk and popular music. He wrote a great deal of music for the stage, including incidental music, ballets, and operas. His other works are discussed in Chapter 30.

Tchaikovsky's two most important operas were both based on novels by Aleksander Pushkin. *Eugene Onegin* (1879) is notable for penetrating the passions of its characters and for the way numerous themes are generated from a germ motive first announced in the orchestral prelude. The opera includes folklike music for the peasant chorus, but also features another kind of national music: its main characters are landed gentry, and they sing in a style modeled on the domestic music-making of that class of Russian society. In *The Queen of Spades* (1890), Tchaikovsky matched the ghoulish atmosphere of Pushkin's story and re-created the spirit of the eighteenth-century Russia of Catherine the Great by borrowing musical ideas from that period. These operas show that the styles and materials composers used in order to provide national flavor were not limited to folk music, although listeners outside Russia may not recognize the allusions to other kinds of Russian music.

Operas

Tchaikovsky won spectacular success with his ballets *Swan Lake* (1876), *The Sleeping Beauty* (1889), and *The Nutcracker* (1892), the most famous and

Ballets

frequently performed ballets in the permanent repertory. Each is a full-length ballet in two or more acts, and together they established Tchaikovsky as the most important composer in the history of ballet. For his ballets, Tchaikovsky found a style that combined hummable melodies with colorful orchestration perfectly suited to the fairy-tale atmosphere of the stories and to the gestures of classical ballet. His collaborations with choreographers Marius Petipa and Lev Ivanov set a high standard for the integration of music and movement within a dramatic framework.

THE MIGHTY FIVE Standing against the professionalism of the conservatories were five composers dubbed *moguchaya kuchka* (mighty little bunch), usually translated as the Mighty Five: Mily Balakirev (1837–1910), Aleksander Borodin (1833–1887), César Cui (1835–1918), Modest Musorgsky (1839–1881), and Nikolay Rimsky-Korsakov (1844–1908). Only Balakirev had conventional training in music, but it would be wrong to call the others amateurs. They admired recent music from western Europe but studied it on their own (see Source Reading), outside the academic musical establishment whose exercises and prizes they scorned. It was because of their enthusiasm for Robert Schumann, Chopin, Liszt, Berlioz, and other progressive composers in western Europe that they sought a fresh approach in their own music. As part of that new approach they incorporated aspects of Russian folk song, modal and exotic scales, and folk polyphony, but they also extended traits from the western European composers they most admired. Their theatrical music is covered here; their songs and instrumental works are treated in Chapter 30.

Mily Balakirev and César Cui   Balakirev was the leader of their circle and an informal teacher for the others, but wrote little for the stage. He published two collections of folk songs

---

SOURCE READING

The Mighty Five

In a 1909 memoir, critic and composer César Cui recalled the gatherings almost fifty years earlier when the circle around Mily Balakirev met to pore over scores and argue about music. They opposed academic correctness, prized the most progressive composers of western Europe, and saw themselves as part of that international current.

❈

We formed a close-knit circle of young composers. And since there was nowhere to study (the conservatory didn't exist) our self-education began. It consisted of playing through everything that had been written by all the greatest composers, and all works were subjected to criticism and analysis in all their technical and creative aspects. We were young and our judgments were harsh. We were very disrespectful in our attitude toward Mozart and Mendelssohn; to the latter we opposed Schumann, who was then ignored by everyone. We were very enthusiastic about Liszt and Berlioz. We worshipped Chopin and Glinka. We carried on heated debates (in the course of which we would down as many as four or five glasses of tea with jam), we discussed musical form, program music, vocal music, and especially operatic form.

From César Cui, "Pervïye kompozitorskiye shagi Ts. A. Kyui," in *Izbrannïye stat'i* (Leningrad: Muzgiz, 1952), 544. Trans. Richard Taruskin in *Defining Russia Musically: Historical and Hermeneutical Essays* (Princeton: Princeton University Press, 1997), xv.

in his own arrangements (1866 and 1899) that were sources for many later composers. Cui completed fourteen operas, including four for children, but none entered the permanent repertory.

Borodin, though devoted to music from a young age, was a chemist by profession and had difficulty finding time to compose. He left many works unfinished, including *Prince Igor* (1869–87), a four-act opera in the French grand opera tradition. It was completed after his death by Rimsky-Korsakov and Aleksander Glazunov and premiered in 1890. In it Borodin contrasted two musical styles to evoke the two ethnic groups, depicting his Russian characters with melodies modeled on Russian folk song and providing the Polovtsians, a central Asian people, with an exotic style laced with vocal melismas, melodic chromaticism and augmented seconds, double-reed instruments, and other signifiers Europeans associated with Asian music. The *Polovtsian Dances* in Act II are often performed separately. Already viewed as exotic in western Europe, Russian composers often found as much success at home and abroad with exoticist works as with nationalist ones.

Aleksander Borodin

MODEST MUSORGSKY Widely considered the most original of the Mighty Five, Musorgsky earned a living as a clerk in the civil service and received most of his musical training from Balakirev. His principal stage works were the operas *Boris Godunov* (1868–69, revised 1871–74), based on a Pushkin play, and *Khovanshchina* (The Khovansky Affair, 1872–80, completed after Musorgsky's death by Rimsky-Korsakov). The realism so prominent in nineteenth-century Russian literature echoes especially in *Boris Godunov,* in the way Musorgsky imitated Russian speech, in his lifelike musical depiction of gestures, and in the sound and stir of the crowds in the choral scenes. Both realism and nationalism are reflected in the composer's famous portrait, shown in Figure 28.15.

Musorgsky's individuality shines through every aspect of his music, as illustrated by the famous Coronation Scene from *Boris Godunov* (NAWM 158), shown in Figure 28.16 as it was staged for the opera's 1874 premiere in St. Petersburg. Example 28.5a shows Boris's first statement in the scene, after he is hailed as the new tsar. The vocal melody exemplifies Musorgsky's approach. He set words naturalistically, following the rhythm and pacing of speech as closely as possible: almost always syllabic, with accented syllables on strong beats, often higher and louder than the surrounding notes. As a result, his vocal music tends to lack lyrical melodic lines and symmetrical phrasing, but at the same time he avoided the conventions of recitative. He sought a melodic profile closer to Russian folk songs, which typically move in a relatively narrow range, rise at the beginning of phrases and sink to cadences, and often repeat one or two melodic or rhythmic motives. All of these characteristics are apparent here.

Musorgsky's harmony is essentially tonal, projecting a clear sense of the key, but in many respects it is highly original, even revolutionary. Some

Harmony

FIGURE 28.15 *Portrait of Modest Musorgsky by Ilya Repin, painted in early March 1881, only two weeks before the composer's death from complications of alcoholism. Artist and composer shared a devotion to nationalism, reflected in the peasant shirt Musorgsky wears, and to realism, evident in the unblinking depiction of his unkempt hair, watery eyes, and red nose.*

FIGURE 28.16 *Set design by Mikhail Il'yich Bocharov for the Coronation Scene from Musorgsky's* Boris Godunov *in its first production at the Mariinsky Theater in St. Petersburg in early 1874.*

passages seem more modal than tonal, and dissonances may be left hanging or resolve in unconventional ways. He often juxtaposes distantly related or coloristic harmonies, usually joined by a common tone. One example is the sequence of C minor, A♭ minor, and G major in Example 28.5a, which includes two pairings that became staples of eerie or gloomy movie music in the twentieth century: two minor triads whose roots are a major third apart (C and A♭ minor, which share E♭), and a minor and a major triad with a common third degree (A♭ minor and G major share C♭/B). Other examples, shown in Example 28.5b and c, are the Coronation Scene's opening chords, two dominant seventh chords that have roots a tritone apart (A♭ and D) and two notes in common (C and G♭/F♯), and three major triads related by thirds (E, C, and A major) that share the common tone E and are used in succession to harmonize it. These types of chord progression are not the result of naive experimentation, as some have imputed to Musorgsky, but show his intellectual approach to composition and his familiarity with Liszt, Glinka, and other composers who had used such progressions.

Block construction   Another trait that is characteristic of Musorgsky and of much Russian music is composition in large blocks of material. This is true of the opera as a whole: rather than continuously developed action, *Boris Godunov* is a series of episodes held together by the central figure of the tsar. Because the story was well known, Musorgsky could condense Pushkin's play into a series of relatively unconnected tableaux and thereby focus more intensely on the title character. Juxtaposition of blocks is also evident in the Coronation Scene. The opening section elaborates the two chords shown in Example 28.5b, twice building to a peak of activity and intensity. Then Example 28.5c begins a section of rapid juxtapositions in which every few measures Musorgsky changes figuration and apparent key, until the chorus sings a folk song in C major accompanied by the first traditional harmony in the scene. Musorgsky rarely uses actual folk melodies; this tune adds an element of realism, as do the bells that ring constantly up to this point, like the church bells of Moscow.

EXAMPLE 28.5 *Excerpts from the Coronation Scene from Modest Musorgsky's* Boris Godunov

a. Boris's speech

My soul suffers. Some kind of involuntary fear has stifled my heart with ominous premonitions.

b. Opening chords (the "Boris" chords)

c. Third-related triads harmonizing a repeated note

Long live Tsar Boris Feodorovich!

NIKOLAY RIMSKY-KORSAKOV Rimsky-Korsakov studied music with private teachers and with Balakirev while pursuing a career in the Russian Navy. In 1871, he became a professor at the St. Petersburg Conservatory, abandoning the anti-academic stance of the Balakirev circle. Quickly realizing how much he still had to learn before he could teach music theory, he burned the midnight oil to keep ahead of his classes; later he joked that he was one of the Conservatory's best students. He also became an active orchestral conductor and a master of orchestration.

Professionalism   Ironically, Rimsky-Korsakov's professionalism guaranteed the continuation of a distinctively Russian school. He edited, completed, and orchestrated works by Glinka, Musorgsky, Borodin, and others, helping to ensure their survival. As a conductor at home and in western Europe, he championed Russian music. He wrote the harmony text most frequently used in Russia and a manual on orchestration, and he taught some of the most important composers of the next generation, including Aleksander Glazunov and Igor Stravinsky.

Operas   Rimsky-Korsakov proved his abiding interest in national music by arranging and editing two collections of folk songs (1875–82) and by incorporating folk tunes and their melodic characteristics into his own compositions. Although best known outside Russia for his orchestral works, he was primarily an opera composer. Several of his fifteen operas draw on Russian history, plays, epics, or folk tales. In many of them, including the epic *Sadko* (1895–97) and the fairy-tale operas *Tsar Saltan* (1899–1900) and *The Golden Cockerel* (1906–7), he alternated a diatonic, often modal style used for the everyday world with a lightly chromatic, "fantastic" style that suggested the world of supernatural beings and magical occurrences.

Whole-tone and octatonic collections   A key element of the fantastic style was the use of scales or pitch collections in which the same sequence of intervals occurs several times, so that there is more than one possible tone center. The simplest such scale is the ***whole-tone scale*** (or *whole-tone collection*), consisting of only whole steps; another is the ***octatonic scale*** (or *octatonic collection*), which alternates whole and half steps. Both are shown in Example 28.6. While each of the twelve major scales contains a unique collection of seven notes, there are only two whole-tone collections and three octatonic collections, shown in the example; any other transposition of these scales will simply reproduce the same notes as one of the scales shown here (assuming enharmonic equivalence). Because they lack the strong gravitation toward a tonic that is characteristic of diatonic

EXAMPLE 28.6 *Scales based on equal divisions of the octave*

a. Whole-tone scales

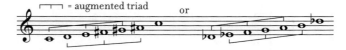

b. Octatonic scales

EXAMPLE 28.7 *From Nikolay Rimsky-Korsakov's* Sadko, *Scene 2*

scales, the whole-tone and octatonic scales create a sense of floating or other-worldliness. Their secret is to divide the octave in equal units; as the example shows, the whole-tone scale comprises two augmented triads (which divide the octave into three major thirds), and the octatonic scale contains two diminished seventh chords (which divide the octave into four minor thirds). These scales are found already in the music of Liszt and other western European composers, deriving from their use of harmonic relationships around the circle of major or minor thirds. Such scales and harmonic relationships became trademarks of Russian music in the late nineteenth and early twentieth centuries.

Example 28.7 shows an example from the second scene of *Sadko,* depicting a fantastic realm under the sea. The rising octatonic scale in the bass is harmonized by the major triads and dominant seventh chords available in the scale, whose roots are related by minor thirds (A, C, Eb, and F♯). The floating harmonies here contrast strongly with the diatonic, folklike song Sadko has just sung, marking him as a human amid the magical surroundings.

RUSSIAN INFLUENCE Tchaikovsky and the Mighty Five developed musical styles that were strongly individual, markedly national, yet suffused with elements from western Europe. In turn, they influenced western European composers of the very late nineteenth and early twentieth centuries, who were especially drawn to the Russians' block construction, orchestral colors, use of modality, and artificial scales. In less than half a century, Russian music went from being peripheral to being a major current in Western music.

OTHER NATIONS

Opera continued to spread to other nations, often—though not always—allied with nationalist movements. The shape that opera took in each nation depended on its individual circumstances. In Poland, which was divided between Russia, Austria-Hungary, and Germany, opera was part of a national cultural revival. Stanisław Moniuszko (1819–1872) inaugurated a tradition of Polish national opera with *Halka* (1848, revised 1858). Britain was dominated by foreign opera, despite repeated attempts to create a national opera tradition in the vernacular. Among the most important British operas were the six of Ethel Smyth (1858–1944), best known for *The Wreckers* (1904); like most of her operas, it was first performed in Germany (where she had studied) before being staged in England. In New York, the Metropolitan Opera Company opened in 1883, performing the entire range of European opera, but almost no native composers attempted opera. The first internationally

FIGURE 28.17
Arthur Sullivan.

recognized composer of opera from the New World was Antônio Carlos Gomes (1836–1896) of Brazil, who had early success with two operas in Portuguese, although neither entered the permanent repertoire. His later operas were written in Italy and in Italian. His masterpiece is *Il Guarany* (1870), on a Brazilian subject centering on reconciliation between the native Indians and the Portuguese colonists, but the style is essentially Italian.

OPERETTA Lighter forms of musical theater flourished in nearly every country. ***Operetta***, a new kind of light opera with spoken dialogue, was manifestly an entertainment, in which nationalism was beside the point. It could be both funny and romantic, spoofing the conventions of opera yet using them sincerely when appropriate. Offenbach had used the term *operetta* for his one-act satirical works of the 1850s, then expanded the concept to a full evening's entertainment in his *opéras bouffes*, which became the models for operettas in other lands. The great masters of operetta in the generation after Offenbach were the Viennese Johann Strauss the younger (1825–1899), known for *Die Fledermaus* (The Bat, 1874), and, in England, the team of W. S. Gilbert (librettist) and Arthur Sullivan (composer, 1842–1900). Sullivan, shown in Figure 28.17, wanted to be known as a serious composer, but his opera on Sir Walter Scott's *Ivanhoe* (1891) was nowhere near as successful as his collaborations with Gilbert, especially *HMS Pinafore* (1878), *The Pirates of Penzance* (1879), and *The Mikado* (1885).

The Pirates of Penzance   The chorus and ensemble *When the foeman bares his steel* from *The Pirates of Penzance* (NAWM 159) illustrates the humor of Gilbert and Sullivan. Everything follows convention yet goes oddly wrong. As the policemen prepare to march on a band of pirates, they sing a rousing chorus set in a martial dotted rhythm. The men, however, freely admit they are terrified at the prospect of battle and are simply covering up their fears. Mabel—a beautiful young woman—and a women's chorus, singing a stirring melody, urge the policemen to suffer death for glory's sake. The police are not happy with this message, but decide it would be too impolite to protest. At the climax, the two choruses sing their melodies in counterpoint, a hilarious juxtaposition of opposing styles and a send-up of the conventions of opera ensembles in which everyone on stage sings together. Indeed, the structure of the scene closely imitates the opening of Act III of *Les Huguenots,* turning Meyerbeer's dramatic opposition of militant Huguenot soldiers and pious Catholic women into farce. When the police continue to sing about marching off to the fray, the Major General notes that they have not left yet ("Yes, but you *don't* go!," he observes with some irritation). The standard roles of men and women in opera, appeals to glory, the tendency to sing at length about taking action before doing it, and other familiar traits are all mocked mercilessly. Throughout, Sullivan matches style and gesture to the text in a satire that shows his command of a wide range of styles.

THE VARIETY OF MUSICAL THEATER In addition to opera and related forms, other kinds of musical theater flourished throughout Europe and the Americas. Ballet in France and Russia has already been mentioned, along with the cabarets, cafés, and nightclubs of Paris.

The particular forms of entertainment varied from place to place, but the variety of musical theater may be illustrated with a snapshot of the United States in the second half of the nineteenth century. European opera was heard in several major cities, both in the original languages and in English translation, and touring companies brought operas to smaller cities across the nation. Minstrel shows continued (see Chapter 27), now including all-black troupes as well as white entertainers in blackface. Operettas were imported from Europe—indeed, *The Pirates of Penzance* was premiered in New York—and homegrown composers wrote their own, including *El capitan* (1896) by John Philip Sousa (1854–1932). A pastiche called *The Black Crook* (1866) combined a melodrama with a visiting French ballet troupe to score a tremendous financial success, and it toured for years, constantly interpolating new material to keep up with fashion. Another great success was *Evangeline* (1874), with music by Edward E. Rice, the first "musical comedy" and an ancestor to the modern musical (see Chapter 31). Singing comics Ned Harrigan (1844–1911) and Tony Hart (1855–1891) collaborated with composer David Braham on comic sketches and musical plays, often focused on Irish, Italian, or other ethnic characters. By bringing variety shows out of the saloons and into music halls that respectable women could attend, New York theater impresario Tony Pastor (1837–1908) invented what became known as **vaudeville**, the major form of theatrical entertainment in the United States until talking movies took over in the late 1920s. Denied the opportunity to perform in opera houses because of segregation, Sissieretta Jones (1868/9–1933) toured the United States and the world singing opera arias and led the Black Patti Troubadours, a traveling variety show that included minstrelsy and vaudeville alongside her excerpts from opera and operetta, making her the highest paid African American performer of her day.

In all these endeavors, the focus was on pleasing the audience and making as much money as possible. In that respect, if in few others, these forms of musical theater could trace their heritage back to the public opera theaters of seventeenth-century Venice (see Chapter 14).

MUSIC FOR THE STAGE AND ITS AUDIENCES

Wagner and Verdi brought the opera of their nations to a peak never surpassed. Even in their lifetimes, they achieved a permanence and centrality in the opera repertory akin to Handel's for oratorio and Beethoven's for the symphony. Since World War II, the works of both Wagner and Verdi have inspired exceptionally innovative and avant-garde stagings, from Wieland Wagner's austerely minimalist productions of his grandfather's operas at Bayreuth in the years 1951–66, which had a profound influence on opera staging in general, to Michael Mayer's 2013 Metropolitan Opera production of Verdi's *Rigoletto,* set in a Las Vegas casino in the 1960s with characterizations based on entertainers from that era. Outside the opera house, excerpts from Wagner operas also became staples of orchestral and band concerts, beginning during his lifetime when full productions were still rare, and several excerpts are still best known in that form.

Of the Italians after Verdi, only Puccini holds a major place in the international opera repertory. Opera composers in other lands found room in their national traditions, and some of their works also entered the permanent international repertory, most notably Gounod's *Faust*, Massenet's *Manon*, Bizet's *Carmen*, Tchaikovsky's *Eugene Onegin* and *The Queen of Spades*, Musorgsky's *Boris Godunov*, and Smetana's *The Bartered Bride*.

Nationalism was a major concern in nineteenth-century opera, and it continues to affect the reception of much of this music in both positive and negative ways. The most nationalist of nineteenth-century composers, Wagner, obscured his nationalism by a claim to universality, and the enthusiastic response of German, English, and even French critics has made it seem that nationalism can be heard only when composers deliberately depart from the German "mainstream." Composers from "peripheral" countries, from Russia to Latin America, are expected to write national music, and those who do are rewarded with an international audience; yet in some respects this keeps their products exotic, and it means that they can never be considered as central as composers from Germany, Austria, France, or Italy.

Meanwhile, the split between elite and popular musical theater became irreparable in this period and has continued to widen. Verdi was still capable of attracting connoisseurs while pleasing the public at large, but the high seriousness of Wagner and much other opera did not aim for popular entertainment and instead inspired a kind of reverence that made attending the *Ring* cycle or *Parsifal* akin to a religious pilgrimage. The popular genres created in reaction, from operetta to vaudeville, became increasingly important and underlie much of the music of the twentieth century. Yet opera is a constant reference as well, since it was for opera that most of the expressive devices in the musical language were first created, and those devices still carry meaning today in music for film, television, and other media. The classic Hollywood film score relies on Wagnerian techniques such as nature imagery and leitmotives, an approach brought over in the late 1920s and early 1930s by emigrés from Austria such as Max Steiner and Erich Wolfgang Korngold (see Chapter 34) and renewed in film scores since the 1970s. The modern movie, especially in the epic genre of *Star Wars* or *Lord of the Rings*, is in many ways a collaborative *Gesamtkunstwerk* in which music plays a crucial role. The movie theater itself is conceptually a descendant of the Bayreuth Festival Theater, with its darkened auditorium and invisible orchestra focusing all our attention on the drama. The influence goes both ways, as film directors and designers create new productions for operas. In these and other ways, the impact of Wagner, Verdi, and other nineteenth-century opera composers has permeated our culture.

Further Reading is available at digital.wwnorton.com/hwm10

LATE ROMANTICISM IN GERMAN MUSICAL CULTURE

During the second half of the nineteenth century, the Western musical world diversified as the audience for music broadened and became more segmented. Increasing interest in music of the past was balanced by the emergence of new styles of concert music, and a growing seriousness in the concert hall and new forms of entertainment music widened the gulf between classical and popular music. This chapter focuses on the classical tradition in German-speaking lands, examining how a debate between partisans of Johannes Brahms and of Richard Wagner crystallized divisions within German music. The following chapter treats national traditions in France and eastern and northern Europe and explores the division into classical and popular streams primarily through musical life in the United States.

DICHOTOMIES AND DISPUTES

Music since 1850 may appear more varied than that of earlier eras simply because the historical evidence is more complete and a wider range of music survives. But that greater diversity is not just an illusion. Several factors combined to make the later nineteenth century the most varied period yet, surpassed only by the even more diverse twentieth and twenty-first centuries.

Before the nineteenth century, most music that was performed had been composed in living memory, except for the chants, chorales, and hymns of the church. By 1850, choral, chamber, and orchestral concerts and solo recitals increasingly focused on a repertoire of musical classics, representing a majority of the pieces on most concerts, and with each decade the proportion of older works grew (see Chapter 26). The establishment of a permanent classical repertoire may be the most important fact about music in the late nineteenth century, for it had many effects beyond concert programming.

In tandem with the rise of the classical repertoire, interest in music

TIMELINE

1848 Frankfurt Assembly votes for parliamentary democracy in Germany

1848–1916 Franz Joseph reigns as emperor of Austria

1851 Complete edition of Johann Sebastian Bach's works begun

1854 Franz Liszt, *Les préludes*

1854 Eduard Hanslick, *On the Musically Beautiful*

1857–59 Richard Wagner, *Tristan und Isolde*

1861 Wilhelm I becomes king of Prussia

1862 Otto von Bismark appointed chancellor of Prussia

1864 Johannes Brahms, Piano Quintet, Op. 34

1867 Austrian Empire reorganized as Austro-Hungarian monarchy

1869 Denkmäler der Tonkunst (Monuments of Musical Art) begins publishing editions of early music

1870–71 Franco-Prussian War

1871 German Empire proclaimed, Wilhelm I becomes emperor

1874–80 Anton Bruckner, Fourth Symphony (*Romantic*)

1885 Brahms, Symphony No. 4 in E Minor

1888 Wilhelm II, last German emperor, crowned

1889 Hugo Wolf, *Mörike Lieder*

1897 Richard Strauss, *Don Quixote*

of the past intensified. The new field of musicology was created in order to study and make available the music of previous generations. Scholars unearthed and published music by the great composers of past eras, issuing editions of the complete works of Bach, Handel, Palestrina, Mozart, Schütz, and Lassus, as well as the early-nineteenth-century masters Beethoven, Mendelssohn, Chopin, Robert Schumann, and Schubert. These editions and numerous less comprehensive performing editions helped to form a canon of composers whose music comprised the center of the repertoire and the mainstream of music history. Most of these composers were German, and their editions were issued by German scholars and publishers, linking the revival of past music to national pride. The German editions of Palestrina and Chopin were notable for granting those composers canonic status despite their nationality. Less widely known music of the Renaissance and Baroque was collected in series such as Denkmäler der Tonkunst (Monuments of Musical Art, begun 1869), Denkmäler deutscher Tonkunst (Monuments of German Music, begun 1892), and Denkmäler der Tonkunst in Österreich (Monuments of Music in Austria, begun 1894). Belatedly, scholars and publishers outside German-speaking regions began to produce editions of music by their own historical masters, including Purcell in England and Grétry and Rameau in France.

Thus in the later nineteenth century, performers and audiences had available to them not only new music and works in the standard repertoire but an increasing supply of older music that was new to them and satisfied some of the desire to hear new pieces as well as familiar ones. A choir's repertoire could include music culled from four centuries, and a pianist might perform works ranging from Bach to the present in a single concert. It is safe to say that nothing approaching this variety of styles had ever before been present simultaneously in the performing tradition.

The preponderance of older music on concert programs posed problems for living composers. How do you craft new works to appeal to an audience that is primarily accustomed to hearing music already familiar to them, most of it composed a generation or more ago? Composers responded in varying ways. Some, like Johannes Brahms, competed with the masters of the past on their own ground, writing symphonies and chamber works worthy of a place next to Beethoven and songs and piano pieces that rival the achievements of Schubert, Robert Schumann, and Chopin. Others, like Wagner and Liszt, saw the legacy of Beethoven as pointing in a different direction, toward genres that combined music with words or with a program. In German-speaking lands, the dispute polarized around Brahms and Wagner and around the dichotomies between absolute and program music, between tradition and innovation, and between classical genres and forms and new ones.

To be sure, the two camps were not so far apart as to foreclose the possibility of mutual respect and influence. Brahms and Wagner admired each other, Anton Bruckner was a Wagnerian in spirit who focused on the traditional genres of the symphony and church music, and both Liszt and Brahms used methods of melodic transformation that derive new musical ideas from existing ones. A number of musicians maintained friendly relations with both sides, including the conductor and pianist Hans von Bülow (see In Performance: Crossing the Divide: Hans von Bülow, p. 714). Moreover, it is clear in retrospect that partisans on both sides shared the common goals of linking themselves to Beethoven, appealing to audiences familiar with the classical masterworks, and securing a place for their own music in the increasingly crowded permanent repertoire.

Although the classical repertoire centered around German-speaking composers, it was performed to varying degrees in concert halls across Europe and the Americas. As a result, composers in other lands also found themselves competing with the classics and addressing issues of national identity.

Nationalism and internationalism

Nationalism was as strong a force in instrumental music, song, and choral music as in opera (see Chapters 27 and 28). National flavor was prized as evidence of a composer's authenticity and distinctiveness. Ethnicity mattered more than political boundaries; in the multinational Austrian Empire, composers increasingly identified with their ethnicity rather than with the imperial state, and German-speaking composers such as Brahms tended to identify with an all-encompassing German tradition wherever they resided. The search for a musical past was in part nationalist. French and German-speaking composers found it in their written tradition as well as in folklore. For example, Brahms drew inspiration from Schütz, Bach, Beethoven, and other German predecessors, but also arranged German folk songs and modeled some melodies on them. Eastern and northern Europeans found a usable past primarily by incorporating aspects of the unwritten tradition of folk music in their own lands (see Chapter 30). Nationalism was not an attempt to break free of the Western tradition, but a way to join it by presenting a distinctive flavor that could be welcomed as part of the international repertoire. Composers everywhere had the choice of whether and how to emphasize their nationality. In the nations farthest from the center, such as Russia and the United States, composers fell at different points on a continuum between nationalist and internationalist orientations, depending on how much they emphasized distinctly national elements in their music.

We saw in Chapter 28 how alongside the venerable tradition of opera, which was growing more expensive and more focused on a standard repertory of operas from the past, lighter forms of theatrical entertainment sprang up, from operetta to cabaret. In instrumental music, song, and choral music, there was likewise a growing gulf between classical music and music intended for popular consumption, both in concert and in publications for music-making at home. The dichotomy has been expressed in various terms, with different shades of meaning: classical versus popular music, serious versus light, cultivated versus vernacular, high versus low. Although at the start of the nineteenth century Beethoven could write both kinds of music—symphonies and string quartets on one side, light rondos and folk-song arrangements on the other—this wide range was rare for composers later in the century, who tended to specialize in one kind of music. While Bruckner was writing his symphonies in Vienna, Johann Strauss the younger, known as "The Waltz King," was in the same city composing hundreds of waltzes, galops, and other

Classical versus popular music

IN PERFORMANCE

Crossing the Divide: Hans von Bülow

Despite heated rhetoric on both sides of the Wagner-Brahms debate, even the most ardent partisans conceded that both composers had a stake in the "music of the future," and most musicians respected both. No one better represents this middle ground, or did more to promote both composers' music, than conductor and pianist Hans von Bülow (1830–1894), shown in Figure 29.1.

Bülow studied piano from age nine with Friedrich Wieck, Robert Schumann's teacher and Clara Schumann's father. Bülow fell under Wagner's spell in 1842, when he attended the premiere of *Rienzi* in Dresden. Convinced that the intense, precociously gifted youth harbored seeds of greatness, Wagner and Liszt took Bülow under their wings. In 1851, he moved to Weimar to study piano with Liszt, and six years later cemented their bond by marrying Liszt's daughter Cosima. His achievements as a pianist were remarkable, including playing the premieres of Liszt's Piano Sonata in B Minor in 1857 and Tchaikovsky's Piano Concerto No. 1 in 1875 and the first complete performance of all thirty-two piano sonatas of Beethoven, all played from memory.

Meanwhile, Bülow had met the twenty-one-year-old Johannes Brahms in 1854 and detected "something really of God's grace, in the best sense, in his talent." That same year he became the first pianist other than Brahms himself to play the composer's music in public, and for the next four decades he steadfastly championed Brahms's works, at both the keyboard and the podium. Although his devotion to Wagner's music never wavered, Bülow came to view Brahms as Beethoven's true successor and the composer best able to continue the great German tradition running from J. S. Bach through Haydn, Mozart, Beethoven, and Schubert to his own time. He coined the phrase "the three Bs," referring to the trinity of Bach, Beethoven, and Brahms.

Bülow conducted the premieres of Wagner's operas *Tristan und Isolde* (1865) and *Die Meistersinger* (1868). These were extraordinarily difficult works, but Bülow was known for his

FIGURE 29.1 *Hans von Bülow, in a portrait by Wilhelm Streckfuss, 1855.*

formidable intellect, rigorous rehearsal procedures, and phenomenal memory. He studied the scores for months, supervised the singers' preparation, and conducted both operas from memory.

Even after his wife Cosima deserted him for Wagner in 1869, having already given birth to two of Wagner's children, Bülow remained loyal to the famously egocentric composer. He contributed generously to the Bayreuth Festival and regularly played his own paraphrases and transcriptions of Wagner's operas on piano recitals.

Bülow's friendship with Brahms deepened after he became conductor of the Meiningen court orchestra in 1880 and turned it into one of the most celebrated in Europe. Brahms's works featured prominently on the orchestra's programs, including his two piano concertos (sometimes with Brahms as soloist or with Bülow conducting from the keyboard) and the premiere of the Fourth Symphony in 1885. But when Brahms insisted on conducting his new symphony on tour, Bülow felt upstaged and resigned in a pique. "I have endured all this once before with Wagner," he told Brahms. "I simply cannot go through it all over again, with you." Saddened to lose Bülow, his employer, Duke Georg, wrote to Brahms that "I shall remain eternally grateful to him for the fame and glory he brought to my orchestra."

FIGURE 29.2 *Scene outside the coffeehouse at the Volksgarten, a large outdoor pleasure garden in Vienna, in 1898. In the background, Johann Strauss the younger leads his orchestra, heard and enjoyed but not attended to with the concentration a classical concert orchestra would have commanded at the time.*

dances to be performed at balls and in concerts, like the open-air concert in Figure 29.2. Popular music was intended purely for entertainment, but classical music was increasingly regarded as a sacred refuge from everyday life. Concerts of classical music became more like going to church; audiences were expected to be quiet and pay reverent attention, and the lights were often dimmed to focus their gaze on the performers—conditions that have prevailed at classical concerts ever since. In contrast to the sacralization of the classical concert hall, audiences for popular music were still allowed to converse, clap during the music or between movements, and pay more or less attention as they wished—in other words, to behave like the audiences who had first heard Haydn's and Mozart's symphonies a century earlier. Classical and popular styles gradually diverged, until there was much less in common between the musical idioms of a symphony and a popular song in the early twentieth century than there had been in Mozart's day.

All of these dichotomies—between old and new musical works and styles, absolute and program music, nationalist and internationalist elements, and classical and popular music—were fault lines in the musical landscape. Listeners and amateurs often enjoyed all the possibilities, piling art songs and popular songs or sonatas and marches side by side on their piano racks, but composers had to make choices. The composers treated here and in the next chapter include the most successful of their day and represent a wide range of strategies for meeting the challenges of their time.

Negotiating the fault lines

JOHANNES BRAHMS

Johannes Brahms (1833–1897; see biography and Figure 29.3) matured as a composer just as the permanent repertoire of musical classics came to dominate concert life. By the time he was twenty, three-fifths of the pieces played

JOHANNES BRAHMS

(1833–1897)

Brahms was the leading German composer of his time in every field except opera and an important influence on twentieth-century music.

He was born in Hamburg to a family of modest means. His father played horn and double bass in dance halls and local ensembles. Brahms studied piano, cello, and horn as a child, and through lessons in piano and music theory developed a love for music of Bach, Haydn, Mozart, and Beethoven. In his teens, he earned money playing popular music at restaurants and private parties. He developed a lifelong taste for folk and popular music. He was especially fond of the Hungarian Romani (Gypsy) style and used it in many compositions.

In 1853, Brahms met the violinist Joseph Joachim and Robert and Clara Schumann, who became his strongest supporters. Robert Schumann praised Brahms in print, launching his career, and helped him secure a publisher. After Robert's suicide attempt and confinement for mental illness, Brahms helped take care of the family while Clara returned to her life as a performer. He often asked for her advice on his compositions and found her a most helpful critic. He fell in love with her, but whether they had more than a platonic relationship, even after Robert's death in 1856, is not known. He had a series of attachments with other women but chose to remain a bachelor, surrounding himself with a close circle of friends.

Brahms made his living by concertizing as a pianist and conductor and from sales of his music to publishers. He conducted the Singakademie in Vienna in 1862–63 and settled there permanently in 1868. From

FIGURE 29.3 *Johannes Brahms in about 1862. Portrait by Carl Jagemann.*

1872 to 1875, he directed the chorus and orchestra of the Gesellschaft der Musikfreunde, programming mostly German music from the sixteenth century through his own day. He was also active as an editor for music by C. P. E. Bach, François Couperin, Robert Schumann, Schubert, and Chopin. In his last two decades he traveled widely as a conductor, performing mostly his own works, and was awarded numerous honors. He died of liver cancer less than one year after Clara Schumann's death and was buried in Vienna's Central Cemetery near Beethoven and Schubert.

MAJOR WORKS 4 symphonies, 2 piano concertos, Violin Concerto, 2 overtures, 2 serenades, 3 string quartets, 21 other chamber works, 3 piano sonatas, numerous piano pieces, *A German Requiem*, choral works, vocal ensembles, and about 200 Lieder

in orchestral concerts were works by dead composers, and by the time he was forty, that proportion had risen beyond three-quarters. Brahms fully understood what it meant to compose for audiences whose tastes were formed by the classical masterpieces of the last two centuries: one had to create pieces that were like those already enshrined in the repertoire in function and aesthetic yet were different enough to offer something new and attractive. He worked slowly and was severely self-critical, knowing that his reputation hinged on the high quality of every piece. He was well versed in music of the past, from Beethoven and the early Romantics back to Renaissance and Baroque composers, both German and non-German, and he synthesized elements from their music with current classical and folk idioms to create a unique personal style. Like Schubert before him, Brahms used virtually all musical languages of his time, from church styles to Hungarian Romani (Gypsy) music, and integrated them into his music to achieve a varied and expressive idiom of his own. At the same time, his erudition was combined with a gift for melody and for direct expression of emotion, so that his music appealed at once to listeners who appreciated its lyrical beauty and sincere expressivity and to connoisseurs who admired its integrity and elegant craft.

ORCHESTRAL WORKS Brahms knew that his symphonies would have to match the standards established by Beethoven. "I shall never compose a symphony!" he exclaimed in 1870. "You have no idea how someone like me feels when he hears such a giant marching behind him all the time." In fact, by his fortieth year, he had completed only four orchestral pieces: two serenades, the Piano Concerto No. 1 in D Minor (1861), and Variations on a Theme of Haydn, Op. 56a (1873). When he did finally produce a symphony, he deliberately invoked Beethoven's model yet carved out a fresh path.

Brahms wrote four symphonies. The first, Symphony No. 1 in C Minor, Op. 68, was completed in 1876, after Brahms worked on it for over twenty years. Its success prompted Brahms immediately to write another, No. 2 in D Major, Op. 73, in 1877. Two more followed: Symphony No. 3 in F Major, Op. 90, in 1883; and Symphony No. 4 in E Minor, Op. 98, in 1885.   *Symphonies*

Brahms's First Symphony carried the weight and history of the genre, yet for every similarity to Beethoven there is a departure. It has the conventional sequence of movements—fast, slow, a light movement, and fast. Yet the third movement is not a scherzo but a lyrical intermezzo, a substitution Brahms repeated in his other symphonies. Brahms echoes Beethoven's Fifth Symphony by moving from C minor to C major and from struggle to triumph, but the overall key scheme of the four movements—C minor, E major, A♭ major, and C minor and major—is characteristic of Schubert and Liszt in defining a circle of major thirds. The presence in both first and last movements of slow introductions that gradually unfold the principal thematic material before the Allegro begins is unlike any Beethoven model but recalls Schumann's Fourth Symphony. The finale's main theme is a hymnlike melody, which immediately suggests a parallel to the finale of Beethoven's Ninth Symphony. Yet there are no voices, as if to say that for Brahms, Beethoven's recourse to words was not necessary. The symphony fully absorbs Beethoven's influence—the conductor Hans von Bülow dubbed it "Beethoven's Tenth"—but also blends in other models and includes much that is new, as it must in order to stand comparison with Beethoven's constant innovations.   *First Symphony*

The opening measures of Symphony No. 3 in Example 29.1 illustrate three traits common in Brahms's music: wide melodic spans; cross-relations between major and minor forms of the tonic triad; and metric ambiguity between triple and duple divisions of the bar. Here rests on the fourth beat invite hearing the theme in $\frac{3}{2}$, but the next phrase makes the $\frac{6}{4}$ meter clear.   *Third Symphony*

EXAMPLE 29.1 *Johannes Brahms, Symphony No. 3, first movement*

EXAMPLE 29.2 *Second theme of Brahms's Symphony No. 3, finale*

The conflict between major and minor recurs in the finale, which begins in
F minor and settles in F major only in the coda. The finale's second theme, in
Example 29.2, features another metric effect that is virtually a Brahms trade-
mark: the clash of simultaneous triple and duple divisions of the beat.

Fourth Symphony   The finale of Brahms's Fourth Symphony (NAWM 160), shown in Figure
29.4, is a chaconne, a form that reflects Brahms's fascination with Baroque
music. It is a set of variations on a bass ostinato and on a harmonic pattern.

FIGURE 29.4 *Auto-
graph score of the opening
of the finale of Brahms's
Symphony No. 4.*

Brahms drew the rising bass figure from the final chorus of Bach's cantata *Nach dir, Herr, verlanget mich,* BWV 150, but he may have had other models in mind as well, such as Buxtehude's Ciacona in E Minor. The use of a variation movement to end a symphony recalls Beethoven's *Eroica* Symphony, one of the few to feature such a finale; like Beethoven, Brahms first presents his bass line as a melody in the upper register and only works it into the bass after several variations. Another possible model is the chaconne finale to Bach's Partita for Unaccompanied Violin in D Minor, which Brahms had transcribed in 1877 as a left-hand exercise for piano; when the ostinato finally reaches the bass, the melodic figuration is a sarabande rhythm exactly like Bach's, and subsequent variations often parallel Bach's, from dotted rhythms to bariolage (rapidly alternating stopped and open strings). All three variation finales are laid out in a broad three-part form with a contrasting middle section, another link between them.

The rich web of allusion is typical of Brahms. To fully understand what he is drawing from the past, we would have to know the music of three centuries as deeply as he did. And yet the Fourth Symphony finale is perfectly clear and coherent without recognizing a single reference to other music. What is most important is that by blending elements from the recent and the more distant past within a contemporary idiom, Brahms was able to create music that sounds wholly original, new, and individual.

Brahms brought the same distinctiveness to his concertos. The Violin Concerto in D Major, Op. 77 (1878), ranks with Beethoven's in scope and popularity. Perhaps his greatest concerto is his Piano Concerto No. 2 in B-flat Major, Op. 83 (1881), whose four movements and close integration between piano and orchestra make it the most symphonic of concertos.

Concertos

CHAMBER MUSIC Brahms's twenty-four chamber works include only three string quartets, a genre where comparison to Beethoven was inescapable. The rest are for a variety of other ensembles: two quintets and two sextets for strings; a quintet for clarinet and strings; three violin sonatas, three cello sonatas, and two clarinet (or viola) sonatas; trios for clarinet, cello, and piano and for violin, natural horn, and piano; and seven works for piano with strings, including three piano trios, three piano quartets, and the Quintet for Piano and Strings in F Minor, Op. 34 (1864).

In the Piano Quintet's first movement (NAWM 161), Brahms's treatment of the opening idea illustrates his use of a method, prevalent throughout his works, of continuously building on germinal ideas, a technique modernist composer Arnold Schoenberg would later—and famously—call ***developing variation*** (see Chapter 33). The theme itself, shown in Example 29.3a, is a series of variants of its opening measure; each measure varies the previous one, and new figures derive from earlier ones (x and y from w, and z from y). In diminution, the theme becomes a piano figure against string chords, telescoping the first and last figures together (motives w and z in Example 29.3b). A transformation of the theme's second measure (motive y) blossoms into a new lyrical melody (Example 29.3c). Then a slower variant of the second measure (drawing only on motive x) is introduced by the piano and imitated in the strings (Example 29.3d). The three ideas in Examples 29.3b, c, and d have little in common, yet all derive from a common ancestor.

Developing variation

EXAMPLE 29.3 *Developing variation in Brahms's Piano Quintet in F Minor, first movement, showing elements of the opening theme that are varied in later themes*

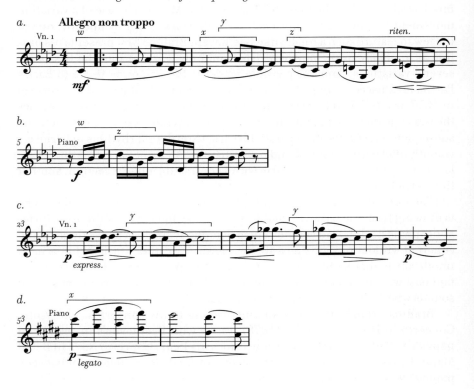

PIANO MUSIC Brahms developed a highly individual piano style characterized by full sonority; broken-chord figuration; frequent doubling of the melodic line in octaves, thirds, or sixths; multiple chordlike appoggiaturas; and frequent use of cross-rhythms. He was extraordinarily imaginative in developing simple ideas into innovative textures, using arpeggiations, repeated notes, contrasting rhythms in different lines, and other means to increase the rhythmic density while maintaining transparent clarity.

As a young man in 1852–53, Brahms wrote three large sonatas in the tradition of Beethoven that also incorporate the chromatic harmony of Chopin and Liszt and the songlike style of Schumann's character pieces. In his twenties and thirties, Brahms began to focus on variations, culminating in the Variations and Fugue on a Theme of Handel, Op. 24 (1861) and the difficult, étude-like Variations on a Theme of Paganini, Op. 35 (1863). Brahms did not simply ornament the melody or change the accompanimental figuration but gave each variation a distinctive character. The twenty-five variations on Handel's theme, for instance, include evocations of Chopin and Mozart, canons, études, character pieces, hunting-horn style, a miniature Hungarian rhapsody, a siciliana, a chromatic fantasia, a musette, a scherzo, and a march, alternating styles of the present with references to eighteenth-century styles, all culminating with a Beethovenian fugue. Brahms's Waltzes, Op. 39 (1865) and Hungarian Dances (1872) were intended for home or concert performance, like Chopin's dances, rather than as music for dancing, but they have a strong popular flavor; Brahms admired Johann Strauss's waltzes, and the two were good friends, shown together in Figure 29.5.

In his last two decades, Brahms issued six sets of intermezzos, rhapsodies, and other short pieces that are perhaps his finest contribution to keyboard literature. Most are in ABA′ form and resemble songs without words or other types of character pieces. The varied textures, surprising harmonies, and deft counterpoint show Brahms's familiarity with keyboard music from Bach to his own time, while the pianistic idiom remains within reach of the amateur performer, and the attractive melodies delight the listener.

SONGS Brahms used Schubert as his model for songwriting, making the voice the primary partner and the piano rich with supporting figuration. Of his more than 200 Lieder, many follow a strophic or modified strophic form, and some, like the familiar *Wiegenlied* (Lullaby, 1868), imitate the style of folk songs. Brahms often chose texts that suggest emotional restraint or an introspective, elegiac mood. Yet he still expresses passion, which becomes all the more effective because it is controlled. The piano is usually varied in texture, changing figuration about every two to four measures; this trait distinguishes Brahms's Lieder from those of Schumann or Schubert while recalling Mozart's frequent changes of figure and topic (see Chapter 23). In his songs, as in his piano music, Brahms was one of the rare composers of the late nineteenth century who wrote music that is both accessible for amateur performers and interesting for connoisseurs, in a parallel to the alchemy of Haydn and Mozart a century earlier.

FIGURE 29.5 *Johann Strauss the younger (left), with Brahms in 1894.*

CHORAL WORKS The same alchemy pervades Brahms's choral music, which was all composed for amateur performers. He arranged German folk songs for chorus and wrote many short, unaccompanied partsongs for women's, men's, or mixed voices, as well as larger pieces for chorus with orchestra.

His greatest choral work is *Ein deutsches Requiem* (A German Requiem, 1868), for soprano and baritone soloists, chorus, and orchestra. Performances of this piece across Europe won enthusiastic responses from audiences and critics and established Brahms as a major composer. The text is not the liturgical words of the Latin Requiem (Mass for the Dead), but rather passages in German, chosen by the composer from the Old Testament, Apocrypha, and New Testament, that speak to universal themes of mortality, loss, comfort, and blessing. Brahms's music draws on Schütz and Bach in its use of counterpoint and expressive text setting. In the *German Requiem,* solemn thoughts are clothed with opulent colors of nineteenth-century harmony, regulated by spacious formal architecture and guided by Brahms's unerring judgment for choral and orchestral effect.

Ein deutsches Requiem

BRAHMS'S PLACE Brahms has often been called conservative, but he was actually a pathbreaker. He was among the first to view the entire range of music of the present and past as material to draw upon in composing his own new and highly individual music—a stance we see repeatedly in composers of the twentieth and twenty-first centuries. By introducing new elements into traditional forms and trying to meet the master composers on their own ground, he was arguably pursuing a more difficult course than those who simply made their mark through innovation. He also developed subtle and complex techniques that were of enormous importance to later composers, from Richard Strauss and Gustav Mahler through Arnold Schoenberg and beyond. Yet he never lost sight of the average listener or musical amateur and succeeded in creating pieces that please on first hearing and continue to engage us after many more.

THE WAGNERIANS

The New German School   In 1859, music critic Franz Brendel proposed the term "New German School" for the composers he felt were leading the new developments, primarily Wagner, Liszt, and Berlioz and their disciples in the next generation. He acknowledged that neither Liszt nor Berlioz was German, but claimed they were German in spirit because they took Beethoven as their model. The term crystallized the polarization among German composers between Liszt, Wagner, and their followers on one side, who believed that music could be linked to the other arts, and on the other side the advocates of absolute music such as Brahms and music critic Eduard Hanslick (see Source Readings).

Composers identified with the Wagnerian side of the debate include Liszt himself; Anton Bruckner, Brahms's contemporary; and two in the next generation, Hugo Wolf and Richard Strauss. Wagner's view that music should engage in a collective artwork (*Gesamtkunstwerk*) with drama, poetry, and other arts posed problems for those who composed orchestral music, songs, and choral works. Each of these four composers found individual solutions to this dilemma—and to the more general problem of how to compose for an audience now steeped in the classical tradition.

FRANZ LISZT In 1848, Liszt retired from his career as a touring pianist (see Chapter 25), became court music director at Weimar, and focused increasingly on composition. From this point on, his music was no longer a vehicle for showing off his virtuosity, and the poetic idea and logical development of the material became more important. Although he still aimed for the stunning immediate effect, he clearly understood the shift toward the classical repertoire (a shift he had aided by including earlier composers in his recitals) and presented himself as a composer worthy of comparison to his peers and predecessors.

Symphonic poems   Between 1848 and 1858, Liszt composed twelve orchestral works he called ***symphonic poems***, adding a thirteenth in 1881–82. Each is a programmatic work in one movement with sections of contrasting character and tempo, presenting a few themes that are developed, repeated, varied, or transformed. These pieces are symphonic in sound, weight, and developmental procedures and are "poems" by analogy to poetry, especially narrative poems. Often the form has vestiges of traditional patterns such as sonata form or the contrasts in mood and tempo found in a four-movement symphony, and some combine the two in a double-function form as in Liszt's Piano Sonata in B Minor (see Chapter 25).

Absolute and Program Music

The most articulate proponent of absolute music was music critic Eduard Hanslick (1825–1904). In his book, *On the Musically Beautiful* (1854), he claimed that music should be understood and appreciated on its own terms rather than for its ties to anything outside music, and that musical content is inseparable from form.

What kind of beauty is the beauty of a musical composition?

It is a specifically musical kind of beauty. By this we understand a beauty that is self-contained and in no need of content from outside itself, that consists simply and solely of tones and their artistic combination. . . .

Nothing could be more misguided and prevalent than the view which distinguishes between beautiful music which possesses ideal content and beautiful music which does not. This view has a much too narrow conception of the beautiful in music, representing both the elaborately constructed form and the ideal content with which the form is filled as self-sufficient. Consequently this view divides all compositions into two categories, the full and the empty, like champagne bottles. Musical champagne, however, has the peculiarity that it grows along with the bottle.

Eduard Hanslick, *On the Musically Beautiful*, trans. and ed. Geoffrey Payzant (Indianapolis: Hackett, 1986), 32, in SR 162 (6:15), p. 1203.

Liszt, on the other hand, argued in defending Berlioz's *Harold in Italy* that a program could clarify the composer's intentions.

The program asks only acknowledgment for the possibility of precise definition of the psychological moment which prompts the composer to create his work and of the thought to which he gives outward form. If it is on the one hand childish, idle, sometimes even mistaken, to outline programs after the event, and thus to dispel the magic, to profane the feeling, and to tear to pieces with words the soul's most delicate web, in an attempt to *explain* the feeling of an instrumental poem which took this shape precisely because its content could not be expressed in words, images, and ideas; so on the other hand the master is also master of his work and can create it under the influence of definite impressions which he wishes to bring to a full and complete realization in the listener. The specifically musical symphonist carries his listeners with him into ideal regions, whose shaping and ornamenting he relinquishes to their individual imaginations; in such cases it is extremely dangerous to wish to impose on one's neighbor the same scenes or successions of ideas into which our imagination feels itself transported. The painter-symphonist, however, setting himself the task of reproducing with equal clarity a picture clearly present in his mind, of developing a series of emotional states which are unequivocally and definitely latent in his consciousness—why may he not, through a program, strive to make himself fully intelligible? . . .

Through song there have always been *combinations* of music with literary or quasi-literary works; the present time seeks a *union* of the two which promises to become a more intimate one than any that have offered themselves thus far.

Franz Liszt (with Carolyne von Sayn-Wittgenstein), "Berlioz und seine Haroldsymphonie," *Neue Zeitschrift für Musik* 43 (1855): 49–50 and 77. Trans. Oliver Strunk, in SR 158 (6:11), pp. 1168–69 and 1171.

The content and form of symphonic poems were usually suggested by a picture, statue, play, poem, scene, personality, or something else, identified by the title and usually by a program. Thus Liszt's *Prometheus* (1850–55) relates to a myth and to a poem by Herder, *Mazeppa* (1852–54) to a poem by Victor Hugo, and *Orpheus* (1853–54) to Gluck's opera *Orfeo ed Euridice* and to an Etruscan vase in the Louvre Museum depicting Orpheus singing to the lyre. The two works that Liszt called symphonies—the *Faust Symphony* (1854) and *Dante Symphony* (1856)—are also programmatic but in more than one movement, essentially consisting of a linked series of symphonic poems. Liszt's symphonic poems thus parallel for orchestral music Wagner's concept of the collective artwork, formulated around the same time.

Thematic transformation

Liszt devised a method of providing unity, variety, and narrative-like logic to a composition by transforming the thematic material to reflect the diverse moods needed to portray a programmatic subject, following the lead of Berlioz's *Symphonie fantastique* (see Chapter 26 and Example 26.5). In his symphonic poem *Les préludes* (The Preludes, 1854), he applied this method, known as **thematic transformation**, with notable artistic success. We can see how this works in Example 29.4. A three-note motive (Example 29.4a) that is initially tentative, like a prelude, is modified and expanded to take on different characters: flowing yet somewhat amorphous (Example 29.4b), resolute (Example 29.4c), lyrical (Example 29.4d), stormy (Example 29.4e

EXAMPLE 29.4 *Thematic transformation in Franz Liszt's* Les préludes

and f), excited (Example 29.4g, an inverted form of the motive), and martial (Example 29.4h). A more distant metamorphosis (Example 29.4i) serves as a contrasting theme and is itself subjected to transformations. Liszt linked *Les préludes* to a poem of that title by Alfonse-Marie de Lamartine, following the same sequence of moods: introductory, with pizzicato chords and arpeggios in the strings and harp to suggest a poet summoning his Muse with lyre and song; amorous (measures 47 and 55, Example 29.4d); troubled and pessimistic about human destiny (measure 131, Example 29.4f); peaceful and pastoral (measure 200); bellicose (measure 344, Example 29.4h); and a return to the initial mood (measure 405). Liszt also used thematic transformation in works without an overt program. The four movements of his Piano Concerto No. 1 in E-flat Major (completed 1855), for example, are played without pauses and linked by themes that are transformed within and between movements.

Choral music

Liszt's choral works offer an accommodation between past and present. Most important are the two oratorios, *St. Elisabeth* (1857–62), on St. Elisabeth of Hungary, and *Christus* (1866–72), on the life of Christ. Both derive much of their thematic material from melodies of plainchants related to their subjects, paraphrased and treated in the style of modern times.

Liszt's influence

Liszt was perhaps even more influential as a composer than he was as a virtuoso. The symphonic poem was taken up by many composers, including Smetana, César Franck, Saint-Saëns, Tchaikovsky, Rimsky-Korsakov, Richard Strauss, Jean Sibelius, and Charles Ives. Liszt's chromatic harmonies helped to form Wagner's style after 1854, and his interest in even divisions of the octave, such as the augmented triad, had a strong impact on Russian and French composers. The process of thematic transformation in Liszt's music has much in common with Berlioz's use of the idée fixe (see Chapter 26) and Wagner's treatment of leitmotives (see Chapter 28), and had many later echoes in the late nineteenth and twentieth centuries. There are also parallels with Brahms's technique of developing variation, although Liszt's approach is less subtle, placing greater emphasis on metamorphosis than on an ongoing, incremental process of organic development from which new themes gradually emerge.

ANTON BRUCKNER If Liszt showed how to compose purely orchestral music in a Wagnerian spirit, Anton Bruckner (1824–1896), shown in Figure 29.6, tried the more daunting tasks of absorbing Wagner's style and ethos into the traditional symphony and of writing church music that united the technical resources of nineteenth-century music with a reverent, liturgical approach to the sacred texts. A devout Catholic, Bruckner was thoroughly schooled in counterpoint and served as organist of the cathedral at Linz, then as court organist in Vienna from 1867 to his death. He was internationally renowned as an organ virtuoso, taught at the Vienna Conservatory, and later lectured at the University of Vienna.

Bruckner wrote nine numbered symphonies and two early unnumbered ones. He frequently revised them,

FIGURE 29.6 *Anton Bruckner in 1891, around the time he was awarded an honorary Doctor of Philosophy by the University of Vienna. Bronzed plaster of Paris sculpture by Viktor Tilgner.*

often in response to criticism from friends and colleagues; as a result most exist in two or three versions, and there is ongoing debate among performers and scholars about which version is best. All but the Ninth are in the conventional four movements, and none is explicitly programmatic, though he did at one time furnish descriptive tags for the Fourth (*Romantic*) Symphony in E-flat Major (1874–80). His devotion to the symphony set him apart from Wagner and Liszt, but his works were championed by a younger generation of Wagnerians.

Influences   Bruckner looked to Beethoven's Ninth Symphony as a model for procedure, purpose, grandiose proportions, and religious spirit. Beethoven's first movement, in which the theme emerges from inchoate intervals and rhythms, suggested an opening gambit, while Beethoven's fourth-movement hymn served as a model for the chorale-like themes in most of Bruckner's finales, although he never used voices. As in Beethoven's Ninth, Bruckner's finales often recycle subjects from earlier movements. Bruckner's debt to Wagner is evident in large-scale structures, the great length of the symphonies, lush harmonies, and sequential repetition of entire passages. Bruckner's experience as an organist informed his orchestration, in which instruments or groups are brought in, opposed, and combined, just like the contrasting keyboards of an organ are, and the massive blocks of sound, piled one on top of the other, suggest an organist's improvisation.

Fourth Symphony   Bruckner's symphonies typically begin, like Beethoven's Ninth, with a vague agitation in the strings out of which a theme gradually coalesces and then builds up in a crescendo, conveying a sense of coming into being. For example, the Fourth Symphony opens with a quiet tonic-triad tremolo in the strings against horn calls with falling and rising fifths (occasionally altered to sixths and octaves) and a triple-dotted rhythm, shown in Example 29.5a. After some striking modulations, the intervals are filled in with scalar passages, and

EXAMPLE 29.5 *Motives from Bruckner, Symphony No. 4 (Romantic), first movement*

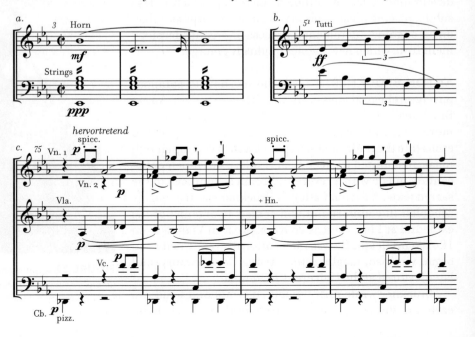

the theme in Example 29.5b emerges *fortissimo,* forcefully proclaiming the tonic with a favorite rhythmic figure that alternates duple and triple divisions. Development of this idea leads to the key of D♭, where a bird call—as Bruckner identified it—is heard in violin 1 against a lyrical melody in the viola, shown in Example 29.5c. The exposition ends in the dominant B♭, creating a three-key exposition like those of Schubert (see Chapters 25 and 26). Both themes are reworked until the development section combines them in a dreamlike sequence resembling Wagner's orchestral interludes. A return to the main key ushers in a recapitulation that reviews material from the exposition in the expected order, with the bird-call section in B major, followed by a long coda. Although we can view this movement in terms of sonata form, the continuous development of musical ideas, characteristic of Beethoven and Wagner, gives the work a monumental dimension.

Choral music

Bruckner's religious choral music blends modern elements with influences from the Cecilian movement, which promoted a revival of the sixteenth-century a cappella style. His motets for unaccompanied chorus reflect these Cecilian ideals, yet their harmonic palette ranges from the strictly modal *Os justi* (1879) to the quickly modulating harmonies of *Virga Jesse* (1885). His Mass No. 2 in E Minor (1866) is a unique neo-medieval work for eight-part chorus and fifteen wind instruments. Bruckner designed his sacred music to function equally well as part of the liturgy or as concert music and to project a sense of timelessness while incorporating up-to-date harmony, balancing these competing requirements perhaps better than any of his contemporaries.

HUGO WOLF Hugo Wolf (1860–1903) is best known for adapting Wagner's methods to the German Lied. He also wrote piano pieces, a string quartet, symphonic works, choruses, and an opera, but none shared the success of his songs.

Lieder

Wolf produced most of his 250 Lieder in short periods of intense creative activity from 1887 until 1897, when he was incapacitated by a mental breakdown, probably caused by syphilis. He published five principal collections of Lieder, each devoted to a single poet or group: Eduard Mörike (1889), Joseph Freiherr von Eichendorff (1889), Goethe (1890), and German translations of Spanish poems (1891) and Italian poems (1892 and 1896). By concentrating on one poet or group at a time and placing the poet's name above his own in the titles of his collections, Wolf indicated a new ideal of equality between words and music, derived from Wagner's approach to opera. Wolf had little use for the folk-song type of melody and strophic structures characteristic of Brahms. Instead, he judiciously applied to the Lied Wagner's notion of a collective artwork (*Gesamtkunstwerk*), achieving a fusion of poetry and music, and of voice and piano, without subordinating either to the other.

A good illustration of Wolf's approach is *Lebe wohl!* from the Mörike songbook, shown in Example 29.6. The vocal line adapts Wagner's arioso style, presenting a speechlike rhythm and pitch contour. As in Wagner's operas, continuity is sustained by the instrumental part rather than the voice, which often parallels melodies in the piano. The chromatic voice-leading, appoggiaturas, anticipations, and wandering tonality are clearly inspired by the idiom of *Tristan und Isolde* (compare NAWM 153). Dissonances resolve to other dissonances, pure triads are rare, and phrases end more often on dissonant than

EXAMPLE 29.6 *Hugo Wolf,* Lebe wohl!

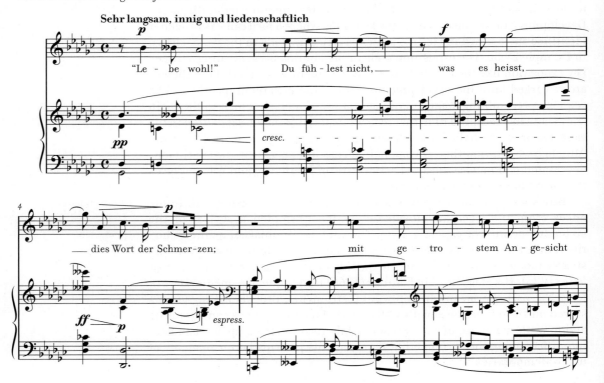

"Farewell!" You are not aware of what it means, this word of pain; with a confident face [and light heart you said it.]

on consonant chords. A measure of the intense chromaticism is that all twelve chromatic notes appear in the first phrase (measures 1–4) and again in measures 5–6, an effect later termed ***chromatic saturation*** (see Chapter 33). The music precisely reflects the text in declamation and in emotion, aptly conveying the despairing feelings of a rejected lover.

RICHARD STRAUSS Richard Strauss (1864–1949), shown in Figure 29.7, was a dominant figure in German musical life for most of his career. He was celebrated as a conductor, holding positions in the opera houses of Munich, Weimar, Berlin, and Vienna, and conducting most of the world's great orchestras during numerous tours. As a composer, he is remembered especially for his ***tone poems*** (his preferred term for symphonic poems), most written before 1900; his operas, all but one of which came later (see Chapter 32); and his Lieder.

Tone poems   Strauss's early compositions emulated Mozart, Beethoven, and Schubert, reflecting the conservative tastes of his father, a renowned horn player. But in his teens, Strauss heard Wagner's operas and studied the score of *Tristan und Isolde,* as a result of which his style soon changed profoundly. Strauss's chief models for program music were Liszt and Berlioz, drawing on their colorful orchestration, transformation of themes, and types of program. Like theirs, some of Strauss's programs are based on literature, including *Don Juan* (1888–89), after a poem by Nikolaus Lenau; *Macbeth* (1888, revised 1891), on Shakespeare; *Also sprach Zarathustra* (Thus Spoke Zoroaster, 1896), after a prose-poem by philosopher-poet Friedrich Nietzsche; and *Don Quixote* (1897), on the picaresque novel by Miguel Cervantes. Other works drew on his personal experience, as Berlioz had done in his *Symphonie fantastique*. The *Symphonia domestica* (1902–3) painted an idealized portrait of his domestic life, and *Ein Heldenleben* (A Hero's Life, 1897–98) is openly autobiographical, caricaturing his critics in cacophonous passages while glorifying his own triumphs with citations from his early works.

Program music covers a broad spectrum, from representing specific events, as in Berlioz's *Symphonie fantastique,* to a more general evocation of ideas and emotional states, as in several of Liszt's symphonic poems. Strauss's tone poems fall at varying places on this spectrum from the representational to the philosophical and typically combine aspects of both.

Don Juan is Strauss's first complete mature work, and its success established his reputation while he was still in his twenties. Events in Don Juan's career as a roving lover are pictured, including wooing a new romantic interest, a rather graphic sexual climax followed by a search for his

FIGURE 29.7 *Richard Strauss in the 1890s, at the peak of his career as a composer of symphonic poems.*

next conquest, and his death at the end. Yet most of the piece evokes general moods of activity, boldness, and romance, rather than following a specific plot.

If *Don Juan* falls in the middle of the spectrum, *Till Eulenspiegels lustige Streiche* (Till Eulenspiegel's Merry Pranks, 1894–95) tends toward the representational, telling the comic tale of a trickster's exploits. The realistic details of Till's adventures are specified by marginal notes the composer added to the printed score. Two themes for Till are used and developed like leitmotives, changing to suggest his activities and situation. Yet the specific events are so thoroughly blended into the musical flow that the work could be heard simply as a character sketch of a particularly appealing rascal, or just as a piece of musical humor. This illustrates an important point about program music in the nineteenth and early twentieth centuries: as in opera, the suggestion of events and ideas outside music allows and explains the use of novel musical sounds, gestures, and forms, but in most cases the music still makes sense on its own terms, presenting, developing, and recalling themes and motives in ways that both parallel and diverge from the processes and forms of earlier music. Strauss indicated that the piece is "in rondeau form." It is not a rondo in the Classic sense, but rondo-like because the two Till themes keep recurring in a variety of guises, enlivened by shrewd touches of instrumentation. Rondo is appropriate for Till, who remains the same fool after each prank.

Also sprach Zarathustra is a musical commentary on Nietzsche's long prose-poem, which proclaimed that the Christian ethic should be replaced by the idea of a superman who is above good and evil. Although the general course of the program is philosophical, moments are directly representational. Zarathustra's address to the rising sun in the poem's prologue inspired the tone poem's splendid opening, with a deep C in the organ pedal and contrabassoon, a rising brass fanfare, opposing C minor and C major triads, thumping

Till Eulenspiegels lustige Streiche

Also sprach Zarathustra

timpani, and triumphant orchestral culmination for full orchestra. The passage became one of Strauss's most famous when it was used in the soundtrack of Stanley Kubrick's 1968 film *2001: A Space Odyssey* to accompany both the sunrise and a scene meant to suggest the birth of reasoning.

Don Quixote

As the rondo suits *Till Eulenspiegel*, so variation form fits the adventures of the knight Don Quixote and his squire Sancho Panza, whose personalities are shaped by their frustrating experiences. We are no longer in a world of merry pranks but in one of split personalities and double meanings. The wry humor and cleverness in *Don Quixote* (see excerpt in NAWM 162) lie not so much in the apt depiction of real things as in the play with musical ideas. Much of this work has a chamber-music sound, because it is conceived in contrapuntal lines, and its themes attach to particular solo instruments, notably the cello for Don Quixote and bass clarinet, tenor tuba, and viola for Sancho Panza. "Variations" here does not mean preserving a melody or harmonic progression and its form through a number of statements. Rather, the themes of the two main characters are transformed so that the beginnings of the themes sprout new melodic characters, building on Liszt's technique of thematic transformation.

REACHING THE AUDIENCE

Each of the composers examined in this chapter pursued a different path, but all succeeded in reaching an audience and securing a permanent place in the classical repertoire. Brahms wrote music in a wide range of traditional forms and genres, and of all late-nineteenth-century composers came closest to achieving the broad appeal to performers, amateurs, listeners, and connoisseurs alike that was characteristic of his great predecessors Bach, Handel, Haydn, Mozart, and Beethoven. Brahms was seen first as a conservative opposed to Wagner and Liszt, then as a cerebral composer of demanding music, but by his death in 1897 he was considered the central figure of classical music in his time, outside the field of opera.

The composers of the Wagnerian wing of the German tradition, like Wagner himself, tended to focus more narrowly on a few genres. The symphonic poems of Liszt and especially of Richard Strauss found a ready audience among lovers of classical music because these works offered something essentially new that was both deeply connected to the symphonic tradition, through procedures of thematic presentation, development, and return, and appealing to first-time listeners, through the programs and novel effects. The choral music of Liszt and Bruckner, Bruckner's symphonies, and Wolf's songs had a harder time competing against the well-established classics in these genres, but they too found a devoted audience of connoisseurs—particularly in German-speaking lands—and now have an enduring place in the repertoire.

From our perspective more than a century later, the dispute between the partisans of Brahms and those of the New German School seems like an argument among close relatives, for all traced their heritage back to Beethoven and the early Romantics and sought to add something of their own to an already rich common tradition.

Further Reading is available at digital.wwnorton.com/hwm10

DIVERGING TRADITIONS IN THE LATER NINETEENTH CENTURY

❖

The fault lines described in the previous chapter between old and new music, absolute and program music, and national and international elements were evident in every corner of the Western classical tradition during the second half of the nineteenth century. We have seen how German-speaking composers responded in different ways to their common heritage and to the gradual development of a permanent repertoire of musical classics, and in the process each created a distinctive personal style. Given the centrality of Bach, Haydn, Mozart, Beethoven, and other German composers in the classical repertoire, composers in other lands who sought a place in that repertoire had to engage with the German tradition as well as with the music and cultural traditions of their own nations. Often—but not always—they sought to assert a specifically national style, as well as an individual one. French composers debated whether to assimilate Bach, Beethoven, Mendelssohn, and Wagner or to pursue a more national idiom. In Russia, Bohemia, Scandinavia, and England, nationalist schools emerged in instrumental music as well as in opera. Yet many composers avoided overt nationalism, choosing instead to speak in what they regarded as the universal common language of music.

All these competing currents contributed to the growing diversity of classical music in the later nineteenth century. But classical music was only one of several streams in musical life, alongside entertainment music, popular song, utilitarian music, and folk music. Through a look at trends in the United States, we can gain a sense of the variety of musical traditions at the time.

FRANCE

Germans had looked to music and other arts to forge a sense of nationhood before the unification of Germany in 1871. But France had been a unified state for centuries and one of the leading musical nations from

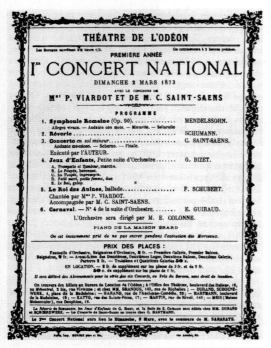

FIGURE 30.1 *Handbill for the first Concert National,
conducted by Edouard Colonne on March 2, 1873. The program is split between German music from earlier generations—Mendelssohn's* Italian Symphony, *a short Robert
Schumann piece, and Schubert's song* Erlkönig—*and new
music by living French composers Saint-Saëns, Bizet, and Ernest Guiraud, all then in their thirties. Many of the seats were
so inexpensive (at one franc or less) that almost anyone could
afford to attend, and audiences were often very large.*

the Middle Ages on. In the second half of the nineteenth century, the challenge for French musicians
was not to use music to create a nation but to position French music in a changed musical landscape in
which classics from the past and the German tradition were both increasing in importance.

In concert music as in opera, Paris was the center of French musical life. Concert-giving institutions balanced increasing interest in German music
with concern for France's musical heritage and
encouragement of its native composers. Beginning
in 1852, an orchestra of the best Paris Conservatoire students gave concerts focused on symphonic
music of Haydn, Mozart, Beethoven, Mendelssohn,
and Robert Schumann, and on new French works in
the same vein, such as Gounod's symphonies. Other
organizations presented a similar repertoire to audiences numbering in the thousands. Figure 30.1 shows
the program of the first Concert National (founded
1873), split equally between German classics and new
French works. Conductor Edouard Colonne focused
his 1885–86 concert series on surveying the history
of music and introduced explanatory program notes,
which became standard in Paris by the end of the century and are now part of classical concerts everywhere.

French music was linked to politics, a tradition
that stretched back to royal control of music in the
seventeenth century (see Chapter 16). The national
government provided significant funding for many
musical institutions, from the Opéra to the Conser-
vatoire, and accordingly these institutions had to respond to political pressure
from those in power. Concert series, composers, and even musical styles were
often associated with political movements. One notable political effect was an
increasing activity in musical life after the Franco-Prussian War of 1870–71,
when the government and the Parisian elite sought to assert the vibrancy of
French culture in the face of an embarrassing defeat. For example, the Société
Nationale de Musique (National Society of Music), founded in 1871, gave concerts of works by French composers and sought to revive the great French
music of the past through editions and performances of Rameau, Gluck, and
sixteenth-century composers. At the same time, somewhat ironically, French
composers were increasingly influenced by German music, from the impact
of Bach on organ music and of the Germanic tradition on symphonic and
chamber works to that of Wagner on vocal and instrumental music alike.

Schools   Music schools reflected competing visions. The Conservatoire stressed
technical training with an emphasis on opera. It was still the most prestigious school, and a first prize there could guarantee a successful career. The
École Niedermeyer, founded in 1853, gave general instruction but focused on
church music; by teaching students to sing Gregorian chant and to accompany
it with modal chords, the school influenced many French composers to use

modal melody and harmony. The Schola Cantorum, founded in 1894 by Vincent d'Indy (1851–1931) and others, emphasized broad historical studies in music, including a focus on counterpoint and composition in classical forms.

The growth in concert activity, proliferation of music schools, revival of past traditions, and encouragement of new music created a stimulating climate for French music. Outside the field of opera and musical theater, two main strands can be identified before the emergence of impressionism (discussed in Chapter 32): a cosmopolitan tradition, transmitted through César Franck (1822–1890) and his pupils, and a more specifically French tradition, embodied in the music of Gabriel Fauré (1845–1924) and passed on to countless twentieth-century composers through his students, especially the famous pedagogue Nadia Boulanger (1887–1979). *Renewal*

CÉSAR FRANCK Franck, shown in Figure 30.2, was born in Belgium, came to Paris to study at the Conservatoire, and became a professor of organ there in 1871. Working mainly in instrumental genres and oratorio, he achieved a distinctive style by blending traditional counterpoint and classical forms with Liszt's thematic transformation, Wagner's harmony, and the Romantic idea of cyclic unification through thematic return.

Typical of Franck's approach is the *Prelude, Chorale, and Fugue* (1884) for piano, which emulates a Baroque toccata in the prelude; introduces a chorale-like melody in distant keys; presents a fugue on a chromatic subject that has been foreshadowed in both previous sections; and closes by combining the opening toccata texture with the chorale melody and fugue subject in counterpoint. It is a piece that could only have been written by someone who had absorbed the thematic and harmonic methods of Liszt and Wagner and also the organ music of Bach and the French Baroque. Franck's organ music took a similar approach, often combining original melodies in chorale style with richly developed fantasias and full chordal finales, as in his *Three Chorales* (1890). His improvisatory style inaugurated a new type of organ music in France, one dominated by lyrical themes, contrapuntal development, and orchestral color. The design of the organ in France changed completely during this period in order to accommodate this new "symphonic" approach. *Keyboard music*

FIGURE 30.2
César Franck.

Franck's Symphony in D Minor (1888) is probably the most popular French symphony after Berlioz. Like Berlioz's *Symphonie fantastique* and *Harold en Italie* (see Chapter 26), it is a model of cyclic form, featuring themes that recur or are transformed in two or more movements. For Berlioz, such thematic links were programmatic, while for Franck they were a fundamental element of his approach to multimovement works, weaving the movements into a unity through continuous development.

Franck has been called the founder of modern French chamber music. His chief chamber works, all cyclic in form, are his Piano Quintet in F Minor (1879), String Quartet in D Major (1889), and Violin Sonata in A Major (1886). The finale of the Violin Sonata (NAWM 163) illustrates Franck's blend of tradition with innovation, from Renaissance and Baroque procedures to Romantic harmony and thematic

TIMELINE

structure. The unique form combines ritornello form, typical of Baroque concertos, with elements of sonata, ternary, and rondo forms. The main theme is marked by an extended canon between violin and piano, thirty-seven measures long at its first appearance, that is reworked in various ways at each later statement of the theme. The harmony meanwhile modulates most often by third, spelling out the tonic triad A–C♯–E for the first three presentations of the main theme, then reaches keys as distant as B♭ minor, E♭ minor, and A♭ minor before working its way back to the tonic. The main theme alternates with themes from the three previous movements. For all this complex interplay, the first impression is of surpassing beauty and emotional power, with songlike themes and expressive climaxes.

GABRIEL FAURÉ AND THE FRENCH TRADITION The other tendency in French music drew primarily on earlier French composers from Couperin to Gounod and approached music more as sonorous form than as expression. Order and restraint are fundamental. Instead of emotional displays and musical depiction, we hear subtle patterns of tones, rhythms, and colors. The music sounds more lyric or dancelike than epic or dramatic. It is economical, simple, and reserved rather than profuse, complex, or grandiloquent.

The refined music of Gabriel Fauré, who is shown in Figure 30.3, embodies the qualities of this French tradition. He studied under Saint-Saëns at the École Niedermeyer, held various posts as an organist, and was a cofounder of the Société Nationale. Although he was considered a radical who composed in an advanced modern style, he became professor of composition at the Paris Conservatoire in 1896 and was its director from 1905 to 1920. Fauré wrote some music in larger forms, including his best-known work, the Requiem (1887), and two operas. But he was primarily a composer of mélodies (songs); of piano music, chiefly preludes, impromptus, nocturnes, and barcarolles; and of chamber music.

Fauré is recognized today as one of the great masters of French song. He wrote dozens of mélodies over a period of six decades, from the early 1860s to the early 1920s. He began by composing mélodies in the manner of Gounod, and lyrical melody, with no display of virtuosity, remained the basis of his style. But in his maturity, from about 1885, he developed a new language in which melodic lines are fragmented and harmony becomes much less directional.

The song cycle *La bonne chanson* (The Good Song), Op. 61 (1892–94) illustrates these characteristics. The poems are by Paul Verlaine (1844–1896), whose focus on suggesting moods through imagery and the sound of language rather than through direct statement became known as *symbolism*. Fauré's approach is similarly indirect. In the sixth song, *Avant que tu ne t'en ailles* (NAWM 164), each poetic image is set to a melodic phrase in its own tonal world, a declamatory fragment joined to the other phrases by subtle motivic echoes. Although they are not modal, the melodies have qualities that reflect Fauré's training in Gregorian chant, moving mostly by step or skip in a gentle arc while avoiding the leading tone and clear harmonic implications.

In the passage shown in Example 30.1, the chords consist mainly of dominant sevenths and ninths, but the tension melts as one chord fades into another, linked through common tones. In each of the first three measures, for example, the dominant seventh on G♯ is succeeded by an E♯-major triad, which neutralizes the leading tone B♯ in the vocal line as the fifth of the new chord and treats the seventh F♯ as an appoggiatura. Such harmonic successions dilute the need for resolution and undermine the pull of the tonic, creating a sense of repose or even stasis that is the opposite of the emotional unrest in Wagner's music. Here the chromaticism that is the lifeblood of so much expressive music in the nineteenth century becomes instead a means to achieve equilibrium and restraint, attributes that have long been esteemed in French music.

FIGURE 30.3 *Gabriel Fauré in a portrait by John Singer Sargent (1889).*

On a larger scale, *La bonne chanson* exemplifies Fauré's innovative approach to traditional genres. He arranged Verlaine's poems to suggest a narrative, as in earlier song cycles (see Chapter 25), but also used recurring themes to create musical unity across the entire cycle and to recall earlier events or emotions. Similar techniques had appeared in Robert Schumann's piano sets and song cycles (see NAWM 133 and 136) and had long been used in opera and symphonic music, in the form of reminiscence motives, leitmotives, or cyclic recollection of themes, but they were new to French art song. The novel harmony and form, along with the heightened role for the piano in

EXAMPLE 30.1 *Excerpt from Gabriel Fauré,* Avant que tu ne t'en ailles

What joy among the fields of ripe wheat!

comparison to most mélodies, provoked resistance from France's conservative musical establishment, who regarded Fauré as an outlier. But by the time he died in 1924, his musical language had become the common currency of modern French musicians, setting French music on a very different course from German music.

EASTERN AND NORTHERN EUROPE

The instrumental repertoire centered on works by German and Austrian composers from Bach to Brahms, but some composers from eastern and northern Europe active in the later nineteenth century were able to secure a place in the classical canon. Inevitably, their works were perceived as offering a different voice, colored as much by their nationality as by their individual character.

TCHAIKOVSKY By far the most successful of these composers was Piotr Il'yich Tchaikovsky (see biography and Figure 30.4), a dominant force in Russian music and a cosmopolitan musician renowned all over Europe and North America. Emblematic of his wide appeal was his First Piano Concerto (1875), premiered in Boston under an American-born conductor with German pianist Hans von Bülow (see Chapter 29) as soloist, and now one of the best-known and most frequently played piano concertos. His theatrical works (discussed in Chapter 28) include the three most popular ballets in the world and two of the most regularly staged Russian operas, and his instrumental works are no less important; his piano concertos, Violin Concerto (1878), and symphonies have won a place near the heart of the repertoire. His best-known symphonies, performed almost as often as Beethoven's, are his last three: No. 4 in F Minor (1877–78); No. 5 in E Minor (1888); and No. 6 in B Minor, the *Pathétique* (1893).

Fourth Symphony   Tchaikovsky wrote his patron Nadezhda von Meck that the Fourth Symphony had a private program in which the horn call from the introduction symbolizes inexorable fate. The horn motive is recalled after the exposition and before the coda of the final movement, unifying the symphony through cyclic return while conveying the program. The outer movements are dramatic, suffused with high emotion; the second movement is wistful, and the third an airy scherzo of a type that became a Russian specialty. Especially novel is the key scheme of the first movement, organized by a circle of minor thirds: the first theme group is in F minor and the second in A♭ major, as expected, but the closing theme appears in B major, a tritone from the tonic; then the recapitulation begins in D minor for the first and second themes, modulates to F major for the closing theme, and returns to F minor for the coda. As we saw in Chapter 28, such circles of minor or major thirds were common in Russian music and ultimately derive from the music of Liszt and Schubert. The three-key exposition and the recapitulation that begins away from the tonic also suggest the influence of Schubert.

Sixth Symphony   The Sixth Symphony (*Pathétique*) also had a private program that Tchaikovsky never specified but whose general outlines can be intuited from its extraordinary sequence of movements. Beginning with a somber slow introduction, the darkly passionate first movement in B minor features a first theme that seems to strive ever upward only to fall back short of the goal, and a consoling, mostly pentatonic second theme. A brief quotation from the

PIOTR IL'YICH TCHAIKOVSKY
(1840–1893)

Tchaikovsky was the most prominent Russian composer of the nineteenth century, in his own country and throughout Europe and the Americas. He combined his Russian heritage with influences from Italian opera, French ballet, and German symphony and song.

Tchaikovsky was born in a distant province of Russia but moved with his family to St. Petersburg, where he graduated from law school at age nineteen, destined for a career in government. After four years as a civil servant, he enrolled at the new St. Petersburg Conservatory, where he studied with its founder Anton Rubinstein and was one of the first students to graduate. He quickly found a position teaching at the new Moscow Conservatory, where he remained for twelve years.

Although Tchaikovsky's professional career was successful, his personal life was in disarray. In addition to bouts of depression and constant worries about money due to overspending, he was troubled by the growing realization of his homosexuality. In 1877, he tried to escape into a hasty marriage to Antonina Milyukova, an attractive and financially independent woman, but it proved disastrous. On the verge of a nervous breakdown and fearing a loss of creativity, he fled back to St. Petersburg after two months, though they never divorced. Around the same time, Tchaikovsky formed another life-changing relationship. Nadezhda von Meck, a wealthy widow who was enthralled by his music, became his financial supporter and intellectual confidante, although the two took care never to meet. Her patronage for over thirteen years enabled him to resign his teaching position in 1878 and devote himself entirely to composition. Reading their voluminous correspondence allows extraordinary insights into Tchaikovsky's thinking and personality.

Tchaikovsky traveled throughout Europe as a

FIGURE 30.4 *Piotr Il'yich Tchaikovsky in 1893, the last year of his life, in an oil portrait by Nikolay Kuznetzov.*

conductor. In the spring of 1891, he made a brief tour of the United States, taking part in the ceremonies inaugurating New York's Carnegie Hall. He was at the peak of his fame when he conducted the premiere of his Sixth Symphony in October 1893. Yet nine days later he died after a brief and unexplained illness, prompting some to see the symphony and other works of his last year as offering a premonition of his death.

MAJOR WORKS 8 operas, including *Eugene Onegin* and *The Queen of Spades*; 3 ballets, *Swan Lake, The Sleeping Beauty*, and *The Nutcracker*; 6 symphonies; 2 piano concertos; a violin concerto; symphonic poems and overtures, including *Romeo and Juliet* and *1812 Overture*; chamber music and songs

---

Russian Orthodox Requiem in the development intensifies the dark mood. The second movement, in D major, is in minuet and trio form, but instead of a minuet uses a dance in $\frac{5}{4}$ meter, one of the many European dances from Switzerland to Russia that combine waltz patterns with pivots or other duple-meter steps (here in the order pivot-waltz, two beats then three beats, in every measure). The dance is graceful and fun, but its B-minor trio has descending gestures that suggest sorrow. The third movement (NAWM 165) in G major begins with a light scherzando character and gradually evolves into a triumphant march, as motivic fragments introduced near the beginning coalesce into a main theme that reaches its definitive form only upon its repetition near the end. So far, the symphony has traced an emotional path from struggle to triumph, familiar from symphonies going back to Beethoven. But Tchaikovsky's *Pathétique* tells another story: it ends extraordinarily with a despairing slow movement, filled with lamenting figures, that fades away at the end over a low pulse in the strings, like the beating of a dying heart. Although Tchaikovsky's unexpected death nine days after the symphony's premiere has led some listeners to interpret the piece in terms of his biography, linking it to his homosexuality, a premonition of death, or the recent deaths of several friends and colleagues his own age, it is more likely that he conceived it as a kind of drama, capturing in instrumental music the tragic arc of many late-nineteenth-century operas in which seeming triumph ends in tragedy.

Reception   Tchaikovsky's symphonies and concertos did not always win immediate or unanimous acclaim from audiences and critics. Listeners only gradually warmed to the Fourth Symphony after its initial cool reception, and the Sixth Symphony was greeted with mixed reactions at its premiere, then praised as a masterpiece when played again soon after the composer's death. Yet both ultimately triumphed because Tchaikovsky met the challenge of his time, blending novel ideas with traditional elements from both the classical tradition and national traditions to create highly individual pieces of music with wide and lasting appeal.

THE MIGHTY FIVE Tchaikovsky was the most prominent Russian composer of his time, but others also found a place in the repertoire. The composers known as the Mighty Five (see Chapter 28)—Balakirev and Cui, as well as Borodin, Musorgsky, and Rimsky-Korsakov (discussed below)—were active in instrumental music as well as in opera, and indeed their instrumental works are more widely known.

Borodin   Borodin's principal instrumental works are his two string quartets (1874–79 and 1881), Symphony No. 2 in B Minor (1869–76), and a symphonic sketch, *In Central Asia* (1880). Alone among the Mighty Five, he was a devotee of chamber music and an admirer of Mendelssohn. Although he seldom quoted folk tunes—as Balakirev and Cui did—his melodies reflect their spirit. His chamber and orchestral works are characterized by song-like themes, transparent instrumental textures, modally tinged harmonies, and his original method of spinning out an entire movement from a single pregnant thematic idea, as in the first movement of the Second Symphony.

Musorgsky   Musorgsky's principal nonoperatic works are a symphonic fantasy, *Night on Bald Mountain* (1867); a set of piano pieces, *Pictures at an Exhibition* (1874; later orchestrated by Ravel); and the song cycles *The Nursery* (1872), *Sunless* (1874), and *Songs and Dances of Death* (1875). *Pictures at an Exhibition* is a suite of ten pieces inspired by an exhibition Musorgsky saw of over four hundred sketches, paintings, and designs by his late friend Viktor Hartmann, who shared with the composer an interest in finding a new artistic language that was uniquely Russian. Several of the paintings are rendered in character pieces, sewn together by interludes that vary a theme meant to represent the viewer walking through the gallery. Figure 30.5 shows Hartmann's design for a commemorative gate to be built at Kiev that combined classical columns, capitals, and arches with decoration modeled on Russian folk art. In the opening theme of the climactic final movement, shown in Example 30.2, Musorgsky translates this image into a grand processional hymn that similarly combines western European and Russian elements, blending classical procedures with a melody that resembles a Russian folk song and harmonies that suggest the modality and parallel motion of folk polyphony. Later, he twice states a Russian Orthodox hymn, which adds a prayerful tone and authentic national element to this majestic concluding movement.

FIGURE 30.5 Design for Kiev City Gate, Main Façade, *by Viktor Hartmann.*

Rimsky-Korsakov is best known for his programmatic orchestral works, although he also wrote symphonies, chamber music, choruses, and songs as well as operas. The *Capriccio espagnol* (1887), the symphonic suite *Scheherazade* (1888), and the *Russian Easter Overture* (1888) display his genius for orchestration and musical characterization. The first two typify exoticism, based on Spanish themes and on tales from the *Arabian Nights* respectively, and the third is nationalist, incorporating Russian Orthodox liturgical melodies. The four movements of *Scheherazade,* each on a different story, are woven together by the themes of the Sultan and his wife Scheherazade, the storyteller, portrayed by a solo violin. These recurring themes lend the work a thematic unity akin to the cyclic symphonies of Franck and Tchaikovsky.

Rimsky-Korsakov

Through a blend of Russian elements with Western conventions, Borodin, Musorgsky, and Rimsky-Korsakov each succeeded in creating instrumental works with a distinctive personality, and ultimately it was their most individual works that have secured a place in the permanent repertoire.

EXAMPLE 30.2 *Modest Musorgsky,* The Great Gate of Kiev, *from* Pictures at an Exhibition

BOHEMIA: SMETANA AND DVOŘÁK As part of the multinational Austro-Hungarian Empire, Bohemia (now the Czech Republic) was close to the German musical tradition but also home to a budding nationalism in music. Like the Russians, Czech composers Bedřich Smetana and Antonín Dvořák are better known outside their native land for their instrumental works than for their operas (discussed in Chapter 28), no doubt because instrumental music can leap over the language barrier. Their operas and tone poems were influenced by the innovations of the New German School (see Chapter 29), and in his symphonies and chamber music, Dvořák was deeply indebted to Brahms, who actively promoted Dvořák's music.

Smetana   Smetana sketched a musical autobiography in his String Quartet No. 1, *From My Life* (1876), and sought to create a national music in his cycle of six symphonic poems collectively titled *Má vlast* (My Country, ca. 1872–79). Of the latter, the best known is *The Moldau,* a picture of the river that winds through the Czech countryside in an ever-broadening current, through forests (represented by hunting music), past a village wedding (represented by a polka), and over rapids on its way to Prague. But the most stirring is *Tábor,* named after the city where followers of radical religious reformer Jan Hus (ca. 1369–1415) built a fortress that became a symbol of Czech resistance to outside oppression. *Tábor* falls into two sections, like the slow introduction and Allegro of a symphonic first movement. In each half, fragments of a Hussite chorale are presented and developed until the entire chorale theme appears in full for the first time at the end. Smetana uses this process to embody the legend that the Hussite warriors will gather strength and emerge from their stronghold in the Czech people's time of need.

Dvořák   Dvořák wrote nine symphonies; four concertos, of which the most popular is the Cello Concerto in B Minor (1894–95); numerous dances and other works for orchestra, including symphonic poems in the Lisztian tradition; and many chamber works, piano pieces, songs, and choral works. Many of his pieces are in an international style. For example, his Symphony No. 6 in D Major (1880), premiered in Vienna, is full of allusions to Beethoven and Brahms symphonies, as Dvořák claimed a place in the Viennese symphonic tradition. Yet in pieces like the *Slavonic Dances* for piano four hands or orchestra (1878 and 1886–87), the dramatic overture *Husitská* (1883), and the *Dumky* Piano Trio (1890–91), Dvořák used elements from Czech traditional music to achieve a national idiom. *Husitská* borrows the same Hussite chorale Smetana used in *Tábor* to invoke nationalistic sentiments, but most often Dvořák avoided quotation of Czech tunes, preferring to invoke national styles by using dance rhythms and his own folklike melodies. The first of the *Slavonic Dances* (NAWM 166) is in the rhythm and style of the *furiant,* a dance in triple meter that begins with hemiolas, as shown in Example 30.3.

EXAMPLE 30.3 *Antonín Dvořák,* Slavonic Dances, *Op. 46, No. 1, opening melody*

By choosing a furiant for the first dance in the set, Dvořák was highlighting his ethnicity: it was one of the most widely known of Czech dances, popularized by Smetana's opera *The Bartered Bride,* and the dance starts with its most idiosyncratic and recognizable feature, the hemiolas that play against the triple meter before we are even sure what the meter is. In other works, such as the Symphonies No. 7 in D Minor (1884–85) and No. 8 in G Major (1889), Dvořák blended folk and national elements with a more broadly international language that drew on older contemporaries from Wagner to Brahms.

Dvořák's best-known symphony is No. 9 in E Minor (*From the New World*), which he wrote in 1893 during an extended sojourn in the United States as artistic director of the National Conservatory of Music in New York. That same year, he conducted at the World's Fair in Chicago, as shown in Figure 30.6. He had been hired to direct the Conservatory with the expectation that as a nationalist composer he would show Americans how to create a new national style of art music for the United States. Believing that a truly national music could derive only from folk traditions, Dvořák looked to the music of Native Americans and African Americans (see Source Readings, pp. 742–43). After studying Native American melodies and hearing an African American student at the Conservatory, Harry T. Burleigh, sing plantation songs and spirituals, Dvořák took the elements of those musical idioms, including pentatonic melodies, syncopated rhythms, drones, and plagal cadences, and applied them to his symphony. Its two middle movements are loosely based on events in Henry Wadsworth Longfellow's epic poem *The Song of Hiawatha.* Similar sounds also suffuse Dvořák's String Quartet No. 12 in F Major (*American*), which he wrote in the summer of 1893 while at a Czech settlement in Spillville, Iowa. As we will see, Americans differed on whether Dvořák's approach was the right one.

FIGURE 30.6 *Antonín Dvořák conducting at the 1893 World's Columbian Exposition in Chicago, in a painting by V. E. Nádherný.*

NORWAY: EDVARD GRIEG At the same time that the Mighty Five were forging a distinct Russian idiom, Edvard Grieg (1843–1907) was writing songs, short piano pieces, and orchestral suites that emulated the modal melodies and harmonies as well as the dance rhythms of his native Norway. An ethnic character emerges most clearly in his songs on Norwegian texts, his *Peer Gynt* Suite (1875), and especially the *Slåtter,* Norwegian peasant dances that Grieg arranged for the piano from transcriptions of country fiddle playing. His piano style, with its delicate grace notes and mordents, owes something to Chopin, but the all-pervading influence in his music is that of Norwegian folk songs and dances, reflected in his modal turns of melody and harmony (Lydian raised fourth, Aeolian lowered seventh, alternating major and minor thirds); frequent drones in the bass or middle register (suggested by the drone strings on Norwegian stringed instruments); and the fascinating combination of $\frac{3}{4}$ and $\frac{6}{8}$ rhythm in the *Slåtter.* His ten sets of *Lyric Pieces* for piano (1867–1901) illustrate the range of his style, from the chromaticism of *Butterfly* in Example 30.4a to the raw folklike *Halling* in Example 30.4b. The latter is particularly

SOURCE READINGS

Dvořák and Paine on an American National Music

Recognized as a nationalist composer, Dvořák was often asked during his sojourn in America about how to create an American national music. This passage is from a magazine article written in 1895, a few months before he returned to Europe, and includes revealing comments about his own situation as well as American music.

✳

A while ago [in an 1893 interview] I suggested that inspiration for truly national music might be derived from the Negro melodies or Indian chants. I was led to take this view partly by the fact that the so-called plantation songs are indeed the most striking and appealing melodies that have yet been found on this side of the water, but largely by the observation that this seems to be recognized, though often unconsciously, by most Americans. All races have their distinctively national songs, which they at once recognize as their own, even if they have never heard them before. . . .

Undoubtedly the germs for the best in music lie hidden among all the races that are commingled in this great country. The music of the people is like a rare and lovely flower growing amidst encroaching weeds. Thousands pass it, while others trample it under foot, and thus the chances are that it will perish before it is seen by the one discriminating spirit who will prize it above all else. The fact that no one has as yet arisen to make the most of it does not prove that nothing is there.

Not so many years ago Slavic music was not known to the men of other races. A few men like Chopin, Glinka, Moniuszko, Smetana, Rubinstein, and Tchaikovsky, with a few others, were able to create a Slavic school of music. Chopin alone caused the music of Poland to be known and prized by all lovers of music. Smetana did the same for Bohemians. Such national music, I repeat, is not created out of nothing. It is discovered and clothed in new beauty, just as the myths and the legends of a people are brought to light

EXAMPLE 30.4 *Edvard Grieg, excerpts from* Lyric Pieces

a. Butterfly, *Op. 43, No. 1*

b. Halling (Norwegian Dance), *Op. 47, No. 4*

and crystallized in undying verse by the master poets. All that is needed is a delicate ear, a retentive memory, and the power to weld the fragments of former ages together in one harmonious whole. . . . The music of the people, sooner or later, will command attention and creep into the books of composers.

Antonín Dvořák, "Music in America," *Harper's* 90 (February 1895), as excerpted in *Composers on Music: Eight Centuries of Writings*, ed. Josiah Fisk (Boston: Northeastern University Press, 1997), 163.

Several American musicians objected to Dvořák's views, including John Knowles Paine (1839–1906), a leading American composer, the first music professor at an American college, and founder of the country's first academic music department, at Harvard.

❖

Even if it be granted that musical style is formed to some extent on popular melodies, the time is past when composers are to be classed according to geographical limits.

It is not a question of nationality, but individuality, and individuality of style is not the result of limitation—whether of folk-songs, negro melodies, the tunes of the heathen Chine[s]e or Digger Indians, but of personal character and inborn originality. During the present century musical art has overstepped all national limits; it is no longer a mere question of Italian, German, French, English, Slavonic or American music, but of world music. Except in opera and church music, the prominent composers of the present day belong to this universal or cosmopolitan school of music, although most of them may express here and there certain characteristics of style, due in part to the influence of airs and dances of their respective countries. The music of Chopin, Grieg and Dvořák, for instance, is distinguished for strong local coloring; on the other hand, the works of Mozart, Mendelssohn, Berlioz, Liszt, [Anton] Rubinstein and others are far less national than individual and universal in character and style.

. . . As our civilization is a fusion of various European nationalities, so American music more than any other should be all-embracing and universal.

From "American Music: Dr. Antonin Dvořák Expresses Some Radical Opinions," *Boston Herald*, May 28, 1893; reprinted in Adrienne Fried Block, "Boston Talks Back to Dvořák," *Institute for Studies in American Music Newsletter* 17, no. 2 (May 1989): 40.

evocative of Norwegian dance music through its imitation of circling melodies with subtle variations, grace notes, open strings, and drone fifths.

Not all of Grieg's music was nationalist. He studied at the Leipzig Conservatory and thoroughly absorbed the tradition of Mendelssohn and Schumann represented there. Among his best-known pieces is the Piano Concerto in A Minor (1868, revised 1907), a bravura work modeled on Robert Schumann's piano concerto in the same key.

BRITAIN: THE "ENGLISH MUSICAL RENAISSANCE" AND ELGAR The question of a national musical tradition was especially acute in Great Britain. England had long been a centralized state, and now it was the heart of a United Kingdom encompassing all of the British Isles, including Wales, Scotland, and Ireland. An economic powerhouse thanks to its leadership in the Industrial Revolution, Britain was the world's leading naval power and had the most far-flung empire the world had ever seen; the slogan that "the sun never sets on the British Empire" expressed the truth that with Canada, New Zealand, Australia, a stretch of Asia from Malaya through India to Afghanistan, large swaths of Africa, and smaller possessions around the globe, it was always daylight somewhere in Queen Victoria's empire. But despite Britain's economic and military might, British intellectuals felt a sense of inferiority in the realm of music. Since the eighteenth century, foreign-born musicians and foreign styles had dominated opera and concert music in Britain, and homegrown composers had failed to match the achievements of Continental composers.

Parry and Stanford   A movement to create a significant independent British musical tradition emerged in the 1880s, dubbed the "English Musical Renaissance" by London critics Joseph Bennett at *The Daily Telegraph* and J. A. Fuller Maitland at *The Times*. They especially praised the music of composers Hubert Parry (1848–1918) and Charles Villiers Stanford (1852–1924) for offering a distinctive national style. Both Parry and Stanford taught composition at the Royal College of Music, established in 1883 with the goal of training young British musicians at the same professional level as conservatories in Paris, Leipzig, and other European centers, and in 1898 both were cofounders of the Folk-Song Society, devoted to the collection and publication of folk songs in the British Isles. Parry, best known for his choral music and five symphonies, developed an individual style that drew on Brahms, Wagner, and Liszt, especially in techniques of development, thematic transformation, and cyclic form, but with a diatonic sound culled from Anglican church music, British folk song, and English composers of the sixteenth and seventeenth centuries such as Tallis and Purcell. The Irish-born Stanford, known for choral music, symphonies, and concertos, similarly blended procedures modeled on Brahms and Mendelssohn with a prevailing diatonic style infused with the flavor of Irish folk tunes, as in his *Irish* Symphony (No. 3 in F Minor, 1887) and six *Irish Rhapsodies* for orchestra (1902–22). But declarations of a Renaissance were premature; neither Parry nor Stanford found a place in the international classical repertoire, although both taught many significant composers of the next generation, including Ralph Vaughan Williams and Gustav Holst, whose reputations eclipsed their own (see Chapter 32).

Considered outsiders to the "Renaissance" were Arthur Sullivan, tainted by his success as a composer of operettas (see Chapter 28), and Edward Elgar (1857–1934), who had no academic training and whose Catholic religion and humble provincial origins barred him from some social circles. Ironically, these are the two British composers best remembered from that era. Elgar, shown in Figure 30.7, was the first English composer in more than two hundred years to enjoy wide international recognition. Unlike Parry and Stanford, he was not interested in folk music or in English music from the Renaissance and Baroque eras and instead forged a personal style made more individual because he was self-taught.

Elgar derived his harmonic approach from Brahms and Wagner and drew from Wagner the system of leitmotives in his oratorios. The oratorio *The Dream of Gerontius* (1900), on a Catholic poem by John Henry Newman, influenced by Wagner's *Parsifal,* gives the orchestra an expressive role as important as the chorus. His symphonic output includes the *Enigma Variations* (1899), which made his reputation, and two symphonies. Among his most popular works are

AKG-IMAGES/NEWSCOM

FIGURE 30.7 *Edward Elgar in about 1901.*

his Violin Concerto (1910), his Cello Concerto (1918–19), now a mainstay of the repertoire, and the five *Pomp and Circumstance Marches* (1901–30), of which the first is familiar to British audiences from its annual performance at the London Promenade Concerts and to every American who ever attended a graduation. Given its primarily Continental influences, if Elgar's music sounds English, it is because it has come to represent British music of his generation.

FINDING A NICHE This sampling of a few composers can give only a taste of the variety of national and individual styles in Europe in the second half of the nineteenth century. Composers often first found a niche for their music within a local, regional, or national performing tradition. A lucky few won a broader audience, often by capitalizing on their national identity, especially when that nation was not yet represented in the international repertoire, or by devising a highly individual musical idiom. This remained true for composers in the early twentieth century, as we will see in Chapters 32, 33, and 35.

THE UNITED STATES

In the United States, national identity was both complicated and enriched by the country's ethnic diversity. Immigrants from many different regions in Europe, Latin America, and Asia, as well as former African American slaves and their descendants, brought their own musical traditions, from folk to classical. American musical life became not exactly a melting pot but perhaps a stewpot, where each group maintained its own music while lending a flavor to the whole.

Superimposed on these ethnic divisions were the rapidly emerging distinctions between classical, popular, and folk music. In theory, these three categories represented different attitudes toward notation, composition, and performance. The classical tradition centered on the composer and the work and required scrupulous adherence to the notated score. Popular music was written down and sold as a commodity but centered on the performer and the performance, allowing considerable leeway in rearranging the notated music. Folk music was independent of notation, passed on through oral tradition. But in practice, the categories overlapped. Folk tunes were written down and sold as popular music, arranged for concert performance, or incorporated into classical pieces; classical works were transcribed and altered for performance in popular venues; and some popular songs (such as *Turkey in the Straw*) became so well known they were passed down orally, like folk songs.

Classical, popular, and folk music

Of all these trends, we will look at four: music in the classical tradition; band music, affected strongly by the growing split between classical and popular music; popular songs; and music of African Americans, drawing on oral traditions but becoming a strand of both popular and classical music.

THE CLASSICAL TRADITION Beginning in the 1840s, crop failures and the 1848 Revolution spurred many Germans to emigrate to the United States, following others who had done so over the previous century. Many of the immigrants were musicians and music teachers with a strong commitment to classical music, and they contributed to an extraordinary growth in

Immigration and institutions

performing institutions, music schools, and university departments of music in the second half of the nineteenth century. German musicians performed widely, filled positions in orchestras, taught music at all levels, and—along with Americans who had studied in Germany—dominated the teaching of composition and music theory in conservatories, colleges, and universities. The new immigrants and the institutions they helped to found fostered an increasingly sharp divide between classical music and popular music. Not surprisingly, German tastes and styles dominated American music in the classical tradition until World War I.

Theodore Thomas   One of the most famous immigrant musicians was Theodore Thomas (1835–1905), who came over with his family in 1845, played violin with the New York Philharmonic and the Academy of Music, conducted the Brooklyn Philharmonic, and in 1865 founded his own professional orchestra. Through constant performing and touring, the Theodore Thomas Orchestra became the best and the most financially successful in the United States. Thomas was devoted to the classical masterworks but recognized that there was not a large enough demand for them to pay his musicians' salaries. So his orchestra gave both concert-hall programs centered on works in the classical tradition and outdoor concerts that interspersed dances and lighter music between overtures and symphonic movements, pleasing the public while introducing them to the classics in small doses. In 1890, he became the first conductor of the Chicago Symphony Orchestra, one of a new breed of full-time professional orchestras backed by wealthy donors and focused almost entirely on classical music.

American composers   As classical music became well established, native-born composers were able to pursue careers that combined composition with performing and teaching, especially in the region from Boston to New York. Among them were John Knowles Paine (1839–1906), trained by a German immigrant, who became Harvard's (and North America's) first professor of music; George Whitefield Chadwick (1854–1931), who studied at the New England Conservatory in Boston and became its director; Chadwick's student Horatio Parker (1863–1919), who taught at Yale and was the first dean of its School of Music; and Edward MacDowell (1860–1908), a New Yorker who was the first professor of music at Columbia University in New York. All studied in Germany as well as the United States, and all pursued styles deeply rooted in the German tradition (primarily the Brahms wing for the Boston composers, Wagner and Liszt for MacDowell).

Attitudes about   However, these composers had varying attitudes about nationalism.
nationalism   Paine argued that the best composers of the day used a universal language that transcended nationality, and as a melting pot of different nations the United States should embrace that transnational approach (see Source Readings, pp. 742–43). Parker believed American composers should simply write the best music they could; his Latin oratorio *Hora novissima* (1893), the piece that made his reputation, is in a universal style modeled on German and English oratorios. Chadwick, on the other hand, developed an idiom laced with American traits such as pentatonic melodies and characteristic rhythms from Protestant psalmody and African-Caribbean dances, used in his Symphony No. 2 in B-flat Major (1883–85) and *Symphonic Sketches* (1895–1904). MacDowell opposed jingoistic nationalism, but like most Europeans he saw

a national identity as an important aspect of any composer's claim to international attention. Among his overtly nationalist works is his Second (*Indian*) Suite for orchestra (1891–95), based on Native American melodies.

Another Boston composer, Amy Beach (1867–1944), shown in Figure 30.8, could not study or teach at the top universities because they excluded women. A child prodigy, she studied piano, harmony, and counterpoint privately, then taught herself to compose by studying and playing works of composers she admired. In 1885 she married a wealthy physician who considered a career as a professional pianist inappropriate for a woman of her social standing, so she restricted her public performances to one solo recital each year and occasional orchestral and chamber concerts, with the proceeds donated

FIGURE 30.8 *Amy Beach in about 1903.*

to charity. Freed of financial concerns and of the demands of performance, and with the strong encouragement of her husband, she devoted herself to composition, publishing her works under her formal married name, Mrs. H. H. A. Beach.

At the time, women were considered incapable of composing in longer forms. As if to prove them wrong, Beach wrote large-scale works such as her Mass in E-flat (1890), *Gaelic* Symphony (Symphony in E Minor, 1894–96), and Piano Concerto (1899), all of them well received. She also wrote about 120 songs and dozens of piano and choral pieces, many of them very popular. After her husband's death in 1910, she resumed her career as a professional performer, while continuing to compose. During a successful three-year residency in Germany in 1911–14, she used the name Amy Beach, but on her return to the United States she decided to revert to her married name, by which she was already well known.

Like her Boston colleagues Paine and Chadwick, Beach engaged the tradition of the German classics in her works and maintained a style rooted in Brahms. Some of her music has an ethnic flavor, including her Variations on Balkan Themes for piano (1904) and String Quartet (1929) on American Indian melodies. Her *Gaelic* Symphony is both ethnic and nationalist, written as a response to Dvořák's *New World* Symphony and to his view that composers in the United States should draw on African American and Native American melodies to establish a national tradition in classical music. Beach believed that a better source was the folk music of the British Isles, which had been popular in the United States for well over a century and had deeply influenced American music, and accordingly based her symphony on four Irish tunes as well as on one of her own songs. The symphony's second movement (NAWM 167) begins with an Irish tune in a slow and lilting $\frac{12}{8}$, then develops it in a fast duple meter, introducing a kaleidoscopic array of paraphrases, fragments, and variations and modulating around two circles of major thirds before returning at the end to the tonic and the source melody.

Gaelic Symphony

Recognized in her day as one of America's leading composers and its most famous woman composer, Beach inspired many women musicians in later generations. Her gender made it harder for her contemporaries to see that she was striving to claim a place on the world stage not only for women but also for American music in the classical tradition.

Reputation

BAND MUSIC While orchestras gradually moved toward greater concentration on the classics, wind and brass bands maintained the mix of serious and popular music that had once been typical for all concerts.

Spread of bands   The earliest American bands were attached to military units, but in the nineteenth century local bands became common everywhere. One important factor was the invention of brass instruments with valves, pistons, or keys, allowing these instruments to play melodies throughout their range (instead of just notes from the harmonic series) and making them easier for amateurs to play (see Chapter 25). Soon the brass were the backbone of the band, either joining or replacing the winds. Amateur bands were formed in communities across the country; some of the earliest are still active, including the Allentown Band (founded 1828) and Repasz Band (1831) in Pennsylvania. Bands played indoors or outdoors, seated or on parade, in concerts but also at dances, holiday celebrations, fairs, picnics, parties, ball games, political rallies, store openings, sales events, weddings, funerals, and other public and private gatherings. The Civil War was called the most musical war in history because almost every regiment on both sides had its own band, which entertained the troops, led marches, performed in parades, and played during battles to hearten the soldiers. After the war, community bands continued to proliferate, becoming such a fixture of American life that by the 1880s there were some ten thousand bands that performed at every opportunity.

Professional bands   The period between the Civil War and World War I was the heyday of professional bands. The Irish-born conductor Patrick S. Gilmore (1829–1892) founded his own band in 1858, enlisted together with them in the Union Army, and led them in concerts after the war. Inspired by patriotism, finances, and fame, he organized two mammoth music festivals: a five-day National Peace Jubilee in Boston in 1869, featuring a thousand-piece band and a chorus of ten thousand, and a World Peace Jubilee in 1872 to celebrate the end of the Franco-Prussian War, with more than twenty thousand performers, including Johann Strauss. Gilmore's Band toured the nation in 1876, traveling from New York to San Francisco, and two years later they made an international tour. His success led to a flood of professional touring bands. The most successful bandmaster was John Philip Sousa (1854–1932), whose years conducting the United States Marine Band (1880–92) raised it to national prominence through tours and savvy promotion. In 1892, he organized his own band, shown in Figure 30.9, which made annual tours of the United States, several European tours, and a world tour.

The repertory of nineteenth-century bands consisted of marches; quicksteps (fast marches); dances including two-steps, waltzes, polkas, galops, and schottisches; arrangements of opera arias and

BROWN BROTHERS, STERLING, PENNSYLVANIA

FIGURE 30.9 *John Philip Sousa with the Sousa Band at a fashionable outdoor concert.*

A. STANDARD MARCH FORM		
March Intro ‖: A :‖: B :‖	Trio (Optional Intro) ‖: C :‖: D :‖	March (da capo) Intro ‖: A :‖: B :‖

B. NON REPETITIVE MARCH FORM				
March Intro ‖: A :‖: B :‖	Trio C	Break Strain ‖: D	Trio C :‖	

FIGURE 30.10 *March forms.*

songs, including medleys; virtuosic display pieces often featuring famous soloists; and transcriptions of pieces by classical composers from Rossini to Wagner. Wagner, Liszt, Bruckner, Brahms, Richard Strauss, and countless other composers encouraged such transcriptions for band, recognizing the value of making their music available to a wider audience through such a popular medium, and some (including Wagner and Strauss) composed original pieces for band. Except for the instrumentation, the band repertory was essentially the same fare played by orchestras in the mid-nineteenth century, such as those conducted by Louis Jullien (see Chapter 26) and Theodore Thomas. Bands, whose first purpose was entertainment, retained this formula far longer. Sousa's programming was especially astute. After every selection listed on the program, the band played an encore, usually a light, quick piece guaranteed to please. Yet he also performed the European classics from Bach to Richard Strauss, introducing Wagner's music to more Americans than anyone else. The same variety is evident in the music Sousa composed for band, which varies from programmatic fantasias to more than a hundred marches, including his most famous march, *The Stars and Stripes Forever* (1897; NAWM 168). Not limited to a single genre or medium, Sousa also wrote more than a dozen operettas and some seventy songs.

Marches

The staple of the band repertory was and still is the ***march***. Figure 30.10a shows the standard march form at midcentury: a brief introduction, usually of four measures; two ***strains*** or periods, each repeated; a trio in a contrasting key, most often in the subdominant, with an optional introduction and two repeated strains; and then a da capo repetition of the march up to the trio. The strains are typically sixteen measures long, and often the second half of a strain varies its first half. The first strain of the trio tends to be soft and lyrical, in contrast to the dynamism of the other strains.

Sousa marches

This form was well suited to parades, when the band may be blocks away by the time the first strain returns, but Sousa sensed that concert performance required a more dramatic effect, building to a climax rather than returning to the beginning. So in most of his marches, including *The Stars and Stripes Forever,* he dropped the da capo repetition and instead alternated the lyrical trio with a more aggressive break strain, producing the form in Figure 30.10b. In performances, if not always in the score, Sousa added countermelodies or increased the instrumentation or dynamic level with each repetition of the trio. As classical composers had been doing for almost a century, Sousa shifted the weight to the end to create a sense of forward progress. This dramatic flair, combined with catchy melodies, lively rhythms, and strong contrasts of instruments and textures, helped to make Sousa marches the most widely known ever throughout Europe and the Americas and to earn him the nickname "The March King" (after Johann Strauss, "The Waltz King").

POPULAR SONG While bands embraced a wide repertoire from marches to classics, the world of song was splintering. Schubert's Lieder and Stephen Foster's parlor songs had served similar purposes, intended primarily for home music-making and occasionally performed in concerts. But in the later nineteenth century, there was a widening gulf between *art songs* and *popular songs*. Art songs, such as those of Gabriel Fauré and Hugo Wolf, had precisely notated piano parts, tended to be through-composed rather than strophic, were meant to engage listeners on a high artistic plane, and required high professional standards of both pianist and singer. Composers of popular songs sought instead to entertain their audience, accommodate amateur performers, and sell as many copies of the sheet music as possible, so immediate appeal and stick-in-your-head catchiness were the most important attributes.

Subjects   Topics for popular songs included love, heartbreak, birth, death, racial and ethnic satire, new inventions like the bicycle and telephone, sentimental thoughts of mother and the old family home, and America's favorite pastime, baseball. Songs were pressed into service for every possible cause: abolition, the Civil War, temperance (the campaign against drunkenness), labor organizing, political campaigns, and evangelism, as in gospel songs such as Joseph P. Webster's *In the Sweet By-and-By* (1868).

Conventions   Popular art depends upon the interplay of convention and novelty, and both are evident in the best popular songs. The standard form remained verse and refrain, with a four- or eight-measure introduction for the piano; an eight-, sixteen-, or thirty-two-measure verse; and a refrain of similar size. Often the refrain was scored in parts for chorus (or four solo singers), so that *chorus* came to be used as a term for refrain. Both verse and refrain typically had internal repetitions, falling into forms such as AABA. In some songs the verse and refrain shared material, and in others the chorus was wholly new, occasionally even in a different meter.

The key to success was creating a catchy phrase, sometimes called the *hook,* that could grab the listener's attention and then be repeated and varied over the course of the song. The chorus of Charles K. Harris's *After the Ball* (1892), shown in Example 30.5, begins with a motive that is simple yet has enough unusual features to make it intriguing: it begins and ends away from the tonic note, avoids stepwise motion, twice rocks back and forth on a minor third, and has its high point early in the phrase on an unstressed beat and syllable. Linked with the waltz rhythm, all these features convey a lack of balance, suggesting the intoxication of dancing at a ball. The motive is varied many times in succession, then is replaced by a more stable, stepwise phrase at the close, producing an AA′A″B form. The lilting waltz suits the subject of the text, and the move from giddiness to steadiness drives home the lesson the words convey.

Tin Pan Alley   Harris's song was enormously popular, selling millions of copies and—

EXAMPLE 30.5 *Chorus from Charles K. Harris,* After the Ball

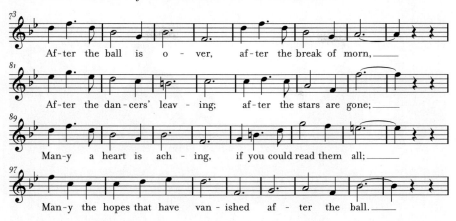

After the ball is o - ver, af - ter the break of morn,___

After the dan - cers' leav - ing; af - ter the stars are gone;___

Man - y a heart is ach - ing, if you could read them all;___

Man - y the hopes that have van - ished af - ter the ball.___

since he had published it himself—making him rich. It typifies the products of **Tin Pan Alley**, the jocular name for a district on West 28th Street in New York where, beginning in the 1880s, numerous publishers specializing in popular songs were located. Harris's strategy for promoting the song also became typical. He paid a singer to introduce the song in a show, and when it became a hit with the audiences, people went out in droves to buy a copy of the sheet music. The link between success on stage and in sales of printed music hearkens back to Baroque opera and the minstrel show tunes of Stephen Foster, and remained important in the twentieth century.

MUSIC OF AFRICAN AMERICANS The one immigrant group that came to the United States against their will was Africans. Enslaved and brought over in inhuman conditions, they came from many ethnic groups with different languages and customs. Mixed together on plantations or as domestic servants, they would have had a difficult time maintaining their original languages and cultures even if slaveholders had not actively worked to prevent this. But elements of their music were easier to preserve, because they had been widely shared among African societies and because white slaveholders did not consider singing a threat. Indeed, work songs were actively encouraged as a way to keep up the pace and the spirits, and many slaveholders required the enslaved people in their household or plantation to sing and dance for their entertainment.

Among the many traits of African American music that have been traced back to Africa are these:

Traits of African American music

- alternating short phrases between a leader and the group, called **call and response**;
- improvisation, usually based on a simple formula that allows wide-ranging variation;
- syncopation;
- repetition of short rhythmic or melodic patterns;

FIGURE 30.11 *The original Fisk Jubilee Singers, photographed in 1873 in London, during their European tour. Founded at Fisk University in Nashville, Tennessee, the group consisted of African American student musicians who performed spirituals and other songs in four-part harmony.*

- multiple layers of rhythm, with beats in some instruments (or hand clapping or foot stomping) and offbeats in others;
- bending pitches or sliding from one pitch to another;
- moans, shouts, and other vocalizations; and
- instruments with African roots such as the banjo, based on a West African stringed instrument.

We will see these and other traits in ragtime, blues, jazz, rhythm and blues, and other twentieth-century styles based on African American traditions.

Spirituals   The African American form of music with the greatest impact in the nineteenth century was the ***spiritual***, a religious song of southern slaves, passed down through oral tradition. The texts were usually based on images or stories from the Bible, but they often carried hidden meanings of enslaved people's yearning for freedom. The first to appear in print was *Go Down, Moses,* which uses the story of Israel's deliverance from Egypt as a symbol for the liberation of the slaves. The song was published in 1861, during the first year of the Civil War, after a missionary heard it sung by refugees from slavery.

The first publications of spirituals tried to document the songs as former slaves sang them, though the editors admitted that they could not notate the bent pitches and other aspects of performance. But soon dozens of spirituals were arranged as songs with piano accompaniments that anyone could play and in four-part harmony for choirs. The Fisk Jubilee Singers, depicted in Figure 30.11, popularized spirituals in the 1870s through polished performances in concert tours on both sides of the Atlantic. By the late 1800s, spirituals were simultaneously folk music for those who had learned them from oral tradition, popular songs for those who bought them in collections or as sheet music or heard them in popular venues, and a source of melodic material for classical composers like Dvořák (see pp. 741–43).

RECEPTION AND RECOGNITION

By the end of the nineteenth century, what seemed in retrospect like a mainstream of musical development in the late eighteenth century had broken into many smaller currents, like a great river forming a delta as it heads toward the sea. The split between classical and popular music had widened and was becoming irrevocable, but even within those two broad traditions there were many competing strands.

Most of the classical composers we have studied found a place in the permanent repertoire. National flavor helped many gain a niche, from Fauré and Dvořák at Europe's center to Tchaikovsky, Grieg, and others on the periphery. Some were admitted into the canon of classical masters on the strength of relatively few works, as were Franck, Smetana, and Elgar. In each case, performers, audiences, and critics tended to favor works that brought a distinctive new personality into the tradition, a trend that would become even stronger in the twentieth century.

Divisions between classical and popular streams existed everywhere in Europe and the Americas, not only in the United States. Yet the American case is especially interesting because the hierarchy of permanence is the opposite of Europe's. In the United States, the late-nineteenth-century composers in the classical tradition won respect and renown in their lifetimes, but then faded from view, and despite recent revivals their music is still relatively little known. The reasons for this are debated: is it simply a question of unfamiliarity, or lesser quality, or prejudice against American composers, or did Paine, Beach, and their contemporaries fail to create music with an identifiable personality because they were overly dependent on a tradition that was not native and thus inauthentic—or does that very question give too much credence to the expectation that all composers outside Germany should be nationalists? By contrast, some popular traditions produced works that have never ceased being played and enjoyed. These pieces—including Sousa's best-known marches, popular songs such as *The Battle Cry of Freedom* and *The Band Played On,* and dozens of African American spirituals—have every reason to be called "classics." Like the works of Handel, Haydn, Mozart, and Beethoven that became the first classics, these works entertained their first audiences but also had an enduring appeal that brought performers and listeners back repeatedly, and their growing familiarity made these pieces even more beloved. The twentieth century in turn saw other types of popular music develop their own repertoires of classics and their own legions of connoisseurs. More than in most other nations, the permanent repertoire of musical classics from the United States grew from indigenous popular traditions, rather than as an offshoot of the international classical mainstream.

Further Reading is available at digital.wwnorton.com/hwm10

PART SIX

THE TWENTIETH CENTURY AND AFTER

We know more about musical culture in the twentieth century than in any earlier period. Recalling the four types of evidence discussed in Chapter 1 for reconstructing the music of the past—physical remains, visual images, writings about music and musicians, and music itself—we have far more of all of these for music since 1900 than for all previous eras combined. The new technologies of sound recording, photography, film, television, and computers have preserved and made available every kind of music-making from almost every nation and social group, giving us a more complete picture than for earlier times, when music survived only in notation. On the other hand, the sheer amount of music from the past century can seem overwhelming, and our historical closeness can make it difficult to discern what is of greatest or most lasting importance.

The music from the twentieth century was also more diverse than in previous generations. Throughout each decade, musicians reexamined their basic assumptions about music and created new works that did astonishing things. New traditions emerged such as ragtime, jazz, musicals, film music, rock, hip hop, and other types of popular music. In the classical realm, some composers continued to write tonal music, while others devised new systems of organizing pitch, such as atonality, polytonality, neotonality, and twelve-tone methods. It was a time of competing styles, from impressionism and expressionism to neoclassicism, minimalism, and neo-Romanticism, and of exploring new sounds and approaches, including experimental music, spatial music, electronic music, indeterminacy, chance, and collage. These trends are still with us in the twenty-first century, and more come each year, making today's musical life the most varied the world has ever known.

PART OUTLINE

THE EARLY TWENTIETH CENTURY: VERNACULAR MUSIC

The early twentieth century was a time of rapid change in technology, society, and the arts, including music. The invention of devices for recording sound began to change the way music was preserved, distributed, and sold, making music in sound as permanent and widely available as music in notation. As a result, the vibrant traditions of ***vernacular music*** loom larger in the history of twentieth-century music than in any earlier era. African American musicians, soon joined by white collaborators and competitors, developed new currents in ***ragtime*** and ***jazz*** that won the world's attention and made popular music more culturally and historically significant than it had ever been. Composers in the classical tradition, forced to compete for space on concert programs with the classics of the past, sought to win an audience in the present and secure a place in the permanent repertoire of the future by offering a unique style and perspective that balanced traditional and novel elements. This chapter will describe the historical background for the last years of the nineteenth century and the first two decades of the twentieth, and then will focus on developments in vernacular music, especially the African American tradition. The next two chapters will examine the first two generations of modern composers in the classical tradition, born between 1860 and 1885.

MODERN TIMES, 1889–1918

The turn of a new century is a convenient and memorable marker for delineating a new historical period, but life rarely follows the calendar so closely. Historians sometimes speak of a "long nineteenth century" from the French Revolution in 1789, which ended the older order, to the start of World War I in 1914, which ended four decades of relative peace in Europe. In other respects, the new age of greater global interconnection and accelerating innovation in science and technology characteristic of the twentieth century already seemed to be under way by the time of the Paris Universal Exposition (World's Fair) of 1889, when people gathered from all over the world and the Eiffel Tower, the tallest structure humans had ever built and a triumph of modern engineering, was opened to the public. Figure 31.1 shows this impressive structure as it appeared in March 1889 at the opening of the Fair.

The period between the Paris Exposition and the end of World War I in 1918 was more self-consciously "modern" than any previous era, so much so that a century later we still think of art, music, and literature from this time as modern. The pace of technological and social change was more rapid than in any previous era, prompting both an optimistic sense of progress and a nostalgia for a simpler past.

One symbol of progress was the electrification of industry, businesses, and homes. Electric lighting increasingly replaced gas lighting, and electrical appliances were produced for the home market. Internal combustion engines fueled by petroleum gradually replaced coal-fueled engines in steamships and factories. By streamlining production and distribution, Henry Ford made his Model T the first widely affordable automobile in 1908, launching the modern world's love affair with the car. Wilbur and Orville Wright flew the first working airplane in 1903, and by the end of the next decade airplanes were used for both military and commercial purposes. New products, improved transportation, and new marketing techniques combined to expand the mass market for manufactured goods. Of crucial importance for music were new technologies for reproducing music, from player pianos to phonographs (see Innovations: Recorded Sound, pp. 758–59). Meanwhile, moving picture shows—the movies—offered a new form of theatrical entertainment with musical accompaniment.

New technologies

COURTESY OF EVERETT COLLECTION

FIGURE 31.1 *The Eiffel Tower and the Champ de Mars as seen at the Paris Exposition of 1889. At the time, it was the tallest structure built by human hands.*

Recorded Sound

The advent of recording technology had the most significant impact on musical culture of any innovation since the printing press. It completely revolutionized the way we experience and share music as listeners, performers, or composers.

When Thomas Edison made the first playable sound recording in his laboratory in Menlo Park, New Jersey, in 1877, using his tinfoil cylinder phonograph shown in Figure 31.2, he intended his new device as a dictation machine for offices. He had no idea that his invention would catapult some musicians to fame and fortune, deliver their product to huge audiences, and spawn a multibillion-dollar industry.

Edison's phonograph recorded sound by a mechanical process. The sound waves, collected by a horn, moved a diaphragm that transmitted its motions to a needle. The needle cut a groove in the cylinder as the latter rotated, turned by a hand crank. The undulations in the groove corresponded to the motions of the diaphragm. To play back the record, the process was reversed: as the crank rotated the cylinder, the shape of the groove made the needle move, which in turn moved the diaphragm, and its vibrations sent the recorded sounds moving through the air.

Edison soon replaced his fragile tinfoil cylinders with wax cylinders, which could be mass-produced by a molding process. Adding a motor to the machine made it possible to maintain a steady speed of rotation, necessary for recording music. Members of John Philip Sousa's band and other artists made recordings that were sold commercially, but quantities were limited because each cylinder had to be recorded separately.

In 1887, Emile Berliner invented a more practical system that recorded on a flat disc, which could be used as a mold to make any number of duplicates. Record players like the one in Figure 31.3 became available in the 1890s, and ten-inch discs with a capacity for four minutes of music on each side were sold for a dollar each, the equivalent of about twenty dollars today.

HULTON ARCHIVE/GETTY IMAGES

FIGURE 31.2 *Thomas Edison with his original phonograph, which recorded sounds through impressions on a tinfoil cylinder.*

The early discs featured famous artists, such as the great Italian tenor Enrico Caruso (1873–1921), who made his first recording in 1902 and whose many records encouraged the medium's acceptance as suitable for opera. Because he became one of the recording industry's earliest superstars, it has been said that "Caruso made the phonograph and it made him." His recordings also preserved his performances beyond the grave. The new technology allowed performers to achieve for the first time the kind of immortality previously available only to composers.

Mechanical recording was well suited for voices, but the limited range of frequencies it could reproduce made orchestral music sound tinny. For years, the only symphony available was Beethoven's Fifth, recorded in 1913 by the Berlin Philharmonic for

FIGURE 31.3 *The "Trademark Model" of the phonograph by His Master's Voice, available beginning in 1898. The firm's name and the dog's pose implied that the device reproduced sound so faithfully that a dog would recognize a recording of his owner's voice*

His Master's Voice. Because it was such a long piece, the company had to issue it on eight discs gathered in an "album," which became the standard format for longer works.

In the 1920s, new methods of recording and reproduction using electricity—including the electric microphone—allowed a great increase in frequency range, dynamic variation, and fidelity, making the medium still more attractive to musicians and music lovers. Falling prices and continuing improvement of the recording process stimulated a growing market for recordings, from popular songs and dance numbers to the classical repertoire. Record companies competed to record the most famous performers, and by the late 1940s most of the better-known orchestral works had been recorded more than ten times each.

Encouraged by competition, companies continued to develop new improvements. In 1948, Columbia Records introduced the long-playing record, or LP, which rotated at 33-1/3 revolutions per minute instead of 78, used smaller grooves, and thus allowed twenty-three minutes of music per side instead of four. Longer pieces could be played without interruption, and as shown in Figure 31.4, LPs took up much less space. Music lovers bought the LPs by the millions and got rid of their old 78s. High-fidelity and stereophonic records were introduced in the 1950s, which also saw the debut of an entirely new recording technology: magnetic tape. Philips introduced cassette tapes in 1963, and by the 1970s tape sales were rivaling those of records, especially among consumers who valued portability more than faithful sound reproduction. Then in 1983, Philips and Sony unveiled the Compact Disc, or CD, which stored recorded sound in digital code

etched onto a four-inch plastic disc and read by a laser. Even as listeners were replacing all their LPs with CDs, new technologies were being developed that made it possible to download music from the Internet onto a personal computer or portable device.

The development of recordings irrevocably altered the way people listen to music. No longer did they have to go to a concert hall or gather around a bandstand. They could now sit in their homes and order up a favorite singer or an entire orchestra at their convenience. The visual element of music-making suddenly disappeared; listeners heard performers without seeing them, and musicians played in recording studios for invisible audiences. Listening to recordings often replaced amateur music-making at home, with the paradoxical effect that people devoted less time and effort to engaging actively with music as participants. For many people, listening to music became no longer a communal activity but a largely solitary pursuit. People increasingly used recorded music as a background to other activities, rather than listening with focused concentration.

Along with performers and listeners, composers too were influenced by the new technologies, being able to avail themselves of musical styles and ideas outside of their ordinary experience. Music from Africa, India, Asia, and elsewhere became available via recording without the hardships or expense of travel, as did the entire history of Western music, from the singing of plainchant by monks in a faraway monastery to the most recent pop tune. Composers since the 1940s have used recorded sounds to make music, allowing them to incorporate an unprecedented variety of sounds.

FIGURE 31.4 *At the unveiling of the new long-playing record, a Columbia Records spokesman compares the foot-high stack of LPs in his hands with the ten-feet-tall pile of 78s needed to record the same amount of music.*

Economy and social conflicts

The growth of industry fostered an expanding economy and rapidly growing cities. The first steel-framed skyscraper was erected in Chicago in 1889, packing more indoor space for people and businesses into a smaller area of land than ever before, and in the coming decades the tall buildings transformed the look of cities around the world. People continued to migrate from rural areas to cities, although not without regret; Tin Pan Alley songs and Mahler symphonies alike expressed nostalgia for the countryside. Economic inequalities prompted workers to organize in labor unions to fight for better conditions, inspired social reformers such as Jane Addams to work with the poor, and aroused revolutionary movements in Russia and elsewhere. International trade continued to increase. European nations grew rich importing raw materials and food, and marketing manufactured goods to the world. The great powers—Britain, France, and the German, Austro-Hungarian, Russian, and Ottoman empires—competed for dominance, while the peoples of eastern Europe, from the Balkans to Finland, agitated for their own freedom. Increasing tensions and complex political issues culminated in World War I. The modern, efficient machinery of war killed millions of soldiers, ending the hope that technological improvements would lead inevitably to the betterment of humankind. The collapse of widespread faith in human progress left deep disillusionment in its wake.

United States

During these years, the United States emerged as a world power. It easily defeated Spain in the Spanish-American War of 1898, taking over Puerto Rico, Cuba, the Philippines, and other Spanish colonies. American industries and overseas trade expanded rapidly, growing to rival the industrial powerhouses of Britain and Germany. The United States' entrance into World War I in April 1917 on the side of Britain and France tipped the scales against Germany and Austria-Hungary, and President Woodrow Wilson played a leading role in negotiating the peace.

As in Europe, rapid economic development brought social conflict. The Progressive movement created reforms to reduce the dominance of large corporations. Immigrants continued to stream to the United States, now increasingly from southern and eastern Europe, and their presence in cities caused strains with earlier immigrant groups. Looking for new opportunities, African Americans from the South moved to the large northern cities but because of racist attitudes settled into segregated neighborhoods. Here a black urban culture began to develop, in which music was a major cultural force.

New views on the human mind

Psychologists raised new questions about what it meant to be human. Sigmund Freud developed psychoanalysis, theorizing that human behavior springs from unconscious desires that are repressed by cultural restraints and that dreams are windows into a person's internal conflicts. Ivan Pavlov showed that dogs accustomed to being fed after a bell was rung would salivate at the sound of the bell even if no food was present and that humans could likewise be conditioned to respond to stimuli in predictable ways. These approaches challenged the Romantic view of individuals as protagonists of their own dramas, seeming instead to portray humans as subject to internal and social forces of which they were only dimly aware. Such changing views of human nature played a strong role in literature and the other arts.

The arts

Sustained by Romantic notions of art as a window on the divine and of the artist as an enlightened visionary, artists increasingly regarded their work as an end in itself to be appreciated for its own sake. Success was measured not by wide popular appeal but by the esteem of intellectuals and fellow artists. Many artists searched for new and unusual content or techniques. For example, symbolist poets such as Paul Verlaine, Stéphane Mallarmé, Paul Valéry, and Stefan George used intense imagery and disrupted syntax to evoke an indefinite, dreamlike state and to suggest feelings and experiences rather than describing them directly. They focused on the senses and on the present moment, opening new possibilities of sensuality that had strong parallels in art and music.

In the late nineteenth century, French painters known as *impressionists*— named after Claude Monet's painting *Impression: Sunrise* (1872), shown in Figure 31.5—inaugurated the first in a series of modern artistic movements that utterly changed styles and attitudes toward art. Rather than depicting things realistically, the impressionists sought to convey atmosphere and sensuous impressions from nature, adopting a stance of detached observation rather than direct emotional engagement. The idea was to capture an instant in time, as one apprehends a scene, before reason can process it. In Monet's paintings, objects and people are suggested by a few brushstrokes, often of starkly contrasting colors, leaving it to the viewer's eyes and mind to blend the colors and fill in the missing details. The effect of light on an object is often as much the subject of a painting as is the object itself, as in Monet's series of paintings

From impressionism to cubism

MUSÉE MARMOTTAN, PARIS/ERICH LESSING/ART RESOURCE, NY

FIGURE 31.5 *Claude Monet,* Impression: Sunrise *(1872). Monet entered this work and eight others in an exhibition he helped to organize in 1874. A critic headlined his mocking review "Exhibition of the Impressionists," picking up on Monet's title and coining a term that would encompass an entire artistic movement. Instead of mixing his colors on a palette, Monet juxtaposed them on the canvas to capture a fleeting moment of the early light of day. Apart from the rowboats and the sun reflecting from the water in the foreground, the tall ships, smokestacks, and cranes blend into the misty blue-gray background against a reddish sky.*

of haystacks (1890–91) and of the Rouen Cathedral (1892–93) captured at different times of day. The distinction between foreground and background is blurred, flattening the perspective and focusing our attention on the overall impression. Although impressionist paintings are widely popular today, they were at first poorly received, derided as lacking in artistic skill and opposed to traditional aesthetics. Such reactions would also greet other modern styles of painting and music.

Each impressionist painter had a highly individual style, and later artists extended their ideas in unique ways. Paul Cézanne depicted natural scenes and figures as orderly arrangements of geometrical forms and planes of color, as in his painting of Mont Sainte-Victoire (1906) in Figure 31.6. Pablo Picasso and Georges Braque further abstracted this idea in *cubism*, a style in which three-dimensional objects are represented on a flat plane by breaking them down into geometrical shapes, such as cubes and cones, and juxtaposing or overlapping them in an active, colorful design. Figure 31.7 shows an example, one of a series Picasso painted in 1912 that used the violin as a subject.

Modernism in art   The revolution begun by impressionism stimulated new ways of making, seeing, and thinking about paintings, giving birth to movements such as expressionism (discussed in Chapter 33), surrealism, and abstract art. All of these movements can be seen as forms of **modernism** in art, paralleling the varied forms of modernism in music that we will encounter in the next two chapters. In most of these new movements, artists and their approving critics

FIGURE 31.6 *Paul Cézanne,* Mont Sainte-Victoire *(1906). Cézanne painted many versions of this scene visible from his house in Aix-en-Provence in southern France, rendering the massive mountain and the details of the city and countryside as juxtaposed blocks of color in geometrical arrangements.*

no longer placed as high a value on attractiveness, immediate comprehensibility, or pleasing the viewer as had painters from the Renaissance to the Romantics. Instead, they sought a deeper engagement, demanding that the viewer work to understand and interpret the image.

We will see all these trends reflected in music in this and the next several chapters. Music was directly affected by the expanding economy, new technologies, the devastation of World War I, the emergence of the United States on the world stage, the role of African American urban culture as a source for new musical styles, new thinking about human nature, and the new modernist artistic movements, with particularly close parallels to symbolism, impressionism, expressionism, and cubism.

VERNACULAR MUSICAL TRADITIONS

The impact of prosperity and technology on music, and the growing importance of the United States and especially African Americans, are apparent in the varied and vibrant musical traditions outside the classical concert hall and opera house. These traditions are sometimes referred to as ***vernacular music***, since they are intended to reach a broad musical public in a widely understood language, rather than appealing to an elite.

FIGURE 31.7 *Pablo Picasso*, Still Life, *1912–13. This cubist painting includes a violin on the right, broken into its various components and planes, and a clarinet on the left, stylized as multiple bars (gray, blue, brown, and black-and-white), most with fingerholes, and concentric circles and a cone to represent the instrument's bell.*

STILL LIFE, 1912–13 (OIL ON CANVAS), PICASSO, PABLO (1881–1973)/PRIVATE COLLECTION/BRIDGEMAN IMAGES

Vernacular traditions assume greater significance in recounting the history of twentieth-century music than in earlier centuries because the advent of recordings has preserved so much more vernacular music. In addition, recordings and other mass media disseminated forms of popular music that otherwise would have remained strictly local.

Impact of recordings

Moreover, much vernacular music of the twentieth century has achieved a permanence rivaling that of classical music. We have seen a few examples of popular music that have endured: dance tunes in John Playford's *The English Dancing Master* (1651), waltzes by Johann Strauss and Joseph Lanner, songs of Stephen Foster and Tin Pan Alley, Sousa marches, and African American spirituals. But in the twentieth century, the trickle becomes a flood, as some popular songs, dance numbers, Broadway shows, film scores, band pieces, piano rags, and jazz performances become classics in their own traditions, widely played and in many cases more familiar a century later than are the classical works of the same era. These traditions must be part of any history of music since 1900, for they are an integral part of musical culture, important in their own right and as influences on composers in the classical tradition. It was in the realm of vernacular music, with ragtime, jazz, and popular song and later film scores, rock, and hip hop, that the United States became the leading exporter of music to the world, matching in music its impact in industry

Lasting importance

TIMELINE

1889 Paris Universal Exposition

1889 First steel-framed skyscraper

1898 Spanish-American War

1899 Scott Joplin, *Maple Leaf Rag*

1899 Sigmund Freud, *The Interpretation of Dreams*

1900 Oil fields discovered in Texas, Persia, and Russia

1902 Enrico Caruso makes his first recording

1902 Will Marion Cook, *In Dahomey*

1903 Wilbur and Orville Wright fly first airplane

1904 George M. Cohan, *Little Johnny Jones*

1905 Franz Lehár, *The Merry Widow*

1906 Paul Cézanne, *Mont Sainte-Victoire*

1907 Georges Braque and Pablo Picasso paint first cubist pictures

1908 Henry Ford introduces the Model T automobile

1909 Gustav Holst, Suite No. 1 in E-flat for band

1913 Berlin Philharmonic records Beethoven's Fifth Symphony

1914–18 World War I

1915 D. W. Griffith's film *The Birth of a Nation* with music by Joseph Carl Breil

1917 United States enters World War I

1917 Original Dixieland Jazz Band recording of *Livery Stable Blues*, first jazz record

and world affairs. And as we will see in Chapters 38 and 39, by the late 1900s and early 2000s performers and composers increasingly bridged the divide between classical and vernacular traditions, interweaving elements from each.

POPULAR SONG AND STAGE MUSIC The most ubiquitous music of the early twentieth century was popular song, performed in cabarets, cafés, music halls, and theaters and sold as sheet music and recordings for the home market. Each linguistic region had its own repertoire and styles of popular song, although growing trade and travel enabled some songs to reach an international market. British songs had found audiences in the United States since the eighteenth century, and in the twentieth century American songs became increasingly popular in Britain. Tin Pan Alley was in its heyday, and some hits of the time became classics that are still familiar, such as *Take Me Out to the Ball Game* (1908) by Jack Norworth and Albert Von Tilzer and *Over There* (1917) by George M. Cohan (1878–1942).

Many of the best-known and best-selling popular songs came from stage shows. Revues spread from Paris to London, New York, and elsewhere, increasingly centered around song and dance numbers, often with flashy costumes and sets. Franz Lehár (1870–1948) continued the Viennese operetta tradition with *The Merry Widow* (1905) and other works, while in the United States Victor Herbert (1859–1924) achieved successes with his operettas *Babes in Toyland* (1903) and *Naughty Marietta* (1910).

A significant new genre, the *musical comedy* or **musical**, featured songs and dance numbers in styles drawn from popular music in the context of a spoken play with a comic or romantic plot. English theater manager George Edwardes established the genre by combining elements of variety shows, comic operas, and plays in a series of productions at the Gaiety Theatre in London in the 1890s. British musicals were soon staged in the United States, and the New York theater district on Broadway became the main center for musicals, along with London's West End. George M. Cohan inaugurated a distinctive style of American musical with his *Little Johnny Jones* (1904), which brought together American subject matter and the vernacular sounds of vaudeville and Tin Pan Alley with the romantic plots and European styles of comic opera and operetta. That show included two of the most famous and enduring popular songs of the era, *Give My Regards to Broadway* and *The Yankee Doodle Boy* (whose chorus begins "I'm a Yankee Doodle Dandy"). From these roots would grow the musicals of Jerome Kern, Irving Berlin, George Gershwin, Rodgers and Hammerstein, and Andrew Lloyd Webber, among many others.

MUSIC FOR SILENT FILMS Moving picture shows began to compete with live theater in the 1890s and became enormously popular in the twentieth century. Films were silent until the late 1920s but were always accompanied by music, just as dance and other spectacles had been. The first such public display was Emile Reynaud's *Pantomimes lumineuses* (Luminous Mime Shows, 1892), presented in Paris, with music by Gaston Paulin. Music covered up the noise of the projector, provided continuity to the succession of scenes and shots, evoked appropriate moods, and marked dramatic events. Often the music was performed by a pianist or organist, who might improvise or play excerpts from memory, drawing on both classical and popular pieces. In larger theaters, small to medium-sized orchestras played music arranged or composed for the film by the resident music director. By the 1920s, tens of thousands of musicians were employed in theaters across Europe and North America, providing music for a variety of entertainments, including silent films.

Opera and operetta were important influences on film music. These genres had already established conventions for enhancing drama through musical accompaniment, and music for films borrowed many of them, including loud, rapid passages for moments of excitement, tremolos to suggest tension or high drama, and soft, romantic themes for love scenes. Strongly contrasting excerpts or styles, from Wagner to popular song, were used side by side to evoke changes of scene or dramatic situation and to delineate characters.

Music, drama, and emotion

Because the music affected the audience's reactions to the movie and thus its profitability, filmmakers made efforts to standardize the music for their films. Beginning in 1909, studios issued cue sheets that showed the sequence of scenes and events in a movie and suggested appropriate music. Music publishers saw a market niche and printed anthologies of pieces and excerpts grouped by mood or situation, of which Giuseppe Becce's *Kinothek* (Berlin, 1919) was among the most widely used. Saint-Saëns's score for *L'assassinat du duc de Guise* (The Assassination of the Duke of Guise, 1908) inaugurated the era of the film score, composed to accompany a particular film. This idea was popularized especially by the orchestral score Joseph Carl Breil (1870–1926) created for D. W. Griffith's *The Birth of a Nation* (1915), in which he interwove excerpts arranged from Wagner, Tchaikovsky, popular songs, and other sources with his own music. Later composers increasingly wrote original scores that evoked the styles and conventions of Romantic or popular composers.

Cue sheets and film scores

BAND MUSIC The tradition of military and amateur wind bands remained strong across Europe and North America. In the United States and Canada, bands increasingly found a home in colleges and schools as well, playing at sporting events and in concerts. Sousa's band continued to tour and became a pioneer in making phonograph recordings. Among the many other professional bands was Helen May Butler's Ladies Brass Band, one of several all-female ensembles formed in response to the exclusion of women from most bands.

The twentieth century saw a growing effort among bandleaders to establish a repertoire of serious works for band worthy of comparison to the orchestral repertoire. Because of the band's long association with the military and with amateur performance, there were very few original pieces for band by the major Classic and Romantic composers, who were represented on band concerts mostly by transcriptions. In the first decades of the century, a new

Concert repertoire

seriousness of purpose emerged in pieces that soon formed the core of a developing classical repertoire for band, notably Suites No. 1 in E-flat (NAWM 175, 1909; discussed in Chapter 32) and 2 in F (1911) by English composer Gustav Holst (1874–1934); *Dionysiaques* (1914–25) by French composer Florent Schmitt (1870–1958); *Irish Tune from County Derry* (1917) and *Lincolnshire Posy* (1937) by Australian composer Percy Grainger (1882–1961); and *English Folk Song Suite* (1923) and *Toccata marziale* (1924) by Ralph Vaughan Williams (1872–1958). Holst, Grainger, and Vaughan Williams drew on folk songs for themes, distributed the melodic content more evenly between winds and brass, used modal harmonies within a tonal context, and developed a symphonic style of instrumentation.

AFRICAN AMERICAN TRADITIONS

African American bands

Brass bands were one of the main training grounds for African American musicians, along with black churches and dance orchestras. During the late nineteenth and early twentieth centuries, black bands occupied an important place in both black and white social life in many big cities, including New Orleans, Baltimore, Memphis, Newark, Richmond, Philadelphia, New York, Detroit, and Chicago. Among the bandleaders and composers who attracted national and international attention were James Reese Europe, Tim Brymn, William H. Tyers, and Ford Dabney. Their bands performed from notation and did relatively little improvising, but they played with a swinging and syncopated style that distinguished them from white bands. Europe's band created a sensation in Paris during and after World War I, and the French Garde Républicaine tried in vain to imitate its sound.

RAGTIME Among the dances played by both brass and concert bands were pieces in ***ragtime***, a style popular from the 1890s through the 1910s that featured syncopated (or "ragged") rhythm against a regular, marchlike bass. This syncopation apparently derived from the clapping *Juba* of African Americans, a survival of African drumming and hand clapping. The emphasis on offbeats in one rhythmic layer against steady beats in another reflects the complex cross-rhythms common in African music.

Cakewalks, rags, and ragtime songs

Ragtime is today known mostly as a style of piano music, but in the late nineteenth and early twentieth centuries the term also encompassed ensemble music and songs. Ragtime was originally a manner of improvising or performing, "ragging" pieces notated in even rhythms by introducing syncopations. One vehicle was the cakewalk, a couples dance derived from slave dances and marked by strutting and acrobatic movements. Music for cakewalks was printed without syncopations until 1897, when syncopated figures characteristic of ragtime began to appear. Beginning that year, instrumental works called ***rags*** were published, especially for piano, and cakewalks and rags were soon among the best-selling forms of instrumental music. Classically trained African American violinist and composer Will Marion Cook (1869–1944) introduced the new rhythms into the Broadway tradition with *Clorindy, or The Origin of the Cakewalk* (1898), and his *In Dahomey,* produced in New York in 1902 and London in 1903, brought the cakewalk and ragtime style to Europe. Many popular songs were also written with ragtime rhythms. Both black and white composers, songwriters, and performers embraced the style; indeed, the Sousa band made some of the first ragtime recordings.

The leading ragtime composer was Scott Joplin (1867–1917), shown in Figure 31.8. Son of a former slave, he studied music in his home town of Texarkana, Texas, and worked in Sedalia and St. Louis, Missouri, before moving to New York in 1907. His most ambitious work was the opera *Treemoni-sha,* published in 1911 though not staged until 1972. But he was best known for his piano rags, which he regarded as artistic works on the level of the European classics for piano. Indeed, Joplin published a ragtime primer in the form of études, the *School of Ragtime* (1908), for the express purpose of legitimizing his craft as composition. His first best-selling rag, and still his best known, is *Maple Leaf Rag* (1899; NAWM 169a). Like most rags, it is in $\frac{2}{4}$ meter and follows the form of a march, with a series of sixteen-measure strains, each repeated. The second strain, excerpted in Example 31.1, shows several rhythmic features typical of ragtime. The left hand keeps up a steady pulse in eighth notes, alternating between bass notes and chords, while the right-hand figures syncopate both within and across the beat. The notes in octaves, which receive extra stress, occur every three sixteenth notes, momentarily creating the impression of $\frac{3}{16}$ meter in the right hand against $\frac{2}{4}$ in the left. Essentially the same rhythmic idea appears in each two-measure unit. Such repetition of a short rhythmic pattern, like syncopation and multiple rhythmic layers, is a characteristic of African American music that can be traced back to Africa. So while the form, left-hand pattern, harmony, and chromatic motion all ultimately derive from European sources, the rhythmic elements have African roots, and the resulting mixture is quintessentially African American.

FIGURE 31.8 *Scott Joplin in a photograph printed on the cover of his rag* The Cascades *(1904).*

EARLY JAZZ The 1910s also saw the early development of another type of music from African American roots: ***jazz***. Jazz evolved into a diverse tradition encompassing many styles, genres, and social roles but seems to have begun as a mixture of ragtime and dance music with elements of the blues (described in Chapter 34).

EXAMPLE 31.1 *Second strain from Scott Joplin's* Maple Leaf Rag

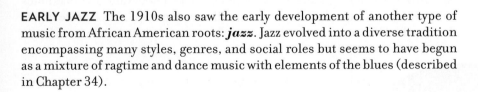

New Orleans

New Orleans has long been considered the "cradle of jazz," although recent research has uncovered early jazz in other regions as well. The cultural and social environment of New Orleans nurtured the development of early jazz. The French and Spanish background of the city gave it a flavor different from other cities in the United States. Before Emancipation, New Orleans was the only place in the South where slaves were allowed to gather in public. As a result, music in New Orleans retained some African traditions that were lost elsewhere. Moreover, the city had close connections to the Caribbean, and rhythms from Haitian, Cuban, and Creole music also influenced early jazz. The dance bands of New Orleans interwove these strands with European styles, gradually producing a new kind of music. Typically, these bands were small ensembles with two or three melody instruments, such as trumpet, clarinet, and trombone; a bass instrument such as a tuba; and snare and bass drums.

The new style had no name at first, or was simply known as the New Orleans style of ragtime. But when bands from New Orleans began playing in Chicago, New York, and elsewhere, they used the term "jazz." Bands who popularized the term included a black group that toured in 1913–18 as the New Orleans Jazz Band, and a white band that in 1917 performed in New York and made recordings there as the Original Dixieland Jazz Band. Their recording for Victor of *Livery Stable Blues*, shown in Figure 31.9, was the first jazz record issued; it was a hit, introducing jazz to a wide audience and inspiring many other bands to form and to make recordings.

FIGURE 31.9 *Label for the first jazz recording released to the public,* Livery Stable Blues *by the* Original Dixieland Jazz Band, *issued by the Victor Talking Machine Co. in May 1917 with* Dixie Jass Band One-Step *on the other side. "Jass" was an early alternate spelling for the new style, but "jazz" became the standard spelling within the next year.*

Jazz differed from ragtime particularly in the way it was performed. Instead of playing the music "straight," observing the rhythms and textures of a fully notated piece, players extemporized arrangements that distinguished one performer or performance from another. Listening to early jazz pianist and composer and New Orleans native Jelly Roll Morton (1890–1941) play Joplin's *Maple Leaf Rag* in a recording from 1938 (NAWM 169b), we recognize that this is unmistakably jazz and not ragtime because of the anticipations of beats; the swinging, uneven rendering of successions of equal note values so that notes on the beat are longer than those on the offbeats; the many added grace notes; the enriched harmony; and the weaving of ragtime's brief motivic units into a more continuous line.

Despite (and at times because of) the wide appeal of ragtime and jazz, they were regarded with suspicion and condescension by many practitioners of classical music. In the United States, the reception of ragtime and jazz was entangled with the racial politics of the period. During this time, the freedoms African Americans had won after the Civil War, like the right to vote, were being taken away all across the South through new state constitutions and Jim Crow laws. Racial discrimination in all parts of the country restricted economic opportunity and forced African Americans into segregated neighborhoods and schools. The long tradition of blackface minstrelsy, and of black musicians performing for white audiences (see Chapters 27 and 30), meant that ragtime and jazz could be welcomed as popular entertainment, but few whites would have agreed with Joplin that his rags were on

HIS MASTER'S VOICE

Victor

For Dancing

Livery Stable Blues—Fox Trot
Original Dixieland 'Jass' Band
18255–B

THE LIBRARY
OF CONGRESS

a par with the waltzes and mazurkas of Chopin. Yet there were also classical composers who admired the new styles and incorporated elements of ragtime or jazz in their own music, including Debussy, Ravel, Satie, Stravinsky, Ives, and Milhaud (see Chapters 32, 33, and 35). For many in Europe, ragtime and jazz represented the raw energy and newness of the United States. As we will see in later chapters, after World War I jazz became an emblem of modernity on both sides of the Atlantic, and by midcentury it was beginning to be accepted as an art music tradition in its own right.

CLASSICS OF VERNACULAR MUSIC

Vernacular music of the early twentieth century was created for immediate consumption as entertainment, and most of it is long forgotten. Yet many of the pieces discussed here became classics in their own traditions, in a process that parallels the development of the classical repertoire in chamber music, orchestral music, and opera during the nineteenth century (see Chapters 26 and 28). Few operettas and virtually no musicals of the time were performed for more than a few seasons, and modern productions are rare. Nonetheless, overtures, waltzes, and songs from operettas and musicals, such as Lehár's *The Merry Widow Waltz* and Cohan's *Give My Regards to Broadway*, have continued to be performed, and so have some of the era's popular songs. Music for silent films was always an art for the moment, not for the ages, but from the 1960s on, the tradition of improvised accompaniment on organ or piano was revived along with silent movies themselves, and in recent decades a few of the full scores have been performed again with their films. The band works of Holst, Vaughan Williams, and Grainger have remained classics of the concert band repertoire. Ragtime fell out of fashion in the 1920s, was revived after World War II, and regained wide popularity in the 1970s after the rags of Scott Joplin and others were brought back to life in print and recordings. Jazz became increasingly popular after World War I and grew into a diverse current widely recognized as one of the twentieth century's most important contributions to musical culture. All of these musical traditions now have a permanent place in musical life and receive increasing attention from historians, as reflected in this book, whose first four editions ignored them completely.

Further Reading is available at digital.wwnorton.com/hwm10

THE EARLY TWENTIETH CENTURY: THE CLASSICAL TRADITION

The rise of a permanent classical repertoire in the nineteenth century created an increasingly difficult challenge for composers at the end of that century and the beginning of the twentieth. Concert programs, opera stages, and other venues for their music were dominated by older works regarded as classics worthy of repeated performance and rehearings, leaving less room for new music than ever before. **Modernist** composers in the classical tradition all sought to solve the same conundrum—how to secure a place in a crowded repertoire—by writing works that offered something new and that musicians, audiences, and critics would deem worthy of performance alongside the classics of the past. To succeed, their music had to meet the criteria established by those classics: to be works of high quality that participated in the tradition of serious art music; that had lasting value, rewarding both performers and listeners through many rehearings and close study; and that proclaimed a distinctive musical personality. This is the central paradox of musical modernism: that it combines a deep respect for the classics with a search for the new, with the ultimate goal of creating fresh works that will themselves become classics.

Faced with common problems, modernist composers created highly individual solutions, differing in what they valued most in the tradition, what they extended, what they discarded, and what innovations they introduced. As a result, music in the classical tradition became increasingly diverse in style and approach, a process that accelerated throughout the twentieth century. This chapter will examine the first generation of modernists, born between 1860 and the mid-1870s. Most continued to use tonality, but many wrote **post-tonal** music. A few composers of this generation were not modernist but **avant-garde**, seeking to overthrow artistic traditions inherited from the past and start fresh. The next chapter will focus on six younger modernists, born between the mid-1870s and mid-1880s, who were among the most famous and influential composers of the twentieth century.

MODERN MUSIC IN THE CLASSICAL TRADITION

By the turn of the twentieth century, an established repertoire of musical classics dominated almost every field of concert music, from piano, song, and
chamber music recitals to operas and orchestral concerts. The change from
a century before was enormous. In the eighteenth century, performers and
listeners demanded new music all the time, and "ancient music" included
anything written more than twenty years earlier. But musicians and audiences
in the early 1900s expected that most concert music they performed or heard
would be at least a generation old, and they judged new music by the standards
of the classics already enshrined in the repertoire. In essence, concert halls
and opera houses had become museums for displaying the musical artworks of
the past two hundred years. The repertoire varied according to the performing
medium and from region to region, but the core was largely the same throughout most of Europe and the Americas, including operas and operatic excerpts
from Mozart through Wagner, Verdi, and Bizet; orchestral and chamber music
from Haydn through the late Romantics; and keyboard music by J. S. Bach,
Haydn, Mozart, Beethoven, and prominent nineteenth-century composers.

The established repertoire

    Living composers increasingly found themselves in competition with the
music of the past. This became the great theme of **modernism** in the classical tradition, especially in the first half of the century: in competing with past
composers for the attention of performers and listeners who loved the classical masterworks, living composers sought to secure a place for themselves
by offering something new and distinctive while continuing the tradition.
There were many possible solutions: extending aspects of past practice to new
extremes, reinterpreting familiar elements in new ways, combining traits
drawn from different traditions or from different past eras, or changing the
balance among musical parameters, to name some of the most common. Each
of these strategies gave listeners something familiar to grasp while offering
musical experiences that were new or more intense.

Modernism

    Writers on music have used the word *modernism* with more than one
meaning. Some reserve it for composers who break radically from the musical language of the past, like those in the next chapter. In this book it will be
used more broadly, to encompass the entire range of composers from the late
nineteenth century through the twentieth century whose music is marked by
a search for a place beside the classics, intertwining innovation with emulation of the past. Their music was and remains modernist, because it has
always been—and perhaps always will be—measured against the older styles
enshrined in the classical repertoire before them, and is still heard as "modern" in relation to the classics of the eighteenth and nineteenth centuries.

    Composers' choices of what to preserve and what to change varied, reflect-
ing differences in what they valued most in the tradition. One result was a
proliferation of contrasting trends, colloquially known as "-isms." Some of
these -isms continued from the nineteenth century, such as Romanticism and
exoticism. But many were new in the twentieth century, including impressionism, expressionism, primitivism, neoclassicism, and serialism—plus, in
the second half of the century, minimalism, postmodernism, polystylism, and
neo-Romanticism. All of these can be seen as aspects of modernism, because
each offers a different combination of traditional elements and novel ones.

TIMELINE

The search for an original, individual style made the use of conventional gestures, including standard cadences and other routines of tonal harmony, problematic. Adhering to traditional harmony could make one's music sound too much like that of earlier generations and therefore unoriginal, while departing too far from common practice risked making the music incomprehensible and thus losing the audience. How to adapt the shared musical language of tonality to achieve a unique style—or how to invent a new, personal language—became a problem facing every composer. Some composers abandoned tonality, while others attenuated it or extended it in new directions, as we will see in this chapter and the next.

That it was still possible to compose tonal music in the twentieth century is clear from the careers of Richard Strauss, Maurice Ravel, Gustav Holst, Ralph Vaughan Williams, Serge Rachmaninoff, and Jean Sibelius, discussed in this chapter, as well as younger composers active through the 1930s and beyond, who found new flavors and possibilities within tonality but never renounced it. Even today, every music student learns the rules of tonal music, and it remains the common language against which others are judged. Yet other composers, including Claude Debussy, Manuel de Falla, Alexander Scriabin, and Leoš Janáček, moved beyond tonal practice in the early 1900s, as each developed a personal musical language that followed its own rules. Even when a pitch center can be identified, it no longer makes sense to describe the music as tonal, because the music diverges too far from the common-practice harmony of the eighteenth and nineteenth centuries. The most general term for such music is ***post-tonal***, which embraces all the new ways composers found to organize pitch, from atonality to neotonality (see Chapter 33). The new possibilities of post-tonal idioms were part of the marvelous diversity of twentieth-century music in the classical tradition, but so were the individual approaches to tonality.

Another issue was nationalism, still a potent force in the arts, in culture, and in politics, where it was responsible for much of the agitation that led to World War I. As part of the heritage from Romanticism, composers were expected to write music that was true to their national identity and drew on regional traditions yet spoke to an international audience. For many composers, their own national traditions had elements they could draw upon that helped to make their music individual, addressing simultaneously the desires for originality and authentic national identity that had been growing since the nineteenth century. Each composer synthesized a personal style from the diverse mix of national and foreign influences and of old and new music that surrounded them.

The result was music of tremendous diversity. The most successful modern composers offered something unique, a style and a viewpoint that were not previously represented in the repertoire. The wide range of styles and approaches produced many currents and unique figures, precluding a single stylistic mainstream of twentieth-century classical music. The following account of some of the best-known composers active early in the century, together with a closer look at six younger modernist composers in Chapter 33, can only suggest the rich variety of the era.

Because the influence of national and regional traditions is so strong, we can highlight the individuality of composers in this generation by comparing composers from the same nation or region and exploring the choices they made to distinguish their music from that of their contemporaries as well as from the classics of the past. We will begin by comparing the two leading composers in the Austro-German tradition at the turn of the twentieth century, Gustav Mahler and Richard Strauss; will continue with Debussy and Ravel from France; and then will briefly survey other national traditions in Europe.

GERMAN MODERNISM: MAHLER AND STRAUSS

German-speaking composers faced a particular challenge because their national tradition was already so central to the repertoire. Indeed, the characteristics of modernism are already apparent a generation earlier in the music of Brahms (see Chapter 29), the first major composer to fully embrace the challenge of writing music for audiences whose tastes were formed by their familiarity with the permanent classical repertoire. The two most successful German composers of the next generation, Gustav Mahler and Richard Strauss, both found ways to intensify elements from their heritage and create music at once familiar and radically new.

GUSTAV MAHLER Gustav Mahler (1860–1911) was the leading Austro-German composer of symphonies after Brahms and Bruckner and one of the great masters of the song for voice and orchestra. Born to Jewish parents in Bohemia, Mahler went to Vienna in his teens to study piano and composition at the Conservatory and later attended classes at the University of Vienna. There he formed friendships with fellow student Hugo Wolf and with Bruckner, who was teaching at the university. He became an avid Wagnerian, although he also respected and was influenced by Brahms. Beginning at the age of twenty, his primary career was as a professional opera and orchestral conductor (see In Performance: Mahler as Conductor).

Composing mainly in the summers between busy seasons of conducting, Mahler completed nine symphonies, leaving a tenth unfinished, and five multimovement works for voice with orchestra (for which he also prepared versions with piano). He revised most of his works repeatedly, including the first seven symphonies, retouching the orchestration but not changing the substance of the music. As a composer, Mahler inherited the Romantic traditions of Berlioz, Robert Schumann, Liszt, Wagner, and especially the Viennese branch of Haydn, Mozart, Beethoven, Schubert, Brahms, and Bruckner, and he was a prime influence on Schoenberg, Berg, Webern, and other modern Viennese composers.

Songs in the symphonies

Mahler the symphonist cannot be separated from Mahler the song composer. Themes from his song cycle *Lieder eines fahrenden Gesellen* (Songs of a Wayfarer, 1884–85, revised 1891–96) appear in the first and third movements of the First Symphony (1884–88, revised 1893–96, 1906, and 1910). Following the example of Beethoven's Ninth Symphony, Mahler used voices in four of his symphonies, most extensively in the Second (1888–94, revised

IN PERFORMANCE

Mahler as Conductor

Although we know Mahler today as a composer, he made his living as a conductor. After conducting at numerous opera houses throughout central Europe, including Prague, Leipzig, Budapest, and Hamburg, he was appointed director of the Vienna Opera in 1897, converting to Catholicism in order to be eligible for the post. In 1898–1901, he was also conductor of the Vienna Philharmonic. In these positions, he gained international renown. Beginning in 1907 he spent most of each year in New York, serving as a conductor of German opera at the Metropolitan Opera from 1907 to 1910, and from 1909 to 1911 as director of the New York Philharmonic, which was reorganized as a full-time professional ensemble especially for him.

Mahler conducted a wide range of repertoire, but especially focused on the operas of Mozart and Wagner and on nineteenth-century German orchestral music from Beethoven to Richard Strauss. It had become standard practice to omit scenes and sections from many operas, but Mahler restored these cuts, believing that it was the performer's duty to respect the integrity of the artwork and its composer. But he was not a purist: Mahler sometimes rescored music he performed, for example adding instruments to Beethoven's symphonies to achieve more striking climaxes.

As a conductor, Mahler was renowned for his dynamism, precision, expressivity, and tyrannical perfectionism—traits that are depicted in Figure 32.1, drawn by Austrian illustrator and caricaturist Han Schliessmann and published in March 1901 in a satirical Munich paper, the *Fliegende Blätter*. The face, eyeglasses, haircut, stature, and motions are all those of Mahler, whose dynamic gestures and expressive style made him a favorite with the public and have influenced many later conductors.

In later years, Mahler streamlined his approach, as recalled by his disciple, the great conductor Bruno Walter, in his biography of Mahler:

> Gradually his stance and gestures became quieter; his conducting technique became so intellectualized that he achieved musicianly freedom combined with unfailing precision quite effortlessly by a simple-looking beat,

1906) and Eighth (1906). The Second, Third (1895–96, revised 1906), and Fourth (1899–1900, revised 1906 and 1910) incorporate melodies from his set of twelve songs on folk poems from the early-nineteenth-century collection *Des Knaben Wunderhorn* (The Boy's Magic Horn, 1892–1901) and introduce texts of some of the songs in the vocal movements.

Symphony as a world   Mahler extended Beethoven's concept of the symphony as a bold personal statement. He once observed that to write a symphony was to "construct a world," and his symphonies often convey a sense of life experience, as if telling a story or depicting a scene. To create the impression of events occurring in a variegated world, he used musical styles as *topics*, just as Mozart had done (see Chapter 23). For example, in the slow introduction to Mahler's First Symphony, the strings softly sustain the note A in seven octaves, producing an effect of vast space, filled in at times by ideas in other instruments—a melody in the winds, clarinets with hunting horn calls, a trumpet fanfare, a cuckoo call, a Romantic horn theme in parallel thirds—like the sounds of humans and nature heard across a great landscape. In this and other works, he often drew on the styles and rhythms of Austrian folk songs and dances, using them at times to suggest his urban audience's nostalgia for rural scenes and simpler times.

PRIVATE COLLECTION/© COSTA/LEEMAGE/BRIDGEMAN IMAGES

FIGURE 32.1 *Caricature of Gustav Mahler as conductor. The German captions (not shown) read (top) "A hypermodern conductor" and (bottom) "Kapellmeister Kappelmann conducts his Diabolical Symphony."*

while keeping almost still. His enormous influence on singers and instrumentalists was conveyed by a look or the sparest of gestures, where before he had exerted himself with impassioned movements. Towards the end his conducting represented the image of an almost eerie calm.

With his performers Mahler was dictatorial, demanding that they subordinate their vision of the music to his own. At the opera, he insisted on hiring singers who could also act, and on stage direction that highlighted the drama of the work. In one orchestral rehearsal, unsatisfied with the players' performance of the opening of Beethoven's Fifth Symphony, he had them repeat it so many times that some became angry and refused to continue. His response: "Gentlemen, save your fury for the performance; then at least we shall have the opening played as it should be." Such exacting standards won his players' respect, delighted his audiences, and became a model for many twentieth-century conductors, including his successor at the Metropolitan Opera, Arturo Toscanini.

Another source of variety is Mahler's instrumentation. His works typically require a large number of performers. The Second Symphony calls for about sixty strings, seventeen woodwinds, twenty-three brasses, six timpani and other percussion, four harps, organ, soprano and alto soloists, and a large chorus; the Eighth demands an even larger array of players and singers, earning its nickname "Symphony of a Thousand." But the size of the orchestra tells only part of the story. Mahler showed great imagination in combining instruments, achieving effects ranging from the most delicate to the gigantic. Often only a few instruments are playing while he creates many different chamber-orchestra groupings from his vast palette of sounds. Mahler was one of the first composers to envision music as an art not just of notes but of sound itself, an approach that became more common over the course of the twentieth century.

Instrumentation and sound

In accord with Mahler's interest in presenting a world, his symphonies often imply a program. For the first four symphonies, he wrote detailed programs in the manner of Berlioz and Liszt but later suppressed them. No such clues exist for the Fifth, Sixth, and Seventh Symphonies (composed between 1901 and 1905), yet the presence of pictorial details and material borrowed from his own songs, combined with the overall plan of each

Programmatic content

work, suggested that the composer had extramusical ideas in mind like those ascribed to Beethoven's Third and Fifth Symphonies. Thus Mahler's Fifth moves from a funereal opening march to triumph in the scherzo and a joyous finale. The Sixth is his "tragic" symphony, culminating in a colossal finale in which heroic struggle seems to end in defeat and death. The Ninth, Mahler's last completed symphony (1909), conjures up a mood of resignation mixed with bitter satire, a strange and sad farewell to life.

Fourth Symphony   The Fourth Symphony, one of Mahler's most popular, illustrates several of his compositional techniques. Each movement strongly differs from the others, exaggerating the contrasts in a traditional four-movement symphony, as if to suggest the world's variety. The work begins in one key (G major) and ends in another (E major), implying that life's adventures do not always bring us back home.

The first movement recalls the late-eighteenth-century symphony, through references to Haydn and Mozart's styles and by using sonata-form conventions, and contrasts it with Romantic styles. The exposition has clearly articulated themes, shown in Example 32.1: a principal theme in the tonic G major, a lyrical second theme in the dominant, and a playful closing theme. In the first theme, Mahler follows Mozart in using contrasting rhythmic and melodic figures (compare Example 23.7), but outdoes him in the number and variety of

EXAMPLE 32.1 *Themes from Gustav Mahler's Symphony No. 4, first movement*

a. First theme

b. Second theme

c. Closing theme

motives. There are surprises and deceptions that recall Classic-era wit: unexpected sforzandos, dynamic changes, and harmonic twists; portions of the theme used to accompany or interrupt other portions; and figures expanded to the point of pomposity (like the dotted figure in measure 6 as extended in measures 8–9), played upside down (that same figure in measure 12, in contrary motion with itself in the cellos), or varied in other surprising ways.

By contrast to these Classic-era elements, the second theme resembles a Romantic song and is introduced in the cellos and later joined by the horn, two quintessentially Romantic instruments. The development is fantasy-like and tonally daring, a Romantic outburst in a Classic frame, as Mahler shows how the two idioms can be blended in a single movement. When motives from the themes are reassigned to different instruments and recombined in new ways, they sound ironic and self-parodying, suggesting a feverish dream in which remembered images pop up from the subconscious in strange and distorted guises. The effect is as if the rational order of the eighteenth-century Enlightenment were displaced by the irrational dreams analyzed by Sigmund Freud. The recapitulation restores lucidity and logic, but there is no going back to the innocence of the opening; the movement achieves balance by embracing all the possibilities it includes rather than trying to resolve all the potential conflicts, in a musical metaphor for the compromises required of us by the complexities and contradictions of modern life. This movement's interweaving of Romantic fantasy and modern style with references to a classical past is typical of the way modernist music combines elements of the past and present into something entirely new and individual, and it has a close counterpart in the paintings of Mahler's fellow Viennese, Gustav Klimt, whose painting entitled *Music* appears in Figure 32.2.

FIGURE 32.2 Music *(1895), by Gustav Klimt (1862–1918), a leader of the Secessionist group of artists in Vienna, who challenged the narrow realism supported by the art establishment. This painting, for the music room of a wealthy industrialist, combines allusions to the classical past—notably the ancient Greek kithara (see Figure 1.9)—with a sensuous modern style influenced by symbolism (see Chapter 31).*

Kindertotenlieder

Irony also haunts the *Kindertotenlieder* (Songs on the Death of Children, 1901–4), an orchestral song cycle on poems of Friedrich Rückert. The first song, *Nun will die Sonn' so hell aufgeh'n* (NAWM 170), achieves the transparency of chamber music through its spare use of instruments. Mahler's characteristic post-Wagnerian harmony intensifies the emotion through stark contrasts of dissonance with consonance and of chromaticism with diatonicism. Thin textures and simple melodies and rhythms produce an effect of understated restraint, ironic for a song about the death of one's child. The irony is heightened at times by an emotional mismatch between text and music: the opening line, "Now will the sun so brightly rise again," is sung to a woeful, descending, D-minor melody, while the next phrase rises chromatically to a sunny D major on the words "as if no misfortune occurred during the night."

Das Lied von der Erde

Das Lied von der Erde (The Song of the Earth, 1908) rivals the Ninth Symphony as the high point of Mahler's late works. Mahler called it "a symphony for a tenor voice and an alto or baritone voice and orchestra," and its six movements alternate between the two soloists. The texts, poems translated from Chinese, alternate between frenzied grasping at the dreamlike whirl of life and sad resignation at having to part from all its joys and beauties. Just as Mahler called on the human voice in his symphonies to complete his musical thought with words, here he calls on the orchestra to sustain and supplement the singers, both in accompaniment and in extensive connecting interludes. The exotic atmosphere of the words is lightly suggested by instrumental color and the use of the pentatonic scale. In no other work did Mahler so perfectly define and balance two extremes of his personality: ecstatic pleasure and deadly foreboding.

Mahler's impact

Although Mahler's early works were products of the late nineteenth century, he had his greatest success in the first decade of the twentieth, his last decade of life. This was also the time of his most radical creations, such as the vast two-movement Eighth Symphony ("Symphony of a Thousand") and the six-movement symphony with voices, *Das Lied von der Erde*. These works stretch the very meaning of the word "symphony," taking elements of the symphonic tradition to new extremes and thereby inspiring us to rethink the whole tradition. So do his other symphonies and orchestral song cycles, each in its own way renovating the tradition in modernist garb. He was an inspiration to and mentor for many in the younger generation, including Arnold Schoenberg and his circle (see Chapter 33).

RICHARD STRAUSS OPERAS While Mahler focused on the symphony and orchestral song cycle, Richard Strauss followed a different course. Having established himself in the 1880s and 1890s as the leading composer of symphonic poems after Liszt (see Chapter 29), Strauss turned to opera, seeking to inherit Wagner's mantle. After an early failure with *Guntram* in 1893 and moderate success with *Feuersnot* (The Fire Famine) in 1901, he scored a triumph in 1905 with *Salome,* and from then on the powers of depiction and characterization that he had honed in his tone poems went primarily into opera. His main models were Wagner and Mozart, composers from the Austro-German tradition whose operas he enjoyed conducting most of all and who—despite the great differences between them—were both adept at using contrasting styles to capture their characters' personalities, articulate their emotions, and convey the dramatic situation. Like Wagner, Strauss heightened both musical coherence and dramatic power through the use of leitmotives and the association of certain keys with particular characters.

Salome is a setting of a one-act play by Oscar Wilde in German translation. Strauss adapted the libretto himself. In this decadent version of the biblical story, the teenaged Salome performs her famous Dance of the Seven Veils and entices her stepfather Herod to deliver the head of John the Baptist on a silver platter so that she can kiss his cold lips, as illustrated in Figure 32.3. The subject, actions, and emotions were stranger than any attempted in opera before, and they stimulated Strauss to create harmonically complex and dissonant music that greatly influenced later composers and helped to spark the expressionist movement in music (see Chapter 33).

In the conclusion of the opera (NAWM 171), Salome speaks to John's head, musing that his lips taste bitter and wondering if they taste of blood or of love, which she has heard has a bitter taste. She concludes that it does not matter, because she has finally kissed his lips. The strange and shocking situation—combining the familiar scene of a young woman murmuring to her lover with the gruesome reality of the life-

FIGURE 32.3 The Climax, *illustration by British artist Aubrey Beardsley from his series of illustrations for Oscar Wilde's* Salome. *Beardsley's decadent style captures the macabre situation as Salome speaks to the severed head of John the Baptist.*

less head and her heartless act—is perfectly matched by Strauss's music, which achieves a high level of dissonance and drama through remarkably simple means. The beginning of the passage features a diminished seventh chord, used to create tension as far back as Alessandro Scarlatti in the late seventeenth century (see Chapter 17), overlaid with elements that are related but augment the dissonance: melodic and harmonic minor triads derived from the minor thirds in the diminished seventh chord itself; a chromatic trill embellishing one note of the chord; and Salome's recitative-like declamation that hovers around notes from the chord. Remarkably, this overwhelmingly dissonant passage, which seems to verge on atonality or polytonality (see Chapter 33), resolves through a familiar tonal progression (i–IV–I$_4^6$ –V^7–I) in a blissful C♯ major, the key associated with Salome throughout the opera. The move from stomach-churning dissonance to untroubled consonance and from tonal ambiguity to a clear tonal cadence—and then back again to dissonance and ambiguity—captures in music the catharsis of erotic ecstasy Salome experiences, framed by our horror at what she has done.

Such fiercely dissonant music as heard at the beginning of this excerpt inspired some later composers to abandon tonality altogether. But the resolution to C♯ and many other passages in this opera sound as sweetly diatonic, consonant, and clearly key-centered as this excerpt's opening passage is chromatic, dissonant, and ambiguous. The intense effect Strauss achieves here is predicated on our expectations that the dissonances will resolve. For his purposes of musical dramatization Strauss needed the polarities inherent in tonal music between dissonance and consonance, chromaticism and diatonicism, instability and stability, tension and resolution, all basic oppositions that composers since the sixteenth century had used to create drama and expression. In this he was the direct heir of Wagner, who relied on the same polarities to convey intense longing in *Tristan und Isolde*.

Elektra

With *Elektra* (1906–8), Strauss began a long and fruitful collaboration with the Viennese playwright Hugo von Hofmannsthal (1874–1929) that would result in seven operas. Adapted from a Greek tragedy by Sophocles, *Elektra* dwells on the emotions of insane hatred and revenge. Accordingly, Strauss intensified the chromaticism, dissonance, and tonal instability at times even beyond *Salome,* offset at other times by serene, diatonic, and tonally stable passages.

Der Rosenkavalier

Der Rosenkavalier (The Cavalier of the Rose, 1909–10) takes us into a sunnier world of elegant eroticism and tender feeling in the aristocratic, powdered-wig milieu of eighteenth-century Vienna. Here deceptively simple diatonic music dominates, while chromaticism, novel harmonic twists, unpredictably curving melodies, and magical orchestral colors suggest sensuality and enchantment. The whole score, with its mingling of sentiment and comedy, overflows with the lighthearted rhythms and melodies of Viennese waltzes—a witty anachronism, since the waltz craze began in the early nineteenth century, well after the events in the opera.

Ariadne auf Naxos

The anachronisms of *Der Rosenkavalier* are multiplied in Strauss's next opera, *Ariadne auf Naxos* (1911–12, revised 1916), which combines characters from Greek tragedy with characters from the eighteenth-century improvised comic *commedia dell'arte* and Mozartean music with Strauss's most Romantic effusions, using the conceit that the richest man in late-eighteenth-century Vienna has ordered up a tragic opera and a light comedy for his banquet and at the last moment, to save time for his guests, orders them both to be performed simultaneously. This self-aware play with past traditions, freely mixing elements from different eras to create something entirely new, is as typical of modernism as Salome's sensuousness or Elektra's howls of hatred.

Style and rhetoric

Strauss's later operas also exhibit his cunning use of musical styles and his intensification of the polarities inherent in tonality to depict characters and convey the drama. Seen as a leader of the radical modernists due to the extreme dissonance and shocking innovations of *Salome* and *Elektra*, Strauss was attacked for what some saw as a retreat to a more moderate and accessible style beginning with *Der Rosenkavalier*. But this is wrong, on two counts. First, his music always suited the situation and characters, and the plot of each opera called for different treatment. And second, his stylistic range did not change; just as there are gloriously diatonic passages in *Salome* and *Elektra*, there are extraordinarily dissonant and chromatic moments in *Der Rosenkavalier*, from the opening graphic depiction of sexual climax (before the curtain comes up to find the two main characters in bed) to the chords of the Rose leitmotive itself. Ultimately, Strauss's art is rhetorical, seeking to engage the audience's emotions directly, as a film composer might do, and he needed just as wide a range of style and effect.

After four decades of operas, Strauss turned in his final works to other *Last works*
genres better suited for expressing his own feelings rather than those of his
characters. His *Metamorphosen* (Metamorphoses, 1945) for string orchestra is
a lament on the disasters brought on Europe and Germany by Hitler and World
War II; only gradually do we realize that its intense outpourings are based on
the theme from the funeral march movement of Beethoven's *Eroica* Symphony,
finally stated near the end. And his *Four Last Songs* for voice and orchestra
(1948) evoke images of autumn and sunset, revisiting the theme from his
early tone poem *Death and Transfiguration* (1888–89) and now accepting death
as a culmination. These works remain tonal, in an age when others were creating electronic music and total serialism, but their tonal language is unlike
anyone else's, and would have sounded utterly radical even forty years before.
Despite—or perhaps because of—his continued use of tonality, all of Strauss's
music is new and highly individual, yet constantly looking to the past.

TRADITION AND DISTINCTION Both Mahler and Strauss claimed a place
in the permanent repertoire next to their great German forebears, but they
staked out different turf. Mahler became the last great Austro-German symphonist, capping the tradition stemming from Haydn and creating the most
significant successors to Beethoven's Ninth Symphony in his own symphonies with voices. Strauss proved to be the great successor to Wagner in German opera, using similar tools from leitmotives to stylistic contrasts and
producing a body of operas with a far greater range of subject than Wagner.
Both Mahler and Strauss also found a place in the tradition of German Lieder
and raised the orchestral song to a new prominence. As we will see in Chapters 33 and 35, their music served as models for younger composers on how
to write music that is welcomed into the museum of musical classics.

FRENCH MODERNISM: DEBUSSY AND RAVEL

While German modernists strove to join the ranks of Bach, Mozart, Beethoven,
and Wagner, French modernists contended with a more conflicted past. The
German classics from Bach to Mendelssohn were well established in the repertoire in France, and Wagner was a dominant figure. But after France's defeat
by German forces in the Franco-Prussian War of 1870–71, French musicians
sought greater independence from German music, seeking a distinctive path
of their own while beginning to revive French music of the sixteenth through
eighteenth centuries as a counterbalance to the German composers who were
at the core of the classical repertoire. By the turn of the century, younger
French composers had to contend not only with the German past, but with
the French past as well, stretching from the Renaissance through the major
figures of the late nineteenth century such as Saint-Saëns, Massenet, Fauré,
and d'Indy, all of whom were still alive (see Chapters 28 and 30).

Drawing elements from their national heritage helped French modernists *Drawing on the past*
to distinguish their music from that of their German contemporaries, and
especially to escape the overwhelming influence of Wagner. The French tradition of the seventeenth and eighteenth centuries (which the French called
"classic" rather than "Baroque") was marked by emotional reserve and under-
statement rather than effusion; as we have seen in the dramatic recitatives

from Lully's opera *Armide* (NAWM 85) and Rameau's opera *Hippolyte et Aricie* (NAWM 100) discussed in Chapters 16 and 18, the most profound emotions could be expressed through simple, direct means rather than by overpowering the audience with vocal gymnastics, scathing dissonance, or loud dynamics. Central to the French tradition was dance music, from Lully's operas and Couperin's suites to Chopin's waltzes. Taste and restraint were valued, as were elements of music that added beauty and gave pleasure, from appropriate decoration of melodies to variety of instrumental color. Reaching even further back, the music of Gregorian chant—the product of collaboration between French kings and Roman popes in the eighth and ninth centuries (see Chapter 2)—and of French Renaissance composers offered models of how to compose using modes rather than the goal-directed harmonic progressions of tonal music. All of these traits were useful to composers seeking a personal style distinct from their immediate predecessors yet informed by French tradition. The two most significant French composers of the early twentieth century, Claude Debussy and Maurice Ravel, found very different solutions.

CLAUDE DEBUSSY While Mahler and Strauss extended Wagnerian harmony to new levels of rhetorical intensity, their French contemporary Claude Debussy (1862–1918; see biography and Figure 32.4) took it in a different direction: toward pleasure and beauty. His admiration for Wagner's works, especially *Tristan* and *Parsifal,* was coupled with revulsion against Wagner's bombast and his attempts to expound philosophy in music. Debussy drew from the French tradition a preference for sensibility, taste, and restraint, admiring particularly his older contemporary Emmanuel Chabrier (1841–1894). He found new ideas in Russian composers, especially Rimsky-Korsakov and Musorgsky; in medieval music, notably parallel organum; and in music from Asia, including Javanese gamelan music and Chinese and Japanese melody. Blending these and other influences, he produced works of striking individuality that had a profound impact on almost all later composers.

Impressionism and symbolism   Debussy's music is often called **impressionist**, by analogy to the impressionist painters, but it is closer to symbolism, a connection reinforced by his friendships with symbolist poets and his use of their texts for songs and dramatic works. One trait shared with both trends is a sense of detached observation: rather than expressing deeply felt emotion or telling a story, as in much Romantic music, Debussy's typically evokes a mood, feeling, atmosphere, or scene. As in symbolist poetry, the normal syntax is often disrupted, so that the chord progressions of common-practice harmony are avoided or attenuated. Our attention is drawn instead to individual musical ideas or images that carry the work's structure and meaning. Debussy creates these musical images through motives, harmony, exotic scales (such as the whole-tone, octatonic, and pentatonic scales), instrumental timbre, and other elements, then composes by juxtaposing them. Motives need not develop, but may repeat with small changes, like an object viewed from different perspectives; dissonances need not resolve; sonorities may move in parallel motion; contrasts of scale type reinforce the articulation of phrases and sections; and instrumental timbres are intrinsic to the musical content rather than simple coloration. Indeed, Debussy's mature works are shaped more by contrasts of timbre and texture than by traditional formal devices or tonal function.

CLAUDE DEBUSSY

(1862–1918)

Debussy exercised an enormous influence on his contemporaries and later generations, creating music of new sounds and delicate colors.

Debussy was born in a suburb of Paris to a middle-class family. He began studying at the Paris Conservatoire at age ten, first piano and then composition. In the early 1880s he worked for Tchaikovsky's patron Nadezhda von Meck and twice traveled to Russia, where he encountered the recent works of Rimsky-Korsakov and others that deeply influenced his style and orchestration. He won the coveted Prix de Rome in 1884 and spent two years in Italy. Returning to Paris in 1887, he became friends with several symbolist poets and other artists. He made the pilgrimage to Bayreuth to hear Wagner's operas in 1888 and 1889, but came away recognizing both the power of the music and his own need to avoid being overly influenced by it.

In the 1890s, Debussy lived with his lover Gabrielle Dupont in Montmartre, the "Bohemian" neighborhood that had become a center for the new artistic movements. He found his own voice in composing a series of songs, his early piano music, the orchestral *Prelude to "The Afternoon of a Faun,"* and especially his opera *Pelléas et Mélisande,* whose 1902 premiere made him a star overnight. He made a living as a music critic and through an income from his publisher.

In 1898, Debussy left Dupont for Lilly Texier, whom he married the next year. But in 1904 he fell in love with Emma Bardac, with whom he had a child in 1905 and whom he married in 1908 after they had both divorced their spouses. By then he was well

FIGURE 32.4 *Portrait of Claude Debussy by Jacques-Emile Blanche, completed in 1902.*

established as France's leading modern composer, producing orchestral works like *La mer* and *Images* and piano pieces that soon entered the standard repertory. Although depressed by World War I and a diagnosis of cancer in 1914, he soon regained his productivity and composed his Études and three chamber sonatas before his death in 1918.

MAJOR WORKS *Pelléas et Mélisande* (opera); *Jeux* (ballet); *Prelude to "The Afternoon of a Faun,"* Nocturnes, La mer, Images, and other orchestral works; Preludes, Études, *Images, Children's Corner,* and many other piano pieces; about 90 songs; string quartet, sonatas, and other chamber works

In all these respects, Debussy deliberately undermines the sense of urgency and desire that underlay tonal music from its beginnings and came to the forefront in German Romanticism from Beethoven to Wagner: the need to resolve, to return to the tonic, to solve the musical problem posed at the beginning of a movement, and to develop the potential of a motive until it is exhausted. In place of all this urgency, Debussy promoted a modernism that focused on what he regarded as the traditionally French values of decoration, beauty, and pleasure (see Source Reading).

These traits are evident in the passage from Debussy's piano piece *L'isle*

SOURCE READING

Debussy on Tradition, Freedom, and Pleasure

Claude Debussy was well trained in the classical tradition and deeply influenced by Wagner. But he sought a new freedom for music that focused on pleasure and beautiful sounds, as he explained to his former teacher at the Paris Conservatoire, New Orleans–born composer Ernest Guiraud (1836–1892), in a conversation around 1890.

✦

Debussy: The tonal scale must be enriched by other scales. . . . Music is neither major nor minor. Minor thirds and major thirds should be combined, modulation thus becoming more flexible. The mode is that which one happens to choose at the moment. It is inconstant. In [Wagner's opera] *Tristan* the themes heard in the orchestra are themes of the action. They do no violence to the action. There must be a balance between musical demands and thematic evocation. Themes suggest their orchestral coloring.

Ernest Guiraud: (*Debussy having played a series of intervals on the piano*): What's that?

Debussy: Incomplete chords, floating. *Il faut noyer: le ton* [one must inundate or obscure the key]. One can travel where one wishes and leave by any door. Greater nuances.

Guiraud: But when I play this it has to resolve.

Debussy: I don't see that it should. Why?

Guiraud: Well, do you find this lovely?

Debussy: Yes, yes, yes!

Guiraud: But how would you get out of this?

I am not saying that what you do isn't beautiful, but it's theoretically absurd.

Debussy: There is no theory. You merely have to listen. Pleasure is the law.

From Edward Lockspeiser, Debussy: *His Life and Mind*, vol. 1 (London: Cassell, 1962), 206–7.

joyeuse (The Joyous Isle, 1903–4) in Example 32.2. Each motive is associated with a particular figuration, chord or succession of chords, scale type, dynamic level, and range on the piano, producing a succession of images that remain distinct from one another even as each flows into the next: (a) a rising major-third motive in a whole-tone environment; (b) an upward sweep in the B-Dorian diatonic scale; (c) a partially chromatic motive based on undulating thirds; (d) a pentatonic filigree; and (e) chromatic lines in contrary motion over a pedal A (combined with c). In the motion from each segment to the next, some notes remain the same and some change, producing the effect of a harmonic progression.

The harmonic styles of Wagner and Liszt influenced Debussy's use of chromatic and whole-tone chords, but the urgency to resolve is absent. Instead, we are content to enjoy each moment as it comes. Debussy usually maintained a tonal focus—a kind of key center, here A—but he defied the conventional tonal relationships between chords and allowed each chord a

EXAMPLE 32.2 *Claude Debussy,* L'isle joyeuse

degree of independence. This changed attitude toward harmony, inviting us to take pleasure in each event rather than yearn for resolution, gives his music a feeling of detached observation. Of course pleasure can lead to exuberance or even ecstasy, as it does in the climactic conclusion of this piece, so it should not be imagined that Debussy's music is without feeling.

Piano music

Many of Debussy's other piano pieces also have evocative titles, often suggesting a visual image, like *Estampes* (Engravings or Prints, 1903) and the two sets of *Images* (1901–5 and 1907). Several of his works evoke distinctive styles of music. *Pagodes* (Pagodas), the first piece in *Estampes,* conveys its Asian atmosphere by imitating the pentatonic melodies, low gongs, and multilayered textures of a Javanese gamelan, an orchestra comprising mostly gongs and percussion, which Debussy had heard at the 1889 Paris Universal Exposition. *Children's Corner* (1906–8), inspired by Debussy's daughter, depicts a child's world, including a sly poke at Clementi and Czerny's piano exercises in *Dr. Gradus ad Parnassum.* The last piece in the set, *Golliwogg's Cake-Walk,* imitates Scott Joplin's ragtime style and juxtaposes it with a middle section that satirically recasts the opening of Wagner's *Tristan und Isolde* in the style of salon music, marked "avec une grande émotion" (with a great show of emotion); in this lighthearted piece, Debussy demonstrates his modernist tastes by showing his familiarity with up-to-date American music and mocking the grandiosity and excessive emotionalism of his German predecessor.

The twenty-four Preludes (two books, 1909–10 and 1911–13) are character pieces whose picturesque titles are placed at the end rather than the beginning of each piece to allow listeners or performers to form their own associations. Other works are relatively abstract, although unmistakably in Debussy's style: *Suite bergamasque* (ca. 1890) and *Pour le piano* (1894–1901) update the French tradition of the keyboard suite, and the late Études (1915) explore pianistic timbre as well as technique in the tradition of Chopin.

Orchestral music

Debussy's orchestral music shows the same characteristics as his piano works, with the added element of instrumental timbre. Often a particular instrument is associated with a certain motive, and different musical layers are separated through tone color. His works require a large orchestra, which is seldom used to make a loud sound but instead offers a great variety of tone colors and textures. Even more than Mahler, Debussy treated music as an art of sound and reveled in the wide range of sounds available in the orchestra.

Debussy based his celebrated *Prélude à "L'après-midi d'un faune"* (Prelude to "The Afternoon of a Faun," 1891–94) on a symbolist poem by Stéphane Mallarmé, and he treats the subject the same way that French symbolist poets did: by evoking a mood through suggestion, connotation, and indirection rather than through intense emotional expression. Debussy's orchestral technique is well represented by the three *Nocturnes* (1897–99), with subdued, imagist instrumentation in *Nuages* (Clouds), the brilliance of the full ensemble in *Fêtes* (Festivals), and the blending of orchestra with wordless female chorus in *Sirènes* (the Sirens of Greek mythology). *La mer* (The Sea, 1903–5), subtitled "three symphonic sketches," captures the movements of the sea through rapidly alternating musical images.

Nuages

Nuages (NAWM 172) from *Nocturnes* exemplifies the interaction of timbre with motive, scale type, and other elements to create a musical image. The piece begins with an oscillating pattern of fifths and thirds, adapted from a Musorgsky song, that conveys an impression of movement but no harmonic direction, an apt analogy for slowly moving clouds. Each time the pattern appears, it features different tone colors or pitches, or both, sometimes changing into a series of parallel triads or seventh or ninth chords. Near the end the pattern practically disappears, giving the impression of dispersing clouds. Juxtaposed with this figure's inconstancy is one that changes little: an English-horn motive that quickly rises and slowly falls through a segment of the octatonic scale. The English horn sometimes omits or repeats some of its final notes, but the motive is never developed, transposed, or given to another instrument, and the English horn never plays anything else; there is complete identification between timbre and motive. The motive is usually answered by horns playing a tritone or other figures from the same octatonic scale or a whole-tone scale. It is not clear what, if anything, these musical gestures represent; they are themselves, lending coherence to the music and helping to convey a sense of stillness and contemplation. The movement unfolds in a series of cycles, each ending with the English-horn motive, that vary the material heard before and introduce new ideas. In one episode near the end, sustained string chords underlie a slow pentatonic melody in the style of Javanese gamelan music or other Asian traditions Debussy had heard at the 1889 Paris Universal Exposition. The gentle cycling through musical ideas that may change, repeat verbatim, or appear only once lends the music a shape somewhat like the recurring cycles of life itself, or of an afternoon spent watching the clouds.

Debussy's lifelong engagement with texts—he was also a music critic— made him particularly interested in the written word. Notable among his songs are settings of several major French poets, including Charles Baudelaire, Paul Verlaine, and the ballades of fifteenth-century poet François Villon. He repeatedly sought out dramatic projects, from incidental music to Gabriele d'Annunzio's mystery play *The Martyrdom of Saint Sebastian* (1910–11) and the ballet *Jeux* (1912–13) to several unfinished works. His only completed opera, *Pelléas et Mélisande* (1893–1902), was his response to Wagner's *Tristan und Isolde,* and it made his reputation when it premiered in 1902 at the Paris Opéra-Comique. The veiled allusions and images of the text, a symbolist play by Maurice Maeterlinck, are matched by the strange, often modal harmonies, subdued colors, and restrained expressiveness of the music. The voices, set in fluent recitative that matches the flow of the French language, are supported but never dominated by a continuous orchestral background, while the instrumental interludes connecting the scenes carry on the mysterious inner drama.

Songs and stage music

The changes that Debussy introduced in harmonic and orchestral usage made him one of the seminal forces in the history of music. The composers who at one time or another came under his influence include nearly every distinguished composer of the early and middle twentieth century, from Ravel, Messiaen, and Boulez in France to Puccini, Janáček, Richard Strauss, Scriabin, Ives, Falla, Bartók, Stravinsky, Berg, and others from many national traditions, as well as American jazz and popular musicians. His emphasis on sound itself as an element of music opened doors to new possibilities later explored by Varèse, Cage, Penderecki, Ligeti, and many postwar composers.

Debussy's influence

MAURICE RAVEL Maurice Ravel (1875–1937), shown in Figure 32.5, is often grouped with Debussy as an impressionist, and some of his works seem to fit the label. But he might better be called a superb assimilator, whose music encompasses a variety of influences while carrying his distinctive stamp marked by consummate craftsmanship, traditional forms, diatonic melodies, and complex harmonies within an essentially tonal language.

Although Ravel spent most of his life in Paris, he was born in a Basque village in the Pyrenees to a Swiss father and Basque mother and always felt a connection to the Basque region and to Spain. He had an independent streak that made him something of an outsider. He studied piano and composition at the Paris Conservatoire but resisted conventional expectations and was dismissed when he failed to win any prizes. Active in a circle of innovative young musicians, writers, and artists in Paris, Ravel was open to all the currents he encountered, from Russian and Asian music to the latest French literature. When in 1905 he was passed over for the fifth time in the competition for the Prix de Rome, the judges' decision caused a scandal because he was already establishing himself as the most interesting and controversial French composer of the generation after Debussy.

Outsider

The impressionist side of Ravel, and some differences from Debussy, are

Distinctive traits

FIGURE 32.5 *Maurice Ravel at the piano.*

illustrated in the piano piece *Jeux d'eau* (Fountains, 1901). In it Ravel drew on Liszt's pianistic techniques and in turn gave Debussy ideas for his own watery music. The passage in Example 32.3 includes many innovative textures, such as parallel dissonant chords under rushing scales, and chords and arpeggiated figures that emphasize opens fifths and fourths. This passage juxtaposes whole-tone with diatonic music, as in *L'isle joyeuse* (Example 32.2). But unlike Debussy, Ravel treats his whole-tone sonorities as dissonant harmonies that must resolve, culminating in a complex reworking of the traditional ii–V–I tonal cadence: a progression from an F♯ ninth chord (drawn from one whole-tone scale) through an F–A–B–D♯ augmented sixth chord (drawn from the other whole-tone scale) to a resolution on the tonic E major. Also characteristic of Ravel are the prominent major sevenths he attaches to the tonic and subdominant chords in measure 7, creating a spiky dissonance that Debussy normally avoided.

Classical models   The descriptive piano pieces in the sets *Miroirs* (Mirrors, 1904–5) and *Gaspard de la nuit* (1908) and the ballet *Daphnis et Chloé* (1909–12) likewise invoke impressionism in their strong musical imagery, brilliant instrumental technique, and colorful harmonies. But Ravel also absorbed ideas from

EXAMPLE 32.3 *Maurice Ravel,* Jeux d'eau

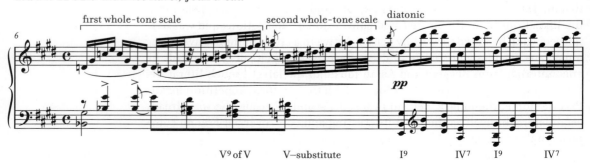

older French music and from the eighteenth-century Classic tradition. His interest in Classic forms and genres is clear in works such as the Sonatine for piano (1903–5), String Quartet in F (1902–3), Piano Trio (1914), and Violin Sonata (1923–27). He borrows from the French tradition of stylized dances and suites in his piano pieces *Menuet antique* (1895), *Pavane pour une infante défunte* (Pavane for a Dead Princess, 1899), and *Le tombeau de Couperin* (Memorial for Couperin, 1914–17), all of which he later orchestrated.

Beyond impressionist traits and classical models, Ravel borrowed ideas from many kinds of music to enrich his own. His songs draw on French art and popular traditions and range in topic from humorous and realistic takes on animal life in *Histoires naturelles* (1906) to three symbolist poems by Mallarmé for voice and chamber ensemble (1913). Ravel's settings closely reflect the natural accents of French, often dropping final syllables that were truncated in normal speech and music-hall songs but had traditionally been set in art songs. He also looked to popular traditions outside France, using Viennese waltz rhythms in the tone poem *La valse* (1919–20); Romani (Gypsy) style in *Tzigane* for violin and piano or orchestra (1924); blues in the Violin Sonata; and jazz elements in the Piano Concerto in G (1929–31) and the Piano Concerto for the Left Hand (1929–30), composed for pianist Paul Wittgenstein, who had lost his right arm in World War I. Many works featured Spanish idioms, including Ravel's famous *Bolero* (1928), an orchestral rumination on a single idea varied by changes of instrumentation and a gradual crescendo. Working in a classical tradition that esteemed originality, Ravel avoided repeating himself by drawing on a wide range of sources and giving each piece its individual stamp.

Varied influences

Although no one piece can represent such a multifaceted composer, the orchestral suite *Rapsodie espagnole* (Spanish Rhapsody, 1907–8; NAWM 173) is characteristic in its combination of multiple influences. Ravel's evocations of Spain are never exaggerated or exoticized, but convey an authentic flavor derived from his lifelong familiarity with Spanish music and culture through his mother. Of the rhapsody's four movements, the most overtly Spanish are the second, *Malagueña* (NAWM 173b), and the third, *Habanera*, both based on Spanish dances and marked by imitations of guitar playing. *Malagueña* evokes both the flashy dancing and the soulful, unmeasured songs associated with flamenco style. The outer movements, *Prélude à la nuit* (Prelude to the Night; NAWM 173a) and *Feria* (Fair, or Market), are mood pieces, summoning up the mysterious stillness of twilight and the boisterous activity of an outdoor marketplace. Their Spanish character comes in part from a play between triple and duple rhythms and meters, and in the first movement from hints of a seguidilla melody. French and Russian influences are also strong. The first two movements follow Debussy in using ostinatos and multiple layers of music set apart by rhythm and timbre, and the first movement's alternation between octatonic and diatonic passages recalls Rimsky-Korsakov's use of the same juxtaposition to contrast magical realms and characters with human ones (see Chapter 28). All four movements show a mastery of orchestration, using a wide variety of timbres from unusual instruments and percussion to string harmonics and muted brass to create an endlessly shifting kaleidoscope of colors that evoke a range of moods, spaces, and images.

Rapsodie espagnole

MODERNISM AND NATIONAL TRADITIONS

The careers and music of Mahler, Strauss, Debussy, and Ravel exemplify the search by those in the first generation of modernist composers for a personal style that absorbed what was useful from the past, was true to their national identity, yet was distinctive and individual. As we survey a number of major composers from other nations across Europe, we will also see this interplay between tradition and innovation and between national identity and personal style at work.

SPAIN: ALBÉNIZ, GRANADOS, AND FALLA German and French composers were heirs to a well-established tradition that had already achieved international distinction. But their contemporaries in other lands, such as Spain, were still engaged in the attempt to define their nations musically. French, Russian, and other composers had often used Spanish elements to create an exotic atmosphere. In the early twentieth century, building on the achievements of Barbieri, Pedrell, and others in the nineteenth century (see Chapter 28), Spanish composers sought to reclaim their national tradition, using authentic native materials in order to appeal to their own people and to gain a foothold in the international repertoire.

Albéniz and Granados   Isaac Albéniz (1860–1909) and Enrique Granados (1867–1916) are best known for their piano music, although both wrote operas and other works. In his *Iberia* (1905–8), a collection of twelve piano pieces in four books, Albéniz blended Spanish melodic traits and dance rhythms with a colorful virtuoso style that drew on Liszt and Debussy. Granados based piano pieces on dances from all over Spain, and his *Goyescas* (1909–12), inspired by sketches by the Spanish artist Francisco Goya (1746–1828), draw on numerous Spanish styles, from the keyboard sonatas of Domenico Scarlatti (see Chapter 22) and eighteenth-century theatrical styles of the *tonadilla* and *zarzuela* to flamenco guitar and Andalusian song.

FIGURE 32.6 *Manuel de Falla.*

The principal Spanish composer of the twentieth century was Manuel de Falla (1876–1946), shown in Figure 32.6, who developed a diverse nationalism that resisted the merely exotic. Like Albéniz and Granados, he studied with Pedrell, who passed along a sense of the Spanish tradition dating back to the Renaissance. Falla collected and arranged national folk songs, introducing a wider public to the variety in the Spanish folk tradition. His earlier works—such as the opera *La vida breve* (Life Is Short, 1904–13) and the ballets *El amor brujo* (Love, the Sorcerer, 1915) and *El sombrero de tres picos* (The Three-Cornered Hat, 1916–19)—are imbued with the melodic and rhythmic qualities of Spanish popular music. His finest mature works are *El retablo de maese Pedro* (Master Pedro's Puppet Show, 1919–23), based on an episode from Miguel de Cervantes's great Spanish novel *Don Quixote,* and the concerto for harpsichord with five solo instruments (1923–26), which harks back to the Spanish Baroque. Both works combine specific national elements with the neoclassical approach popular after World War I (see Chapters 33 and 35) to produce music that is both nationalist and more broadly modernist.

Falla's *Homenaje* (Homage; NAWM 174) for solo guitar illustrates his combination of national with international traits, and of folk elements with modernist ones. He composed the piece in 1920 as an homage to Debussy, who had died two years earlier, and to the guitar, the instrument that was an emblem of Spanish music. Falla came to know Debussy and his music during seven years in Paris just before World War I, and he respected the French composer's ability to evoke Spanish music in ways that went beyond exoticism. *Homenaje* quotes Debussy's piano piece *Soirée dans Grenade* (Evening in Granada) near the end, and uses many of the same Spanish elements as Debussy, from habanera rhythm to melodic and harmonic gestures of flamenco music. Falla also uses sounds and techniques typical of guitar music to foreground its unique qualities: strumming, plucking, harmonics, and especially the sound of open strings tuned in fourths, resulting in dissonant harmonies using stacked fourths. The result is a modernist tapestry that does not sound like traditional Spanish guitar music, or like Debussy, but pays homage to both.

Homenaje

BRITAIN: VAUGHAN WILLIAMS AND HOLST The English musical renaissance begun in the late nineteenth century (see Chapter 30) took flight in the twentieth, as composers sought a distinctive voice for English art music after centuries of domination by foreign styles. Cecil Sharp (1859–1924), Ralph Vaughan Williams (1872–1958), and others collected and published hundreds of folk songs, leading to the use of these melodies in compositions such as Vaughan Williams's *Norfolk Rhapsodies* (1905–6) and *Five Variants of "Dives and Lazarus"* (1939) as well as Gustav Holst's *Somerset Rhapsody* (1906–7). These two composers, shown together in Figure 32.7, had become close friends while students of Parry and Stanford at the Royal Conservatory of Music, and they became the leaders of a new English school.

FIGURE 32.7 *Gustav Holst (seated) and Ralph Vaughan Williams in 1921, during a walking tour of the scenic Malvern Hills in the English Midlands.*

Vaughan Williams composed nine symphonies, other orchestral pieces, film scores, works for band, songs, operas, and many choral pieces. He drew inspiration from folk song, English hymnody, and earlier English composers such as Thomas Tallis and Henry Purcell. He also studied with Ravel and absorbed strong influences from Debussy, Bach, and Handel.

Vaughan Williams exemplified a trait common to several modern English composers: he wrote both art music and practical or utilitarian music, using elements from each tradition in the other. He gained a profound knowledge of hymnody as musical editor of the new *English Hymnal* in 1904–6, writing later that "Two years of close association with some of the best (as well as some of the worst) tunes in the world was a better musical education than any amount of sonatas and fugues." He also composed a half-dozen hymn tunes, arranged over forty folk songs

TOPFOTO/THE IMAGE WORKS

as hymns, and resurrected forgotten sixteenth-century tunes for the hymnal. Throughout his long career, he conducted local amateur singers and players, for whom he wrote a number of pieces. Such links with amateur music-making kept Vaughan Williams and other English composers from cultivating an esoteric style addressed only to educated listeners.

The national quality of Vaughan Williams's music comes from his incorporation or imitation of British folk tunes and his assimilation of the modal harmony of sixteenth-century English composers. One of his most popular works, *Fantasia on a Theme of Thomas Tallis* (1910) for double string orchestra and string quartet, is based on a Tallis hymn in the Phrygian mode that Vaughan Williams had revived for the *English Hymnal.* The piece introduces fragments of the tune, states it simply once, and develops motives from it in a free fantasy, using antiphonal sonorities and triads in parallel motion in a modal framework. Like his teacher Ravel, Vaughan Williams found ways to write varied but always national and recognizably individual music.

Gustav Holst   Gustav Holst (1874–1934) came from a musical family—his father, grandfather, and great-grandfather all had careers as performers and piano teachers—and he made his living as a trombonist and later as a music teacher at St. Paul's Girls' School in Hammersmith and at Morley College. He won renown with works for orchestra, for band, and for chorus, notably *Choral Hymns from the Rig Veda* (1908–12) on Hindu sacred texts and *The Hymn of Jesus* (1917) on texts from the apocryphal Acts of John, both to his own English translations. His greatest success and enduring reputation came with the orchestral suite *The Planets* (1914–16), which became the source for many conventions of scoring for movies and television shows set in space.

Suite No. 1 in E-flat   Holst's two suites for band combine the British military band tradition with elements from the classical tradition and English folk music. His Suite No. 1 in E-flat (1909) begins with a chaconne, whose sixteen variations over a ground bass theme gradually build to a climactic close. Some of the variations place the chaconne bass in the middle or top of the texture, as in the chaconne finale of Brahms's Fourth Symphony (NAWM 160), and two use the theme in inversion. The other two movements of the suite feature themes derived from the chaconne theme through thematic transformation, as in the music of Liszt. The two main themes of the second movement, titled Intermezzo (NAWM 175), reshape the first half of the chaconne theme into modal melodies that have the character of an English country dance tune and a folk song respectively, and a secondary idea is based on the second half of the chaconne theme. The finale is a march whose primary strain resembles the inverted form of the chaconne theme, while the trio recasts the chaconne tune into a melody as long, beautiful, and uplifting as the Jupiter theme from *The Planets.* The latter two movements both end with their themes in contrapuntal combination. Through the modal flavor of the melodies and references to the English traditions of folk song, country dance, march, and ground bass variations (as in Purcell's *Dido and Aeneas,* NAWM 90), Holst makes the suite quintessentially national, at the same time that his use of classical procedures from counterpoint to cyclic form link it to the international tradition of art music.

RUSSIA: RACHMANINOFF AND SCRIABIN The works of Rachmaninoff and Scriabin illustrate the wide variety of personal styles in the early twentieth century. Classmates at the Moscow Conservatory, each developed an individual idiom that drew both on Russian traditions and on the pan-European heritage of the virtuoso pianist-composer.

Serge Rachmaninoff (1873–1943), shown in Figure 32.8, made his living primarily as a pianist, especially after leaving Russia in 1917 in the wake of the Russian Revolution and making his home in the United States. His notable works include three symphonies, the symphonic poem *The Isle of the Dead* (1907), and the choral symphony *The Bells* (1913). But his most characteristic music is for piano, especially the twenty-four preludes (1892–1910) and two sets of *Etudes-Tableaux* (1911 and 1916–17) for piano solo, four piano concertos, and his *Rhapsody on a Theme of Paganini* for piano and orchestra (1934), a salute from one great virtuoso to another. His music combines influences from composers active in western Europe, such as Mendelssohn and Chopin, with Russian elements from Orthodox liturgical music to Tchaikovsky.

Rachmaninoff is renowned for his passionate, melodious idiom. Some have dismissed his music as old-fashioned, but like other composers of his generation, he sought a way to appeal to listeners enamored of the classics by offering something new and individual yet steeped in tradition. Rather than introduce innovations in harmony, as did Strauss, Debussy, and Scriabin—which would have violated both his temperament and the demands of the audience for touring virtuosos—he focused on other elements of the Romantic tradition, creating melodies and textures that sound both fresh and familiar. As in the best popular music, or long-standing traditions such as Italian opera, Rachmaninoff made his mark not by stark departures from convention but by doing the conventional in a way no one had done before.

FIGURE 32.8 *Serge Rachmaninoff, in a portrait by Boris Chaliapin.*

GLINKA MUSEUM OF MUSIC CULTURE, MOSCOW, RUSSIA/BRIDGEMAN IMAGES

The excerpts in Example 32.4 from Rachmaninoff's Prelude in G Minor, Op. 23, No. 5 (1901; NAWM 176), illustrate his ability to create innovative textures and melodies within traditional harmonies and ABA′ form. The first measure is just a decorated arpeggiation of a G-minor triad, but a triad had never been presented exactly like this; the pattern of rhythm and alternating registers is distinctive. That pattern develops throughout the A sections, with constant small changes to provide variety. The bass has the melody, modal and slightly awkward, which is revealed in retrospect as a decorated descent to the dominant. We expect a contrasting key, probably in major, for the middle section (Example 32.4b), but instead Rachmaninoff dwells on the dominant seventh chord, as if the major third were enough of a contrast. The melody here sounds Russian and characteristic of Rachmaninoff because of its close intervals, straining to rise, then falling back, with a diminished fourth for a mournful touch. Both the diminished fourth, marked by a bracket, and the rising figure in a middle voice at the end of this excerpt, marked by a brace, echo elements from the opening theme in Example 32.4a, linking the two themes. The melodic character of the middle section is strongly influenced

Prelude in G Minor

EXAMPLE 32.4 *Themes from Serge Rachmaninoff's Prelude in G Minor, Op. 23, No. 5*

a. Opening

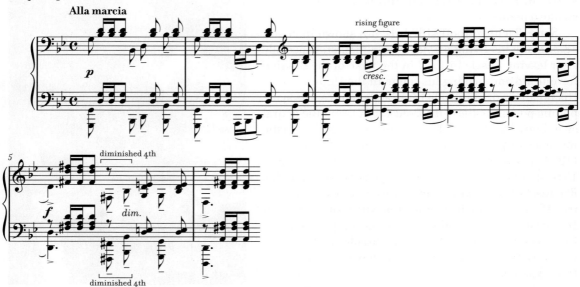

b. Middle section

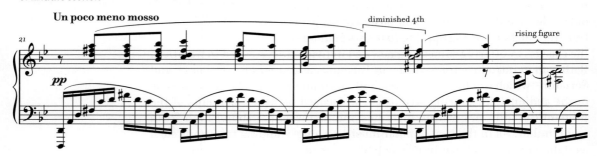

by the harmonic context and the new, flowing accompanimental figure. This melodic idea is developed through a series of slight variations, typical of Rachmaninoff in that one cannot predict the melody's progress but it sounds right in retrospect. Such qualities were not enough for those who demanded innovation in harmony, but Rachmaninoff's music ultimately won a place in the permanent repertoire most of his contemporaries would have envied.

Alexander Scriabin   Alexander Scriabin (1872–1915), shown in Figure 32.9, traveled a different path. He began by writing nocturnes, preludes, études, and mazurkas in the manner of Chopin, then gradually absorbed the chromaticism of Liszt and Wagner; the octatonic scale and other exotic elements from Rimsky-Korsakov; and the juxtapositions of texture, scale, and figuration from Debussy and Russian composers. He gradually evolved a complex harmonic vocabulary all his own, using chords featuring tritones and drawn from the octatonic and whole-tone scales, often mixing the two. Such a language, with its symmetrical scales that provide colorful dissonance while evading conventional tonal resolution, was perfectly suited to Scriabin's notion of music as a means to transcend daily existence and offer a glimpse of the divine, an otherworldly truth, an experience of ecstasy. Besides piano music, he wrote symphonies and other orchestral works, notably *Poem of Ecstasy* (1908) and *Prometheus* (1910). During performances of the latter, the composer wanted the concert hall to be flooded with changing colored light; his own synesthesia caused him to link particular pitches to colors, and he aspired to a synthesis of all the arts with the aim of inducing states of mystic rapture.

The changes in his musical language can be followed in his ten piano sonatas, of which the last five, composed 1911–13, dispense with key signatures and tonality. He replaced conventional tonal harmony by choosing for each work a complex chord that serves as a kind of tonic and as the source of a work's melodic and harmonic material. The referential chord typically contains one or two tritones and is usually part of an octatonic scale, sometimes with one added note. These chords resemble Wagner's Tristan chord (see Chapter 28), yet they are treated as static objects and do not project a yearning toward resolution; instead of the desire Wagner sought to invoke, they suggest a transcendence of desire, which can be read as erotic or mystic depending on the context. Scriabin creates a sense of harmonic progression by transposing and altering the referential chord, enlivening the texture with vigorous figuration, until the chord returns at the end, sometimes with alterations. Through this process of harmonic and textural change, together with a gradual increase in dynamics and range, the music typically traces a course from an enigmatic beginning, through increasing dynamism, to ecstatic transcendence. Such pieces cannot be described as tonal, but the novel harmony serves most of the functions of tonality, establishing a home tonal region, departing from it, and returning.

Example 32.5 illustrates this process in *Vers la flamme* (Toward the Flame), Op. 72 (1914; NAWM 177), a one-movement tone poem for piano. The opening in Example 32.5b establishes a referential sonority of two tritones, E–A♯–G♯–D, decorated melodically by C♯ and F♯. With the exception of F♯, these are all notes from the octatonic scale shown in Example 32.5a. When the sonority is transposed up a minor third in measure 5, the remaining notes of the scale appear, and the whole passage repeats in the new position. Such octatonic sonorities and chord successions occur throughout, interspersed with other types of harmonies. As shown in Example 32.5c–e, the opening chord returns periodically in new guises, acquiring B as well as C♯ and F♯ along the way; all these variants also appear in transposition, usually by major or minor third or tritone. At the climactic ending (Example 32.5f), the D becomes D♯, creating a resonant chord based mostly on fourths that serves as a final tonic equivalent. Instead of resolving the initial tritones E–A♯ and G♯–D as tritones normally do in tonal music—inward to a third or outward to a sixth—both of these tritones "resolve" over the course of the movement by expanding to form the perfect fifths E–B and G♯–D♯, a harmonic embodiment of the journey toward transcendence implied by the title. The predominant figuration changes from section to section, producing an effect of static

FIGURE 32.9 *Alexander Scriabin, in a portrait by A. Y. Golovin.*

EXAMPLE 32.5 *Excerpts from Alexander Scriabin,* Vers la flamme

a. Octatonic scale on E–F

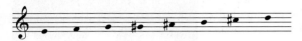

b. Opening

c. Measures 41–42

d. Measures 77–78

e. Measures 107–8

f. Measure 125

blocks of sound that are juxtaposed, as in Musorgsky's and Debussy's music. Coordinated with the gradual transformations of the referential chord is a vast expansion in range and increase in dynamic level and density of attacks, leading to the ecstatic conclusion.

Of all the composers surveyed in this chapter, Scriabin traveled the furthest from common-practice tonal harmony, Rachmaninoff the least, yet both came from a similar heritage as virtuoso pianist-composers in the Russian tradition. Their differences exemplify the range of choices open to modernist composers and the variety of paths they pursued.

EASTERN AND NORTHERN EUROPE: JANÁČEK AND SIBELIUS Spain, Britain, and Russia were independent nations for whom nationalism was primarily a cultural issue. But for the peoples of eastern Europe and the Baltic region under the Austro-Hungarian and Russian Empires, it was also an urgent political concern. Music that reflected a people's language and traditions was valuable at home as an assertion of an independent national identity and abroad as an appeal for international recognition as a nation.

The leading twentieth-century Czech composer, Leoš Janáček (1854–1928), worked in the genres of Western art music, especially opera, but sought a specifically national style. Beginning in the 1880s, he collected and edited folk music from his native region of Moravia, studied the rhythms and inflections of peasant speech and song, and devised a highly personal idiom based on them. Particularly distinctive is his use of melodies and rhythms derived from the inflections and rhythms of spoken words. This is an idea that we have seen repeatedly in vocal music, from Peri's recitative in the early seventeenth century to Musorgsky's settings of Russian in *Boris Godunov,* but Janáček applied it to instrumental music as well. The particular patterns of the Czech language—especially its long and short vowels, independent of the stress accent that usually falls at the beginning of a word—give his music a highly individual character. Janáček asserted his independence from Austria not only in melodic style but also in his characteristic procedures. His music relies on contrasting sonorities, harmonies, motives, and tone colors, and it proceeds primarily by repeating and juxtaposing ideas in a manner akin to Musorgsky or Debussy rather than developing them as in the Germanic tradition.

Leoš Janáček

After winning local renown for his collections of folk songs and dances and for choral music in Czech, Janáček gained wider prominence in his sixties when his opera *Jenůfa,* based on a Moravian subject and premiered in Brno in 1904, was performed in Prague in 1916 and again in Vienna in 1918, the year that Czechoslovakia gained independence after the dissolution of Austria-Hungary. With new confidence from both personal and political triumphs, in his last decade Janáček produced a string of operas that dominated the Czech stage between the world wars and later became part of the international repertory, including *Kát'a Kabanová* (1921), *The Cunning Little Vixen* (1924), *The Makropulos Affair* (1925), and *From the House of the Dead* (1928). In his operas, strongly contrasting ideas are used to delineate diverse characters and situations. His instrumental works, such as the flashy orchestral *Sinfonietta* (1926) and two late string quartets (1923 and 1928), depend on similar contrasts.

Finland was part of the Russian Empire from 1809 until it gained independence in 1917, but it was culturally dominated by Sweden, which had

Jean Sibelius

FIGURE 32.10 *Jean Sibelius around 1904, in a drawing by Albert Edelfelt.*

ruled it for centuries. Jean Sibelius (1865–1957), shown in Figure 32.10, was raised speaking Swedish, then as a young man became a committed Finnish patriot, learning the language and changing his name from the Swedish Johan to the French Jean. Fascinated with the Finnish national epic, the *Kalevala*, he mined it for texts to set in his vocal works and for subjects to treat in his symphonic poems. He modeled many themes on recitation formulas for the epic, repetitive melodies on the first five notes of the minor scale.

Sibelius established his reputation as Finland's leading composer in the 1890s with a series of symphonic poems, including *Kullervo* (in five movements with soloists and chorus), *En saga, The Swan of Tuonela, Lemminkäinen's Return*, and his most famous (and political), *Finlandia*. From 1897 to the end of his life, he was supported by the Finnish government as a national artist. Around 1900, he turned to the international audience with publication and performances of his symphonic poems and with his first two symphonies (1899 and 1901–2) and Violin Concerto (1903–4), followed by five more symphonies through 1924. Sibelius devised a personal style marked by modal melodies, uncomplicated rhythms, insistent repetition of brief motives, ostinatos, pedal points, and strong contrasts of orchestral timbres and textures, all designed to create a distinctive sound and musical discourse far removed from the nineteenth-century academic tradition in which he had been trained.

Form   Especially original is Sibelius's treatment of form. In addition to reworking sonata form in novel ways, he used devices that James Hepokoski has called "rotational form," repeatedly cycling through a series of thematic elements that are varied each time, and "teleological genesis," a goal-directed process of generating a theme from motivic fragments, sometimes over an entire movement or symphony. The former was anticipated in the Prelude to Wagner's *Tristan und Isolde* (NAWM 153a) and used independently by Debussy in *Nuages* (see NAWM 172), and the latter builds on Liszt's thematic transformation and Brahms's developing variation. Both rotational form and teleological genesis are exemplified in the slow third movement of Sibelius's Fourth Symphony (1910–11; NAWM 178), which rotates several times through three main ideas. Example 32.6 shows one of these ideas at three different stages: (a) its first appearance; (b) a statement midway, when the first half of the theme is clear but the second half has not yet found its footing; and (c) the final, definitive form.

Reception   Sibelius saw his style as modern, a radical departure from traditional procedures. But by the 1910s, he was regarded in some circles as conservative because he continued to use diatonic melodies and tonal harmonies, even if in a novel, personal idiom. These traits helped to make his music popular in his own country, Britain, and the United States, but hurt his reputation on the Continent, and he stopped composing by the late 1920s. Moreover, while audiences and critics on the Continent welcomed his early works as representatives of a new nation in the classical repertoire, they resisted his

EXAMPLE 32.6 *Jean Sibelius, Symphony No. 4 in A Minor, thematic transformations*

a. First appearance

b. A middle stage

c. Final statement in definitive form

subsequent turn to a more universal style in his symphonies, showing that for composers on Europe's periphery a strong national identity could be as much of a trap as it was a blessing. Sibelius's search to reconcile his status as an outsider with the classical heritage, to blend nationalism with international appeal, and to balance innovative with traditional elements reveals many of the fault lines in twentieth-century music.

THE AVANT-GARDE

While modernist composers were devising ways to say something new within the classical tradition, the years before World War I also brought the first stirrings of a movement that directly challenged that tradition and would grow in importance over the course of the century: the ***avant-garde***. The French military used the term to describe an advance group that prepared the way for the main army. The term was then adopted in the mid-nineteenth century for and by French artists who saw themselves as a vanguard exploring new territory. Although sometimes applied to anyone who departs from convention, or to modernists such as Schoenberg (see Chapter 33), the term is most helpful when used more narrowly for art that is iconoclastic, irreverent, antagonistic, and nihilistic—for art that seeks to overthrow accepted aesthetics and start fresh. Rather than attempt to write music suited for the classical repertoire, avant-garde composers have challenged the very concept of deathless classics, asking their listeners to focus instead on what is happening in the present. Their movement is marked not by shared elements of style but by shared attitudes, particularly an unrelenting opposition to the status quo.

ERIK SATIE One side of the avant-garde is exemplified by the music of Erik Satie (1866–1925), which wittily upends conventional ideas. Satie was a French nationalist in a similar vein to Debussy and Ravel, but made a more radical break from the entire classical tradition. His set of three *Gymnopédies* (1888) for piano, for example, challenged the Romantic notions of expressivity and individuality. Instead of offering variety, as expected in a set of pieces, they are all ostentatiously plain and unemotional, using the same slow tempo, the same accompanimental pattern, virtually the same melodic rhythm, and similar modal harmonies and puzzling dynamics. Satie's use of modal and unresolved chords opened new possibilities for Debussy and Ravel, who turned them to different uses but did not follow his avant-garde tendencies.

Piano works   Between 1900 and 1915, Satie wrote several sets of piano pieces with surrealistic titles like *Three Pieces in the Form of a Pear* (1903, which actually has seven pieces) and *Automatic Descriptions* (1913). Most had running commentary and tongue-in-cheek directions to the player, such as "withdraw your hand and put it in your pocket," "that's wonderful!," or "heavy as a sow." These satirized the titles and expressive directions of Debussy, Scriabin, and other composers of descriptive and programmatic music. Moreover, by printing the commentary on the music rather than in a program, so that only the player was aware of it, Satie critiqued the idea of concert music and reclaimed the fading tradition of music for the player's own enjoyment. But the comic and critical spirit resides also in the music itself—spare, dry, capricious, brief, repetitive, parodistic, and witty in the highest degree. The classical masterworks are a particular target: the second of the three *Embryons desséchés* (Dried Embryos, 1913) includes a mocking "quotation from the celebrated mazurka of Schubert" (actually Chopin's funeral march), marked "they all begin to cry," and the third (NAWM 179) satirizes Wagnerian leitmotives and ends with a long "obligatory cadenza (by the composer)" that pounds on the tonic repeatedly, a jibe at the similar passages that close several Beethoven symphonies. Clearly Satie was not out to create masterpieces that would take their place in the great tradition; rather, he was challenging the very foundations of that tradition.

Larger works   In his larger pieces, Satie sought to create music that would fix our attention on the present. His "realistic ballet" *Parade* (1916–17), with a scenario by the writer Jean Cocteau, choreography by Léonide Massine, and scenery and costumes by Picasso, introduced cubism to the stage, as illustrated in Figure 32.11. The ballet satirizes the aspirations of high art forced to compete with popular entertainment: trying to draw an audience into their theater, managers use circus performers to attract a crowd, but the spectators are so entranced with the circus acts they refuse to go inside to see the show. In the cubist spirit of including fragments of everyday life, Satie's score drew on the sounds of the music hall and cabaret, recast through mangled syntax and overlapping rhythms into a kind of musical nonsense, and incorporated ragtime, jazz elements, a whistle, a siren, and a typewriter. *Parade* caused a scandal, as did Satie's later ballet with film, *Relâche* (No Show Tonight, 1924). His "symphonic drama" *Socrate* (1920), for soloists and chamber orchestra on texts from Plato, attains in its last scene, on the death of Socrates, a poignancy that is intensified by the stylistic monotony and the studied avoidance of a direct emotional appeal. Satie composed his *Musique d'ameublement*

(Furniture Music, 1920) to be played during the intermissions of a play, intending it as background music that should *not* be listened to.

Each work by Satie questioned the listener's expectations, no two pieces were alike, and whenever he gained followers, he abandoned them by doing something radically different. His biting, anti-sentimental spirit, economical textures, and severe harmony and melody influenced the music of his younger compatriots Darius Milhaud and Francis Poulenc, among others, and he was a significant inspiration for the American avant-garde, notably John Cage.

FUTURISM   Although Satie questioned traditional assumptions about expressivity, individuality, seriousness, masterworks, and the very purpose of music, he used traditional instruments and musical pitches. The Italian ***futurists*** rejected even those. In *The Art of Noises: A Futurist Manifesto* (1913; see Source Reading, p. 802), the futurist painter Luigi Russolo argued in dead earnest that musical sounds had become stale and that the modern world of machines required a new kind of music based on noise. He divided noises into six families, then he and his colleagues built new instruments called *intonarumori* (noise-makers), each capable of producing a particular kind of noise over a range of at least an octave and a half. They composed pieces for these instruments, alone or with traditional instruments, and presented them in concert between 1913 and 1921 in Italy, London, and Paris.

In opposition to the constant recycling of classics in the concert halls, futurist music was impermanent, perhaps deliberately so; only one fragment of Russolo's music survives in a recording by Russolo's brother, and the instruments were destroyed during World War II. But the movement continued in various forms in Italy, France, and Russia during the 1920s and 1930s, and it anticipated or stimulated many later developments, including electronic music, microtonal composition, and the pursuit of new instrumental timbres.

As different as futurist music was from Satie's, they shared a focus on the experience of listening in the present moment and an iconoclastic rejection of the music and aesthetics of the past, both attributes that remained central to avant-garde music throughout the twentieth century.

FIGURE 32.11 *Costume for the Paris Manager in the first production of Satie's ballet* Parade *(1917). The sets and costumes for this ballet, designed by Pablo Picasso, brought his cubist style to the stage.*

LATE ROMANTIC OR MODERN?

The music of early-twentieth-century composers in the classical tradition was remarkably diverse, and its reception has been equally varied.

These composers' position between the lions of late Romanticism, discussed in Chapters 28–30, and the more radical composers discussed in the next chapter can make their music hard to classify. The first edition of this book in 1960 treated Debussy as a late-Romantic figure, but by the 1973 second edition he was regarded as a seminal force for modern music. All the composers of this generation have aspects of both eras, combining nineteenth-century training and traits with twentieth-century sensibilities.

The Art of Noises

Futurism began in 1909 as a literary and artistic move-ment in Italy celebrating the dynamism, speed, ma-chines, and violence of the twentieth century. Luigi Russolo (1885–1947) was a futurist painter who turned his attention to music in 1913. In *The Art of Noises: A Fu-turist Manifesto*, Russolo laid out his argument for music based on noise rather than musical pitches.

❀

The art of music at first sought and achieved pu-rity and sweetness of sound; later, it blended di-verse sounds, but always with intent to caress the ear with suave harmonics. Today, growing ever more complicated, it seeks those combinations of sounds that fall most dissonantly, strangely, and harshly upon the ear. We thus approach nearer and nearer to the *music of noise*.

This musical evolution parallels the growing multiplicity of machines, which everywhere are assisting mankind. Not only amid the clamor of great cities but even in the countryside, which until yesterday was ordinarily quiet, the machine today has created so many varieties and combinations of noise that pure musical sound—with its poverty and monotony—no longer awakens any emotion in the hearer. . . .

We must break out of this narrow circle of pure musical sounds, and conquer the infinite variety of noise-sounds.

Everyone will recognize that every musical sound carries with it an incrustation of familiar and stale sense associations, which predispose the

hearer to boredom, despite all the efforts of in-novating musicians. We futurists have all deep-ly loved the music of the great composers. Beethoven and Wagner for many years wrung our hearts. But now we are satiated with them and derive much greater pleasure from ideally com-bining the noises of street-cars, internal-combus-tion engines, automobiles, and busy crowds than from re-hearing, for example, the "Eroica" or the "Pastorale." . . .

Every manifestation of life is accompanied by noise. Noise is therefore familiar to our ears and has the power to remind us immediately of life itself. Musical sound, a thing extraneous to life and independent of it, an occasional and unne-cessary adjunct, has become for our ears what a too familiar face is to our eyes. Noise, on the other hand, which comes to us confused and ir-regular as life itself, never reveals itself wholly but reserves for us innumerable surprises. We are convinced, therefore, that by selecting, co-ordinating, and controlling noises we shall enrich mankind with a new and unsuspected source of pleasure. Despite the fact that it is characteristic of sound to remind us brutally of life, the Art of Noises must not limit itself to reproductive imi-tation. It will reach its greatest emotional power through the purely acoustic enjoyment which the inspiration of the artist will contrive to evoke from combinations of noises.

Translated by Stephen Somervell in Nicolas Slonimsky, *Music Since 1900*, 4th ed. (New York: Charles Scribner's Sons, 1971), 1299–1301. In SR 177 (7:8), 1330–32.

Perhaps that is why so much of this music—especially that of Mahler, Strauss, Debussy, Ravel, Vaughan Williams, Holst, Rachmaninoff, and Sibelius—has proven extremely popular with listeners.

Critical disputes about what is most valuable in music have been especially acute in the twentieth century, and as a result, critical esteem for these com-posers has changed over time, often dramatically. For example, Mahler during his lifetime was known outside Vienna mostly as a conductor. In the last years of his life and the decades after his death, the advocacy of conductors such as

Bruno Walter and Willem Mengelberg began to establish his reputation as a composer, and Austria promoted him as a native son, until the ban on performance of music by Jewish composers during the Nazi regime in Germany and Austria cut the boomlet short. After World War II, the long-playing record made his long symphonies more accessible, performances and recordings by Leonard Bernstein and others around the time of Mahler's centenary in 1960 brought his music to a wider audience, and soon his symphonies and orchestral songs were firmly established in the international repertoire. Similar efforts after World War II raised Janáček from local to international fame. Meanwhile, when critics and scholars increasingly came to view tonality as old-fashioned, the reputations of Strauss and Sibelius declined, only to be rescued later in the twentieth century when their innovations became better understood and when increasing numbers of living composers turned back to the sounds and methods of tonal music. While some music by composers of this generation may sound late Romantic in spirit or technique, what makes all of it modernist is this overwhelming sense of measuring oneself against the past.

Further Reading is available at digital.wwnorton.com/hwm10

RADICAL MODERNISTS

The first wave of modernist composers discussed in the previous chapter secured an enduring place in the classical repertoire by combining elements from the classical tradition with something new to create an individual, distinctive, and original body of music. In the years just before and after World War I, a younger group of modernist composers carried out a more radical break from the musical language of the past than their predecessors had, while maintaining strong links to the same traditions. These composers reassessed inherited conventions as profoundly as the modernists in art who pioneered expressionism, cubism, and abstract art. Rather than please viewers or listeners on first sight or first hearing, an attribute that had always been considered essential in both art and music, modernists of their generation sought to challenge our perceptions and capacities, providing an experience that would be impossible through traditional means. They offered an implicit critique of mass culture and easily digested art, and their writings often make that critique explicit. These composers saw no contradiction in claiming the masters of the past as models. In fact, they saw their own work as continuing what the pathbreaking classical composers had started, not as overthrowing that tradition, and their music is often most radical in the ways they interpret and remake the past.

Rather than taking up the topics in this chapter one by one, we will introduce them in the context of discussing six modernist composers who are among the best known and most influential of the entire century. Arnold Schoenberg and Igor Stravinsky were leaders of two branches of modernism that often seemed to be at opposite poles but that faced common concerns. Schoenberg's students Alban Berg and Anton Webern took their teacher's ideas in individual directions. Béla Bartók and Charles Ives both developed unique combinations of nationalism and modernism within the classical tradition. Born between 1874 and 1885, all six began by writing tonal music in late Romantic styles, then devised new and distinctive post-tonal idioms that won them a central place in the world of modern music.

ARNOLD SCHOENBERG

Arnold Schoenberg (1874–1951; see biography and Figure 33.1) was committed to continuing the German classical tradition, and for that very reason he felt compelled to move beyond tonality to *atonality*—a term for music that avoids establishing a tonal center—and then to the *twelve-tone method*, a form of atonality based on systematic orderings of the twelve notes of the chromatic scale. His innovations made him famous in some quarters and—because the resulting music was both dissonant and difficult to follow—notorious in others.

TONAL WORKS Like other modernists of his generation, Schoenberg began by writing tonal music in late Romantic style. The chromatic idiom of his first important work, a tone poem for string sextet titled *Verklärte Nacht* (Transfigured Night, Op. 4, 1899), grew from that of Wagner's *Tristan und Isolde,* while the symphonic poem *Pelleas und Melisande*, Op. 5 (1902–3) draws on Gustav Mahler and Richard Strauss. The huge cantata *Gurrelieder* (Songs of Gurre, 1900–1, orchestration completed 1911) outdoes Wagner in emotional fervor, and Mahler and Strauss in the complexity of its scoring.

Schoenberg soon turned away from late Romantic gigantism and toward chamber music, merging the Brahmsian side of German music with the Wagnerian. Central to his thinking was the principle he called ***developing variation***, a process of continuously building on germinal ideas so that each new idea is derived from what has come before. As he wrote in one essay, developing variation "means that variation of the features of a basic unit produces all the thematic formulations which provide for fluency, contrasts, variety, logic, and unity, on the one hand, and character, mood, expression, and every needed differentiation, on the other hand—thus elaborating the *idea* of the piece." He found precedents for this method in the music of composers from Mozart to Brahms (see Chapter 29), arguing in a famous essay that Brahms was a progressive composer, not a conservative. Schoenberg applied developing variation in his own works, such as the String Quartet No. 1 in D Minor, Op. 7 (1904–5). In the quartet all the themes and most subsidiary voices evolve from a few germinal motives through variation and combination. The form of the one-movement work, combining an enlarged sonata form with the four standard movements of a quartet, owes much to Liszt's Piano Sonata in B Minor, demonstrating Schoenberg's willingness to blend influences in order to create something new.

The principle of developing variation

The quartet exemplifies Schoenberg's intertwined goals for his music: to continue the tradition and to say something that had never been said before (see Source Reading, p. 807). He believed that the great composers of the past had all contributed something new and therefore of permanent significance, while preserving and extending what was of highest value in the music of their predecessors. He sought to do likewise, hoping to achieve similar immortality. In essence, his entire career was a process of developing variation on the ideas and procedures he found in the Austro-German tradition of classical music from Bach to Mahler and Strauss. He asked of each work that it not simply repeat but build on the past. Remarkably, he required the same *within* each piece: except for marked repeats in binary forms, nothing should repeat exactly. As he wrote, "With me, variation almost completely takes the place of

The principle of nonrepetition

ARNOLD SCHOENBERG
(1874–1951)

Schoenberg was one of the most influential compos-ers of the twentieth century, best known for his atonal and twelve-tone music.

Schoenberg was born in Vienna, the son of a Jew-ish couple who had a shoe shop. He began violin les-sons at age eight, then taught himself to compose by imitating the music he played. When his father died in 1891, Schoenberg had to leave school and work as a bank clerk. His instruction in theory and composition was minimal, although the composer Alexander von Zemlinsky served for a time as a sounding board and teacher.

Schoenberg married Zemlinsky's sister Mathilde in 1901, and they moved to Berlin, where he worked at a cabaret until Richard Strauss got him a job teach-ing composition at the Stern Conservatory. Two years later he returned to Vienna and taught privately, at-tracting his two most famous students, Alban Berg and Anton Webern. He had the support of Mahler and other progressive musicians, but his works met stormy receptions, especially after he adopted ato-nality in 1908. He took up painting in an expressionist style—see Figures 33.1 and 33.3 and Music in Context, pp. 810–11—and developed friendships with several expressionist painters (one of whom had an affair with Mathilde, who briefly left him before returning for the sake of their two children).

After World War I, Schoenberg founded and di-rected the Society for Private Musical Performances in Vienna, which between 1919 and 1921 gave about 350 performances of music by himself and his stu-dents and colleagues. After a creative impasse, he formulated the twelve-tone method used in the Piano Suite (1921–23) and most of his later works.

Mathilde died in 1923, and a year later Schoen-berg married Gertrud Kolisch, with whom he had

FIGURE 33.1 *A self-portrait by Arnold Schoenberg from around 1910, showing his interest in expressionism in painting, which paralleled his interest in expressionism in music.*

three more children and moved back to Berlin. But in 1933 the Nazis came to power and announced their intention to remove all Jewish instructors from faculty appointments. Although he had become a Lutheran when he was twenty-four to avoid anti-Semitism, he converted back to Judaism after moving with his fam-ily to France. He then traveled on to the United States, finally arriving in Los Angeles in 1934. He was appoint-ed to a professorship at UCLA and retired in 1944 at age seventy. He died in Los Angeles in 1951 on July 13, having always feared the number 13.

MAJOR WORKS 4 operas: *Erwartung, Die glückliche Hand, Von heute auf morgen,* and *Moses und Aron; Pierrot lunaire, Gurrelieder,* and numerous songs and choral works; 2 chamber symphonies, Five Orchestral Pieces, Variations for Orchestra, and other orches-tral works; 5 string quartets, *Verklärte Nacht,* Wind Quintet, and other chamber works; Piano Suite and several sets of piano pieces

repetition." This principle of *nonrepetition* between and within pieces helps explain how Schoenberg's music would evolve.

ATONAL MUSIC In 1908, Schoenberg began to compose pieces that avoided establishing any note as a tonal center. Others called such music ***atonal***,

New Music and Tradition

Arnold Schoenberg saw no contradiction between tradition and innovation. For him, the tradition of classical music was a legacy of innovation, and it was his job as a composer to weave threads from the past and the present into something truly new. He returned to this theme constantly in his writings.

✣

In higher art, only that is worth being presented which has never before been presented. There is no great work of art which does not convey a new message to humanity; there is no great artist who fails in this respect. This is the code of honor of all the great in art, and consequently in all great works of the great we will find that newness which never perishes, whether it be of Josquin des Prés, of Bach or Haydn, or of any other great master.

Because: Art means New Art.

✣

My teachers were primarily Bach and Mozart, and secondarily Beethoven, Brahms, and Wagner. . . .

I also learned much from Schubert and Mahler, Strauss and Reger too. I shut myself off from no one, and so I could say of myself:

My originality comes from this: I immediately imitated everything I saw that was good, even when I had not first seen it in someone else's work.

And I may say: often enough I saw it first in myself. For if I saw something I did not leave it at that; I acquired it, in order to possess it; I worked on it and extended it, and it led me to something new.

I am convinced that eventually people will recognize how immediately this "something new" is linked to the loftiest models that have been granted us. I venture to credit myself with having written truly new music which, being based on tradition, is destined to become tradition.

From "New Music, Outmoded Music, Style and Idea" and "National Music (2)," in *Style and Idea: Selected Writings of Arnold Schoenberg,* ed. Leonard Stein, trans. Leo Black (London: Faber & Faber, 1975), 114–15 and 173–74.

although Schoenberg disliked the term. He felt compelled to abandon tonality in part because the heightened chromaticism, distant modulations, and prolonged dissonances of late-nineteenth-century music had weakened the pull of the tonic, making its declaration at the end of a piece seem increasingly arbitrary. Schoenberg emulated Richard Strauss and others in devising novel progressions and avoiding conventional cadences, as the principle of nonrepetition demanded, but it became harder and harder to find new ways to arrive at the tonic convincingly. Moreover, in music with complex chromatic chords, we cannot easily determine which notes are the dissonant ones that have to resolve. The ambiguities led Schoenberg to what he called "the emancipation of the dissonance"—freeing dissonance from its need to resolve to consonance, so that any combination of tones could serve as a stable chord that did not require resolution. Once this idea was accepted, he believed that atonality was inevitable.

Without a tonal backbone, how was music to be organized? Schoenberg relied on three principles: developing variation, the integration of harmony and melody, and chromatic saturation. All had been used in tonal music, but now he drew on them more fully to provide structure. In addition, he often used gestures from tonal music, forging links to tradition and making his music easier to follow.

Coherence in atonal music

Saget mir

One of Schoenberg's first entirely atonal pieces, dating from March 1908, will illustrate: *Saget mir, auf welchem Pfade* (Tell me on which path), the fifth song from a cycle of fifteen on poems from *The Book of the Hanging Gardens* by symbolist poet Stefan George (Op. 15, 1908–9). The sense of floating in tonal space created by music that does not gravitate to a tonic is perfectly suited to the vague eroticism of the poetry, which expresses, through outward symbols, the inner feelings of a love affair.

Traditional features

Example 33.1 shows the first two phrases. Much about the music is familiar from earlier German Lieder, including the texture of voice with piano, the rise and fall of the vocal melody, the division into phrases, the use of dynamics to shape each phrase, and the descending gestures to mark the ends of phrases. As in nineteenth-century Lieder, most notes in the voice are also present in the accompaniment, either in the piano's topmost melody (as at the beginning of measures 1 and 2) or in the harmony (like the B and C♯ in measure 1, supported by the B and D♭ in the chord below them).

Developing variation

Developing variation is apparent in both voice and accompaniment. The opening vocal motive of a descending semitone changes in measure 2 to a falling whole tone, is inverted in measure 3 as a rising major seventh, and reappears in measure 4 as a descending semitone, though in a new rhythm. Similar development of a semitone motive can be traced in the piano. Meanwhile, the chords in measure 1 are varied in measure 2, and elements from them—such as the combination of a tritone with a perfect fourth or major third—are echoed in measures 3 and 4. Everything that follows is derived in some way from these opening measures. A variant of measures 3–4 closes the piece, providing a traditional sense of return and closure despite the lack of a key.

Pitch-class sets

Schoenberg integrated melody and harmony through a process he called "composing with the tones of a motive," a kind of developing variation in which he manipulated the notes and intervals of a motive to create chords and new melodies. One way this worked was to treat the notes of a motive containing three or more pitches just as we might a triad or other tonal chord: as a collection of pitches that could be transposed, inverted, and arranged in any order and register to generate melodies and harmonies. Theorists later termed such a collection a **set** or, more formally, **pitch-class set**, using **pitch-class** to mean one of the twelve notes of the chromatic scale and its enharmonic equivalents in any octave. A convenient way to label sets is to arrange the notes in the most compact array from lowest to highest and number each pitch-class by the number of semitones above the first one. In this song, the first three notes in the vocal line form the set 016 (counting F as 0, F♯ as 1 semitone higher, and B as 6 semitones higher). In the example, this and all later occurrences of this set are enclosed in red boxes. The first chord in the piano also contains this set, transposed (to F♯, G, and C) and arranged as a perfect fourth and tritone within a major seventh. The set reappears, often transposed or inverted, in several later chords and melodically in the bass. For example, an inverted form (F, E, B) appears as the top three notes of the chord on the downbeat of measure 2, followed by bass motion drawn from a transposed form (B, C, F) and an inverted form (A♭, G, D), each presenting the intervals in a different order. Other sets are used in similar fashion. Using a limited number of sets gives the music a consistent sound,

EXAMPLE 33.1 *Arnold Schoenberg,* Saget mir, auf welchem Pfade, *No. 5 from* The Book of the Hanging Gardens, *Op. 15*

Red boxes indicate set 016 as melody or harmony.

Tell me, on which path she stepped along today,

while changing the order of intervals within each set provides variety, creating the combination of unity and contrast that is the hallmark of developing variation. Schoenberg tended to use sets that formed strong dissonances, because those sets are most distinctive and therefore easier to follow as the music unfolds. This integration of melody and harmony hearkens back to music of earlier eras.

Atonal music can also be shaped through **chromatic saturation**, the appearance of all twelve pitch-classes within a segment of music. We saw this method at work in Example 29.6, a song by Hugo Wolf that is highly chromatic but still tonal, where all twelve chromatic notes are stated in the first phrase and again in the next two measures. The appearance of a note that has not recently been sounded can give a sense of moving forward harmonically. As a corollary, once the twelfth chromatic note has appeared, there can be a sense of fullness and completion, which Wolf in a tonal context and Schoenberg in an atonal context used to reinforce the feeling of completing a phrase. In Example 33.1, all twelve notes occur in the first two-measure phrase, the last two (D and A♯) stated in the piano chord on the second beat of measure 2. Simultaneously, the other notes in that sonority (C and F♯ in the piano and E in the voice) initiate another round of all twelve, completed at the end of the next phrase with the arrival of A and A♭ in the piano. The coordination of chromatic saturation with phrasing is not always this exact; sometimes one or more notes are saved for the next phrase, helping to create longer spans.

Chromatic saturation

Through these means, Schoenberg sought to write atonal music that was as logical as tonal music. In 1909, he completed *The Book of the Hanging Gardens*; Three Piano Pieces, Op. 11; Five Orchestral Pieces, Op. 16; and *Erwartung* (Expectation), Op. 17, a monodrama (one-character opera) for soprano. In the works with orchestra, he followed Mahler in treating instruments soloistically and in swiftly alternating timbres to produce a great variety of colors. *Erwartung*, the height of **expressionism** in music, uses exaggerated gestures, angular melodies, and unrelenting dissonance to convey the tortured emotions of the protagonist (see Music in Context: Expressionism).

Atonal works

MUSIC IN CONTEXT

Expressionism

In the early twentieth century, several groups of German and Austrian painters embraced an international movement called *expressionism,* which also extended to literature, music, dance, theater, and architecture. Expressionism developed from the subjectivity of Romanticism but differed from it in the introspective experience it aimed to portray and how it chose to portray it.

Expressionist painters such as Ernst Ludwig Kirchner, Oskar Kokoschka, and Egon Schiele rejected traditional Western aesthetic values by representing real objects or people in grossly distorted ways, characterized by an intensely expressive use of pure colors and dynamic brushstrokes as in Kokoschka's poster for his own expressionist play *Mörder, Hoffnung der Frauen* (Murderer, Hope of Women, 1909) in Figure 33.2. These artists and others drew on contemporary themes involving the dark side of city life, in which people lived under extreme psychological pressure, as well as bright scenes from the circus and music halls that masked a more gloomy reality. They aspired to represent inner experience, to explore the hidden world of the psyche and to render visible the stressful emotional life of the modern person—isolated; helpless in the grip of poorly understood forces; prey to inner conflict, tension, anxiety, and

FIGURE 33.2 *Oskar Kokoschka, poster for* Mörder, Hoffnung der Frauen *(Murderer, Hope of Women), from 1909, the same year as Schoenberg's* Erwartung.

In this opera, Schoenberg pushed nonrepetition to an extreme: the work is not only atonal, it has no themes or motives that return and lacks any reference to traditional forms. The fluid, constantly changing music suits the nightmare-like text.

Turn back to tradition   Composers can go only so far in avoiding repetition: Schoenberg could not write another piece like *Erwartung* without repeating himself. Instead, he turned back to tradition, using motives, themes, and long-range repetition and evoking traditional forms and the functions of tonality in new ways.

Pierrot lunaire   Early stages of this return can be seen in *Pierrot lunaire*, Op. 21 (Moonstruck Pierrot, 1912), a cycle of twenty-one songs drawn from a larger poetic cycle by the Belgian symbolist poet Albert Giraud. Schoenberg scored the text, translated into German, for a woman's voice with a chamber ensemble of five performers who play nine different instruments. In keeping with the principle of nonrepetition, each movement features a different combination

fear; and tormented by elemental, irrational drives, including an eroticism that often had morbid overtones. That is also how the Viennese doctor Sigmund Freud, founder of psychoanalysis, described the deepest level of memory and emotional activity in his *Interpretation of Dreams* (1900). In short, expressionism sought to capture the human condition as it was perceived in the early twentieth century.

Arnold Schoenberg and his pupil Alban Berg were two leading exponents of expressionism in music, which paralleled expressionist art by adopting a similarly desperate and revolutionary style. Its characteristics are evident in Schoenberg's *Erwartung* (1909), an opera in which a lone protagonist—emblematic of the artist's alienation from society and its conventions—gives voice to what the composer described as a dream of *Angst*, an overwhelming feeling of dread or anxiety. Its distorted melodies, fragmented rhythms, violently graphic musical images, and dissonant harmonies create the quasi-hysterical atmosphere typical of the style. In none of Schoenberg's expressionist pieces, nor in Berg's opera *Wozzeck*, did these composers try to create music that is pretty or naturalistic (as the impressionists did); rather, they deployed the most direct—even drastic—means, no matter how unappealing, to convey extreme and irrational states of mind.

Schoenberg was also an amateur painter

FIGURE 33.3 *Arnold Schoenberg*, The Red Stare *(1910)*.

and took lessons from Richard Gerstl, a young exponent of expressionism in Vienna, who in 1908 had an affair with Schoenberg's wife Mathilde and committed suicide after she returned to Schoenberg. Schoenberg's most impressive pictures, a series of "gazes" in the form of faces, including Figure 33.3, not only emphasize the act of looking but also suggest the same feelings of claustrophobia and *Angst* as those portrayed in *Erwartung*.

of instruments. The voice declaims the text in **Sprechstimme** ("speaking voice"), approximating the written pitches in the gliding tones of speech, while following the notated rhythm exactly—an innovative idea that blends the traditional notions of song and melodrama. The inexact pitches evoke an eerie atmosphere for the symbolist text, in which the clown Pierrot suffers gruesome visions provoked by a moonbeam that takes many shapes.

Expressionist features of the work aside, Schoenberg highlights many traditional elements. Each thirteen-line poem has two refrain lines in the pattern ABcd efAB ghijA, and Schoenberg typically sets the repeated lines with a variant of their original music at the same pitch level, creating a sense of departure and return as in tonal music. We find varied repetition at all levels, from motives and chords to themes, sections, and one entire song: No. 7 is recast as an instrumental epilogue at the end of No. 13, *Enthauptung* (Beheading; NAWM 180b). The cycle includes several traditional forms and genres, including a waltz, a serenade, a barcarolle, and an aria over a walking bass, reminiscent of Bach. Schoenberg called No. 8, *Nacht* (Night; NAWM 180a), a passacaglia, but it is an unusual one because the unifying motive—a rising minor third followed by a descending major third—reappears in various note values in all parts, often treated in canon. The constant repetition of this motive, whose contour in original and inverted forms resembles wings, fittingly illustrates Pierrot's obsession with the giant moths that enclose him in a frightening trap and shut out the sun. Even *Enthauptung,* which appears to abandon thematic development for anarchic improvisation, unfolds by constantly varying the initial ideas to capture the images and feelings in the text.

TWELVE-TONE METHOD Schoenberg still faced a problem: with his atonal methods, he could not match the formal coherence of tonal music and had to rely on a text to sustain pieces of any length. He found the solution in the ***twelve-tone method***.

Row forms and usage   He formulated what he called his "method of composing with twelve tones that are related only to one another" (rather than to a tonic) in the early 1920s, after several years during which he published no music. The basis of a twelve-tone composition is a ***row*** or ***series*** consisting of the twelve pitch-classes of the chromatic scale arranged in an order chosen by the composer and producing a particular sequence of intervals. In composing a piece with a twelve-tone row, the tones of the series may be used both successively, as melody, and simultaneously, as harmony or counterpoint, in any octave and with any desired rhythm. The row may be used not only in its original, or ***prime***, form but also in ***inversion***, in ***retrograde*** order (backward), and in ***retrograde inversion***, and may appear in any of the twelve possible transpositions of any of the four forms. The twelve-note series is often broken into segments of three, four, or six notes, which are then used as sets to create melodic motives and chords. As a rule, the composer states all twelve pitches of the series before going on to use the series in any of its forms again (unless two or more statements occur simultaneously).

Sets, saturation,   Stated this way, the method may sound arbitrary. But for Schoenberg, it
and structure   was a systematic way to accomplish what he was already doing in his atonal music: integrating harmony and melody by composing with a limited number of sets (here, those defined by segments of the row), marking off phrases and subphrases with chromatic saturation (regulated by the appearance of all twelve notes in each statement of the row), and relying on developing variation. Moreover, Schoenberg re-created by analogy what he called "the structural functions of tonality," using the transposition of his rows as an analogue to modulation in tonal music. After focusing on vocal works in his atonal period, he turned to traditional instrumental forms, as if to demonstrate the power of his method to reconstitute tonal forms in a new musical language. Among these works, composed between 1921 and 1949, are the Piano Suite, Op. 25, modeled on the keyboard suites of Bach; Variations for Orchestra, Op. 31; Third and Fourth String Quartets, Opp. 30 and 37; Violin Concerto, Op. 36; and Piano Concerto, Op. 42. In these pieces, motives and themes are presented and developed, using the tonal forms and genres of Classic and Romantic music, but twelve-tone rows stand in for the keys.

The Piano Suite (excerpts in NAWM 181) illustrates some of Schoenberg's *Piano Suite* methods. Throughout the work, the row appears in only eight forms, shown in Example 33.2a: the untransposed prime form (P–0); the prime transposed up six semitones (P–6); the inversion in the same two transpositions (I–0 and I–6); and their retrogrades (R–0, R–6, RI–0, and RI–6). Schoenberg designed the row so that each of these begins on either E or B♭ and ends on the other, and all the prime forms and inversions have G and D♭ as the second pair of notes (see orange box in Example 33.2a). The recurrence of E, B♭, G, and D♭ in the same places creates a consistency that Schoenberg saw as an analogue to staying in a single key throughout, the normal practice in a Baroque keyboard suite. He often emphasizes these notes by placing them at the beginning or end of phrases or by other means, making the consistency of pitch level more apparent than one might expect, given the regular appearance of all twelve notes, although it is still harder for a listener to hear than is the key in tonal music. The first four notes of R–0 give a nod to Schoenberg's model, J. S. Bach, by spelling his name: B♭-A-C-B♮ (B-A-C-H, in German nomenclature).

Example 33.2b shows the rows deployed at the beginning of the Prelude (NAWM 173a). P–0 is in the right hand as melody, divided into motives of four notes each (in red, orange, and green boxes respectively). Twelve-tone theorists call such groups of four consecutive notes from the row **tetrachords**, using the ancient Greek term in a new sense (see Chapter 1). In the left hand as accompaniment we find P–6, using the same division into tetrachords and presenting the last two simultaneously. Each tetrachord is a different type of set, containing different intervals, so in featuring them Schoenberg continued his earlier practice of composing with sets. There is an intervallic canon between the two hands, recalling Bach's contrapuntal practice. At the end of measure 3, I–6 begins, presenting all three tetrachords simultaneously, each in its own rhythm. The last two notes of its first tetrachord overlap the statement of R–6 in measure 5, which also presents the tetrachords simultaneously. Here the left-hand texture is less contrapuntal and more like accompanimental chords.

In the Minuet (NAWM 181b), shown in Example 33.2c, P–0 in the first two measures is answered by I–6 in the second two. Again both are divided into tetrachords, with the first tetrachord accompanying the others. But Schoenberg starts the melody before the accompaniment, so that the first note of the row does not appear first, and he sometimes reorders the notes within the tetrachords. Thus he was still composing with motives and sets, as in his atonal music. Again, the end of each two-measure phrase is coordinated with the end of a row, so that chromatic saturation is still helping to demarcate phrasing. Developing variation is clearly at work, since the second phrase varies the first and develops its dotted rhythmic motive. Also, there are many references to tonal music, including the meter of the dance, the foursquare phrasing, and the leading-tone melodic gestures at the end of each two-measure phrase. All the factors we saw in the atonal music are just as important here. These evocations of tonal music and the constant development of a small number of motives make it possible for listeners to follow the music without any awareness of the rows or the twelve-tone structure that holds it all together.

The Piano Suite stays in the same "key" throughout, but for a sonata form *Twelve-tone regions* or other Classic-era form Schoenberg had to find an analogue to modulation. *and modulation*

EXAMPLE 33.2 *Schoenberg, Piano Suite, Op. 25*

a. Row forms

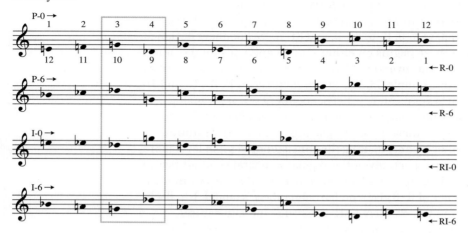

b. Prelude

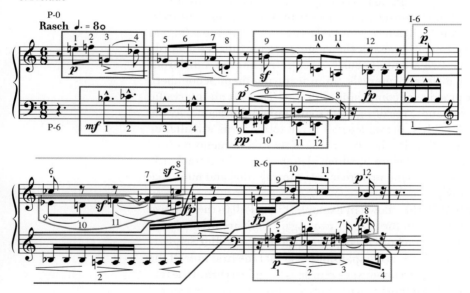

c. Minuet

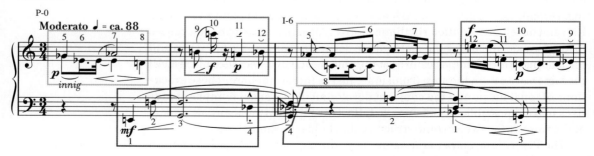

EXAMPLE 33.3 *Row forms used in Schoenberg's Fourth String Quartet, Op. 37*

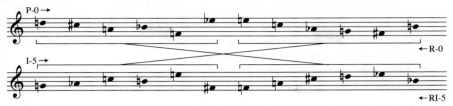

He created it in his Fourth String Quartet and many other works by devising a way to establish twelve-tone regions containing only one transposition of each row form. Example 33.3 shows the row for the quartet. Schoenberg designed it so that the last six notes—the second **hexachord**—constitute an inverted form of the first six notes, in a different order. As a result, there is one inversion of the row, I–5, whose first hexachord has the same notes as the second hexachord of P–0, and vice versa. If P–0 and I–5 are combined contrapuntally, by the time the first half of each has been stated, all twelve chromatic notes will have been heard exactly once. Rows that can combine with their inversion this way are called *combinatorial*. This special relationship prompted Schoenberg to treat each transposition of the prime form, its related inversion, and their retrogrades as a tonal region analogous to a key. In the first movement of the quartet, a sonata form, the P–0/I–5 region serves as "tonic"—the region in which the movement begins and ends, which occupies the largest number of measures, and which is used for the first theme in the exposition and at its final reprise in the coda. The region a fifth higher is used for the second theme in the exposition, serving as a sort of "dominant" region, and the other ten transpositions are used as contrasting "keys." Thus through his twelve-tone method, Schoenberg sought to re-create the forms of tonal music in an entirely new language.

LATE TONAL WORKS Twelve-tone music was not Schoenberg's only strategy for looking back at the tradition. Some of his works from the 1930s and 1940s are tonal, and in two works he "recomposed" eighteenth-century music, by Matthias Georg Monn and by Handel. These "arrangements" highlight the wide stylistic gulf between Schoenberg's modernism and the tonal tradition by juxtaposing them directly. In their own way, these works are as radical as the twelve-tone music.

SCHOENBERG AS MODERNIST We have discussed Schoenberg at much greater length than his place in the repertoire seems to warrant. Yet he merits the space, not only because his music is complex, takes time to understand, and influenced others enormously, but because the problems he chose to address as a modernist composer and the way he faced them did much to shape the course of musical practice in the twentieth century. His desire to match the achievements of his forebears pressed him both backward—to reclaim the genres, forms, procedures, and gestures of the past—and onward toward a new musical language. Ironically, although his music won him a central place in the modernist tradition, it also earned an enduring unpopularity with most listeners and a great many performers, who valued the familiar musical language and conventions that he felt compelled to abandon. The disconnection between audiences and connoisseurs in their evaluation of music, evident already in the reception of Beethoven's late string quartets, reached a new intensity with Schoenberg and many other modernists and became a principal theme of twentieth-century music.

The Second Viennese School   Schoenberg attracted many devoted students. The two most notable, Alban Berg and Anton Webern, were both natives of Vienna and are often grouped with Schoenberg as members of the Second Viennese School, drawing an implicit connection to the first Viennese threesome, Haydn, Mozart, and Beethoven.

ALBAN BERG

Alban Berg (1885–1935), shown in Figure 33.4, began studies with Schoenberg in 1904 at age nineteen. Although he adopted his teacher's atonal and twelve-tone methods, listeners found his music more approachable. He achieved much greater popular success than his teacher, especially with his opera *Wozzeck,* premiered in 1925. His secret lay in infusing his post-tonal idiom not only with the forms and procedures of tonal music, as Schoenberg had done, but also with its expressive gestures, characteristic styles, and other elements that quickly conveyed meanings and feelings to his hearers. In this respect he was a direct heir of Gustav Mahler and Richard Strauss.

Wozzeck is the outstanding example of expressionist opera. The libretto, arranged by Berg from a fragmentary play by Georg Büchner (1813–1837), presents the soldier Wozzeck as a hapless victim of his environment, despised by his fellow men, forced by poverty to submit to a doctor's experiments, betrayed in love, and driven finally to murder and madness. The music is atonal, not twelve-tone, and includes Sprechstimme in some scenes. Each of the three acts has continuous music, with the changing scenes (five in each act) linked by orchestral interludes.

Berg highlights the drama and organizes the music through the use of leitmotives, pitch-class sets identified with the main characters, and traditional forms that wryly comment on the characters and situation. Wozzeck's outburst in the first scene, "Wir arme Leut!" (We poor people!), shown in Example 33.4a, is one of his leitmotives and contains his characteristic set. The first act includes a Baroque suite, suggesting the formal manners of Wozzeck's captain; a rhapsody, suiting Wozzeck's fantastic visions; a march and lullaby for a scene with his common-law wife Marie and their child; a passacaglia for the doctor's constant prattling about his theory; and a rondo for Marie's seduction by a rival suitor, the Drum Major, who tries repeatedly—like the ever-returning theme of the rondo—until she gives in. The second act, the heart of the drama, is a symphony in five movements, including a sonata form, a fantasia and fugue, a ternary slow movement, a

FIGURE 33.4 *Alban Berg around 1910, in a portrait by Arnold Schoenberg.*

EXAMPLE 33.4 *Motives from Alban Berg's* Wozzeck

a. Wozzeck's leitmotive and characteristic set, from Act I, Scene 1

b. Tavern piano in Act III, Scene 3, with rhythmic pattern and Wozzeck's set

scherzo, and a rondo. The third act comprises six inventions, each on a single idea. The most traditional is the invention on a theme (seven variations and a fugue) in Scene 1, when Marie reads from the Bible and is consumed by guilt. In the rest of the act, the inventions are more unusual, on more specific or abstract ideas: a note, a rhythm, a chord, a key, and a duration. These inventions reflect Wozzeck's growing obsessions—or, in the last two, the response to the tragedy by those left behind—and they illustrate Berg's approach that combines atonal organization with allusions to tonality.

Act III, Scene 2

In Act III, Scene 2 (NAWM 182a), Marie and Wozzeck walk at dusk on a forest path by a pond. He asks her how long they have been together and how long it will last, and she grows anxious at his odd behavior. The vocal lines and accompaniment are atonal, angular, and dissonant, but are underpinned by the invention on a single note, B. It begins sounding low in the contrabasses as the curtain rises and is passed from instrument to instrument and from one octave to another throughout the scene, by turns sustained, trilled, repeated, embellished by its chromatic neighbors, tremoloed, and flutter-tongued. When the moon rises red, the B is sustained in all octaves, then hammered in the timpani over thirty times as Wozzeck shouts "If not me, Marie, then no other either!" and slits her throat with a knife. Her cry for help, on her highest B and lowest B, lends that note new significance. Yet despite the near constant presence of B, the music is not "in B" or tonal in any sense; rather, the B sounds throughout like a fixed idea, a perfect musical parallel to Wozzeck's fixation on revenge for Marie's infidelity.

Act III, Scene 3

In Scene 3 (NAWM 182b), Wozzeck is in a tavern drinking and singing, then dances briefly with Marie's friend Margret; she sits on his lap and sings a song, but when she spies blood on his hand, Wozzeck becomes agitated and rushes out. The scene begins with an onstage, out-of-tune tavern piano playing a wild polka, shown in Example 33.4b. The music is atonal—the notes in the first two measures comprise the set associated with Wozzeck—but it instantly conveys the impression of a popular dance tune, through triadic accompaniment under a melody that moves by step and by skip. Just as the singers on stage are acting their parts, so too the atonal music is acting the part of tonal music, and its meaning is immediately clear. The melody lays out the rhythmic theme for the scene, which is then obsessively reiterated at various levels of augmentation and diminution, so that it is almost always present. By constantly repeating the rhythm, Berg unifies the scene through developing variation and also reveals Wozzeck's preoccupation with his guilt, which he cannot escape. When Wozzeck sings a folk song and Margret a popular song with piano accompaniment, Berg imitates recognizable tonal styles in an atonal idiom. The almost constant references to tonality and to familiar styles and genres help to keep listeners engaged, while the atonality heightens the dramatic impact.

The rest of the act is just as sharply etched with musical effects appropriate to the plot. In Scene 4, Wozzeck returns to the pond to dispose of the knife, throws it in, then goes after it to throw it still farther, and drowns. The whole scene is an invention on a six-note chord, incessantly repeated and arpeggiated like Wozzeck's obsession with the knife, then rising and falling in parallel motion as Wozzeck drowns. The invention on a key is the last and longest interlude between scenes, when, as Berg put it, the composer steps in front of the curtain and comments on the tragedy we have witnessed. It sounds at times like a highly dissonant Mahler slow movement in D minor, especially at the beginning and end (indeed, Berg adapted those portions from a sonata movement in that key he had sketched around 1909). But not a single triad appears, and the interlude asserts its "key" through melodic or bass motions that simulate tonality rather than through functional harmonic progressions, in a masterly demonstration of Berg's ability to touch the hearts of his listeners with familiar gestures and sounds while speaking in an atonal language. The final scene, the invention on a duration, is heart-rending in its simplicity. A constantly flowing eighth-note pulse signals that life will go on despite the deaths of Marie and Wozzeck. As children sing ring-around-the-rosy and Marie's child rides his hobby horse, older children rush in and shout that his mother is dead. All run to see the body; the boy, not understanding, keeps playing and singing, notices he is alone, then runs after the others, leaving an empty stage.

Soon after *Wozzeck* was premiered, Berg adopted twelve-tone methods, turning them to his own ends. He often chose rows that allowed for tonal-sounding chords and chord progressions, connecting the new style with the past and investing his music with immediate emotional impact. His chief twelve-tone works are his *Lyric Suite* for string quartet (1925–26), his Violin Concerto (1935), and a second opera, *Lulu* (1928–35), whose orchestration was not quite complete when he died.

Berg designed the row of the Violin Concerto with four interlocking minor and major triads, marked with square brackets in Example 33.5a, which permits frequent references to tonal chords while using twelve-tone procedures. The piece includes evocations of a violin tuning its open strings (using notes 1, 3, 5, and 7 of the

EXAMPLE 33.5 *Row from Berg's Violin Concerto and Bach's* Es ist genug

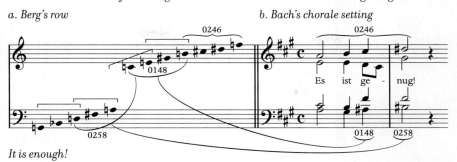

a. Berg's row   *b. Bach's chorale setting*

It is enough!

row), tonal chord progressions, Viennese waltzes, a folk song, and a Bach chorale. The last of these, *Es ist genug* (It is enough), which ends Bach's Cantata No. 60, alludes to the death of Manon Gropius, to whose memory the concerto is dedicated; she was the daughter of Berg's close friend Alma Mahler (widow of Gustav Mahler) and died at eighteen of polio. As shown in Example 33.5b, the chorale melody begins with three rising whole steps, like the last four notes of Berg's row, and Bach's harmonization highlights chords that can be derived from the row. Thus the quotation of the chorale is not something foreign, but stems directly from the row itself.

Berg's concerto can be understood on first hearing by anyone familiar with tonal music, yet its structure is wholly determined by twelve-tone procedures. Berg understood that because twelve-tone music was unfamiliar, it could be incomprehensible to the listener, yet it also had the capacity to imitate any style or emotional gesture, just as an actor may play any role. Thus his music accommodates innovation with the past, reworking the music's inner structure just as radically as in Schoenberg's music but keeping more of the familiar on the surface of the music.

ANTON WEBERN

Anton Webern (1883–1945), shown in Figure 33.5, began lessons with Schoenberg in 1904, at the same time as Berg. He was already studying musicology under Guido Adler at the University of Vienna, where he received a Ph.D. in 1906 and absorbed ideas about music history that influenced his own (and perhaps also Schoenberg's) development.

Webern believed that music involves the presentation of ideas that can be expressed in no other way; that it operates according to rules of order based on natural law rather than taste; that great art does what is necessary, not arbitrary; that evolution in art is also necessary; and that history, and thus musical idioms and practices, can move only forward, not backward. After Schoenberg had formulated, and Webern and Berg had adopted, the twelve-tone method, Webern argued in a series of lectures published posthumously as *The Path to the New Music* that twelve-tone music was the inevitable result of music's evolution because it combined the most advanced approaches to pitch (using all twelve chromatic notes), musical space (integrating the melodic and harmonic dimensions), and the presentation of musical ideas (combining Classic forms with polyphonic procedures and unity with variety, deriving

View of music history

FIGURE 33.5
Anton Webern in 1908,
in a portrait by Max
Oppenheimer.

every element from the thematic material). With his view of history, Webern regarded each step along the way from tonality to atonality to twelve-tone music as an act of discovery, not invention. This gave him—and Schoenberg—total confidence in their own work, despite the incomprehension and opposition they encountered from performers and listeners. Webern's concept of the composer as an artist expressing new ideas, yet also as a researcher making new discoveries, sprang from his training in musicology, and it became enormously influential in the middle to late twentieth century. The contrast to the servant-artisan composer of the fifteenth to eighteenth centuries, or the nineteenth-century composer working to satisfy the public taste, is huge—and very complimentary to composers.

Webern, like Schoenberg and Berg, passed through the stages of late Romantic chromaticism, atonality, and twelve-tone organization, the last beginning in 1925 with the three songs of Op. 17. His works, about equally divided between instrumental and vocal, are mostly for small chamber ensembles.

Webern was at heart a Romantic who sought to write deeply expressive music. Yet because he believed great art should do only what is necessary, his music is extremely concentrated. When writing his Six Bagatelles for String Quartet, Op. 9 (1911–13), he remarked that once he had incorporated all twelve notes, he often felt that the piece was finished. Another atonal work, No. 4 of his Five Pieces for Orchestra, Op. 10, runs to only six measures, and the last of his Three Little Pieces for Cello and Piano, Op. 11, to just twenty notes. Even larger works, like the Symphony, Op. 21 (1927–28), and the String Quartet, Op. 28 (1936–38), are only eight or nine minutes long, and his entire mature output takes less than four hours to play. Textures are stripped to the bare essentials; his music has sometimes been described as pointillistic, since it often features only one to three or four notes at once or in the same instrument in succession. The dynamics, specified down to the finest gradations, seldom rise above *forte*. Perhaps influenced by his musicological studies—for his dissertation he edited volume 2 of Henricus Isaac's *Choralis Constantinus,* which begins wiith Isaac's setting of *Puer natus est* (NAWM 40)—he often used techniques of Renaissance polyphony, including canons in inversion or retrograde. Unlike Berg, he avoided using sets or rows with tonal implications.

Symphony, Op. 21   The first movement of the Symphony, Op. 21 (NAWM 183), illustrates Webern's use of twelve-tone procedures, canons, instrumentation, and form. The entire movement is a double canon in inversion. Example 33.6 shows the beginning, with canon 1 in the top two staves and canon 2 in the bottom two staves. Instead of highlighting the canonic lines by setting each as a continuous melody in a distinctive timbre and range, Webern deliberately integrates them. Each line is filled with rests, changes timbre frequently, and weaves back and forth through the same three-octave range. The succession of timbres is as much part of the melody as are the pitches and rhythms, and

EXAMPLE 33.6 *Double canon at the opening of Anton Webern's Symphony, Op. 21*

the changes of instrument in the leading voice of each canon are echoed in the following voice: for example, in canon 1, horn, clarinet, and cello in the leading voice are imitated by horn, bass clarinet, and viola, producing a similar series of timbres. Here Webern applies Schoenberg's concept of **Klangfarbenmelodie** (tone-color melody), in which changes of tone color are perceived as parallel to changing pitches in a melody.

The double canon is nestled within a reinterpretation of sonata form, showing Webern's integration of Classic formal principles with procedures from Renaissance polyphony. The exposition contains not two contrasting themes, but a contrast of character between canon 1 and canon 2. After the exposition repeats exactly, the development is a palindrome, and the recapitulation presents the same succession of rows as the exposition, but in new rhythms and registers. The development and recapitulation then repeat, as in an early Classic symphony (compare NAWM 118a). Thus through analogy, Webern recreates the tonal structure of a Classic symphonic first movement in twelve-tone terms. Like Schoenberg's twelve-tone analogies to tonal structure, Webern's is beyond the capacity of most listeners. What can be heard more readily is the exact repetition of each half of the movement; given the origins of twelve-tone music in the principles of nonrepetition and developing variation, such deliberate repetition makes a strong reference to the forms of the past.

Influence   Although Webern received little acclaim during his lifetime and his music has never gained wide popularity, recognition of his work among scholars and composers grew steadily after World War II. His systematic approach to composition, his focus on structure and unity, the distinctive sound of his music, and his unwillingness to compromise for the sake of popular appeal made his music seem pure, individual, and fresh at a time when many other styles were tainted by political associations. His music had an abiding influence on some composers in Germany, France, Italy, and the United States, especially in the first two decades after the war.

IGOR STRAVINSKY

While Schoenberg, Berg, and Webern worked inside the Austro-German tradition, Igor Stravinsky (1882–1971; see biography and Figure 33.6) started as a Russian nationalist and became a cosmopolitan—and arguably the most important composer of his time. He created an individual voice by developing several style traits, most derived from Russian traditions, into his distinctive trademarks: undermining meter through unpredictable accents and rests or through rapid changes of meter; frequent ostinatos; layering and juxtaposition of static blocks of sound; discontinuity and interruption; dissonance based on diatonic, octatonic, and other collections; and dry, anti-lyrical, but colorful use of instruments. He forged these traits during his "Russian" period (to about 1918) and used them again in his later periods. Through Stravinsky, elements of Russian music became part of a common international modernist practice.

RUSSIAN PERIOD Stravinsky wrote his most popular works early in his career: the ballets *The Firebird* (1910), *Petrushka* (1910–11), and *The Rite of Spring* (*Le sacre du printemps*, 1911–13), all commissioned by Sergei Diaghilev for the Ballets Russes in Paris.

The Firebird   *The Firebird,* based on Russian folk tales, stems from the Russian nationalist tradition and especially from the exoticism of Rimsky-Korsakov, Stravinsky's principal teacher. Throughout, humans are characterized by diatonic music, while supernatural creatures and places are cast in octatonic or chromatic realms, following Rimsky-Korsakov's standard practice. Some of the sounds, rhythms, harmonies, and orchestral effects also echo Ravel's *Rapsodie espagnole* (NAWM 173) from a couple of years earlier.

Petrushka   In *Petrushka,* Stravinsky introduced several of the stylistic traits that became closely identified with him. The opening scene of the ballet depicts a fair in St. Petersburg during the final week of carnival season. Here we find Stravinsky's characteristic blocks of static harmony with repetitive melodic and rhythmic patterns as well as abrupt shifts from one block to another. Each group of dancers receives its distinctive music: a band of tipsy revelers, an organ grinder with a dancer, a music-box player with another dancer, the puppet theater where Petrushka stars. Seemingly unconnected musical events interrupt each other without transition and then just as suddenly return,

IGOR STRAVINSKY

(1882–1971)

Stravinsky participated in most significant trends in modern music during his lifetime, wrote some of the most successful and enduring music of the twentieth century, and had an enormous influence on four generations of composers.

Stravinsky was born in Orianenbaum, near St. Petersburg in Russia, to a well-to-do musical family. He began piano lessons at age nine and studied music theory in his later teens but never attended the Conservatory. His most important teacher was Rimsky-Korsakov, with whom he studied composition and orchestration privately. In 1906, Stravinsky married his cousin Catherine Nosenko, with whom he had four children.

Stravinsky demonstrated his command of his teacher's rich, colorful style in *Scherzo fantastique* and *Fireworks*. After hearing these two pieces in 1909, the impresario Sergei Diaghilev commissioned Stravinsky to compose for his company the Ballets Russes (Russian Ballet), a hotbed of artistic innovation in Paris from 1909 to 1929. For Diaghilev, Stravinsky wrote the ballets that made him famous and that are still his most popular works: *The Firebird, Petrushka,* and *The Rite of Spring*. He collaborated on them with choreographers Mikhail Fokine, founder of the modern ballet style, and Vaslav Nijinsky, one of the greatest dancers of the early twentieth century.

Stravinsky moved to Paris in 1911, then to Switzerland in 1914. Six years later, after becoming stranded in western Europe by World War I and the 1917 Russian Revolution, he returned to France, having already begun to compose in the neoclassical idiom that would characterize his music for the next three decades. The commotion at the premiere of *The Rite of Spring* bestowed on him a delicious notoriety, and because he performed tirelessly, first as a pianist and then as a conductor, Stravinsky was well known in 1920s Europe and America. He continued to work with the Ballets Russes but also wrote abstract instrumental works. One of his favorite collaborators was the choreographer George Balanchine, whose renewal of classical ballet in modern terms paralleled Stravinsky's music and who later founded the New York City Ballet.

FIGURE 33.6
Photograph of Igor Stravinsky in Paris in May 1913, the month of the premiere of The Rite of Spring.
HULTON-DEUTSCH/ CONTRIBUTOR/GETTY IMAGES

In the mid-1920s, health crises and his wife's devout faith reawakened Stravinsky's own interest in religion, inspiring works such as *Symphony of Psalms*. Catherine died of tuberculosis in March 1939. In September, just weeks after the outbreak of World War II, Stravinsky moved to the United States. In March 1940, he married Vera Sudeikin, with whom he had been having an affair since the early 1920s. He settled in Hollywood, not far from Schoenberg and Rachmaninoff, and wrote several pieces that referred to American styles, such as the *Ebony Concerto* for the jazz clarinetist Woody Herman and his band. His last major neoclassical work was the opera *The Rake's Progress*, premiered in Venice in 1951.

In 1948 Stravinsky met Robert Craft, who became his assistant. Craft was enthusiastic about the twelve-tone music of Schoenberg and Webern. By the mid-1950s, Stravinsky had absorbed twelve-tone methods into his own idiom. Most of his late works are serial and many are religious, from *Canticum sacrum* in 1955 through the *Requiem Canticles* in 1965–66. Stravinsky and his wife moved to New York in 1969. He died there two years later and was buried in Venice.

MAJOR WORKS *The Firebird, Petrushka, The Rite of Spring, L'histoire du soldat, Symphonies of Wind Instruments, Les noces,* Octet for Wind Instruments, *Oedipus rex, Symphony of Psalms,* Symphony in C, Symphony in Three Movements, *The Rake's Progress, Agon, Requiem Canticles*

EXAMPLE 33.7 *Igor Stravinsky, passage from* Petrushka *based on Russian folk song*

creating a sharp juxtaposition of diverse textures that has been compared to cubism (see Chapter 31 and Figure 31.7). The interruption and juxtaposition of blocks, which Stravinsky absorbed from the Russian practice of Musorgsky and Rimsky-Korsakov, is here linked to the visual juxtapositions of ballet.

Stravinsky enhanced the Russian and popular carnival atmosphere throughout the ballet by borrowing and elaborating several Russian folk tunes, a popular French song, and Viennese waltzes. Rather than smoothing out these borrowings, Stravinsky preserved their contexts, heightening the differences between their styles to make each block of sound as distinctive as possible. The passage in Example 33.7, which accompanies the drunken merrymakers, is based on a folk song from Rimsky-Korsakov's 1877 collection of traditional songs. But Stravinsky avoids the dominant-tonic harmony of Rimsky-Korsakov's version; instead, he places the melody in the bass and simulates folk harmony, in which voices sing in parallel fifths and octaves, often against drones. In contrast to the diatonic folk songs, Stravinsky uses octatonic music for the supernatural characters, but the harmony is now more biting than in *The Firebird*. The puppet Petrushka, who has been brought to life by a magician, is characterized in the famous "Petrushka chord" that combines F♯- and C-major triads, both part of the same octatonic scale, as shown in Example 33.8.

Stravinsky's distinctive style crystallized in *The Rite of Spring*. The subject was still Russian, but now it was an imagined fertility ritual set in prehistoric Russia, during which an adolescent girl is chosen for sacrifice and must dance herself to death. Although Stravinsky again borrowed folk melodies, the scenario, choreography, and music were marked by ***primitivism***, a deliberate representation of the elemental, crude, and uncultured, and cast aside the sophistication and stylishness of modern life and trained artistry. Figure 33.7 shows one of the costumes from the original production. The audience at the premiere was shocked, breaking out in a notorious riot

FIGURE 33.7 *Costume sketch by Nikolai Roerich of a peasant girl from the original production of Stravinsky's* The Rite of Spring.

EXAMPLE 33.8 *"Petrushka" chord, with octatonic scale from which it derives*

The Premiere of *The Rite of Spring*

The first performance of Igor Stravinsky's *The Rite of Spring* on May 29, 1913, was greeted by a riot. As he told the story almost half a century later, he was as shocked by the audience's reaction as some listeners were by the spectacle. It was Vaslav Nijinsky's choreography, far more than the music, that provoked the audience, and ever since the piece has usually been performed in concert rather than as a ballet.

❖

That the first performance of *Le Sacre du printemps* was attended by a scandal must be known to everybody. Strange as it may seem, however, I was unprepared for the explosion myself. The reactions of the musicians who came to the orchestra rehearsals were without intimation of it and the stage spectacle did not appear likely to precipitate a riot. . . .

Mild protests against the music could be heard from the very beginning of the performance. Then, when the curtain opened on the group of knock-kneed and long-braided Lolitas jumping up and down [*Danses des adolescentes*], the storm broke. Cries of "Ta gueule" ["Shut up!"] came from behind me. I heard Florent Schmitt shout "Taisez-vous garces du seizième" ["Be quiet, you bitches of the sixteenth"]; the "garces" of the sixteenth arrondissement [the most fashionable residential district of Paris] were, of course, the most elegant ladies in Paris. The uproar continued, however, and a few minutes later I left the hall in a rage; I was sitting on the right near the orchestra, and I remember slamming the door. I have never again been that angry. The music was so familiar to me; I loved it, and I could not understand why people who had not yet heard it wanted to protest in advance. I arrived in a fury backstage, where I saw Diaghilev flicking the house lights in a last effort to quiet the hall. For the rest of the performance I stood in the wings behind Nijinsky holding the tails of his *frac*, while he stood on a chair shouting numbers to the dancers, like a coxswain.

From Igor Stravinsky and Robert Craft, *Expositions and Developments* (New York: Doubleday, 1962), 159–64.

(see Source Reading). Later, the piece became one of the most frequently performed compositions of its time.

The characteristics of Stravinsky's mature idiom can be heard in the first scene, *Danse des adolescentes* (Dance of the Adolescent Girls; NAWM 184a), whose opening measures are shown in Example 33.9.

Stravinsky trademarks

Despite the regular barring, each pulse in the first two measures is played with the same strength, negating the hierarchy of beats and offbeats that is essential to meter. Then accented chords, doubled by eight horns, create an unpredictable pattern of stresses that destroy any feeling of metrical regularity. Yet while the listener is utterly disoriented metrically and rhythmically, the music is cleverly conceived for ballet; the passage makes an eight-measure period, and the dancers can count four-measure phrases. This reduction of meter to mere pulsation was the element that most strongly conveyed a sense of primitivism in the music. In the final dance of the ballet, the *Danse sacrale* (Sacrificial Dance; NAWM 184b), Stravinsky adopted two additional strategies that reduce meter to pulse: rapidly changing meters, and unpredictable alternation of notes with rests.

Undermining meter

The entire passage in Example 33.9 is built from ostinatos, including pounded or arpeggiated chords and the melodic ostinato in the English

Ostinatos and juxtaposed blocks

EXAMPLE 33.9 *Opening of* Danse des adolescentes, *from Stravinsky's* The Rite of Spring

horn. Stravinsky uses these repeating figures to create static blocks of sound, which he juxtaposes. Here one block is replaced by another, then returns. Within each block, and indeed throughout the piece, there is no development of motives or themes as traditionally understood, but rather repetition and unpredictable variation.

Layering   Often Stravinsky builds up textures by layering two or more independent strands of music on top of each other. The material at measure 9 is composed of three layers distinguished by timbre and figuration, with the top line also set off by register and pitch collection.

Discontinuity and   In typical Stravinsky fashion, the patterns within successive blocks are
connection   quite different, creating discontinuity. Yet the collection of pitches being used differs by only one new note (*c*), lending a strong sense of continuity. Stravinsky plays off the obvious surface discontinuities of his music with more subtle connections, somewhat like Mozart did when he joined a varied series of topics by using harmony and form (see Chapter 23).

Most dissonance in Stravinsky's music is based on the scales used in Russian classical music, such as the diatonic and octatonic collections. Here the dissonant chords in measures 1–8 combine an F♭-major triad in the lower strings with a first-inversion dominant seventh chord on E♭ in the upper strings to produce a sonority that has all seven notes of the A♭ harmonic minor scale. *Dissonance*

Stravinsky often identified a musical idea with a particular timbre. Here the pounding chords are always in the strings with horn reinforcements, and the English horn ostinato recurs only in that instrument throughout the first half of the dance. In the second half, it migrates through several other instruments. In music without motivic development, such changes of timbre are one means to provide variety, a technique Stravinsky learned from Glinka and Rimsky-Korsakov. *Timbre linked with motive and variation*

Stravinsky's preference for dry rather than lush or resonant timbres is reflected in his use of instruments. Here this sound is evident in the staccato string chords, which are all played with a down-bow to create even emphasis and natural separations; in the pizzicato cellos; and in the staccato English horn and bassoons.

Having developed these techniques, Stravinsky continued to use them throughout his career. During World War I, the wartime economy forced him to turn away from the large orchestra of his early ballets toward small combinations of instruments to accompany stage works. For *L'histoire du soldat* (The Soldier's Tale, 1918), he called for six solo instruments in pairs (violin and double bass, clarinet and bassoon, cornet and trombone) and one percussionist to play interludes framed by a spoken narration and dialogue. In the marches, tango, waltz, and ragtime movements of *L'histoire,* and in *Ragtime* (1917–18), shown in Figure 33.8, Stravinsky discovered ways to imitate familiar styles while using the devices that had become his trademarks. Stranded in western Europe by the war and then by the Bolshevik Revolution in his home country, he began to move away from Russian topics while retaining the distinctive traits that stemmed largely from his Russian training.

FIGURE 33.8 *Title page designed by Picasso for Stravinsky's piano arrangement of* Ragtime, *originally for eleven instruments.*

NEOCLASSICAL PERIOD In 1919, Diaghilev asked Stravinsky to orchestrate pieces by the eighteenth-century composer Pergolesi (including music erroneously attributed to him) to accompany a new ballet, *Pulcinella.* Stravinsky applied his distinctive stylistic traits to the music, reworking a number of pieces so that they retained the original music faithfully yet sounded more like Stravinsky than Pergolesi. He later spoke of this experience as his "discovery of the past, the epiphany through which the whole of my late work became possible." In the same year of 1920, he completed the *Symphonies of Wind Instruments,* which applied the methods distilled in *The Rite of Spring* to an entirely abstract composition.

Thus was launched a new stage in Stravinsky's career that became known as his **neoclassical** period. The word **neoclassicism** was first applied to *Neoclassicism* music around 1903 and originally used by French writers to disparage German composers such as Brahms who wrote instrumental music in eighteenth-century forms and genres, accusing them of pedantically imitating obsolete structures and thereby lacking originality and substance. But it was recast as a term of praise in 1923 when Parisian music critic Boris de Schloezer applied it to Stravinsky's recent music, characterizing neoclassicism as "one of the dominant forces of the moment" in which "rigorous forms subdue and purify the emotions." Since then, neoclassicism has come to represent a broad movement from the late 1910s to the 1950s in which composers revived, imitated, or evoked the styles, genres, and forms of pre-Romantic music, especially those of the eighteenth century, then called "Classic" ("Baroque" as a term for early-eighteenth-century music became widely used only after 1940). Neoclassicism was in part a rejection of Romanticism, whose associations with intense emotions, irrationality, yearning, individualism, and nationalism were all suspect in the wake of the wanton destruction of World War I. But as we will see in Chapter 35, it also stemmed from a reaction among younger French composers against the overwhelming influence of Debussy, countering what they saw as his focus on exotic imagery, colorful harmonies, and a wash of orchestral sound with a renewed emphasis on absolute music, melody, counterpoint, incisive timbres, and clear forms—traits that became known as neoclassical. Stravinsky was the most prominent composer associated with neoclassicism and the one most closely identified with it. His neoclassical period, from 1919 to 1951, marks a turn away from Russian folk music and toward earlier Western art music as a source for imitation, quotation, or allusion.

Uses of
neoclassicism
This step was useful to Stravinsky because the fashion in western Europe for Russian nationalism was beginning to fade, in part because the political and cultural ties between France and Russia had dissolved after the 1917 Bolshevik Revolution. In technical terms, imitating and alluding to music in the classical tradition was hardly different from what he had been doing all along in making use of folk and popular materials, so neoclassicism in effect gave him new subject matter without requiring him to retool completely. Neoclassicism also addressed the dilemma of establishing a place in the crowded classical repertoire. Stravinsky had already solved the problem of creating an individual style. He now used his distinctive idiom, forged in the Russian traditions, to establish fresh links to the western European classical tradition, just as Schoenberg used his modernist twelve-tone procedures to resurrect the forms and genres of the classical past. Yet even as Stravinsky became thoroughly cosmopolitan, he always remained something of an outsider, and instead of Schoenberg's expressionism, we find in Stravinsky's music an emotional detachment. Thus his neoclassical music adopts an anti-Romantic tone, reflecting a preference for balance, coolness, objectivity, and absolute (as opposed to program) music.

Range of reference
In his neoclassical works, Stravinsky borrowed from or alluded to a wide range of composers, styles, forms, and genres. Many pieces recall the Classic era, including the Piano Sonata (1924), Symphony in C (1939–40), Symphony in Three Movements (1942–45), and *The Rake's Progress* (1947–51), modeled on Mozart's comic operas and with a libretto based on a series of engravings by the eighteenth-century English artist William Hogarth. But some works

use other sources: J. S. Bach's concertos in the Concerto for Piano and Winds (1923–24) and *Dumbarton Oaks* Concerto (1937–38), Rossini and Glinka in the opera *Mavra* (1921–22), Tchaikovsky in the ballet *The Fairy's Kiss* (1928), Baroque oratorios in *Symphony of Psalms* (1930) for mixed chorus and orchestra, and even Monteverdi and ancient Greek modes in *Orpheus* (1947). Often Stravinsky alludes to more than one style, and always he remakes the material in his own personal idiom. He uses the styles he evokes as touchstones that transform his own signature style in fresh ways, so that every piece has a unique personality.

The Octet for Wind Instruments (1922–23), for example, combines Classic-era forms with Baroque figuration and Bach-like counterpoint, while projecting a distinctive Stravinskian sound. The major triads, scales, walking basses, canons, and other eighteenth-century features are mixed with modern dissonances, octatonic melodies, meter changes, and interruptions, so that the music rarely sounds like Classic or Baroque music. The ensemble of flute, clarinet, two bassoons, two trumpets, and two trombones offered Stravinsky a wide range of instrumental colors while avoiding what he called the "emotive" nature of string instruments in favor of the "objective" character of winds and brass.

Octet for Wind Instruments

The first movement (NAWM 185) is in sonata form with a slow introduction. The first theme, shown in Example 33.10a, has many Classic-era features: a leap up followed by stepwise descent; a unison statement that opens up into multiple voices; sequential treatment of a motive in the upper voice; a cadence at the end of the first phrase; and then a repetition of the opening idea, now in imitation over chordal accompaniment. But Mozart would never have written this music: there are parallel fifths and fourths (measures 44–45), frequent changes of meter, and casual dissonances between voices (measures 47–48 and 50–54) that make what looks like counterpoint on the page sound at times like the superimposed layers of Stravinsky's *Rite*, especially when the parts seem to be in different meters based on their rhythmic groupings (measures 53–54). The second theme in Example 33.10b features a cantabile melody in trumpet I accompanied by counterpoint in the other voices, like a Bach chorale setting. Yet again the modernist features predominate: the melody is syncopated, the meter changes, and the accompanying voices form dissonances with the melody almost constantly and with each other in measures 75–76. This music alludes to eighteenth-century styles but is Stravinsky through and through.

In his neoclassical works, Stravinsky avoids the routines of common-practice tonality. In this movement, the tonal motion in the exposition is not from tonic to dominant but down a semitone (E♭ to D), balanced by a complementary motion in the recapitulation (E to E♭, with the second theme recapitulated before the first).

Neotonality

The tonal centers are established not through functional harmonic progressions but by other means. The first phrase of the first theme in Example 33.10a (measures 42–48) begins on E♭, uses exclusively notes of the E♭-major scale, and ends on E♭, making the tonal center clear through simple assertion. Yet what sounds like a cadence in measure 48 is not a functional progression. The "dominant" chord on the first two beats of measure 48 lacks the leading tone D, substituting a dissonant E♭ to create a chord made of fifths and

EXAMPLE 33.10 *Stravinsky, Octet, first-movement themes*

a. First theme

b. Second theme

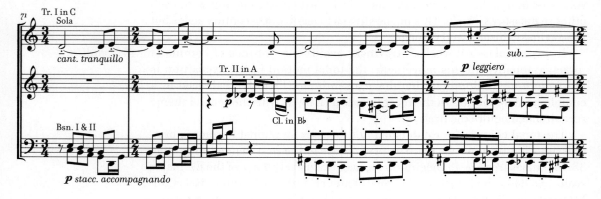

seconds (B♭–F–A♭–B♭–E♭). The melody in trumpet I cadences on the down-beat, arriving on E♭ from D in the previous measure. Instead of harmonizing D with a dominant chord and E♭ with a tonic chord, melody and harmony are out of synchronization, as frequently happens in Stravinsky's music, robbing the harmony of its traditional function: reinforcing melodic motion. The second theme in Example 33.10b defines its tonal center through a melody that begins on D and constantly returns to it, accompanied by other voices drawn from the D-Mixolydian diatonic collection (D major with a lowered seventh). Once again, there is no functional harmony, and the melody and other voices move independently. The contrast between first and second themes is not one of key but of pitch collection, like the contrasts between adjacent sections in Debussy's *Nuages* or Stravinsky's *Rite*, as well as of tonal center.

The assertion of a tonal center through reiteration and other means, evident in these two themes, is very different from Schoenberg's atonality. Yet this music cannot be described as tonal, since it does not follow the rules of traditional harmony. Music like this is ***neotonal***—the composer is finding new ways to establish a single pitch as a tonal center. In this as in other ways, Stravinsky is not reviving older styles but alluding to them in order to create something new, a unique combination of the modern and the familiar.

Partly because his music was based on tonal centers as well as on recognizable genres and styles, performers and audiences found Stravinsky's neoclassical works easier to play and to follow than Schoenberg's twelve-tone compositions. Both composers attracted supporters, who argued about music's need to adhere to tradition versus the need to find new methods, in an echo of the Brahms-Wagner disputes of the nineteenth century. In recent decades, musicians and scholars have come to see how much the two composers had in common, especially in their music of the 1920s–1940s, when both sought to revivify traditional forms in an entirely new and personal musical language.

Schoenberg and Stravinsky

SERIAL PERIOD After Schoenberg's death in 1951, the twelve-tone methods he had pioneered were as much a part of past history as sonata form. They were also becoming popular with younger composers, who extended the principles to series in parameters other than pitch, such as rhythm (see Chapter 37). Such music based on series was no longer simply twelve-tone, and it became known as ***serial music***, a term that has also been applied retrospectively to Schoenberg and his students.

In part to encompass yet another branch of the classical tradition, and in part to keep up with the times, Stravinsky—already in his seventies—adapted serial techniques in his music from about 1953 on. His best-known serial works include the song cycle *In memoriam Dylan Thomas* (1954), which uses a series of only five notes; *Threni* (1957–58), for voices and orchestra on texts from the Lamentations of Jeremiah; and *Movements* (1958–59), for piano and orchestra. All of them show his characteristic idiom of juxtaposed blocks, disrupted meter, and his other signature traits, although the pitch content is increasingly chromatic.

Stravinsky's particular genius lay in finding stylistic markers, derived from Russian sources yet distinctly his own, that proved so recognizable and adaptable that he could assimilate or allude to any style while putting his personal stamp on the music. By drawing on everything from early music to the serial music of his time, he claimed the entire tradition as his own.

INFLUENCE Stravinsky's impact on other composers was in a league with that of Wagner and Debussy, making him among the most influential composers of all time. Through Stravinsky, elements that had been nurtured in Russian music (ostinatos, juxtaposition of blocks, interruption, lack of development) and traits he had introduced (such as frequent changes of meter, unpredictable accents and rests, and dry orchestration) became commonplaces of modern music, used by composers employing many different styles. Stravinsky's neoclassical works set an example that many others imitated. His serial music was less well known, but his support for serialism helped it gain a strong following among composers and academics. His willingness to change styles encouraged others to do the same, though few if any matched his ability to project a single personality in any style he adopted. His writings were also important, including his *Poetics of Music* and a series of conversation books written with Robert Craft between 1959 and 1972. The anti-Romantic stance of objectivity and emotional detachment articulated in his essays and embodied in his neoclassical music had a profound impact on the next two generations of composers. For some, his pronouncements on music had the effect of words and ideas handed down from an oracle.

BÉLA BARTÓK

As we have seen, many modernists, from Falla to Stravinsky, found elements in their own national music that allowed them to create a distinctive voice while continuing the classical tradition. Two of the most significant, the Hungarian Béla Bartók and the American Charles Ives, did so in part by paying attention to musical traditions and qualities that had been ignored or disdained even in their own countries.

Béla Bartók (1881–1945; see biography and Figure 33.9) created an individual modernist idiom by synthesizing elements of Hungarian, Romanian, Slovak, and Bulgarian peasant music with elements of the German and French classical tradition. He arrived at this synthesis only after thorough grounding in both classical and peasant music and exposure to several modern trends.

Classical and modern influences   Born in the Austro-Hungarian Empire and trained as a pianist, Bartók started composing at a young age, progressing from short character pieces to longer works modeled on the music of Bach, Mozart, Beethoven, Brahms, and Liszt. Encounters with the tone poems of Richard Strauss in 1902, with Debussy's music over the following decade, and with Schoenberg's and Stravinsky's works in the 1910s and 1920s inspired Bartók to write music that emulated and ultimately absorbed their idioms.

Peasant music   Bartók's search for an innately Hungarian music led him to collect and study peasant music, often in collaboration with fellow composer Zoltán Kodály (1882–1967). Bartók published nearly two thousand Hungarian, Romanian, Slovak, Croatian, Serbian, and Bulgarian song and dance tunes—only a small part of the music he had collected in expeditions ranging over central and southeastern Europe, Turkey, and North Africa. As shown in Figure 33.10,

BÉLA BARTÓK

(1881–1945)

Bartók was a virtuoso pianist, piano teacher, and ethnomusicologist, and is renowned as one of the leading composers of the early twentieth century.

Bartók was born in the Austro-Hungarian Empire, in a small Hungarian city now in Romania. His parents were teachers and amateur musicians, and he took piano lessons from age five and composed from age nine. He studied piano and composition at the Hungarian Royal Academy of Music in Budapest, returning there in 1907 to teach piano. As a virtuoso pianist, he performed all over Europe and edited keyboard music of Bach, Scarlatti, Haydn, Mozart, Beethoven, and others.

In 1904, Bartók overheard the singing of a woman from Transylvania (a region then in Hungary and now in Romania), which sparked a lifelong interest in folk music of Hungary, Romania, and nearby lands. He collected thousands of songs and dances, edited them in collections, and wrote books and articles about folk music. He arranged many folk tunes, wrote pieces based on them, and borrowed elements from various folk traditions for use in his concert music.

In 1909, Bartók married his student Márta Ziegler, who assisted him in his work. Their son Béla was born in 1910. In 1923, he divorced Márta and married Ditta Pásztory, who gave birth to a second son, Péter, the next year.

In 1934, Bartók left the Academy of Music and moved to a full-time position as ethnomusicologist at the Academy of Sciences, where he joined Zoltán Kodály and others in preparing a critical edition of Hungarian folk music. His compositions over the next five years, including the last two string quartets

FIGURE 33.9 *Béla Bartók in 1936.*

and *Music for Strings, Percussion and Celesta,* marked the high point of his career. Yet the rise of the Nazis in Germany and their 1938 takeover of Austria brought the threat of fascism in Hungary. Bartók arranged to send his manuscripts to the United States, then followed with his family in 1940, settling in New York. His last years were difficult financially and physically. Friends procured jobs and commissions for him, sometimes without his knowledge, but he was already suffering from leukemia, which took his life in 1945.

MAJOR WORKS *Bluebeard's Castle, The Miraculous Mandarin, Dance Suite,* Concerto for Orchestra, *Music for Strings, Percussion and Celesta,* 3 piano concertos, 2 violin concertos, 6 string quartets, 2 violin sonatas, 1 piano sonata, *Mikrokosmos,* numerous other works for piano, songs, choral works, and folk-song arrangements

he used the new technology of audio recording, which preserved the unique and unfamiliar characteristics of each folk singer and style far better than the older method of transcribing music by ear into conventional notation. He then analyzed the collected specimens using techniques developed in the new discipline of ethnomusicology, and he edited collections and wrote books and articles that established him as the leading scholar of this music. Bartók argued that Hungarian peasant music represented the nation better than the

FIGURE 33.10
*Bartók in 1907, recording
Slovakian folk songs
on an acoustic cylinder
machine in the village of
Zobordarázs.*

urban popular music that had long been identified as "Hungarian." This position was politically radical at a time when Hungary was still ruled by an urban,
German-speaking elite, but his views eventually prevailed.

Bartók felt that peasant music offered modern composers a fresh start,
free from Romantic sentimentality and bombast (see Source Reading). He
arranged many peasant tunes and created original works based on them, and
he imitated peasant melodies in some of his themes. But most important, he
drew a new vocabulary of rhythmic, melodic, and formal characteristics from
peasant music and blended them with those of classical and modern music.

Stylistic evolution   Bartók first achieved a distinctive personal style around 1908, with compositions such as the First String Quartet and the one-act opera *Bluebeard's
Castle,* composed in 1911 and premiered in 1918, which combines Hungarian folk elements with influences from Debussy's *Pelléas et Mélisande.* His
Allegro barbaro (1911) and other piano works introduced a new approach to the
piano, treating it more as a percussive instrument than as a spinner of cantabile melodies and resonant accompaniments. His compositions from the
decade after World War I show him pushing toward the limits of dissonance
and tonal ambiguity, reaching the furthest point with his two Violin Sonatas of
1921 and 1922. Other works of this decade include the expressionist panto-
mime *The Miraculous Mandarin* and the Third and Fourth String Quartets. His
later works, which seem in comparison more accessible to a broad audience,
have become the most widely known, including the Fifth and Sixth String
Quartets, *Music for Strings, Percussion and Celesta* (1936), and the Concerto for
Orchestra (1943). His *Mikrokosmos* (1926–39)—153 piano pieces in six books
of graded difficulty—is a work of great pedagogical value that also summarizes
Bartók's own style and presents, in microcosm, the development of European
music in the first third of the twentieth century.

BARTÓK'S SYNTHESIS In synthesizing peasant with classical music, Bartók
emphasized what the traditions have in common and, at the same time, what

Peasant Music and Modern Music

In his essay *The Influence of Peasant Music on Modern Music,* Bartók argued that peasant music offered composers a way to create a truly modern music, whether by borrowing or imitating peasant melodies or, more abstractly, absorbing elements of peasant music into one's own personal style.

❖

At the beginning of the twentieth century there was a turning point in the history of modern music.

The excesses of the Romanticists began to be unbearable for many. There were composers who felt: "this road does not lead us anywhere; there is no other solution but a complete break with the nineteenth century."

Invaluable help was given to this change (or let us rather call it rejuvenation) by a kind of peasant music unknown till then.

The right type of peasant music is most varied and perfect in its forms. Its expressive power is amazing, and at the same time it is devoid of all sentimentality and superfluous ornaments. It is simple, sometimes primitive, but never silly. It is the ideal starting point for a musical renaissance, and a composer in search of new ways cannot be led by a better master. What is the best way for a composer to reap the full benefits of his studies in peasant music? It is to assimilate the idiom of peasant music so completely that he is able to forget all about it and use it as his musical mother tongue. . . .

The question is, what are the ways in which peasant music is taken over and becomes transmuted into modern music?

We may, for instance, take over a peasant melody unchanged or only slightly varied, write an accompaniment to it and possibly some opening and concluding phrases. . . . It is of the greatest importance that the musical qualities of the setting should be derived from the musical qualities of the melody, from such characteristics as are contained in it openly or covertly, so that melody and all additions create the impression of complete unity. . . .

The frequent use of fourth-intervals in our old melodies suggested to us the use of fourth chords. Here again what we heard in succession we tried to build up in a simultaneous chord.

Another method by which peasant music becomes transmuted into modern music is the following: the composer does not make use of a real peasant melody but invents his own imitation of such melodies. . . .

There is yet a third way in which the influence of peasant music can be traced in a composer's work. Neither peasant melodies nor imitations of melodies can be found in his music, but it is pervaded by the atmosphere of peasant music. In this case we may say, he has completely absorbed the idiom of peasant music which has become his musical mother tongue.

From *Béla Bartók Essays,* ed. Benjamin Suchoff (London: Faber & Faber, 1976), 340–44. In SR 198 (7:29), 1437–41.

is most distinctive about each. In both traditions, pieces typically have a single pitch center, use diatonic and other scales, and feature melodies built from motives that are repeated and varied. Then, from the classical tradition, Bartók retained its elaborate contrapuntal and formal procedures, such as fugue and sonata form. From the peasant tradition, he drew rhythmic complexity and irregular meters, common especially in Bulgarian music; modal scales and mixed modes; and specific types of melodic structure and ornamentation. By intensifying these distinctive qualities, Bartók wrote music that can be simultaneously more complex in its counterpoint than Bach's and more ornamented and rhythmically complex than his folk models. In addition, Bartók's use of dissonance, his harmony, and his love of symmetry result partly from mixing concepts and materials taken from the two traditions; for instance, his frequent use of seconds and fourths in chords derives both from their prominence in folk melodies and from the practice of his fellow modernists. His synthesis preserves the integrity of both traditions. He never used folk elements merely for color, nor did he compromise their individuality for smoothness, yet his music always remains grounded in the classical tradition.

Many of the pieces in *Mikrokosmos* exemplify this synthesis. For example, *Staccato and Legato* (NAWM 186) is like a Bach two-part invention, with imitation between the hands, use of inversion and invertible counterpoint, and a tonal structure reminiscent of Bach. Yet the shape of the melody adapts the structure of many Hungarian songs, built from a short phrase that rises and falls within the span of a fourth, repeats transposed up a fifth, is varied, and finally falls back to the tonic. Many elements, from its mixture of diatonic and chromatic motion to its ornamentation, draw from both traditions.

Use of neotonality

Music for Strings, Percussion and Celesta offers a fuller illustration of Bartók's synthesis and several characteristics of his personal style. The combination of peasant and classical elements to create a modernist idiom is seen in his use of neotonality. Each of the four movements establishes a tonal center by methods analogous to the modal melodies of folk song and to the chordal motion and tonic-dominant polarities of classical music, while avoiding common-practice harmony. The tonal center of the first and last movements is A, with an important secondary center at the tritone Eb/D♯, a post-tonal analogue to the conventional dominant E. The second movement is in C, with a similar tritone pole on F♯, those two tones being each a minor third on either side of A; the slow third movement (NAWM 187) has the opposite arrangement, centering on F♯ with C as the competing pole. Some of the principal themes of the four movements and all of the final cadences clearly bring out this tritone relationship, as shown in Example 33.11. In addition, the cadences evoke standard procedures in tonal music, from counterpoint in contrary motion (Example 33.11b) to a mock dominant-tonic cadence (Example 33.11d). There are also strong similarities to peasant music. Peasant melodies often rise from and return to the tonal center, as in the theme of the first movement (Example 33.11a); center around a tone, as in the opening theme of the second movement (Example 33.11c); or descend to the tonal center from its upper octave, as in the finale (Example 33.11f). Here the synthesis of the two traditions to create a modernist idiom is rich in allusions to music in both traditions.

Melodic structure

The themes are created by varying small motives, a typical procedure both in classical music, from Bach and Haydn to Schoenberg and Stravinsky, and in the peasant music of central and southeastern Europe. Many Hungarian tunes use short phrases and repeat motives with slight variations, like the AA'BB' pattern of the first-movement theme (Example 33.11a), while Bulgarian dance tunes typically spin out a rhythmic-melodic motive, as in the finale's theme (Example 33.11f). The latter is diatonic, like many classical themes, but clearly in the Lydian mode, which is used in some peasant songs. Hungarian songs can mix modes, an effect Bartók borrows at the end of the second-movement theme (Example 33.11c), where the melodic rise and fall suggests first Lydian and then Phrygian modes.

EXAMPLE 33.11 *Béla Bartók,* Music for Strings, Percussion and Celesta

a. Theme of first movement

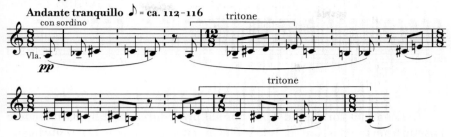

b. Final cadence of first movement

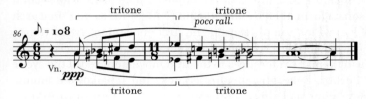

c. Second movement, opening theme

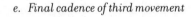

d. Final cadence of second movement   *e. Final cadence of third movement*

f. Fourth movement, opening theme

g. Final cadence

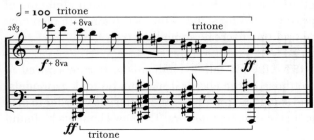

EXAMPLE 33.12 *Xylophone solo from opening of third movement*

Form and counterpoint

The complex forms and contrapuntal procedures used by Bartók come strictly from the classical tradition. The first movement is an elaborate fugue, with entrances that successively rise and fall around the circle of fifths in both directions, meeting in a climax at the opposite pole of E♭. The second movement is a sonata form; the third movement (NAWM 187) a modified arch form (ABCB′A′) in which the phrases of the first-movement fugue theme are embedded; and the finale a rondo that includes a modified reprise of the fugue theme. Such thematic references to the first movement recall the cyclic symphonies of Berlioz, Robert Schumann, Franck, and Tchaikovsky, among others. Each movement includes canon and imitation, often in inversion. The palindromic form of the third movement is foreshadowed in the opening xylophone solo, shown in Example 33.12, which from the midpoint at the beginning of measure 3 is identical going in both directions. Bartók was very fond of such symmetries, as we can see in the mirror counterpoint at the end of the first movement (Example 33.11b).

Peasant elements

Elements from traditional peasant styles are also evident. Bulgarian dance meters feature long and short beats rather than strong and weak beats, with the long beats half again as long as the short beats. In Western notation, this translates into irregular groupings of twos and threes, as in, for example, the 2 + 3 pattern of a *paidushka*, 3 + 2 + 2 of a *chetvorno*, or 2 + 2 + 2 + 3 of a *svornato*. Bartók adopts this effect in the 2 + 3 + 3 pattern in the opening theme of the fourth movement (Example 33.11f) and, more abstractly, in the groups of twos and threes in the first-movement fugue theme (Example 33.11a). The heavily ornamented, partly chromatic type of Serbo-Croatian song in Example 33.13a, which Bartók described as *parlando-rubato* (speech-like, in free tempo), is echoed near the beginning of the third movement, shown in Example 33.13b. Melodies over drones, as in this example, are also a feature of peasant music. String glissandos, snapped pizzicatos, percussive chords laced with dissonant seconds, and other characteristics of Bartók's personal style do not derive directly from peasant music but can convey a rough, vibrant effect that suggests a source other than art music.

Rarely in *Music for Strings, Percussion and Celesta* does anything actually *sound* Hungarian or folklike. Rather, Bartók has extrapolated elements of Hungarian and other peasant traditions and combined them with elements drawn from the classical tradition to create something truly new.

BARTÓK AS MODERNIST Like his fellow modernists, Bartók aspired to create masterpieces like those of the classical masters he took as models, emulated their music, and sought new methods and materials in order to distinguish his music from that of other composers. The new elements he found

EXAMPLE 33.13 *Evocation of peasant ornamentation in the third movement*

a. Serbo-Croatian song

b. Passage near beginning of third movement

were those of another tradition, the peasant music of his and other nations. Through his synthesis of both traditions, he created new works with a strong personal identity and a rich connection to the music of the past.

CHARLES IVES

Charles Ives (1874–1954; see biography and Figure 33.11), like Bartók, created a personal modernist idiom by synthesizing international and regional musical traditions. Ives was a fluent composer in four distinct spheres: American vernacular music, Protestant church music, European classical music, and experimental music, of which he was the first major exponent. In his mature music, he combined elements from all four, using the multiplicity of styles as a rhetorical device to convey rich musical meanings.

Vernacular music

Ives grew up surrounded by American vernacular music, from parlor songs and minstrel show tunes to the marches and cornet solos his father performed as leader of the town band. In his teens and his college years at Yale, Ives wrote numerous marches and parlor songs in the styles of the day, including a presidential campaign song for William McKinley and a march played at McKinley's inauguration in 1897. At Yale he also composed part-songs for the glee club and stage music for fraternity shows.

Church music

Ives sang and heard hymns in church and at revival meetings, and he played them as a professional church organist for most of his teens and twenties (1889–1902). During those years, he improvised organ preludes and postludes, and composed solo songs and sacred choral works representing all

CHARLES IVES

(1874–1954)

Like the archetypal artist in countless movies, Ives worked in obscurity for most of his career but lived to be recognized as one of the most significant classical-music composers of his generation.

Ives was born in Danbury, a small city in Connecticut where his father, George, was a bandmaster, church musician, and music teacher. Ives studied piano and organ, showing prodigious talent —at age fourteen he became the youngest professional church organist in the state. His father taught him theory and composition and encouraged an experimental approach to sound.

In college at Yale, he took liberal arts courses and studied music theory and composition with composer, teacher, and organist Horatio Parker. While in college, Ives wrote marches and songs for his fraternity brothers and church music for his position as organist at Centre Church in New Haven.

After graduating in 1898, he settled in New York, where he worked as a church organist, got a job in the insurance business, and lived with fellow Yale graduates in an apartment they called "Poverty Flat." When his cantata The Celestial Country failed to garner strongly positive reviews, Ives quit his organist position and focused on insurance. His firm, Ives & Myrick, became one of the most successful agencies in the nation, as Ives pioneered the training of agents (his classes are one source for the modern business school) and the idea of estate planning.

His courtship with Harmony Twichell, whom he married in 1908, inspired a new confidence, and the next decade brought an outpouring of music, including most of the pieces that later made Ives's reputation. Composing evenings and weekends, he prepared finished copies of his less radical pieces, such as the first three symphonies and the violin sonatas, and sought

FIGURE 33.11
Charles Ives in New York, around 1913.
AKG-IMAGES

to get them performed, but published nothing and left many works in sketch or partial score.

After trying vainly for over a decade to interest performers and publishers in his music, Ives was spurred in 1918 by a health crisis to edit and self-publish *114 Songs* and his Second Piano Sonata (*Concord, Mass., 1840–1860*), which was accompanied by a book, *Essays Before a Sonata*. He devoted the 1920s to completing several large pieces, including his Fourth Symphony. The remaining three decades of his life saw the premieres and publication of most of his major works. Although accused— despite his thorough musical training—of amateurism because he was a businessman, Ives won a number of advocates among younger composers, performers, and conductors, who promoted his music. By the time of his death at age seventy-nine, he was widely regarded as the first to create a distinctly American body of art music, and his reputation has continued to grow.

MAJOR WORKS 4 symphonies, *Holidays Symphony, Three Places in New England, The Unanswered Question*, 2 string quartets, piano trio, 4 violin sonatas, 2 piano sonatas, about 200 songs

---

Classical music

the styles then prominent in American Protestantism, from simple hymnody to the cultivated manner of his composition teacher at Yale, Horatio Parker. As a teenager, Ives played major organ works by Bach, Mendelssohn, and contemporary French and American composers, along with transcriptions from sonatas and symphonies of Beethoven, Schubert, Brahms, and other composers in the classical tradition. With Parker, he intensified his study of art music, writing exercises in counterpoint, fugue, and orchestration and composing in genres from art song to symphony. His First Symphony, which he began in his last year in college, was directly modeled on Dvořák's *New World* Symphony, with elements from the first movement of Schubert's *Unfinished* Symphony, the scherzo from Beethoven's Ninth, and the third movement of Tchaikovsky's *Pathétique* (NAWM 165).

In his ***experimental music***, Ives's typical approach was to preserve most of the traditional rules but change others to see what would happen. As a youth, he practiced drumming on the piano, devising dissonant chords that would suggest the sound of drums. In his teens, he wrote several pieces that were ***polytonal***, with the melody in one key and the accompaniment in another, or with four imitative voices, each in its own key, asking "If you can play a tune in one key, why can't a feller, if he feels like [it], play one in two keys?" Polytonality was later developed independently by other composers, but Ives was the first to use it systematically.

Experimental works

After his studies with Parker sharpened his craft, Ives wrote numerous short pieces whose main purpose was to try out new techniques. Two are excerpted in Example 33.14. *Processional* for chorus and organ, sketched around 1902, is an essay in possible chord structures. As shown in the excerpt from the organ part in Example 33.14a, Ives presents over a C pedal point a series of chords, each a stack of one or two intervals, gradually expanding from seconds to thirds, fourths, fifths, sixths, and sevenths and finally resolving to octaves at the end of the phrase. *Scherzo: All the Way Around and Back* (ca. 1908) for chamber ensemble is an almost perfect palindrome, building up layers of dissonant ostinatos until at the climax in Example 33.14b units of two, three, five, seven, and eleven equal divisions of the measure are sounding simultaneously, then proceeding in retrograde. The choice of these units was not arbitrary; they represent the first five prime numbers—numbers not divisible by any other—so the attacks coincide only on the downbeat of each measure. Over all this, a bugle plays a fanfare in C major. Like many of his experiments, these pieces introduced unprecedented levels of dissonance and rhythmic complexity, although they usually preserved the idea of a tonal center.

None of Ives's experimental pieces was published or performed in public until long after they were written; they were essentially ways of trying out ideas, and they made Ives aware of new possibilities that he could use in other, less systematic pieces for purposes of expression or representation. But one experimental work became one of Ives's best-known pieces because his novel means fit the inspired program so perfectly: *The Unanswered Question* (ca. 1906–8; NAWM 188). Slowly moving strings in G major represent "The Silences of the Druids—Who Know, See and Hear Nothing," while over them a trumpet poses "The Perennial Question of Existence" and four flutes attempt ever more energetic and dissonant answers until they give up in frustration, leaving the question to sound once more, unanswered. The trumpet and flute parts are atonal, making Ives one of the first composers to use atonality (roughly contemporary with Schoenberg but independent of him) and the first to combine tonal and atonal layers in the same piece.

The Unanswered Question

EXAMPLE 33.14 *New techniques in Charles Ives's experimental compositions*

a. Organ chords in Processional *made of stacked similar intervals*

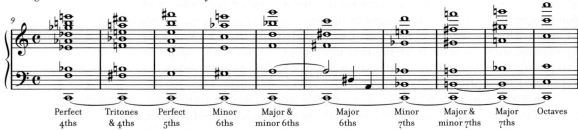

| Perfect 4ths | Tritones & 4ths | Perfect 5ths | Minor 6ths | Major & minor 6ths | Major 6ths | Minor 7ths | Major & minor 7ths | Major 7ths | Octaves |

b. Climax of Scherzo: All the Way Around and Back, *with six rhythmic layers*

SYNTHESES From 1902 on, Ives wrote only in classical genres, but he brought into his music the styles and sounds of the other traditions he knew. Typically, he employed them to suggest extramusical meanings, whether in a character piece or programmatic work. In his Second Symphony, Ives used themes paraphrased from American popular songs and hymns, borrowed transitional passages from Bach, Brahms, and Wagner, and combined all of these in a symphonic form and idiom modeled on Brahms, Dvořák, and Tchaikovsky. Through this synthesis, Ives proclaimed the unity of his own experience as an American familiar with the vernacular, church, and classical traditions and claimed a place for distinctively American music in the symphonic repertoire. Doing so was a radical act, for although classical audiences welcomed folk melodies as sources for concert works, they tended to regard the hymn tunes and popular songs Ives used as beneath notice and entirely out of place in the concert hall.

Ives's Third Symphony, four violin sonatas, and First Piano Sonata all feature movements based on American hymn tunes. Here Ives uses procedures of thematic fragmentation and development from European sonata forms and symphonies, but reverses the normal course of events so that the development happens first and the themes appear in their entirety only at the end. This procedure, akin to Smetana's structure in *Tábor* (see Chapter 30) and Sibelius's teleological genesis (see Chapter 32 and NAWM 178), is called **cumulative form**. In the Second Symphony, Ives had paraphrased the American melodies so they would work well as themes in standard European forms. In these later works, he reshapes the form so the simple American tune appears as the culmination of the previous development, making a place for American melody within the European tradition. While not overtly programmatic, these pieces suggest the coming together of individual voices and the fervent spirit of hymn singing at the camp-meeting revivals of Ives's youth. In these works, Ives is a musical nationalist, but he is also asserting the universal value of his country's music (see Source Reading).

Cumulative form

Many of Ives's later pieces are programmatic, celebrating aspects of American life. *Three Places in New England* presents orchestral pictures of the first African American regiment in the Civil War, a band playing at a Fourth of July picnic, and a walk by a river with his wife during their honeymoon. *A Symphony: New England Holidays* captures the sounds, events, and feelings of Washington's Birthday, Decoration Day (later renamed Memorial Day), the Fourth of July, and Thanksgiving. His Piano Sonata No. 2, titled *Concord, Mass., 1840–1860,* characterizes in music the literary contributions of writers who lived in that town at that time: Ralph Waldo Emerson, Nathaniel Hawthorne, Louisa May Alcott and her family, and Henry David Thoreau. Other works are more philosophical, such as the Fourth Symphony, an extraordinary, complex work that poses and seeks to answer "the searching questions of What? and Why?" In all of these, Ives uses references to American tunes or musical styles, from Stephen Foster to ragtime, to suggest the meanings he wanted to convey. In some pieces he uses multiple tunes, layered on top of each other in a musical *collage* or woven together like a patchwork quilt, to invoke the way experiences are recalled in memory. He also uses techniques developed in his experimental music, often to represent certain kinds of sounds or motions, such as exploding fireworks or mists over a river.

American program music

With such a wide range of styles at his command, Ives frequently mixed styles—whether traditional or newly invented—within a single piece. Like Mozart's use of contrasting topics (see Chapter 23), Mahler's references to various styles, and the juxtapositions of different blocks of material in the music of Debussy, Scriabin, and Stravinsky, this heterogeneity of styles provided a way for Ives to evoke a wide range of extramusical references and also to articulate the musical form, distinguishing each phrase, section, or passage from the next through stylistic contrast. He also used style, alongside timbre, rhythm, figuration, register, and other more traditional means, to differentiate layers heard simultaneously, as we saw in *The Unanswered Question.*

Heterogeneity of styles

A virtuoso example of using heterogeneous styles as topics is *The Alcotts*

The Alcotts

Americanism in Music

Dvořák had advised American composers to use African American or American Indian music as sources for a distinctively national music, and many did so. Charles Ives felt that for himself, as a white New Englander, a more appropriate source was the music regularly heard and sung by people in his own region, from hymns to popular song. No matter what sources are used, he argued, the composer must understand the music from the inside and know what it meant to the people who heard and performed it.

✣

If a man finds that the cadences of an Apache war-dance come nearest to his soul—provided he has taken pains to know enough other cadences, for eclecticism is part of his duty; sorting potatoes means a better crop next year—let him assimilate whatever he finds highest of the Indian ideal so that he can use it with the cadences, fervently, transcendentally, inevitably, furiously, in his symphonies, in his operas, in his whistlings on the way to work, so that he can paint his house with them, make them a part of his prayer-book—this is all possible and necessary, if he is confident that they have a part in his spiritual consciousness. With this assurance, his music will have everything it should of sincerity, nobility, strength, and beauty, no matter how it sounds; and if, with this, he is true to none but the highest of American ideals (that is, the ideals only that coincide with his spiritual consciousness), his music will be true to itself and incidentally American, and it will be so even after it is proved that all our Indians came from Asia.

The man "born down to Babbitt's Corners" may find a deep appeal in the simple but acute Gospel hymns of the New England "camp meetin'" of a generation or so ago. . . . If the Yankee can reflect the fervency with which "his gospels" were sung—the fervency of "Aunt Sarah," who scrubbed her life away for her brother's ten orphans, the fervency with which this woman, after a fourteen-hour work day on the farm, would hitch up and drive five miles through the mud and rain to "prayer meetin'," her one articulate outlet for the fullness of her unselfish soul—if he can reflect the fervency of such a spirit, he may find there a local color that will do all the world good. If his music can but catch that spirit by being a part with itself, it will come somewhere near his ideal—and it will be American too—perhaps nearer so than that of the devotee of Indian or negro melody. In other words, if local color, national color, any color, is a true pigment of the universal color, it is a divine quality, it is a part of substance in art—not of manner.

From Charles Ives, *Essays Before a Sonata, The Majority, and Other Writings*, ed. Howard Boatwright (New York: W. W. Norton, 1970), 79–81.

(NAWM 189), the third movement of his *Concord* Sonata. Example 33.15 shows some of the contrasting styles in this movement: hymnlike melody and harmonization (Example 33.15a); polytonal, the melody in B♭ major over A♭-major triads (Example 33.15b); layered with diatonic chords over whole-tone accompaniment (Example 33.15c); melody and accompaniment in the style of a parlor song by Stephen Foster (Example 33.15d); and pounding chords (Example 33.15e), in a texture reminiscent of the opening of Beethoven's *Hammerklavier* Sonata (Piano Sonata in B-flat Major, Op. 106). There are also passages that are octatonic, feature modernist counterpoint, or refer to the styles of Scottish songs, marches, and minstrel songs.

Ives uses these stylistic references to convey the spirit of the Alcott family, encompassing the domestic life and home music-making described by Louisa May Alcott in her autobiographical novel *Little Women* and also the

EXAMPLE 33.15 *Ives, contrasting styles in* The Alcotts

a. Hymnlike

b. Polytonal

c. Layered, diatonic over whole-tone

d. Parlor song

e. Pounding chords as in Beethoven's Hammerklavier Sonata

transcendentalist philosophy of her father, Bronson Alcott. The hymnlike opening in Example 33.15a is based on a nineteenth-century American hymn tune, *Missionary Chant*, which coincidentally resembles the opening motives of Beethoven's Fifth Symphony and *Hammerklavier* Sonata, both alluded to in Example 33.15e. The movement is in cumulative form, gradually building up to a complete statement of a theme that incorporates both Beethoven allusions, and over the course of the movement Ives reveals the close parallels between hymn and Beethoven, transforming one into the other. Framed within this process is a middle section that begins with Example 33.15d and includes the other references to nineteenth-century styles. As Ives explains in his program, the movement evokes "that home under the elms—the Scotch songs and the family hymns that were sung at the end of each day" and links them to a transcendental theme of "an innate hope—a common interest in common things," "a conviction in the power of the common soul" that the Concord writers expressed with a "Beethovenlike sublimity." By juxtaposing diverse styles—from hymns and parlor songs to art music and from traditional tonality to the new sounds of his own day—and weaving them all into a unified movement, Ives lifts up the commonplace, connects the present to the past, and celebrates American life and culture.

IVES'S PLACE Ives was isolated as a composer. Among his contemporaries, he was influenced by the music of Richard Strauss, Debussy, and Scriabin, but he encountered that of Stravinsky only late in his career, after arriving independently at similar methods, and that of Schoenberg and other modernists only after he had ceased to compose. Nor did they know his music; except for some early vernacular and church works, most of his pieces were performed and published only long after he had written them. Thus his direct influence was felt mostly after World War II, when his departures from the conventional were taken as an example by postwar composers, encouraging them to experiment and providing models for some novel procedures. He could justifiably be called the founder of the experimental music tradition in the United States that includes, among others, Henry Cowell, Edgard Varèse, and John Cage (see Chapters 35 and 37). In most of his works, Ives was a modernist who, like Bartók, Stravinsky, and Berg, drew on his own nation's music to develop a distinctive idiom within the classical tradition. In all of these ways, his work has been of incalculable importance to younger generations of American musicians.

COMPOSER AND AUDIENCE

The music of these six composers and of other modernists intensified the split between popular and classical music that had emerged in the nineteenth century. One secret of Haydn, Mozart, and Beethoven was their ability to appeal both to inexperienced listeners, who enjoyed the music's surface features on first hearing, and to well-trained connoisseurs, who could fully understand its intricacies. Modernism tipped the balance toward the latter, with music targeted especially to those willing to study it, hear it repeatedly, and explore its rich structure and references to other music. Such works have become favorites of composers themselves, adventurous performers, theorists, and historians. The composers discussed in this chapter have a central place in the canon of music, but on the whole—with the exception of Stravinsky's early ballets and several of Bartók's later works, which have enjoyed an enduring popularity—their music is more admired by critics, composers, and scholars than it is loved by audience members, who tend to prefer their less radical contemporaries such as Strauss, Sibelius, and Rachmaninoff. Some of the canonic works of musical modernism still arouse disdain or incomprehension among certain performers and concertgoers, who find them "too modern" even now, a century after they were composed.

On the other hand, the dissonance, atonality, multiple layers, sudden juxtapositions, unpredictability, and startling stylistic contrasts that offended audiences generations ago are now familiar from repeated performances and recordings, and from their use in more recent music, especially music for films. Bartók's *Music for Strings, Percussion and Celesta* turns up in *The Shining*, Webern's Five Pieces for Orchestra in *The Exorcist*, and Ives's *The Unanswered Question* in *The Thin Red Line,* but a much longer list of film scores use sounds and techniques pioneered by these six composers for their strong emotional effect.

The music of all six composers discussed in this chapter has found a small but growing and apparently permanent niche in the repertoire. All are performed and recorded more and more, and interest in their music has tended to increase with every passing decade.

Further Reading is available at digital.wwnorton.com/hwm10

BETWEEN THE WORLD WARS: JAZZ AND POPULAR MUSIC

The period between World Wars I and II saw a remarkable series of changes in musical life and continued diversification in musical styles. The spread of phonographs, improved recording techniques, and the new technologies of radio and sound films fostered a mass market for music in sound as well as in notation. Classical concert music and opera remained the most prestigious musical traditions, but the varieties of popular music were better known and usually more lucrative. Especially prominent were trends from the United States, notably jazz. Music, always an accompaniment to "silent" movies, became an integral part of sound films, and composers of opera, classical concert music, musicals, and popular songs all found a place in the movie industry. Styles of classical music grew ever more varied, as composers responded in individual ways to musical trends from modernism to the avant-garde, and to political and economic conditions in their respective nations. After examining the historical background to the period, we will focus in this chapter on developments in popular music, jazz, and film music between the wars, especially in the United States. In the next chapter, we will address the classical tradition.

BETWEEN THE WARS

When World War I began in 1914, most Europeans and North Americans had enjoyed a generation of peace and increasing prosperity and had a strong faith in progress and the benefits of modernity. By the time the war ended in 1918, they had been profoundly disillusioned. New technologies of warfare, from artillery to poison gas, produced staggering losses of human life and material resources. More than nine million soldiers were killed, and economies across Europe were wrecked. The losses were compounded by a worldwide influenza epidemic in 1918 that killed fifty million people. Modern life no longer seemed benign, and music and other forms of entertainment provided an escape. In this context, popular music and jazz flourished as never before. So did interest in music of earlier times, manifest in neoclassicism and in a growing movement to revive music from before 1750.

The war brought an end to the Austro-Hungarian, German, Russian, and Ottoman empires, and independence to Finland, Estonia, Latvia, Lithuania, Poland, Czechoslovakia, Hungary, and Yugoslavia. In Russia, a revolution in the spring of 1917 forced the tsar to abdicate and sought to replace autocratic rule with a democracy, but late that year the Bolsheviks—radical Marxist revolutionaries—seized power and set up a dictatorship, forming the Soviet Union. In several other nations, democratic governments gave way to totalitarian rule. Benito Mussolini and the fascists took over the Italian government in 1922, and the Spanish Civil War (1936–39) brought Francisco Franco to power. In Germany, the democracy formed after World War I, known as the Weimar Republic for the city where the constitution was drafted, proved too weak to deal with mounting economic problems. After the National Socialists (Nazis) won an electoral plurality, their leader Adolf Hitler was appointed chancellor in 1933 and soon established a dictatorship. In a fierce anti-Semitic campaign, the Nazis passed laws to deprive people of Jewish background of their citizenship and all other rights, driving into exile countless writers, artists, composers, and scholars, many of whom—like Arnold Schoenberg—settled in the United States.

After World War I, the nations of Europe were faced with war debt, crippling inflation, and a shattered infrastructure. The United States and Canada, which suffered far fewer casualties, enjoyed a financial boom. Increased prosperity and leisure time helped make this a golden age for music in America, both popular and classical. American culture and music, especially jazz, had a profound influence on Europeans during the 1920s. But in October 1929, the New York stock market crashed, sparking a worldwide collapse known as the Great Depression. Unemployment approached fifty percent in some areas, producing unprecedented turmoil. In response, governments in Europe and the Americas undertook relief and public works programs, such as the New Deal in the United States. The economies in most nations were still recovering when Germany invaded Poland in September 1939, beginning World War II.

During the 1920s, women increasingly took their place in the public sphere. The need during World War I to replace men in staffing offices and factories had brought women new freedom of movement and economic independence. After the war, women won the right to vote in Britain, the United States, and Germany. Birth control and rising levels of education gave women greater access to careers. The 1930s, however, saw a backlash in some countries against women's freedoms on economic and ideological grounds, especially under the Nazis and other totalitarian regimes.

TIMELINE

1913–27 Marcel Proust, *Remembrance of Things Past*

1914–18 World War I

1917 Russian Revolution

1919 Women win right to vote in United States

ca. 1920 King Oliver forms the Creole Jazz Band

1922 T. S. Eliot, *The Waste Land*

1922 James Joyce, *Ulysses*

1922 First sponsored radio broadcast in United States

1925 Electric recording introduced

1927 Jerome Kern, *Show Boat*

1927 Bessie Smith, *Back Water Blues*

1927 *The Jazz Singer*, first talking picture

1927–31 Duke Ellington at the Cotton Club

1928 Louis Armstrong and His Hot Five record *West End Blues*

1929 New York stock market crash begins Great Depression

1930 George Gershwin, *Girl Crazy*

1930–31 Thomas Hart Benton, *America Today*

1933 Adolf Hitler comes to power in Germany

1933 Max Steiner, score for *King Kong*

1933–45 Franklin Delano Roosevelt, president of United States

1939 John Steinbeck, *The Grapes of Wrath*

1939–45 World War II

1940 Ellington, *Cotton Tail*

The Great Migration   In the United States, African Americans moved in increasing numbers from rural areas of the South to urban areas in the Northeast and Midwest, lured by work in northern factories and service industries and seeking to escape the lynchings, Jim Crow laws, and institutional racism in southern states. Now known as the Great Migration, this was among the largest movements of any group of people in a short time, swelling from over 200,000 in the first decade of the century to over a million people from World War I through the Great Depression. Commemorated in the sixty-panel *Migration Series* (1940–41) by painter Jacob Lawrence (1917–2000), the Great Migration stimulated the Harlem Renaissance, a flowering of African American writers, artists, and intellectuals centered in the Harlem neighborhood of upper Manhattan. The influx of African American musicians from the South helped to create vibrant traditions of jazz and blues in northern cities from New York and Philadelphia to Chicago, Detroit, Indianapolis, and Kansas City.

THE ARTS The 1920s were a time of freewheeling experimentation in the arts. We have already encountered the avant-garde efforts of Satie, the twelve-tone music of Schoenberg, and the neoclassicism of Stravinsky; other new trends in classical music are described in the next chapter. In literature, the decade saw T. S. Eliot's modernist poem of disillusionment, *The Waste Land,* with its many references to literature of the past; James Joyce's stream-of-consciousness novel *Ulysses*; Marcel Proust's multivolume novel of time and memory, *Remembrance of Things Past*; the politically engaged plays of Bertolt Brecht; and the feminist novels and essays of Virginia Woolf. Surrealist painters like Salvador Dalí and René Magritte explored the dreamlike world of the unconscious opened up by Freud. Architects from Walter Gropius in Germany to Frank Lloyd Wright in the United States were pioneering new, less decorated forms with an insistence that the function of a building be reflected in its design.

Impelled by the worldwide depression of the 1930s, many artists reexamined their role and sought to make their work more relevant to the economic and social problems of the time. John Steinbeck, in his novel *The Grapes of Wrath,* wrote about farmers impoverished by the Dust Bowl in the American plains and by exploitation in California. Artists such as George Grosz and Käthe Kollwitz in Germany, Diego Rivera in Mexico, and Thomas Hart Benton in the United States pictured social conditions in simple, direct, yet modern styles that could be understood by all, as in Figure 34.1. Many classical composers likewise sought to write music that was accessible to all, hoping to catch the imagination of ordinary working people.

FIGURE 34.1 City Building, *panel from* America Today *(1930–31)* by American painter Thomas Hart Benton *(1889–1975), a series of murals for the board room of the New School for Social Research in New York. This panel celebrates workers in the construction and shipbuilding industries.*

NEW TECHNOLOGIES The rapid growth of diverse musical styles between the world wars was due in part to new technologies. Recordings, radio broadcasting, and the introduction of sound to film enabled the preservation and rapid distribution of music in performance, not just in score. Now a musical performance, formerly as impermanent as a moment in time, could be preserved, admired, and replayed many times. This change created a new mass market and new commercial possibilities, allowed performers to share in the benefits of mass distribution, and vaulted some performers—whether of classical music, popular music, or jazz—to international stardom.

Recordings

The popular music industry had revolved around sheet music from the 1890s through the 1910s, but after the war, publishers realized that recordings offered a market of potentially unlimited size. Songwriters and bandleaders also turned to recordings, often tailoring their pieces to fit the three-to-four-minute limit of a record side. New technology affected performance styles. For example, before 1925, recording technology was acoustic, and only opera singers and "shouters" could make an effective vocal recording. The introduction of electric recording in 1925 allowed for more sensitive recording of "crooners," encouraging songwriters to compose songs suitable for a more intimate singing style and leading to the rise of singers like Bing Crosby and Frank Sinatra. The new electric microphones were also more sensitive to the nuances of orchestral music.

Radio

Musicians profited from exposure over the radio, since music was a good way of filling large periods of airtime. Radio caught on quickly; by 1924 there were over 1,400 radio stations around North America, and during the 1920s national broadcasting systems were developed in all the major European nations. Recordings were still too poor in quality to be played successfully over the radio, so stations relied primarily on live performers in their own studios and on regional or national transmissions of live shows. Stations in Europe and the Americas sponsored orchestras, such as the BBC Symphony Orchestra (founded 1930) in London and the NBC Symphony Orchestra (1937) in New York. Dance bands also made use of the new medium to gain wider exposure. Benny Goodman and his band, for example, hosted two radio shows, *Let's Dance* (1934–35) and *The Camel Caravan* (1936–39).

Diffusion of music

Recordings and radio spawned an unparalleled growth in the size of the audience for all kinds of music. Music was now available to almost everyone, no matter what their level of musical training. These technologies brought about widespread dissemination of the classical repertoire from Bach to Bartók and began to make available less well-known music from the remote past to the present. They also furthered the growth of a huge body of popular music, blues, and jazz. Most of the latter originated in the United States, and it is there our story will focus for most of this chapter.

AMERICAN MUSICAL THEATER AND POPULAR SONG

The period between the two world wars, and especially the 1920s, was a rich time for American popular music. Music for stage shows of all kinds enjoyed great popularity: vaudeville troupes toured the continent, and operettas, revues, and musicals attracted large audiences. Popular songs from Tin Pan

Alley also proliferated (see Chapter 30). The period roughly from 1920 to 1955—before the advent of rock and roll and the decline of the sheet music industry—is known as the "Golden Age" of Tin Pan Alley.

In the 1920s, as in the previous two decades, popular song and music for theater were inextricably linked. In large part, it was the attractiveness of the songs that drove the popularity of a musical and its composer. Many of the best-known songs, made familiar in hit shows, were then sold as sheet music, often with a picture of the performer who introduced the song on the cover. Yet there were changes in the popular song industry. Sheet music of Tin Pan Alley songs still circulated in American parlors, but publishers and songwriters increasingly counted on recordings to popularize their tunes. And with the arrival of sound technology for films in the late 1920s, the Hollywood musical was born, creating another important venue for popular songwriters. The most successful songwriters of this period—such as Irving Berlin (1888–1989), Jerome Kern (1885–1945), George Gershwin (1898–1937), Harold Arlen (1905–1986), and Richard Rodgers (discussed in Chapter 36)—were equally at home writing music for Tin Pan Alley, musical theater, and Hollywood musicals.

Revues   **MUSICAL THEATER** Vaudeville shows, loose collections of variety acts, were still very popular, but the craze in larger cities such as New York was for revues, conceived as complete shows made up primarily of musical numbers that often included many performers. The premier series of revues was the Ziegfeld Follies, assembled each year by producer Florenz Ziegfeld, which included variety entertainment, star performers, and troupes of beautiful female dancers. Important popular song composers such as Irving Berlin wrote music for these shows. Berlin's contributions to the 1919 Ziegfeld Follies included *A Pretty Girl Is Like a Melody,* which was sung by a bevy of scantily clad women, each costumed as a particular piece of classical music.

Musicals   Several new operettas were successful in the 1920s, such as Sigmund Romberg's *The Student Prince,* but the genre was rapidly being replaced by the musical. Like all forms of musical theater, musicals were complex collaborations, with different artists responsible for the music, lyrics (the texts set to music), book (the spoken words of the play), choreography, staging, sets, and costumes. Some musicals were primarily vehicles for star entertainers, featuring new popular songs that were framed by a loose plot, a structure reminiscent of the singer-centered and aria-focused Italian opera of the late seventeenth to early eighteenth centuries. Yet there was an increasing interest in creating integrated musicals, shows in which the musical numbers are closely related to the story, which is plot-driven rather than focused on the performers. Like reform opera of the late eighteenth century (see Chapter 21), such integrated musicals were valued for their dramatic impact, in addition to their appeal as entertaining spectacle.

Show Boat   Jerome Kern's masterpiece, *Show Boat* (1927), with book and lyrics by Oscar Hammerstein II, exemplifies this new integrated approach. *Show Boat* brings together a number of traditions (such as opera, operetta, musical comedy, revues, and vaudeville) and musical styles (including ragtime, spirituals, sentimental ballads, and marches), and the multiple styles all serve dramatic ends. The score is operatic in scope, with interwoven referential themes

FIGURE 34.2: *The opening scene from the 1946 revival of* Show Boat *at the Ziegfeld Theatre in New York.*

and motives, much like the operas of Richard Wagner (which Kern greatly admired). Based on a novel by Edna Ferber, *Show Boat* captured recent historic events, such as the 1893 Chicago World's Fair, and addressed serious social issues, including racism, the economic and social oppression of African Americans, and the animus against interracial marriage. The realistic situations, and the appearance on stage of white and African American performers side by side, were striking departures from earlier musicals. *Show Boat* was a tremendous success, toured the country after its Broadway run, and enjoyed numerous revivals, among them the 1946 New York production shown in Figure 34.2.

TIN PAN ALLEY: THE GOLDEN AGE By the 1910s, several types of Tin Pan Alley songs had solidified, including waltz, ragtime, and novelty songs. Most Tin Pan Alley songs followed a standard form of one or more verses followed by a thirty-two-measure chorus in an AABA, ABAB, or ABAC pattern. The focus was increasingly on the chorus, where songwriters placed their catchiest rhythms and melodic ideas. Many songwriters worked with lyricists as songwriting teams, although some composers, such as Irving Berlin, wrote both words and music for their songs.

Irving Berlin's lengthy career and prodigious output position him as one of America's most prolific and best-loved popular songwriters. Widely known for his sentimental and patriotic tunes that seem to capture the American spirit, like *God Bless America* and *White Christmas,* Berlin mastered all current popular song genres and was involved in every aspect of the music business. It was said that America could not fight a war or celebrate a holiday without a song from this Russian-born son of a Jewish cantor. Many of his songs were written for revues, such as *Face the Music* and *As Thousands Cheer*; movies, like *Top Hat* and *Holiday Inn*; or musicals, such as *Call Me Madam*.

Irving Berlin

Cole Porter (1891–1964), like Irving Berlin, wrote both lyrics and music for his songs. Born in Indiana to a wealthy family and educated in music at Yale, Harvard, and the Schola Cantorum in Paris, Porter is remembered for

Cole Porter

ARCHIVE PHOTOS/GETTY IMAGES

his suave, urbane, sophisticated lyrics that revel in innuendo and double-entendre and for his irresistibly catchy and memorable tunes. Examples in which the music greatly complements the inventive text include *Let's Do It, I Get a Kick Out of You, It's De-lovely,* and *You're the Top.* Porter wrote exclusively for theater and Hollywood musicals, producing gems such as *Night and Day* from the theater production *Gay Divorce,* which later became a Hollywood musical, *The Gay Divorcee. Night and Day* was popularized by dancer and singer Fred Astaire, who starred in many theater and film productions of Porter's musicals.

George Gershwin   George Gershwin, shown in Figure 34.3, was both a composer of jazz-influenced classical music (see Chapter 35) and a writer of popular songs and musicals. Most of his best-known songs feature lyrics by his brother, Ira Gershwin. Like Irving Berlin, Gershwin got his start writing for revues in New York. And like Kern and Porter, Gershwin moved increasingly toward integrated musicals throughout the 1920s, even venturing into social satire with a few of his shows. *Strike Up the Band* (1927) satirized war and big business, and *Of Thee I Sing* (1931), a spoof of the American presidential election process, was the first musical to win the Pulitzer Prize for Drama. Gershwin's musicals catapulted several new performers to fame; *Lady, Be Good!* (1924) featured the singing and dancing brother-and-sister team of Fred and Adele Astaire, while *Girl Crazy* (1930) made stars of Ethel Merman and Ginger Rogers.

In *Girl Crazy,* Ethel Merman sang the song *I Got Rhythm* (NAWM 190), which became an instant hit. Like most Tin Pan Alley and Broadway songs of the 1920s and 1930s, it has only one verse, shifting the main interest to the chorus. The chorus is in the typical AABA′ form. Comparing Gershwin's chorus to that of Charles K. Harris's *After the Ball* (see Example 30.5, p. 751) illustrates both continuity and change in popular song styles since the 1890s. Both choruses start with a catchy phrase, marked by a striking rhythm and beguiling melodic contour, and vary it throughout, balanced with enough contrast to keep the tune engaging. Like Harris, Gershwin tends to grab our attention with the most unusual features at the beginning, then gradually returns to more conventional rhythms and stepwise contours at the ends of phrases, creating a satisfying emotional arc. But *I Got Rhythm* is much more syncopated, drawing on rhythms of ragtime. Example 34.1 shows the rhythm of the first two phases of the chorus, whose syncopations create the same pattern of accents as in the opening section of Joplin's *Maple Leaf Rag* (NAWM 169), producing interesting cross-accents against the underlying duple meter. Gershwin's harmony changes more

BETTMANN/CONTRIBUTOR/GETTY IMAGES

FIGURE 34.3 *George Gershwin seated at the piano in 1937, during rehearsals for the film* Shall We Dance? *His brother, lyricist Ira Gershwin, is to his left. Seated, to his right, are Fred Astaire and Ginger Rogers.*

EXAMPLE 34.1 *Chorus from George Gershwin's* I Got Rhythm, *compared to Scott Joplin's* Maple Leaf Rag

rapidly, is more chromatic and wide-ranging, and features numerous seventh and ninth chords, raising the overall level of dissonance. While both songs are in part about the power of music to carry us away, Gershwin's reflects the energy of jazz and the optimism of Broadway musicals, while *After the Ball* uses waltz meter and style to convey a sentimental message typical of its time.

Both the style and the carefree attitude of *I Got Rhythm* are drawn in part from jazz. Soon jazz musicians returned the compliment, using the song as a vehicle for jazz improvisation. The chorus's harmonic progression (in jazz terminology, its "changes") was adopted for so many new jazz tunes that this progression itself came to be known simply as "rhythm changes" (see pp. 865 and 903 and NAWM 193 and 205).

THE JAZZ AGE

Revues, musicals, and Tin Pan Alley songs continued traditions that had been imported from Europe or arose among Americans of European descent. But African American music and musicians played an increasingly influential role in American musical life, and in the 1920s two related traditions of African American origin gained wide currency: blues and jazz. Indeed, the 1920s became known as "The Jazz Age," and jazz became the emblematic music for that period when a new generation was cultivating a spirit of social liberation.

The tremendous popularity of blues and jazz from the 1920s onward opened new opportunities for African American musicians, some of whom became nationally or internationally famous. In contrast to the world of classical music, where they encountered obstacles due to racism in conservatories, concert halls, and professional employment, blues and jazz offered economic rewards and a chance to participate in a tradition with African American roots. A recurring theme in the biographies of great black musicians, from James Reese Europe, Scott Joplin, and Will Marion Cook (see Chapter 31) to Fletcher Henderson, Duke Ellington, and Miles Davis (this chapter and Chapter 36), is classical training in their youth, followed by a career in popular music. Dvořák had predicted in the 1890s that the music of African Americans could be the "inspiration for truly national music" of the United States, if composers would incorporate it into their art music (see Chapter 30). In an ironic reversal, the most widely recognized national music of the United States, from jazz to rock and hip hop, has sprung from African American traditions, often absorbing elements of the classical tradition rather than the other way around.

Racism and opportunity

FIGURE 34.4 *Bessie Smith,*
"Empress of the Blues," in the mid-1920s,
when she was the most successful and
prominent African American musician
of the decade.

BLUES One of the most influential genres of music to come out of early-twentieth-century America was the ***blues***. The origin of the blues is obscure, likely stemming from a combination of rural work songs and other African American oral traditions. The lyrics typically speak of disappointments, mistreatment, or other troubles that produce the state of mind known since the early nineteenth century as "the blues." Yet the words also convey defiance and a will to survive abandonment by a faithless lover, a lost job, oppression, or disaster. Often touches of humor suggest the knife-edge separation between sorrow and laughter, tragedy and comedy. The music expresses the feelings implied by the words through melodic contours, freely syncopated rhythms, and distinctive vocal or instrumental effects (such as a slide, rasp, or growl) that evoke the sound of a person expressing pain, sorrow, or frustration. Blues often feature flatted or bent (slightly lowered or sliding) notes, sometimes called ***blue notes***, on the third, fifth, and seventh scale degrees, which add to the emotional intensity. Besides expressing feelings, the blues allows performers to display their artistry, in a musical parallel to the defiance implied in the lyrics. Ultimately the blues are not about *having* the blues, but about *conquering* them through a kind of catharsis embodied in the music.

Two distinct blues traditions can be heard in recordings beginning in the 1920s, now known as *classic blues* and *delta blues*. Classic blues, an urban style influenced by the popular music industry, was the first to be recorded, although delta blues, one of the rural traditions collectively known as *country blues*, was regarded as an older style that remained closer to the oral traditions from which the blues developed.

Classic blues

Classic blues was performed primarily by African American women singers such as Ma Rainey (1886–1939); Bessie Smith (1894–1937), shown in Figure 34.4; and Alberta Hunter (1895–1984). Typically accompanied by a piano or small ensemble, these women popularized the blues on black variety circuits, on minstrel circuits, in clubs, and on many recordings. The recording by Mamie Smith (1883–1946) of *Crazy Blues* (1920), the first recording by an African American singer of a blues song, sold 75,000 copies in a few months, earning her a small fortune. Her success prompted record companies to begin marketing their products to black audiences, in the same way they were already targeting other ethnic groups, selling Irish records to Irish audiences and Yiddish records to Jewish audiences. Records targeted to blacks became known as "race records."

Sexuality and feminist themes

As Angela Davis has pointed out, blues lyrics often addressed issues of sexuality and relations between the sexes that rarely appeared in other forms of popular song. Emancipation did not bring African Americans economic equality, but it did give them control over their own relationships that they did not have under slavery, when marriage was forbidden, couples were separated, and women were sexually exploited by their masters or forced to have sex with men chosen for them in order to produce more slaves. The openness with which Bessie Smith's *Sam Jones Blues* mocks a man who returns home after an affair to discover his wife has divorced him, or Ma Rainey hints at

EXAMPLE 34.2 *First stanza of Bessie Smith's* Back Water Blues

lesbian relationships in *Prove It On Me Blues*, symbolizes the new freedom of black women to choose their own destinies, as well as the independent paths they had to forge in order to survive in an economy that devalued the contributions of both women and African Americans.

The classic blues singers joined aspects of oral tradition with elements of popular song, thanks in part to W. C. Handy (1873–1958), known as the "father of the blues." Handy did not invent the blues, but as a publisher, he introduced blues songs in sheet music form as early as 1912, thus taking advantage of both the genre's new popularity and the booming sheet music industry. With his publications, Handy solidified what we now think of as standard **twelve-bar blues** form. In this form, illustrated by Bessie Smith's *Back Water Blues* (1927; NAWM 191) in Example 34.2, each poetic stanza has three lines; the second line typically restates the first, and the third completes the thought or offers a twist. Each line of text is sung to four measures of music over a set harmonic pattern, in which the first four-measure phrase remains on the tonic chord; the second phrase begins on the subdominant and ends on the tonic; and the third phrase starts on the dominant and moves back to the tonic, as illustrated in Figure 34.5.

Twelve-bar blues

After a brief piano introduction, each of the seven stanzas of *Back Water Blues* follows the same form and general melodic outline. The form may be simple, but in Smith's recorded performance, the musical possibilities seem infinite. She enlivens each stanza with unique timbres, phrasing, and melodic

MEASURE:	1	2	3	4	5	6	7	8	9	10	11	12
HARMONY:	I	I(IV)	I	I	IV	IV	I	I	V	V(IV)	I	I
POETIC STRUCTURE:	A				A				B			

FIGURE 34.5 *Twelve-bar blues form.*

sensibility. The melody shows typical traits of the blues, with prominent blue notes on the third and seventh degrees of the scale (E/E♭ and B/B♭) and a tendency to place stressed syllables just before rather than on the strong beats of the measure. The typical blues phrase centers around a relatively high note, usually the fifth degree of the scale, repeats or decorates it, and then descends to the tonic. All three phrases in Example 34.2 follow this pattern but in different ways: the first phrase curves above and below G before sinking to C; the second twice rises to G and descends; and the last hammers G and the B above it, descending only on the last three syllables. The vocal melody cadences in the third measure of each phrase, allowing a call-and-response interchange between the voice and the piano accompaniment, played by African American composer and pianist James P. Johnson (1891–1955). In its use of improvisation on a simple formula, syncopation, repetition of short patterns, bent pitches, and call and response, this song embodies many of the characteristics of African American music that apparently originated in Africa (see Chapter 30).

Delta blues   Delta blues came primarily from the delta region of Mississippi and is usually associated with male African American singers and guitarists. In comparison to classic blues, which tended to conform to the conventions of popular song genres, delta blues is more directly rooted in oral traditions, resulting in greater flexibility of textual and musical form and harmonic choices. Blues singers gained national exposure through collectors such as Alan Lomax, who traveled to rural parts of the south and recorded blues artists as they sang and accompanied themselves on guitar. Delta blues recordings from the 1920s and 1930s reveal a wealth of expressive devices. The singing style is rough, rich in timbre and nuance, and rhythmically flexible, and each section of a blues song features alternation between the voice and accompanying guitar in the style of call and response. As in classic blues, sexuality and relationships are constant themes, as strongly focused on the male perspective as classic blues is on the female.

During the first half of the twentieth century, when an unprecedented number of African Americans moved from the rural south to northern urban centers, in the Great Migration, many blues singers followed the same path. Many of the delta blues singers landed in Chicago, already a burgeoning center of new recording technology, which would greatly extend their influence on future performers. Legendary bluesman Robert Johnson (1911–1938), for example, recorded only twenty-nine songs in his brief career, yet his musical legacy extended well into the 1960s, when British rock musicians rediscovered his recordings and recorded new versions of his songs.

JAZZ IN THE 1920S Jazz was already established and growing in popularity during the late 1910s (see Chapter 31). The essence of 1920s jazz was syncopated rhythm, combined with novel vocal and instrumental sounds and an unbridled spirit that seemed to mock earlier social and musical proprieties. Improvisation was an important element of jazz, but often melodies in the style of an improvisation were worked out in rehearsals, played from memory, or written down and played from notation. Jazz was very much a player's art, so the rise of the recording industry and of radio played a key role in fostering its growth and dissemination.

The leading style of jazz in the period just after World War I is now known as **New Orleans jazz**. This style, named after the city where it originated, centers on group variation of a given tune, either improvised or in the same spontaneous style. The result is a counterpoint of melodic lines, alternating with solos during which the rest of the ensemble provides a rhythmic and harmonic background. It incorporates the African idiom of call and response, as well as the ecstatic outpourings of the African American gospel tradition. The development of the style in New Orleans was enhanced by the healthy rivalry between musically literate Creoles (descendants of immigrants from the West Indies, often of mixed race) and musically untutored African Americans, who possessed great improvisational skill. Leading musicians, including cornetist Joe "King" Oliver (1885–1938), trumpeter Louis Armstrong (1901–1971), and pianist Jelly Roll Morton (1890–1941), developed the style playing in clubs in Storyville, the city's red-light district. In the late 1910s, many New Orleans jazz performers left the city when professional opportunities elsewhere in the country beckoned during the Great Migration, spreading the style to other regions.

New Orleans jazz

King Oliver moved north to Chicago in 1918 and formed his own band in 1920. In 1922, Oliver invited Louis Armstrong, whom he had mentored in New Orleans, to come north and join his band, by then named King Oliver's Creole Jazz Band. The next year the band began recording for OKeh Records in Chicago and for Gennett in Richmond, Indiana, both among the most important record labels in jazz history, and posed for the publicity photograph in Figure 34.6. Armstrong later assembled his own band for making recordings, calling it the Hot Five or Hot Seven, depending on the current number

King Oliver and Louis Armstrong

FIGURE 34.6 *King Oliver's Creole Jazz Band in a 1923 publicity photograph. Left to right: Honoré Dutrey, trombone; Baby Dodds, drums; King Oliver, cornet; Louis Armstrong (kneeling), slide trumpet; Lillian Hardin (later Armstrong's wife), piano; Bill Johnson, banjo; and Johnny Dodds, clarinet. The drums, piano, and banjo served as a rhythm section.*

Jazz conventions

of musicians. With these groups he cut several dozen recordings for OKeh between 1925 and 1928.

The recordings of these two bands embody the classic New Orleans style. Armstrong's recording of Oliver's tune *West End Blues* (NAWM 192), recorded with his Hot Five in Chicago in 1928, exemplifies the conventions of the style and showcases Armstrong's emphasis on solo improvisation. The ensemble is small and is divided into two groups: the "front line" of melodic instruments—trumpet, clarinet, and trombone—and the **rhythm section** that keeps the beat and fills in the background—drums, piano, and banjo. New Orleans jazz typically takes twelve-bar blues, a sixteen-measure strain from ragtime, or a thirty-two-bar popular song form (usually AABA) as a starting point. A tune is presented at the beginning over a particular harmonic progression, then that same progression repeats several times while various soloists or combinations of instruments play over it. Each such repetition is called a **chorus** (not to be confused with the chorus in a song with verse and chorus). Typically each chorus features different instruments and some new musical ideas, producing a kind of variation form.

West End Blues

As the title suggests, *West End Blues* is built on twelve-bar blues form. The published sheet music (NAWM 192a) adapts the blues to Tin Pan Alley verse-refrain form, presenting the blues progression once in the verse, shown in Example 34.3a, and twice in the refrain. But the recording (NAWM 192b) follows the conventions of jazz, presenting a blazing trumpet introduction by Armstrong and five choruses of the twelve-bar blues pattern. In the first, Armstrong varies the published verse as shown in Example 34.3b, progressing from a fairly straight performance of the tune to increasingly fanciful acrobatics. He embellishes the tune rhythmically—with delays, syncopations, triplets, and sixteenth notes—and melodically, with neighboring and passing tones. For example, in measure 7, he approaches every note of the E♭ triad from its upper neighbor, then in the next measure plays all the notes in the E♭ scale but one, holding back the A♭ to emphasize its appearance in measure 9 as the seventh of the dominant seventh chord. At the end of his solo, he climbs upward in a fanfare-like arpeggiation and ends on a high B♭. In the second chorus, the trombonist plays off the first half of the published refrain and then improvises freely. The third chorus features the clarinet alternating in call and response with Armstrong who, to tenderly expressive effect, sings syllables rather than playing notes on his instrument, a technique known as **scat singing**. After the piano takes the fourth chorus, everyone joins in on the final chorus, backing Armstrong as he returns to the high B♭ that ended his first solo, sustains it for four measures, and then unleashes an extraordinary torrent of notes, obsessively repeating and then varying a descending figure as if to balance the rising arpeggiation that closed his first chorus. Through inspired solos such as those in this recording, Armstrong helped to create a new focus in jazz on the art of solo improvisation, replacing the ensemble improvisation that was characteristic of earlier New Orleans jazz.

BIG BANDS AND SWING Although Armstrong's feats as a soloist inspired virtuosity and expressivity in other jazz musicians, the main function of jazz was to accompany dancing. A fashion for larger bands began in the 1920s,

EXAMPLE 34.3 *Verse of King Oliver's* West End Blues *with Louis Armstrong's variation*

propelled partly by the availability of larger performance spaces for jazz, including supper clubs, ballrooms, auditoriums, and theaters. African American band leaders, such as Armstrong, Fletcher Henderson (1898–1952), Duke Ellington (1899–1974), and Count Basie (1904–1984), as well as white musicians like Paul Whiteman (1890–1967) and Benny Goodman (1909–1986), organized **big bands**. By 1930, the typical dance band was divided into three sections: brass, reeds, and rhythm. Brasses might include three trumpets and two trombones; the reed section was made up of clarinets and saxophones; and the rhythm section consisted of piano, guitar (replacing the banjo), double bass, and drums. These sections interacted as units and alternated with soloists, providing a great variety of sounds.

Although solos might still be improvised, the piece was written down by an arranger, who was sometimes the leader (as in the case of Ellington) but more often a member of the band or a skilled orchestrator. Successful arrangers captured in notation the spontaneous spirit of improvised playing. Preparing

Arrangers and composers

arrangements in advance made possible a wider variety of effects, including rhythmic unisons of the entire band or of a section, coordinated dialogue between sections and soloists, and more complex chromatic harmonies, all of which added to the emotional impact and polished sound of the music. With the creation of fully or largely notated jazz pieces, jazz composers who made their own arrangements came increasingly to resemble their counterparts in the classical music world. They also borrowed sounds from modern classical music, especially the four-note sonorities (such as seventh chords and added sixth chords) and chromatic harmonies of Debussy and Ravel.

Singers   In addition to playing instrumental pieces, the typical big band also featured a vocalist, who might sing through the entire piece, sing only at the beginning and end, or come in on one of the later choruses. Much of the big-band repertory consisted of popular songs in which the band both accompanied a singer and elaborated on the song through clever, harmonically adventurous arrangements that highlighted one or more of the band's sections.

The swing era   The combination of stylish, well-executed arrangements with hard-driving jazz rhythms produced a music that became known as **swing**. The name derived from swing rhythm, in which notes on the beat are given extra time and those on offbeats are delayed and shortened, producing an effect like triplets alternating quarter and eighth notes, much like the *notes inégales* of seventeenth-century France (see Chapter 16). Swing was an energetic and optimistic style that became the musical background to the United States' gradual recovery from the Great Depression. It was an immediate hit with the American public, igniting a dance craze across the country. Swing dances such as the Lindy Hop were more bouncy and vigorous than earlier ballroom dances, matching the style of the music. Swing was the most popular music from the 1930s through the late 1940s. With swing, jazz attained a popularity that it never had before, nor would have in later years.

Swing and race   The new music broke down racial barriers, attracting legions of young white fans who became interested in black musicians and their art. The number of swing bands exploded during the 1930s, boosted by new white bands entering the jazz world, especially those led by Tommy Dorsey (1905–1956) and Glenn Miller (1904–1944). In an era still marked by racial prejudice and segregation, the white bands had an easier time establishing themselves; they did not have to worry about playing to segregated audiences and had greater access to performance venues and radio time. Some big-band leaders integrated their bands, hiring both black and white performers; Benny Goodman was the most prominent white band leader to do so, bringing on Fletcher Henderson as an arranger and playing with vibraphonist Lionel Hampton, pianist Teddy Wilson, and drummer Gene Krupa (who was white) in the Benny Goodman Quartet, one of the first racially integrated jazz groups to play in public. Black or white, band leaders like Ellington, Basie, Goodman, Dorsey, and Miller—and many of their star players—were celebrities, known across the continent and abroad, and their music was heard on millions of radios and phonographs.

JAZZ IN EUROPE Jazz spread quickly in the 1920s throughout North America, Latin America, and Europe. European musicians and music lovers encountered American jazz through imported recordings, sheet music, and traveling jazz ensembles. African American musician-soldiers serving in Europe during World War I, such as the band led by James Reese Europe (see Chapter 31), had helped to introduce the new style. By the 1920s, jazz groups were forming in Europe, and a European jazz tradition was well established by the 1930s. Jazz also became a frequent topic in European literature and arts, as illustrated by Figure 34.7.

In 1934, Roma (Gypsy) guitarist Django Reinhardt (1910–1953) formed one of the most successful and musically innovative European jazz bands, the Quintette du Hot Club de France, along with violinist Stéphane Grappelli (1908–1997). The group toured throughout Europe until the outbreak of World War II. The first European to become an outstanding jazz performer and composer, Reinhardt demonstrated the international potential of the American-born tradition, blending it with his own Roma heritage to create a highly individual and appealing style.

FIGURE 34.7 The Three Musicians *(1920), by Henri Hayden (1883–1970). Born in Poland, Hayden came to Paris in 1907 and painted in a cubist style for many years. The three instruments—banjo, saxophone, and guitar—mark the music of this group as jazz, all the rage in Paris after World War I.*

DUKE ELLINGTON

One of the leading composers of the Jazz Age and after, and one of the most influential American composers ever, was Duke Ellington (see biography and Figure 34.8).

Ellington developed his individual style and began to garner national attention during the years 1927–31, when his group was house band at the Cotton Club in Harlem, the vibrant and famous African American area in New York. The Cotton Club was Harlem's preeminent nightclub, offering alcohol (illegal because of Prohibition, yet readily available) and entertainment. It featured black performers, including Ellington's band and a bevy of beautiful, light-skinned female dancers, but its clientele was white. The Cotton Club period was crucial to the development of Ellington's sound. Because his was the house band, the personnel was relatively stable, they had time to rehearse, and Ellington could use the band as a workshop to try out new pieces and new effects, testing the unusual timbres and voicings that became his trademark. He started experimenting with longer jazz works, such as *Creole Rhapsody* and *Reminiscing in Tempo*.

Cotton Club years

Rather than relying primarily on improvisation, the group moved more and more to arrangements worked out in advance that contrasted ensemble passages with solos, whether scored or improvised. When hiring players, Ellington looked for excellent musicians with very individual sounds, then capitalized on the unique talents of his band members by writing specifically

DUKE ELLINGTON

(1899–1974)

Edward Kennedy ("Duke") Ellington, the most important composer of jazz to date, was an influential innovator who expanded the boundaries in jazz and sought to break down barriers between it and art music. He admired the great jazz musicians, but his favorite composers were Debussy, Stravinsky, and Gershwin.

Born in Washington, D.C., Ellington was the son of a White House butler. He studied piano, including ragtime, from the age of seven and received a good education in music and other subjects. A school friend gave him the nickname "Duke" for his aristocratic bearing and stylish clothing. By the age of seventeen, Ellington was playing throughout the Washington area with his own group. In 1923, he moved to New York with his band the Washingtonians, playing at clubs on Broadway and at the Cotton Club in Harlem and making recordings.

During the 1930s and early 1940s, Ellington was the leading figure in jazz, and in later years he continued to play a prominent role, especially in efforts to have jazz recognized as a kind of art music, not merely as entertainment. He and his band made several international tours in the 1950s and 1960s, sponsored by the State Department and intended to create good will toward the United States. By the 1960s he was regarded as a national treasure. He won thirteen Grammy awards, was awarded seventeen honorary degrees, was granted the Presidential Medal of Honor

FIGURE 34.8 *Duke Ellington at the piano in the mid-1930s.*

in 1969, and in the early 1970s was named a member of the National Institute of Arts and Letters and of the Swedish Royal Academy of Music, the first jazz musician to be so honored. He played and toured with his band until his death at age seventy-five, when his son, Mercer Ellington, took over the band and continued to tour.

MAJOR WORKS *East St. Louis Toodle-oo; Black and Tan Fantasy; Mood Indigo; Creole Rhapsody; Concerto for Cootie; Ko-Ko; Cotton Tail; Black, Brown and Beige;* and more than 1,300 other compositions, including songs, choral works, tone poems, suites, musicals, and ballet and film scores

---

for them or collaborating with them, as in *Black and Tan Fantasy* (1927) with trumpeter Bubber Miley and *Mood Indigo* (1930) with clarinet and saxophone player Barney Bigard. His band grew from ten to twelve players, made about two hundred recordings, and appeared regularly on radio broadcasts.

Touring   From 1931 on, Ellington and his band spent most of their time on the road. The band continued to grow, reaching fourteen players in the late 1930s and eighteen in 1946. The group's repertoire consisted largely of Ellington's own tunes, but they also played popular songs and dance favorites. Many of Ellington's tunes were given lyrics and sold as popular songs, including *Sophisticated Lady* and *Don't Get Around Much Anymore*. Ellington often wrote and recorded smaller ensemble pieces to highlight the skills of individual players, keeping his stars happy by giving each a piece of the limelight.

The early 1940s is widely considered the peak of Ellington's creative abilities and of the performing rapport among the band members. In 1939–40, he added three important new members: Jimmie Blanton on bass, Ben Webster on tenor saxophone, and Billy Strayhorn as second pianist, composer, and arranger. Ellington took advantage of their talents and wrote a number of new pieces to display their gifts. *Cotton Tail* (1940; NAWM 193) was written for Webster, and his solo became a classic. Strayhorn shared composing duties with Ellington, producing standards such as *Take the A Train* (1941), which became one of the band's signature tunes.

Cotton Tail illustrates Ellington's music from this era. It follows the typical form for jazz performances, with a tune at the beginning followed by a series of choruses over the same progression. *Cotton Tail* is a **contrafact**, a new tune composed over a harmonic progression borrowed from a particular song—in this case, the chorus of Gershwin's *I Got Rhythm* (NAWM 190). Ellington's melody—fast, angular, highly syncopated, and full of unexpected twists—has little resemblance to Gershwin's, even though the harmonic progression is the same. The first two choruses feature Ben Webster soloing on tenor saxophone accompanied by the rhythm section with occasional punctuation from the rest of the band. Example 34.4 compares the opening measures of Ellington's tune with those of Webster's choruses. The solo plays off the same chord progression as the tune but does not vary or develop the tune. Rather, the music at each chorus presents new ideas and may or may not use melodic or rhythmic ideas from earlier in the piece. The remaining three choruses feature various combinations of instruments playing together or in call-and-response fashion, and the final bars of Ellington's tune return to bring the piece to a close.

Throughout his career, Ellington fought the label "jazz composer," preferring to consider his music (and all good music) "beyond category." He believed that jazz could serve not only as dance or entertainment music but also as art music, listened to for its own sake. He frequently pushed against

The 1940s

Cotton Tail

Beyond category

EXAMPLE 34.4 *Duke Ellington's* Cotton Tail *and Ben Webster's solo*

the boundaries of technology and convention. Until the introduction of long-playing records in the late 1940s, a piece could only be about three to four minutes long in order to fit on one side of a 78-rpm record; longer pieces had to be split up on several record sides, making them more difficult to market. Ellington composed longer pieces anyway and convinced the record companies to record the pieces on multiple sides. Later in his career, he composed suites, such as *Black, Brown and Beige* (1943), *Harlem* (1950), and *Suite Thursday* (1960), and collaborated with Billy Strayhorn in rescoring for jazz band classical favorites such as Tchaikovsky's *Nutcracker Suite* and Grieg's *Peer Gynt Suite.* In asserting the value of jazz as an art music, he was declaring it worthy of attentive listening and of a permanent place in American culture. In both respects, his view has won out.

FILM MUSIC

Sound in film   In the same way that recordings and radio fostered the explosive growth of jazz, new technologies transformed film music. In the late 1920s, methods were invented to synchronize recorded sound with film, opening up new possibilities for the use of music as part of a film, not merely as live accompaniment to it. The first "talking picture" (so called because it featured recorded dialogue) was *The Jazz Singer* (1927) starring Al Jolson, which included scenes of Jolson singing and other scenes in which music was used to accompany the action, as in earlier silent films. These two types of scene exemplify the two categories of music in film that have continued to the present:

1. music that is heard or performed by the characters themselves, known as **diegetic music** or **source music**, and
2. background music that conveys to the viewer a mood or other aspects of a scene or character, known as **nondiegetic music** or **underscoring**.

On-screen performances   The advent of sound film put thousands of theater musicians out of work, an economic downturn made disastrous by the Great Depression that began in 1929. Yet it did open a new window of opportunity. By the mid-1930s, the major Hollywood studios each employed composers, orchestrators, arrangers, and editors to create music for films and orchestras to perform it, and filmmakers abroad assembled similar units. Both dramas and comedies often included musical numbers as interludes or for dramatic reasons. One of the earliest movies to use music dramatically was the Austrian film *Der blaue Engel* (simultaneously released in English as *The Blue Angel,* 1930). In it Marlene Dietrich as a cabaret singer performs songs by Friedrich Hollaender (a.k.a. Frederick Hollander), among them her signature song, *Falling in Love Again,* which in the German version has entirely different and racier words.

Movie musicals   Beginning in 1929, Hollywood studios produced numerous musicals composed for film. During the 1930s, the "Golden Age" of the Hollywood musical, many of Broadway's best-known composers wrote music for movie musicals, including Romberg (*Viennese Nights*), Gershwin (*Delicious* and *Shall We Dance?*), Berlin (*Top Hat*), Kern (*Swing Time*), and Porter (*Born to Dance*). The spectacular choreography of Busby Berkeley enlivened *Gold Diggers of 1933* and many other films, and the singing and dancing of Bing Crosby, Fred Astaire, and Ginger Rogers in many movie musicals made them international stars. Movie musicals were enormously popular. They offered escape from the Great Depression, their level of talent was high, and ticket prices were inexpensive compared to Broadway shows. A parallel development in Germany was the film operetta, including scores by Franz Lehár (*Where Is This Lady?*) and other prominent composers, but the rise of the Nazis in 1933 forced many of the leading figures to emigrate.

The Hollywood studios also fostered the rise of film scores that were fully integrated into the dramatic action, like the music for an opera—"opera without singing," in the memorable phrase of composer Erich Wolfgang Korngold. Many of the composers working in Hollywood were European immigrants, and they applied the language of Wagner, Richard Strauss, and Debussy to music for film. Max Steiner (1888–1971), an immigrant from Vienna who had worked on Broadway for fifteen years as an arranger, orchestrator, and composer, established the model for the Hollywood film score with his music for *King Kong* (1933). The movie, whose poster is shown in Figure 34.9, centered on a giant gorilla discovered in Africa and brought to New York, where it threatens the city. Steiner's score is organized around leitmotives for characters and ideas, as in a Wagner opera, and coordinates the music with actions on screen, often marking particular movements with musical effects. The music conveys mood, character, and place through styles with strong associations, from primitivism for the African setting to orchestral Romanticism for dramatic moments, and it uses modernist techniques when appropriate, such as intense dissonance for fright and other extreme emotions. All of these traits became characteristic of film scoring.

FIGURE 34.9 *Poster for* King Kong *(1933), whose score by Max Steiner set the paradigm for Hollywood film music.*

Steiner continued writing film scores through the 1960s, his credits including *Gone with the Wind* (1939) and *Casablanca* (1943). Other leading Hollywood film composers include Erich Wolfgang Korngold (1897–1957), who brought his experience as a Viennese composer of opera and classical concert works to scores for the Errol Flynn swashbucklers *Captain Blood* (1935) and *The Adventures of Robin Hood* (1938), and Alfred Newman (1900–1970), the first major native-born American film composer, known for scores to *Wuthering Heights, The Song of Bernadette, How the West Was Won, Airport,* and more than two hundred other films. Music also played a prominent role in animated films, from shorts like Walt Disney's pioneering cartoon *Steamboat Willie* (1928) and the Bugs Bunny cartoons scored by Carl Stalling (1891–1972) to full-length features, beginning with Disney's *Snow White and the Seven Dwarfs* (1937) with a score by Frank Churchill (1901–1942). Music became integral to all these types of film, guiding the viewer's emotional responses and giving depth to the events on screen.

MASS MEDIA AND POPULAR MUSIC

Through the new technologies of recordings, radio, and sound on film, American popular music, jazz, and film music reached audiences throughout the Western world. Music could now be preserved and enjoyed year after year, for decades to come. As a result, much of this music maintained its popularity, and within a generation or two many of these pieces achieved the status of classics: widely known, heard and reheard, and highly valued. By the 1970s, canons of classics had developed for popular song, blues, jazz, and film music, in parallel with the canon of classical music that had emerged in the nineteenth century. The central core of those canons—parallel to Bach, Mozart, and Beethoven in the classical world—is in most cases formed by composers and performers whose music was popular between the world wars, including Berlin, Kern, Gershwin, Porter, Bessie Smith, King Oliver, Armstrong, Ellington, Basie, Goodman, Steiner, Korngold, and Newman.

Today, in addition to recordings and movies, live ensembles perform Tin Pan Alley songs, Broadway musicals, blues, New Orleans jazz, swing, big-band jazz, and even movie scores from the 1910s, 1920s, and 1930s. This music is admired both for its original value as entertainment and because it is considered artful, worth listening to with attention, and capable of offering musical experiences available nowhere else—the same reasons that music of earlier generations was preserved and revived in the nineteenth century. There are now many traditions of musical classics, and all have a share in our richly varied musical life.

Further Reading is available at digital.wwnorton.com/hwm10

BETWEEN THE WORLD WARS: THE CLASSICAL TRADITION

❖

Music in the classical tradition continued to diversify in style and concept between the world wars, as composers sought individual solutions to the common problem of finding a place in the crowded classical repertoire. In all nations and regions, music composition became increasingly—or perhaps only more overtly—tied to political concerns and ideologies. Government regulation of music was especially strong in the Soviet Union and Nazi Germany. Some composers in the classical tradition—reacting to social and political pressures, to the economic crisis of the Great Depression, to their older modernist colleagues, or to the perceived loss of a listening public for modern music—sought to reconnect with a large audience, while others pursued new ideas with little concern for popularity. Throughout the Americas a growing number of composers won international reputations with music that represented their nations on the world stage. An experimental or "ultramodernist" tradition emerged in the United States alongside a growing nationalist trend, both representing assertions of independence from Europe.

MUSIC, POLITICS, AND THE PEOPLE

Music has long been linked to politics. Aristotle discussed music in his *Politics,* and he and Plato described the appropriate uses of music for the ideal society. Charlemagne's desire to unify his large empire led to the codification of Gregorian chant. Louis XIV asserted control through dance and opera. And Verdi's operas rallied support for Italian unification and freedom from foreign rule.

But in the nineteenth century, some writers claimed that classical music was an autonomous art that transcended politics and should be composed, performed, experienced, and admired for its own sake, separate from political or social concerns. The new "science" of musicology that emerged during the nineteenth century reinforced this view, focusing more on the styles and procedures of past music than on its social functions. To some extent, treating music on its own terms

TIMELINE

1914–18 World War I

1923 Darius Milhaud, *La création du monde*

1923 Edgard Varèse, *Hyperprism*

1924 George Gershwin, *Rhapsody in Blue*

1925 Henry Cowell, *The Banshee*

1925–26 Ernst Krenek, *Jonny spielt auf*

1928 Kurt Weill, *The Threepenny Opera*

1929 New York stock market crash begins Great Depression

1930 William Grant Still, *Afro-American Symphony*

1931 Ruth Crawford Seeger, *String Quartet 1931*

1933 Adolf Hitler comes to power in Germany

1933 Franklin D. Roosevelt institutes New Deal in USA

1933 Union of Soviet Composers founded

1933–34 Paul Hindemith, *Symphony Mathis der Maler*

1934 Doctrine of socialist realism adopted in Soviet Union

1936 Dmitri Shostakovich's opera *Lady Macbeth* attacked in Soviet press

1937 Shostakovich, Fifth Symphony

1938 Sergey Prokofiev, *Alexander Nevsky*

1938–45 Heitor Villa-Lobos, *Bachianas brasileiras No. 5*

1939–45 World War II

1943–44 Aaron Copland, *Appalachian Spring*

was an admirable ideal, allowing many listeners to enjoy music for its own sake and as a respite from the concerns of the day. But in other respects, from its cultivation by the economic and social elite to its association with nationalism, classical music never escaped politics.

The period between the world wars brought new links between music and politics. In democracies such as Britain, France, Germany under the Weimar Republic, and the United States, economic troubles and political conflicts led many composers to believe that art which set itself apart from social needs was in danger of becoming irrelevant to society at large. As the gap widened between the unfamiliar sounds of modernist music and the ability of listeners to understand it, composers tried to bring contemporary music closer to the general public by crafting widely accessible concert works or by writing music for films, theater, and dance. Convinced that music performed by amateurs and school groups was as important as art music, some composers wrote works that were within the capabilities of amateurs and rewarding to perform, yet were modern in style. Many composers used music, especially musical theater, to engage current social, political, and economic issues. Nationalism continued as a strong force in most countries, exemplified in the musical styles of individual composers and in efforts to edit, publish, and perform music of the nation, including both folk music and the written music of earlier times.

Most governments sponsored musical activities directly. Public schools increasingly included music in the curriculum. Hungarian composer Zoltán Kodály devised a method of teaching music to children through the use of folk songs, musical games, and graded exercises—a method that was eventually adopted by many schools across Europe and North America. Throughout most of Europe, radio was controlled by the government and was a major employer of composers and performers. During the New Deal in the United States, the federal government established programs to employ out-of-work musicians and composers. Totalitarian governments insisted that music under their regimes support the state and its ideologies. In the 1930s, the Soviet Union and Nazi Germany attempted to suppress the composition and performance of modernist music, which was condemned in one country as bourgeois decadence, in the other as cultural Bolshevism. This last example illustrates a point worth bearing in mind. Although musical styles were often identified with particular ideologies, these links were contingent on the unique political situation in each nation; the same style, even the same piece, could be seen as progressive or socialist in one place and conservative or fascistic in another.

FRANCE

In France, and especially in Paris, musical life had long been intertwined with politics. Since the Franco-Prussian War in 1870–71, strong anti-German sentiment had led to an increased focus on French music as an embodiment of French national character and culture, but people of different political stripes disagreed about what qualities French culture, and thus French music, should have. Groups across the political spectrum sponsored concerts that supported their points of view. In the early 1900s, the conservative nationalist Ligue de la Patrie Française (League of the French Homeland) joined with Vincent d'Indy and his Schola Cantorum to present concerts and lectures that showcased the French tradition—particularly composers from the Middle Ages to the 1789 Revolution and the classically oriented composers since Franck—as the embodiment of authentic French culture based on religious principles and respect for authority. In response, the government, then dominated by left-wing parties, promoted French composers since the Revolution, especially those like Berlioz and Saint-Saëns who, their advocates argued, freed French music from the bonds of tradition. In this way, not only new music but the music of the past was politically contested.

World War I and its aftermath brought a new wave of anti-German sentiment and a renewed opposition to German influences in French culture. During and after the war, nationalists asserted that French music was intrinsically classic, as opposed to the Romanticism of the Germans. But exactly how "classic" was to be defined was a point of contention. Conservatives like d'Indy identified it with balance, order, discipline, and tradition, contrasting with the irrationality and individualism of Romanticism. Composers on the left, like Ravel (see Chapter 32), saw the classic as encompassing the universal and not merely the national. His music included elements from Viennese waltzes (*La valse*), Spain (*Bolero*), Roma style (*Tzigane*), blues (Violin Sonata), and jazz (Concerto for the Left Hand), all rejected by the conservative nationalists. *Notions of classicism*

The turn away from Romanticism was also linked to a new interest in popular music, from cabarets to the music of African Americans. Maurice Chevalier (1888–1972) sang in cafés and music halls from the age of twelve and starred in the Folies-Bergère in the 1910s and 1920s, the most famous among dozens of singers who enlivened the Parisian popular traditions. James Reese Europe's band of African American soldiers was the toast of Paris at the end of the war (see Chapter 31), and from 1925 on the performances of St. Louis–born singer and dancer Josephine Baker (1906–1975) at the Folies-Bergères made her among the most acclaimed musicians in France. Many writers and musicians saw the energy of this music as affording a way out of Romanticism, an escape from Wagnerism, a path forward after Debussy, and a fresh beginning after the shock of the war. As Jean Cocteau wrote in his essay *Cock and Harlequin* (1918), "Enough of music in which one lies and soaks. . . . What we need is a music of the earth, every day music." He held up "the music hall, the circus, and American Negro bands" as stimulants for a new art music that would be anti-Romantic and fully French in its clarity, accessibility, and emotional restraint, while moving beyond the recent past: "Impressionism has fired its last fine fireworks at the end of a long fête. It is up to us to set the rockets for another fête." *Popular influences*

According to recent research by Marianne Wheeldon, Cocteau's farewell to impressionism was part of a larger anti-Debussyist ferment that led to both French neoclassicism and the growing interest in popular music. Younger critics and composers, while acknowledging their esteem for Debussy's *Anti-Debussyism* music, sought to move beyond what they saw as his overemphasis on vertical sonorities, his blurred timbres and colorful orchestral effects, and his reliance on extramusical imagery and exotic associations. Instead they promoted counterpoint, more pungent dissonance, precise timbres, more use of winds and percussion, formal clarity, and absolute music that suggests associations with the everyday world of popular music or with the historical past of the classics, rather than with dreams, visions, or distant places. These are the characteristics that coalesced in French music of the 1920s and became identified as neoclassical. Thus neoclassicism—the use of counterpoint, eighteenth-century forms and genres, and neotonal harmony, allied with emotional restraint and a rejection of Debussyism and Romanticism—became the prevailing trend in France after World War I.

LES SIX A younger group of composers absorbed these new attitudes but sought to escape the old political dichotomies. Arthur Honegger (1892–1955), Darius Milhaud (1892–1974), Francis Poulenc (1899–1963), Germaine Tailleferre (1892–1983), Georges Auric (1899–1983), and Louis Durey (1888–1979) were dubbed "Les Six" (The Six), in a parallel to the Mighty Five in Russia (see Chapters 28 and 30), by a French journalist writing in 1920 who saw them as seeking to free French music from foreign domination. They drew inspiration from Erik Satie (see Chapter 32) and were hailed by Cocteau.

The group, pictured in Figure 35.1, collaborated in joint concerts, an album of piano music, and Cocteau's absurdist play-with-ballet *Les mariés de la tour Eiffel* (Newlyweds on the Eiffel Tower, 1921). But the group did not remain together long—Durey left before the ballet project started—and none of them fully conformed to Cocteau's program. Instead, they each wrote highly individual works that drew on a wide range of influences, including but not limited to neoclassicism. Tailleferre was the most in tune with neoclassical ideals, drawing on Couperin and Rameau (see Chapter 18) in her Piano Concerto (1923–24) and other works. Auric was the most taken with Satie's avant-garde approach. But the most individual were Honegger, Milhaud, and Poulenc, who achieved success independent of the group and found ways to make their music distinctive within the broad outlines of neoclassicism.

Honegger excelled in music of dynamic action and graphic gesture, expressed in short-breathed melodies, strong ostinato rhythms, bold colors, and dissonant harmonies. His symphonic movement *Pacific 231* (1923), a translation into music of the visual and physical impression of a speeding locomotive, was hailed as a sensational piece of modernist descriptive music. Honegger won an international reputation in

FIGURE 35.1 The Group of the Six (Hommage à Satie) *by Jacques-Emile Blanche (1922–23). This group portrait shows five of the composers known as Les Six and three of their collaborators. Clockwise from bottom left are Germaine Tailleferre, Darius Milhaud, Arthur Honegger, conductor Jean Wiéner, pianist Marcelle Meyer, Francis Poulenc, writer Jean Cocteau, and Georges Auric. Not shown is Louis Durey, who left the group in 1921.*

1923 with his oratorio *King David,* which combined the tradition of music for amateur chorus with allusions to styles from Gregorian chant to Baroque polyphony to jazz. The evocations of pre-Romantic styles, use of traditional forms and procedures, and prevailing diatonic language all reveal the impact of neoclassicism.

Milhaud produced an immense quantity of music, including piano pieces, chamber music, suites, sonatas, symphonies, film music, ballets, songs, cantatas, operas, and music for children. His works are diverse in style and approach, ranging from the comic frivolity of the ballet *Le boeuf sur le toit* (The Ox on the Roof, 1919) to the earnestness of the opera-oratorio *Christophe Colomb* (Christopher Columbus, 1928) and the religious devotion of the *Sacred Service* (1947), which reflects Milhaud's Jewish heritage. He was especially open to sounds and styles from the Americas, where he traveled often. During World War II, after France fell to the Germans in 1940, he fled to the United States to escape Nazi persecution of Jews. He accepted a teaching position at Mills College in Oakland, California, and continued to teach there until 1971, dividing his time between there and France after the war.

Darius Milhaud

Milhaud grew familiar with the popular music of Brazil during a two-year stay there in 1917–18, and upon his return to Paris he incorporated Brazilian melodies and rhythms in *Le boeuf sur le toit* and in the suite of dances *Saudades do Brasil* (Longing for Brazil, 1920–21), illustrated in Example 35.1. In addition to the syncopated rhythms and diatonic melodies of Brazilian dance, the latter uses polytonality, in which two lines of melody and planes of harmony, each in a distinct and different key, sound simultaneously—here, B major in the upper register over G major in the accompaniment. This procedure would become associated with Milhaud, although many used it before and since.

Inspired by jazz and blues he heard in Harlem during a concert tour in the United States, Milhaud imitated the sounds and styles of jazz in his ballet *La création du monde* (The Creation of the World, 1923). Saxophone, piano, and soloistic treatment of the instruments evoke the sound of jazz bands. In the first scene (NAWM 194), elements of jazz such as blue notes, blues melodies, syncopations, riffs, and ensemble textures are stylized and synthesized with neoclassic and other modernist features, including a fugue, polytonality, and polyrhythms. In all his music, Milhaud blended ingenuity, freshness, and variety with the clarity and logical form he had absorbed from neoclassicism. Yet his openness to foreign influences, from jazz to Schoenberg, was a far cry from the program of nationalist classical purity favored by d'Indy.

La création du monde

Poulenc drew especially on Parisian popular song traditions from cabarets and revues. This too violated the strictures of d'Indy, who rejected influence from "lower" forms of music. Poulenc's compositions revel in an ingratiating

Francis Poulenc

EXAMPLE 35.1 *Darius Milhaud, "Copacabana," from* Saudades do Brasil

harmonic idiom, draw grace and wit from popular styles, and wed satirical mimicry to fluent melody, as in his early ballet *Les biches* (The Darlings, 1923) for Diaghilev's Ballets Russes or his surrealist opera *Les mamelles de Tiresias* (The Breasts of Tiresias, 1940). The *Concert champêtre* (Pastoral Concerto) for harpsichord or piano and small orchestra (1928), commissioned by harpsichordist Wanda Landowska, evokes the spirit of Rameau and Domenico Scarlatti, and his sonatas and chamber works for various groups of instruments bring an expressive, song-influenced melodic idiom and fresh, mildly dissonant harmonies into classical genres and forms. His three-act opera *Dialogues of the Carmelites* (1956) is an affecting meditation on the execution of Carmelite nuns during the French Revolution, raising issues of religion, politics, allegiance, and personal choice that had deep resonances in French political life.

GERMANY

Germany under the Weimar Republic (1919–1933) was a hotbed of political contention. The German Empire had ended in November 1918 when the kaiser abdicated two days before the end of World War I. Before the new government could hold elections, radical factions formed on both the left and the right, battling each other in the streets and opposing the centrist government. The new constitution ratified in Weimar guaranteed universal suffrage for women and men, civil liberties, social welfare, and a democratic framework. Yet the Treaty of Versailles punished the defunct empire instead of supporting the new democracy: Germany was forced to accept responsibility for the war and pay enormous reparations to other nations. Runaway inflation was one result, wiping out savings and impoverishing millions; by the end of 1923 a bag of groceries cost trillions of marks. The government was able to stabilize the currency and renegotiate reparations in 1924, and the economy improved, aided by investments from the United States. That ended when the New York stock market crashed in October 1929, launching the Great Depression. Mass unemployment and a contracting economy led to falling tax revenues, forcing cuts in benefits and services in a spiral of increasing misery. The National Socialist (Nazi) Party exploited the crisis, winning a plurality in the 1932 election. Their leader Adolf Hitler was appointed chancellor in January 1933, and later that spring he assumed unlimited powers and established the Third Reich, a name chosen to claim a place as successor to the Holy Roman Empire and the German Empire of the kaisers.

Weimar culture and music   The liberal ideals of the Weimar Republic and the ongoing political ferment echoed in the musical world. The capital, Berlin, became a center of cultural innovation, from fashion and art to music. The government helped to subsidize ticket prices so people from all social classes could attend operas and orchestral concerts. Some composers sought wider audiences by creating music in accessible styles, incorporating jazz and popular music, or writing pieces for amateurs to sing or play. The openness of Weimar culture allowed music of all kinds to thrive, from Schoenberg's twelve-tone music to the mass songs his former student Hanns Eisler (1898–1962) composed for working-class choruses and left-wing political groups. But after the Nazis came to power in 1933, they attacked most modern music as decadent, banned the political left and Jews from participating in public life, and persecuted Jews and other minorities. As a result, many leading musicians, including Schoenberg and Eisler, took refuge abroad.

We can see the effects of the intellectual and political currents under the Weimar Republic and Third Reich in the careers and music of leading German composers of the time, including Ernst Krenek, Kurt Weill, Paul Hindemith, and Carl Orff.

NEW OBJECTIVITY In opposition to the emotional intensity of the late Romantics and the expressionism of Schoenberg and Berg, a new trend emerged in the 1920s under the slogan *Neue Sachlichkeit,* meaning **New Objectivity**, New Realism, or "New Matter-of-Factness." The phrase was first used in art criticism and quickly adopted by musicians. As articulated by the composer Ernst Krenek (1900–1991) and others, the New Objectivity opposed complexity and promoted the use of familiar elements, borrowing from popular music and jazz or from Classical and Baroque procedures. In their view, music should be objective in its expression, as in the Baroque concept of the affections (see Chapters 13 and 17), rather than subjective or extreme. The notion of music as autonomous was rejected. Instead, it should be widely accessible, communicate clearly, and draw connections to the events and concerns of the time.

Krenek's *Jonny spielt auf* (Johnny Strikes Up the Band), premiered in Leipzig in 1927, was the embodiment of these ideals, an opera set in the present time that used the interaction of a European composer and an African American jazz musician to examine dichotomies between contemplation and pleasure and between a seemingly exhausted and inward-looking European tradition and a new and energetic American one. The music drew on jazz and on a simplified harmonic language. The opera was an immediate success, was produced on over seventy stages during the next three years, and established Krenek's reputation. But almost from the start it was vociferously attacked by the Nazis as "degenerate" for its use of African American elements. Krenek later adopted the twelve-tone method and emigrated to the United States after Nazi Germany absorbed his native Austria in 1938.

Ernst Krenek

KURT WEILL Kurt Weill (1900–1950), an opera composer in Berlin, was also an exponent of the New Objectivity. Sympathetic to the political left, he sought to offer social commentary and to entertain everyday people rather than the intellectual elites.

Weill collaborated with the playwright Bertolt Brecht on the allegorical opera *Aufstieg und Fall der Stadt Mahagonny* (Rise and Fall of the City of Mahagonny, premiered 1930). In the opera, fugitives from justice build a town dedicated to pleasure, free of legal or moral taboos, but soon find that they have created a hell rather than a paradise on earth. Weill's score incorporates elements of popular music and jazz and makes witty references to a variety of styles. The pit orchestra includes instruments typical of jazz bands—two saxophones, piano, banjo, and bass guitar—as well as winds and timpani, while three saxophones, zither, a bandoneon (a kind of accordion), strings, and brass play in the stage orchestra. Through satire in both libretto and music, Brecht and Weill sought to expose what they regarded as the failures of capitalism, which the city of Mahagonny exemplified.

Mahagonny

FIGURE 35.2 *Lotte Lenya as Jenny in the 1931 film version of Kurt Weill's* The Threepenny Opera.

The most famous collaboration between Weill and Brecht was *Die Dreigroschenoper* (The Threepenny Opera, premiered 1928). Brecht based the libretto on *The Beggar's Opera* by John Gay (see Chapter 21 and NAWM 112), although Weill borrowed only one air from the score. The cast included Lotte Lenya, shown in Figure 35.2, whom Weill had married in 1926; she became his favorite interpreter and after his death a champion of his work. The music parodied rather than imitated American hit songs, then the rage in Europe. Weill juxtaposed in a surreal manner the eighteenth-century ballad texts, European dance music, and American jazz. The opening song, *Die Moritat von Mackie Messer* (The Ballad of Mack the Knife; NAWM 195), lists the murderous deeds of Macheath, the central character, a gang leader in London. The lilting melody undercuts the brutal imagery, conveying Macheath's easygoing charm, and creating a disturbing sense that we are meant to sympathize with the criminal underclass rather than with the power structure. As the verses go by and the body count rises, the accompaniment changes from a harmonium, imitating the barrel organ of an eighteenth-century street singer, to a jazz band with piano, banjo, percussion, trombone, trumpet, and saxophones; the effect is to gradually bring the story into the present day and to suggest its relevance as a parable for modern society.

The original Berlin production ran for over two years, and within five years *The Threepenny Opera* enjoyed more than ten thousand performances in nineteen languages. The Nazis banned it as decadent in 1933, and Weill and Lenya left for Paris, then in 1935 for the United States.

Career on Broadway   In New York, Weill began his second career as a composer for Broadway musicals. The most successful were *Knickerbocker Holiday* (1938), *Lady in the Dark* (1941), and the musical tragedy *Lost in the Stars* (1948), about apartheid in South Africa. The spirit of the New Objectivity lived on in these works, crafted by a classically trained modernist yet addressed to a broad musical public and meant to be immediately grasped by mind and heart.

PAUL HINDEMITH   Paul Hindemith (1895–1963) was among the most prolific composers of the century. At the Berlin School of Music (1927–37), Yale University (1940–53), and the University of Zurich (1951–57), he taught two generations of musicians. He thought of himself primarily as a practicing musician, performing professionally as violinist, violist, and conductor and able to play many other instruments. The experience of performance became central to his music, whether intended for amateurs or professionals.

Works of the Weimar period   In the fragmented world of new music between the wars, Hindemith changed his approach several times. He began composing in a late Romantic style, then developed an individual expressionist language in works like the one-act opera *Mörder, Hoffnung der Frauen* (Murderer, Hope of Women, 1919), based on Oskar Kokoschka's play (see Figure 33.2). Soon he adopted the aesthetic stance later dubbed the New Objectivity, which in his music was exemplified by an avoidance of Romantic expressivity and a focus on purely musical procedures, especially motivic development and a polyphony of independent lines. The seven works he titled simply *Kammermusik* (Chamber Music, 1922–27) include a piece for small orchestra and six concertos for solo instrument and chamber orchestra, which encompass a variety of movement types from neo-Baroque ritornello forms to military marches and dances. All his music is neotonal, establishing pitch centers through techniques from simple reiteration of a note to complex contrapuntal voice-leading.

By the late 1920s, Hindemith was disturbed by the widening gulf between modern composers and an increasingly passive public. In response, he began composing what was known as **Gebrauchsmusik**—"music for use," as distinguished from music for its own sake. His goal was to create for young or amateur performers music that was high in quality, modern in style, and challenging yet rewarding to perform. An example is his musical play for children, *Wir bauen eine Stadt* (We Build a Town, 1930), in which children build a town of their own and govern it without adults, offering a lesson in civic virtues through singing and playing music that is entertaining and appropriate for young amateurs.

Gebrauchsmusik

After the Nazis came to power, they attacked Hindemith in the press and banned much of his music as "cultural Bolshevism." He began to examine the role of the artist in relation to politics and power, and from his questioning emerged the opera *Mathis der Maler* (Mathis the Painter, 1934–35; premiered 1938 in Zurich) and *Symphony Mathis der Maler* (1933–34), his best-known work, comprising the overture and other material for the opera composed while he was writing the libretto. The opera is based on the life of Matthias Grünewald (Mathis Neithardt, ca. 1470–1528), painter of the famous Isenheim Altarpiece shown in Figure 35.3. Grünewald was little known until the late nineteenth and early twentieth centuries, when he was rediscovered and enthusiastically embraced for the dramatic, almost expressionist qualities of his altarpiece, for his distinctively German style, and for his political sympathies with the peasantry. In the opera, Mathis leaves his calling as a painter to join the peasants in their rebellion against the nobles during the German Peasants' War of 1525. In despair after their defeat, he comes to realize that by abandoning his art he betrayed his gift and his true obligation to society, which is to paint. Yet Hindemith does not portray art as entirely autonomous, since Mathis's experiences inform his moral vision. The opera can be read as an allegory for Hindemith's own career.

Mathis der Maler

For *Mathis* and his other works from the 1930s on, Hindemith developed a more accessible neo-Romantic style, with less dissonant linear counterpoint and more systematic tonal organization. He devised a new harmonic method that he called "harmonic fluctuation": fairly consonant chords progress toward combinations containing greater tension and dissonance, which are then resolved either suddenly or by slowly moderating the tension until consonance is again reached. We can see this technique in Example 35.2, the beginning of the second movement of the symphony (NAWM 196), representing Mathis's painting of the entombment of Christ shown in Figure 35.3. From an open fifth, the harmony adds fourths and major seconds, with

FIGURE 35.3 *Three panels from the* Isenheim Altarpiece, *painted by Matthias Grünewald between 1512 and 1516 for the chapel of a hospital and monastery in Colmar, Alsace. On the top right is the* Nativity *with Mary holding the newborn Jesus; on the left is the* Concert of Angels, *the inspiration for the first movement of Hindemith's* Symphony Mathis der Maler, *and below is the* Entombment, *evoked in the second movement. Both movements were reused in the opera* Mathis der Maler, *about Grünewald's life.*

some parallel-fourth motion leading to a cadence on a sonority of open fifths and octaves. An answering phrase in the winds adds minor thirds, reaching a height of dissonance on a minor ninth before returning to the initial sonority with octave doublings. Such progressions were at once novel, distinctive, and easy for listeners to understand.

Later works   In 1936, the Nazi government forbade performances of Hindemith's music. *Mathis der Maler* had to be premiered in Switzerland, and Hindemith moved there in 1938. He emigrated to the United States in 1940 after the outbreak of World War II and stayed for over a decade, returning to Switzerland in 1953. Having found his mature style in *Mathis,* he applied it to a series of sonatas for almost every orchestral instrument (1935–55). *Ludus tonalis* (Tonal Play, 1942) for piano evokes the model of Bach's *Well-Tempered Clavier* with twelve fugues, each centered on a different note in the chromatic scale, linked by modulating interludes and framed by a prelude and postlude.

EXAMPLE 35.2 *Paul Hindemith,* Symphony Mathis der Maler, *opening of second movement*

Other notable later works include *Symphonic Metamorphosis after Themes of Carl Maria von Weber* (1943) and the Symphony in B-flat for band (1951).

MUSIC UNDER THE NAZIS Schoenberg, Krenek, Weill, and Hindemith all fled to the United States, but other composers stayed in Germany during the Nazi era. The Nazis established a Reich Chamber of Culture under Joseph Goebbels, which included a Reich Music Chamber to which all musicians had to belong. Richard Strauss, the grand old man of German music, was appointed its first president, but was soon forced to resign when he continued to collaborate on operas with a Jewish librettist, Stefan Zweig.

The Nazis' requirements for music were mostly expressed in negatives: music must not be dissonant, atonal, twelve-tone, "chaotic," intellectual, Jewish, jazz-influenced, or left-wing, which excluded most modernist music. Composers had to cooperate with the regime in order to have their music performed, and most did. But many German composers continued to write in personal idioms influenced by Schoenberg, Stravinsky, Hindemith, or Weill, whose works the Nazis had attacked as decadent or banned outright, and were permitted to do so if the authorities happened to like their music; for example, Hitler hailed Werner Egk (1901–1983) as a worthy heir to Wagner after seeing Egk's opera *Peer Gynt* (1938), although the music drew on Weill, Berg, Stravinsky, and jazz more than on Wagner. As a result, no coherent Nazi style of new music emerged. Rather, the government focused more on performance than on composition, exploiting the great German composers of the nineteenth century from Beethoven to Bruckner as symbols of the alleged superiority of the German people. They especially fostered a cult of Wagner, Hitler's favorite composer, whose anti-Semitic views supported their own and whose *Ring* cycle embodied a German mythology they could embrace.

The one German composer who won an international reputation during the Nazi era was Carl Orff (1895–1982), who was far from sympathetic

Nazi policies for music

Carl Orff

with the regime but, perhaps naively, believed that music was autonomous from politics and stayed in Germany when others had left. His best-known work, *Carmina burana* (1936) for chorus and orchestra, was an immediate success at its 1937 premiere in Frankfurt, despite a hostile review in the Nazi Party paper. In this piece, Orff set medieval poems akin to goliard songs (see Chapter 4) in an attractive, deceptively simple neo-modal idiom. Drawing on Stravinsky, folk songs, chant, and medieval secular song, he created a monumental pseudo-antique style based on drones, ostinatos, harmonic stasis, and strophic repetition. His *Carmina burana* is distinctive yet immediately comprehensible and has been much imitated, especially by composers for film and television.

Orff approach to teaching music

Like Kodály, Orff also developed in the 1920s methods and materials for teaching music in schools, calling for movement, singing, and playing on percussion and other instruments, leading children in a natural way to experience a great variety of scales and rhythms and to arrive at a broadly based understanding of music. The Orff system, which embodied the egalitarian ideals of the Weimar Republic, continues to be used widely in schools and group lessons for children, making it one of the most significant legacies of Weimar musical culture.

THE SOVIET UNION

In the Soviet Union, the government controlled the arts along with every other realm of life. The arts were seen as ways to indoctrinate the populace in Marxist-Leninist ideology, enhance their patriotism, and venerate the country's leaders. Soon after the Bolshevik Revolution, theaters, conservatories, concert halls, performing ensembles, publishers, and other musical institutions were all nationalized, and concert programming and the opera and ballet repertories were strictly regulated.

Composers' organizations

Civil war in 1918–20 and an economic crisis through the early 1920s preoccupied the government and forced some relaxation of state control over the arts. During this period of relative freedom, divergent tendencies emerged among composers and crystallized in two organizations founded in 1923. The Association for Contemporary Music sought to continue the modernist trends established by Scriabin and others before the war and promoted contacts with western Europe, sponsoring performances of music by Stravinsky, Schoenberg, Berg, Hindemith, and others. The Russian Association of Proletarian Musicians, on the other hand, considered such music elitist and instead encouraged simple tonal music with wide appeal, especially "mass songs" (songs for group unison singing) to socialist texts. After Joseph Stalin consolidated total power in 1929, dissent was quashed. The competing composers' groups were replaced in 1933 by a single new organization, the Union of Soviet Composers.

Socialist realism versus formalism

A 1934 writers' congress promulgated **socialist realism** as the ideal for Soviet arts. In literature, drama, film, and painting, this doctrine called for using a realistic style (as opposed to abstraction, expressionism, or symbolism) in works that portrayed socialism in a positive light, showing signs of progress for the people under the Soviet state and celebrating revolutionary ideology and its heroes. What this meant for music was the use of a relatively simple, accessible language, centered on melody, often drawing on folk or folklike styles, and used for patriotic or inspirational subject matter. Interest in music for its own sake or in modernist styles was condemned as "formalism." But the definitions of socialist realism and formalism were so vague and arbitrary that composers often ran afoul of the authorities, including the two leading Soviet composers of the time, Sergey Prokofiev and Dmitri Shostakovich.

SERGEY PROKOFIEV Prokofiev (1891–1953), shown in Figure 35.4, made his initial reputation before 1918 as a radical modernist, combining striking dissonance with driving rhythms. He wrote in his autobiography that his music encompasses five main tendencies—classical, modern, motoric, lyric, and grotesque—and these are evident early on, from the grotesque parallel minor ninths of his *Suggestion diabolique* (1910–12) and the relentlessly motoric Toccata (1912) to the affectionate and witty evocation of Haydn in his Classical Symphony (1918). He left Russia after the Revolution and spent almost two decades residing and touring in North America and western Europe, composing solo piano works and concertos for himself to play, and fulfilling commis-

FIGURE 35.4 *Sergey Prokofiev in 1934, in a painting by Pyotr Konchalovsky.*

sions for larger compositions, among them an opera for Chicago with a slyly absurd plot, *The Love for Three Oranges* (1921), and ballets for Serge Diaghilev's Ballets Russes in Paris.

His career at a low ebb, Prokofiev succumbed to promises from the Soviet regime of commissions and performances. He returned to Russia permanently in 1936, having already fulfilled Soviet commissions for the film *Lieutenant Kijé* (1933) and for the ballet *Romeo and Juliet* (1935–36). His symphonic fairy tale for narrator and orchestra, *Peter and the Wolf* (1936), was one of many pieces he wrote in response to the Soviet demand for high-quality music for children, and his music for Sergei Eisenstein's film *Alexander Nevsky* (1938) became one of the most celebrated film scores of the era. Prokofiev's pieces for state occasions, like his cantatas for the twentieth and thirtieth anniversaries of the Russian Revolution, were less successful and were ignored outside of the Soviet Union.

In keeping with a practice common in Europe, Prokofiev reworked most of his theatrical pieces and film scores into concert works. Although Hollywood composers sometimes made such arrangements from their film music, for Prokofiev and other European composers the concert pieces were often as important as the film score itself. The orchestral suites Prokofiev drew from *Romeo and Juliet* and *Lieutenant Kijé* became among his most popular works and entered the standard repertory. So did his cantata *Alexander Nevsky*, which he adapted in 1939 from the music for the film. The fourth movement (NAWM 197), drawn from a scene in which the people of Russia are summoned to arise and take up arms against German invaders, works well as film music: stirring choral melodies in folklike style, sung in unison or simple two-part

Alexander Nevsky

homophony, suggest the unity and determination of the people, giving emotional depth to what is depicted on screen; mostly diatonic melodies and harmonies make the music immediately accessible, while occasional dissonance and unexpected turns make it engaging and distinctive as well; and the modal melodies and orchestration convey a Russian sound, evoking both the strumming of seven-string Russian guitars and the clanging bells and prominent brass and percussion of the Coronation scene from Musorgsky's *Boris Godunov* (NAWM 158). But these same qualities make it well suited as concert music that conforms to the doctrine of socialist realism. Moreover, although Prokofiev sometimes chafed at the restrictions imposed by the Soviet state, the widely appealing style he used in pieces like this brought him greater success with audiences than his more modernist pieces of the 1920s.

Later works   World War II again brought a relaxation of government control, and Prokofiev turned to absolute music in classical genres, notably the Piano Sonatas Nos. 6–8 (1939–44) and the Fifth Symphony (1944). These works are largely tonal, with the unexpected harmonic juxtapositions and the alternation of acerbic dryness, lyricism, and motoric rhythms that had been features of his personal style since the 1910s. But after the war, the authorities again cracked down in a 1948 resolution that condemned the works of Prokofiev and other leading composers as "formalist." He tried to write more simply, but never recovered the balance of wit with feeling and of convention with surprise that marks his best music. He died in 1953—ironically, on the same day as Stalin, whose brutal regime had so circumscribed his freedom.

DMITRI SHOSTAKOVICH Dimitri Shostakovich (1906–1975), shown in Figure 35.5, received his education and spent his entire career within the Soviet system. He studied at the Conservatory in Petrograd (formerly St. Petersburg, later Leningrad, now St. Petersburg again), cultivating a combination of traditional discipline with experimentation. In the 1920s, he was more aligned with the modernist than with the proletarian wing in Russia. The premiere of his First Symphony in 1926, when he was nineteen, and subsequent performances in western Europe rocketed him to international prominence.

Shostakovich's opera *Lady Macbeth of the Mtsensk District* was premiered in 1934 in both Leningrad and Moscow and scored a great success, with subsequent performances throughout the Soviet Union and abroad. But Stalin saw it in January 1936 and was angered by its discordant modernist music and surrealistic, often grotesque, portrayal of violence and sex. Shortly thereafter, the newspaper *Pravda* printed an unsigned article attacking the opera as "Chaos Instead of Music" (see Source Reading). In its wake the production was closed down and the opera withdrawn. Shostakovich temporarily lost his favored status and may have feared for his life: the previous year Stalin had begun a campaign of repression known as

FIGURE 35.5 *Portrait of Dmitri Shostakovich by Tair Salakhov.*

Censuring Shostakovich

After Shostakovich's opera *Lady Macbeth of the Mtsensk District* had been performed widely to great acclaim, Stalin's government singled it out for censure with a negative review in *Pravda* (Truth), the Communist Party newspaper. Through this attack on the nation's leading composer, they signaled a crackdown on composers' artistic freedoms.

❖

From the first minute, the listener is shocked by deliberate dissonance, by a confused stream of sounds. Snatches of melody, the beginnings of a musical phrase, are drowned, emerge again, and disappear in a grinding and squealing roar. To follow this "music" is most difficult; to remember it, impossible.

Thus it goes practically throughout the entire opera. The singing on the stage is replaced by shrieks. If the composer chances to come on the path of a clear and simple melody, then immediately, as though frightened at this misfortune, he throws himself back into a wilderness of musical chaos—in places becoming cacophony. The expression which the listener demands is supplanted by wild rhythm. Passion is here supposed to be expressed by musical noise. All this is not due to lack of talent, or to lack of ability to depict simple and strong emotions in music. Here is music turned deliberately inside out in order that nothing will be reminiscent of classical opera, or have anything in common with symphonic music or with simple and popular musical language accessible to all. . . . The power of good music to infect the masses has been sacrificed to a petty-bourgeois, "formalist" attempt to create originality through cheap clowning. It is a game of clever ingenuity that may end very badly.

From "Chaos Instead of Music," as translated in Victor Seroff, *Dmitri Shostakovich: The Life and Background of a Soviet Composer* (New York: Alfred A. Knopf, 1943), 204–5. In SR 188 (7:19), 1397–98.

the Purges, during which many political figures, intellectuals, and artists were executed or banished to prison camps.

It is hard not to see the Fifth Symphony, written and premiered to great acclaim in 1937, as his response to the criticism of his opera; indeed, he endorsed a description of the work as "a Soviet artist's reply to just criticism." The symphony embodies a new approach Shostakovich had been developing, inspired by close study of Mahler's symphonies, that encompassed a wide range of styles and moods, from lyricism to dynamism and from deep feeling and high tragedy to bombast and the grotesque. It is framed as a heroic symphony in the grand manner of Beethoven and Tchaikovsky and in the traditional four movements. A dynamic opening movement in sonata form, suggestive of struggle, is followed by a scherzo-like Allegretto (NAWM 198), an intensely sad slow movement, and a boisterous finale. The symphony outwardly conformed to the tenets of socialist realism, infusing the most prestigious nineteenth-century instrumental genre with an optimistic, populist outlook and adopting a clear, easily understood tonal language. For these reasons, it provided the vehicle for Shostakovich's rehabilitation with the state. Yet it was also possible to hear in it messages of bitterness and mourning in the face of totalitarian repression. The Allegretto adopts the jarring contrasts of a Mahler scherzo, juxtaposing passages that evoke a variety of popular styles

Fifth Symphony

from waltz to fanfare. The sorrowful slow movement evokes traditional Russian funeral music; it prompted open tears at the premiere and has been seen by some as expressing sorrow at the Purges. The triumphalism of the final movement could also be interpreted as false enthusiasm. Such double meanings do not mean that Shostakovich was a dissident—there was no room for dissidence under Stalin—but by composing multivalent music, he could at once please the Party bosses and provide an outlet for emotions that had to remain unspoken.

Seventh Symphony   All of Shostakovich's works were created in a politicized context, and the search for double meanings has been widespread in western Europe, in the United States, and in Russia since the fall of the Soviet Union. The Seventh Symphony (*Leningrad,* 1941) deals programmatically with the heroic defense of Leningrad against Hitler's armies, although some hear in its depiction of the totalitarian invaders a complaint against Stalin's repression as well. It was performed in London and New York in 1942 and immediately became a symbol of the war against Nazi Germany, in which the United States, Britain, and the Soviet Union were allies.

Later works   In the 1948 crackdown, Shostakovich was denounced along with Prokofiev and others, and he had to write patriotic film scores and choral paeans to the regime to gain rehabilitation. He wrote some of his music "for the drawer"—with no expectation of performance until the political atmosphere changed. In an assertion of individuality, he musically signed the third movement of the Tenth Symphony (1953, the year of Stalin's death) with a motive drawn from the German spelling of his name, D–E♭–C–B—in German nomenclature, D–Es–C–H, or D–S–C–H, from **D**mitri **SCH**ostakovich. He used the same motive in the Fifth and Eighth String Quartets (1952 and 1960) and the concertos for violin and for cello.

The ambivalence in Shostakovich's music reflects the accommodations he had to make to survive in a state where one could never say precisely what one felt, and thus where the arts—especially music—offered an outlet for what was otherwise inexpressible. The relative accessibility of his music combined with its impression of giving voice to inner feelings has won Shostakovitch many devoted listeners not only in Russia but throughout the world.

THE AMERICAS

In the New World, the interwar period saw the emergence of composers who gained prominence in their own countries and recognition in Europe, placing their homelands on the international stage for the first time. As with composers in the "peripheral" nations of Europe, these composers of the Americas found that creating a distinctive national style was often the only way to gain attention from an international audience. Their nationalism was sometimes infused with national politics but always linked to the cultural politics of securing for themselves and their countries a niche in the performing repertoire.

CANADA Canada had a thriving musical life that developed along patterns similar to those in the United States. In both nations, performance of the European classical repertoire was far more central than playing music of homegrown composers in the classical tradition. Performing spaces, concert societies, bands, professional chamber ensembles, choral societies, and conservatories all emerged in Canada during the nineteenth century, and the twentieth century brought the founding of orchestras in most large cities, beginning with Quebec (1903) and Toronto (1906).

A key figure in Canadian music was Ernest MacMillan (1893–1973), who for many years was head of the Toronto conservatory and the University of Toronto Faculty of Music as well as conductor of the Toronto Symphony Orchestra. He collected and arranged music of native peoples, edited an anthology of Canadian songs used in schools, conducted numerous premieres of works by Canadian composers, and edited the first book on music in Canada. He composed many works that drew on national materials, especially French Canadian folk songs, including *Two Sketches for Strings* (1927).

Ernest MacMillan

The first Canadian composer to achieve an international reputation was Claude Champagne (1891–1965). He learned French-Canadian fiddle music and dance tunes in his youth, then as a young man was deeply influenced by Russian composers, from Musorgsky to Scriabin. During studies in Paris in 1921–28, he encountered Renaissance polyphony, Fauré, and Debussy, and saw in their modal practice links to the folk tunes of Canada. He developed a distinctive nationalist style in his *Suite canadienne* (Canadian Suite, 1927) for chorus and orchestra, blending elements from French-Canadian folk music and polyphonic French chansons with the symphonic tradition. His best-known piece, *Dance villageoise* (Village Dance, 1929), evokes both French-Canadian and Irish folk styles, acknowledging another ethnic strain in Canada and in his own heritage.

Claude Champagne

BRAZIL Art music was well established in Brazil by the late nineteenth century, with successful operas by Gomes (see Chapter 28) and others and with several composers of concert music who developed their own nationalist styles.

The most important Brazilian composer was Heitor Villa-Lobos (1887–1959), shown in Figure 35.6, who drew together traditional Brazilian elements with modernist techniques. He spent the years 1923–30 mostly in Paris, where performances of his music won widespread praise and established him as the most prominent Latin American composer. He returned to Brazil in 1930 and, with government support, instituted a national effort to promote music in the schools and through choral singing. He was criticized for his collaboration with Brazil's nationalist dictatorship, akin to the totalitarian regimes of Europe at the time, but it is not clear whether he shared its ideology.

Heitor Villa-Lobos

The series of fourteen pieces titled *Chôros* (1920–28), after a type of popular ensemble music Villa-Lobos played in the streets of Rio de Janeiro in his youth, are among his most characteristic works. For various media, from solo guitar or piano to orchestra with chorus, each *Chôros* blends one or more vernacular styles of Brazil, typified by syncopated rhythms and unusual timbres, with modernist techniques such as ostinatos, polytonality, polyrhythms, and vivid orchestration to create a remarkably distinctive sound. A later series, the nine *Bachianas brasileiras* (1930–45), pays

FIGURE 35.6 *Heitor Villa-Lobos, photographed in Paris in the 1920s by Max Eschig.*

FIGURE 35.7 The Day of the Dead Man (1923–24),
a fresco by Diego Rivera (1886–1957) for the Ministry of
Public Instruction in Mexico City. This picture portrays
a Mexican festival in a style that draws on pre-Colum-
bian art.

tribute to Bach and thus to the neoclassical trend of the
times. Each is a suite of two to four movements combining elements of Baroque harmony, counterpoint, genres,
and styles with Brazilian folk elements and long, lyrical melodic lines. This unique blend is exemplified in
Villa-Lobos's most famous work, *Bachianas brasileiras
No. 5* (1938–45) for solo soprano and orchestra of cellos.
The first movement (NAWM 199) invokes the spirit of a
Bach aria, spinning out a long-breathed cantabile melody from a few initial motives, and alludes to the typical
da capo form of Baroque arias through a modified ABA
structure and a suggestion of an instrumental ritornello.
At the same time, it draws on styles of improvisation
in Brazilian popular song and on vocal embellishment
in Italian opera, a tradition that was as strong in Brazil
as in Europe. The result, simultaneously neoclassical,
national, and modernist, exemplifies how the Western
musical tradition has become a transatlantic culture.

MEXICO Beginning in 1921, the Mexican government
began to support bringing the arts to a wide public and
promoted a new nationalism that drew on native Indian
cultures, especially from before the Spanish Conquest.
As part of this effort, Diego Rivera and other artists were
commissioned to paint murals in public buildings that
illustrated Mexican life, such as the fresco shown in
Figure 35.7.

The first composer associated with the new nationalism was Carlos Chávez (1899–1978), who also served
as conductor of Mexico's first professional orchestra
and director of the national conservatory. He wrote two
ballets on Aztec scenarios, and his *Sinfonía india* (Indian Symphony, 1935–
36) uses Indian melodies in a modernist, primitivist idiom also apparent
in his Piano Concerto (1938–40). Other works are not overtly nationalist,
including his *Sinfonía romantica* (Symphony No. 4, 1953).

Silvestre Revueltas   Silvestre Revueltas (1899–1940) studied in Mexico and in the United
States before returning to assume the post of assistant conductor under
Chávez. His compositions do not use folk songs but combine melodies,
rhythms, gestures, and timbres modeled on Mexican folk and popular music
with a modernist idiom. Characteristic is his *Homenaje a Federico García
Lorca* (Homage to Federico García Lorca, 1936), written in memory of one of
Spain's most important poets and playwrights, killed by a Nationalist mili-
tia in the early days of the Spanish Civil War (1936–39). The first movement, *Baile* (Dance), begins and ends with a muted trumpet playing a slow,
recitative-like melody that evokes the style of *cante jondo,* a Spanish flamenco
song tradition Lorca celebrated in his poetry. The main body of the movement is a lively dance that recalls the timbres, characteristic rhythms, melodies in parallel thirds, and group improvisation of Mexican mariachi band
music. Yet modernist elements, such as strong dissonance, glissandos, and
grotesque combinations like piccolo and E♭ clarinet in parallel ninths over a

chromatic line in the tuba, make clear that this is concert music *about* popular culture rather than popular entertainment itself. The evocation of popular and folk styles within a modernist idiom is characteristic of Revueltas and an appropriate homage to Lorca, who did the same in his own work.

THE UNITED STATES

The United States emerged from World War I as one of the world's most powerful economies and most influential nations. We have already seen the impact in this era of American popular music and jazz, and music in the classical tradition was vibrant as well. The new technologies of the electric microphone, radio, and sound film made classical as well as popular music widely available across the country. Conductors like Leopold Stokowski, Walter Damrosch, and Arturo Toscanini became nationally known figures, issuing recordings of the classical masterworks and conducting live concerts on the radio. Metropolitan Opera radio broadcasts on Saturday afternoons beginning in 1931 reached millions of listeners. Stokowski at the Philadelphia Orchestra and Serge Koussevitzky with the Boston Symphony Orchestra were important advocates for American composers, premiering over a hundred new works, and patrons like Elizabeth Sprague Coolidge commissioned new music. Damrosch gave radio lecture-demonstrations to children on how to appreciate classical music. Music education continued to expand in schools, colleges, and communities, with many young people singing in choirs, learning piano or other instruments, and playing in orchestras or bands. In these and other respects the period between the wars marked a new peak of interest in classical music in the United States.

After the stock market crash of 1929, the economy collapsed in the Great Depression, lowering incomes and throwing millions out of work. In 1932, Franklin Delano Roosevelt was elected president promising "a new deal for the American people." His administration's New Deal policies brought banking and monetary reform; assistance for agriculture; Social Security, a new program providing support for the elderly, disabled, and dependent children; improved conditions for workers, including a minimum wage, the forty-hour workweek, unemployment compensation, and a ban on child labor; and work for the unemployed, hiring them to build roads, bridges, dams, schools, hospitals, parks, and other infrastructure through the Public Works Administration and Works Progress Administration. The latter included support for writers, artists, and musicians, marking the first time the federal government had supported the arts beyond military bands. Between 1935 and 1939 the Federal Music Project employed over fifteen thousand performing musicians in dozens of orchestras, bands, choruses, and opera groups, along with music teachers, copyists, and scholars, and more than one hundred million people attended their concerts. The FMP supported composers through programs like the Composers' Forum Laboratory, which presented concerts of new music followed by a question-and-answer session with the composers, allowing them to hear feedback directly from the public.

Between the wars, composers and performers in the United States developed new links with Europe, due in part to the immigration of many of Europe's leading composers for political or professional reasons. By the early 1940s, these included Rachmaninoff, Schoenberg, Stravinsky, Bartók, Milhaud,

The New Deal

New links with Europe

Krenek, Weill, and Hindemith. Americans had studied in Germany since the mid-nineteenth century, but World War I helped to foster a reorientation of American music away from Germany and toward France. After the war, American conductor Walter Damrosch joined with French organist and composer Charles-Marie Widor and others to found the American Conservatory at Fontainebleau, whose purpose was to provide the best of French musical training to American students. Starting in the early 1920s, a steady stream of Americans went to France to study with Nadia Boulanger (1887–1979), renowned pedagogue and promoter of Fauré and Stravinsky, who taught classes in Paris and at Fontainebleau until her death. Among those studying with her were Aaron Copland, Virgil Thomson, Roy Harris, Walter Piston, and Elliott Carter.

Ultramodernist and Americanist trends

The interwar period also saw new currents among American composers. Two of the most salient were an experimentalist or **ultramodernist** trend, focused on developing new musical resources, and an Americanist trend that incorporated national styles and sounds into European genres. The former group included Edgard Varèse, Henry Cowell, and Ruth Crawford Seeger, and the latter encompassed George Gershwin, Aaron Copland, William Grant Still, Virgil Thomson, Roy Harris, Cowell's later works, and many others. Both currents asserted independence from Europe while still drawing on the European tradition, and in the 1930s the latter group blended nationalism with a new populism inspired by the Great Depression and by President Roosevelt's New Deal policies. In order to secure performances for their music in a concert culture that focused on European masterworks, American composers formed their own organizations, including the International Composers' Guild cofounded by Varèse, the League of Composers headed by Claire Reis, and Cowell's *New Music*.

EDGARD VARÈSE The French-born Edgard Varèse (1883–1965), shown in Figure 35.8, studied at the Schola Cantorum and Conservatoire, had a brief career in Paris and Berlin as a composer and as a conductor of early and contemporary music, and then moved to New York in 1915. Varèse celebrated his adopted country in his first major work, *Amériques* (1918–21). Its fragmentary melodies and loose structure show links to Debussy. He was also influenced by Schoenberg, notably in the use of strong dissonance and chromatic saturation, and by Stravinsky, including the association of a musical idea with a specific instrumental color, the avoidance of linear development, and the juxtaposition of disparate elements through layering and interruption.

FIGURE 35.8
Edgard Varèse.

Next came a series of works that laid down a new agenda: *Offrandes* (1921), *Hyperprism* (1922–23), *Octandre* (1923), *Intégrales* (1924–25), *Ionisation* (percussion only, 1929–31), and *Ecuatorial* (1932–34). In these works, he aimed to liberate composition from conventional melody, harmony, meter, regular pulse, and traditional orchestration. For Varèse, sounds as such were the essential structural components of music, which he defined as "organized sound," and he considered all sounds acceptable as raw material. He imagined music as *spatial*, akin to an aural ballet in which what he called **sound masses** moved through musical space, changing and interacting. A sound mass is a body of sounds characterized by a particular timbre, register, rhythm, and melodic gesture, which may be stable or may gradually be transformed. In Varèse's compositions, these sound masses collide, intersect, speed up, slow down, combine, split up, diffuse, and expand and contract in range, volume, and timbre. A great variety of percussion instruments, some drawn from non-Western cultures and others (such as the siren) from city life, play key roles, acting independently as equals to the winds and strings. For Varèse, form was not something you start with, but what results as you work with the material. Typically, his pieces are organized in a series of sections, each centered around a few sound masses, some of which may carry over to later sections.

The passage from *Hyperprism* (NAWM 200) in Example 35.3 illustrates how pitch, instrumental color, gesture, and rhythm interact to suggest sound masses colliding and changing. The trombone has introduced and embellished the pitch C♯, and now the horns (notated here at sounding pitch) take

Hyperprism

EXAMPLE 35.3 *Edgard Varèse, passage from* Hyperprism

it up with flutter-tonguing (fast tongue motions) and sforzandos, both effects that produce brassy sounds excluded from traditional music. The trombone returns, decorating the C♯ with glissandos (another nontraditional effect), and exchanges short phrases with the horns. The horns ultimately take over the note and the glissando, as if the sound mass has gradually changed timbre. Meanwhile a low D in bass trombone, a strong dissonance against the C♯, swells and fades in alternation with a siren, forming another sound mass that changes color. In the percussion, a gesture produced by bass drum, tam-tam (a flat gong), cymbals, snare drum, and tambourine alternates with another using Indian drum, triangle, and rattles and adding sleigh bells on its repetition, like two contesting sound masses. Every combination of sounds is unusual, so that it is heard as a sound mass rather than as melody, harmony, or accompaniment.

In Varèse's entirely new spatial conception of music, the listener must put aside expectations that music will be rhetorical or will develop organically, as in earlier styles, and must simply observe the interaction of what he called "intelligent bodies of sound moving in space." His ideas and his music had an enormous influence on younger composers, including Cage and Feldman in the United States and Boulez and Stockhausen in Europe (see Chapter 37).

Electronic music   Since his music depended on sound itself, especially unusual timbres, Varèse sought new instruments from the 1920s on. Only after World War II did the new resources of electronic sound generation and the tape recorder make possible the realization of the sounds he heard in his mind, in his *Déserts* (1950–54) for winds, percussion, and tape, and in the tape piece *Poème électronique* (1957–58; NAWM 214, discussed in Chapter 37).

Experimental music   **HENRY COWELL** A native Californian, Henry Cowell (1897–1965) began composing as a teenager with little training in European music, and from the start he sought out new resources for music. Many of his early pieces are experimental, designed to try out a new technique. *The Tides of Manaunaun* (ca. 1917) uses ***tone clusters***, chords of diatonic or chromatic seconds produced by pressing the keys with the fist or forearm, to represent the tides moved by Manaunaun, the legendary Irish sea god. Figure 35.9 shows Cowell playing both kinds of clusters. He used the technique so often, including in his Piano Concerto (1928), that it became identified as his invention, and Bartók once wrote Cowell asking permission to use clusters. In *The Aeolian Harp* (1923), the player strums the piano strings while holding down three- and four-note chords on the keyboard, as if playing a grand autoharp. In *The Banshee* (1925; NAWM 201), an assistant holds the damper pedal down so that the strings can resonate freely while the pianist strums the strings, plucks some, and rubs along the length of the lower, wire-wound strings with the fingertips or fingernails to create an eerie, voicelike howl similar to that of a banshee, a spirit in Irish legend. Besides new playing techniques, Cowell also explored new textures and procedures, such as giving each voice or instrument a different subdivision of the meter. He summarized his new ideas in his book *New Musical Resources* (1930).

Eclectic influences   Throughout his career, Cowell was interested in non-Western musics. He taught courses on music from around the world at the New School for Social Research in New York and at other institutions, doing a great deal to encourage the study of world music and ethnomusicology. He took an eclectic

FIGURE 35.9 *Henry Cowell at the piano, playing clusters with his fist and forearm.*

approach to composition, trying out everything that interested him rather than developing a single identifiable method or style. During and after the 1930s, Cowell turned from experimentalism to a more accessible language, often incorporating American, Irish, or Asian elements. He wrote a series of works called *Hymn and Fuguing Tune* for band or for orchestra, modeled on the style of William Billings and his contemporaries, alongside symphonies and other traditional genres. In the years after World War II, several pieces show his interest in Asian music and incorporate instruments such as the Indian tabla and the Japanese koto.

Cowell promoted music by his contemporaries as well as his own through concerts and through the periodical *New Music,* in which he published scores by Ives, Schoenberg, and other modernist and ultramodernist composers. His adventurous search for new resources and his interest in non-Western music had an enormous impact on younger composers, especially in the United States.

Impact

RUTH CRAWFORD SEEGER Among the composers whose works Cowell published was Ruth Crawford (1901–1953), shown in Figure 35.10, the first woman to win a Guggenheim Fellowship in music. She was most active as a composer in Chicago between 1924 and 1929 and in New York between 1929 and 1933. In New York, she studied composition with the composer and musicologist Charles Seeger, whom she married in 1932. Seeger had developed theories about dissonant counterpoint, rhythmic freedom between contrapuntal voices, and other modernist techniques that Crawford helped to refine and then applied in her own music. In her New York period she experimented with serial techniques, including their application to parameters other than pitch. Influenced by the New Deal, she became convinced that preserving folk songs would be a greater contribution to the nation's musical life than writing modernist works that few would hear or appreciate. She collaborated

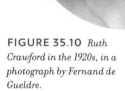

with the writer Carl Sandburg, folklorists John and Alan Lomax, and her husband, editing American folk songs from field recordings. She also published many transcriptions and arrangements in which she sought to be faithful to the songs' native contexts. Crawford stands out for her advocacy in preserving American traditional music and for being one of the very few women in the ultramodernist group.

Crawford's best-known work is her *String Quartet 1931*, composed while she was in Europe on a Guggenheim Fellowship. Each movement is different, embodying Crawford's constant search for new procedures. In the first movement, four thematic ideas unfold in dissonant counterpoint; rarely do two instruments attack a note at the same time, creating a sense of great independence between the parts. The second movement develops a short motive through counterpoint and convergence, creating rapid changes of accent and implied meter. The third movement features "heterophony of dynamics": while all four instruments sustain long tones, one instrument at a time comes to the fore through a crescendo, and the dynamically prominent notes are heard as a composite melody that builds to an intense climax. The finale (NAWM 202), shown in Example 35.4, is laid out in two-part counterpoint, pitting the first violin against the three other instruments playing in parallel octaves with mutes on. The first violin plays a single note, then two, three, four, and so on, adding one note with each phrase until it reaches twenty-one, gradually getting softer. In between its phrases, the other instruments, using a ten-note series, play rapid eighth notes in groups that decline from twenty notes to one, gradually getting louder, so that the two voices head in opposite directions in density and dynamics. At the end of this process, each part sustains its last tone, and then the entire musical fabric is repeated in retrograde, transposed up a semitone, to create a nearly perfect palindrome. Through four highly contrasting movements, Crawford simultaneously embraces the tradition of the string quartet and satisfies the ultramodernist desire for something truly new.

FIGURE 35.10 *Ruth Crawford in the 1920s, in a photograph by Fernand de Gueldre.*

PHOTO COURTESY JUDITH TICK

EXAMPLE 35.4 *Opening of the finale of Ruth Crawford's* String Quartet 1931

GEORGE GERSHWIN George Gershwin (1897–1938) first made his reputation as a composer of popular songs and Broadway shows (see Chapter 34), but in the late 1920s and 1930s he also established himself as the most famous and frequently performed American composer in classical genres. For Gershwin, this was no contradiction, because he saw no firm line between popular and classical music. He always had a foot in both camps: he studied classical piano as a teenager, including works of Chopin, Liszt, and Debussy; took private lessons in harmony, counterpoint, form, and orchestration from 1915 to 1921; and later studied composition with several teachers, including Cowell. Gershwin recognized the potential of jazz and blues to add new dimensions to art music, and he used his familiarity with those traditions to create a distinctively American modernist style.

Gershwin's most famous piece, *Rhapsody in Blue* (1924), billed as a "jazz concerto," had its premiere as the centerpiece of an extravagant concert organized by bandleader Paul Whiteman as "An Experiment in Modern Music." Scored for solo piano and jazz ensemble, and incorporating stylized popular song forms, blue notes, and other elements of jazz and blues, *Rhapsody in Blue* met with immediate approval. Along with Milhaud's *La création du monde* from the year before, Gershwin's *Rhapsody* pointed the way for other composers to incorporate jazz, blues, and popular music into their art music, suggesting that such a blend could produce music that was at once truly modern, truly American, and broadly appealing.

Rhapsody in Blue

Gershwin himself continued to fuse the seemingly disparate traditions, producing compositions like the Piano Concerto in F (1925), the second movement of which is constructed over a twelve-bar blues harmonic pattern stretched to fit a sixteen-measure theme, and the three Preludes for Piano (1926), which bring elements of blues, jazz, and Latin dance rhythms into preludes influenced by Chopin and Debussy. Gershwin's *Porgy and Bess* (1935), which he called a folk opera, has been produced both as an opera and as a musical, and it draws from both genres. The music is continuous and features recurring motives like those in Verdi or Wagner operas. Yet in part because the characters are African American, the musical style is heavily influenced by African American idioms such as spirituals, blues, and jazz. This blending of traditions is part of Gershwin's appeal, and it makes his music especially rich in reference and in meaning. Because of his early death from a brain tumor, his output of classical works was relatively small, but he remains the most familiar American composer of the century.

Other works

AARON COPLAND Aaron Copland (1900–1990), shown in Figure 35.11, moved from stringent dissonance in the 1920s to a streamlined style in the 1930s and 1940s that combined modernism with national American idioms. Copland's Jewish faith, his homosexuality, and his leftist politics made him something of an outsider, yet he became the most important and central American composer of his generation through his own compositions and his work for the cause of American music. He organized concert series and composer groups and promoted works of his predecessors and contemporaries, including Ives, Chávez, and Virgil Thomson. Through encouragement, counsel, and by example, he influenced many younger American composers, among them Leonard Bernstein, Elliott Carter, and David Del Tredici.

FIGURE 35.11 *American composer Aaron Copland shown conducting, December 9, 1962.*

Growing up in a Jewish immigrant family in Brooklyn, Copland was exposed to ragtime and popular music from a young age, while studying piano, theory, and composition in the European tradition. He was the first of many American composers to study in France with Nadia Boulanger, from whom he learned to write music that was clear, logical, and elegant. While in Paris he heard the newest music, from Stravinsky's Octet to Honegger's *Pacific 231* and Milhaud's *La création du monde*, and assimilated the French anti-Romantic and neoclassical aesthetics. Jazz elements and strong dissonances figure prominently in his early works, such as *Music for the Theatre* (1925) and the Piano Concerto (1927).

Recognizing the growing number of radio and record listeners, Copland sought to appeal to a larger audience. At about the same time, the Great Depression deepened his belief in socialism, and he turned to writing music in a language the broad masses of people could understand, on subjects that were relevant to their lives and concerns. He developed a new style by reducing his modernist technique to its essence of counterpoint, dissonance, and juxtaposition, then combining it with simple textures and diatonic melodies and harmonies. In some works, he borrowed traditional songs to suggest place and atmosphere. He incorporated Mexican folk songs in the orchestral suite *El Salón México* (1932–36), inspired by a visit to Mexico at the invitation of Chávez, and cowboy songs in the ballets *Billy the Kid* (1938) and *Rodeo* (1942), which reflected the American frontier experience. His opera *The Second Hurricane* (1936)—written for schools—and his scores for a number of films including *Of Mice and Men* (1939) and *Our Town* (1940) represent music composed specifically "for use."

Appalachian Spring   Copland's Americanist idiom is exemplified in *Appalachian Spring* (1943–44), first written as a ballet with an ensemble of thirteen instruments but better known in the arrangement as an orchestral suite (excerpt in NAWM 203). The work incorporates variations on the Shaker hymn *'Tis the Gift to Be Simple*. Example 35.5 shows two variations on the hymn's third phrase, one set simply against syncopated sustained tones, the other in widely separated three-part counterpoint with a variant of the song's first phrase in the middle voice. The song is subtly transfigured and its essence is absorbed in music that conveys the spirit of rural life in American terms. Copland's use of transparent, widely spaced sonorities, empty octaves and fifths, and diatonic dissonances creates a distinctive sound that has been frequently imitated and has become the quintessential musical emblem of America, used especially in music for film and television.

Later works   Copland's later works embraced a variety of styles. His Americanist idiom continued in the Third Symphony (1946), but in the Piano Quartet (1950), the Piano Fantasy (1957), and the orchestral *Inscape* (1967), he adopted some features of twelve-tone technique. Perhaps he sought to cultivate a more

EXAMPLE 35.5 *Passages from Aaron Copland's* Appalachian Spring, *showing two variations of the Shaker hymn's third phrase*

abstract language during the 1950s, when the left-wing political sympathies that lay behind his Americanist music came under attack. Despite the range of styles he employed, Copland retained an unmistakable artistic identity. His music preserves a sense of a tonal center, though seldom by traditional means. His rhythms are lively and flexible, and he was adept at obtaining new sounds from simple chords by exploiting instrumental color and spacing.

WILLIAM GRANT STILL William Grant Still (1895–1978), shown in Figure 35.12, also incorporated specifically American idioms into art music. He drew on a diverse musical background, including composition studies with George Whitefield Chadwick and Edgard Varèse and work as an arranger for W. C. Handy's dance band. Still's success as a composer, when blacks were still largely excluded from the field of classical music, earned him the sobriquet "Dean of Afro-American Composers." He broke numerous racial barriers and earned many "firsts" for his race—the first African American to conduct a major symphony orchestra in the United States (the Los Angeles Philharmonic, 1936); the first to have an opera produced by a major company in the United States (*Troubled Island* at New York's City Center, 1949); and the first to have an opera televised over a national network. He completed over 150 compositions, including operas, ballets, symphonies, chamber works, choral pieces, and solo vocal works.

FIGURE 35.12 *American composer William Grant Still holds pages from one of his own compositions, 1950s.*

Afro-American
Symphony

Still established his reputation with the *Afro-American Symphony* (1930), the first symphonic work by an African American composer to be performed by a major American orchestra. The symphony encompasses African American musical elements within the traditional framework of a European four-movement symphony. The opening movement (NAWM 204) is in sonata form, with a first theme in twelve-bar blues structure and a second theme that suggests a spiritual. It also features numerous other traits from African American traditions: call and response, syncopation, varied repetition of short melodic or rhythmic ideas, jazz harmonies, dialogue between groups of instruments as in a jazz arrangement, and instrumental timbres common in jazz, such as trumpets and trombones played with Harmon mutes.

DIVERSITY OF STYLES   In addition to the composers mentioned here, the interwar period saw the publications and performances of the mature music of Charles Ives (see Chapter 33), who was seen both as an ultramodernist and as an Americanist and thus was promoted by both Cowell and Copland. Other composers wrote in styles ranging from Romanticism to neoclassicism to serialism. The variety of American idioms between the wars illustrates the general point we have already seen in Chapters 32 and 33. Most composers of art music sought a place in the crowded classical repertoire by writing music that was individual and distinctive yet drew on past traditions and genres. Meanwhile, the most radical composers—like Varèse, Cowell, and Crawford—each forged a new concept of music. For them, the best solution to the problem of competing with the past was to ignore it and focus on creating something fundamentally new.

WHAT POLITICS?

Art music between the wars includes some of the most widely performed classical works of the twentieth century. By now, listeners and musicians have largely forgotten the political circumstances in which most of this music was created. Audiences enjoy Orff's *Carmina burana*, Shostakovich's Fifth Symphony, or Copland's Americanist ballets without regard to the politics that shaped their creation. Indeed, the insistence on immediate wide appeal by authorities in totalitarian states seems to have helped the popularity of some works such as Prokofiev's *Romeo and Juliet* and *Peter and the Wolf*, which lack the dissonance and satire of his earlier pieces. Today Milhaud, Poulenc, and Weill are admired for their wit and clarity, Hindemith for his summation of the German tradition from Bach through Brahms in a novel musical language, Shostakovich and Prokofiev for their highly emotional and passionate symphonic styles, and composers in the Americas for giving their nations a place in the classical tradition—all with little thought to the ideologies that swirled around these composers and the constraints under which they labored. Yet politics still shapes the reception of some of this music, as shown by the continuing controversy about whether Shostakovich meant his music to convey a dissident message.

The postwar depoliticizing of art music composed between the wars resulted in part from the Romantic idea that classical music is a thing apart, an idealized, autonomous art (see Chapter 25), a notion that continues today but has come under increasing scrutiny from historians and musicians. With historical distance comes a greater focus on the music itself and fading memories of the circumstances in which it was born. Moreover, the period after World War II saw a reaction in western Europe and the Americas against not only Nazism but also communism and political ideologies in general, making overt links to politics a potentially embarrassing distraction for listeners. Copland's turn from populist Americanism to abstract twelve-tone music in the 1950s illustrates this reaction. Indeed, the least overtly political trend discussed in this chapter, the experimental tradition exemplified by Varèse, Cowell, and Crawford, grew in strength after the war, leading directly to post-war trends in North America and Europe.

In the long run, what seems most important about classical music between the wars, including that of the composers previously discussed in Chapters 32 and 33, is its great variety. Most composers still sought a place in the permanent repertoire and tried to secure it by combining elements from the classical tradition with individual and innovative traits that distinguished their music from that of their peers. The varied styles that emerged resulted in part from different views of what was valuable in the past classics and in part from composers' differing circumstances. They transformed their ways of thinking, from the political to the personal, into music of unprecedented diversity. Among their works, there are riches for every taste.

Further Reading is available at digital.wwnorton.com/hwm10

POSTWAR
CROSSCURRENTS

❖

The central theme of Western music history since the mid-nineteenth century is a growing pluralism. With each generation, new popular traditions emerged in response to changes in society, and the heirs to the classical tradition created more diverse styles of art music at an ever increasing rate.

This process accelerated in the twenty-five years after the end of World War II, propelled by an economic boom in the United States and most of western Europe, by ever more rapid communications, and by a desire among younger generations to explore new possibilities. Technological improvements increased the reach of radio and the quality of recordings, which became the primary means of distributing and listening to music. These changing patterns of production and consumption breached long-standing geographic, regional, and social boundaries, fostering interest in music of other cultures and social groups and opening new markets for all kinds of music.

During this period, musicians developed new styles, trends, and traditions, including styles of jazz that demanded more concentrated listening, from **bebop** to **free jazz**; types of popular music aimed principally at young people, such as **rock and roll** and its offshoots, or at particular communities, from **country music** to **salsa**; musicals that aimed for greater dramatic depth, integrated dance and music more closely with the plot, and incorporated styles from jazz, rock, and other traditions; film music that drew on a wider diversity of sounds and styles; and music for band and **wind ensemble** intended to match the depth, seriousness, and permanence of the orchestral repertoire. In varying ways, some musicians in each of these traditions sought to gain for their own music the respect long accorded to art music. All of these styles will be explored in this chapter, focusing on the United States, where most of these trends began. In the next chapter, we will consider new trends in classical music on both sides of the Atlantic during this era, and how they reflected the new sense of postwar pluralism.

Amidst the pluralism, there are also common themes. As we

proceed, we will encounter some tendencies shared by music across these traditions, including a growth of ambition that placed increasing demands on performers and listeners; a greater focus on music for attentive listening; experimentation with new techniques from novel sounds and textures to uses of the recording studio as a musical element; and borrowing or evoking styles from other traditions, both Western and non-Western. All of these arose from the new circumstances of the postwar era, the most technologically advanced and globally interwoven time the world had yet known, when almost any kind of music could be heard almost anywhere.

THE COLD WAR AND THE POSTWAR BOOM

The postwar expansion was achieved by generations who had suffered through the Great Depression and the most global and destructive war the world had ever seen. Germany, Italy, and Japan were defeated by the Allies, but at great cost. Tens of millions were dead: soldiers killed in action, civilians in bombing raids, and Jews and other victims in the Nazi death camps. Much of Europe lay in ruins, and many of the buildings, artworks, and musical scores Europeans had created over the centuries were destroyed. Musicians from all the combatant countries were displaced, imprisoned, or killed during the war: among many others, Stravinsky, Bartók, Milhaud, and Hindemith fled to the United States; Glenn Miller formed the Army Air Forces Band and played hundreds of concerts for the troops before dying in a plane crash; and prominent Jewish musicians perished in the Nazi camps, including Czech composers Erwin Schulhoff (1894–1942), whose music ranged from atonality and jazz to folk-influenced modernism, and Viktor Ullmann (1898–1944), whose orchestral and dramatic works have been rediscovered and revived in recent decades.

The Atomic Age

The destructive power of armaments in the war surpassed anything the world had ever seen, and much of it was aimed at civilians, from German rocket attacks on London during the Blitz to the Allies' massive bombing of German cities. By dropping atomic bombs on Hiroshima and Nagasaki in August 1945, the United States forced Japan to capitulate but inaugurated the Atomic Age. In response the Soviet Union, the United Kingdom, France, and other nations developed their own nuclear arsenals. The horrors of war, the Holocaust, and nuclear weapons provoked a wide range of cultural reactions, from the French existentialist literature of Jean-Paul Sartre and Albert Camus to a growing fashion for horror and science fiction films.

Occupation and recovery

At war's end, the Soviet Union occupied most of eastern Europe. By 1948, it reabsorbed Lithuania, Latvia, and Estonia, which were independent between the wars, and installed communist regimes under its control in Poland, Czechoslovakia, Hungary, Romania, and Bulgaria. Communist governments also took power in Yugoslavia, Albania, and China. Western democracies responded with attempts to contain the expansion of communism. Rather than impose reparations on Germany, Italy, and Japan, as they had done to Germany after World War I, the Allies sought to remake them as democracies, rebuild their economies, and turn them into trading partners. The United States invested billions in western Europe through the Marshall Plan, named after Secretary of State George C. Marshall, who saw economic recovery and prosperity as key to political stability in the region and preventing the spread of communism. Similar investments in Japan during the

United States occupation (1945–52) reshaped that nation as a strong ally with a growing economy and constitutional monarchy.

The Cold War   International relations for the next two generations were framed by the political conflict, known as the Cold War, between the United States and the Soviet Union and their respective allies. Figure 36.1 shows the map of postwar Europe, divided between the North Atlantic Treaty Organization—an alliance of the United States, Canada, and European democracies—and the Soviet Union's parallel organization, the Warsaw Pact. Symbolic of the conflict was the division of Germany between a democratic government in West Germany and a communist government in East Germany.

New international institutions such as the United Nations, founded in 1945, furthered cooperation but could not defuse all tensions. At times the Cold War heated up, as in the Korean War (1950–53), Cuban missile crisis (1962), and Vietnam War (1954–75). It also played out in other types of competition, such as the race into space, in which the Soviet Union took an early lead with the 1957 launch of Sputnik 1, the first man-made satellite put into orbit around the Earth; this spurred an energetic response from the United States, who won the race to the moon with the first moon landing in 1969. Music performance and composition, along with Olympic sports, chess, and other cultural fields, were used by both sides as arenas for competition. While communist regimes all over eastern Europe encouraged folk-dance and

FIGURE 36.1 *Europe during the Cold War (1945–91).*

folk-music ensembles in a combination of nationalism with pro-letarian ideology, the presence of American soldiers, diplomats, and businesspeople across western Europe brought a new wave of interest not only in jazz but in other forms of American music, popular and classical. The American occupying forces in Germany sought both to oppose communism and to denazify German musi-cal culture by funding performing groups, concerts of American symphonic music and jazz, and the International Summer Courses for New Music at Darmstadt, a school to promote new composi-tion through performances and lectures, whose focus on trends suppressed by the Nazis encouraged a new wave of twelve-tone music in Europe (see Chapter 37). The Department of State funded American composers from Cowell to Ellington to travel through-out Europe and Asia as cultural ambassadors. The United States occupation of Japan and military presence in Korea also stimulated interest there in American culture, from baseball to jazz, popular music, and Western classical music.

The United States, least damaged by the war among the active participants, enjoyed rapid economic growth and became the lead-ing economic power in the world. Technological innovations and expanded manufacturing capacity boosted productivity, resulting in historically high incomes for factory and office workers that lifted most Americans into the middle class. A second wave of the Great Migration brought many more African Americans from the South to northern cities, attracted first by wartime industries and then by the postwar expansion. Returning soldiers created both a baby boom and a housing boom, raising consumer demand. The G.I. Bill paid for veterans to go to college, producing a tremen-dous expansion of colleges and universities and of the numbers of citizens with university degrees, which further fueled economic growth. The number of families owning their own homes soared, and they bought cars, furniture, household appliances, and other goods at growing rates. Western Europe and Japan underwent similar economic growth, aided by investments from the United States. Cooperation through the Common Market and NATO wove western Europe together, making old nationalist tensions increas-ingly obsolete.

The expansion of higher education in North America and Europe was linked with growing access to the arts, and attendance at museums, concerts, and other cultural venues rose along with government and private support. Television and home stereo sys-tems increasingly brought entertainment and music into the home. The 78-rpm records (discs rotating 78 times per minute) that were the mainstay of recordings before the war were replaced by 33-rpm long-playing records (LPs), which could accommodate more than twenty minutes of music per side, and 45-rpm "singles" became the main medium for popular songs. The invention of the transis-tor led to miniature, portable radios that could go anywhere, bring-ing broadcast music into cars and the outdoors. "Disc jockeys" played recordings of popular songs on the radio, replacing most

TIMELINE

1939–1945 World War II

1943 Rodgers and Hammerstein, *Oklahoma!*

1945 Charlie Parker and Dizzy Gillespie, *Anthropology*

1945 First use of atomic bombs

1949 North Atlantic Treaty Organization formed

1949 *Billboard* begins country and rhythm and blues charts

1950–53 Korean War

1953 USA and USSR both test hydrogen bombs

1956 Chuck Berry, *Roll Over Beethoven*

1957 Leonard Bernstein, *West Side Story*

1957 Sputnik I launched

1958 European Common Market formed

1959 Miles Davis, *So What*

1959 John Coltrane, *Giant Steps*

1960 Bernard Herrmann, film score to *Psycho*

1960 Ornette Coleman, *Free Jazz*

1962 Bob Dylan, *Blowin' in the Wind*

1962 Cuban missile crisis

1964 The Beatles' first American tour

1967 The Beatles, *Sgt. Pepper's Lonely Hearts Club Band*

1969 Half a million people attend Woodstock outdoor rock festival

1969 Neil Armstrong and Buzz Aldrin are first humans on the moon

of the live-music shows of previous decades. Tape recorders, invented during the 1930s and widely available from the 1950s on, improved the sound of recorded music, made electronic music possible, and put into the hands of individuals the tools for preserving and manipulating sounds. Amplified musical instruments, especially the electric guitar and electric bass, transformed the sound of popular music and gave countless teenagers the means to form their own performing groups.

Independence and civil rights

Starting with British India in 1947, European colonies throughout Asia and Africa won independence and emerged as new nations. The growing political and economic significance of Asia and Africa encouraged cultural exchanges, leading to a rising interest in music of the non-Western world in the West and in American popular music throughout the world, facilitated by widespread distribution of recordings and radio. The nonviolent strategies Mohandas Gandhi developed to win independence for India were adopted by Martin Luther King Jr. and others in the effort to win equal civil rights for African Americans, a movement in which music played a significant role as unifier and inspiration. The Civil Rights movement in turn inspired others in the 1960s and 1970s, from student organizations and protests against the Vietnam War to the women's and gay liberation movements.

Musical pluralism

The victory over fascism, the economic boom, new technologies, and the winds of freedom helped to inspire a period of unprecedented experimentation and diversification in music. New trends in jazz led to a rapid proliferation of styles. Popular music splintered into traditions for different regions, ethnicities, affinity groups, and ages, each owing something to earlier popular song, blues, jazz, or swing while forging a distinctive identity. From musicals to band music, traditions that had focused on entertainment sought a new seriousness and encompassed a widening variety of sounds and styles. Composers of art music went in numerous directions, sharing less common ground as they explored new possibilities. Urban centers, mass media, and colleges and universities allowed musicians to find a small but devoted audience that would support specialized types of music, creating niche markets in which everything from early music groups to avant-garde rock bands could thrive. Musicians, critics, and listeners engaged in strident debates about music: whether jazz should hold to its traditions or search out new methods, whether rock music was a bad influence on the young or a source of freedom, whether classical composers should seek to appeal to a broad public or pursue a hermetic ideal in isolation.

Among the dizzying number and variety of trends in this period, this chapter and the next will describe some of the most important and distinctive. We will focus first on traditions outside the classical tradition, and primarily on the United States, which was the dominant force especially in jazz, popular music, musicals, film music, and band music. In the next chapter, we will take up the new streams in classical music, in which the United States for the first time competed with Europe as an equal partner.

FROM BEBOP TO FREE JAZZ

The three decades from 1940 to 1970 witnessed the emergence of several new styles of jazz, the continuation of older styles, and a growing consciousness of jazz history and desire to preserve it. Jazz lost its role as a form of popular music, replaced by rhythm and blues and other new traditions (see pp. 908–13). Instead, jazz was increasingly regarded as music that demanded concentrated listening, lessening the conceptual distance between jazz and classical music. Although most of the major jazz artists were African American, many of the performers and the great majority of the audience for jazz were white.

In the years immediately following the end of World War II, financial support for big bands declined sharply. More musicians now joined smaller groups, called *combos.* But a few big bands, including those of Count Basie, Duke Ellington, and other stars of the swing era, continued to tour, and younger artists like Stan Kenton (1911–1979) formed big bands that mixed mainstream jazz with progressive elements.

BEBOP A new style of jazz built around virtuosic soloists fronting small combos, known as ***bebop*** or ***bop***, emerged in the early 1940s during the waning years of the swing craze. In New York City, soloists playing with swing bands began to meet in after-hours clubs after their regular engagements finished for the evening. Clubs such as Minton's Playhouse and Monroe's Uptown House offered these musicians the opportunity to pit their skills against each other in "cutting contests," playing standards at blistering speed or in difficult keys to weed out the less virtuosic musicians. Out of these cutting contests grew a new musical language that became known as bebop.

Bebop was rooted in standards from the swing era, in blues progressions, and in other popular sources for contrafacts, but it was newly infused with extreme virtuosity, harmonic ingenuity, unusual dissonances, chromaticism, complicated rhythms, and a focus on solo voices and improvisation. A typical bebop combo featured a rhythm section of piano, bass, and drums, plus one or more melody instruments, such as trumpet or saxophone. In contrast to big-band music, bebop was meant not for dancing but for attentive listening. The focus was on the star performers and their prowess as improvisers. Performances in which one of the players was essentially the composer are preserved on recordings that have become classics, listened to over and over again, transcribed, analyzed, and reviewed in critical essays.

Characteristics

A characteristic example of bebop is *Anthropology* (NAWM 205), by alto saxophonist Charlie Parker (1920–1955, nicknamed "Bird") and trumpeter Dizzy Gillespie (1917–1993), shown in Figure 36.2. Like many other bebop standards, *Anthropology* is a contrafact on the "rhythm changes"; that is, it features a new melody over the chord progression for Gershwin's *I Got Rhythm* (see Chapter 34 and NAWM 190 and 193). A bebop performance normally begins with an introduction and then the *head,* the primary tune, played in unison or octaves by the melody instruments. Players perform from an abbreviated score called a lead sheet (shown in NAWM 205a), which includes only the head, with chord symbols indicating the harmony. The tune for *Anthropology* is typical in consisting of short, rapid bursts of notes separated by surprising rests, creating a jagged, unpredictable melody. The head is then followed by several choruses, solo improvisations over the harmony, and the piece ends with a final statement of the head. In the classic recording of *Anthropology,* Parker played a sizzling solo of unusual length (transcribed in NAWM 205b), taking up three choruses and surrounding the chord changes with a flurry of

Anthropology

HULTON ARCHIVE/GETTY IMAGES

FIGURE 36.2 *Alto saxophonist Charlie Parker and trumpeter Dizzy Gillespie performing with bassist Tommy Potter and tenor saxophonist John Coltrane, in a photograph taken on stage at the legendary Birdland jazz club in New York City, ca. 1950.*

chromatic alterations. This solo has been learned by countless younger saxophonists seeking to emulate Parker's sound and style.

In addition to Gillespie and Parker, prominent bebop musicians included classically trained jazz trumpeter Miles Davis (1926–1991) and, in their early careers, saxophonist John Coltrane (1926–1967), pianists Thelonious Monk (1917–1982) and Bud Powell (1924–1966), and drummers Kenny Clarke (1914–1985) and Max Roach (1924–2007).

Cool jazz   **AFTER BEBOP** Many of these musicians pioneered new jazz styles in the 1950s, seeking paths for individual expression by extending the methods and ideas of bebop. Miles Davis, as shown in Figure 36.3, was behind a series of innovations, beginning with his album *Birth of the Cool* (1949–50). Its softer timbres, more relaxed pace, and rhythmic subtleties inaugurated the trend that became known as **cool jazz**, soon taken up by the Modern Jazz Quartet, Dave Brubeck (1920–2012), and many others. Whereas bebop had begun as music dominated by improvising soloists, *Birth of the Cool* put the composer-arranger front and center.

Hard bop   A contrasting style was **hard bop**, which emerged in the mid-1950s as players incorporated into bebop elements from blues, gospel, and rhythm and blues. Among the pioneers were pianist Horace Silver (1928–2014) and drummer Art Blakey (1919–1990), who sought to recapture a wide audience for jazz with catchy melodies, slower tempos, and hard-driving rhythms, while emphasizing its African American roots. Significant recordings include their collaborations on *A Night at Birdland* (1954) and *Horace Silver and the Jazz Messengers* (1956), as well as Miles Davis's *Walkin'* (1954).

In *Kind of Blue* (1959), Miles Davis explored yet another new style that became known as **modal jazz**, which featured slowly unfolding melodies over stable, relatively static modal harmonies. Davis had grown interested in modal music through encounters with African music, the jazz pianist George Russell, and works by Ravel. The first track on the album, and among the most famous examples of modal jazz, is *So What* (NAWM 206). After an introduction for piano and bass that recalls the whole-tone music of Debussy, the tune is in the expected AABA form, but nothing else is ordinary: the A phrases are in the Dorian mode on D; the B phrase features almost the same music transposed up a half step to E♭ Dorian, so that changes of pitch collection delineate phrases as in the music of Debussy and Ravel (see Chapter 32); the harmony in each phrase is static, meaning there are only two chord changes in the entire tune, from D minor seventh to E♭ minor seventh and back; and the bass states the melody, which consists mostly of repetitions of a single idea, punctuated every two bars by parallel dissonant sonorities

FIGURE 36.3 *Miles Davis in about 1959, the year he recorded* Kind of Blue.

in the other instruments. In his solo, Davis repeatedly touches the tonal center to make the mode clear, playing at a relaxed pace far from the intense speed of bebop. *Kind of Blue* became the best-selling jazz record ever and is often cited as the greatest and most influential. Davis also collaborated with pianist Gil Evans (1912–1988) on a series of albums that incorporated elements of Spanish and classical music, including adaptations of classical works by Spanish composers on *Sketches of Spain* (1959–60) and *Miles Davis at Carnegie Hall* (1961).

John Coltrane

Tenor saxophonist John Coltrane played with Charlie Parker and Dizzy Gillespie (see Figure 36.2) and was part of Miles Davis's sextet for *Kind of Blue*, but also led groups on his own. He developed a personal jazz style based on very fast playing, motivic development, new sonorities, and greater dissonance and density of sound. His approach is evident in his solo on *So What*, which is much more virtuosic than Davis's, introduces and develops new motives, and cascades through the entire range of his instrument in rolling waves of arpeggios and scale patterns that a critic called "sheets of sound." Coltrane's album *Giant Steps* (1960), recorded soon after *Kind of Blue*, exemplifies his exploration of new resources in harmony. The title track (NAWM 207) is based on a harmonic progression that moves around a circle of chords whose roots are a major third apart: B, G, and E♭. Each is preceded by its dominant in the first half of the tune and by a ii–V–I motion in the second half. For the most part the melody also moves by thirds—"giant" steps instead of the usual whole or half steps, hence the tune's title. Circles of major thirds were used by nineteenth-century composers such as Schubert and Liszt (see Chapters 25 and 26) but were novel in popular music and jazz, and Coltrane's use of them was imitated by many later players.

Modern jazz   Cool jazz, hard bop, and modal jazz were all attempts to temper the extremes of bebop, through mellowness, the use of elements from rhythm and blues, or more freedom for melodic and harmonic improvisation. Coltrane's approaches to harmony likewise opened up new possibilities. The new jazz styles from bebop on, collectively known as **modern jazz**, have been compared by some historians to the multiplicity of modern styles in twentieth-century classical music. They derive from a similar source: a desire to say something new in a distinctive style that remained rooted in the tradition. And like modern classical music, modern jazz did not displace older styles but developed alongside them.

Free jazz   In the 1960s, alto saxophonist Ornette Coleman (1930–2015) and his ensemble introduced a radically new jazz language known as **free jazz**, named after their landmark album *Free Jazz* (1960), which contained a single thirty-seven-minute-long group improvisation. This experimental style moved away from jazz standards and familiar tunes, turning instead to a language built of melodic and harmonic gestures, innovative sounds, atonality, and free forms using improvisation that was carried on outside the strictures and structures of standard jazz forms.

Avant-garde jazz   Free jazz was part of a broader movement called **avant-garde jazz**, which blurred distinctions between avant-garde art music and jazz and between composition and spontaneous improvisation, and which left behind the conventions of bebop and modern jazz. Prominent avant-garde jazz artists include pianist Cecil Taylor (1929–2018), composer and bandleader Sun Ra (1914–1993), and the Chicago-based group the Association for the Advancement of Creative Musicians (founded 1965). Like avant-garde composers of art music, creators of free jazz and other avant-garde jazz styles question some of the basic assumptions of the tradition yet clearly draw from it.

JAZZ AS A CLASSICAL MUSIC While some jazz performers were pursuing new alternatives, others maintained older styles, reviving ragtime and New Orleans jazz or continuing to play swing. In a striking parallel to the rise of the classical concert repertoire over a century earlier, by 1970 the jazz world had developed its own roster of classics that were treasured on recordings and kept alive in performance. A sense of history was inculcated by written histories and recorded historical anthologies of jazz. At the same time, audiences for jazz were shrinking; swing was no longer the most popular kind of music, and the newer jazz styles from bebop to free jazz were more esoteric, aimed at connoisseurs. As younger listeners turned to rhythm and blues and other new traditions, jazz increasingly became music for the well-informed listener. Jazz critics and historians began to describe jazz as a kind of classical music. Jazz ensembles were formed at many schools, colleges, and universities beginning in the 1950s and 1960s, and jazz history became part of the curriculum. Now respected as an art music, jazz nonetheless retained some of the aura of the rebellious popular music it had been half a century before.

We have seen in bebop, modern jazz, and avant-garde jazz examples of the themes mentioned at the beginning of this chapter: a growing ambition for the music itself, reflected in heightened demands on both players and listeners; a focus on listening with concentration to the music for its own sake rather than using it for dancing or background music; experimenting with new techniques, sounds, and textures; and borrowing styles from other traditions. As we will see, these same themes are also apparent in popular music of the time.

POPULAR MUSIC

In the interwar years, popular music in the United States had been closely allied to jazz and to Broadway musicals. But after the war, musicians took popular music in several separate directions.

Economic growth in the postwar years gave young people greater leisure time and more disposable income. For the first time, teenagers became significant for the marketing industry, and clothing, cosmetics, magazines, movies, and entertainment were designed for and marketed to them. Increasingly, young people had their own radios and record players, and they listened to and bought recordings of music that reflected their own tastes. Record companies responded by marketing specific kinds of music to the teen and young adult market that became known as ***pop music***. Some types of music, like rock and roll, united most teenagers in the late 1950s and early 1960s, creating a "generation gap" between them and older generations. But as popular music continued to split into niche markets oriented to different groups of listeners, people of all ages found that the music they listened to marked their identity as strongly as the clothes they wore and the ways they behaved. Each type of music had its own stars, fans, and radio programs, and the popularity of songs in each category was tracked on ***charts***, weekly rankings by sales of 45-rpm singles. The varieties of popular music surveyed here, from country music to rock to salsa, are sometimes referred to as *genres* of music; to avoid confusion with the use of that word for a type of composition, such as a symphony or ballad, we will refer to them as traditions or styles of music.

Identity through music

COUNTRY MUSIC One tradition, associated primarily with white southerners, was ***country music*** (also called *country-and-western*), a type of popular music with folk-music roots that began between the wars, spread through radio shows and recordings, and grew in popularity after World War II. Like "race records" in the 1920s (see Chapter 34), country music was viewed within the music industry as a market demographic, a sector of the music-buying public who shared characteristics and favored certain styles; the name was codified by editors at the industry magazine *Billboard*, who tracked sales of what they called "hillbilly music" until 1944, then changed the name to "folk songs and blues," and in 1949 adopted the term "country" or "country and western." Country music was a blend of many sources: the hill-country music of the southeast, based on traditional Anglo-American ballads and fiddle tunes; western cowboy songs and styles popularized by Gene Autry (1907–1998) and other movie cowboys; popular songs of the nineteenth and early twentieth centuries; blues, banjo music, and other African American traditions; big-band swing; and gospel songs. Such a combination of traditions across social and ethnic lines is typically American.

Country music was valued for its energy, its witty wordplay (part of its heritage from Tin Pan Alley), and its ability to articulate the experience of rural and working-class Americans in a rapidly changing world. Most country

Characteristics

songs told stories, often first-person narratives of heartbreak, hard times, or nostalgia for home, that were especially appealing to people from rural backgrounds who were now in urban areas. Country music established itself as a kind of popular music in the 1920s and 1930s, the period when the United States population shifted from mainly rural to primarily urban, and grew steadily in popularity as the move to cities and suburbs intensified after World War II. The distinctive characteristics of country music include markers of rural speech, from word choice to a southern twang, and signals of sadness and nostalgia, from breaks in the voice to bending notes on the steel guitar that have been compared to sobs.

Typically country music centers on a singer strumming or picking a guitar accompaniment, often joined by others singing in close harmony or backed by a band dominated by fiddles and guitars (eventually electric and pedal steel guitars). Several distinctive styles developed, including *western swing,* a style of dance music that blends country fiddling with cowboy music, jazz, and big-band swing, and *bluegrass,* an up-tempo amalgam of old-time fiddling and banjo picking with blues and jazz, marked by impressive virtuosity and by solo improvisations on new or traditional melodies, and, like bebop, intended more for focused listening than for dancing. Two stars of postwar country music, Hank Williams (1923–1953) and Johnny Cash (1932–2003), reached both country and mainstream audiences. Nashville became the center of country music in part because of important venues such as the Grand Ol' Opry, made famous through radio and later television broadcasts. By the 1970s, there were country music stations all over the United States, and country became a nationwide style with continuing regional, racial, and class associations, much as New Orleans jazz had done fifty years earlier.

Electric blues **RHYTHM AND BLUES AND ROCK AND ROLL** The war and postwar years saw a continuation of the Great Migration of African Americans to northern cities, seeking greater economic opportunities. As bluesmen moved from the rural south to the urban north, many began to play electric guitars and developed a new style known as *electric blues.* Chicago was an important center for the development of electric blues, personified by the music of Muddy Waters (McKinley Morganfield, 1915–1983).

Rhythm and blues In 1949, Jerry Wexler, a reporter for the record-industry journal *Billboard,* coined the term "rhythm and blues" to replace "race music" as the name for the magazine's weekly chart of music marketed chiefly to African Americans, and it was adopted the same week as "country music" (see p. 907). Soon ***rhythm and blues*** (or *R&B*) wase being used as the name of a new sound that developed in urban areas in the years just after World War II. Rhythm-and-blues groups typically included a vocalist or vocal quartet, a piano or organ, saxophone or electric guitar, bass, and drums, and they performed mostly new songs built on twelve-bar blues or thirty-two-bar popular song formulas. In the 1950s, electric guitar and electric bass became increasingly common, gradually displacing the saxophone and acoustic bass. Rhythm and blues is distinguished from traditional blues by insistent rhythm, with emphasis on the second and fourth beats—called the *back beats*—in $\frac{4}{4}$ meter; whining electric guitar; and a repetitive amplified bass line.

At first intended for an African American audience, rhythm and blues reached white teenagers through radio and recordings. The teens were attracted to the sexual themes of the lyrics, the strong rhythms, and the intensity of the performances. Recognizing an opportunity, record companies produced *covers*, new recordings by different artists of songs that had been previously released—in this case, recordings by white singers of songs already popular in performances by black singers. For example, *Hound Dog*, a twelve-bar blues by the white songwriting duo Jerry Leiber and Mike Stoller, was a hit for black blues-singer Willie Mae "Big Mama" Thornton (1926–1984) in 1952, but sold millions more copies in the 1956 recording by Elvis Presley (1935–1977). In a time when African Americans were struggling for equal rights, the popularity of a black urban style of music among white teenagers was a force for change.

Alan Freed, a popular radio disc jockey in Cleveland, is credited with coining ***rock and roll*** as a name for a new style that blended black and white traditions of popular music. Rock and roll combined the driving beat of rhythm and blues with the milder guitar background of country music and drew on numerous elements in both traditions, from rhythm to timbre. The instrumentation consisted of amplified or electric guitars for both rhythm and melody, backed by electric bass and drums and sometimes augmented by other instruments. Song forms drew on Tin Pan Alley as well as blues, and rhythms and vocal styles encompassed everything from boogie-woogie to country twangs and gospel shouts. The words, most often concerned with love or sex, were often delivered in a raucous, sometimes wailing voice, although there were also gentle romantic ballads sung in a deliberately subdued tone. Both the words and the varied styles spoke directly to teens' experiences, creating a close identification between the listeners and their music.

Rock and roll

Rock and roll was launched nationally in the 1955 film *Blackboard Jungle* with the hit song *Rock Around the Clock* by Bill Haley and His Comets, an up-tempo song based on the twelve-bar blues progression first released in 1954 and chosen for the film's opening credits to illustrate what teenagers were listening to at the time. The first megastar was Elvis Presley, who enjoyed phenomenal success with his hip-swiveling blend of country and rhythm and blues. By 1960, rock and roll—soon simply called ***rock***—was being heard all over the world, especially in English-speaking areas, and was outselling every other kind of music. Black singer-songwriter Chuck Berry (1926–2017), one of the pioneers in blending country music with rhythm and blues to create rock and roll, caught the bravado of the young displacing their elders in his 1956 hit *Roll Over Beethoven*: "Roll over Beethoven and dig these rhythm and blues."

THE SIXTIES By the early 1960s, many of rock's earliest stars had fallen off the pop charts. Into the void stepped the Beatles, a quartet from Liverpool, England, composed of two creative singer-songwriters, John Lennon (1940–1980) and Paul McCartney (b. 1942); guitarist and songwriter George Harrison (1943–2001); and drummer Ringo Starr (b. 1940). All four were thoroughly versed in current American popular music, which had been circulating on recordings and radio throughout the British Isles since World War II, and especially in American rock and roll, which had as profound an impact on music and youth culture in Britain beginning in the mid-1950s as it did in the United States. Beginning as a group playing *skiffle*, a British amalgam of

The Beatles

FIGURE 36.4 *The British rock group the Beatles performing on the television series* The Ed Sullivan Show *on February 9, 1964. Already well known in the United Kingdom, the Beatles became a worldwide cultural phenomenon. Their appearance on American television ushered in what became known as Beatlemania.*

BERNARD GOTFRYD/HULTON ARCHIVE/GETTY IMAGES

jazz, blues, and folk, and mastering rock at clubs in Hamburg and Liverpool, they developed under the guidance of record producer George Martin into the leading rock group in Britain. "Beatlemania," already taking hold in the United Kingdom in 1963, reached America in February 1964 when the Beatles, shown in Figure 36.4, began a tour of the United States. After a few years of touring, the Beatles began devoting their energy to studio recordings, experimenting with novel instrumental combinations and techniques of sound manipulation that were impossible to produce in a live setting. The resulting albums, especially *Sgt. Pepper's Lonely Hearts Club Band* (1967), embraced a wide variety of musical styles, from British music-hall songs to Indian sitar music, in songs whose level of interest to connoisseurs began to rival that of classical music. Their example encouraged other rock bands to experiment with recording technology and to create rock-based music of depth.

Rock branches out   The Beatles' 1964 American tour began the "British Invasion," an influx into North America of British bands such as the Rolling Stones, the Kinks, the Animals, the Who, and Cream. Many of these bands were blues-based, influenced by African American bluesmen such as Robert Johnson. The emphasis on blues and an increasing focus on electric guitar solos gave rock a harder edge. Guitar virtuosos such as Seattle-born Jimi Hendrix (1942–1970) and Cream's Eric Clapton (b. 1945) became for the electric guitar what Paganini and Liszt were for the nineteenth-century violin and piano. Hendrix's stunning solo improvisation on *The Star-Spangled Banner* in front of an audience of half a million people at the outdoor rock festival Woodstock (1969) in upstate New York was both a protest against knee-jerk patriotism and an assertion of virtuosic prowess. As bands sought an individual sound, they developed many new styles within the broad tradition of rock: the California surf style of the Beach Boys, combining rock with close vocal harmonies and experimental effects (like the electronic sounds used in *Good Vibrations*) to salute the good times of sun and summer; the *acid rock* or *psychedelic rock* of Jefferson Airplane and the Grateful Dead, evoking the mind-altering effects of psychedelic drugs through surreal lyrics, extended solo improvisations, electronic sounds, manipulations of sound in the recording studio, and use of Indian instruments such as sitar and tabla; the loud and aggressive *hard rock* of Led Zeppelin and Aerosmith, marked by a heavy, distorted electric guitar sound and driving backbeat drum rhythms; and the *avant-garde rock* of Frank Zappa (1940–1993), who drew on influences from Varèse, Ives, and Stravinsky to rhythm and blues and on techniques from group improvisation to sound collages. Music and lyrics often expressed opposition to the prevailing political culture or social expectations. Except for a few singers like Janis Joplin (1943–1970), rock stars were overwhelmingly male, setting rock apart from classic blues (see Chapter 34) and most other popular music traditions.

By the late 1960s, rock music was aimed not just at teenagers but at listen-   *Rock grows up*
ers in their twenties and thirties, who had been teenagers in the 1950s and had stayed with rock as it grew up with them. Although some rock could still be danced to, most rock music, like bebop or other modern jazz, was intended and used primarily for attentive listening rather than for dancing; fans typically bought the latest album, took it home, and listened to it repeatedly, like art music. Concerts, however, were raucous affairs, with high levels of amplification and audience response, and none of the sit-quietly decorum of classical concerts.

In the postwar decades, rising interest in American folk songs led to a new   *Folk and protest*
kind of popular music that drew on folk traditions. Groups like the Weavers   *music*
and Peter, Paul, and Mary performed genuine folk songs alongside new songs in similar styles. Although the latter by definition were popular songs (newly composed by known authors and sold through sheet music and recordings) rather than folk songs (which have unknown origins and are passed down orally), the whole tradition became known as ***folk music***. In opposition to the increasing sophistication and professionalism of most other popular music, folk music was deliberately simple, featuring one or more singers with guitar or banjo accompaniment, and often the audience was encouraged to join in the singing.

Like rock and roll, folk music was an important musical voice for express-ing identity and ideology. Since the nineteenth century, singer-songwriters had adapted folk, popular, and hymn tunes to political ends by writing new texts in support of labor unions and other social causes. Many such songs were adopted by or created for the Civil Rights movement, including the move-ment's anthem *We Shall Overcome,* adapted from a hymn. In the 1940s and 1950s, Woody Guthrie (1912–1967) and Pete Seeger (1919–2014), stepson of Ruth Crawford Seeger, were especially prominent as singers and songwriters of folk and protest songs.

In the 1960s, the struggles for civil rights and against the Vietnam War galvanized younger musicians such as Joan Baez (b. 1941) and Bob Dylan (b. 1941) who voiced the protests of their generation in their songs. Dylan's songs *Blowin' in the Wind* (1962) and *The Times They Are A-Changin'* (1963) combined traditional folk styles with simple guitar harmonies, a rough voice, blues harmonica, and a keen sense of poetry. By the mid-sixties, Dylan was using electric guitar in a blend of folk and rock traditions. His complex lyrics, marked by unusual rhymes, puns, alliteration, and apparently deep or hidden meanings, captivated a generation and inspired many other pop artists.

FIGURE 36.5 *Ray Charles shown performing at the piano, in a photograph taken around 1960.*

The leading African American tradition of popular music in the 1960s was **soul**, a descendant of rhythm and blues in which the intense expression, melismas, and ecstatic vocalizations of gospel singing were brought over to songs on love, sex, and other secular subjects. Among the leading exponents were singer-songwriter Ray Charles (1930–2004), shown in Figure 36.5, who popularized the new trend from the mid-1950s on; James Brown (1933–2006), the "Godfather of Soul"; Otis Redding (1941–1967); and Aretha Franklin (1942–2018). Soul became closely associated with the struggle for African American equality through songs like Brown's *Say It Loud—I'm Black and I'm Proud* (1968) and Franklin's recording of Redding's *Respect* (1967).

The sounds of Motown—a Detroit-based record company founded and owned by African American entrepreneur Berry Gordy (b. 1929)—dominated the soul charts of the 1960s and often crossed over to top the pop charts as well. Knowing that the mainstream pop music market was much larger than the traditional demographic for rhythm and blues, Gordy sought to create popular music in the African American tradition that would appeal to both black and white audiences. To do so he synthesized the traits shared by black artists and songs that were most successful on the pop charts, and trained his songwriters, performers, and producers to combine them in a distinctive Motown style. In-house songwriting teams and studio musicians produced a consistent, groomed sound for groups like Smokey Robinson and the Miracles, the Supremes, the Temptations, the Four Tops, and Martha and the Vandellas. Other significant performer-composers who got their start at Motown include Marvin Gaye (1939–1984), Stevie Wonder (b. 1950), and Michael Jackson (1958–2009).

Tex-Mex and salsa

Latino-Americans produced their own styles of music, drawing on traditions from Central or Latin America. In Texas and the southwestern United States, *Tex-Mex* or *Tejano music* combined elements of Mexican mariachi music with folk styles such as German and Czech polka style and American country music. In New York City and Puerto Rico, a distinctive type of dance music called **salsa** emerged in the 1960s. Salsa is a mix of Cuban dance styles with jazz, rock, and Puerto Rican musical elements. A typical salsa ensemble includes ten to fourteen members on vocals, piano, Cuban percussion (such as timbales, claves, and conga drums), bass, and brass. Each instrument plays a distinctive rhythm, forming a driving dance beat of interlocking, polyrhythmic ostinatos. Championed by Tito Puente (1923–2000) and other performers, salsa embodied the rich ethnic mix of New York's music scene and offered the Puerto Rican immigrant community a distinct musical identity.

Pluralism and hybrids

The diversity of popular traditions shows the pluralism of modern society but also its common threads. Although identified with a particular group of people, each of these traditions represents a blend of elements from several sources, including common roots in prewar popular song, jazz, and blues, and attracted fans across a wide spectrum of the public. Popular music in other nations likewise blended local and regional traditions with elements absorbed from American popular styles. Although the traditional music of a culture or region once helped provide a sense of common identity for all generations, the emergence of new styles and types of popular music in each region reflected and reinforced tensions between older and younger generations and between rural and urban populations.

BROADWAY AND FILM MUSIC

Broadway musicals after World War II strengthened the emphasis on integrated musicals that began with *Show Boat*, in which all aspects of the production support the plot. As in the past, most Broadway shows were collaborations, and the great songwriting teams produced hit tunes well into the 1960s. Composer Richard Rodgers (1902–1979) initially collaborated with lyricist Lorenz Hart (1895–1943) and later with Oscar Hammerstein II (1895–1960), and Frederick Loewe (1904–1988) wrote music for the books and lyrics of Alan Jay Lerner (1918–1986). Irving Berlin was still active, producing classics such as *Annie Get Your Gun* (1946) and *Call Me Madam* (1950), and Cole Porter had one of his biggest hits with *Kiss Me, Kate* (1948), based on Shakespeare's *The Taming of the Shrew*. Successful musicals tended to find their way to Hollywood films within a few years and were also quickly disseminated to the public through recordings and productions by touring, amateur, and, in later years, high school theater groups.

Musicals

Rodgers and Hammerstein produced some of Broadway's best-loved shows, including *Oklahoma!* (1943), *Carousel* (1945), *South Pacific* (1949), *The King and I* (1951), and *The Sound of Music* (1959). Their first collaboration, *Oklahoma!*, not only enjoyed a record-breaking run of over two thousand performances but also marked a pivotal moment in the development of the integrated musical. Set in the Oklahoma territory around 1900, the story is richly textured, filled with both dramatic and comedic subplots. The characters are developed not only through dialogue but also through song. Dance, choreographed by famed dancer Agnes de Mille, also played a crucial dramatic role. The story's emphasis on American folk history and the simple pleasures of rural life appealed greatly to Americans during war time and the early postwar years. Rodgers and Hammerstein also explored innovative themes of racial prejudice and encounters between Polynesia or Asia and the West in several shows that use elements of non-Western music to evoke a sense of place: *South Pacific*, set on a Pacific island during World War II; *The King and I*, about an English governess in Siam (modern-day Thailand); and *Flower Drum Song* (1958), a story of Chinese immigrants and Asian Americans in San Francisco's Chinatown, which also featured a song in rock style to depict a young, thoroughly assimilated son of an immigrant.

Rodgers and Hammerstein

Leonard Bernstein (1918–1990) was a major presence both on Broadway and in classical music. Initially known as a classical composer, he became an overnight celebrity in 1944 after brilliantly conducting the New York Philharmonic as a last-minute replacement. That same year, his Broadway musical *On the Town* opened for a run of 463 performances. In addition to his

Leonard Bernstein

FIGURE 36.6 *Jerome Robbins leads dancers in a rehearsal of* Cool, *for the 1961 movie of Leonard Bernstein's* West Side Story.

career as a conductor and composer of symphonies and vocal music, Bernstein enjoyed enormous success with his musical *West Side Story* (1957), with lyrics by Stephen Sondheim (b. 1930), book by Arthur Laurents, and choreography by Jerome Robbins. Set in New York City in the 1950s, *West Side Story* is a retelling of Shakespeare's *Romeo and Juliet,* substituting rival gangs for the warring families of the original. The setting provided Bernstein with rich opportunities for including a variety of musical styles, including Afro-Caribbean dance styles, jazz, and soaring melodies in Tin Pan Alley AABA formulas.

West Side Story   *Cool* from Act I of *West Side Story* (NAWM 208) exemplifies his approach, mixing traditions and styles in order to convey the pent-up energy of one of the gangs before a fight. Figure 36.6 shows Jerome Robbins rehearsing the dancers in this scene, where the Jets are trying to "cool" down before meeting with their rivals, the Sharks. In *Cool*, modern styles of jazz symbolize the urban American setting and the youthful vigor of the characters, alternating between cool jazz, as the Jets attempt to calm their nerves, and the tense energy of bebop. These styles mix with elements of modernist classical music embodied in a fugue on a twelve-tone theme, representing for Bernstein the confusion and anxiety of modern life (through atonality) and the typically American blending of old and new and of high and low (modern sounds in a neoclassical fugue in the middle of a jazz song in a Broadway show).

The music of *West Side Story* shows how much Bernstein was under the sway of the integrated musical of Rodgers and Hammerstein, a genre Bernstein described at the time as the true American form of opera. *West Side Story* is typical of his compositions in blurring genres—comedy with tragedy, and musical with opera—and juxtaposing highly contrasting styles for a meaningful purpose. His blend of jazz and classical elements resonates both with earlier such combinations, like Milhaud's *La création du monde* and Gershwin's *Rhapsody in Blue,* and with the tendency of modern jazz musicians like Duke Ellington and Miles Davis to draw on classical music and to conceive of themselves as artists rather than entertainers.

Later Broadway   In the 1960s, Broadway musicals further diversified their subject matter and therefore continued to adapt styles from other traditions. Jerry Bock evoked several types of Jewish music for *Fiddler on the Roof* (1964), set in a Russian Jewish village, and Galt MacDermot's *Hair* (1967), a picture of urban hippie life, used a rock band and emulated Motown, acid rock, and folk music alongside traditional Broadway styles.

FILM MUSIC Film music also diversified in the postwar era, as composers chose styles and sounds that were appropriate to the subject and mood. Miklós Rózsa (1907–1995) developed several different styles, from an angular, contrapuntal, yet tonal modernism that helped to define the urban crime drama genre known as *film noir* to a mock-ancient style for historical epics such as *Ben Hur* (1959). The score to *A Streetcar Named Desire* (1951) by Alex North (1910–1991) popularized the use of jazz to represent urban settings, sexual situations, and social ills from alcoholism to crime. Leonard Bernstein used a dissonant modernist style in his score for *On the Waterfront* (1954), and others adopted atonal and serial music where their tense emotional qualities were appropriate. Bernard Herrmann (1911–1975), whose dissonant tonal language drew on Ives, Berg, Hindemith, and other modernists, became famous for his scores to Orson Welles's *Citizen Kane* (1941) and Alfred Hitchcock's *Vertigo* (1958), *North by Northwest* (1959), and *Psycho* (1960). Westerns often featured music in the diatonic Americanist style championed by Copland in his ballets and film scores, but the Italian composer Ennio Morricone (b. 1928) created a new, pop-influenced style for his Western scores, including *The Good, the Bad and the Ugly* (1967). National and ethnic traditions helped to establish place and atmosphere, from Mikis Theodorakis's score for *Zorba the Greek* (1964) to the blend of traditional and Western elements in the film music of India, China, and Japan. Electronic music was used frequently for psychologically upsetting events, the strange or supernatural, and space aliens.

Popular music continued to be a strong element in postwar film. In his jazz-influenced score to *Laura* (1944), David Raksin (1912–2004) introduced a theme song that was woven throughout the film and became a hit song in its own right. Many later films also featured theme songs, whose presence on the pop charts could earn additional income and advertise the film. Rock and other forms of pop music appeared in movies aimed at the teen market, from *Blackboard Jungle* and a series of films starring Elvis Presley to the beach movies of the 1960s. The Beatles' *A Hard Day's Night* (1964) was a financial success both as a film and as a soundtrack recording, and many other movies followed a similar model of marketing the film and soundtrack together.

Popular songs and film

BAND AND WIND ENSEMBLE MUSIC

Band music, traditionally viewed as a kind of popular music, underwent a striking transformation in the postwar era with the creation of a large repertoire of serious works for winds, especially in North America. This change in focus resulted from the convergence of several factors.

Over the previous century, the wind band had grown in popularity to become one of the fixtures of American life. There were amateur bands in most towns of any size, along with several professional bands. The most famous bandmaster after Sousa was Edwin Franko Goldman (1878–1956).

Variety of bands

FIGURE 36.7 *The Grambling University marching band performs their pregame show on January 14, 1968, before Super Bowl II between the Green Bay Packers and the Oakland Raiders.*

He and his son, Richard Franko Goldman (1910–1980), continued the tradition of outdoor band concerts through the nationally broadcast Goldman Band summer series from New York's Central Park.

School bands   Bands were especially important in the schools; virtually every high school, college, and university had one, and by the 1960s there were fifty thousand wind bands in schools across the country. School bands served multiple functions, giving concerts, playing as pep bands at games and rallies, or performing as marching bands in parades and at football games. From the first football halftime show, staged in 1907 by the Marching Illini of the University of Illinois, through the creation of Drum Corps International in the early 1970s, such performances spread to universities, colleges, and high schools across the United States and grew progressively more elaborate, combining music with choreographed movements on the field, adding more varied percussion, and supplementing the show with pageantry from baton twirling to flag-waving color guards. The tradition was especially vibrant at historically black colleges and universities such as Grambling University, whose band is shown in Figure 36.7 performing at the Super Bowl in 1968. The music for such shows drew on everything from college fight songs and pop songs to excerpts from Broadway musicals, movie scores, and well-known classical works, all in crisp arrangements that featured the various sections of the band and the power of massed sound.

Concert bands   Town bands, the Goldman Band, and marching bands all continued the tradition of band music as popular entertainment. But at the same time, there was a growing interest in presenting music for attentive listening. The American Bandmasters Association (founded 1930) and College Band Directors National Association (CBDNA, founded 1942) promoted bands and band music, including professional training for conductors and standardization of ensembles. Most important, they promoted the concept of the ***concert band*** (or *symphonic band*) as a vehicle for serious concert music. In purpose, role, performing context, and repertoire, a concert band is more like an orchestra than like the marching bands of parades and football games.

Goldman, the CBDNA, and various conductors were eager to broaden the repertoire for winds, building on the foundation laid by Holst, Schmitt, Grainger, and Vaughan Williams early in the century (see Chapters 31 and 32) to create a body of works parallel in weight and seriousness to music for orchestra. They embarked on ambitious programs to commission works for concert band. Major composers contributed pieces for the medium, including Schoenberg's *Theme and Variations,* Op. 43a (1943), Milhaud's *Suite Française* (1944), and Hindemith's Symphony in B-flat (1951).

Commissioning serious works

Then in 1952, Frederick Fennell (1914–2005) founded the Eastman Wind Ensemble at the Eastman School of Music in Rochester, New York. The **wind ensemble** was a group dedicated solely to serious music, rather than the mix of marches and other fare typically played by bands. Band pieces like Holst's Suite No. 1 in E-flat (NAWM 175) were traditionally scored for multiple players on each instrumental part and with each musical line in more than one instrument so that substitutions could be made to suit the available players. But the wind ensemble was different: each instrumental part became essential, and all or most were played by soloists, as in a large chamber ensemble. Wind ensembles quickly spread to other schools, and there are now several professional wind ensembles such as the Detroit Winds. The notion of specific rather than variable instrumentation influenced band scoring as well.

Wind ensemble

The presence of serious concert ensembles, well-funded commissions, and the prospect of enjoying widespread performances and earning continuing income from their music attracted many composers to write for winds, particularly at a time when orchestras were playing few works by living composers. Many composers who worked in a variety of media achieved their most frequent performances and most enduring success with music for winds, including Vincent Persichetti (1915–1987; *Divertimento*, 1950, and Symphony for Band, 1956) and William Schuman (1910–1992; *George Washington Bridge*), or have written one or more pieces that are now part of the permanent repertoire of serious classical music for winds; such works include Copland's *Emblems* (1964), Krzysztof Penderecki's *Pittsburgh Overture* (1967), *Music for Prague 1968* (1968) by Karel Husa (1921–2016), and *. . . and the mountains rising nowhere* (1977) by Joseph Schwantner (b. 1943). As a group, these works for band or wind ensemble reflect the same wide range of styles and concerns as do contemporary orchestral works, from neoclassicism to twelve-tone methods, new sounds and textures, and avant-garde effects.

Works for winds

Composing for band or wind ensemble was attractive for classical composers, because the wind repertoire was much more open to new works than the crowded repertoire of music for orchestra, string quartet, or piano. As Persichetti commented, "Band music is virtually the only kind of music in America today (outside the pop field) which can be introduced, accepted, put to immediate wide use, and become a staple of the literature in a short time." But there was a downside as well. Despite the tremendous growth in quantity and quality of the repertoire, wind music still lacks the status of music for strings or orchestra, due to its long-standing associations with marches, entertainment music, and amateur performers. For example, although Husa's *Music for Prague 1968* has received over eight thousand performances, more than any other Husa work and more than the great majority of twentieth-century classical compositions, Husa's music in standard classical genres has won him more prestige,

The problem of prestige

including prizes for his String Quartet No. 3 (awarded the Pulitzer Prize in 1969) and his Cello Concerto (winner of the Grawemeyer Award for 1983).

ROLL OVER, BEETHOVEN

In this brief survey of postwar developments, we have seen a proliferation of new styles and traditions in jazz, popular music, musicals, film music, and band music. All of these were introduced in earlier chapters as types of vernacular music, yet in each we have seen in the postwar era a desire to reach the status of art music. Traditions as disparate as bebop, bluegrass, rock music, Broadway, and concert-band music made increasing demands on performers, making a virtue of virtuosity, and on listeners, requiring the same focused attention expected of listeners to classical music. We have seen jazz artists, rock musicians, and band composers experimenting with new techniques, and have encountered musicians in all of these traditions who borrow or evoke other styles, from the use of classical and avant-garde elements in modern jazz, to the incorporation of Asian instruments and sounds in rock music, to the assimilation of jazz, classical, rock, and non-Western traditions in Broadway musicals. The eclecticism of the music of this time is in part a reflection of the people hearing it, most of whom listened to and loved more than one type of music. We will see these same themes played out in the classical arena, discussed in the next chapter.

In the years since 1970, popular music has grown ever more central to musical life. The teenagers who listened to Elvis Presley, the Beatles, Bob Dylan, or Aretha Franklin grew up but held onto the music they loved. There are now classics in pop music as surely as in classical music—nurtured and introduced to new generations by the "golden oldies" radio stations that emerged in the 1970s—and it is the music of the 1950s and 1960s that lies at the heart of that repertoire.

Repertoires of classics emerged also in jazz, Broadway, film music, and band music. Jazz numbers by Charlie Parker, Miles Davis, and John Coltrane have become as standard as earlier works by Armstrong and Ellington. Musicals by Rodgers and Hammerstein, Bernstein, and others from the postwar decades are staged every year by touring companies and in schools, and are occasionally revived on Broadway. Film music has of course endured in its role as accompaniment to the movies themselves, but in recent years it has received attention for its own sake as well. The campaign to create a repertoire of art music for concert band and wind ensemble succeeded by the 1970s and forever changed the nature of band concerts. In each of these musical traditions, the music from the postwar era has never ceased being played (at least in recorded form) and is now among the most frequently heard and deeply loved of the entire tradition. As these new canons of musical classics have become established, the first such canon—classical music itself—has seen its share of the market and of the concert audience shrink in proportion. Chuck Berry's mocking suggestion that Beethoven roll over and make way for a new kind of music now seems prophetic.

Further Reading is available at digital.wwnorton.com/hwm10

POSTWAR HEIRS TO THE CLASSICAL TRADITION

❧

The tradition of classical music performance became stronger than ever during the years after World War II. Audiences grew, government support in many nations rose, schools of music expanded, and music education in primary and secondary schools increased in quantity and quality. But the living composers who saw themselves as participants in the classical tradition shared less and less common ground, with little consensus on style, aesthetic, or purpose. Some composers sought to preserve and extend particular aspects of the tradition, from audience appeal to modernist complexity, while others focused on the new. After two world wars, nationalism seemed to many like a dangerous relic of the past, and although governments on both sides of the Cold War used music to promote their agendas, socialist realism or overt flag-waving proved less effective than support for a wide range of idioms. In every nation there was a diversity of styles and approaches, and ideas that began in one place were often imitated elsewhere. Thus it makes sense to divide our survey not by nation but by large trends, using individual composers as case studies while recognizing that some composers participated in several different trends, reflecting the diversity of the time in their own music.

DIVERSITY AND COMMON THEMES

There were many competing approaches in the postwar decades to the problem of composing new music that fit the times, and no brief survey is able to describe them all. The following can only begin to suggest the range, from the extensions of tradition to the radical avant-garde. This spectrum includes tonal and neotonal music; post-tonal styles drawing on composers from earlier in the century; increasingly complex approaches to twelve-tone and *serial* composition; a new virtuosity that engaged and challenged the best performers; applications of *indeterminacy* and *chance* in composition and performance; music that explored sound itself by employing new instruments, *electronic music*, or new sounds on existing instruments; incorporation of elements from other traditions such as jazz and non-Western music; and pieces based on *quotation* and *collage* of past music.

Yet amid all this diversity, there are also commonalities. In much of this music we will encounter the same themes we observed in other traditions in the previous chapter, including increasing demands on performers and listeners; a continued focus on attentive listening; experimentation with new techniques, sounds, textures, and technology; and borrowing elements from other traditions, both Western and non-Western.

We will turn first to composers who sought a place in the permanent classical repertoire alongside the masterpieces of the past and designed their works to function in the same way as the established classics had, drawing on the art music tradition, proclaiming a distinctive musical personality, and rewarding the listener at each rehearing. These composers pulled the goals of modernism into a new generation. As we will see, these individuals span a broad spectrum—from those who aimed to contribute something new that listeners could immediately understand, such as Samuel Barber and Benjamin Britten, to others, such as Milton Babbitt, Pierre Boulez, Luciano Berio, and Elliott Carter, who pushed the twelve-tone method, atonality, or performer capabilities to new extremes, creating pieces that were very hard to perform and struck their first listeners as radically new and often difficult to comprehend.

Then we will examine composers of the avant-garde, who sought to remake music from the ground up. As noted in the discussion of Satie and futurism in Chapter 32, avant-garde composers challenge accepted aesthetics, even the very concept of permanent classics, and invite listeners to focus on what is happening in the present. The central figure from the 1950s on was John Cage, who questioned the role of the composer and demanded attentive listening even to unintended sounds, and whose work has had a greater impact than any other postwar composer.

The next section considers composers who focused on new sounds and textures, including the new technologies of electronic sound creation, recording, and manipulation. Many of their works were experimental, designed to try out new methods for their own sake, while others were modernist or avant-garde.

The final section addresses stylistic mixtures, borrowing from non-Western music, and quotation. All of these trends blur the boundaries between modern art music and other traditions, and some also blur the lines between modernism and other trends. Together they set the stage for new developments in the late twentieth and early twenty-first centuries.

In some discussions of twentieth-century music, all of the radical new approaches in the postwar era are lumped together as manifestations of the avant-garde. But this obscures important differences. The distinctions between modernism, the avant-garde, and experimentalism do not lie in what techniques are used but in the music's purpose: is it to create new music that will find a place alongside older classics, to challenge listeners' preconceptions of music, or to try something new with little reference to the past? While these distinctions are useful, we will also find that increasingly in the postwar era these broad currents intermingle. Some composers, such as Karlheinz Stockhausen, participated in all of them; there are aspects of his work that are experimental, trying out new resources, or avant-garde, intended to shock his audience and raise questions, yet ultimately he sought a permanence for his music that marks him as a modernist. It can be hard to figure out a composer's motivations: did Krzysztof Penderecki intend his *Threnody for the Victims of Hiroshima* (see pp. 947–48) as an experiment in new musical sounds and resources, as a challenge to the basic concepts of concert music, or as a piece to be heard repeatedly, admired, and played alongside the classics? That it has been performed and recorded many times suggests the last, but the very question shows how entangled the three streams have become in postwar music.

THE NEW PATRONAGE As always, how composers made a living is part of the story. A few of them, such as Stravinsky and Copland, were able to support themselves with commissions, royalties, and income from conducting or performances. Other composers required patronage, but without the kings and aristocracy of earlier centuries, it had to come in new forms. In Europe, composers often were supported by the state, through radio stations, annual subsidies, grants, arts agencies, or educational institutions. In some countries, such as the United Kingdom and most communist nations, government support tended to make composers responsive to public tastes. Yet in others, such as West Germany, France, and Poland, the government sponsored the most radical new music, as part of its responsibility to support the nation's culture. The situation varied from country to country on both sides of the Cold War: for instance, in the Soviet Union, the thaw after Stalin's death allowed Shostakovich to set anti-Stalinist poems in his Symphony No. 13 (1962), yet his student Galina Ustvolskaya (1919–2006) was unable to secure performances for her radical modernist music, while in Poland the communist government funded the Warsaw Autumn Festival of Contemporary Music (founded 1956), where the astonishing new music of Polish composers like Krzysztof Penderecki was first performed.

The university as patron

In the United States and Canada, many composers were employed as teaching faculty in universities, colleges, and conservatories, giving them time to compose, a ready audience, and access to performing organizations, including ensembles set up to perform new music. Since colleges and universities prize academic freedom, the music coming from academic composers has been diverse, varying from traditional styles to avant-garde and experimental. Indeed, the safety of tenure and the ivory tower tended to isolate composers from the public and make them independent of its support. Some saw that as a virtue, allowing music to advance in its own terms, without having to please the untutored listener (see Source Reading).

To a great extent, the type of music encouraged at a school varied with the composers who taught there. Among many refugees from Europe, Schoenberg

Composition as Research

Milton Babbitt, professor of music and of mathematics at Princeton University, argued that composers, like scientists, engage in research that advances knowledge and should be supported for that work, even if it lies beyond most people's comprehension. His view extends in new terms the nineteenth-century view of music as an autonomous art to be pursued for its own sake. This excerpt is from an essay he wrote under the title "The Composer as Specialist," changed by an editor at the magazine where it first appeared to the more provocative "Who Cares If You Listen?"

❋

Why should the layman be other than bored and puzzled by what he is unable to understand, music or anything else? It is only the translation of this boredom and puzzlement into resentment and denunciation that seems to me indefensible. After all, the public does have its own music, its ubiquitous music: music to eat by, to read by, to dance by, and to be impressed by. Why refuse to recognize the possibility that contemporary music has reached a stage long since attained by other forms of activity? The time has passed when the normally well-educated man without special preparation can understand the most advanced work in, for example, mathematics, philosophy, and physics. Advanced music, to the extent that it reflects the knowledge and originality of the informed composer, scarcely can be expected to appear more intelligible than these arts and sciences to the person whose musical education usually has been even less extensive than his background in other fields. But to this, a double standard is invoked, with the words "music is music," implying also that "music is *just* music." Why not, then, equate the activities of the radio repairman with those of the theoretical physicist, on the basis of the dictum that "physics is physics"? . . .

. . . I dare suggest that the composer would do himself and his music an immediate and eventual service by total, resolute, and voluntary withdrawal from this public world to one of private performance and electronic media, with its very real possibility of complete elimination of the public and social aspects of musical composition. By so doing, the separation between the domains would be defined beyond any possibility of confusion of categories, and the composer would be free to pursue a private life of professional achievement, as opposed to a public life of unprofessional compromise and exhibitionism.

But how, it may be asked, will this serve to secure the means of survival for the composer and his music? One answer is that after all such a private life is what the university provides the scholar and the scientist. It is only proper that the university, which—significantly—has provided so many contemporary composers with their professional training and general education, should provide a home for the "complex," "difficult," and "problematical" in music.

From Milton Babbitt, "Who Cares If You Listen?," *High Fidelity* 8, no. 2 (February 1958): 39–40. In SR 174 (7:5), 1305–11.

taught at the University of California at Los Angeles; Milhaud at Mills College in Oakland, California; and Paul Hindemith at Yale. Walter Piston, a Nadia Boulanger student who taught at Harvard, encouraged a neoclassical approach, while Princeton was dominated by approaches derived from Schoenberg and Webern, particularly through the influence of Roger Sessions and his student and colleague Milton Babbitt. The Universities of Illinois and Michigan were also important centers, where annual festivals of contemporary music served as forums for both avant-garde and traditional approaches.

EXTENSIONS OF TRADITION

Although critical discussion has often focused on new sounds and techniques, most postwar composers used traditional means. Like their forebears, they sought an individual voice within the classical tradition.

TONAL TRADITIONALISM Many twentieth-century composers developed individual styles without departing radically from the past. Tonality or neotonality often, though not necessarily, characterizes their music. Seeking to communicate with as varied a public as possible, these composers offered listeners a thread that can be followed through identifiable themes, readably audible forms, or programmatic subjects or titles. The most successful also discovered the secret of inspiring performers to champion their music, creating works that musicians are eager to play more than once. Among such composers were Leonard Bernstein, whom we encountered in the previous chapter; Prokofiev, Shostakovich, and other Soviet composers affected by the expectations of the state that music should have wide appeal; Poulenc, Hindemith, and other composers who established their reputations between the world wars; and Richard Strauss, who was still composing tonal music in his own personal idiom in the late 1940s, culminating with his *Four Last Songs* (1948).

Of the American composers who remained committed to tonality, one of the most successful was Samuel Barber (1910–1981). His tonal romanticism is fully expressed in his best-known work, *Adagio for Strings* (arranged from the slow movement of his String Quartet, 1936), and in his Violin Concerto (1939) and Piano Concerto (1962). He often incorporated modernist resources into his tonal music; for example, his Piano Sonata (1949) uses twelve-tone rows in a tonal framework. Barber was renowned for his vocal music, including *Dover Beach* (1931) for voice and string quartet, *Knoxville: Summer of 1915* (1950) for voice and orchestra, and three operas. The songs in his cycle *Hermit Songs* (1952–53), on texts by medieval Irish monks and hermits, are always tonally centered, yet each offers a novel blend of traditional tonality with modern techniques. For instance, *The Monk and His Cat*, shown in Example 37.1, is solidly in F major yet features almost no consonant harmonies. Barber uses open fifths in the bass line to suggest a medieval atmosphere and dissonant augmented unisons (B♭–B♮ and E–E♭) in the piano to suggest the cat. Against the steady rhythm of the piano, the vocal melody projects the natural text accentuation in a syncopated, flexible line, whose rise and fall roughly parallels the contour of the piano's chantlike melody a perfect fourth higher, like an embellished style of medieval parallel organum. This song shows Barber's ability to write music that sounds fresh, like no other music, while using only traditional resources.

Samuel Barber

BENJAMIN BRITTEN The most prominent composer in the tonal or neotonal tradition to win an international reputation in the postwar decades was English composer Benjamin Britten (1913–1976). After studying privately and at the Royal College of Music, Britten spent several years in the late 1930s writing music for films, an experience that shaped his style by teaching him to communicate through the simplest means. Like Copland, he tempered modernism with simplicity to achieve a clear and widely appealing idiom. As a

EXAMPLE 37.1 *Samuel Barber,* The Monk and His Cat, *from* Hermit Songs

*Notes marked (–) in these two measures should be slightly longer, pochissimo rubato.

young man in the 1930s, he was deeply influenced by humanitarian concerns and ideals of public service, manifest in his interest in writing music for children and amateurs, his allegorical pleas for tolerance, and his pacifism.

Music for amateurs   The English choral tradition was nurtured in church and cathedral choirs, schools, and amateur choruses. Most of Britten's choral music was conceived for such groups, and works such as *Hymn to St. Cecilia* (1941–42), *A Ceremony of Carols* (1942), and *Missa brevis* (1959) have become standards. His one-act opera *Noye's Fludde* (Noah's Flood, 1957–58), on the text of a medieval miracle play, is intended for a mixture of professional performers with children of various ages and includes hymns that the audience is invited to sing. These and his other works for nonprofessionals are melodious, challenging pieces that suit their performers' abilities yet are not limited by them.

Homosexuality   Britten was a homosexual and was the life partner of the tenor Peter Pears (1910–1986). Shown in Figure 37.1, the two met in 1936 and lived together until Britten's death four decades later. Britten wrote most of his tenor roles for Pears, and the two collaborated as performers and as producers of the annual music festival at Aldeburgh in England that they cofounded in 1948. Several of Britten's operas have themes that relate to homosexuality, including *Billy Budd* (1950–51) and *Death in Venice* (1971–74).

Peter Grimes   *Peter Grimes* (1944–45), which established Britten's reputation and became the first English opera since Purcell to enter the international repertory, centers on a fisherman who is disliked by the other residents of his village, pursued by mobs, and ultimately driven to suicide. The theme of the individual persecuted by the crowd can be read as an allegory for the condition of homosexuals in a hostile society. Tellingly, Grimes is not a sympathetic character; we are meant to see ourselves, not in him, but in the ugly crowd that unthinkingly persecutes outsiders on the basis of suspicions and misinformation, forcing a poignant catharsis in the final tragedy. In the last scene (NAWM 209), as a search party pursues him calling his name, Grimes raves and mocks them in an unmeasured recitative, until his friend Balstrode urges him to sail his boat out to sea and sink it. The opera ends with a stunning depiction of the uncaring sea and equally uncaring townsfolk in a most successful application of bitonality: strings, harp, and winds arpeggiate thirds that encompass all the notes of the C-major scale, depicting the shimmering sea, as the town's citizens go about their business, singing a slow hymn to the sea in A major, each key stubbornly ignoring the other. The entire scene displays the eloquent dramatic effects Britten creates out of simple means.

FIGURE 37.1
Benjamin Britten (right) playing the piano as Peter Pears follows the score.

Britten's pacifism—his conscientious objection to war in any form—is expressed in his choral masterpiece, the *War Requiem* (1961–62). Commissioned for the consecration of the new cathedral at Coventry, a city destroyed in a German bombing raid during World War II, the work weaves together the Latin text of the Requiem Mass with anti-war verses by Wilfred Owen, English soldier and poet killed in France in 1918 just days before the end of World War I. The contrast of texts is highlighted by contrasts of performing forces; the Latin texts are set for soprano soloist, chorus, and full orchestra, with sections for boys' choir and organ, and the Owen poems are scored for alternating tenor and baritone soloists with chamber orchestra. Ironies abound. As the chorus sings "Requiem aeternam" (Grant them eternal rest), they hammer home a tritone (F♯–C), the least restful of intervals but the tonal axis of the entire work. Britten interleaves the English texts so that they comment on the Latin, and vice versa, as in the "Lacrimosa," where the melodic links between the soprano's tearful plea for mercy and the tenor's English verses highlight the futility a soldier feels at the death of a friend in battle.

Britten's commitment—to pacifism, to tolerance, to including all ages and talents in music-making—gives his music a quality of social engagement that has attracted many performers and listeners and has inspired later composers. Its enduring success shows the continuing power of music with a tonal center to move audiences and earn a place in the permanent repertoire.

OLIVIER MESSIAEN While Britten used a tonal or neotonal idiom that drew on English traditions and communicated social meanings, Olivier Messiaen (1908–1992) extended techniques from Debussy and Stravinsky to create a personal post-tonal musical language based on nondiatonic modes, harmonic stasis, nonmetric rhythms, and colorful harmonies and timbres, and used it to create music that inspired contemplation.

FIGURE 37.2
Olivier Messiaen.

Shown in Figure 37.2, Messiaen was the most important French composer born in the twentieth century. A native of Avignon in southern France, he studied organ and composition at the Paris Conservatoire, was organist at Saint Trinité in Paris from 1931 until his death more than six decades later, and became professor of harmony at the Conservatoire in 1941. After the war, he taught many important composers of the younger generation, including his fellow Frenchman Pierre Boulez, the German Karlheinz Stockhausen (both discussed on pp. 930–32), and the Netherlander Ton de Leeuw (1926–1996). It is a tribute to the quality and impartiality of Messiaen's teaching that each pupil went his own way.

A devout Catholic, Messiaen composed many pieces on religious subjects, such as the *Quatuor pour la fin du temps* (Quartet for the End of Time) for violin, clarinet, cello, and piano, written at a German military prison camp in 1940–41 for performance by the composer and three fellow prisoners; *Vingt regards sur l'Enfant-Jésus* (Twenty Looks at the Infant Jesus, 1944) for piano; his opera *Saint Francis of Assisi* (1975–83); and numerous works for his own instrument, the organ. Other principal compositions include the *Turangalîla* Symphony (1946–48) for orchestra and *Catalogue d'oiseaux* (Catalogue of Birds, 1956–58) for piano.

Music as contemplation

Messiaen sought to embody in music a stance of ecstatic contemplation. His works typically present an experience of concentrated meditation on a few materials, like a musical mantra. Rather than developing themes, he juxtaposes static ideas, showing his heritage from Debussy and Stravinsky. Messiaen used several characteristic devices, described in his book *The Technique of My Musical Language* (1944), that helped him achieve his goal of writing meditative music. The opening movement of the *Quatuor pour la fin du temps,* titled *Liturgie de cristal* (Crystal Liturgy; NAWM 210), illustrates several of them, as shown in Example 37.2.

Bird songs

Messiaen often wrote down birdsongs in musical notation and used them in several compositions, where they convey a sense of contemplating the gifts of nature and the divine. In Example 37.2, both the violin and clarinet play figures that suggest birdcalls (marked "comme un oiseau," like a bird), repeating them at irregular intervals.

Modes of limited transposition

What Messiaen called *modes of limited transposition* are collections of notes, like the whole-tone and octatonic scales, that do not change when transposed by certain intervals; for example, an octatonic scale transposed a minor third, tritone, or major sixth will yield the same set of notes. Such scales lack the differentiation of diatonic scales and so do not create a strong desire for resolution, making them well suited for music designed to suggest contemplation and a negation of desire. In *Liturgie de cristal,* the cello notes are all from a single whole-tone scale, in a repeating sequence of five notes (C–E–D–F♯–B♭).

Harmonic stasis

Messiaen's harmony also avoids moving forward to a resolution. Rather, chord series are simply repeated to create a sense of stasis or meditation. In this movement, the piano plays a succession of twenty-nine chords six times (the last incomplete); the second statement begins in measure 8.

EXAMPLE 37.2 *Olivier Messiaen, opening of* Liturgie de cristal *from* Quatuor pour la fin du temps

* *Glissando bref; id. aux passages similaires.*

EXAMPLE 37.3 *Durational patterns in* Liturgie de cristal

a. In piano   *b. In cello, with nonretrogradable rhythms*

Duration, not meter   Messiaen treats rhythm as a matter of duration, not meter. Rejecting traditional Western meters based on strong and weak beats, he drew inspiration from systems based on duration, including ancient Greek poetic meters that alternate long and short syllables rather than stressed and unstressed ones; the French Renaissance practice of *musique mesurée* (see Chapter 10), itself based on ancient Greek poetry; and the durational system of Indian music, known as *tala.* Meter, as a series of beats organized in measures, is a human or worldly thing, associated with dance and heartbeats. When we respond to music metrically, we are in our bodies, but when we attend instead to durations we are in the realm of time, ruled by the divine. In Example 37.2, the changing note lengths in the cello and piano do not create a sense of syncopation against a metric framework; instead, the smooth, legato playing style makes us hear patterns of shorter and longer durations. Throughout the movement both piano and cello play repeated patterns of durations that resemble the *talea,* or repeating rhythmic pattern, of medieval isorhythm (see Chapter 6). The piano features a series of seventeen durations played ten times, of which the first two statements appear in Example 37.2. Against this talea, the twenty-nine-chord series acts like the *color* (repeating segment of melody) in medieval isorhythm. Similarly, the cello has a talea of fifteen durations, framing its five-note color. These repeating pitch and rhythmic series create cyclic repetition, which again invites contemplation.

Additive and nonretrogradable rhythms   Example 37.3 shows the piano and cello taleae written out in integral note values (without ties). The piano talea features a device Messiaen used to emphasize duration over meter: what he called *added values,* such as the dotted eighth note amid even eighths or the lone sixteenth note, which add a small durational value to produce units of irregular length. The cello part includes another Messiaen trademark that he dubbed *nonretrogradable rhythms,* which are the same forward and backward; as shown by brackets, the first three notes form one such rhythm, the next twelve another. Such patterns preserve their identity outside of time—whether heard in normal time or reverse time, they are the same—and thus symbolize the eternal, that which exists outside of time.

Beautiful sounds   Finally, Messiaen preferred beautiful timbres and colorful harmonies. Here, the cello plays in high harmonics (sounding two octaves above the notated pitches), creating an ethereal sound, augmented by the gentle birdcalls in the high violin and clarinet, over soft dissonances in the piano. Messiaen invites us to meditate on these sonorous objects as they constantly recombine in new ways yet remain the same, like colorful shapes in a kaleidoscope.

The spread of serialism   **SERIALISM** Alongside extensions of tonality and individual post-tonal idioms such as Messiaen's, another prominent current in the postwar era was **_serial music,_** based on the twelve-tone method or similar approaches that use series of pitches or other elements. Following Schoenberg's invention of twelve-tone music in the early 1920s, several composers in Europe and the

United States adopted serial methods in at least some of their works, as we have seen with Berg, Webern, Krenek, and Crawford. Schoenberg's methods were introduced to the United States in 1927 by Adolph Weiss (1891–1971), who had gone over to study with Schoenberg in Vienna and Berlin and subsequently taught several American composers. The influx of composers fleeing the Nazi regime, including Schoenberg himself in 1933 and Krenek in 1938, reinforced interest in serial techniques, and during and after World War II the number and prominence of twelve-tone composers in the Americas continued to grow. Established composers like Stravinsky, Copland, and Barber took up serialism in the 1950s, as did many in the generation of composers who were just beginning their careers at the end of the war.

The situation was quite different in Europe, where the most prominent twelve-tone composers had died or fled during the Nazi era. But after the war, young composers in Germany and elsewhere embraced music that the Nazi regime had condemned, especially that of Schoenberg and Webern. By the early 1950s, many composers had adopted serial methods, adapting them to their own purposes. Their interest was partly musical, reflecting enthusiasm for new possibilities suggested by music they had been kept from hearing, and partly political, expressing a rejection of the Nazi and communist ideologies that had suppressed such music.

The new developments were encouraged by government-sponsored musical institutions, such as the International Summer Courses for New Music held in Darmstadt, Germany, each summer beginning in 1946. The United States' occupying forces supported the Darmstadt courses as a way to draw younger musicians away from styles and aesthetics promoted by the Nazis. At first Hindemith, Schoenberg, and American composers like Ives were all performed, but soon serialism became the predominant focus. At a memorial concert of his works at Darmstadt in 1953, Webern was hailed as the father of a new movement. Some composers adopted serialism as a way to achieve a music free of nationalist, fascist, or leftist ideology and thus escape the taint of politics many styles had acquired during the 1930s and early 1940s. Only in recent years have scholars argued that the government support through institutions like Darmstadt made serial music no less political, functioning as part of Cold War efforts to demonstrate the greater freedom for artists and citizens in noncommunist countries.

Politics and institutional support

The ideas fostered at Darmstadt and other centers for new music inspired composers in many countries. But every composer who embraced serialism worked independently, striking out in new directions, cultivating a personal language and style, and using serial methods in a unique way.

Individual approaches

Beginning in the late 1940s, some composers applied the principle of Schoenberg's tone rows to musical parameters other than pitch, giving rise to what has sometimes been called ***total serialism***. If the twelve notes of the chromatic scale could be serialized, so could durations, dynamics, timbres, or other elements. Despite its name, total serialism is never total; typically only some nonpitch elements are treated serially, often only duration, and the rest are used to highlight the serial structure. Other new extensions included methods of deriving subsidiary rows from the main series of a work, using fragments of a row, and subjecting rows to various other transformations. In these new developments, Milton Babbitt (1916–2011; see Figure 37.10 on p. 945) became the leading composer and theorist in the United States, and

Extensions of serialism

EXAMPLE 37.4 *Basic pitch row and number row from Milton Babbitt's String Quartet No. 3 (1970)*

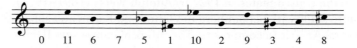

Pierre Boulez of Paris and Karlheinz Stockhausen of Cologne, both pupils of Messiaen and associated with the Darmstadt summer courses, became the principal exponents in Europe.

Milton Babbitt   In Babbitt's Three Compositions for Piano (1947), the first piece to apply serial principles to duration, he used combinatorial twelve-tone rows (see Chapter 33) and a four-number durational row and manipulated them by the usual operations of inversion and retrograde. His music quickly grew more complex, as he went beyond the practices of Schoenberg and his circle to realize new potentials of serialism. From 1947 to about 1961, Babbitt focused on combinatorial rows and derived rows related by trichords (three-note groupings within the row), and organized duration through number rows. In the early 1960s, he began to use "all-partition arrays" of interrelated rows using all possible ways of segmenting the row into groups of various lengths. Around the same time, he developed a "time point" approach to duration, in which each measure of music is divided into twelve equal units of time, numbered from 0 to 11, and notes are assigned to begin at particular points on this time grid using number rows. Babbitt converted a pitch row into a number row by indicating the number of semitones each note lies above the first note, as in Example 37.4. In this way, at least in concept, the same row that is used for the pitches also determines the rhythm. Babbitt once commented, "I want a piece of music to be literally as much as possible," and he pursued this goal by making the relationships between notes as numerous and intricate as possible.

European composers   Composers in Europe explored similar ideas, independent of Babbitt. In *Mode de valeurs et d'intensités* (Mode of Durations and Intensities), the third of *Quatre études de rythme* (Four Rhythmic Studies, 1949) for piano, Messiaen created a "mode" comprising thirty-six pitches, each assigned a specific duration, dynamic level, and articulation to be used every time that pitch occurred. Although the pitches were arranged in three divisions, each including all twelve chromatic notes, the piece itself was not serially organized. But it inspired Boulez and Stockhausen to write the first European works of total serialism.

Karlheinz Stockhausen   Stockhausen (1928–2007), shown in Figure 37.3, heard *Mode de valeurs* at Darmstadt in 1951 and composed his *Kreuzspiel* (Cross-Play) for piano, oboe, bass clarinet, and percussion that fall. In the first section, the pitch row is permuted through a complex process of rotation, in which notes are shifted from the ends of the row to the middle to create a derived row, and subsequent rows are derived by similar procedures. Each of the row forms is stated only once in Part 1, which is over after all have been stated. Each note of the chromatic scale is linked to a certain duration and dynamic level, creating rows of duration and dynamics that permute with the pitch rows. A similar process of rotation occurs in the percussion, using two different rows of duration. Meanwhile, another serial process controls the register in which each pitch is heard: half of the notes begin in the lowest register and rise to the highest over the course of Part 1, the other half move from highest to lowest. Stockhausen sets up these processes of change in pitch, duration, dynamic, and register so that they all cross at precisely the same point in the middle, hence the title, *Kreuzspiel*.

Stockhausen continued to develop serial procedures in *Kontra-Punkte* (1952–53) and other works, but also moved in many other directions, combining serialism with other methods while creating a body of work as diverse as any composer of the time. We will encounter him several times in this chapter and the next, in relation to electronic music, indeterminacy, quotation, and other trends. In *Kontakte* (1958–60) and later works, Stockhausen used *moment form,* in which formal units of contrasting character follow each other without necessarily suggesting a process, direction, or narrative, creating a sense of timelessness. Serial ideas continued to inform many of Stockhausen's works, but his music was also marked by a constant search for new procedures.

Boulez (1925–2016), shown in Figure 37.4, was also inspired by Messiaen's *Mode de valeurs* to apply serialism to both pitch and duration. His *Structures* (1951–52) for two pianos used the first of Messiaen's three twelve-note divisions as the pitch row; transformed both pitch and duration rows through retrograde, inversion, and other methods; and used dynamics and articulation to distinguish rows from one another. Boulez noticed that the work could give a listener an impression of randomness, because the piece lacked readily perceived themes, a distinct rhythmic pulse, or a sense of progression toward points of climax, and instead presented a sequence of unrepeated and unpredictable musical events. Seeking a more expressive language, but convinced that composition must be logical and systematic, Boulez developed new methods of deriving related rows from a basic row that provided him with enormous flexibility and expressive potential.

His best-known piece is *Le marteau sans maître* (The Hammer without a Master, 1953–55), in which he fused his pointillist style and serial methods with sensitive musical realization of the text. This work in nine short movements is a setting of verses from a cycle of surrealist poems by René Char, interleaved with instrumental movements that comment on the vocal ones by realizing the same material in different ways. The ensemble—a different combination in each movement, as in Schoenberg's *Pierrot lunaire*—comprises alto voice, alto flute, xylorimba (a large xylophone), vibraphone, guitar, viola, and a variety of soft percussion instruments. The ensemble produces a translucent scrim of sound, all in the middle and high registers, with effects sometimes suggestive of Balinese gamelan

FIGURE 37.3 *Karlheinz Stockhausen.*

FIGURE 37.4 *Pierre Boulez.*

music. The vocal line is characterized by wide melodic intervals, glissandos, and occasional Sprechstimme. The sixth movement, a setting of Char's *Bourreaux de solitude* (Executioners of Solitude; NAWM 211), is typical in that the complex serial procedures Boulez used are almost impervious to analysis, yet the musical surface is attractive and always changing in interesting ways—no doubt because of those very procedures. Moreover, the general shape is clear. The instrumental prelude and postlude rapidly and repeatedly circulate all twelve chromatic notes and the entire set of durations, dynamic levels, and timbres that Boulez is using. The central portion with the song setting has a completely different character, with a thinner texture, longer melodic lines, and frequent unisons or repeated pitches between voice and instruments.

The diversity of serial music   These composers and works should not be taken as representative of postwar serial music. They are very different from each other, and in that sense alone they are typical: virtually every composer who used serial procedures, from Schoenberg on, did so in a unique way, devising individual approaches and, in many cases, using different techniques from piece to piece. The diversity of serial music is a reflection of the basic condition of twentieth-century classical music we have observed since Chapter 32: that each composer seeks to create music that is individual, distinctive, and innovative, yet linked in essential ways to the music of the past.

THE NEW VIRTUOSITY   The music of total serialism was extraordinarily difficult to perform. For the structure to be clear in a work like Boulez's *Le marteau sans maître*, not only must the pitches and rhythms be absolutely accurate, but the dynamics must be exact—every *ff* exactly that and not *f* or *fff*. In the postwar years, a new generation of technically proficient performers emerged who were capable of playing such works and who made careers as champions of the newest music. Their presence encouraged composers to write pieces to challenge the skills of these new virtuosos. Much of this new music was not serial, but drew on sounds and textures like those explored in serial music.

Luciano Berio   The new virtuosity is well represented by the series of works titled *Sequenza* by Italian composer Luciano Berio (1925–2003; see Figure 37.13 on p. 952). Each *Sequenza* is for an unaccompanied solo instrument, from flute (1958) to cello (2002), and each was composed for a specific performer. The excerpt from *Sequenza IV* for piano (1965–66) in Example 37.5 shows the rapid gestures and sudden changes of register and dynamic level that are typical of the work. The atonal language, figuration, and textures Berio uses here resemble those of his earlier serial music. Throughout this passage, he uses the sostenuto pedal (which holds the dampers off the strings for notes that are being held when the pedal is pressed) to allow open strings to continue sounding or to catch harmonics from other notes, creating an unusual effect. The title *Sequenza* (Sequence) refers to a sequence of harmonic fields explored over the course of the piece. In this excerpt, the second chord is derived from the first (transposing the top and bottom portions by whole step and tritone respectively), and most of what follows is drawn from one or both chords.

Elliott Carter   The American composer Elliott Carter (1908–2012) wrote for virtuoso performers as well, using a complex, nonserial style characterized by innovations in rhythm and form. Beginning with his Cello Sonata (1948), Carter developed what he called *metric modulation,* in which a transition is made from one tempo and meter to another through an intermediary stage that

EXAMPLE 37.5 *Luciano Berio, passage from* Sequenza IV *for piano*

shares aspects of both, resulting in a precise proportional change in the value of a durational unit.

The passage from his String Quartet No. 2 (1959) in Example 37.6 illustrates Carter's methods. In this work, each instrumental part takes on a distinctive personality that interacts with the others as if in a dramatic work. The instruments are differentiated by their most prominent intervals: the first

EXAMPLE 37.6 *Elliot Carter, metric modulation in String Quartet No. 2*

violin dwells on minor thirds and perfect fifths, the second violin on major sixths and sevenths, the viola on tritones and ninths, the cello on perfect fourths and minor sixths. They are also distinguished by rhythm: rapid, even notes in the first violin, regular punctuations in the second violin, triplets in the viola, and a notated accelerando in the cello, with a dotted arrow indicating license to speed up smoothly rather than exactly as notated. The first violin effects the metric modulation: what was a sixteenth-note quintuplet in measures 57–58 is renotated as a sixteenth note in measure 59, then in measure 60 the dotted eighth (equal to three sixteenths) becomes the beat, creating a 3:5 proportion in tempo, from 112 beats per minute to 186.7. There is also a proportion of 8:5 between the first violin and the second violin, whose chords articulate a tempo of 70 attacks per minute. The result is a counterpoint of sharply differentiated lines, inspired in part by the multilayered textures in the music of Ives, whom Carter knew in his youth.

The performance difficulties of works like these have meant that they are seldom performed and are known mainly through recordings. Yet, like nineteenth-century virtuoso showpieces, the best of these pieces attract some of the top performers and are likely to endure. The extraordinary virtuosity they represent has parallels in jazz and popular music of the same era, from the blistering solos of Charlie Parker, John Coltrane, and other bebop and modern jazz artists to the feats of rock guitarists like Eric Clapton and Jimi Hendrix (see Chapter 36). Performers in all of these traditions were willing to go to new extremes to make an impact and claim listeners' attention.

Demands on listeners

The demands on performers by composers like Berio and Carter, or by serial composers such as Babbitt, Stockhausen, and Boulez, were matched by their demands on listeners. Each piece was difficult to understand in its own right, using a novel musical language even more distant from the staples of the concert repertoire than earlier modernist music had been. Compounding listeners' difficulties was that each composer and often each piece used a unique approach, so that even after getting to know one such work, encountering the next one could be like starting from scratch. Again there are parallels with the rising demands on the listener imposed in the same decades by modern and avant-garde jazz or by the most adventurous artists in popular music. Such challenges had tremendous appeal to some members of the audience for classical music, the modern equivalents to the connoisseurs of the eighteenth and nineteenth centuries. But many listeners, like many players, found the new music harder to grasp than anything they had ever encountered.

JOHN CAGE AND THE AVANT-GARDE

The music we have examined so far, from Barber's tonal works and Britten's neotonal music to the complex sounds of Messiaen, Babbitt, Boulez, and Berio, can all be regarded as modernist in essence, because each composer extended aspects of existing music in new directions. But the music of John Cage and other avant-garde composers raises more fundamental questions. What *is* music? What counts as musical sound? How should we listen, and to what? What is a composition, and what is the role of the composer? Where is the boundary between art and life—or is there any?

JOHN CAGE Over the course of a long and influential career, John Cage (1912–1992), shown in Figure 37.5, created sounds, approaches, and ideas that previously had been excluded from music. After studying with Cowell and Schoenberg, he composed serial music in the mid-1930s, worked in the experimentalist tradition through the 1940s, then turned in the 1950s and 1960s to ever more radical reconceptions of music that made him the leading composer and philosopher of the postwar avant-garde. Throughout his career, he worked closely with artists in other fields, from painters to dancers. His most frequent collaborator was modern dancer and choreographer Merce Cunningham (1919–2009), who was his life partner from the mid-1940s until Cage's death almost five decades later.

In the late 1930s and early 1940s, Cage wrote numerous works for percussion ensemble, following the lead of Varèse's all-percussion work *Ionisation.* Cage's search for new sounds, part of his heritage from Cowell, is evident in his use of untraditional instruments, such as tin cans of varying size and pitch in *Third Construction in Metal* (1941), and an electric buzzer and electronically amplified noises in *Imaginary Landscape No. 3* (1942). Composing for percussion raised the question of form, since traditional forms based on pitch, themes, and development were not suitable. While Schoenberg had impressed upon Cage the need for musical structure that relates the whole to the parts, Cowell had introduced him to the concept of *tala,* or organization by duration, in Indian music. Combining these ideas, Cage devised structures based on duration in which the proportions of the whole were reflected in each part: a movement is divided into as many units as each unit has measures, and the grouping of units into sections is the same as the grouping of measures within each unit. For example, *First Construction in Metal* (1939) has sixteen units of sixteen measures each; the units are grouped into contrasting sections in the pattern 4+3+2+3+4, and within each unit the measures are grouped in the same pattern, with contrasting material in each group of measures to make the durational pattern audible. Cage sometimes called such a structure *square root form,* since the number of measures in each unit is the square root of the total in the movement. The organization of music in terms of units of time rather than pitch and rhythmic relationships was one of Cage's most important innovations and continued to underlie much of his later work.

FIGURE 37.5 *John Cage working on his* Sonatas and Interludes *for prepared piano, 1947.*

Cage's experimentation with timbre culminated in his invention of the ***prepared piano***, in which various objects—such as pennies, bolts, screws, or pieces of wood, rubber, plastic, weather stripping, or slit bamboo—are inserted between the strings, resulting in delicate, complex percussive sounds when the piano is played from the keyboard. Essentially, the prepared piano is a one-person percussion ensemble, with sounds that resemble drums, woodblocks, gongs, and other standard or unusual instruments. Cage's best-known work for prepared piano is *Sonatas and Interludes* (1946–48),

Prepared piano

consisting of sixteen "sonatas"—relatively brief movements, most in binary form without thematic returns—and four interludes. The pianist prepares the piano in advance, following detailed instructions concerning what objects to place between the strings and where to put them. Each movement explores a different set of timbres and figurations. Sonata V (NAWM 212) illustrates the contrasts Cage achieves between wood, drum, gong, and unaltered piano sounds, and the interactions he creates between the content—the succession of sounds—and the durational structure—the units of time determined by binary and square root forms.

1950s and 1960s   Cage's pieces for percussion and prepared piano continued in the tradition of experimental music of his former teacher Henry Cowell. But in 1950, Cage met composer Morton Feldman (1926–1987), and the two became the nucleus of a small group of like-minded musicians in New York. Their conversations, together with Cage's growing interest in Zen Buddhism and in the art of Robert Rauschenberg (1925–2008), moved Cage in new directions that were no longer experimentalist but were unmistakably avant-garde. In his lectures and writings, he strongly opposed the museum-like preservation of music from the past and argued for music that focused the listener's attention on the present moment. He did not seek to write works that expressed emotions, conveyed images, developed material, revealed a coherent structure, or unfolded a logical series of events, as music had done for centuries. Instead, influenced by Zen Buddhism, he created opportunities for experiencing sounds as themselves, not as vehicles for the composer's intentions (see Source Reading). His three main strategies for accomplishing this were ***chance***, ***indeterminacy***, and the blurring of boundaries between music, art, and life.

Chance   By leaving some of the decisions normally made by a composer to chance, Cage created pieces in which the sounds did not convey his intentions, but simply were. His approach varied from piece to piece but typically involved choosing a gamut of elements to be included, planning how they were to be selected and deployed, and then using chance operations to do the selection. *Music of Changes* for piano (1951; Book I in NAWM 213) took its name from the ancient Chinese book of prophecy *I-Ching* (*Book of Changes*), which offers a method of divination by tossing coins six times to determine the answer from a list of sixty-four possibilities. For *Music of Changes,* Cage devised charts of possible sounds (half were silences), dynamics, durations, and tempos and used the method from the *I-Ching* to select which were to be used, filling in a formal structure based on units of time. The result is a piece in which sounds occur (and may recur) randomly and at random volumes, durations, and speeds. Perhaps surprisingly, because humans naturally find patterns even in random events—think of the constellations, randomly scattered stars in which ancient cultures found images of animals and mythological beings—listeners can hear even chance-determined music as interesting and beautiful, full of intriguing changes in density, register, and sound. Thus we may find a chance composition appealing, even while recognizing that it does not convey an emotion, story, or other intention. Cage hoped that listeners would find his chance works engaging precisely because they offer the opportunity to hear sounds simply as themselves, not as vehicles of communication or mysteries to puzzle out.

Indeterminacy   Chance is a way to determine certain aspects of the music without

SOURCE READING

Music in the Present Moment

John Cage articulated his views about music in a series of lectures given at Darmstadt, Germany, in 1958, and published in his first book of writings, *Silence* (1961). The lecture "Changes," from which the following is excerpted, was interleaved in its presentation with excerpts from Cage's *Music of Changes*.

❖

[In my recent works,] the view taken is not of an activity the purpose of which is to integrate the opposites, but rather of an activity characterized by process and essentially purposeless. The mind, though stripped of its right to control, is still present. What does it do, having nothing to do? And what happens to a piece of music when it is purposelessly made?

What happens, for instance, to silence? That is, how does the mind's perception of it change? Formerly, silence was the time lapse between sounds, useful towards a variety of ends, among them that of tasteful arrangement, where by separating two sounds or two groups of sounds their differences or relationships might receive emphasis; or that of expressivity, where silences in a musical discourse might provide pause or punctuation; or again, that of architecture, where the introduction or interruption of silence might give definition either to a predetermined structure or to an organically developing one. Where none of these or other goals is present, silence becomes something else—not silence at all, but sounds, the ambient sounds. The nature of these is unpredictable and changing. These sounds (which are called silence only because they do not form part of a musical intention) may be depended upon to exist. The world teems with them, and is, in fact, at no point free of them. He who has entered an anechoic chamber, a room made as silent as technologically possible, has heard there two sounds, one high, one low—the high the listener's nervous system in operation, the low his blood circulation. There are, demonstrably, sounds to be heard and forever, given ears to hear. Where these ears are in connection with a mind that has nothing to do, that mind is free to enter into the act of listening, hearing each sound just as it is, not as a phenomenon more or less approximating a preconception. . . .

The early works have beginnings, middles, and endings. The later ones do not. They begin anywhere, last any length of time, and involve more or fewer instruments and players. They are therefore not preconceived objects, and to approach them as objects is to utterly miss the point. They are occasions for experience. . . . The mind may be used either to ignore ambient sounds, pitches other than the eighty-eight [keys on a piano], durations which are not counted, timbres which are unmusical or distasteful, and in general to control and understand an available experience. Or the mind may give up its desire to improve on creation and function as a faithful receiver of experience.

From John Cage, "Changes," in *Silence: Lectures and Writings* (Middletown, CT: Wesleyan University Press, 1961), 22–23 and 31–32.

imposing the composer's intentions. Another approach Cage pioneered is what he called *indeterminacy*, in which the composer leaves certain aspects of the music unspecified. He drew the idea in part from the work of his friend Morton Feldman, who in pieces such as *Projection I* for cello (1950) used graphic notation to indicate register in general terms rather than specifying precise notes (see discussion on pp. 938–39). Cage's *Concert* for piano and orchestra (1957–58) includes sixty-three pages containing various kinds of graphic notation, intended to be realized by the players according to instructions in the score; the exact sounds produced vary considerably from one

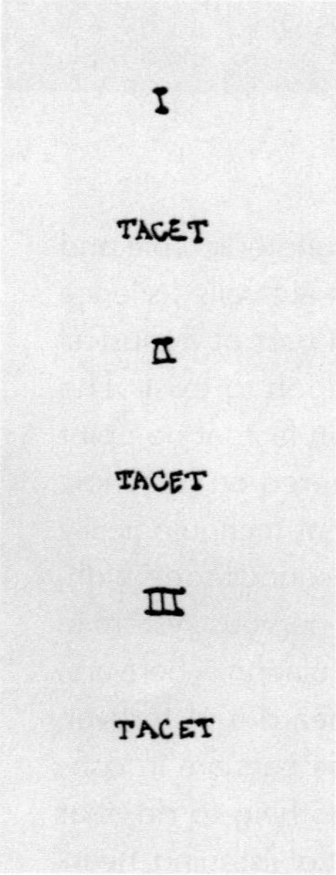

I

TACET

II

TACET

III

TACET

FIGURE 37.6 *The score of John Cage's three-movement work 4′33″ as published by Edition Peters. "Tacet" means "be silent" and is normally used in orchestral parts when an instrument is silent for an entire movement.*

performance to another. Cage's most extreme indeterminate work—and his most famous piece—was *4′33″* (Four Minutes Thirty-Three Seconds, 1952), shown in Figure 37.6, in which the performer or performers sit silently at their instruments for a span of time specified in the title (subdivided into three "movements"), while whatever noises can be heard in the concert hall or from outside constitute the music. The piece implies that silence is simply openness to ambient sound and that there are always environmental sounds worth contemplating.

In chance music, some elements are determined by chance; in indeterminate music, some elements are left unspecified by the composer. In both, Cage invites the listener simply to hear sounds as sounds, whether notated in the music or not, whether generated by the performers or occurring as part of the ambient sounds, experiencing each sound as it comes along, not trying to connect it to what precedes or follows it, not expecting the music to communicate feelings or meanings of any kind, but listening as intently as we would listen to any art music, so that we learn to extend our attention beyond music to the world itself. We saw in the previous chapter that postwar musicians in jazz, popular music, Broadway, and band music often demanded more attentive listening from their audiences, the same kind of close attention expected from listeners to classical music; Cage's music asks that we give that same level of attention not only to musical sounds but to all the sounds we hear.

Beginning in the late 1950s, Cage moved toward complete openness in every aspect of composition and performance. *Variations IV* (1963), for instance, uses both indeterminacy and chance (transparent plastic sheets with lines, dots, and other symbols are superimposed randomly and then read as graphic notation) to create a piece "for any number of players, any sounds or combinations of sounds produced by any means, with or without other activities." The "other activities" might include speech, theater, dance, and activities of daily life. Including these in "musical" works blurred the boundaries between music, other arts, and the rest of life. *Musicircus* (1967) is an open-ended "happening," consisting of any number of musicians and ensembles, each performing different music, all playing at once in a large space while the audience wanders freely. Through such events, Cage sought to focus our attention on whatever is happening in the present, experiencing it without prejudice.

Later works

In his later years, Cage continued to innovate, but chance and indeterminacy remained constant tools. Several of these later works submit music composed by others to chance procedures that transform the sources in unexpected ways. For example, *Cheap Imitation* (1969) takes the entirety of Satie's *Socrate* and transposes melodic segments of random length by random intervals. Another group of pieces, titled by the number of players (with a superscript for each new piece for that number, such as *Two²* for two pianos, 1989), present a succession of notes, chosen by chance, to be played within specified time ranges; these pieces combine chance, indeterminacy, and structure based on duration with a new simplicity of material.

Morton Feldman

INDETERMINACY IN WORKS OF OTHER COMPOSERS As we have seen, Cage was inspired to use indeterminacy in part because of Morton Feldman's example. Feldman was closely associated with the New York abstract expressionist painters, including Jackson Pollock, Mark Rothko, and Philip Guston, who inspired him to trust instinct, reject compositional systems and traditional forms of expression, and compose in a manner analogous to their flat, abstract images. His *Projection I* for solo cello uses boxes rather than noteheads to indicate approximate register, leaving the specific pitches up to the player. But timbre and rhythm are specified (although shown by graphic rather than standard notation), and the pattern of sounds and silences and of changing timbres and densities of attack will be the same no matter what pitches are chosen. By deemphasizing pitch, Feldman focuses our attention on other aspects of the music. In other pieces, Feldman notated specific pitches but left the durations indeterminate, and in some he used conventional notation. However notated, his pieces are generally sparse in texture, quiet, atonal, and pointillistic, showing the influence of Webern (whose Symphony, NAWM 183, sparked Feldman's first meeting with Cage) but with a completely distinctive sound.

Another member of the New York group around Cage and Feldman was Earle Brown (1926–2002). His *December 1952* (1952), shown in Figure 37.7, is a piece in graphic notation in which nothing is specified. He offers lines and rectangles of various sizes, some vertical and others horizontal, and explains in a note that the score can be placed in any orientation, read in any direction, and performed for any length of time by any number of instruments or other sound-makers. It is up to the performers to determine how to translate the signs on the page into sounds. Inspired by the mobiles of Alexander Calder, Brown took another approach to indeterminacy in his "open form" pieces *Available Forms I* (1961) for eighteen players and *Available Forms II* (1962) for large orchestra, in which the musicians play completely scored fragments—with some leeway in the choice of pitches—in the order and tempos determined by the conductor. In such works the piece will vary considerably from performance to performance, while its overall character remains within a certain range.

Earle Brown

Encounters with Cage or his music prompted several European contemporaries to adopt chance procedures or indeterminacy. Among them was Stockhausen, who used indeterminacy in pieces such as *Klavierstuck XI* (Piano Piece XI, 1956). The score is a single large sheet with nineteen short segments of music that are to be played in succession as the player's eye happens to light on one after another. Not all need be played, any may be repeated, and the piece ends after the pianist plays any segment for a third time. Many other composers, even Britten, called for brief periods of indeterminacy in their music in order to achieve a certain sound, gesture, or effect.

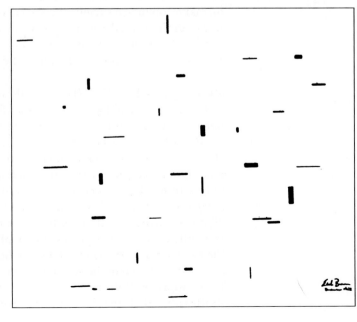

FIGURE 37.7 *Earle Brown*, December 1952.

Witold Lutosławski   The Polish composer Witold Lutosławski (1913–1994) made selective use of indeterminacy, while insisting on his authorship of the entire composition—a stance quite at odds with Cage's, suggesting an orientation more modernist than avant-garde. In his String Quartet (1964), pitches and rhythms are specified but not the coordination of parts; the players begin a section together, but each plays independently, changing tempo as desired, until the next checkpoint is reached, when at a signal from one of the players they begin together again. Symphony No. 3 (1983) applies this method with great subtlety. Some sections invite individual players to dwell upon a figure in the manner of a soloist playing a cadenza; at other times, eight stands of violins, guided by prescribed pitches but only approximate durations, go their own ways like tendrils of a vine. These passages achieve a freedom and eloquence hardly possible through precise notation and show the power of limited indeterminacy within a traditional genre.

Significance of   Many other composers adopted indeterminacy in some form under the
indeterminacy   influence of Cage or his associates. One by-product of indeterminacy is the variety of new kinds of notation. Scores range all the way from fragments of conventional staff notes through purely graphic suggestions of melodic curves, dynamic ranges, rhythms, and the like to even more slippery and meager directives. Another consequence of indeterminacy is that no two performances of a piece need use the same pitches or rhythms, as performances of a traditionally notated piece would do. In effect, a composition does not exist as such, but only as a performance, or as the sum of possible performances. The more the composer leaves undetermined, the more the performers become co-composers, having to make decisions—either during performance or in advance—about how to translate the notation or instructions into sounds and actions. Through the reconsideration of "the musical work" that indeterminacy and related notions stimulated, musicians in the late twentieth century became increasingly aware of the openness of early music as well, coming to understand that a medieval song or a Baroque aria is also a platform for performance open to a variety of choices within a stylistically appropriate range, not a rigidly defined, unchanging work. A similar openness characterized free jazz (see Chapter 36), whose freedom from the set harmonic progressions and conventions of earlier jazz parallels the free spontaneity of indeterminacy.

MUSIC AS THEATER AND PERFORMANCE ART   Cage's embrace of indeterminacy and of all types of sounds and actions as possible material for composition inspired others to challenge accepted definitions of music and art.

Fluxus   **Performance art**, in which performing an action in a public place constitutes a work of art, came into its own in the 1960s, spearheaded by Fluxus, a loose group of avant-garde artists in Europe and the United States who cooperated to produce concerts and publications of their pieces. For example, *Composition 1960 No. 2* by La Monte Young (b. 1935) instructs the performer to "Build a fire in front of the audience." *Grapefruit* (1964) by Yoko Ono (b. 1933) is a collection of such pieces, many of them conceptual, aimed as much at the performer as at any observers; in her *Earth Piece* (1963), the performer is directed to "listen to the sound of the earth turning." Ono brought her avant-garde approach into rock music in collaboration with John Lennon of the Beatles after their marriage in 1969. Some Fluxus pieces were never intended to be performed, but their very composition challenges our conceptions of music, the concert, performance, and the audience. Such a piece is *An anti-personnel CBU-Type cluster bomb unit will be thrown into the audience* (1969) by Philip Corner (b. 1933), which is listed on the concert publicity and program and then "performed" by canceling its performance at the last moment, saving the audience from apparently imminent danger; the bomb mentioned in the title was a type used in the Vietnam War, against which the piece obliquely protests. One of the central figures of the Fluxus movement, Korean-born Nam June Paik (1932–2006), devised exhibits with multiple television sets that blended music, video, performance art, and sculpture.

Performance art is intended to be temporary, experienced in the moment and essentially unrepeatable. Such pieces had no place in the concert repertoire because they proceeded from wholly different assumptions. But they left lingering questions about what music is and what purposes it serves, opening up possibilities that are still being explored.

Temporary art

NEW SOUNDS AND TEXTURES

A prominent strand throughout twentieth-century music was the exploration of new musical resources, including new sounds and new conceptions of music. Particularly active in this respect were composers of experimental music such as Cowell and Varèse, but composers of all stripes explored new resources, from the *intonarumori* (noisemakers) of the futurists to the Sprechstimme in Schoenberg's *Pierrot lunaire* and the sound effects in Bartók's *Music for Strings, Percussion and Celesta*. In the postwar period, the search for new resources intensified, including the use of new instruments, sounds, and scales; electronic music; and music of texture and process.

NEW INSTRUMENTS, SOUNDS, AND SCALES In their effort to offer something new and distinctive in art music, many composers sought out new sounds, sometimes building new instruments or reconfiguring traditional ones, and some explored scales featuring intervals smaller than a semitone. We have already seen several examples of postwar composers exploring new sounds, in Cage's percussion music and prepared piano pieces and in the novel combinations of instruments in the chamber works of Stockhausen and Boulez.

One composer who combined the exploration of new instrumental sounds with a new approach to pitch was Harry Partch (1901–1974), who undertook an individualistic, single-minded search for new sonic media. He repudiated equal temperament and Western harmony and counterpoint to seek a wholly new system inspired partly by Chinese, Japanese, Native American, African, and rural American music. His writings speak of a "monophonic" musical ideal, hearkening back to the ancient Greeks. Partch devised a new scale with forty-three notes to the octave based on just intonation, in which notes relate to each other through pure intervals from the harmonic series. As shown in Figure 37.8, he then built new instruments that could play using this scale, including modified guitars, marimbas, tuned cloud-chamber bowls (large glass containers used in early particle physics), a large string instrument like the ancient Greek kithara, and the gourd tree. In his multimedia works of the

Harry Partch

FIGURE 37.8 *Harry Partch with several of the instruments he invented to realize his music based on his forty-three-note untempered scale. The cloud-chamber bowls are on the far left, and the gourd tree is on the far right.*

1950s and 1960s, these instruments accompany speaking and chanting voices and dancing by singer-actor-dancers. In *Oedipus—A Music-Dance Drama* (1951) and *Revelation in the Courthouse Park* (1962), based on Euripides's *The Bacchae,* Partch aspired to the ideal of Greek tragedy.

George Crumb   George Crumb (b. 1929) has been most imaginative in coaxing new sounds out of ordinary instruments and objects. In *Ancient Voices of Children* (1970), a cycle of four songs on poems by Federico García Lorca with two instrumental interludes, unusual sound sources include toy piano, musical saw, harmonica, mandolin, Tibetan prayer stones, Japanese temple bells, and electric piano. He obtained special effects also from conventional instruments: for example, players must bend the pitch of the piano by applying a chisel to the strings, thread paper in the harp strings, and tune the mandolin a quarter tone flat. In *Black Angels* (1970), a string quartet is electronically amplified to produce surrealistic dreamlike juxtapositions. The composer explored unusual means of bowing, such as striking the strings near the pegs with the bow and bowing between the left-hand fingers and the pegs. The new and unusual effects in Crumb's music always have a musical purpose, providing material for juxtaposition and variation, and usually evoke extramusical associations as well. In *Black Angels*, they help to express his reactions to the Vietnam conflict, the social unrest in the United States, and the horrors of war.

ELECTRONIC MUSIC As new technologies developed, musicians explored their potential. No technology promised more far-reaching changes for music than the electronic recording, production, and transformation of sounds. These technologies were first exploited in art music but ultimately became more significant for film and popular music beginning in the 1960s.

Musique concrète   One approach was to work with recorded sounds, taking the entire world of sound as potential material for music, manipulating the chosen sounds through mechanical and electronic means, and assembling them into collages. Pierre Schaeffer (1910–1995), who pioneered music of this type at Radiodiffusion Française (French Radio) in Paris in the 1940s, named it ***musique concrète*** because the composer worked with concrete sounds themselves rather than with music notation. Schaeffer's first experiments, *Cinq études de bruits* (Five Studies of Noises) for phonograph, were premiered at a concert in Paris in 1948. He then collaborated with Pierre Henry (1927–2017) to create the first major work of musique concrète, *Symphonie pour un homme seul* (Symphony for One Man), premiered in a 1950 radio broadcast.

Tape recorders, which became widely available around that year, made it possible to record, amplify, and transform sounds, then superimpose, juxtapose, fragment, and arrange them as desired to produce pieces of music. The tape on which sounds were recorded had glossy plastic on one side and a thin layer of iron oxide on the other. It ran at a regular speed past electromagnetic heads that used magnetism to record sounds on the iron oxide or, when playing back previously recorded sounds, to translate the magnetic signature already on the tape. Running the tape by the playback heads at different speeds changed the pitch and often the tone color (the pattern of harmonics associated with a pitch). Many other playback effects were possible, and the tape itself could be cut and respliced to juxtapose fragments of sound. Composers used all these tools to manipulate the sounds they had recorded, creating music by a process that often physically as well as artistically resembled collage.

Tape recorders

Another source for new sounds was to produce them electronically. Most electronic sounds are created by oscillators, invented in 1915. The first successful electronic instrument was the Theremin, invented around 1920 by Lev Termen, which changed pitch according to the distance between the instrument's antenna and the performer's hand. The Ondes Martenot, invented in 1928 by Maurice Martenot, was controlled by a wire, ribbon, or keyboard. Both instruments produced only one note at a time, were capable of glissandos along the entire pitch continuum, and projected a haunting, almost voicelike sound. Featured in some orchestral works, such as Messiaen's *Turangalîla* Symphony, they became common in film scores like Hitchcock's *Spellbound* (1945), where they lent an eerie or futuristic effect, and in some popular songs such as the Beach Boys' *Good Vibrations* (1966), but they were not used in electronic music itself.

Electronic sound

Between 1951 and 1953, studios to create electronic music were founded at Columbia University in New York and at radio stations in Cologne (Germany), Milan (Italy), and Tokyo (Japan), followed by many others across Europe and the Americas. These studios were funded by governments and grants because they were very expensive and time-consuming to equip and to run; at Cologne, for example, Karlheinz Stockhausen had a dedicated team of technicians, and his electronic compositions took hundreds of hours to create. At most studios, composers focused on producing sounds electronically and manipulating them through electronic devices and on tape. A whole new realm of possible sounds became available, including sounds that could not be produced by any "natural" means.

Electronic music studios

Stockhausen and others often used recorded sounds alongside electronic ones, as in his *Gesang der Jünglinge* (Song of the Youths, 1955–56), which incorporated a boy's voice. This was the first major electronic piece to use

Gesang der Jünglinge

FIGURE 37.9 *The Philips Pavilion at the 1958 World's Fair in Brussels, Belgium. Edgard Varèse collaborated with the architect Le Corbusier to fill this building with the sound of* Poème électronique, *composed at the Philips laboratories at Eindhoven in the Netherlands.*

multiple tracks, played in concert through several loudspeakers placed in various positions relative to the audience, which created a sense of the music coming from numerous directions and moving through space.

Varèse's *Poème électronique* (Electronic Poem, 1957–58; NAWM 214) also combined electronic sounds with recorded ones, from noises to a singer, and represented a pinnacle of his concept of spatial music. Commissioned by the Philips Radio Corporation for the Brussels World's Fair in 1958, the eight-minute piece was projected by 425 loudspeakers ranged all about the interior space of the pavilion designed by Le Corbusier, shown in Figure 37.9, accompanied by moving colored lights and projected images. Fifteen thousand people a day experienced this multimedia piece over a six-month period.

Electronic music was at first produced by combining, modifying, and controlling in various ways the output of oscillators, then recording these sounds on tape. The composer had to splice the tapes and mix their output, sometimes in combination with recorded sounds of physical objects in motion or of musicians, speakers, or singers. Electronic sound **synthesizers** were developed to make the process much easier. The composer could call on pitches from a music keyboard and with switches and knobs control harmonics, waveform (which determines timbre), resonance, and location of sound sources. The first programmable synthesizer was the RCA Mark II Sound Synthesizer, shown in Figure 37.10, which was developed at the joint Columbia-Princeton Electronic Music Center in the late 1950s and used by many composers from the United States and abroad.

Moog and Buchla synthesizers

In the mid-1960s, Robert Moog and Donald Buchla each developed synthesizers that were far simpler and more compact, based on transistors and voltage-controlled oscillators. Moog worked at the Columbia-Princeton Center alongside Walter Carlos (later Wendy Carlos, b. 1939), and Buchla designed his first synthesizer for the San Francisco Tape Music Center, cofounded in 1962 by Pauline Oliveros (1934–2016), Morton Subotnick (b. 1933), and Ramon Sender (b. 1934). When the Moog and Buchla synthesizers became commercially available in 1966, they were adopted by electronic music studios and individual composers around the world. The new synthesizers reduced the time needed to create electronic music and were much less expensive, allowing composers to buy and use them at home. One of the early works created on the Buchla synthesizer was Subotnick's *Silver Apples of the Moon* (1967), the first electronic piece to be commissioned by a record company, designed to fill two sides of an LP and to be played at home rather than in concert. The next year Carlos released *Switched-On Bach*, an LP of pieces by J. S. Bach performed on the Moog synthesizer. Both albums were surprise hits; *Silver Apples* was a best-seller for the classical label Nonesuch,

FIGURE 37.10 *Composers Mario Davidovsky, Milton Babbitt, and Vladimir Ussachevsky with the RCA Mark II Sound Synthesizer, the first programmable synthesizer, at the Columbia-Princeton Electronic Music Center in New York.*

and *Switched-On Bach* sold more than a million copies and topped the *Billboard* classical music chart for three years running. Their success established the synthesizers as legitimate and useful instruments. The new synthesizers were also adopted by popular artists such as the Beatles, and electronic synthesizers soon became a familiar sound in pop music.

The electronic medium gave composers complete, unmediated control over their compositions. Much of the new music already demanded complex rhythms and minute shadings of pitch, intensity, and timbre that could barely be realized by human performers, but in the electronic studio, every detail could be accurately calculated and recorded. This is one reason practitioners of total serialism embraced electronic music. Yet the absence of performers hindered the acceptance of purely electronic music, since audiences expect to have performers to watch and respond to, and since performers are the main promoters and advocates for new music.

Role of performers

Recognizing this, composers soon began to create works that combined prerecorded tape with live performers. One of the most moving early examples was Milton Babbitt's *Philomel* (1964; first section in NAWM 215), for soprano soloist with a tape that includes altered recorded fragments of the singer as well as electronic sounds. The live voice and the voice on tape engage in dialogue, accompanied by synthesized sounds, all worked out according to Babbitt's usual serial procedures.

Tape and live performance

Electronic music, whether played in concert or distributed in the form of recordings for private listening, attracted a relatively small, devoted audience without gaining broad popularity. Yet it became a potent tool in music for film and television, and most of the music produced today, especially popular music, uses technology developed by the pioneers of electronic music.

MUSIC OF TEXTURE AND PROCESS Varèse's conception of music as spatial, with sound masses moving through musical space and interacting with each other like an abstract ballet in sound, opened the door to music that centered not on melody, harmony, or counterpoint but on sound itself. More-over, the exploration of electronic sounds stimulated the invention of new sound effects obtainable from conventional instruments and voices, often imitating electronic music. Composers now wrote pieces whose material con-sists primarily of striking sound combinations that create interesting and novel textures, organized by gradual or sudden processes of change.

Iannis Xenakis　　One of the first to write such music for acoustic instruments was Iannis Xenakis (1922–2001). A Greek who spent most of his career in France, Xena-kis was an engineer and architect as well as a composer. Like the ancient Greeks, he saw mathematics as fundamental to both music and architecture, so he based his music on mathematical concepts. In *Metastaseis* (1953–54), he gave each string player in the orchestra a unique part to play. In many sec-tions of the work, each player has a glissando, moving slowly or quickly in comparison to the other parts. In Figure 37.11, Xenakis plotted out the glis-sandos as straight lines on a graph that add up to create an effect of curves in musical space. He then transferred the lines to standard musical notation. The resulting motions, of a chromatic cluster gradually closing to a unison or

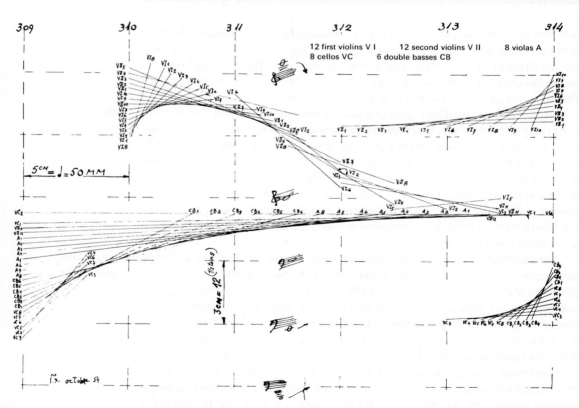

FIGURE 37.11 *Iannis Xenakis's graph for a passage in* Metastaseis, *with pitch as the vertical axis and time as the horizontal axis. The lower half of the graph represents the lower strings attacking a chromatic cluster together, then curving upward as the lowest pitches in the cluster rise in rapid glissandos and the higher ones move progressively more slowly. A measure later, the upper strings enter on another cluster, then rise and fall in their own pattern. Toward the end of the passage, groups of strings enter on the same note one after another, each successively rising in a faster glissando until all end together in a chromatic cluster. The combined effect of these overlapping glis-sandos moving at different speeds is to create a sense of curves in musical space, akin to the curves created by the combination of straight lines on the graph.*

a unison expanding to a cluster, resemble changes achievable in electronic music through the use of pitch filters. The overall effect is very strongly visual, although the materials are musical. Indeed, Xenakis later applied the same idea of straight lines creating a curving effect in the design for the Philips Pavilion (see Figure 37.9), on which he worked with Le Corbusier.

One of the best-known pieces based on texture and process is *Threnody for the Victims of Hiroshima* (1960; NAWM 216) for fifty-two string instruments, by Polish composer Krzysztof Penderecki (b. 1933). The score gives few definite pulses or note values, and instead measures time by seconds. Again each instrument has a unique part to play. Each section focuses on a particular kind of sound, using newly invented notation that shows the effect graphically but not imprecisely. At the beginning, four to six instruments enter at a time, each playing its highest possible note, like a scream of very high clusters. This gradually gives way to a section in which each player rapidly repeats a series of sound effects—such as bowing or arpeggiating behind the bridge (producing high pitches), striking the soundboard, or bowing or plucking the highest possible note. The players may choose one of four patterns, they may move at different speeds (each as fast as possible), and the exact sounds each produces are indeterminate, but the overall effect is essentially the same in each performance, creating a prickly, interesting texture. Next is a section based on sustained tones, quarter-tone clusters, and glissandos between them, shown graphically in the score in Example 37.7 and notated precisely in the parts. The entire pitched and unpitched world, animate and inanimate, wailing and weeping at once, often in polychoral and antiphonal calls and responses, seems to mourn in this dirge. Remarkably, Penderecki originally conceived the work as a purely abstract play of sound and titled it *8'37"* (its timing); the evocative final title has won it a much larger audience than it would otherwise have had by connecting the new musical resources it uses to the tradition of expressive instrumental music extending back to the seventeenth century.

Penderecki used similar techniques in many other pieces, including the *St. Luke Passion* (1963–66) and his opera *The Devils of Loudun* (1968), which show how the new resources can be used dramatically. But in these works he already began to incorporate elements of more traditional styles, and in the mid-1970s he turned to a personal style of neo-Romanticism (see Chapter 38).

The music of Hungarian composer György Ligeti (1923–2006) achieved world renown through Stanley Kubrick's science fiction film *2001: A Space Odyssey,* which uses excerpts from four of his works: *Atmosphères* (1961), *Requiem* (1963–65), *Lux aeterna* (1966), and *Aventures* (1962–63, used in electronically altered form). This music is in constant motion, yet static both harmonically and melodically. *Atmosphères* begins with fifty-six muted strings, together with a selection of woodwinds and horns, playing simultaneously all the chromatic notes through a five-octave range. Instruments imperceptibly drop out until only the violas and cellos remain, imitating an effect Ligeti had experimented with in an earlier unfinished electronic piece, *Pièce électronique No. 3* (Electronic Piece No. 3, 1957). An orchestral tutti follows with a similar panchromatic layout, but out of it emerge two clusters: one, in the strings, made up of the seven notes of a diatonic scale, contrasts with the other, a pentatonic cluster of the remaining five

Krzysztof Penderecki

György Ligeti

EXAMPLE 37.7 *Krzysztof Penderecki*, Threnody for the Victims of Hiroshima

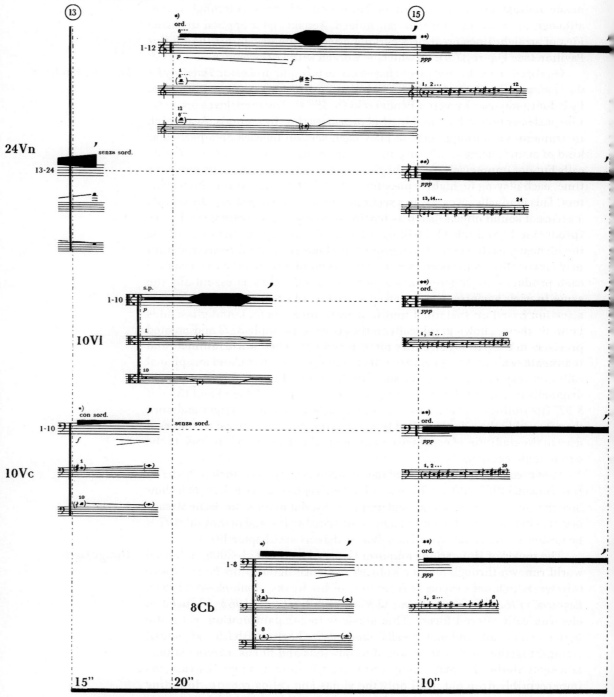

notes of the chromatic scale, in the woodwinds and horns. While one group crescendos, the other diminuendos, then the two reverse, creating changing sonorities that suggest the play of light and shadow on clouds. At times Ligeti uses what he called "micropolyphony," with many lines moving at different rates to create the effect of a mass of sound slowly moving through space; this too is a technique from the electronic piece. In one spectacular passage, these lines gradually rise until they reach the top of the orchestra, with four piccolos sounding *fortissimo* notes a half-step apart high in their range; at such a high register, the differences in pitch create resultant tones octaves lower. This eerily electronic-sounding effect is then cut off by a low cluster in the basses.

NEW THINKING Whether using new instruments, traditional instruments, modified instruments (such as prepared piano or amplified string quartet), electronic instruments, or tape, composers using new sounds had to make choices about how to construct their music to incorporate the new materials. The spectrum of choices earlier composers had made, from the novel pitch structures of Schoenberg's twelve-tone music to Varèse's use of sound masses, inspired the younger generation to explore these and other possibilities. Much of this music requires listeners to forego traditional expectations for melody, harmony, and form and to engage each work instead as an experience of sound itself. These pieces demand new thinking about music from their listeners as much as from their composers, and the questions and new insights they stimulate are part of what many have valued in these works.

MIXING STYLES AND TRADITIONS

While some postwar composers explored new resources in the realm of abstract sound, others continued doing what Western musicians have done for centuries: absorb elements from other musical traditions into their own. The wide dissemination of music from all over the world encouraged composers to mix styles and traditions. Some stayed close to home, blending their own national or regional traditions with international ones, as previous generations had done. But many shared the same interest in music of Asia that we have seen in popular music, and still others turned back to earlier periods in the Western classical tradition through quotation.

Alberto Ginastera (1916–1983) of Argentina, the most prominent Latin American composer in the generation after Villa-Lobos, drew on both national and international sources. He divided his career into three periods. His "objective nationalism" (to 1947), typified in *Danzas argentinas* for piano (1937), is characterized by tonal music infused with traditional Argentine folk elements. In the second period, "subjective nationalism" (1947–57), he forged an original style through a Bartók-like synthesis of native and international elements, as in *Pampeanas No. 1* for violin and piano (1947) and *No. 2* for cello and piano (1950). His "neo-expressionism" (after 1957) combines earlier traits with twelve-tone and avant-garde techniques, as in his operas *Don Rodrigo* (1963–64), *Bomarzo* (1966–67), and *Beatrix Cenci* (1971). Ginastera's turn from nationalism to a more abstract style is typical

Alberto Ginastera

of the postwar era, as musical nationalism came to have too many unwelcome resonances with the kind of music promoted by fascist or communist governments.

Third Stream   In the 1950s and 1960s, as jazz was being taken more and more seriously, some American composers who were conversant with both jazz and classical music sought consciously to merge the two. One of the most successful of these, Gunther Schuller (1925–2015), called this combination "third stream." In his *Transformation* (1957), a pointillistic twelve-tone context with elements of Schoenberg's *Klangfarbenmelodie* is transformed into a full-blown modern jazz piece. Leonard Bernstein also incorporated jazz elements in his classical music, including *Prelude, Fugue and Riffs* for clarinet and jazz ensemble (1949), Symphony No. 2 "The Age of Anxiety" (1949), and the opera *Candide* (1956).

Michael Tippett   Englishman Michael Tippett (1905–1998) represents a different kind of synthesis, remarkably open to historical, ethnic, and non-Western styles and materials. The rhythmic and metrical independence Tippett assigned to instrumental parts derived partly from English Renaissance music. The Piano Concerto (1953–55) and the Triple Concerto for violin, viola, and cello (1979) reveal Tippett's admiration for Javanese gamelan music, the first in its textures and instrumental combinations, the second in its use of a Javanese melody with rippling figuration and sounds such as gongs in the accompaniment of the slow movement.

Asian influences   Tippett's respectful approach to Javanese music is typical of the postwar era, in which growing sensitivity to the perspectives of other cultures led to an exploration of their music with respect for its uniqueness, rather than invoking the "foreign" for its sheer otherness as in nineteenth-century exoticism. We have seen that Messiaen, Cage, and Partch drew on ideas from Asian music and that jazz, pop, and Broadway composers did as well. Canadian-American composer Colin McPhee (1900–1964) studied music in Bali in the 1930s, transcribed gamelan music for Western instruments, and composed *Tabuh-tabuhan* (1936) for orchestra and many other pieces that drew on Balinese materials. McPhee introduced Balinese gamelan music to Britten, who visited Bali in 1956 and echoed gamelan sounds in works like the ballet *The Prince of the Pagodas* (1955–56) and the church parable *Curlew River* (1964). Henry Cowell's lifelong interest in Asian music grew after World War II, and travels to Iran, India, and Japan led to several works that blend Asian and Western elements, such as *Persian Set* (1957) for chamber orchestra, Symphony No. 13 "Madras" (1956–58), *Ongaku* (1957) for orchestra, and two concertos for the Japanese koto (a plucked string instrument) and orchestra (1961–62 and 1965). His student and friend Lou Harrison (1917–2003) combined interests in just intonation and inventing new instruments, inspired by Partch, with enthusiasm for the music of Asia. After visiting Korea and Taiwan in 1961–62, Harrison wrote several works that combine Western and Asian instruments, including *Pacifika Rondo* (1963) and *La Koro Sutro* (1972), and beginning in the 1970s he composed dozens of pieces for traditional Javanese gamelan.

Tōru Takemitsu   Interest in linking Asian and Western traditions extended as well to Asian composers familiar with European styles. Western music, both classical and popular, became well known in Asia over the course of the twentieth century, and by midcentury many Asians were writing music in the European classical tradition. Among the most inventive and best known was Japanese composer Tōru Takemitsu (1930–1996), shown in Figure 37.12. Western music had been banned in Japan during the war, but Takemitsu grew familiar with it in his teen years during the American occupation of Japan and decided to become a composer. He wrote for Western ensembles and was inspired by European influences, as in his *Requiem* for strings (1957), before turning in the 1960s to the music of his native country and blending the two traditions. His *November Steps* (1967) is a sort of double concerto, contrasting the sonorities of the Japanese shakuhachi (a bamboo flute) and biwa (a pear-shaped lute) with those of a Western orchestra. Takemitsu often combined Japanese and Western instruments and techniques in his many film scores, such as the score for Akira Kurosawa's *Ran* (1985), a retelling of *King Lear* in a Japanese setting.

FIGURE 37.12 *Tōru Takemitsu.*

QUOTATION AND COLLAGE A resource used by many composers of varying orientations was *quotation* of existing music, including a *collage* of multiple quotations. The ways earlier composers from Bach and Handel to modernists like Schoenberg, Ives, and Stravinsky had reworked borrowed material served as inspiration, as did quotations in modern poetry and collage in modern art. But postwar composers turned borrowing to new purposes, using evocations of older music to carry meanings that were not available by other means.

English composer Peter Maxwell Davies (1934–2016) drew on chant and English Renaissance music for many works, emphasizing the gulf between modern times and the distant past by distorting the source material or transforming it through modern procedures. His opera *Taverner* (1962–70), on the life of Renaissance composer John Taverner, reworks the latter's *In Nomine* (see Chapter 12) in a variety of ways before finally presenting it in recognizable form at the end, recalling Ives's cumulative form.

Peter Maxwell Davies

American composer George Rochberg (1918–2005), who had written mostly serial music, found it inadequate to express his feelings on the death of his son in 1964, and turned the next year to works based on borrowed material. *Contra mortem et tempus* (Against Death and Time) quotes passages from Boulez, Berio, Varèse, and Ives, and *Music for a Magic Theater* incorporates music of Mozart, Beethoven, Mahler, Webern, Varèse, Stockhausen, and his own earlier works, seeking in both pieces to evoke "the many-layered density of human existence." *Nach Bach* (After Bach, 1966) for harpsichord is a "commentary" on Bach's Keyboard Partita No. 6 in E Minor, BWV 830, in which fragments of the Bach, altered to varying degrees, emerge from Rochberg's own atonal music to create a dialogue between composers and styles. A similar work is *Baroque Variations* (1967) by Lukas Foss (1922–2009), whose three movements subject pieces by Handel, Domenico Scarlatti, and Bach respectively to a variety of transformations from adding clusters to fading out to inaudibility, creating what the composer called "'dreams' about these pieces." George Crumb also often reflects on music of the past; for example, his *Black Angels* quotes the chant *Dies irae* and Schubert's *Death and the Maiden* Quartet for their affective associations.

Rochberg, Foss, and Crumb

FIGURE 37.13
Luciano Berio.

Stockhausen used borrowed material in several works, notably *Gesang der Jünglinge, Telemusik* (1966), *Hymnen* (1967), and *Opus 1970* (1970). *Hymnen* incorporates words and melodies of many different national anthems in a performance combining electronic sounds with voices and instruments. The intention, Stockhausen claimed, was "not to interpret, but to hear familiar, old, preformed musical material with new ears, to penetrate and transform it with a musical consciousness of today." This aim represents a new way of relating music of the present to that of the past. *Opus 1970,* written for the Beethoven bicentenary in that year, includes transformed but recognizable fragments from Beethoven's works, assembled on tape and played from four loudspeakers alongside live music; the older composer's music is distorted and overwhelmed in an act more of violent conquest than of homage.

One of the richest pieces based on borrowed material is the third movement of Luciano Berio's *Sinfonia* (Symphony, 1968–69). Berio, shown in Figure 37.13, incorporated most of the scherzo movement of Mahler's Second Symphony and superimposed on it an amplified verbal commentary by an eight-voice ensemble and a musical commentary by a large orchestra. The bar-to-bar continuity of the Mahler is mostly maintained, although at times it disappears temporarily or appears with parts of the texture omitted. Overlaid on the Mahler are quotations from over one hundred other works, including Richard Strauss's *Der Rosenkavalier,* Ravel's *La valse,* Berg's *Wozzeck,* and Debussy's *La mer.* Each quotation connects in some way to the Mahler or to the spoken texts, drawn mostly from Samuel Beckett's *The Unnamable,* an interior monologue of a man who has just died. Both words and music suggest a stream of consciousness, as the memories of a lifetime emerge and slip away.

Role of the familiar   Music based on quotation can carry many meanings, but often it gives the audience something familiar to grasp—either the quoted piece itself or the style or type of piece it represents—and provides a new experience drawing on what the listener already knows. As a result, many listeners find it much more approachable than the unfamiliar sounds of serialism, the avant-garde, electronic music, and other postwar trends. For some composers, using borrowed material has been a way to rediscover styles and methods of the past, including tonality. This is one origin for the recent trends of neo-Romanticism and postmodernism, discussed in the next chapter.

NEW PATHS

In the postwar period, composers of every stripe were trying to create something new, from the new flavors of tonal music in Barber and Britten, of post-tonal music in Messiaen, and of serialism in Babbitt and Boulez to the radical rethinking of music in Cage's works, the new sounds of electronic music, the incorporation of Asian elements, and the new approach to quotation. Like jazz, popular music, musicals, and band music of the same era, postwar classical music borrowed from other traditions, experimented with new techniques and technology, and made increasing demands on performers and listeners, in some cases demanding unprecedented levels of attention and comprehension.

In part because of this great diversity of sound and approach and the greater difficulty it poses for the audience, much of the music by postwar composers in the classical tradition still seems new and unfamiliar to most listeners, even while works by their contemporaries in jazz, popular music, and Broadway have become among the most familiar and well-known pieces in those traditions. Some works have become established in the permanent classical repertoire, such as the postwar symphonies and quartets of Shostakovich and the operas and choral music of Britten, and a few others are part of the canon that most well-educated classical musicians and listeners know, including Messiaen's *Quartet for the End of Time*, Boulez's *Le marteau sans maître*, and Penderecki's *Threnody for the Victims of Hiroshima*. But most art music of the era, whether traditional or innovative, still remains less well known than works from earlier in the century. Some of the experiments in total serialism, indeterminacy, performance art, electronic music, and other new ideas now seem dated, and works whose impact depended in part on the unfamiliarity of their sounds or techniques do not always stand up well to rehearings.

Yet the impact of this music should not be underestimated. Many of those sounds and techniques have become common currency for later composers of classical, popular, and film music, from electronics and Asian instruments to variegated textures and quotation, and Cage's philosophy of music has opened up new possibilities that have borne fruit in recent decades, from minimalism to dance theater events like *STOMP*. Virtually everything is fair game now.

Further Reading is available at digital.wwnorton.com/hwm10

CHAPTER

38

THE LATE TWENTIETH CENTURY

In the last three decades of the twentieth century, the Western musical tradition continued to diversify. New institutions were created to preserve and study the history of jazz and popular music, while new types of popular music such as punk and hip hop emerged to serve specific audiences. Boundaries between traditions blurred or became irrelevant as musicians created hybrids between popular and classical traditions or Western and non-Western ones. Digital synthesizers and computers provided new resources for electronic music in both classical and popular traditions. New forms of **mixed media** challenged old distinctions between art and popular music and between music, theater, dance, and other arts. Among composers in the classical tradition, an increased interest in reaching a broad audience produced a number of new currents, including **minimalism** and **neo-Romanticism**. At the same time, almost all the trends discussed in the previous chapter continued, and many composers pursued individual paths.

Because this chapter cannot do justice to all the varied music of this era, we will look at only a few salient issues. We will begin with a survey of the changing world of music, noting especially the broadening conception of music as an art, the cross-fertilization of traditions, the influence of new digital technologies, and the increasing importance of mixed media. We will then examine five trends that seem especially prominent in these decades: the fragmentation of popular music; minimalism and its offshoots; the continuing strength of modernism in new and individual idioms; **polystylism**, the juxtaposition of contrasting styles from different historical eras; and, overlapping with these other trends, a rising concern among classical composers for writing immediately accessible music.

A GLOBAL CULTURE

The late 1960s and 1970s brought a series of political and economic shocks to Western nations. Student protests symbolized a growing gulf between younger and older generations. In the United States, urban riots, discord over the Vietnam War, and the assassinations of Martin Luther King Jr. and Robert F. Kennedy in 1968 marked increasing social strife. The Organization of Petroleum Exporting Countries (OPEC) cut oil production in 1973 to force up prices, leading to economic disruptions and inflation for the next decade. The Watergate scandal, over a political burglary and subsequent cover-up, led to the impeachment and resignation of President Richard Nixon in 1974 and greatly diminished Americans' faith in their government.

Meanwhile, Cold War tensions began to ease during the 1970s. Under the policy of *detente,* the United States and the Soviet Union sought greater cultural contacts and signed treaties to reduce nuclear arms. European leaders reached across the divide between NATO and the Warsaw Pact. President Nixon initiated diplomatic relations with the communist government in China after years without formal contact. Authoritarian regimes in Spain and Portugal, the last dictatorships in western Europe, were peacefully replaced by democratic governments.

Detente and democracy

Increasing contacts with western Europe and the election in 1978 of Polish pope John Paul II, the first pope from a communist country, helped to inspire movements for change in eastern Europe. Beginning with the 1980 strike by the Solidarity movement in Poland, and climaxing with the fall of the Berlin Wall in 1989 and the union of East and West Germany the following year, the people of central and eastern Europe freed themselves from Soviet domination with remarkably little bloodshed. In the Soviet Union itself, Mikhail Gorbachev's policies of *glasnost* (openness) and *perestroika* (restructuring) encouraged freer expression and a more entrepreneurial economy. Although he sought to reform the Soviet Union, the ultimate result was its dissolution in 1991. Its fifteen constituent republics, from massive Russia to tiny Armenia, became independent nations, with governments ranging from democratic to authoritarian.

Collapse of European communism

The Soviet Union's collapse ended the Cold War that had defined the postwar world. It did not end the fear of a nuclear attack, however, because the knowledge and technology for manufacturing nuclear weapons was spreading. In the post-Soviet era, regional conflicts from the Middle East to the Korean peninsula became more urgent, and civil wars proliferated from the Balkans and Africa to the Philippines. Extremists increasingly turned to terror as a tactic, whether directed at their own government, as in the 1995 Oklahoma City bombing, or other lands, as in Al Qaeda's attacks on United States embassies in Kenya and Tanzania in August 1998.

New conflicts

Yet it was also a time of growing equality. In the United States, legal discrimination against African Americans had ended and economic opportunities were increasing, aided by new programs in education, college admissions, and hiring. Around the world, women were breaking through barriers and gaining more economic and political power, becoming doctors, lawyers, judges, business leaders, politicians, and prime ministers, including Indira Gandhi in India (1966–77 and 1980–84), Golda Meir in Israel (1969–74), and Margaret Thatcher in the United Kingdom (1979–90).

Growing equality

In the economic realm, the end of the Cold War encouraged a trend toward integration across national boundaries. The Common Market became the European Union, absorbing new members from eastern Europe and pursuing a unified European economic system. Asian countries enjoyed rapid

Global economy

TIMELINE

growth, sustained by increasing trade with the rest of the world. Reductions in trade barriers and new technologies led to rising productivity in the Western democracies, producing an economic boom in the 1990s. By then, almost every country was part of an interwoven global economy, so that a stock market crash in one place had ripple effects around the world.

News, entertainment, and the arts became global as well. The spread of communications satellites and cable television, and the advent in the 1980s and 1990s of personal computers, fax machines, cell phones, and the Internet, put people around the world in immediate touch with one another. Many issues, from the environment to the drug trade to terrorism, crossed national boundaries, requiring countries to work together. With easy travel, diseases from flu to AIDS spread rapidly across the globe, prompting international cooperation in response.

Improved communications and travel also fostered a global market for the arts. Many forms of entertainment reached audiences all over the world, from Hollywood movies to touring groups of traditional artists such as the Bulgarian Women's Choir and Tuvan throat-singers. From conductor Seiji Ozawa to composer Tan Dun, Asians became prominent as musicians in the Western classical tradition, while some Americans and Europeans became proficient performers of Indian, Javanese, or other Asian musics. Music from around the world became increasingly accessible through recordings, the Internet, and live performances. The diversity of the world's music brought a growing awareness in Europe and the Americas that each musician's work is but one strand in a global tapestry.

THE CHANGING WORLD OF MUSIC

In the multidimensional world of music since the 1970s, most people cross musical boundaries every day. A person might attend live concerts and collect recordings of classical music, jazz, rock, and non-Western music, and hear pop songs at the gym, country music on the radio, and background music of various types in shops, elevators, and offices. Musicians live in the same fluid environment, and their work reflects it; for example, country musicians who grew up in the 1960s and 1970s and began professional careers in the 1980s and 1990s found it natural to incorporate sounds and styles from the rock music they heard in their youth. Crossing and blending traditions became commonplace.

BROADENING THE MEANING OF "ART MUSIC" The idea of art music—music listened to with rapt attention, valued for its own sake, and preserved in a repertoire of classics—began in the tradition of concert music, but by the late twentieth century it had spread to other traditions.

Each style of jazz continued to attract performers and listeners even after the "next" style emerged, so that jazz of all eras remained available in performance and on recordings, just like classical music. The reissuing of old recordings on LPs and compact discs (see Music in Context, p. 966) made the entire history of jazz readily accessible, and books and courses on jazz history have proliferated since 1970. Increasingly, jazz musicians have been trained at conservatories, schools of music, and universities, in the same way as classical musicians, and while at school perform in jazz ensembles that play music from the entire jazz tradition.

In the 1980s and 1900, new institutions were created to preserve and present classic jazz of former times. The Smithsonian Jazz Masterworks Orchestra, established by Congress in 1990 and founded by Gunther Schuller and David Baker (1931–2016) under the auspices of the Smithsonian Institution in Washington, D.C., offers live performances of jazz from past generations, scrupulously transcribed from recordings or reconstructed from the original charts. Jazz at Lincoln Center, founded by Wynton Marsalis in 1987 as an ensemble and concert series for historically inspired jazz performances at the complex shared by the New York Philharmonic and Metropolitan Opera, got its own hall in 2004, a short walk from Lincoln Center. By then it was widely accepted that jazz was an art music with its own repertory of classics. But there has been controversy, especially about Marsalis's dismissal of avant-garde jazz and other recent styles as departures from jazz tradition, his efforts to preserve earlier types, and his own compositions in traditional jazz idioms. Many jazz musicians viewed Jazz at Lincoln Center as locking jazz in a museum. The strong views on both sides exemplify the conflicts that can result from constructing a repertoire of musical classics in any tradition.

Historically inspired jazz ensembles

In a similar vein, academic musicians from the generation that grew up listening to rock music began in the 1980s to teach courses on rock history and embrace rock as a subject for study alongside classical music and jazz, focusing both on the roles rock music played in the culture at large and on the meanings and understandings that can be gained from attentive listening. Teachers and scholars of rock engaged issues of race, gender, class, age, and marketing; addressed aspects of record production, from the collaborative processes involved to the ways artists use technology, timbre, texture, rhythm, and sound itself; and analyzed well-known recordings as closely as any Beethoven symphony. Wealthy donors funded new institutions dedicated to preserving the rock legacy, notably the Rock and Roll Hall of Fame and Museum in Cleveland, shown in Figure 38.1, and the Experience Music Project Museum in Seattle, both of which hired musicologists, gathered materials, created museum exhibits with artifacts and interactive displays, and sponsored scholarly conferences on the history of rock and its predecessors and offshoots. These institutions, along with the enduring popularity of rock and pop songs from the 1950s on as shown by sales figures, "golden oldies" radio stations, and live performances by the artists themselves or by tribute bands, indicated that this music had become a tradition of classics, akin to jazz and classical music. Hit songs of the Beatles and Motown artists remained familiar across generations, often better known than the current Top 40, available in recordings and played by countless cover bands, serving both a continuing role as popular music (nothing gets all ages on the dance floor at a wedding reception better than Motown) and a growing function as music listened to for

Rock courses, research, and museums

FIGURE 38.1 *The Rock and Roll Hall of Fame and Museum in Cleveland, Ohio. The building, on the shores of Lake Erie, was designed by internationally famous architect I. M. Pei and opened in September 1995.*

its own sake and admired for its artfulness. Country music was not far behind; the Country Music Hall of Fame and Museum, which dates back to the 1960s, opened a spectacular new building in Nashville in 2001, and interest in preserving older styles continued to grow.

Musicals   The musical, too, became recognized as a tradition of classics, marked by academic books and courses if not yet by museums or performing institutions. New productions of shows by Rodgers and Hammerstein, Lerner and Loewe, Kern, Porter, Berlin, and others were staged on Broadway and around the world. Musicals that had not been seen since their original runs decades earlier were revived with the same commitment shown by those who rediscovered, edited, and performed works of earlier centuries.

New musicals often aspired to the status of art music as well as entertainment. The dominant figure in the American musical in the late twentieth century was Stephen Sondheim (b. 1930), whose musicals include the plotless social commentary of *Company* (1970); the melodramatic *Sweeney Todd* (1979), about a murderous London barber; *Sunday in the Park with George* (1984), based on a famous pointillist painting by Georges Seurat; and *Assassins* (1991), featuring successful and would-be assassins of American presidents—all subjects earlier musicals would not likely have touched. As a teenager, Sondheim studied privately with lyricist Oscar Hammerstein II, who coached him on how to create the book, lyrics, and music for musicals. Sondheim's lyrics are witty and poetic, and his songs draw on Broadway and popular styles while often breaking from convention, sounding a bit like art songs in a semipopular idiom. Andrew Lloyd Webber (b. 1948) was the leading English composer of musicals, including *Jesus Christ Superstar* (1970–71), a rock-music retelling of Jesus's life; *Evita* (1976–78), about Eva Perón, wife of Argentinian dictator Juan Perón; *Cats* (1981), on poetry by T. S. Eliot; and *The Phantom of the Opera* (1986) and *Sunset Boulevard* (1993), two of the first musicals to be based on classic films, reversing the usual direction taken by adaptation. Like film composers, Lloyd Webber drew on a wide range of styles to suit the dramatic situation, while retaining the musical's traditional focus on lyrical, affecting melody. Also remarkably successful with audiences were the musicals of French composer Claude-Michel Schönberg (b. 1944), notably *Les Misérables* (1980; English version, 1985), a setting of Victor Hugo's novel of poverty in Paris, and *Miss Saigon* (1989), retelling Puccini's *Madama Butterfly* in the context of the Vietnam War. Other musicals based on operas followed, such as *Rent* (1996) by Jonathan Larson (1960–1996), which adapted the plot of Puccini's *La bohème* to the pop music styles of New York in the era of AIDS, and *Aida* (1998–2000) by pop star Elton John (b. 1947) and lyricist Tim Rice, based on the story of Verdi's opera. Many of these musicals resemble operas in their serious tone, use of spectacle, and almost continuous music.

Western listeners increasingly became aware of Asian classical tra- *Other traditions* ditions, including those of Japan, China, Indonesia, India, and Iran. At the same time, a continuing trend toward passive listening and away from active music-making gave most young people in Europe and the Americas a more attenuated connection to the Western classical tradition than in past generations. Now Western classical music is no longer the only, or even the most, prestigious musical tradition, but one of many.

BLURRING THE LINES In a world where musicians are aware of such a wide range of music, the boundaries between traditions naturally begin to blur, especially for those who value music from more than one tradition and seek to create comparable music of their own. While many musicians have stayed within their own traditions, others cross over from one to another or blend aspects of several, so that for them and their listeners the existing boundaries for all intents and purposes disappear. If the splintering of the classical tradition into a variety of currents since the mid-nineteenth century can be compared to the delta of a great river approaching the sea, a similar metaphor of streams coming together and becoming one river can suggest the convergence of traditions.

Prominent in this convergence have been commercial pop musicians who *Pop and classical* create music for classical ensembles, genres, or record labels. Paul McCartney *hybrids* brought classical influences from Baroque music to John Cage and electronic music into his work with the Beatles, and later brought his pop sensibilities to classical genres in works like the *Liverpool Oratorio* (1991) and the orchestral and choral piece *Standing Stone* (1997). Elvis Costello (b. 1954), a British singer-songwriter whose albums range from rock to country, collaborated with the Brodsky Quartet on *The Juliet Letters* (1993), a song cycle for voice and string quartet, and wrote the orchestral score for the ballet *Il Sogno,* premiered in Bologna in 2000, which rose to the top of the *Billboard* classical music chart. Ryuichi Sakamoto (b. 1952), trained in classical composition and ethnomusicology in his native Japan, achieved international success as songwriter, keyboard player, and singer with the electronic pop group Yellow Magic Orchestra and as a solo artist, pioneering new trends from electropop to techno and incorporating music from traditional Japanese songs to Brazilian bossa nova. Since the 1980s, Sakamoto has composed award-winning film scores, including *The Last Emperor* (1987), that encompass orchestral music, extended playing techniques, and musique concrète, and created *Discord* (1998), an orchestral work that blends popular melodic styles with sounds and procedures from modern classical music. Some classically trained composers have absorbed pop styles to create similar blends, such as Christopher Rouse (b. 1949), whose *Bonham* (1988) for percussion ensemble celebrates John Bonham (drummer for the rock band Led Zeppelin) and quotes several of his drumbeats, and Steven Mackey (b. 1956), whose experience as a rock and jazz guitarist in his teens resonates in pieces like *TILT* (1992) for orchestra and *Troubadour Songs* (1991) for electric guitar and string quartet. In hybrid works like these the old distinctions between popular and classical traditions can seem irrelevant.

Frank Zappa   The music of American guitarist and composer Frank Zappa (1940–1993) exemplifies the convergence of traditions. As a teenager in the 1950s, he was fascinated by the modernist music of Varèse, Stravinsky, and Webern as well as by rock and roll, and he found them all useful for annoying his parents when he played them on the family phonograph. He made his reputation in the 1960s and 1970s with avant-garde rock that broke down distinctions between rock, jazz, and classical music, and he blended the traditions in *200 Motels* (1970) for rock band and orchestra. In the 1980s and 1990s, he also produced a series of orchestral and chamber works recorded by the London Symphony Orchestra (1983–87), the Ensemble InterContemporain conducted by Pierre Boulez (*The Perfect Stranger*, 1984), and the contemporary music group Ensemble Modern (*The Yellow Shark*, 1993). Several of his pieces for classical ensembles include transcriptions of material first devised for his touring rock bands. Zappa's work often constitutes a critique of the music business, of its manipulation of pop music consumers, and of the pretensions of classical music supporters. One of his wittiest barbs, highlighting scholars' deliberate ignorance of contemporary popular music in preference for the music of the past, was his 1984 album of faithful electronic performances on the Synclavier digital synthesizer of works by Francesco Zappa (1717–1803), an obscure composer who was included in the *New Grove Dictionary of Music and Musicians* (1980), the mammoth English-language encyclopedia of music, while Frank Zappa (who must have tried looking himself up in it) was not.

FIGURE 38.2 *Ástor Piazzolla playing the bandoneon in Rome, 1999.*

Another hybridizer was Argentine composer Ástor Piazzolla (1921–1992), shown in Figure 38.2, who combined the Argentine tradition of the tango with elements of jazz and classical music to create a new style, *nuevo tango* (new tango). He encountered jazz during his childhood in New York, became a professional tango musician in Argentina, and studied composition with Alberto Ginastera and Nadia Boulanger, so he was well schooled in all three traditions. His nuevo tango incorporated improvisation from jazz and drew several elements from the classical tradition, including the Baroque procedures of counterpoint, fugue, and passacaglia; modern chromaticism, dissonance, and angular melodies; and the ideas of extended forms and of music worth listening to for its own sake. After developing the new style playing with his ensemble in his club in Buenos Aires, Piazzolla moved in 1974 to Rome, writing more-ambitious pieces

ELIGIO PAONI/CONTRASTO/REDUX

like *Libertango* (1974), the three-movement *La Camorra* (1989), and *Five Tango Sensations* (1991) on commission from the Kronos Quartet. In works like his tango opera *María de Buenos Aires* (1968) and his Double Concerto for guitar, bandoneon, and string orchestra (1985), Piazzolla drew on a living popular tradition to create music in classical genres, like Gershwin in his *Rhapsody in Blue* and *Porgy and Bess*.

Jazz musicians have also crossed boundaries to produce hybrids, as the tensions between jazz as an art music and jazz as a popular music played out in new forms of jazz. Having pioneered cool jazz and modal jazz in the 1950s (see Chapter 36), Miles Davis launched a new trend called *fusion* (or *jazz fusion*) in 1970 with his best-selling album *Bitches Brew,* his greatest commercial success. Fusion joined jazz with elements of other traditions, especially the electric guitar sound and propulsion of rock and the rhythms and character of soul and of rhythm and blues, in a new style of instrumental music. Fusion was seen as a way to renew jazz and appeal to a wider public than the more esoteric styles since bebop had done. Some fusion artists, like pianists Herbie Hancock (b. 1940) and Chick Corea (b. 1941), earned the respect of jazz fans with their inventive improvisations while also reaching a broader audience. But a 1980s offshoot of fusion that blended jazz with pop music, known as *smooth jazz,* was seen by purists as a sellout to easy-listening commercialism, despite (or because of) the popularity of artists such as saxophonists Kenny G (Kenneth Gorelick, b. 1956) and David Sanborn (b. 1945). At the opposite end of the spectrum was the avant-garde jazz of the Art Ensemble of Chicago, formed in the late 1960s by members of the Association for the Advancement of Creative Musicians; the ensemble combines multiple styles of jazz with elements from non-Western music and performance art, including costumes, face paint, and socially conscious humor, while their name makes clear their devotion to jazz as an art music for a select audience of connoisseurs.

Fusion and other jazz blends

The career of John Zorn (b. 1953) epitomizes the work of musicians who transcend categorization. His eclectic tastes were formed as a youth growing up in New York in a family whose members listened to a range of music from classical and jazz to rock, country, and music from around the world. As a teenager, he encountered avant-garde and experimental music, which became the core of his approach. After studying composition in school and taking up jazz saxophone as his main instrument, he established himself in New York as an avant-garde performer and composer who drew on elements of jazz, rock, classical music, film music, popular styles, and klezmer (a Jewish popular style that originated in central Europe), among others. His music is unclassifiable and very diverse, represented on a series of albums of film scores, titled *Filmworks* (1990–2008); recordings with his avant-garde rock bands Naked City and Painkiller; hundreds of tunes drawing on klezmer and other traditional Jewish styles, collected in the *Masada Books* (1993–2004); several collaborations with jazz artists; and numerous pieces for classical chamber groups and orchestra, including the chamber work *Kristallnacht* (1993), about the 1938 Nazi attack on Jews known as the Night of Broken Glass, and *Aporias: Requia for Piano and Orchestra* (1998).

John Zorn

The old boundaries that separate jazz, popular, classical, avant-garde, modernist, and experimental music do not apply to Zorn or to other musicians who have similar all-embracing tastes. But all of what Zorn does is art

Breaking boundaries, making art

music at heart, music one listens to with full attention and values for itself rather than for any other purpose it may serve. Such music shows how interconnected all these branches of the Western tradition ultimately are.

Multiple fusions

Each of the musicians and pieces mentioned in this section offers one possible response to the diversity of musical culture in the late twentieth century, one way to join together two or more currents from the multivalent heritage of Western music. There are many such fusions, each an expression of the unique background and ideas of the artists who created it. The ones discussed here only illustrate some of the possibilities, and there are countless others worth exploring.

Institutions and ensembles

The blending of traditions is evident also in musical institutions and ensembles that make it a priority to feature diverse fare and encourage border crossings. One such institution is the Meltdown Festival, held in London since 1993, which brings together a varied mix of performers, chosen by the director for that year; directors have ranged from pop artists Elvis Costello and David Bowie (1947–2016) to free jazz pioneer Ornette Coleman, performance artist Laurie Anderson (see pp. 967–68), and classical composers Magnus Lindberg (b. 1958) and Louis Andriessen (see pp. 980–81). Bang on a Can, founded in 1987 and directed by composers Julia Wolfe (b. 1958), David Lang (b. 1957), and Michael Gordon (b. 1956), is another diverse group who put on an annual Marathon concert in New York highlighting innovative music from a variety of traditions, from Cage and Zorn to electronic pop to new sounds from Bulgarian folk ensembles and Balinese gamelan orchestras, with the goal of breaking down barriers between musical communities. The Kronos Quartet, founded in 1973, is a classically trained string quartet whose repertoire embraces the diversity of music in the late twentieth and early twenty-first centuries, ranging from newly commissioned works and modernist classics to jazz, rock, and early music (see In Performance: Kronos Quartet). Such eclectic programming also blurs the lines between traditions.

Despite all this blurring and blending, many musicians adhere to their own traditions, and for them the lines between traditions have not collapsed. In this and the next chapter, we will continue to refer to the various types of music as separate entities, while remembering that just how separate—or how connected—they are is a choice that must be made by each musician, now that the possibilities of cross-fertilization and hybridization are always present.

INTERACTIONS WITH NON-WESTERN MUSIC Crossing and hybridization of traditions was taking place not just within Western music but also between Western and non-Western traditions, as people on all continents became more familiar with each other's music. As Americans and the technologies of radio and recording spread across the globe after World War II, American popular music could be heard in almost every corner of the planet, influencing popular music everywhere else. Simultaneously, both traditional and popular music from around the world was increasingly available in the last third of the twentieth century on recordings and in live performances by touring groups, marketed in Western nations as *world music*. This broad category includes Asian classical traditions from India, Indonesia, China, Japan, Korea, and other lands; ethnic traditions and folk music from all over; and popular musical idioms from non-Western or Latin American nations, which often blend local

IN PERFORMANCE

Kronos Quartet

The Kronos Quartet is both one of the leading string quartets in the world and one of the classical ensembles most dedicated to performing a wide range of music. Formed in Seattle in 1973, they underwent several changes of personnel, then took up residence in San Francisco in 1978 with the players shown in Figure 38.3.

While the members of the quartet are expert performers on their instruments, they approach music with an eclecticism that is far from traditional string quartets, and with the energy and informal garb of a rock band. They have become the most widely known and heard ensemble for contemporary classical music, in part because they appeal to audiences outside the worlds of classical music or "new music" and perform such a diverse array of pieces.

Kronos came to prominence in the 1980s with recordings that included rock star Jimi Hendrix's *Purple Haze*; jazz by Thelonious Monk and Bill Evans; modernist works from earlier in the century by Bartók, Ives, Webern, Shostakovich, and Crumb; and music—much of it commissioned by Kronos— by contemporary composers from John Zorn and

Ástor Piazzolla to Terry Riley, Steve Reich, Philip Glass, Arvo Pärt, and Alfred Schnittke (discussed later in this chapter). Later albums include medieval music by Perotinus (*Viderunt omnes*, NAWM 19) and Machaut (Kyrie from his mass, NAWM 25a), blues by Willie Dixon, Mexican music, movie soundtracks, Indian movie music (known as Bollywood), music of central Asia, and works by Sigur Rós, a post-rock band from Reykjavík, Iceland. The quartet has also performed on recordings by the Dave Matthews Band, Nine Inch Nails, Nelly Furtado, and many others.

The quartet has commissioned and premiered over seven hundred new works. In 2003, in celebration of the quartet's thirtieth anniversary, they initiated a new program that commissions works from composers under the age of thirty. In association with the quartet, the Kronos Performing Arts Association "continually re-imagines the string quartet experience." Through the association, Kronos mentors and collaborates with other artists and includes educational concerts and activities in its touring schedule. The quartet has become one of the most influential and formidable groups of our time.

FIGURE 38.3 *The Kronos Quartet at New York's Central Park SummerStage, 1992, with group founder David Harrington, first violin; John Sherba, second violin; Hank Dutt, viola; and Joan Jeanrenaud, cello.*

singing styles, instruments, scales, or other elements with sounds and styles from American or European popular music. Since the 1980s, all these kinds of music have been heard at festivals of world music held across Europe, the Americas, Africa, and Asia. The widespread availability of music from almost everywhere has facilitated cross-fertilization of all kinds.

World beat   Closely linked to the globalization of music was *world beat,* a term referring to African popular musics that reached international audiences. African musicians like the Nigerian Fela Kuti (1938–1997) merged popular styles from the United States and elsewhere with local traditions to create new sounds. In the 1980s, their music in turn began to be heard worldwide, and pop artists in Europe and America incorporated world beat into their own music. Paul Simon (b. 1941), who first came to prominence in the 1960s as the songwriter half of the pop duo Simon and Garfunkel, celebrated African popular music in his Grammy Award–winning album *Graceland* (1986); one hit song from that album, *Diamonds on the Soles of Her Shoes,* featured Simon on lead vocals backed by Ladysmith Black Mambazo, a South African unaccompanied men's chorus in the *isicathamiya* singing tradition, and on several tracks Simon mixed together contributions recorded by musicians from around Africa.

Glocalization   Kuti's creation of a local style that drew on American popular music can be seen as an example of *glocalization*, a term popularized in the 1990s to indicate the adaptation of global forces to local needs, forging something that is both localized and the product of globalization. Through such processes of adaptation, local traditions have merged with the amplification and propulsive beat of rock or other internationally distributed types of popular music to create hybrids that carry a strongly regional flavor. In turn, some of these local adaptations, from the Swedish folk-pop groups Väsen and Nordman to the music of Senegalese singer Youssou N'Dour (b. 1959), have found a global audience, in a feedback loop that constantly brings new flavors to the smorgasbord of music around the world.

Asian hybrids   Cross-cultural hybridization takes place in classical as well as in popular music. Several composers born and trained in China and later active in the United States have created music in the Western classical tradition that represents a hybrid with Asian traditions.

Bright Sheng (b. 1955), shown in Figure 38.4, studied piano as a boy in his native Shanghai. Sent to the province of Qinghai in his teens during the Cultural Revolution, he learned and collected folk music there. He then earned degrees in composition at the Shanghai Conservatory and in New York, where he studied with Leonard Bernstein and Chou Wen-chung (b. 1923), a student of Varèse. He has made his career in the United States. He seeks to integrate elements of Asian and Western music while respecting the integrity of each, inspired by the attempts of Bartók to do the same with eastern European folk and Western classical music. In the solo cello suite *Seven Tunes Heard in China* (1995), Sheng joins the European tradition of the Bach cello suites—with sequences, double stops, and implied polyphony—to the playing style of Chinese bowed string instruments, marked by grace notes, glissandos, sudden dynamic changes, and flexible rhythm. In the first movement, *Seasons* (NAWM 217), the mostly pentatonic Chinese tune used as a source is fragmented and spun out using both Baroque and modernist methods, including polytonality. The result blends together fundamental aspects of Chinese, Western classical, and modern music.

Several other composers have pursued parallel paths, including Chen Yi (b. 1953) and Zhou Long (b. 1953). The best known of this group is Tan Dun (b. 1957), who learned to play traditional string instruments in his native China, then—like Sheng and the others—moved to New York in the 1980s and studied with Chou Wen-chung at Columbia University. Influenced by John Cage and other experimental composers, he has combined Chinese instruments and non-Western vocal timbres with Western techniques in works such as the film score for *Crouching Tiger, Hidden Dragon* (2000) as well as *Water Passion after St. Matthew* (2000) for soloists, chorus, and orchestra, commissioned to commemorate the 250th anniversary of the death of Johann Sebastian Bach.

FIGURE 38.4
Bright Sheng.

Other blends

A similar union of Western and non-Western styles and sensibilities can be found in other composers' works. *White Man Sleeps* (1985) for string quartet by South African native Kevin Volans (b. 1949) draws on African traditions, and *Songs of Sea and Sky* (1987) for clarinet and piano by Australian composer Peter Sculthorpe (1929–2014) incorporates or imitates Aboriginal melodies.

In the final analysis, all the works described in this section are at the same time hybrids and quintessentially Western, representing new instances of the centuries-old capacity of the Western tradition to absorb foreign elements and arrive at a new synthesis, as in the merging of French, Italian, and English styles into an international language in the fifteenth century (see Chapter 8) or of various styles and habits into the cosmopolitan idiom of the Classic era (see Chapters 20–23). These recent works go beyond nineteenth-century exoticism in the respect they show for the intrinsic value of the non-Western traditions on which they draw.

NEW TECHNOLOGIES New connections across traditions since the 1970s were accompanied by new technologies that have altered the ways musicians work with music and listeners consume it. Among the most important inventions were the ***digital*** synthesis, recording, and reproduction of sound (see Music in Context: Digital Technologies in the 1980s), which have given creators of music new tools and listeners new flexibility. Digital synthesizers, first widely available in the 1980s, were much cheaper, smaller, and easier to use than previous synthesizers. As a result, they were adopted by a wide range of musicians, amateur and professional alike, working in traditions from classical to popular music.

Sampling

One significant technique is ***sampling***, a process of creating new compositions by patching together digital chunks of previously recorded music. Although sampling raises copyright concerns, it has been used extensively in hip hop (see p. 970) and other forms of pop music, as well as in experimental, avant-garde, and classical concert music.

MUSIC IN CONTEXT

Digital Technologies in the 1980s

In the 1970s and early 1980s, music joined the digital revolution. Inventors devised a method for translating sound into a coded series of on-off pulses, or 1s and 0s, in the same way that computers stored and transmitted data. Soon digital processes were replacing older ones, known as *analog* because they rely on creating an analogue of the sound waves, such as the undulations in the groove of a record.

By the 1980s, musicians were using digital synthesizers instead of the older analog devices that produced sounds generated from or processed by electrical circuits, and were recording and manipulating digital samples of musical instruments and other sounds with sampling synthesizers like the one in Figure 38.5. Because digital processes produced and recorded sounds as streams of numbers, musical sounds could be reproduced and controlled precisely. Musicians could control all the parameters of pitch, timbre, dynamics, and rhythm, and the characteristics thus digitally encoded could be translated directly into music through MIDI (Musical Instrument Digital Interface).

Some musicians combined live performers with synthesized or computer-generated music. Using software programs that respond to music, the composer devises formulas that are then played on a synthesizer, digital piano, or acoustic instrument. In this way, a musician can generate imitative or nonimitative polyphony, rhythmic or melodic ostinatos, heterophony, and a variety of other textures by playing on a synthesizer keyboard in "real time"—that is, as actually played and heard, rather than laboriously prepared in advance and tape-recorded, as electronic music was in the 1950s.

Vinyl records, the primary means of distribution for decades, gave way in the 1980s to compact discs (CDs), which were smaller, more durable, and able to reproduce music digitally, offering greater fidelity. Thousands of recordings first released on 78- or 33-rpm records were reissued on CDs, making an entire century of recorded sound more widely accessible than ever before. Portable playback devices with headphones or earbuds made it possible to carry music of one's own choice everywhere.

FIGURE 38.5 *Keyboard console of the E-Mu Emulator II digital sampling synthesizer from 1984.*

Computer music   Advances in computing and the miniaturization of the computer have offered many new possibilities, explored by composers whose music is part experimentation with technology and part sound sculpture. One of the pioneers of computer music is Charles Dodge (b. 1942), whose *Speech Songs* (1972) features computer-synthesized vocal sounds, mixing lifelike imitations of speech with transformations that change vowels into noise or natural inflections into melodies to create a word-based music well suited to the surrealistic poetry he uses as a text. Paul Lansky (b. 1944) developed his own software to create computer works. He manipulates recorded sounds, such as speech in *Six Fantasies on a Poem by Thomas Campion* (1979) and *Smalltalk*

(1988) or highway traffic noises in *Night Traffic* (1990), transforming them beyond immediate recognition and using them as a kind of pitched percussion. Despite the unusual sound sources, his music draws on pop traditions, with tonal harmonies, regular meter, propulsive beat, and layered syncopated rhythms. A very different aesthetic is pursued at the Institut de Recherche et Coordination Acoustique/Musique (Institute for Acoustic and Musical Research and Coordination) in Paris, one of the premier centers for computer music in Europe, founded by Pierre Boulez and opened in 1977. In *Inharmonique* (1977) and other works written during his time as director of the IRCAM department of computer music, Jean-Claude Risset (1938–2016) used the computer to mediate between live voices or acoustic instruments and synthesized or electronically processed sound. He continued to design new sounds, exploring the interaction of sound waves, harmonics, timbre, and other basic elements of sound. The work of these three composers only begins to illustrate the potential of computer music. In addition, computer software for notating and publishing music, such as Finale and Sibelius, became available in the late 1980s and 1990s and is now widely used by composers and arrangers in all branches of music.

MIXED MEDIA Music in the late twentieth century grew closer to other performance arts, as it increasingly became part of ***mixed media*** artworks.

Pop music concerts in the early 1960s, like those of the Beatles, typically consisted of a group playing music, perhaps with some exaggerated physical gestures to charge up the audience. But by the 1970s and 1980s, stage shows for performers like Kiss, Michael Jackson, or Madonna, though still called concerts, involved elaborate sets and costumes, intricate choreography, and visual effects such as lighting, fog machines, and pyrotechnics. The spectacle was almost as important as the music, which was only one component in a multimedia extravaganza. ***Music videos***, short films that provide a visual accompaniment to songs, came of age in the early 1980s, serving as the mainstay of the cable channel MTV (Music Television) and quickly becoming a primary form of contact for popular music consumers. Most were elaborate productions, with sets, costumes, dancing, and rapid-fire editing all calculated to catch the eye, draw attention to the song, and promote sales. In line with the tendency of some works in all traditions to be experienced and valued as art music, a good number of music videos came to be considered works of art, and some have been collected and exhibited by museums such as the Museum of Modern Art in New York. Both spectacular stage shows and artistic music videos continue to be significant as visual companions to popular music.

Stage shows and music videos

While pop music was becoming more visual, performance art was becoming more musical. One of the leading performance artists, Laurie Anderson (b. 1947), shown in Figure 38.6, incorporated a wide range of media, including singing, violin playing, poetry, speaking, electronics, film, slides, and lighting. Her single *O Superman* (1981), which featured her synthesizer-processed voice in a simple, repetitive song with light electronic accompaniment, was an unexpected pop hit, winning her additional audiences and reinforcing the musical element in her work. She released several albums of songs, but the heart of her art remained in her stage shows. Most ambitious was *United States I–IV* (1983), a seven-hour extravaganza that used all the

Laurie Anderson

FIGURE 38.6 *Performance artist Laurie Anderson playing an electronic violin during a concert.*

tools of modern media to comment ironically on the alienation and social ills of the culture that invented them.

A new genre of musical theater emerged in the 1990s in which the process of making music itself became a visual spectacle. *STOMP* (1991), created by Luke Cresswell and Steve McNicholas in England and on Broadway and on tour since 1994, has no dialogue or plot, but consists entirely of a troupe of performers using everyday objects from matchbooks to brooms to garbage-can lids to produce elaborate percussion music carried out with stunning choreography, as in Figure 38.7. Blue Man Group, formed in New York in 1987 by Chris Wink, Matt Goldman, and Phil Stanton and presenting full-length shows around the world since 1991, features percussion-based experimental music using unusual instruments played by musician-mimes dressed in identical clothing and wearing light blue makeup on their hands and heads, like blue-skinned space aliens. Jim Mason's *Blast!* (2001) took the routines of a marching band halftime show and drum corps performance, souped them up with new choreography, and put them on the Broadway stage.

Film music   Film is a multimedia format of long standing, and although music played an important role from the start—so-called silent films always had piano, organ, or orchestral accompaniment—its significance in recent decades has heightened. In a growing number of movies after 1970, music no longer served as background accompaniment but became as much a part of the total art work as the music in an opera or musical. Many films used existing music; George Lucas's *American Graffiti* (1973) set a pattern by employing pop music of the late 1950s and early 1960s to accompany a teen drama set in that era. But most striking was the return to full-scale symphonic scores organized around leitmotives. The music by John Williams (b. 1932) for the first six *Star Wars* movies (1977–2005) was arguably as important as the actors

FIGURE 38.7 *Scene from the London production of* STOMP.

in conveying the dramatic action. Symphonic movie soundtracks became hot-selling recordings, outpacing all other orchestral music and raising the stature of film composers. Some composers arranged their film scores as concert works. Among the most ambitious was *The Lord of the Rings: Symphony in Six Movements* (2004) by Howard Shore (b. 1946), drawn from his scores for the movie trilogy *The Lord of the Rings* (2001–3).

TRENDS The broadening conception of music as an art, the convergence of formerly distinct types of music, the blending of Western and non-Western elements, the application of new technologies, and the growing interaction of music with other media are just a few of the trends apparent in recent music, but they are characteristic in crossing or weakening boundaries between traditions.

Other trends resulted from pressures *within* traditions. The strong identification of 1950s and 1960s teenagers with rock and pop music prompted a search by smaller social groups for a music to call their own. They were abetted by a popular music industry that was eager, as always, to exploit new markets. As a result, the popular tradition became fragmented. Meanwhile, in the classical tradition, modernism and the search for individual styles—the central theme of twentieth-century classical music—continued strong, prompting new approaches. The study of sound color led to the new trend of *spectral music* (see p. 979), and an awareness of the continuing presence of historical styles combined with the breakdown of a common musical language stimulated a new self-conscious *polystylism* (see pp. 981–83). At the same time, the desire of some composers to connect with listeners who were unsympathetic to modernist or avant-garde music prompted a search for more accessible languages, including *minimalism* (see pp. 971–77) and *neo-Romanticism* (see pp. 986–87). Thus, ironically, while in many musicians' work popular and classical music were converging, in other respects each tradition continued to break apart into more and more diverse streams.

NICHES IN POPULAR MUSIC

As the supply of music has increased and choices have became more varied, the amount of music common to all members of a society has diminished. The days are over when all of America heard the songs of Irving Berlin, or the Beatles were famous around the world. Instead, popular music has splintered into niche markets and competing trends, each identified with particular social groups. Some trends won widespread, though usually short-lived, popularity, while others remained the property of specific groups. The following sampling of a few popular music trends in North America and Europe after 1970 is not an attempt to survey the whole of popular music, which would be beyond the scope of this book, but may begin to suggest the ways various segments of society built a group identity by sharing a common music.

In the 1970s, a new style of dance music known as *disco* developed in New York clubs that catered primarily to African Americans, Latinos, and gay men, then became an international craze. Club goers valued the steady $\frac{4}{4}$ meter and uniform dance tempo of disco songs, which allowed disc jockeys to move smoothly from song to song and the dancers to keep moving

Disco

without interruption. Lush orchestrations and slick production pleased the ear while the relentless beat moved the body, joining glamour, fun, and sexuality in an intoxicating brew. Disco reached its height of popularity with the film *Saturday Night Fever* (1977) and the accompanying soundtrack by the Bee Gees.

Punk, New Wave, indie rock, and grunge

Another 1970s trend was *punk,* a hard-driving style voicing teenage alienation. The most notorious punk band, the Sex Pistols, popularized edgy fashions such as safety pins through flesh and preached nihilism in their lyrics. Most punk musicians were largely untutored, preferring raw, unskilled sounds to the virtuosity and smooth production of rock and disco. *New Wave* musicians like Blondie and Talking Heads followed closely on the heels of punk, sharing some of its nihilism without disdaining musical skill, and won wider commercial success. *Indie rock* (or independent rock), a catchall term for rock music set apart from the mainstream, was nurtured by college and independent radio stations and performing venues, then came to dominate in the early 1990s thanks to *grunge* rockers from Seattle, such as Nirvana, Soundgarden, and Pearl Jam. Grunge combined the nihilism of punk and the electric-guitar-laden sound of heavy metal with intimate lyrics and dressed-down fashions (especially flannel). Nirvana's 1991 song *Smells Like Teen Spirit* brought grunge to national attention. Each of these styles became an emblem for youth of a certain age, while offending or being incomprehensible to most of their elders.

Hip hop

Hip hop, also called *rap,* emerged in the 1970s as the music of hip-hop culture, an African American urban youth culture that originated at block parties in the South Bronx neighborhood of New York. DJs (disc jockeys) isolated the percussive break passages on soul, funk, and disco recordings and looped them (played them repeatedly, using two turntables) for dancers, stimulating the elaborate and athletic dance style known as breaking or breakdancing. Over these breaks a rapper or MC (master of ceremonies) recited or improvised lyrics, in a tradition with roots in earlier African American, African, and West Indian practices. From these origins hip hop developed into a style with rapped (or sometimes sung) lyrics over music mostly composed of samples from earlier recordings. As it spread to other cities and recordings, hip hop branched into multiple types, including *gangsta rap,* celebrating lawlessness, and *political hip hop* or *conscious rap,* which voiced the woes of inequality and racism and addressed social and political issues. With songs like *Fight the Power,* the rap group Public Enemy, shown in Figure 38.8, led the ranks of conscious rap in the late 1980s and early 1990s. By the mid-1990s, mainstream pop radio stations increasingly played rap records. In a parallel to the discovery of rhythm and blues by white teens in the 1950s, rap became the popular music of a generation of white suburban teenagers, especially males attracted to its heavy beat and themes of male dominance, and artists like Snoop Dogg (b. 1971) and Eminem (b. 1972) crossed over onto the pop charts. By the late 1990s, styles related to hip hop were practiced around the world from France to Bangladesh, some derived directly from African American rap music, others part of a larger continuum of African, West Indian, and Latin American music-making. Hip hop has proven much more enduring than other trends such as disco or grunge, and in the twenty-first century has moved to a central position in popular music.

Musical subcultures

Other types of music served to foster group feeling among particular

FIGURE 38.8 *Rap group Public Enemy, featuring soloists Flavor Flav (seated left, with his trademark giant watch), Chuck D (seated next to Flavor Flav), and Terminator X (behind them).*

segments of society but rarely attracted the attention of outsiders. For example, the movement called *women's music* encompasses songs in various styles, often folk-influenced, with texts that reflect a feminist perspective. Nurtured by concert circuits organized by women outside the usual venues and by annual festivals like the National Women's Music Festival, the movement developed its own roster of headliners beginning in the 1970s, including singer-songwriters Cris Williamson (b. 1947) and Holly Near (b. 1949) and classical composer Kay Gardner (1941–2002), and its own recording companies such as Olivia Records. More widely known is *contemporary Christian music,* which uses current popular styles to convey evangelical Christian themes. As is true for women's music, the message is more important than the style in defining this type of music. Performing at youth revivals and festivals, pop singers like Amy Grant (b. 1960) and rock bands such as Third Day dress, play, and sing like secular pop artists, seeking to capture the interest of youth through the music and let the words carry the religious content.

The types of popular music listed here are only a few of the many varieties current between 1970 and 2000, which ranged from the acoustically overwhelming *heavy metal* of Judas Priest to the gentle sounds of *ambient music,* pioneered by Brian Eno (b. 1948). Wherever there was a group with distinctive tastes or needs, there was a market niche and musicians to fill it, from polka bands in Milwaukee to Bollywood singers in India. Equally significant is that unlike the 1960s, when almost every teenager in the English-speaking world listened to the Beatles, Bob Dylan, and Aretha Franklin, popular music in the last quarter of the twentieth century was fragmented into niche audiences, and no one achieved the same broad popularity.

Niche markets

MINIMALISM AND POSTMINIMALISM

Composers of art music also cultivated a varied range of styles and approaches. One of the most prominent trends since the 1970s has been ***minimalism***, in which materials are reduced to a minimum and procedures simplified so that

FIGURE 38.9 Hyena Stomp *by Frank Stella (b. 1936). Stella reduced painting to its fundamentals, intending that his work be understood as only a play of form and color, not as an expression of feelings. The title, from a jazz piece by Jelly Roll Morton, reflects Stella's interest in translating syncopation into visual form in this painting.*

what is going on in the music is immediately apparent. Minimalism began in the early 1960s as an avant-garde aesthetic focused on the musical processes themselves but over time became a widely used and popular technique, capable of a wide range of expressive content. Composers of minimalist works absorbed influences from rock, African music, Asian music, tonality, and finally Romanticism, to create what has been called the leading musical style of the late twentieth century.

Art critic Richard Wollheim coined "minimal art" in 1965 as a term for art that reduced materials and form to fundamentals and was not intended to express feelings or convey the artist's state of mind. It represented a reaction against the complexity, density, irregularity, and expressive intensity of postwar abstract expressionism, in favor of simplicity, clarity, and regularity in artworks that do not require interpretation. Minimalist artworks often feature a repetitive pattern of simple elements. For example, Carl Andre's *64 Copper Squares* (1969) consists of sixty-four square copper plates laid on the floor in a square, and Frank Stella's painting *Hyena Stomp* (1962), shown in Figure 38.9, forms a spiral pattern from straight lines and bands of bright color. Such art focused on its materials, making it part of the avant-garde concept art of the 1960s.

Early minimalism in music   A parallel movement was nurtured among musicians in New York City and in the California counterculture. Links between early minimalist composers and artists were very strong, and performances often took place in art galleries and lofts rather than traditional concert venues. In parallel with minimalist art, minimalist composers were reacting against the complexity, density, and sheer difficulty of recent modernist music, from the chance music of Cage to the serialist music of Babbitt, Stockhausen, and Boulez and the virtuoso works of Carter and Berio. Instead of overwhelming the listener with unfamiliar content and a rapidly changing musical surface, minimalist composers reduced the amount of material and the pace of change to a minimum and invited listeners to focus on the small changes that do occur.

La Monte Young   One of the pioneers of musical minimalism was La Monte Young (b. 1935), whose music centers on a small number of pitches that are sustained at great length. *Composition 1960 No. 7* consists simply of the notes B and F♯ "to be held for a long time." While challenging traditional concepts of music in an avant-garde spirit, the piece also directs the listener's attention to the minute changes in pitch and timbre that inevitably happen as a musician sustains a pitch. *The Tortoise: His Dreams and Journeys* (1964) was an improvisation in which instrumentalists and singers come in and out on various harmonics over a fundamental played as a drone by a synthesizer. Among his later projects is *The Dream House* (1996), a sound and light environment open to the public at his house in New York, with light installations by his wife and collaborator, sculptor Marian Zazeela. Giant speakers project drones of thirty-two different frequencies tuned in just intonation that interact in different ways at different points in the room, so that the sound is static if one stays still, but changes as the listener moves through the space, creating a dreamlike experience.

While Young reduced music to sustained tones, Terry Riley (b. 1935), who once performed in Young's ensemble, explored patterns created through repetition. He began while at the San Francisco Tape Music Center by experimenting with **tape loops**, short segments of magnetic tape spliced into loops that when fed through a tape recorder play the same recorded sounds again and again. His tape piece *Mescalin Mix* (1962–63) piled up many such loops, each repeating a short phrase, over a regular pulse. His most famous work, *In C* (1964), uses a similar procedure with live instruments. It can be performed by any number of instruments, each playing the same series of brief repeated figures against the backdrop of a quickly pulsing high octave C, with the number of repetitions in each part and the coordination of parts left indeterminate. The resulting sound combines a steady pulsation with a process of slow change from consonance to diatonic dissonance and back. The concept and materials are simple and the process immediately audible, but the multilayered texture is complex and like nothing ever heard before.

Terry Riley

FROM AVANT-GARDE TO WIDESPREAD APPEAL
While Young remained an avant-garde experimentalist and Riley moved toward rock music, three other Americans brought minimalist procedures into art music intended for a broad audience.

Steve Reich (b. 1936), shown in Figure 38.10, developed a quasi-canonic procedure in which musicians play the same material out of phase with each other. Like Riley, he began in the electronic studio. He created *Come Out*

Steve Reich

FIGURE 38.10 *Steve Reich practicing at his apartment in New York. On the shelf behind him can be seen earlier editions of this book and its accompanying anthology.*

EXAMPLE 38.1 *Steve Reich,* Piano Phase, *opening*

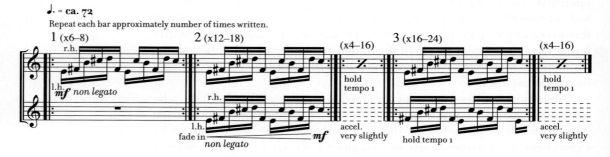

(1966; NAWM 218) by superimposing tape loops of a spoken phrase ("come out to show them") in such a way that one loop was slightly shorter and thus gradually moved ahead of the other, an effect called *phasing*. As the texture grows from two to four to eight simultaneous loops, each out of phase with the others, we can no longer hear the words, only their constituent vocal sounds (especially the consonants "k," "m," and "sh" and the vowels "uh" and "oh"), each endlessly repeating in its own plane of sound.

Piano Phase   In *Piano Phase* (1967), whose opening measures are shown in Example 38.1, Reich applied a similar idea to a work for two pianos. Both pianists repeat the same figure in unison several times, then one gradually pulls ahead until that performer is exactly one eighth note ahead of the other (at measure 3 in the example), and they repeat the figure several times in rhythmic synchronization but melodically out of phase. This process is repeated twelve times, producing a different series of harmonic combinations each time the parts slip into synchrony, until the two parts are again in melodic unison; then the same process is used for a figure of eight notes and then one of four notes. As the opening melody repeats and moves out of phase with itself, it seems to split into two planes, the notes in its upper range (*b′, c♯″,* and *d″*) moving in one melodic stream, its lower notes (*e′* and *f♯′*) in another, each rippling in constant variation. The fascination in music like this lies in observing gradual changes and the many possible permutations of very simple ideas. The processes that underlie the composition are revealed for every listener to hear and experience. Such music is not intended to be expressive, but the moments when the melodies click into phase can be enormously satisfying, like a resolution to consonance after a long dissonance.

Drumming   Reich formed his own ensemble and was able to make a living by performing, touring, and recording his works. Much of his music in the 1970s, such as *Drumming* (1970–71), was percussive, superimposing layers of figuration in ways that parallel African drumming, one source of his inspiration. He attracted a wide range of listeners, drawing audiences accustomed to jazz, rock, and pop music as well as classical music, as the diatonic material and rapid pulsation gave his music wide appeal.

Tehillim   By the 1980s, Reich no longer subscribed to a minimalist aesthetic, instead using minimalist techniques to create large-scale works with significant emotional content, often drawing on his Jewish heritage. *Tehillim* (1981) is a setting of psalm texts in the original Hebrew for four singers and orchestra, using rhythmic and melodic canons at the unison in constantly changing meters over pulsing percussion and sustained diatonic but dissonant harmonies. Each of the first three sections uses different procedures, and the fourth section combines all these techniques, adding layers and building to a climactic conclusion. In the first and last sections, as melodies first heard alone are treated in two-part and then four-part canons at the unison in repeating loops, it becomes progressively harder to follow a single part, and we begin to hear the repeating melodic high points as a separate plane of sound in a way that parallels the effects of phasing in *Come Out* and *Piano Phase.*

A piece as rich and complex as this can hardly be called minimalist, yet it shows the application of minimalist techniques in the realm of art music. For this reason, Reich's music since 1980 is sometimes called ***postminimalist***, reflecting the influence of minimalist procedures while moving beyond the original minimalist aesthetic to include traditional methods (such as canon and harmonic motion), more varied material, and renewed expressivity. His later works include *Different Trains* (1988) for string quartet and tape, a moving reflection on the Holocaust, and *The Cave* (1993) for voices, ensemble, and video, which explores the relationship of Judaism, Christianity, and Islam to each other and to their common patriarch Abraham. Over the course of his career, Reich has moved from avant-garde experimentation to a focus on construction in the 1970s and finally to using the tools he had developed in works that convey meaning and are intended to find a permanent place in the repertoire.

Later works

Philip Glass (b. 1937) had published twenty works by the time he completed degrees at the University of Chicago and The Juilliard School and finished studies with Nadia Boulanger, but withdrew all of them after working with the Indian sitarist Ravi Shankar in Paris. Glass's works since the mid-1960s have been deeply influenced by the rhythmic organization of Indian music. They emphasize melodiousness, consonance, and the simple harmonic progressions and abundant amplification of rock music, and have won Glass a large and diverse following from rock enthusiasts to classical listeners. Like Reich, he initially wrote mainly for his own ensemble, but he secured his reputation with a series of major works, including operas, symphonies, concertos, and film scores.

Philip Glass

Glass's one-act, four-and-a-half-hour opera *Einstein on the Beach,* premiered at the Avignon Festival in France in 1976, was a collaboration with avant-garde director Robert Wilson, who wrote the scenario. The opera avoids narrative, has no sung text other than solfège syllables (the modern descendants of solmization syllables; see Chapter 2), and involves repetitious and commonplace stage gestures that play with the viewer's sense of time and concepts of art. The music consists primarily of repeated figures, mostly arpeggiated triads, performed by an orchestra of electronic keyboard instruments, woodwinds, and a solo violinist. The work offered a completely different experience from traditional opera, raising fundamental questions about the nature of opera, and became one of the most influential works of music theater in the past several decades. Other operas followed, including *Satyagraha* (1980), about Gandhi's nonviolent struggle for Indian independence, and *Akhnaten* (1984), about an Egyptian pharaoh martyred for his monotheistic worship of the sun god. *The Voyage* (1992), commissioned by the

Operas

FIGURE 38.11 *American composer and conductor John Adams conducting the BBC Symphony Orchestra in London.*

Metropolitan Opera to commemorate the five hundredth anniversary of Columbus's voyage to the New World, blends his signature style of multilayered ostinatos, rapid pulse, and slowly changing tonal or modal harmonies with the standard orchestra, recitatives, and arias of the operatic tradition. Glass's approach to opera served as a model for many later composers.

Glass also exercised a profound influence on film music. His focus on repetition was perfectly suited to Godfrey Reggio's film trilogy, *Koyaanisqatsi* (1982), *Powaqqatsi* (1988), and *Naqoyqatsi* (2002), a critique of modern social and environmental conditions composed of images without dialogue or narration. With modifications, the concept works equally well for narrative movies, and it has been adopted by other composers. Glass has scored over two dozen films, garnering Academy Award nominations for *Kundun* (1997), *The Hours* (2002), and *Notes on a Scandal* (2006). He adapted music from some of his films for chamber works, and has also written a series of symphonies, two of which—No. 1, *Low* (1992) and No. 4, *Heroes* (1996)—are based on themes from albums by experimental pop musicians David Bowie and Brian Eno.

John Adams   John Adams (b. 1947), shown in Figure 38.11, has traced a path from minimalism to a personal postminimalist style that blends minimalist techniques with a variety of other approaches. His first major composition, *Phrygian Gates* for piano (1977–78), is representative of the period when minimalism was moving beyond its avant-garde origins to become a style rather than an aesthetic. Except for a middle section of shifting sustained chords, this twenty-four-minute piece relies almost entirely on quick repetitive figurations, primarily in diatonic modes. The music goes through what Adams calls *gates*, changing from one set of notes to another: from the Lydian scale on A to the Phrygian scale on A, as shown in Example 38.2, then the Lydian and Phrygian scales on E, and so on. These changes give the work its title, and they convey the sense of a journey through a gradually changing environment.

Adams continued to use minimalist techniques in his later works, but

EXAMPLE 38.2 *A gate change from John Adams's* Phrygian Gates

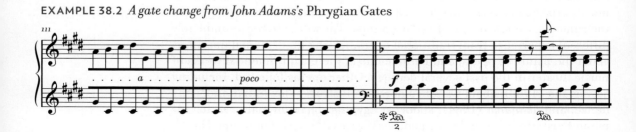

also embraced elements from popular and classical music. The first move-ment of *Harmonielehre* (1985), a symphonic suite that draws on Romantic and modernist styles, begins with loud, repeated E-minor chords, then moves through a minimalist landscape to arrive at a middle section in which twitter-ing ostinatos in the upper register accompany a tragic, almost expressionist, long-breathed melody that recalls late Mahler or Berg. Adams's opera *Nixon in China* (1987), on President Nixon's 1972 trip to China to open relations with the communist regime, treats its up-to-date subject with the formality of a Baroque historical opera while applying minimalist techniques. Short, driv-ing, pulsating ideas, insistently repeated, constantly evolve, using an orches-tra dominated by brass, winds, and percussion. Typical of this idiom from the 1980s is the orchestral fanfare *Short Ride in a Fast Machine* (1986; NAWM 219), which has become one of Adams's most frequently played pieces. A sense of harmonic progression, activated by ostinatos and repeating chords, moves the music forward, and wide-ranging melodies emerge to dominate the tex-ture, culminating in expansive three-part counterpoint over slowly changing but rapidly pulsing harmonies.

The melodic element that emerged in Adams's works of the 1980s has grown stronger over time. In *The Wound Dresser* (1988) for baritone and orchestra, the poem by Walt Whitman relates his experiences as a nurse caring for wounded soldiers in the Civil War. The instruments provide a background of modal harmonies, slowly repeating figures, and gates between pitch collec-tions, drawing on the minimalist techniques of Adams's earlier music. But the focus is on the singer's melody, alternating with melodic orchestral interludes, and the slow pace and Romantic harmonies and orchestral palette convey a mood very different from his previous works. The Violin Concerto (1993) has a similar texture, with a rhapsodic melody in the solo violin unfolding over more regular, endlessly moving figuration in the orchestra. The traditional elements, including virtuoso playing, cadenzas, and the chaconne and toc-cata in the latter two movements, are more prominent than the minimalist techniques. By integrating traditional harmonic and contrapuntal procedures with minimalist ones, Adams has developed a personal style of great flex-ibility and emotional power, marked by greater variety and range than most of his contemporaries. The diversity and depth of both his style and his subject matter have won Adams a broad and enthusiastic audience.

Minimalism has had a profound influence. Since the music of Reich, *Influence* Glass, and Adams achieved popularity in the 1970s and 1980s, minimal-ist techniques have grown increasingly common in popular music and film music, leading some to claim that minimalism is the common musical lan-guage of the late twentieth and early twenty-first centuries. Many composers in the classical tradition have adopted some elements of minimalism, such as repetition, drones, gradual processes of change, reduction in complexity, or modal harmonies, while rejecting others. For some, the greatest impact of minimalism was the permission it gave to write music that was comprehen-sible and appealing. By refuting (or simply ignoring) the nineteenth-century idea of progress in musical style—a notion that underlay the strand of mod-ernism that led from the New German School through Schoenberg to Babbitt, Stockhausen, and Boulez—minimalism helped to create an atmosphere in which anything was possible.

MODERNISM AND INDIVIDUALISM

Among the possibilities, of course, were continuations of modernism, in a variety of directions. Composers of the generation who dominated modernist and avant-garde composition in the 1950s and 1960s were still active, and a younger generation born during or after World War II explored new ideas and developed highly individual approaches.

The older generation   Several postwar modernists extended their personal idioms into the late twentieth or early twenty-first centuries. Milton Babbitt developed further extensions of serialism, becoming more prolific than ever after devising "superarrays" of interrelated rows in the early 1980s. Karlheinz Stockhausen spent his later years composing *Licht* (Light, 1977–2003), a massive cycle of seven operas named for the days of the week and composed using serial melody-formulas associated with the three main characters, Eve, Lucifer, and the archangel Michael. Pierre Boulez focused on elaborating several of his older pieces in new guises and on work with IRCAM on music for acoustic instruments with live electronics that transform the sounds of the instruments as they play, as in *Répons* (1980–84) for six soloists, chamber orchestra, and electronics.

György Ligeti   But some in the older generation changed their approach more radically. György Ligeti, shown in Figure 38.12, had been a leader in the postwar exploration of texture and process (see Chapter 37). He felt his compositional options constrained by the doctrines of modernism and the avant-garde but found new possibilities in the music of minimalists like Riley and Reich and in reclaiming aspects of the nineteenth-century heritage, including Chopin; all three are cited in the title of his 1976 piece for two pianos *Self Portrait with Reich and Riley (and Chopin is also there)*. Between 1985 and 2001, Ligeti wrote a series of études for solo piano that combined elements of his earlier music, which focused on dissonant textures that gradually change, with repetitive procedures inspired by minimalism and with aspects of the virtuoso tradition of the nineteenth century.

FIGURE 38.12
György Ligeti.

In his Étude No. 9, *Vertige* (Vertigo, 1990; NAWM 220), the ideas are essentially simple and familiar: descending chromatic scale segments that enter in succession and overlap to form chordal sonorities. But they move so quickly that they fuse together into an undulating texture in which the individual lines become difficult to hear, recalling the micropolyphony of Ligeti's *Atmosphères* (see Chapter 37). Ligeti varies the texture through the number of simultaneous lines, the interval between them, their range, and the dynamics, and at times overlays melodies and chords. The constant repetition of simple material reflects the influence of minimalism, while the texture of overlapping continuous lines comes from electronic music concepts designed by Jean-Claude Risset at IRCAM (see NAWM 220 commentary). The piece is novel, thoroughly modernist, and consistent with Ligeti's previous work, but at the same time it is dramatic, emotionally expressive, and immediately comprehensible. This combination of the most engaging aspects from modernism, minimalism, and Romantic virtuoso music has given Ligeti's études a wide appeal to audiences and to performers, who find these études a formidable but rewarding challenge.

Among younger composers, research at IRCAM and elsewhere on analysis of timbre and sound spectra led to a new trend known as **spectral music** or **spectralism**, which is not a style but an approach to sound and to composition. In reaction to the abstraction of serial music, spectralism focuses on perception, acoustics, and tone color. The timbre of a musical pitch is a combination of a fundamental note and its overtones, each at a specific frequency and intensity in comparison to the fundamental and to each other; a violin sounds different from a clarinet playing the same note because the combination of overtones is different. Because each frequency and level of intensity can be represented numerically, a timbre can be depicted by a sound spectrum or sonogram and analyzed mathematically, and complex sounds can be created by juxtaposing spectra through processes characteristic of electronic music, such as ring modulation. Spectral music centers on the properties of sound identified by such analysis, using acoustic instruments to re-create the harmonic relationships within the sounds analyzed.

Spectralism

Spectralism was first developed by French composers including Gérard Grisey (1946–1998) and Tristan Murail (b. 1947), cofounders of Ensemble L'Itinéraire in 1973. Grisey's *Partiels* (1975) begins with a low E on trombone followed by a chord on other instruments derived from the sonogram representing the timbre of that low E, and alternates this with chords that simulate electronic sounds produced by ring modulation. Another group of spectralist composers centered in Cologne, including former students of Stockhausen, used similar techniques of harmony but combined them with a greater emphasis on melody, notable in *Lonely Child* for soprano and orchestra by Canadian composer Claude Vivier (1948–1983). Spectralism influenced composers elsewhere who adapted it in personal ways, including Magnus Lindberg and Kaija Saariaho (see Chapter 39) from Finland and British composer Jonathan Harvey (1939–2012).

Minimalism and spectralism were among the last "-isms" of the twentieth century, which spawned more such competing schools of composition than any previous era (see Chapter 32, and pp. 981–83 and 986–87 for three more -isms). But most younger composers resisted conforming to a school or group, and sought a unique voice. One of the most hermetic was Brian Ferneyhough (b. 1943), whose use of microtones and astonishingly complex durations makes his music extraordinarily difficult to play, like an Ars Subtilior for the late twentieth century (see Chapter 6). For others, like Sofia Gubaidulina, Louis Andriessen, and R. Murray Schafer, what was most important was to find expressive means that conveyed a personal vision.

Individualists

Sofia Gubaidulina (b. 1931), shown in Figure 38.13, was born in the Tatar Republic, an autonomous region in central Russia, four hundred miles east of Moscow. Her childhood there, together with her combined Tatar, Russian, Polish, and Jewish heritage, led to a profound interest in blending sounds and influences. She once said, "I am the place where East and West meet." Despite the official atheism of the Soviet Union, almost all her works have

Sofia Gubaidulina

FIGURE 38.13

Composer Sofia Gubaidulina.

MATTHIAS HOENIG/PICTURE-ALLIANCE/DPA/AP IMAGES

a spiritual dimension. She came to international prominence with her violin concerto *Offertorium* (1980, revised 1982 and 1986), written for violinist Gidon Kremer, which captures the concept of self-sacrifice—paralleling that of Jesus on the cross, or of the composer for the sake of her music—by presenting, deconstructing, and reconstructing, note by note, the theme Frederick the Great offered to Johann Sebastian Bach, who made it the central idea of his *Musical Offering* (see p. 433 and Example 19.3). The five movements of her sonata for violin and cello, *Rejoice!* (1981), were inspired by eighteenth-century devotional texts. According to the composer, the sonata expresses the transcendence from ordinary reality to a state of joy and relies particularly on the passage from a fundamental note to its harmonics to embody this journey of consciousness. The fifth movement (NAWM 221), inscribed with the text "Listen to the still small voice within," is a study in chromatics, tremolos, and harmonics, particularly glissandos from low fundamental notes in the cello to their higher harmonics. In these and other pieces, Gubaidulina's music is both modernist, in its combination of a highly individual musical personality with evocations of the classical tradition, and immediately appealing through its spiritual resonances and beautiful surface textures and timbres.

Louis Andriessen

A different flavor is conveyed by the music of Louis Andriessen (b. 1939), the most significant Dutch composer of the postwar era and a major influence on younger composers in Europe and the United States such as the Bang on a Can group. After early mentoring by his father and older brother, who were also composers, he studied composition at the Royal Conservatory in The Hague and then with Luciano Berio in Berlin and Milan. Committed to left-wing politics, he participated in 1969 in disrupting a performance by Amsterdam's Concertgebouw Orchestra as a protest against its conservative programming. He turned his back on orchestral music and writes instead for ensembles that combine orchestral instruments with sounds from big-band jazz and rock music, such as saxophones, synthesizer, electric guitars and bass guitars, and drum sets. Often his music is put together by juxtaposing contrasting blocks of energetically pulsing sound, as in the music of Stravinsky, and layering disparate musical strands as in Ives's orchestral works; Stravinsky was an early and fundamental influence on his music, and Ives a passion in the late 1960s and early 1970s. In works like *De staat* (The Republic, 1972–76, with texts from Plato's *Republic*) for four female voices and large ensemble and the four-part music theater piece *De materie* (Matter, 1984–88), Andriessen interweaves European and American procedures and popular and classical sounds, including minimalist repetition; canon, hocket, passacaglia, and other traditional devices; nonfunctional diatonic melodies and harmonies contrasted with stringent chromatic dissonance; sonorities modeled on Claude Vivier's spectralism; and references to familiar styles from Bach toccata style to boogie-woogie. His subject matter reflects both his social concerns and an interest in abstract philosophical issues, as in *De staat, De materie,* and *De tijd* (Time, 1980–81) for female chorus and large ensemble on texts by St. Augustine.

R. Murray Schafer (b. 1933), the leading Canadian composer of the era, *R. Murray Schafer* traversed a wide variety of styles from neoclassical to avant-garde, yet most of his pieces are based on extramusical inspirations. His orchestral works *Dream Rainbow Dream Thunder* (1986) and *Manitou* (1995), for example, reflect ideas from the culture of the Inuits, natives of Canada. His most striking innovation is what he calls *environmental music,* pieces that break out of the concert hall and require more than passive attention from listeners. *Music for Wilderness Lake* (1979) is to be performed at sunrise and sunset at a small lake away from human settlements, with twelve trombonists positioned around its shores playing meditative melodies to one another across the water, cued by a conductor in a raft, and joined by animal sounds. Ideally, listeners would participate in the event by experiencing the lake, its stillness, its sounds, and its surrounding wilderness as the music is performed; in fact, most can only watch the event on film.

Pursuing different aims, Ligeti, the spectralists, Ferneyhough, Gubaidulina, Andriessen, and Schafer arrived at very different ends, each developing a unique musical language. Yet they have at least one thing in common: each is an individualist with roots in modernism and ultimately in the classical tradition itself.

POLYSTYLISM

The profusion of individual idioms in the twentieth century had as a corollary the breakdown of any common musical language. Composers in earlier eras shared a fund of musical resources, styles, and procedures, but all that musicians as diverse as Sheng, Adams, Ligeti, and Gubaidulina had in common was their heritage as composers in the classical tradition. At the same time, countless musical idioms of the past were also part of the musical present, in performances and recordings of music from all eras.

In the face of such stylistic profusion, some composers responded by *Postmodernism* combining past and present styles. Such blending of old and new styles in music has been compared to the architecture of Philip Johnson, Robert Venturi, Cesar Pelli, and others, who left behind the bare glass façades of mid-twentieth-century modernism by incorporating elements of earlier styles into essentially modern designs as in Figure 38.14, a mixture that came to be called ***postmodernism***. A central aspect of postmodernism is a turning away from the belief, crucial to modernist thought, that history progresses irreversibly in one direction. In music, this idea means abandoning the notion that musical idioms develop continuously, as if according to a plan or some inner necessity. To the postmodernist, history gives the artist more freedom than that; the styles of all epochs and cultures are equally available as musical material, to be employed as the composer sees fit.

A composer who borrowed past styles effectively was Alfred Schnittke *Alfred Schnittke* (1934–1998). He worked in the Soviet Union, where he was known chiefly for his film music, before moving to Germany in 1990 after the fall of the Berlin Wall. The Soviet government began to relax its control over culture in the 1960s under Nikita Khrushchev, exposing Schnittke and other young composers

FIGURE 38.14 *The AT&T building (1984) in New York City, later renamed the Sony Tower. The architect, Philip Johnson, blended elements from the past, such as the columns and slanted roofline, together with modern elements of glass and concrete in his design. This blending of elements from different periods, sometimes called* postmodernism, *rejects the stark glass walls and undecorated façades of many mid-twentieth-century buildings.*

to trends such as serial, chance, and electronic music. After writing several works based on serialism, indeterminacy, and new instrumental sounds, Schnittke turned to what he called **polystylism**, a combination of new and older styles created through quotation or stylistic allusion. His Symphony No. 1 (1969–72) incorporates passages from works by Haydn, Beethoven, Chopin, Tchaikovsky, Grieg, Johann Strauss, and Schnittke himself. For listeners familiar with works of these composers, such music embodies a contrast not only of styles but of historical periods.

Schnittke's Concerto Grosso No. 1 (1976) juxtaposes styles of the eighteenth century with modern atonal and popular styles, through allusion rather than quotation. The second movement (NAWM 222) includes sections that evoke Vivaldi concertos, galant style, twelve-tone music, and a hymnlike popular style, but Schnittke defamiliarizes each style through canons and polytonality. In the final section, all the themes are combined at once, resolving the stylistic conflicts by forcing all into a dense modernist polyphony. Such stylistic contrasts have precedents in Mozart's use of topics (see Chapter 23) and Ives's stylistic heterogeneity (see Chapter 33), and like them can serve both formal and expressive ends. But because the styles Schnittke uses cross centuries and traditions, his music violates listener expectations and thus raises fascinating questions for analysis and interpretation.

Like Schnittke, the American composer John Corigliano (b. 1938) often juxtaposes styles to convey meanings, drawing on a stylistic continuum from Baroque and Classic to avant-garde. His opera *The Ghosts of Versailles* (1987) centers around ghosts in the French royal palace, including Queen Marie Antoinette and others slain during the Revolution, and a play staged for their entertainment; the ghosts are rendered with modern serial music and timbral effects, while the play is set in a style based on Mozart operas, which were composed in Marie Antoinette's own time and in her native Austria. The range of styles and influences evoked in this opera is immense, including chant, Broadway, Schoenberg, Stravinsky, and opera composers from Rossini to Penderecki. Corigliano's Symphony No. 1 (1989), a memorial to friends who died of AIDS, incorporates quotations from some of their favorite pieces framed by deeply expressive, often angry or tragic music drawing on a variety of modern techniques. In his Academy Award–winning score for the film *The Red Violin* (1998), which follows a violin from its maker through a series of owners to its auction in the present, Corigliano created a leitmotive for the violin and developed it into a series of pieces representing the era and style of each owner, from an eighteenth-century concerto to Roma (Gypsy) music and a nineteenth-century virtuoso improvisation. Corigliano adapted the music for concert use in the *Red Violin Chaconne* (1997) and *Red Violin Concerto* (2007).

The wittiest and most popular composer to use stylistic allusion is Peter Schickele (b. 1935). His works, such as his five string quartets (1983–98), are mostly tonal. They draw on a wide variety of styles, from Stravinsky to jazz and rock, and create form and expression through contrasts of style, mood, texture, figuration, timbre, dynamics, and other factors, sometimes using quotation for humorous effect. His String Quartet No. 4 (1992) exemplifies his eclectic tastes; subtitled "Inter-Era Dance Suite," it includes not only the overture, minuet, and sarabande one would expect to find in a Bach orchestral suite, but also a jig (instead of gigue), waltz, tango, and fox trot, encompassing dances of every century from the seventeenth to the twentieth.

Peter Schickele and P. D. Q. Bach

Schickele is best known for his music under the guise of P. D. Q. Bach, the supposed youngest son of J. S. Bach who inherited none of his father's talent. This persona allows Schickele to spoof old music, its performing practice, and musicologists. Performing conventions go awry, as in the long-winded continuo accompaniment in the cantata *Iphigenia in Brooklyn* (1964); bizarre instruments are featured, like the double-reed slide music stand, parodying the unfamiliar instruments called for in early music; and every stylistic expectation is violated, with hilarious results. For example, in the *"Howdy"* Symphony (1982)—a response to Haydn's *Farewell* Symphony—the first movement Allegro uses contrasts of style to delineate form, as in Classic-era music (see Chapter 23), but here the styles range from Classic to vaudeville, big-band jazz, and modernist dissonance; the witty incongruities and surprises typical of Haydn become burlesque.

Whether used for comic effect, to convey meanings through associations carried by existing music, to upend listener expectations, or to create disjunctions that comment on our experience of time and history, allusions to past styles gave audiences something familiar to hold onto, often even more directly than the use of quotation and collage (discussed in Chapter 37). For many listeners, such allusions made this music more engaging and easier to follow than the unfamiliar sounds of modernist composers. In another sense, however, polystylism—even if considered an aspect of postmodernism—was yet another kind of modernism, and another way for composers to engage the past while creating a distinctive voice of their own.

THE NEW ACCESSIBILITY

In the late twentieth century, composers in the classical tradition faced a new reality. While they were able to make a living teaching at universities or conservatories, obtaining performances for their music was increasingly difficult. It was often easier to win a commission for a new piece than to secure a second or third performance of an existing work. Few new compositions entered the repertory, and few listeners heard a recently composed classical piece live more than once. In some respects, the situation was like that of the eighteenth century, when a concerto or symphony was seldom heard twice by the same listeners. Moreover, at a time when music was growing more plentiful and easy to access, the audience for classical music seemed to be shrinking.

Some composers, such as Babbitt and Ferneyhough, took this situation as the price of artistic freedom and remained committed to complex and hermetic styles. But many and perhaps most composers of the time sought to attract wider audiences by writing music that could be appreciated on first hearing. Rouse, Mackey, Zorn, and others found one solution by incorporating elements of popular music. Reich, Glass, and Adams found another in minimalism. Other composers used a variety of approaches, often in tandem: modifying their modernist idiom to make it more accessible; radically simplifying their material and procedures; invoking extramusical imagery and meanings; or renovating nineteenth-century tonal Romanticism.

Ellen Taaffe Zwilich

ACCESSIBLE MODERNISM Some composers writing in a modernist idiom have made their music accessible by keeping the ideas and procedures relatively simple and easy to grasp. For example, Ellen Taaffe Zwilich (b. 1939) joins continuous variation with older formal devices of recurrence and contrast. Like Schoenberg, she presents the main idea at the outset, then elaborates it through developing variation in which everything grows logically from the initial seed. Yet the basic idea is usually simple and the textures clear, making her music much easier to follow than Schoenberg's. A prime example is her Symphony No. 1 (1982), which won the first Pulitzer Prize in Music awarded to a woman. In the first movement, all the melodic material derives through variation from the initial interval of a rising minor third, and the harmonies combine thirds to produce dissonant sonorities. The soft opening gesture, a threefold rising third with an accelerando, serves as a motto that generates a gradual increase in tempo, dynamics, and density to a central allegro section, then toward the end the music slows and thins to a quiet close. The gradual process of development is easy to hear, and the experience of listening is both intellectually and emotionally satisfying.

FIGURE 38.15
Arvo Pärt.

RADICAL SIMPLIFICATION Other composers combined a radical simplification of material and procedures with a return to diatonic music. One strain can be found in minimalism, but not all music of this type fits the minimalist category.

Estonian composer Arvo Pärt (b. 1935), shown in Figure 38.15, forged a highly individual, instantly recognizable style using the simplest materials. Following early neoclassical and serial works, and others that contrasted modernist with Baroque styles, he turned to a study of Gregorian chant and early polyphony. In the 1970s, he devised a method he called *tintinnabuli,* after the bell-like sonorities it produced. Its essence lies in counterpoint between a pitch-centered, mostly stepwise diatonic melody and one or more other voices that sound only notes of the tonic triad, with the placement of each note determined by a preset system. Pärt established his international reputation with instrumental works in tintinnabuli style, notably *Tabula rasa, Fratres* (Brothers), and *Cantus in memorium Benjamin Britten* (all 1977), then increasingly focused on religious

EXAMPLE 38.3 *Arvo Pärt,* O König aller Völker, *No. 6 of* Seven Magnificat Antiphons

O king of all peoples, their expectation [and hope]

choral music, especially after leaving the Soviet Union in 1980. With its calm, steady tempo, quiet surface, gentle diatonic dissonances, and stylistic features reminiscent of medieval chant and early church polyphony, his music suggests an aura of mysticism and embodies a simple beauty many listeners find deeply satisfying.

Pärt's tintinnabuli technique and choral style are exemplified in his *Seven Magnificat Antiphons* (1988, revised 1991; excerpts in NAWM 223) and illustrated in Example 38.3, which shows the opening of No. 6, *O König aller Völker.* The second tenor (the lower part on the tenor staff) presents a plain modal tune that is centered on A and that moves no more than a fourth away in either direction. Its rhythm is restricted to quarter and half notes, and measures change length to fit the text accentuation. The tenor melody is echoed by the second soprano to form an augmentation canon. The altos recite the text, phrase by phrase, on D. The other parts sound notes of the D-minor triad, following strict but simple rules reminiscent of early polyphony (see Chapter 5). The bass and first tenor surround the second-tenor melody, each singing the note of the D-minor triad that is second closest to the melody note: thus, at the outset, we find the D below and the F above the melody's opening A. Meanwhile, the first soprano sings the note from the triad that is nearest above the second-soprano melody. The resulting texture alternates between consonance and diatonic dissonance, allowing for variety and dramatic climaxes within a stripped-down, pitch-centered style.

EXTRAMUSICAL IMAGERY AND MEANINGS Using simpler material and processes that were easier to follow was one strategy composers used to make their music more accessible, appealing, and meaningful. Another was to invoke extramusical imagery, hoping that listeners would accept unusual sounds if their meanings were clear.

Many works by American composer Joan Tower (b. 1938) are based on images. *Silver Ladders* (1986) for orchestra features rising lines (the "ladders" of the title), either stepwise or leaping by fourths, moving at different

Joan Tower

speeds amid a variety of textures. The "silver" in the title is meant to evoke the metal in both its solid state, embodied in the dense orchestral sections, and its molten state, represented through freely flowing solos for clarinet, oboe, marimba, and trumpet. The piece offers an abstract play of musical ideas, but the imagery offers the listener a welcome hook that makes the work easier to follow. Tower's *Made in America* (2005) is based not on a visual image but on a sonic one. Commissioned by small-budget orchestras and played in all fifty states during the two years after its composition, the piece is a fantasy on *America the Beautiful,* gradually revealing more of the tune over time without ever stating it in full.

John Tavener　　Evocations of spirituality can give listeners an immediate connection to new music, continuing music's long association with religion and the transcendent. This is part of the appeal of Reich's *Tehillim,* Gubaidulina's *Rejoice!,* and Pärt's *Magnificat Antiphons,* and it runs counter to the tendency of much twentieth-century music to focus on secular concerns or on the abstract play of musical parameters. English composer John Tavener (1944–2013) was one whose music centered on spiritual concerns. After writing works influenced by Stravinsky's serialism and block construction, he joined the Orthodox Church in 1977 and began to incorporate elements from its liturgical music, as in *Liturgy of St. John Chrysostom* (1977) for unaccompanied chorus. He made his reputation with sacred choral works in a harmonically simple, chant-derived idiom, then applied a similar style in a series of instrumental works on religious subjects that won international renown, of which *The Protecting Veil* for cello and string orchestra (1987) is best known.

NEO-ROMANTICISM In their search for expressive tools that connect directly with listeners, some composers adopted the familiar tonal idiom of nineteenth-century Romanticism or incorporated its sounds and gestures, a trend known as **neo-Romanticism**.

Krzysztof Penderecki　　For example, after making his reputation with pieces based on texture and process (see Chapter 37), Krzysztof Penderecki focused increasingly on melody and drew on past styles, genres, and harmonic practice in neo-Romantic works of the mid-1970s and beyond, such as the Violin Concerto No. 1 (1976–77) and the opera *Paradise Lost* (1975–78). The struggles of the trade union Solidarity to achieve democracy in Poland inspired the *Polish Requiem* (1980–84), in which Penderecki combined neo-Romanticism, elements from Renaissance and Baroque styles, and his signature textures from the 1960s in a new synthesis of styles.

George Rochberg　　Having turned from serialism to quotation in the 1960s (see Chapter 37), George Rochberg moved on in the 1970s to use Romantic and early modernist styles for their expressive potential. His String Quartet No. 5 (1978) is neo-Romantic in three of its five movements. Each movement is written in a consistent style, but the styles differ considerably between movements. The first movement is a sprightly sonata form in A major reminiscent of late Beethoven or Schubert; the second, a sad E♭-minor slow movement whose canons and loosely dissonant harmonies recall early Bartók; the third, a Beethovenian scherzo in A minor with a Mahlerian trio; the fourth, an atonal serenade that resembles works of Schoenberg or Berg; and the finale, an energetic, constantly developing, rapidly modulating yet tonal rondo in late Romantic style,

EXAMPLE 38.4 *"The Accusation," from David Del Tredici's* Final Alice

"The Queen of Hearts, she made some tarts, All on a sum-mer day:___ The Knave of Hearts, he stole those tarts And took them quite a - way!"___

akin to Schoenberg's First Quartet. The mixture of idioms challenged the traditional expectation that music be stylistically uniform, but even more radical was Rochberg's choice to reclaim styles of the past and use them in a wholehearted effort to make their resources his own without the distancing effects notable in Stravinsky's neoclassicism or Schnittke's polystylism.

David Del Tredici (b. 1937) embraced neo-Romanticism for a different reason. After using atonal and serial methods in the 1960s, he changed his style radically when he started to set excerpts from Lewis Carroll's stories for children, feeling that their whimsy called for a direct, comprehensible presentation. *Final Alice* (1975), to a text from the final chapters of *Alice's Adventures in Wonderland,* is scored for amplified soprano and orchestra, with a contrasting "folk group" of banjo, mandolin, accordion, and two soprano saxophones. The lush orchestration gives the music a Romantic sound, as do the diatonic melodies, rich harmonies, and expressive use of dynamics and rhythm to create exhilarating waves of music that build, climax, and dissolve. The soprano narrates, plays all the characters, and sings a series of arias. The central motive of the piece, a rising major sixth introduced by the saxophones, is taken up by other instruments and becomes the fundamental interval of "The Accusation" sung by the White Rabbit, shown in Example 38.4; a greater concentration of rising sixths in a melody is hard to imagine. Through this and other arias, the orchestra and folk group accompany in a kind of nonsense tonality, with slightly off-kilter dance rhythms and multiple layers in differing tempos. Most of the music is tonal, ranging from folklike episodes to an idiom reminiscent of Richard Strauss. But when Alice begins to grow larger, Del Tredici suggests the strange occurrence with atonal music, a twelve-tone motive, and the electronic sounds of the Theremin. By using tonal and atonal styles side by side for their expressive effect, Del Tredici renounced the modernist ideology of progress. In its place, he returned to eighteenth- and nineteenth-century ideals of music, mixing diverse styles in a coherent whole that is comprehensible on first hearing to an untrained listener yet holds hidden delights for the connoisseur. The result was music that was immediately appealing to audiences but provoked a strong reaction from some of Del Tredici's modernist colleagues (see Source Readings).

David Del Tredici

DIRECT COMMUNICATION The pieces discussed here represent only a few of the many strategies composers have used to communicate directly with listeners. By the 1990s, most composers sought to write music that nonspecialist audiences could grasp on first hearing, by employing familiar idioms,

On Reaching an Audience

David Del Tredici's *Final Alice* won immediate praise from listeners, as noted in the reviews of its premiere in October 1976.

✤

When the last stroke of *Final Alice* died away at the Chicago Symphony concert, the audience broke into sustained applause which quickly grew into a standing ovation. Cheers and bravos mingled with the handclaps. . . . It was the most enthusiastic reception of a new work that I have ever heard at a symphony concert.

Thomas Willis, *Chicago Tribune*, October 9, 1976.

But some of his fellow composers viewed the piece as a betrayal of the tenets of modernism, and Del Tredici found himself having to defend his success.

✤

About halfway through [composing] the piece, I thought, "Oh my God, if I just leave it like this, my colleagues will think I'm crazy." But then I thought, "What else can I do? If nothing else occurs to me I can't go against my instincts." But I was terrified my colleagues would think I was an idiot. . . . People think now that I wanted to be tonal and have a big audience. But that was just not true. I didn't want to be tonal. My world was my colleagues—my composing friends. . . . The success of *Final Alice* was very defining as to who my real friends were. I think many composers regard success as a kind of threat. It's really better, they think, if nobody has any success, to be all in one boat. Composers now are beginning to realize that if a piece excites an audience, that doesn't mean it's terrible. For my generation, it is considered vulgar to have an audience really, really like a piece on a first hearing. But why are we writing music except to move people and to be expressive? To have what has moved us move somebody else?

Right now, audiences just reject contemporary music. But if they start to like one thing, then they begin to have perspective. That will make a difference, it always has in the past. The sleeping giant is the audience.

From an interview with John Rockwell, in *The New York Times*, Sunday, October 26, 1980, Section D, 23, 28.

gestures, and other elements drawn from the entire range of music history, popular styles, and musics of the world. These familiar elements were often juxtaposed or blended in unprecedented ways in order to provide a new experience and achieve a distinctive profile. Thus, composers sought to uphold the high value placed on individuality since the nineteenth century while seeking to reclaim the immediate appeal that, many felt, had been lost in the modernist era.

FINDING AN AUDIENCE

The trends explored in this chapter are still with us, many of them just as characteristic of the early twenty-first century as of the late twentieth, as we will see in the next chapter. By now it seems obvious that classical music is not the only art music, and that all kinds of music can be valued for their own sake. The discipline of musicology, founded in the nineteenth century to unearth, edit, and describe the music of the past and to curate the growing canon of classics, now embraces every sort of music in the Western tradition. Fusions and hybrids between popular and classical music, rock and jazz, or Western and non-Western music have grown ever more common, calling the very boundaries between traditions into question. Popular trends that once had millions of fans, then seemed to fade, endure on recordings and are eventually revived; disco, punk, and grunge, all passé by the 1990s, came back again after 2000. Other styles like hip hop and electronic pop have spread all over the planet. Postminimalist sounds and textures are everywhere, from pop to concert music to film scores, no longer the center of attention but now a framework for all manner of musical styles and approaches. Modernism is still a force, as it was a century ago, appealing to a small but passionate audience, while the movements formed in reaction to modernism, from polystylism to neo-Romanticism, have also found their niche.

The diverse music of the late twentieth century is still with us as well. The tendency we have seen for classics to emerge in each tradition as it develops has kept in circulation pathbreaking music of the past, in every realm, from classical concert works to film scores and pop music. In the tradition of classical music, the composers and pieces we have surveyed in this chapter are not household names like Bach or Beethoven, but they have found performers to promote them and listeners who value their music deeply. There is no longer one mainstream, one taste for music, but many streams and tastes. In this diverse musical culture, each new sound of the late 1900s has a special appeal, a unique sound that sets it apart, and has found an audience.

Further Reading is available at digital.wwnorton.com/hwm10

THE TWENTY-FIRST CENTURY

Time and historical distance will tell whether or not the year 2000 marked the beginning of a new era in music. From our current vantage point, there seems to be as much continuity as change from the final decades of the last century through the second decade of our own, since most of the trends discussed in the previous chapter have continued, and what new styles and types of music emerged were often linked to the past. The most significant changes have been in new technologies for making and distributing music, which have put unprecedented capabilities in the hands of anyone who wants to produce and distribute music, thereby decentralizing the marketplace and weakening the influence of gatekeepers such as record companies. One new technology, the *mashup*, is an appropriate metaphor for the most characteristic feature of today's musical life, the mixing of elements from disparate sources to create something new. Another technology, *streaming*, is transforming the market for music from selling commodities—music in print or recordings—to offering musicians' services on a vast scale, and reflects a growing focus, especially among the young, on having experiences rather than owning things.

THE NEW MILLENNIUM

Images of an interconnected global culture were captured on New Year's Eve and New Year's Day 2000, when television showed celebrations of the new millennium arriving around the world as midnight crept across time zones from South Pacific nations to Alaska, and fireworks went off from Australia's Sydney Opera House to the Eiffel Tower in Paris, shown in Figure 39.1. The only worry was that computer codes designed in the middle to late 1900s with dates that allowed just two digits for the year would suddenly stop functioning when 2000 dawned, taking down electric grids and other basic services, but most institutions and corporations addressed the "Y2K problem" in advance and no such chaos occurred.

Less than two years later, the dream of global understanding was shattered when, in the name of distancing the Islamic world from the West, Al Qaeda terrorists flew hijacked passenger planes into the World Trade Center in New York City and the Pentagon in Washington, D.C. on September 11, 2001. Responses to that event, from wars to debating the proper balance between security and liberty, continue to shape society and politics today. Meanwhile, governments were slow to react to a new potential threat, when scientists concluded that the atmosphere and oceans were gradually warming because of human activity and that changing climate patterns would likely cause flooding to coastal areas, heighten the strength and severity of storms, and affect food production. Yet hopes for a better world continued to emerge, in the increasing freedom for women and young people around the globe; the replacement of some dictatorships with democratic governments, from Latin America to Africa and the Middle East; and the growing numbers of people studying and working abroad, from Asian students at American universities to American businesspeople in Asia. One sign of how much has changed in the twenty-first century—and how quickly—is same-sex marriage, which was recognized in the law nowhere in the world until 2001, when the Netherlands became the first nation to do so, and now is legal in over two dozen countries, from South Africa and Argentina to Australia and Ireland.

FIGURE 39.1 *Fireworks going off from the Eiffel Tower just after midnight on New Year's Day, 2000, to celebrate the new millennium.*

ALEXIS KOMENDA/GETTY IMAGES

The integration of the global economy continued, as factories in Asia became the prime suppliers of manufactured goods for Europe and North America, and as food from all continents was shipped thousands of miles to make formerly seasonal fruits and vegetables available almost everywhere in almost any season. The European Union introduced a new shared currency, the euro, adopted by most member nations in 1999 for accounting purposes and circulating in coins and banknotes beginning in 2002. Despite such international ties, national economies did not move in lockstep. As China, India, and Brazil boomed, the first decade of the century brought new economic problems to the United States, including the declining value of the dollar, increasing oil prices, stagnant income for the great majority of households, expensive wars in Iraq and Afghanistan, and the collapse of major corporations from airlines to financial institutions, culminating in 2008 in the Great Recession, the worst worldwide downturn since the 1930s.

In the economic recovery since 2009, the United States, thanks to government spending and tax cuts, recovered sooner than Europe, whose leaders compounded their problems with austerity measures that shrank their economies. Yet the sense of crisis continued on both sides of the Atlantic. The

Growing inequality and isolationism

TIMELINE

2000 New millennium celebrated worldwide

2000 Jennifer Higdon, *blue cathedral*

2000 Kaija Saariaho, *L'amour de loin*

2000 Osvaldo Golijov, *La Pasión según San Marcos*

2001 Wikipedia launched

2001 Terrorist attack on World Trade Center and Pentagon

2002 Euro circulates as currency in European Union

2003 War in Iraq begins

2003 Project to map human genome completed

2004 DJ Danger Mouse, *The Grey Album*

2005 John Adams, *Doctor Atomic*

2005 YouTube launched

2005 Thomas Adès, Violin Concerto

2006 One billionth song downloaded from iTunes

2008 Spotify launched

2008 Great Recession begins

2008 Barack Obama elected first African American president of USA

2009–11 Caroline Shaw, *Partita for 8 Voices*

2011 Jeremy Sams, *The Enchanted Island*

2011 Global population reaches 7 billion

2015 Lin-Manuel Miranda, *Hamilton*

2016 Donald Trump elected president of USA

election of the first African American president in 2008 did not mark the end of racism or bring the resolution of partisan differences, as many had hoped; political polarization continued, making it difficult to address the nation's problems, and racial conflict reemerged as a major concern, from the Black Lives Matter movement protesting police killings of black men to a resurgence of overt white nationalism. In the United States, Russia, and many other countries, wealth became more concentrated in the hands of a few while most people's incomes were level with inflation or declined, producing a growing inequality. Although global supply chains and cultural exchanges seem likely to endure, resistance to globalization grew in the century's second decade, evident in rising nationalist and isolationist movements across Europe and the Americas. For the first time since World War II, the number of functioning democracies fell, replaced in several nations by strongmen who encouraged a cult of personality rather than reliance on democratic institutions. Civil wars in Africa and Syria led to a flood of refugees to Europe; after a generous initial response, some countries reacted by closing their borders, and immigration became a vexing political question exploited by right-wing nationalist parties. As Russia flexed its muscles, stimulating proxy wars in Georgia and Ukraine and annexing Crimea, the European Union was weakened by political turmoil in Greece and Italy, rising authoritarianism in Hungary and Poland, and the 2016 vote in the United Kingdom to leave the European Union, known as Brexit. That same year saw the election of an American president who was deeply suspicious of multilateral agreements and actively criticized NATO, the World Trade Organization, and other institutions. All these developments seemed to threaten the whole postwar international structure that the United States and its allies had painstakingly built over more than seventy years.

COMMUNICATIONS TECHNOLOGY Among the greatest and most significant changes in the early twenty-first century were new communications technologies that are now so much a fabric of everyday life around the world that it is hard to remember how new they are. Digital cameras, first marketed in 1995, virtually replaced film cameras by 2005. Cell phones, once a vision of the future on the 1960s television show *Star Trek*, became ubiquitous around the world after the development of 3G (third generation) systems in 2001, and now mobile phones serve over six billion subscribers, almost 90 percent of the world's population. The iPhone, introduced by Apple in 2007, and other smartphones put the power of a computer in anyone's pocket, with more computing power than the largest computer in the world fifty years earlier. Flat screens using liquid crystal displays or plasma panels replaced cathode ray tubes in televisions and computer monitors, and the continued miniaturization of computer components led to the development of tablet computers like the iPad, introduced in 2010.

These new devices linked users into a global web of communication and information, both privately through direct personal exchanges and publicly through the Internet. Email, used widely in schools and businesses since the early 1990s on desktop computers, was now accessible on smartphones and tablet computers as well. Young people used their phones more often for sending text messages and photos than making calls, and it became easy to stay in constant touch with friends, which could be a boon or a distraction.

Global communication

By the early 2000s, the once freewheeling Internet was dominated by a few corporations that provided tools adopted by a rapidly growing world of users. Facebook, launched in 2004, became the world's largest social networking service, with over two billion members making contacts, exchanging messages, posting updates, and participating in group conversations, replacing email for many users. Google, created in the late 1990s, and other search engines allowed quick access to anything on the Internet; knowledge about almost everything was immediately available, but so was misinformation and disinformation, and it could be difficult to gauge which sources were reliable. Print media like newspapers and broadcast media like radio stations and television networks greatly increased their presence online, and their open comment sections allowed hundreds of readers to post responses to every news story, article, or opinion piece and to engage in debate with each other that could range from civil to snarky. New web publishing tools such as Blogger and WordPress fostered a proliferation of blogs (web logs), so that everyone could be a journalist or pundit, or could post pictures of and stories about their children or pets for their family and friends to read. YouTube debuted in 2005 and made it easy to post videos, including music videos and concerts, that could be viewed worldwide; by the 2010s both corporate content providers and individual users were establishing their own channels on YouTube that reached thousands or millions of viewers, posting original content, winning recognition, and earning income from advertising. Twitter has become instrumental in getting news and photographs out quickly to the world, from the demonstrations in the Arab Spring of 2010 to the latest celebrity scandal or political controversy. People increasingly stay in touch by sharing pictures or videos rather than words, using resources like instant messaging, Instagram, Tumblr, or Snapchat. In the first two decades of the twenty-first century, all of these technologies changed communication immensely, allowing anyone to share their thoughts or photos with the world, without passing through the filter of publishers or print media.

Internet tools and corporations

THE NEW WORLD OF MUSIC

NEW TECHNOLOGY AND THE MUSIC INDUSTRY By giving people everywhere the means to access, produce, and distribute digital material through the Internet, these new devices and software programs radically changed the music industry. The iPod portable media player, introduced by Apple in 2001, put an entire library of recorded music in a pocket-sized device using digital audio files. iTunes, launched in 2002, was one of the first services to allow listeners to purchase pieces of music as audio files rather than on CDs, LPs, or tapes, after Napster (1999–2001) and other peer-to-peer file sharing programs had popularized illegal file sharing. Listeners could download audio files as podcasts (from "iPod" and "broadcast") or listen online to audio webcasts (from "World Wide Web" and "broadcast"). In recent years, high-speed connections have made it viable to deliver music (and other audio and visual materials) over the Internet through **streaming**, with which a user can listen to digital audio content directly via a website or application without having to download the audio file. Many users now access music from streaming services like Pandora, Spotify, or Tidal rather than buying it as downloads (see Innovations: Music Technology for Everyone, pp. 996–97), and stream music videos from websites like Vevo and YouTube. The recorded anthology that accompanies NAWM illustrates the changes: available on LPs in the 1980s, cassettes in the late 1980s and 1990s, CDs from the late 1980s through the early 2010s, and audio files and streaming since 2014.

Effects on record companies and stores   As a result of the greater portability and availability of audio files and streaming, sales of CDs plummeted; according to the Recording Industry Association of America, CD album sales in the United States dropped from 942.5 million in 2000 to 99.4 million in 2016. Recording companies were hard hit financially and became increasingly dependent on sales of audio files through online distributors like iTunes and Amazon, then more recently on streaming services. The falloff in sales also led to the closure of thousands of record stores. Yet older formats like cassettes and vinyl LPs have staged a surprising comeback, with LP sales rising from one million in 2005 to 14.3 million in 2017, stimulated in part by fans who prefer the sound of analog recording and playback over digital sound. And independent record stores are holding on. Record Store Day, inaugurated in 2008, is an annual event in North America, Europe, Australia, and Japan that supports independent record stores, in part through recordings released on that day by dozens of artists and sold only in those stores.

DECENTRALIZING MUSIC PRODUCTION The new digital technologies also have made it possible for anyone to create, record, produce, and distribute music (see Innovations: Music Technology for Everyone, pp. 996–97). Amateurs and professionals alike can bypass the recording companies and make their music available by posting it to YouTube or Facebook or on their own websites as podcasts, webcasts, or streaming audio or video. Professionals sometimes offer their music for free, as advertising for their concert tours, or find ways to sell the online content. Aspiring musicians promote their music online with profiles on Bandcamp, SoundCloud, or ReverbNation and by posting videos on YouTube or other websites, hoping to be discovered: Lily Allen (b. 1985) and Sean Kingston (b. 1990) had popular MySpace pages before being signed to major labels; Justin Bieber (b. 1994) rocketed to worldwide fame after a talent manager saw him singing in videos his mother posted to YouTube; and Shawn Mendes (b. 1998) first gained a following on the video-sharing application Vine, was signed by a manager and label at age fifteen, and by the age of twenty had released three albums, which all debuted at number one on the *Billboard* charts. Both industry-produced content and self-created music are available side by side on YouTube and other sites, creating a freewheeling marketplace where anything can happen.

It is still true that the greatest financial rewards for musicians in popular or classical traditions come through established institutions of recording companies and concert management, and working musicians are often unable to earn a living through online sales and royalties. But making the means of production widely available has decentralized the music industry and has opened new paths to success.

One such path is crowdsourcing. Using online platforms such as Kick- *The new patronage* starter or Patreon, a number of popular and classical artists have asked fans to invest financially in their forthcoming projects in turn for a certain stake, ranging from a single audio file for a 99-cent donation to backstage passes and face time with the artist for a five-hundred-dollar donation. Jazz composer Maria Schneider (b. 1960) was one of the first musicians to use ArtistShare to fund an entire album, her *Concert in the Garden* (2004), which won a Grammy Award the following year. Not unlike the way Prince Lobkowitz, Prince Kinsky, and Archduke Rudolph gave Beethoven a stipend to prevent him from leaving Vienna and were rewarded by dedications on his future compositions (see Chapter 24), artists achieve greater security through crowdsourcing and repay their financial indebtedness with creative contributions and new works of art. Through such distributed financing, patronage—the mainstay of musicians from the Middle Ages through the nineteenth century—has returned in a new guise.

TRENDS IN POPULAR MUSIC In response to all these changes, all corners of the music industry have been forced to reinvent themselves. In popular music, with the decline in CD sales, there is a renewed focus on live performances. People born since the 1980s, accustomed to the Internet and streaming services, tend to value having experiences more than owning things; for many, sharing a concert or music festival with friends, in person or through social media like Facebook, Instagram, or Snapchat, is more rewarding than assembling a collection of recordings. Major artists can demand very high ticket prices in large venues and make more from a concert tour than from an entire year's royalties on CDs, downloads, or streaming, and other performers can also make a living by touring. The interest in hearing music live has fostered a growing number of annual music festivals such as South by Southwest (Austin, Texas), Donauinselfest (Vienna), Rock in Rio (Brazil), Lollapalooza (international), Przystanek Woodstock (Poland), Fuji Rock Festival (Japan), Coachella (California), and Bonnaroo (Tennessee), each attracting a range of artists and over a hundred thousand attendees, as well as festivals focused on individual traditions, from the Bill Monroe Bean Blossom Music Festival (Indiana) for bluegrass to Electric Zoo (New York) for all types of electronic music. Television shows like *American Idol* and *The X Factor* promote new interest through elaborate competitions that allow amateurs to aspire to stardom like that achieved by contestants Kelly Clarkson (b. 1982) and the boy band One Direction. Even many record stores emphasize experience over acquisition, with booths for listening, coffee shops, and live performances. The focus on concerts, festivals, and competitions marks a reversal from the previous four decades, and a return to conditions before record sales took off in the mid-1960s and became the most lucrative part of the music business.

The splintering of the pop music audience has continued, encouraged by *The splintering pop* easy access to many different kinds of music. Every niche repertoire has its *music audience* own websites and YouTube channels, as musicians and fans create an online

Music Technology for Everyone

In the first decades of the twenty-first century, the constantly improving capabilities of personal computers have had a profound impact on the creation and consumption of music. As was true for several innovations in earlier times, such as notation and the printing press (see Chapters 6 and 7), or sound recording and the wax cylinder (see Chapter 31), the technologies powering changes today combine a new means of capturing music—digital audio files—with a new method of distribution—broadband Internet. The result is virtually limitless access to music for listeners, and unprecedented access to audiences for musicians.

The first audio format to combine fidelity with small file size—the MP3—appeared in 1995 after a decade of development, and more-sophisticated formats soon followed. Wired and wireless networks date back to the 1980s, but widespread access to high-speed data transfers is comparatively recent. Although neither the digital audio file nor the Internet is new in the twenty-first century, their combination has been potent. And with the growth of social media and streaming music services, a new musical landscape has emerged.

Smartphones and tablets connected to enormous music libraries have become the default method of consumption for most listeners. As the listening experience has centered on these devices, it has become both more portable and more personal. Thousands of radio stations from around the world are available online, while streaming

FIGURE 39.2 *Screenshot of Philip Glass's opera* Akhnaten, *as performed at the Indiana University Opera Theater and streamed live over the Internet.*

services such as Pandora (launched in 2000), Spotify (2008), Tidal (2014), and Apple Music (2015) allow people to listen to music they do not own. Someone with a smartphone and a wireless connection has access to—as Ben Ratliff summed it up in the title of his 2016 book—*Every Song Ever.* The earlier technologies of music printing and recording transformed music from a service offered by live musicians to a commodity that could be sold; the new technology of streaming is turning it back into a service, now provided on a mass scale.

One of the most significant aspects of this change is how it takes the job of curating music out of the hands of disc jockeys, record labels, and other tastemakers and gives it to the individual listener and the service provider. With so much music to choose from—Spotify alone has more than 35 million tracks—listeners now often rely on computer algorithms to help sift through all the possibilities, granting these corporations and algorithms the power to guide individuals' taste and choices. Many streaming music services enlist Echo Nest (founded 2005), a "music intelligence community" that continually identifies musical microgenres, presenting users with new music that matches their prior listening preferences with a remarkable degree of precision. Rather than recommending a complete album—the traditional method of distributing both classical and popular music since the mid-twentieth century—these algorithms assemble playlists of songs recorded by different musicians but with similar musical characteristics. And although Apple Music and Tidal briefly experimented with securing exclusive rights to albums like Taylor Swift's *1989* (2014) and Beyoncé's visual album *Lemonade* (2016), the industry has moved toward a one-stop-shopping model, where streaming services generally have the same catalogue, and listeners decide which service they want to use.

Much as streaming services have given listeners greater autonomy, musicians can now bypass traditional gatekeepers like record labels and producers to create, record, and distribute their work. In the past, musicians had to buy their digital instruments, audio processors, and recording equipment separately as pieces of hardware, but software equivalents now exist that are as good as or better than their predecessors. Digital audio workstations (DAWs), originally hardware devices created in the late 1970s as an alternative to recording, mixing, and editing with tape, are now available as software like Pro Tools (released in 1989),

Logic Pro (1993), Audacity (2000), and GarageBand (2004). Today, a musician with a computer and a microphone can produce a recording that rivals the quality of a professional studio.

To find an audience for their work, musicians and bands rely on the Internet and social media. Since its launch in 2005, YouTube has become the primary online resource for audiovisual material, including music. Videos of performances from opera companies to local bands can be viewed online, whether on YouTube, Vevo, or other sites, or streaming on their own websites as in Figure 39.2. Professionals and amateurs alike can upload their music for the world to hear. Social networking tools such as Facebook, Instagram, and Twitter offer opportunities for musicians to promote their work at little to no cost.

Audio platforms such as ReverbNation (established 2006), SoundCloud (2007), and Bandcamp (2008) let musicians distribute their music and communicate directly with fans, promoters, festivals, and record labels. These sites also allow users to collaborate with other musicians they have never met. A singer can purchase an instrumental track from a producer and add her own lyrics, or post a voice track in pursuit of a producer to create an accompaniment for it. All of these developments give musicians a greater amount of independence, making it easier for them to win an audience, and potentially earn a living, without management or a record contract.

With production and marketing capabilities in the hands of artists themselves, major labels have less control over the marketplace. Musical acts that once relied on live tours to promote their records now use their recordings to promote their live tours. Classical music institutions like the Metropolitan Opera stream high-definition performances into movie theaters to expand their audience and find new sources of revenue.

Collectively, these changes in the way we listen to, record, distribute, and profit from music have profoundly reshaped the landscape for audiences and musicians in this new century. Tools that once were expensive and restricted to recording studios and record companies are now available to individual musicians, both professional and amateur. In the nineteenth century, millions of amateurs played the piano or sang for their friends and family or for their own pleasure. Today, millions can use digital software to create music for their own enjoyment and share it with the entire world.

community for themselves. Hip hop, once a niche market, has taken center stage, as rappers like Snoop Dogg, Eminem, Jay-Z (b. 1969), and Kanye West (b. 1977) have become household names, and Kendrick Lamar (b. 1987) won the 2018 Pulitzer Prize for his album *DAMN.*, the first time the Pulitzer was awarded for hip hop or any kind of popular music. Pop artists like Beyoncé (b. 1981), who gained fame as the lead singer of the female rhythm and blues group Destiny's Child before striking out on her own, mix a wide variety of styles in their music, blending funk, soul, and hip hop with pop. Rock music is no longer at the center of popular music as it was in the 1960s, but it endures in the realm of indie rock; in tours of older bands like the Rolling Stones; in local cover bands who play a variety of classic songs; and in tribute bands who play live shows that re-create performances by famous groups, such as Rain (for the Beatles) and Led Zepagain (for Led Zeppelin). Some radio stations maintain a focus on mainstream pop, but golden oldies and mixed formats have proliferated, including mixtures of current and older music on both pop and country stations. Hits from the 1960s through the 1990s have sold well alongside newer songs. Some artists have recorded remakes of vintage songs or have included long samples from older records as parts of new songs, creating a kind of collaboration between generations that was pioneered by Natalie Cole (1950–2015) in her 1991 recording of *Unforgettable* as a duet with her father Nat King Cole (1919–1965), combining her voice with his recording from 1952.

Retrospective styles   The growing presence of older music is not the only retrospective trend. Hip hop has continued to draw on sampled music from earlier decades, enlarging its reach to include jazz and earlier hip-hop recordings themselves. And paralleling the references to the past we have seen in modern classical music, pop musicians have revived and renewed sounds from the 1960s through the 1980s. Among the first revival movements was *neo soul,* combining 1960s soul and R&B with jazz, funk, hip hop, and African influences and exemplified in D'Angelo albums *Brown Sugar* (1995) and *Voodoo* (2000); Erykah Badu's *Baduizm* (1997); and Lauryn Hill's *The Miseducation of Lauryn Hill* (1998), which won five Grammy Awards. The *disco revival* movement joins the dance beat and vocals of disco with the new sounds of records produced after 2000, as in Madonna's single *Hung Up* (2005), based on a sample from the 1980s group ABBA, and Lady Gaga's first hit, *Just Dance* (2008). The harder styles of the 1970s were also resurrected in the *post-punk revival* or *garage rock revival,* exemplified by the White Stripes' *White Blood Cells* (2001) and the Strokes' *This Is It* (2001), which drew on blues, new wave, and grunge.

MASHUPS Another form of recycling is the **mashup** (also called *bootleg*), created by combining elements of two or more recordings, such as the vocal line from one song with the instrumental track of another. The idea goes back to the *quodlibet,* a Renaissance and Baroque genre based on combining borrowed melodies in counterpoint, and to the 1989 album *Plunderphonic* by Canadian composer John Oswald (b. 1953), in which he created each track by manipulating existing recordings in various ways, from overdubbing an Elvis Presley recording with other samples to cutting up Michael Jackson's song *Bad* into brief segments and reordering them. Since the material mashups use is copyrighted, most are distributed online for free, avoiding the legal liability a commercial release would entail. New software tools such as Ableton Live, introduced in 2001, made it possible to isolate certain layers from recorded music and automatically synchronize samples to match tempo and pitch. Such tools allowed users with relatively little training, working on a laptop or desktop computer, to overlay elements from different songs in much less time or expense than was possible using previous techniques such as tape splicing or professional studio mixing. The result was an explosion of mashups such as *A Stroke of Genie-Us* (2001) by Freelance Hellraiser, which layers pop star Christina Aguilera's voice on *Genie in a Bottle* over the loud guitars from *Hard to Explain* by the neo-garage rock band the Strokes, and 2ManyDJs' *Smells Like Teen Booty* (2002), which combines the angst-ridden guitar, bass, and drums of grunge band Nirvana's *Smells Like Teen Spirit* (see Chapter 38) with the bubble-gum pop vocal line of Destiny's Child's *Bootylicious.* Mashups like these often aim to undermine the seriousness of either or both source tracks, by interchanging the components of either, and to erase the lines between high and low popular music, treating songs by revered artists with the same lack of respect as the music of artists perceived to be more frivolous.

Over time, many mashup producers moved beyond simply matching vocal and instrumental lines from different songs to a more complicated process of combining many small fragments from a variety of different songs. A notable example is the *United State of Pop* series that DJ Earworm has created every year since 2007, comprising a mashup of the music and videos for the top twenty-five songs on the *Billboard* chart for that year.

Perhaps the most ambitious mashup is *The Grey Album* (2004) by DJ Danger Mouse, which blended the a cappella version of rapper Jay-Z's 2003 *The Black Album* with the Beatles' 1968 album known as *The White Album* (because its cover was all white with no text but the band's name). Danger Mouse extracted hundreds of sonic fragments from the Beatles' songs and wove together a new accompaniment for Jay-Z's lyrics from tiny slivers of sound from guitars, clapping, voices, drums, and even harpsichord. Despite (and perhaps because of) threats of lawsuits from the owners of the Beatles' copyrights, *The Grey Album* has been downloaded over one million times. It has become a prime example for those who argue that intellectual property laws are outdated and inhibit creation of new music. In response, those who support copyright laws argue that they protect the original artists from having their music used in ways they do not approve, and that without adequate copyright protection artists would lose control of their work—and any right to profit by it—as soon as it was released. It is a debate that is typical of our age, as the ideal that information should be widely available for free on the Internet collides with the truth that those who create that information, or that music, are giving away something of value without getting paid.

The Grey Album

FUSIONS The trend toward blurring and dissolving lines between musical traditions in the 1980s and 1990s (see Chapter 38) gathered momentum after the turn of the century. More and more organizations, festivals, and venues encourage mixing of artists and audiences by programming a diversity of music. For example, Le Poisson Rouge, a multimedia art cabaret in New York that opened in 2008 (motto: "serving art and alcohol"), presents groups playing contemporary jazz, folk music, indie rock, classical music, hip hop, electronica, Broadway, and other types of music, or free mixtures of several types. The shows change daily and provide a wide range of music, and the audience is equally eclectic in their tastes, filled with young people who take in Webern, Messiaen, Boulez, and Ligeti as music of interest in the same way they listen to avant-garde rock or electronica. Traditional venues have also broadened their offerings. Many orchestras are showing movies with live performances of the film score and are exploring ways to incorporate music from other traditions. The Seattle Symphony's Sonic Evolution series was launched in 2011 with a tribute to Nirvana's Kurt Cobain, a Seattle native, and has included collaborations like the symphony's 2014 performance with rapper Sir Mix-A-Lot (b. 1963) of his *Baby Got Back*, captured on a video that has been viewed more than 5.5 million times on YouTube.

Beyond category   Duke Ellington saw his own music as "beyond category" (see Chapter 34), and increasingly that is true of a wide range of today's musicians. Composers like Edgar Meyer (b. 1960), Christian Fennesz (b. 1962), Nico Muhly (b. 1981), and Ty Braxton (b. 1978) easily blend classical and popular traditions in music that defies categorization. Pop star Tori Amos (b. 1963), who is classically trained, is now composing for the classical label Deutsche Grammophon, beginning with *Night of Hunters* (2011), a song cycle with chamber music accompaniment that is also a set of variations on a theme. Pop groups like Radiohead create music that attracts the attention of classical musicians and critics. With indie rock and electronic pop music, popular music has its own avant-garde and modernist trends; the intricacy of the music interests a diverse range of listeners and musicians, further blurring the lines between new art music and these pop styles. Many individual artists mix materials and influences in innovative ways. Janelle Monáe (b. 1985) blends funk, rhythm and blues, and hip hop with science fiction themes and film scoring in her albums *Metropolis* (2007, based on the 1927 German expressionist science fiction film *Metropolis*), *The ArchAndroid* (2010), and *Dirty Computer* (2018). Jazz pianist and composer Uri Caine (b. 1956) has collaborated with klezmer, funk, and hip-hop artists, and his reworkings of Mahler's Fifth Symphony (1998), Bach's *Goldberg Variations* (2000), Beethoven's *Diabelli Variations* (2002), Verdi's *Otello* (2008), and Vivaldi's *The Four Seasons* (2011) are not mere transcriptions but are fundamentally reimagined as up-to-date idiomatic works of fusion. Jason Moran (b. 1975) is a jazz pianist whose music combines the influences of Thelonius Monk and avant-garde jazz with modern popular sounds, sampling, and hip hop, mixing old and new in an appealing new fusion. Singer and bassist Esperanza Spalding (b. 1984) and pianist Robert Glasper (b. 1978) are also jazz artists who not only incorporate elements of hip hop but work with hip-hop artists including Q-Tip (b. 1970) and Kanye West to explore new avenues. Such collaborations inspire a high level of artistry and allow the music to reach a wider audience, including fans of all the musicians involved. These fusions of popular music, jazz, and contemporary art music can be seen equally as enriching each of these traditions and breaking down barriers between them, especially for younger listeners.

Fusions on Broadway   Musicals have been absorbing other styles for decades, from ragtime and African American spirituals in *Show Boat* (1928; see Chapter 34) to cool jazz and bebop in *West Side Story* (1957), Jewish music in *Fiddler on the Roof* (1964), and rock and Motown in *Hair* (1967; see Chapter 36). The trend shows no

FIGURE 39.3 *A scene from* Hamilton *on Broadway in 2015, with Lin-Manuel Miranda, left, as Alexander Hamilton and Leslie Odom Jr. as Aaron Burr.*

signs of stopping, as recent musicals infused with opera, world music, and popular styles have scored successes on Broadway, in London's West End, and on tour. *The Light in the Piazza* (2005) by Adam Guettel (b. 1965), grandson of Richard Rodgers, features the sound and feel of opera, with a lush score marked by neo-Romanticism, extended operatic melodies, and a classical orchestra. *Mamma Mia!* (1999) wove a new plot, about a young woman trying to discover which of her mother's lovers from twenty years ago is her biological father, around the two-decade-old dance and disco hits of the Swedish pop group ABBA by Benny Andersson and Björn Ulvaeus. *Fela!* (2008–9) brought world beat to Broadway through the music and life of Nigerian singer and composer Fela Kuti (see Chapter 38). *The Band's Visit* (2016–17), winner of ten Tony Awards including Best Musical, depicts an Egyptian band stuck overnight in an Israeli town where they traveled by mistake, and the songs and music by David Yazbek (b. 1961) invoke the sounds of Egyptian popular music, including the legendary singer Umm Kulthum (ca. 1904–1975). The biggest hit musical of the early twenty-first century is *Hamilton* (2015) by Lin-Manuel Miranda (b. 1980), which won the Pulitzer Prize for Drama as well as eleven Tony Awards. Based on the life of Alexander Hamilton, the first American secretary of the treasury, the musical inverts racial and cultural hierarchies by casting Hispanic and African American actors as the founding fathers, as shown in Figure 39.3, and adopting hip hop as its primary musical style, blending in others from rhythm and blues to Broadway-style show tunes. In each of these musicals, the characters are brought to life and the message is conveyed in large part through musical styles that carry deep and significant cultural associations.

CLASSICAL MUSIC: DYING OR VIBRANT? We have seen that the new technologies for producing, distributing, and consuming music are making all kinds of music more accessible than ever; that many artists are forging fusions between traditions, including classical music as well as pop, jazz, and hip hop;

and that some are creating music that challenges these very divisions between categories. Given these trends, how are performance and composition in the classical tradition itself faring in the new millennium?

A dying tradition?   In the early twenty-first century, a flurry of newspaper articles and blogs in the United States argued that classical music was in a critical situation and in danger of dying out. The number of radio stations playing classical music is dwindling, as is the proportion of younger listeners and concertgoers; the recording industry is being supplanted by digital downloads, streaming, and self-recording, which can affect musicians' income; and several major orchestras have experienced financial hardships. The League of American Orchestras reported a steep drop in the number of professional orchestras and performances in the United States in the aftermath of the Great Recession, from more than 300 professional orchestras and nearly 4,750 concerts in the 2007–8 season to fewer than 150 professional orchestras performing just under 2,000 concerts in the 2009–10 season.

A golden age?   But others have argued in response that we live at the best time for classical music (see Source Reading). More classical music is available, and more people listen to it worldwide, than ever before. Familiar classics pop up in commercials, video games, and movies, like the appearance of Verdi's *Requiem* in *Mad Max: Fury Road* (2015). Publishers and recording companies are issuing reams of music by composers who were little known until recently (NAWM includes several examples), as well as previously neglected works by well-known composers. Every medium from concerts to recordings to YouTube videos is more accessible than ever. The level of performance has never been higher. And we have access to the entire range of music from the past, often in outstanding performances informed by new understandings of how that music was originally performed—or, conversely, taking a new and individual approach.

There is truth in both perspectives. The crisis in professional orchestras is fostering a generation of musical entrepreneurs who are discovering new ways to make a living, suggesting that what we are witnessing is not the death of classical music but a process of deinstitutionalizing, democratizing, and decentering classical music that is creating a new musical culture, just as the invention of opera and the emergence of star singers did in the early seventeenth century (see Chapters 14–15), and the decline of patronage and the rise of the musical marketplace did in the early nineteenth century (see Chapter 25). Listeners eager to explore music from chant to a piece premiering this evening have more available to them than ever, and performers and composers can use the new media to get their music out to the entire world. But when the Internet offers so much for free, getting paid for making music can be a challenge. And unless people are introduced to a type of music by their families, in school, by friends, or by others around them, they may never care about it or even know it exists. The same media that allow us to find and listen to any music from anywhere in the world also provide so much of each type of music that we can focus on a single kind, disappear down a rabbit hole, and never come out.

Responses   Many institutions are meeting these challenges with innovative programming and marketing. Orchestras and chamber groups sponsor education and outreach programs, give concerts for targeted audiences from teens to

A Golden Age for Classical Music?

In response to opinion pieces in *The New York Times* and elsewhere claiming that classical music is dying, political commentator Heather Mac Donald suggests it is thriving.

✣

In many respects, we live in a golden age of classical music. Such an observation defies received wisdom, which seizes on every symphony budget deficit to herald classical music's imminent demise. But this declinist perspective ignores the more significant reality of our time: never before has so much great music been available to so many people, performed at levels of artistry that would have astounded Berlioz and his peers. Students flock to conservatories and graduate with skills once possessed only by a few virtuosi. More people listen to classical music today, and more money gets spent on producing and disseminating it, than ever before. . . .

The declinists who proclaim the death of classical music might have a case if musical standards were falling. But in fact, "the professional standards are higher everywhere in the world compared to 20 or 40 years ago," says James Conlon, conductor of the Los Angeles Opera. . . .

The radical transformation of how people consume classical music [due to recordings] puts the current hand-wringing over an inattentive, shrinking audience in a different perspective. Beethoven's *Eroica* Symphony premiered before an audience of 100 at most. These days, probably 10,000 people are listening to it during any given 24-hour period, either live or on record, estimates critic Harvey Sachs. Recordings have expanded the availability of music in astounding ways. . . .

Recordings have also, it is true, taken a toll on the communal, participatory aspect of music-making. But the explosion of classical music on the Internet has revived some of that communal element. The ever-expanding offerings of performances on YouTube, uploaded simply out of love, demonstrate the passion that unites classical-music listeners. A listener can compare 15 different interpretations of "Là ci darem la mano" [from Mozart's opera *Don Giovanni*] at the click of a mouse, all—amazingly—for free. Organized websites, such as the live classical-concert site InstantEncore.com, are creating new ways of disseminating music that will undoubtedly reach new audiences. Even with recording technology's impetus for passive, private listening, the percentage of amateur musicians studying classical music has risen 30 percent over the last six years, from an admittedly small 1.8 percent to 3 percent. Many of those nonprofessional musicians, as well as their children, are uploading their own performances onto the Web.

Contrary to the standard dirge, the classical recording industry is still shooting out more music than anyone can possibly take in over a lifetime. Has the pace of Beethoven symphony cycles slowed down? We'll survive. In the course of one month arrive arias by Nicola Porpora, an opera by Federico Ricci, a symphony by Ildebrando Pizzetti—three composers previously known only to musicologists—Cherubini's *Chant sur la Mort de Joseph Haydn*, and Haydn's *The Storm*. This cornucopia of previously lost works is more than any of us has a right to hope for.

The much-publicized financial difficulties of many orchestras during the current recession also need to be put into historical perspective. More people are making a living playing an instrument than ever before, and doing so as respected and well-paid professionals, not lowly drones.

From Heather Mac Donald, "Classical Music's New Golden Age," *City Journal* 20 (Summer 2010).

toddlers, offer pre-concert lectures and post-concert discussions, collaborate with pop and multimedia artists, and find other ways to engage audiences and cultivate fans. The BBC Proms and other music festivals attract large audiences in person, on television and radio, and through podcasts and streaming. The Metropolitan Opera in New York reaches thousands of viewers through live high-definition broadcasts in movie theaters, and universities stream their own concerts and opera productions on the Internet. Conservatories and schools of music are adding courses in music business, entrepreneurship, and technology to enable their students to create careers for themselves. All these types of institutions have programs in public schools to encourage engagement with classical music and broaden their audience.

Meanwhile, outside the United States classical music remains vibrant. In Europe, the old traditions of home music-making have endured, more than in the United States. In Latin America, classical music is being used as a way to engage young people from disadvantaged backgrounds, developing their self-discipline through training in performance and thereby improving their educational and economic prospects, as in the Venezuelan initiative El Sistema. The number of Asians pursuing training and careers in Western music continues to grow, from international stars like pianist Lang Lang to the Afghan Youth Orchestra, the rising prominence of Asian students in conservatories around the world, and the fifty million children studying Western classical music in China, who will also be avid listeners for the rest of their lives. All told, it seems that the classical tradition has a lot of life left in it.

MUSIC IN CLASSICAL GENRES That vibrancy is reflected in the continuing output of new music, in a bewildering variety of styles. Composers who work in the classical tradition in our century have an unprecedented range of choices before them. Most of the approaches discussed in Chapter 38, from serialism to simplification to hybrids with popular or non-Western music, are still current. Many composers continue the modernist tradition, others adopt an avant-garde or experimentalist stance, and still others abandon old orthodoxies to focus on direct engagement with listeners in the present, whether that be a small circle of connoisseurs or a wider public. Really, anything is possible.

Within this great variety, we will examine a few pieces that share one overarching characteristic: they extend one or more of the late-twentieth-century trends we examined in Chapters 37 and 38, while also directly evoking music of the more distant past. We make no claim that such pieces are representative of all contemporary music in the classical tradition. But their combination of retrospection with an up-to-date approach echoes what we saw throughout the twentieth century, when composers sought to create music that could find a place in the permanent repertoire next to the classics of the past while saying something new and individual. Such pieces also seem characteristic of our time, paralleling the fusions, mashups, hybrids, and blends in popular music and jazz with a similar spirit of combining very different musics. And in reflecting on music of the past, from the Middle Ages to the twentieth century, these works provide an apt conclusion to our survey of the entire Western tradition.

Kaija Saariaho,
L'amour de loin

Kaija Saariaho (b. 1952), shown in Figure 39.4, studied composition in her native Finland, then in 1982 moved to Paris to work at IRCAM. There she was deeply influenced by spectral music composers Gérard Grisey and Tristan Murail (see Chapter 38). She made her reputation in the 1980s and 1990s with works in the spectralist tradition that focused on timbre, deriving harmonies from computer analysis of instrumental sounds and combining live electronics with acoustic instruments, as in *Lichtbogen* (1985–86) and *Nymphea* (1987, written for the Kronos Quartet).

In her opera *L'amour de loin* (2000), Saariaho applied her spectralist-influenced musical style to the story of twelfth-century troubadour Jaufré Rudel (fl. 1120–1147), who sang of an idealized love from afar. In the last tableau of Act IV (NAWM 224), Jaufré is at sea on his way to meet his beloved, of whom he has only heard descriptions. During a storm, he is overtaken by regret for making the voyage instead of keeping his love at a distance and therefore pure. The melodic material is thoroughly modernist, using cells based on arrays of semitones and tritones within perfect fifths. But the form of Jaufré's lament, alternating variants of three phrases of melody in a distinctive pattern, evokes the patterns of repeating phrases found in troubadour songs, and the melodic style of short phrases focused around certain pitches has similarities to troubadour melodies (see Chapter 4 and NAWM 8 and 9). The melodies in the dialogue that precedes the lament, as well as the storm music and other orchestral material, are derived from melodic cells in Jaufré's lament, drawing together the troubadour-shaped melody and spectralist-flavored orchestral harmonies in a unique fusion of twelfth- and twentieth-century ideas.

FIGURE 39.4 *Kaija Saariaho.*

Caroline Shaw (b. 1982), shown in Figure 39.5, became the youngest person to win the Pulitzer Prize for Music in 2013 for her *Partita for 8 Voices* (2009–11). A performing violinist and singer from North Carolina who lives in New York, Shaw sings in and wrote the piece for Roomful of Teeth, an a cappella group that cultivates a wide range of vocal sounds and draws on singing traditions from around the world.

Partita continues the twentieth-century trends of exploring new sounds and techniques; incorporating aspects of non-Western music, here elements of singing styles from Korea in east Asia, Tuva in the Siberian steppes, Georgia in the Caucasus, and the Inuit peoples in Greenland, Canada, and Alaska; and evoking the past of Western music, with sections that echo the sounds and styles of Gregorian chant, imitative polyphony, William Billings, and shape-note singing, among others. The title recalls the partitas of J. S. Bach, which were suites of dances, and each movement is named for a Baroque dance or instrumental genre: Allemande, Sarabande, Courante, and Passacaglia. The Allemande (NAWM 225) is in $\frac{4}{4}$ meter and begins with an upbeat motive, constant motion, and contrapuntal texture, all typical of Baroque allemandes, but with unpitched recitation of texts that include the American square dance call "allemande left," weaving together the

FIGURE 39.5 *Caroline Shaw.*

dance traditions of two continents and four centuries. The movement is in five sections, each less dancelike and more songlike than the previous one, until the final section blossoms into unmeasured, chantlike melodies in unison and in imitation over resonant major triads, culminating a magical journey from dance to song. The piece is a compelling fusion of Baroque, medieval, American, and non-Western elements with the modern classical tradition.

Jeremy Sams, The Enchanted Island

A literal mashup in a classical genre is *The Enchanted Island,* which premiered in December 2011 at the Metropolitan Opera in New York. Composer and librettist Jeremy Sams (b. 1957) devised a plot that brings together characters from two Shakespeare plays, as the pairs of lovers from *A Midsummer Night's Dream* are shipwrecked on Prospero's island from *The Tempest.* Sams drew the music from Baroque composers: the arias mostly from Handel's operas, oratorios, and cantatas and from vocal works of Vivaldi, and choruses and descriptive instrumental interludes from Rameau, Leclair, and other French composers. In one sense, the work is a pastiche opera, a common type of the Baroque era, when it was often easier and more profitable to assemble a new opera from existing music than to hire a composer to write one from scratch. But in another sense, *The Enchanted Island* is a work of quotation and collage, fully at home in the postwar tradition of such works (see Chapter 37), and it calls into question ideas of authorship and originality, making it a thoroughly postmodern work. Yet it is also utterly enjoyable as entertainment, combining lovely music with a fun comedic plot that has serious philosophical overtones. The appeal to spectacle in the staging and costumes is also typical of Baroque opera, yet no less typical of modern opera houses, pop concerts, music videos, and movies.

Osvaldo Golijov, St. Mark Passion

Osvaldo Golijov (b. 1960) grew up in Argentina in a Jewish immigrant family hearing classical music, Piazzolla's nuevo tango, synagogue music, and klezmer, and has drawn on all of them in his music. After studying with George Crumb, he has made his career in the United States. Among his best-known works is his Grammy Award–winning opera *Ainadamar: Fountain of Tears* (2005), on the 1936 murder of Spanish poet Federico García Lorca by the fascists. The spellbinding score combines computer music, musique concrète, and modernist dissonance with elements from Spanish flamenco music, Cuban rhythms, and Latin American popular music. Such blending of classical, modern, and popular traditions is a vital trend in music of the last fifty years, as is the pointed juxtaposition of contrasting styles within a single piece (see Chapter 38), and both are typical of Golijov.

A similar fusion and polystylism is found in Golijov's *La Pasión según San Marcos* (The Passion according to St. Mark), composed for the Passion 2000 project, through which the International Bach Academy in Stuttgart commemorated the 250th anniversary of the death of Johann Sebastian Bach by commissioning settings of the Passion by four composers from around the world: Golijov from the Americas, Sofia Gubaidulina from Russia, Tan Dun from China, and Wolfgang Rihm (b. 1952) from Bach's native Germany. As a Latin American and a Jew, Golijov offers an outsider's take on the Passion story, drawing on African-influenced traditions from Cuba and Brazil to create a piece that enacts the story as a kind of ritual through voices, dance, and theatrical movement, as shown in Figure 39.6, rather than simply narrating it. In the passage when Jesus is taken and tried, and Peter denies knowing

HIROYUKI ITO/THE NEW YORK TIMES/REDUX

FIGURE 39.6 *Scene from* La Pasión según San Marcos *by Osvaldo Golijov as performed by singers and instrumentalists from Venezuela and New York at Carnegie Hall on March 10, 2013.*

him (NAWM 226), Golijov omits the narration that Bach gave to the Evangelist in his *St. Matthew Passion* (compare the parallel section in NAWM 106) and has the chorus play all the roles, distilling the events into the words and feelings of the people involved. The varied timbres of Latin American percussion instruments, each playing a distinctive rhythm, lay down a complex bed of sound. As in Bach's *St. Matthew Passion,* Peter's remorse at betraying his friend is captured in a lyrical, beautifully embellished aria in dialogue with a solo violin, evoking at once the sounds of Bach and other early music and the vocal styles of flamenco and folk song.

British composer Thomas Adès (b. 1971) was born in London, trained at the Guildhall School and Cambridge University, became Britten Professor of Composition at the Royal Academy of Music, and in 1999–2009 served as artistic director of the Aldeburgh Festival of Music and the Arts, founded by Benjamin Britten and Peter Pears. He also performs as a pianist and conductor, often conducting his own works, as in Figure 39.7. Best known for his operas, orchestral works, and chamber music, Adès shares in some respects the broad approach of Britten, joining modernist techniques with an ability to appeal to a wide audience.

Thomas Adès, Violin Concerto

Adès's Violin Concerto, subtitled *Concentric Paths* (2005), combines the Romantic virtuoso tradition with the new virtuosity and the interest in texture and process of the late twentieth century. The first movement, *Rings* (NAWM 227), shares the perpetual motion of Ligeti's Étude No. 9, *Vertige* (NAWM 220), another tribute to Romantic virtuoso music, and is structured around a cycle of fifths (G–D, B–F♯, E♭–B♭) whose roots are related by major thirds, echoing in a post-tonal context the circles of keys a major third apart in pieces like Liszt's étude *Un sospiro* (NAWM 140) and Schubert's String Quintet (NAWM 144). There are Baroque resonances as well: for much of the movement, the harmony gradually sinks as each note in the chord takes a turn moving down a half step, like a chain of suspensions and resolutions in a Corelli sonata (see

FIGURE 39.7

Thomas Adès conducting a rehearsal of his opera The Tempest *at the Royal Opera House in 2004.*

CLIVE BARDA/ARENAPAL © ARENAPAL/TOPHAM/THE IMAGES WORKS

NAWM 96), reflected in continuous sixteenth-note arpeggiated figuration as in Bach's organ prelude in A minor (NAWM 102a).

John Adams, Doctor Atomic

John Adams began as a composer in the minimalist tradition, then synthesized it with other styles (see Chapter 38) and engaged the twenty-first-century trend of fusions and hybrids. He has continued to embrace a wide range of topics in his recent music, from celebrating Jesus's Nativity in the oratorio *El Niño* (1999–2000), to mourning the deaths in the 2001 terrorist attack on the World Trade Center in *On the Transmigration of Souls* (2002), to his opera *Doctor Atomic* (2005), about the pressures on Robert Oppenheimer and other scientists as they prepared for the first test of the atomic bomb in the summer of 1945. Oppenheimer's aria *Batter my heart* (NAWM 228) exemplifies the blending of postminimalist techniques, which dominate the orchestral interludes, with the singer's slowly unfolding, expressive vocal line, whose tonality, arching shapes, and emotive power recall nineteenth-century opera arias by Verdi and others. Adams is able to fuse two such different styles as minimalism and Romantic opera by finding the points of contact between them, including sectional forms, tonal melodies, slow-moving harmonies animated by repeating figuration, and strong contrasts in sound, tempo, dynamic level, and other parameters that can convey powerful emotions.

Jennifer Higdon, blue cathedral

Finally, Jennifer Higdon's *blue cathedral* (2000) exemplifies accessible modernism, one of the trends we observed in Chapter 38, while reaching back to the trademark procedures of one of the first and most beloved modernists, Debussy. Higdon (b. 1962), shown in Figure 39.8, grew up listening to popular music and bluegrass, taught herself to play the flute at fifteen, then discovered classical music in college at Bowling Green State University. After studying at the Curtis Institute in Philadelphia and with George Crumb at the University of Pennsylvania, she returned to Curtis to teach. The 2002 premiere of her Concerto for Orchestra by the Philadelphia Orchestra put her on the map as a composer, followed by the 2010 Pulitzer Prize for her Violin Concerto and a Grammy Award for her Percussion Concerto.

Her *blue cathedral* (NAWM 229), a one-movement orchestral tone poem, has been performed hundreds of times, ranking among the most widely performed orchestra works composed in the last twenty-five years. In the words of her program note, the piece represents a "journey through a glass cathedral in the sky." Higdon wrote the piece in memory of her brother, and the piece features the flute, her instrument, and the clarinet, his instrument, as they dance in dialogue in their upper registers, later joined by solo violin and other instruments. Undergirding the soloists are effects that are typical of Debussy. The strings and brass play triads in parallel motion, as in *Nuages* (NAWM 172) and other works, and changes of pitch collection, in this case different transpositions of the diatonic scale, demarcate phrases or smaller musical units and provide a sense of harmonic motion as in Debussy's music (compare Example 32.2). Although there are no tonal progressions, the triads and diatonic fields are familiar, and together with coloristic orchestration inspired by Debussy they create a sheer beauty of sound that is part of the piece's wide appeal.

FIGURE 39.8
Jennifer Higdon.

These seven pieces are too few to be fully representative of the very diverse music being created in classical genres in our century. But each represents a vital current among today's composers, including spectralism, new sound resources, hybridization, quotation, polystylism, the new virtuosity, focus on texture and process, and minimalism, and together they illustrate the range of modernism from astringent dissonance to accessible diatonicism. Each also evokes significant music of the past, from the twelfth to the early twentieth centuries. Like other fusions, mashups, and blends within and between traditions, these pieces recycle old material into new forms and link familiar sounds, structures, and ideas to create new combinations. That, if anything, may be what is most characteristic of the music of our age.

THE FUTURE OF WESTERN MUSIC

The popularity of fusions, mashups, mixtures, and blends in recent years is only the latest manifestation of a long-standing trait in the Western tradition: combining multiple influences to create something new. Ancient Greek writers said that different harmoniae or modes came from different regions, but together they made up the Greek system (see Chapter 1). Gregorian chant, the liturgical chant of the Western church, had roots in Jewish and Byzantine practice and combined elements from local chant traditions like Roman and Gallican (Chapters 2–3). The musical language of the Renaissance came from a union of French, Italian, and English elements and spread all over Europe from Spain to Poland (Chapters 8–9). Opera was invented as a blend of ancient Greek drama, Italian pastoral drama, and current musical genres like the air, madrigal, and canzonetta, and then opera in turn infused new vocal styles into church and chamber music (Chapters 14–15). French composers in the seventeenth century remade Italian genres in new French styles, keyboard composers borrowed from lute style, and the English drew on both Italian and French models (Chapter 16). German composers like Bach and Handel blended French, Italian, and German traditions (Chapters 17 and 19). Mozart's music was so diverse in style, both between and within works, because he traveled so widely as a youth and learned so many different styles, which he later combined in his mature compositions (Chapter 23). In the nineteenth century, French opera composers borrowed ideas from Italian opera, German composers used both Italian and French operas as models, and Russian composers adapted ideas from all three regions (Chapters 27–28). Once the music of the past began to be widely available, composers drew on older styles and procedures as well (Chapters 26 and 29). Jazz is a blend of African American traditions with Caribbean and European elements (Chapter 31). Stravinsky and others combined eighteenth-century and modern sounds and procedures in neoclassicism, and Bartók, Ives, and other composers integrated international traits with stylistic features from their own region to produce music in completely new styles (Chapters 32, 33, and 35). Rhythm and blues, rock, country, hip hop, and most other postwar popular styles are blends from multiple sources, as are the music of Ástor Piazzolla, John Zorn, Bright Sheng, and others who create hybrids that are beyond categorization (Chapters 36 and 38). Again and again, in all corners of Western music history, we encounter people creating new genres, styles, and traditions by incorporating aspects of other music.

Often what makes the difference in which strands are interwoven with each other is access. The contributions of the English to the Continental style in the fifteenth century, of Italians to music in Germany, Poland, England, and Russia, and of Africans and their descendants to jazz and other traditions in North America would not have happened without those people visiting or living in those regions. And now, of course, through digital recordings and the Internet, there is instant access around the world to almost everything. In such a world every type of music and every piece of music is fair game for being reused in novel ways. The only limit is our imagination.

This ability to absorb other musics and create new blends has been a defining characteristic of the Western tradition from its beginnings to now, and it sets Western music apart from many other musical traditions. Japanese composer Tōru Takemitsu once observed that he could use Japanese instruments, sounds, and techniques in a work in a Western genre such as a concerto, but he could not use Western tunes or techniques within a Japanese tradition such as music for the Noh drama or for shakuhachi, because those traditions did not permit outside influences; any hybrid belonged to the Western tradition. Much the same is true for the gamelan music of Java and Bali or the classical music of India or Persia. But this capability to absorb influences is at the very core of the Western tradition in all of its branches, from church music to classical concert music to jazz, pop, and hip hop. We may well wonder whether the term "Western music" is still appropriate when Western culture has spread around the world, and when some of the most practiced performers and interesting new composers come from China, Japan, and Korea. Given its global reach, it may be time to rename this tradition, but as eclectic and diverse as it has become, its roots are still in Western culture reaching back through Europe to ancient Greece.

Just as classical music is not isolated from popular music or jazz, and

Western music is no longer isolated from other musical traditions, there is a renewed understanding in our century that music itself is not isolated: it is connected to the world around it, shaped by that world and helping to shape it. As musicologists explore the interactions between music, social contexts, and the history of ideas, psychologists are exploring how music affects the brain, and social scientists are examining how music can draw people together and influence society. The new field of sound studies focuses on how all the sound we hear, including music, affects us: for example, how music, speech, and other human and environmental noises combine in a movie soundtrack to convey meanings. In classical, jazz, and popular music traditions as well as in film music, musicians increasingly are thinking about *sound* rather than notes, using the recording studio itself as an instrument, and treating the audio or video recording as the text. This growing awareness of music's place in larger contexts from sound to society may guide the future of music more than any innovation in style or technology.

It is too early to know what music from the late twentieth or early twenty-first century will be remembered, performed, and listened to in the future or will influence later music. Trends change too quickly to give a balanced or complete overview of recent music. But it seems clear that there is a continuing tension in all forms of music between finding a niche of committed listeners whose support will endure and finding a wide audience. There are few pieces that everyone knows; perhaps national anthems and scores for blockbuster films come closest to providing the shared musical experiences that seem to have been more common in the past. The great success enjoyed by Beethoven in orchestral music, Verdi in opera, Duke Ellington in jazz, or the Beatles in popular music seems no longer possible, because the audience is so divided that such unanimity of opinion is unlikely to be achieved.

Yet perhaps the relative lack of giants may be a good thing. Music of the past and of the entire world is more available now than ever. Thanks to radio, recordings, the Internet, and marketing, most of the music we have studied in this book is heard by more people each year today than heard it during the composer's entire lifetime. There is no need to focus our interest on a few great composers when there is so much variety to enjoy. The choices we have for music to listen to or perform have become almost limitless. So too are the possibilities for new music. With new computer software and techniques of sampling and synthesis found in traditions from art music to hip hop, it is now possible for people with access to technology to make their own music, without training in performance. In some respects, we are surrounded by more music than we can ever consume. But perhaps we are also returning to something akin to the practice of music long ago, when every singer sang their own song.

Further Reading is available at digital.wwnorton.com/hwm10

GLOSSARY

Within a definition, terms that are themselves defined in this glossary are printed in SMALL CAPITALS. Terms defined in general dictionaries are not included here. Pronunciation of foreign words is approximate and is given only when the spelling makes mispronunciation likely; "nh" stands for a final "n" in French, which nasalizes the preceding vowel (as in "chanson," rendered here as "shanh-SONH").

absolute music Music that is independent of words, drama, visual images, or any kind of representational aspects.

a cappella (Italian, "in chapel style") Manner of singing without instrumental accompaniment.

accidental Sign that calls for altering the pitch of a NOTE: a sharp (♯) raises the pitch a semitone, a flat (♭) lowers it a semitone, and a natural (♮) cancels a previous accidental.

accompanied recitative RECITATIVE that uses ORCHESTRAL accompaniment to dramatize the text.

act Main division of an OPERA. Most operas have two to five acts, although some have only one.

affections Objectified or archetypal emotions or states of mind, such as sadness, joy, fear, or wonder; one goal of much BAROQUE music was to arouse the affections.

Agnus Dei (Latin, "Lamb of God") Fifth of the five major musical items in the MASS ORDINARY, based on a litany.

agrément (French, "charm"; pronounced ah-gray-MANH) ORNAMENT in French music, usually indicated by a sign.

air English or French song for solo voice with instrumental accompaniment, setting rhymed poetry, often STROPHIC, and usually in the METER of a DANCE.

air de cour (French, "court air") Type of song for voice and accompaniment, prominent in France from about 1580 through the seventeenth century.

Alberti bass Broken-CHORD accompaniment common in the second half of the eighteenth century and named after Domenico Alberti, who used the FIGURATION frequently.

Alleluia Item from the MASS PROPER, sung just before the Gospel reading, comprising a RESPOND to the text "Alleluia," a verse, and a repetition of the respond. CHANT alleluias are normally MELISMATIC in style and sung in a RESPONSORIAL manner, one or more soloists alternating with the CHOIR.

allemande (French for "German dance") Highly stylized DANCE in BINARY FORM, in moderately slow quadruple METER with almost continuous movement, beginning with an upbeat. Popular during the RENAISSANCE and BAROQUE; appearing often as the first dance in a SUITE.

alta (Italian, "loud") Fifteenth- and early-sixteenth-century term for an ENSEMBLE of HAUT instruments, usually two or three SHAWMS and a SACKBUT.

alto (from ALTUS) (1) Relatively low female voice, or high male voice. (2) Part for such a voice in an ENSEMBLE work.

altus (Latin, "high") In fifteenth- and sixteenth-century POLYPHONY, a part in a RANGE between the TENOR and the SUPERIUS; originally CONTRATENOR ALTUS.

answer In the EXPOSITION of a FUGUE, the second entry of the SUBJECT, normally on the DOMINANT if the subject was on the TONIC, or vice versa. Also refers to subsequent answers to the subject.

anthem A POLYPHONIC sacred work in English for Anglican religious services.

antiphon (1) A LITURGICAL CHANT that precedes and follows a PSALM or CANTICLE in the OFFICE. (2) In the MASS, a chant originally associated with ANTIPHONAL PSALMODY; specifically, the COMMUNION and the first and final portion of the INTROIT.

antiphonal Adjective describing a manner of performance in which two or more groups alternate.

Aquitanian polyphony Style of POLYPHONY from the twelfth century, encompassing both DISCANT and FLORID ORGANUM.

aria (Italian, "air") (1) In the late sixteenth and early seventeenth centuries, any section of an Italian STROPHIC poem for a solo singer. (2) Lyrical monologue in an OPERA or other vocal work such as CANTATA and ORATORIO.

arioso (1) RECITATIVO ARIOSO. (2) Short, ARIA-like passage. (3) Style of vocal writing that approaches the lyricism of an ARIA but is freer in form.

arpeggio (from Italian *arpa*, "harp") Broken-CHORD FIGURE.

Ars Nova (Latin, "new art") Style of POLYPHONY from fourteenth-century France, distinguished from earlier styles by a new system of rhythmic NOTATION that allowed duple or triple division of NOTE values, SYNCOPATION, and great rhythmic flexibility.

Ars Subtilior (Latin, "more subtle art") Style of POLYPHONY from the late fourteenth or very early fifteenth centuries in southern France and northern Italy, distinguished by extreme complexity in rhythm and NOTATION.

art music Music that is (or is meant to be) listened to with rapt attention, for its own sake. Compare POPULAR MUSIC.

art song A song intended to be appreciated as an artistic statement rather than as entertainment, featuring precisely notated music, usually THROUGH-COMPOSED, and requiring professional standards of performance. Compare POPULAR SONG.

atonal, atonality Terms for music that avoids establishing a central pitch or tonal center (such as the TONIC in TONAL music).

augmentation The uniform lengthening of a MELODY using longer NOTE values, for example by doubling the length of each note.

aulos Ancient Greek reed instrument, usually played in pairs.

authentic mode A MODE (2) in which the RANGE normally extends from a STEP below the FINAL to an octave above it. See also PLAGAL MODE.

avant-garde Term for music (and art) that is iconoclastic, irreverent, antagonistic, and nihilistic, seeking to overthrow established aesthetics.

avant-garde jazz A trend beginning in the 1960s that blended JAZZ with AVANT-GARDE ART MUSIC and blurred distinctions between COMPOSITION and IMPROVISATION.

balanced binary form Binary form in which the latter part of the first section returns at the end of the second section, but in the TONIC.

ballad (1) Long narrative poem, or musical setting of such a poem. (2) Late-eighteenth-century German poetic form that imitated the folk ballad of England and Scotland and was set to music by German composers. The ballad expanded the LIED in both FORM and emotional content.

ballad opera GENRE of eighteenth-century English comic play featuring songs in which new words are set to borrowed tunes.

ballade (1) French FORME FIXE, normally in three stanzas, in which each stanza has the musical FORM aabC and ends with a REFRAIN (C). (2) Instrumental piece inspired by the GENRE of narrative poetry.

ballata (from Italian *ballare*, "to dance"; pl. *ballate*) Fourteenth-century Italian song GENRE with the FORM AbbaA, in which A is the *ripresa* or REFRAIN, and the single stanza consists of two *piedi* (bb) and a *volta* (a) sung to the music of the ripresa.

ballet In sixteenth- and seventeenth-century France, an entertainment in which both professionals and guests danced; later, a stage work danced by professionals.

balletto, ballett (Italian, "little dance") Sixteenth-century Italian (and later English) song GENRE in a simple, dancelike, HOMOPHONIC style with repeated sections and "fa-la-la" refrains.

band Large ENSEMBLE of winds, brass, and percussion instruments, or of brass and percussion instruments without winds.

bar form Song FORM in which the first section of MELODY is sung twice with different texts (the two *Stollen*) and the remainder (the *Abgesang*) is sung once.

bard Medieval poet-singer, especially of epics.

Baroque period (from Portuguese *barroco*, "a misshapen pearl") PERIOD of music history from about 1600 to about 1750, overlapping the late RENAISSANCE and early CLASSIC periods.

bas (French, "low"; pronounced BAH) In the fourteenth through sixteenth centuries, term for soft instruments such as VIELLES and HARPS. See HAUT.

bass (from BASSUS) (1) The lowest part in an ENSEMBLE work. (2) Low male voice. (3) Low instrument, especially the string bass or bass VIOL.

basse danse (French, "low dance") Type of stately couple DANCE of the fifteenth and early sixteenth centuries.

basso continuo (Italian, "continuous bass") (1) System of NOTATION and performance practice, used in the BAROQUE PERIOD, in which an instrumental BASS line is written out and one or more players of keyboard, LUTE, or similar instruments fill in the HARMONY with appropriate CHORDS or IMPROVISED MELODIC lines. (2) The bass line itself.

basso ostinato (Italian, "persistent bass") or **ground bass** A pattern in the BASS that repeats while the MELODY above it changes.

bassus (Latin, "low") In fifteenth- and sixteenth-century POLYPHONY, the lowest part; originally CONTRATENOR BASSUS.

bebop (or **bop**) A style of JAZZ developed in New York in the 1940s that had a diversified rhythmic texture, enriched HARMONIC vocabulary, and an emphasis on IMPROVISATION with rapid MELODIES and asymmetrical PHRASES.

bel canto (Italian, "beautiful singing") Elegant Italian vocal style of the early nineteenth century marked by lyrical, embellished, and florid MELODIES that show off the beauty, agility, and fluency of the singer's voice.

benefice Appointment granting a priest a stipend to perform certain duties, often with permission to pay another a lesser amount to perform those duties and keep the difference; used to supplement pay for CHAPEL musicians in the RENAISSANCE.

big band Type of large JAZZ ENSEMBLE popular between the world wars, featuring brass, reeds, and RHYTHM SECTIONS, and playing prepared arrangements that included rhythmic unisons and coordinated dialogue between sections and soloists.

binary form A FORM composed of two complementary sections, each of which is repeated. The first section usually ends on the DOMINANT or the relative major, although it may end on the TONIC or other KEY; the second section returns to the tonic. Types include SIMPLE BINARY FORM, BALANCED BINARY FORM, and ROUNDED BINARY FORM.

blue note Slight drop or slide in pitch on the third, fifth, or seventh degree of a MAJOR SCALE, common in BLUES and JAZZ.

blues (1) African American vocal GENRE that is based on

a simple repetitive formula and characterized by a distinctive style of performance. (2) TWELVE-BAR BLUES.

bop See BEBOP.

breve (from Latin *brevis*, "short") In medieval and RENAISSANCE systems of RHYTHMIC NOTATION, a NOTE that is normally equal to half or a third of a LONG.

burden (1) In English medieval POLYPHONY, the lowest voice. (2) In the English CAROL, the REFRAIN.

Byzantine chant The repertory of ecclesiastical CHANT used in the Byzantine RITE and in the modern Greek Orthodox Church.

cabaletta In the operatic scene structure developed by Gioachino Rossini in the early nineteenth century, the last part of an ARIA or ENSEMBLE, which was lively and brilliant and expressed active feelings, such as joy or despair. See also CANTABILE, SCENA, TEMPO D'ATTACCO, and TEMPO DI MEZZO.

cabaret Type of nightclub, first introduced in nineteenth-century Paris, that offered serious or comic sketches, DANCES, songs, and poetry.

caccia (Italian, "hunt"; pronounced CAH-cha; pl. *cacce*) Fourteenth-century Italian FORM featuring two voices in CANON over a free untexted TENOR.

cadence MELODIC or HARMONIC succession that closes a musical PHRASE, PERIOD, section, or COMPOSITION.

cadenza (Italian, "cadence") Highly embellished passage, often IMPROVISED, at an important CADENCE, usually occurring just before the end of a piece or section.

café-concert Type of dining establishment, prominent in late-nineteenth- and early-twentieth-century Paris, that combined the food and drink of a café with musical entertainment, usually songs on sentimental, comic, or political topics.

call and response Alternation of short PHRASES between a leader and a group; used especially for music in the African American tradition.

cambiata (Italian, "changed") Figure in sixteenth-century POLYPHONY in which a voice skips down from a DISSONANCE to a CONSONANCE instead of resolving by STEP, then moves to the expected NOTE of resolution.

Camerata (Italian, "circle" or "association") Circle of intellectuals and amateurs of the arts that met in Florence, Italy, in the 1570s and 1580s.

canon (Latin, "rule") (1) Rule for performing music, particularly for deriving more than one voice from a single line of notated music, as when several voices sing the same MELODY, entering at certain intervals of time or singing at different speeds simultaneously. (2) COMPOSITION in which the voices enter successively at determined pitch and time intervals, all performing the same MELODY.

canso TROUBADOUR song about FINE AMOUR (courtly love).

cantabile (Italian, "songlike") (1) Songful, lyrical, in a songlike style. (2) In the operatic scene structure developed by Gioachino Rossini in the early nineteenth century, the first section of an ARIA or ENSEMBLE, somewhat slow and expressing a relatively calm mood. See

also CABELETTA, SCENA, TEMPO D'ATTACCO, and TEMPO DI MEZZO.

cantata (Italian, "to be sung") (1) In the seventeenth and eighteenth centuries, a vocal CHAMBER work with CONTINUO, usually for solo voice, consisting of several sections or MOVEMENTS that include RECITATIVES and ARIAS and setting a lyrical or quasi-dramatic text. (2) Form of Lutheran church music in the eighteenth century, combining poetic texts with texts drawn from CHORALES or the Bible, and including RECITATIVES, ARIAS, chorale settings, and usually one or more CHORUSES. (3) In later eras, a work for soloists, CHORUS, and ORCHESTRA in several MOVEMENTS but smaller than an ORATORIO.

canticle HYMN-like or PSALM-like passage from a part of the Bible other than the Book of Psalms.

cantiga Medieval MONOPHONIC song in Spanish or Portuguese.

cantilena (Latin, "song") Polyphonic song not based on a CANTUS FIRMUS; used especially for polyphonic songs by English composers of the late thirteenth through early fifteenth centuries.

cantillation Chanting of a sacred text by a solo singer, particularly in the Jewish synagogue.

cantional style (from Latin *cantionale*, "songbook") Manner of setting CHORALES in CHORDAL HOMOPHONY with the MELODY in the highest voice.

cantor In the medieval Christian church, the leader of the CHOIR. In Jewish synagogue music, the main solo singer.

cantus (Latin, "melody") In POLYPHONY of the fourteenth through sixteenth centuries, the highest voice, especially the texted voice in a polyphonic song.

cantus firmus (Latin, "fixed melody") An existing MELODY, often taken from a GREGORIAN chant, on which a new POLYPHONIC work is based; used especially for melodies presented in long NOTES.

cantus-firmus mass POLYPHONIC MASS in which the same CANTUS FIRMUS is used in each MOVEMENT, normally in the TENOR.

cantus-firmus/imitation mass POLYPHONIC MASS in which each MOVEMENT is based on the same polyphonic work, using that work's TENOR (sometimes the SUPERIUS) as a CANTUS FIRMUS, normally in the tenor, and borrowing some elements from the other voices of the model to use in the other voices of the mass.

cantus-firmus variations Instrumental GENRE of the late 1500s and early 1600s, comprising a set of VARIATIONS in which the MELODY repeats with little change but is surrounded by different CONTRAPUNTAL material in each variation.

canzona (canzon) (Italian, "song") (1) Sixteenth-century Italian GENRE, an instrumental work adapted from a CHANSON or composed in a similar style. (2) In the late sixteenth and early seventeenth centuries, an instrumental work in several contrasting sections, of which the first and some of the others are in IMITATIVE COUNTERPOINT.

canzonetta, canzonet (Italian, "little song") Sixteenth-century Italian (and later English) song GENRE in a simple, mostly HOMOPHONIC style. Diminutive of CANZONA.

capriccio (Italian, "whim") (1) In the BAROQUE PERIOD, a FUGAL piece in continuous IMITATIVE COUNTERPOINT. (2) In the nineteenth century, a short COMPOSITION in free FORM, usually for PIANO.

carol English song, usually on a religious subject, with several stanzas and a BURDEN, or REFRAIN. From the fifteenth century on, most carols are POLYPHONIC.

carole Medieval circle or line dance, or the MONOPHONIC song that accompanied it.

castrati (sing. *castrato*) Male singers who were castrated before puberty to preserve their high vocal RANGE, prominent in the seventeenth and early eighteenth centuries, especially in OPERA.

catch English GENRE of CANON, usually with a humorous or ribald text.

cauda (Latin, "tail"; pl. *caudae*) MELISMATIC passage in a POLYPHONIC CONDUCTUS.

chacona (Italian, **ciaccona**) A vivacious dance-song imported from Latin America into Spain and then into Italy, popular during the seventeenth century.

chaconne (or **ciaccona**) BAROQUE GENRE derived from the CHACONA, consisting of VARIATIONS over a BASSO CONTINUO.

chamber One of the three divisions of musicians at court, serving the ruler's personal needs and family with music for relatively small ENSEMBLES and audiences. Compare CHAPEL.

chamber music Music for small ENSEMBLE.

chamber sonata See SONATA DA CAMERA.

chance Approach to composing music pioneered by John Cage, in which some of the decisions normally made by the composer are instead determined through random procedures, such as tossing coins. Chance differs from INDETERMINACY but shares with it the result that the sounds in the music do not convey an intention and are therefore to be experienced only as pure sound.

chanson (French, "song"; pronounced shanh-SONH) Secular song with French words; used especially for POLYPHONIC songs of the fourteenth through sixteenth centuries.

chanson de geste (French, "song of deeds") Type of medieval French epic recounting the deeds of national heroes, sung to MELODIC formulas.

chansonnier (French, "songbook") Manuscript collection of secular songs with French words; used both for collections of MONOPHONIC TROUBADOUR and TROUVÈRE songs and for collections of POLYPHONIC songs.

chant (1) Unison unaccompanied song, particularly that of the Latin LITURGY (also called PLAINCHANT). (2) The repertory of unaccompanied liturgical songs of a particular RITE.

chapel A group of salaried musicians and clerics employed by a ruler, nobleman, church official, or other patron, who officiate at and furnish music for religious services.

character piece A piece of CHARACTERISTIC MUSIC, especially one for PIANO.

characteristic (or **descriptive**) **music** Instrumental music that depicts or suggests a mood, personality, or scene, usually indicated in its title.

charts In postwar POPULAR MUSIC, weekly rankings of songs by sales or other measures of popularity.

choir A group of singers who perform together, singing either in unison or in parts. Used especially for the group that sings in a religious service.

choral society Amateur CHORUS whose members sing for their own enjoyment and may pay dues to purchase music, pay the CONDUCTOR, and meet other expenses.

chorale (pronounced ko-RAL) STROPHIC HYMN in the Lutheran tradition, intended to be sung by the congregation.

chorale motet CHORALE setting in the style of a sixteenth-century MOTET.

chorale prelude Relatively short setting for organ of a CHORALE MELODY, used as an introduction for congregational singing or as an interlude in a Lutheran church service.

chorale variations A set of VARIATIONS on a CHORALE MELODY.

chord Three or more simultaneous NOTES heard as a single entity. In TONAL music, three or more notes that can be arranged as a succession of thirds, such as a TRIAD.

choreography (1) The art of designing dance. (2) The design for a particular dance, indicating the steps and movements to be performed by the dancers.

chorus (1) Group of singers who perform together, usually with several singers on each part. (2) A MOVEMENT or passage for such a group in an ORATORIO, OPERA, or other multimovement work. (3) The REFRAIN of a POPULAR song. (4) In JAZZ, a statement of the HARMONIC PROGRESSION of the opening tune, over which one or more instruments play variants or new musical ideas.

chromatic (from Greek *chroma*, "color") (1) In ancient Greek music, adjective describing a TETRACHORD comprising a minor third and two SEMITONES, or a MELODY that uses such tetrachords. (2) Adjective describing a melody that uses two or more successive semitones in the same direction, a SCALE consisting exclusively of semitones, an INTERVAL or CHORD that draws NOTES from more than one DIATONIC scale, or music that uses many such melodies or chords.

chromatic saturation The appearance of all twelve PITCH-CLASSES within a segment of music.

chromaticism The use of many NOTES from the CHROMATIC SCALE in a passage or piece.

church calendar In a Christian RITE, the schedule of days commemorating special events, individuals, or times of year.

church sonata See SONATA DA CHIESA.

ciaccona See CHACONA and CHACONNE.

Classic period In music history, the era from about 1730 to about 1815, between and overlapping the BAROQUE and ROMANTIC PERIODS.

classical music (1) Common term for ART MUSIC of all PERIODS, as distinct from POPULAR MUSIC or FOLK MUSIC. (2) Music in the tradition of the repertoire of musical masterworks that formed in the nineteenth century, including lesser works in the same GENRES (such as OPERA, ORATORIO, SYMPHONY, SONATA, STRING QUARTET, and

ART SONG) or for the same performing forces and newly composed works intended as part of the same tradition. (3) Music in the CLASSIC PERIOD.

classical style Musical idiom of the middle to late eighteenth century, generally characterized by an emphasis on MELODY over relatively light accompaniment; simple, clearly articulated harmonic plans; PERIODIC phrasing; clearly delineated FORMS based on contrast between THEMES, between KEYS, between stable and unstable passages, and between sections with different functions; and contrasts of mood, style, and figuration within MOVEMENTS as well as between them.

clausula (Latin, "clause," pl. *clausulae*) In NOTRE DAME POLYPHONY, a self-contained section of an ORGANUM that closes with a CADENCE.

clavecin French term for HARPSICHORD.

clavecinist A person who performs on or composes works for the CLAVECIN.

clavichord Keyboard instrument popular between the fifteenth and eighteenth centuries. The loudness, which depends on the force with which a brass blade strikes the strings, is under the direct control of the player.

clos See OPEN AND CLOSED ENDINGS.

coda (Italian, "tail") A supplementary ending to a COMPOSITION or MOVEMENT; a concluding section that lies outside the FORM as usually described.

collage Work or passage that uses multiple QUOTATIONS without following a standard procedure for doing so, such as a medley.

collegium musicum (1) An association of amateurs, popular during the BAROQUE PERIOD, who gathered to play and sing together for their own pleasure. (2) Today, an ENSEMBLE of university students that performs early music.

color (Latin rhetorical term for ornament, particularly repetition, pronounced KOH-lor) In an ISORHYTHMIC COMPOSITION, a repeated MELODIC pattern, as opposed to the repeating rhythmic pattern (the TALEA).

coloratura Florid vocal ORNAMENTATION.

Communion Item in the MASS PROPER, originally sung during communion, comprising an ANTIPHON without verses.

composition The act or process of creating new pieces of music, or a piece that results from this process and is substantially similar each time it is performed; usually distinguished from IMPROVISATION and performance.

concert band Large ENSEMBLE of winds, brass, and percussion instruments that performs seated in concert halls, like an ORCHESTRA.

concert étude See ÉTUDE.

concert overture Nineteenth-century GENRE for ORCHESTRA in one MOVEMENT, typically in SONATA FORM, with a descriptive title that is reflected in the music.

concertato medium or **concertato style** (from Italian *concertare*, "to reach agreement") In seventeenth-century music, the combination of voices with one or more instruments, where the instruments do not simply double the voices but play independent parts.

concerted madrigal Early-seventeenth-century type of MADRIGAL for one or more voices accompanied by BASSO CONTINUO and in some cases by other instruments.

concertino (1) In a CONCERTO GROSSO, the small ENSEMBLE that is contrasted with the larger group. (2) A one-MOVEMENT instrumental CONCERTO (also called *Konzertstück*, "concert piece").

concerto (from Italian *concertare*, "to reach agreement") (1) In the seventeenth century, ENSEMBLE of instruments or of voices with one or more instruments, or a work for such an ensemble. (2) COMPOSITION in which one or more solo instruments (or instrumental group) contrasts with an ORCHESTRAL ENSEMBLE. See also CONCERTO GROSSO and ORCHESTRAL CONCERTO.

concerto grosso Instrumental work that exploits the contrast in sonority between a small ENSEMBLE of solo instruments (CONCERTINO), usually the same forces that appeared in the TRIO SONATA, and a large ENSEMBLE (RIPIENO or *concerto grosso*).

concitato genere See STILE CONCITATO.

conductor A person who leads a performance, especially for an ORCHESTRA, BAND, CHORUS, or other large ENSEMBLE, by means of gestures.

conductus A serious medieval song, MONOPHONIC or POLYPHONIC, setting a rhymed, rhythmic Latin poem.

conjunct (1) In ancient Greek music, adjective used to describe the relationship between two TETRACHORDS when the bottom NOTE of one is the same as the top note of the other. (2) Of a MELODY, consisting mostly of STEPS.

connoisseur (French, "one who knows") A term coined in the early eighteenth century to indicate an informed listener who cultivates a taste for the best in music and art.

conservatory School that specializes in teaching music.

consonance INTERVAL or CHORD that has a stable, harmonious sound. Compare DISSONANCE.

consort English name (current ca. 1575–1700) for a group of instruments.

consort song RENAISSANCE English GENRE of song for voice accompanied by a CONSORT of VIOLS.

contenance angloise (French, "English guise") Characteristic quality of early-fifteenth-century English music, marked by pervasive CONSONANCE with frequent use of HARMONIC thirds and sixths, often in parallel motion.

continuo BASSO CONTINUO.

continuo instruments Instruments used to REALIZE a BASSO CONTINUO, such as HARPSICHORD, organ, LUTE, or THEORBO.

contrafact In JAZZ, a new MELODY composed over a HARMONIC PROGRESSION borrowed from another song.

contrafactum (Latin, "counterfeit"; pl. *contrafacta*) The practice of replacing the text of a vocal work with a new text while the music remains essentially the same; or the resulting piece.

contrapuntal Employing COUNTERPOINT, or two or more simultaneous MELODIC lines.

contratenor (Latin, "against the tenor") In fourteenth- and fifteenth-century POLYPHONY, voice composed after or in conjunction with the TENOR and in about the same RANGE, helping to form the HARMONIC foundation.

contratenor altus, contratenor bassus (Latin) In fifteenth-century POLYPHONY, CONTRATENOR parts that lie relatively high (ALTUS) or low (BASSUS) in comparison to the TENOR. Often simply written as "altus" or "bassus," these are the ancestors of the vocal ranges ALTO and BASS.

cool jazz A style in JAZZ characterized by softer TIMBRES, more relaxed pace, and rhythmic subtleties, first heard in *Birth of the Cool* (1949–50) by Miles Davis.

cornett Wind instrument of hollowed-out wood or ivory, with finger holes and a cup mouthpiece, blown like a brass instrument.

counterpoint The combination of two or more simultaneous MELODIC lines according to a set of rules.

countersubject In a FUGUE or RICERCARE, a secondary theme designed to combine well in counterpoint with the SUBJECT. In the initial EXPOSITION of a fugue, each voice typically states the countersubject immediately after the subject, as the next voice enters with the subject; later in a fugue, or in a ricercare, the countersubject may be handled more freely.

country music (also known as *country-and-western*) A type of POPULAR MUSIC associated primarily with white southerners, that blends elements of FOLK MUSIC, POPULAR SONG, and other traditions.

couplet In a RONDO or seventeenth- or eighteenth-century RONDEAU, one of several PERIODS or passages that alternate with the REFRAIN.

courante A DANCE in BINARY FORM, in compound METER at a moderate tempo and with an upbeat, featured as a standard MOVEMENT of the Baroque dance SUITE.

court ballet Seventeenth-century French GENRE, an extensive musical-dramatic work with costumes, scenery, poetry, and DANCE that featured members of the court as well as professional dancers.

courtly love See FINE AMOUR.

Credo (Latin, "I believe") Third of the five major musical items in the Mass ORDINARY, a creed or statement of faith.

crumhorn RENAISSANCE wind instrument, with a double reed enclosed in a cap so the player's lips do not touch the reed.

cumulative form Form used by Charles Ives and others in which the principal THEME appears in its entirety only at the end of a work, preceded by its DEVELOPMENT.

cycle A group of related works, comprising MOVEMENTS of a single larger entity. Examples include cycles of CHANTS for the Mass ORDINARY, consisting of one setting each of the KYRIE, GLORIA, SANCTUS, and AGNUS DEI (and sometimes also *Ite, missa est*); the POLYPHONIC MASS cycle of the fifteenth through seventeenth centuries; and the SONG CYCLE of the nineteenth century.

cyclic form Form of a multimovement work created by the recollection of THEMES from one or more earlier MOVEMENTS in later ones.

da capo aria ARIA FORM with two sections. The first section is repeated after the second section's close, which carries the instruction *da capo* (Italian, "from the head"), creating an ABA FORM.

dances Pieces in stylized dance rhythms, whether independent, paired, or linked together in a SUITE.

descriptive music See CHARACTERISTIC MUSIC.

developing variation Term coined by Arnold Schoenberg for the process of deriving new THEMES, accompaniments, and other ideas throughout a piece through variations of a germinal idea.

development (1) The process of reworking, recombining, fragmenting, and varying given THEMES or other material. (2) In SONATA FORM, the section after the EXPOSITION, which MODULATES through a variety of KEYS and in which THEMES from the exposition are presented in new ways.

diatonic (1) In ancient Greek music, adjective describing a TETRACHORD with two WHOLE TONES and one SEMITONE. (2) Name for a SCALE that includes five whole tones and two semitones, where the semitones are separated by two or three whole tones. (3) Adjective describing a MELODY, CHORD, or passage based exclusively on a single diatonic scale.

diegetic music or **source music** In film, music that is heard or performed by the characters themselves.

digital Relating to methods for producing or recording musical sounds by translating them into a coded series of on-off pulses, or 1s and 0s, in the same way that computers store and transmit data.

diminution (1) Uniform reduction of NOTE values in a MELODY or PHRASE, for instance by halving the length of each note. (2) Type of IMPROVISED ORNAMENTATION in the sixteenth and seventeenth centuries, in which relatively long notes are replaced with SCALES or other FIGURES composed of short notes.

direct Pertaining to a manner of performing CHANT without alternation between groups (see ANTIPHONAL) or between soloist and group (see RESPONSORIAL).

discant (Latin, "singing apart") (1) Twelfth-century style of POLYPHONY in which the upper voice or voices have about one to three NOTES for each note of the lower voice. (2) TREBLE part.

disjunct (1) In ancient Greek music, adjective used to describe the relationship between two TETRACHORDS when the bottom NOTE of one is a WHOLE TONE above the top note of the other. (2) Of a MELODY, consisting mostly of skips (thirds) and leaps (larger INTERVALS) rather than STEPS.

dissonance (1) Two or more NOTES sounding together to produce a discord, or a sound that needs to be resolved to a CONSONANCE. (2) A NOTE that does not belong to the CHORD that sounds simultaneously with it; a nonchord TONE.

diva A leading and successful female OPERA singer. See also PRIMA DONNA.

divertissement In TRAGÉDIE EN MUSIQUE, a long interlude of BALLET, solo AIRS, choral singing, and spectacle, intended as entertainment.

division Another term for DIMINUTION (2).

dominant In TONAL music, the NOTE and CHORD a perfect fifth above the TONIC.

double-function form A combination of single-MOVEMENT and multimovement structures, such as SONATA FORM superimposed over four movements of a SONATA or SYMPHONY that are played without breaks between them.

double leading-tone cadence CADENCE popular in the fourteenth and fifteenth centuries, in which the bottom voice moves down a WHOLE TONE and the upper voices move up a SEMITONE, forming a major third and major sixth expanding to an open fifth and octave.

Doxology A formula of praise to the Trinity. Two forms are used in GREGORIAN CHANT: the Greater Doxology, or GLORIA, and the LESSER DOXOLOGY, used with PSALMS, INTROITS, and other chants.

dramatic opera Seventeenth-century English mixed GENRE of musical theater, a spoken play with an OVERTURE and four or more MASQUES or long musical interludes. Today often called SEMI-OPERA.

drone NOTE or notes sustained throughout an entire piece or section.

duplum (from Latin *duplus*, "double") In POLYPHONY of the late twelfth through fourteenth centuries, second voice from the bottom in a four-voice TEXTURE, above the TENOR.

dynamics Level of loudness or softness, or intensity.

echos (Greek; pl. *echoi*) One of the eight MODES associated with BYZANTINE CHANT.

electronic music Music based on sounds that are produced or modified through electronic means.

empfindsam style (German, "sensitive style") Close relative of the GALANT STYLE, featuring surprising turns of HARMONY, CHROMATICISM, nervous RHYTHMS, and speechlike MELODIES.

enharmonic (1) In ancient Greek music, adjective describing a TETRACHORD comprising a major third and two quarter tones, or a MELODY that uses such tetrachords. (2) Adjective describing the relationship between two pitches that are notated differently but sound alike when played, such as G♯ and A♭.

ensemble (1) A group of singers or instrumentalists who perform together. (2) In an OPERA, a passage or piece for more than one singer.

episode (1) In a FUGUE, a passage of COUNTERPOINT between statements of the SUBJECT. (2) In RONDO FORM, a section between two statements of the main THEME. (3) A subsidiary passage between presentations of the main thematic material.

equal temperament A TEMPERAMENT in which the octave is divided into twelve equal SEMITONES. This is the most commonly used tuning for Western music today.

estampie Medieval instrumental DANCE that features a series of sections, each played twice with two different endings, OUVERT and CLOS.

ethos (Greek, "custom") (1) Moral and ethical character or way of being or behaving. (2) Character, mood, or emotional effect of a certain TONOS, MODE, METER, or MELODY.

étude (French, "study") An instrumental piece designed to develop a particular skill or performing technique. Certain nineteenth-century études that contained significant artistic content and were played in concert were called CONCERT ÉTUDES.

exoticism Nineteenth-century trend in which composers wrote music that evoked feelings and settings of distant lands or foreign cultures.

experimental music A trend in twentieth-century music that focused on the exploration of new musical sounds, techniques, and resources.

exposition (1) In a FUGUE, a set of entries of the SUBJECT. (2) In SONATA FORM, the first part of the MOVEMENT, in which the main THEMES are stated, beginning in the TONIC and usually closing in the DOMINANT (or relative major).

expressionism, expressionist Early-twentieth-century term derived from art, in which music avoids all traditional forms of "beauty" in order to express deep personal feelings through exaggerated gestures, angular MELODIES, and extreme DISSONANCE.

faburden English style of IMPROVISED POLYPHONY from the late Middle Ages and RENAISSANCE, in which a CHANT in the middle voice is joined by an upper voice moving in parallel a perfect fourth above it and a lower voice that follows below the chant mostly in parallel thirds, moving to a fifth below to mark the beginning and end of phrases and the ends of most words.

fantasia (Italian, "fantasy"), **fantasy** (1) Instrumental COMPOSITION that resembles an IMPROVISATION or lacks a strict FORM. (2) IMITATIVE instrumental piece on a single SUBJECT.

fauxbourdon (pronounced FOH-boor-donh) Continental style of POLYPHONY in the early RENAISSANCE, in which two voices are written, moving mostly in parallel sixths and ending each PHRASE on an octave, while a third unwritten voice is sung in parallel perfect fourths below the upper voice.

figuration, figure MELODIC pattern made of commonplace materials such as SCALES or ARPEGGIOS, usually not distinctive enough to be considered a MOTIVE or THEME.

figured bass A form of BASSO CONTINUO in which the BASS line is supplied with numbers or flat or sharp signs to indicate the appropriate CHORDS to be played.

final The main NOTE in a MODE; the normal closing note of a CHANT in that mode.

finale Last MOVEMENT of a work in three or more movements, or the closing portion of an ACT in an OPERA.

fine amour (French, "refined love"; pronounced FEEN ah-MOOR; *fin' amors* in Occitan; also called **courtly love**) An idealized love for an unattainable woman who is admired from a distance. Chief subject of the TROUBADOURS and TROUVÈRES.

first practice See PRIMA PRATICA.

florid organum Twelfth-century style of two-voice

POLYPHONY in which the lower voice sustains relatively long NOTES while the upper voice sings note groups of varying length above each note of the lower voice.

folk music (1) Music of unknown authorship from a particular region or people, passed down through oral tradition. (2) In the decades after World War II, a type of POPULAR MUSIC that drew on folk traditions, which included both genuine FOLK SONGS and POPULAR SONGS.

folk song Song of unknown authorship from a particular region or people, passed down through oral tradition.

form The shape or structure of a COMPOSITION or MOVEMENT.

formes fixes (French, "fixed forms"; pronounced form FEEX) Schemes of poetic and musical repetition, each featuring a REFRAIN, used in late medieval and fifteenth-century French CHANSONS; in particular, the BALLADE, RONDEAU, and VIRELAI.

fortepiano Type of PIANO from the eighteenth or early nineteenth centuries, distinguished from later pianos by a variety of features, notably a smaller range and strings attached to a wooden rather than metal frame.

Franconian notation System of NOTATION described by Franco of Cologne around 1280, using note shapes to indicate durations.

free jazz An experimental JAZZ style introduced in the 1960s by Ornette Coleman, using IMPROVISATION that disregards the standard forms and conventions of jazz.

French overture Type of OVERTURE used in TRAGÉDIE EN MUSIQUE and other GENRES, that opens with a slow, HOMOPHONIC, and majestic section, followed by a faster second section that begins with IMITATION.

frottola (pl. *frottole*) Sixteenth-century GENRE of Italian POLYPHONIC song in mock-popular style, typically SYLLABIC, HOMOPHONIC, and DIATONIC, with the MELODY in the upper voice and marked rhythmic patterns.

fugal Resembling a FUGUE; featuring fugue-like IMITATION.

fuging tune Eighteenth-century American type of PSALM or HYMN tune that features a passage in free IMITATION, usually preceded and followed by HOMOPHONIC sections.

fugue (from Italian *fuga*, "flight") COMPOSITION or section of a composition in IMITATIVE TEXTURE that is based on a single SUBJECT and begins with successive statements of the subject in voices.

fundamental bass Term coined by Jean-Philippe Rameau to indicate the succession of the ROOTS or fundamental TONES in a series of CHORDS.

futurism, futurists Twentieth-century movement that created music based on noise.

galant style (French, "elegant") Eighteenth-century musical style that featured songlike MELODIES, short PHRASES, frequent CADENCES, and light accompaniment.

galliard Sixteenth-century dance in fast triple METER, often paired with the PAVANE and in the same FORM (AABBCC).

gamut The entire range of pitches normally written in the Middle Ages.

gavotte BAROQUE duple-meter DANCE in BINARY FORM, with a half-measure upbeat and a characteristic rhythm of short-short-*long*.

Gebrauchsmusik (German "utilitarian music" or "music for use") Term from the 1920s to describe music that was socially relevant and useful, especially music for amateurs, children, or workers to play or sing.

genre Type or category of musical COMPOSITION, such as SONATA or SYMPHONY.

genus (Latin, "class"; pronounced GHEH-noos; pl. *genera*) In ancient Greek music, one of three forms of TETRACHORD: DIATONIC, CHROMATIC, and ENHARMONIC.

Gesamtkunstwerk (German, "total artwork" or "collective artwork") Term coined by Richard Wagner for a dramatic work in which poetry, scenic design, staging, action, and music all work together toward one artistic expression.

gigue (French for "jig") Stylized DANCE movement of a standard BAROQUE SUITE, in BINARY FORM, marked by fast compound METER such as $\frac{6}{4}$ or $\frac{12}{8}$ with wide MELODIC leaps and continuous triplets. The two sections usually both begin with IMITATION.

Gloria (Latin, "Glory") Second of the five major musical items in the MASS ORDINARY, a praise formula also known as the Greater DOXOLOGY.

goliard songs Medieval Latin songs associated with the goliards, who were wandering students and clerics.

Gradual (from Latin *gradus*, "stairstep") Item in the MASS PROPER, sung after the Epistle reading, comprising a RESPOND and VERSE. CHANT graduals are normally MELISMATIC in style and sung in a RESPONSORIAL manner, one or more soloists alternating with the CHOIR.

grand motet French version of the large-scale SACRED CONCERTO, for soloists, double CHORUS, and ORCHESTRA.

grand opera A serious form of OPERA, popular during the ROMANTIC era, that was sung throughout and included BALLETS, CHORUSES, and spectacular staging.

Greater Doxology See **Gloria**.

Greater Perfect System In ancient Greek music, a system of TETRACHORDS spanning two octaves.

Gregorian chant The repertory of ecclesiastical CHANT used in the Roman Catholic Church.

ground bass BASSO OSTINATO.

guitar A string instrument, related to the LUTE, which has a flat back, fretted fingerboard, and inward curves on the sides and is played by plucking or strumming the strings.

half step (or **semitone**) The smallest INTERVAL normally used in Western music, equivalent to the interval between any two successive NOTES on the PIANO keyboard; half the size of a WHOLE STEP.

hard bop A style of JAZZ developed in the middle 1950s that combined BEBOP with elements from BLUES, RHYTHM AND BLUES, and African American gospel music.

harmonia (pl. *harmoniai*) Ancient Greek term with multiple meanings: (1) the union of parts in an orderly whole; (2) INTERVAL; (3) SCALE type; (4) style of MELODY.

harmonic progression A logical succession of CHORDS with a sense of direction; especially, the succession of chords used to accompany a MELODY or used as the basis for VARIATIONS.

harmony Aspect of music that pertains to simultaneous combinations of NOTES, the INTERVALS and CHORDS that result, and the correct succession of chords.

harp Plucked string instrument with a resonating soundbox, neck, and strings in roughly triangular shape. The strings rise perpendicular from the soundboard to the neck.

harpsichord Keyboard instrument in use between the fifteenth and eighteenth centuries. It was distinguished from the CLAVICHORD and the PIANO by the fact that its strings were plucked, not struck.

haut (French, "high"; pronounced OH) In the fourteenth through sixteenth centuries, term for loud instruments such as CORNETTS and SACKBUTS. See BAS.

head-motive Initial passage or MOTIVE of a piece or MOVEMENT; used especially for a motive or PHRASE that appears at the beginning of each movement of a MOTTO MASS or CANTUS-FIRMUS MASS.

heighted neumes In an early form of NOTATION, NEUMES arranged so that their relative height indicated higher or lower pitch.

hemiola (from Greek *hemiolios*, "one and a half") A metrical effect in which three duple units substitute for two triple ones, such as three successive quarter NOTES within a MEASURE of ⁶⁄₈, or three two-beat groupings in two measures of triple METER. Hemiola may occur between voices or over successive measures.

heterophony Music or musical TEXTURE in which a MELODY is performed by two or more parts simultaneously in more than one way, for example, one voice performing it simply, and the other with embellishments.

hexachord (from Greek, "six strings") (1) A set of six pitches. (2) In RENAISSANCE solmization, the six NOTES represented by the syllables *ut, re, mi, fa, sol, la*, which could be transposed to three positions: the "natural" hexachord, C–D–E–F–G–A; the "hard" hexachord, G–A–B–C–D–E; and the "soft" hexachord, F–G–A–B♭–C–D. (3) In TWELVE-TONE theory, the first six or last six notes in the ROW.

historia In Lutheran music of the sixteenth to eighteenth centuries, a musical setting based on a biblical narrative. See PASSION.

hocket (French *hoquet*, "hiccup") In thirteenth- and fourteenth-century POLYPHONY, the device of alternating rapidly between two voices, each resting while the other sings, as if a single MELODY is split between them; or, a COMPOSITION based on this device.

homophony Musical TEXTURE in which all voices move together in essentially the same RHYTHM, as distinct from POLYPHONY and HETEROPHONY. See also MELODY AND ACCOMPANIMENT.

homorhythmic Having the same RHYTHM, as when several voices or parts move together.

humanism Movement in the RENAISSANCE to revive ancient Greek and Roman culture and to study things pertaining to human knowledge and experience.

hurdy-gurdy An instrument with MELODY and DRONE strings, bowed by a rotating wheel turned with a crank, with levers worked by a keyboard to change the pitch on the melody string(s).

hymn Song to or in honor of a god. In the Christian tradition, song of praise sung to God.

idée fixe (French, "fixed idea" or "obsession") Term adopted by Hector Berlioz for the MELODY he used throughout his *Symphonie fantastique* to represent his beloved.

imitate (1) To repeat or slightly vary in one voice part a segment of MELODY just heard in another, at pitch or transposed. (2) To follow the example of an existing piece or style in composing a new piece.

imitation (1) In POLYPHONIC music, the device of repeating (imitating) a MELODY or MOTIVE announced in one part in one or more other parts, often at a different pitch level and sometimes with minor melodic or rhythmic alterations. Usually the voices enter with the element that is imitated, although sometimes imitation happens within the middle of a segment of melody. (2) The act of patterning a new work after an existing work or style; especially, to borrow much of the existing work's material.

imitation mass (or **parody mass**) POLYPHONIC MASS in which each MOVEMENT is based on the same polyphonic model, normally a CHANSON or MOTET, and all voices of the model are used in the mass, but none is used as a CANTUS FIRMUS.

imitative counterpoint CONTRAPUNTAL TEXTURE marked by IMITATION between voices.

imperfect (or **minor**) **division** In medieval and RENAISSANCE NOTATION, a division of a NOTE value into two of the next smaller units (rather than three). See MODE, TIME, AND PROLATION.

impresario During the BAROQUE PERIOD, a businessman who managed and oversaw the production of OPERAS; today, someone who books and stages operas and other musical events.

impressionism, impressionist Term derived from art, used for music that evokes moods and visual imagery through colorful HARMONY and instrumental TIMBRE.

improvisation, improvising Spontaneous invention of music while performing, including devising VARIATIONS, embellishments, or accompaniments for existing music.

indeterminacy An approach to COMPOSITION, pioneered by John Cage, in which the composer leaves certain aspects of the music unspecified. Should not be confused with CHANCE.

instrumental family Set of instruments, all of the same

type but of different sizes and RANGES, such as a VIOL CONSORT.

intabulation Arrangement of a vocal piece for LUTE or keyboard, typically written in TABLATURE.

intermedio Musical interlude on a pastoral, allegorical, or mythological subject performed before, between, or after the acts of a spoken comedy or tragedy.

intermezzo Eighteenth-century GENRE of Italian comic OPERA, performed between acts of a serious opera or play.

interval Distance in pitch between two NOTES.

Introit (from Latin *introitus*, "entrance") First item in the MASS PROPER, originally sung for the entrance procession, comprising an ANTIPHON, PSALM verse, Lesser Doxology, and reprise of the ANTIPHON.

inversion (1) In a MELODY or TWELVE-TONE ROW, reversing the upward or downward direction of each INTERVAL while maintaining its size; or the new melody or row form that results. (2) In HARMONY, a distribution of the NOTES in a CHORD so that a note other than the ROOT is the lowest note. (3) In COUNTERPOINT, reversing the relative position of two melodies, so that the one that had been lower is now above the other.

isorhythm (from Greek *iso-*, "equal," and *rhythm*) Repetition in a voice part (usually the TENOR) of an extended pattern of durations throughout a section or an entire COMPOSITION.

jazz A type of music developed mostly by African Americans in the early part of the twentieth century that combined elements of African, POPULAR, and European music, and that has evolved into a broad tradition encompassing many styles.

jongleur (French) Itinerant medieval musician or street entertainer.

jubilus (Latin) In CHANT, an effusive MELISMA, particularly the melisma on "-ia" in an ALLELUIA.

just intonation A system of tuning NOTES in the SCALE, common in the RENAISSANCE, in which most (but not all) thirds, sixths, perfect fourths, and perfect fifths are in perfect tune.

key In TONAL music, the hierarchy of NOTES, chords, and other pitch elements around a central note, the TONIC. There are two kinds of keys, major and minor.

kithara Ancient Greek instrument, a large LYRE.

Klangfarbenmelodie (German, "tone-color melody") Term coined by Arnold Schoenberg to describe a succession of TIMBRES that is perceived as analogous to the changing pitches in a MELODY.

Kyrie (Greek, "Lord") One of the five major musical items in the MASS ORDINARY, based on a BYZANTINE litany.

Landini cadence (named for Francesco Landini) In POLYPHONY of the fourteenth and fifteenth centuries, a decorated sixth-to-octave CADENCE in which the upper

voice moves down a STEP, then rises a third as the TENOR descends by step.

lauda (pl. *laude*; from Latin *laudare*, "to praise") Italian devotional song.

Leitmotiv, leitmotive (German, "leading motive") In an OPERA or film score, a MOTIVE, THEME, or musical idea associated with a person, thing, mood, or idea, which returns in original or altered form throughout.

Lesser Doxology A formula of praise to the Trinity, used with PSALMS, INTROITS, and other chants.

libretto (Italian, "little book") Literary text for an OPERA or other musical stage work.

Lied (German, "song"; pl. *Lieder*) Song with German words, whether MONOPHONIC, POLYPHONIC, or for voice with accompaniment; used especially for polyphonic songs in the RENAISSANCE and songs for voice and PIANO in the eighteenth and nineteenth centuries.

ligature NEUME-like note shape used to indicate a short RHYTHMIC pattern in twelfth- to sixteenth-century NOTATION.

liturgical drama Dialogue on a sacred subject, set to music and usually performed with action, and linked to the LITURGY.

liturgy The prescribed body of texts to be spoken or sung and ritual actions to be performed in a religious service.

long In medieval and RENAISSANCE systems of RHYTHMIC NOTATION, a NOTE equal to two or three BREVES.

lute Plucked string instrument popular from the late Middle Ages through the BAROQUE PERIOD, typically pear- or almond-shaped with a rounded back, flat fingerboard, frets, and one single and five double strings.

lute song English GENRE of solo song with LUTE accompaniment.

lyre Plucked string instrument with a resonating soundbox, two arms, crossbar, and strings that run parallel to the soundboard over a bridge and attach to the crossbar.

lyric opera ROMANTIC OPERA that lies somewhere between light OPÉRA COMIQUE and GRAND OPERA.

madrigal (Italian *madrigale*, "song in the mother tongue") (1) Fourteenth-century Italian poetic form and its musical setting, having two or three stanzas followed by a RITORNELLO. (2) Sixteenth-century Italian poem having any number of lines, each of seven or eleven syllables. (3) POLYPHONIC or CONCERTATO setting of such a poem or of a sonnet or other nonrepetitive VERSE form. (4) English polyphonic work imitating the Italian GENRE.

madrigal comedy, madrigal cycle In the late sixteenth and early seventeenth centuries, a series of MADRIGALS that represents a succession of scenes or a simple plot.

madrigalism A particularly evocative—or, if used in a disparaging sense, a thoroughly conventional—instance of TEXT DEPICTION or word-painting; so called because of the prominent role of word-painting in MADRIGALS.

major scale DIATONIC succession of NOTES with a major third and major seventh above the TONIC.

march A piece in duple or $\frac{6}{8}$ METER comprising an introduction and several STRAINS, each repeated. Typically there are two strains in the initial key followed by a TRIO in a key a fourth higher; the opening strains may or may not repeat after the trio.

mashup Combination of elements from two or more recordings, such as the vocal line from one song with the instrumental track of another.

masque Seventeenth-century English entertainment involving poetry, music, dance, costumes, CHORUSES, and elaborate sets, akin to the French COURT BALLET.

Mass (from Latin *missa*, "dismissed") (1) The most important service in the Roman Church. (2) A musical work setting the texts of the ORDINARY of the Mass, typically KYRIE, GLORIA, CREDO, SANCTUS, and AGNUS DEI. In this book, as in common usage, the church service is capitalized (the Mass), but a musical setting of the Mass Ordinary is not (a mass).

mazurka A type of Polish folk dance (and later ballroom dance) in triple METER, characterized by accents on the second or third beat and often by dotted figures on the first beat, or a stylized PIANO piece based on such a dance.

mean-tone temperament A type of TEMPERAMENT in which the fifths are tuned small so that the major thirds sound well; frequently used for keyboard instruments from the RENAISSANCE through the eighteenth century.

measure (1) A unit of musical time consisting of a given number of beats; the basic unit of METER. (2) Metrical unit set off by barlines.

Meistersinger (German, "master singer") Type of German amateur singer and poet-composer of the fourteenth through seventeenth centuries, who was a member of a guild that cultivated a style of MONOPHONIC song derived from MINNELIEDER.

melisma A long MELODIC passage sung to a single syllable of text.

melismatic Of a MELODY, having many MELISMAS.

mélodie French ART SONG, the French counterpart to the LIED.

melodrama A GENRE of musical theater that combined spoken dialogue with background music.

melody (1) Succession of tones perceived as a coherent line. (2) Tune. (3) Principal part accompanied by other parts or CHORDS.

melody and accompaniment A kind of HOMOPHONIC TEXTURE in which there is one main MELODY, which is accompanied by CHORDS or other FIGURATION.

mensuration canon A CANON in which voices move at different rates of speed by using different MENSURATION SIGNS.

mensuration signs In ARS NOVA and RENAISSANCE systems of rhythmic NOTATION, signs that indicate which combination of time and prolation to use (see MODE, TIME, AND PROLATION). The predecessors of TIME SIGNATURES.

meter Recurring patterns of strong and weak beats, dividing musical time into regularly recurring units of equal duration.

metrical psalm Metric, rhymed, and STROPHIC vernacular translation of a PSALM, sung to a relatively simple MELODY that repeats for each strophe.

mezzo carattere (Italian for "middle character") In OPERA of the late eighteenth century, a term for characters who fall between the categories of serious and comic.

minim In ARS NOVA and RENAISSANCE systems of rhythmic NOTATION, a NOTE that is equal to half or a third of a SEMIBREVE.

minimalism One of the leading musical styles of the late twentieth century, in which materials are reduced to a minimum and procedures simplified so that what is going on in the music is immediately apparent. Often characterized by a constant pulse and many repetitions of simple RHYTHMIC, MELODIC, or HARMONIC patterns.

Minnelieder (German, "love songs") Songs of the MINNESINGERS.

Minnesinger (German, "singer of love") A poet-composer of medieval Germany who wrote MONOPHONIC songs, particularly about love, in Middle High German.

minor scale DIATONIC SCALE that begins with a WHOLE STEP and HALF STEP, forming a minor third above the TONIC. The sixth and seventh above the tonic are also minor in the natural minor scale but one or both may be raised.

minstrel (from Latin *minister*, "servant") Thirteenth-century traveling musician, some of whom were also employed at a court or city.

minstrelsy Popular form of musical theater in the United States during the mid-nineteenth century, in which white performers blackened their faces and impersonated African Americans in jokes, skits, songs, and dances.

minuet DANCE in moderate triple METER, two-measure units, and BINARY FORM.

minuet and trio form Form that joins two BINARY-FORM MINUETS to create an ABA pattern, where A is the minuet and B the TRIO.

mixed media Trend of the late twentieth century that combines two or more of the arts, including music, to create a new kind of PERFORMANCE ART or musical theater.

mixed parallel and oblique organum Early form of ORGANUM that combines parallel motion with oblique motion (in which the ORGANAL VOICE remains on the same NOTE while the PRINCIPAL VOICE moves) in order to avoid TRITONES.

modal Making use of a MODE. Compare TONAL.

modal jazz A style of JAZZ developed in the late 1950s based on MODES and changes of SCALE or pitch collection rather than HARMONIC PROGRESSIONS.

mode (1) A SCALE or MELODY type, identified by the particular INTERVALLIC relationships among the NOTES in the mode. (2) In particular, one of the eight (later twelve) scale or melody types recognized by church musicians and theorists beginning in the Middle Ages, distinguished from one another by the arrangement of WHOLE TONES and SEMITONES around the FINAL, by the RANGE relative to the final, and by the position of the TENOR or RECITING TONE. (3) RHYTHMIC MODE. See also MODE, TIME, AND PROLATION.

mode, time, and prolation (Latin *modus, tempus, prolatio*) The three levels of rhythmic division in ARS NOVA

NOTATION. Mode is the division of LONGS into BREVES; time the division of breves into SEMIBREVES; and prolation the division of semibreves into MINIMS.

modern jazz Collective term for BEBOP, COOL JAZZ, HARD BOP, and MODAL JAZZ.

modernism, modernist General term for music, art, and literature from the late nineteenth century through the twentieth century whose creators sought to offer something new and distinctive while maintaining strong links to tradition, intertwining innovation with emulation of past classics. Compare AVANT-GARDE.

modified strophic form Variant of STROPHIC FORM in which the music for the first stanza is varied for later stanzas, or in which there is a change of KEY, RHYTHM, character, or material.

modulation In TONAL music, a gradual change from one KEY to another within a section of a MOVEMENT.

monody (1) An accompanied solo song. (2) The musical TEXTURE of solo singing accompanied by one or more instruments.

monophonic Consisting of a single unaccompanied MELODIC line.

monophony Music or musical TEXTURE consisting of unaccompanied MELODY.

motet (from French *mot*, "word") POLYPHONIC vocal COMPOSITION; the specific meaning changes over time. The earliest motets add a text to an existing DISCANT CLAUSULA. Thirteenth-century motets feature one or more voices, each with its own sacred or secular text in Latin or French, above a TENOR drawn from CHANT or other MELODY. Most fourteenth- and some fifteenth-century motets feature ISORHYTHM and may include a CONTRATENOR. From the fifteenth century on, any polyphonic setting of a Latin text (other than a MASS) could be called a motet; from the late sixteenth century on, the term was also applied to sacred compositions in German and later in other languages.

motive Short MELODIC or RHYTHMIC idea that recurs throughout a piece or section in the same or altered form.

motto mass POLYPHONIC MASS in which the MOVEMENTS are linked primarily by sharing the same opening MOTIVE or PHRASE.

movement Self-contained unit of music, complete in itself, that can stand alone or be joined with others in a larger work. Some types of COMPOSITION typically consist of several movements (such as the four movements common in the SYMPHONY).

music video Type of short film popularized in the early 1980s that provides a visual accompaniment to a POP SONG.

musica ficta (Latin, "feigned music") (1) In early music, NOTES outside the standard GAMUT, which excluded all flatted and sharped notes except B♭. (2). In POLYPHONY of the fourteenth through sixteenth centuries, the practice of raising or lowering by a SEMITONE the pitch of a written note, particularly at a CADENCE, for the sake of smoother HARMONY or motion of the parts.

musica mundana, musica humana, musica instrumentalis (Latin, "music of the universe," "human music,"

and "instrumental music") Three kinds of music identified by Boethius (ca. 480–ca. 524), respectively the "music" or numerical relationships governing the movement of stars, planets, and the seasons; the "music" that harmonizes the human body and soul and their parts; and audible music produced by voices or instruments.

musical GENRE of musical theater that features songs and DANCE numbers in styles drawn from POPULAR MUSIC in the context of a spoken play with a comic or romantic plot.

musical figure In BAROQUE music, a MELODIC pattern or CONTRAPUNTAL effect conventionally employed to convey the meaning of a text.

musique concrète (French, "concrete music") Term coined by composers working in Paris in the 1940s for music composed by assembling and manipulating recorded sounds, working "concretely" with sound itself rather than with music NOTATION.

musique mesurée (French, "measured music") Late-sixteenth-century French style of text setting, especially in CHANSONS, in which stressed syllables are given longer NOTES than unstressed syllables (usually twice as long).

nationalism (1) In politics and culture, an attempt to unify or represent a particular group of people by creating a national identity through characteristics such as common language, shared culture, historical traditions, and national institutions and rituals. (2) Nineteenth- and twentieth-century trend in music in which composers were eager to embrace elements in their music that claimed a national identity.

neoclassicism, neoclassical Trend in music from the 1910s to the 1950s in which composers revived, imitated, or evoked the styles, GENRES, and FORMS of pre-ROMANTIC music, especially those of the eighteenth century.

neo-Romanticism, neo-Romantic A trend of the late twentieth century in which composers adopted the familiar TONAL idiom of nineteenth-century ROMANTIC music and incorporated its sounds and gestures.

neotonal, neotonality Term for music since the early 1900s that establishes a single pitch as a tonal center, but does not follow the traditional rules of TONALITY.

neumatic In CHANT, having about one to six NOTES or so (or one NEUME) sung to each syllable of text.

neume A sign used in NOTATION of CHANT to indicate a certain number of NOTES and general MELODIC direction (in early forms of notation) or particular pitches (in later forms).

New Objectivity Term coined in the 1920s to describe a kind of new REALISM in music, in reaction to the emotional intensity of the late ROMANTICS and the EXPRESSIONISM of Schoenberg and Berg.

New Orleans jazz Leading style of JAZZ just after World War I, which centers on group VARIATION of a given tune, either IMPROVISED or in the style of IMPROVISATION.

nocturne Type of short PIANO piece popular during the ROMANTIC PERIOD, marked by highly embellished

MELODY, sonorous accompaniments, and a contemplative mood evocative of night.

nondiegetic music or **underscoring** In film, background music that conveys to the viewer a mood or other aspect of a scene or character but is not heard by the characters themselves. Compare DIEGETIC MUSIC.

notation A system for writing down musical sounds, or the process of writing down music. The principal notation systems of European music use a staff of lines and signs that define the pitch, duration, and other qualities of sound.

note (1) A musical TONE. (2) A symbol denoting a musical tone.

note-against-note organum Style of ORGANUM in which the ORGANAL VOICE moves in a free mixture of contrary, oblique, parallel, and similar motion against the CHANT, usually above the chant and mostly with one note for each note of the chant.

notes inégales (French, "unequal notes"; pronounced NUTS an-ay-GALL) Seventeenth-century convention of performing French music in which passages notated in short, even durations, such as a succession of eighth notes, are performed by alternating longer notes on the beat with shorter offbeats to produce a lilting rhythm.

Notre Dame polyphony Style of POLYPHONY from the late twelfth and thirteenth centuries, associated with Notre Dame Cathedral of Paris.

octatonic scale (or **octatonic collection**) A SCALE that alternates WHOLE and HALF STEPS.

Offertory Item in the MASS PROPER, sung while the COMMUNION is prepared, comprising a RESPOND without VERSES.

Office (from Latin *officium*, "obligation" or "ceremony") A series of eight prayer services of the Roman Church, celebrated daily at specified times, especially in monasteries and convents; also, any one of those services.

open and closed endings (French, *ouvert* and *clos*) In an ESTAMPIE, BALLADE, or other medieval form, two different endings for a repeated section. The first ("open") closes on a pitch other than the FINAL, and the second ("closed") ends with a full CADENCE on the final.

opera (Italian, "work") Drama with continuous or nearly continuous music, staged with scenery, costumes, and action.

opera buffa (Italian, "comic opera") Eighteenth-century GENRE of Italian comic OPERA, sung throughout.

opéra bouffe ROMANTIC operatic GENRE in France that emphasized the smart, witty, and satirical elements of OPÉRA COMIQUE.

opéra comique (French, "comic opera") (1) In the eighteenth century, light French comic OPERA, which used spoken dialogue instead of RECITATIVES. (2) In nineteenth-century France, opera with spoken dialogue, whether comic or tragic.

opera seria (Italian, "serious opera") Eighteenth-century GENRE of Italian OPERA, on a serious subject but normally with a happy ending, usually without comic characters and scenes.

operetta Nineteenth-century kind of light OPERA with spoken dialogue, originating in OPÉRA BOUFFE.

opus (Latin, "work") Work or collection of works in the same GENRE, issued as a publication.

oratorio GENRE of dramatic music that originated in the seventeenth century, combining narrative, dialogue, and commentary through ARIAS, RECITATIVES, ENSEMBLES, CHORUSES, and instrumental music, like an unstaged OPERA. Usually on a religious or biblical subject.

orchestra ENSEMBLE whose core consists of strings with more than one player on a part, usually joined by woodwinds, brass, and percussion instruments.

orchestral concerto Orchestral GENRE in several MOVEMENTS, originating in the late seventeenth century, that emphasized the first VIOLIN part and the BASS, avoiding the more CONTRAPUNTAL TEXTURE of the SONATA.

orchestral suite Late-seventeenth-century German SUITE for ORCHESTRA patterned after the groups of DANCES in French BALLETS and OPERA.

Ordinary of the Mass (from Latin *ordinarium*, "usual") Texts of the MASS that remain the same on most or all days of the CHURCH CALENDAR, although the tunes may change.

organ mass Setting for organ of all sections of the MASS for which the organ would play, including ORGAN VERSES and other pieces.

organ verse Setting for an organ of an existing MELODY from the Roman Catholic LITURGY.

organal voice (Latin, *vox organalis*) In an ORGANUM, the voice that is added above or below the original CHANT MELODY.

organic Describes a musical work in which all the parts relate to each other and to the whole like the parts of a single organism, derived from a common source.

organicism Concept that pieces of music should be ORGANIC.

organum (Latin; pronounced OR-guh-num) (1) One of several styles of early POLYPHONY from the ninth through thirteenth centuries, involving the addition of one or more voices to an existing CHANT. (2) A piece, whether IMPROVISED or written, in one of those styles, in which one voice is drawn from a CHANT. The plural is *organa*.

organum duplum In NOTRE DAME POLYPHONY, an ORGANUM in two voices.

ornament A brief, conventional formula, such as a TRILL or turn, written or IMPROVISED, that adds expression or charm to a MELODIC line.

ornamentation The addition of embellishments to a given MELODY, either during performance or as part of the act of COMPOSITION.

ostinato (Italian, "obstinate") Short musical pattern that is repeated persistently throughout a piece or section. See BASSO OSTINATO.

ouvert See OPEN AND CLOSED ENDINGS.

ouverture (French, "opening") (1) OVERTURE, especially FRENCH OVERTURE. (2) SUITE for ORCHESTRA, beginning with an OVERTURE.

overdotting Performing practice in French BAROQUE music in which a dotted NOTE is held longer than written, while the following short note is shortened.

overture (1) An ORCHESTRAL piece introducing an OPERA or other long work. (2) Independent ORCHESTRAL WORK in one movement, usually descriptive, such as a CONCERT OVERTURE.

parallel organum Type of POLYPHONY in which an added voice moves in exact parallel to a CHANT, normally a perfect fifth below it. Either voice may be doubled at the octave.

paraphrase Technique in which a CHANT or other MELODY is reworked, often by altering rhythms and adding NOTES, and placed in a POLYPHONIC setting.

paraphrase mass POLYPHONIC MASS in which each MOVEMENT is based on the same MONOPHONIC MELODY, normally a CHANT, which is PARAPHRASED in most or all voices rather than being used as a CANTUS FIRMUS in one voice.

parlor song Song for home music-making, sometimes performed in public concerts as well.

parody mass IMITATION MASS.

partbook A manuscript or printed book containing the music for one voice or instrumental part of a POLYPHONIC COMPOSITION (most often, an anthology of pieces); to perform any piece, a complete set of partbooks is needed, so that all the parts are represented.

partita or **partite** BAROQUE term for a set of VARIATIONS on a MELODY or BASS line.

partsong (1) A song for more than one voice. (2) In the nineteenth century, a song for CHORUS, parallel in function and style to the LIED or PARLOR SONG.

passacaglia BAROQUE GENRE of VARIATIONS over a repeated BASS line or HARMONIC PROGRESSION in triple METER.

Passion A musical setting of one of the biblical accounts of Jesus's crucifixion, the most common type of HISTORIA.

pastoral, pastoral drama Play in verse with incidental music and songs, normally set in idealized rural surroundings, often in ancient times; a source for the earliest OPERA LIBRETTOS.

pavane (pavan) Sixteenth-century dance in slow duple METER with three repeated sections (AABBCC). Often followed by a GALLIARD.

perfect (or **major**) **division** In medieval and RENAISSANCE NOTATION, a division of a note value into three (rather than two) of the next smaller unit. See MODE, TIME, AND PROLATION.

perfection (1) What we all strive for. (2) In medieval systems of NOTATION, a unit of duration equal to three TEMPORA, akin to a MEASURE of three beats.

performance art A type of art that first came to prominence in the 1960s, based on the idea that performing a prescribed action in a public place constitutes a work of art.

period (1) In music history, an era whose music is understood to have common attributes of style, conventions, approach, and function, in contrast to the previous and following eras. (2) In musical FORM, especially since the eighteenth century, a complete musical thought concluded by a CADENCE and normally containing at least two PHRASES.

periodic Organized in discrete PHRASES or PERIODS.

periodicity The quality of being PERIODIC, especially when this is emphasized through frequent resting points and articulations between PHRASES and PERIODS.

petit motet (French, "little motet") French version of the SMALL SACRED CONCERTO, for one, two, or three voices and CONTINUO.

phrase A unit of MELODY or of an entire musical TEXTURE that has a distinct beginning and ending and is followed by a pause or other articulation but does not express a complete musical thought. See PERIOD (2).

Phrygian cadence CADENCE in which the bottom voice moves down a SEMITONE and upper voices move up a WHOLE TONE to form a fifth and octave over the cadential NOTE.

piano or **pianoforte** A keyboard instrument invented in 1700 that uses a mechanism in which the strings are struck, rather than plucked as the HARPSICHORD was, and which allowed for crescendos, diminuendos, and other effects.

pipe and tabor Two instruments played by one player, respectively a high whistle fingered with one hand and a small drum beaten with a stick or mallet.

pitch-class Any one of the twelve NOTES of the CHROMATIC SCALE, including its ENHARMONIC equivalents, in any octave.

pitch-class set (or **set**) A collection of PITCH-CLASSES that preserves its identity when transposed, inverted, or reordered and used MELODICALLY or HARMONICALLY.

plagal mode A MODE (2) in a which the RANGE normally extends from a fourth (or fifth) below the FINAL to a fifth or sixth above it. See also AUTHENTIC MODE.

plainchant, plainsong A unison unaccompanied song, particularly a LITURGICAL song to a Latin text.

plainsong mass A MASS in which each MOVEMENT is based on a CHANT to the same text (the KYRIE is based on a chant Kyrie, the GLORIA on a chant Gloria, and so on).

plica In medieval NOTATION, a NOTE with a tail attached, sung as two pitches, the main note and the note a step down (if the tail goes down) or up (if the tail goes up).

point of imitation Passage in a POLYPHONIC work in which two or more parts enter in IMITATION.

polonaise A stately Polish processional DANCE in triple METER, or a stylized piece in the style of such a dance.

polychoral For more than one CHOIR.

polychoral motet MOTET for two or more choirs.

polyphony Music or musical TEXTURE consisting of two or more simultaneous lines of independent MELODY. See also COUNTERPOINT.

polystylism Term coined by Alfred Schnittke for a combination of newer and older musical styles created through QUOTATION or stylistic allusion.

polytonal, polytonality The simultaneous use of two or more KEYS, each in a different layer of the music (such as MELODY and accompaniment).

pop music Term coined in the 1950s for music that reflected the tastes and styles popular with the teen and young adult market.

popular music Music, primarily intended as entertainment, that is sold in printed or recorded form. It is distinguished from FOLK MUSIC by being written down and marketed as a commodity, and from CLASSICAL MUSIC by being centered on the performer and the performance, allowing great latitude in rearranging the notated music.

popular song Song that is intended primarily to entertain an audience, accommodate amateur performers, and sell as many copies as possible. Compare ART SONG.

portative organ Medieval or RENAISSANCE organ small enough to be carried, played by one hand while the other worked the bellows.

positive organ Organ from the medieval through BAROQUE PERIODS that was small enough to be moved, usually placed on a table.

postminimalism, postminimalist Musical style that uses techniques of MINIMALISM in combination with traditional methods, more varied material, and greater expressivity.

postmodernism, postmodernist Trend in the late twentieth century that blurs the boundaries between high and popular art, and in which styles of all epochs and cultures are equally available for creating music.

post-tonal General term for music after 1900 that does not adhere to TONALITY but instead uses any of the new ways that composers found to organize pitch, from ATONALITY to NEOTONALITY.

prelude Introductory piece for solo instrument, often in the style of an IMPROVISATION, or introductory MOVEMENT in a multimovement work such as an OPERA or SUITE.

prepared piano An invention of John Cage in which various objects—such as pennies, bolts, screws, or pieces of wood, rubber, plastic, or slit bamboo—are inserted between the strings of a PIANO, resulting in complex percussive sounds when the piano is played from the keyboard.

prima donna (Italian, "first lady") A SOPRANO (1) singing the leading female role in an OPERA. See also DIVA.

prima pratica (Italian, "first practice") Claudio Monteverdi's term for the style and practice of sixteenth-century POLYPHONY, in contradistinction to the SECONDA PRATICA.

prime In TWELVE-TONE music based on a particular ROW, the original form of the row, transposed or untransposed, as opposed to the INVERSION, RETROGRADE, or RETROGRADE INVERSION.

primitivism Musical style that represents the primitive or elemental through pulsation (rather than METER), static repetition, unprepared and unresolved DISSONANCE, dry TIMBRES, and other techniques.

principal voice (Latin, *vox principalis*) In an ORGANUM, the original CHANT MELODY.

program Text to accompany an instrumental work of PROGRAM MUSIC, describing the sequence of events depicted in the music.

program music Instrumental music that tells a story or follows a narrative or other sequence of events, often spelled out in an accompanying text called a PROGRAM.

prolation See MODE, TIME, AND PROLATION.

Proper of the Mass (from Latin *proprium*, "particular" or "appropriate") Texts of the MASS that are assigned to a particular day in the CHURCH CALENDAR.

psalm A poem of praise to God, one of 150 in the Book of Psalms in the Hebrew Scriptures (the Christian Old Testament). Singing psalms was and is a central part of Jewish, Christian, Catholic, and Protestant worship.

psalm tone A MELODIC formula for singing PSALMS in the OFFICE. There is one psalm tone for each MODE.

psalmody The singing of PSALMS.

psalter A published collection of METRICAL PSALMS.

psaltery A plucked string instrument whose strings are attached to a frame over a wooden sounding board.

Pythagorean intonation A system of tuning NOTES in the SCALE, common in the Middle Ages, in which all perfect fourths and fifths are in perfect tune.

quadruplum (Latin, "quadruple") (1) In POLYPHONY of the late twelfth through fourteenth centuries, the fourth voice from the bottom in a four-voice TEXTURE, added to a TENOR, DUPLUM, and TRIPLUM. (2) In NOTRE DAME POLYPHONY, an ORGANUM in four voices.

quotation Direct borrowing of one work in another, especially when the borrowed material is not reworked using a standard musical procedure (such as VARIATIONS, PARAPHRASE, or IMITATION MASS) but is set off as a foreign element.

rag Instrumental work in RAGTIME style, usually in the FORM of a MARCH.

ragtime Musical style that features SYNCOPATED rhythm against a regular, marchlike BASS.

range A span of NOTES, as in the range of a MELODY or of a MODE.

realism Nineteenth-century movement in art, literature, and OPERA that sought to depict the reality of everyday life, including common people and their concerns. See also VERISMO.

realization Performing (or creating a performable edition of) music whose NOTATION is incomplete, as in playing a BASSO CONTINUO or completing a piece left unfinished by its composer.

recapitulation In SONATA FORM, the third main section, which restates the material from the EXPOSITION, normally all in the TONIC.

recital Term popularized by Franz Liszt for his solo PIANO performances and used today for any presentation given by a single performer or a small group.

recitation formula In CHANT, a simple outline MELODY used for a variety of texts.

recitative A passage or section in an OPERA, ORATORIO, CANTATA, or other vocal work in RECITATIVE STYLE.

recitative style (from Italian *stile recitativo*, "recitational style") A type of vocal singing that approaches speech and follows the natural rhythms of the text.

recitativo arioso A passage or selection in an OPERA or other vocal work in a style that lies somewhere between RECITATIVE STYLE and ARIA style.

reciting tone The second most important NOTE in a MODE (after the FINAL), often emphasized in CHANT and used for reciting text in a PSALM TONE.

recorder End-blown wind instrument with a whistle mouthpiece, usually made of wood.

refrain In a song, a recurring line (or lines) of text, usually set to a recurring MELODY.

reminiscence motive In an OPERA, a MOTIVE, THEME, or MELODY that recurs in a later scene, in order to recall the events and feelings with which it was first associated. Compare LEITMOTIV.

Renaissance (French, "rebirth") PERIOD of art, cultural, and music history between the Middle Ages and the BAROQUE PERIOD, marked by HUMANISM, a revival of ancient culture and ideas, and a new focus on the individual, the world, and the senses.

respond The first part of a RESPONSORIAL CHANT, appearing before and sometimes repeated after the PSALM verse.

responsorial Pertaining to a manner of performing CHANT in which a soloist alternates with a group.

responsory RESPONSORIAL CHANT used in the OFFICE. Matins includes nine Great Responsories, and several other Office services include a Short Responsory.

retransition In a SONATA FORM, the passage at the end of the DEVELOPMENT that leads to and emphasizes the DOMINANT in preparation for the return of the TONIC at the RECAPITULATION.

retrograde Backward statement of a previously heard MELODY, passage, or TWELVE-TONE ROW.

retrograde inversion Upside-down and backward statement of a MELODY or TWELVE-TONE ROW.

revue Type of musical theater that includes a variety of DANCES, songs, comedy, and other acts, often united by a common theme.

rhythm (1) The pattern of music's movement in time. (2) A particular pattern of short and long durations.

rhythm and blues African American style of POPULAR MUSIC, originating in the 1940s, that featured a vocalist or vocal quartet, PIANO or organ, electric guitar, bass, and drums, and songs built on TWELVE-BAR BLUES or POPULAR SONG formulas.

rhythm section In a JAZZ ENSEMBLE, the group of instruments that keeps the beat and fills in the background.

rhythmic modes System of six durational patterns (for example, mode 1, long-short) in POLYPHONY of the late twelfth and thirteenth centuries, used as the basis of the rhythmic NOTATION of the Notre Dame composers.

ricercare (ricercar) (Italian, "to seek out" or "to attempt") (1) In the early to mid-sixteenth century, a PRELUDE in the style of an IMPROVISATION. (2) From the late sixteenth century on, an instrumental piece that treats one or more SUBJECTS in IMITATION.

ripieno (Italian, "full") In a CONCERTO or CONCERTO GROSSO, designates the full ORCHESTRA. Also called TUTTI.

rite The set of practices that defines a particular Christian tradition, including a CHURCH CALENDAR, a LITURGY, and a repertory of CHANT.

ritornello (1) In a fourteenth-century MADRIGAL, the closing section, in a different METER from the preceding stanzas. (2) In sixteenth- and seventeenth-century vocal music, instrumental introduction or interlude between sung stanzas. (3) In an ARIA or similar piece, an instrumental passage that recurs several times, like a REFRAIN. Typically, it is played at the beginning, as interludes (often in modified form), and again at the end, and it states the main THEME. (4) In a fast MOVEMENT of a CONCERTO, the recurring thematic material played at the beginning by the full ORCHESTRA and repeated, usually in varied form, throughout the movement and at the end.

ritornello form Standard FORM for fast MOVEMENTS in CONCERTOS of the first half of the eighteenth century, featuring a RITORNELLO (4) for full ORCHESTRA that alternates with EPISODES (3) characterized by virtuosic material played by one or more soloists.

rock and roll (or **rock**) A musical style that emerged in the United States in the mid-1950s as a blend of black and white traditions of POPULAR MUSIC, primarily RHYTHM AND BLUES, COUNTRY MUSIC, POP MUSIC, and TIN PAN ALLEY.

Romantic Term applied to music of the nineteenth century. Romantic music had looser and more extended FORMS, greater experimentation with HARMONY and TEXTURE, richly expressive and memorable MELODIES, improved musical instruments, an interest in musical NATIONALISM, and a view of music as a moral force, in which there was a link between the artists' inner lives and the world around them.

rondeau (pl. *rondeaux*) (1) French FORME FIXE with a single stanza and the musical FORM ABaAabAB, with uppercase letters indicating lines of REFRAIN and lowercase letters indicating new text set to music from the refrain. (2) FORM in seventeenth- and eighteenth-century instrumental music in which a repeated STRAIN alternates with other strains, as in the pattern AABACA.

rondellus Technique in medieval English POLYPHONY in which two or three PHRASES of music, first heard simultaneously in different voices, are each sung in turn by each of the voices.

rondo Piece or MOVEMENT in RONDO FORM.

rondo form Musical FORM in which the first or main section recurs, usually in the TONIC, between subsidiary sections or EPISODES.

root The lowest NOTE in a CHORD when it is arranged as a succession of thirds.

rota FORM of medieval English POLYPHONY in which two or more voices sing the same MELODY, entering at different times and repeating the melody until all stop together. See CANON.

rounded binary form BINARY FORM in which the beginning or all of the first section returns in the TONIC in the latter part of the second section.

row In TWELVE-TONE MUSIC, an ordering of all twelve PITCH-CLASSES that is used to generate the musical content.

rubato (from Italian *tempo rubato*, "stolen time") Technique common in ROMANTIC music in which the performer holds back or hurries the written NOTE values.

sackbut RENAISSANCE brass instrument, an early form of the trombone.

sacred concerto In the seventeenth century, a COMPOSITION on a sacred text for one or more singers and instrumental accompaniment.

salsa A type of DANCE music that emerged in the 1960s combining elements of Cuban dance styles with JAZZ, ROCK, and Puerto Rican music.

sampling A process of creating new COMPOSITIONS by patching together snippets of previously recorded music.

Sanctus (Latin, "Holy") One of the five major musical items in the MASS ORDINARY, based in part on Isaiah 6:3.

sarabande (1) Originally a quick dance-song from Latin America. (2) In French BAROQUE music, a slow DANCE in BINARY FORM and in triple METER, often emphasizing the second beat; a standard MOVEMENT of a SUITE.

saxophone Single-reed wind instrument invented by Adolphe Sax in about 1840.

scale A series of three or more different pitches in ascending or descending order and arranged in a specific pattern.

scat singing Technique in JAZZ in which the performer sings nonsense syllables to an IMPROVISED or composed MELODY.

scena (Italian, "scene") In the operatic scene structure developed by Gioachino Rossini in the early nineteenth century, the first section of an ARIA or ENSEMBLE after the orchestral introduction, usually in RECITATIVE accompanied by the ORCHESTRA. See also CABALETTA, CANTABILE, TEMPO D'ATTACCO, and TEMPO DI MEZZO.

schema (pl. **schemata**) Robert O. Gjerdingen's term for any of the conventional formulas used in the GALANT STYLE. Each schema coordinates a specific outline in the MELODY with a particular motion in the BASS line.

scherzo (Italian, "joke") A joking or particularly fast MOVEMENT in MINUET AND TRIO FORM.

score notation A type of NOTATION in which the different voices or parts are aligned vertically to show how they are coordinated with each other.

seconda pratica or **second practice** Monteverdi's term for a practice of COUNTERPOINT and COMPOSITION that allows the rules of sixteenth-century counterpoint (the PRIMA PRATICA) to be broken in order to express the feelings of a text. Also called STILE MODERNO.

semibreve In medieval and RENAISSANCE systems of rhythmic NOTATION, a NOTE that is normally equal to half or a third of a BREVE.

semiminim In ARS NOVA and RENAISSANCE systems of rhythmic NOTATION, a NOTE that is equal to half of a MINIM.

semi-opera Modern term for DRAMATIC OPERA.

semitone (or **half step**) The smallest INTERVAL normally used in Western music; half of a TONE (2).

sequence (from Latin *sequentia*, "something that follows") (1) A category of Latin CHANT that follows the ALLELUIA in some MASSES. (2) Restatement of a pattern, either MELODIC or HARMONIC, on successive or different pitch levels.

serenata (Italian, "serenade") A semidramatic piece for several singers and small ORCHESTRA, usually written for a special occasion.

serial, serial music Music that uses the TWELVE-TONE METHOD; used especially for music that extends the same general approach to SERIES in parameters other than pitch.

series (1) A ROW. (2) An ordering of specific durations, dynamic levels, or other nonpitch elements, used in SERIAL MUSIC.

Service A setting of Anglican service music, encompassing specific portions of Matins, Holy Communion, and Evensong. A *Great Service* is a MELISMATIC, CONTRAPUNTAL setting of these texts; a *Short Service* sets the same text in SYLLABIC, CHORDAL style.

set PITCH-CLASS SET.

shape-note singing A tradition of group singing that arose in nineteenth-century America, named after the NOTATION used in song collections in which the shape of the noteheads indicates the SOLMIZATION syllables, allowing for easy sight-reading in parts.

shawm Double-reed instrument, similar to the oboe, used in the medieval, RENAISSANCE, and BAROQUE PERIODS.

simple binary form BINARY FORM in which the two sections are roughly equal in length and feature musical material that is different or only loosely related.

simple recitative Style of RECITATIVE scored for solo voice and BASSO CONTINUO, used for setting dialogue or monologue in as speechlike a fashion as possible, without dramatization.

sinfonia (1) Generic term used throughout the seventeenth century for an abstract ENSEMBLE piece, especially one that serves as an introduction to a vocal work. (2) Italian OPERA OVERTURE in the early eighteenth century. (3) Early SYMPHONY.

Singspiel (German, "singing play") German GENRE of OPERA, featuring spoken dialogue interspersed with songs, CHORUSES, and instrumental music.

sketch General term for a compositional idea jotted down in a notebook, or an early draft of a work.

slow-movement sonata form Classic-era variant of SONATA FORM that omits the DEVELOPMENT.

small sacred concerto Seventeenth-century GENRE of sacred vocal music featuring one or more soloists accompanied by organ CONTINUO (or modest instrumental ENSEMBLE).

socialist realism A doctrine of the Soviet Union, begun in the 1930s, in which all the arts were required to use a realistic approach (as opposed to an abstract or symbolic one) that portrayed socialism in a positive light. In music this meant use of simple, accessible language, centered on MELODY, and patriotic subject matter.

solmization A method of assigning syllables to STEPS in a SCALE, used to make it easier to identify and sing the WHOLE TONES and SEMITONES in a MELODY.

solo madrigal In the late sixteenth and early seventeenth centuries, a THROUGH-COMPOSED setting of a nonstrophic poem for solo voice with accompaniment, distinguished from an ARIA and from a MADRIGAL for several voices.

solo sonata SONATA for one featured instrument, usually accompanied by BASSO CONTINUO, HARPSICHORD, or PIANO. Compare TRIO SONATA.

sonata (Italian, "sounded") (1) A piece to be played on

one or more instruments. (2) BAROQUE instrumental piece with contrasting sections or MOVEMENTS, often with IMITATIVE COUNTERPOINT. (3) GENRE in several movements for one or two solo instruments.

sonata da camera or **chamber sonata** BAROQUE SONATA, usually a SUITE of stylized DANCES, scored for one or more TREBLE instruments and CONTINUO.

sonata da chiesa or **church sonata** BAROQUE instrumental work intended for performance in church; usually in four MOVEMENTS—slow-fast-slow-fast—and scored for one or more TREBLE instruments and CONTINUO.

sonata form FORM typically used in first MOVEMENTS of SONATAS, instrumental CHAMBER works, and SYMPHONIES during the CLASSIC and ROMANTIC PERIODS. An expansion of ROUNDED BINARY FORM, it was described in the nineteenth century as consisting of an EXPOSITION, DEVELOPMENT, and RECAPITULATION based on a limited number of THEMES.

sonata-rondo A FORM that blends characteristics of SONATA FORM and RONDO FORM. One frequent structure is ABACABA, in which A and B correspond to the first and second THEMES of sonata form and B appears first in the DOMINANT and returns in the TONIC.

song cycle A group of songs performed in succession that tells or suggests a story.

soprano (from SUPERIUS) (1) High female voice. (2) Part for such a voice in an ENSEMBLE work.

soul The leading African American tradition of POPULAR MUSIC in the 1960s that combined elements of RHYTHM AND BLUES and gospel singing in songs on love, sex, and other secular subjects.

sound mass Term coined by Edgard Varèse for a body of sounds characterized by a particular TIMBRE, register, RHYTHM, or MELODIC gesture, which may remain stable or may be transformed as it recurs.

source music See DIEGETIC MUSIC.

spatial Pertaining to a conception of music as sounds moving through musical space, rather than as the presentation and VARIATION of THEMES or MOTIVES.

species The particular ordering of WHOLE TONES and SEMITONES within a perfect fourth, fifth, or octave.

spectral music or **spectralism** Late-twentieth-century approach to composition that focuses on perception, acoustics, TIMBRE, and the properties of sound.

spiritual African American type of religious song that originated among southern slaves and was passed down through oral tradition, with texts often based on stories or images from the Bible.

Sprechstimme (German, "speaking voice") A vocal style developed by Arnold Schoenberg in which the performer approximates the written pitches in the gliding tones of speech, while following the notated rhythm.

Stadtpfeifer (German, "town pipers") Professional town musicians who had the exclusive right to provide music within city limits.

step INTERVAL between two adjacent pitches in a DIATONIC, CHROMATIC, OCTATONIC, or WHOLE-TONE SCALE; WHOLE STEP or HALF STEP.

stile antico (Italian, "old style") Style used in music written after 1600, in imitation of the old CONTRAPUNTAL style of Palestrina, used especially for church music.

stile concitato (Italian, "excited style") Style devised by Claudio Monteverdi to portray anger and warlike actions, characterized by rapid reiteration of a single NOTE, whether on quickly spoken syllables or in a measured string tremolo.

stile moderno (Italian, "modern style") Seventeenth-century term for the up-to-date style that used BASSO CONTINUO and applied the rules of COUNTERPOINT freely; used most often for church music in contradistinction to STILE ANTICO.

stop (1) Mechanism on an organ to turn on or off the sounding of certain sets of pipes. (2) The particular set of pipes controlled by such a mechanism.

strain In a MARCH or RAG, a PERIOD, usually of sixteen or thirty-two measures.

streaming Process of delivering DIGITAL music or other media directly through a website or application without having to download a digital audio file.

stretta In nineteenth-century Italian OPERA, a fast section that concludes the FINALE at the end of an ACT, akin to the CABALETTA at the end of an ARIA or ENSEMBLE.

stretto In a FUGUE, overlapping entrances of the SUBJECT that enter more quickly after one another than in the opening EXPOSITION.

string quartet (1) Standard CHAMBER ENSEMBLE consisting of two VIOLINS, viola, and cello. (2) Multimovement composition for this ensemble.

strophic Of a poem, consisting of two or more stanzas that are equivalent in form and can each be sung to the same MELODY; of a vocal work, consisting of a strophic poem set to the same music for each stanza.

strophic variation Early seventeenth-century vocal GENRE, a setting of a STROPHIC poem, in which the MELODY of the first stanza is varied but the HARMONIC plan remains essentially the same, although the duration of harmonies may change to reflect the accentuation and meaning of the text.

style luthé (French, "lute style") or **style brisé** (French, "broken style") Broken or ARPEGGIATED TEXTURE in keyboard and LUTE music from seventeenth-century France. The technique originated with the lute, and the FIGURATION was transferred to the HARPSICHORD.

subdominant In TONAL music, the NOTE and CHORD a fifth below the TONIC.

subject THEME, used especially for the main MELODY of a RICERCARE, FUGUE, or other IMITATIVE work.

substitute clausula In NOTRE DAME POLYPHONY, a new CLAUSULA (usually in DISCANT style) designed to replace the original polyphonic setting of a particular segment of a CHANT.

suite A set of pieces that are linked together into a single work. During the BAROQUE PERIOD, a suite usually referred to a set of stylized DANCE pieces.

superius (Latin, "highest") In fifteenth- and sixteenth-century POLYPHONY, the highest part (compare CANTUS).

suspension DISSONANCE created when a NOTE is sustained while another voice moves to form a dissonance with it; the sustained voice descends a STEP to resolve the dissonance.

syllabic Having (or tending to have) one NOTE sung to each syllable of text.

symphonic poem Term coined by Franz Liszt for a one-movement work of PROGRAM MUSIC for orchestra that conveys a poetic idea, story, scene, or succession of moods by presenting THEMES that are repeated, varied, or transformed.

symphonie concertante A CONCERTO-like GENRE of the late eighteenth and early nineteenth centuries for two or more solo instruments and ORCHESTRA, characterized by its lightheartedness and MELODIC variety.

symphony Large work for ORCHESTRA, usually in four MOVEMENTS.

swing A style of JAZZ originating in the 1930s that was characterized by large ENSEMBLES and hard-driving jazz rhythms.

syncopation Temporary disruption of METER by beginning a long NOTE on an offbeat and sustaining it through the beginning of the next beat.

synthesizer Electronic instrument that generates and processes a wide variety of sounds.

tablature A system of NOTATION used for LUTE or other plucked string instrument that tells the player which strings to pluck and where to place the fingers on the strings, rather than indicating which NOTES will result. Tablatures were also used for keyboard instruments until the seventeenth century.

tabor See PIPE AND TABOR.

talea (Latin, "cutting"; pronounced TAH-lay-ah) In an ISORHYTHMIC COMPOSITION, an extended rhythmic pattern repeated one or more times, usually in the TENOR. Compare COLOR.

tape loop (1) Segment of magnetic recording tape spliced to form a loop that can run continuously through a tape recorder and thus play the recorded sounds repeatedly. (2) The continually repeating set of sounds that results.

temperament Any system of tuning NOTES in the SCALE in which pitches are adjusted to make most or all INTERVALS sound well, though perhaps not in perfect tune.

tempo (Italian, "time") Speed of performance, or relative pace of the music.

tempo d'attacco (Italian, "opening section") In the operatic scene structure for duets or ENSEMBLES developed by Gioachino Rossini in the early nineteenth century, a section after the SCENA and before the CANTABILE, in which the characters trade melodic phrases. See also CABALETTA and TEMPO DI MEZZO.

tempo di mezzo (Italian, "middle movement") In the operatic scene structure developed by Gioachino Rossini in the early nineteenth century, the middle section of an ARIA or ENSEMBLE, usually an interruption or a TRANSI-TION, that falls between the CANTABILE and the CABALETTA. See also SCENA and TEMPO D'ATTACCO.

tempus (Latin, "time"; pl. *tempora*) In medieval systems of NOTATION, the basic time unit. See also MODE, TIME, AND PROLATION.

tenor (from Latin *tenere*, "to hold") (1) In POLYPHONY of the twelfth and thirteenth centuries, the voice part that has the chant or other borrowed MELODY, often in long-held NOTES. (2) In POLYPHONY of the fourteenth and fifteenth centuries, the fundamental voice that together with the CANTUS determines the musical structure. (3) In vocal music from the sixteenth century on, part for a relatively high male voice. (4) Male voice of a relatively high range.

ternary form A FORM in three main sections, in which the first and third are identical or closely related and the middle section is contrasting, creating an ABA pattern.

tetrachord (from Greek, "four strings") (1) In Greek and medieval theory, a SCALE of four NOTES spanning a perfect fourth. (2) In modern theory, a SET of four pitches or PITCH-CLASSES. (3) In TWELVE-TONE theory, the first four, middle four, or last four notes in the ROW.

text depiction Using musical gestures to reinforce or suggest images in a text, such as rising on the word "ascend."

text expression Conveying or suggesting through musical means the emotions expressed in a text.

texture The combination of elements in a piece or passage, such as the number and relationship of independent parts (as in MONOPHONY, HETEROPHONY, POLYPHONY, or HOMOPHONY), groups (as in POLYCHORAL MUSIC), or musical events (as in relatively dense or transparent sonorities).

thematic transformation A method devised by Franz Liszt to provide unity, variety, and a narrative-like logic to a COMPOSITION by transforming the thematic material into new THEMES or other elements, in order to reflect the diverse moods needed to portray a PROGRAMMATIC subject.

theme Musical subject of a COMPOSITION or section, or of a set of VARIATIONS.

theorbo or **chitarrone** Large LUTE with extra BASS strings, used especially in the seventeenth century for performing BASSO CONTINUO as accompaniment to singers or instruments.

through-composed Composed throughout, as when each stanza or other unit of a poem is set to new music rather than in a STROPHIC manner to a single MELODY.

tiento Spanish IMPROVISATORY-style instrumental piece that features IMITATION, akin to the sixteenth-century FANTASIA.

timbre or **tone color** Characteristic color or sound of an instrument or voice.

time See MODE, TIME, AND PROLATION.

time signature Sign or numerical proportion, such as $\frac{3}{4}$, placed at the beginning of a piece, section, or MEASURE to indicate the METER.

Tin Pan Alley (1) Jocular name for a district in New York where numerous publishers specializing in POPULAR SONGS were located from the 1880s through the 1950s. (2) Styles of American POPULAR SONG from that era.

toccata (Italian, "touched") Piece for keyboard instrument or LUTE resembling an IMPROVISATION that may include IMITATIVE sections or may serve as a PRELUDE to an independent FUGUE.

tonal Operating within the system of TONALITY.

tonality The system, common since the late seventeenth century, by which a piece of music is organized around a TONIC NOTE, CHORD, and KEY, to which all the other notes and keys in the piece are subordinate.

tone (1) A sound of definite pitch. (2) See WHOLE STEP.

tone cluster Term coined by Henry Cowell for a CHORD of DIATONIC or CHROMATIC seconds.

tone color See TIMBRE.

tone poem SYMPHONIC POEM, or a similar work for a medium other than ORCHESTRA.

tonic (1) The first and central NOTE of a MAJOR or MINOR SCALE. (2) The main KEY of a piece or MOVEMENT, in which the piece begins and ends and to which all other keys are subordinate.

tonos (pl. *tonoi*) Ancient Greek term used with different meanings by various writers; one meaning is a particular set of pitches within a certain RANGE or region of the voice.

topics In music from the CLASSIC PERIOD on, term for the different and contrasting styles that serve as subjects for musical discourse.

total serialism The application of the principles of the TWELVE-TONE METHOD to musical parameters other than pitch, including duration, intensities, and TIMBRES. See SERIAL MUSIC.

Tract (from Latin *tractus*, "drawn out") Item in the MASS PROPER that replaces the ALLELUIA on certain days in Lent, whose text comprises a series of PSALM VERSES.

tragédie en musique (French, "tragedy in music"; later **tragédie lyrique**, "lyric tragedy") French seventeenth- and eighteenth-century form of OPERA, pioneered by Jean-Baptiste Lully, that combined the French classic drama and BALLET traditions with music, DANCES, and spectacles.

transcription Arrangement of a piece for an instrumental medium different from the original, such as a reduction of an ORCHESTRAL score for PIANO.

transition (1) In the EXPOSITION of a MOVEMENT in SONATA FORM, the passage between the first and second THEMES that effects the MODULATION to a new KEY. (2) More generally, a passage between two MOVEMENTS or SECTIONS of a work.

transverse flute Flute blown across a hole in the side of the pipe and held to one side of the player; used for medieval, RENAISSANCE, and BAROQUE forms of the flute to distinguish it from the RECORDER, which is blown in one end and held in front.

treble (French, "triple") (1) A high voice or a part written for high voice, especially the highest part in three-part POLYPHONY of the fourteenth and fifteenth centuries. (2) Pertaining to the highest voice.

treble-dominated style Style common in the fourteenth and fifteenth centuries, in which the main MELODY is in the CANTUS, the upper voice carrying the text, supported by a slower-moving TENOR and CONTRATENOR.

Trecento (Italian, short for *mille trecento*, "one thousand three hundred"; pronounced treh-CHEN-toh) The 1300s (the fourteenth century), particularly with reference to Italian art, literature, and music of the time.

triad CHORD consisting of two successive thirds (for instance, C–E–G), or any INVERSION of such a chord.

trill Rapid alternation between a NOTE and another a HALF STEP or WHOLE STEP above.

trio (1) Piece for three players or singers. (2) The second of two alternating DANCES, as in the Classic-era MINUET AND TRIO FORM. (3) The second main section of a MARCH.

trio sonata Common instrumental GENRE during the BAROQUE period, a SONATA for two TREBLE instruments (usually VIOLINS) above a BASSO CONTINUO. A performance featured four or more players if more than one was used for the continuo part.

triplum (from Latin *triplus*, "triple") (1) In POLYPHONY of the late twelfth through fourteenth centuries, third voice from the bottom in a three- or four-voice TEXTURE, added to a TENOR and DUPLUM. (2) In NOTRE DAME POLYPHONY, an ORGANUM in three voices.

tritone INTERVAL spanning three WHOLE TONES or six SEMITONES, such as F to B.

trobairitz (from Occitan *trobar*, "to compose a song") A female TROUBADOUR.

trope Addition to an existing CHANT, consisting of (1) words and MELODY; (2) a MELISMA; or (3) words only, set to an existing melisma or other melody.

troubadour (from Occitan *trobar*, "to compose a song") A poet-composer of southern France who wrote MONOPHONIC songs in Occitan (*langue d'oc*) in the twelfth or thirteenth century.

trouvère (from Old French *trover*, "to compose a song") A poet-composer of northern France who wrote MONOPHONIC songs in Old French (*langue d'oïl*) in the twelfth or thirteenth century.

tuba (1) In ancient Rome, a long, straight trumpet. (2) Low brass instrument invented in the 1830s, used as the BASS of the brass section of the ORCHESTRA.

tutti (Italian, "all") (1) In both the CONCERTO and the CONCERTO GROSSO, designates the full ORCHESTRA. Also called RIPIENO (Italian, "full"). (2) Instruction to an ENSEMBLE that all should play.

twelve-bar blues Standard formula for the BLUES, with a HARMONIC PROGRESSION in which the first four-measure PHRASE is on the TONIC, the second phrase begins on the SUBDOMINANT and ends on the tonic, and the third phrase starts on the DOMINANT and returns to the tonic.

twelve-tone method A form of ATONALITY based on the systematic ordering of the twelve notes of the CHROMATIC SCALE into a ROW that may be manipulated according to certain rules.

ultramodernism Current in American music between the world wars that focused on developing new musical resources.

underscoring See NONDIEGETIC MUSIC.

unmeasured prelude A French BAROQUE keyboard GENRE, usually the first MOVEMENT in a SUITE, whose nonmetric NOTATION gives a feeling of IMPROVISATION.

variation The process of reworking a given MELODY, song, THEME, or other musical idea, or the resulting varied FORM of it.

variations (variation form) FORM that presents an uninterrupted series of variants (each called a VARIATION) on a THEME; the theme may be a MELODY, a BASS line, a HARMONIC plan, or other musical subject.

vaudeville In late-nineteenth- and early-twentieth-century America, a type of variety show including musical numbers, but without the common theme of a REVUE.

verismo (Italian, "realism") (1) Nineteenth-century operatic movement that presents everyday people in familiar situations, often depicting sordid or brutal events. (2) More broadly, term used in the late nineteenth and early twentieth centuries for OPERAS that turned away from Romantic idealism and reliance on conventions. See also REALISM.

vernacular music General term encompassing POPULAR MUSIC, FOLK MUSIC, JAZZ, and other traditions outside CLASSICAL music.

verse (1) Line of poetry. (2) Stanza of a HYMN or STROPHIC song. (3) Sentence of a PSALM. (4) In GREGORIAN CHANT, a setting of a Psalm verse or similar text, such as the verses that are part of the INTROIT, GRADUAL, and ALLELUIA.

verse-refrain form A FORM in vocal music in which two or more stanzas of poetry are each sung to the same music (the VERSE) and each is followed by the same REFRAIN.

versus (Latin, "verse") A type of Latin sacred song, either MONOPHONIC or POLYPHONIC, setting a rhymed, rhythmic poem.

vielle Medieval bowed string instrument, early form of the fiddle and predecessor of the VIOLIN and VIOL.

vihuela Spanish relative of the LUTE with a flat back and guitar-shaped body.

villancico (from Spanish *villano*, "peasant"; pronounced vee-yan-SEE-co or vee-yan-THEE-co) Type of POLYPHONIC song in Spanish, with several stanzas framed by a REFRAIN; originally secular, the FORM was later used for sacred works, especially associated with Christmas or other important holy days.

villanella Type of sixteenth-century Italian song, generally for three voices, in a rustic HOMOPHONIC style.

viol (viola da gamba) Bowed, fretted string instrument popular from the mid-fifteenth to the early eighteenth centuries, held between the legs.

violin Bowed, fretless string instrument tuned in fifths $(g-d'-a'-e')$.

virelai French FORME FIXE in the pattern A bba A bba A bba A, in which a REFRAIN (A) alternates with stanzas with the musical FORM bba, the a using the same music as the refrain.

virginal (1) English name for HARPSICHORD, used for all types until the seventeenth century. (2) Type of HARPSICHORD that is small enough to place on a table, with a single keyboard and strings running at right angles to the keys rather than parallel with them as in larger harpsichords.

virtuoso Performer who specializes in one instrument and dazzles audiences with his or her technical prowess.

voice exchange In POLYPHONY, technique in which voices trade segments of music, so that the same combination of lines is heard twice or more, but with different voices singing each line.

walking bass Bass line in BAROQUE music—and later in JAZZ—that moves steadily and continuously.

waltz Type of couple DANCE in triple METER, popular in the late eighteenth and nineteenth centuries, or a short, stylized work for the PIANO in the style of such a dance.

whole step (or **whole tone**) An INTERVAL equivalent to two SEMITONES.

whole-tone scale (or **whole-tone collection**) A SCALE consisting of only WHOLE STEPS.

wind ensemble Large ENSEMBLE of winds, brass, and percussion instruments, mostly with one player per part, dedicated solely to serious music, rather than to the mix of MARCHES and other fare typically played by BANDS.

word-painting TEXT DEPICTION.

zarzuela Spanish GENRE of musical theater that alternates between sung and spoken dialogue and various types of ENSEMBLE and solo song.

CREDITS

ART

pp. iii, xiv, **754, 756, 770, 804, 848, 898, 919, 954, 990**: Private Collection/Bridgeman Images. **pp. vi, 2, 4, 20, 42, 63, 80, 106**: Monasterio de El Escorial, El Escorial, Spain/Index/Bridgeman Images. **pp. vii, 134, 136, 159, 180, 205, 229, 254**: National Gallery, London, UK/Bridgeman Images. **pp. viii, 276, 278, 297, 317, 339, 371**: Harold Samuel Collection, City of London/Bridgeman Images. **pp. ix, 400, 402, 426, 454, 471, 494, 514**: Yale Center for British Art, Paul Mellon Collection, USA/Bridgeman Images. **pp. x, 552, 554, 580, 618, 646, 671, 711, 731**: Private Collection/Photo © O. Vaering/Bridgeman Images.

MUSIC AND TEXT

Example 4.1: Melody transcribed by Hendrik van der Werf, *The Extant Troubadour Melodies* (Rochester: Author, 1984), 13. Gerald A. Bond, text editor. **Example 6.1**: Philippe de Vitry, *Complete Works*, ed. Leo Schrade, with new introduction and notes by Edward H. Roesner (Monaco: Éditions de l'Oiseau-Lyre, 1984, 26–28. *Polyphonic Music of the Fourteenth Century*, vol. 1, 82–84). Reprinted by kind permission of l'Oiseau-Lyre at the University of Melbourne. **Example 9.9**: Edited by Alejandro Enrique Planchart. Reprinted from Allan W. Atlas, *Anthology of Renaissance Music* (New York: W. W. Norton, 1998), 159–65. Reprinted with permission of the author. **Example 16.5**: From Tomás de Torrejón y Velasco and Juan Hidalgo, *La púrpura de la rosa*, ed. Louise K. Stein, *Musica Hispana*, ser. A, vol. 25 (Madrid: Instituto Complutense de Ciencias Musicales, 1999), 74–80. **Chapter 21, p. 488**: Dedication for *Alceste* (1769), trans. Eric Bloom. From Alfred Einstein, *Gluck* (London: J. M. Dent & Sons, 1936), 98–100. In SR 136 (5:15), pp. 933–34. **Example 33.6**: Webern Symphony, Op. 21 © 1929 Universal Edition A.G., Wien. © Renewed. All rights reserved. Used by permission of European American Music Distributors Company, agent for Universal Edition A.G., Wien. **Example 33.7**: *Petrushka* by Igor Stravinsky © Copyright 1912, 1947 by Hawkes & Son (London) Ltd. Copyright renewed. Reprinted by permission of Boosey & Hawkes, Inc., an Imagem company. **Example 33.9**: *The Rite of Spring* by Igor Stravinsky © 1912, 1921 by Hawkes & Son (London) Ltd. U.S. Copyright renewed. Used with permission. All rights reserved. **Example 33.11**: From Béla Bartók, *Music for String Instruments, Percussion and Celesta* (New York: Boosey & Hawkes, 1939), 66–94. © Copyright 1937 for the USA by Boosey & Hawkes, Inc. Copyright renewed. Reprinted by permission of Boosey & Hawkes, Inc. All rights reserved. Used in the territory of the world excluding the United States by permission of European American Music Distributors LLC, agent for Universal Edition A.G., Vienna. **Example 33.12**: From Béla Bartók, *Music for String Instruments, Percussion and Celesta* (New York: Boosey & Hawkes, 1939), 66–94. © Copyright 1937 for the USA by Boosey & Hawkes, Inc. Copyright renewed. Reprinted by permission of Boosey & Hawkes, Inc. All rights reserved. Used in the territory of the world excluding the United States by permission of European American Music Distributors LLC, agent for Universal Edition A.G., Vienna. **Example 33.13**: From Béla Bartók, *Music for String Instruments, Percussion and Celesta* (New York: Boosey & Hawkes, 1939), 66–94. © Copyright 1937 for the USA by Boosey & Hawkes, Inc. Copyright renewed. Reprinted by permission of Boosey & Hawkes, Inc. All rights reserved. Used in the territory of the world excluding the United States by permission of European American Music Distributors LLC, agent for Universal Edition A.G., Vienna. **Example 34.2**: *Back Water Blues* by Bessie Smith © 1927 (Renewed), 1974 Frank Music Corp. All rights reserved. Reprinted by permission of Hal Leonard LLC. **Example 34.3**: *West End Blues*. Words and music by Joe Oliver and Clarence Williams. Copyright © 1928 Universal Music Corp. and Great Standard's Music Publishing Co. Copyright renewed. All rights reserved. Used by permission. **Example 34.4**: *Cotton Tail* by Duke Ellington. Copyright © 1940 Sony/ATV Music Publishing LLC in the U.S.A. Copyright renewed. All rights administered by Sony/ATV Music Publishing LLC, 424 Church Street, Suite 1200, Nashville, TN 37219. Rights for the world outside the U.S.A. administered by EMI Robbins Catalog Inc. (publishing) and Alfred Music (print). International copyright secured. All rights reserved. **Example 35.3**: From Edgard Varèse, *Hyperprism* (New York: G. Ricordi, 1961). Used by permission of Universal Music MGB Publications. **Example 35.4**: *String Quartet 1931* by Ruth Crawford Seeger. Copyright © 1941 by Merion Music Inc. **Example 35.5**: *Appalachian Spring* by Aaron Copland. © 1945 The Aaron Copland Fund for Music, Inc. Copyright renewed. Boosey & Hawkes, Inc., used with permission. All rights reserved. **Example 37.2**: *Liturgie de crista I* (n. 1 de "Quatuor pour 10 fin du temps"). Music by Olivier Messiaen. Copyright © 1942 by Editions Durand–Paris. All rights reserved. Reproduced by kind permission of Hal Leonard Europe S.r.l.–Italy. **Figure 37.6**: Excerpt from John Cage *4'33"*. Copyright © 1960 by Henmar Press, Inc. Used by permission. All rights reserved. **Figure 37.7**: *December 1952* by Earle Brown. Copyright © 1961 (Renewed) by Associated Music Publishers, Inc. (BMI). International copyright secured. All rights reserved. Reprinted by permission. **Figure 37.11**: *Metastaseis* by Iannis Xenakis © 1967 By Boosey & Hawkes Music Publishers Limited. Used with permission. All rights reserved. **Example 37.7**: From Krzysztof Penderecki, *Ofiarom Hiroszimy: Tren na 52 Instrumenty Smyczkowe* (Warsaw: Polskie Wydawnictwo Muzyczne, 1961). © 1961 (Renewed) EMI DESHON MUSIC, INC. All rights controlled and administered by EMI DESHON MUSIC, INC. (Publishing) and ALFRED PUBLISHING CO., INC. (Print). All rights reserved. Used by permission. **Chapter 39, p. 1003**, Source Reading, from Heather Mac Donald, "Classical Music's New Golden Age," *City Journal* 20 (Summer 2010).

INDEX